"No other guide has as much to offer . . . these books are a pleasure to read." Gene Shalit on the *Today Show*

". . . Excellently organized for the casual traveler who is looking for a mix of recreation and cultural insight."
Washington Post

★★★★★ (5-star rating) "Crisply written and remarkably personable. Cleverly organized so you can pluck out the minutest fact in a moment. Satisfyingly thorough."
Réalités

"The information they offer is up-to-date, crisply presented but far from exhaustive, the judgments knowledgeable but not opinionated." *New York Times*

"The individual volumes are compact, the prose succinct, and the coverage up-to-date and knowledgeable . . . The format is portable and the index admirably detailed."
John Barkham Syndicate

". . . An abundance of excellent directions, diversions, and facts, including perspectives and getting-ready-to-go advice — succinct, detailed, and well organized in an easy-to-follow style." *Los Angeles Times*

"They contain an amount of information that is truly staggering, besides being surprisingly current."
Detroit News

"These guides address themselves to the needs of the modern traveler demanding precise, qualitative information . . . Upbeat, slick, and well put together."
Dallas Morning News

". . . Attractive to look at, refreshingly easy to read, and generously packed with information." *Miami Herald*

"These guides are as good as any published, and much better than most." *Louisville* (Kentucky) *Times*

Stephen Birnbaum Travel Guides

Acapulco
Bahamas, and Turks & Caicos
Barcelona
Bermuda
Boston
Canada
Cancun, Cozumel & Isla Mujeres
Caribbean
Chicago
Disneyland
Eastern Europe
Europe
Europe for Business Travelers
Florence
France
Great Britain
Hawaii
Honolulu
Ireland
Italy
Ixtapa & Zihuatanejo
Las Vegas
London
Los Angeles
Mexico
Miami & Ft. Lauderdale
Montreal & Quebec City
New Orleans
New York
Paris
Portugal
Puerto Vallarta
Rome
San Francisco
South America
Spain
Toronto
United States
USA for Business Travelers
Vancouver
Venice
Walt Disney World
Washington, DC
Western Europe

ADVISORY EDITOR
Claire Hardiman

CONTRIBUTING EDITORS
Cathy Beason
Janet Bennett
Lois Brett
Kevin Causey
Ben Harte
Brian McCallen
Richard John Pietschmann
Dee Prather

MAPS Etta Jacobs
SYMBOLS Gloria McKeown

A Stephen Birnbaum Travel Guide

Birnbaum's HAWAII 1993

Alexandra Mayes Birnbaum
EDITOR

Lois Spritzer
EXECUTIVE EDITOR

Allan Seiden
AREA EDITOR

Laura L. Brengelman
Managing Editor

Mary Callahan
Jill Kadetsky
Susan McClung
Beth Schlau
Dana Margaret Schwartz
Associate Editors

Gene Gold
Assistant Editor

HarperPerennial
A Division of HarperCollins*Publishers*

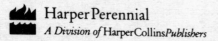

To Stephen, who merely made all this possible.

FIRST EDITION

ISSN 0749-2561 (Stephen Birnbaum Travel Guides)
ISSN 0883-2471 (Hawaii)
ISBN 0-06-278048-4 (pbk.)

92 93 94 95 96 CC/WP 10 9 8 7 6 5 4 3 2 1

Contents

Sources and Resources

PERSPECTIVES

A cultural and historical survey of Hawaii's past and present, its people, politics, and heritage.

ISLAND-BY-ISLAND HOPPING

Thorough, qualitative guides to the islands. Designed to be used on the spot, each section offers a comprehensive report on the island's most compelling attractions and amenities. Directions and recommendations are immediately accessible because each report is presented in consistent form.

DIVERSIONS

A selective guide to over 20 active and cerebral vacations, including the places to pursue them where the quality of experience is likely to be highest.

A Word from the Editor

My husband Stephen Birnbaum was a major fan of islands. My travel trail usually led from Los Angeles and San Francisco to New York, and then on through London, Paris, Rome, and Hong Kong, with a fair number of other urban rest stops in between. The constant in my journeying was a surfeit of asphalt and concrete, which I evidently found as relaxing as most people do hammocks and palm trees.

So it took some substantial effort for Steve to get me motivated to meander around any atoll, no matter how attractive. I shared a not uncommon (and admittedly narrow) view that one island was pretty much like any other, and that when you've seen one pristine strand of sand you've pretty much experienced what beaches in general have to offer. That was, until I saw Hawaii.

I won't bore you with a long description of the Hawaiian experiences that left me wide-eyed and a bit slack-jawed, but on island after island, I found myself entranced and enchanted by natural wonders and extraordinary vistas that a first-time visitor to Hawaii just doesn't believe possible. My infatuation proved enduring, as my editorship of this volume attests.

Still, all is not swaying palms and shimmering sands even in this idyllic Pacific paradise. As with world news in general, headlines about Hawaii have described some troubles in Eden, and there's no denying that these exist. On the whole, however, Hawaii's remarkably multi-ethnic and polyglot population has confronted most of the malaise of civilization as intelligently as it is possible to in a world that sometimes seems to defy sense and sanity.

Among these problems are tourists by the jumbo-jetful, and the islands' economy, which has come more and more to rely on a sizable, constant influx of tourist currency. Inevitably, the sheer numbers of these visitors have affected island life — and not always for the better. For example, certain segments of Waikiki Beach in Honolulu on Oahu and parts of the Kaanapali coast on Maui bear the scars of overzealous development. But these are really the only two areas that can be cited as being significantly marred. Other areas — like Hana (on Maui) and Hanalei (on Kauai) and Hilo (on the Big Island) — remain just about as immune from contemporary commercial crassness as ever.

In recent years, the nature of travel to and through the Hawaiian archipelago has altered somewhat to reflect changing travel tastes. More and more visitors are leaving Honolulu in their jet trail to spend more time on other, less crowded islands. The newly updated guide to Hawaii which you hold in your hand hopes to expand this trend by directing prospective Hawaii visitors to those special corners of the islands that are not necessarily part of the most publicized package tours. A burgeoning number of money-saving package programs and excursion airfares, plus subsidized inter-island flights, make travel among the islands affordable and extremely easy. So there's no excuse for any visitor to remain anchored in some less than desirable high-rise hotel. The real wonders of Hawaii glisten along the cliffs of the Na Pali coast on Kauai, among the steaming craters of Hawaii Volcanoes National Park on the Big Island, and in dozens of other similarly magical places. The pages that follow contain as many leads to Hawaii's enduring magic as can be found anywhere.

Obviously, any guidebook to Hawaii must keep pace with and answer the real needs of today's travelers. That's why we've tried to create a guide that's specifically organized, written, and edited for the more demanding modern traveler, one for whom qualitative information is infinitely more desirable than mere quantities of unappraised data. We think that this book, along with all the other guides in our series, represent a new generation of travel guides — one that is especially responsive to modern needs and interests.

For years, dating back as far as Herr Baedeker, travel guides have tended to be encyclopedic, seemingly much more concerned with demonstrating expertise in geography and history than with a real analysis of the sorts of things that actually concern a typical modern tourist. But today, when it is hardly necessary to tell a traveler where Honolulu is (in many cases, the traveler has been there nearly as often as the guidebook editors), it becomes the responsibility of those editors to provide new perspectives and to suggest new directions in order to make the guide genuinely valuable.

That's exactly what we've tried to do in this series. I think you'll notice a different, more contemporary tone to the text, as well as an organization and focus that are distinctive and more functional. And even a random reading of what follows will demonstrate a substantial departure from the standard guidebook orientation, for we've not only attempted to provide information of a more compelling sort, but we also have tried to present the data in a format that makes it particularly accessible.

Needless to say, it's difficult to decide just what to include in a guidebook of this size — and what to omit. Early on, we realized that giving up the encyclopedic approach precluded our listing every single route and restaurant, a realization that helped define our overall editorial focus. Similarly, when we discussed the possibility of presenting certain information in other than strict geographic order, we found that the new format enabled us to arrange data in a way that we feel best answers the questions travelers typically ask.

Large numbers of specific questions have provided the real editorial skeleton for this book. The volume of mail we regularly receive emphasizes that modern travelers want very precise information, so we've tried to organize our material in the most responsive way possible. Readers who want to know the best restaurants in Poipu or the best golf courses on the Big Island will have no trouble extracting that data from this guide.

Travel guides are, understandably, reflections of personal taste, and putting one's name on a title page obviously puts one's preferences on the line. But I think I ought to amplify just what "personal" means. Like Steve, I don't believe in the sort of personal guidebook that's a palpable misrepresentation on its face. It is, for example, hardly possible for any single travel writer to visit thousands of restaurants (and nearly as many hotels) in any given year and provide accurate appraisals of each. And even if it were physically possible for one human being to survive such an itinerary, it would of necessity have to be done at a dead sprint, and the perceptions derived therefrom would probably be less valid than those of any other intelligent individual visiting the same establishments. It is, therefore, impossible (especially in a large, annually revised and updated guidebook *series* such as we offer) to have only one person provide all the data on the entire world.

I also happen to think that such individual orientation is of substantially less value to readers. Visiting a single hotel for just one night or eating one hasty meal in a random restaurant hardly equips anyone to provide appraisals that are of more than passing interest. No amount of doggedly alliterative or oppressively onomatopoeic text can camouflage a technique that is essentially specious. We have, therefore, chosen what I like to describe as the "thee and me" approach to restaurant and hotel evaluation and, to a somewhat more limited degree, to the sites and sights we have included in the other sections of our text. What this really reflects is personal sampling tempered by intelligent counsel from informed local sources, and these additional friends-of-the-editors are almost always residents of the city and/or area about which they are consulted.

Despite the presence of several editors, writers, researchers, and local contributors, very precise editing and tailoring keep our text fiercely subjective. So what follows is the gospel according to Birnbaum, and represents as much of our own taste and instincts as we can manage. It is probable, therefore, that if you like your beaches largely unpopulated and your mountainsides mostly uncrowded, prefer small hotels with personality to huge high-rise anonymities, and can't tolerate fresh fish that's been relentlessly overcooked, we're likely to have a long and meaningful relationship. Readers with dissimilar tastes may be less enraptured.

I should also point out something about the person to whom this guidebook is directed. Above all, he or she is a "visitor." This means that such elements as restaurants have been specifically picked to provide the visitor with a representative, enlightening, stimulating, and above all, pleasant experience. Since so many extraneous considerations can affect the reception and service accorded a regular restaurant patron, our choices can in no way be construed as an exhaustive guide to island dining. We think we've listed all the best places, in various price ranges, but they were chosen with a visitor's enjoyment in mind.

Other evidence of how we've tried to tailor our text to reflect modern travel habits is most apparent in the section we call DIVERSIONS. Where once it was common for travelers to spend an island visit nailed to a single spot, the emphasis today is more likely to be directed toward pursuing some sport or special interest while seeing the surrounding countryside. So we've organized every activity we could reasonably evaluate and arranged the material in a way that it is especially accessible to activists of either athletic or cerebral bent. It is no longer necessary, therefore, to wade through a pound or two of superfluous prose just to find the very best surfing spot or the supreme scenic vista within a reasonable distance of your destination.

If there is a single thing that best characterizes the revolution in and evolution of current holiday habits, it is that most travelers now consider travel a right rather than a privilege. No longer is a family trip to the far corners of the world necessarily a once-in-a-lifetime thing; nor is the idea of visiting exotic, faraway places in the least worrisome. Travel today translates as the enthusiastic desire to sample all of the world's opportunities, to find that elusive quality of experience that is not only enriching but comfortable. For that reason, we've tried to make what follows not only helpful and enlightening, but the sort of welcome companion of which every traveler dreams.

Finally, I also should point out that every good travel guide is a living enterprise; that is, no part of this text is carved in stone. In our annual revisions, we refine, expand, and further hone all our material to serve your travel needs better. To this end, no contribution is of greater value to us than your personal reaction to what we have written, as well as information reflecting your own experiences while using the book. We earnestly and enthusiastically solicit your comments about this guide *and* your opinions and perceptions about places you have recently visited. In this way, we will be able to provide the most current information — including the actual experiences of recent travelers — and to make those experiences more readily available to others. Please write to us at 10 E. 53rd St., New York, NY 10022.

We sincerely hope to hear from you.

ALEXANDRA MAYES BIRNBAUM

How to Use This Guide

A great deal of care has gone into the organization of this guidebook, and we believe it represents a real breakthrough in the presentation of travel material. Our aim has been to create a new, more modern generation of travel books and to make this guide the most useful and practical travel tool available today.

Our text is divided into four basic sections, in order to present information in the best way on every possible aspect of a Hawaii vacation. This organization itself should alert you to the vast and varied opportunities available in these islands — as well as indicate all the specific data necessary to plan a successful visit. You won't find much of the conventional "swaying palms and shimmering sand" text here; we've chosen instead to deliver more useful and practical information. Prospective Hawaiian itineraries tend to speak for themselves, and with so many diverse travel opportunities, we feel our main job is to highlight what's where and to provide basic information — how, when, where, how much, and what's best — to assist you in making the most intelligent choices possible.

Here is a brief summary of the four basic sections and what you can expect to find in each. We believe that you will find both your travel planning and on-island enjoyment enhanced by having this book at your side.

GETTING READY TO GO

This mini-encyclopedia of practical travel facts is a sort of know-it-all companion with all the precise information necessary to create a successful journey to and through Hawaii. There are entries on more than 2 dozen separate topics, including how to get where you're going, what preparations to make before leaving, what to expect on the different islands, what your trip is likely to cost, and how to avoid prospective problems. The individual entries are specific, realistic, and, where appropriate, cost-oriented.

We expect you to use this section most in the course of planning your trip, for its ideas and suggestions are intended to simplify this often confusing period. Entries are intentionally concise, in an effort to get to the meat of the matter with the least extraneous prose. These entries are augmented by extensive lists of specific sources from which to obtain even more specialized data, plus some suggestions for obtaining travel information on your own.

PERSPECTIVES

Any visit to an unfamiliar destination is enhanced and enriched by an understanding of the cultural and historical heritage of that area. We have, therefore, provided just such an introduction to Hawaii — its history, people, music and dance, food and drink, folklore and myths, and language.

ISLAND-BY-ISLAND HOPPING

Individual reports on the eight major islands have been prepared with the aid of researchers, contributors, professional journalists, and other experts on the spot. Although useful at the planning stage, ISLAND-BY-ISLAND HOPPING is really designed to be taken along and used on the spot. Each report offers a short-stay guide to its island within a consistent format: an essay introduces the island as a historic entity and a functioning contemporary place to live and visit; *Sources and Resources* is a concise, island-wide listing of pertinent tourist information, meant to answer myriad potentially pressing questions as they arise — from simple things such as the address of the local tourist office, how to get around, which sightseeing tours to take, and when the island's special events occur to something more difficult like where the best golf, tennis, fishing, and swimming are to be found. *Around the Island* is an area-by-area analysis of each island, with emphasis on the most important sights to see and things to do, the best places to eat and sleep, the savviest places to shop, and the liveliest nightspots to try.

DIVERSIONS

This section is designed to help travelers find the best places in which to pursue a wide range of physical and cerebral activities, without having to wade through endless pages of unrelated text. This very selective guide lists the broadest possible range of activities, including all the best places to pursue them.

We start with a list of special places to stay and eat, and move to activities that require some perspiration — sports preferences and other rigorous pursuits — and go on to report on a number of more cerebral and spiritual vacation opportunities. In every case, our suggestion of a particular location — and often our recommendation of a specific resort — is intended to guide you to that special place where the quality of experience is likely to be the highest. Whether you want to surf, swim, or sail, dine elegantly, or shop wisely, each category is the equivalent of a comprehensive checklist of the absolute best in Hawaii.

Although each of the book's sections has a distinct format and a special function, they have all been designed to be used together to provide a complete inventory of travel information. To use this book to full advantage, take a few minutes to read the table of contents and random entries in each section to get a firsthand feel for how it all fits together.

Pick and choose needed information. Assume, for example, that you have always wanted to explore Hawaii's volcanoes, but you never really knew how to organize it or where to go. Turn first to the hiking section of GETTING READY TO GO, as well as the chapters on planning a trip, accommodations, and climate and clothes. These short, informative entries provide plenty of practical information. But where to go? Turn next to ISLAND-BY-ISLAND HOPPING. Perhaps you choose to watch the famous sunrise at Haleakala on

Maui or examine the fissures in the crater of still-steaming Kilauea on the Big Island. Your trip will almost certainly include a stopover in Waikiki, and for a complete rundown on that complex area, read the Waikiki section of the Oahu chapter. Finally, turn to DIVERSIONS to peruse the sections on sports, hotels, restaurants, museums, historic sites, and other activities in which you are interested to make sure don't miss anything in the neighborhood.

In other words, the sections of this book are building blocks designed to help you put together the best possible trip. Use them selectively as a tool, a source of ideas, a reference work for accurate facts, and a guidebook to the best buys, the most exciting sights, the most pleasant accommodations, the tastiest food — *the best travel experience* that you can possibly have.

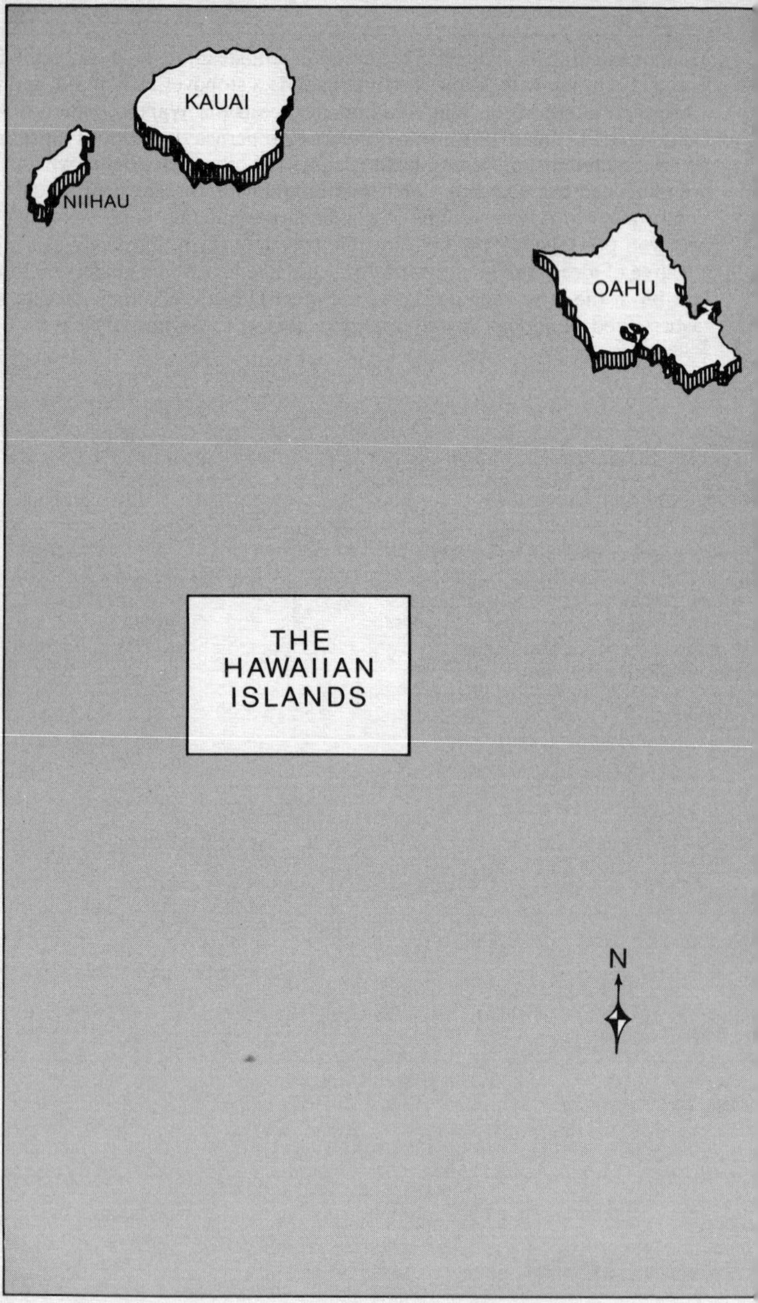
KAUAI
NIIHAU
OAHU
THE HAWAIIAN ISLANDS
N

PACIFIC OCEAN
MOLOKAI
LANAI
MAUI
KAHOOLAWE
THE
BIG ISLAND

GETTING READY TO GO

When and How to Go

What's Where

Hawaii's geographic isolation is awesome. Lying in the central Pacific, its nearest neighbor is the minuscule Christmas Island chain, some 2,000 miles to the south. North America, the nearest continent, is 2,400 miles to the east, and it's necessary to travel almost 3,000 miles to the west before hitting any land larger than a big rock in the ocean. Given Hawaii's remoteness, it's not surprising that human beings didn't stumble upon this string of perfect isles until around the 6th century, or that it would be another millennium before the rest of the world discovered what are now among the best known and most visited 6,425 square miles on earth.

What we think of as the Hawaiian islands — eight major islands lying at about the same latitude as Mexico City — are in fact only the youngest of a chain of over 100 islands, reefs, and atolls that stretch nearly 2,000 miles to the northwest. The first of these, Kure Atoll, now a semicircle of coral reef, was pushed up from the sea floor about 25 million years ago. As the earth's plates shifted slightly to the northwest, the stationary volcanic vent broke through other weak spots in the earth's crust, thrusting up a succession of lava mountains. The latest of these to break the surface of the sea is the Big Island, whose continuing growing pains fascinate geologists and laypeople alike.

The oldest of the major islands is **Kauai**. Over the eons, the smooth-sloped volcano that formed this roughly circular island has been transformed by wind, rain, and the sea into craggy peaks creased with steep and narrow valleys and brimming with rich tropical life. At the heart of the island is 5,240-foot-high Mt. Waialeale, which catches an average of 500 inches of rain a year and feeds the many rivers, streams, and waterfalls that bejewel the island. To the northwest, along the Na Pali Coast, Kauai meets the sea with towering cliffs and vertical valleys of heart-stopping beauty. To the west is Waimea Canyon, a long, deep gorge of pale greens and pinks. To the east, south, and southwest, the island levels out into gentle slopes of sugarcane fields and ends in a chain of beaches about as perfect as one could imagine.

Seventeen miles southwest of Kauai is **Niihau**, a small, dry island whose central plateau of gently rolling grasslands supports sheep and cattle ranching. As on most of the islands, the windward side ends in black lava cliffs and the leeward side in a long strand of sandy beaches. Lying just off the north coast of Niihau, like a diacritical mark, is **Lehua**, a crescent of shiny black rock left from an ancient volcanic explosion.

Shaped a bit like an old-fashioned boot, **Oahu**, about 80 miles southeast of Kauai, is made up of two parallel mountain ranges — the Koolau and the Waianae — with a saddle of agricultural fields (the era of pineapple plantations is all but over) suspended between them. Honolulu and its environs occupy most of the southeast, from Pearl City at the instep to Koko Head at the tip of the boot. As the city outgrew the coastal plain, it spread up into the Koolau Mountains behind it, and at night the lights scattered in the upper reaches of the black valleys blink like low-slung stars. Along the south coast are all the familiar landmarks — Waikiki, Diamond Head, and the Punchbowl. The southeast coast is rocky, with lava cliffs sculpted in multi-leveled terraces that conceal caves and blowholes, lava tubes and rock pools. Farther up the east side, the coast tempers down into swimmable beaches, while the famed surfing beaches — Sunset Point, the Banzai Pipeline, Pupukea — line the North Shore.

The geographic center of the Hawaiian chain is **Molokai**, about 25 miles southeast of Oahu. A long, narrow island about the size of Manhattan, Molokai breaks into two distinct regions: the upland plateau of grazing and agricultural land in the west and the deep gorges of rain forest in the east. Molokai's most spectacular feature is its northeast coast, where sea cliffs 2,000 feet high jut out into the blue Pacific like so many flying buttresses of kelly green. Isolated at the foot of these cliffs is the beautiful lava plain of Makanalua Peninsula, where Kalaupapa, the well known (and once infamous) leper colony, has existed since the 19th century.

It's a little less than 10 miles from the eastern tip of Molokai to **Maui**, an island created by two separate volcanoes whose lava flows ran together to create a low-lying plain of remarkable fertility. The central core of West Maui, the older and smaller of the two sections, is carved into steep, nearly inaccessible, wildly beautiful valleys. But as the slopes smooth out near the coast, sugarcane and tourism take over. West Maui's beaches are long, lovely, and world famous. Dominating East Maui is Haleakala, the 10,023-foot volcano whose 7½-mile-long and 2½-mile-wide crater is a national park. Its gentle west slope is covered with vegetable and flower farms, while the south face is dry and cut by numerous deep ravines. Along the north coast, as far as the eastern tip of the island, is scenery so lush that the name of the district, Hana, is almost always (and accurately) preceded by the adjective "heavenly."

Due west of Maui and tucked south of Molokai is **Lanai**, a small tear-shaped island devoted mostly to farming. Deeply etched valleys are drawn along the eastern side, but past the central plateau the land slopes easily to the sea. Slightly southwest of Maui is **Kahoolawe**, an arid, desolate island that swelters in the shadow of Haleakala, which blocks any rain or cooling trade winds. Heavily populated by wild goats, Kahoolawe has not had a human resident since the navy began using the island for artillery and bombing target practice in 1941 (firing was stopped in 1990).

Dropping like a heavy pendant from a delicate chain is **Hawaii**, the Big Island. Unlike the older islands, the Big Island doesn't have an abundance of spectacular cliffs and hidden valleys, and little of its shore has been pulverized into sandy beaches. But with at least two active volcanoes, the Big Island boasts scenery that delights and amazes. The east central coast is hot and humid, a perfect climate for the wild orchids that carpet its meadows and hillsides. Farther up the east coast, sugarcane fields cover the lower slopes of Mauna Kea, the 13,796-foot dormant volcano of the north, which is capped with snow in the winter. Between Mauna Kea and the northwest-facing peninsula of the Kohala Mountains is the high grassy plateau of the Parker cattle ranch, which is as close to country-style mainland landscape as any ranch in Texas.

As Mauna Kea dominates the north, so active Mauna Loa, called the long mountain, curves to embrace the southeast part of the island. Kilauea, the Big Island's other, intensely active volcano, sits in the shadow of Mauna Loa and is the center of Hawaii Volcanoes National Park. Covering 230,000 acres, the park encompasses scenery of startling variety — sterile landscapes of shiny black lava newly laid down; a barren and blasted desert where not even the sturdy kiawe tree grows; black sand beaches lined with majestic coco palms; and thick jungle where giant ferns grow in greens of incandescent intensity. The entire west coast exhibits signs of the volcanic process, too. Between patches of land denuded by lava flows is the lush greenery of resort cultivation. What resort-style beaches exist on the Big Island are here, but the sand on some is so shallow that it often gets carried away with the tide, leaving the rock shelf as exposed as a new layer of lava from Mauna Loa, which looms in the background.

Although these islands constitute the Hawaii currently available to visitors, the Hawaiian islands are not "finished." Even as you stand on the shore just south of Hawaii Volcanoes National Park, with Kilauea crackling and sputtering at your back, another Hawaiian island is being formed under the Pacific, only about 30 miles south of the spot on which you are standing. It's called **Loihi**, and this active volcanic cone, rising over 10,000 feet from the ocean floor, is gradually adding to its own size. Scientists say that it won't be too many centuries before another Hawaiian island begins to take shape *above* the surface, and who knows how many visitors will then have the opportunity to enjoy this as-yet-invisible atoll.

When to Go

There really isn't a "best" time to visit Hawaii. The winter months have long been — and remain — the peak travel period, traditionally the most popular time for an island getaway. It is important to emphasize, however, that due to the near-perfect weather year-round, more vacationers have begun to visit Hawaii during the so-called off-season; that is, in the spring, the fall, and — to some degree — the summer.

For some, the most convincing argument in favor of off-season travel is the economic one. Although the seasonal variance is less marked in Hawaii than in most other vacation destinations, getting there and staying there still is somewhat less expensive during the off-season. Airfares, hotel rooms, and car rental rates go down, less expensive package tours become available, and the independent traveler can go farther on less, too. What's more, major tourist attractions and facilities tend to be less crowded during the off-season, and — throughout the islands — life proceeds at a more leisurely pace.

It also should be noted that the months immediately before and after the peak winter months — what the travel industry refers to as the shoulder season (in Hawaii, around April and October) — often are sought out because they offer fair weather and somewhat smaller crowds. But be aware that very near high-season prices can prevail during these periods, especially in the most popular resort areas.

CLIMATE: In Hawaii, the four seasons are virtually indistinguishable, with good weather persisting throughout much of the year. Although readings as low as 30F have been recorded in Hawaii's mountainous regions, pleasant temperatures in the 80s and balmy trade wind breezes are more typical. Only the winter season (November to March) sees frequent, but normally passing, showers and temperatures that may drop into the 70s — and possibly the 60s. At any time of year an uncomfortable Kona wind may blow in from the south or west, bringing with it high humidity and clammy air, but like the rain, it passes quickly. And unlike the Caribbean islands, Hawaii has no formal hurricane season.

Travelers can get current readings and extended forecasts through *The Weather Channel Connection,* the worldwide weather report center of *The Weather Channel,* a cable television station. By dialing 900-WEATHER and punching in either the first four letters of the city — or, for the state of Hawaii, in some cases, the island — name or the area code for over 600 cities in the US, an up-to-date recording will provide such information as current temperature, barometric pressure, relative humidity, and wind speed, as well as a general 2-day forecast. (Seven-day extended forecasts, which are provided for some US cities, are not currently available for Hawaii.) Beach, boating, and highway reports are also provided for some locations. Callers also can access information on weather patterns for any time of the year in the area requested. For instance, to obtain the weather report for Honolulu, punch in HONO, the first four letters of the city name; alternatively, you could enter 808 (the area code for all of Hawaii) and then select from a list of islands and cities for which reports are available. Weather reports in Hawaii are available for the cities of Hilo, Honolulu, and Kahului, and by island for Lanai and Molokai. This 24-hour service can be accessed from any touch-tone phone in the US, and costs 95¢ per minute. The charge will show up on your phone bill. For additional information, contact *The Weather Channel Connection,* 2600 Cumberland Pkwy., Atlanta, GA 30339 (phone: 404-434-6800).

SPECIAL EVENTS: Travelers may want to schedule a trip to Hawaii to coincide with some special event, and Hawaii's benevolent climate ensures a full calendar of happenings that will enhance any vacation. In addition to the usual national holidays observed by the rest of the United States, Hawaiians enjoy many athletic competitions, music festivals, parades, ethnic fairs, and horticultural exhibits.

Listed below, according to the months in which they usually occur, are some of the most important festivities. For specific dates (and to guard against inevitable scheduling changes), it's best to check with the Hawaii Visitors Bureau, which regularly issues a comprehensive list. (For a list of the offices of the Visitors Bureau, see *Tourist Information Offices,* in this section.) More specific information also can be found in the chapters on the individual islands. It's always wise to call and reconfirm dates for the most current information.

January

Narcissus Festival: Lion dances, fireworks, a beauty contest, and a coronation ball in Honolulu's Chinatown. Celebrates the Chinese New Year. Oahu.

Hula Bowl Game: College football classic at *Aloha Stadium,* Honolulu, Oahu.

Opening of the State Legislature: Legislative sessions begin with speeches, hula demonstrations, leis, and Hawaiian music. Honolulu, Oahu.

Cherry Blossom Festival: A 4-month-long Japanese cultural celebration in Honolulu with tea ceremonies, flower arranging and cooking demonstrations, a fashion show, beauty contest, and coronation ball. Honolulu, Oahu.

Hawaiian Open International Golf Tournament: Part of the PGA tour, at *Waialae Golf and Country Club,* Honolulu, Oahu.

February

Maui Marine Art Expo: Top artists nationwide gather to display their marine works at *Maui Inter-Continental Wailea* hotel, Maui.

Pro Bowl: Annual football game featuring National Football League all-stars at *Aloha Stadium,* Honolulu, Oahu.

March

Hawaii Ski Cup/Mauna Kea Ski Meet: Open, international, and club downhill snow skiing races on the Big Island.

Maui Marathon: Annual marathon from Kahului to the *Kaanapali Whalers Village Shopping Complex* in Lahaina, Maui.

St. Patrick's Day: A parade plus Irish-flavored activities in Waikiki, Oahu.

Prince Kuhio Festival: One week of celebrations throughout the state commemorating Prince Jonah Kuhio Kalanianaole (1871–1922), Hawaii's first representative to Congress, with music and dance dating from his time.

Easter Sunrise Service: At the Punchbowl National Memorial Cemetery of the Pacific, in Honolulu, Oahu.

April

Merrie Monarch Festival: Competition among Hawaii's best hula schools, held in honor of Hawaii's last king, David Kalakaua (1836–1891). Hilo, the Big Island of Hawaii.

Na Mele O Maui: Hawaiian festival in Lahaina and Kaanapali with arts and crafts shows, luaus, and music and dance demonstrations. Maui.

Buddha Day: Various festivals held the first week in April at temples throughout the islands celebrate the birth of Buddha.

Tin Man Biathlon: A 2.7-mile run and an 800-meter swim at Ala Moana Beach Park. Honolulu, Oahu.

Annual Hawaiian Invitational International Music Festival: In Honolulu, a competition drawing international and island entrants, performing music from many genres — jazz, swing, symphonic, rock. Oahu.

Carol Kai Bed Race: Charity fund-raiser with decorated beds racing through the streets of Waikiki, Oahu.

Marui O'Neil International Windsurfing Tournament: Top international windsurfers compete at Maui's Hookipa Beach.

May

Lei Day: Everyone sports a lei on this holiday (*May Day* on the mainland) and enjoys lei making contests and exhibits. Honolulu, Oahu.

Pacific Handcrafters Guild Spring Fair: Crafts displays from Hawaii's finest artists. Ala Moana Park, Honolulu, Oahu.

Kona Gold Jackpot Tournament: Three-day game fishing competition for men on the Big Island.

Kona Golden Goddess Tournament: Two-day game fishing competition for women, also on the Big Island.

50th State Fair: An exposition featuring commercial exhibits, produce, food stalls, and entertainment. Honolulu, Oahu.

Steinlager Keauhou-Kona Triathlon: Tenth annual contest of athletic stamina including a 1.2-mile swim, 56-mile bicycle race, and 13.1-mile run held on the Big Island's west coast.

June

Kapalua Music Festival: Chamber music performed by the country's finest musicians. Kapalua, Maui.

Festival of the Pacific: A celebration of Pacific culture, including music, song, dance, and athletic competitions. Honolulu, Oahu.

King Kamehameha Celebration: State holiday honoring Kamehameha, who conquered and consolidated the Hawaiian islands and reigned as king at the turn of the 19th century; events include parades, arts and crafts exhibits, and hula and chant demonstrations. All islands.

Kona Stampede: A 26-year-old tradition of rodeo events in Honaunau on the Big Island is occasionally scheduled; check before you go.

July

Big Island Bonsai Show: Exhibitions and demonstrations of the Japanese art of the diminutive garden. Hilo, the Big Island.

July Victoria to Maui Yacht Race: Yacht race from Victoria, British Columbia, Canada, to Maui's *Lahaina Yacht Club.*

Makawao, Naalehu, and Parker Ranch Rodeos: Hawaiian cowboys — *paniolos* — do their stuff at these competitions on Maui and the Big Island.

Tin Man Triathlon: Triathletes gather at Ala Moana Park (Honolulu) to swim 800 meters, bike 25 miles, and complete a 6.2-mile run around Diamond Head to Queen Kapiolani Park (near Waikiki). Oahu.

Prince Lot Hula Festival: Traditional Hawaiian dances honor King Kamehameha V. Monalua Gardens, Honolulu, Oahu.

Koloa Plantation Days: Cultural celebration featuring parades, games, crafts, and luau. Kauai.

August

Hawaiian International Billfish Tournament: Marlin fishing competition held at Kailua-Kona on the Big Island.

Queen Liliuokalani Keiki Hula Competition: Hawaiian children participate in hula, costume, and native language competitions. Honolulu, Oahu.

Haleakala Run to the Sun: A 36-mile uphill run from Kahului to the top of Haleakala Crater on Maui.

September

Aloha Week Festival: Successive festivals on each island add up to a full month of activities and events, including luaus, parades, crafts shows, a royal ball, and the famous 27½-mile canoe race from Molokai to Oahu.

Waikiki Annual Rough Water Swim: A 2-mile swim meet from Oahu's Sans Souci Beach to Duke Kahanamoku Beach, open to all ages and levels of skill.

October

Ironman World Triathlon Championship: One of two triathlons (the other is in Nice, in the south of France) that claims to be the "world" championship, this grueling competition — a 2.4-mile swim, a 112-mile bike ride, and a 26.2-mile run — begins and ends at Kailua-Kona on the Big Island.

Bankoh Molokai Hou: About 50 teams race canoes across the rough Molokai channel to Oahu, finishing at Fort DeRussy in Waikiki.

Waimea Falls Makahiki Festival: Hawaiian foods, crafts, games, music, and hula exhibitions on Oahu's North Shore.

Annual Orchid Plant & Flower Show: Largest orchid exhibition in the islands, in *Blaisdell Center,* Honolulu, Oahu.

Pearl Harbor Aloha Festival: Largest military fair of its kind. Pearl Harbor, Oahu.

Peter Stuyvesant Aloha Classic: Wave surfing at Maui's Hookipa Beach.

November

Maui Invitational: College basketball's finest in a pre-season tournament. Lahaina, Maui.

Academy Folk Art Bazaar: Pre-holiday sale of folk art pieces and ornaments from around the world. *Honolulu Academy of Arts,* Oahu.

Christmas Fair: At the *Mission Houses Museum* in Honolulu, crafts including *Christmas* items are sold in an open market. Oahu.

December

Triple Crown of Surfing: World's top pros compete — dates and time depend on wave action. Oahu.

Bodhi Day: Ceremonies at Buddhist temples throughout the islands commemorate the "Day of Enlightenment."

Pearl Harbor Day: A service at the USS *Arizona* memorial and a veteran's parade honor those killed on December 7, 1941. Honolulu, Oahu.

Annual Honolulu Marathon: A 26-mile race beginning at Aloha Tower and ending at Kapiolani Park. Honolulu, Oahu.

Hawaiian Pro Surfing Championships: The islands' most important surfing competition, at the Banzai Pipeline on Oahu's North Shore.

Eagle Aloha Bowl: Collegiate football at *Aloha Stadium,* Oahu.

Traveling by Plane

For the traveler who lacks a rich uncle willing to lend his private yacht, it's probable that flying will be the mode of transportation used to get to the 50th state. Despite recent attempts at price simplification by a number of major US carriers, the airlines offering flights to Hawaii continue to sell seats at a variety of prices under a vast spectrum of requirements and restrictions. Since you probably will spend more for your airfare than for any other single item in your travel budget, try to take advantage of the lowest fares offered by either scheduled or charter companies. You should know what kinds of flights are available, the rules under which air travel operates, and all the special package options.

SCHEDULED FLIGHTS: Airlines offering regularly scheduled flights from the mainland to Hawaii, most on a daily basis, are: *American, America West, Continental, Delta, Hawaiian Airlines, Northwest, TWA,* and *United.* In addition, new discount carriers frequently enter the market for a brief period, then disappear.

As of this writing, direct flights — usually with no change of plane between the originating and terminating US cities (though the flight may not be nonstop) depart from Atlanta, Boston, Chicago, Dallas/Fort Worth, Denver, Detroit, Houston, Los Angeles, Minneapolis/St. Paul, New York/Newark, St. Louis, Salt Lake City, San Diego, San Francisco/Oakland, Seattle/Tacoma, and Washington, DC. This lineup is, however, subject to frequent change, so check current schedules carefully before making final arrangements. (Occasionally, an airline will require a change of aircraft, but as long as the flight number is the same, the flight still is considered a direct one.) Nonstop flights depart from all of the West Coast cities noted above.Elsewhere, only Anchorage, Atlanta, Chicago, Cincinnati, Dallas/Fort Worth, Denver, Las Vegas, Phoenix, and St. Louis have nonstop service.

Most flights land at Honolulu International Airport on Oahu, though direct service from the mainland to the neighbor islands, especially Maui, has been increasing steadily. For example, *United* flies to the four major islands with nonstop or connecting service via Honolulu and flies nonstop to Kahului on Maui from Los Angeles and San Francisco, and to Kailua-Kona on the Big Island from San Francisco. *American* also flies nonstop and direct to Maui from Los Angeles, and direct from Salt Lake City and Atlanta.

The flying time from Los Angeles to Honolulu is about 5½ hours; nonstop flights from Atlanta and Chicago take about 8½ hours each. Nonstop flights from Dallas/Fort Worth will be in the air a little under 7½ hours; from Denver, 7½ hours. Although, at the time of this writing, nonstop service from New York to Honolulu was not available, a one-stop flight from New York usually spends approximately 11 hours in the air, to which about 1½ hours on the ground at an intermediate stop should be added. Return flights (west to east) are slightly shorter due to tail winds.

A number of foreign airlines stop in Honolulu on Oahu on their way from the mainland US to foreign cities, but they are prohibited by law (the Jones Act of 1896, which originally was intended to be applied only to ships) from carrying passengers solely between two points in the US. You are permitted to fly to Hawaii aboard a foreign carrier if your visit there is a stop en route to a foreign destination, however, and you may use a foreign carrier to fly to Hawaii from a foreign city. If you live closer to Vancouver, Canada, than to any US gateway, there's no reason not to fly *Air Canada*'s, *Canadian Airlines International*'s, or *Quantas*'s nonstop service to Honolulu. As of this writing, *Canadian Air* also flies direct from Toronto to Honolulu.

Tickets – When traveling on one of the many regularly scheduled flights, a full-fare ticket provides maximum travel flexibility (although at considerable expense) because there are no advance booking requirements. A prospective passenger can buy a ticket for a flight right up to the minute of takeoff — if a seat is available. If your ticket is for a round trip, you can make the return reservation whenever you wish — months before you leave or the day before you return. (Tickets generally are good for a year and can be renewed if not used.) On some airlines, you may be able to cancel your flight at any time without penalty, on others, cancellation — even of a full-fare ticket — may be subject to a variety of restrictions. It pays to check *before* booking your flight. In addition, while it is true that this category of ticket can be purchased at the last minute, it is advisable to reserve well in advance during popular vacation periods and around holiday times.

Fares – Airfares continue to change so rapidly that even the experts find it difficult to keep up with them. This ever-changing situation is due to a number of factors, including airline deregulation, volatile labor relations, increasing fuel costs, and vastly increased competition.

Perhaps the most common misconception about fares on scheduled airlines is that the cost of the ticket determines how much service will be provided on the flight. This is true only to a certain extent. A far more realistic rule of thumb is that the less you pay for your ticket, the more restrictions and qualifications are likely to come into play before you board the plane (as well as after you get off). These qualifying aspects relate to the months (and the days of the week) during which you must travel, how far in advance you must purchase your ticket, the minimum and maximum amount of time you may or must remain away, your willingness to decide on a return date at the time of booking — and your ability to stick to that decision. It is not uncommon for passengers sitting side by side on the same wide-body jet to have paid fares varying by hundreds of dollars, and all too often the traveler paying more would have been equally willing (and able) to accept the terms of the far less expensive ticket.

In general, the great variety of airfares to Hawaii can be reduced to four basic categories, including first class, coach (also called economy or tourist class), and excursion or discount fares. A fourth category, called business class, has been added by many airlines in recent years. In addition, Advance Purchase Excursion (APEX) fares offer savings under certain conditions.

A **first class** ticket is your admission to the special section of the aircraft, with larger seats, more legroom, sleeperette seating on some wide-body aircraft, better (or more elaborately served) food, free drinks and headsets for movies and music channels, and above all, personal attention. First class fares are about twice those of full-fare economy, although both first class passengers and those paying full-fare economy fares are entitled to reserve seats and are sold tickets on an open reservation system. An additional advantage of a first class ticket is that if you're planning to visit other cities in the US, you may include any number of stops en route to or from Hawaii, provided that these cities are regular stopovers on flights to Hawaii. For instance, if you book a flight between New York and Hawaii and the flight normally includes a stopover in Los Angeles, you may stay in Los Angeles for several days before continuing on to the islands.

Not too long ago, there were only two classes of air travel, first class and all the rest, usually called economy or tourist. Then **business class** came into being — one of the most successful recent airline innovations. At first, business class passengers were merely curtained off from the other economy passengers. Now a separate cabin or cabins — usually toward the front of the plane — is the norm. While standards of comfort and service are not as high as in first class, they represent a considerable improvement over conditions in the rear of the plane, with roomier seats, more leg and shoulder space between passengers, and fewer seats abreast. Free liquor and headsets, a choice of meal entrées, and a separate counter for speedier check-in are other inducements. As in first class, a business class passenger may travel on any scheduled flight he or she wishes, may buy a one-way or round-trip ticket, and have the ticket remain valid for a year. There are no minimum or maximum stay requirements, no advance booking requirements, and no cancellation penalties, and the fare allows the same free stopover privileges as first class. Airlines often have their own names for their business class service — such as Medallion Class on *Delta* and Ambassador Class on *TWA*.

The terms of the **coach** or **economy** fare may vary slightly from airline to airline, and, in fact, from time to time airlines may be selling more than one type of economy fare. Coach or economy passengers sit more snugly, as many as 10 in a single row on a wide-body jet, behind the first class and business class sections. Normally, alcoholic drinks are not free, nor are the headsets. If there are two economy fares on the books, one (often called "regular economy") still may include several free stopovers. The other, less expensive fare (often called "special economy") may limit stopovers to one or two, with a charge (typically $25) for each one. Like first class passengers, travelers paying the full coach fare are subject to none of the restrictions that usually are attached to less expensive excursion and discount fares. There are no advance booking requirements, no minimum stay requirements, and (often) no cancellation penalties — but beware, the rules regarding cancellation vary from carrier to carrier. Tickets are sold on an open reservation system: They can be bought for a flight right up to the minute of takeoff (if seats are available), and if the ticket is round-trip, the return reservation can be made any time you wish. Both first class and coach tickets generally are good for a year, after which they can be renewed if not used, and if you ultimately decide not to fly at all, your money may be refunded (again, policies vary). The cost of economy and business class tickets to Hawaii does not vary much in the course of the year, though on some routes they may vary from a basic (low-season) price in effect most of the year to a peak (high-season) price during the winter.

Excursions and other **discount** fares are the airlines' equivalent of a special sale and usually apply to round-trip bookings only. These fares generally differ according to the season and the number of travel days permitted. They are only a bit less flexible than full-fare economy tickets, and are, therefore, often useful for both business and holiday travelers. Most round-trip excursion tickets include strict minimum and maximum stay requirements and can be changed only within the specified time limits. So don't count on extending a ticket beyond the prescribed time of return or staying less time than required. Different airlines may have different regulations concerning the number of stopovers permitted, and sometimes excursion fares are less expensive during midweek. The availability of these reduced-rate seats is most limited at busy times such as holidays. Discount- or excursion-fare ticket holders sit with the coach passengers and, for all intents and purposes, are indistinguishable from them. They receive all the same basic services, even though they may have paid anywhere between 30% and 55% less for the trip. Obviously, it's wise to make plans early enough to qualify for this less expensive transportation if possible.

These discount or excursion fares may masquerade under a variety of names, they may vary from city to city (from the East Coast to the West Coast, especially), but they invariably have strings attached. A common requirement is that the ticket be purchased a certain number of days — usually between 7 and 21 days — in advance of departure, though it may be booked weeks or months in advance (it has to be "ticketed," or paid for, shortly after booking, however). The return reservation usually has to be made at the time of the original ticketing and often cannot be changed later than a certain number of days (again, usually 7 to 21 days) before the return flight. If events force a change in the return reservation after the date allowed, the passenger may have to pay the difference between the round-trip excursion rate and the round-trip coach rate, although some carriers permit such scheduling changes for a nominal fee. In addition, some airlines may allow passengers to use their discounted fares by standing by for an empty seat, even if they don't otherwise have standby fares. Another common condition is a minimum and maximum stay requirement; for example, 1 to 6 days or 6 to 14 days (but including at least a Saturday night). Last, cancellation penalties of up to 50% of the full price of the ticket have been assessed — if a refund is offered at all — so check the specific penalty in effect when you purchase your discount/excursion ticket.

On some airlines, the ticket bearing the lowest price of all the current discount fares is the ticket where no change at all in departure and/or return flights is permitted, and where the ticket price is totally nonrefundable. If you do buy such a nonrefundable ticket, you should be aware of a policy followed by some airlines that may make it easier to change your plans if necessary. For a fee — set by each airline and payable at the airport when checking in — you *may* be able to change the time or date of a return flight on a nonrefundable ticket. However, if the nonrefundable ticket price for the replacement flight is higher than that of the original (as often is the case when trading in a weekday for a weekend flight), you will have to pay the difference. Any such change must be made a certain number of days in advance — in some cases as little as 2 days — of either the original or the replacement flight, whichever is earlier; restrictions are set by the individual carrier. (Travelers holding a nonrefundable or other restricted ticket who must change their plans due to a family emergency should know that some carriers may make special allowances in such situations; for further information, see *Staying Healthy,* in this section.)

■ **Note:** Due to recent changes in many US airlines' policies, nonrefundable tickets are now available that carry none of the above restrictions. Although passengers still may *not* be able to obtain a refund for the price paid, the time or date of a departing or return flight may be changed at any time (assuming seats are available) for a nominal service charge.

There also is a newer, often less expensive, type of excursion fare, the **APEX**, or **Advance Purchase Excursion,** fare. As with traditional excursion fares, passengers paying an APEX fare sit with and receive the same basic services as any other coach or economy passenger, even though they may have paid up to 50% less for their seats. In return, they are subject to certain restrictions. In the case of flights to Hawaii, the ticket usually is good for a minimum of 7 days in the islands and a maximum, currently, of 2 to 6 months (depending on the airline and destination); and as its name implies, it must be "ticketed," or paid for in its entirety, a certain period of time before departure — usually 14 to 21 days.

The drawback to some APEX fares is that they penalize travelers who change their minds — and travel plans. Usually the return reservation must be made at the time of the original ticketing, and if for some reason you change your schedule while traveling, you will have to pay a penalty of $100 or 10% of the ticket value, whichever is greater, as long as you travel within the validity period of your ticket. More flexible APEX fares recently have been introduced, which allow travelers to make changes in the date or time of their flights for a nominal charge (as low as $25).

With either type of APEX fare, if you change your return to a date less than the minimum stay or more than the maximum stay, the difference between the round-trip APEX fare and the full round-trip coach rate will have to be paid. There also is a penalty of anywhere from $75 to $125 or more for canceling or changing a reservation *before* travel begins — check the specific penalty in effect when you purchase your ticket. APEX fares to Hawaii are sold at basic (off-season) and peak (winter) rates, and may include surcharges for weekend flights.

Standby fares, at one time the rock-bottom price at which a traveler could fly to Hawaii, have become elusive. At the time of this writing, most major scheduled airlines did not regularly offer standby fares on direct flights to Hawaii. Because airline fares and their conditions constantly change, however, bargain hunters should not hesitate to ask if such a fare exists at the time they plan to travel.

While the definition of standby varies somewhat from airline to airline, it generally means that you make yourself available to buy a ticket for a flight (usually no sooner than the day of departure), then literally stand by on the chance that a seat will be empty. Once aboard, however, a standby passenger has the same meal service and frills (or lack of them) enjoyed by others in the economy class compartment.

Something else to check is the possibility of qualifying for a **GIT** (Group Inclusive Travel) fare, which requires that a specific dollar amount of ground arrangements be purchased, in advance, along with the ticket. The requirements vary as to the number of travel days and stopovers permitted, and the minimum number of passengers required for a group. The actual fares also vary, but the cost will be spelled out in brochures distributed by the tour operators handling the ground arrangements. In the past, GIT fares were among the least expensive available from the established carriers, but the prevalence of discount fares has caused group fares to all but disappear from some air routes. Travelers reading brochures on group package tours to Hawaii will find that, in almost all cases, the applicable airfare given as a sample (to be added to the price of the land package to obtain the total tour price) is an APEX fare, the same discount fare available to the independent traveler.

The major airlines serving Hawaii from the mainland also may offer individual excursion-fare rates similar to GIT fares, which are sold in conjunction with ground accommodation packages. Previously called ITX, and sometimes referred to as individual tour-basing fares, these fares generally are offered as part of "air/hotel/car/transfer packages," and can reduce the cost of an economy fare by more than a third. The packages are booked for a specific amount of time, with return dates specified; rescheduling and cancellation restrictions and penalties vary from carrier to carrier. At the time of this writing, this type of fare was offered to Hawaii by *American, America West, Continental, Delta, Northwest, TWA,* and *United,* and although their offerings did not represent substantial savings over standard economy fare, it is worth checking at the time you plan to travel. (For further information on package options, see *Package Tours,* in this section.)

Travelers looking for the least expensive possible airfares should, finally, scan the pages of their hometown newspapers (especially the Sunday travel sections) for announcements of special promotional fares. Most airlines offer their most attractive special fares to encourage travel during slow seasons, and to inaugurate and publicize new routes. Even if none of these factors applies, prospective passengers can be fairly sure that the number of discount seats per flight at the lowest price is strictly limited, or that the fare offering includes a set expiration date — which means it's absolutely necessary to move fast to enjoy the lowest possible price.

Among other special airline promotional deals for which you should be on the lookout are discount or upgrade coupons sometimes offered by the major carriers and found in mail order merchandise catalogues. For instance, airlines sometimes issue coupons that typically cost around $25 each and are good for a percentage discount or an upgrade on an international or domestic airline ticket — including flights to Hawaii. The only requirement beyond the fee generally is that a coupon purchaser must buy at least one item from the catalogue. There usually are some minimum airfare restrictions before the coupon is redeemable, but in general these are worthwhile offers. Restrictions often include certain blackout days (when the coupon cannot be used at all), usually imposed during peak travel periods. These coupons are particularly valuable to business travelers who tend to buy full-fare tickets, and they can be used by others who are traveling on the same itinerary.

It's always wise to ask about discount or promotional fares and about any conditions that might restrict booking, payment, cancellation, and changes in plans. Check the prices from neighboring cities. A special rate may be offered in a nearby city but not in yours, and it may be enough of a bargain to warrant your leaving from that city. Ask if there is a difference in price for midweek versus weekend travel, or if there is a further discount for traveling early in the morning or late at night. Also be sure to investigate package deals, which are offered by virtually every airline. These may include a car rental, accommodations, and dining and/or sightseeing features, in addition to the basic airfare, and the combined cost of packaged elements usually is considerably less than the cost of the exact same elements when purchased separately.

If in the course of your research you come across a deal that seems too good to be true, keep in mind that logic may not be a component of deeply discounted airfares — there's not always any sane relationship between miles to be flown and the price to get there. More often than not, the level of competition on a given route dictates the degree of discount, and don't be dissuaded from accepting an offer that sounds irresistible just because it also sounds illogical. Better to buy that inexpensive fare while it's being offered and worry about the sense — or absence thereof — while you're flying to your desired destination.

When you're satisfied that you've found the lowest possible price for which you can conveniently qualify (you may have to call the airline more than once, because different airline reservations clerks have been known to quote different prices), make your booking. Then, to protect yourself against fare increases, purchase and pay for your ticket as soon as possible after you've received a confirmed reservation. Airlines generally will honor their tickets, even if the operative price at the time of your flight is higher than the price you paid; if fares go up between the time you *reserve* a flight and the time you *pay* for it, you likely will be out of luck. Finally, with excursion or discount fares, it is important to remember that when a reservations clerk says that you must purchase a ticket by a specific date, this is an absolute deadline. Miss the deadline and the airline may automatically cancel your reservation without telling you.

■ **Note:** Another wrinkle in the airfare scene is that if the fares go *down* after you purchase your ticket, you *may* be entitled to a refund of the difference. However, this is only possible in certain situations — availability and advance purchase restrictions pertaining to the lower rate are set by the airline. If you suspect that you may be able to qualify for such a refund, check with your travel agent or the airline.

Frequent Flyers – Most of the leading carriers serving Hawaii offer offer a bonus system to frequent travelers. After the first 10,000 miles, for example, a passenger might be eligible for a first class seat for the coach fare; after another 10,000 miles, he or she might receive a discount on his or her next ticket purchase. The value of the bonuses continues to increase as more miles are logged.

Bonus miles also may be earned by patronizing affiliated car rental companies or hotel chains, or by using one of the credit cards that now offer this reward. In deciding whether to accept such a credit card from one of the issuing organizations that tempt you with frequent flyer mileage bonuses on a specific airline, first determine whether the interest rate charged on the unpaid balance is the same as (or less than) possible alternate credit cards, and whether the annual "membership" fee also is equal or lower. If these charges are slightly higher than those of competing cards, weigh the difference against the potential value in airfare savings. Also ask about any bonus miles awarded just for signing up — 1,000 is common, 5,000 generally the maximum.

For the most up-to-date information on frequent flyer bonus options, you may want to send for the monthly newsletter *Frequent.* Issued by Frequent Publications, it provides current information about frequent flyer plans in general, as well as specific data about promotions, awards, and combination deals to help you keep track of the profusion — and confusion — of current and upcoming availabilities. For a year's subscription, send $33 to Frequent Publications, 4715-C Town Center Dr., Colorado Springs, CO 80916 (phone: 800-333-5937).

There also is a monthly magazine called *Frequent Flyer,* but unlike the newsletter mentioned above, its focus is primarily on newsy articles of interest to business travelers and other frequent flyers. Published by Official Airline Guides (PO Box 58543, Boulder, CO 80322-8543; phone: 800-323-3537), *Frequent Flyer* is available for $24 for a 1-year subscription.

Low-Fare Airlines – Increasingly, in today's economic climate, the stimulus for special fares is the appearance of new airlines associated with bargain rates. On these airlines, all seats generally sell for the same price, which tends to be somewhat below the lowest discount fare offered by the larger, more established airlines. It is important to note that tickets offered by these smaller companies frequently are not subject to the same restrictions as some of the discounted fares offered by the more established carriers. They may not require advance purchase or minimum and maximum stays, may involve no cancellation penalties, and may be available one way or round-trip. A disadvantage to many of the low-fare airlines, however, is that when something goes wrong, such as delayed baggage or a flight cancellation due to equipment breakdown, their smaller fleets and fewer flights mean that passengers may have to wait longer for a solution than they would on one of the equipment-rich major carriers.

Inter-Island Air Travel – The cost of the round trip across the Pacific is not the only air travel expense to consider. The airplane also is the quickest means of island-hopping in Hawaii and, although relatively inexpensive, the cost of these flights can add up. Two inter-island carriers — *Hawaiian Airlines* and *Aloha Airlines* — connect major island airports with numerous flights daily, and other smaller commuter lines serve both the large and small airports with frequent flights.

There's not a lot of variation in the fares charged by the various inter-island carriers, and fares on the smaller lines, which used to be among the best bargains in the islands, generally are comparable to those offered by the major airlines, though they may be a few dollars lower. Still, if you plan to do a lot of traveling between islands, it would pay to look into the various discounts offered by inter-island carriers. *Aloha* and *Hawaiian* both have discount fares that are about 10% to 30% less expensive than full fares. These low fares usually are available for a limited number of seats on selected flights — often the first or last flight of the day. Both carriers have also recently introduced economical air passes which permit unlimited inter-island travel over a specified period of time. For example, *Hawaiian Airlines* offers the Hawaiian AirPass, which is valid for periods of 5, 7, 10, and 14 days. Discounts for children are available on most airlines, while discounts for senior citizens are less common and less generous. Note: Joint fares, once available to passengers holding a round-trip ticket on a scheduled flight between Hawaii and the continental US or Canada, have been discontinued.

A roundup of the airlines operating within Hawaii, and the routes they fly, follows. Keep in mind that the smaller of these lines probably won't get you to your destination as quickly as the biggest carrier, but the smaller planes generally used fly at lower altitudes and will provide a more scenic view en route. Also, be aware that the baggage allowance on small aircraft may not be as generous as on larger planes.

Aloha Airlines (phone: 800-367-5250). This carrier provides extensive service between and within Oahu, the Big Island, Maui, and Kauai aboard 737s. It offers service to Molokai and Lanai through its sister carrier, *Aloha IslandAir.*

Hawaiian Airlines (phone: 800-367-5320). The oldest of the major inter-island carriers flies to more island airports than its competitors, using mainly DC-9s. Its service to and from Molokai and Lanai and on some flights to Maui uses 50-passenger De Havilland Dash-7 turboprops.

Panorama Air (phone: 800-367-2671). Links Honolulu and Molokai aboard 9-passenger Piper Chieftains.

Reservations – For those who don't have the time and patience to investigate personally all possible air departures and connections for a proposed trip, a travel agent can be of inestimable help. A good agent should have all the information on which flights go where and when, and which categories of tickets are available on each. Most have computerized reservation links with the major carriers, so that a seat can be reserved and confirmed in minutes. An increasing number of agents also possess fare-comparison computer programs, so they often are very reliable sources of detailed competitive price data. (For more information, see *How to Use a Travel Agent,* in this section.)

When making reservations through a travel agent, ask the agent to give the airline your home phone number, as well as your daytime business phone number. All too often the agent uses the agency number as the official contact for changes in flight plans. Especially during the winter, weather conditions hundreds or even thousands of miles away can wreak havoc with flight schedules. Aircraft are constantly in use, and a plane delayed in the Orient or on the East Coast can miss its scheduled flight from the West Coast the next morning. The airlines are fairly reliable about getting this sort of information to passengers if they can reach them; diligence does little good at 10 PM if the airline has only the agency's or an office number.

Reconfirmation is not usually required on domestic flights. However, it is still a good idea to call ahead to make sure that the airline did not slip up in entering your original reservation, or in registering any changes you may have made since, and that it has your seat reservation and/or special meal request in the computer. If you look at the printed information on your ticket, you'll see the airline's reconfirmation policy stated explicitly. Don't be lulled into a false sense of security by the "OK" on your ticket next to the number and time of the flight. This only means that a reservation has been entered; a reconfirmation still may be necessary. If in doubt — call.

If you plan not to take a flight on which you hold a confirmed reservation, by all means inform the airline. Because the problem of "no-shows" is a constant expense for airlines, they are allowed to overbook flights, a practice that often contributes to the threat of denied boarding for a certain number of passengers (see "Getting Bumped," below).

Seating – For most types of tickets, airline seats usually are assigned on a first-come, first-served basis at check-in, although some airlines make it possible to reserve a seat at the time of ticket purchase. Always check in early for your flight, even with advance seat assignments. A good rule of thumb for domestic flights is to arrive at the airport *at least* 1 hour before the scheduled departure to give yourself plenty of time in case there are long lines.

Most airlines furnish seating charts, which make choosing a seat much easier, but there are a few basics to consider. You must decide whether you prefer a window, aisle, or middle seat. On domestic flights longer than 6 hours where smoking is permitted, you also should indicate if you prefer the smoking or nonsmoking section.

The amount of legroom provided (as well as chest room, especially when the seat in front of you is in a reclining position) is determined by something called "pitch," a measure of the distance between the back of the seat in front of you and the front of the back of your seat. The amount of pitch is a matter of airline policy, not the type of plane you fly. First class and business class seats have the greatest pitch, a fact that figures prominently in airline advertising. In economy class or coach, the standard pitch ranges from 33 to as little as 31 inches — downright cramped.

The number of seats abreast, another factor determining comfort, depends on a combination of airline policy and airplane dimensions. First class and business class have the fewest seats per row. Economy generally has 9 seats per row on a DC-10 or an L-1011, making either one slightly more comfortable than a 747, on which there normally are 10 seats per row. Charter flights on DC-10s and L-1011s, however, often have 10 seats per row and can be noticeably more cramped than 747 charters, on which the seating normally remains at 10 per row.

Airline representatives claim that most aircraft are more stable toward the front and midsection, while seats farthest from the engines are quietest. Passengers who have long legs and are traveling on a wide-body aircraft might request a seat directly behind a door or emergency exit, since these seats often have greater than average pitch, or a seat in the first row of a given section, which offers extra legroom — although these seats are increasingly being reserved for passengers who are willing (and able) to perform certain tasks in the event of emergency evacuation. It often is impossible, however, to see the movie from these seats, which are directly behind the plane's exits. Be aware that the first row of the economy section (called a "bulkhead" seat) on a conventional aircraft (not a widebody) does *not* offer extra legroom, since the fixed partition will not permit passengers to slide their feet under it, and that watching a movie from this first-row seat can be difficult and uncomfortable. These bulkhead seats do, however, provide ample room to use a bassinet or safety seat and often are reserved for families traveling with children.

A window seat protects you from aisle traffic and clumsy serving carts and also provides a view, while an aisle seat enables you to get up and stretch your legs without disturbing anyone. Middle seats are the least desirable, and seats in the last row are the worst of all, since they seldom recline fully. If you wish to avoid children on your flight or if you find that you are sitting in an especially noisy section, you usually are free to move to any unoccupied seat — if there is one.

If you are overweight, you may face the prospect of a long flight with special trepidation. Center seats in the alignments of wide-body 747s, L-1011s, and DC-10s are about 1½ inches wider than those on either side, so larger travelers tend to be more comfortable there.

Despite all these rules of thumb, finding out which specific rows are near emergency exits or at the front of a wide-body cabin can be difficult because seating arrangements on two otherwise identical planes vary from airline to airline. There is, however, a quarterly publication called *Airline Seating Guide* that publishes seating charts for most major US airlines and many foreign carriers as well. Your travel agent should have a copy, or you can buy the US edition for $39.95 per year. Order from Carlson Publishing Co., Box 888, Los Alamitos, CA 90720 (phone: 800-728-4877 or 213-493-4877).

Simply reserving an airline seat in advance, however, actually may guarantee very little. Most airlines require that passengers arrive at the departure gate at least 45 minutes (sometimes more) ahead of time to hold a seat reservation. They may cancel seat assignments and may not honor reservations of passengers who have not checked in some period of time — usually around 45 minutes, depending on the airline and airport — before the scheduled departure time, and they *ask* travelers to check in at least 1 hour before all domestic flights. It pays to read the fine print on your ticket carefully and plan ahead.

A far better strategy is to visit an airline ticket office (or one of a select group of travel agents) to secure an actual boarding pass for your specific flight. Once this has been issued, airline computers show you as checked in, and you effectively own the seat you have selected (although some carriers may not honor boarding passes of passengers arriving at the gate less than 10 minutes before departure). This also is good — but not foolproof — insurance against getting bumped from an overbooked flight and is, therefore, an especially valuable tactic at peak travel times.

Smoking – One decision regarding choosing a seat has been taken out of the hands of most travelers who smoke. Effective February 25, 1990, the US government imposed a ban that prohibits smoking on all flights scheduled for 6 hours or less within the US and its territories. The new regulation applies to both domestic and international carriers serving these routes.

In the case of flights to Hawaii, only those with a *continuous* flight time of over 6 hours between stops in the US or its territories are exempt. Smoking is not permitted on flights where the flight time between US landings is under 6 hours — for instance, flights that include a stopover (even with no change of plane), or connecting flights. To further complicate the situation, several individual carriers are banning smoking altogether on certain routes.

On those flights that do permit smoking, the US Department of Transportation has determined that nonsmoking sections must be enlarged to accommodate all passengers who wish to sit in one. The airline does not, however, have to shift seating to accommodate nonsmokers who arrive late for a flight or travelers flying standby. Cigar and pipe smoking are prohibited on all flights, even in the smoking sections.

For a wallet-size guide, which notes in detail the rights of nonsmokers according to these regulations, send a self-addressed, stamped envelope to *ASH (Action on Smoking and Health),* Airline Card, 2013 H St. NW, Washington, DC 20006 (phone: 202-659-4310).

Meals – If you have specific dietary requirements, be sure to let the airline know well before departure time. The available meals include vegetarian, seafood, kosher, Muslim, Hindu, high-protein, low-calorie, low-cholesterol, low-fat, low-sodium, diabetic, bland, and children's menus (not all may be available on every carrier). There is no extra charge for this option. It usually is necessary to request special meals when you make your reservations — check-in time is too late. It's also wise to reconfirm that your request for a special meal has made its way into the airline's computer — the time to do this is 24 hours before departure.

Baggage – Though airline baggage allowances vary slightly, in general all passengers are allowed to carry on board, without charge, one piece of luggage that will fit easily under a seat of the plane or in an overhead bin and whose combined dimensions (length, width, and depth) do not exceed 45 inches. (If you prefer not to carry it with you, most airlines will allow you to check this bag in the hold.) A reasonable amount of reading material, camera equipment, and a handbag also are allowed. In addition, all passengers are allowed to check two bags in the cargo hold: one usually not to exceed 62 inches when length, width, and depth are combined, the other not to exceed 55 inches in combined dimensions. Generally no single bag may weigh more than 70 pounds. Note that the weight restriction, however, may be lower on small inter-island carriers — it pays to check in advance.

Charges for additional, oversize, or overweight bags usually are made at a flat rate; the actual dollar amount varies from carrier to carrier. If you plan to travel with any special equipment or sporting gear, be sure to check with the airline beforehand. Most have specific procedures for handling such baggage, and you may have to pay for transport regardless of how much other baggage you have checked. Golf clubs may be checked through as luggage (most airlines are accustomed to handling them), but tennis rackets should be carried onto the plane. Aqualung tanks, depressurized and appropriately packed with padding, and surfboards (minus the fin and padded) also may go as baggage. Snorkeling gear should be packed in a suitcase, duffel bag, or tote bag. Some airlines require that bicycles be partially dismantled and packaged (see *Camping and RVs, Hiking and Biking,* in this section).

Airline policies regarding baggage allowances for children vary and usually are based on the percentage of full adult fare paid. Although on many US carriers children who are ticket holders are entitled to the same baggage allowance as a full-fare passenger, some carriers allow only one bag per child, which sometimes must be smaller than an adult's bag (around 39 to 45 inches in combined dimensions). Often there is no luggage allowance for a child traveling on an adult's lap or in a bassinet. It's always wise to check ahead. (For more information, see *Hints for Traveling with Children,* in this section.)

To reduce the chances of your luggage going astray, remove all airline tags from previous trips, label each bag inside and out — with your business address rather than your home address on the outside, to prevent thieves from knowing whose house might be unguarded. Lock everything and double-check the tag that the airline attaches to make sure that it is coded correctly for your destination: HNL for Honolulu International Airport on Oahu and OGG for Kahului Airport on Maui, for instance.

If your bags are not in the baggage claim area after your flight, or if they're damaged, report the problem to airline personnel immediately. Keep in mind that policies regarding the specific time limit within which you have to make your claim vary from carrier to carrier. Fill out a report form on your lost or damaged luggage and keep a copy of it and your original baggage claim check. If you must surrender the check to claim a damaged bag, get a receipt for it to prove that you did, indeed, check your baggage on the flight. If luggage is missing, be sure to give the airline your destination and/or a telephone number where you can be reached. Also, take the name and number of the person in charge of recovering lost luggage.

Most airlines have emergency funds for passengers stranded away from home without their luggage, but if it turns out your bags are truly lost and not simply delayed, do not then and there sign any paper indicating you'll accept an offered settlement. Since the airline is responsible for the value of your bags within certain statutory limits ($1,250 per passenger for lost baggage on a domestic US flight), you should take some time to assess the extent of your loss (see *Insurance,* in this section). It's a good idea to keep records indicating the value of the contents of your luggage. A wise alternative is to take a Polaroid picture of the most valuable of your packed items just after putting them in your suitcase.

Considering the increased incidence of damage to baggage, it's now more than ever a good idea to keep the sales slips that confirm how much you paid for your bags. These are invaluable in establishing the value of damaged baggage and eliminate any arguments. A better way to protect your precious gear from the luggage-eating conveyers is to try to carry it on board wherever possible.

Airline Clubs – US and some foreign carriers often have clubs for travelers who either pay for membership or are awarded membership based on a combination of miles flown and/or class of service chosen. (These clubs are not solely for first class passengers, although a first class ticket *may* entitle a passenger to a club's lounge privileges.) Membership entitles the traveler to use of the private lounges at airports along their route, to refreshments served in these lounges, and to check-cashing privileges at most of their counters. Extras include special telephone numbers for individual reservations, embossed luggage tags, and a membership card for identification. Airlines serving Hawaii that offer membership in such clubs include the following:

American: The *Admirals Club.* Single yearly membership $225; $125 yearly thereafter; spouse an additional $70 per year.

Delta: The *Crown Club.* Single yearly membership $150; spouse an additional $50 per year.

Northwest: The *World Club.* Single yearly membership $190 for the first year; $140 yearly thereafter; spouse an additional $50 per year; 3-year and lifetime memberships also available.

TWA: The *Ambassador Club.* Single yearly membership $150; spouse an additional $25 per year; lifetime memberships also available.

United: The *Red Carpet Club.* There is a onetime $100 initiation fee; single yearly membership $125; spouse an additional $50; 3-year and lifetime memberships also available.

Note that such companies do not have club facilities in all airports. Other airlines also offer a variety of special services in many airports.

Getting Bumped – A special air travel problem is the possibility that an airline will accept more reservations (and sell more tickets) than there are seats on a given flight. This is entirely legal and is done to make up for "no-shows," passengers who don't show up for a flight for which they have made reservations and bought tickets. If the airline has oversold the flight and everyone does show up, there simply aren't enough seats. When this happens, the airline is subject to stringent rules designed to protect travelers.

In such cases, the airline first seeks ticket holders willing to give up their seats voluntarily in return for a negotiable sum of money or some other inducement, such as an offer of upgraded seating on the next flight or a voucher for a free trip at some other time. If there are not enough volunteers, the airline may bump passengers against their wishes.

Anyone inconvenienced in this way, however, is entitled to an explanation of the criteria used to determine who does and does not get on the flight, as well as compensation if the resulting delay exceeds certain limits. If the airline can put the bumped passengers on an alternate flight that is *scheduled to arrive* at their original destination within 1 hour of their originally scheduled arrival time, no compensation is owed. If the delay is more than 1 hour but less than 2 hours on a domestic US flight, they must be paid denied-boarding compensation equivalent to the one-way fare to their destination (but not more than $200). If the delay is more than 2 hours after the original arrival time on a domestic flight, the compensation must be doubled (not more than $400). The airline also may offer bumped travelers a voucher for a free flight instead of the denied-boarding compensation. The passenger may be given the choice of either the money or the voucher, the dollar value of which may be no less than the monetary compensation to which the passenger would be entitled. The voucher is not a substitute for the bumped passenger's original ticket; the airline continues to honor that as well.

Keep in mind that the above regulations and policies are for flights leaving the US only, and do *not* apply to charters or to inbound flights originating abroad, even on US carriers.

To protect yourself as best you can against getting bumped, arrive at the airport early, allowing plenty of time to check in and get to the gate. If the flight is oversold, ask immediately for the written statement explaining the airline's policy on denied-boarding compensation and its boarding priorities. If the airline refuses to give you this information, or if you feel it has not handled the situation properly, file a complaint with both the airline and the appropriate government agency (see "Consumer Protection," below).

Delays and Cancellations – The above compensation rules also do not apply if the flight is canceled or delayed, or if a smaller aircraft is substituted due to mechanical problems. Each airline has its own policy for assisting passengers whose flights are delayed or canceled or who must wait for another flight because their original one was overbooked. Most airline personnel will make new travel arrangements if necessary. If the delay is longer than 4 hours, the airline may pay for a phone call or telegram, a meal, and, in some cases, a hotel room and transportation to it.

■ **Caution:** If you are bumped or miss a flight, be sure to ask the airline to notify other airlines on which you have reservations or connecting flights. When your name is taken off the passenger list of your initial flight, the computer usually cancels all of your reservations automatically, unless *you* take steps to preserve them.

CHARTER FLIGHTS: By booking a block of seats on a specially arranged flight, charter operators offer travelers air transportation for a substantial reduction over the full coach or economy fare. These operators may offer air-only charters (selling transportation alone) or charter packages (the flight plus a combination of land arrangements such as accommodations, meals, tours, or car rentals). Charters are especially attractive to people living in smaller cities or out-of-the-way places, because they frequently leave from nearby airports, saving travelers the inconvenience and expense of getting to a major gateway.

From the consumer's standpoint, charters differ from scheduled airlines in two main respects: You generally need to book and pay in advance, and you can't change the itinerary or the departure and return dates once you've booked the flight. In practice, however, these restrictions don't always apply. Today, although most charters still require advance reservations, some permit last-minute bookings (when there are unsold seats available), and occasionally charter seats may be offered on a standby basis. Though charters almost always are round-trip, and it is unlikely that you would be sold a one-way seat on a round-trip flight, on rare occasions one-way tickets on charters are offered.

Some things to keep in mind about the charter game include the following:

1. It cannot be repeated often enough that if you are forced to cancel your trip, you can lose much (and possibly all) of your money unless you have cancellation insurance, which is a *must* (see *Insurance,* in this section). Frequently, if the cancellation occurs far enough in advance (often 6 weeks or more), you may forfeit only a $25 or $50 penalty. If you cancel only 2 or 3 weeks before the flight, there may be no refund at all unless you or the operator can provide a substitute passenger.
2. Charter flights may be canceled by the operator up to 10 days before departure for any reason, usually underbooking. Your money is returned in this event, but there may be too little time for you to make new arrangements.
3. Most charters have little of the flexibility of regularly scheduled flights regarding

refunds and the changing of flight dates; if you book a return flight, you must be on it or lose your money.

4. Charter operators are permitted to assess a surcharge, if fuel or other costs warrant it, of up to 10% of the airfare up to 10 days before departure. Note, however, that a surcharge of *more* than 10% up to 10 days before departure and *any* surcharge less than 10 days before departure entitle passengers to a full refund if they choose.
5. Because of the economics of charter flights, your plane almost always will be full, so you will be crowded, though not necessarily uncomfortable. (There is, however, a new movement among charter airlines to provide flight accommodations that are more comfort-oriented, so this situation may change in the near future.)

To avoid problems, *always* choose charter flights with care. When you consider a charter, ask your travel agent who runs it and carefully check the company. The Better Business Bureau in the company's home city can report on how many complaints, if any, have been lodged against it in the past. Protect yourself with trip cancellation and interruption insurance, which can help safeguard your investment if you or a traveling companion is unable to make the trip and must cancel too late to receive a full refund from the company providing your travel services. (This is advisable whether you're buying a charter flight alone or a tour package for which the airfare is provided by charter or scheduled flight.)

Bookings – If you do fly on a charter, read the contract's fine print carefully and pay particular attention to the following:

Instructions concerning the payment of the deposit and its balance and to whom the check is to be made payable. Ordinarily, checks are made out to an escrow account, which means the charter company can't spend your money until your flight has safely returned. This provides some protection for you. To ensure the safe handling of your money, make out your check to the escrow account, the number of which must appear by law on the brochure, though all too often it is on the back in fine print. Write the details of the charter, including the destination and dates, on the face of the check; on the back, print "For Deposit Only." Your travel agent may prefer that you make out your check to the agency, saying that it will then pay the tour operator the fee minus commission. It is perfectly legal to write the check as we suggest, however, and if your agent objects too vociferously (he or she should trust the tour operator to send the proper commission), consider taking your business elsewhere. If you don't make your check out to the escrow account, you lose the protection of that escrow should the trip be canceled. Furthermore, recent bankruptcies in the travel industry have served to point out that even the protection of escrow may not be enough to safeguard a traveler's investment. More and more, insurance is becoming a necessity. The charter company should be bonded (usually by an insurance company), and if you want to file a claim against it, the claim should be sent to the bonding agent. The contract will set a time limit within which a claim must be filed.

Specific stipulations and penalties for cancellations. Most charters allow you to cancel up to 45 days in advance without major penalty, but some cancellation dates are 50 to 60 days before departure.

Stipulations regarding cancellation and major changes made by the charterer. US rules say that charter flights may not be canceled within 10 days of departure except when circumstances — such as natural disasters or political upheavals — make it physically impossible to fly. Charterers may make "major changes," however, such as in the date or place of departure or return, but you are entitled to cancel and receive a full refund if you don't wish to accept these changes. A price increase of more than 10% at any time up to 10 days before departure is considered a major change; no price increase at all is allowed during the last 10 days immediately before departure.

At the time of this writing, only one company, *MLT Vacations* (5130 Hwy. 101,

Minnetonka, MN 55345; phone: 800-328-0025), was offering charter flights to Hawaii. Another, *MTI Vacations* (1220 Kensington, Oakbrook, IL 60521; phone: 800-323-7285), which has offered such flights in the past, had not yet finalized its plans for 1993. Call to check availability when you are planning your trip. For the most current information on charter flight options, the travel newsletter *Jax Fax* regularly features a list of charter companies and packagers offering seats on charter flights. For a year's subscription send a check or money order for $12 to *Jax Fax* (397 Post Rd., Darien, CT 06820; phone: 203-655-8746).

DISCOUNTS ON SCHEDULED FLIGHTS: Promotional fares often are called discount fares because they cost less than what used to be the standard airline fare — full-fare economy. Nevertheless, they cost the traveler the same whether they are bought through a travel agent or directly from the airline. Tickets that cost less if bought from some outlet other than the airline do exist, however. While it is likely that the vast majority of travelers flying to Hawaii in the near future will be doing so on a promotional fare or charter rather than on a "discount" air ticket of this sort, it still is a good idea for cost-conscious consumers to be aware of the latest developments in the budget airfare scene. Note that the following discussion makes clear-cut distinctions among the types of discounts available based on how they reach the consumer; in actual practice, the distinctions are not nearly so precise.

Courier Travel – There was a time when traveling as a courier was a sort of underground way to save money and visit otherwise unaffordable destinations, but more and more, this once exotic idea of traveling as a courier is becoming a very "establishment" exercise. "Courier" means no more than a traveler who accompanies freight of one sort or another, and typically that freight replaces what otherwise would be the traveler's checked baggage. Be prepared, therefore, to carry all your own personal travel gear in a carry-on bag. In addition, the so-called courier usually pays only a portion of the total airfare — the freight company pays the remainder — and the courier also may be assessed a small registration fee. Note that many courier flights can be booked in advance (sometimes as much as 3 months), and that flights usually are round trip.

There are dozens of courier companies operating actively around the globe, and several publications provide information on courier opportunities:

A Simple Guide to Courier Travel, by Jesse L. Riddle, is a particularly good reference guide to courier travel. Published by the Carriage Group (PO Box 2394, Lake Oswego, OR 97035; phone: 800-222-3599), it's available for $15.95, including postage and handling.

Travel Secrets (PO Box 2325, New York, NY 10108; phone: 212-245-8703). Provides information useful to those considering traveling as a courier and often lists specific US and Canadian courier companies. Monthly; a year's subscription costs $33.

Travel Unlimited (PO Box 1058, Allston, MA 02134-1058; no phone). Lists courier companies and agents worldwide. Monthly; for a year's subscription send $25.

World Courier News (PO Box 77471, San Francisco, CA 94107; no phone). Provides information on courier opportunities, as well as useful tips. Each issue highlights a different destination. Monthly; for a year's subscription send $20.

Net Fare Sources – The newest notion for reducing the costs of travel services comes from travel agents who offer individual travelers "net" fares. Defined simply, a net fare is the bare minimum amount at which an airline or tour operator will carry a prospective traveler. It doesn't include the amount that normally would be paid to the travel agent as a commission. Traditionally, such commissions amount to about 10% on domestic fares — not counting significant additions to these commission levels that are paid retroactively when agents sell more than a specific volume of tickets or trips for a single supplier. At press time, at least one travel agency in the US was offering travelers the opportunity to purchase tickets and/or tours for a net price. Instead of earning income from individual commissions, this agency assesses a fixed fee that may or may not provide a bargain for travelers; it requires a little arithmetic to determine whether to use the services of a net travel agent or those of one who accepts conventional commissions. One of the potential drawbacks of buying from agencies selling travel services at net fares is that some airlines refuse to do business with them, thus possibly limiting your flight options.

Travel Avenue is a fee-based agency that rebates its ordinary agency commission to the customer. For domestic flights, an agent will find the lowest retail fare, then rebate 7% to 10% (depending on the airline selected) of that price minus a $10 ticket-writing charge. The ticket-writing charge is imposed per ticket; if the ticket includes more than eight separate flights, an additional $10 fee is charged. Customers using free flight coupons pay the ticket-writing charge, plus an additional $20 coupon-processing fee.

Travel Avenue will rebate its commissions on all tickets, including heavily discounted fares and senior citizen passes. Available 7 days a week, reservations should be made far enough in advance to allow the tickets to be sent by first class mail, since extra charges accrue for special handling. It's possible to economize further by making your own airline reservation, then asking *Travel Avenue* only to write/issue your ticket. For travelers outside the Chicago area, business may be transacted by phone and purchases charged to a credit card. For information, contact *Travel Avenue* at 641 W. Lake St., Suite 201, Chicago, IL 60606-1012 (phone: 312-876-1116 in Illinois; 800-333-3335 elsewhere in the US).

Consolidators and Bucket Shops – Other vendors of travel services can afford to sell tickets to their customers at an even greater discount because the airline has sold the tickets to them at a substantial discount (usually accomplished by sharply increasing commissions to that vendor), a practice in which many airlines indulge, albeit discreetly, preferring that the general public not know they are undercutting their own "list" prices. Airlines anticipating a slow period on a particular route sometimes sell off a certain portion of their capacity at a very great discount to a wholesaler, or consolidator. The wholesaler sometimes is a charter operator who resells the seats to the public as though they were charter seats, which is why prospective travelers perusing the brochures of charter operators with large programs frequently see a number of flights designated as "scheduled service." As often as not, however, the consolidator, in turn, sells the seats to a travel agency specializing in discounting. Airlines also can sell seats directly to such an agency, which thus acts as its own consolidator. The airline offers the seats either at a net wholesale price, but without the volume-purchase requirement that would be difficult for a modest retail travel agency to fulfill, or at the standard price, but with a commission override large enough (as high as 50%) to allow both a profit and a price reduction to the public.

Travel agencies specializing in discounting sometimes are called "bucket shops," a term fraught with connotations of unreliability in this country. But in today's highly competitive travel marketplace, more and more conventional travel agencies are selling consolidator-supplied tickets, and the old bucket shops' image is becoming respectable. Agencies that specialize in discounted tickets exist in most large cities, and usually can be found by studying the smaller ads in the travel sections of Sunday newspapers.

Before buying a discounted ticket, whether from a bucket shop or a conventional, full-service travel agency, keep the following considerations in mind: To be in a position to judge how much you'll be saving, first find out the "list" prices of tickets to your destination. Then do some comparison shopping among agencies. Also bear in mind that a ticket that may not differ much in price from one available directly from the airline may, however, allow the circumvention of such things as the advance-purchase requirement. If your plans are less than final, be sure to find out about any other restrictions, such as penalties for canceling a flight or changing a reservation. Most discount tickets are non-endorsable, meaning that they can be used only on the airline that issued them, and they usually are marked "nonrefundable" to prevent their being cashed in for a list price refund.

A great many bucket shops are small businesses operating on a thin margin, so it's a good idea to check the local Better Business Bureau for any complaints registered against the one with which you're dealing before parting with any money. If you still do not feel reassured, consider buying discounted tickets only through a conventional travel agency, which can be expected to have found its own reliable source of consolidator tickets — some of the largest consolidators, in fact, sell only to travel agencies.

A few bucket shops require payment in cash or by certified check or money order, but if credit cards are accepted, use that option. Note, however, if buying from a charter operator selling both scheduled and charter flights, that the scheduled seats are not protected by the regulations — including the use of escrow accounts — governing the charter seats. Well-established charter operators, nevertheless, may extend the same protections to their scheduled flights, and when this is the case, consumers should be sure that the payment option selected directs their money into the escrow account.

Among the consolidators offering discount fares to Hawaii are the following:

Bargain Air (655 Deep Valley Dr., Suite 355, Rolling Hills, CA 90274; phone: 800-347-2345 in California; 213-377-2919 elsewhere in the US).

International Adventures (60 E. 42nd St., New York, NY 10165; phone: 212-599-0577).

Maharaja/Consumer Wholesale Travel (34 W. 33rd St., Suite 1014, New York, NY 10001; phone: 212-213-2020 in New York State; 800-223-6862 elsewhere in the US).

TFI Tours International (34 W. 32nd St., 12th Floor, New York, NY 10001; phone: 800-TAKE-TFI or 212-736-1140).

■ **Note:** Although rebating and discounting are becoming increasingly common, there is some legal ambiguity concerning them. Strictly speaking, it is legal to discount domestic tickets but not international tickets. On the other hand, the law that prohibits discounting, the Federal Aviation Act of 1958, is consistently ignored these days, in part because consumers benefit from the practice and in part because many illegal arrangements are indistinguishable from legal ones. Since the line separating the two is so fine that even the authorities can't always tell the difference, it is unlikely that most consumers would be able to do so, and in fact it is not illegal to *buy* a discounted ticket. If the issue of legality bothers you, ask the agency whether any ticket you're about to buy would be permissible under the above-mentioned act.

OTHER DISCOUNT TRAVEL SOURCES: An excellent source of information on economical travel opportunities is the *Consumer Reports Travel Letter,* published monthly by Consumers Union. It keeps abreast of the scene on a wide variety of fronts, including package tours, rental cars, insurance, and more, but it is especially helpful for its comprehensive coverage of airfares, offering guidance on all the options from scheduled flights on major or low-fare airlines to charters and discount sources. For a year's subscription, send $37 ($57 for 2 years) to *Consumer Reports Travel Letter* (PO Box 53629, Boulder, CO 80322-3629; phone: 800-234-1970). For information on other travel newsletters, see *Books, Magazines, and Newsletters,* in this section.

Last-Minute Travel Clubs – Still another way to take advantage of bargain airfares is open to those who have a flexible schedule. A number of organizations, usually set up as last-minute travel clubs and functioning on a membership basis, routinely keep in touch with travel suppliers to help them dispose of unsold inventory at discounts of between 15% and 60%. A great deal of the inventory consists of complete package tours and cruises, but some clubs offer air-only charter seats and, occasionally, seats on scheduled flights.

Members pay an annual fee and receive a toll-free hotline telephone number to call for information on imminent trips. In some cases, they also receive periodic mailings with information on bargain travel opportunities for which there is more advance notice. Despite the suggestive names of the clubs providing these services, last-minute travel does not necessarily mean that you cannot make plans until literally the last minute. Trips can be announced as little as a few days or as much as 2 months before departure, but the average is from 1 to 4 weeks' notice.

Among the organizations regularly offering such discounted travel opportunities to Hawaii are the following:

Encore Short Notice (4501 Forbes Blvd., Lanham, MD 20706; phone: 800-638-0930 or 301-459-8020). Annual fee: $48 per family.

Last Minute Travel (1249 Boylston St., Boston, MA 02215; phone: 800-LAST-MIN or 617-267-9800). No fee.

Moment's Notice (425 Madison Ave., New York, NY 10017; phone: 212-486-0500). Annual fee: $45 per family.

Spur-of-the-Moment Tours and Cruises (10780 Jefferson Blvd., Culver City, CA 90230; phone: 213-839-2418 in California; 800-343-1991 elsewhere in the US). No fee.

Traveler's Advantage (3033 S. Parker Rd., Suite 1000, Aurora, CO 80014; phone: 800-548-1116). Annual fee: $49 per family.

Vacations to Go (2411 Fountain View, Suite 201, Houston, TX 77057; phone: 800-338-4962). Annual fee: $19.95 per family.

Worldwide Discount Travel Club (1674 Meridian Ave., Miami Beach, FL 33139; phone: 305-534-2082). Annual fee: $40 per person; $50 per family.

Generic Air Travel – Organizations that apply the same flexible-schedule idea to air travel only and arrange for flights at literally the last minute also exist. The service they provide sometimes is known as "generic" air travel, and it operates somewhat like an ordinary airline standby service except that the organizations running it do not guarantee flights to a specific destination, but only to a general region, and offer seats on not one but several scheduled and charter airlines.

One pioneer of generic flights is *Airhitch* (2790 Broadway, Suite 100, New York, NY 10025; phone: 212-864-2000), which offers flights to Hawaii from the West Coast through its Hawaiihitch program. (Passengers from the East Coast can travel to the West Coast with the company's Calhitch program.) Prospective travelers stipulate a range of at least five consecutive departure dates and their desired destination, along with alternate choices, and pay the fare in advance. They are then sent a voucher good for travel *on a space-available basis* on flights to Hawaii during this time period. The week before this range of departure dates begins, travelers must contact *Airhitch* for specific information about flights on which seats may be available and instructions on how to proceed for check-in. (Return flights are arranged in the same manner as the outbound flights — a specified period of travel is decided upon, and a few days before this date range begins, prospective passengers contact *Airhitch* for details about flights that may be available.) If the client does not accept any of the suggested flights or cancels his or her travel plans after selecting a flight, the amount paid may be applied toward a future fare, or the flight arrangements can be transferred to another individual (although, in both cases, an additional fee may be charged). No refunds are offered unless the prospective passenger does not ultimately get on any flight in the specified date range; in such a case, the full fare is refunded. (Note that *Airhitch*'s slightly more expensive Target program, which provides confirmed reservations on specific dates to specific destinations, offers passengers greater — but not guaranteed — certainty regarding destinations and other flight arrangements.)

Bartered Travel Sources – Suppose a hotel buys advertising space in a newspaper. As payment, the hotel gives the publishing company the use of a number of hotel rooms in lieu of cash. This is barter, a common means of exchange among hotels, airlines, car rental companies, cruise lines, tour operators, restaurants, and other travel service companies. When a bartering company finds itself with empty airline seats (or excess hotel rooms, or cruise ship cabin space, and so on) and offers them to the public, considerable savings can be enjoyed.

Bartered travel clubs often offer discounts of up to 50% to members who pay an annual fee (approximately $50 at press time) which entitles them to select the flights, cruises, hotel rooms, or other travel services that the club obtained by barter. Members usually present a voucher, club credit card, or scrip (a dollar-denomination voucher negotiable only for the bartered product) to the hotel, which in turn subtracts the dollar amount from the bartering company's account.

Selling bartered travel is a perfectly legitimate means of retailing. One advantage to club members is that they don't have to wait until the last minute to obtain flight or room reservations.

Among the companies specializing in bartered travel, those that frequently offer members travel services to and in Hawaii include the following:

Travel Guild (18210 Redmond Way, Redmond, WA 98052; phone: 206-861-1900). Annual fee: $48 per family.

Travel World Leisure Club (225 W. 34th St., Suite 2203, New York, NY 10122; phone: 800-444-TWLC or 212-239-4855). Annual fee: $50 per family.

Although another company, *IGT (In Good Taste) Services* (1111 Lincoln Rd., 4th Floor, Miami Beach, FL 33139; phone: 800-444-8872 or 305-534-7900), offers discounts on a variety of travel services, and occasionally sells bartered travel arrangements as well, at press time, they were offering only dining discounts in Hawaii. Their annual fee is $48 per family.

CONSUMER PROTECTION: Consumers who feel that they have not been dealt with fairly by an airline should make their complaints known. Begin with the customer service representative at the airport where the problem occurs. If he or she cannot resolve your complaint to your satisfaction, write to the airline's consumer office. In a businesslike, typed letter, explain what reservations you held, what happened, the names of the employees involved, and what you expect the airline to do to remedy the situation. Send copies (never the originals) of the tickets, receipts, and other documents that back your claims. Ideally, all correspondence should be sent via certified mail, return receipt requested. This provides proof that your complaint was received.

Passengers with consumer complaints — lost baggage, compensation for getting bumped, violations of smoking and nonsmoking rules, deceptive practices by an airline, charter regulations — who are not satisfied with the airline's response should contact the US Department of Transportation (DOT), Consumer Affairs Division (400 Seventh St. SW, Room 10405, Washington, DC 20590; phone: 202-366-2220). DOT personnel stress, however, that consumers initially should direct their complaints to the airline that provoked them.

Remember, too, that the federal Fair Credit Billing Act permits purchasers to refuse payment for credit card charges where services have not been delivered, so the onus of dealing with the receiver for a bankrupt airline falls on the credit card company. Do not rely on another airline to honor the ticket you're holding, since the days when virtually all major carriers subscribed to a default protection program that bound them to do so are long gone. Some airlines may voluntarily step forward to accommodate the stranded passengers of a fellow carrier, but this is now an entirely altruistic act.

The deregulation of US airlines has meant that the traveler must find out for himself or herself what he or she is entitled to receive. The US Department of Transportation's informative consumer booklet, *Fly Rights,* is a good place to start. To receive a copy, send $1 to the Superintendent of Documents, US Government Printing Office (Washington, DC 20402-9325; phone: 202-783-3238). Specify its stock number, 050-000-00513-5, and allow 3 to 4 weeks for delivery.

■ **Note:** Those who tend to experience discomfort due to the change in air pressure while flying may be interested in the free pamphlet *Ears, Altitude and Airplane Travel;* for a copy send a self-addressed, stamped, business-size envelope to the *American Academy of Otolaryngology* (One Prince St., Alexandria, VA 22314; phone: 703-836-4444). And for when you land, *Overcoming Jet Lag* offers some helpful tips on minimizing post-flight stress; it is available from Berkeley Publishing Group (PO Box 506, Mail Order Dept., East Rutherford, NJ 07073; phone: 800-631-8571) for $6.95, plus shipping and handling.

Traveling by Ship

There was a time when traveling by ship was extraordinarily expensive, time consuming, utterly elegant, and was utilized almost exclusively for getting from one point to another. No longer primarily pure transportation, cruising currently is riding a wave of popularity as a leisure activity in its own right, and the host of new ships (and dozens of rebuilt old ones) testifies dramatically to the attraction of vacationing on the high seas.

Even if you have the time, the money, and the inclination to treat yourself to the luxury of an ocean voyage, and you wish to see Hawaii as well, your choices are somewhat limited. At the time of this writing, only one company (*Holland America Line;* see below) scheduled regular cruises between the US mainland and the Hawaiian islands. Several cruise lines do, however, offer cruises between the Hawaiian islands and Mexican or other foreign ports.

Those interested in sailing to Hawaii also can reserve a stateroom on one of the several foreign cruise ships that frequently include Hawaii as a port of call on their long Pacific or around-the-world cruises. Or you can go along as a passenger on a freighter plying the same routes. Both alternatives have drawbacks: They are expensive; they require a fair hunk of time, anywhere from 16 to 90 days; and the stopover in Hawaii usually is very brief, as little as 12 hours, never more than 2 days. Another option for those wishing to cruise Hawaiian waters is to fly to Honolulu and embark from there on one of the oceangoing passenger liners calling at ports on the major islands. Although relatively few travelers first set foot on Hawaiian soil with sea legs developed during an ocean voyage, more and more people are cruising *around* the islands.

Many modern-day cruise ships seem much more like motels-at-sea than the classic liners of a couple of generations ago, but they are consistently comfortable and passengers often are pampered. Cruise prices can be quite reasonable, and since the single cruise price covers all the major items in a typical vacation — transportation, accommodations, all meals and entertainment, and a full range of social activities, sports, and recreation — a traveler need not fear any unexpected assaults on the family travel budget.

There are a number of moments in the cruise-planning process when discounts are available from the major cruise lines, so it may be possible to enjoy some diminution of the list price almost anytime you book passage on a cruise ship. For those willing to commit early — say 4 to 6 months before sailing — most of the major cruise lines routinely offer a 10% reduction off posted prices, in addition to the widest selection of cabins. For those who decide to sail rather late in the game — say, 4 to 6 weeks before departure — savings often are even greater — an average of 20% — as steamship lines try to fill up their ships. The only negative aspect is that the choice of cabins tends to be limited, although it is possible that a fare upgrade will be offered to make this limited selection more palatable. In addition, there's the option of buying from a discount travel club or a travel agency that specializes in last-minute bargains; these discounters and other discount travel sources are discussed at the end of *Traveling by Plane,* above.

Although there are less expensive ways to see the islands, the romance and enjoyment of a sea voyage remain irresistible for many, so a few points should be considered by such sojourners before they sign on for a seagoing vacation (after all, it's hard to get off in mid-ocean). Herewith, a rundown on what to expect from a cruise, a few suggestions on what to look for and arrange when purchasing passage on one, and some representative sailings to and around Hawaiian waters.

CABINS: The most important factor in determining the price of a cruise is the cabin. Cabin prices are set according to size and location. The size can vary considerably on older ships, less so on newer or more recently modernized ones, and may be entirely uniform on the very newest vessels.

Shipboard accommodations utilize the same pricing pattern as hotels. Suites, which consist of a sitting room–bedroom combination and occasionally a small private deck that could be compared to a patio, cost the most. Prices for other cabins (interchangeably called staterooms) usually are more expensive on the upper passenger decks, less expensive on lower decks; if the cabin has a bathtub instead of a shower, the price probably will be higher. The outside cabins with portholes cost more than inside cabins without views and generally are preferred — although many experienced cruise passengers eschew the more expensive accommodations for they know they will spend very few waking hours in their cabins. As in all forms of travel, accommodations are more expensive for single travelers. If you are traveling on your own but want to share a double cabin to reduce the cost, some ship lines will attempt to find someone of the same sex willing to share quarters (see *Hints for Single Travelers,* in this section).

FACILITIES AND ACTIVITIES: You may not use your cabin very much — organized shipboard activities are geared to keep you busy. A standard schedule might consist of swimming, sunbathing, and numerous other outdoor recreations. Evenings are devoted to leisurely dining, lounge shows or movies, bingo and other organized games, gambling, dancing, and a midnight buffet. Your cruise fare includes all of these activities — except the cost of drinks.

Most cruise ships have at least one major social lounge, a main dining room, several bars, an entertainment room that may double as a discotheque for late dancing, an exercise room, indoor games facilities, at least one pool, and shopping facilities, which can range from a single boutique to an arcade. Still others have gambling casinos and/or slot machines, card rooms, libraries, children's recreation centers, indoor pools (as well as one or more on open decks), separate movie theaters, and private meeting rooms. Open deck space should be ample, because this is where most passengers spend their days at sea.

Usually there is a social director and staff to organize and coordinate activities. Evening entertainment is provided by professionals. Movies are mostly first-run and drinks are moderate in price (or should be) because a ship is exempt from local taxes when at sea.

■ **Note:** To be prepared for possible illnesses at sea, travelers should get a prescription from their doctor for medicine to counteract motion sickness. All ships with more than 12 passengers have a doctor on board, plus facilities for handling sickness or medical emergencies.

Shore Excursions – These side trips almost always are optional and available at extra cost. Before you leave, do a little basic research about the island ports you'll be visiting and decide what sights will interest you. If several of the most compelling of these are some distance from the pier where your ship docks, chances are that paying for a shore excursion will be worth the money.

Shore excursions usually can be booked through your travel agent at the same time you make your cruise booking, but this is worthwhile only if you can get complete details on the nature of each excursion being offered. If you can't get these details, better opt to purchase your shore arrangements after you're on board. Your enthusiasm for an excursion may be higher once you are on board because you will have met other passengers with whom to share the excitement of "shore leave." And depending on your time in port, you may decide to eschew the guided tour and venture out on your own.

Meals – All meals on board almost always are included in the basic price of a cruise, and the food generally is abundant and quite palatable. Evening meals are taken in the main dining room, where tables are assigned according to the passengers' preferences. Tables usually accommodate from 2 to 10; specify your preference when you book your cruise. If there are two sittings, you also can specify which one you want at the time you book or, at the latest, when you board the ship. Later sittings usually are more leisurely. Breakfast frequently is available in your cabin, as well as in the main dining room. For lunch, many passengers prefer the buffet offered on deck, usually at or near the pool, but again, the main dining room is available.

DRESS: Most people pack too much for a cruise on the assumption that their daily attire should be chic and every night is a big event. Comfort is a more realistic criterion. Daytime wear on most ships is decidedly casual. Evening wear for most cruises is dressy-casual. Formal attire probably is not necessary for 1-week cruises, optional for longer ones. For information on choosing and packing a basic wardrobe, see *How to Pack,* in this section.

TIPS: Tips are a strictly personal expense, and you *are* expected to tip — in particular, your cabin and dining room stewards. The general rule of thumb (or palm) is to expect to pay from 10% to 20% of your total cruise budget for gratuities — the actual amount within this range is based on the length of the cruise and the extent of personalized services provided. Allow $2 to $5 a day for each cabin and dining room steward (more if you wish), and additional sums for very good service. (*Note:* Tips should be paid by and for each individual in a cabin, whether there are one, two, or more.) Others who may merit tips are the deck steward who sets up your chair at the pool or elsewhere, the wine steward in the dining room, porters who handle your luggage (tip them individually at the time they assist you), and any others who provide personal service. On some ships you can charge your bar tab to your cabin; throw in the tip when you pay it at the end of the cruise. Smart travelers tip twice during the trip: about midway through the cruise and at the end; even wiser travelers tip a bit at the start of the trip to ensure better service throughout.

Although some cruise lines do have a no-tipping policy and you are not penalized by the crew for not tipping, naturally, you aren't penalized for tipping, either. If you can restrain yourself, it is better not to tip on those few ships that discourage it. However, never make the mistake of not tipping on the majority of ships, where it is a common, expected practice. (For further information on calculating gratuities, see *Tipping,* in this section.)

SHIP SANITATION: The US Public Health Service (PHS) currently inspects all passenger vessels calling at US ports, so very precise information is available on which ships meet its requirements and which do not. The further requirement that ships immediately report any illness that occurs on board adds to the available data.

The problem for a prospective cruise passenger is to determine whether the ship on which he or she plans to sail has met the official sanitary standard. US regulations require the PHS to publish actual grades for the ships inspected (rather than the old pass or fail designation), so it's now easy to determine any cruise ship's status. Nearly 4,000 travel agents, public health organizations, and doctors receive a copy of each monthly ship sanitation summary, but be aware that not all travel agents fully understand what this ship inspection program is all about. The best advice is to deal with a travel agent who specializes in cruise bookings, for he or she is most likely to have the latest information on the sanitary conditions of all cruise ships (see "A final note on picking a cruise," below). To receive a copy of the most recent summary or a particular inspection report, contact Chief, Vessel Sanitation Program, Center for Environmental Health and Injury Control, 1015 N. America Way, Room 107, Miami, FL 33132 (phone: 305-536-4307).

PACIFIC CRUISES TO HAWAII: At least six foreign steamship lines continue to call at Hawaiian ports as part of Pacific or around-the-world itineraries: *Crystal Cruises, Cunard, Holland America Line, Princess Cruises, Royal Cruise Line,* and *Royal Viking Lines.* These major cruise lines also offer passengers the option of joining the Pacific leg of longer cruises that include stopovers in Hawaii. Although some of these cruises allow passengers to join just the Hawaiian portion of the cruise, passengers more commonly begin or end the cruise at the port of Ensenada, Mexico, or at other foreign ports.

For seagoing enthusiasts, *Cunard*'s *Queen Elizabeth 2,* one of the largest and most comfortable vessels afloat, each year includes Hawaiian ports of call as part of its around-the-world itinerary. *Cunard* also offers a 28-day cruise between the US, Mexico, and Hawaii aboard the *Vistafjord,* which calls at Honolulu (Oahu), Kona (the Big Island), and Lahaina (Maui). Air/sea packages also are available. For information, contact *Cunard,* 555 Fifth Ave., New York, NY 10017 (phone: 800-221-4770).

Other cruises visiting the Hawaiian islands include the following:

Crystal Cruises (2121 Ave. of the Stars, Los Angeles, CA 90067; phone: 800-446-6645). Offers a 48-day round-trip sailing from Honolulu to Australia aboard the *Crystal Harmony,* with stops at several Hawaiian islands before continuing its South Pacific voyage. Also offered is a 6-day sailing from Ensenada (Mexico) to Honolulu calling at Lahaina (Maui).

Holland America Line (300 Elliot Ave. W., Seattle, WA 98119; phone: 800-426-0327). Offers a 16-day round-trip cruise aboard the *Rotterdam* between Los Angeles and Hawaii. Ports of call include Kona and Hilo (the Big Island), Nawiliwili (Kauai), Honolulu (Oahu), and Lahaina (Maui).

Princess Cruises (10100 Santa Monica Blvd., Santa Monica, CA 90067; phone: 800-421-0522). Offers 10-day sailings aboard the *Island Princess* and the *Pacific Princess* between Hawaii and Vancouver, British Columbia. Ports of call include Hilo (the Big Island), Kapaa (Kauai), and Lahaina (Maui). These ships also offer 11-day sailings between Honolulu and French Polynesia that visit several Hawaiian islands. In addition, the *Pacific Princess* makes 17-day cruises from San Diego to French Polynesia, visiting several Hawaiian islands en route.

Royal Cruise Line (One Maritime Plaza, Suite 1400, San Francisco, CA 94111; phone: 800-227-5628 or 415-956-7200). Regularly offers cruises to and from the Hawaiian islands. Among its offerings last year were "Pacific Hawaiian Odyssey" cruises aboard the *Crown Odyssey* and *Royal Odyssey.* These 8- and 16-day cruises began in Ensenada, Mexico, sailed on to Kailua-Kona (the Big Island),

Kahului and Lahaina (Maui), and Honolulu (Oahu), and included a visit at Nawiliwili (Kauai), before returning to Ensenada.

Royal Viking Lines (95 Merrick Way, Coral Gables, FL 33134; phone: 800-422-8000). This line usually offers 11-day cruises aboard the *Royal Viking Sky* between Ensenada, Mexico, and Honolulu (Oahu), including stops on the Big Island, Kauai, and Maui. At press time, however, the complete schedule for 1993 had not yet been set, so call for current information when planning your trip.

INTER-ISLAND CRUISES: The cruise ship industry among the islands of Oahu, Maui, Kauai, and the Big Island has grown into a very big business, although at the time of this writing, there was only one major cruise line offering luxury liner cruises solely in Hawaiian waters (not as a portion of an extended trip).

American Hawaii Cruises' SS *Constitution* leaves Honolulu on Saturday nights year-round; cruises by Molokai, Lanai, and Kahoolawe; docks at Kahului (Maui), at Hilo and Kailua-Kona (on the Big Island), and at Nawiliwili (Kauai); and arrives at Honolulu again on Saturday morning. Its sister ship, the SS *Independence,* sails on Saturday nights in the opposite direction, docking first at Kauai, then at Kailua-Kona and Hilo (on the Big Island), then Maui, before cruising by Molokai on its way home to Honolulu. Optional group shore excursions are offered in each port of call; car rentals also are available. Back aboard, there's dining, dancing, and Hawaiian-style entertainment. Week-long and several day packages are offered and hotel or condo packages also are available for those who wish to extend their stay. *American Hawaii Cruises* also offers two economical standby air/sea programs: the "Hono-Low-Low" program and the "A-Low-Ha" program (available to those who live in or near a gateway city for *American Airlines,* the air partner for these packages). For information, contact *American Hawaii Cruises,* 550 Kearny St., San Francisco, CA 94108 (phone: 800-765-7000).

FREIGHTERS: An alternative to conventional cruise ships is travel by freighter. These are cargo ships that also take a limited number of passengers (usually about 12) in reasonably comfortable accommodations. The idea of traveling by freighter has long appealed to romantic souls, but there are a number of drawbacks to consider before casting off. Once upon a time, a major advantage of freighter travel was its low cost, but this is no longer the case. Though freighters usually are less expensive than cruise ships, the difference is not as great as it once was. Accommodations and recreational facilities vary, but freighters were not designed to amuse passengers, so it is important to appreciate the idea of freighter travel itself. Schedules are erratic, and travelers must fit their timetable to that of the ship. Passengers have found themselves waiting as long as a month for a promised sailing, and because freighters follow their cargo commitments, it is possible that a scheduled port could be omitted at the last minute or a new one added.

Although there are no freighters regularly carrying passengers to Hawaiian ports at the present time, this situation may change. Anyone contemplating a freighter trip should be aware that there are specialists who deal only (or largely) in this type of travel. They provide information, schedules, and, if you decide to sail, booking services. Among these agencies are the following:

Freighter World Cruises (180 S. Lake Ave., Suite 335, Pasadena, CA 91101; phone: 818-449-3106). A freighter travel agency that acts as general agent for several freighter lines. Publishes the twice-monthly *Freighter Space Advisory,* listing space available on sailings worldwide. A subscription costs $27 a year, $25 of which can be credited toward the cost of a cruise.

Pearl's Travel Tips (9903 Oaks La., Seminole, FL 34642; phone: 813-393-2919).

Run by Ilse Hoffman, who finds sailings for her customers and sends them off with all kinds of valuable information and advice.

TravLtips Cruise and Freighter Travel Association (PO Box 188, Flushing, NY 11358; phone: 800-872-8584 or 718-939-2400). A freighter travel agency and club ($15 a year or $25 for 2 years) whose members receive the bimonthly *TravLtips* magazine of cruise and freighter travel.

Those interested in freighter travel also may want to subscribe to *Freighter Travel News,* a publication of the *Freighter Travel Club of America.* A year's subscription to this monthly newsletter costs $18. To subscribe, write to the club at 3524 Harts Lake Rd., Roy, WA 98580.

Another monthly newsletter that may be of interest to those planning to cruise Hawaiian waters is *Ocean and Cruise News,* which offers comprehensive coverage of the latest on the cruise ship scene. A year's subscription costs $24. Contact *Ocean and Cruise News,* PO Box 92, Stamford, CT 06904 (phone: 203-329-2787).

■ **A final note on picking a cruise:** A "cruise-only" travel agency can best help you choose a cruise ship and itinerary. Cruise-only agents are best equipped to tell you about a particular ship's "personality," the kind of person with whom you'll likely be traveling on a particular ship, what dress is acceptable (it varies from ship to ship), and much more. Travel agencies that specialize in booking cruises usually are members of the *National Association of Cruise Only Agencies (NACOA).* For a listing of the agencies in your area (requests are limited to three states), send a self-addressed, stamped envelope to *NACOA,* PO Box 7209, Freeport, NY 11520, or call 516-378-8006.

Touring by Car

Although it may seem that a car is unnecessary for an island stay, the automobile is the most popular means of transportation in and around Hawaii. While you may be able to get around Honolulu and the island of Oahu easily enough on *TheBus,* the island's one-fare public transportation system, or see Hilo and travel to some other spots on the Big Island of Hawaii via the *Hele-On Bus,* the same is not true of the remaining islands, where public transportation is limited — or nonexistent. So a car is a genuine necessity if you plan to venture any distance from your hotel, or see more than the sights included on the traditional organized sightseeing excursion. And even where a car is not essential, driving still is a highly desirable way to explore the state. It will allow you to take the scenic stretches at your own pace, satisfy your curiosity about some out-of-the-way corner, and stop for a snack, a swim, or a photograph at will.

RENTING A CAR: Visitors who want to drive in Hawaii rent a car through a travel agent or national rental firm before leaving home or from a local company once they are in Hawaii. Another possibility, also arranged before departure, is to rent the car as part of a larger travel package.

Renting a car in Hawaii is not inexpensive, but it is possible to economize by determining your own needs and then shopping around among the car rental companies until you find the best deal. As you comparison shop, keep in mind that rates vary considerably from location to location on the same island. For instance, it might be less expensive to rent a car from an office near the center of Honolulu rather than at the airport. Ask about special rates or promotional deals, such as weekend or weekly rates, bonus coupons for airline tickets, or 24-hour rates that include gas and unlimited mileage.

Rental car companies operating in the Hawaiian islands can be divided into three basic categories: large national or international companies; statewide or regional companies; and several-island locals, some of them with catchy names such as *Sunshine of Hawaii Rent-A-Car* (phone: 808-871-6222) and *Rainbow Rent-A-Car* (phone: 808-661-8734), which offer rentals on Maui. In addition, there are agencies that rent convertibles, minivans for camping (see "Recreational Vehicles," in this section), or four-wheel-drive vehicles (see below). Because of aggressive local competition, the cost of renting a car can be less expensive once a traveler arrives in Hawaii, compared to the prices quoted in advance from the mainland. Local companies usually are less expensive than the national giants.

Given this situation, it's tempting to wait until arriving to consult the yellow pages and scout out the lowest-priced rental from the company located the farthest from the airport high-rent district and offering no pick-up services. But if your arrival coincides with a holiday or a peak travel period, you may be disappointed to find that even the most expensive car in town was spoken for months ago. Whenever possible, it is best to reserve in advance, anywhere from a few days in slack periods to a month or more during the busier seasons.

If you do decide to wait until you arrive and let your fingers do the walking through the local island phone books, you'll find more than 80 car rental firms on Oahu alone (give or take a few as they appear or disappear with the ebb and flow of the commercial tide), about 50 or more on Maui, more than 30 on Hawaii and nearly as many on Kauai, several on Molokai, and even 2 on Lanai. Often the best guide to sorting through the options is the local tourist board, and the Hawaii Visitors Bureau *Accommodation Guide* contains a partial list of car rental firms, with their local phone numbers (all in area code 808). Information on local car rental companies, as well as sources for the more unusual types of motorized transport, can be found in the *Sources and Resources* section of the individual island reports in ISLAND-BY-ISLAND HOPPING.

Travel agents can arrange rentals for clients, but it is just as easy to call and rent a car yourself. Listed below are the major national rental companies represented in Hawaii, along with some of the statewide ones that have information and reservations numbers that can be dialed toll-free from the mainland.

Alamo Rent-A-Car (phone: 800-327-9633). Rentals on the Big Island of Hawaii, Kauai, Maui, and Oahu.

Avis (phone: 800-331-1212). Rentals on Hawaii, Kauai, Maui, Molokai, and Oahu.

Budget (phone: 800-527-0707). Rentals on Hawaii, Kauai, Maui, Molokai, and Oahu.

Dollar Rent A Car (phone: 800-367-7006 for Hawaii information and reservations; 800-800-4000 for general inquiries). Rentals on Hawaii, Kauai, Lanai, Maui, Molokai, and Oahu.

Hertz (phone: 800-654-3131 in Oklahoma; 800-654-8200 elsewhere in the US). Rentals on Hawaii, Kaui, Maui, and Oahu.

National Car Rental (phone: 800-CAR-RENT). Rentals on Hawaii, Kauai, Maui, and Oahu.

Thrifty Rent-A-Car (phone: 800-FOR-CARS). Rentals on Hawaii, Kauai, Maui, and Oahu.

Tropical Rent-A-Car (phone: 800-678-6000). Rentals on Hawaii, Kauai, Lanai, Maui, Molokai, and Oahu.

Requirements – Whether you decide to rent a car in advance from a large national rental company with Hawaiian branches or wait to rent from a local company, you should know that renting a car is rarely as simple as signing on the dotted line and roaring off into the night. If you are renting for personal use, you must have a valid driver's license and will have to convince the renting agency that (1) you are personally creditworthy, and (2) you will bring the car back at the stated time. This will be easy if you have a major credit card; most rental companies accept credit cards in lieu of a cash deposit, as well as for payment of your final bill. If you prefer to pay in cash, leave your credit card imprint as a "deposit," then pay your bill in cash when you return the car.

If you are planning to rent a car once in Hawaii, *Avis, Budget, Hertz,* and other US rental companies usually *will* rent to travelers paying in cash and leaving either a credit card imprint or a substantial amount of cash as a deposit. This is not necessarily standard policy, however, as some of the other national chains and a number of local Hawaiian companies will *not* rent to an individual who doesn't have a valid credit card. In this case, you may have to call around to find a company that accepts cash.

Also keep in mind that although the minimum age to drive a car in Hawaii is 18 years, the minimum age to rent a car is set by the rental company. Many firms have a minimum age requirement of 21 years, some raise that to 23 or 25 years, and for some models of cars it rises to 30 years. The upper age limit at many companies is between 69 and 75; others have no upper limit or may make drivers above a certain age subject to special conditions.

Costs – Finding the most economical car rental will require some telephone shopping on your part. As a *general* rule, expect to hear lower prices quoted by the smaller, strictly local companies than by the well-known international names, with those of the statewide and regional companies falling somewhere between the two.

Comparison shopping always is advisable, however, because the company that has the least expensive rentals on one island may not have the least expensive cars on another, and even the international giants offer discount plans whose conditions are easy for most travelers to fulfill. For instance, *Budget* and *National* offer discounts of anywhere from 10% to 30% off their usual rates (according to the size of the car and the duration of the rental), provided that the car is reserved a certain number of days before departure (usually 7 to 14 days, but it can be less), is rented for a minimum period (5 days or, more often, a week), is paid for at the time of booking, and, in most cases, is returned to the same location that supplied it or to another on the island. Similar discount plans include *Hertz*'s Leisure Rates and *Avis*'s Supervalue Rates.

If you are driving short distances for only a day or two, the best deal may be a per-day, per-mile rate: You pay a flat fee for each day you keep the car, plus a per-mile charge. An increasingly common alternative is to be granted a certain number of free miles each day and then be charged on a per-mile basis over that number.

Most companies also offer a flat per-day rate with unlimited free mileage. Make sure that the low, flat daily rate that catches your eye, however, is indeed a per-day rate: Often the lowest price advertised by a company turns out to be available only with a minimum 3-day rental — fine if you want the car that long, but not the bargain it appears if you really intend to use it no more than 24 hours. Flat weekly rates also are available, and some flat monthly rates that represent a further saving over the daily rate. If the company does business on several islands, it may offer a multiple- or all-island weekly rate that can be applied to shorter rentals on a combination of those islands, say 4 days on Maui, followed by 3 days on Kauai. Some companies charge even less for this weekly "touring" rate than they do for a week-long single-island rental, but it also can cost the same or more.

Another factor influencing cost is the type of car you rent. Rentals generally are based on a tiered price system, with different sizes of cars — variations of budget, economy, regular, and luxury — often listed as A (the smallest and least expensive) through F, G, or H, and sometimes even higher. Charges may increase by only a few dollars a day through several categories of subcompact and compact cars — where most of the competition is — then increase by great leaps through the remaining classes of full-size and luxury cars and passenger vans. The larger the car, the more it costs to rent and the more gas it consumes, but for some people the greater comfort and extra luggage space of a larger car (in which bags and sporting gear can be safely locked out of sight) may make it worth the additional expense. Also more expensive are sleek sports cars, but, again, for some people the thrill of driving such a car — for a week or a day — may be worth it.

Electing to pay for collision damage waiver (CDW) protection will add considerably to the cost of renting a car. You may be responsible for the *full value* of the vehicle being rented, but you can dispense with the possible obligation by buying the offered waiver at a cost of around $10 to $13 a day for rentals in Hawaii. Before making any decisions about optional collision damage waivers, check with your own insurance agent and determine whether your personal automobile insurance policy covers rented vehicles; if it does, you probably won't need to pay for the waiver. Be aware, too, that increasing numbers of credit cards automatically provide CDW coverage if the car rental is charged to the appropriate credit card. However, the specific terms of such coverage differ sharply among individual credit card companies, so check with the credit card company for information on the nature and amount of coverage provided. Business travelers also should be aware that, at the time of this writing, *American Express* had withdrawn its automatic CDW coverage from some corporate *Green* card accounts — watch for similar cutbacks by other credit card companies.

When inquiring about CDW coverage and costs, you should be aware that a number of the major international car rental companies now are automatically including the cost of this waiver in their quoted prices. This does not mean that they are absorbing this cost and you are receiving free coverage — total rental prices have increased to include the former CDW charge. The disadvantage of this inclusion is that you probably will not have the option to refuse this coverage, and will end up paying the added charge — even if you already are adequately covered by your own insurance policy or through a credit card company.

Additional costs to be added to the price tag include drop-off charges or one-way service fees. The lowest price quoted by any given company may apply only to a car that is returned to the same location from which it was rented. A slightly higher rate may be charged if the car is to be returned to a different location on the island.

A further consideration: Don't forget that car rentals are subject to the 4.16% state sales tax, or that the price of gas, on the whole, is higher in Hawaii than on the mainland. Rental cars usually are delivered with a full tank of gas. (This is not always the case, however, so check the gas gauge when picking up the car, and have the amount of gas noted on your rental agreement if the tank is not full.) Remember to fill the tank before you return the car or you will have to pay to refill it, and gasoline at the car rental company's pump is always much more expensive than at a service station. This policy may vary for smaller, regional companies; ask when picking up the vehicle. Before leaving the lot, also check that the rental car has a spare tire and jack in the trunk.

Particularly if you're staying in Waikiki, you might want to add parking costs to your calculations. Some of the large hotels and condominiums have free parking for guests, but just as many charge for it. Parking isn't as much of a problem in the rest of the state.

Fly/Drive Packages – Airlines, charter companies, car rental companies, and tour operators have been offering fly/drive packages for years, and even though the basic components of the package have changed somewhat — return airfare, a car waiting at the airport, and perhaps a night's lodging all for one inclusive price used to be the rule — the idea remains the same. You rent a car *here* for use *there* by booking it along with other arrangements for the trip. These days, the very minimum arrangement possible is the result of a tie-in between a car rental company and an airline, which entitles customers to a rental car for less than the company's usual rates, provided they show proof of having booked a flight on that airline. For information on available packages, check with the airline or your travel agent.

■ **Note:** When reserving and picking up a rental car, always ask for any available maps and information on the areas in which you will be driving; some companies also may offer brochures outlining scenic driving routes.

RENTING A JEEP: The main roads on almost all the islands are in good condition and most travelers will not need anything sturdier than the ordinary rental car. Four-wheel-drive vehicles, though not plentiful, can be rented on all the islands, but they are a necessity only if you intend to explore Lanai. You can rent one for about $99 per day on Lanai (less on other islands) plus gas from the island's gas station–cum–car rental agency *Oshiro Service and U-Drive* (850 Fraser Ave., Lanai City, HI 96763; phone: 808-565-6952). Note that *Oshiro* also rents cars, but they are of little use to sightseers on this island of largely unpaved roads.

The southern route on East Maui and the northern route on West Maui, plus parts of West Molokai, are other areas where a four-wheel-drive vehicle will be of value to the adventuresome. Of the car rental companies with toll-free numbers listed above, *Alamo, Budget,* and *Dollar* rent jeeps on the Big Island, Kauai, Maui, and Oahu (*Dollar* also rents jeeps on Lanai); and *Avis* rents GEO Trackers (a four-wheel-drive vehicle similar to a jeep) on these islands, as well as Molokai. Other companies renting jeeps — including specialists such as *Rent-A-Jeep* (phone: 808-877-6626) for Maui — are listed in the yellow pages of the respective island phone books. Jeep rentals tend to cost more than car rentals, but you'll still have to reserve well in advance to get one.

Package Tours

If the mere thought of buying a package for travel to and around Hawaii conjures up visions of a trip spent marching in lockstep with a horde of frazzled fellow travelers, remember that packages have come a long way. For one thing, not all packages necessarily are escorted tours, and the one you buy does not have to include any organized touring at all — nor will it necessarily include traveling companions. If it does, however, you'll find that people of all sorts — many just like yourself — are taking advantage of packages today because they are economical and convenient, save you an immense amount of planning time, and exist in such variety that it's virtually impossible not to find one that fits at least the majority of your travel preferences. Given the high cost of travel these days, packages have emerged as a particularly wise buy.

In essence, a package is just an amalgam of travel services that can be purchased in a single transaction. A package (tour or otherwise) to and around the Hawaiian islands may include any or all of the following: round-trip transpacific transportation, local transportation (and/or car rentals), accommodations, some or all meals, sightseeing, entertainment, transfers to and from the hotel at each destination, taxes, tips, escort service, and a variety of incidental features that might be offered as options at additional cost. In other words, a package can be any combination of travel elements, from a fully escorted tour offered at an all-inclusive price to a simple fly/drive booking allowing you to move about totally on your own. Its principal advantage is that it saves money: The cost of the combined arrangements invariably is well below the price of all the same elements if bought separately, and particularly if transportation is provided by charter or discount flight, the whole package could cost less than just a round-trip economy airline ticket on a regularly scheduled flight. A package provides more than economy and convenience: It releases the traveler from having to make individual arrangements for each separate element of a trip.

Tour programs generally can be divided into two categories — "'escorted" (or locally hosted) and "independent." An escorted tour means that a guide will accompany the group from the beginning of the tour through to the return flight; a locally hosted tour means that the group will be met upon arrival at each location by a different local host. On independent tours, there generally is a choice of hotels, meal plans, and sightseeing trips, as well as a variety of special excursions. The independent plan is for travelers who do not want a totally set itinerary, but who do prefer confirmed hotel reservations. Whether choosing an escorted or independent tour, always bring along complete contact information for your tour operator in case a problem arises, although tour operators often have local affiliates who can give additional assistance or make other arrangements on the spot.

To determine whether a package — or, more specifically, *which* package — fits your travel plans, start by evaluating your interests and needs, deciding how much and what you want to spend, see, and do. Gather whatever package tour information is available for your schedule. Be sure that you take the time to read the brochure *carefully* to determine precisely what is included. Keep in mind that travel brochures are written to entice you into signing up for a package tour. Often the language is deceptive and devious. For example, a brochure may quote the lowest prices for a package tour based on facilities that are unavailable during the off-season, undesirable at any season, or just plain nonexistent. Information such as "breakfast included" or "plus tax" (which can add up) should be taken into account. Note, too, that the prices quoted in brochures almost always are based on double occupancy: The rate listed is for each of two people sharing a double room, and if you travel alone, the supplement for single accommodations can raise the price considerably (see *Hints for Single Travelers,* in this section).

In this age of erratic airfares, the brochure most often will *not* include the price of an airline ticket in the price of the package, though sample fares from various gateway cities usually will be listed separately as extras to be added to the price of the ground arrangements. Before figuring your actual cost, check the latest fares with the airlines, because the samples invariably are out of date by the time you read them. If the brochure gives more than one category of sample fares per gateway city — such as an individual tour-basing fare, a group fare, an excursion, APEX, or other discount ticket — your travel agent or airline tour desk will be able to tell you which one applies to the package you choose, depending on when you travel, how far in advance you book, and other factors. (An individual tour-basing fare is a fare computed as part of a package that includes land arrangements, thereby entitling a carrier to reduce the air portion almost to the absolute minimum. Though it always represents a saving over full-fare coach or economy, lately the individual tour-basing fare has not been as inexpensive as the excursion and other discount fares that also are available to individuals. The group fare usually is the least expensive fare, and it is the tour operator, not you, who makes up the group.) When the brochure does include round-trip transportation in the package price, don't forget to add the cost of round-trip transportation from your home to the departure city to come up with the total cost of the package.

Finally, read the general information regarding terms and conditions and the responsibility clause (usually in fine print at the end of the descriptive literature) to determine the precise elements for which the tour operator is — and is not — liable. Here the tour operator frequently expresses the right to change services or schedules as long as equivalent arrangements are offered. This clause also absolves the operator of responsibility for circumstances beyond human control, such as hurricanes or volcanic eruptions, or injury to you or your property. While reading, ask the following questions:

1. Does the tour include airfare or other transportation, sightseeing, meals, transfers, taxes, baggage handling, tips, or any other services? Do you want all these services?

2. If the brochure indicates that "some meals" are included, does this mean a welcoming and farewell dinner, two breakfasts, or every evening meal?
3. What classes of hotels are offered? If you will be traveling alone, what is the single supplement?
4. Does the tour itinerary or price vary according to the season?
5. Are the prices guaranteed; that is, if costs increase between the time you book and the time you depart, can surcharges unilaterally be added?
6. Do you get a full refund if you cancel? If not, be sure to obtain cancellation insurance.
7. Can the operator cancel if too few people join? At what point?

One of the consumer's biggest problems is finding enough information to judge the reliability of a tour packager, since individual travelers seldom have direct contact with the firm putting the package together. Usually, a retail travel agent is interposed between customer and tour operator, and much depends on his or her candor and cooperation. So ask a number of questions about the tour you are considering. For example:

- Has the travel agent ever used a package provided by this tour operator?
- How long has the tour operator been in business? Check the Better Business Bureau in the area where the tour operator is based to see if any complaints have been filed against it.
- Is the tour operator a member of the *United States Tour Operators Association* (*USTOA;* 211 E. 51st St., Suite 12B, New York, NY 10022; phone: 212-944-5727)? The *USTOA* will provide a list of its members on request; it also offers a useful brochure, *How to Select a Package Tour.*
- How many and which companies are involved in the package?
- If air travel is by charter flight, is there an escrow account in which deposits will be held; if so, what is the name of the bank?

This last question is very important. US law requires that tour operators place every charter passenger's deposit and subsequent payment in a proper escrow account. Money paid into such an account cannot legally be used except to pay for the costs of a particular package or as a refund if the trip is canceled. To ensure the safe handling of your money, make your check payable to the escrow account — by law, the name of the depository must appear in the operator-participant contract, and usually is found in that mass of minuscule type on the back of the brochure. Write the details of the charter, including the destination and dates, on the face of the check; on the back, print "For Deposit Only." Your travel agent may prefer that you make your check out to the agency, saying that it will then pay the tour operator the fee minus commission. But it is perfectly legal to write your check as we suggest, and if your agent objects too strongly (the agent should have sufficient faith in the tour operator to trust him or her to send the proper commission), consider taking your business elsewhere. If you don't make your check out to the escrow account, you lose the protection of that escrow should the trip be canceled or the tour operator or travel agent fail. Furthermore, recent bankruptcies in the travel industry have served to point out that even the protection of escrow may not be enough to safeguard your investment. Increasingly, insurance is becoming a necessity (see *Insurance,* in this section), and payment by credit card has become popular since it offers some additional safeguards if the tour operator defaults.

■ **A word of advice:** Purchasers of vacation packages who feel they're not getting their money's worth are more likely to get a refund if they complain in writing to the operator — and bail out of the whole package immediately. Alert the tour operator or resort manager to the fact that you are dissatisfied, that you will be leaving for home as soon as transportation can be arranged, and that you expect a refund. They may have forms to fill out detailing your complaint; otherwise, state your case in a letter. Even if difficulty in arranging immediate transportation home detains you, your dated, written complaint should help in procuring a refund from the operator.

SAMPLE PACKAGES TO HAWAII: It is doubtful whether anyone has ever seen a "packaged" traveler emerge from Honolulu International Airport without a string of plumeria, orchids, hibiscus, or other blossoms around his or her neck, because the traditional lei greeting is the first experience a tour operator figures into any package to Hawaii. Beyond that fixed feature, however, you can get nearly anything you want in a Hawaiian package, and for as long as you want it. The keynote is flexibility. Some packages include several of the islands, while other explore only a selected island or visit only a major city or resort area.

Perhaps the most common arrangement — especially for the first-time visitor — is a week-long stay at a Waikiki hotel, including transfers between the airport and the hotel, baggage handling, taxes and tips, a limited amount of Honolulu sightseeing, and very few, if any, meals. Nearly every tour operator offers such a basic package, which usually can be prolonged by the addition of extra days or even extra weeks at the same place. Those who have already been to Honolulu, or who wish to get beyond the hustle and bustle of a city straightaway, will find the same sort of week-long, stay-put package available at resort areas on other islands — Kailua-Kona on Hawaii, or the Kaanapali Beach area on Maui, for instance.

There is a do-it-yourself quality to Hawaiian tour offerings, and the basic package is immediately subject to variation. The week in Waikiki becomes a 10-day, 2-island holiday with the addition of a 3-day neighbor island "extension," or it becomes a 2-week, 3-island holiday with the addition of a second neighbor island extension. In fact, most packagers offer a series of 2-, 3-, or 4-day mini-packages at various islands that travelers may string together at will, adding them to a block of time spent in one place or island-hopping for the entire length of their stay. You rarely will see Lanai listed among the extensions or mini-packages available, but all the other major islands, including Molokai, can be seen this way.

Another common variation is the marketing of any one package in two versions — a sightseeing version and a U-drive version. In the latter instance, a rental car will be waiting at the airport, and transfers to and from the hotel will be eliminated from the package ingredients, along with any organized sightseeing that might have been included. An operator with a hefty catalogue of tours may offer both options on all of the islands it packages, providing the opportunity to explore on your own on some islands and be driven and guided on others. When selections are more limited, it's most likely that the Honolulu portions of tours will be the ones set up for organized sightseeing, while visits to the neighboring islands will tend to include a rental car. Because driving yourself is such a popular way of seeing Hawaii, and because rental cars are relatively inexpensive, nearly every company that offers tours to Hawaii has a certain number of wholly U-drive plans available. Even in the most basic stay-put package, a "car for a day" may be a feature.

A rental car also is part of most condominium packages, a type of vacation that is becoming more and more important in the overall Hawaiian tourism picture. The package usually includes nothing more than daily car rental and accommodations, which are in privately owned condominiums whose rates for a couple compare very favorably with double-occupancy hotel rates, and they become even more attractive when two couples or a family travel together. In addition, fully equipped kitchens or kitchenettes allow travelers to save money by preparing many meals themselves, breakfast in particular. Some condominium developments offer all the amenities and services of a hotel, whereas others stress simplicity and seclusion; in either case, the spaciousness and frequent luxury of the premises, together with the often prime locations of the properties, prevent their being considered as mere cost-cutting alternatives to hotel rooms.

A number of tour operators include condominium holidays among their regular offerings; these packages also can be booked through travel agents and condominium rental specialists (see *Accommodations,* in this section). For instance, *Hawaii Land Vacations* (550 Kearny St., San Francisco, CA 94108; phone: 800-765-7000), a subsidiary of *American Hawaii Cruises,* offers 52 land vacation packages which include lodging at a selection of condominium properties (or hotels) throughout the islands, rental car (except for stays in Waikiki, which instead include transfers), lei greeting, and inter-island airfare. Unlike other operators with similar offerings, however, *Hawaii Land Vacations* offers these packages only to customers who take one of the parent company's inter-island cruises (see *Traveling by Ship,* in this section).

Most of the foregoing packages could be described as independent tours or, at the most, hosted tours. Having gotten you to your destination and having provided a place to stay, they leave you by yourself, free to do as you want. A representative of the tour company may be available at a local office to answer questions, or a company host may be stationed at a desk in the hotel or condominium development, again to answer questions, handle problems, or assist in arranging activities or optional excursions.

Not everyone prefers lack of structure, however. While fully escorted, all-inclusive group sightseeing tours to and through Hawaii are not as common as they are to some other destinations, they do exist. Hotel accommodations in these packages usually are characterized as first class or better, although more than a few tour packagers offer less expensive alternatives by providing more modest lodgings. Breakfast almost always is included, whereas the number of lunches and dinners may vary considerably, and meals include wine (or other alcoholic beverages) only when the tour literature clearly states so. Also included are transfers between airport and hotel, baggage handling, tips to maids and waiters, local transportation, and sightseeing excursions and admission fees, as well as any featured evening entertainment, personal expenses for laundry, incidentals and souvenirs, and tips to the motorcoach driver and to the tour escort, who remains with the group from beginning to end — almost everything, in fact, except round-trip airfare between the mainland and Hawaii (which generally is shown separately).

Among the companies offering this type of all-inclusive package are the following:

American Express Vacations (3400 Robards Court, Louisville, KY 40218; phone: 800-241-1700). Offers 7-, 9-, and 13-day, two-, three-, and four-island escorted tours.

Cartan Tours (2809 Butterfield Rd., Oakbrook, IL 60521; phone: 800-422-7826). Offers 8-, 11-, and 13-day, two-, three-, and four-island escorted tours with many meals included. This tour operator is a wholesaler, so use a travel agent.

Collette Tours (162 Middle St., Pawtucket, RI 02860; phone: 800-752-2655). Offers 9-, 12-, and 14-day, two-, three-, and four-island escorted (or independent) tours, including some meals.

Cosmos/Globus Gateway Tours (95-25 Queens Blvd., Rego Park, NY 11374; phone: 718-268-1700 or 718-268-7000 in New York State; 800-221-0090 elsewhere in the US). Offers 10- and 13-day, four-island escorted tours, including most meals.

Grandtravel (6900 Wisconsin Ave., Suite 706, Chevy Chase, MD 20815; phone: 800-247-7651 or 301-986-0790). This company, which specializes in packages for grandparents traveling with their granchildren, offers a 12-day cruise of four Hawaiian islands.

Maupintour (PO Box 807, Lawrence, KS 66044; phone: 800-255-4266). Offers 9- and 12-day, three- and four-island escorted tours with many meals included.

Mayflower (1225 Warren Ave., Downers Grove, IL 60515; phone: 708-960-3430). Offers a 13-day, four-island tour.

Tauck Tours (PO Box 5027, Westport, CT 06881; phone: 203-226-6911). Offers a 13-day Complete Tour of Hawaii that visits Oahu, Molokai, Maui, the Big Island, and Kauai, with daily sightseeing by motorcoach or helicopter. Most meals are included. Also offers a 9-day, three-island tour with many of the same features.

Special-Interest Packages – Special-interest tours are a growing sector of the travel industry, and prominent among these are packages built around sports or those designed to bring nature lovers as close as possible to the beauty of the Hawaiian landscape. One thing to note about special-interest packages is that they tend to be quite structured arrangements rather than independent ones, and often are not created with the budget traveler in mind.

Among the companies offering wilderness and adventure packages in Hawaii are the following:

American Wilderness Experience (PO Box 1486, Boulder, CO 80306; phone: 800-444-0099 or 303-444-2622). Offers several itineraries exploring these tropical islands, many focusing on ocean wildlife and natural history. Accommodations are in tents, cabins, lodges, or aboard yachts.

The Challenges (PO Box 5489, Glendale, AZ 85312; phone: 800-448-9816 or 602-878-7071). Offers a Maui Challenge package, featuring luxurious oceanfront estate accommodations, for travelers seeking outdoor adventure with an emphasis on physical fitness

Eye of the Whale (*Marine Wilderness Adventures,* PO Box 1269, Kapa'au, HI 96755; phone: 800-657-7730 or 808-889-0227). Offers tours led by naturalist guides focusing on Hawaiian ecosystems on or around the Big Island, Kauai, and Molokai. Depending on the itinerary, accommodations may be in cabins, bed and breakfast establishments, inns, or on yachts.

International Expeditions (One Environs Park, Helena, AL 35080; phone: 800-633-4734 or 205-428-1700). Offers expeditions visiting the Big Island, Kauai, and Maui that focus on the undisturbed wildlife of Hawaii.

Mountain Travel/Sobek Expeditions (6420 Fairmount Ave., El Cerrito, CA 94530-3606; phone: 800-227-2384 or 510-527-8100). Offers several Hawaiian itineraries, focusing on the exploration of its rain forests, volcanoes, and coral reefs.

Nature Expeditions International (PO Box 11496, Eugene, OR 97440; phone: 503-484-6529). Offers a 15-day natural history study tour of the Big Island, Kauai, Maui, and Oahu that includes lectures and tours focusing on plant and marine life, bird watching, and other aspects of the islands' natural — as well as cultural — history.

Oceanic Society Expeditions (Fort Mason Center, Building E, San Francisco, CA 94123; phone: 800-326-7491). Offers a number of whale watching trips throughout the islands.

Pacific Quest (PO Box 205, Haleiwa, HI 96712; phone: 800-367-8047, ext. 523, or 808-638-8338). Offers a 13-day package exploring the volcanoes, tropical forests, and ancient temples of the Big Island, Kauai, and Maui.

Questers Worldwide Nature Tours (257 Park Ave. S., New York, NY 10016; phone: 212-779-3480). Offers a 15-day venture that visits the Big Island, Kauai, Lanai, Maui, Molokai, and Oahu, focusing on the islands' natural history and wildlife that includes activities such as bird watching, hiking, and snorkeling.

Victor Emanuel Nature Tours (PO Box 33008, Austin, TX 78764; phone: 800-328-VENT). This nature specialist offers a 15-day trip to Hawaii featuring bird watching on Kauai, Maui, and Oahu.

Wildlife Adventures (3516 NE 155th St., Seattle, WA 98155; phone: 800-345-4453). Offers 8-day and 11-day explorations of Kauai, Molokai, and Oahu focusing on the wildlife of the islands and surrounding waters.

For further information on outdoor adventures and activities, see *Camping and RVs, Hiking and Biking* below, DIVERSIONS, and the individual island reports elsewhere in this guide.

It is not unusual for Hawaii to be packaged in concert with other domestic destinations to be visited en route to or from the islands. These "stopover" packages are especially appealing to Easterners and Midwesterners who can thus visit one or more western city, such as Las Vegas, Los Angeles, San Francisco, or San Diego, usually for no additional airfare. For instance, *Liberty Travel* offers a 2-week package that combines 3 days in San Francisco and 7 in Honolulu with a choice of 3 days in either Las Vegas or Los Angeles on the return trip. *Liberty Travel* has over 100 retail outlets; for the one nearest you, contact the central office at 69 Spring St., Ramsey, NJ 07446 (phone: 201-934-3500).

Hawaii itself, finally, may be offered as a stopover or extension on packages to more distant destinations in the Far East or the South Pacific. For instance, *Cosmos/Globus Gateway Tours* (95-25 Queens Blvd., Rego Park NY 11374; phone: 718-268-1700 or 718-268-7000 in New York State; 800-221-0090 elsewhere in the US) has designed 4- and 8-day Hawaiian extensions, visiting Honolulu and Oahu, which can be added to any of its escorted tours to Australia, New Zealand, the South Pacific Islands, and the Orient. If you are considering booking such a package, ask your travel agent whether the applicable airfare allows a stopover.

Camping and RVs, Hiking and Biking

CAMPING: Hawaii's year-round warm climate and splendid scenery can make for delightful adventures. Camping is very popular in the Hawaiian islands, which boast numerous parks that are open year-round and offer camping facilities, hiking trails, fishing, swimming, and other amenities. You can sleep in an RV, a tent, or with nothing between you and the outdoors but your bedroll.

Directors of campgrounds often have a great deal of information about their island, and some even will arrange local tours or recommend the best restaurants, shops, beaches, or attractions in the immediate area. Campgrounds also provide the atmosphere and opportunity to meet other travelers and exchange useful information. Too much so, sometimes — the popularity of the Hawaiian campgrounds causes them to be quite crowded during the winter, and campsites can be so close together that any attempt at privacy or getting away from it all is sabotaged. As campgrounds fill quickly throughout the season, and the more isolated sites always go first, it's a good idea to arrive early in the day and reserve your chosen spot — which leaves you free to explore the area for the rest of the day. (Whenever possible, try to call ahead and arrange a "pitch" in advance. At the height of the season, however, if you do not have advance reservations, you may be lucky to get even a less desirable site.) Those interested in camping in more remote areas should be aware that permits often are required. Many facilities also have maximum length of stay restrictions — generally from 3 to 7 days.

For detailed information on the top camping sites in the state, permit and reservation requirements, and the best sources of information on each facility, see *Camping from Crater to Coastline* in DIVERSIONS. You'll also find discussions of camping facilities in the individual island chapters.

Information on the national, state, and county campgrounds in the Hawaiian islands also is available from the following sources:

National

Haleakala National Park: Superintendent, PO Box 369, Makawao, HI 96718 (phone: 808-572-9177).

Hawaii Volcanoes National Park: Superintendent, PO Box 52, Hawaii Volcanoes National Park, HI 96718-0052 (phone: 808-967-7311).

State

Hawaii: Division of State Parks, PO Box 936, Hilo, HI 96721 (phone: 808-933-4200).

Kauai: Division of State Parks, PO Box 1671, Lihue, HI 96766 (phone: 808-241-3444).

Maui and Molokai: Division of State Parks, 54 South High St., Wailuku, HI 96793 (phone: 808-243-5354).

Oahu: Division of State Parks, PO Box 621, Honolulu, HI 96809 (phone: 808-587-0300).

County

Hawaii: Department of Parks and Recreation, 25 Aupuni St., Hilo, HI 967201 (phone: 808-961-8311).

Kauai: Division of Parks and Recreation, County of Kauai, 4193 Hardy St., Lihue, HI 96766 (phone: 808-245-8821).

Maui: Department of Recreation, War Memorial Gym, 1580 Kaahumanu Ave., Wailuku, HI 96793 (phone: 808-243-7230).

Molokai: County Parks Department, Kaunakakai, HI 96748 (no phone; write).

Oahu: Department of Parks and Recreation, 650 S. King St., Honolulu, HI 96813 (phone: 808-523-4182).

Brief descriptions of the individual parks, campgrounds, and their facilities may be found in the following sources:

Allstate Motor Club RV and Campground Directory (Prentice Hall; nationwide edition, $14.95).

The National Parks: Index, 1989 (doc. #024-005-01056-4; $3). Write to the Superintendent of Documents, US Government Printing Office, Washington, DC 20402 (phone: 202-783-3238).

Sierra Club Guides to the National Parks: Pacific Southwest and Hawaii (*Sierra Club;* $16.95).

Woodall's Campground Directory, Western Edition (Woodall; $10.95, including postage and handling).

For a more thorough discussion of Hawaiian campgrounds, as well as advice on a number of related topics, look in the travel section of your local bookstore for *Hawaii, Naturally,* by David Zurick. It also is available for $12.95 from Wilderness Press, 2440 Bancroft Way, Berkeley, CA 94704 (phone: 510-843-8080).

Camping Equipment – Although it's often best to bring along your own, as on the mainland, camping equipment is available for sale or rent throughout Hawaii, and rentals can be booked in advance through any number of outfitters. The above-mentioned guides, park authorities, and the local tourist offices all are good sources for information on reliable dealers.

■ **Note:** Two good sources for renting camping gear are *Jungle Bob's* on Kauai (PO

Box 1245, Hanalei, HI 96714; phone 808-826-6664) and *Omar the Tent Man* (650A Kakoi St., Honolulu, HI 96819; phone: 808-836-8785).

Organized Camping Trips – A packaged camping tour in Hawaii is a good way to have your cake and eat it, too. The problems of advance planning and day-to-day organizing are left to someone else, yet you still reap the benefits that shoestring travel affords and can enjoy the insights of experienced guides and the company of other campers. Be aware, however, that these packages usually are geared to the young, with ages 18 to 35 as common limits. Transfer from place to place often is by bus or van (as on other sightseeing tours), overnights are in tents, and meal arrangements vary. Often there is a kitty that covers meals in restaurants or in the camps; sometimes there is a chef, and sometimes the cooking is done by the participants themselves. When considering a packaged camping tour, be sure to find out if equipment is included and what individual participants are required to bring. (For information on companies and associations offering package tours that include camping, see "Sample Package Tours," below.)

RECREATIONAL VEHICLES: The term recreational vehicles — RVs — is applied to all manner of camping vehicles, whether towed or self-propelled. RVs will appeal most to the kind of person who prefers the flexibility of accommodation and enjoys camping with a little extra comfort.

As none of the campgrounds in Hawaii provide RV hookups (and RVs are restricted within the islands, see below), the only models available for rent are minivans — vans customized in various ways for camping, often including elevated roofs. An RV undoubtedly saves a traveler a great deal of money on accommodations; in-camp cooking saves money on food as well. However, it is important to remember that renting an RV is a major expense, and minivans get relatively low gas mileage — a consideration in Hawaii, where gasoline is more expensive than on the mainland.

Note that RVs are permitted *only* on the Big Island of Hawaii — in Hawaii Volcanoes National Park — and in some of the state parks on Kauai. RV rental rates in Hawaii generally vary depending on the number of days rented, and often include customer pick-up and drop-off services at the airport. At the time of this writing, there were no companies specializing in RV rentals in the Hawaiian islands, but a common source of minivans is the car rental companies listed in *Touring by Car,* in this section, although you may have to do some calling around to find one. The tourist board offices should be able to provide information on RV rental sources, as well as where RVs are permitted.

Useful information on RVs is available from the following sources:

Living on Wheels by Richard A. Wolters. Provides useful information on how to choose and operate a recreational vehicle. As it's currently out of print, check your library.

Recreational Vehicle Industry Association (*RVIA;* Dept. RK, PO Box 2999, Reston, VA 22090-0999). Issues a useful complimentary package of information on RVs, as well as a 24-page magazine-size guide, *Set Free in an RV* ($3), and a free catalogue of RV sources and consumer information. Write to the association for these and other publications.

Recreational Vehicle Rental Association (*RVRA;* 3251 Old Lee Hwy., Suite 500, Fairfax, VA 22030; phone: 800-336-0355 or 703-591-7130). This RV dealers group publishes an annual rental directory, *Who's Who in RV Rentals* ($7.50).

TL Enterprises (29901 Agoura Rd., Agoura, CA 91301; phone: 818-991-4980) publishes two monthly magazines for RV enthusiasts: *Motorhome* and *Trailer Life.* A year's subscription to *Motorhome* costs $17.98; a subscription to *Trailer Life* costs $14.98. Members of the *TL Enterprises' Good Sam Club* can subscribe to *Motorhome* for $12 and to *Trailer Life* for $11, and also receive discounts on a variety of other RV services; Membership costs $19 per year.

Trailblazer (1000 124th Ave. NE, Bellevue, WA 98005; phone: 206-455-8585). A recreational vehicle and motorhome magazine. A year's subscription costs $24.

HIKING: If you would rather eliminate all the gear and planning and take to the outdoors unencumbered, park the car and go for a day's hike. There are fabulous trails all over Hawaii. For information on exploring Hawaii afoot, see *Hiking the Hawaiian Wilderness,* in DIVERSIONS.

For those who are hiking on their own, without benefit of a guide or group, a map of the trail is a must. Preliminary information on where to hike is available from the Hawaiian Visitors Bureau both on the mainland and in the Hawaiian islands, and most parks provide maps of the trails in their domains.

For information and maps for Hawaii's State Forest Reserves, write ahead to the individual island's Department of Land and Natural Resources, Division of Forestry and Wildlife, at the following addresses:

Hawaii: PO Box 4849, Hilo, HI 96720.
Kauai: PO Box 1671, Lihue, HI 96766.
Maui: PO Box 1015, Wailuku, HI 96793-0330.
Oahu: 1151 Punchbowl St., Honolulu, HI 96813.

The *US Geologial Survey Maps of the National Parks* ($5.75 each), published by the Department of the Interior, provide detailed information on topography, trails, roads, and other features of the national parks. The *National Forest Maps* ($7.95), published by the Department of Agriculture, provides the same details on national forests. A wealth of other useful maps is available from *Map Link* (25 E. Mason St., Suite 201, Santa Barbara, CA 93101; phone: 805-965-4402), one of the best sources for detailed topographical maps and just about any other type of map (of just about anywhere in the world). Their comprehensive guide *The World Map Directory* ($29.95) includes a host of sources for travelers afoot, and if they don't stock a map of the area in which you are interested (or the type of map best suited to your outdoor exploration), they will order it for you. (For information on companies and associations offering package tours that include hiking, see "Sample Package Tours," below.)

Other sources for those intent on getting about on their own steam include the following:

Hawaii: A Walker's Guide, by Rodney Smith, takes you on a guided tour of some of the most idyllic spots in the islands. It is available for $13.95 from Hunter Publishing, 300 Raritan Center Parkway, Edison, NJ 08818 (phone: 908-225-1900).

Hawaiian Hiking Trails by Craig Chisholm; available for $14.95, plus $1.50 for shipping and handling, from Fernglen Press (473 6th St., Lake Oswego, OR 97034; phone: 503-635-4719). Features 49 trails on the five major islands, along with useful, detailed information on difficulty, time, altitude, and average calories expended on each hike.

Hiking Hawaii, Kauai, Maui, Oahu series ($8.95 each), by Robert Smith, discusses each island's trails in detail, including permit requirements. To order, write to Hawaii Outdoor Adventures Press (PO Box 869, Huntington Beach, CA 92648).

Hawaii's Best Hiking Trails ($12.95), also by Robert Smith, combines the highlights of his *Hiking* series and gives additional information on Molokai and Lanai. This book also can be ordered by writing to Hawaii Outdoor Adventure Press (address above).

Hawaiian Trail and Mountain Club (PO Box 2238, Honolulu 96804; phone:

808-247-3922). This nonprofit hiking club offers day hikes throughout the islands. For information on upcoming excursions, send a self-addressed, stamped envelope to the club.

BIKING: For young and/or fit travelers, a bicycle offers a marvelous tool for exploring. The Oahu coast is ideal for bicycling, with no dramatic hills, and services never too far away (except for along the northern corner of the Waianae Coast). Top beaches and attractions are accessible via half-day treks from Waikiki. Cyclists seeking a gentler ride prefer to take the coastal routes, while those in top condition may take on the challenge of the steeper routes both north and south up the central plateau. Note, however, that bike lanes are few and traffic can be heavy.

As home of the annual *Ironman Triathlon,* the Big Island sees more than its share of bicycling. The tougher route that heads north up the Kohala Coast to Waimea should be tackled only by experienced riders.

Detailed maps of these and other routes are available from a number of sources, including the local tourist authorities (see *Tourist Information Offices,* in this section, for addresses), which often can offer recommendations on popular scenic routes. *Map Link* (see "Hiking," above) also is a good source for maps suitable for cyclists planning Hawaiian routes.

The book *American Biking Atlas & Touring Guide* by Sue Browder (Workman) describes 3 tour routes in Hawaii; *Bicycling in Hawaii* by Robert Immler (Wilderness Press) outlines 20 tours around all the islands and rates them according to distance, difficulty, and traffic. Both of these books are out of print, but are worth trying to find in your library. For general biking information, consult *The Complete Book of Bicycling* by Eugene A. Sloane (Simon & Schuster; $15.95) and *Anybody's Bike Book* by Tom Cuthberson (Ten Speed Press; $8.95).

■ **Note:** When biking, wear bright clothes and use lights or wear reflective material to increase your visibility at dusk or at night. Above all, even though many cyclists don't, always wear a helmet.

Renting a Bike – Bicycle rental agencies are listed in the individual island sections of ISLAND-BY-ISLAND HOPPING; you also can consult the yellow pages of the island phone directory. Bicycles usually must be picked up and dropped off at the same point; the available models include basic (one-gear), 10-speed, and mountain bikes. As there is no guarantee, however, of the availability or condition of rentals, serious cyclists may prefer to bring their own bikes.

Airlines generally allow bicycles to be checked as baggage; they require that the pedals be removed, handlebars be turned sideways, and the bike be in a shipping carton (which some airlines provide, subject to availability — call ahead to make sure). If buying a shipping carton from a bicycle shop, check the airline's specifications and also ask about storing the carton at the destination airport so that you can use it again for the return flight. Airlines serving Hawaii from the mainland, however, generally charge a fee of between $30 and $50 each way to transport a bicycle (inter-island carriers charge around $20), regardless of whether you already have checked two pieces of baggage. As regulations vary from carrier to carrier, be sure to call well before departure to find out your airline's specific regulations. If you plan to transport your bike inter-island, it is particularly important to check in advance with the inter-island carrier, as the smaller commuter planes may have limited baggage facilities. As with other baggage, make sure that the bike is thoroughly labeled with your name, a business address and phone number, and the correct airport destination code.

Organized Biking Trips – A number of organizations offer bike tours in Hawaii. Linking up with a bike tour is more expensive than traveling alone, but with experienced leaders, an organized tour often becomes an educational, as well as a very social, experience.

One of the attractions of a bike tour is that the shipment of equipment — the bike — is handled by the organizers, and the shipping fee is included in the total tour package. Travelers simply deliver the bike to the airport, already disassembled and boxed; shipping cartons can be obtained from most bicycle shops with little difficulty. Bicyclists not with a tour must make their own arrangements with the airline, and there are no standard procedures for this (see above). Although some tour organizers will rent bikes, most prefer that participants bring a bike with which they are already familiar. Another attraction of *some* tours is the existence of a "sag wagon" to carry extra luggage, fatigued cyclists, and their bikes, too, when pedaling another mile is impossible.

Tours vary considerably in style and ambience, so request brochures from several operators in order to make the best decision. When contacting groups, be sure to ask about the maximum number of people on the trip, the maximum number of miles to be traveled each day, and the degree of difficulty of the biking; these details should determine which tour you join and can greatly affect your enjoyment of the experience. Planning ahead is essential because trips often fill up 6 months or more in advance. (For information on companies and associations offering package tours that include biking, see "Sample Package Tours" below.)

One of the most unusual bicycling adventures in Hawaii is Maui's bike ride down the slopes of Haleakala Crater. A 38-mile guided excursion from the 10,000-foot summit features van pick-up and a ride to the top of the crater. Coasting downhill, riders view the neighboring islands, pineapple and sugarcane fields and more. All equipment and meals are provided. Some of the local companies offering this ride are: *Cruiser Bob's Original Haleakala Downhill* (PO Box B, Paia, HI 96779; phone: 800-654-7717), *Maui Downhill* (199 Dairy Rd., Kahului, HI 96732; phone: 800-535-BIKE), and *Maui Mountain Cruisers* (353 Hanamau St., Kahului, HI 96732; phone: 800-232-MAUI). Most companies offer two tours daily; the average price is $90 per person.

SAMPLE PACKAGE TOURS – A number of companies offer tours that feature camping, hiking, and biking, as well as other outdoor activities. While many of these companies specialize in outdoor adventure packages, others include these activities as part of broader tour programs. Among such companies are the following:

American Wilderness Experience (PO Box 1486, Boulder, CO 80306; phone: 800-444-0099 or 303-444-2622). Offers a 14-day, four-island camping trip in Hawaii, as well as a variety of hiking trips suitable for both novice and experienced hikers. Hiking trips explore one or several islands, and range in length from 5 to 14 days.

Backroads Bicycle Touring (1516 5th St., Berkeley, CA 94710-1713; phone: 800-245-3874 or 510-527-1555). Offers an 8-day inn-to-inn cycling tour of the Big Island of Hawaii.

The Challenges (PO Box 5489, Glendale, AZ 85312; phone: 800-448-9816 or 602-878-7071). Offers an adventure package on Maui with an emphasis on physical fitness, including windsurfing, snorkeling, hiking and other outdoor activities.

Charley's Trail Rides and Pack Trips (Charles Aki, Jr., c/o Kaupo Store, Hana, Maui 96713; phone: 808-248-8209). Offers guided horseback rides up the slopes of Haleakala Crater which include a night of camping inside the crater. Meals and all equipment are included.

Eye of the Whale (*Marine Wilderness Adventures,* PO Box 1269, Kapa'au, HI 96755; phone: 800-657-7730 or 808-889-0227). Offers a 7-day Earth, Fire, and Sea hiking trip on the Big Island with naturalist guides and a 10-day Hiking Odyssey tour to Kauai, Molokai, and Hawaii.

Hawaiian Bicycle Experience Tours (PO Box 1874, Kihei, HI 96753; phone:

808-874-1929). Offers 7-day hiking/biking/sailing trips on the Big Island and Maui, as well as customized day trips for individuals and groups. Several of their packages include accommodations at bed and breakfast establishments.

Mountain Travel/Sobek Expeditions (6420 Fairmount Ave., El Cerrito, CA 94530-3606; phone: 800-227-2384 or 510-527-8100). This adventure package specialist offers a variety of packages combining camping, hiking, and other outdoor activities, with an emphasis on appreciation of an area's natural history and wildlife. Trips usually cover several islands, including Kauai, Hawaii, Maui, and Molokai. The company also offers several hiking trips on the Big Island and Kauai, exploring these islands' rain forests, volcanoes, and coral reefs.

MountainFit (350 Fifth Ave., Suite 3304, New York, NY 10118; phone: 800-926-5700). Offers 1-week fitness packages on Maui, featuring day hikes of 5 to 15 miles, as well as snorkeling, sea kayaking, and windsurfing. Amenities include massage, sauna, and yoga classes.

New England Hiking Holidays (PO Box 1648, North Conway, NH 03860; phone: 603-356-9696). Offers a 7-day hiking trip that traverses the Big Island, including Hawaii Volcanoes National Park, with stays at hotels along the way.

North Shore Bike, Cruise, & Snorkel (PO Box 1192, Kapaa, HI 96746; phone: 808-822-1582). Offers full-day guided bicycle/snorkel excursions along the north shore of Kauai, including a 6-mile bike excursion with support van, all equipment, and barbecue lunch on the beach.

On the Loose Bicycle Vacations (1030 Merced St., Berkeley, CA 94707; phone: 510-527-4005). Offers two Hawaiian tours: 10 days exploring the Big Island, including the Kona Coast and Hawaii Volcanoes National Park; 7 days on the Big Island and 3 days on Maui. Both tours feature first class accommodations.

Outdoor Woman's School–Call of the Wild (2519 Cedar St., Berkeley, CA 94708; phone: 510-849-9292). Offers a 9-day camping/hiking trip on the Na Pali Coast of Kauai — for women only.

Outfitters Kauai (PO Box 1149, Poipu Beach, HI 96756; phone: 808-742-9667). Offers 1-day biking trips on Kauai, above the Waimea Canyon.

Overseas Adventure Travel (349 Broadway, Cambridge, MA 02139; phone: 800-221-0814 or 617-876-0533). Offers two 14-day hiking trips focusing on the natural history and culture of several islands.

Wilderness Travel (801 Allston Way, Berkeley, CA 94710; phone: 800-247-6700 or 510-548-0420). This adventure packager, known for expeditions in the wild, regularly offers hiking tours in Hawaii. Offerings include a 14-day hiking trip on the Big Island, Maui, and Kauai.

Wildland Adventures (3516 NE 155th St., Seattle, WA 98155; phone: 800-345-4453 or 206-365-0686). Offers an 11-day hiking trip on Kauai, Molokai, and the Big Island.

An alternative to dealing directly with the above companies is to contact *All Adventure Travel,* a specialist in hiking and biking trips worldwide. This company, which acts as a representative for numerous special tour packagers offering such outdoor adventures, can provide a wealth of detailed information about each packager and programs offered. They also will help you design and arrange all aspects of a personalized itinerary. This company operates much like a travel agency, collecting commissions from the packagers. Therefore, there is no additional charge for these services. For information, contact *All Adventure Travel,* PO Box 4307, Boulder, CO 80306 (phone: 800-537-4025 or 303-499-1981.)

Also, the *Specialty Travel Index* (305 San Anselmo Ave., Suite 313, San Anselmo, CA 94960; phone: 415-459-4900 in California; 800-442-4942 elsewhere in the US) is a special-interest travel directory and an invaluable resource. Listings include tour operators specializing in camping, as well as myriad other activities that combine nicely with a camping trip, such as biking, horseback riding, scuba diving, and other water sports. The index costs $6 per copy, $10 for a year's subscription of two issues.

ADDITIONAL RESOURCES – Other useful sources of information on camping, hiking, and biking in the Hawaiian islands include the following organizations, most of which also sponsor tours of their own.

American Youth Hostels (PO Box 37613, Washington, DC 20013-7613; phone: 202-783-6161). This nonprofit organization and its local chapters regularly sponsor hiking and biking trips. Membership is open to all ages and departures are geared to various age groups and levels of skill and frequently feature accommodations in hostels — along with hotels for adults and campgrounds for younger participants.

The Hawaii Bicycling League (Box 4403, Honolulu, HI 96812-4403; phone: 808-735-5756). This local bicycle club sponsors weekend rides — not tours. Although these are mainly for local residents, visiting cyclists may be permitted to join.

International Bicycle Touring Society (*IBTS;* PO Box 6979, San Diego, CA 92166-0979; phone: 619-226-TOUR). Regularly sponsors low-cost bicycle tours led by member volunteers. Participants must be over 21. For information, send them $2 plus a self-addressed, stamped envelope.

League of American Wheelmen (190 W. Ostend St., Suite 1208, Baltimore, MD 21230; phone: 301-539-3399). This organization publishes *Tourfinder,* a list of organizations that sponsor bicycle tours of the US and abroad. The list is free with membership ($25 individual, $30 family) and can be obtained by non-members who send $5. The *League* also can put you in touch with biking groups in your area.

Sierra Club (Outing Dept., 730 Polk St., San Francisco, CA 94109; phone: 415-776-2211). Dedicated to preserving and protecting the natural environment, this nonprofit organization also offers a variety of trips each year to the Big Island, Kauai, and Maui. These include walking tours and camping trips that involve other outdoor activities such as biking and sea kayaking. Some are backpacking trips, moving to a new camp each day; others make day hikes from a base camp.

Preparing

Calculating Costs

A realistic appraisal of travel expenses is the most crucial bit of planning you will undertake before any trip. It also is, unfortunately, one for which it is most difficult to give precise, practical advice.

In Hawaii, estimating travel expenses depends on the mode of transportation you choose, the part or parts of the Hawaiian islands you plan to visit, how long you will stay, and, in some cases, what time of year you plan to travel. In addition to the basics of transportation, hotels, meals, and sightseeing, you have to take into account seasonal price changes that apply on certain air routings and in popular resort areas.

DETERMINING A BUDGET: When calculating costs, start with the basics, the major expenses being transportation, accommodations, and food. However, don't forget such extras as local transportation, shopping, and such miscellaneous items as laundry and tips. The reasonable cost of these items usually is a positive surprise to your budget. Ask about special discount passes that provide tourists with unlimited travel by the day or the week on local public transportation. For instance, an economical monthly pass is available for bus travel on Oahu. Entries in the individual island reports in ISLAND-BY-ISLAND HOPPING also give helpful information on local transportation options.

Other expenses, such as the cost of local sightseeing tours and other excursions, will vary from island to island. Tourist information offices are plentiful throughout Hawaii, and most of the better hotels will have someone at the front desk to provide a rundown on the costs of local tours and full-day excursions on and off the island. Travel agents also can provide this information.

Savings can be found in the more remote areas of the islands; budget-minded families also can take advantage of some of the more economical accommodations options to be found in Hawaii (see our discussion of accommodations in *On the Islands,* in this section). Campgrounds are particularly inexpensive and they are located throughout the Hawaiian islands (see *Camping and RVs, Hiking and Biking,* in this section.) Picnicking is another way to cut costs, and Hawaii abounds with well-groomed parks, beaches, and idyllic tropical settings. A stop at a delicatessen or market can provide a feast of delicacies at a surprisingly economical price compared to the cost of a restaurant lunch.

In planning any travel budget, it also is wise to allow a realistic amount for both entertainment and recreation. Are you planning to spend time sightseeing and visiting local tourist attractions? Do you intend to rent a catamaran or take windsurfing lessons? Is daily golf or tennis a part of your plan? Will your children be disappointed if they don't take a helicopter ride (an expensive but exciting way to see the sights in Hawaii) or a whale watching cruise? Finally, don't forget that if haunting discotheques or other nightspots is an essential part of your vacation, or you feel that one luau and/or Polynesian dinner show may not be enough, allow for the extra cost of nightlife. This one item alone can add a great deal to your daily expenditures, whether in Honolulu or on neighboring islands.

If at any point in the planning process it appears impossible to estimate expenses, consider this suggestion: The easiest way to put a ceiling on the price of all these elements is to buy a package tour. A totally planned and escorted one, with almost all transportation, rooms, meals, sightseeing, local travel, tips, and a dinner show or two included and prepaid, provides a pretty exact total of what the trip will cost beforehand, and the only surprise will be the one you spring on yourself by succumbing to some irresistible, expensive souvenir.

Planning a Trip

Travelers fall into two categories: those who make lists and those who do not. Some people prefer to plot the course of their trip to the finest detail, with contingency plans and alternatives at the ready. For others, the joy of a voyage is its spontaneity; exhaustive planning only lessens the thrill of anticipation and the sense of freedom.

For most travelers, however, any week-plus trip to Hawaii can be too expensive for an "I'll take my chances" type of attitude. Even perennial gypsies and anarchistic wanderers have to take into account the time-consuming logistics of getting around, and even with minimal baggage, they need to think about packing. Hence, at least some planning is crucial.

This is not to suggest that you work out your itinerary in minute detail before you go; but it's still wise to decide certain basics at the very start: where to go, what to do, and how much to spend. These decisions require a certain amount of consideration. So before rigorously planning specific details, you might want to establish your general travel objectives:

1. How much time will you have for the entire trip, and how much of it are you willing to spend getting where you're going?
2. What interests and/or activities do you want to pursue while on vacation? Do you want to visit one, a few, or several different places?
3. At what time of year do you want to go?
4. What kind of topography would you prefer?
5. Do you want peace and privacy or lots of activity and company?
6. How much money can you afford to spend for the entire vacation?

You now can make almost all of your own travel arrangements if you have time to follow through with hotels, airlines, tour operators, and so on. But you'll probably save considerable time and energy if you have a travel agent make arrangements for you. The agent also should be able to advise you of alternate arrangements of which you may not be aware. Only rarely will a travel agent's services cost a traveler any money, and they may even save you some (see *How to Use a Travel Agent,* below).

Pay particular attention to the dates when off-season rates go into effect. In major resort areas, accommodations may cost less during the off-season (and the weather often is perfectly acceptable at this time). Off-season rates frequently are lower for other facilities, too, although don't expect to save much on car rental costs during any season. In general, it is a good idea to be aware of holiday weeks, as rates at hotels generally are higher during these periods and rooms normally are heavily booked.

Make plans early. For a trip to Hawaii, make hotel reservations for a winter visit as far in advance as possible. Several months is advisable and as early as a year in advance is not too soon to reserve for the holidays, especially during *Easter Week* and the *Christmas/New Year* period. If you are flying at these times and want to benefit from the savings of discount fares or charter programs, purchase tickets as far ahead as possible. The less flexible your schedule requirements, the earlier you should book. Many hotels require deposits before they will guarantee reservations, and this most often is the case during peak travel periods. (Be sure to request a receipt for any deposit or use a credit card.)

Before your departure, find out what the weather is likely to be at your destination — in Hawaii, relatively fair all year long. See *When to Go,* in this section, for a brief description of climatic variations in the islands; see *How to Pack,* also in this section, for some suggestions on how to decide what clothes to take. Also see the individual island chapters for information on special events that may occur during your stay, as well as for essential information on local transportation and other services and resources.

Make a list of any valuable items you are carrying with you, including credit card numbers and the serial numbers of your traveler's checks. Put copies in your purse or pocket and leave other copies at home. Put a label with your name and home address on the inside of your luggage for identification in case of loss. Put your name and business address — *never your home address* — on a label on the outside of your luggage. (Those who run businesses from home should use the office address of a friend or relative.)

Review your travel documents. If you are traveling by air, check that your ticket has been filled in correctly. The left side of the ticket should have a list of each stop you will make (even if you are only stopping to change planes), beginning with your departure point. Be sure that the list is correct, and count the number of copies to see that you have one for each plane you will take. If you have confirmed reservations, be sure that the column marked "status" says "OK" beside each flight. Have in hand vouchers or proof of payment for any reservation for which you've paid in advance; this includes hotels, transfers to and from the airport, sightseeing tours, car rentals, and tickets to special events.

Although policies vary from carrier to carrier, it's still smart to reconfirm your flight 48 to 72 hours before departure, both going and returning. Reconfirmation is particularly recommended for inter-island flights within Hawaii. If you will be driving while in the islands, bring your driver's license.

Finally, you always should bear in mind that despite the most careful plans, things do not always occur on schedule. If you maintain a flexible attitude and try to accept minor disruptions as less than cataclysmic, you will enjoy yourself a lot more.

How to Use a Travel Agent

T.A. A reliable travel agent remains the best source of service and information for planning a trip, whether you have a specific itinerary and require an agent only to make reservations or you need extensive help in sorting through the maze of airfares, tour offerings, hotel packages, and the scores of other arrangements that may be involved in a trip to Hawaii.

Know what you want from a travel agent so that you can evaluate what you are getting. It is perfectly reasonable to expect your agent to be a thoroughly knowledgeable travel specialist, with information about your destination and, even more crucial, a command of current airfares, ground arrangements, and other wrinkles in the travel scene.

Most travel agents work through computer reservations systems (CRS). These are used to assess the availability and cost of flights, hotels, and car rentals, and through them they can book reservations. Despite reports of "computer bias," in which a computer may favor one airline over another, the CRS should provide agents with the entire spectrum of flights available to a given destination and the complete range of fares in considerably less time than it takes to telephone the airlines individually — and at no extra cost to the client.

Make the most intelligent use of a travel agent's time and expertise; understand the economics of the industry. As a client, traditionally you pay nothing for the agent's services; with few exceptions, it's all free, from hotel bookings to advice on package tours. Any money the travel agent makes on the time spent arranging your itinerary — booking hotels, resorts, or flights, or suggesting activities — comes from commissions paid by the suppliers of these services — the airlines, hotels, and so on. These commissions generally run from 10% to 15% of the total cost of the service, although suppliers often reward agencies that sell their services in volume with an increased commission, called an override. In most instances, you'll find that travel agents make their time and experience available to you at no charge, and you do not pay more for an airline ticket, package tour, or other product bought from a travel agent than you would for the same one bought directly from the supplier.

Exceptions to the general rule of free service by a travel agency are the agencies that practice net pricing. In essence, such agencies return their commissions and overrides to their customers and make their income by charging a flat fee per transaction instead (thus adding a charge after a reduction for the commission has been made). Net fares and fees are a growing practice, though hardly widespread.

Even a conventional travel agent sometimes may charge a fee for special services. These chargeable items may include long-distance telephone or cable costs incurred in making a booking, for reserving a room in a place that does not pay a commission (such as a small, out-of-the way hotel), or for special attention such as planning a highly personalized itinerary. A fee also may be assessed in instances of deeply discounted airfares.

Choose a travel agent with the same care with which you would choose a doctor or lawyer. You will be spending a good deal of money on the basis of the agent's judgment, so you have a right to expect that judgment to be mature, informed, and interested. At the moment, unfortunately, there aren't many standards within the travel agent industry to help you gauge competence, and the quality of individual agents varies enormously.

At present, only nine states have registration, licensing, or other forms of travel agent–related legislation on their books. Rhode Island licenses travel agents; Florida, Hawaii, Iowa, and Ohio register them; and California, Illinois, Oregon, and Washington have laws governing the sale of transportation or related services. While state licensing of agents cannot absolutely guarantee competence, it can at least ensure that an agent has met some minimum requirements.

Perhaps the best-prepared agents are those who have completed the CTC Travel Management program offered by the *Institute of Certified Travel Agents (ICTA)* and carry the initials CTC (Certified Travel Counselor) after their names. This indicates a relatively high level of expertise. For a free list of CTCs in your area, send a self-addressed, stamped, #10 envelope to *ICTA,* 148 Linden St., Box 56, Wellesley, MA 02181 (phone: 617-237-0280 in Massachusetts; 800-542-4282 elsewhere in the US).

An agent's membership in the *American Society of Travel Agents (ASTA)* can be a useful guideline in making a selection. But keep in mind that *ASTA* is an industry organization, requiring only that its members be licensed in those states where required; be accredited to represent the suppliers whose products they sell, including airline and cruise tickets; and adhere to its Principles of Professional Conduct and Ethics code. *ASTA* does not guarantee the competence, ethics, or financial soundness of its members, but it does offer some recourse if you feel you have been dealt with unfairly. Complaints may be registered with *ASTA* (Consumer Affairs Dept., PO Box 23992, Washington, DC 20026-3992; phone: 703-739-2782). First try to resolve the complaint directly with the supplier. For a list of *ASTA* members in your area, send a self-addressed, stamped, #10 envelope to *ASTA,* Public Relations Dept., at the address above.

There also is the *Association of Retail Travel Agents (ARTA),* a smaller but highly respected trade organization similar to *ASTA.* Its member agencies and agents similarly agree to abide by a code of ethics, and complaints about a member can be made to *ARTA*'s Grievance Committee, 1745 Jeff Davis Hwy., Arlington, VA 22202-3402 (phone: 800-969-6069 or 703-553-7777).

Perhaps the best way to find a travel agent is by word of mouth. If the agent (or agency) has done a good job for your friends over a period of time, it probably indicates a certain level of commitment and competence. Always ask not only for the name of the company, but also for the name of the specific agent with whom your friends dealt, for it is that individual who will serve you, and quality can vary widely within a single agency. There are some superb travel agents in the business, and they can facilitate vacation or business arrangements.

Insurance

It is unfortunate that most decisions to buy travel insurance are impulsive and usually are made without any real consideration of the traveler's existing policies. Therefore, the first person with whom you should discuss travel insurance is your own insurance broker, not a travel agent or the clerk behind the airport insurance counter. You may discover that the insurance you already carry — homeowner's policies and/or accident, health, and life insurance — protects you adequately while you travel and that your real needs are in the more mundane areas of excess value insurance for baggage or trip cancellation insurance.

TYPES OF INSURANCE: To make insurance decisions intelligently, however, you first should understand the basic categories of travel insurance and what they cover. Then you can decide what you should have in the broader context of your personal insurance needs, and you can choose the most economical way of getting the desired protection: through riders on existing policies; with onetime short-term policies; through a special program put together for the frequent traveler; through coverage that's part of a travel club's benefits; or with a combination policy sold by insurance companies through brokers, automobile clubs, tour operators, and travel agents.

There are seven basic categories of travel insurance:

1. Baggage and personal effects insurance
2. Personal accident and sickness insurance
3. Trip cancellation and interruption insurance
4. Default and/or bankruptcy insurance
5. Flight insurance (to cover injury or death)
6. Automobile insurance (for driving your own or a rented car)
7. Combination policies

Baggage and Personal Effects Insurance – Ask your insurance agent if baggage and personal effects are included in your current homeowner's policy, or if you will need a special floater to cover you for the duration of a trip. The object is to protect your bags and their contents in case of damage or theft anytime during your travels, not just while you're in flight and covered by the airline's policy. Furthermore, only limited protection is provided by the airline. Baggage liability varies from carrier to carrier, but generally speaking, on domestic flights, luggage usually is insured to $1,250 — that's per passenger, not per bag. This limit should be specified on your airline ticket, but to be awarded any amount, you'll have to provide an itemized list of lost property, and if you're including new and/or expensive items, be prepared for a request that you back up your claim with sales receipts or other proof of purchase.

If you are carrying goods worth more than the maximum protection offered by the airline, consider excess value insurance. Additional coverage is available from airlines at an average, currently, of $1 to $2 per $100 worth of coverage, up to a maximum of $5,000. This insurance can be purchased at the airline counter when you check in, though you should arrive early to fill out the necessary forms and to avoid holding up other passengers.

Major credit card companies also provide coverage for lost or delayed baggage — and this coverage often also is over and above what the airline will pay. The basic coverage usually is automatic for all cardholders who use the credit card to purchase tickets, but to qualify for additional coverage, cardholders generally must enroll.

American Express: Provides $500 coverage for checked baggage; $1,250 for carry-on baggage; and $250 for valuables, such as cameras and jewelry.

Carte Blanche and Diners Club: Provide $1,250 free insurance for checked or carry-on baggage that's lost or damaged.

Discover Card: Offers $500 insurance for checked baggage and $1,250 for carry-on baggage — but to qualify for this coverage cardholders first must purchase additional flight insurance (see "Flight Insurance," below).

MasterCard and Visa: Baggage insurance coverage set by the issuing institution.

Additional baggage and personal effects insurance also is included in certain of the combination travel insurance policies discussed below.

■ **A note of warning:** Be sure to read the fine print of any excess value insurance policy; there often are specific exclusions, such as cash, tickets, furs, gold and silver objects, art, and antiques. And remember that insurance companies ordinarily will pay only the depreciated value of the goods rather than their replacement value. The best way to protect the items you're carrying in your luggage is to take photos of your valuables and keep a record of the serial numbers of such items as cameras, typewriters, laptop computers, radios, and so on. This will establish that you do, indeed, own the objects. If your luggage disappears en route or is damaged, deal with the situation immediately. If an airline loses your luggage, you will be asked to fill out a Property Irregularity Report before you leave the airport. If your property disappears at other transportation centers, tell the local company, but also report it to the police (since the insurance company will check with the police when processing the claim).

Personal Accident and Sickness Insurance – This covers you in case of illness during your trip or death in an accident. Most policies insure you for hospital and doctor's expenses, lost income, and so on. In most cases, it is a standard part of existing health insurance policies, though you should check with your insurance broker to be sure that your policy will pay for any medical expenses incurred abroad. If not, take out a separate vacation accident policy or an entire vacation insurance policy that includes health and life coverage.

Two examples of such comprehensive health and life insurance coverage are the travel insurance packages offered by *Wallach & Co:*

HealthCare Global: This insurance package, which can be purchased for periods of 10 to 180 days, is offered for two age groups: Men and women up to age 75 receive $25,000 medical insurance and $50,000 death benefit; those from age 76 to 84 are eligible for $12,500 medical insurance and $25,000 death benefit. For either policy, the cost for a 10-day period is $25, with decreasing rates up to 75 days, after which the rate is $1.50 a day.

HealthCare Abroad: This program is available to individuals up to age 75. For $3 per day (minimum 10 days, maximum 90 days), policy holders receive $100,000 medical insurance and $25,000 death benefit.

Both of these basic programs also may be bought in combination with trip cancellation and baggage insurance at extra cost. For further information, write to *Wallach & Co.,* PO Box 480, Middleburg, VA 22117-0480 (phone: 703-687-3166 in Virginia; 800-237-6615 elsewhere in the US).

Trip Cancellation and Interruption Insurance – Most charter and package tour passengers pay for their travel well before departure. The disappointment of having to miss a vacation because of illness or any other reason pales before the awful prospect that not all (and sometimes none) of the money paid in advance might be returned. So cancellation insurance for any package tour is a must.

Although cancellation penalties vary (they are listed in the fine print of every tour brochure, and before you purchase a package tour you should know exactly what they are), rarely will a passenger get more than 50% of this money back if forced to cancel within a few weeks of scheduled departure. Therefore, if you book a package tour or charter flight, you should have trip cancellation insurance to guarantee full reimbursement or refund should you, a traveling companion, or a member of your immediate family get sick, forcing you to cancel your trip or *return home early.*

The key here is *not* to buy just enough insurance to guarantee full reimbursement for the cost of the package or charter in case of cancellation. The proper amount of coverage should be sufficient to reimburse you for the cost of having to catch up with a tour after its departure or having to travel home at the full economy airfare if you have to forgo the return flight of your charter. There usually is quite a discrepancy between a charter fare and the amount charged to travel the same distance on a regularly scheduled flight at full economy fare.

Trip cancellation insurance is available from travel agents and tour operators in two forms: as part of a short-term, all-purpose travel insurance package (sold by the travel agent); or as specific cancellation insurance designed by the tour operator for a specific charter tour. Generally, tour operators' policies are less expensive, but also less inclusive. Cancellation insurance also is available directly from insurance companies or their agents as part of a short-term, all-inclusive travel insurance policy.

Before you decide on a policy, read each one carefully. (Either type can be purchased from a travel agent when you book the charter or package tour.) Be certain that your policy includes enough coverage to pay your fare from the farthest destination on your itinerary should you have to miss the charter flight. Also, be sure to check the fine print for stipulations concerning "family members" and "pre-existing medical conditions," as well as allowances for living expenses if you must delay your return due to bodily injury or illness.

Default and/or Bankruptcy Insurance – Although trip cancellation insurance usually protects you if *you* are unable to complete — or begin — your trip, a fairly recent innovation is coverage in the event of default and/or bankruptcy on the part of the tour operator, airline, or other travel supplier. In some travel insurance packages, this contingency is included in the trip cancellation portion of the coverage; in others, it is a separate feature. Either way, it is becoming increasingly important. Whereas sophisticated travelers have long known to beware of the possibility of default or bankruptcy when buying a charter flight or tour package, in recent years more than a few respected airlines have unexpectedly revealed their shaky financial condition, sometimes leaving hordes of stranded ticket holders in their wake. Moreover, the value of escrow protection of a charter passenger's funds lately has been unreliable. While default/bankruptcy insurance will not ordinarily result in reimbursement in time to pay for new arrangements, it can ensure that you will get your money back, and even independent travelers buying no more than an airplane ticket may want to consider it.

Flight Insurance – US airlines' liability for injury or death to passengers on domestic flights currently is determined on a case-by-case basis in court — this means potentially unlimited liability. But remember, this liability is not the same thing as an insurance policy; every penny that an airline eventually pays in the case of death or injury likely will be subject to a legal battle.

But before you buy last-minute flight insurance from an airport vending machine, consider the purchase in light of your total existing insurance coverage. A careful review of your current policies may reveal that you already are amply covered for accidental death, sometimes up to three times the amount provided for by the flight insurance you're buying at the airport.

Be aware that airport insurance, the kind typically bought at a counter or from a vending machine, is among the most expensive forms of life insurance coverage, and that even within a single airport, rates for approximately the same coverage vary widely. Often policies sold in vending machines are more expensive than those sold over the counter, even when they are with the same national company.

If you buy your plane ticket with a major credit card, you generally receive automatic insurance coverage at no extra cost. Additional coverage usually can be obtained at extremely reasonable prices, but a cardholder must sign up for it in advance. (Note that rates vary slightly for residents of some states.) As we went to press, the travel accident and life insurance policies of the major credit cards were as follows:

American Express: Automatically provides $100,000 in insurance to its *Green, Gold,* and *Optima* cardholders, and $500,000 to *Platinum* cardholders. With *American Express,* $4.50 per ticket buys an additional $250,000 worth of flight insurance; $7 buys $500,000 worth; and $14 provides an added $1 million worth of coverage.

Carte Blanche: Automatically provides $125,000 flight insurance. An additional $250,000 is available for $4. $500,000 costs $6.50.

Diners Club: Provides $350,000 free flight insurance. An additional $250,000 worth of insurance is available for $4; $500,000 costs $6.50.

Discover Card: Provides $500,000 free flight insurance. An additional $250,000 worth of insurance is available for $4.50; $500,000 costs $6.50.

MasterCard and Visa: Insurance coverage set by the issuing institution.

Automobile Insurance – If you have an accident in a state that has "no fault" insurance — as does Hawaii — each party's insurance company pays his or her expenses up to certain specified limits. When you rent a car, the rental company is required to offer you collision protection.

In your car rental contract, you'll see that for about $10 to $13 a day, you may buy optional collision damage waiver (CDW) protection. (If partial coverage with a deductible is included in the rental contract, the CDW will cover the deductible in the event of an accident, and can cost as much as $25 per day.) If you do not accept the CDW coverage, you may be liable for as much as the full retail value of the rental car, and by paying for the CDW you are relieved of all responsibility for any damage to the car. Before agreeing to this coverage, however, check with your own broker about your own existing personal automobile insurance policy. It very well may cover your entire liability exposure without any additonal cost, or you automatically may be covered by the credit card company to which you are charging the cost of your rental. To find out the amount of rental car insurance provided by major credit cards, contact the issuing institutions.

You also should know that an increasing number of the major international car rental companies automatically are including the cost of the CDW in their basic rates. Car rental prices have increased to include this coverage, although rental company ad campaigns may promote this as a new, improved rental package "benefit." The disadvantage of this inclusion is that you may not have the option to turn down the CDW — even if you already are adequately covered by your own insurance policy or through a credit card company.

Combination Policies – Short-term insurance policies, which may include a combination of any or all of the types of insurance discussed above, are available through retail insurance agencies, automobile clubs, and many travel agents. These combination policies are designed to cover you for the duration of a single trip.

Policies of this type include the following:

Access America International: A subsidiary of the Blue Cross/Blue Shield plans of New York and Washington, DC, now available nationwide. Contact *Access America,* 600 Third Ave, PO Box 807, New York, NY 10016 (phone: 800-424-3391 or 212-949-5960).

Carefree: Underwritten by The Hartford. Contact *Carefree Travel Insurance,* Arm Coverage, PO Box 310, Mineola, NY 11501 (phone: 800-645-2424 or 516-294-0220).

NEAR Services: In addition to a full range of travel services, this organization offers a comprehensive travel insurance package. An added feature is coverage for lost or stolen airline tickets. Contact *NEAR Services,* 450 Prairie Ave., Suite 101, Calumet City, IL 60409 (phone: 708-868-6700 in the Chicago area; 800-654-6700 elsewhere in the US and Canada).

Tele-Trip: Underwritten by the Mutual of Omaha Companies. Contact *Tele-Trip Co.,* PO Box 31685, 3201 Farnam St., Omaha, NE 68131 (phone: 402-345-2400 in Nebraska; 800-228-9792 elsewhere in the US).

Travel Assistance International: Provided by Europ Assistance Worldwide Services, and underwritten by Transamerica Occidental Life Insurance. Contact *Travel Assistance International,* 1133 15th St. NW, Suite 400, Washington, DC 20005 (phone: 202-331-1609 in Washington, DC; 800-821-2828 elsewhere in the US).

Travel Guard International: Underwritten by The Insurance Company of North America, it is available through authorized travel agents, or contact *Travel Guard International,* 1145 Clark St., Stevens Point, WI 54481 (phone: 715-345-0505 in Wisconsin; 800-826-1300 elsewhere in the US).

Travel Insurance PAK: Underwritten by The Travelers. Contact *The Travelers Companies,* Ticket and Travel Plans, One Tower Sq., Hartford, CT 06183-5040 (phone: 203-277-2319 in Connecticut; 800-243-3174 elsewhere in the US).

How to Pack

No one can provide a completely foolproof list of precisely what to pack, so it's best to let common sense, space, and comfort guide you. Keep one maxim in mind: Less is more. You simply won't need as much clothing as you think, and you are far more likely to need a forgotten accessory — or a needle and thread or scissors — than a particular piece of clothing.

As with almost anything relating to travel, a little planning can go a long way.

1. Where are you going — beach, mountains, or both?
2. How many total days will you be gone?
3. What's the average temperature likely to be during your stay?

The goal is to remain perfectly comfortable, neat, clean, and fashionable, but to pack as little as possible. Learn to travel light by following two firm packing principles:

1. Organize your travel wardrobe around a single color — blue or beige, for example — that allows you to mix, match, and layer clothes. Holding firm to one color scheme will make it easy to eliminate items of clothing that don't harmonize.
2. Never overpack to ensure a supply of fresh clothing — shirts, blouses, underwear — for each day of a long trip. Use hotel laundry services to wash and dry clean clothes; if these are too expensive, opt for local self-service laundries and dry cleaners.

CLIMATE AND CLOTHES: Exactly what you pack for your trip will be a function of where you are going and when, and the kinds of things you intend to do. A few degrees can make all the difference between being comfortably attired and very real suffering, so your initial step should be to find out what the general weather conditions are likely to be in the areas you will visit.

Generally speaking, the weather in the islands is warm and dry from May to October, and slightly cooler and wetter from November to March. Temperatures average in the low 80s in summer and the high 70s in winter, usually varying little from day to night. Hawaii is an informal place and calls for a casual style of dress.

Keeping temperature and climate in mind, consider the problem of luggage. Plan on one suitcase per person (and in a pinch, remember it's always easier to carry two small suitcases than to schlepp one that is roughly the size of downtown Detroit). Standard 26- to 28-inch suitcases can be made to work for 1 week or 1 month, and unless you are going for no more than a weekend, never cram wardrobes for two people into one suitcase. Hanging bags are best for dresses, suits, and jackets.

Before packing, lay out every piece of clothing you think you might want to take. Select clothing on the basis of what can serve several functions (wherever possible, clothes should be chosen that can be used for both daytime and evening wear). Pack clothes that have a lot of pockets for traveler's checks, documents, and tickets. Eliminate items that don't mix, match, or coordinate with your color scheme. If you can't wear it in at least two distinct incarnations, leave it at home. Accessorize everything beforehand so you know exactly what you will be wearing with what.

Layering is a good way to prepare for atypical temperatures or changes in the weather. For unexpectedly cool days or for outings in the mountains (where it may be cooler), recommended basics are a T-shirt and a lightweight cotton turtleneck, shirt, or sweater, which can be worn under another shirt and perhaps a third layer, such as a pullover sweater, jacket, or windbreaker. As the weather changes, you can add or remove clothes as required. And finally, as some of the best touring of the islands is often done on foot, be sure to bring comfortable shoes.

Your carry-on luggage should contain a survival kit with the basic things you will need in case your luggage gets lost or stolen: a toothbrush, toothpaste, all medications, a sweater, nightclothes, and a change of underwear. With these essential items at hand, you will be prepared for any sudden, unexpected occurrence that separates you from your suitcase. Also, if you have many 1- or 2-night stops scheduled, you can live out of your survival case without having to unpack completely at each hotel.

Sundries – For vacationing beneath the strong sun of the Pacific isles, be sure to take along a sun hat (to protect hair as well as skin) and sunscreen. Other items you might consider packing are a pocket-size flashlight with extra batteries, a small sewing kit, a first-aid kit (see *Staying Healthy,* in this section, for recommended components), binoculars, and a camera or camcorder (see *Cameras and Equipment,* also in this section).

■ **Note:** For those on the go, *Travel Mini Pack* offers numerous products — from toilet articles to wrinkle-remover spray — in handy travel sizes, as well as travel accessories such as money pouches, foreign currency calculators, and even a combination hair dryer/iron. For a catalogue, contact *Travel Mini Pack* (PO Box 571, Stony Point, NY 10980; phone: 914-429-8281). *Pacific Traveler's Supply* (529 State St., Santa Barbara, CA 93101; phone: 805-963-4438) also carries a variety of similar items, as well as an extensive collection of travel guides and maps.

PACKING: The basic idea of packing is to get everything into the suitcase and out again with as few wrinkles as possible. Simple, casual clothes — shirts, jeans and slacks, permanent press skirts — can be rolled into neat, tight sausages that keep other packed items in place and leave the clothes themselves amazingly unwrinkled. However, for items that are too bulky or delicate for even careful rolling, a suitcase can be packed with the heaviest items on the bottom, toward the hinges, so that they will not wrinkle more perishable clothes. Candidates for the bottom layer include shoes (stuff them with small items to save space), a toilet kit, handbags (stuff them to help keep their shape), and an alarm clock. Fill out this layer with articles that will not wrinkle or will not matter if they do, such as sweaters, socks, a bathing suit, and underwear.

If you get this first, heavy layer as smooth as possible with the fill-ins, you will have a shelf for the next layer — the most easily wrinkled items, like slacks, jackets, shirts, dresses, and skirts. These should be buttoned and zipped and laid along the whole length of the suitcase with as little folding as possible. When you do need to make a fold, do it on a crease (as with pants), along a seam in the fabric, or where it will not show (such as shirttails). Alternate each piece of clothing, using one side of the suitcase, then the other, to make the layers as flat as possible. Make the layers even and the total contents of your bag full and firm to keep things from shifting around during transit. On the top layer put the things you will want at once: nightclothes, a bathing suit, a sweater.

With men's two-suiter suitcases, follow the same procedure. Then place jackets on hangers, straighten them out, and leave them unbuttoned. If they are too wide for the suitcase, fold them lengthwise down the middle, straighten the shoulders, and fold the sleeves in along the seam.

While packing, it is a good idea to separate each layer of clothes with plastic cleaning bags, which will help preserve pressed clothes while they are in the suitcase. Unpack your bags as soon as you get to your hotel. Nothing so thoroughly destroys freshly cleaned and pressed clothes as sitting for days in a suitcase. Finally, if something is badly wrinkled and can't be professionally pressed before you must wear it, hang it for several hours in a bathroom where the bathtub has been filled with very hot water; keep the bathroom door closed so the room becomes something of a steamroom. It really works miracles.

SOME FINAL PACKING HINTS: Apart from the items you pack as carry-on luggage (see above), always keep all necessary medicines, valuable jewelry, and travel or business documents in your purse, briefcase, or carry-on bag — *not in the luggage you will check.* Tuck a bathing suit into your handbag or briefcase, too; in the event of lost baggage, it's frustrating to be without one. And whether in your overnight bag or checked luggage, cosmetics and any liquids should be packed in plastic bottles or at least wrapped in plastic bags and tied.

Golf clubs may be checked through as luggage (most airlines are accustomed to handling them), but tennis rackets should be carried onto the plane. Aqualung tanks (appropriately packed with padding and depressurized) and surfboards (minus the fin and padded) also may go as baggage. Snorkeling gear should be packed in a suitcase, duffel, or tote bag. Some airlines require that bicycles be partially dismantled and packaged (see *Camping and RVs, Hiking and Biking,* in this section). Check with the airline before departure to see if there is a specific regulation concerning any special equipment or sporting gear you plan to take.

Hints for Handicapped Travelers

From 40 to 50 million people in the US alone have some sort of disability, and over half this number are physically handicapped. Like everyone else today, they — and the uncounted disabled millions around the world — are on the move. More than ever before, they are demanding facilities they can use comfortably, and they are being heard.

Those who have chosen to visit Hawaii are in luck. More and more disabled travelers are returning from this most luscious of destinations bearing tales of ramped sidewalks, a style of warm-weather architecture that erects fewer barriers between the indoors and the outdoors, and sightseeing tours designed especially for them. The island of Oahu is rated as particularly accessible for travelers with disabilities.

PLANNING: Collect as much information as you can about your specific disability and facilities for the disabled in Hawaii. Make your travel arrangements well in advance, and specify to all services involved the exact nature of your condition or restricted mobility, as your trip will be much more comfortable if you know that there are accommodations and facilities to suit your needs. The best way to find out if your intended destination can accommodate a handicapped traveler is to write or call the local tourist authority or hotel and ask specific questions. If you require a corridor of a certain width to maneuver a wheelchair or if you need handles on the bathroom walls for support, ask the hotel manager. A travel agent or the local chapter or national office of the organization that deals with your particular disability — for example, the *American Foundation for the Blind* or the *American Heart Association* — will supply the most up-to-date information on the subject. The following organizations offer general information on access:

ACCENT on Living (PO Box 700, Bloomington, IL 61702; phone: 309-378-2961). This information service for persons with disabilities provides a free list of travel agencies specializing in arranging trips for the disabled; for a copy send a self-addressed, stamped envelope. Also offers a wide range of publications, including a quarterly magazine ($10 per year; $17.50 for 2 years) for persons with disabilities.

Information Center for Individuals with Disabilities (Fort Point Pl., 1st Floor, 27-43 Wormwood St., Boston, MA 02210; phone: 800-462-5015 in Massachusetts; 617-727-5540/1 elsewhere in the US; both numbers provide voice and TDD — telecommunications device for the deaf). The center offers information and referral services on disability-related issues, publishes fact sheets on travel agents, tour operators, and other travel resources, and can help you research your trip.

Mobility International USA (*MIUSA;* PO Box 3551, Eugene, OR 97403; phone: 503-343-1284; both voice and TDD). This US branch of *Mobility International* (the main office is at 228 Borough High St., London SE1 1JX, England; phone: 44-71-403-5688), a nonprofit British organization with affiliates worldwide, offers members advice and assistance — including information on accommodations and other travel services, and publications applicable to the traveler's disability. *Mobility International* also offers a quarterly newsletter and a comprehensive sourcebook, *A World of Options for the 90s: A Guide to International Education Exchange, Community Service and Travel for Persons with Disabilities* ($14 for members; $16 for non-members). Membership includes the newsletter and is $20 a year; subscription to the newsletter alone is $10 annually.

National Rehabilitation Information Center (8455 Colesville Rd., Suite 935, Silver

Spring, MD 20910; phone: 301-588-9284). A general information, resource, research, and referral service.

Paralyzed Veterans of America (*PVA;* PVA/ATTS Program, 801 18th St. NW, Washington, DC 20006; phone: 202-416-7708 in Washington, DC; 800-424-8200 elsewhere in the US). The members of this national service organization all are veterans who have suffered spinal cord injuries, but it offers advocacy services and information to all persons with a disability. *PVA* also sponsors *Access to the Skies (ATTS),* a program that coordinates the efforts of the national and international air travel industry in providing airport and airplane access for the disabled. Members receive several helpful publications, as well as regular notification of conferences on subjects of interest to the disabled traveler.

Royal Association for Disability and Rehabilitation (*RADAR;* 25 Mortimer St., London W1N 8AB, England; phone: 44-71-637-5400). Offers a number of publications for the handicapped, including *Holidays and Travel Abroad 1992/93 — A Guide for Disabled People,* a comprehensive guidebook focusing on international travel, but including helpful advice applicable to domestic travel. This publication can be ordered by sending payment in British pounds to *RADAR.* As we went to press, this publication cost just over £6; call for current pricing before ordering.

Society for the Advancement of Travel for the Handicapped (*SATH;* 347 Fifth Ave., Suite 610, New York, NY 10016; phone: 212-447-7284). To keep abreast of developments in travel for the handicapped as they occur, you may want to join *SATH,* a nonprofit organization whose members include consumers, as well as travel service professionals who have experience (or an interest) in travel for the handicapped. For an annual fee of $45 ($25 for students and travelers who are 65 and older) members receive a quarterly newsletter and have access to extensive information and referral services. *SATH* also offers two useful publications: *Travel Tips for the Handicapped* (a series of informative fact sheets) and *The United States Welcomes Handicapped Visitors* (a 48-page guide covering domestic transportation and accommodations); to order, send a self-addressed, #10 envelope and $1 per title for postage.

Travel Information Service (Moss Rehabilitation Hospital, 1200 W. Tabor Rd., Philadelphia, PA 19141-3099; phone: 215-456-9600 for voice; 215-456-9602 for TDD). This service assists physically handicapped people in planning trips and supplies detailed information on accessibility for a nominal fee.

Blind travelers should contact the *American Foundation for the Blind* (15 W. 16th St., New York, NY 10011; phone: 800-829-0500 or 212-620-2147) and *The Seeing Eye* (Box 375, Morristown, NJ 07963-0375; phone: 201-539-4425); both provide useful information on resources for the visually impaired. *Note:* All dogs arriving in the Hawaiian islands from the mainland US must be quarantined, and Seeing Eye dogs are *not* exempt. (For information on quarantine restrictions, see *Hints for Traveling with Pets,* in this section.)

In addition, there are a number of publications — from travel guides to magazines — of interest to handicapped travelers. Among these are the following:

Access America: An Atlas and Guide to the National Parks for Visitors with Disabilities is a comprehensive 464-page guide to accessibility in national parks throughout the US — including Hawaii. To order send a check or money order for $49.95 (includes postage) to Northern Cartographic, Inc., PO Box 133, Burlington, VT 05402 (phone: 802-860-2886).

Access to the World, by Louise Weiss, offers sound tips for the disabled traveler. Information on Hawaii is included in several sections. Published by Facts on File (460 Park Ave. S., New York, NY 10016; phone: 212-683-2244 in New York State; 800-322-8755 elsewhere in the US; 800-443-8323 in Canada), it costs

$16.95. Check with your local bookstore; it also can be ordered by phone with a credit card.

Access Travel: A Guide to the Accessibility of Airport Terminals, published by the Airport Operators Council International, provides information on more than 500 airports worldwide — including information on the Honolulu, Hilo, Kailua-Kona, Kahului, Lihue, and Lanai airports in Hawaii — with ratings according to 70 features, including accessibility to bathrooms, corridor width, and parking spaces. For a free copy, write to the Consumer Information Center (PO Box 100, Pueblo, CO 81002) and request publication #580Y, 2-A.

Air Transportation of Handicapped Persons is a booklet published by the US Department of Transportation, and will be sent at no charge upon written request. Ask for "Free Advisory Circular #AC-120-32" from the US Dept. of Transportation, Distribution Unit, Publications Section, M-443-2, 400 Seventh St. SW, Washington, DC 20590.

Aloha Guide to Accessibility for Persons with Mobility Impairments in the State of Hawaii details accessibility on Oahu, Maui, Kauai, and the Big Island, and provides useful information and resources for disabled visitors. To order this pamphlet, write to the Commission on Persons with Disabilities, 5 Waterfront Plaza, Suite 210, 500 Ala Moana Blvd., Honolulu, HI 96813 (phone: 808-586-8121; both voice and TDD), and include $3 for shipping and handling.

The Diabetic Traveler (PO Box 8223 RW, Stamford, CT 06905; phone: 203-327-5832) is a useful quarterly newsletter. Each issue highlights a single destination or type of travel and includes information on general resources and hints for diabetics. A 1-year subscription costs $15. When subscribing, ask for the free fact sheet including an index of special articles; back issues are available for $4 each.

Guide to Traveling with Arthritis, a free brochure available by writing to the Upjohn Company (PO Box 307-B, Coventry, CT 06238), provides lots of good, commonsense tips on planning your trip and how to be as comfortable as possible when traveling by car, bus, cruise ship, or plane.

Handicapped Travel Newsletter is regarded as one of the best sources of information for the disabled traveler. It is edited by wheelchair-bound Vietnam veteran Michael Quigley, who has traveled to 93 countries around the world. Issued every 2 months (plus special issues), a subscription is $10 per year. Write to *Handicapped Travel Newsletter,* PO Box 269, Athens, TX 75751 (phone: 903-677-1260).

Handi-Travel: A Resource Book for Disabled and Elderly Travellers, by Cinnie Noble, is a comprehensive travel guide full of practical tips for those with disabilities affecting mobility, hearing, or sight. To order this book, send $12.95, plus shipping and handling, to the *Canadian Rehabilitation Council for the Disabled,* 45 Sheppard Ave. E., Suite 801, Toronto, Ont. M2N 5W9, Canada (phone: 416-250-7490; both voice and TDD).

The Itinerary (PO Box 2012, Bayonne, NJ 07002-2012; phone: 201-858-3400). This quarterly travel magazine for people with disabilities includes information on accessibility, listings of tours, news of adaptive devices, travel aids, and special services, as well as numerous general travel hints. A subscription costs $10 a year.

The Physically Disabled Traveler's Guide, by Rod W. Durgin and Norene Lindsay, rates accessibility of a number of travel services and includes a list of organizations specializing in travel for the disabled. It is available for $9.95, plus $2 for shipping and handling, from *Resource Directories,* 3361 Executive Pkwy., Suite 302, Toledo, OH 43606 (phone: 419-536-5353 in the Toledo area; 800-274-8515 elsewhere in the US).

Ticket to Safe Travel offers useful information for travelers with diabetes. A reprint of this article is available free from local chapters of the *American Diabetes Association.* For the nearest branch, contact the central office at 505 Eighth Ave., 21st Floor, New York, NY 10018 (phone: 212-947-9707 in New York State; 800-232-3472 elsewhere in the US).

Travel for the Patient with Chronic Obstructive Pulmonary Disease, a publication of the George Washington University Medical Center, provides some sound practical suggestions for those with emphysema, chronic bronchitis, asthma, or other lung ailments. To order, send $2 to Dr. Harold Silver, 1601 18th St. NW, Washington, DC 20009 (phone: 202-667-0134).

Traveling Like Everybody Else: A Practical Guide for Disabled Travelers, by Jacqueline Freedman and Susan Gersten, offers the disabled tips on traveling by car, cruise ship, and plane, as well as lists of accessible accommodations, tour operators specializing in tours for disabled travelers, and other resources. It is available for $11.95, plus postage and handling, from Modan Publishing, PO Box 1202, Bellmore, NY 11710 (phone: 516-679-1380).

Travel Tips for Hearing-Impaired People, a free pamphlet for deaf and hearing-impaired travelers, is available from the *American Academy of Otolaryngology* (One Prince St., Alexandria, VA 22314; phone: 703-836-4444). For a copy, send a self-addressed, stamped, business-size envelope to the academy.

Travel Tips for People with Arthritis, a 31-page booklet published by the *Arthritis Foundation,* provides helpful information regarding travel by car, bus, train, cruise ship, or plane, planning your trip, medical considerations, and ways to conserve your energy while traveling. It also includes listings of helpful resources, such as associations and travel agencies that operate tours for disabled travelers. For a copy, contact your local *Arthritis Foundation* chapter, or send $1 to the national office, PO Box 19000, Atlanta, GA 30326 (phone: 404-872-7100).

The Wheelchair Traveler, by Douglass R. Annand, lists accessible hotels, motels, restaurants, and other sites by state, including the major islands of Hawaii. This valuable resource is available directly from the author. For the price of the most recent edition, contact Douglass R. Annand, 123 Ball Hill Rd., Milford, NH 03055 (phone: 603-673-4539).

A few more basic resources to look for are *Travel for the Disabled,* by Helen Hecker ($19.95), and by the same author, *Directory of Travel Agencies for the Disabled* ($19.95). *Wheelchair Vagabond,* by John G. Nelson, is another useful guide for travelers confined to a wheelchair (hardcover, $14.95; paperback, $9.95). All three titles are published by Twin Peaks Press, PO Box 129, Vancouver, WA 98666 (phone: 800-637-CALM or 206-694-2462). The publisher offers a catalogue of 26 other books on travel for the disabled for $2.

PLANE: The US Department of Transportation (DOT) has ruled that US airlines must accept all passengers with disabilities. As a matter of course, US airlines were pretty good about accommodating handicapped passengers even before the ruling, although each airline has somewhat different procedures.

Disabled passengers should always make reservations well in advance, and should provide the airline with all relevant details of their condition. These details include information on mobility and equipment that you will need the airline to supply — such as a wheelchair for boarding or portable oxygen for in-flight use. Be sure that the person to whom you speak fully understands the degree of your disability — the more details provided, the more effective help the airline can give you.

On the day before the flight, call back to make sure that all arrangements have been prepared, and arrive early on the day of the flight so that you can board before the rest of the passengers. It's a good idea to bring a medical certificate with you, stating your specific disability or the need to carry particular medicine.

Because most airports have jetways (corridors connecting the terminal with the door of the plane), a disabled passenger usually can be taken as far as the plane, and sometimes right onto it, in a wheelchair. If not, a narrow boarding chair may be used to take you to your seat. Your own wheelchair, which will be folded and put in the baggage compartment, should be tagged as escort luggage to assure that it's available at planeside upon landing rather than in the baggage claim area. Travel is not quite as simple if your wheelchair is battery-operated: Unless it has non-spillable batteries, it might not be accepted on board, and you will have to check with the airline ahead of time to find out how the batteries and the chair should be packaged for the flight. Usually people in wheelchairs are asked to wait until other passengers have disembarked. If you are making a tight connection, be sure to tell the attendant.

Passengers who use oxygen may not use their personal supply in the cabin, though it may be carried on the plane as cargo (the tank must be emptied) when properly packed and labeled. If you will need oxygen during the flight, the airline will supply it to you (there is a charge) provided you have given advance notice — 24 hours to a few days, depending on the carrier.

Useful information on every stage of air travel, from planning to arrival, is provided in the booklet *Incapacitated Passengers Air Travel Guide.* To receive a free copy, write to Publications Sales Department, International Air Transport Association, 2000 Peel St., Montreal, Quebec H3A 2R4 Canada (phone: 514-844-6311).

The following airlines serving Hawaii have TDD toll-free lines in the US for the hearing-impaired:

Aloha: 800-554-4833 from the mainland; 800-486-9321 on Oahu
American: 800-582-1573 in Ohio; 800-543-1586 elsewhere in the US
America West: 800-526-8077
Continental: 800-343-9195
Delta: 800-831-4488
Northwest: 800-692-2105 in Minnesota; 800-328-2298 elsewhere in the US
TWA: 800-252-0622 in California; 800-421-8480 elsewhere in the US
United: 800-942-8819 in Illinois; 800-323-0170 elsewhere in the US

SHIP: Among the ships calling at Hawaiian ports, *Crystal Cruises' Crystal Harmony, Cunard*'s *Queen Elizabeth 2, Holland America Line*'s *Rotterdam,* and *Royal Cruise Line*'s *Crown Odyssey* are considered the best-equipped vessels for the physically disabled. Handicapped travelers are advised to book their trip at least 90 days in advance to reserve specialized cabins.

For those in wheelchairs or with limited mobility, one of the best sources for evaluating a ship's accessibility is the free chart issued by the *Cruise Lines International Association* (500 Fifth Ave., Suite 1407, New York, NY 10110; phone: 212-921-0066). The chart lists accessible ships and indicates whether they accommodate standard-size or only narrow wheelchairs, have ramps, wide doors, low or no doorsills, handrails in the rooms, and so on. (For further information on ships cruising Hawaiian waters, see *Traveling by Ship,* in this section.)

GROUND TRANSPORTATION: Perhaps the simplest solution to getting around is to travel with an able-bodied companion who can drive. If you are accustomed to driving your own hand-controlled car and want to rent one in the islands, you are in luck. Both *Avis* and *Hertz* rent cars with hand controls. *Avis* (phone: 800-331-1212), with offices on Oahu, Maui, the Big Island of Hawaii, Kauai, and Molokai, can convert a car to hand controls with as little as 24 hours' notice, though it's a good idea to arrange for one earlier. *Hertz* (phone: 800-654-3131), which has offices on Oahu, Maui, Hawaii, and Kauai, requires a minimum of 48 hours to install the controls, and makes the additional stipulation that the car be returned to the office from which it was rented.

Neither company charges extra for hand controls, but *Avis* will fit them only on a full-size car, and both request that you bring your handicapped driver's permit with you.

The *American Automobile Association (AAA)* publishes a useful book, *The Handicapped Driver's Mobility Guide.* Contact the central office of your local *AAA* club for availability and pricing, which may vary at different branch offices.

There are a number of companies that offer specialized transportation services (usually by van) for persons with disabilities. Most require that passengers call and make arrangements 1 to several days in advance. Among these companies are the following:

On the Big Island of Hawaii

Coordinated Services for the Elderly (127 Kamana St., Hilo HI 96720; phone: 808-961-3418). This county agency provides van services for elderly and/or disabled individuals. Note that the agency's primary function is transporting those requiring medical attention; however, visitors may be accommodated if a van is available.

On Kauai

Akita Enterprises, Ltd. (3018 Aukele St., Lihue, HI 96766; phone: 808-245-5344). This schoolbus service transports travelers in wheelchairs in a specially adapted bus for a small fee during off-hours (mornings until noon and evenings during the week, and on weekends).

Kauai Bus (Transportation Office, Office of Elderly Affairs, 4193 Hardy St., #2, Lihue, HI 96766; phone: 808-246-4622). In addition to regular service, provides scheduled and on-call bus and van transportation for elderly and/or disabled individuals.

On Maui

Maui Accessible Transfers and Tours (641 Komo Place, Kahului, HI 96732; phone: 808-871-6843). Provides van transportation for persons with disabilities; local tours also may be offered.

On Oahu

Handicabs of the Pacific, Inc. (PO Box 22428, Honolulu, HI 96823; phone: 808-524-3866). This taxi and tour company caters to travelers in wheelchairs.

Honolulu has another unusual institution, the city- and county-subsidized *Handi-Van,* which provides inexpensive curb-to-curb service for those unable to use the regular bus; 24-hour notice is required. It is not designed for the tourist, but you may use it if you have a Handi-Van pass; the pass also is valid on regular city buses. For particulars on how to obtain one, contact the City and County of Honolulu Department of Transportation Services, 650 S. King St., Honolulu, HI 96813 (phone: 808-523-4083).

TOURS: Programs designed for the physically impaired are run by specialists who have researched hotels, restaurants, and sites to be sure they present no insurmountable obstacles. The following travel agencies and tour operators specialize in making group and individual arrangements for travelers with physical or other disabilities.

Access: The Foundation for Accessibility by the Disabled (PO Box 356, Malverne, NY 11565; phone: 516-887-5798). A travelers' referral service that acts as an intermediary with tour operators and agents worldwide, and provides information on accessibility at various locations.

Accessible Journeys (412 S. 45th St., Philadelphia, PA 19104; phone: 215-747-0171). Arranges for traveling companions who are medical professionals — registered or licensed practical nurses, therapists, or doctors (all are experienced travelers). Several prospective companions' profiles and photos are sent to the client for perusal, and if one is acceptable, the "match" is made. The client usually pays all travel expenses for the companion, plus a certain amount in "earnings" to replace wages the companion would be making at his or her usual job. This company also offers tours and cruises for people with special needs, although you don't have to take one of their tours to hire a companion through them.

Accessible Tours/Directions Unlimited (720 N. Bedford Rd., Bedford Hills, NY 10507; phone: 914-241-1700 in New York State; 800-533-5343 elsewhere in the continental US). Arranges group or individual tours for disabled persons traveling in the company of able-bodied friends or family members. Accepts the unaccompanied traveler if completely self-sufficient.

Beehive Business and Leisure Travel (1130 W. Center St., N. Salt Lake, UT 84054; phone: 800-777-5727 or 801-292-4445). John Warner runs Dialysis in Wonderland, a guided tour program for dialysis patients, which includes arrangements for treatment en route. Hawaii is among the destinations offered.

Evergreen Travel Service (4114 198th St. SW, Suite 13, Lynnwood, WA 98036-6742; phone: 800-435-2288 or 206-776-1184 throughout the continental US and Canada). Offers worldwide tours and cruises for the disabled (Wings on Wheels Tours), sight impaired/blind (White Cane Tours), and hearing impaired/deaf (Flying Fingers Tours). Most programs are first class or deluxe, and include a trained escort.

Flying Wheels Travel (143 W. Bridge St., Box 382, Owatonna, MN 55060; phone: 800-535-6790 or 507-451-5005 throughout the continental US and Canada). Handles both tours and individual arrangements.

The Guided Tour (613 W. Cheltenham Ave., Suite 200, Melrose Park, PA 19126; phone: 215-782-1370). Arranges tours for people with developmental and learning disabilities and sponsors separate tours for members of the same population who also are physically disabled or who simply need a slower pace.

Sprout (893 Amsterdam Ave., New York, NY 10025; phone: 212-222-9575). Arranges travel programs for mildly and moderately developmentally disabled teens and adults.

USTS Travel Horizons (11 E. 44th St., New York, NY 10017; phone: 800-487-8787 or 212-687-5121). Travel agent and registered nurse Mary Ann Hamm designs trips for individual travelers requiring all types of kidney dialysis and handles arrangements for the dialysis.

Whole Person Tours (PO Box 1084, Bayonne, NJ 07002-1084; phone: 201-858-3400). Handicapped owner Bob Zywicki travels the world with his wheelchair and offers a lineup of escorted tours (many conducted by him) for the disabled. *Whole Person Tours* also publishes *The Itinerary,* a quarterly newsletter for disabled travelers (see the publication source list above).

Travelers who would benefit from being accompanied by a nurse or physical therapist also can hire a companion through *Traveling Nurses' Network,* a service provided by Twin Peaks Press (PO Box 129, Vancouver, WA 98666; phone: 800-637-CALM or 206-694-2462). For a $10 fee, clients receive the names of three nurses, whom they can then contact directly; for a $125 fee, the agency will make all the hiring arrangements for the client. Travel arrangements also may be made in some cases — the fee for this further service is determined on an individual basis.

A similar service is offered by *MedEscort International* (ABE International Airport, PO Box 8766, Allentown, PA 18105; phone: 800-255-7182 in the continental US; elsewhere call 215-791-3111). Clients can arrange to be accompanied by a nurse, paramedic, respiratory therapist, or physician through *MedEscort.* The fees are based on the disabled traveler's needs. This service also can assist in making travel arrangements.

Hints for Single Travelers

Just about the last trip in human history on which the participants were neatly paired was the voyage of Noah's Ark. Ever since, passenger lists and tour groups have reflected the same kind of asymmetry that occurs in real life, as countless individuals set forth to see the world unaccompanied (or unencumbered, depending on your outlook) by spouse, lover, friend, or relative. Unfortunately, traveling alone can turn a traveler into a second class citizen.

The truth is that the travel industry is not very fair to people who vacation by themselves. People traveling alone almost invariably end up paying more than individuals traveling in pairs. Most travel bargains, including package tours, accommodations, resort packages, and cruises, are based on *double occupancy* rates. This means that the per-person price is offered on the basis of two people traveling together and sharing a double room (which means they each will spend a good deal more on meals and extras). The single traveler will have to pay a surcharge, called a single supplement, for exactly the same package. In extreme cases, this can add as much as 35% — and sometimes more — to the basic per-person rate.

Don't despair, however. Throughout Hawaii, there are scores of smaller hotels and other hostelries where, in addition to a cozier atmosphere, prices still are quite reasonable for the single traveler.

The obvious, most effective alternative is to find a traveling companion. Even special "singles' tours" that promise no supplements are usually based on people sharing double rooms. Perhaps the most recent innovation along these lines is the creation of organizations that "introduce" the single traveler to other single travelers, somewhat like a dating service. Some charge fees, others are free, but the basic service offered is the same: to match an unattached person with a compatible travel mate, often as part of the company's own package tours. Among such organizations are the following:

Partners-in-Travel (PO Box 491145, Los Angeles, CA 90049; phone: 213-476-4869). Members receive a list of singles seeking traveling companions; prospective companions make contact through the agency. The membership fee is $40 per year and includes a chatty newsletter (6 issues per year).

Travel Companion Exchange (PO Box 833, Amityville, NY 11701; phone: 516-454-0880). This group publishes a newsletter for singles and a directory of individuals looking for travel companions. On joining, members fill out a lengthy questionnaire and write a small listing (much like an ad in a personal column). Based on these listings, members can request copies of profiles and contact prospective traveling companions. It is wise to join well in advance of your planned vacation so that there's enough time to determine compatibility and plan a joint trip. Membership fees, including the newsletter, are $36 for 6 months or $60 a year for a single-sex listing; $66 and $120, respectively, for a complete listing.

In addition, a number of tour packagers cater to single travelers. These companies offer packages designed for individuals interested in vacationing with a group of single travelers or in being matched with a traveling companion. Among the better established of these agencies are the following:

Cosmos: This tour operator offers a number of package tours — including year-round trips to Hawaii — with a guaranteed-share plan whereby singles who wish to share rooms (and avoid paying the single supplement) are matched by the tour escort with individuals of the same sex and charged the basic double-occupancy tour price. Contact the firm at one of its three North American branches: 95-25 Queens Blvd., Rego Park, NY 11374 (phone: 800-221-0090 from the eastern US); 150 S. Los Robles Ave., Pasadena, CA 91101 (phone: 800-556-5454 or 818-449-0919 from the western US); 1801 Eglinton Ave. W., Suite 104, Toronto, Ont. M6E 2H8, Canada (phone: 416-787-1281).

Grand Circle Travel (347 Congress St., Boston, MA 02210; phone: 800-221-2610 or 617-350-7500). Arranges extended vacations, escorted tours, and cruises for the over-50 traveler, including singles. Membership, which is automatic when you book a trip through *Grand Circle,* includes travel discounts and other extras, such as a Pen Pals service for singles seeking traveling companions.

Marion Smith Singles (611 Prescott Place, North Woodmere, NY 11581; phone: 516-791-4852, 516-791-4865, or 212-944-2112). Specializes in tours for singles ages 20 to 50, who can choose to share accommodations to avoid paying single-supplement charges.

Saga International Holidays (120 Boylston St., Boston MA 02116; phone: 800-343-0273 or 617-451-6808). A subsidiary of a British company specializing in older travelers, many of them single, *Saga* offers a broad selection of packages for people age 60 and over or those 50 to 59 traveling with someone 60 or older. Recent offerings included a 17-day round-trip cruise from Los Angeles to Hawaii on the *Holland America Line.* Although anyone can book a *Saga* trip, a $15 club membership includes a subscription to their newsletter, as well as other publications and travel services — such as a matching service for single travelers.

Singles in Motion (545 W. 236th St., Suite 1D, Riverdale, NY 10463; phone: 718-884-4464). Offers a number of packages for single travelers, including tours, cruises, and excursions focusing on outdoor activities such as hiking and biking.

Singleworld (401 Theodore Fremd Ave., Rye, NY 10580; phone: 800-223-6490 or 914-967-3334 in the continental US). For a yearly fee of $25, this club books members on tours and cruises, and arranges shared accommodations, allowing individual travelers to avoid the single-supplement charge; members also receive a quarterly newsletter. *Singleworld* also offers package tours for singles with departures categorized by age group.

Solo Flights (127 S. Compo Rd., Westport, CT 06880; phone: 203-226-9993). Represents a number of packagers and cruise lines and books singles on individual and group tours.

Travel in Two's (239 N. Broadway, Suite 3, N. Tarrytown, NY 10591; phone: 914-631-8409). This company books solo travelers on packages offered by a number of companies (at no extra cost to clients), offers its own tours, and matches singles with traveling companions. Many offerings are listed in their quarterly *Singles Vacation Newsletter,* which costs $7.50 per issue or $20 per year.

A good book for single travelers is *Traveling on Your Own,* by Eleanor Berman, which offers tips on traveling solo and includes information on trips for singles, ranging from outdoor adventures to educational programs. Available in bookstores, it also can be ordered by sending $12.95, plus postage and handling, to Random House, Order Dept., 400 Hahn Rd., Westminster, MD 21157 (phone: 800-733-3000).

Single travelers also may want to subscribe to *Going Solo,* a newsletter that offers helpful information on going on your own. Issued eight times a year, a subscription costs $36. Contact Doerfer Communications, PO Box 1035, Cambridge, MA 02238 (phone: 617-876-2764).

Those interested in a particularly cozy type of accommodation should consider going the bed and breakfast route. Though a single person will likely pay more than half of the rate quoted for a couple even at a bed and breakfast establishment, the prices still are quite reasonable, and the homey atmosphere will make you feel less conspicuously alone.

Considering Hawaii's near-perfect year-round temperatures, one of the most inexpensive accommodations options could be your own tent. Campsites are plentiful everywhere on the islands, and many of the campgrounds have showers, public phones, eating facilities, and shops. (For more information, see *Camping and RVs, Hiking and Biking,* in this section.)

WOMEN AND STUDENTS: Two specific groups of single travelers deserve special mention: women and students. Countless women travel by themselves in Hawaii, and such an adventure need not be feared.

One lingering inhibition many female travelers still harbor is that of eating alone in public places. The trick here is to relax and enjoy your meal and surroundings; while you may run across the occasional unenlightened waiter, dining solo is no longer uncommon.

For students (and singles in general) traveling to Hawaii on a strict budget, there are several accommodation options. There are two *American Youth Hostels (AYH)* in the Hawaiian islands: both in Honolulu. The main one will accommodate members of both *AYH* and its parent organization, the *International Youth Hostel Federation,* for a nightly fee of $9. Members can make advance reservations for 3-night stays, which can be extended if there is room. (Non-members can stay on a night-by-night basis for $12 per night.) Because it is in Honolulu and very popular, there often isn't a room available, so reservations are highly recommended (write-in reservations that include a 1-night's deposit will be held until 11 PM). For reservations and information, contact the *Honolulu International AYH Hostel,* 2323A Seaview Ave., Honolulu, HI 96822 (phone: 808-946-0591).

The other *AYH* hostel in Honolulu, the *Hale Aloha AYH Hostel* (2417 Prince Edward St., Honolulu, HI 96815; phone: 808-926-8313), is open to *AYH* members only. Here the nightly rate is $12, and guests may reserve up to 3 nights, with extensions possible when space permits.

An *American Youth Hostels* membership card, recognized internationally at over 5,000 hostels worldwide, is available from the main Honolulu hostel on Seaview Avenue (see above) or from *American Youth Hostels* (PO Box 37613, Washington, DC 20013-7613; phone: 202-783-6161), or the local *AYH* council nearest you. As we went to press, the following membership rates were in effect: $25 for adults (between 18 and 54), $10 for youths (17 and under), $15 for seniors (55 and up), and $35 for family membership. *Hosteling North America,* which lists hostels in the US and Canada, comes with your *AYH* card (non-members can purchase this book for $5, plus postage and handling). The *Guide to Budget Accommodations,* Volume 2, covers hostels in the US, including Hawaii and must be purchased (Volume 1 covers Europe and the Mediterranean); each volume costs $10.95, plus postage and handling.

Honolulu also has a *YWCA* and several *YMCA* residences. The *Fernhurst YWCA Residence* (1566 Wilder Ave., Honolulu, HI 96822; phone: 808-941-2231), for women only, is midway between downtown Honolulu and Waikiki, and has double rooms joined to one another by shared baths, as well as a few singles, at daily and weekly rates. At the time of this writing, the daily rate was $20 for a double room and $28 for a single for members, $25 and $33, respectively, for non-members, which included breakfast and dinner (except on Sundays and certain holidays). Single rooms are available only from April through November. The residence has an outdoor swimming pool, and though the doors are locked at 11 PM for security reasons, the night watchman will let you in later. A reservation can be made at *Fernhurst Residence* by writing and enclosing a 1-night's deposit in the form of a money order; call in advance to check availability. Note that *YWCA* membership — which costs $25 at any *YWCA* in the US — is required for stays exceeding 3 nights.

There are two *YMCA* residences for men only: the *Central Branch,* just outside Waikiki (401 Atkinson Dr., Honolulu, HI 96814; phone: 808-941-3344), and the *Nuuanu Branch,* in downtown Honolulu (1441 Pali Hwy., Honolulu, HI 96813; phone: 808-536-3556). The *Central Branch* has single rooms with private baths for $34.50; singles and doubles using communal showers are available for $28 and $20, respectively. The *Nuuanu Branch* has singles only at $32 a night for a room with private bath (there are two) and at $27 a night with use of the communal showers. Both have outdoor pools; only the *Nuuanu Branch* accepts reservations (you must send a deposit equal to 1-night's lodging at least 3 weeks in advance of your stay).

The *Atherton Branch YMCA* (1810 University Ave., Honolulu, HI 96822; phone: 808-946-0253), generally open only to students at the nearby University of Hawaii at Manoa, offers a few dormitory-type rooms to non-student visitors during the summer. Full advance payment and a substantial deposit are required, and rates change frequently, so it's best to call for information.

The *YMCA*'s *Camp Keanae,* on Maui, offers members and non-members duplex accommodations with communal showers and kitchen facilities. At the time of this writing, the nightly rate was $8, with a maximum stay of 3 nights. Contact the *Maui Family YMCA* (250 Kanaloa Ave., Kahului, HI 96792; phone: 808-242-9007) for current rates, reservations, and further information.

Travelers who are (or have been) students of accredited colleges and universities elsewhere might consider taking some courses at the *University of Hawaii at Manoa.* The university offers two 6-week summer sessions, and anyone enrolled in a course carrying 3 or more credit hours qualifies for campus housing. Least expensive are the residence halls, where rooms are shared and meal plans mandatory (single rooms sometimes are available). One- and two-bedroom apartments on the university grounds cost more, but meal plans aren't required. Summer semester bulletins go out in March and, in addition to curriculum listings, the summer activities program for students is announced. For more information and application forms, contact the Summer Session Office, University of Hawaii at Manoa, 2500 Dole St., Krauss Hall 101, Honolulu, HI 96822 (phone: 808-956-7221).

Those who are interested in a "learning vacation" also may be interested in *Travel and Learn* by Evelyn Kaye. This guide to educational travel discusses a wide range of opportunities — everything from archaeology to whale watching — and provides information on organizations that offer programs in these areas of interest. The book is available in bookstores for $23.95; or you can send $26 (which includes shipping charges) to Blue Penguin Publications (3031 Fifth St., Boulder, CO 80304; phone: 800-800-8147 or 303-449-8474). *Learning Vacations* by Gerson G. Eisenberg also provides extensive information on seminars, workshops, courses, and so on — in a wide variety of subjects. Available in bookstores, it also can be ordered from Peterson's Guides (PO Box 2123, Princeton, NJ 08543-2123; phone: 800-338-3282 or 609-243-9111) for $11.95, plus shipping and handling.

Hints for Older Travelers

Special discounts and more free time are just two factors that have given Americans over age 65 a chance to see the world at affordable prices. Senior citizens make up an ever-growing segment of the travel population, and the trend among them is to travel more frequently and for longer periods of time.

PLANNING: When planning a vacation, prepare your itinerary with one eye on your own physical condition and the other on a topographical map. Keep in mind variations in climate, terrain, and altitudes, which may pose some danger for anyone with heart or breathing problems.

Older travelers may find the following publications of interest:

The Discount Guide for Travelers Over 55, by Caroline and Walter Weintz, is an excellent book for budget-conscious older travelers. Published by Penguin USA, it is currently out of print; check your local library.

Going Abroad: 101 Tips for Mature Travelers offers tips on preparing for your trip, commonsense precautions en route, and some basic travel terminology. This concise, free booklet is available from *Grand Circle Travel,* 347 Congress St., Boston, MA 02210 (phone: 800-221-2610 or 617-350-7500).

The International Health Guide for Senior Citizen Travelers, by Dr. W. Robert Lange, covers such topics as trip preparations, food and water precautions, adjusting to weather and climate conditions, finding a doctor, motion sickness, jet lag, and so on. Also includes a list of resource organizations that provide medical assistance for travelers. It is available for $4.95 postpaid from Pilot Books, 103 Cooper St., Babylon, NY 11702 (phone: 516-422-2225).

The Mature Traveler is a monthly newsletter that provides information on travel discounts, places of interest, useful tips, and other topics of interest for travelers 49 and up. To subscribe, send $24.50 to GEM Publishing Group, PO Box 50820, Reno, NV 89513 (phone: 702-786-7419).

The Senior Citizen's Guide To Budget Travel In The US And Canada, by Paige Palmer, provides specific information on economical travel options for senior citizens. To order, send $3.95, plus postage and handling, to Pilot Books (address above).

Take a Camel to Lunch and Other Adventures for Mature Travelers, by Nancy O'Connell, offers offbeat and unusual adventures for travelers over 50. Available at bookstores or directly from Bristol Publishing Enterprises (PO Box 1737, San Leandro, CA 94577; phone: 800-346-4889 or 510-895-4461) for $8.95, plus shipping and handling.

Travel Tips for Older Americans is a useful booklet that provides good, basic advice. This US State Department publication (stock number: 044-000-02270-2) can be ordered by sending a check or money order for $1 to the Superintendent of Documents (US Government Printing Office, Washington, DC 20402) or by calling 202-783-3238 and charging the order to a credit card.

Unbelievably Good Deals & Great Adventures That You Absolutely Can't Get Unless You're Over 50, by Joan Rattner Heilman, offers travel tips for older travelers, including discounts on accommodations and transportation, as well as a list of organizations for seniors. It is available for $7.95, plus shipping and handling, from Contemporary Books, 180 N. Michigan Ave., Chicago, IL 60601 (phone: 312-782-9181).

HEALTH: The traveler to Hawaii will find health facilities as readily available and of the same quality as those found elsewhere in the US. In addition, a number of organizations exist to help travelers avoid or deal with a medical emergency while traveling. For information on these services, see *Staying Healthy,* in this section.

Pre-trip medical and dental checkups are strongly recommended. In addition, be sure to take along any prescription medication you need, enough to last *without a new prescription* for the duration of your trip; pack all medications with a note from your doctor for the benefit of airport authorities. If you have specific medical problems, bring prescriptions and a "medical file" composed of the following:

1. A summary of your medical history and current diagnosis.
2. A list of drugs to which you are allergic.
3. Your most recent electrocardiogram, if you have heart problems.
4. Your doctor's name, address, and telephone number.

DISCOUNTS AND PACKAGES: Since guidelines change from place to place, it is a good idea to inquire in advance about discounts on transportation, hotels, concerts, movies, museums, and other activities.

Many US hotel and motel chains, airlines, car rental companies, bus lines, and other travel suppliers offer discounts to older travelers. Some US airlines offer those age 62 (and often one traveling companion per senior) discounts on flights to Hawaii. Contact the individual carriers for information on advance purchase restrictions, availability, and current fares.

Some of these discounts, however, are extended only to bona fide members of certain senior citizens organizations. For instance, although *Sheraton* offers a 25% discount to any senior citizen, participating *Hilton* hotels offer 10% discounts for *AARP* members — in both cases, these discounts may not apply during certain "blackout" periods. (See listings below for more information on *AARP* benefits.) Because the same organizations frequently offer package tours to both domestic and international destinations, the benefits of membership are twofold: Those who join can take advantage of discounts as individual travelers and also reap the savings that group travel affords. In addition, because the age requirements for some of these organizations are quite low (or nonexistent), the benefits can begin to accrue early.

In order to take advantage of these discounts, you should carry proof of your age (or eligibility). A driver's license, membership card in a recognized senior citizen's organization, or a Medicare card should be adequate. Among the organizations dedicated to helping older travelers see the world are the following:

American Association of Retired Persons (*AARP;* 601 E St. NW, Washington, DC 20049; phone: 202-434-2277). The largest and best known of these organizations. Membership is open to anyone 50 or over, whether retired or not; dues are $5 a year, $12.50 for 3 years, or $35 for 10 years, and include spouse. The *AARP* Travel Experience Worldwide program, available through *American Express Travel Related Services,* offers members tours, cruises, and other travel programs worldwide designed exclusively for older travelers. Members can book these services by calling *American Express* at 800-927-0111 for land and air travel, or 800-745-4567 for cruises.

Mature Outlook (Customer Service Center, 6001 N. Clark St., Chicago, IL 60660; phone: 800-336-6330). Through its *TravelAlert,* tours, cruises, and other vacation packages are available to members at special savings. Hotel and car rental discounts and travel accident insurance also are available. Membership is open to anyone 50 years of age or older, costs $9.95 a year, and includes a bimonthly newsletter and magazine, as well as information on package tours.

National Council of Senior Citizens (1331 F St. NW, Washington, DC 20004; phone: 202-347-8800). Here, too, the emphasis is on keeping costs low. This nonprofit organization offers members a different roster of package tours each year, as well as individual arrangements through its affiliated travel agency *(Vantage Travel Service).* Although most members are over 50, membership is open to anyone (regardless of age) for an annual fee of $12 per person or couple. Lifetime membership costs $150.

Certain travel agencies and tour operators offer special trips geared to older travelers. Among them are the following:

Evergreen Travel Service (4114 198th St. SW, Suite 13, Lynnwood, WA 98036-6742; phone: 800-435-2288 or 206-776-1184 throughout the continental US and Canada). This specialist in trips for persons with disabilities recently introduced Lazybones Tours, a program offering leisurely tours for older travelers. Most programs are first class or deluxe, and include an escort.

Gadabout Tours (700 E. Tahquitz, Palm Springs, CA 92262; phone: 619-325-5556 or 800-521-7309 in California; 800-952-5068 elsewhere in the US). Offers escorted tours and cruises to a number of destinations, including Hawaii.

Grand Circle Travel (347 Congress St., Boston, MA 02210; phone: 800-221-2610 or 617-350-7500). Caters exclusively to the over-50 traveler and packages a large variety of escorted tours, cruises, and extended vacations. Membership, which is automatic when you book a trip through *Grand Circle,* includes discount certificates on future trips and other travel services, such as a matching service for single travelers and a helpful free booklet, *Going Abroad: 101 Tips for Mature Travelers* (see the source list above).

Saga International Holidays (120 Boylston St., Boston MA 02116; phone: 800-343-0273 or 617-451-6808). A subsidiary of a British company catering to older travelers, *Saga* offers a broad selection of packages for people age 60 and over or those 50 to 59 traveling with someone 60 or older. Recent offerings included a 17-day, round-trip cruise from Los Angeles that visited Oahu, Maui, and the Big Island. Although anyone can book a *Saga* trip, a $15 club membership includes a subscription to their newsletter, as well as other publications and travel services.

Many travel agencies, particularly the larger ones, are delighted to make presentations to help a group of senior citizens select destinations. A local chamber of commerce should be able to provide the names of such agencies. Once a time and place are determined, an organization member or travel agent can obtain group quotations for transportation, accommodations, meal plans, and sightseeing. Larger groups usually get the best breaks.

Another choice open to older travelers is a trip that includes an educational element. *Elderhostel,* a nonprofit organization, offers programs at educational institutions throughout the US and worldwide, including several universities in Hawaii. The domestic programs generally last about 1 week, and include double occupancy accommodations in hotels or student residence halls and all meals, but participants must make their own travel arrangements. Elderhostelers must be at least 60 years old (younger if a spouse or companion qualifies), in good health, and not in need of special diets. For a free catalogue describing the program and current offerings, write to *Elderhostel* (75 Federal St., Boston, MA 02110; phone: 617-426-7788). Those interested in the program also can borrow slides at no charge or purchase an informational videotape for $5.

Hints for Traveling with Children

What better way to encounter the world's variety than in the company of the young, wide-eyed members of your family? Their presence does not have to be a burden or an excessive expense. The current generation of discounts for children and family package deals can make a trip together quite reasonable.

A family trip will be an investment in your children's future, making geography and history come alive to them, and leaving a sure memory that will be among the fondest you will share with them someday. Their insights will be refreshing to you; their impulses may take you to unexpected places with unexpected dividends.

PLANNING: Here are several hints for making a trip with children easy and fun.

1. Children, like everyone else, will derive more pleasure from a trip if they know something about their destination before they arrive. Begin their education about a month before you leave. Using maps, travel magazines, and books, give children a clear idea of where you are going and how far away it is.
2. Children should help to plan the itinerary, and where you go and what you do should reflect some of their ideas. If they already know something about the sites they'll visit, they will have the excitement of recognition when they arrive.
3. Children also will enjoy learning some Hawaiian phrases — such as *aloha* (a greeting) and *mahalo* (thank you) — and it's a good idea to familiarize them with the flora, fauna, and sea life they will encounter.
4. Give children specific responsibilities: The job of carrying their own flight bags and looking after their personal things, along with some other light chores, will give them a stake in the journey.
5. Give each child a travel diary or scrapbook to take along.

Children's books about Hawaii provide an excellent introduction to the islands. Some particularly good titles include the following:

Kidding Around the Hawaiian Islands: A Young Person's Guide, by Sarah Lovett, is a good introduction to the state for older children and includes a historical overview and descriptions of current attractions. It can be ordered for $9.95, plus shipping and handling, from John Muir Publications, PO Box 613, Santa Fe, NM 87504 (phone: 800-888-7504 or 505-982-4078 in the continental US).

My Travels in Hawaii, a magazine-size softcover book for younger children, includes descriptions of Hawaiian sights, drawings for coloring, games and puzzles, and a Hawaiian travel diary. To order, send $2.95, plus shipping and handling, to *Havin' Fun,* PO Box 70468, Eugene, OR 97401-0124 (phone: 503-344-6207).

Other books that provide an introduction to Hawaii include the outstanding publications of the University of Hawaii Press (2840 Kolowalu St., Honolulu, HI 96822; phone: 808-956-8255). When ordering these books, call to find out how much to include for shipping and handling.

A Is For Aloha ($8.95), by Stephanie Feeney, is a charming introduction to the alphabet — Hawaiian style.

Hawaii Is a Rainbow ($12.95), also by Stephanie Feeney, is a vibrant lesson in island colors.

Sand to Sea: Marine Life of Hawaii ($12.95), by Stephanie Feeney and Ann Fielding, introduces younger children to the inhabitants of the Pacific's crystal waters.

These and other children's books can be found at many general bookstores and libraries. (For sources of travel books, many suitable for young readers, also see *Sources and Resources,* in this section.) Bookstores specializing in children's books include the following:

Books of Wonder (132 7th Ave., New York, NY 10011; phone: 212-989-3270; or 464 Hudson St., New York, NY 10014; phone: 212-645-8006). Carries both new and used books for children.

Cheshire Cat (5512 Connecticut Ave. NW, Washington, DC 20015; phone: 202-244-3956). Specializes in books for children of all ages.

Eeyore's Books for Children (2212 Broadway, New York, NY 10024; phone: 212-362-0634; or 25 E. 83rd St., New York, NY 10028; phone: 212-988-3404). Carries an extensive selection of children's books; features a special travel section.

Reading Reptile, Books and Toys for Young Mammals (4120 Pennsylvania St., Kansas City, MO 64111; phone: 816-753-0441). Carries books for children and teens to age 15.

Red Balloon (891 Grand Ave., St. Paul, MN 55105; phone: 612-224-8320). Carries both new and used books for children.

White Rabbit Children's Books (7755 Girard Ave., La Jolla, CA 92037; phone: 619-454-3518). Carries books and music for children (and parents).

And for parents, *Travel With Your Children* (*TWYCH;* 80 Eighth Ave., New York, NY 10011; phone: 212-206-0688) publishes a newsletter, *Family Travel Times,* that focuses on families with young travelers and offers helpful hints. An annual subscription (10 issues) is $35 and includes a copy of the "Airline Guide" issue (updated every other year), which focuses on the subject of flying with children. This special issue and an issue featuring Hawaiian attractions, activities, and services for families (July/August 1990) are available separately, for $10 each.

Another newsletter devoted to family travel is *Getaways.* This quarterly publication provides reviews of family-oriented literature, activities, and useful travel tips. To subscribe, send $25 to *Getaways,* Att. Ms. Brooke Kane, PO Box 11511, Washington, DC 20008 (phone: 703-534-8747).

Also of interest to parents traveling with their children is *How to Take Great Trips with Your Kids,* by psychologist Sanford Portnoy and his wife, Joan Flynn Portnoy. The book includes helpful tips from fellow family travelers, tips on economical accommodations and touring by car, recreational vehicle, and train, as well as over 50 games to play with your children en route. It is available for $8.95, plus shipping and handling, from Harvard Common Press, 535 Albany St., Boston, MA 02118 (phone: 617-423-5803); when ordering provide the ISBN: 0-916782-51-4. Another title worth looking for is *Great Vacations with Your Kids,* by Dorothy Jordan (Dutton; $12.95).

Another book on family travel, *Travel with Children,* by Maureen Wheeler, offers a wide range of practical tips on traveling with children, and includes accounts of the author's family travel experiences. It is available for $10.95, plus shipping and handling, from Lonely Planet Publications, Embarcadero West, 112 Linden St., Oakland, CA 94607 (phone: 510-893-8555).

Finally, parents arranging a trip with their children may want to deal with an agency specializing in family travel such as *Let's Take the Kids* (1268 Devon Ave., Los Angeles, CA 90024; phone: 800-726-4349 or 213-274-7088). In addition to arranging and booking trips for individual families, this group occasionally organizes trips for single-parent families traveling together. They also offer a parent travel network, whereby parents who have been to a particular destination can evaluate it for others.

GETTING THERE AND GETTING AROUND: Begin early to investigate all available discount and charter flights, as well as any package deals and special rates offered by the major airlines. Booking is sometimes required up to 2 months in advance. You may well find that charter plans offer no reductions for children, or not enough to offset the risk of last-minute delays or other inconveniences to which charters are subject. Some of the major scheduled airlines, on the other hand, do provide hefty discounts for children. If traveling by ship, note that children under 12 usually travel at a considerably reduced fare on cruise lines. When using local transportation such as island buses, ask about lower fares for children or family rates.

Plane – When you make your reservations, tell the airline that you are traveling with a child. Children ages 2 through 11 generally travel at about 80% of the adult fare on domestic flights. As a general rule, children under 2 travel free in a plane if they sit on an adult's lap. A second infant without a second adult would pay the fare applicable to children ages 2 through 11.

Although some airlines will, on request, supply bassinets for infants, most carriers encourage parents to bring their own safety seat on board, which then is strapped into the airline seat with a regular seat belt. This is much safer — and certainly more comfortable — than holding the child in your lap. If you do not purchase a seat for your baby, you have the option of bringing the infant restraint along on the off chance that there might be an empty seat next to yours — in which case some airlines will let you use that seat at no charge for your baby and infant seat. However, if there is no empty seat available, the infant seat no doubt will have to be checked as baggage (and you may have to pay an additional charge), since it generally does not fit under airplane seats or in the overhead racks. The safest bet is to pay for a seat.

Be forewarned: Some safety seats designed primarily for use in cars do not fit into plane seats properly. Although nearly all seats manufactured since 1985 carry labels indicating whether they meet federal standards for use aboard planes, actual seat sizes may vary from carrier to carrier. At the time of this writing, the FAA was in the process of reviewing and revising the federal regulations regarding infant travel and safety devices — it was still to be determined if children should be *required* to sit in safety seats and whether the airlines will have to provide them.

If using one of these infant restraints, you should try to get bulkhead seats, which will provide extra room to care for your child during the flight. You also should request a bulkhead seat when using a bassinet — again, this is not as safe as strapping the child in. On some planes bassinets hook into a bulkhead wall; on others they are placed on the floor in front of you. (Note that bulkhead seats often are reserved for families traveling with children.) As a general rule, babies should be held during takeoff and landing.

Request seats on the aisle if you have a toddler or if you think you will need to use the bathroom frequently. Carry onto the plane all you will need to care for and occupy your children during the flight — formula, diapers, a sweater, books, favorite stuffed animals, and so on. Dress your baby simply, with a minimum of buttons and snaps, because the only place you may have to change a diaper is at your seat or in a small lavatory. The flight attendant can warm a bottle for you.

On most US carriers, you also can ask for a hot dog or hamburger instead of the airline's regular dinner if you give at least 24 hours' notice. Some, but not all, airlines have baby food aboard. While you should bring along toys from home, also ask about children's diversions. Some carriers have terrific free packages of games, coloring books, and puzzles.

When the plane takes off and lands, make sure your baby is nursing or has a bottle, pacifier, or thumb in its mouth. This sucking will make the child swallow and help to clear stopped ears. A piece of hard candy will do the same thing for an older child.

Parents traveling by plane with toddlers, children, or young teenagers may want to consult *When Kids Fly,* a free booklet published by Massport (Public Affairs Department, 10 Park Plaza, Boston, MA 02116-3971; phone: 617-973-5600), which includes helpful information on airfares for children, infant seats, what to do in the event of overbooked or canceled flights, and so on.

■ **Note:** Newborn babies, whose lungs may not be able to adjust to the altitude, should not be taken aboard an airplane. And some airlines may refuse to allow a pregnant woman in her 8th or 9th month to fly. Check with the airline ahead of time, and carry a letter from your doctor stating that you are fit to travel — and indicating the estimated date of birth.

Ship – Some shipping lines offer cruises that feature special activities for children, particularly during periods that coincide with major school holidays like *Christmas, Easter,* and the summer months. On such cruises, children may be charged special cut-rate fares, and there are youth counselors to organize activities. Occasionally, a shipping line even offers free passage during the summer months for children under age 16 occupying a stateroom with two (full-fare) adult passengers. Your travel agent should know which cruise lines offer such programs.

Car – Touring by car allows greater flexibility in traveling and packing. You may want to stock the car with a variety of favorite snacks. Games and simple toys, such as magnetic checkerboards or drawing pencils and pads, also provide a welcome diversion. And frequent stops so that children can run around make car travel much easier.

ACCOMMODATIONS AND MEALS: Often a cot for a child will be placed in a hotel room at little or no extra charge. If you wish to sleep in separate rooms, special rates sometimes are available for families; some places do not charge for children under a certain age. In many of the larger chain hotels, the staffs are more used to children. These hotels also are likely to have swimming pools or gamerooms — both popular with most youngsters. Many large resorts also have recreation centers for children.

The many resort condominium apartments available for rent in Hawaii provide excellent accommodations for families. The apartment becomes a "home away from home" and a considerable sum can be saved by preparing meals yourself rather than taking the entire crew out to restaurants three times a day. In addition, many complexes do not charge for children under 12, and a few permit anyone under 18 to stay with his or her family free. (On the other hand, some condos don't allow children, so before you set your heart on a particular one, find out all the details of its rental policy.)

Many of the condominium vacation packages include a rental car; these combination deals can be quite economical. Hotels and condominium complexes also often recommend baby-sitters (whether the sitter is hired directly or through an agency, ask for and check references), and some have activities programs especially for children (although these may be seasonal only).

Among the least expensive options is a camping facility; many are situated in beautiful, out-of-the-way spots, and generally are good, well equipped, and less expensive than any hotel. For further information on accommodations options for the whole family, see our discussions in *On the Islands,* and for information on camping facilities, see *Camping and RVs, Hiking and Biking,* both in this section.

At mealtime, don't deny yourself or your children the delights of a new style of cooking. Encourage them to try new things. Children like to know what kind of food to expect, so it will be interesting to look up Hawaiian dishes before leaving. And don't forget about picnics and luaus.

Things to Remember

1. If you are spending your vacation touring several islands, pace the days with children in mind. Break the trip into half-day segments, with running around or "doing" time built in.
2. Don't forget that a child's attention span is far shorter than an adult's. Children don't have to see every sight or all of any sight to learn something from their trip; watching, playing with, and talking to other children can be equally enlightening.
3. Let your children lead the way sometimes; their perspective is different from yours, and they may lead you to things you would never have noticed on your own.
4. Remember the places that children love to visit: aquariums, zoos, beaches, nature trails, and so on. Among the attractions that may pique their interest are:
   - **The Big Island:** At Hawaii Volcanoes National Park, explore the Thurston Lava Tube and other volcanic formations and marvel at active Kilauea's

red-hot lava flow. Go horseback riding at Parker Ranch. Take the *Atlantis Submarine* for a view of the colorful inhabitants of the coral reefs.

- **Lanai:** Go snorkeling in the calm waters of the Manele-Hulopoe Marine Life Conservation District and beachcombing along peaceful stretches of sand.
- **Kauai:** Tour the lagoons by launch or Polynesian-style canoe. Search for native wildlife at the Kilauea Point National Wildlife Refuge. Go spelunking in the caves at Haena State Park.
- **Maui:** See the 3-story-high film at the domed *Hawaii Experience/Omni Theater.* Learn about whales at the *Whalers Village Museum.* Take a ride aboard the *Lahaina-Kaanapali and Pacific Railroad* or the *Kaanapali Trolley.* Marvel at exotic birds, spider monkeys, and pygmy goats at Maui's *Zoological and Botanical Gardens.*
- **Molokai:** Take a tour of the restored *R.W. Meyer Sugar Mill.* Join a safari at the *Molokai Ranch Wildlife Park* and see ibex, oryx, zebras, and other animals native to Africa and India.
- **Oahu:** View underwater mammals — sea lions, dolphins, and whales — and fish from above and below at *Sea Life Park.* Handle aquatic creatures in the Touch Tank exhibit at the *Waikiki Aquarium* and pet furry friends at the *Honolulu Zoo.* Try on historical Hawaiian costumes at the *Bernice Pauahi Bishop Museum.* Visit the *Hawaii Children's Museum of Arts, Culture, Science & Technology* and the USS *Bowfin/Pacific Submarine Museum and Park.*

Hints for Traveling with Pets

You may wish to bring your pet along on your vacation in Hawaii. Although there are no restrictions on traveling with your pet throughout the continental US, when traveling from the mainland to the Hawaiian islands, stringent requlations apply.

DOGS AND CATS: Hawaii strictly enforces its anti-rabies laws. Therefore, all dogs and cats entering Hawaii (except those coming from Australia, New Zealand, and Great Britain) must be quarantined for 120 days. This includes dogs and cats from the mainland, and Seeing Eye dogs are *not* exempt. Animals generally are held at the Airport Animal Quarantine Holding Facility (at the Honolulu airport; phone: 808-836-3228) and then transferred to the State of Hawaii Animal Quarantine Station (99-770 Moanalua Rd., Aiea, HI 96701; phone: 808-488-8462).

Quarantine fees are $466 for dogs, $412 for cats. You also must provide a valid Interstate Health Certificate from the pet's state of origin, signed by an accredited veterinarian and dated no more than 10 days prior to shipping. (Your pet's veterinarian will supply this form.)

According to the Hawaiian Department of Agriculture authorities, you won't need any special permits to bring your dog or cat — or even a dog or cat you purchased on the Hawaiian islands — back to the mainland. Other paperwork — such as a health certificate — may be required by some states.

The American Society for the Prevention of Cruelty to Animals (ASPCA) offers a very useful booklet, *Traveling with Your Pet,* which lists inoculation and other requirements by state, and also includes a number of helpful hints. It is available for $5 (which includes postage and handling). Send check or money order to the *ASPCA* (Education Dept., 441 E. 92 St., New York, NY 10128; phone: 212-876-7700). For further information on interstate pet transportation contact the US Department of Agriculture Veterinary Services (Animal and Plant Health Inspection Service, Veterinary Services, Federal Center Building, 6505 Belcrest Rd., Room 769, Hyattsville, MD 20782; phone: 301-436-6954).

Other publications of interest to those traveling with pets include *The Complete Book of Dog Care,* by Ulrich Klever, and *The Complete Book of Cat Care,* by Monika Wegler. Both contain a variety of tips on traveling with your four-footed friends and can be ordered for $8.95 each, plus postage and handling, from Barrons Educational Series (250 Wireless Blvd., Hauppauge, NY 11788; phone: 800-645-3476 or 516-434-3311). *The Portable Pet,* by Barbara Nicholas, covers such topics as traveling by car, plane, bus, and ship; first aid for your pet; travel supplies that you'll need; quarantine regulations; and airport kennel facilities. It is available for $5.95, plus shipping and handling, from Harvard Common Press, 535 Albany St., Boston, MA 02118 (phone: 617-423-5803).

■ **Note:** Before considering taking any wild animal home as a "pet" check with the local branch of the US Department of Agriculture for state regulations, as well as health and safety considerations. The best advice is: Don't.

PLANE AND CAR: Many airlines require a health certificate for your pet. *Northwest, TWA,* and *United,* for example, all require submission of an Interstate Health Certificate signed by an accredited veterinarian and dated no more than 30 days before travel. Check with your air carrier well before your departure.

It's a good idea to buy a traveling kennel. Most pet stores sell them, as do some airlines. Any animal must be boxed for the plane trip; a kennel also is a good safety measure when touring by car.

If your pet is traveling by plane, label the kennel with your name, address, destination, pet's name, and special handling instructions. Remove the animal's collar before putting it in the kennel. Dogs should not be muzzled. Put a few toys and familiar objects in the kennel to acquaint the animal with its box before the start of the trip.

Some airlines (such as *TWA* and *United*) allow kenneled pets to fly in the passenger compartment — if there is room and the kennel falls within the dimension restrictions of carry-on baggage. A common restriction is that the pet must be kept in the kennel during takeoff and landing and when food is being served. On most airlines, however, the animal must fly in a special area reserved for live cargo. Whether the pet travels in the passenger or cargo compartment, the airline will charge a fee for transport.

■ **Note:** For the majority of travelers to Hawaii who choose to leave their pets at home, the *American Boarding Kennels Association* (4575 Galley Rd., Suite 400A, Colorado Springs, CO 80915; phone: 719-591-1113) publishes a roster of member boarding kennels throughout the US, as well as an informative pamphlet, *How to Select a Boarding Kennel* (available for $3.50).

On the Islands

Credit Cards and Traveler's Checks

It may seem hard to believe, but one of the greatest (and least understood) costs of travel is money itself. Your one single objective in relation to the care and retention of your travel funds is to make them stretch as far as possible. When you do spend money, it should be on things that expand and enhance your travel experience, with no buying power lost due to carelessness or lack of knowledge. This requires more than merely ferreting out the best airfare or the most charming budget hotel. It means being canny about the management of money itself. Herewith, a primer on making money go as far as possible in the islands.

TRAVELER'S CHECKS: It's wise to carry traveler's checks while on the road instead of (or in addition to) cash, since it's possible to replace them if they are stolen or lost; you usually can receive partial or full replacement funds the same day if you have your purchase receipt and proper identification. Issued in various denominations, with adequate proof of identification (credit cards, driver's license, passport), traveler's checks are as good as cash in most hotels, restaurants, stores, and banks.

Don't assume, however, that restaurants, small shops, and other establishments are going to be able to change checks of large denominations. Worldwide, more and more establishments are beginning to restrict the amount of traveler's checks they will accept or cash, so it is wise to purchase at least some of your checks in small denominations — say, $10 and $20.

Every type of traveler's check is legal tender in banks around the world, and each company guarantees full replacement if checks are lost or stolen. After that the similarity ends. Some charge a fee for purchase, others are free; you can buy traveler's checks at almost any bank, and some are available by mail. Most important, each traveler's check issuer differs slightly in its refund policy — the amount refunded immediately, the accessibility of refund locations, the availability of a 24-hour refund service, and the time it will take for you to receive replacement checks. For instance, *American Express* guarantees replacement of lost or stolen traveler's checks in under 3 hours at any *American Express* office — other companies may not be as prompt. (Note that *American Express*'s 3-hour policy is based on a traveler's being able to provide the serial numbers of the lost checks. Without these numbers, refunds can take much longer.)

We cannot overemphasize the importance of knowing how to replace lost or stolen checks. All of the traveler's check companies have agents around the world, both in their own name and at associated agencies (usually, but not necessarily, banks), where refunds can be obtained during business hours. Most of them also have 24-hour toll-free telephone lines, and some even will provide emergency funds to tide you over on a Sunday.

Be sure to make a photocopy of the refund instructions that will be given to you by the issuing institution at the time of purchase. To avoid complications should you need to redeem lost checks (and to speed up the replacement process), keep the purchase receipt and an accurate list, by serial number, of the checks that have been spent or cashed. You may want to incorporate this information in an "emergency packet," also including the numbers of the credit cards you are carrying and any other bits of information you shouldn't be without. Always keep these records separate from the checks and the original records themselves (you may want to give them to a traveling companion to hold).

Several of the major traveler's check companies charge 1% for the acquisition of their checks. To receive fee-free traveler's checks you may have to meet certain qualifications — for instance, *Thomas Cook*'s checks issued in US currency are free if you make your travel arrangements through its travel agency. *American Express* traveler's checks are available without charge to members of the *American Automobile Association (AAA).* Holders of some credit cards (such as the *American Express Platinum* card) also may be entitled to free traveler's checks. The issuing institution (e.g., the particular bank at which you purchase them) may itself charge a fee. If you purchase traveler's checks at a bank in which you or your company maintains significant accounts (especially commercial accounts of some size), the bank may absorb the 1% fee as a courtesy.

■ **Note:** *American Express* cardholders now can order traveler's checks by phone through a new service called *Cheques on Call.* By dialing 800-55-FOR-TC, *Green* cardholders can order up to $1,000, *Gold* cardholders, $2,500, and *Platinum* cardholders, $10,000 in *American Express* traveler's checks during any 7-day period. In addition, the usual 1% acquisition fee is waived for *Gold* and *Platinum* cardholders. There is no shipping charge if the checks are sent by first class mail; *Federal Express* delivery is available for a fee.

American Express, Bank of America, Citicorp, Thomas Cook, MasterCard, and *Visa* all offer traveler's checks. Here is a list of the major companies issuing traveler's checks and the numbers to call in the event that loss or theft makes replacement necessary:

American Express: To report lost or stolen checks in the US and Canada, call 800-221-7282. Elsewhere call 801-964-6665, collect.

Bank of America: To report lost or stolen checks in the US, call 800-227-3460. Elsewhere call 415-624-5400 or 415-622-3800, collect.

Citicorp: To report lost or stolen checks in the continental US and Hawaii, call 800-645-6556. Elsewhere worldwide, call 813-623-1709 or 813-626-4444, collect.

MasterCard: Note that *Thomas Cook MasterCard* (below) is now handling all *MasterCard* traveler's check inquiries and refunds.

Thomas Cook MasterCard: To report lost or stolen checks in the US, call 800-223-7373. In Hawaii, call 212-974-5696 or 609-987-7300, collect, and they will direct you to the nearest branch of *Thomas Cook.*

Visa: To report lost or stolen checks in the continental US and Canada, call 800-227-6811. In Hawaii, call 415-574-7111, collect.

CREDIT CARDS: Some establishments you encounter during the course of your travels may not honor any credit cards and some may not honor all cards, so there is a practical reason to carry more than one. The following is a list of credit cards that enjoy wide domestic and international acceptance:

American Express: Cardholders can cash personal checks for traveler's checks and cash at *American Express* or its representatives' offices in the US up to the following limits (within any 21-day period): $1,000 for *Green* and *Optima* cardholders; $5,000 for *Gold* cardholders; and $10,000 for *Platinum* cardholders. Check cashing also is available to cardholders who are guests at participating hotels (up to $250) and for holders of airline tickets at participating airlines (up to $50). Free travel accident, baggage, and car rental insurance if ticket or rental is charged to the card; additional insurance also is available for additional cost. For further information or to report a lost or stolen *American Express* card, call 800-528-4800 throughout the continental US; elsewhere, call 212-477-5700, collect.

Carte Blanche: Free travel accident, baggage, and car rental insurance if ticket or rental is charged to card; additional insurance also is available at additional cost. For medical, legal, and travel assistance worldwide, call 800-356-3448 throughout the US; elsewhere, call 214-680-6480, collect. For further information or to report a lost or stolen *Carte Blanche* card, call 800-525-9135 throughout the US; elsewhere, call 303-790-2433, collect.

Diners Club: Emergency personal check cashing for cardholders staying at participating hotels and motels (up to $250 per stay). Free travel accident, baggage, and car rental insurance if ticket or rental is charged to card; additional insurance also is available for an additional fee. For medical, legal, and travel assistance worldwide, call 800-356-3448 throughout the US; elsewhere, call 214-680-6480, collect. For further information or to report a lost or stolen *Diners Club* card, call 800-525-9135 throughout the US; elsewhere, call 303-790-2433, collect.

Discover Card: Offered by a subsidiary of Sears, Roebuck & Co., it provides cardholders with cash advances at numerous automatic teller machines and *Sears* stores throughout the US. For further information or to report a lost or stolen *Discover* card, call 800-DISCOVER.

MasterCard: Cash advances are available at participating banks worldwide. Check with your issuing bank for information. *MasterCard* also offers a 24-hour emergency lost card service; call 800-826-2181 throughout the US; 314-275-6690, collect, from abroad.

Visa: Cash advances are available at participating banks worldwide. Check with your issuing bank for information. *Visa* also offers a 24-hour emergency lost card service; call 800-336-8472 throughout the US; elsewhere, call 415-574-7700, collect.

SENDING MONEY: If you have used up your traveler's checks, cashed as many emergency personal checks as your credit card allows, drawn on your cash advance line to the fullest extent, and still need money, have it sent to you via one of the following services:

American Express (phone: 800-543-4080). Offers a service called "MoneyGram," completing money transfers in anywhere from 10 minutes to 2 days. The sender can go to any *American Express* office in the US and can transfer money by presenting cash, a personal check, money order, or credit card — *Discover, MasterCard, Visa,* or *American Express Optima Card* (no other *American Express* or other credit cards are accepted). *American Express Optima* cardholders also can arrange for this transfer over the phone. The minimum transfer charge is $25, which rises with the amount of the transaction; the sender can forward funds of up to $10,000 per transaction (credit card users are limited to the amount of pre-established credit line). To collect at the other end, the receiver must show identification (passport, driver's license, or other picture ID) at a local *American Express* office. In Hawaii, this service is offered on the Big Island, Kauai, Maui, Molokai, and Oahu.

Western Union Telegraph Company (phone: 800-325-4176). To send money to Hawaii, a friend or relative can go, cash in hand, to any *Western Union* office in the US, where for a *minimum* charge of $13 (it rises with the amount of the transaction), the funds will be wired directly to one of their branch offices. When the money arrives in the islands — in the case of Hawaii, generally within 24 hours — you can go to any *Western Union* branch office to pick up the transferred funds; for an additional fee of $2.95 you will be notified by phone when the money is available. For a higher fee, the sender may call *Western Union* with a *MasterCard* or *Visa* number to send up to $2,000, although larger transfers will be sent to a predesignated location. In Hawaii, *Western Union* branch offices are located on the Big Island, Kauai, Maui, and Oahu.

CASH MACHINES: Automatic teller machines (ATMs) are increasingly common worldwide. If your bank participates in one of the international ATM networks (most do), the bank will issue you a "cash card" along with a personal identification code or number (also called a PIC or PIN). You can use this card at any ATM in the same electronic network to check your account balances, transfer monies between checking and savings accounts, and — most important for a traveler — withdraw cash instantly. Network ATMs generally are located in banks, commercial and transportation centers, and near major tourist attractions.

Some financial institutions offer exclusive automatic teller machines for their own customers only at bank branches. At the time of this writing, ATMs that *are* connected generally belong to one of the following two international networks:

Cirrus: Has over 70,000 ATMs worldwide, including over 100 locations in the Hawaiian islands. *MasterCard* holders also may use their cards to draw cash against their credit lines. For further information on the *Cirrus* network, call 800-4-CIRRUS.

Plus System: Has over 70,000 automatic teller machines worldwide, including over 150 locations in Hawaii. *MasterCard* and *Visa* cardholders also may use their cards to draw cash against their credit lines. For further information on the *Plus System* network, call 800-THE-PLUS.

Information about the *Cirrus* and *Plus* systems also is available at member bank branches, where you can obtain free booklets listing the locations of machines worldwide. Note that a recent change in banking regulations permits financial institutions in the US (including Hawaii) to subscribe to *both* the *Cirrus* and *Plus* systems, allowing users of either network to withdraw funds from ATMs at participating banks.

Accommodations

Deciding where to stay in Hawaii isn't easy, thanks to what some might call an embarrassment of riches. There are, first of all, a great many hotels, and standards of quality and service throughout the industry are quite high. Travelers who want the finest in resort living — and can afford it — will not be disappointed, while others can be safe in assuming that they will find a clean and comfortable hotel in an acceptable price range. What's more, hotels are not the only lodgings available. About a third of the state's 74,000 plus rooms (or rental units) are in resort and urban condominiums, a type of accommodation that provides the ordinary traveler with the extraordinary opportunity to live for a while in the kind of vacation home that only the very wealthy can afford to own. In addition, there are more choices — from bed and breakfast accommodations to the possibility of exchanging your own home for the home of a Hawaiian family — that will appeal to those traveling on a shoestring, those in search of something a little bit different, or both.

HOTELS: Grand and gracious older establishments — in the tradition of the *Royal Hawaiian* — still exist in Hawaii, but most visitors stay at hotels that are only a few years old, the products of a rampant building surge that has only recently subsided. A fair number of these are high-rise towers that provide guests with grand views, but tend to be crowded together. At the other extreme are low-slung, but equally modern, properties scattered over the landscape in forms and finishes reminiscent of the indigenous architecture. Both types, as well as all the other structures in between, come in deluxe and more economical versions.

Large, luxury hotels — which can be independent or part of familiar national or international chains — provide comfortable to opulent accommodations, and often function as self-contained resorts, offering a wide range of modern services and recreation. Hotels of this kind can be found on all the major islands, and often operate in conjunction with condominiums and residences in the newer resort developments. Moderately priced and inexpensive — but perfectly acceptable — hotels also can be found on all the islands, offering fewer amenities and located on less prized plots of real estate. Another economical accommodation option is an apartment hotel — offering studio or 1- or 2-bedroom units with kitchenettes.

The most comprehensive list of accommodations in Hawaii is the *Accommodation Guide,* an annual publication of the Hawaii Visitors Bureau. Although it includes only those hotels (and apartment hotels and condominiums) that belong to the bureau, and, therefore, not all the establishments in the state, it nevertheless includes most of them, from luxury to low-cost choices, and lists basic facilities, addresses, phone numbers, and approximate room rates.

For your quick reference, following are the major hotel chains represented in Hawaii:

Best Western (phone: 800-528-1234). Has 2 properties on Oahu.
Embassy Suites (phone: 800-362-2779). Has 1 property on Maui.
Four Seasons (phone: 800-332-3442). Has 1 property on Maui; another hotel is scheduled to open on the Big Island in 1993.
Hilton (the US chain; phone: 800-445-8667). Has 3 properties on Oahu, and 1 each on the Big Island and Kauai.
Holiday Inn (phone: 800-465-4329). Has 1 property on Oahu.
Hyatt Regency (phone: 800-233-1234). Has 2 properties on Maui and 1 each on the Big Island, Kauai, and Oahu.
Inter-Continental (phone: 800-327-0200). Has 1 property on Maui.
Marriott (phone: 800-228-9290). Has 1 property on Maui.
Ritz Carlton (phone: 800-241-3333). Has 1 property on the Big Island, and recently opened another on Maui.
Sheraton (phone: 800-325-3535). Has 5 properties on Oahu, 3 on Kauai, and 2 on Maui.

CONDOMINIUMS AND OTHER RENTAL PROPERTIES: Hawaii continues to see rapid growth in the number of resort condominiums that are available to visitors — an increasingly popular alternative to hotels. The difference between a condominium complex and an apartment hotel is that apartment hotels are designed entirely for transient rental, whereas condominium complexes are designed to be sold to private owners as an investment, a permanent residence, or part-time vacation home. In the past, travelers renting such condominiums sight unseen could not always be sure of what they would get. But today, the development of properties in prime locations and the handling of day-to-day operations by professional management companies have imposed standards of quality and introduced a certain consistency in the facilities and services offered.

Resort condominium complexes vary from high-rise blocks to cottage clusters. Some may provide all the facilities of a hotel — including restaurants, lobbies, and lounges — and others may stress quiet or seclusion, with a definite lack of bustle. All come fully furnished.

The cost of all this for one traveler alone — or even one couple — is not inexpensive.

But for a family, two or more couples, or a group of friends, the per-person cost can be quite reasonable. Weekly and monthly rates are available to reduce costs still more. But best of all is the amount of space that no conventional hotel room can equal. As with hotels, the rates at some condominium resorts are seasonal, rising from approximately mid-December to mid-April, while at others they remain the same year-round. To have your pick of the properties available, you should begin to make arrangements for a rental at least 6 months in advance.

There are several ways of finding a suitable condominium. They are listed along with the other accommodations in the Hawaii Visitors Bureau *Accommodation Guide,* and it is also possible to find them through a travel agent. Many tour wholesalers regularly include condominium packages among their offerings. In addition, certain companies specialize in condominium vacations. Their plans typically include a rental car and rental of the condominium (at as many resorts on as many islands as you like, but usually for a minimum 2- or 3-day stay per resort), to which can be applied an excursion, individual tour-basing, or group airfare (whichever is least expensive when and from where you travel), just as it could be combined with any other package.

Other rental options in Hawaii include apartments, houses, or cottages. These rentals also can be substantially less expensive than staying in a first class hotel for the same period of time (particularly for a family), although very luxurious and expensive properties are available, too. Furthermore, it gives a sense of island life that a large hotel often cannot. Some of these rentals (especially the luxury ones) come with a maid, but most don't. (If you want this service, arrangements often can be made with a nearby service.)

The companies listed below rent condominiums and other properties in the Hawaiian islands. They handle the booking and confirmation paperwork, and can be expected to provide more information about the properties than that which might ordinarily be gleaned from a short listing in an accommodations guide.

Condo Resorts Hawaii (2222 Kalakaua Ave., Suite 1100, Honolulu, HI 96815; phone: 800-854-3823). Handles over 40 condominium properties on the Big Island, Kauai, Maui, and Oahu.

Creative Leisure (951 Transport Way, Petaluma, CA 94954; phone: 800-4-CONDOS in the US and Canada). Offers over 60 apartments and condominiums on the Big Island, Kauai, Maui, Molokai, and Oahu.

Hideaways International (PO Box 1270, Littleton, MA 01460; phone: 800-843-4433 or 508-486-8955). Rents several hundred properties on the Big Island, Kauai, Maui, and Oahu.

Hometours International (1170 Broadway, Suite 614, New York, NY 10001; phone: 800-367-4668 or 212-689-0851). Rents several hundred condominium properties throughout the islands. Also represents bed and breakfast establishments (see list below).

Rent a Home International (7200 34th Ave. NW, Seattle, WA 98117; phone: 800-488-RENT or 206-789-9377). Rents houses and villas on all the major islands, including Lanai and Molokai. Most rentals include a full housekeeping staff.

VHR, Worldwide (235 Kensington Ave., Norwood, NJ 07648; phone: 800-NEED-A-VILLA or 201-767-9393). Represents over 100 properties on the Big Island, Kauai, Maui, Molokai, and Oahu.

Villa Leisure (PO Box 209, Westport, CT 06881; phone: 800-526-4244 or 203-222-7397). This agency rents private homes and villas on the Big Island, Maui, and Oahu. Minimum stay is 1 week during the high season (2 weeks during *Christmas),* and 4 days during the summer. Villa rentals include car, transfers, staff, and private pool or beach. The well-informed staff personally inspects the properties and is a good source of information; the firm has local management on the islands.

Villas International Ltd. (605 Market St., San Francisco, CA 94105; phone:

800-221-2260 or 415-281-0910). Rents villas and private homes on the Big Island, Maui, and Oahu (also rents condos on Oahu). Some villas and condos include maid service and other staff. Minimum 1-week stay.

In addition, a useful publication, the *Worldwide Home Rental Guide,* lists private villas and cottages in Hawaii, as well as the managing agencies. Issued twice annually, single copies may be available at newsstands for $10 an issue. For a year's subscription (two issues), send $18 to *Worldwide Home Rental Guide,* PO Box 2842, Sante Fe, NM 87504 (phone: 505-988-5188).

When considering a particular vacation rental property, look for answers to the following questions:

- How do you get from the airport to the condominium?
- How far is the nearest beach? Is it sandy or rocky and is it safe for swimming?
- What size and number of beds are provided?
- How far is the property from whatever else is important to you, such as a golf course or nightlife?
- If there is no grocery store on the premises (which may be comparatively expensive, anyway), how far is the nearest market?
- Are baby-sitters, cribs, bicycles, or anything else you may need for your children available?
- Is maid service provided daily?
- Is air conditioning and/or a phone provided?
- Is a car rental part of the package? Is a car necessary?

Before deciding which rental is for you, make sure you have satisfactory answers to all your questions. Ask your travel agent to find out or call the company involved directly.

Accommodation Discounts – Several discount travel organizations provide a substantial savings — up to 50% off list prices — on condominimum and other rental accommodations (and some hotels) throughout the Hawaiian islands. Reservations are handled by the central office of the organization or members may deal directly with the rental agencies or individual property owners. To take advantage of the full selection of properties, these organizations often require that reservations be made as much as 6 months in advance — particularly for stays during peak travel periods.

Concierge (1600 Wynkoop St., Suite 102, Denver CO 80202; phone: 303-623-6775 in Colorado; 800-346-1022 elsewhere in the US). Offers up to 50% discounts on week-long condominium stays on the Big Island, Kauai, Maui, Molokai, and Oahu. Annual membership fee is $69.95 per couple.

Discount Travel International (Ives Bldg., 114 Forrest Ave., Suite 205, Narberth, PA 19072; phone: 800-334-9294 or 215-668-7184). Offers up to 50% discounts on hotel stays on the Big Island, Kauai, Maui, Molokai, and Oahu. Annual membership fee is $45 per household.

Entertainment Publications (2125 Butterfield Rd., Troy MI 48084; phone: 800-521-9640 or 313-637-8400). The company's Travel America at HalfPrice program offers up to 50% discounts on stays at over 60 hotels and up to 50% off condominium rentals on the Big Island, Kauai, Maui, Molokai, and Oahu. Their Bed & Breakfast Plus Club offers 25% discounts on stays in 3 bed and breakfast establishments in Hawaii, one each on the Big Island, Kauai, and Maui. Purchase of one of the national or regional discount coupon books published by this firm includes membership. Either the Hawaii or the national edition costs about $30.

Hotel Express (3052 El Cajon Blvd., San Diego, CA 92104; phone: 800-634-6526 or 619-280-2582). Offers up to 50% off on rental accommodations in Hawaii (the Big Island, Kauai, Maui, and Molokai). One week is the standard minimum stay; shorter rentals may also be available during the off-season. Annual membership fee of $49.95 per family provides discounts on other travel services, but membership is not required for bargains on rental accommodations.

IntlTravel Card (6001 N. Clark St., Chicago, IL 60660; phone: 800-342-0558 or 312-465-8891). Offers an ITC-50 discount program which provides 50% off on stays of 1 night (or longer) at hotels on Kauai. Members also receive discounts on dining, car rentals, and other travel services. The $36 annual membership fee includes spouse.

Privilege Card (PO Box 629, Duluth, GA 30136; phone: 800-359-0066 or 404-623-0066). Up to 50% discounts available on condominium rentals (and other travel services) on the Big Island, Kauai, Maui, Molokai, and Oahu; minimum length of stay depends on availability. Annual membership fee is $49.95 per family.

Quest International (Chinook Tower, Box 4041, Yakima, WA 98901; phone: 800-325-2400 or 509-248-7512). Condominium stays for 1 night to 1 week (or longer, depending on the availability of the property) at variable discounts on the Big Island, Kauai, Maui, Molokai, and Oahu. The annual membership fee is $99 per card, and a spouse card is included. The basic membership card is good for one 1-bedroom condominium unit per stay — the spouse card entitles a family to a second bedroom.

BED AND BREAKFAST ESTABLISHMENTS: Bed and breakfast establishments (commonly known as B&Bs) provide exactly what their name implies. It is unusual for a bed and breakfast establishment to offer the extra services found in conventional hostelries, so the bed and breakfast route often is the least expensive way to go.

Beyond the obvious fundamentals, nothing else is predictable about bed and breakfast establishments. The bed may be in an extra room in a family home, in an apartment with a separate entrance, or in a free-standing cottage elsewhere on the host's property. A private bath isn't always offered, so check before you reserve. In Hawaii, you may not even have a bed, but a sleeping pad (futon) in a Japanese-style house. Some homes have only one room to let, whereas others may be large enough to have another party or two in residence at the same time.

Breakfast probably will be a Hawaiian version of the continental variety: tropical fruit plus juice, toast or roll or homemade bread and preserves, and coffee or tea. And as often as not, breakfast will be served along with some helpful tips on what to see and do. If you're in a studio with a kitchenette, you may be furnished with the makings and have to prepare it for yourself. Despite their name, some B&Bs offer an evening meal as well — by prior arrangement and at extra cost.

Some hosts enjoy helping guests with tips on what to see and do and even serve as informal tour guides, while in other places your privacy won't be disturbed. Whichever the case, the beauty of bed and breakfast establishments is that you'll always have a warm reception and the opportunity to meet many more Hawaiians than you otherwise would, which means you'll experience the hospitality of the 50th state in a special fashion.

Bed and breakfast accommodations are found on all the islands, in beach, mountain, and town locations. Although some hosts may be contacted directly, most prefer that arrangements be made through a reservations organization. The general procedure for making reservations through bed and breakfast services is that you contact them with your requirements, they help find the right place, and confirm your reservations upon receipt of a deposit. Any further information needed will be provided by either the service or the owner of the bed and breakfast establishment. The best rule of thumb is to find out as much as you can before you book.

Among the bed and breakfast reservations services handling establishments in Hawaii are the following:

All Islands Bed & Breakfast (823 Kainui Dr., Kailua, HI 96734; phone: 808-263-2342 in Hawaii; 800-542-0344 elsewhere in the US). Represents numerous bed and breakfast establishments throughout the islands.

Bed & Breakfast Connection Maui Style (PO Box 98, Puunene, HI 96784; phone: 808-879-7865 in Hawaii; 800-848-5567 elsewhere in the US). Represents over 100 bed and breakfast establishments throughout the islands.

Bed & Breakfast Hawaii (Box 449, Kapaa, HI 96746; phone: 800-733-1632 from the mainland US and Alaska; 808-536-8421 on Oahu; 808-822-7771 elsewhere in the islands). Represents over 150 bed and breakfast establishments throughout the islands.

Bed & Breakfast Honolulu Statewide (3242 Kaohinani Dr., Honolulu, HI 96817; phone: 808-595-7533 in Hawaii; 800-288-4666 elsewhere in the US). Represents over 350 bed and breakfast establishments throughout the islands.

Pacific Hawaii Bed & Breakfast (970 N. Kalaheo, Suite A218, Kailua, HI 96734; phone: 800-999-6026, 808-262-6026, or 808-254-5030). Represents over 250 bed and breakfast establishments throughout the islands.

A useful source of information on bed and breakfast reservations services and establishments is the *Bed & Breakfast Reservations Services Worldwide* (PO Box 39000, Washington, DC 20016; phone: 800-842-1486), a trade association of B&B reservations services, which provides a list of its members for $3. *Bed & Breakfast: The National Network* also offers a list of bed and breakfast reservations services throughout the US, including Hawaii. For a copy, send a self-addressed, stamped envelope to the network (PO Box 4616, Springfield, MA 01101; no phone — the company requests that all inquiries be made in writing). The *American Bed and Breakfast Association* (1407 Huguenot Rd., Midlothian, VA 23113; phone: 804-379-2222) also can send you information.

For true bed and breakfast aficionados, there are publications that highlight noteworthy establishments. The bimonthly *Country Inns: Bed & Breakfast* includes feature articles on special bed and breakfast and similar inn-type establishments across the country, as well as advertisements placed by organizations and individual properties. To subscribe, send $15 to *Country Inns Magazine* (PO Box 457, Mount Morris, IL 61054; phone: 800-435-0715 or 815-734-1114). *Gracious Stays & Special Places* is a newsletter focusing on guesthouses and bed and breakfast establishments set in historic and architecturally significant buildings. Published by a nonprofit organization, *Person to Person Travel Productions, Inc.* (2856 Hundred Oaks, Baton Rouge, LA 70808; phone: 504-343-0672), the annual membership fee, which starts at $20, includes six issues of the newsletter.

HOME EXCHANGES: Still another alternative for travelers who are content to stay in one place during their Hawaiian vacation is a home exchange: The Smith family from Vermont moves into the home of the Opaka family in Honolulu, while the Opakas enjoy a stay in the Smiths' home. The home exchange is an exceptionally inexpensive way to ensure comfortable, reasonable living quarters with amenities that no hotel could possibly offer; often the trade includes a car. Moreover, it allows you to live in a new community in a way that few tourists ever do: For a little while, at least, you will become something of a *kamaaina* (native).

Several companies publish directories of individuals and families willing to trade homes with others for a specific period of time. In some cases, you must be willing to list your own home in the directory; in others, you can subscribe without appearing in it. Most listings are for straight exchanges only, but each directory also has a number of listings placed by people interested in either exchanging or renting (for instance, if they own a second home). Other arrangements include exchanges of hospitality while owners are in residence or youth exchanges, where your teenager is received as a guest in return for your welcoming their teenager at a later date. A few house-sitting opportunities also are available. In most cases, arrangements for the actual exchange take place directly between you and the foreign host. There is no guarantee that you will find a listing in the area in which you are interested, but each of the organizations noted below includes Hawaiian homes (mostly on Oahu, Hawaii's most populous island) among hundreds or even thousands of foreign and domestic properties.

Intervac US/International Home Exchange Service (Box 190070, San Francisco, CA 94119; phone: 415-435-3497). For $45 (plus postage) subscribers receive copies of the three directories published yearly, and are entitled to list their home in one of them; a black-and-white photo may be included with the listing for an additional $10. A $5 discount is given to travelers over age 62.

Loan-A-Home (2 Park Lane, Apt. 6E, Mt. Vernon, NY 10552; phone: 914-664-7640). Specializes in long-term (4 months or more — excluding July and August) housing arrangements worldwide for students, professors, businesspeople, and retirees, although its two annual directories (with supplements) carry a small list of short-term rentals and/or exchanges. $35 for a copy of one directory and one supplement; $45 for two directories and two supplements.

Vacation Exchange Club (PO Box 820, Haleiwa, HI 96712; phone: 800-638-3841). Offers some 10,000 listings, about half of which are in the US, including Hawaii. For $50, the subscriber receives four quarterly directories, and is listed in one.

Worldwide Home Exchange Club (13 Knightsbridge Green, London SW1X 7Q1, England; phone: 44-71-589-6055; or 806 Brantford Ave., Silver Spring, MD 20904; phone: 301-680-8950). Handles over 1,500 listings a year worldwide, including homes in Hawaii. For $25 a year, you will receive two listings yearly, as well as supplements.

Better Homes and Travel (formerly *Home Exchange International*), with offices in New York, and representatives in Los Angeles, London, Paris, and Milan, functions differently in that it publishes no directory and shepherds the exchange process most of the way. Interested parties supply the firm with photographs of themselves and their homes, information on the type of home they want and where, and a registration fee of $50. The company then works with its other offices to propose a few possibilities, and only when a match is made do the parties exchange names, addresses, and phone numbers. For this service, *Better Homes and Travel* charges a closing fee, which ranges from $150 to $500 for switches from 2 weeks to 3 months in duration, and from $300 to $600 for switches longer than 3 months. Contact *Better Homes and Travel,* 33 E. 33rd St., New York, NY 10016 (phone: 212-689-6608).

HOME STAYS: If the idea of actually staying in a private home as the guest of a Hawaiian family appeals to you, check with the *United States Servas Committee,* which maintains a list of hosts throughout the world willing to throw open their doors to visitors entirely free of charge. The primary aim of this nonprofit cultural program is to promote international understanding and peace (although domestic stays are possible), and every effort is made to discourage freeloaders. *Servas* will send you an application form and the name of the nearest of some 200 interviewers around the US for you to contact. After the interview, if you're approved, you'll receive documentation certifying you as a *Servas* traveler. There is a membership fee of $45 for an individual, and there also is a deposit of $15 to receive the host list, refunded on its return. The list gives the name, address, age, occupation, and other particulars of the hosts, including languages spoken. From then on, it is up to you to write to prospective hosts directly, and *Servas* makes no guarantee that you will be accommodated.

Servas stresses that you should choose only people you really want to meet, and that during your stay (which normally lasts between 2 nights and 2 weeks) you should be interested mainly in your hosts, not in sightseeing. It also suggests that one way to show your appreciation once you've returned home is to become a host yourself. The minimum age of a *Servas* traveler is 18 (however, children under 18 may accompany their parents), and though quite a few are young people who have just finished college, there are travelers (and hosts) in all age ranges and occupations. Contact *Servas* at 11 John St., Room 706, New York, NY 10038-4009 (phone: 212-267-0252).

Time Zones, Business Hours, and Public Holidays

TIME ZONES: Hawaii operates on Hawaiian Standard Time; clocks in the islands read 2 hours earlier than those on the mainland's West Coast (Pacific Standard Time). This time lapse increases by 1 hour as you move eastward across the three other US time zones. Therefore, if it's 7 AM Hawaiian Standard Time, it's 9 AM Pacific, 10 AM Mountain, 11 AM Central, and noon Eastern time.

Since Hawaii never suffers from a lack of daylight hours at any time of year, it does not change to Daylight Savings Time in the spring. This means that from the first Sunday in April until the last Sunday in October, the above time differences increase by 1 hour (except in Arizona and parts of Indiana, where they also don't observe the time change). Hence, if it is 7 AM in Honolulu, it's 10 AM in Los Angeles and 1 PM in New York City during those months.

BUSINESS HOURS: Most businesses in Hawaii are open from 8 AM to 5 PM, Mondays through Fridays. There are many exceptions to the blanket rule covering business hours, however, especially in the case of banks and retail stores. The traditional Hawaiian banker's hours are 8:30 AM to 3 or 3:30 PM. But, like the rest of the US, island banks are following the trend toward longer hours and most have later closings — about 6 PM at week's end, usually on Fridays. In addition, Saturday hours are becoming increasingly common. Shopping malls, also like those on the mainland, stay open late.

HOLIDAYS: This year, banks and a great many businesses in Hawaii are closed on the following days:

New Year's Day (January 1)
Martin Luther King, Jr., Day (January 18)
Presidents' Day (February 15)
Prince Kuhio Day (March 26)
Easter Sunday (April 11)
Memorial Day (May 30)
King Kamehameha Day (June 11)
Independence Day (July 4)
Admission Day (observed on the Friday or Monday closest to August 21 — the date had not been set at press time)
Labor Day (September 7)
Columbus Day (generally called *Discover's Day* in Hawaii; October 11)
Election Day (November 2)
Veterans' Day (November 11)
Thanksgiving Day (November 25)
Christmas Day (December 25)

■ **Note:** Be advised that "Aloha Friday" is not a holiday but a delightful local custom. It occurs any Friday when someone who might otherwise feel compelled to wear a business suit or mainland-style dress to work shows up in an aloha shirt or a muumuu, the ladies with flowers in their hair. This also is the day when any gentleman visitor who left his jacket at home, but nevertheless has his heart set on dining in a fancy restaurant where jackets are "suggested," is least likely to be embarrassed. The aloha spirit in aloha attire is irresistible.

Mail, Telephone, and Electricity

MAIL: Post offices in Hawaii generally are open from 8 or 8:30 AM to 4:30 PM, Mondays through Fridays, with only morning hours on Saturdays. The General Delivery section of the Main Post Office at Honolulu International Airport (3600 Aolele St., Honolulu, HI 96820) is open from 8 AM to 7:30 PM on weekdays and from 8 AM to 2:30 PM on Saturdays.

There are several places that will receive and hold mail for travelers in Hawaii. Mail sent to you at a hotel and clearly marked "Guest Mail, Hold for Arrival" is one safe approach. Hawaii's main post offices will extend this service to you if the mail is sent to you in care of General Delivery. These post offices include the Honolulu post office mentioned above (zip code: 96820); the Lahaina post office on Kauai (zip code: 96766); and the Hilo (zip code: 96720), Kailua-Kona (zip code: 96740), and Kamuela (zip code: 96743) post offices on the Big Island of Hawaii. (Note that other Hawaiian post offices will *not* accept general delivery mail.) Ask the sender to put "Hold for 30 Days" (the maximum time that the US Postal Service will hold correspondence), as well as a return address on the envelope so that the post office can return it if you are unable to pick it up. The post office will keep it for only 30 days. To claim this mail, go to the post office, ask for General Delivery, and present identification (driver's license, credit cards, birth certificate, or passport). Mail must be collected in person.

If you are an *American Express* customer (a cardholder, a carrier of *American Express* traveler's checks, or traveling on an *American Express Travel Service* tour) you can have mail sent to the *American Express* Honolulu client's mail office at the *Hyatt Regency Waikiki* (2424 Kalakaua Ave., Honolulu, HI 96815; phone 808-922-4718). Letters are held free of charge — registered mail and packages are not accepted. You must be able to show an *American Express* card, traveler's checks, or a voucher proving you are on one of the company's tours to avoid paying for mail privileges. Those who aren't clients must pay a nominal charge each time they inquire if they have received mail, whether or not they actually have a letter. There also is a forwarding fee, for clients and non-clients alike. Mail should be addressed to you, care of *American Express,* and should be marked "Client Mail Service." Additional information on this mail service is listed in the pamphlet *Services and Offices,* available from any US branch of *American Express.*

Members of the *American Automobile Association (AAA)* also can have mail held free of charge at any *AAA* office in the US. The Hawaiian branch office is in Honolulu (590 Queen St., Honolulu, HI 96813; phone: 808-528-2600). Instruct the sender to mark the envelope "Hold for Arrival." For more information regarding *AAA*'s mail service and branch locations, contact your local chapter or the national office (1000 AAA Dr., Heathrow, FL 32746-5063; phone: 407-444-8544).

TELEPHONE: The area code for the entire state is 808. As on the mainland, public telephones are available just about everywhere On the islands, it costs 25¢ to make a local call, which is defined as a call placed to a number on the same island from which you are calling. Although you can use a telephone company credit card number on any phone, particularly in transportation and tourism centers, pay phones that take major credit cards (*American Express, MasterCard, Visa,* and so on) are increasingly common.

Inter-island phone calls, as well as those to the mainland, are considered long distance — and as in some parts of the mainland, you will need to dial 1 before any long distance call. Long-distance rates are charged according to when the call is placed: weekday daytime; weekday evenings; and nights, weekends, and holidays. Least expensive are the calls you dial yourself from a private phone at night and on weekends and holidays. It generally is more expensive to call from a pay phone and you must pay for a minimum 3-minute call. If the operator assists you, calls are more expensive. This includes credit card, bill-to-a-third-number, collect, and time-and-charge calls, as well as person-to-person calls, which are the most expensive. Rates are fully explained in the front of the white pages of every telephone directory.

Hotel Surcharges – Before calling from your room, inquire about any surcharges the hotel may impose. These can be excessive, but can be avoided by calling collect, using a telephone credit card (free from phone companies), or calling from a public pay phone. Another way to keep down the cost of calling from Hawaii is to leave a copy of your itinerary and telephone numbers with people at home so that they can call you instead. (Note that when calling from your hotel room, even if the call is made collect or charged to a credit card number, some establishments still may add on a nominal line usage charge — so ask before you call.)

Emergency Number – Throughout the Hawaiian islands, 911 is the number to dial in the event of an emergency. Operators at this number will get you the help you need from the police, fire department, or ambulance service. It is, however, a number that should be used for real emergencies only.

Other Resources – Particularly useful for planning a trip is *AT&T*'s *Toll-Free 800 Directory,* which lists thousands of companies with 800 numbers, both alphabetically (white pages) and by category (yellow pages), including a wide range of travel services — from travel agents to transportation and accommodations. Issued in a consumer edition for $9.95 and a business edition for $14.95, both are available from *AT&T Phone Centers* or by calling 800-426-8686. Other useful directories for use before you leave and on the road include the *Toll-Free Travel & Vacation Information Directory* ($4.95 postpaid from Pilot Books, 103 Cooper St., Babylon, NY 11702; phone 516-422-2225) and *The Phone Booklet,* which lists the nationwide, toll-free (800) numbers of travel information sources and suppliers — such as major airlines, hotel and motel chains, car rental companies, and tourist information offices (send $2 to *Scott American Corporation,* Box 88, W. Redding, CT 06896).

ELECTRICITY: Hawaii has the same electrical current system as that on the mainland: 110 volts, 60 cycles, alternating current (AC). Appliances running on standard current can be used throughout the islands without adapters or convertors.

Staying Healthy

The surest way to return home in good health is to be prepared for medical problems that might occur on vacation. Below, we've outlined some things you need to think about before your trip begins.

BEFORE YOU GO: Older travelers or anyone suffering from a chronic medical condition, such as diabetes, high blood pressure, cardiopulmonary disease, asthma, or ear, eye, or sinus trouble, should consult a physician before leaving home. Those with conditions requiring special consideration when traveling should consider seeing, in addition to their regular physician, a specialist in travel medicine. For a referral in a particular community, contact the nearest medical school or ask a local doctor to recommend such a specialist. Dr. Leonard Marcus, a member of the *American Committee on Clinical Tropical Medicine and Travelers' Health,* provides a directory of more than 100 travel doctors across the country. For a copy, send a 9-by-12-inch self-addressed, stamped envelope, to Dr. Marcus at 148 Highland Ave., Newton, MA 02165 (phone: 617-527-4003).

Also, be sure to check with your insurance company ahead of time about the applicability of your hospitalization and major medical policies away from home. If your medical policy does not protect you while you're traveling, there are comprehensive combination policies specifically designed to fill the gap. (For a discussion of medical insurance and a list of inclusive combination policies, see *Insurance,* in this section.)

First Aid – Put together a compact, personal medical kit including Band-Aids, first-aid cream, antiseptic, nose drops, insect repellent, aspirin, an extra pair of prescription glasses or contact lenses (and a copy of your prescription for glasses or contact lenses), sunglasses, over-the-counter remedies for diarrhea, indigestion, and motion sickness, a thermometer, and a supply of those prescription medicines you take regularly.

In a corner of your kit, keep a list of all the drugs you have brought and their purpose, as well as duplicate copies of your doctor's prescriptions (or a note from your doctor). As brand names may vary in different parts of the US, it's a good idea to ask your doctor for the generic name of any drugs you use so that you can ask for their equivalent should you need a refill.

It also is a good idea to ask your doctor to prepare a medical identification card that includes such information as your blood type, your social security number, any allergies or chronic health problems you have, and your medical insurance information. Considering the essential contents of your kit, keep it with you, rather than in your checked luggage.

MINIMIZING THE RISKS: At least one of the typical health problems suffered by tourists when traveling in the tropics is of little concern in Hawaii — gastrointestinal upset. Because, as on the mainland, tap water is thoroughly purified, none of the precautions which must be taken in this regard when traveling to areas such as Mexico or South America are necessary. Fruit, vegetables, and dairy products are likewise safe — and delicious. However, avoid swimming in or drinking water from freshwater streams, rivers, or pools, as they may be contaminated with Leptospira, a bacterium which causes a disease called leptospirosis (its symptoms resemble influenza). In campgrounds, water usually is indicated as potable or for washing only — if you're not sure, ask.

Sunburn – The burning power of the sun can quickly cause severe sunburn or sunstroke. This is especially important to remember when traveling to Hawaii, where much time may be spent out of doors and on the beach. To protect yourself against these ills, wear sunglasses, take along a broad-brimmed hat and cover-up, and, most important, use a sunscreen lotion.

Water Safety – Hawaiian beaches are so beautiful, with sands so caressing and waters so crystalline, that it's hard to remember that the waters of the Pacific also can be treacherous. A few precautions are necessary. Beware of the undertow, that current of water running back down the beach after a wave has washed ashore; it can knock you off your feet and into the surf. Even more dangerous is the riptide, a strong current of water running against the tide, which can pull you out to sea. If you get caught offshore, don't panic or try to fight the current, because it will only exhaust you; instead, ride it out while waiting for it to subside, which usually happens not too far from shore, or try swimming away parallel to the beach.

Sharks are sometimes sighted, but they usually don't come in close to shore, and they are well fed on fish. Should you meet up with one, just swim away as quietly and smoothly as you can, without shouting or splashing. Although not aggressive, eels can be dangerous when threatened. If snorkeling or diving, beware of crevices where these creatures may be lurking. The tentacled Portuguese man-of-war and other jellyfish may drift in quiet salt waters for food and often wash up onto the beach; the long tentacles of these creatures sting whatever they touch — a paste made of household vinegar and unseasoned meat tenderizer is the recommended treatment.

Shell collectors should be aware that the inhabitants of the conical brown or black patterned Hawaiian cone shells have a poisonous "dart." If you are stung, soak the wound in very hot water.

Hawaii's coral reefs are extensive and razor sharp. Treat all coral cuts with an antiseptic, and then watch carefully since coral is a living organism with bacteria on the coral surface which may cause an infection. If you step on a sea urchin, you'll find that the spines are very sharp, pierce the skin, and break off easily. Like splinters, the tips left embedded in the skin are difficult to remove, but they will dissolve in a week or two; rinsing with vinegar may help to dissolve them more quickly. To avoid these hazards, keep your feet covered whenever possible.

Insects – Although relatively free of insects, Hawaii does have its share of flies and mosquitoes. Mosquitoes can be a particular nuisance and it is a good idea to use some form of topical insect repellent — those containing DEET (N,N-diethyl-m-toluamide) are among the most common and effective. The US Environmental Protection Agency (EPA) stresses that you should not use any pesticide that has not been approved by the EPA (check the label) and that all such preparations should be used in moderation. (Use solutions containing no more than a 15% concentration of DEET on children, for example, and apply only to clothing, not directly to the skin.) If picnicking or camping, burn mosquito coils or candles containing allethrin, pyrethrin, or citronella, or use a pyrethrum-containing flying-insect spray. For further information about active ingredients in repellents, call the *National Pesticide Telecommunications Network*'s 24-hour hotline number: 800-858-7378.

If you do get bitten — by mosquitoes or other bugs — the itching can be relieved with baking soda, topical first-aid cream, or antihistamine tablets. Should a bite become infected, treat it with a disinfectant or antibiotic cream. *Note:* Antihistamines should not be combined with alcohol or taken by those who will be driving.

If complications, allergic reactions (such as breathlessness, fever, or cramps), or signs of serious infection result from any of the above circumstances, *see a doctor.*

Other Pests – Though rarer, bites from scorpions, centipedes, or spiders can be serious. If possible, always try to catch the villain for identification purposes. If bitten by these creatures or *any* wild animal, the best course of action may be to head directly to the nearest emergency ward or outpatient clinic of a hospital.

Cockroaches and termites thrive in warm climates, but pose no serious health threat. There are no poisonous snakes in Hawaii; garden snakes and geckos (small lizards) are common and quite harmless.

Following all these precautions will not guarantee an illness-free trip, but should minimize the risk. For more information regarding preventive health care for travelers, contact the *International Association for Medical Assistance to Travelers* (*IAMAT;* 417 Center St., Lewiston, NY 14092; phone: 716-754-4883). This organization also assists travelers in obtaining emergency medical assistance while abroad (see list of such organizations below).

MEDICAL ASSISTANCE IN THE ISLANDS: You will discover, in the event of an emergency, that most tourist facilities — transportation companies, hotels, and resorts — are equipped to handle the situation quickly and efficiently. The hospitals in the Hawaiian islands all are prepared for emergency cases, and all — except for the smallest islands, Niihau (which is private) and Kahoolawe (which is uninhabited) — have at least some sort of medical facility. Patients on islands without hospitals who require special medical attention are transferred via *Medivac* helicopter to a hospital on a neighboring island.

In An Emergency – If a bona fide emergency occurs, dial the free "emergency" number 911 or "0" (for Operator) and immediately state the nature of your problem and your location. If you are able to, another alternative is to go directly to the emergency room of the nearest hospital — if there is one on the island.

Non-Emergency Care – If a doctor is needed for something less than an emergency, there are several ways to find one. If you are staying in a hotel or at a resort, ask for help in reaching a doctor or other emergency services, or for the house physician, who may visit you in your room or ask you to visit an office. When you register at a hotel, it's not a bad idea to include your home address and telephone number; this will facilitate the process of notifying friends, relatives, or your own doctor in case of an emergency.

Pharmacies and Prescriptions – There should be no problem finding a drugstore on most of the islands. Unlike on the mainland, however, none are open round-the-clock. In an emergency, call 911 — the local emergency number — or go directly to a hospital emergency room.

ADDITIONAL SOURCES: Medical assistance also is available from various organizations designed for travelers who have chronic ailments or whose illness requires them to return home:

International Health Care Service (New York Hospital–Cornell Medical Center, 525 E. 68th St., Box 210, New York, NY 10021; phone: 212-746-1601). This service provides a variety of travel-related health services, including a complete range of immunizations at moderate per-shot rates. A pre-travel counseling and immunization package costs $255 for the first family member and $195 for each additional member; a post-travel consultation is $175 to $275, plus lab work. Consultations are by appointment only, from 4 to 8 PM Mondays through Thursdays, although 24-hour coverage is available for urgent travel-related problems. In addition, sending $4.50 (with a self-addressed, stamped envelope) to the address above will procure the service's publication, *International Health Care Traveler's Guide,* a compendium of facts and advice on health care and diseases around the world.

International SOS Assistance, Inc. (PO Box 11568, Philadelphia, PA 19116; phone: 800-523-8930 or 215-244-1500). Subscribers are provided with telephone access — 24 hours a day, 365 days a year — to a worldwide, monitored, multilingual network of medical centers. A phone call brings assistance ranging from a telephone consultation to transportation home by ambulance or aircraft, or, in some cases, transportation of a family member to wherever you are hospitalized. Individual rates are $35 for 2 weeks of coverage ($3.50 for each additional day), $70 for 1 month, or $240 for 1 year; couple and family rates also are available.

Medic Alert Foundation (2323 N. Colorado, Turlock, CA 95380; phone: 800-ID-ALERT or 209-668-3333). If you have a health condition that may not be readily perceptible to the casual observer — one that might result in a tragic error in an emergency situation — this organization offers identification emblems specifying such conditions. The foundation also maintains a computerized central file from which your complete medical history is available 24 hours a day by phone (the telephone number is clearly inscribed on the emblem). The onetime membership fee (between $25 and $45) is based on the type of metal from which the emblem is made — the choices range from stainless steel to 10K gold-filled.

■ **Note:** Those who are unable to take a reserved flight due to personal illness or who must fly home unexpectedly due to a family emergency should be aware that airlines may offer a discounted airfare (or arrange a partial refund) if the traveler can demonstrate that his or her situation is indeed a legitimate emergency. Your inability to fly or the illness or death of an immediate family member usually must be substantiated by a doctor's note or by the name, relationship, and funeral home from which the deceased will be buried. In such cases, airlines often will waive certain advance purchase restrictions or you may receive a refund check or voucher for future travel at a later date. Be aware, however, that this bereavement fare may not necessarily be the least expensive fare available and, if possible, it is best to have a travel agent check all possible flights through a computer reservations system (CRS).

Helpful Publications – A useful publication, *Health Hints for the Tropics,* offers tips on preventing illnesses and staying healthy in tropical regions, including Hawaii, and provides practical information on immunizations, trip preparation, as well as a list of resources. It is available for $4 postpaid from Dr. Karl A. Western at the *American Society of Tropical Medicine and Hygiene,* 6436 31st St. NW, Washington, DC 20015-2342 (phone: 301-496-6721).

Practically every phase of health care — before, during, and after a trip — is covered in *The New Traveler's Health Guide,* by Drs. Patrick J. Doyle and James E. Banta. It is available for $4.95, plus postage and handling, from Acropolis Books Ltd., 13950 Park Center Rd., Herndon, VA 22071 (phone: 800-451-7771 or 703-709-0006).

The *Traveling Healthy Newsletter,* which is published six times a year, also is brimming with health-related travel tips. For a year's subscription, which costs $24 (sample issues are available for $4), contact Dr. Karl Neumann, 108-48 70th Rd., Forest Hills, NY 11375 (phone: 718-268-7290). Dr. Neumann also is the editor of the useful free booklet *Traveling Healthy,* which is available by writing to the *Travel Healthy Program* (Clark O'Neill Inc., 1 Broad Ave., Fairview, NJ 07022; phone: 215-732-4100).

Legal Help in the Islands

The best way to begin looking for legal aid in an unfamiliar area is to call your own lawyer. If you don't have, or cannot reach, your own attorney, most cities offer legal referral services (sometimes called attorney referral services) maintained by county bar associations. Such referral services see that anyone in need of legal representation gets it. (Attorneys also are listed in the yellow pages under Attorney or Lawyer.) The referral service is almost always free. If your case goes to court, you are entitled to court-appointed representation if you can't get a lawyer or can't afford one.

Drinking and Drugs

DRINKING: In Hawaii, the legal drinking age is 21. The state has no dry areas, and you should have no trouble finding a place to have a drink. However, the exact hours during which liquor is served depends on the type of establishment. Under Hawaii's liquor laws, hotels may serve alcohol from 6 AM to 2 AM or 4 AM (with a license); discos, cabarets, and other places with dancing, from 10 AM to 4 AM; and bars where there is no dancing, from 6 AM to 2 AM. Unlicensed restaurants may allow patrons to bring their own wine or other alcoholic beverage, but don't count on this — it's best to check ahead.

There are no state liquor stores in the Hawaiian islands. Beer, wine, and other spirits are available in numerous shops and markets. On Oahu, and especially in Honolulu, many shops are open as late as 11 PM. Since restrictions on Sunday sales have been lifted, liquor may be purchased on any day on any island.

As in the rest of the US, national taxes on alcohol affect the prices of liquor in the islands, and as a general rule, mixed drinks made from imported liquors (such as whiskey and gin) are more expensive than on the mainland. If you like a drop before dinner, a good way to save money is to bring a bottle of your favorite brand from home and enjoy it in your hotel before setting out.

- **Note:** It is illegal to drink anything alcoholic on the beaches or in any other public place in Hawaii.

DRUGS: Despite the US government's intensified and concerted effort to stamp out drugs, illegal narcotics still are prevalent in Hawaii, as on the mainland. Enforcement of drug laws is becoming increasingly strict throughout the US, and local narcotics officers are renowned for their absence of understanding and lack of a sense of humor.

The Hawaiian word for marijuana is *pakalolo.* Although grown in abundance throughout the islands — some well-informed wags contend that marijuana is Hawaii's largest cash crop — *pakalolo* is just as illegal in Hawaii as it is in any other part of the US, and penalties for selling, growing, and smoking it are just as severe.

Opiates and barbiturates, and other increasingly popular drugs — "'white powder" substances like heroin, cocaine, and "crack" (the cocaine derivative) — also are a problem in Hawaii, as elsewhere. Of particular concern to narcotics officials in the islands is the substance called ICE (a crystallized amphetamine). **Warning: Authorities warn those traveling with children that this substance is virtually indistinguishable from rock salt or rock candy, so it is particularly important to stress to children not to accept anything from strangers.**

The best advice we can offer is this: Don't carry, use, buy, or sell illegal drugs.

To avoid difficulties during an inspection of your luggage at the airport, those who carry medicines that contain a controlled drug such as codeine should be sure to have a current doctor's prescription with them.

- **Be forewarned:** US narcotics agents warn travelers of the increasingly common ploy of drug dealers asking travelers to transport a "gift" or other package for them. In other words, do not, under any circumstances, agree to take anything back to the mainland for a stranger.

Tipping

While tipping is at the discretion of the person receiving the service, 50¢ is the rock-bottom tip for anything, and $1 is the current customary minimum for small services. In restaurants, tip between 10% and 20% of the bill. For average service in an average restaurant, a 15% tip to the waiter is reasonable, although one should never hesitate to penalize poor service or reward excellent and efficient attention by leaving less or more.

Although it's not necessary to tip the maître d' of most restaurants — unless he or she has been especially helpful in arranging a special party or providing a table (slipping him something in a crowded restaurant *may* get you seated sooner or procure a preferred table) — when tipping is desirable or appropriate, the least amount should be $5. In the finest restaurants, where a multiplicity of servers are present, plan to tip 5% to the captain. The sommelier (wine waiter) is tipped approximately 10% of the price of the bottle of wine.

In allocating gratuities at a restaurant, pay particular attention to what has become the standard credit card charge form, which now includes separate places for gratuities for waiters and/or captains. If these separate boxes are not on the charge slip, simply ask the waiter or captain how these separate tips should be indicated.

In a large hotel or resort, where it is difficult to determine just who out of a horde of attendants actually performed particular services, it is perfectly proper for guests to ask to have an extra 10% to 15% added to their bill, to be distributed among those who served them. For those who prefer to distribute tips themselves, a chambermaid is generally tipped at the rate of around $1 a day per person. Tip the concierge or hall porter for specific services only, with the amount of such gratuities dependent on the level of service provided. For any special service you receive in a hotel, a tip is expected — $1 being the minimum for a small service.

Bellhops, doormen, and porters at hotels and transportation centers generally are tipped at the rate of around $1 per piece of luggage, along with a small additional amount if a doorman helps with a cab or car. Taxi drivers should get about 15% of the total fare.

Sightseeing tour guides should be tipped. If you are traveling in a group, decide together what you want to give the guide and present it from the group at the end of the tour ($1 per person is a reasonable tip). If you have been individually escorted, the amount paid should depend on the degree of your satisfaction, but it should not be less than 10% of the total tour price. Museum and monument guides also are usually tipped a few dollars.

Miscellaneous tips: In barbershops and beauty salons, tip as you would at home, keeping in mind that the percentages vary according to the type of establishment — 10% in the most expensive salons; 15% to 20% in less expensive establishments. (As a general rule, the person who washes your hair should get a small additional tip.) The washroom attendants in these places, or wherever you see one, should get a small tip — they usually set out a little plate with a coin already on it indicating the suggested denomination. Coat checks are worth about 50¢ to $1 a coat. For information on tipping aboard ships, see *Traveling by Ship,* in this section.

Tipping always is a matter of personal preference. In the situations covered above, as well as in any others that arise where you feel a tip is expected or due, feel free to express your pleasure or displeasure. Again, never hesitate to reward excellent and efficient attention or to penalize poor service. Give an extra gratuity and a word of thanks when someone has gone out of his or her way for you. Either way, the more personal the act of tipping, the more appropriate it seems. And if you didn't like the service — or the attitude — don't tip.

Religion in the Islands

The surest source of information on religious services in an unfamiliar community is the desk clerk of the hotel or motel in which you are staying; the local tourist information office also may be able to provide this information. For a full range of options, joint religious councils often print circulars with the addresses and times of services of all the local churches, synagogues, and temples. These often are printed as part of general tourist guides provided by the local tourist and convention center, or as part of a "what's going on" guide to the island. Many newspapers also print a listing of religious services in their area in weekend editions.

You may want to use your vacation to broaden your religious experience by joining an unfamiliar faith in its service. This can be a moving experience, especially if the service is held in a church, synagogue, or temple that is historically significant or architecturally notable. You almost always will find yourself made welcome and comfortable.

Sources and Resources

Tourist Information Offices

The Hawaii Visitors Bureau is the best source of local travel information, and most of their publications are free for the asking. For the best results, request information on specific islands, as well as publications relating to your particular areas of interest: accommodations, restaurants, special events, tourist attractions, guided tours, and facilities for specific sports and other activities. There is no need to send a self-addressed, stamped envelope with your request, unless specified.

Below is a list of the Hawaii Visitors Bureau offices on both the mainland and the islands. On the mainland, these offices usually are open Mondays through Fridays, 9 AM to 5PM; on the islands they tend to close around 4:30.

Mainland Offices

Chicago: 180 N. Michigan Ave., Suite 1031, Chicago, IL 60601 (phone: 312-236-0632).

Los Angeles: 3440 Wilshire Blvd., Suite 502, Los Angeles, CA 90010 (phone: 213-385-5301).

New York: 441 Lexington Ave., Room 1003, New York, NY 10017 (phone: 212-986-9203).

San Francisco: 50 California St., Suite 450, San Francisco, CA 94111 (phone: 415-392-8173).

Washington, DC: 1511 K St. NW, Suite 519, Washington, DC 20005 (phone: 202-393-6752).

Island Offices

Big Island of Hawaii: 180 Kinoole St., Suite 105, Hilo, HI 96720 (phone: 808-961-5797); 75-5719 W. Alii Dr., Kailua-Kona, HI 96740 (phone: 808-329-7787).

Kauai: 3016 Umi St., Suite 207, Lihue, HI 96766 (phone: 808-245-3971).

Maui: 250 Alamaha St., Kahului, HI 96732 (phone: 808-871-8691).

Oahu: 2270 Kalakaua Ave., Suite 801, Honolulu, HI 96815 (phone: 808-923-1811).

■ **Note:** The Hawaii Visitors Bureau does not have offices on Lanai or Molokai. For information on these islands contact the main office on Oahu (address above). Also, *Destination Molokai* (PO Box 960, Kaunakakai, HI 96748; phone: 808-367-4756), a public relations firm, provides tourist information for Molokai.

Theater and Special Event Tickets

In more than one section of this book you will read about events that may spark your interest — everything from theater performances to sporting championships — along with telephone numbers and addresses to which to write for descriptive brochures, reservations, or tickets. The Hawaii Visitors

Bureau also can supply information on these and other special events, though they cannot in all cases provide the actual program or detailed information on ticket prices. Since many of these occasions often are fully booked well in advance, you should think about having your reservation in hand before you go. Tickets usually can be reserved over the phone and charged to a credit card, or you can send a check or money order.

Books, Magazines, and Newsletters

BOOKS: Throughout GETTING READY TO GO, numerous books and brochures have been recommended as good sources of further information on a variety of topics.

Those interested in further reading may want to write for *What to Read About Hawaii: A Bibliography,* the catalogue of the Hawaii State Library (Hawaii and Pacific Section, 478 S. King St., Honolulu, HI 96813), which lists approximately 200 recommended titles. A large and varied selection of books is available from the University of Hawaii Press; their catalogue, *Hawaii and the Pacific,* is available by writing to the University of Hawaii Press (2840 Kolowalu St., Honolulu, HI 96822).

The following is a list of books recommended for travelers headed for Hawaii. It includes books that provide information about the islands' past, discussions of life in the islands today and aspects of Hawaiian culture, and books intended to foster an appreciation of the rich endowment of plant and animal life for which the islands are renowned.

GENERAL TRAVEL

Birnbaum's Honolulu, edited by Alexandra Mayes Birnbaum (HarperCollins; $11).

Hawaii, by Robert Wenkam (Tradewinds; $34.95).

Hawaii for Free: Hundreds of Things to Do in Hawaii, by Frances Carter (Mustang Publishing; $6.95).

Hawaiian National Parks: The Site-by-Site Guide, edited by Nicky Leach (Sunrise; $5.95).

How to Get Lost and Found in Our Hawaii, (original title, ***Our Hawaii***), by John and Bobbye McDermott (ORAFA; $9.95).

Kauai, Hawaii's Garden Island, by Robert Wenkam (Rand McNally; currently out of print — check your library).

Maui No Ka Oi, by Robert Wenkam (Tradewinds; $34.95).

Smithsonian Guide to Historic America: The Pacific States (Stewart, Tabori & Chang; $18.95).

FOOD AND DRINK

Aunty Pua's Keiki Cookbook, by Ann K. Corum (Bess Press; $6.95).

Best Tested Recipes of Hawaii, by Margaret Stone (Aloha; $4.95).

Hawaii Cooks Throughout the Year, by Mali Yardley (Editions, Ltd.; $18.95).

How to Use Hawaiian Fruit, by Agnes Alexander (Petroglyph; $4.95).

Joys of Hawaiian Cooking, by Judith and Martin Beeman (Petroglyph; $6.95).

HISTORY AND CULTURE

The Curse of Lono, by Hunter S. Thompson (Bantam; $14.95).

Damien the Leper, by John Farrow (Doubleday; $8.95).

Explorations of Captain James Cook in the Pacific, as Told by Selections of His Own Journals, 1768–1779, edited by A. Grenfell Price (Dover; $7.95).

Feathered Gods and Fishhooks: An Introduction to Hawaiian Archeology and Prehistory, by Patrick V. Kirch (University of Hawaii Press; $26.00).

Hawaiian Music and Musicians, by George Kanahele (University of Hawaii Press; $15.00).

Holy Man: Father Damien of Molokai, by Gavan Daws (University of Hawaii Press; $9.95).

How to Make Your Own Hawaiian Musical Instruments, by Jerry Hopkins (Bess Press; $6.95).

Kalakaua: Hawaii's Last King, by Kristin Zambucka (Mana Publications; $12.-95).

Music of Ancient Hawaii, by Dorothy Kahananui (Petroglyph; $3.95).

Pele, Goddess of Hawaii's Volcanoes, by Herb K. Kane (Kawaiinui Press; $7.95).

Shoal of Time: A History of the Hawaiian Islands, by Gavan Daws (University of Hawaii Press; $9.95).

Six Months in the Sandwich Islands, by Isabella Bird (Charles Tuttle; $9.95).

Travels in Hawaii, by Robert Louis Stevenson (University of Hawaii Press; $10.-50).

WhaleSong: A Pictorial History of Whaling and Hawaii, by Simpson Mackinnon (Island Heritage; $24.95).

LANGUAGE AND LITERATURE

Hawaii, by James Michener (Ballantine Books; $6.95).

Legends of Hawaii, by Padraic Colum (Yale University Press; $30 cloth, $11.95 paperback).

Ole lo No'eau: Hawaiian Proverbs and Poetical Sayings, edited by Mary K. Pakui (University of Washington Press; $35.00).

Poetry of Hawaii: A Contemporary Anthology, edited by Frank Stewart and John Unterecker (University of Hawaii Press; $5.95).

Spoken Hawaiian, by Samuel H. Elbert (University of Hawaii Press; $9.95).

Unwritten Literature of Hawaii: The Sacred Songs of the Hula, by Nathaniel B. Emerson (C.E. Tuttle; $6.75).

FLORA AND FAUNA

Hawaiian Birdlife, by Andrew J. Berger (University of Hawaii Press; $29.95).

Hawaiian Fish Watcher's Field Guide, by Idaz Greenberg (Seahawk Press; $5).

Hawaiian Reef Animals, edited by Edmund Hobson and E. H. Chave (University of Hawaii Press; $19.95).

Plants and Flowers of Hawai'i, by S. H. Sohmer and R. Gustafson (University of Hawaii Press; $15.95).

An Underwater Guide to Hawai'i, by Ann Fielding and Ed Robinson (University of Hawaii Press; $15.95).

The books listed above may be ordered directly from the publishers or found in the travel section of any good general bookstore or sizable public library. If you still can't find something, the following stores and/or mail-order houses also specialize in travel literature. They offer books on Hawaii along with guides to the rest of the world, and in some cases, even an old Baedeker or two.

Book Passage (51 Tamal Vista Blvd., Corte Madera, CA 94925; phone: 415-927-0960 in California; 800-321-9785 elsewhere in the US). Travel guides and maps to all areas of the world. A free catalogue is available.

The Complete Traveller (199 Madison Ave., New York, NY 10016; phone: 212-685-9007). Travel guides and maps. A catalogue is available for $2.

Forsyth Travel Library (PO Box 2975, Shawnee Mission, KS 66201-1375; phone: 800-367-7984 or 913-384-3440). Travel guides and maps, old and new, to all parts of the world, including Hawaii. Ask for the "Worldwide Travel Books and Maps" catalogue.

Phileas Fogg's Books and Maps (87 *Stanford Shopping Center,* Palo Alto, CA 94304; phone: 800-533-FOGG or 415-327-1754). Travel guides, maps, and language aids.

Powell's Travel Store (Pioneer Courthouse Sq., 701 SW 6th Ave., Portland, OR 97204; phone: 503-228-1108). A wealth of travel-related books (over 15,000 titles) and reference materials (globes, an extensive selection of maps, language aids, etc.), as well as luggage and travel accessories (travel irons, electrical converters, etc.). There is even a travel agency on the premises.

The Reader's Catalog (250 West 57th St., Suite 1330, New York, NY 10107; phone: 800-733-BOOK or 212-262-7198). This general mail-order bookstore will make recommendations on travel — and all other — books and literature and ship books anywhere in the world.

Tattered Cover (2955 E. First Ave., Denver, CO 80206; phone: 800-833-9327 or 303-322-7727). The travel department alone of this enormous bookstore carries over 7,000 books, as well as maps and atlases. No catalogue is offered (the list is too extensive), but a newsletter, issued three times a year, is available on request.

Thomas Brothers Maps & Travel Books (603 W. Seventh St., Los Angeles, CA 90017; phone: 213-627-4018). Maps (including road atlases, street guides, and wall maps), guidebooks, and travel accessories.

Traveller's Bookstore (22 W. 52nd St., New York, NY 10019; phone: 212-664-0995). Travel guides, maps, literature, and accessories. A catalogue is available for $2.

MAGAZINES: You may want to subscribe to magazines that specialize in information about Hawaii:

Hawaii, a bimonthly, highlights customs, history, art, and sports; it also publishes events calendars, restaurant listings, and gallery dates. For a year's subscription, send $12.99 to *Hawaii* (PO Box 485, Mount Morris, IL 61054; phone: 815-734-6083).

Honolulu, a monthly, focuses on life in the capital, with articles on home design, fashion, politics, restaurants, and the like. For a year's subscription, residents of the continental US should send $21 ($15 for Hawaii residents) to *Honolulu Magazine* (36 Merchant St., Honolulu, HI 96813; phone: 808-524-7400).

NEWSLETTERS: Throughout GETTING READY TO GO we have mentioned specific newsletters which our readers may be interested in consulting for further information. One of the very best sources of detailed travel information is *Consumer Reports Travel Letter.* Published monthly by Consumers Union (PO Box 53629, Boulder, CO 80322-3629; phone: 800-999-7959), it offers comprehensive coverage of the travel scene on a wide variety of fronts. A year's subscription costs $37; 2 years' costs $59.

The following travel newsletters also provide useful up-to-date information on travel services and bargains, as well as what's happening and where to go in the Hawaiian islands.

Aloha (49 S. Hotel St., Suite 309, Honolulu, HI 96813; phone: 808-523-9871). Spotlights places of interest in the islands and includes a calendar of special events. $17.97 for six issues per year.

Big Island Update, Kauai Update, Maui Update (Paradise Publications, 8110 SW Wareham, Portland, OR 97223; phone: 503-246-1555). These three quarterly newsletters provide detailed information on their respective island beats. $6 for each island letter per year.

The Hideaway Report (Harper Associates, Subscription Office: PO Box 300, Whitefish, MO 59937; phone: 406-862-3480; Editorial Office: PO Box 50, Sun

Valley, ID 83353; phone: 208-622-3193). This monthly source highlights retreats — including island idylls — for sophisticated travelers. A year's subscription costs $90.

Romantic Hideaways (217 E. 86th St., Suite 258, New York, NY 10028; phone: 212-969-8682). This monthly newsletter leans toward those special places made for those traveling in twos. A year's subscription costs $65.

Travel Smart (Communications House, 40 Beechdale Rd., Dobbs Ferry, NY 10522; phone: 914-693-8300 in New York State; 800-327-3633 elsewhere in the US). This monthly covers a wide variety of trips and travel discounts. A year's subscription costs $44.

■ **Computer Services:** Anyone who owns a personal computer and a modem can subscribe to a database service providing everything from airline schedules and fares to restaurant listings. Two such services of particular use to travelers are *CompuServe* (5000 Arlington Center Blvd., Columbus, OH 43220; phone: 800-848-8199 or 614-457-8600; $39.95 to join, plus usage fees of $6 to $12.50 per hour) and *Prodigy Services* (445 Hamilton Ave., White Plains, NY 10601; phone: 800-822-6922 or 914-993-8000; $12.95 per month's subscription, plus variable usage fees).

Before using any computer bulletin-board services, be sure to take precautions to prevent downloading of a computer "virus." First install one of the programs designed to screen out such nuisances.

Cameras and Equipment

Vacations are everybody's favorite time for taking pictures and home movies. After all, most of us want to remember the places we visit — and show them off to others. Here are a few suggestions to help you get the best results from your travel photography or videography. Also, see *A Shutterbug's Hawaii* in DIVERSIONS for further suggestions on photographing in the Hawaiian islands.

BEFORE THE TRIP

If you're taking your camera or camcorder out after a long period in mothballs, or have just bought a new one, check it thoroughly before you leave to prevent unexpected breakdowns or disappointing pictures.

1. Still cameras should be cleaned carefully and thoroughly, inside and out. If using a camcorder, run a head cleaner through it. You also may want to have your camcorder professionally serviced (opening the casing yourself will violate the manufacturer's warranty). Always use filters to protect your lens while traveling.
2. Check the batteries for your camera's light meter and flash, and take along extras just in case yours wear out during the trip. For camcorders, bring along extra Nickel-Cadmium (Ni-Cad) batteries; if you use rechargeable batteries, a recharger will cut down on the extras.
3. Using all the settings and features, shoot at least one test roll of film or one videocassette, using the type you plan to take along with you.

EQUIPMENT TO TAKE ALONG

Keep your gear light and compact. Items that are too heavy or bulky to be carried comfortably on a full-day excursion will likely remain in your hotel room.

1. Invest in a broad camera or camcorder strap if you now have a thin one. It will make carrying the camera much more comfortable.
2. A sturdy canvas, vinyl, or leather camera or camcorder bag, preferably with padded pockets (not an airline bag), will keep your equipment organized and easy to find. If you will be doing much shooting around the water, a waterproof case is best.
3. For cleaning, bring along a camel's hair brush that retracts into a rubber squeeze bulb. Also take plenty of lens tissue, soft cloths, and plastic bags to protect equipment from dust and moisture.

FILM AND TAPES: If you are concerned about airport security X-rays damaging undeveloped film (X-rays do not affect processed film) or tapes, store them in one of the lead-lined bags sold in camera shops. This possibility is not as much of a threat as it used to be, however. In the US and Canada, incidents of X-ray damage to unprocessed film (exposed or unexposed) are few because low-dosage X-ray equipment is used virtually everywhere. If you're traveling without a protective bag, you may want to ask to have your photo equipment inspected by hand. One type of film that should never be subjected to X-rays is the very high speed ASA 1000. The walk-through metal detector devices at airports do not affect film, though the film cartridges may set them off.

You'll have no trouble getting any standard film in Hawaii; it's sold everywhere. Most Waikiki hotels and other resort areas charge a premium for film. If you want to buy a lot of film, try *City Art Works* (1133 Nuuanu Ave.; phone: 808-536-4066) or *Super Save Camera* (1334 Young St.; phone: 808-536-6431). *Long's,* a chain of drugstores with outlets in Hilo (the Big Island), Lihue (Kauai), Kahului and Lahaina (Maui), and Kailua (Oahu), also sells discounted film and handles processing. On Kauai, Maui, and Oahu, *Fox Photo* stores offer a full range of photo supplies and 1-hour film processing; all branches sell disposable underwater cameras and several also rent 35mm models. For the nearest *Fox Photo* location (there are over 20), call 808-667-7737. Other shops offering 1-hour processing are now found on all the major islands. *Kodak* even has a processing lab in Honolulu. For equipment, check the daily newspaper for increasingly common discount prices. Should your camera need repairs while in the islands, on Oahu call *Photocine* (738 Kaheka St., Room 305; phone: 808-941-4133), which provides warranty and out-of-warranty service for almost all models.

Tapes and video equipment rentals are now available on all islands. On Maui, try *Point and Shoot* (phone: 808-661-1212) or *Rainbow Video* (phone: 808-879-8905) in Kihei, and *Wave Video* (phone: 808-661-5885) in Lahaina. On Oahu, it's *King Video Camera Rentals* on Royal Hawaiian Ave. (phone: 808-922-6510) and *Video Camera Rentals* at 1860 Ala Moana Blvd. (phone: 808-942-2866), which offers delivery service.

PERSPECTIVES

History

As many as 25 million years ago, volcanic eruptions 19,000 feet below the surface of the Pacific began to build up mountains of lava that emerged from the water one by one and eventually presented themselves to the world as a chain of islands.

The isolated and slowly weathering mountain peaks we think of as Hawaii lie approximately 2,400 miles off the coast of North America, but the archipelago's eight major islands — Kauai, Niihau, Oahu, Molokai, Maui, Lanai, Kahoolawe, and Hawaii — are only the southernmost and youngest of a chain of 132 islands and atolls that stretch another 1,500 miles to the northwest. Kure Atoll, at the far end of the chain and now eroded to a semicircle of reef, is the oldest of the family. The approximately 2- to 3-million-year-old Big Island of Hawaii, with its active volcanoes, is, for the moment at least, the baby.

Geologists used to think that the islands were born when a fissure opened in a northwest-southeast direction across the floor of the ocean. According to this theory, volcanism progressed southeastward along the fissure so that volcanoes at the northwestern end ceased activity ages ago. A newer theory, however, propounds that the entire archipelago was created by a single "hot spot" that squeezed lava up, assembly-line fashion, through successive weak spots in the earth's crust as the sea floor slid north, then west, over the course of millions of years. The hot spot is presently under the Big Island, but this theory predicts that just as the other islands were carried away from their birthplace, the Big Island, too, will eventually move westward, its volcanic fires extinguished, and a new island will arise to take its place.

So much for geology. The Hawaiians have always basically understood this, because the correct geological sequence of events has long been pinpointed in Hawaiian myth and attributed to none other than that celebrated personage Pele, the explosive fire goddess who lives in the very heart of the Big Island, in the bubbling white heat of the constantly shifting molten lava of Kilauea volcano. Before taking up residence in Kilauea, Pele is credited with having created volcanoes first on Kauai, then on Oahu, then on the other islands, and finally on Maui, while continuously searching for the perfect home as well as the perfect lover. She brought the handsome high chief Lohiau with her to Kilauea, but when he fell in love with her younger sister, Hiiaka, and the pair tried to escape, the lovers were engulfed in molten lava sent after them by the jealous and angry fire goddess. With his last breath Lohiau called Pele's name, and the goddess, as the story goes, vowed, "Someday I will build for us a new island, a new land, where we will live in harmony."

Thus, both science and mythology have set the scene for Hawaii's latest volcanic island, and, indeed, 30 miles south of Kilauea, at 3,000 feet below the surface of the blue Pacific, is the cone of a volcano rising almost 16,000 feet from the ocean floor. It is called Loihi and has erupted as recently as 1980.

THE POLYNESIANS

Legend has it that Hawaii was named for the great Polynesian chief Hawaii Loa, who is believed by some to have been its discoverer. Today's consensus indicates that whoever led the initial expedition, the islands' first settlers came from the Marquesas Islands and from the Society Islands (Tahiti, Raiatea, and Bora Bora) as early as the 3rd century (and possibly earlier), with another wave of migration during the 11th and 12th centuries directly from Tahiti.

Long before Christopher Columbus ventured out of sight of land and discovered that the world was not flat after all, Polynesians were freely sailing the Pacific without compass or sextant in double-hulled canoes (*waakauluas*) connected by a deck that could carry 50 passengers with their household goods, food, animals, plants, and their gods. These voyaging canoes, equipped with masts, sails, paddles, bailers, and stone anchors, were actually two canoes lashed together with connecting booms to support the deck, or *polu.* On this platform was a shelter, a firepit built of rocks on a base of sand, and an altar to the god Kane, whose aid was invoked by offerings during the long journey.

The Polynesians set their course by the stars, the prevailing winds, familiar cloud formations, and a sixth sense, logging 100 miles a day and voyaging thousands of miles from their home. In feats of navigation that are still fascinating and impressive, these people sailed and settled the whole eastern Pacific just as they had probably sailed centuries earlier from the Malay Peninsula and Indonesia to settle the western Pacific.

Most historians maintain that Hawaii's first settlers, the Marquesans, arrived on the Big Island of Hawaii, at South Point. While it remains uncertain on which island these great voyaging canoes landed, these earliest settlers thought to be descendants of the mysterious race of people called Menehunes, who are depicted in Hawaiian legend as an ancient race of industrious elves, were famous for undertaking and finishing large engineering projects overnight. If judged by the fishponds, walls, and irrigation canals said to be their work, they were not only busy, they were brilliant. No one knows how they arrived or what became of them, but if they were indeed the Marquesans, it seems probable that they were driven out or absorbed by the later Polynesians, who began to arrive during the 11th century from Tahiti.

Many great canoes followed this first wave of immigration. There is also evidence in the Hawaiian tradition that for some time after their arrival, perhaps as late as the 15th or 16th century, the new settlers voyaged back and forth between their new and their old homelands, probably to pick up more relatives, animals, and plants — the Polynesians were responsible for bringing pigs, dogs, and chickens, plus breadfruit, yams, taro, bananas, sugarcane, coconuts, ti plants, and the paper mulberry, from which cloth was made, to

Hawaii. Eventually, they seemed content to stay put in their ever more bountiful Hawaiian islands and sailed out the Kealaikahiki Channel (between Lanai and Kahoolawe; it means "the way to Tahiti") no more, isolated until the coming of the white man.

CAPTAIN COOK

There are indications that Spanish explorers sailed in and out of Hawaiian waters several times during the 16th century, loading provisions and water and leaving behind the pineapple, perhaps, and one or two shipwrecked sailors. They did not announce their discovery, if they considered it such, to the world, however, leaving that feat to the British explorer Captain James Cook. On his first two voyages, Cook had disproved the existence of a southern continent in the Pacific and explored or discovered several South Pacific lands. The object of his third voyage was to find a Northwest Passage from the Pacific to the Atlantic.

In December 1777, Cook and his two ships, HMS *Resolution* and HMS *Discovery,* headed north from the Society Islands to cross the equator and search the west coast of North America for the supposed passage to the Atlantic. On January 18, 1778, he sighted the island of Oahu and then Kauai, where he sailed into Waimea Bay and was ceremoniously welcomed by the natives, who believed him to be Lono, the god of agriculture and fertility, fulfilling a vow to return one day. Cook spent 2 weeks trading on Kauai and Niihau before sailing north on his original assignment, naming his discovery the Sandwich Islands in honor of the Earl of Sandwich, who had sponsored the expedition.

After a fruitless search for the Northwest Passage, Captain Cook returned to the Sandwich Islands in November of the same year. This time, his ships stood off the east coast of Maui, where the aged high chief of Hawaii, Kalaniopuu, who was waging war with Kahekili, the high chief of Maui, spent the night as a guest aboard the *Resolution,* along with his young warrior nephew, Kamehameha.

The British explorer then sailed south and discovered the island of Hawaii. Weeks of cruising for a safe anchorage followed, but when it was finally found at Kealakekua Bay in mid-January 1779, Cook was again welcomed as a god. Relations remained pleasant throughout the *makahiki* season (the 4-month fall festival, during which war was *kapu,* forbidden by law) while the British ships were repaired and provisioned.

On February 4, 1779, Cook resumed his journey, but from that moment, fate was against him. His ships ran into gale winds and the *Resolution* sprang her foremast, forcing a return to Kealakekua Bay for repairs. Strangely, there was no greeting for the ships on this occasion; in fact, the bay appeared deserted — the *makahiki* season was over and the natives no longer looked upon the captain as anything more than a mortal man. On February 14, 1779, a cutter from the *Discovery* was stolen and dismantled by Hawaiians eager for its highly prized iron nails. Cook and his men went after the boat, and in the pitched battle that ensued, he and 17 Hawaiians were killed. Cook's bones were claimed for burial by his sailing master, Captain Bligh, who later commanded the *Bounty.* A monument to Cook stands on the north side of the bay at Kaawaloa on the Big Island.

KAMEHAMEHA I AND UNIFICATION

At the time Captain Cook visited the islands, the Hawaiian populace was divided into a rigid class system made up of a hereditary group of nobles or chiefs called *alii;* of priests, *kahunas;* of the commoners, *makaainanas;* and of the outcasts or slaves, *kauwas.* At the top of the heap were the high chiefs (*moi*) who held court, collected taxes, led the soldiery, consecrated the temples (*heiaus*), oversaw religious rites, and upheld the *kapu* (taboo) system that was both religion and law, the foundation of society. Cook had not discovered a peaceful paradise by any means; life under the *kapus* was as difficult for the mass of commoners as the life of a European serf under feudalism, and warfare among chiefs was frequent.

The night Kamehameha spent aboard Captain Cook's ship had been the young chief's introduction to Western civilization and to firearms. No doubt his imagination was stirred, reinforcing his resolve to rule more than a chief's section of Hawaii. When his uncle, Kalaniopuu, died in 1782, Kamehameha seized the opportunity to expand his domination of the Big Island. Though his cousin Kiwalao had been made heir to the throne, Kamehameha had become the keeper of the family war god, Kukailimoku. Kamehama soon defeated Kiwalao, but his struggle against another cousin and rival, Keoua, went on for a full 9 years. Finally, Kamehameha built a huge *heiau,* Puukohola, sacred to the war god, on a hill above Kawaihae on the North Kohala coast. When it came time to dedicate Puukohola, Kamehameha enticed his cousin to the ceremony, slew him, and offered him as the ultimate sacrifice on the altar of the temple. Kamehameha's consecration was complete; he was now ruler of all the island of Hawaii, and he soon would rule over the entire chain.

The year before, Kamehameha had won an important battle over the high chief of Maui, Kahekili, who also controlled Molokai and Lanai. After Kahekili's death in 1794, it was not long before Kamehameha disposed of his successor. Oahu fell in the Battle of the Pali in 1795, and with that decisive victory, no major island remained to be conquered except Kauai, which capitulated in 1810, won by diplomacy.

Kamehameha I is recorded in Hawaiian history as Kamehameha the Great, the creator of a united Hawaiian kingdom. A fierce and fearless fighter, he also proved a master statesman, maintaining power by appointing royal governors who had no ties of kinship with the islands they served. After so many years of devastation and impoverishment by war, he quickly restored the kingdom to peace and prosperity.

In his conquest, he had used foreign weapons and advisers — as did other island chiefs — and he kept these advisers with him, adopting their new ideas. Trade between Honolulu and Europe and America became increasingly important during this time, and Kamehameha took eagerly to it, establishing a royal monopoly. Though the sandalwood trade with China, which began in earnest around 1810 and continued for about 20 years, did not, in the end, prove beneficial to Hawaii (it depleted the forests), in other ways he encouraged agriculture and industry. Above all, he advocated hard work and a religious way of life.

Kamehameha had 21 wives, all high-born chiefs, but only two of them stand out in history. Queen Keopuolani, of Maui, was his "sacred" wife, so called because she was a *niaupio,* a child of a brother and sister union of great chiefs. Under the *kapu* system, such people represented an intensification of the power of their parents and were so sacred that all who came into their presence had to prostrate themselves. Keopuolani outranked Kamehameha and thus assured him of the noblest of offspring. She bore him two sons, Liholiho and Kauikeaouli, and a daughter, Nahienaena.

Queen Kaahumanu, a chief of high rank from Maui, was Kamehameha's "favorite" wife. A native 19th-century historian described her as a "handsome woman, six feet tall, straight, and well-formed." Kaahumanu was intelligent, headstrong, and politically astute, and though she had no children, she became Hawaii's first *kuhina nui* (regent) for the two sons of Keopuolani who succeeded Kamehameha to the throne.

Kamehameha died in Kailua, on the Big Island of Hawaii, in May 1819, at about age 60. (His actual birth date is unknown.) He was accorded all of the *kapus* and funeral rituals of the ancient Hawaiian religion — the last Hawaiian king to be so honored. During a lengthy and complicated mourning, his body was prepared for burial, and at the end of the 10 days needed to clean the bones, they were wrapped in black tapa cloth and placed in a basketwork container. After prayers and incantations spoken at his *heiau,* two close companions cached his bones in a safe spot where they could not be found (and have not to this day). It is said that "only the stars of the heavens know the resting place of Kamehameha."

KAMEHAMEHA II AND THE BREAKING OF THE KAPU

Kamehameha was succeeded by his son Liholiho, who became Kamehameha II at the age of 22 and had a brief but eventful rule. The powerful Queen Kaahumanu immediately named herself his regent — whether by command of the departed king or by her own initiative, it is not known — and at once urged him to abandon the ancient *kapu* system. The spirited queen had already broken several *kapus* and escaped retribution from the gods, but there were *kapus* of greater importance that she wished to challenge. One of the strictest barred women from the *luakini heiaus,* where political and religious decisions were made. As a high female chief in her own right, a wife of one king and regent to another, Kaahumanu occupied a position of great rank, but her sex prevented her from exercising its authority to the fullest.

Kaahumanu enlisted the aid of Liholiho's mother, Queen Keopuolani, another chief who did not fear the retribution of the gods. Together they arranged a special public feast and insisted that the young king eat with them, thus breaking a most conspicuous *kapu* — the one preventing men and women from eating together no matter what their rank — and, symbolically, all of them.

Liholiho did not acquiesce without a great deal of thought, but acquiesce he did, and on the third or fourth day of October 1819, the eating *kapu* was broken. The following day, messengers were sent to all the islands informing the people that the *kapus* were no more and ordering the *heiaus* and the images of the gods destroyed. Surprisingly, few besides the king's cousin Kekuaokalani, protector of the war god, rebelled at these orders, but his and other uprisings were soon quieted.

The spectacle of a society in a few short weeks doing away with a system of religion and law that had served it for centuries was a strange one. In part, the arrival of foreigners was to blame: Not only did the chiefs see *haoles* (white men) violating *kapus* without punishment from the gods, but commoners also saw them go unpunished by the chiefs, whose duty it was to uphold the system. In this confusion, it seemed perhaps to all levels of society that the gods had lost their power or at least their interest in the Hawaiian people.

That it was two women who led the revolution does not surprise historians. From the beginning, Hawaiian women, who were condemned to an exceedingly subordinate role in their society, had had the closest and most frequent contacts with the *haoles* and consequently the greatest exposure to a liberated life, without *kapus.* But commoners of both sexes, who could be burned, strangled, or stoned to death for so much as allowing their shadow to fall upon the house of a high chief, had cause to rejoice in emancipation, even though the breaking of the *kapus* left a void at the heart of society.

Liholiho still ruled after the *kapus* were gone, though no longer by divine right. And in less than 5 years, both he and his favorite wife, Queen Kamamalu, would be dead as the result of an ill-fated trip to London. Since the days of the first Kamehameha, Hawaiian royalty had felt a particular affection for England. During the 1790s, Kamehameha the Great had been friends with the British explorer Captain George Vancouver, who had advised him on government and military matters and had presented him with sheep and cattle, thereby introducing them to the islands. Vancouver became so respected that the king accorded him the singular honor of "ceding" the island of Hawaii to Great Britain in 1794 and hoisting the British flag at Kealakekua Bay. (Recognition that the island was a British protectorate never came from London, however, and so the islands remained — for the time being — independent.)

Because England had a king and queen, a court, and nobles, just as the Hawaiians did after Kamehameha's successful unification of the islands into a single kingdom, Liholiho had a great desire to visit them. Once in London, he and his queen were caught up in the social whirl, and their official presentation was imminent when both of them suddenly fell ill. The court physician diagnosed the illness as measles, a simple enough disease as far as Londoners were concerned, but not for the Hawaiians, who had never encountered it before. Kamamalu and Liholiho both died there in July 1824, and a small, sad, and weary party of Hawaiian *alii* returned to the islands to announce the news. Liholiho's younger brother, Kauikeaouli, not yet in his teens, became Kamehameha III, with Kaahumanu again as *kuhina nui.*

THE MISSIONARIES AND WHALERS

The breaking of the *kapus* set the stage for the arrival of the missionaries, who, at the very moment the gods were being thrown from their pedestals all over Hawaii, were sailing the high seas with the islands as their destination. They had been inspired by a particularly devout young Hawaiian convert, Henry Obookiah (Opukahaia), who had worked his way aboard ship to New England during Kamehameha's reign and enrolled in a mission school. Stories of his home impressed two young students, Hiram Bingham and Asa Thurston, who, after Henry's death, volunteered to take Christianity to the Sandwich Islands.

They gathered a dedicated Calvinist group in Boston and on October 23, 1819, set sail aboard the brig *Thaddeus.* In the group were the two missionaries, a doctor, two teachers, a printer, and a farmer, along with their wives and children. Also aboard were four young Hawaiian boys who had been attending the mission school and who spent the 5 months at sea teaching the small band Hawaiian.

The impact of the missionaries on Hawaiian society began immediately. Within a few short years, they and subsequent missions had "clothed the naked," created an alphabet for Hawaiian and produced a written language, printed Bibles and hymnals in Hawaiian, established schools on all the islands, banned the hula, and become involved in commerce and politics. They introduced the seeds of their own foods along with the seeds of Christianity, and soon they replaced grass houses with clapboard saltboxes and built churches in the image of the ones left behind in New England.

Their progress was remarkable, considering their relatively small numbers, but the missionaries had several things in their favor: the mood of the islands, for instance, ripe for change, and the presence of the missionary wives and doctors. The wives labored as hard as their husbands and impressed the Hawaiian women with their skills in needlework and nursing. The physicians performed operations, fought epidemics, and established patterns of hygiene formerly unknown to the Hawaiians.

Finally, the missionaries' desire to teach as well as preach stood them in good stead. The shrewd and powerful Kaahumanu, who had been wary of the missionaries at first, learned to read and write and immediately recognized the importance of education to her people. When she was won over by the content of her reading and converted to Christianity, she supported the American missions even more forcefully.

After Liholiho's departure for England, Kaahumanu ordered the strict observance of the Sabbath, and soon afterward, with the concurrence of the council of chiefs, she issued a code of laws against drunkenness, fighting, theft, and murder. Another law decreed that as schools were established, all Hawaiians should learn to read and write. These were the first laws to fill the vacuum left by the breaking of the *kapus,* and her subjects accepted the new code without protest.

The schools decreed by Kaahumanu grew rapidly. In 1824, there were 2,000 pupils. By 1831, 50,000 students filled 1,100 schools. At first, only adults were taught, but at about this time, adult attendance fell off and the children had their chance at *palapala* (writing). Lahainaluna School, the first high school west of the Rockies, was established in 1831 on Maui by the American Board of Commissioners for Foreign Missions (it is now the public high school for West Maui). Ten years later, the private Punahou School was opened in Honolulu for the children of missionaries and other foreigners. Such was the reputation of these schools that as the Gold Rush brought families to California, those who struck it rich sent their children to Hawaii to be educated.

A major thorn in the missionaries' side was the "drunken, roistering, iniquitous" behavior of the crews of the whaling ships. The first whalers had arrived in Hawaiian waters in 1819, the year before the arrival of the missionaries. Fishing grounds for the sperm whale had been discovered off Japan, and Hawaii was a convenient mid-Pacific station for refitting the whaleships and taking on stores. The number of ships increased rapidly. In 1822, more than 60 whaleships stopped in Hawaiian ports, and by 1830, an average of 150 a year, mostly American, were dropping anchor. In the 1840s and 1850s, they averaged several hundred — almost 600 in the peak year of 1846. Naturally, the crews of the ships raised hell in every port. They favored Honolulu in the beginning, but after the death in 1840 of Maui's native governor, Hoapili, a Christian convert who was an ally of the missionaries in banning brothels and grog shops, they found that Lahaina had all they needed.

The whaling crews and captains were in some ways the benefactors of the missions. They brought many of the missionaries to the islands and then brought mail from home as well as the famous "missionary barrels" of clothes and hand-me-downs. They brought supplies for schools, materials for housing, and even such luxuries as pianos. But mostly the whalers brought torment and anguish to the missionaries. For all their preaching, debauchery and prostitution still flourished, endangering not only the souls of the Hawaiians but their bodies, too. The first *haoles* aboard Captain Cook's ships had brought venereal disease to the islands; now it reached epidemic proportions. Other diseases entered the native bloodstream at Lahaina and Honolulu, and with the Hawaiians' limited resistance to infection, their population was shrinking.

The beginning of the end of whaling was signaled in 1859 by the discovery in Pennsylvania of the oil that would henceforth replace whale oil. Some whaling ships were lost in the Civil War, but the final blow was a major catastrophe in 1871, when a particularly good whaling season tempted the fleet to remain too long in the Arctic, which had supplanted the more southerly hunting grounds. The encroaching winter caused 33 ships to be abandoned and crushed in the ice floes; only 14 survived. In succeeding years, the few whaling ships still calling at Hawaiian ports were retired one by one.

KAMEHAMEHA III AND CONSTITUTIONAL GOVERNMENT

The king during the early half of the whaling era was Kauikeaouli, who had succeeded his brother in 1825, with Queen Kaahumanu again as regent. When Kaahumanu died in 1832, another high chief, Kinau (Kauikeaouli's half-sister), was named *kuhina nui,* but the king sensed her lack of power and assumed his duties and his title as Kamehameha III the following year.

At 20, the young king had yet to show any sign that he would make an impressive ruler. All the cultural confusion accompanying the transition of Hawaiian society from its old Polynesian ways to its new Western ways was apparent in the disarray of his private life. He drank to excess and was known as an inveterate womanizer. He was also known to have a strong attachment to his younger sister, Princess Nahienaena, whom he wanted to marry. In the old days, their marriage would have been expected of them and would have produced a child of the very highest — sacred — rank. In the new order, their relationship was merely incest.

Neither Kauikeaouli nor Nahienaena withstood the thwarting of their desires and the mental strain of the cultural clash very well, and Kauikeaouli attempted suicide in 1834. Nahienaena, vacillating between a dissipated life and repeated returns to the missionaries' Christian fold, married a Big Island chief at their urging, then bore a child who many suspected was her brother's, not her husband's. The child lived only a few hours, and Nahienaena, ill and exhausted, lived only a few months longer, dying at the age of 20 in December 1836.

His sister's tragic death had a sobering effect on Kamehameha III. In 1838, he and his chiefs began to take instruction in "political economy" from the American missionary William Richards. A series of political innovations based on the Western model followed. In 1839, the king issued a declaration of rights and an edict of religious tolerance. In 1840, he gave his people a voice in the government by signing Hawaii's first written constitution, which provided for a bicameral legislature (with an upper house of hereditary chiefs and appointed nobles and a lower house of elected representatives) and a supreme court. In 1852, a revised constitution granted almost universal male suffrage.

Probably his most far-reaching move was the land reform of 1848, known as the Great Mahele (division). Previously, Hawaii's kings had owned the land, which was administered by their chiefs, who held it in fief, and worked by the commoners. The Great Mahele introduced the Western principle of private ownership of land, dividing it among the king (crown lands), the government (public lands), the chiefs, and the commoners. This division was welcomed as a great boon, especially to the common people, who were allowed a share of the land for the first time in their history. Shortly afterward, however, foreigners were also given the right to buy land, and they proved to be more experienced property owners than the natives. Many Hawaiian commoners lost their land by neglecting to register their titles or pay taxes; others realized that they could sell it, and did — mainly to the foreigners. In the end, the native Hawaiian land holdings were insignificant compared to those of the *haoles,* and the way was paved for the great plantations that were to come.

The question of national sovereignty was another important issue during Kamehameha III's reign. In 1842, he dispatched a diplomatic mission (including his adviser William Richards) to the United States, Great Britain, and France, attempting to extract from them recognition of Hawaii's independence. President John Tyler, in an extension of the Monroe Doctrine to the Pacific, did recognize the islands as an independent kingdom, and Britain and France eventually did so, too, but not before Lord George Paulit, commanding the British frigate *Carysfort,* forced the king to cede the islands to Great

Britain in February 1843. Paulit presumably acted to protect British interests, but without the approval of the British government. Nevertheless, it was 5 months before Admiral Sir Richard Thomas of the British navy arrived to repudiate his action.

Kamehameha III is credited with having spoken what is now the motto of the State of Hawaii — *Ua mau ke ea o ka aina i ka pono* ("The life of the land is perpetuated in righteousness") — in Honolulu's Kawaiahao Church at a thanksgiving service for the restoration of the island's independence after this incident.

The 29-year reign of Kamehameha III proved to be the longest of the Hawaiian monarchs. When he died in December 1854, at the age of 41, his nephew saluted him as a "great national benefactor" who had given Hawaiians a "constitution and fixed laws . . . title to their lands . . . a voice in his councils and in the making of laws by which they are governed." Because he died without an heir, that same nephew, Prince Alexander Liholiho, succeeded him.

THE LAST OF THE KAMEHAMEHAS

Kamehameha IV was a handsome, elegant young man who had had all the advantages of an excellent education and a world tour. His queen was the cultured and educated Emma Rooke, the granddaughter of the first Kamehameha's English adviser, John Young. Their reign was aristocratic and ceremonial, but pursued by calamity. In 1859, the king shot and severely wounded his friend and secretary, Henry Neilson, in a jealous rage over unfounded reports of Neilson's misconduct with the queen. Kamehameha suffered agonizing remorse as Neilson slowly died, and his cabinet had difficulty restraining him from abdicating. Only 3 years later, his son, 4-year-old Prince Albert, died of a fever several days after his father had held him in a cold shower to stop a childish tantrum. The following year, the 29-year-old king himself died of an asthmatic attack or, it was said, of a broken heart.

The overriding concern of Kamehameha IV's reign was the decimation of the Hawaiian population by imported diseases: venereal disease, cholera, and smallpox, in particular, and the new scourge of leprosy from an unknown source. At the time that Captain Cook visited the islands, Hawaii is thought to have had from 250,000 to 300,000 inhabitants; by Kamehameha IV's time, the number of native Hawaiians had dwindled to less than 100,000. Referring to the "wasting hand" that was destroying the people, the king pleaded with the legislature for funds for a public hospital; when the money was not forthcoming, he and Queen Emma personally raised it. By 1860, Queen's Hospital, Hawaii's first hospital for Hawaiians, was a reality.

Kamehameha IV was decidedly pro-British rather than pro-American, even to the point of naming his son after the consort of Queen Victoria, who was the child's godmother. Several reasons have been given for his stance, including a predilection for the life of the British and French courts, which he had visited as a teenager and where he had been treated as royalty, versus bitterness over an incident in Washington, DC, where he had been mistaken for a black and asked to leave a train. His stringent missionary upbringing had constrained him as a child, and as an adult he feared that the missionary influence on the Hawaiian government would lead to the loss of independence. He married his wife, an Anglican, in an elaborate Anglican ceremony, and later he brought the Church of England to Hawaii to upstage the missionaries' Congregationalism.

Kamehameha V was Lot Kamehameha, the older brother of Alexander Liholiho. He had accompanied his brother on their world tour as youths and shared his pro-British attitude; he exceeded his brother in anti-republicanism, and he was more of a nativist, believing that a strong monarchy was the only institution that could save Hawaii from the *haoles.*

His first act as king was to refuse to take the oath to uphold Hawaii's constitution of 1852 — the first of several royal revolts, actually protests against the loss of royal prerogatives, that would occur in the next 30 years. Instead, after abrogating the constitution, he enacted a new, less liberal, British-influenced document that gave more power to the crown than the previous one, which had reflected America's influence. His constitution of 1864 remained in effect for 23 years, longer than any other Hawaiian constitution.

Kamehameha V was a stubborn, forceful ruler for 9 pivotal years while whaling came to a halt and the sugar industry gradually became the islands' major source of revenue. When he died in 1872, he was a childless bachelor, the last of the Kamehameha line to rule. Because he had named no successor, the next ruler was elected by the legislature from the ranks of the *alii.* The very popular "Prince Bill," described by Mark Twain as "affable, gentlemanly, open, frank . . . intelligent, shrewd, sensible . . . a man of first-rate abilities," became King William Lunalilo and ruled for 13 months before he died in 1874 of tuberculosis complicated by alcoholism. He, too, had been a bachelor.

KING SUGAR

Sugarcane, brought to the islands by the Polynesians, had been grown in quantity in Hawaii from about the 1830s, but it was not until the Civil War, which cut the rest of the United States off from its Confederate sugar supply, that a demand for Hawaiian sugar was created in the American market. After the war, the price of sugar fell and Hawaii was threatened with the loss of this new market unless it could negotiate a favorable trade treaty, allowing its sugar to enter American ports without paying duty. In return, specified American goods entering Hawaiian ports would enjoy the same privilege. Reciprocity became a prime issue, but one fraught with political implications. Hawaii's *haole*-dominated (and largely American) sugar interests favored such a treaty, but Hawaiian natives, king and commoners alike, while admitting its economic necessity, were wary: It could either avert the dread possibility of annexation or hasten it.

Both Kamehameha IV and Kamehameha V tried to work out an acceptable agreement, but it wasn't until 1876, in the reign of David Kalakaua, who followed Lunalilo as king, that the reciprocity treaty was approved and passed. It came up for renewal in 1884 but was not ratified until 1887, when an amendment — granting US warships exclusive right of entrance to Pearl Harbor as a refueling and repair base — was the price of its extension.

Reciprocity caused such a boom in the sugar business that both the planters and the government were forced to come to terms with the islands' labor shortage: The native Hawaiian population had not been and would never be equal to the task of working the increasing number of plantations. As early as 1852, the first Chinese contract laborers had made their appearance in Hawaii, and thousands more followed them. A single shipload of Japanese had arrived in 1868. But after 1876, the need for immigrant labor became pressing. Arrangements were made to import Portuguese workers from the Azores and Madeira islands, with the first contingent of 180 arriving in 1878. Seven years later, nearly a thousand Japanese contract workers arrived, the spearhead of tens of thousands of their countrymen to come in the next quarter of a century.

Hawaii's social fabric was as changed by the influx of immigrant labor as it had been by the first wave of foreigners. Already, more and more control of the kingdom was passing into the hands of *haole* merchants and planters, among them the sons of missionaries, who had gone into commerce and would build themselves empires. Now, as the contracts of the plantation workers expired, most of them remained in their new home. Some married into Hawaiian families, thus acquiring their own tracts of land; some settled in the towns and went into their own businesses. The native population continued to decrease, so it was not difficult to make room for the newcomers.

THE END OF THE MONARCHY

In 1874, the Hawaiian legislature had elected the high chief David Kalakaua to succeed Lunalilo. Kalakaua was not pro-American, but he was not against reciprocity, either: Before the year was out, he paid a visit to Washington to negotiate the terms of the treaty. Island businessmen were reassured by the trip, and when reciprocity became a fact in 1876, they were pleased.

Kalakaua was an educated and sociable gentleman, an accomplished poet and musician, and a scholar. He was conscious of the loss of Hawaii's traditional culture and tried to reclaim and revitalize it. He had the "Kumulipo," the Hawaiian creation chant, transcribed for the first time, and he collected the Hawaiian legends and myths into a book that is still a classic of the literature. Public performances of the hula, which had been suppressed by the missionaries, were reinstated during his reign. He wrote many new hula chants himself and is credited with having rescued at least 300 ancient ones from the brink of extinction. With the bandmaster of the *Royal Hawaiian Band* (an innovation of Kamehameha V), he co-wrote Hawaii's national anthem, "Hawaii Ponoi." He collected the feathered cloaks of former chiefs and helped to promote the nearly lost art of featherwork by encouraging the production of new ones. He formed a secret society, the Hale Naua, to revive the ancient sciences. As far as the *haole* community was concerned, all of this activity was nativism and tolerable. But his attempts to rally Hawaiians to vote as a bloc and to fill appointive positions with men of Hawaiian blood were, in their eyes, racism.

Kalakaua's extravagance also got him into trouble. He lived on a grand scale, signing his name "Kalakaua Rex." At great expense, he rebuilt the royal residence, Iolani, into the properly royal Iolani Palace, and while it was under construction, he became the first reigning monarch of any nation to travel around the world, calling on the royalty of Europe and Asia, the pope, and the American president. When he returned, he invited his subjects to Hawaii's first — and last — coronation, a 2-week celebration at which the feathered cloak of Kamehameha I was placed on his shoulders and a jeweled crown, fashioned for him in England, was placed on his head, matched by another for his queen, Kapiolani. Among some of his subjects, such displays helped to earn him a reputation as "the Merrie Monarch," but they did not endear him to the white men whose sugar lands were paying most of the kingdom's taxes.

Ironically, Kalakaua came to grief because of his relationship with two white men. One was his American adviser, Walter Murray Gibson, whose sentiments lay more with native Hawaiians than with foreigners, and who was prone to encourage the king's grandiose schemes, including his dream of a federation of Pacific islands with himself as its head. The other was Claus Spreckels, a powerful California sugar magnate, who gained a foothold in the islands by lending the king money in return for favorable water rights to newly acquired sugar lands, and who ended up with a stranglehold on the king's treasury.

By January 1887, *haole* planters and businessmen had had enough. Led by Lorrin Thurston, a grandson of one of the first missionaries, they formed a secret reform organization, the Hawaiian League, with a military wing in the form of a volunteer militia. By July 1887, using intimidation rather than actual firepower, they had forced the king to dismiss his cabinet and sign a new constitution — the so-called Bayonet Constitution — which severely curtailed his powers and denied the right to vote to most Hawaiians by basing the franchise on ownership of property.

Kalakaua lived out his last years as a figurehead. One of the first accomplishments of the new *haole*-dominated cabinet was the renegotiation of the reciprocity treaty, which had been renewed yearly since 1883, but now was extended by Congress only on the condition that the US be granted exclusive use of Pearl Harbor. Kalakaua, who had always been against the concession, was forced to ratify it nevertheless. An attempted counterrevolution in 1889, led by a part-Hawaiian, Robert Wilcox, failed to overthrow the *haoles* and their Bayonet Constitution (it is not known whether the king played any part in the insurrection), and in 1890, an ailing Kalakaua left for San Francisco to nurse his health. He died there in January 1891, shortly before the US government replaced tariffs on foreign sugar with a bounty for domestic producers, thereby negating the advantages of reciprocity. The Hawaiian sugar industry faced collapse unless something could be done, and the Americans in Hawaii considered annexation the best solution.

Kalakaua's sister, Liliuokalani, was Hawaii's first reigning queen and its last monarch. She was as musically talented as her brother and added many songs to the Hawaiian repertoire, including the beautiful and famous farewell song "Aloha-Oe." She was also as strong-willed as he and as much a believer in Hawaii for the Hawaiians. From the start, she resolved to restore power to the monarchy, but her efforts brought about its downfall a mere 2 years after her accession to the throne.

On January 14, 1893, the queen dissolved the legislature and told her cabinet of her intention to proclaim a new constitution that would remove the checks to her power according to the Bayonet Constitution and that would allow only true Hawaiians to vote, whether property owners or not. Sheer political chaos ensued. A secret Annexation Club, which had been formed the year before with much the same *haole* membership as the old Hawaiian League, hastily set up a Committee of Safety to study the formation of a provisional government to replace the monarchy. The US Minister to Hawaii, John L. Stevens, and Captain G. C. Wiltse, the commander of the troops aboard the visiting USS *Boston,* were both approached by the committee to enlist their support and aid in "protecting American lives and property," should that become necessary. On January 16, the troops were posted at strategic locations around Honolulu, and on January 17, the provisional government declared itself in power, with Sanford B. Dole, another descendant of missionaries, as president. In order to avoid bloodshed, Queen Liliuokalani surrendered her royal authority, but under protest, certain that the US government would repudiate the actions of its representatives and reinstate her.

In fact, upon hearing of the events in Hawaii, President Grover Cleveland did send an investigator, who reported back that "a great wrong has been done to the Hawaiians." Cleveland sought congressional action but was ignored, just as a request to restore the queen was ignored by the provisional government. Instead, it proclaimed a republican constitution on July 4, 1894, and Sanford Dole became the President of the new Republic of Hawaii.

Later that year, followers of the deposed queen (led again by Robert Wilcox) staged one last abortive attempt to return her to the throne. Liliuokalani was linked to the plot and was put under house arrest in Iolani Palace on January 16, 1895. She was charged with treason, tried, and found guilty, but her sentence — 5 years at hard labor plus a $5,000 fine — was not enforced. She was paroled and, in late 1896, regained her complete freedom, which she used to go to Washington to plead the cause of the monarchy. By now, however, the US government was in an expansionist frame of mind, and the issue of Hawaii's annexation was caught up in the larger question of the country's Manifest Destiny.

Liliuokalani retired to her home, Washington Place (now the governor's mansion), to write music and poetry; she put aside her bitterness and led her people as loyal residents of the Republic and then the Territory of Hawaii until her death in 1917. Among her writings, her memoir, *Hawaii's Story by Hawaii's Queen,* was an exceptional farewell to the independent island kingdom.

FROM ANNEXATION TO STATEHOOD

As president of the republic, Sanford Dole negotiated for the annexation of the islands by the US, which became a fact by joint resolution of Congress in July 1898, during the administration of President William McKinley. Hawaii's flag flew over Iolani Palace for the last time on August 12, 1898, and its lowering, to the tune of "Hawaii Ponoi," played for the last time as the national anthem, was a solemn and dramatic occasion. Then the American flag was raised and the *Royal Hawaiian Band* struck up "The Star-Spangled Banner."

The islands officially became a US territory in 1900, when the passage of the Organic Act extended the US Constitution across the Pacific and automatically made American citizens of those who had been citizens of the Hawaiian republic. Sanford Dole was appointed governor of the territory, while the firebrand and revolutionary Robert Wilcox was elected its first delegate to Congress. Hawaii's next delegate to Congress was its greatest modern *alii,* Prince Jonah Kuhio Kalanianaole, a nephew of Queen Liliuokalani, who had also taken part in the attempted coup of 1895 and been imprisoned for it.

Prince Kuhio was elected to Congress for the first of ten times in 1902, and though he was the candidate of the Republican party — the party of *haole* business interests, which dominated Hawaiian elections until World War II — he was a tireless fighter for the rights of the Hawaiian people. He introduced the first statehood bill to Congress in 1919 (it was submitted biennially for the next 40 years before meeting with success), and worked to restore dispossessed Hawaiians to their land by sponsoring the Hawaiian Homes Commission Act of 1920, which set aside 200,000 acres of government land to be leased as small plots by Hawaiians of more than half native blood. He founded the Hawaiian Civic Club to encourage his people to take an active role in public affairs and to preserve and promote Hawaiian culture. The "citizen prince" died in 1922, but because of his devotion to the cause of native Hawaiians, his birthday, March 26, was made a territorial, then a state, holiday. Only one other Hawaiian, Kamehameha I, is so honored.

The period between annexation and World War II saw the continued growth of the sugar industry and the emergence of the pineapple industry as a second income producer. (In 1922, James D. Dole — a distant cousin of Sanford Dole — bought almost the entire island of Lanai, on which to raise pineapples.) The same period also saw five major sugar companies — Castle & Cooke, Alexander & Baldwin, C. Brewer and Company, Theo H. Davies and Company, and American Factors — become Hawaii's Big Five, as they grew to control 95% of the sugar crop by the early 1930s and simultaneously succeeded in monopolizing other sectors of the economy by expanding into refining, transportation and shipping, retail and wholesale merchandising, banking, insurance, and utilities. (Another company, Dillingham Corporation, not founded on sugar, made the Big Five the Big Six.)

Not surprisingly, the boards of these companies were sprinkled with men descended from the early missionaries and from businessmen who had been active in the annexation movement of the 19th century, and their power flowed into the politics of the 20th century. The *haole* plantation elite voted Republican, and they had enough money for campaign contributions to ensure that 80% of the candidates voted into the territorial legislature before World War II were also Republicans, and beholden to them.

The islands' population became increasingly multiracial as the influx of immigrants to work the vast plantations continued. Before annexation became official, the plantation owners, knowing they would be subject to US immigration laws, rushed to bring in as much labor as possible. Between 1896 and 1900, the Japanese population of the islands rose from 25,000 to 60,000, and 40,000 more arrived before an agreement with Japan in 1907 stopped the flow of workers, though women and children continued to come until Congress passed the Japanese Exclusion Act in 1924. By then, the Japanese had reached a peak of 42% of the population.

Still, more workers were needed. Labor recruited in Puerto Rico began to arrive in 1900, and from Korea in 1903, but the next massive influx came from the Philippines, which had been an American dependency since the Spanish-American War. Between 1906 and World War II, more than 100,000 Filipinos were brought to Hawaii. They eventually outnumbered the Japanese in Hawaii's fields and mills, though they never outnumbered them in the larger Hawaiian melting pot. Others who migrated to Hawaii included Samoans and residents from other Pacific islands.

Another presence, the US military, was making itself felt. In 1908, Congress approved a bill for the establishment of a giant naval base at Pearl Harbor, to be the home of America's Pacific Fleet. In the mid-1930s, Hickam Field, adjacent to Pearl Harbor, became the largest American military airfield, and Schofield Barracks, in central Oahu, became the largest American army post. If the existence of these installations raised hopes that Hawaii would soon gain statehood (a movement that gathered momentum in the islands after 1934, when Congress passed a law detrimental to Hawaiian sugar interests), the existence of Hawaii's large Japanese population served to dampen them. The United States was on the brink of war with Japan, and as far as Congress was concerned, the Japanese in Hawaii were the enemy in the backyard, even though the majority of them were second- and third-generation Japanese Americans and already US citizens.

It took the attack on Pearl Harbor at 7:55 AM on December 7, 1941, to prove the loyalty of Hawaii's Japanese population. In the 2-hour surprise attack, the United States suffered 3,435 casualties, the loss of 188 planes, and the loss of or damage to 18 ships. Pearl Harbor was the greatest military and naval disaster in US history and the direct cause of America's entry into World War II.

Martial law was immediately declared against the threat of a possible Japanese invasion of Hawaii, an invasion that might be abetted by local Japanese. It never came, but a distrust of Japanese Americans continued, preventing them from enlisting in the armed services until mid-1942, when the 1,400-strong 100th Infantry Battalion was formed, and early 1943, when the call went out for 1,500 Japanese volunteers to become the 442nd Regimental Combat Team. More than 9,000 men answered the call; 3,000 were chosen. The 442nd absorbed the 100th, fought in Italy and France, and emerged from the war as the most highly decorated unit of the armed forces: The "Go for Broke" Japanese won seven presidential unit citations and nearly 6,000 individual awards.

The Japanese were not the only Hawaiians who fought in World War II.

The islands' other ethnic groups — pure and part-Hawaiians, Chinese, Filipinos, Koreans, Portuguese — as well as the dominant *haoles,* largely of American and British descent, had all participated, and Hawaiian society was significantly changed by their experience. As long as Hawaii was a territory rather than a state, its residents were not first class US citizens, and their ancestry made some of them decidedly more second class than others. Yet they had all fought for the same principles of equality and democracy.

Even before the war, plantation workers had begun to question the paternalistic plantation system, and the militant International Longshoremen's and Warehousemen's Union (ILWU) had begun to organize the waterfront. After martial law was lifted, the labor movement developed rapidly. In 1946, the ILWU called a major strike against the sugar industry: 21,000 workers walked off the job for 79 days, winning, in the end, a wage increase and an end to the perquisite system by which they had received some of their pay in the form of company housing and vouchers to be used at the company store. The value of the perquisites would now be received in cash, granting greater freedom of decision to the formerly passive work force. In 1949, a 178-day strike of 2,000 longshoremen crippled the islands' economy and demonstrated once again the strength of organized workers.

Concomitant to the rise of labor was the rise of the Democratic party. Until the war, the party in power was the party of property, of planters and businessmen, of the Big Five. After so many years of staunch *haole* Republican rule, it was only natural that as more and more Orientals, particularly Japanese, took their university degrees under the GI Bill and became active in politics, they would join the ranks of the opposition, the Democrats. It was also only natural that the newly politicized and mainly Oriental working class should vote for them. In 1954, the Democratic party reversed a precedent of 50 years and swept both houses of the territorial legislature. Not incidentally, half of the legislative seats went to Japanese Americans.

By 1954, very little stood between Hawaii and statehood. The extreme tactics used by the ILWU, seen in the light of the Cold War of the early 1950s, had led to accusations that the Communists ran the territory, and these charges momentarily retarded progress. Then, too, Hawaii was still seen by some as too far away and too different to be a part of the Union, but when Alaska became the 49th state in January 1959, these objections were put to rest.

On January 7, 1959, the last of a long line of Hawaii statehood bills was announced. Appropriately numbered S-50, it went before the Senate on March 11 and passed overwhelmingly with no debate. The House passed it on March 12, and at 10:04 AM Hawaiian Standard Time, the church bells of Honolulu rang out; newspapers, already typeset, shouted STATEHOOD! in big, red headlines; and the Hawaiian population quit work for the day to dance and sing in the streets. An American flag with 50 stars flew over Hawaii, and that it was greeted with greater and more sincere enthusiasm than the one raised over Iolani Palace in 1898 was proved in June, when the people of Hawaii ratified the decision of Congress by a ratio of 17 to 1. Only the island of Niihau rejected statehood.

In the same special election, the islanders celebrated their diversity by giving one Senate seat to Democrat Oren Long, a native Kansan and a former territorial governor, and the other to Republican Hiram Fong, a Harvard Law School graduate and the son of a Chinese plantation laborer. The state's seat in the House of Representatives went to Democrat Daniel Inouye, a territorial legislator of Japanese ancestry who had lost an arm fighting with the 442nd Regimental Combat Team in Italy. Hawaii's first elected governor was the appointed incumbent, Republican William Quinn, a former New Yorker; its first elected lieutenant governor was Republican James Kealoha, a territorial senator of Hawaiian-Chinese ancestry. It remained only for President Dwight D. Eisenhower to proclaim Hawaii the 50th state on August 21, 1959.

THE ALOHA STATE

Statehood brought boom times. It coincided with the advent of regular jet service between the mainland and the islands, and gave tourism such a big boost that by the 1970s it became necessary to pose the question of how far development should go. It's a question that remains unanswered as the number of tourists increases each year (over 6.5 million visitors annually as of 1990) and hotel and condominium development explodes. Tourism is Hawaii's principal industry (filling state coffers with approximately $10 billion a year), followed by defense and, finally, agriculture (mostly sugar, macadamia nuts, papaya, and cut flowers — pineapples are almost a fruit of the past), a distant third. Statehood also brought a new influx of immigrants, this time a second migration of mainland *haoles.* As a result, Caucasians now rank as Hawaii's largest group (close to 25% of the population), followed by Japanese (27%), and Filipinos (more than 10%). As Hawaii's immigration increases and intermarriage continues, "pure-blooded" Hawaiians are becoming more and more rare. Today they represent less than one-quarter of one percent of Hawaii's total population.

And although approximately 30% of Hawaii's 1.2 million people have some Hawaiian blood, cultural assimilation continues to dilute the islands' "Hawaiianness." Even the resurgence of interest in Hawaiian language, music, traditions, and beliefs may not be enough to preserve the 50th state's distinctive Polynesian past. With the lowest unemployment rate of any state, Hawaii is experiencing labor shortages that will probably encourage additional migration from the mainland and Pacific Rim nations, further altering Hawaii's racial and ethnic mix.

As a result of the billions of dollars being pumped into the state by foreign investors — particularly the Japanese — during the 1980s, Hawaii will continue to be a cultural and economic hybrid. For example, a great many of Hawaii's major hotels are now owned by Japanese, as are tens of thousands of acres zoned for resort, residential, and commercial development. In the opening years of this decade, locals are questioning whether Hawaii is economically the westernmost extension of the US or the easternmost outpost of Japan. The impact of foreign investment has already emerged as one of the state's major issues, particularly as crucial decisions have to be made as to the best use of Hawaii's critical resources, such as water.

Other environmental concerns have carried over from the 1980s into this decade. Environmental activists have focused their efforts on state government plans to develop geothermal energy on the Big Island's volcanically active lands, as an alternative to the high cost and pollution potential of imported oil. But some have expressed concern over the environmental impact of geothermal energy. Opponents feel it is economically unfeasible (they believe solar energy provides a more reliable and less costly alternative), as well as an affront to native Hawaiians' belief in the sacred fires of the goddess Pele.

Environmentalists and Pele believers have joined forces to stop further drilling. Protesters have been arrested at drilling sites just outside the boundaries of Hawaii Volcanoes National Park, and lawsuits dealing with environmental impact and religious beliefs are likely to haunt geothermal energy production for years to come.

At the same time, environmental and cultural concerns have halted runaway tourism development (to say nothing of recent economic times, which have sorely slowed the influx of tourist dollars). Concern for the preservation of ancient burial grounds has halted at least two hotel resort developments, while pollution problems — water, land, and noise — have spawned bans and referendums relating to the future operation of such tourism staples as Zodiac tour boats and flightseeing helicopters. The continued construction of vast golf course complexes has also come under close scrutiny. The resolution of these questions are among the thorny decisions that will determine the character of the Aloha State in the 21st century.

Music and Dance

She came dancing upon the waves
Her feet lightly tripping over the froth,
Her flesh glistening with the wild blowing sea spray.
She came with beauty shining in her eyes,
Wreathed in golden blossoms, her loins girdled with mountain vines.
And in her hair were ferns of the valley, fragile and fragrant.
She was Laka, child of music, goddess of the dance.
— Samuel Crowningburg Amalu

The origin of the hula is lost in Hawaiian legend. One story says that two gods named Laka — one male, one female — arrived from beyond the Great Western Sea in a canoe and danced for the people of Hawaii. After a time the male disappeared, but the female remained. The Hawaiians worshiped her, and she taught them the hula. It is said that the ruins of the *heiau* (temple) and dancing pavilion of Laka can be seen at Haena on the Na Pali Coast of Kauai.

For whatever reasons now obscured by time, the hula was originally danced only by men and used only in religious rituals. Later, it evolved into a method of teaching, a form of entertainment, and the foundation for the art of *lua,* a style of hand-to-hand self-defense known only to Hawaiians. (*Lua* involved paralyzing nerves, breaking bones, leaping, quick thrusts with the spear, and swinging clubs, all of which was practiced with the *hula kui,* sham battle dance. Today's *hula kui* still incorporates steps of the war dance that were part of *lua.*) It is thought that as time went on and the island civilization became more complex, wars and governing and tax-collecting duties kept the men too busy to spare the years for the hula's rigid training. Women were then allowed to assume some of the chanting and dancing ritual.

Candidates for the supreme honor of hula training were required to enter the *halau* (house of hula instruction) to be supervised by a *kumu hula* (hula teacher), rather like a novice entering a convent. The selection of dancers was made at an early age on the basis of physical beauty, health, grace, agility, quickness of wit, and liveliness of imagination. Every aspect of the dancers' training was strictly regulated by *kapus* (taboos), and throughout their novitiate, generally from ages 3 to 16, they were seldom allowed beyond the school enclosure and no villager could speak with them. Only after the *uniki* (graduation) were they permitted to mingle with outsiders.

People with an oral tradition, such as the Hawaiians, often coupled chanted stories with dances. The hula movements and hand gestures reinforced for the audience the meaning and feeling of the story.

For example, graceful hand motions above the head of the dancer depict the sun, moon, stars, or creation. An abrupt arm thrust at shoulder level tells of a thrown spear or club; raised arms, bent at the elbow and with closed fists, show strength or bravery; a high, forceful kick may indicate battle. A knee bounce may mean billowing waves, a rough canoe ride, or riding a horse, or when combined with a hip-swiveling motion, it can be an allusion to sex. Foot movements can show ritual, coquetry, a journey, or boldness.

The stories narrated in the chants, the *meles,* were for commoners or for chiefs; they told of the origin of the islanders, the adventures of great island rulers, and about the gods and their exploits. There were name songs composed at the birth of chiefs as well as prayer chants, nature chants, prophecies, war chants, love songs, funeral chants, and lullabies. In fact, from its start as a strictly religious expression, the hula gradually expanded into the opera of old Hawaii, with dancers and singers combining to tell its history and folk tales.

The chants were mostly accompanied by rhythm instruments, although "voice extenders," which had a short range of tones, were also used. The *ipu* was a drum made from a large gourd or two gourds fastened together; one played it by stamping it on a mat and then slapping it with the fingers of the right hand. The *pahu* is the largest of the Hawaiian drums; it's about 26 inches tall when used normally to accompany the hula and can be as tall as 46 inches when set on a carved base for use in temples. Made of a hollowed coconut or breadfruit tree log covered with a sharkskin membrane, it is played with one or both hands, and different parts of the drumhead are struck to produce varying depths of sound. The *punui,* half a coconut shell covered with a fish membrane, is struck with a flexible stick. Frequently played in counterpoint to the *ipu* for the hula, the *punui* is depicted in early sketches tied to the player's knee or thigh.

Uliuli are gourds or coconuts that have been filled with shells or pebbles and decorated along the handles with feathers, tapa, or woven disks. Hit against the dancer's hips or hand, *uliuli* produce a continuous rhythm and are now frequently used in *hapa haole* (half-foreign, meaning not traditional Hawaiian) songs.

Puili is a length of bamboo split into narrow strips at one end. The hula dancers hold two *puili* and hit them against their shoulders, hips, or each other, making a rattling, swishing sound.

Kaekeeke, the bamboo organ, is varying lengths of bamboo stamped on the ground to produce different tonal qualities.

Kupee niho ilio was the dog's-tooth rattle male dancers wore on their ankles in the old days. With the renaissance of traditional dances, men today often wear rattles made of seashells.

Ohe hano ihu, the nose flute, is a length of bamboo with a nosehole and several fingering holes on the upper side. Played by expelling breath from the right nostril, it functions as a "voice extension" to the chant.

The costume of the hula dancer was much the same for both sexes and hardly elaborate. Male dancers wore a simple, short wrap of tapa about their loins, large boar's-tusk bracelets on their arms, and rattles of dog's teeth around their ankles. Sketches by the traveler and novelist Jacques Arago in 1819 show female dancers in opulent wrapped skirts of colorful tapa and little else except, perhaps, a tattoo and a necklace. Garlands made of the plants and flowers sacred to Laka, the scarlet or white ohia lehua, maile, halapepe, and many fragrant ferns, were often worn around the head, wrists, and ankles.

This was the hula that so horrified the Protestant missionaries who arrived in Hawaii in 1820 and immediately began an intense campaign to suppress the ancient art form. First, they put the naked dancers into clothes — bulky middy blouses and long, voluminous skirts. Next, they introduced the Hawaiians to religious hymns and started classes to teach them the Western musical scale. It must have been a difficult task for the Hawaiians, who, after all, had their own quite different musical system, but curiosity and love of music bent them to the task, and they mastered scales fairly quickly. To the hymns they gave full and enthusiastic voice.

The first hymnal in Hawaiian, *Na Himeni Hawaii: He Me Ori Ia Iehova, Ke Akua Mau* (Hawaiian Hymns and Songs to Jehovah the Eternal God), was printed on the Honolulu mission press in 1823. It had words but no music; tunes were either memorized or interchangeable. The hymnal was an instant best seller; 52,000 were printed and distributed to several hundred schools by 1853. Under the direction of the Reverends Hiram Bingham in Honolulu and Lorenzo Lyons in Waimea on the Big Island, whole congregations were soon singing day and night.

In the years that followed the missionary invasion, the Hawaiian islands saw the arrival of many other groups, each one with its own musical instruments. The guitar made its way to Hawaii on the New England whaling ships during the early 19th century. The slack key guitar, a style of playing devised by the Hawaiians, refers to the tuning of the instrument. The six strings are loosened (or slacked) to the lower registers and chord tuning is determined by the player's preference. The chant tradition is reflected in slack key play, with bass notes corresponding to *ipu* beats. Variations, including slapping strings, sliding into the next note, and beating the guitar body, all imitate *ipu* beats.

Hawaii is the birthplace of the steel guitar, but exactly who invented it, and when, are open to debate. The nod is generally given to Joseph Kekuku, who as a schoolboy experimented with sliding a railroad bolt across the strings of his guitar. He later tried a penknife and a metal comb to produce the sweet sound; finally he designed and made a special steel bar. He then switched from gut to wire strings and raised the strings so the steel bar did not touch the neck frets. Later modifications in the bar, metal finger and thumb picks, and electric amplification produced the steel guitar as we know it today.

Hawaiians adapted the *ukulele* from the Portuguese *braguinha,* introduced to Hawaii in 1878 by immigrants who brought their favorite music from the island of Madeira, where it is still played today. During its early days in Honolulu, it was called the *pila liilii,* which means "little fiddle." Sometime in the late 19th century, the name became ukulele, which, freely translated, means "jumping flea." Queen Liliuokalani preferred a more romanticized translation: *uku* (gift) *lele* (that came). The little instrument was easy to tune and to play, with just four strings, and it was easier to carry and hold than the larger guitar. It was tremendously popular.

One of the very greatest influences on Hawaiian music appeared in the person of Henry Berger, who was brought to the islands from Germany in

1872 by King Kamehameha V to set up a Hawaiian brass band similar to those in Germany. A great admirer of 19th-century Hawaiian music, "unique and of a type not known elsewhere in the world," Berger helped the Hawaiians make the transition to Western scales and instruments, organized the *Royal Hawaiian Band and Orchestra,* and wrote and arranged many popular songs. He later collaborated with King David Kalakaua and his sister, Queen Liliuokalani, on much memorable music, including such songs as "Sweet Lei Lehua," "Koni Au I Ka Wai," "Kiss Me My Darling," "Hilo March," and — that most famous Hawaiian melody — "'Aloha-Oe."

David Kalakaua, who reigned from 1874 to 1891, is fondly remembered for his interest in reviving traditional Hawaiian music and dance. He believed that "the hula is the language of the heart and, therefore, the heartbeat of the Hawaiian people." Under his patronage, more than 300 ancient hulas were saved from extinction, and he created a number of hula chants. Many new dances and songs were written to honor the king, whose spontaneous good spirits earned him the sobriquet of the Merrie Monarch. The music and dance renaissance thus begun is still under way and is celebrated annually by the *Merrie Monarch Festival,* held each April in Hilo, at which the state's greatest hula troupes compete.

In this century, Hawaiian music was greatly popularized by the *Panama-Pacific Exposition* in San Francisco in 1915. Since the Hawaii Pavilion was one of its main attractions and hula shows were held several times a day, many of the 17 million visitors went away singing "On the Beach at Waikiki." And in 1916 there were more Hawaiian recordings sold on the mainland than any other popular music. Broadway's *Bird of Paradise,* starring Laurette Taylor, ran for a year in New York and toured for several years throughout the US and Canada.

Johnny Noble's *Moana Hotel Orchestra* played for tourists and naval personnel from 1917 to 1933 and started dancers singing his compositions, "My Little Grass Shack" and "Hawaiian War Chant." Next door at the "pink palace of the Pacific," the *Royal Hawaiian* hotel, Harry Owens and his *Royal Hawaiian Orchestra* kept visitors dancing under the stars to "Princess Poopooly Has Plenty Papaya" and his biggest hit, "Sweet Leilani," from 1934 through the start of World War II. This genre of Hawaiian music came to be known as *hapa haole* (half-foreign), or Hawaiian by way of Tin Pan Alley.

One of the country's best-known and longest-running radio shows, "Hawaii Calls," brought the music of the islands to an estimated 2 billion listeners during the 2,083 programs that were broadcast from 1935 to 1975. For 4 decades the popular show, featuring the best songs and best singers of each generation, was transmitted from the Banyan Court of the *Moana* hotel. Each program began with the sound of the "waves at Waikiki," bringing a nostalgic tear to the eye of anyone who had visited Hawaii. At its peak, in 1952, "Hawaii Calls" was broadcast to 750 stations on the mainland, Canada, Japan, Korea, Europe, Latin America, New Zealand, and Australia. It can still be heard on the 28 "Hawaii Calls" records produced by the show's originator and director, Webley Edwards.

After World War II, Hilo Hattie and Ray Kinney took their special songs, "When Hilo Hattie Does the Hilo Hop" and "Song of the Islands," from the

Mural Room in San Francisco's *St. Francis* hotel, to the Hawaiian Room of the *Lexington* hotel in New York, and across the length and breadth of Canada and the United States. Until rock came in, everybody was singing their songs.

And that's because Hollywood was putting Hawaiian music and dance on the silver screen. There was *Waikiki Wedding* (1937), with Bing Crosby; *Moonlight in Hawaii* (1942); *Song of the Islands* (1941), with Betty Grable; *Bird of Paradise* (1951), with Jeff Chandler and Debra Paget; *From Here to Eternity* (1953); *The Revolt of Mamie Stover* (1956); *Gidget Goes Hawaiian* (1961); *Paradise Hawaiian Style* and *Hawaii* (1966); and the greatest, all-time most popular Hawaiian movie of them all — *Blue Hawaii* (1961), with Elvis Presley. Though a few Hawaiians, music and dance purists, were affronted by the cellophane skirts and the "wiggle" hulas of some of the early movies, most islanders laughed, enjoyed the movies, and felt that the public would remember the good and forget the bad.

The year 1959 ushered in the jet plane and statehood for the islands, followed closely by mainland hotel chains building luxurious resorts along the beach at Waikiki, and within a decade on the Neighbor Islands — Kauai, Maui, and the Big Island — as well. This brought to Hawaii thousands of first-time visitors and introduced the era of the showroom star.

A holdover from the 1950s, with a magnificent baritone voice, Alfred Apaka kept female hearts beating to the old Hawaiian songs until his untimely death in 1961.

The stars of the 1960s were Ed Kenney, soprano Emma Veary, contralto Haunani Kahalewai, Danny Kaleikini, and Hawaiian crooner Don Ho, who still occasionally performs. They sang Hawaiian songs, mainland songs, Japanese songs — ranging from the traditional "Ke Kali Nei Au," to the celebrated "Hawaiian Wedding Song" to the relatively recent "I'll Remember You."

The 1960s saw the birth of the only radio station — KCCN AM–1420 — that plays only Hawaiian music. Still broadcasting today, KCCN also features interviews with musicians who sing or play Hawaiian tunes, as well as news of interest to Hawaiians.

During the 1970s, both hula music and Hawaiian music experienced a renaissance as a result of the creative efforts of new *kumu hula* (hula teachers), and such talented musicians and singers as Peter Moon and the *Sunday Manoa,* Gabby Pahinui and the *Sons of Hawaii,* Auntie Genoa Keawe, Eddie Kamae, and the *Makaha Sons of Niihau.* The recognition of hula as a valid cultural art form was enhanced by the growing popularity of major competitions such as Hilo's *Merrie Monarch Festival* (named after Hawaii's musically gifted king, David Kalakaua), where both *kahiko* (traditional) and *auwana* (contemporary) hulas are performed.

By the mid-1970s, a new generation of singers and musicians surfaced, lending a more contemporary air to Hawaiian music. Most influential among these performers were *Cecelio and Kapono,* and Jerry Santos and Robert Beaumont of Olomana, whose lyric melodies quickly became Hawaiian standards. Others, such as Melveen Leed, helped popularize Hawaiian country music. The 1980s brought the *Beamer Brothers* (Keola and Kapono), the

Cazimero Brothers (Roland and Robert), Nohelani Cypriano, Jay Larrin, Audy Kimura, and Karen Keawehawaii to the list of those blending the musical traditions of old Hawaii with modern styling and beat. While the music scene today is a bit less innovative than it was during the 1970s and 1980s, Hawaiian music is still widely performed in the islands. It offers both visitors and residents a wide repertoire of melodies, encompassing more than a century of creativity.

Food and Drink

Eating with your fingers while sitting on the floor in your bare feet might sound unorthodox, but it isn't if you're doing it at a traditional Hawaiian luau. Not simply a three-course meal but a major banquet that often lasted a whole day, this famed feast has a history as ancient as the islands themselves and an experience that has delighted practically every visitor to Hawaii since Captain Cook. All major occasions were celebrated with a luau, and the season of *makahiki,* a period of thanksgiving and rest in the fall, was virtually a 4-month luau. Even warring was called to a halt to celebrate this season.

In the old days, elaborate preparations were necessary for the luau, and villagers broke up into groups to share the tasks. Some gathered the *limu* or seaweed, a luau delicacy. Others combed the searocks for tiny shellfish called *opihi* and *pupu inu* (the latter of which gave its name to Hawaiian hors d'oeuvres). Still others caught fish, dug taro and pounded poi, and gathered coconuts, guava, and bananas. Finally, the *imu,* underground oven, was prepared.

Still used today, for no other cooking method is really better, the *imu* was a shallow, oblong hole dug in the ground that was flat on the bottom. It was lined with stones, upon which a fire of kiawe wood was built. When the stones were heated through, the wood and ashes were removed and a thick layer of ti or banana leaves laid over the stones to create steam. The food was placed on top of the leaves, and more leaves and banana stalks were spread over it. Often bunches of leaves were woven into a flat, circular lid, which was then covered with earth. All feasts included a pig (*puaa*), set in the center of the *imu,* where the heat was greatest. The other foods went around it — sweet potatoes, bananas, breadfruit, bundles of taro or sweet potato leaves wrapped in ti leaves, large fish, and perhaps a dog. The cooking time was from 2 to 8 hours, depending upon the amount of food. When the process was considered *pau* (finished), a careful uncovering took place and the meal was served.

The men tended the *imu* in ancient times and still do today, although the *kapu* (taboo) against women was lifted long ago. Since antiquity, however, women have done the serving.

At a traditional luau, mats of woven *lau hala* (pandanus leaves) covered the ground and the eating area was strewn with ti leaves. Large wooden calabashes (bowls) and gourds served as communal dishes. If there were individual plates at all, they were simply sturdy banana leaves. A place of honor was always left for the large koa wood tray, which held the pig when the *imu* was opened. Following the seating of the chief, guests were positioned around the eating area according to the strict rules of Hawaiian protocol. All sat cross-legged on the ground or partly reclined.

Poi was the Hawaiians' principal food. A paste made from the root of the taro plant, it is cooked, pounded into a powder, then mixed with water. One of the world's most nutritious foods, it has a rather insipid taste that is somewhat improved by allowing it to ferment for a day or two. To give it flavor, poi was always eaten with something else — the minced kernel of the oily kukui nut, fresh or dried fish, seaweed, or even salt crystals that were collected from slightly hollowed rocks. Poi had to be made fresh daily since it was consumed in great quantities and there was no means of preserving it for more than a few days.

After taro, sweet potatoes were the major starch staple and were served often. Another starch, breadfruit, brought to Hawaii from south of the equator, did not do as well in the islands' cooler climate, and the fruit was seasonal. Eating or cooking bananas, wild or cultivated, were available year-round.

Coconut palms thrived in ancient Hawaii as they do today. The Hawaiians drank coconut milk and ate the flesh, but they did not grate and squeeze the meat to make coconut cream as did other Polynesians. The only sweets were sugarcane, cut into small sections for chewing, and baked ti root.

Chickens were brought into Hawaii from Tahiti and may have been eaten at certain times, but they were more prized for their feathers than for their meat. Dogs were not readily available and therefore were considered a delicacy for chiefs. They were carefully fed and fattened with poi and other starchy foods and cooked when very young. Fish was usually wrapped in ti leaves and broiled or steamed in the *imu,* but any that was left over could be salted and dried for future use.

Inu, liquid refreshments, were limited to water; the milk of young coconuts; a commoners' drink made from fermented ti roots, later known as *okolehao;* and *awa.* Basically a ceremonial drink, *awa* was supposed to be served to the gods as an offering. What the gods didn't drink, the priests did, and some chiefs and priests became addicted to it and drank it whenever and wherever they pleased. Commoners seldom had a chance even to taste it.

Prepared from the chewed root of a type of pepper plant and mixed with water, the effects of *awa* vary. A non-intoxicating drink, it is generally a benign narcotic that induces deep sleep and leaves no hangover — that is, in small amounts; overindulgence could present problems. A "safe" quantity for quaffing was gauged by the eye. When the light of a kukui nut candle seemed to be the light of two kukui nut candles, one had had enough. Excessive drinking caused arm and leg muscles to weaken, the eyes to become bloodshot, and the skin scaly. However, when the victim went on the wagon, the symptoms disappeared.

Bananas, guava, and sweet gourd or melon provided a "sorbet," a pause before the feasting began anew.

There are still luaus in Hawaii, great wonderful feasts for birthdays, anniversaries, church benefits, weddings, and other special occasions. However, just as Hawaii has changed in the centuries since Captain Cook, so too has the luau and for the same reason: The melange of races and peoples who came to the islands over the years brought along their own foods and added them to the traditional Hawaiian table.

Pineapple immediately comes to mind at the first mention of Hawaii. It is unclear when the fruit was brought to the islands, but the prevailing opinion is that it came some time after Captain Cook arrived in 1778. Hawaiians called the fruit "*halakahiki,*" which means "screw-pine from a foreign land." After a short time, pineapple started growing all over the islands — both wild and in cultivated plots. At the end of the century, James Dole arrived in Hawaii and turned the harvesting of pineapple into an industry. He subsequently started canning the fruit and exporting it throughout the world.

By the end of this year, however — due to decreasing profitability — all but the last vestiges of pineapple cultivation will be obliterated. On the island of Lanai, the vast, sprawling plantation fields once devoted solely to pineapple planting have dwindled to a few acres, but still enough to grow a small amount of the fruit for the island's burgeoning hotel and tourist industry. Undoubtedly, its history for over half a century as the "Pineapple Island" will be romanticized in Hawaiian annals.

The missionaries and whalers arrived in 1820 with molasses, popcorn, gingerbread, corn, carrots, cabbage, salt salmon, corned beef, and ship's bread. In 1852 the Chinese began to work on the sugar plantations; they contributed ginger root and spices, rice and soy sauce, bean sprouts and bok choy, duck and Mongolian barbecue, and new ways of cooking. With an 1868 shipload of Japanese workers came noodles, *mochi,* pickled cucumbers and turnips, rice tea, tempura and sushi, octopus and squid. The Portuguese, who settled here in 1878, shared their sweetbreads and *malasadas,* spicy sausages and omelettes, hearty fish stews and bean soups; and the Filipinos, who docked in Honolulu Harbor in 1906, offered sweet limes and sour oranges, lemon grass and fish sauces. Later waves of Koreans added *kim chi* and *kal bi* beef, and in the past 10 years exotic dishes from the cuisines of Indonesia and Vietnam have become part of the Hawaiian culinary scene. There's a dish for every taste in Hawaii.

Luaus are a special kind of party endemic to Hawaii, and most certainly all visitors should attend at least one, if only to be able to say that they tried poi and that once is enough. Luaus are relaxed and comfortable — wear a muumuu or aloha shirt — and are usually held in beautiful locations. The entertainment — Hawaiian melodies and hulas performed by young men and women — is rollicking and energetic, although sometimes romantic, and guests are often asked to participate.

Commercial luaus usually begin with a selection of Hawaiian specialty drinks aptly called exotic, which are a blend of various fruit juices and rum or other liquor. (Rum was the drink of the 19th-century whalers and seafaring men who came here from all climes and has remained a favorite in the islands.) Some of Hawaii's famous exotic drinks are the *blue Hawaii,* vodka and blue curaçao; *mai tai,* light and dark rum, orange curaçao, orgeat, and lemon juice; *planter's punch,* light rum, lemon juice, Angostura bitters, and grenadine; *Singapore sling,* gin, cherry brandy, and lemon juice; *tropical itch,* bourbon, rum, orange curaçao, Angostura bitters, and passion fruit juice; and *chi chi,* vodka, pineapple juice, and coconut syrup.

When the pig comes out of the *imu* it is called kalua (roasted) pork. It is then shredded and served as the centerpiece of the luau buffet, which may have from 10 to 16 courses and will certainly include poi, laulau, chicken luau (see list below), and lomilomi salmon, and may also include such dishes as teriyaki steak, broiled chicken, mahimahi, various salads, tempura, pickled vegetables, sushi, homemade banana and coconut bread, fresh pineapple and papaya or bananas, several desserts, and Kona coffee. Even Mark Twain bragged about Hawaii's Kona coffee, the only coffee grown in the US, claiming, "It has a richer flavor than any other." And he was right; it's as habit forming as a Kona sunset.

Once Hawaii's food production was limited almost exclusively to sugarcane and pineapple. In recent years, however, because of the Aloha State's benign climate, reputation, and a tourist trade that expects traditionally native taste treats, there has been an increase in Hawaiian products. For example, Tedeschi Vineyards manufactures wines both from grapes grown at its Maui vineyards and from pineapple grown on Haleakala's up-country slopes. On Kauai, *poha* berries, guava, and *lilikoi* (passion fruit) are harvested for expensive jams, jellies, preserves, and juices, while on the Big Island, papaya and pineapple are slow-dried to create natural treats. Maui has turned the simple potato chip into a classic snack, and on Oahu and the Big Island (where Kona coffee has become a classic among caffeine connoisseurs), half a dozen candy companies add chocolate coating to macadamia nuts grown on Hawaii and Maui plantations. In fact, during the 1980s, the macadamia nut in a variety of forms — roasted, glazed, and baked into cookies — became a major export.

Hawaii is also famous for its beer. Koolau Lager, 100 percent malt beer (no corn or rice is used), is made from water from Oahu's Koolau Range. Expatriate Germans, who adhere to that country's strict beer purity laws, produce Koolau Lager using the best Canadian malted barley and German yeast and hops.

The origin and ingredients of many of the dishes included in the luau and served by island restaurants are noted in the following glossary.

CONTEMPORARY HAWAIIAN FOODS

chicken luau: Chicken simmered slowly with taro leaves and coconut milk.

crackseed: Chinese preserved fruit, eaten like candy by island children (and adults).

haupia: Tender, sweet, white pudding made from coconut cream and arrowroot.

kim chi: Korean, *highly* spiced pickled vegetables.

laulau: Butterfish, pork, and taro leaves wrapped and steamed in fresh ti leaves.

lomilomi salmon: Salt salmon shredded and lomied (mixed) with chopped green onions, tomatoes, and crushed ice.

mahimahi: A local favorite fish, delicately flavored. (It's dolphin *fish* — not related to the mammal.)

malasadas: Portuguese sugared doughnuts (with no hole) that are eaten hot.

manapua: Chinese, called *dim sum* everywhere but Hawaii, it's a steamed, yeast dough bun filled with *char siu* (sweet roasted) pork.

poi: Very Hawaiian, mashed taro root, it replaces potatoes as the local starch. Takes some getting used to; islanders like it a day or two old and slightly sour.

saimin: Noodles cooked in a chicken or shrimp broth; replaces the hot dog at baseball and football games. Garnished with fish cake and *char siu,* it's filling and inexpensive.

sashimi: Japanese, thinly sliced, very fresh, raw fish, served with a hot sauce of shoyu and Chinese mustard. Pick it up with chopsticks or a fork and dip into the sauce. Worth trying.

shave ice: An island confection. A large paper cone is generously mounded with finely shaved ice, which is flavored with delicious and wildly colored syrups — red, purple, orange, green — and eaten with a wooden or plastic spoon.

sushi: Japanese, for snacks or meals. Small patties of rice mixed with mirin vinegar and formed around bits of pickled vegetables or fish. Cone sushi is wrapped in a golden soybean skin.

tempura: Japanese, fish, shellfish, or vegetables dipped in delicious light batter and deep fried.

teriyaki: A steak or strips of beef marinated in a local sauce of fresh ginger, sugar, and soy sauce.

Gods, Myths, and Legends

Hawaiian *moolelo* (legend) often depicts the gods as great chiefs who dwell in the heavens or in distant lands but who occasionally visit particular places or groups of people in the islands. In the broad pantheon of the thousands worshiped by the ancient Hawaiians, four gods were considered the most powerful: Ku, Kane, Kanaloa, and Lono. Each one was noted for specific interests and talents, as illustrated in the following legend of creation:

> One day, Kane, often called the "leading god among the great gods," removed the cover of a great gourd calabash and, throwing it high into space, he formed the sky. He then plucked out the white seeds and, tossing them into the sky, he made the clouds, the rain, and the wind. With more seeds, Kane produced the stars, the moon, and the sun. Pulling the flesh from the gourd, he molded it with his fingers to make mountains, valleys, and plains.
>
> After Kane had done this, Lono, the god of verdure, came and planted colorful flowers, tall trees, and swaying grasses to make the hills and valleys fragrant and beautiful.
>
> Next came the god Ku, who looked this way and that to see what more could be done and concluded that man was necessary; he therefore created him and the strife over right and wrong that is part of his existence.

Ku was the expression of the male generating power, the first parent by whom the race was made fertile and reproduced from a single stock. Hina, his wife, was the expression of female fecundity, the power of growth and reproduction. Together, they were invoked as ancestors of all mankind, past and future.

Ku's help was sought in producing bountiful crops, good fishing, a large family, long life, and national prosperity. There were at least 18 different manifestations of Ku, gods of taro, farming, mountains, and trees, but the two most feared and propitiated were the war gods Kukailimoku (Ku, the snatcher of land) and Kuwahailo (Ku of the mouthful of maggots). *Heiaus* (temples) were built in their honor and human sacrifices offered to win their assistance in battle. Their effigies were carried into war, sometimes in the form of great heads woven from sennit and covered with red or yellow feathers, with glaring mother-of-pearl eyes and fierce rows of dog's teeth, or sometimes represented by a simple ohia log, blessed and wrapped in yellow tapa cloth.

Kamehameha's battle effigy of Kukailimoku, which traveled with him at all times, was a small, roughly carved figure with a headdress of yellow feathers. It was said to cry out so fiercely in battle as to cause fear in the enemy and turn the tide in Kamehameha's favor.

Kane, who formed the three worlds — the upper heaven of the gods, the lower heaven above the earth, and the earth itself — was venerated as the great creator and patron of light and life. Thus, human sacrifices were not offered to him. Kane was usually coupled with the god Kanaloa, about whom little is known. In some stories he seems cast as a Polynesian Poseidon, god of the sea, although Martha Beckwith, a scholar of Hawaiian chants and traditions, has said there is a tendency for Hawaiians to equate Kanaloa with the Christian devil, noting that there are several legends in which Kanaloa and his evil spirits rebelled against Kane and were sent to the nether regions.

Lono, worshiped as the god of clouds and rain, crops and agriculture, games and celebrations, was also never offered human sacrifices. Instead, each Hawaiian house had an *ipu,* or gourd, of Lono hanging by the door, in which were kept bits of food, fish, and fruit; morning and evening the head of the household took down the gourd, placed it in the doorway, and prayed for the king, chiefs, commoners, and for his own family.

The fall *makahiki,* a harvest festival that lasted about 4 months, from October to February, was dedicated to Lono. It was a time when everyone ceased work, there were athletic games and feasting, all regular *kapu* (taboo) days were suspended, and rituals of thanksgiving were held. A royal procession moved through each district, collecting taxes out of the abundance provided by the god Lono in response to the prayers and offerings of the people. In these processions, Lono was represented by a straight wooden mast about a foot around and 10 to 15 feet tall. Close to the top, a crosspiece was tied to the mast from which were hung birds, feather leis, bundles of taro leaves, and, at each end, a long streamer of wide, white tapa cloth.

It was the legend of the *makahiki* that made the Hawaiians first mistake Captain Cook for Lono, and it was their discovery that he and his men were mortal that ultimately led to his death.

According to the legend, Lono sent two of his brothers from heaven to seek out a fair wife for him on earth. They traveled through each island and, finally, in the beautiful valley of Waipio on the Big Island beside the white-veiled falls of Hiilawe, they found the lovely Kaikilani, dwelling with colorful birds in a breadfruit forest.

Lono descended to her on a rainbow, made her his wife and a goddess, and took her to live at Kealakekua. One day Lono heard a mortal singing a wooing song to Kaikilani, and although she assured him that she loved him and had been faithful to him, beat her to death.

In remorse, Lono then instituted the *Makahiki Games* in her memory and traveled about the islands like a madman, challenging every human he met to a wrestling match. When he could no longer bear to live in Hawaii, he built a canoe, which was filled with great piles of provisions and required 40 men to carry it to the launching place. As Lono prepared to sail away, he said to his people, "I will return again to you, I promise. Not by canoe but on a floating island with tall trees and with many people and many birds and pigs."

Thus, when Cook sailed into Kealakekua Bay in January 1779 during the *makahiki* season, the Hawaiians naturally assumed he was Lono returned.

In addition to these four major gods — Ku, Kane, Kanaloa, and Lono — two other gods are of special interest — Maui and Pele.

Maui, a bit of a rogue and known as "the trickster," is celebrated throughout all Polynesia. Ethnologists have pointed out that one of the strongest pieces of evidence that Hawaiians, Tahitians, Samoans, and the Maoris of New Zealand sprang from a common ethnic root is the consistency with which stories of Maui's exploits are heard in the islands of all these people.

Maui's greatest deed was snaring the sun from atop Haleakala, the large crater that dominates the eastern part of the island of Maui (not, however, named after him). The legend goes that Hina, Maui's mother, complained that because the sun traveled so quickly through the heavens, the tapa cloth, which she produced from the paper mulberry, did not have time to dry.

Maui promptly fashioned a lasso from the fiber of coconut husks, journeyed to Haleakala, caught the sun by its rays (some versions say genitals), and extracted a promise that it would henceforth travel more slowly over the islands. The promise, it is said, has never been broken.

Another Maui legend — this one involving his mother's sister — tells how he tried to pull the Hawaiian islands together. Said the glib Maui (according to the story), "Oh beautiful Hinaopuhalakoa, I must have the strongest fishhook there ever was if I am to pull the islands together."

His aunt therefore changed herself into a long, hard, coral reef from which Maui broke a curved portion. Using a great rock from Kapalua to sharpen the point, he then fashioned a sturdy line from coconut palm fibers and, leaping over Molokai to the island of Oahu, he raced to Kaena Point.

With one mighty heave he threw the fishhook so far he caught the edge of Na Pali on Kauai. With all his human and godly strength he braced his feet and pulled and pulled. Suddenly, the fishhook came springing back to shatter the rocks at Kaena. Kauai had not moved one hand's breadth, although some say that Waimea Canyon was created as the great hook dragged across the island. Somewhat sheepishly, Maui decided bringing the islands together couldn't be done and went on to other adventures, leaving the broken fishhook at Kaena Point.

Although Pele, goddess of volcanoes, is not one of the four major gods, she is perhaps the most revered Hawaiian god today. It is said that Pele was originally a human, who traveled to Hawaii with her brothers and sisters sometime in the 12th century. She became known on the islands of Oahu, Maui, and Hawaii as a beautiful and powerful sorceress who was killed by a cataclysmic outpouring of lava and returned as the very spirit of that red-hot lava. She is now said to reside in Kilauea Crater on the Big Island, and the various lava flows and eruptions that have taken place during recent years have been attributed to her wrath.

For example, when development of the Warm Springs resort area in the Puna District on the Big Island began, old-timers claimed that Pele was angered. They warned that the beautiful beach and *waiapele* (waters made warm by Pele) were given to the Hawaiians to enjoy without charge and forecast the destruction of the cottages and souvenir shops. Most people thought the possibility highly unlikely, for no eruption had disturbed the tranquillity of the beautiful district southeast of Hilo in hundreds of years. Early in 1955, however, before the area could become a real tourist destination, the peace of Puna was shattered by 88 days of volcanic fountaining.

When the eruption ended, enchanting Warm Springs was under 15 feet of lava.

Visitors to Volcanoes National Park who cart away "souvenir" rocks also risk incurring Pele's disfavor. When they return home, they may find themselves suffering a streak of bad luck, ranging from broken china to broken legs. Hawaiians say this is because each volcanic rock is a part of Pele — a finger, lock of hair, ankle, eyebrow, and so on — and the fiery goddess wants them returned. As a result, park rangers receive dozens of boxes of rocks each month sent back by repentant thieves.

To this tempestuous and irritable Pele, the early Hawaiians offered the young leaves of the taro plant and the sweet ohelo berries, which grow only on the summits of active volcanoes and are considered sacred to the goddess. Choice branches were tossed into Halemaumau firepit at Kilauea Crater before the rest of the berries were eaten. Today, believers still offer ohelo berries in respect, although of late it is rumored that Pele, a timely as well as timeless goddess, prefers a gift of gin.

Language

ALOHA
MAHALO
WAHINE
KANE

A visitor to the Hawaiian islands may hear as many as nine languages — Chinese, English, Filipino, Hawaiian, Japanese, Korean, Portuguese, Samoan, and a smattering of Spanish — spoken during even a brief stay. This diversity simply adds to the romance of the visit and does not cause problems, because English has been the spoken language of Hawaii since the 1850s and is the language taught in all island schools, even though certain conversations liberally laced with "pidgin" may belie this fact at times.

Unfortunately, a fluent speaker of Hawaiian is a rare bird, and usually an elderly one. Hawaiian is a language that is gradually disappearing, scarcely spoken at home, taught in only a few schools and at the University of Hawaii, and transmitted to the new generation as a mother tongue only on the tiny, isolated, private island of Niihau (whose population is less than 250).

Visitors will, however, hear many Hawaiian words and phrases animating ordinary English sentences. In addition, because of the present cultural renaissance, many songs are sung in the Hawaiian language only, most major choirs sing in Hawaiian, and several churches, particularly Kawaiahao Church in Honolulu, present sermons in Hawaiian. All but a few street names and the names of most public buildings are in Hawaiian. Therefore, a traveler with some small knowledge of what Hawaiian is all about and able to pronounce the names of new native friends will be more comfortable in this paradise of the Pacific and, homeward bound, will have something to show off.

The Hawaiian language, as written today, has the shortest alphabet in the world, with only twelve letters. Five of them are vowels — *a, e, i, o,* and *u* — and seven are consonants — *h, k, l, m, n, p,* and *w.* All vowels are pronounced, there is a vowel at the end of each syllable, and a vowel always appears between consonants. Some words contain a glottal stop (") rather than a written consonant. The glottal stop, which could be considered the eighth consonant, is pronounced the way the breathy pause in "oh-oh" is pronounced.

Most words are stressed on the next to last syllable and some words have an even stress. Consonants are pronounced as in English except for *w.* When it is the first letter of a word, as in Waikiki, it is pronounced like a *w;* when it follows the vowels *e* or *i,* it is pronounced like a *v,* as in Ewa or Iwalani.

Anyone familiar with Spanish will have no trouble with Hawaiian vowels in general (and beginners shouldn't worry about exceptions). They are pronounced as follows:

a like *a* in far
e like *e* in bed

i like *ee* in see
o like *o* in sole
u like *oo* in moon

Spoken, Hawaiian is melodious and dramatic, with a lilting, romantic sound. Its vocabulary, as passed down through the written language, has only about 20,000 words, and considering how lately it became a written language — the early-19th-century missionary era — it has generated an overwhelming number of books, manuscripts, and other writings. The language is ingenious and sophisticated, often figurative in meaning, and tales and poems are filled with symbolism and plays on words. Given this complexity, it is sometimes difficult to read correctly unless glottal stops are stressed or accented vowels are marked in the text as they would be heard in speech; words otherwise pronounced the same way can have several different meanings: *ka"u* is mine, *"kau* is yours; *pua"a* is pig or pork and *pu"a"a* is confused or frightened. (These refinements in transcription do not appear in this guidebook because the only Hawaiian words included are those few, easily recognized words in almost universal use in Hawaii or the names of people or places. Glottal stops are not used on Hawaiian street signs, incidentally.)

Hawaiian differs from the Polynesian languages of other Pacific islands principally in the use of *k* for *t, l* for *r, n* for *nd* or *ng,* and *h* for *f* or *s,* and in its ambivalence about *w* for *v* (that is, using the written *w* and pronouncing it both ways).

Most Pacific sociologists and phylogenists believe that the languages of the Pacific islands derived from the root languages of Indonesia and Malaya. There are many similar words of everyday use and meaning. Coconut in Indonesian is *niur;* in Hawaiian, Samoan, and Tongan it is *niu.* Fire in Indonesian is *api,* in Hawaiian it is *ahi,* and in Samoan and Tongan it is *afi.* Sky in Indonesian is *langit,* in Samoan and Tongan it is *langi,* and in Hawaiian it is *lani.* If the missionaries who created the Hawaiian alphabet had not been so arbitrary in their choice of letters to represent the sounds they heard, these root words might even be closer in spelling and pronunciation.

The early Hawaiians carved their messages to posterity in the smooth lava rocks of their islands. Excellent petroglyph examples are on the Big Island of Hawaii at Puuloa near Kalapana Beach, at Kaupulehu near Kona Village, and at Puako near Kawaihae, South Kohala. Though each island has areas of petroglyphs, Hawaii seems to have more of them, probably because it is so much bigger.

Petroglyphs were once highly rated by romantic scholars and were considered transported derivatives of Egyptian hieroglyphics. In recent years they have been accepted for what they appear to be — stick pictures of people, animals, fish, canoes, battles, maps — depictions of a variety of aspects of ancient Hawaiian life. Some students say the pictures' deep and real meanings still have not been established, but most historians feel they are no more than what they seem, that they record a king's death, a good fish catch, the arrival of a great canoe from Tahiti, a family tree, or a war party.

This does not negate their importance as primitive art nor diminish the interest of the stories they tell. But it is obvious they are neither remnants of a forgotten written language nor the beginnings of one.

The Hawaiians did not have a written language until missionaries to the Sandwich Islands produced one so that the "pagans" could be taught to read the Bible. In January 1822, every *alii* (noble) in Honolulu was invited to watch the first book printed in Hawaiian, a little four-page primer, come off the small mission press. A number of the stalwart chiefs even gave printer Elisha Loomis a hand in turning the level of the old Rampage.

A full year and 9 months' work had gone into the little book, all of it spent in creating an alphabet for the Hawaiian language. Each minister, doctor, carpenter, and missionary wife had given the project every available moment. Before a sentence could be written, speech variations had to be tabulated; before speech variations could be tabulated, sounds had to be distinguished. A spelling system had to be conceived, and before any of the problems could be solved, an alphabet had to be devised.

In the beginning, this diligent company identified 90 different sounds and for a few brief weeks was tempted to create an alphabet to match. But they thought it was hardly likely that the illiterate Hawaiians would be able to master an alphabet if they themselves couldn't, so they cut it as much as possible and wound up with just twelve letters, with "nine biblical consonants reserved for biblical names and Sunday school books."

Beginning with Captain James Cook, who was the first person known to have transliterated the Hawaiian spoken word, explorers and traders had given the language a confusing variety of spellings. But the phonetic decisions made by the missionaries were final. Hanarooru, Whyteetee, Owahoo, and Owhyhee became Honolulu, Waikiki, Oahu, and Hawaii forever, and *pule* (prayer) and *palapala* (writing) became the basis of the new kingdom.

Kaahumanu, a widow of Kamehameha I and the regent for the absent Liholiho (King Kamehameha II), quickly issued a decree that everyone in the kingdom was obliged to learn reading and writing. She herself ably demonstrated that the Hawaiians had the intellect to do so.

During this period only adults went to school. There wasn't room for the youngsters, whose turn, most Hawaiians felt, would come later. Besides, the alphabet was so simple that even the dullest citizen could master it. As fast as the students graduated, they were sent to organize other schools. Some classes were held under banyan trees, some under palm frond lean-tos, and some simply on the open plains, where students held their slates as often above their heads to ward off rain and sun as on their laps.

Twenty thousand copies of the Old Testament came off the presses in Honolulu and Lahaina in 1831 and 50,000 copies of the New Testament in 1832. By 1844, more than half of the adult Hawaiian population had been taught to read.

In their extreme simplification of the alphabet, the missionaries created difficulties for Hawaiians of the 20th century, for a major part of their cultural renaissance is the attempt to reclaim the rich linguistic expressiveness of their ancestors. The Hawaiian language was one of great descriptive beauty, with many nuances, but during these early "learning" years, much was lost, dual meanings were abandoned, and some words were irreparably forgotten. Today's Hawaiian scholars are making every effort to record the speech of their *kupunas* (elders) before these last few contacts with the past are gone.

This undertaking is described by Mary Kawena Pukui and Samuel H. Elbert in the introduction to the second edition of their definitive *Hawaiian Dictionary,* which begins with the saying *He loa ka"imina o ke ala o Hawai"i "imi loa* ("Long is the search for the way of Hawaii's thinkers").

There's a tenth language spoken to a degree by everyone in Hawaii — pidgin. Pidgin is the catalyst of many Hawaiian conversations, and although it is now basically a language of fun and the peer language in all island schools, it also crops up in many a business dialogue, where it is the common medium of exchange. Hawaiian pidgin developed as a mixture of English and the various immigrant patois, to which schoolchildren have added the refinements of their own colloquial dialect. It varies not only from one island to another but from one school to another.

The ubiquitous pidgin expression is *da kine,* which can be used anywhere to describe anything. More expressive than whatchamacallit, *da kine* can cover weather, cars, lost articles, gadgets, and so on, and it can also be a flattering or a derogatory description depending upon the tone of voice. It is used when other people know what you mean and when you can't remember the name of something. Other expressions used in everyday conversations include:

an' den: and then what? so what else? I'm bored!
brah: friend, buddy, as in "Howzit, brah?"
cockaroach: steal or sneak away with
geev um: go for it, beat them, give it all you've got; similar to "go for broke," which is about the same exhortation
li' dat: like that, and so; used to explain something one doesn't want to bother explaining
mo' bettah: better, best, a good idea
shaka: very good, right on, this is really OK; combined with a hand signal, with the thumb and little finger extended, is a "Howzit?" greeting
s'koshi: a small thing or person, just a little bit
talk story: gossip, shooting the breeze, bull session

The current dictionary of pidgin in Hawaii is *Pidgin to da Max,* by Peppo, found in most Hawaiian bookstores. It is lovingly done, interesting, amusing, and informative.

Pidgin is a very personal thing with the people of Hawaii, who use it every day. It's not an affectation and doesn't mix well with mainland English. Visitors can avoid embarrassing themselves and the Hawaiians by saving pidgin practice for friends and the tour escort and not including it in conversations with strangers. Using it does not make one an instant *kamaaina,* anyway. Mo' bettah to listen for it, sit back and enjoy it, but not try to get involved.

USEFUL, COMMON HAWAIIAN EXPRESSIONS

aikane (eye-*kah*-nay): friend
akamai (ah-kah-my): smart, clever
ala (ah-lah): road or pathway
alii (ah-*lee*-ee): chief, nobility

aloha (ah-*loh*-hah): welcome, love, greetings, sympathy, farewell
auwe (ow-way): too bad, oh damn
ewa (*eh*-vah): toward Ewa or westerly direction
haole (*hah*-oh-lay): Caucasian, foreigner
hapa (hah-pah): half
hapa haole (hah-pah *hah*-oh-lay): half- or part-Caucasian
holoku (*ho*-loh-koo): long fitted dress with a train
hoolaulea (ho-oh-lah-oo-lay-ah): celebration
hoomalimali (ho-oh-mah-lee-mah-lee): flattery, blarney
huhu (hoo-*hoo*): miffed, angry
kai (kah-ee): sea
kamaaina (kah-mah-*aye*-nah): native, local resident
kane (*kah*-ney): man, sign on men's room
keiki (kay-*ee*-kee): child
kokua (koh-*koo*-ah): help, assistance, aid
lanai (lah-*nye*): balcony or patio
lei (lay): necklace or garland of flowers
lua (loo-ah): bathroom, not to be confused with luau
luau (loo-*ow*): party, feast, cooked taro leaves
mahalo (mah-*hah*-low): thank you
makai (mah-*kah*-ee): direction toward the sea
malihini (mah-lih-*hee*-nee): newcomer, visitor
mauka (*mau*-kah): direction toward the mountains
mele (*meh*-lay): chant, song
muumuu (moo-oo-moo-oo): very loose, long dress for all occasions
ohana (oh-*hah*-nah): family, extended family
okole (oh-koh-leh): butt, rear, bottom
okolemaluna (oh-koh-leh-mah-*loo*-nah): as in a toast "bottoms up"; literally "bottom to the moon" (luna)
ono (*oh*-noh): tastes good
opu (oh-*poo*): stomach
pahu (pah-hoo): drum
pali (*pah*-lee): cliff, escarpment
paniolo (pah-nee-*oh*-loh): cowboy
pau (pow): the end, finished
pehea oe (peh-hay-ah *oh-ee*): how are you?
pilikia (pee-lee-*key*-ah): trouble
poi (poy-ee): cooked taro corm pounded into paste
puka (*poo*-kah): doorway, entrance, hole, parking space
pupule (poo-*poo*-ley): crazy, pixilated
wahine (wah-*hee*-ney): girl, woman, sign on ladies' room
wai (wah-ee): water
wikiwiki (*wee*-kee-*wee*-kee): be quick, hurry, quickly

Hauoli la hanau (hah-oo-*oh*-lee lah hah-*nah*-oo): Happy Birthday
Mele Kalikimaka (meh-lay kah-lee-*kee*-mah-kah): Merry Christmas
Hauoli makahiki hou (hah-oo-*oh*-lee mah-kah-*hee*-kee ho-oo): Happy New Year

ISLAND-BY-ISLAND HOPPING

OAHU

What Oahu means to you probably depends on how old you are. If you are over 60, chances are that it conjures up images of Japanese fighter planes strafing Schofield Barracks and Pearl Harbor. If you're younger, the island's iconography is more likely to consist of surfboards, blue seas, and the concrete exclamation marks along the Waikiki shoreline. Both images are valid, but they are recent motifs on a canvas that is much older and far more complex.

Two million years ago, Oahu was two separate islands focused on the Koolau volcano in the east and the Waianae volcano in the west. Today, these once-turbulent volcanoes are relatively serene mountain ranges and for the most part little known except to forest rangers, a few hikers, and soldiers and air personnel engaged in military exercises. Like the other Hawaiian islands, Oahu was first settled over 1,000 years ago by the Marquesans, who sailed the Pacific in huge canoes fitted with thatch roofs to ward off the glare of the sun. Tahitian immigrants followed, and as they mingled with the Marquesans, a distinct Hawaiian culture eventually developed, with its own language, traditions, and rituals. One is tempted to think of the islands as an earthly paradise, and in terms of beauty and climate, they probably were. Yet it was not entirely a simple life: There were such refinements as a complicated system of *kapus* (taboos), elegant feathered costumes and headdresses and tall *kahilis* (feather-decorated staffs carried by Hawaiian royalty), and intricate leis whose design symbolized the strict divisions in society. There was, too, a dark side to this life — one of internecine skirmishes and human sacrifice, as the chiefs of the various islands sought to extend their hegemony.

In the late 18th century, Kamehameha, a chief from the Big Island of Hawaii, began his ambitious campaign to conquer all of the Hawaiian islands. He took Oahu in 1795 in one of the last and bloodiest battles. All along, Kamehameha had been conducting a healthy business in firearms with Western ships arriving in Hawaii; and as the islands were consolidated, the traders discovered that Honolulu had the largest deepwater harbor in the islands. Ships began to sail here from all over the world, particularly Europe and America. In 1820, New England missionaries arrived, eager to convert and "civilize" the natives, and soon after came the great whaling ships, full of randy and hard-drinking seamen who made Honolulu their base. By the 1840s, at the decree of Kamehameha III, the nomadic Hawaiian royal court was permanently settled in Honolulu, and the island began to live up to its name, *O"a"hu,* or "the gathering place."

Most of the first Kamehameha's successors — including Kamehameha II (reigned 1819–24), Kamehameha IV (1855–63), Kamehameha V (1863–72), and King David Kalakaua (1874–91) — traveled to Europe, where they were notably impressed by the lifestyle of the court at Windsor Castle. Hawaiian women of fashion took to wearing bustles, and gentlemen donned epaulets.

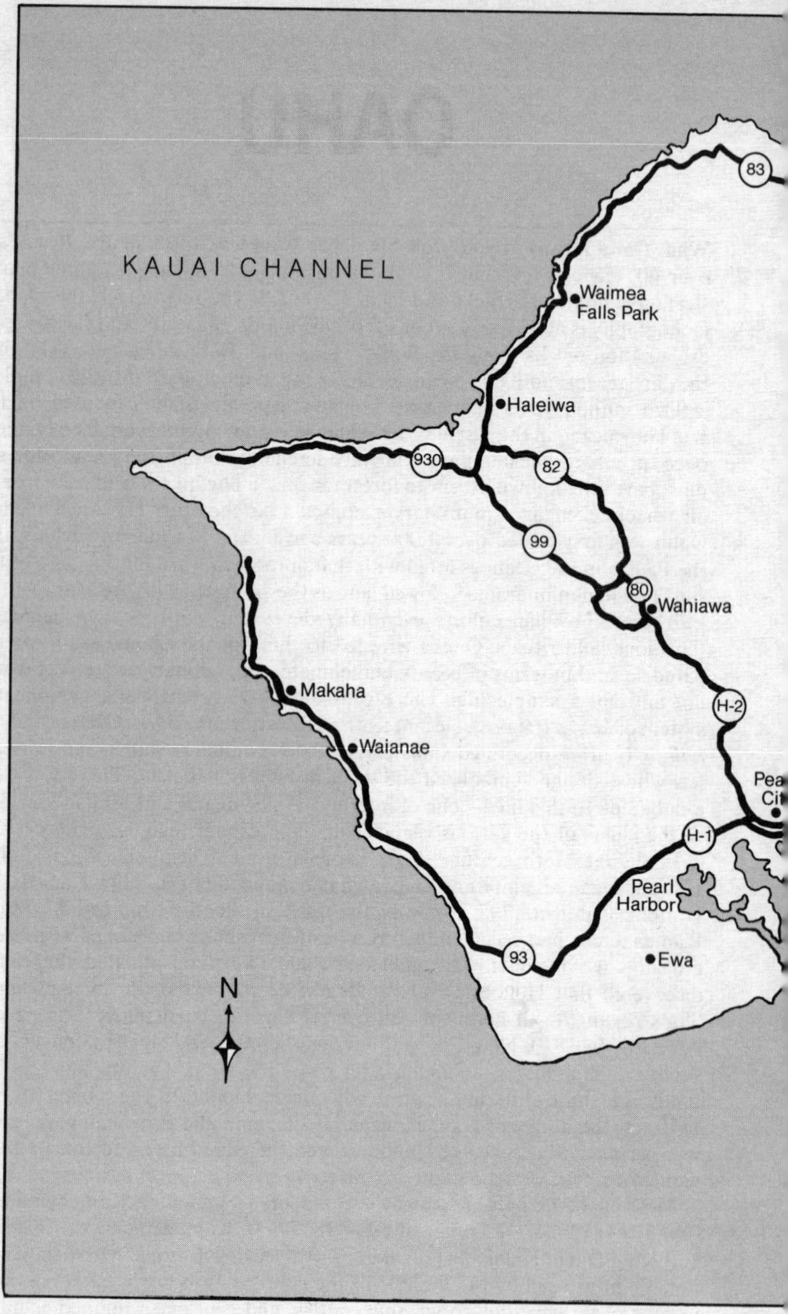
KAUAI CHANNEL
83
Waimea Falls Park
Haleiwa
930
82
99
80
Wahiawa
H-2
Makaha
Waianae
H-1
Pearl Harbor
93
Ewa
N

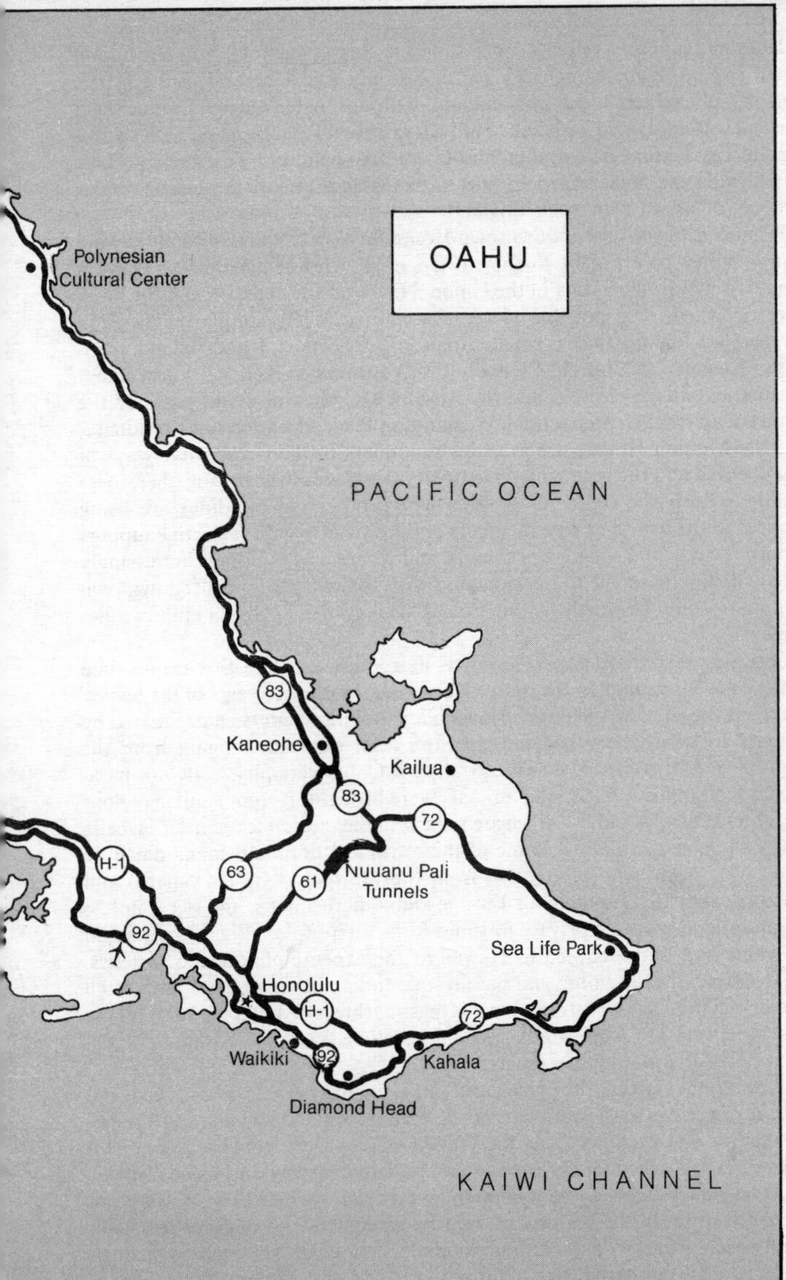
OAHU
Polynesian Cultural Center
PACIFIC OCEAN
83
Kaneohe
Kailua
83
72
H-1
63
61
Nuuanu Pali Tunnels
92
Sea Life Park
Honolulu
H-1
72
Waikiki
92
Kahala
Diamond Head
KAIWI CHANNEL

Palaces and summer retreats more suited to Surrey were built in the humid island capital. Kamehameha IV called his only son Albert, after the prince consort; played excellent cricket; and with his wife, Queen Emma, held musical soirées. David Kalakaua built a new Iolani Palace replete with sweeping staircases, stone balustrades, and Corinthian columns. To crown it all, he embellished the palace gardens with a bandstand, one of the most familiar symbols of life in provincial England.

Whatever the virtues of downtown Honolulu may be today — and they are many — they owe a debt to the royal family, who bequeathed to Oahu a capital as handsome as any in the Union. Now that the captains and the kings have departed, it is possible to see the comparatively simple buildings in perspective. Iolani Palace is smaller than some Newport, Rhode Island, mansions; Kawaiahao Church, "Honolulu's Westminster Abbey," looks like a prosperous village church; and St. Andrew's Cathedral could pass for the chapel of an English prep school. Washington Place, the governor's residence, and the Mission Houses are gracious reminders in their respective ways of how the rich and the bourgeois lived in New England. In scale, together, these buildings form the center of an area where other old buildings are being restored at the behest of wise members of the citizenry with the active support of both the city and state governments, and where new buildings increasingly are erected with an eye to harmonizing with the old. As a result, downtown Honolulu would be worth visiting even if Waikiki Beach were a million miles away.

Certainly this architectural legacy is more pleasant than that bequeathed by the early white men to the native Hawaiians. Within 20 years of the *haoles*' arrival in the islands, the native Hawaiian population had been decimated by illnesses to which they had never before been exposed, ranging from the common cold to venereal disease. And, as if Oahu were physically not paradise enough, plants, birds, and animals were brought in from similar regions to gild what was already — if we are to believe the insatiable recorder Isabella Bird — a considerable lily. Some of these tropical flora and fauna did little harm. The sugarcane (brought in from the Marquesas by Hawaiians) and pineapple provided produce for Europe and America, jobs, and (let it not be forgotten) considerable private fortunes for some people. Other imports had less value and have adapted to Hawaii at the expense of endemic varieties. For example, the charming and picturesque Indian mongoose is a pest, often destroying the eggs and the young of nesting birds. And trees such as the poinciana, brought from Madagascar, have flourished in the islands, sometimes displacing native specimens.

Some would say that the presence of strangers has been damaging, too, and that the muggings in the dark corners of Waikiki and the assaults and vandalism that have made news along the Waianae Coast stem from the resentment *kamaainas* feel when *haoles* (foreigners) buy up property and fence it in. To the Hawaiian psyche, these compounds, especially when they are large or priced to suit only the budgets of wealthy foreigners and mainlanders — or equally rich locals — are chilling reminders of what are seen as historic abuses against the native Hawaiian at the hands of outsiders. Whatever the cause, crime is a problem on Oahu, though not nearly serious enough to deter the more than 3 million visitors who annually swell Honolulu's 435,000 resident population.

But this is the debit side, and whether you put Waikiki here or on the credit side is strictly a matter of taste. The area has been called colorful and exciting as well as crass and commercial, and some tourists never venture beyond its boundaries. Yet it is in the country, outside Honolulu, that the Oahu that is Hawaiian can most easily be found.

If the natural and spontaneous Hawaii fascinates you, go up to the Tantalus Drive and exult in the wonderland of a tropical rain forest; hike into the heart of Koko Crater and look at the weird and wonderful shrubs and plants that fight and survive in a wilderness of volcanic debris; walk around Kaena Point — it's hard on the feet — in the northwest of the island and look for whales spouting in the water; go to the North Shore on a rainy afternoon when the beachboys are sleeping or riding the surf silhouetted against the setting sun, recapturing the freedom of simpler times. At Kaaawa Beach, you may even spot a lone fisherman spearing squid for his family's table.

Ko Olina, a new resort near Ewa Beach, is being constructed on land once used to raise sugarcane. Eventually, the complex will include marinas, golf courses (one is already open), beaches, condos, houses, and hotels; for now, it means a lush, palm-dotted golf course and clubhouse, the *Ihilani* hotel (which will open this year), and the Paradise Cove luau grounds. The once rural feel of the Ewa plains seems destined for history as plans for the development of Kapolei, a satellite city of 200,000 people, are also under way. Still, places of quiet beauty remain even as Oahu continues intense development. It's still common to see fishermen returning at sunset along the beach-lined Waianae Coast, as well as flurries of partridge and screeching peacocks in the dry clefts way up in Makaha Valley. Within a few minutes of Honolulu's urban core are the lushly landscaped gardens of the Lyon Arboretum, a dense rain forest. And don't forget to ride *TheBus,* the surest way of coming into contact with *kamaainas* all around the island. Simply get off when you want to savor some fresh tropical fruits from a run-down mom-and-pop store. If you make even a few of these outings, you will experience the remnants of Oahu's quieter past, a serenity that endures despite Honolulu's position as the eleventh-largest US metropolitan area.

SOURCES AND RESOURCES

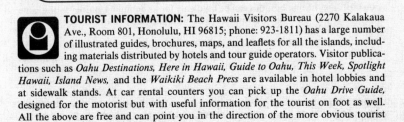

TOURIST INFORMATION: The Hawaii Visitors Bureau (2270 Kalakaua Ave., Room 801, Honolulu, HI 96815; phone: 923-1811) has a large number of illustrated guides, brochures, maps, and leaflets for all the islands, including materials distributed by hotels and tour guide operators. Visitor publications such as *Oahu Destinations, Here in Hawaii, Guide to Oahu, This Week, Spotlight Hawaii, Island News,* and the *Waikiki Beach Press* are available in hotel lobbies and at sidewalk stands. At car rental counters you can pick up the *Oahu Drive Guide,* designed for the motorist but with useful information for the tourist on foot as well. All the above are free and can point you in the direction of the more obvious tourist attractions and places to eat. In addition, they sometimes contain discount coupons.

Local Coverage – The *Honolulu Advertiser,* a morning daily, and the *Honolulu Star-Bulletin,* an afternoon paper, are major newspapers that cover world, national, and local events. They combine to produce a Sunday newspaper, which has a week-long review of events and a dining section containing restaurants, including some lesser-known "ethnic" places, and entertainment (editorial coverage is largely influenced by advertisers). Check the *Advertiser*'s Honolulu Calendar or the *Star-Bulletin*'s Pulse of Paradise for listings of the city's often overlooked selection of movies, concerts, and shows. (Top name performers frequently include a Honolulu stopover on Asia or Australia tours.) The *Los Angeles Times* and *USA Today* are usually available in Honolulu by 9 AM on the day of publication; *The New York Times* generally arrives a day after publication. They are sold in the sundries stores of most large hotels. *Honolulu,* a monthly magazine, covers island topics, people, and places, and also features a useful calendar of events. *Aloha* (bimonthly) also publishes a calendar of statewide events; *Aloha* features a restaurant directory and listing of gallery exhibits. You can also pick up a copy of our brand-new *BIRNBAUM'S Honolulu 1993.*

TELEPHONE: The area code for Hawaii is 808.

GETTING AROUND: While some of the other islands have as many as three airfields to service them, Oahu has only one — Honolulu International Airport. The largest in the state, it handles all international flights to Hawaii, and most of the ones from the mainland. Travelers can make connections to the other Hawaiian islands at either the main terminal or the new inter-island terminal. Airlines that fly to the other islands from Oahu are *Hawaiian Airlines, Aloha IslandAir, Aloha Airlines, Air Molokai,* and *Panorama Air.*

Honolulu International is about 6 miles from downtown Honolulu, and nearly 10 miles from Waikiki. Rental cars, taxis, and shuttle buses to all parts of the island are available from both terminals.

Bus – *TheBus:* TheMarvel! A proofreader's and typographer's nightmare, *TheBus* is a dream come true for everyone else. It not only circulates through all the suburban veins of Honolulu but runs along most of the coastline and through central Oahu, too. Whether you go one stop or 80 miles around the island, it costs the same, 60¢ (at press time), which you must pay with exact change. *TheBus* is painted in shades of yellow, black, and gray. The main terminus on Oahu is at the *Ala Moana Shopping Center* on the Kona Street side of the ground-floor parking lot. The No. 8 bus is a shuttle between Kapiolani Park, near Diamond Head, and the *Ala Moana Center,* and passes through the main Waikiki hotel district en route. If you are coming from Waikiki, it will drop you on the *makai* (ocean) side of the shopping center. To reach the terminus, walk through the parking lot. Passengers proceeding by another bus can ask for a transfer upon boarding the first bus; this can be used only for a continuing journey in the same direction. If you are making several stops along a particular route, ask for a transfer each time you pay a fare.

A favorite trip on *TheBus* is the journey around the island: For 60¢ it's an extraordinary way to see a great deal of Oahu, besides being one of the best ways to meet local people. If you stay on the bus, the trip takes 4 hours. There are two ways to go: north across central Oahu, eastward along the North Shore, and south down the Windward Coast on bus No. 52, marked Wahiawa/Kaneohe or Wahiawa/Circle Island; or north along the Windward Coast, west along the North Shore, and south through central Oahu on bus No. 52, marked Kaneohe/Wahiawa or Kaneohe/Circle Island. Either way, the ride is splendid. Waimea Falls and the Polynesian Cultural Center are served by these routes; take the former for the falls and the latter for the center. To get to Pearl Harbor direct from Waikiki, take bus No. 20, marked Airport. You can also ride the No. 8 bus to Ala Moana and change to bus No. 50, 51, or 52, marked Wahiawa/Kaneohe or Wahiawa/Circle Island. Some buses that pass through Waikiki but do not require a trip to Ala Moana are the No. 58 Hawaii Kai bus, which can be boarded on Kuhio Avenue and makes stops at the entrance to Diamond Head Crater and Sea Life Park, and the No. 2 School Street bus, which passes the *Bishop Museum. TheBus* No. 19 Airport runs between Waikiki and Honolulu International Airport; however, there is no room for luggage on board, and what cannot be carried on your lap cannot be brought on. Telephone information lines provide route information at *Ala Moana Center.* Two publications that can be purchased for a couple of dollars are *TheBus Guide,* with details on 71 destinations and a great deal of other useful information, and *Honolulu and Oahu by TheBus,* which contains maps of Oahu, Greater Honolulu, and Waikiki showing every bus route as well as 35 small maps indicating the bus stops at some of the most frequently visited points of interest. For further information, contact the Honolulu Department of Transport, Mass Transit Lines (MTL), 811 Middle St., Honolulu, HI 96819 (phone: 848-4444).

A private enterprise, *Airport Motorcoach* (phone: 926-4747), provides hotel/airport transfers for $5 (it's possible to reserve seats in advance) and makes runs to the Arizona Memorial for $4 per person, round-trip.

Taxi – Technically, taxis are not allowed to cruise or pick up passengers on the street. However, most cabs will stop if they are not on radio call, and if the cabs are not creating a nuisance, the police usually turn a blind eye. Generally, to be sure of finding a cab, it is wise to call one yourself or through a hotel bell captain. *SIDA (State Independent Drivers Association)* taxis are owner-driven and have a good reputation for reliability (phone: 836-0011). Other major companies are *Aloha State Taxi* (phone: 847-3566), which serves the whole island and is especially popular with military personnel; and *Charley's* (phone: 955-2211; 531-1333), which will take you to any point on the island from the airport or drive you around the island in a Cadillac Fleetwood for about $55 an hour, with a 2-hour minimum. If you want to show up at your hotel in a Rolls-Royce, call *Cloud Nine* (phone: 524-7999). *Handicabs* (phone: 524-3866) specializes in transport for handicapped people and operates vehicles that will accommodate passengers in their wheelchairs. Best to call a day in advance.

Car Rental – This is a big business in Hawaii, with more firms coming up with different deals all the time. Generally speaking, the national and statewide firms are more expensive than the purely local agencies, many of which have been driven out of business in recent years by high insurance premiums. If you are traveling during July or August, in the couple of year-end weeks that include *Christmas* and *New Year's,* or in February, book your car ahead because auto rentals become very scarce in these periods. Prices decline in the late spring and the fall, but even then, it is never smart to listen to the auto rental shills who parade along Waikiki's main thoroughfares. *Alamo* (phone: 833-4585; 800-327-9633), *Avis* (phone: 834-5536; 800-831-8000), *Budget* (phone: 922-3600; 800-527-0700), *Dollar* (phone: 944-1544; 800-367-7006), *Hertz* (phone: 831-3800; 800-654-3131), *National* (phone: 836-2655; 800-227-7368), *Thrifty Rent-A-Car* (phone: 836-2388; 800-367-2277), and *Tropical Rent-A-Car* (phone: 957-0800; 800-678-6000) are the major national firms represented at the airport. *Budget*'s coupon book features many free and discount options. Some regional firms include *Robert's Hawaii* (phone: 523-9323); *Courtesy Car and Truck Rental* (phone: 831-2277); *Travelers Rent-A-Car* (phone: 834-1093); and *World* (phone: 833-1866), which offers the lowest rates for no-frills rentals. Whereas most of the Waikiki hotels have car rental desks that will deliver automobiles to the front door for their clients, an airport pickup will save the cost of airport-hotel transfers. *Classic Car Rentals* (phone: 951-8331) has a vintage fleet that includes models that span the 1920s through the 1960s.

Bicycle Rental – Ideal for getting around town and along the coast, where there are no really intimidating hills, bikes are not good for the mountainside suburbs. *Island Triathlon & Bike* (569 Kapahulu Ave., near Waikiki; phone: 732-7227) offers quality lightweight rentals for $25 for the first day; $10 a day thereafter.

Moped and Motorcycle – They're a breezy way to see the island or just to cruise around Waikiki and the southeast. Be careful: Pickup truck drivers on the Waianae Coast tend to look askance at riders of these motorized "toys," and driving them on newly wet surfaces can be tricky if you're not completely accustomed to them. *Aloha Funway Rentals* (1778 Ala Moana Blvd.; phone: 942-9696) is the best-known motorcycle/moped rental outfit in Honolulu. In Haleiwa, you can rent from *Fantasy Cycles* (66-134 Kam Hwy.; phone: 637-3221).

Trolley – *Waikiki Trolley* (phone: 599-2561) has launched a fleet of motorized, open-air reproductions of the horse-drawn trolleys that operated at the turn of the century. Today, they provide tour and point-to-point service between Waikiki and such shopping and cultural attractions as Kewalo Basin, *Ala Moana Center,* Chinatown, and the Aloha Tower. The trolleys run from 8:30 AM to 4 PM, and tours run between 9 AM and 4 PM; all-day passes cost $10.

Ferry – A new passenger ferry connecting downtown Honolulu and west Oahu during rush hours — and offering service between Oahu, Maui, and Kauai at other times — began operating at press time. The Barbers Point–downtown Honolulu run will take 27 minutes, the trips between Oahu and Maui about 1½ hours, and those between Oahu and Kauai will take 2 hours. *San Diego Shipbuilding and Repair* (phone: 619-691-1091).

SIGHTSEEING TOURS: Boat – *Paradise Cruises*'s 1,600-passenger *Star of Honolulu* (phone: 536-3641) takes guests on a daily Pearl Harbor cruise. Also offered by *Paradise* are daily sunset dinner cruises. *RoyalHawaiian Cruises* (phone: 848-6360) operates the *Navatek* and the *Stardancer* on dinner cruises along the Waikiki coast. A free bus carries passengers from and back to pick-up points in Waikiki. *Aikane Catamarans* (phone: 522-1533) has twin-hulled Polynesian boats offering sunset and moonlight dinner sails, with live music and dancing. All of these cruises leave from the Kewalo Bay Boat Basin. *Windjammer Cruises* (phone: 521-0036) features sunset and dinner cruises aboard their 1,000-passenger *Rella Mae,* which sets out from Honolulu Harbor. Waikiki pickups are provided. On Friday nights, *Windjammer* also offers a 2-hour sunset cocktail and pupu cruise ($25, including hotel pickup) that departs from Kewalo Basin at 5:30 PM. The *Mani Kai* departs daily at 5 or 5:30 PM (March through September) from the beach fronting the *Hyatt Regency Waikiki* hotel (2424 Kalakaua Ave.; phone: 923-1234) for a 1½-hour cocktail sail ($20). *Royal Hawaiian Cruises*' state-of-the-art *Navatek,* which is powered by underwater jets, offers first-rate cruises of Waikiki. Although the plush setting and steak and lobster dinner ($130) are impressive, a less expensive option is the buffet luncheon cruise ($45) or a ride on the 400-passenger *Stardancer.* The *Navatek* departs from Pier 9, adjacent to the Hawaii Maritime Center. For information, call *Royal-Hawaiian Cruises* (phone: 947-9971). For individual trips by sea, hire one of the privately owned catamarans that depart from Waikiki beaches.

Bus or Van – Whether you choose one of the full-size coaches or a minibus, the driver is going to introduce himself as "Uncle X" or "Cousin Y." It's an island tradition that all *kamaainas* are part of one big family, and on these tours they expect passengers to adopt the spirit. If you're gregarious, it's fine; if you're misanthropic, you'll find it cloying. The information the drivers spout is generally — but not always — accurate. If you like traveling in large groups, *Robert's Tours of Hawaii* (phone: 947-3939) and *Gray Line* (phone: 834-1033) operate large buses accommodating 30 or more people. The minibus tours, carrying a maximum of 16 people, are more personal and more popular with most visitors traveling alone or in couples. The Arizona Memorial Tour offered by *Polynesian Adventure Tours* (phone: 922-0888) takes in not only Pearl

Harbor but Punchbowl National Memorial Cemetery of the Pacific as well. On its Grand Circle Island Tour, admission to Waimea Falls Park and Byodo-In Buddhist Temple and a lunch stop are included; its Circle Island Beach & Picnic Tour has a beach picnic instead of the restaurant stop. *E Noa Tours* (phone: 599-2561) has a Circle Island Beach and Waterfall Tour that features Hanauma Bay, the Mormon Temple, North Shore surfing beaches, and a return to Waikiki over central Oahu's pineapple fields. A stop at Paradise Cove provides time for snorkeling. For active people, *Action Hawaii Adventures* (phone: 732-4453) offers day trips led by Hawaii-born-and-raised guides; the agenda includes a fully narrated island tour by van, hiking to the summit of Diamond Head, Boogie boarding (using a small surfboard, or Boogie board), and snorkeling from Waimanalo's exquisite beach (accompanied by certified lifeguards) for $69 (lunch extra). The *Moanalua Gardens Foundation* (phone: 839-5334) offers 4½-hour strolls through one of Oahu's most interesting valleys on the second Saturday and fourth Sunday of each month. Reservations required. *Charley's Sightseeing Tours* (phone: 531-2333) offers personalized limousine tours for $35 to $62 per hour, with a 2-hour minimum required. *Hawaiian Safari* (phone: 988-3999) offers 4-wheel-drive excursions ($60) of backwoods Oahu.

Plane and Helicopter – This is the only way, other than walking, to catch sight of many of Oahu's hidden mountains, cleft valleys, and waterfalls. Flying also provides a magnificent new perspective on favorite spots such as Hanauma Bay, Pearl Harbor, and Waimea Falls. *Papillon Hawaiian Helicopters* (phone: 836-1566; 800-367-7095) conducts tours ranging from 20 to 90 minutes. The shortest tour covers Waikiki to Makapuu, and a flight over the *pali* ($79). The Oahu Epic includes Windward Oahu, Haleiwa, the beaches of the North Shore, Pearl Harbor, as well as Waikiki ($187). The 90-minute Oahu-Molokai Experience starts at Waikiki and eastern Oahu before heading over to Molokai for a look-see at the Kalaupapa peninsula and the sea cliffs of the North Coast ($275). Departures are from Honolulu International. Prices include taxes and Waikiki hotel pickups. *Helicopters Hawaii* (phone: 836-3315) and *Hawaii International Helicopters* (phone: 839-5509) both depart Honolulu International Airport on charters (half-hour minimum) at $250 an hour for two, with four-passenger tours priced at $550 an hour. If you're on your own, *Makani Kai Helicopters* (phone: 834-5813), which departs Honolulu International, offers the best charter rates at $175 an hour for a one-passenger chopper. *Cherry Helicopters* (phone: 833-4339) operates charters from Honolulu International, and scheduled flightseeing tours from the *Turtle Bay Hilton,* including a 15-minute surfing tour ($50) and a half-hour Sacred Falls scenic tour ($100). For a quite different and infinitely pleasing experience in aerodynamics, drive to Dillingham Field in Mokuleia on the North Shore and take a ride in a bubble-top glider under the auspices of the *Honolulu Soaring Club* (phone: 677-3404), which charges $45 per person. *Hawaiian Airlines* (phone: 537-5100) has a multi-island day tour called Islands in the Sky; excursions are included on Maui and Kauai. The $275 cost includes all transfers, land tours, breakfast, and lunch. *Robert's* (phone: 523-9323) also feature overnight room and car excursions to the neighbor islands. Check the Sunday *Star Bulletin*'s Advertiser Travel Section for a full range of inter-island travel specials.

Submarine – *Atlantis Submarine* (phone: 536-2694; 800-548-6262) offers 45-minute excursions to the ocean floor in a state-of-the-art submarine from which spectators can view reefs and sea life through portholes. Groups depart the *Hilton Hawaiian Village* hotel in a catamaran for transfer to the 46-passenger submarine ($74; $48 for children under 12). Although the charge is hefty, the thrill the ride provides is worth it.

SPECIAL EVENTS: The *Hula Bowl,* played when you thought you could finally forget all about college football, takes place on the first or second Saturday in January at *Aloha Stadium,* Halawa Heights, and features all-stars from mainland college teams. The *Chinese New Year,* in mid-January to late February, is celebrated with traditional lion dances, drums, and firecrackers in Chinatown, downtown Honolulu. The Irish and would-be Irish celebrate with a lot of green and the traditional (and not so traditional) varieties of good cheer along Kalakaua Avenue, Waikiki, on *St. Patrick's Day,* March 17. A sunrise service is held each year at the Punchbowl National Memorial Cemetery of the Pacific on *Easter* morning. On May 1, a *Lei Day* queen is crowned at the *Waikiki Band Shell* in Kapiolani Park, where there is also a lei making contest and, at sunset, a hula show. In early June, there is a week-long *Festival of the Pacific,* highlighting the songs, dances, arts and crafts, and competitive sports of more than 40 Pacific Rim nations. The most spectacular annual parade in the islands is seen each June 11 on *Kamehameha the Great Day,* when King Kamehameha I's statue, opposite the Judiciary Building in downtown Honolulu, is festooned with 40-foot leis. The *50th State Fair* also takes place on weekends from late May to mid-June; it features foods, crafts, livestock shows, and entertainment and is held in the *Aloha Stadium.* July's *State Farm Fair,* held on McKinley High School grounds near the *Neal S. Blaisdell Center* downtown, provides a similar round of activities and a chance to mingle with locals. During the last 2 weeks of July (of even-numbered years), competitors in the *Transpacific Yacht Race,* who set off from San Pedro, California, on July 4, can be seen crossing the finish line off Diamond Head. The *Honolulu Symphony* begins its season at the *Blaisdell Concert Hall* in mid-September, with performances running through late April. Internationally renowned soloists are a highlight of the season, which also includes a December performance of Handel's *Messiah. Aloha Week,* the famous statewide celebration that on Oahu occupies the third or fourth week of September, sees a flower parade march from downtown to Waikiki as well as balls and luaus across the island. The *Honolulu Orchid Society Show,* held in October at the *Blaisdell Center,* offers lei-making and flower-arranging demonstrations as well as stunning floral displays. Also in October, there are the Hawaiian festivities of *makahiki* at Waimea Falls Park and the *Bud Light Championship Rodeo* in Waimea. If you're in town during the last week of November or the first week of December, check out the free films offered as part of the impressive, annual *Hawaii International Film Festival.* The *Honolulu Marathon* is held in early December, with competitors running a 26-mile course from the Aloha Tower to the band shell in Kapiolani Park. December 7, *Pearl Harbor Day,* is commemorated with a service at the Arizona Memorial. It is especially moving to see veterans of the attack who still make the pilgrimage here each December, some from as far away as New England and Florida. It is ironic, too, to see the numbers of curious Japanese tourists who visit Pearl Harbor that day. For a very special *Christmas* experience, go to the *Christmas Eve* Midnight Service at Kawaiahao Church (957 Punchbowl St.), where you can hear carols sung in Hawaiian. On *New Year's Eve* you can rub elbows with the locals at the *First Night* street fair, which is held on December 31 in downtown Honolulu from late afternoon through midnight.

SPORTS: The conventional sports and games enjoyed across America have their adherents here, too, and whether you come to watch or participate, you will find plenty to do.

FOR THE SPECTATOR

Oahu and surfing are synonymous, but if you think that surfing is the major spectator sport on the island, try again. Here, as elsewhere across America, football draws the largest crowds and stirs the strongest passions. Hearts are frequently broken, and small fortunes lost, on the results of the University of Hawaii *Rainbows'* games, whose home turf is the *Aloha Stadium* at Halawa Heights (phone: 486-9300). The classic *Rainbows'* confrontation is the Western Collegiate Conference game against Brigham Young University (the Utah division, not the small Oahu branch at Laie). *Aloha Stadium* is the site of the *Hula Bowl,* which features top players from US colleges. The *Pro Bowl,* featuring the all-stars from the National Football League, and the invitational collegiate *Aloha Bowl* are often held here as well. Local prep school and high school games also draw fanatical support. To observe island residents in action, it's worth going to a game between, for instance, St. Louis High and one of the tougher Western Oahu high schools, when the colorful behavior in the stands often outshines that on the field.

The *Rainbow Warriors,* the University of Hawaii's basketball team, also has its supporters, whose loyalty sometimes excels that of the football team's in quality if not in quantity. The *Warriors* play at the *Neal S. Blaisdell Center* (777 Ward Ave., Honolulu; phone: 521-2911), which also houses such events as horse and dog shows and wrestling and boxing matches on an irregular basis.

Hawaii's best-known surfing competitions are held during the Pro Tour season in December. The three major events of the *Corona Triple Crown* are the *Hard Rock Café* competition (late November to early December), the *Billabong Hawaiian Pro* (early December), and the *Marui Masters* (mid- to late December), all held at North Shore beaches. Other events also crop up frequently during the prime winter surf season, and good noncompetitive surfing is available just about any time the surf is up, particularly off North Shore or Makaha beaches.

Other aquatic events that attract spectators are the *Waikiki Annual Rough Water Swim,* in which men, women, and children of varying levels of ability race from Sans Souci Beach, on the Diamond Head side of Kapiolani Park, to Duke Kahanamoku Beach, in front of the *Hilton Hawaiian Village,* sometime during September; and the *Transpacific Yacht Races,* which start at San Pedro, California, on July 4 and reach the finish line at Diamond Head sometime between July 12 and 24, depending on the class of boat. Yachts race in odd-numbered years, multihulled boats such as catamarans and trimarans in even years.

Windsurfing competitions are also held throughout the year off Diamond Head Beach, where the ample lookouts from Diamond Head Road and Kailua Beach Park provide spectators with excellent viewing.

The island's golf classic is the *Hawaiian Open International Golf Tournament,* usually held in February at the ritzy *Waialae Golf and Country Club* (4997 Kahala Ave., Kahala; phone: 734-2151). Many people come to the *Hawaiian Open* for the aesthetic pleasure of watching the world's greatest golfers ease little white balls over what some experts consider Hawaii's finest greens. Others come simply because it is the only way they will ever be admitted to these hallowed grounds, where membership is as keenly prized by some as inclusion in East Coast social registers.

Head out to Mokuleia on the North Shore any Sunday between March and early December to catch first-rate polo at the *Hawaii Polo Club* (68-411 Farrington Hwy., Waialua; phone: 949-0061). The gates open at 11 AM for picnickers, who can set up their blankets before the match begins at 2 PM. Local teams often pit themselves against mainland or foreign competition, and Prince Charles is among those who have played in exhibition matches here. Food is available, or you can bring a picnic basket. Admission to the polo grounds is $5. The *Honolulu Polo Club* (phone: 533-7656), with its field fronting the Kalanianaole Highway in Waimanalo (25 minutes from Waikiki by car), also offers team play between April and October. The grounds open at 12:30 PM for picnicking. Matches start at 1 PM. There's a $5 admission charge and plenty of space to picnic.

Somewhat more esoteric events are outrigger canoe races and regattas held at various island beaches in the summer (check local newspapers) and off Haleiwa Beach during the *Haleiwa Sea Spree* in February; windsurfing and sailing regattas that take place off

Diamond Head Beach and Kailua Beach; cockfights, held at times and places that can be discovered only by personal inquiry; and darts tournaments, which take place occasionally at *Anna Banana's* bar, 2440 S. Beretania St., Honolulu (phone: 946-5190).

FOR THE PARTICIPANT

Bicycling – Except for parts of the desolate lava trail around Kaena Point, where you have to push a bike for a while, the Oahu coast is ideal for bicycling. There are no traumatic hills, and except for the northern corner of the Waianae Coast, food and refreshment are never too far away. All the best beaches and many sights of interest, such as the *Bishop Museum* and Waimea Falls Park, are accessible by bike. Some easy half-day or day rides out of Waikiki are Hanauma Bay, *Sea Life Park,* Makapuu Beach, the Kahala beaches, and Pearl Harbor. The routes through central Oahu climb from both north and south up to the central plateau, and unless you're in top condition, they would require walking a few miles. However, there is little to attract the tourist along these routes, and people coming to Haleiwa, for instance, from Waikiki via the Windward Coast might wish to return the same way. Two cautionary notes: Traffic on all the coast roads, especially on the Windward Coast and Southeast Oahu, is bad, and bike lanes, even though they do exist, are few. Thefts and vandalism of bicycles have been reported all over Oahu; the North Shore and the Waianae Coast seem to be spots where bikes and sometimes their riders are especially vulnerable.

For casual weekend outings with reliable guides, contact *Hawaii Bicycling League* (PO Box 4403, Honolulu, HI 96813; phone: 735-5756) for a schedule of its programs and excursions. Information about them is usually available in bike shops. If you're planning a stay of several months, check *Goodwill Vocational Training Centers,* where there are occasionally good bargains in standard secondhand bikes. Two locations are in downtown Honolulu (780 S. Beretania St.; phone: 536-4115; and 2028 Dillingham; phone: 842-1000).

Boating – Although dozens of operators are anxious to sail you down to Pearl Harbor or along the Waikiki shore with a mai tai in hand, surprisingly few places offer boat rentals or instruction. *Jada Yacht Charters* (phone: 955-0772) and *Honolulu Sailing Company* (phone: 239-3900) offer skippered yacht charters.

Body-Surfing – The Diamond Head end of Prince Kuhio Beach in the 2400 block of Kalakaua Avenue offers some of the best body-surfing in Waikiki. Kalama Beach, in Kailua between Kalaka Place and Kaione Place where large surfboards are forbidden, is another favorite spot. Makapuu Beach, on Kalanianaole Highway just beyond Koko Head, is one of the loveliest places on Oahu to while away an afternoon, and it is also the most famous body-surfing beach on the island. Although Makapuu lies between two rocky points, there are no exposed rocks on the beach in the summer (they do appear after the erosion caused by the winter surf), and there is no offshore reef. These conditions mean that when you ride in on a strong but slow-rolling wave, you land — with luck, not too heavily — on firm sand. Here again a caveat is in order: Easy as it might look when you see people performing nonchalantly all around, if you have no experience of body-surfing, this is not the place to learn. Those waves are not always the gentle giants they appear to be. Note that body-surfing here in the winter is lethal and that boards — except for the small *paipo* kind — are forbidden at any time of the year.

Fishing – Au, ahi, ono, mahimahi, opakapaka, aku: If these names are music to your ears, head for the Kewalo Boat Basin on Ala Moana Boulevard across from the *Ward Warehouse.* Here you will find boats ranging in size from 35 feet to over 60 feet available for charter by the day, half day, or for several days. They are chartered mostly by groups of six and sometimes more, but it is not unusual to be able to buy one or two shares in a cruise. If you're not quite sure what you want, your best bet is to go to the basin in the late afternoon when the boats return and talk to passengers and owners to decide who is offering the trip that suits you best. If you are commandeering the complete boat, then the outing is tailored according to your needs. Among the better-known operations, all of which supply tackle and bait (lunch and beverage may be supplied at extra charge), are *Island Charters* (phone: 536-1555); *Coreene C's Sport Fishing* (phone: 247-2040 or 226-8421), whose deluxe vessel, the *Coreene C,* once brought back to shore a 1,805-pound marlin, the largest ever caught off Oahu; *Ocean Adventures* (phone: 487-9060); *Golden Eagle Marine Charter Services* (phone: 531-4966); and *Ilima V* (phone: 521-2087), all in Kewalo Basin. Pokai Bay, on the Waianae Coast, and Haleiwa, on the North Shore, are other places where you can find charters.

At Haleiwa you will also find people fishing for mullet from the bridge across the Anahulu River. At Kaiaka Bay, about a half mile west, crabs can be found where Paukauila Stream empties into the ocean. At Kaaawa, on the Windward Coast, people seek out squid with spears. Pole fishing is popular all along the Waianae Coast, at the Haleiwa beaches, and along the North Shore between Waialee Beach and Kaihalulu Beach. Oio (bonefish) and moi (threadfish) are some of the catches you might make. For information on fishing in Hawaii, get a copy of the monthly *Hawaiian Charter Fishing Guide* by writing PO Box P, Kailua-Kona, HI 96745 (phone: 800-367-8014).

Football – For those who dream of trampling a 250-pound lineman underfoot, NFL Properties and Dream Week, Inc. now offer a football fantasy camp. The "NFL Pro Bowl Dream Week" will take place during *Pro Bowl Week* in Honolulu for a week at the end of January. Participants will receive football instruction from such NFL legends as Gale Sayers, Don Maynard, Paul Warfield, Mel Blount, and Ted Hendricks. Everyone will compete at the end of the week in a big pre-Pro Bowl game of flag football (your bones should remain reasonably intact) at *Aloha Stadium* — and survivors will attend the Pro Bowl game itself the next day. The Dream Week costs $4,995, which includes 6 nights at the *Hilton Hawaiian Village,* transportation to all activities, continental breakfast, lunch, a luau, uniforms, commemorative personal football cards and video, and reserved seating at the Pro Bowl game, along with the former pros. Information: Dream Week, Inc., 2617 Huntingdon Pike, Huntingdon Valley, PA 19006 (phone: 215-938-1200; 800-888-4376).

Golf – If you're serious about golf in Honolulu, you move to Kahala or Diamond Head, fill out an application form for the *Waialae Country Club* (4997 Kahala Ave.; phone: 734-2151), and wait for a member to die so that you can move up a place on the waiting list. It has the most prestigious greens and the swankiest 19th hole on Oahu, and people have been known to divorce and remarry just to be able to say they belong. Non-members have to make do with the 15 other courses on the island that are open to the public (regardless of pedigree or bank balance), but require greens fees of anywhere from $4 at some municipal courses to $120 at a few resorts (cart included). In addition to the municipal, private, and resort golf courses, several of the military facilities on Oahu have their own. If you're glued to Waikiki, the place to head is the *Ala Wai* golf course (404 Kapahulu Ave.; phone: 296-4653), constructed on what once were waterlogged taro fields. *Ala Wai* is very flat and not particularly challenging. However, it is a pleasant place to stand around looking at the Koolau Range and Diamond Head, which is what a lot of people do while waiting to start on this very busy course. Statistics for the course are 18 holes, 6,000 yards, par 70. Other municipal courses include *Pali* golf course (18 holes, 6,950 yards, par 72; 45-050 Kamehameha Hwy., Kaneohe; phone: 261-9784), which is the one you look down on from the Pali Lookout; and *Kahuku* golf course (9 holes, 2,700 yards, par 35; Kahuku; phone: 293-5842), which is right on the ocean in the northeast section of the island, but has neither a pro shop nor carts. At press time, 40 new courses were being planned all around the island, including a municipal course next to the *Pali* golf course. Controversy over land use and water supplies, however, and high development fees and zoning restrictions will likely quash many of these tee-off proposals.

Three resorts with first class golf are the *Sheraton Makaha* resort, the *Turtle Bay Hilton,* and *Ko Olina*. The *Sheraton Makaha* course (18 holes, 6,398 yards, par 72; phone: 695-9511) straddles the low, rolling hillside between the imperious walls of the Makaha Valley. It is bisected by the Makaha Stream and has reputedly the highest stroke rating in Hawaii. If you hear shrieking here, it's not the pro making critical comments but peacocks looking for attention in the undergrowth. Adjacent to the *Makaha* course is the *Makaha Valley Country Club's East* course (18 holes, 6,369 yards, par 71; phone: 695-7111), whose hilly grounds appear deceptively simple. The championship course at the *Turtle Bay Hilton* (18 holes, 6,400 yards, par 70; phone: 293-8574) is another oceanside challenge. Opened late in 1992, the new Arnold Palmer–designed course (18 holes, 7,084 yards, par 72) provides flat fairways made redoubtable by water hazards on the front nine, as well as water hazards and windbreak trees on the back nine. The hotel's original 18-hole course designed by George Fazio (currently closed), will be reborn as a second Palmer-designed course (18 holes, 6,873 yards, par 72); the *Turtle Bay* makeover is likely to open for play late next year. *Ko Olina* (18 holes, 6,867 yards, par 72; phone: 676-5300), owned by a subsidiary of *Japan Airlines,* opened near the Ewa district, west of Honolulu, in 1990. The course's designer, Ted Robinson, put water hazards on eight of its holes, making a round here much more interesting. All resorts have fully equipped pro shops. The *Makaha Valley Country Club* (phone: 695-9578), adjacent to the *Sheraton Makaha* resort, was formerly a private enclave but is now open to the public (the course is 18 holes, 6,369 yards, par 71). *Hawaii Kai Championship Course* and par 3 holes of the *Hawaii Kai Executive Course* (both at 8902 Kalanianaole Hwy.; phone: 395-2358) have magnificent views of the Kaiwi Channel to distract you. There is a pro shop attached and lessons are available (*Championship* course: 18 holes, 6,350 yards, par 72; *Executive* course: 18 holes, 2,386 yards, par 55). At *Mililani Golf Club* (18 holes, 6,360 yards, par 72; Mililani Town; phone: 623-2222), instruction is available for the whole family. Other courses include *Moanalua Golf Club* (9 holes, 2,972 yards, par 36; 1250 Ala Aolani; phone: 839-2411), on the *ewa* (west) side of Moanalua Valley, near the bubble gum pink Oahu landmark, Tripler Army Medical Center; the *Olomana Golf Links* (18 holes, 6,081 yards, par 72; 41-1801 Kalanianaole Hwy., Waimanalo; phone: 259-7926); and *Pearl Country Club* (18 holes, 6,750 yards, par 72; 98-535 Kaonohi St., Honolulu; phone: 487-3802), where you need to call for a starting time.

Golf tours, which include in their cost hotel pickup, clubs, greens fees, and carts, are available from *Kato's Golf* (phone: 947-3010).

Hang Gliding – *The Fall of Icarus* is the name of a painting by Pieter Brueghel the Elder, and modern Icaruses still occasionally fall to their death along the Windward Coast in spite of the steadily increasing amount of know-how and streamlined equipment available. The ridges above *Sea Life Park* are a popular takeoff point in southeastern Oahu, and when the wind conditions are right, colorful airborne flotillas drift between Kailua and Makapuu Point. If you want to have a go, *Tradewinds Hang Gliding Center* (phone: 396-8557) has certified instructors who urge beginners from sand dunes and lead advanced fliers soaring over the *palis.* Tandem flights with a certified instructor are also offered.

Hiking – It is entirely possible to see and appreciate Oahu's coastline by car, assuming that you stop here and there to savor the beaches and the mountain peaks more fully. To penetrate what remains of "hidden Oahu" — the rain forests, a crater or two, and the back reaches of Makaha Valley — walking is the only way. Many of the trails that are marked on maps belong to the federal government or the military or are privately owned. All the hikes referred to below require only will power, varying degrees of stamina, a good pair of hiking boots, and in some cases, supplies of fresh water. (Diamond Head also requires a permit for groups of 25 or more.)

Manoa Falls: This is the most accessible and one of the easiest trails in the Honolulu area, leading through dense, brooding rain forests in the mountains and valleys that can be seen from Waikiki. On either side of the trail, which for part of the way is a stone footpath, are flaming ti leaves, brilliant ginger, mountain apple, hau trees, and colorful thimbleberry and passion fruit vines. You can cool off by dangling your feet in the Manoa Stream, at the bottom of the falls, though if the rains have been particularly heavy — 200 inches in 1 year is not unheard of — it is wise to stand clear in case boulders come tumbling over the cataract. To reach the trail, drive to the end of Manoa Road just past Paradise Park and the Lyon Arboretum. Park close to the chain strung across the road; the trail begins on the other side of it in front of a high stone wall.

Mount Tantalus: This 1,200-foot peak provides a lush backdrop for Honolulu, with many excellent forest and ridgeline trails. Some trails, 15 minutes from the road and winding their way to within 150 feet of the summit, are reminiscent of those along the Na Pali Coast on Kauai. Some popular options include the West Manoa Cliffs Trail (full circuit, 4½ miles) and the Makiki Loop Trail (full circuit, 2½ miles).

Diamond Head: Just about everybody knows what it looks like from the outside, but not many people have explored it from within. The crater was a major installation in the defense of the Pacific in World War II and is still part of Fort Ruger and used by the Hawaiian National Guard. Bunkers, shelters, and gun redoubts are still in evidence, and part of the climb up to Point Leahi, the highest point on the crater rim, leads you through gun emplacements and up steel stairways and ladders. From the top, the view of Honolulu, Waikiki, and the ocean is memorable. The crater is open from 6 AM to 6 PM daily. To reach the trail head, drive up Monsarrat Avenue into Diamond Head Road and take the right turn into the crater just beyond the junction with Makapuu Avenue. The trail begins at the parking area by the firing range in the middle of the crater and is paved much of the way. The escorted tours of *Action Hawaii Adventures* (phone: 944-6754) feature hikes to the summit of Diamond Head.

Lanipo Trail: This hike is for the physically fit. It takes about 6 hours and runs along the crest of Mauumae Ridge to an elevation of almost 2,500 feet through groves of koa and ohia trees reminiscent of the Big Island. Around the tree trunks you will see the small white flowers of the *kopiko* shrub, and here and there are dense growths of red *ieie* and wildernesses of tropical ferns. You may even glimpse Kaau Crater, seen by few islanders and fewer tourists. These southeastern reaches of the Koolau Range also have abundant birdlife, and you will most likely see Japanese white-eye (small and greenish, with yellow throat and broad white ring around the eye), apapane (deep red with black wings and tail), and amakihi (yellowish green with a curved bill). If you are lucky, you may catch sight of an elepaio (brown uppers, white hindquarters, cocked tail) or a shama (shiny black with a reddish brown belly, white hindquarters, and a black and white tail). If you don't see the shama you may hear it; its song is lovely. The trail starts at Maunalani Circle at the top of Wilhelmina Rise.

Some other Oahu hikes are Makaha Valley: Easy trails lead up to the back reaches of the valley from the *Sheraton Makaha,* where partridge and wild turkey can be heard and/or seen. Koko Head Cliff Walk: A rocky shelf between the ocean and the road leads from Hanauma Bay to the Blowhole. It is a beautiful, 2-mile seaside ramble above tidal pools and past caves. Waves along the coast can be very deceptive even on calm days, and someone has to keep an eye on the surf at all times. If you're walking alone, that means you. This trail is not recommended for children. Makua Gulch: A pool of refreshing mountain water awaits you at the end of this densely overgrown canyon on the northern windward slopes of the Koolau Range. The State Division of Forestry (1151 Punchbowl St., Honolulu, HI 96814; phone: 587-0166) issues permits for hiking trails that cross state lands. The division also has a selection of trail maps that cover the island. Office hours are from 7:45 AM to 4:30 PM, with maps and permits available in Room 325. This is an excellent source of information for serious hikers on Oahu and the Neighbor Islands.

If you want to hike Oahu with people familiar with the island's trails, check with the *Hawaiian Trail and Mountain Club* (PO Box 2238, Honolulu, HI 96804), the *Hawaii Nature Center* (2131 Makiki Heights Dr., Honolulu, HI 96822; phone 973-0100), and the Hawaiian chapter of the *Sierra Club* (PO Box 2577, Honolulu, HI 96803; phone: 538-6616), all of which conduct hikes at fairly regular intervals. Before venturing forth, you might read Craig Chisholm's *Hawaiian Hiking Trails* (Touchstone Press; $9.95) or *Hiking Oahu, The Capital Island,* by Robert Smith, both of which are jammed with facts and make delightful reading whether you set foot on a trail or not.

Horseback Riding – Some of the best riding on Oahu is up into the wilderness in the little-known back reaches of Makaha Valley: The *Sheraton Makaha* (phone: 695-9511) conducts hour-long escorted rides for guests ($20) as well as the public ($22). The *Turtle Bay Hilton* (in Kahuku; phone: 293-8811) offers escorted rides to its guests ($24) and the public ($25) through palm and ironwood groves along beautiful deserted beaches. In the southeast of the island, lessons are available from *Koko Crater Stables* (408 Kealahou St., Honolulu; phone: 395-2628). The *Kualoa Ranch* (49-560 Kamehameha Hwy., Honolulu; phone: 237-8515) features 1- and 2-hour trail rides ($20 and $30, respectively) into the undeveloped valleys that stretch inland from the Windward Coast.

Hunting – Wild pig, wild goat, pheasant, quail, partridge, and wild turkey are all present on Oahu. Although there are 12 designated hunting areas on the island, most fairly inaccessible, there are no guides or tourist services available for the visitor who would like a day's rough shooting. Hunting activities and the issuing of licenses are controlled by the State of Hawaii Department of Land and Natural Resources, Conservation and Resources Division, 1151 Punchbowl St., Room 330, Honolulu, HI 96813 (phone: 548-5919).

Kayaking – *Go Bananas,* near Waikiki (732 Kapahulu Ave.; phone: 737-9514), offers hour-long lessons for $20. Rentals are available for experienced kayakers only. *Twogood Kayak Hawaii* (171-B Hamakua Dr., Kailua; phone: 262-5656) offers lessons ($45 an hour), rentals ($20 for a half day; $25 full day; and $40 weekend), as well two-person tandem kayaks ($35 for a half day; $45 full day). *Twogood* also offers escorted kayak tours ($65) that travel through Kailua Bay and the Mokulua islands 1 mile off Oahu. *Ocean Kayak* (phone: 239-9803), in windward Kahulu, offers half-day rentals for $15, full-day rentals for $25 for kayaking on Kaneohe Bay. Closed Sundays. Kayaking fans can contact *Hui Waa Kaukahi* (*hui* is Hawaiian for fellowship, or club) for information on conditions or planned excursions (phone: 263-6249).

Parasailing – *Aloha Parasail* (phone: 521-2446) will transport its clients from Waikiki hotels to its takeoff site at Pier 2. Another parasail company is *Waikiki Beach Services* (phone: 924-4941).

Polo – The *Hawaii Polo School* (phone: 637-7656; 949-0061) offers private instruction on the grounds of the *Hawaii Polo Club* and packages that include lessons, play, horses, equipment, and accommodations in a cottage at the *Mokuleia Beach Colony,* adjacent to the polo field. Cost per student is $90 for a 1½-hour lesson, $2,400 for the week-long package.

Scuba Diving – Hanauma Bay, a marine life conservation park, is a good place for beginners. The coral formations, marine plants, marine life, and shells here are more interesting than those found along the Waikiki reefs. An illustrated board on the beach shows you the best spots for diving and what you can expect to find. Several dive shops along the bay operate Mondays through Fridays. Another good spot for beginners is Sans Souci Beach, Waikiki, just *ewa* (west) of the *Kaimana Beach* hotel. More experienced divers can choose more glamorous locations. Divers off Manana Island, popularly known as Rabbit Island, off the Windward Coast, can descend to 60 feet to examine the corals covering the Koolau basalt on the ocean bottom. Fantasy Reef, off Waialae Beach at Kahala, is accessible only by boat. Divers like to come here to see giant sea turtles and watch huge manta rays show off by swimming upside down and turning somersaults. There is more good diving at Laie Beach, on the northern section of the Windward Coast, especially in the reefs between Laie and Laniloa Point. You may find lobster ambling around here as well as the usual dazzling array of tropical fish. In the summer, when the ocean thereabouts is very calm, Haleiwa Beach can be rewarding for the diver.

There are a number of professional operations in Honolulu to help the diver and the would-be diver. Among the best known are *Dan's Dive Shop* (660 Ala Moana Blvd., Honolulu; phone: 536-6181), *Steve's Diving Adventures* (1860 Ala Moana Blvd., Honolulu; phone: 947-8900), *Aloha Dive Shop* (Koko Marina, Hawaii Kai, Honolulu; phone: 395-5922), *Ocean Adventures* (98-406 Kam Hwy., Pearl City; phone: 487-9060); and *Waikiki Diving* (1734 Kalakaua Ave., Honolulu; phone: 955-5151), all of which offer instruction for ingenues and brush-up courses for those with some experience. *Aquaventure* (phone: 734-2211) offers in-pool introductory lessons and charter dives from the *Kahala Hilton.* Free van transfers are provided to and from Waikiki. *South Seas Aquatics* (870 Kapahulu Ave., Honolulu; phone: 735-0437; and 2155 Kalahaua Ave., Waikiki Beach; phone: 922-0852) offers two-tank dives off the Waianae Coast out of Waianae boat harbor. Divers can explore coastal sea caves and inspect a World War II boat that rests on the sandy bottom 85 feet below the surface. All these operators make Waikiki hotel pickups and returns. The *Leeward Dive Center* (87-066 Farrington Hwy., Maili; phone: 696-3414) explores some of the most fascinating waters along the rocky north Waianae Coast. (Give them a day's advance notice.) Guests at the *Turtle Bay Hilton* (Kahuku; phone: 293-8811) can avail themselves of free scuba instruction in the hotel pool. Those who take to the pastime can arrange for ocean dive tours (for certified or non-certified divers) through the LRS Pool Services desk at the hotel.

Snorkeling – This is not the poor or timid man's version of scuba diving, but a quite separate experience — gentle, meditative, and occasionally thrilling. Hanauma Bay, once again, is the paradise among snorkeling spots on Oahu. Friendly fish really will rub noses with you, though enticing them with a crust of bread or cookie crumbs is a no-no even though the habit appears to be growing. Check the display board on the beach for the best snorkeling areas. In Waikiki, Sans Souci Beach is the best place for snorkeling. The North Shore beaches, deadly to all but the most expert surfers in the winter, are ideal for snorkeling on calm summer days, especially Waimea Bay Beach, Sunset Beach, and Pupukea Bay Beach. At Pupukea, from a panoramic vantage point on the surface of the lovely tidal pools known collectively and erroneously as Shark's Cove, you can glimpse some quite large fish cruising idly over the sponges on the ocean bottom. Kahe Beach Park and Nanakuli Beach, off the Farrington Highway on the Waianae Coast, provide interesting snorkeling right along the shoreline. If you are a snorkeling buff, it might be worth comparing experiences of the windward side of the island, with its abundant offshore reefs, to those of the Waianae side, where offshore reefs are extremely scarce.

Hanauma Bay day trips are offered by *Hanauma Bay Snorkeling Tours* (phone: 944-8828), which includes hotel or condo transfers and equipment. In addition, most beach hotels in Waikiki and many off-beach hotels rent snorkeling equipment to guests. *Waikiki Beach Services* (phone: 924-4941) is one of a number of equipment rental concessions along Waikiki Beach. *Captain Bob's* (phone: 926-5077) makes hotel pick-ups before heading to Kaneohe Bay for a picnic snorkel cruise ($65; $45 for children 17 and under) with the Windward Coast as a backdrop. *Barefoot Catamaran Cruises* (phone: 532-3150; 800-522-1538) departs Kewalo Basin for the marine preserve just off Diamond Head. It offers a half-day excursion ($80) that uses the catamaran as a reef-side base. Zodiac raft excursions use the reef for snorkeling which is the equal of that offered at Hanauma Bay. Deepwater options closer to the catamaran include an on-board water slide, easy-access ladder, and scuba-style viewing of sea life that includes spinner dolphins and sea turtles.

Surfing – This is Oahu's top "glamour" sport, the one that brings visitors to the islands the way skiing brings them to Colorado and grouse shooting to Scotland. In the popular imagination, Waikiki Beach is, along with Bondi Beach near Sydney, Australia, one of the two most famous surfing spots in the world. Hawaiian royalty surfed here generations ago, and the 2- to 5-foot waves that are standard along the celebrated shoreline for much of the year are perfect for novices and amateurs. On the few days in the summer when they reach 15 feet, Waikiki's waves should be avoided by all but experts. There are many concessions on the beach that rent surfboards and have licensed instructors on hand. *Beach Boys Inc.* (phone: 923-0711; ask for beach services) and *Waikiki Beach Services* (phone: 924-4940/4941) both offer equipment rental and lessons ($25 an hour) for surfing, jet skis, outriggers, and so on. A major drawback for surfers on Waikiki Beach is that it is almost always crowded. The nearest beach off the strip that is safe enough for the casual surfer is Ala Moana Beach Park, just *ewa* (west) of the Ala Wai Canal between the ocean and the 1200 block of Ala Moana Boulevard. Farther afield, Haleiwa Beach Park, in the 6200 block of Kamehameha Highway, on the North Shore, is good for beginners when the surf is low between April and October. Kalama Beach, reached by the public right of way at the end of L'Orange Place or Kalaka Place, off North Kalaheo Avenue in Kailua, is one of the most beautiful surfing spots on Oahu for novices and casual surfers. Board surfing, except on *paipo* boards less than 3 feet long, is forbidden on Kalama Beach between Kalaka Place and Kai One Place. Expert and champion surfers head for Makaha Beach and Yokohama Beach, Farrington Highway on Oahu's Waianae Coast, which have some of the most impressive surf in Hawaii during the winter, and for such notorious North Shore spots as Sunset Beach, Ehukai Beach Park, home of the legendary Banzai Pipeline, and Waimea Bay Beach Park, all of which are along the Kamehameha Highway east of Haleiwa.

If you're traveling without equipment, *Local Motion Surfboards* (1714 Kapiolani Blvd., near the *Ala Moana Shopping Center* in Honolulu; phone: 955-7873) sells and rents used surfboards and Boogie boards. The store also has experts on duty to advise newcomers on what particular kind of equipment suits which particular area. Surfers who are pretty sure of what they want in terms of size, shape, weight, and skegs (fins), should try one of the following businesses in Honolulu, all of which supply custom surfboards along with whatever esoteric details may be requested: *Blue Hawaii* (1960 Kapiolani Blvd.; phone: 947-5115), *Downing Hawaii* (3021 Waialae Ave.; phone: 737-9696), or *Hawaiian Island Creations* (*Ala Moana Shopping Center;* phone: 941-4491).

Swimming and Sunning – High surf and strong currents are characteristic of every beach on Oahu at some time or another. It may not be very romantic or particularly intrepid, but the smart thing to do is to stick to beaches where there are lifeguards. If you're uncertain about the water conditions on any particular day, ask them; they can tell you whether those gently rolling waves are disguising a mischievous (or worse) current. Other hazards to look out for are surfboards; rare raids by Portuguese man-of-war jellyfish when the wind is in the right direction; and coral, a living organism that can cause nasty gashes and infections. Sharks pose no threat in Hawaiian waters except under the most unusual conditions.

Waikiki Beach, from Duke Kahanamoku Lagoon in front of the *Hilton Hawaiian Village* to the *Outrigger Canoe Club* at the Diamond Head end, is the most popular — and one of the safest — swimming areas on the island. The area in front of Waikiki Beach Center is considered ideal for the casual swimmer. Queen's Surf Beach, a few hundred yards south of Waikiki Beach Center, is popular because it has lawns behind it on which to relax after exercising. *Kamaainas* like Ala Moana Beach Park. On the windward side of the island, Kailua Beach Park, at the very end of Kailua Road in Kailua, is a beautiful white strand that slopes gently into deep waters that are calm most (but not all) days of the year. At Kalama Beach, also in Kailua, the shoreline is steeper and the currents stronger; however, for experienced ocean swimmers, there should be no problem. The bonus here is the absence by law of all surfboards (except the small, *paipo* kind) within a restricted area of about a half mile. Farther north, Kahana Bay Beach Park is another place where a gentle slope to deeper waters makes for safe, pleasant bathing. When the waters are quiet in the summer you can swim at Ehukai Park, home of the Banzai Pipeline, and at Waimea Bay on the North Shore; then, later, at home, you can say "I swam there!" as the huge winter surf rolls across your television screen. For a quite different experience, hike up to Sacred Falls from Plantation Road, which turns off the Kamehameha Highway between Punaluu and Hauula. At the end of the hour-long trek, at the bottom of the falls, there is a lovely swimming hole that can be downright bracing.

Tennis – There are public courts at 40 places around Oahu, all under the supervision of the County of Honolulu Department of Parks and Recreation, Tennis Division (3908 Paki Ave., Honolulu, HI 96815; phone: 971-2500), which will supply a complete list of addresses to anyone requesting it with a self-addressed, stamped envelope. Public courts in the Waikiki area are *Ala Moana Tennis Center* (1201 Ala Moana Blvd.; phone: 522-7031), 10 lighted courts; *Diamond Head Tennis Center* (3908 Paki Ave.; phone: 971-7150), 9 courts; and *Kapiolani Tennis Courts,* at 2748 Kalakaua Ave., which has 4 courts. Play is on a first-come, first-served basis. *Honolulu Tennis Club* (2220 S. King St.; phone: 944-9696) has 4 courts and an instructor for lessons.

Waikiki hotels with tennis facilities are the *Hawaiian Regent* (2552 Kalakaua Ave.; phone: 922-6611), with 1 court, professional instruction, and a pro shop; the *Outrigger Malia* (2211 Kuhio Ave.; phone: 923-7621), with 1 court; and the *Pacific Beach* (2490 Kalakaua Ave.; phone: 922-1233), with 2 courts. The *Ilikai* (in Waikiki at 1777 Ala Moana Blvd.; phone: 949-3811) has complete tennis facilities, with a resident pro, a pro shop, 4 day courts, 1 lighted court, and 1 lesson court, and offers instruction for singles, couples, or groups. *Peter Burwash International* (phone: 946-1236) also offers private lessons at the *Ilikai.* Outside Waikiki, the *Sheraton Makaha* in Makaha (phone: 695-9511) has 4 courts, a pro shop, and professional instruction; and the *Turtle Bay Hilton* (in Kahuku; phone: 293-8811) has 10 courts (4 lighted for night play) operated by tennis coach Nick Bollettieri, who provides a director for single or group instruction. Bollettieri also offers tennis camp programs at the *Turtle Bay Hilton* (phone: 800-USA-NICK).

Water Skiing – The novice to the advanced water skier will find fine opportunities in the Koko Marina Lagoon in Hawaii Kai by contacting the *Water Ski Center* (phone: 395-3773).

Windsurfing – After racquetball, windsurfing may be the fastest growing sport in the US. Kailua Beach Park and Diamond Beach Park see most of the action; you can occasionally spot equipment designers and practice teams testing new equipment here. *Naish Hawaii* (155A Hamakua Dr., Kailua; phone: 261-3539), owned by windsurfing champion Robbie Naish, has a wide selection of boards for people just learning as well as for windsurfing whizzes. The same organization runs the *Kailua Beach School,* which promotes windsurfing tours for beginners and advanced sailors on the Windward Coast, where whales are sometimes spotted, and has a 3-hour introductory course. Private lessons ($50 for 1½ hours) are also available for people eager to master the skill of wave jumping.

AROUND THE ISLAND

Oahu looks vaguely like a square with an appendage off the lower right-hand corner. It has six distinct geographic areas: the southern flatlands, including the Ewa district, Pearl Harbor, and Honolulu; southeast Oahu, a triangle, with Honolulu, Kailua, and Koko Head forming its three points; the wet and very green narrow strip known as the Windward Coast in the east; the North Shore; central Oahu, a broad valley between the Koolau Range in the east and the Waianae Mountains in the west; and the Waianae Coast, on the dry, leeward side of the Waianae Mountains. The highest point in the Koolau Range is Puu Konahuanui, at 3,105 feet, and the tallest peak in the Waianaes is Kaala, at 4,025 feet. The words *north, south, east,* and *west* are heard on Oahu, but the island has some special terms to indicate directions that are not just picturesque but are in constant daily use. The two that are common throughout the islands are *mauka,* which means inland or toward the mountains (from Waikiki, for instance, the *Ala Wai Golf Course* is *mauka* the Ala Wai Canal; "go *mauka* along Kapahulu Avenue to the golf course"); and *makai,* toward the sea (from the golf course, Waikiki is *makai* of the Ala Wai Canal; "go *makai* along Kapahulu Avenue to Waikiki"). Two terms that are used only on Oahu and more precisely in the Honolulu area are *ewa,* which indicates west (Ewa is a district west of Honolulu); and Diamond Head, which is Honolulu talk for east. (*TheBus* goes *ewa* along Kalakaua Avenue; "walk two blocks Diamond Head.") Between Diamond Head and Koko Head, east becomes "Koko Head;" west is either still *ewa* or Diamond Head. It is not nearly so difficult as it sounds and is really rather exotic, one of the traditions on Oahu that has not been tainted by commercialism.

Waikiki

From ancient times, Oahu's chiefs made Waikiki something of a royal playground. Then, in the early 19th century, Kamehameha I, the warrior king, built a *pili* (grass shack) on Waikiki Beach for his favorite wife, Queen Kaahumanu. This lovely and serene stretch of sand, with its backdrop of coconut groves, luminous rainbows, and the romantic Koolau Mountains, was already a favorite swimming and surfing spot for Oahu's *alii* (nobility) long before Kamehameha conquered the island. Subsequent monarchs built cottages; and eventually two hotels, the white, New England–style *Moana* and the raffish and roseate hacienda-style *Royal Hawaiian,* both still flourishing, were constructed to accommodate the mainlanders who had been attracted by Mark Twain's *Letter from the Sandwich Islands* and Isabella Bird's *Six Months in the Sandwich Islands.*

Military personnel who knew Hawaii only in the uncertain days of World War II tell of the long and lonely stretches of beach that remained in Waikiki even then. The great building boom started in the 1950s, and today the *Royal Hawaiian* and the *Moana* are dwarfed and obscured by concrete high-rises that have mushroomed around them, with dozens along the beach and Kalakaua Avenue alone. The coconut groves that used to merge with the taro fields and swamp between the beach and the mountains are all but gone. The swamp in turn has been drained, and Waikiki is now defined on its *ewa* (west) and *mauka* (inland) sides by the Ala Wai Canal, a moat shaped like a hockey stick, with the handle pointing toward Diamond Head and the blade into the Yacht Harbor across from Ala Moana Park. The canal and Diamond Head provide Waikiki with neat boundaries encompassing an area about 2 miles long and a half-mile wide.

This small space, chock full of hotels, condominiums, and shopping malls, is for many people what Hawaii is all about. It has been compared to Coney Island, Miami Beach, Babylon, and Paradise. It is none of these, though it does have touches of them all, especially the first three. This may be the island tropics, but Waikiki is every bit an urban resort — a situation that prompted the city and state to create landscaped pedestrian malls on both sides of Kalakaua Avenue at a cost of $10 million. In recent years, nearly a billion dollars have been spent to keep Waikiki up-to-date and competitive, with the upgrading of nearly all its numerous high-rise hotels.

The most controversial issue at the moment revolves around plans for a mass-transit line. Recently, it was excluded from master plans for development in Waikiki into the 21st century (along with a new convention center) in an attempt to contain Waikiki's already heavily developed half-square-mile area. Although a year-long moratorium on new construction in Waikiki came to an end early last year, Waikiki's suburban image is long gone.

First, it should be said that the mountains, which are never far away and seldom out of sight, the rainbows, the constant presence of Diamond Head, and the often spectacular sunsets are reminders that there is something more special about the place than just the high-rises that line Kalakaua and Kuhio Avenues. There is an occasional touch of drama, class, or elegance; a glimpse inside the *Hyatt Regency, Royal Hawaiian, Hilton Hawaiian Village,* the *Hawaii Prince, Sheraton Moana Surfrider,* or *Halekulani* will confirm that. There are also a dozen restaurants in the area that can deservedly be labeled first class — a claim that can be made for few other tropical resort areas in the US — and there are quiet, sophisticated places where intimacy is possible to the accompaniment of soft music. There are narrow streets where tall coconut palms grow, not straight and sentinel as city planners might like them to be, but slightly bent and wobbly. And then there are the beaches, safe for swimming, where waters are usually clear and smooth. There are surfboards for riding the waves; outrigger canoes; catamarans for day and evening sails; and the dazzling cascades of bejeweled lights as seen from the *Sheraton Waikiki's Hanohano Room; Annabelle's,* atop the *Ilikai;* and *Nicholas Nickolas,* atop the *Ala Moana* hotel.

Then there is the other side — seamy, commercial, and aesthetically offensive. Street-cruising prostitutes peddle their wares. Touts offer a tour, luau, and extravaganza tickets at one-third the regular price, the snag being that beforehand the buyer must attend a cocktail party where time-sharing accommodations are being hawked. And the shopping malls often feature a mix of designer boutiques, art galleries, and kitsch souvenir shops. After a few days or a week of this commercial overkill and street crowds, Waikiki may no longer seem much of a Polynesian paradise.

Beaches – Waikiki consists of not one but a series of beaches, stretching from Duke Kahanamoku Beach on the *ewa* (west) fringe of Waikiki to Sans Souci Beach at the

Diamond Head end of Kalakaua Avenue. Swimming is good for almost the entire length of the beach, the exception being from the western end of Kuhio Beach Park to the Kapahulu Wall, an easily identifiable landmark along the shoreline. Some features of the beaches, going from east to west, are these: At Duke Kahanamoku Beach, in front of the *Hilton Hawaiian Village,* there is a manmade lagoon of clear waters with a soft sandy bottom. Fort DeRussy Beach Park, just beyond, is a popular sunning spot for military personnel staying at the *Hale Koa,* a hotel for armed forces staff and their families. The next small stretch of sand is called Gray's Beach, with a swimming area known as Gray's Channel. The palm-fringed strand running from the two original hotels and now called the Royal Hawaiian Beach is the most famous stretch of sand in Hawaii. Canoeing, snorkeling, and sailing are just as popular here as swimming or just plain lolling in the sun. At Kuhio Beach Park, farther on, a wall has been built parallel to the beach to retain sand. Although the eastern end here is good for swimming, the wall has a slick covering of marine growth and is best avoided, the nonchalant youngsters running up and down it notwithstanding. At Sans Souci Beach, the reef-sheltered waters draw weekend crowds of *kamaainas.* With Diamond Head as a backdrop, for many Sans Souci represents Waikiki at its best. At press time, plans had been announced for a multimillion-dollar rebuilding of Waikiki's beaches, which will add almost 50% to the present swath of sand, with a series of offshore sea walls designed to limit the erosion that has washed away portions of Waikiki over the years.

Duke Kahanamoku Statue – Duke Kahanamoku, the *Olympic* gold medalist swimmer and Hawaiian surfer, was honored on the 100th anniversary of his birth with a beachfront statue in the Kuhio Beach section of Waikiki. The larger-than-lifesize bronze figure provides a fitting memorial to a native son who continues to serve as an example of athletic skill and Hawaiian aloha spirit.

IMAX Theater Waikiki – This 420-seat, wide-screen, high-tech theater offers an exhilarating look at Hawaii. Its 35-minute film, called "Hawaii: Born in Paradise," includes breathtaking views of Hawaii at its most remote and spectacular. A must see. Open daily from 10 AM to 8 PM. Admission charge. 325 Seaside Ave. (phone: 923-4629).

Fort DeRussy Army Museum – Weapons used by ancient Hawaiians, weapons captured from the Japanese, and weapons used by US soldiers in campaigns from the Spanish-American War to the Korean War are on display here. In addition, there are uniforms worn at various times by US forces as well as uniforms worn by the enemy. The most fascinating items are the Hawaiian weapons made in times long past from sharks' teeth and the blowups of the Honolulu newspapers describing the early days of the US involvement in World War II following the bombing of Pearl Harbor. Open from 10 AM to 4:30 PM. Closed Mondays. Kalia Rd. (phone: 438-2821).

International Market Place – Open-air stalls and open-front stores dominated by a huge banyan tree are some of the features that lure people to this famous shopping mall. Occasionally there are mimes and puppeteers here as well as Polynesian mat weavers, and hammerers of gold and silver. If you are somewhat retiring, you may find the place bohemian; if you are bohemian, you will find it rather tame. At press time, plans were still being completed for a major convention center at the site. 2330 Kalakaua Ave. (phone: 923-9871).

Royal Hawaiian – This place is still lively, even though most of its garden has been usurped by the architecturally characterless *Sheraton-Waikiki* next door and the view of its façade obliterated by the *Royal Hawaiian Shopping Center.* The theme is pink inside as well as out, and there is an overdose of rose this-and-that everywhere. It is worth a visit to see through the haze of time how travelers to Waikiki lived 50 years ago. 2259 Kalakaua Ave. (phone: 923-7311).

Sheraton Moana Surfrider – Waikiki's oldest hotel (it opened in 1901 and was listed on the National Register of Historic Places in 1972) has been returned to Victorian elegance following a $50-million restoration. The result is a match for the nearby

Royal Hawaiian in terms of quality and historic appeal. Mementos from the *Moana* through the decades are displayed on the second floor. 2365 Kalakaua Ave. (phone: 922-3111).

Honolulu Zoo – It's not a major zoo, but millions have been spent to upgrade and re-landscape this 42-acre preserve. It's easily accessible and a good place to see some unusual animals, such as Galápagos tortoises, and a fine collection of rare Asian birds. Open daily from 8:30 AM to 4 PM. Admission charge. Kapiolani Park (phone: 971-7171).

Waikiki Aquarium – A seaside setting, with Diamond Head in the background, adds to well-displayed tanks and exhibits ranging from the exotic chambered nautilus to the history of fishing in Hawaii. The newest addition is the outdoor Touch Tank exhibit. Open daily from 9 AM to 5 PM. Admission charge. In Kapiolani Park, 2777 Kalakaua Ave. (phone: 923-9741).

Kapiolani Park – This 220-acre park separating Waikiki from the small residential area on the southwest side of Diamond Head is famous for its joggers, rose garden, golden shower trees, and for the Kodak Hula Show (phone: 833-1661) that takes place Tuesdays through Thursdays from 10 to 11:15 AM. No admission charge. In addition, look for the distinguished-looking red-crested, gray-mantled Brazilian cardinal birds, who strut fussily around the park, reluctant to acknowledge the presence of human beings. Other quite untouristy sights are the small, carefully tended garden plots where fruit, vegetables, and flowers are grown. City farmers are assisted in their efforts by the manure that is made easily obtainable by the nearby zoo (phone: 971-7171).

Kualoa Ranch – A working ranch along the windward coast, it is now open to the public. Activities include horseback riding, catamaran sails, windsurfing, helicopter touring, and scuba diving. A five-activity ticket book and lunch costs $95, which includes Waikiki pickups. You need two tickets for each activity, with the exception of the helicopter ride and scuba, which require three. There is an additional $35 charge for scuba diving. *Kualoa Ranch,* 49-560 Kam Hwy., Kaawa, HI 96730 (phone: 237-7321).

SHOPPING: Waikiki shopping is done, with few exceptions, in hotel arcades and malls. Many of the latter have an architectural or commercial theme, usually Oriental or Hawaiian, and are occasionally outdoors. The emphasis is on high-priced, designer goods, aloha- and other resortwear; vacation sundries such as lotions, beach towels and mats, and dark glasses; and Polynesian handicrafts and other gift items. Mixed in are some boutiques that carry famous international names like Courrèges and Gucci, and high-fashion sportswear. In general, it's a bit on the mundane side — gaudy, commercial, and overdone. It could be said that when you've seen one banyan-shaded bazaar selling seashell leis, you've seen them all, but browsing can nonetheless be fun. It is worth noting that prices are generally steeper in Waikiki than in the *Ala Moana Center* and in the *Pearlridge Center.* At *Woolworth's,* for example, a pair of running shorts that costs $16 in the Kalakaua Avenue store might cost only $14 at *Ala Moana.* Family-style grocery shopping for those people living in condominiums is not very convenient unless you're near Hobron Lane or the large supermarket on Kuhio off Kaiulani. The best bet if you're staying for a while is to head to a supermarket outside Waikiki for decent prices and quality produce. The basics are also available in many places described as sundry stores, but at outrageous prices. The *ABC* stores, with locations all over Waikiki, are the best places for buying suntan lotion, picture postcards, and liquor. The major merchandising centers with a selection of stores worth noting include the following:

ROYAL HAWAIIAN SHOPPING CENTER

This ultramodern, 4-story arcade of boutiques and restaurants covers 6½ acres. The shopping center (phone: 922-0588) runs along the south side of Kalakaua Avenue east from Lewers Street in front of the *Sheraton* and *Royal Hawaiian* hotels. This is where some of Waikiki's best shops have moved, which lends a Rodeo Drive elegance to the area. The center also has numerous restaurants and fast-food kiosks, and sponsors a wide range of free musical and cultural presentations throughout the year.

Center Art Gallery – The store has signed prints by Chagall, Dali, and some other prolific printmakers, but its specialty is pictures by celebrities such as Elke Sommer and Red Skelton. If you would like an original painting of Woody Woodpecker commanding an outrigger canoe by his creator, Walt Lantz, hurry on over (phone: 926-2727).

Chanel – Everything from cosmetics to fragrances to ready-to-wear Chanel chic for the well-heeled, fashion-conscious crowd (phone: 923-0255).

Chaumet – More than 200 years after the first shop opened in Paris, a branch of this fine jewelry store now can be found in Waikiki. The collection includes one-of-a-kind watches, accessories, and objets d'art (phone: 923-8055).

Hermès of Paris – An elegant shop, featuring the finest silk scarves, leatherware, fragrances, bath accessories, jewelry, watches, and riding gear from the famous French maker (phone: 922-5780).

Little Hawaiian Craftshop – For one of Hawaii's best collections of carved wood objects and museum-quality reproductions of Hawaiian sculpture, try this store. It's also known for handicrafts made from such materials as nuts, gourds, bones, fossil ivory, and seaweed, and for jewelry, ornaments, and "conversation pieces" made from cowrie shells (phone: 926-2662).

Loewe – This Spanish leather goods shop focuses on high quality, high fashion, and high pricing. Worth a browse, if not a buy (phone: 922-1950).

McInerny Galleria – A small department store that's one of the best places in town for designer clothing for men, women, and children. Some of the labels sold in the store include Giorgio Armani and Ferragamo (phone: 971-4200).

Real Estate Showcase – The place to get an idea of what it costs to buy a piece of paradise. Displays highlighting condominium options on all islands make for interesting browsing and comparing. The Japanese are the big buyers here (phone: 926-5677).

Royal Hawaiian Shooting Gallery – Hunting enthusiasts and would-be cowboys can practice their quick draw with weapons ranging from pistols to semiautomatics (phone: 922-4122).

Van Brugge House – Designer labels from the land down under — Australia, that is — as well as a cache of that country's pink, champagne, and cognac-colored diamonds (phone: 971-6678).

Yokohama-Okadaya – The chief reason for stopping in this international gift shop is its fine collection of designer leather goods (phone: 922-5731).

WAIKIKI SHOPPING PLAZA

The merchandise in this complex (2270 Kalakaua Avenue; phone: 923-1191) has to compete with a 5-story water display that is part fountain and part Plexiglas sculpture. There are a few shops of interest as well as some fine restaurants on the upper floors. Among the stores worth a look are the following:

Betty's Imports – The largest of the semi-wholesale outfits on the fifth floor, it offers real bargains on all kinds of jewelry and imported bric-a-brac, often at prices 30% to 50% lower than at street-level shops (phone: 922-3010).

Eureka M's – Plenty of discounted costume jewelry at bargain prices. Suite 504 (phone: 923-5633).

Lowe's Rare Coins – If you're numismatically inclined, this an interesting place to browse (phone: 923-3372).

Sawada Golf – Fill all your golf needs at this large duffer's shop (phone: 923-0144).

Villa Roma – It has a nice selection of contemporary women's fashions (phone: 923-4447).

Waldenbooks – Most of the sundries stores have pulp romances and spy novels, but if it's the new Paul Theroux or Tom Clancy (or Birnbaum guide) you're after, head here. The shop receives shipments barely days after mainland stores, and if you're staying a month or so, the staff will order anything not in stock (phone: 922-4154).

Yokohama-Okadaya – It's a second branch of the Japanese retailer and features high-priced sportswear by Lacoste and Fila, as well as fine luggage and leather goods (phone: 922-5731).

HYATT REGENCY CENTER

The first three floors of the *Hyatt* complex are dominated by more than 70 shops that surround a 3-tier waterfall and pool. A fashion show is held each Wednesday at 4 PM outside *Harry's Bar* beside the pool. 2424 Kalakaua Ave. (phone: 923-1234).

Chapman's – A rare find in Waikiki, it has good men's clothing, including such helpful basics as lightweight cotton slacks (phone: 923-7010).

Circle Gallery – For a comprehensive selection of serigraphs, lithographs, and other graphics by Erté and other, lesser-known artists (phone: 923-6040).

Coral Grotto – If it's coral jewelry you're after, this shop (part of a chain) is known for its quality merchandise. The rings are particularly lovely — in pink, black, and gold coral — and start at about $80 (phone: 923-3454). There's another shop in the *Ala Moana Shopping Center* (phone: 955-6760).

Cotton Cargo – This shop offers a refreshing change from alohawear, featuring 100% cotton fashion for women. The clothes have style; most are imported from India, Bali, Turkey, Greece, and Central America (phone: 923-5811).

Gucci – One of two branches of this exclusive chain in Honolulu (the other is at *Ala Moana Center* (phone: 942-1148), it carries the usual fine line of leather goods and fashionable clothing (phone: 923-2968).

KING'S VILLAGE

This pastel complex of quaint townhouse-style buildings and cobblestone walkways at the back of the *Hyatt Regency* hotel is designed to resemble urban Honolulu in the days of the 19th-century monarchs. The result is slightly reminiscent of *Disneyland,* although the *Rose and Crown Pub* (phone: 923-5833), with its horse brasses, etched-glass mirrors, and timber beams, manages to be a fair replica of an English country pub. The Changing of the Guard occurs nightly at 6:15 PM.

Chapman's – This once traditional men's clothing chain has added a line of contemporary, high-fashion designs (phone: 923-5920).

The Fossil Shop – Unique fossilized and crystalized items made from minerals and shells can be found here (phone: 924-9314).

Kitamura's – An exquisite collection of antique Japanese dolls. Call in advance for an appointment (phone: 293-1725).

WAIKIKI TRADE CENTER

An architecturally distinctive office building at 2255 Kuhio Avenue (at the juncture of Kuhio and Royal Hawaiian; phone: 922-7444), it has several stories of shops and restaurants. *Bebe* (phone: 926-7888) features ultrahigh-fashion unisex clothing designs, while *C. June Shoes* (phone: 926-1574) offers a marvelous selection of chic footwear.

ELSEWHERE IN WAIKIKI

Alfred Dunhill – Located in the elegantly restored Moana wing of the *Moana Surfrider* hotel, its cherrywood fixtures, plush velvet, and who-can-afford-it prices are as awesome as the jewelry, leather goods, and accessories that carry the Dunhill imprint (phone: 971-2020).

Down Under Honolulu – One of the best sources for men's swimwear in Hawaii, with designer labels as well as merchandise designed in-house. Everything from nearly revealing to very revealing, plus a fine selection of generic shorts and T-shirts. 2139 Kuhio Ave. (phone: 922-9229).

Duke's Lane – In this alley are a couple of dozen narrow stalls teeming with leis made from plumeria, seashells, kukui nuts, and plastic; carved ivory; fancy, embroidered Oriental slippers; Chinese-style cloisonné; tapa wall hangings; and coral jewelry. Much of the merchandise is without distinction. Between Kalakaua Ave. and Kuhio Ave. (no phone).

International Market Place – Famous for its huge banyan tree, it's a bustling, noisy bazaar of shops and booths, including South Seas and Hawaiian products, such as bamboo and rattanwork, baskets woven of *lau hala* or pandanus leaves, and tikis, platters, and bowls carved from monkeypod and other woods. Almost every store has its racks of alohawear and shelves of straw hats, and you'll find that quality, styles, and prices vary little from place to place. Numerous kiosks are draped with earrings, necklaces, and bracelets made of shell and semiprecious stones, including amethyst, coral, jade, opal, puka, and so on. You can bargain with these dealers, and very often a feigned disinterest can drop the asking price by half. At press time, plans were under way to close the *Market Place* and convert the site into a major convention center. 2330 Kalakaua Ave. (phone: 923-9871).

Kuhio Mall – Behind the *International Market Place* is this relatively unchic and unrenowned collection of shops with, nevertheless, very attractive prices. If plans for a convention center come to pass, the mall will also be eliminated.

Louis Vuitton – Located in the historic Gump Building, this is the Waikiki flagship for luggage, wallets, and other leather goods imprinted with the famous intertwining initials. *2201 Kalakaua Ave.,* in the *Royal Hawaiian Shopping Center* (phone: 926-0621).

Rainbow Bazaar – A collection of 30 or so boutiques selling ethnic handicrafts and antiques from Polynesia and Asia. On the whole, it is expensive, but several shops worth a browse include the *Pagoda Shop* (phone: 944-2935) and *China Treasure* (phone: 946-5752). There is also a substation of the post office here (phone: 949-4321; ext. 74129), which is open from 8 AM to 4 PM. *Rainbow Bazaar* is at the *Hilton Hawaiian Village* (phone: 949-4321).

Tiffany & Co. – The Waikiki branch of this world-renowned jeweler offers unique pieces as well as simpler items, all examples of Tiffany quality and style. In the *Sheraton Moana Surfrider* (phone: 922-2722).

NIGHTLIFE: "The most fabulous array of shows outside of Las Vegas," Waikiki publicists like to tell you. Maybe, but if it's stars you're after, better try Las Vegas or Atlantic City. Nightlife in Waikiki usually begins with a drink on your lanai and an exquisite sunset, followed by excellent pupus for dinner. Down in the cocktail lounges there is almost always a pianist, guitarist, or, if it's a classy place, a harpist. Many restaurants discourage conversation by providing live background music. A prime exception is the *Halekulani*'s *House Without a Key* (2199 Kalia Rd.; phone: 923-2311), where mellow Hawaiian music and hula complement the Waikiki sunset. The *Veranda,* with its soothing background piano or violin music, is a lovely place to have cocktails, people watch, and catch the nightly torch lighting ceremony. Another noteworthy spot is the *Beach Bar* where cocktails are served under the stars. Both are at the *Sheraton Moana Surfrider* (2365 Kalakaua Ave.; phone: 922-3111). There's piano music during dinner at the *Hanohano Room* of the *Sheraton Waikiki* (2255 Kalakaua Ave.; phone: 922-4422). A lively crowd frequents the *Esprit* bar in the hotel (phone: 922-4422), with nightly music from 9 PM to 1 AM. Popular island singer Jimmy Borges performs mellow ballads nightly at the *Paradise Lounge* of the *Hilton Hawaiian Village,* Fridays and Saturdays starting at 8 PM (2005 Kalia Rd.; phone: 949-4321). Illusionist and magician John Hirokawa stars in Magic of Polynesia, a spectacular David Copperfield–style show that mixes magic, illusions, and Hawaiian music and song. Nightly in the *Hilton Dome,* at 5 PM for the dinner show ($44.50), and at 6 PM for the cocktail show ($25). For the twentyish set, the action is at *Moose McGillicuddy's* (310 Lewers St.; phone: 923-0751) or try the *Maharaja* club in the *Waikiki Trade Center* (on Kuhio Ave.; phone: 922-3030). On the outskirts of Waikiki, the *Hard Rock Café* (1837 Kapiolani Blvd.; phone: 955-7383) has established itself as an "in" spot with the twenties and thirties crowd. Lots of mingling and noise at the bar. The Flashback show at the *Hula Hut* offers a different kind of fun twice nightly, with entertainers impersonating Elvis, Diana Ross, and Madonna ($42 dinner show; $22 cocktail seating). Closed Sundays. *Waikiki Terrace* hotel (2045 Kalakaua Ave.; phone: 955-8444). For Waikiki's best selection of contemporary Hawaiian music, head to *Malia's Cantina,* 311 Lewers St. (phone: 922-7808), where performers like Kapena, Olomana, and Moe Keala are the nightly attractions from 10 PM to 1 AM.

Headliners in Hawaii usually mean entertainers who have made their name in the islands. The most famous is Don Ho, who has been performing at Waikiki's top showplace, the *Hilton Dome* in the *Hilton Hawaiian Village,* since late 1981. Ho's performances can be sickly and erratic and sometimes downright unpleasant. They are best on Fridays and Saturdays, when he attracts a good number of *kamaainas* who will request songs that the stranger does not know. Also, Charo stars in a good, Vegas-style revue at the *Hilton Hawaiian Village*'s *Tropic Room,* evenings except Sundays. Dinner and cocktail seatings available. Another Waikiki favorite is the *Society of Seven,* a group performing a mix of contemporary music and comedy at the *Outrigger Waikiki* showroom (2335 Kalakaua Ave.; phone: 923-0711). Check the entertainment guides for details. The *Brothers Cazimero,* Roland and Robert, are also very popular. They have a great respect for the music of the islands and their show in the *Royal Hawaiian's Monarch Room* (phone: 923-7311) is one of Hawaii's best. Again, check newspapers and guides to find out where they are appearing. At *Trapper's* at the *Hyatt Regency,* the sound ranges from top-40 tunes to the best of the 50s and 60s (2424 Kalakaua Ave.; phone: 923-1234). Fans of stand-up comedy can head to the *Honolulu Comedy Club* Tuesdays through Sundays at the *Ilikai* hotel. Reservations advised; $10 cover (177 Ala Moana Blvd.; phone: 922-5998). Check Oahu newspapers to find out where a favorite local funny man, Frank Delima, is appearing. His Imelda Marcos impression is priceless.

Waikiki's Polynesian spectaculars (dinner, luau, or cocktail options) provide Hollywood-cum-Broadway versions of Pacific island music and dance and are usually of most interest to first-time visitors to the islands. The best location is the beachside luau and revue at the *Outrigger* hotel (2335 Kalakaua Ave.; phone: 923-0711), Tuesdays, Fridays, and Sundays. At the *Sheraton Princess Kaiulani* (2342 Kalakaua Ave.; phone: 922-5811) there is a nightly show, and the *Royal Hawaiian* (2259 Kalakaua Ave.; phone: 923-7311) is the site for a luau and revue on Mondays. *Voyage* is the latest variation on the theme. The *Aloha Showroom* (on the fourth floor of the *Royal Hawaiian Shopping Center*) features Waikiki's largest and most extravagant showroom. The setting is a Hollywood vision of Hawaii, complete with waterfalls, streams, a rain forest, and "erupting volcanoes," with performers telling the story of a missionary's arrival in 19th-century Hawaii in music and dance. Tickets to the show can be purchased independently ($25) or in conjunction with many dinner packages in restaurants in the *Royal Hawaiian* complex.

Dinner cruises have been part of the Waikiki scene for years. *Royal Hawaiian Cruises* (phone: 947-9971) departs Kewalo Basin on the *Navatek,* a jet-propelled catamaran, on sunset and moonlight cruises. Although the cost, which includes an elegant steak and lobster dinner along with first class entertainment, is high ($130), it is a fine choice for a very romantic evening. *Paradise Cruises* (phone: 536-3641) leaves from Kewalo Basin (hotel pickups are provided), and offers drinks and food during the sail back along

Waikiki Beach to Diamond Head. *Aikane Catamarans* (phone: 522-1533) and *Windjammer Cruises* (phone: 521-0036) also offer popular sunset sails, with drinks, dinner, and all-too-often noisy entertainment. Cruises include transfers between Kewalo Basin and Waikiki.

Another Waikiki and island-wide tradition is the luau, an ancient Hawaiian ceremony of cooking a pig in an *imu,* an earthen pit lined with lava rock and heated by burning kiawe wood. The pig is stuffed with red-hot rocks, wrapped in wet ti and banana leaves, and covered with earth. Other ingredients such as yams, taro, fish, breadfruit, and whatever is available are placed in the *imu* beside the pig. Hours later, the pig is removed, at which time it is referred to as kalua pork. Removing the pig from the *imu* is a ceremony in itself, often accompanied by songs. There are a number of commercial luaus that include the removal ceremony and a torchlighting ritual, a heavy meal of pork and accompanying traditional foodstuffs, "all you can drink," and Polynesian entertainment. In Waikiki there's a Monday luau at the *Royal Hawaiian* hotel (2259 Kalakaua Ave.; phone: 923-7311). Other luaus take place on beaches out of town but with pick-up buses serving all the Waikiki hotels. At the *Paradise Cove Luau* there is an *imu* ceremony, torchlighting ritual, beachfront *hukilau* (communal net fishing), Hawaiian arts and crafts displays, and a Polynesian review (phone: 973-5828). *Paradise Cove* and *Germaine's Luau* both take place on beaches near Ewa, about 40 minutes from Waikiki (transportation provided). *Germaine's* features a net-throwing demonstration during which, for a brief moment, there's the splendid sight of a fishing net extended in silhouette against the late evening sky. Before the removal of the pig, there is also a procession, with young people modeling costumes worn by ancient Hawaiian royalty. In the Polynesian extravaganza that follows ($40), the audience is invited to participate in various dances and songs in an exhibition that may turn even strong stomachs after a generous number of free mai tais and blue Hawaiis (phone: 949-6626).

Sea Life Park (phone: 923-1531) has exhibits and shows from 7 to 10 PM on Thursday, Friday, and Sunday evenings. At the *Bishop Museum* (phone: 848-4129 or 847-8200), a state-of-the-art planetarium show is presented at 7 PM Fridays and Saturdays; admission $2.50. Pack a picnic and seat yourself on the lawn for one of the symphonic, jazz, or Hawaiian shows often presented at the *Waikiki Shell* (box office phone: 521-2911), with Diamond Head as a backdrop. Gates open at 5:30 PM; showtime is usually 7:30 PM. When the moon is full, consider the free escorted walks at Waimea Falls Park (phone: 638-8511).

For something a little more sophisticated, visit *Spats* disco, which has a kind of swank Bonnie and Clyde atmosphere, in the *Hyatt Regency* (2424 Kalakaua Ave.; phone: 923-1234), or *Annabelle's,* atop the *Ilikai,* where, apart from the glitter of the decor, you can also enjoy the glitter of Honolulu spread out below (1777 Ala Moana Blvd.; phone: 949-3811). Those who prefer their music loud and rocking can head next door to *Wave Waikiki,* a popular dance spot that tends to draw a young crowd (1877 Kalakaua Ave.; phone: 941-0424); others are *Bobby McGee's Conglomeration* (2885 Kalakaua Ave.; phone: 922-1282); *Cillys* (1909 Ala Wai Blvd.; phone: 942-2952); *Pink Cadillac* (478 Ena Rd.; phone: 942-5282); and *Rumours* at the *Ramada Renaissance Ala Moana* (phone: 955-4811). The newest and most extravagant addition to the disco scene is the $6-million *Majaraja Restaurant and Disco* (in the Waikiki Trade Center, 2255 Kuhio Ave.; phone: 922-3030). *Hula's,* an open-air disco, the centerpiece of which is a light-festooned banyan tree, attracts a crowd of both sexes and sexual persuasions (2130 Kuhio Ave.; phone: 923-0669). At neighboring *Hamburger Mary's,* the crowd is definitely gay (phone: 922-6722).

CHECKING IN: "We've lost our hotel," a young couple was heard to lament on *TheBus* one night. Was it the *Surf* or the *Surfrider* for which they were looking, the *Surfsider* or the *Outrigger Surf?* Not long ago, most hotels in Waikiki (apart from the older *Royal Hawaiian* and *Moana* and a handful of modern luxury hotels, such as the *Hyatt Regency*) not only sounded the same, they looked the same, inside and out. With nearly a billion dollars spent to upgrade the individual hotels, this is no longer the case, and room quality overall is generally excellent. Standard accommodations consist of double beds or twins; pastel-colored decor; thick wall-to-wall carpeting; wicker armchairs and a table; a TV set; and a lanai, or balcony. Then there are the views which could be, in descending order of desirability and price, of the ocean, Diamond Head, the mountains, or the city. (This is all in the eye of the beholder; the sun rising behind Diamond Head is a pretty inspiring sight, and the rainbows that splay over the mountainsides on many an afternoon can be quite spectacular.)

When making reservations, think carefully about what's most important to you. As a rule, if you plan to spend a lot of time in your hotel, choose a more expensive room with something to look at outside. If all you need is a dormitory while you sunbathe and explore, far less expensive accommodations will likely do nicely. Expect to pay $250 and up for a double room in a hotel listed as very expensive, between $160 and $245 in a hotel listed as expensive, from $75 to $160 in a property listed as moderate, and under $75 in a hotel listed as inexpensive. Unless otherwise stated, all rooms in these categories will include a lanai or terrace, though the size and the view will vary. As elsewhere in the islands, most hotels and condos offer high-season (late December to *Easter*) and low-season rates.

There are also condominiums in Waikiki and adjacent residential neighborhoods, many of which are available for short-term rentals. Most offer front-desk services, restaurants, and daily maid service. And while most condos are a few blocks from the beach, nothing in Waikiki is beyond easy walking distance. The condominiums listed below are all within a 15-minute walk of the ocean; the most convenient store for groceries is the *Food Pantry* supermarket on Kuhio, off Kaiulani. With 24-hour advance reservations, *Terminal Transportation* (phone: 926-4777) and *Airport Motorcoach* (phone: 926-4747) offer $5 airport shuttle service.

The main attraction of a condominium is economic: For a "superior double" — a large 1-bedroom apartment with a living room in which there's a sofa bed — expect to pay around $90 to $135 a night. Unless otherwise stated, the same rate applies for one to four people, though there is often a nominal (under $10) charge for each person after the first two. Thus, it's possible for a family or two couples to save up to 60% over the price of comparable accommodations in a hotel, and for stays extending into weeks or months, the savings are even higher. (For further information on condominium prices and discounts, see *Accommodations,* GETTING READY TO GO.)

Note that some condos, especially those used to long-term renters, do not have telephones, although almost all have jacks for easy phone installation. Telephones are obtained by going to the nearest *Phone Mart,* picking up the equipment, obtaining a number, and filling in the relevant forms. Service usually starts in less than 24 hours. The nearest *Phone Mart* to Waikiki is in the *Ward Warehouse* shopping mall, across from the Kewalo Boat Basin on Ala Moana Boulevard.

Bed and breakfast establishments are another option. *Bed & Breakfast Goes Hawaiian,* published by *Bed & Breakfast Hawaii,* lists nearly 40 such private homes where tourists are welcome. For a copy of the guide, send $8.50 to *Bed & Breakfast Hawaii* (PO Box 449, Kapaa, HI 96746; phone: 822-7771, 536-8421, or 800-733-1632). *Bed & Breakfast Honolulu* (3242 Koahinani Dr., Honolulu, HI 96817; phone: 595-7533; 800-288-4666) and *Pacific Hawaii Bed & Breakfast* (970 N. Kalaheo, Kailua, HI 96734; phone: 254-5030, 262-6026, 800-999-6026) also list Oahu accommodations.

All telephone numbers are in the 808 area code unless otherwise indicated.

HOTELS

Aston Waikiki Beachside – Small and sumptuous, this luxurious establishment is perfect for those who appreciate lovely surroundings. Inside, European and Oriental period pieces add to the elegant ambience, while the service is undeniably impeccable. A minor drawback for those who crave lots of space are the guestrooms, some of which are fairly small, albeit appealingly appointed. In-room VCRs are just one of the extras, as are French toiletries. Although there are no restaurants on the premises, it's merely a 5-minute walk to the *Hyatt Regency* or other resort complexes in the area. Conveniently located just across Kalakaua from the beach. 2452 Kalakaua Ave. (phone: 931-2100; 800-922-7866). Very expensive to expensive.

Halekulani – This contemporary, recently refurbished mid-rise incorporates the old Lewers home, which served as the original hotel. Among its features are 456 rooms, a fitness room, and an open-air, oceanfront lounge — *House Without a Key* — featuring Hawaiian music and fine views of Diamond Head and sunsets. Its restaurants, *Orchids* and *La Mer* (see *Eating Out*), are among Honolulu's best. The hotel, designed to reestablish Waikiki as a destination for the carriage trade, is the essence of contemporary elegance. This is a place for which the adjective "luxury" is no exaggeration. 2199 Kalia Rd. (phone: 923-2311; 800-367-2343). Very expensive to expensive.

Hawaii Prince – Waikiki's newest luxury hotel is the second Hawaii property for Japan's Prince Hotel chain (the other is on Maui). Attention to detail, carefully prepared cuisine at the hotel's five restaurants, including the *Prince Court* (see *Eating Out*), and panoramic views of the neighboring Ala Wai Yacht Tower are the main justifications for top-of-the-scale rates. Guests are also offered complimentary shuttle service to golf courses, a nearby health spa, downtown, and Waikiki. Located on the western edge of Waikiki, it is a short walk from either Ala Moana Beach or Waikiki Beach. Business travelers can receive special rates on oceanfront rooms, along with 24-hour room service and secretarial services. 100 Holomoana St. (phone: 956-1111; 800-321-6284). Very expensive to expensive.

Hilton Hawaiian Village – With close to 2,600 rooms and 22 acres (plans to build a new high-rise tower were recently announced), it is Hawaii's largest hotel, and the western terminus of Waikiki Beach. Standing between the Duke Kahanamoku Lagoon and the beach, it boasts a colorful shopping center, its own post office, and a catamaran that offers both day and night cruises. The Rainbow Tower, famed for its 30-story rainbow mosaic, and the Tapa Tower, with 250 corner suites, have the best views. The Alii Tower is the hotel's most elegant segment, and features its own pool and full concierge services. The village has lots that visitors want from a Hawaiian vacation — pools, beaches, fine dining, luaus, and Polynesian extravaganzas featuring Don Ho — but lacks much peace and serenity. The hotel did a $100-million renovation in 1988 that brought all the parts of the village together around a pool area that also highlights the beach, rather than obscuring it. "Aloha Friday," a weekly celebration dedicated to King David Kalakaua, features crafts displays, hula dancing, and a luau-style dinner from 5 to 9:30 PM at the *Rainbow Lanai.* The evening is capped off by fireworks starting at 7:30 PM, or after dark, whichever is later. 2005 Kalia Rd. (phone: 949-4321; 800-445-8667). Very expensive to expensive.

Hawaiian Regent – Just across the road from the beach, the two tall towers possess little architectural distinction. The interiors, however, are a bit more appealing, with inner courtyards paved in tile and marble, and an outdoor-café atmosphere in the main lobby. The Ocean Terrace pool area is also inviting, and the rooms are large and comfortable. There are several first class restaurants in the hotel, including the prestigious *The Secret,* which boasts a 6,000-bottle wine room (see *Eating Out*). *The Library,* where there's not a book in sight, has some unusually good soft music starting at 8:30 PM. 2552 Kalakaua Ave. (phone: 922-6611; 800-367-5370). Expensive.

Sheraton Moana Surfrider – This beautifully restored Victorian hostelry has been standing at the edge of the Waikiki surf since 1901. The Japanese firm that owns it (Sheraton manages it) finished a $50-million renovation in 1989 that brought back the glow of its early days. Until its exotic neighbor, the *Royal Hawaiian,* was opened in 1927, the *Moana* was the only hotel in the area. Brass headboards, white wicker chairs, antique lamps, and Victorian armoires adorn many of the rooms. These touches, and in many cases a ceiling fan, help to obscure the more modern iconography of Waikiki outside. When making reservations, it is wise to specify a room in the old building, if that is what you want, as the Surfrider wing is more contemporary in style and decor. 2365 Kalakaua Ave. (phone: 922-3111; 800-325-3535). Expensive.

Hawaiian Waikiki Beach – Although the rooms at the recently renamed *Holiday Inn Waikiki Beach* provide the chain's standard level of style and comfort, this hotel boasts magnificent views of the ocean and Diamond Head. It also has a terrific site: just outside the hustle-bustle of the strip, next door to Kapiolani Park and the Honolulu Zoo, and across the street from the loveliest stretch of Waikiki Beach. Its *Captain's Table,* an easygoing eatery that looks out at the sea, is a good place to sample your first mahimahi. 2570 Kalakaua Ave. (phone: 922-2511; 800-877-7666). Expensive to moderate.

Hyatt Regency – The hotel's two octagonal towers are a visual landmark among the concrete blocks along Kalakaua Avenue. The Great Hall, with its outdoor tropical garden, 3-story waterfall, and massive hanging sculpture, is a sightseeing spot in its own right. Each of its 1,230 rooms is handsomely furnished, and the art on the walls is invariably worth looking at. The suites feature some exceptional Japanese and European antiques. Guests in the Regency Club, as the 39th- and 40th-floor accommodations are known, have their own private, complimentary bar and a concierge. The pool deck is one of the most attractive in Honolulu, and the bars, cafés, and restaurants in the complex — they include *Ciao Mein, Spats* (see *Eating Out* for both), *Trapper's,* and *Harry's* — are among the very best in Waikiki. The service here is exemplary. 2424 Kalakaua Ave. (phone: 923-1234; 800-233-1234). Expensive to moderate.

Ilikai – Located at the western edge of Waikiki, this 800-room property recently underwent a multimillion-dollar face-lift, sprucing up its spacious guestrooms (some with kitchenettes; many have panoramic views) and public areas. The hotel has Waikiki's best tennis facilities, with 6 courts and pros available to provide instruction. The open area at the lobby level has pools, terraces, and fountains. The beach, Duke Kahanamoku Lagoon, and the yacht marina are just a stone's throw away. Atop the hotel sits *Annabelle's,* a disco reached via a spectacular ride in an exterior elevator that opens up vast panoramas of the Pacific as you ascend. 1777 Ala Moana Blvd. (phone: 949-3811; 800-367-8434). Expensive to moderate.

Outrigger Reef – With 885 rooms, this is the largest moderately priced beachfront hotel in Waikiki. All rooms and public areas have been nicely upgraded, resulting in somewhat higher rates. Popular with young couples and singles traveling in pairs, it's right on the beach, with most of the rooms facing either toward Diamond Head or across Fort DeRussy Beach Park to the ocean. Guests here seem to use their lanais more than those at any other hotel in the neighborhood; it's a friendly sight. 2169 Kalia Rd. (phone: 923-3111; 800-367-5170). Expensive to moderate.

Pacific Beach – Standing on the site of the summer home of Queen Liliuokalani, this property is famous for its 280,000-gallon indoor oceanarium, which can be viewed from the hotel's bars and restaurants. Along with the swimming pool, there are tennis courts and a Jacuzzi. Recently renovated, this place is a good buy. 2490 Kalakaua Ave. (phone: 922-1233; 800-367-6060). Expensive to moderate.

Royal Hawaiian – "The Pink Lady," as this flamingo-colored, 6-story landmark of

Spanish-Moorish design is best known, is flanked by two other Sheraton properties that seem to stand in an adversary, rather than a neighborly, stance. And indeed, rumor has it along the beach that there are entrepreneurs who would not object to seeing the Lady deposed in favor of something more modern (and anonymous). Never mind. While it lasts — and one hopes it will last a long time — this is one of the two grand old hotels in Waikiki (the *Moana* is the other). The pink color scheme runs, perhaps a smidgin too obviously, throughout the hotel. Most of the rooms have either a pink sofa, quilt, or drapes. Usually it works, sometimes it doesn't. In any case, once away from the bustle of the lobby, which attracts ten times more spectators than guests, this remains the most charming hotel in Waikiki. Reservations through the *Sheraton Waikiki,* 2259 Kalakaua Ave. (phone: 923-7311; 800-325-3535). Expensive to moderate.

Sheraton Waikiki – With 1,852 rooms, this establishment, the second largest in Waikiki (surpassed only by the *Hilton Hawaiian Village*), still has the greatest number of units in one building of any hotel on the beach. Lanais on the Pacific side loom over the ocean as precipitously as a cliff. It's a splendid sensation if you don't suffer from vertigo, and the sunsets can be memorable. Happily, subtle tans and casually tropical styling have replaced the garish greens and floral designs that made the rooms and lobby rather hard on the eyes. This place has all that's expected from a big hotel: There is never a dearth of taxis, it's a pick-up point for every major tour operator, *TheBus* stops nearby, and there is just about every kind of restaurant you could crave, except a truly first class one. 2255 Kalakaua Ave. (phone: 922-4422; 800-325-3535). Expensive to moderate.

Waikiki Joy – Upscale and contemporary, this hostelry has a pleasant marble entry and lounge. Steer clear of the studios on the lower level floors, as they can be a bit noisy. The suites on the upper floors boast wonderful views of Waikiki. Fine continental fare is served at *Cappucino's* restaurant. A complimentary continental breakfast is served in the lobby each morning. 320 Lewers St. (phone: 923-2300; 800-733-5569). Expensive to moderate.

Ilima – Near the Ala Wai Canal, about 3 blocks from the *Royal Hawaiian Beach,* it offers the additional convenience of full kitchens in all rooms, as well as a restaurant, cocktail lounge, sauna, and pool. 445 Nohonani St. (phone: 923-1877; 800-367-5172). Moderate.

Outrigger Prince Kuhio – Quietly set on Kuhio Avenue, just 1 block from the beach, it manages to feel like a small hotel despite its 620 rooms on 37 floors. There are a maximum of 18 rooms to a floor, and each room is individually decorated and furnished, with its own wet bar and marble bathroom. The lobby is a graceful and airy place where complimentary coffee is poured from a silver samovar every morning. Rooms high on the Diamond Head side have stunning views of the crater. The top 3 floors are part of the exclusive Kuhio Club (where guests can take advantage of concierge and other special services). 2500 Kuhio Ave. (phone: 922-0811; 800-733-7777). Moderate.

Outrigger Reef Lanais – A small gem, with 54 rooms (some with kitchenettes) that look out over the expanse of Fort DeRussy and the beach. Recent renovations have transformed this place into a stylish, well-priced alternative to the big hotels that predominate in Waikiki. One block from the beach and convenient to shops and restaurants. 225 Saratoga Ave. (phone: 923-3881; 800-737-7777). Moderate.

Outrigger Reef Towers – Although it is hard to believe that a street of concrete blocks can have character, the section of Lewers Street between Kalia Road and Kalakaua Avenue does — it's narrow and shaded by very tall, spindly coconut palms. One of the concrete blocks is this hotel. Though gorgeous vistas are not a selling point here, some people find it an excellent buy. Rooms with kitchenettes are available. 227 Lewers St. (phone: 923-3111; 800-733-7777). Moderate.

Waikiki Beachcomber – Whether you look toward the ocean, Diamond Head, or downtown, the lanais here are a pleasant spot for breakfast or cocktails. For the price, its rooms are surprisingly large, with separate dressing areas and capacious closets, and their layout and color scheme give them a feeling of coolness and comfort. The lobby has facilities for booking tours, and the hotel is a short walk from the beach. 2300 Kalakaua Ave. (phone: 922-4646; 800-622-4646). Moderate.

Waikiki Gateway – Looking like an unfinished pyramid, it stands sentinel at the western end of Kalakaua Avenue, about 5 minutes' walk from the beach. Rooms, which tend to get smaller the higher up you go, have recently been renovated. Its restaurant, *Nick's Fishmarket* (see *Eating Out*), is one of Honolulu's most famous. 2070 Kalakaua Ave. (phone: 955-3741; 800-633-8799). Moderate.

Waikiki Parc – Opened by the same Japanese company that owns the neighboring *Halekulani,* this hotel focuses its attention on service and high-tech features like computer-coded room locks on its 298 rooms. It's an easy walk to Waikiki Beach, a fact that isn't immediately obvious from its towering proximity to the *Halekulani* and the *Sheraton Waikiki.* 2233 Helumoa Rd. (phone: 921-7272; 800-422-0450). Moderate.

Waikiki Shores – By a stroke of luck, this apartment hotel stands next to the *Fort DeRussy Army Museum* and has an unobstructed view across the museum grounds. From each wide lanai there is a panorama of both ocean and mountains. Under Aston management, some apartments have been refurbished; others are a little worse for wear. Linen, cooking utensils, and dishes are provided. There are fully equipped kitchens and weekly maid service. Cost and location combine to make this one of the best buys on the beach, especially for families. 2161 Kalia Rd. (phone: 926-4733; 800-922-7866). Moderate.

Waikiki Terrace – Reopened in 1990 after a major overhaul, its decor has made use of grays, greens, and mauves in appealing and innovative ways. Surrounded by Fort DeRussy, most of the 255 rooms have gorgeous views from their lanais. Downstairs, the *Mezzanine* restaurant serves tasty fare. 2045 Kalakaua Ave. (phone: 956-6000; 800-445-8811). Moderate.

Waikikian – For many returning visitors, the torches that blaze outside each night signal that they are once more entering the fabled resort area. More torches line the narrow path that passes between the Polynesian cabanas that are the hotel's salient feature. These are decorated in Hawaiian motifs, with ceiling fans, exposed timber ceilings, and wooden lanais, all contributing to the South Seas atmosphere. Some units also have kitchenettes. An adjacent 6-story contemporary building offers more conventional accommodations. The beach, a romantic lagoon, and a particularly attractive palm-fringed poolside area with a popular outdoor café called the *Tahitian Lanai* complete the amenities. 1811 Ala Moana Blvd. (phone: 949-5331; 800-922-7866). Moderate.

Hawaii Dynasty – Set on the extremely busy Ala Moana Boulevard, on the western perimeter of Waikiki (where the high-rises are), this property is within walking distance of the beach and the more hectic attractions of Kalakaua strip. The accommodations are large but not luxurious, and the swimming pool is one of the biggest in Waikiki. 1830 Ala Moana Blvd. (phone: 955-1111; 800-421-6662). Moderate to inexpensive.

Ocean Resort Hotel Waikiki – Just 1 block from 220-acre Kapiolani Park at the foot of Diamond Head, the formerly named *Quality Inn Waikiki* has always enjoyed a good reputation for service and comfort. Some rooms in the older Diamond Head Tower and all the rooms in the newer Pali Tower have kitchenettes, although the newer accommodations tend to be larger and more subdued in decor. There are 2 swimming pools for people who find the 3-minute stroll to the beach too strenuous. 175 Paoakalani Ave. (phone: 922-3861; 800-228-5151). Moderate to inexpensive.

Outrigger Edgewater – This small hostelry manages to look more like a seaside apartment house than a hotel and exudes an air of calm and quiet. For those who find the hurly-burly of large establishments either intimidating or just plain exhausting, this is the ideal spot at an ideal price. An added attraction is the *Trattoria,* a well-regarded Italian restaurant. 2168 Kalia Rd. (phone: 922-6424; 800-733-7777). Moderate to inexpensive.

Outrigger Waikiki Village – Brightly decorated with an emphasis on greens and blues, this member of the Outrigger chain is popular with young couples making a first visit to Hawaii. The poolside area is, if anything, busier than many others in the district, considering that the ocean is just 2 blocks away. Perhaps what attracts so many is its underwater viewing area. Some rooms have kitchenettes. 240 Lewers St. (phone: 923-3881; 800-733-7777). Moderate to inexpensive.

Pleasant Holiday Isle – Right in the heart of Waikiki and just a block from the beach, this is a compact hotel, though it's beginning to look a bit faded. The rates are reasonable, which more than compensates for the fact that from most of the lanais, the view is less than indelible, and the street noise is occasionally audible. 270 Lewers St. (phone: 923-0777). Moderate to inexpensive.

Royal Islander – Another stopping place where smallness is an advantage. The front desk personnel usually manage to remember guests' names. Recently renovated rooms are on the small side, though not oppressively so, and each has a lanai, refrigerator, and coffee makers on request. Street noise may prove bothersome. The property is now managed by the Outrigger chain and is opposite the *Reef* hotel, behind which is the beach. 2164 Kalia Rd. (phone: 922-1961; 800-733-7777). Moderate to inexpensive.

Waikiki Parkside – Overlooking Fort DeRussy and Ala Moana Boulevard, it offers indoor parking ($4), with shopping, restaurants, and the beach minutes away. 1850 Ala Moana Blvd. (phone: 955-1567; 800-237-9666). Moderate to inexpensive.

Royal Grove – This is a small apartment hotel with personality. Like the *Royal Hawaiian,* it is painted pink. There are very comfortable, cheerful studios as well as 1-bedroom units. Although the ocean, a block and a half away, is visible from some of the lanais, many people prefer to look out on the pool and tropical gardens. Most rooms have air conditioning and kitchenettes. There is maid service but no room service. 151 Uluniu Ave. (phone: 923-7691). Inexpensive.

Waikiki Surf – This is one of the "finds" of Honolulu. In a semi-residential part of Waikiki, it's friendly, clean, decorated in blue and green, quiet, and delightfully inexpensive. Some rooms have kitchenettes. Perhaps best of all, the 288-room hotel has two companions — the 102-room *Waikiki Surf East* (422 Royal Hawaiian Ave.) and the 110-room *Waikiki Surf West* (412 Lewers St.) — owned and run by the same very friendly people. The original *Waikiki Surf* is at 2200 Kuhio Ave. (switchboard for all three properties: 923-7671; 800-733-7777). Inexpensive.

CONDOMINIUMS

Aston Waikiki Beach Tower – With only four 2-bedroom apartments to a floor, this is Waikiki's most exclusive rentable condominium. The views, particularly on floors 25 to 40, are magnificent, with large lanais offering front-row seats as the sun slides into the Pacific. Another prime asset is privacy — the perfect antidote to the street energy of Waikiki. Full concierge service, with the beach just across the street. 2470 Kalakaua Ave. (phone: 926-6400; 800-922-3368). Very expensive to expensive.

Aston's Waikiki Sunset – Recent renovations and refurbishing have added to the appeal of this high-rise property, which is convenient to Waikiki Beach and Kapiolani Park. Besides swimming in the large pool, guests can play tennis or shuffleboard. Daily maid service. 229 Paoakalani Ave. (phone: 922-0511; 800-922-7866). Expensive to moderate.

Coconut Plaza Waikiki – This 84-studio unit condominium faces a small landscaped garden and the Ala Wai Canal. The ambience is relaxed, with complimentary continental breakfast served alfresco. Some units have kitchenettes; the complex also has a restaurant and a pool. A good buy. 450 Lewers St. (phone: 923-8828; 800-882-9696). Expensive to moderate.

Foster Tower – For location alone — right across Kalakaua Avenue from the beach — this is one of Waikiki's better buys. All rooms have color television sets, and on the property are a pool and shops. No maid service. 2500 Kalakaua Ave. (phone: 523-7785; 800-367-7040). Moderate.

Island Colony – Another luxury high-rise looking out on the Koolau Mountains and the canal, it is decorated with bleached-wood furniture, light brown walls and textiles, and beige carpets, giving it a pleasantly restful appearance. It also has a restaurant, pool, sauna, and hydromassage facilities, as well as a Jacuzzi. Daily maid service. 445 Seaside Ave. (phone: 923-2345; 800-92-ASTON). Moderate.

Pacific Monarch – Close to the *Kings Alley* shopping bazaar and a few minutes from the beach, the property offers spectacular views from its upper-floor 1-bedroom and studio units and the rooftop pool area. Laundry facilities and daily maid service. 142 Uluniu Ave. (phone: 923-9805; 800-367-6046 or 800-777-1700). Moderate.

Royal Kuhio – Two blocks away from the beach and the *International Market Place*, it has upper-floor units that offer some of the best views of Diamond Head in Waikiki. On the 7th-floor deck, there is a pool and shuffleboard. Maid service. 2240 Kuhio Ave. (phone: 923-0555; 800-367-8047). Moderate.

Waikiki Banyan – One of the largest condos in Waikiki, it's a short walk from the beach, zoo, and the *Ala Wai* golf course. The living rooms are handsomely decorated and have attractive breakfast counters that separate them from the kitchen. The building contains a sauna, a large recreation area with tennis courts and a swimming pool, laundry facilities on each floor, and daily maid service. From the top floor on the Diamond Head side you see beyond the crater to Maunalua Bay. 201 Ohua Ave. (phone: 922-0555; 800-366-7765). Moderate.

Waikiki Lanais – With its attractively furnished 1- and 2-bedroom apartments on one of Waikiki's quieter streets, this well-maintained condominium features a mix of vacation rentals and full-time residences that adds to its appeal, as does its location near the beach and the commercial heart of Waikiki. 2452 Tusitala St. (phone: 923-0994; 800-367-7042; or call Condo Rentals of Waikiki; phone: 923-0555). Moderate.

EATING OUT: There are numerous excellent restaurants in Waikiki. There are also many that are quite ordinary. Seafood houses of varying quality are abundant, as are familiar fast-food names. Tucked away in hotels on Kalakaua and Kuhio Avenues (and on various side streets) are restaurants serving Italian, Chinese, Japanese, Korean, and continental cuisines — even a couple of English pub–style places serving fish and chips and steak and kidney pie. What is impossible to find is a restaurant of note serving Hawaiian food (the few in Honolulu that do are dealt with in our *Greater Honolulu* section). With some notable exceptions, the best restaurants are not right on the beach, and most of the ones that are serve indifferent food and watered-down drinks. As a rule, dress is informal — which means alohawear, not bathing suits — and some tonier spots "prefer" gentlemen to wear jackets. A couple insist on it. For a meal for two, excluding wine, tips, and drinks, expect to pay more than $100 in a place listed as very expensive, $60 to $95 in a place listed as expensive, between $25 and $55 in a place listed as moderate, and under $25 in an inexpensive place. (*Note:* For a discussion of dining within a short distance of Waikiki, see *Diamond Head.*) While in Honolulu, don't miss the ice cream at the many stores of *Lappert's Ice Cream,* or the flavored, crushed ice over red bean paste that is served at the *Goodie Goodie Drive-In* chain. All telephone numbers are in the 808 area code unless otherwise indicated.

La Mer – The distinctive menu suits one of Hawaii's most refined restaurants. Start with an appetizer of grilled filet of salmon with steamed asparagus and orange sauce, then move on to roast duck with cherries marmalade and port wine sauce. The service is excellent and the decor an appealing blend of Oriental styles. Open daily from 6 to 9:30 PM. Reservations necessary. In the *Halekulani Hotel,* 2199 Kalia Rd. (phone: 923-2311). Very expensive to expensive.

The Secret – One of the top dining rooms in Honolulu, it has consistently won prizes for its cooking. Guests dine in a setting of high-backed rattan chairs with red velvet cushions, strolling musicians, a carp pool, and a fountain. Among the house specialties are medallions of veal *forêt noire* and rack of spring lamb. For dessert there are Polynesian fruits with kirsch, followed by well-made Irish coffee. Oenophiles can select a rare vintage or two from the vast 6,000-bottle wine room. Open daily for dinner from 6:30 to 9 PM; there is a $15 minimum charge. Reservations advised. In the *Hawaiian Regent Hotel,* 2552 Kalakaua Ave. (phone: 922-6611). Very expensive to expensive.

Bali by the Sea – Contemporary elegance, enhanced by a mix of cool whites and Mediterranean pastels, sets the scene for seaside dining. The food is excellent, with appetizers like *coquille* of shrimp and scallops with ginger sauce, enticing entrées such as Kaiwi Channel opakapaka with fresh basil, and a concluding irresistible dessert tray. Open daily for dinner from 6 to 9:30 PM. Reservations advised and valet parking is available. *Hilton Hawaiian Village Rainbow Tower,* 2005 Kalia Rd. (phone: 949-4321). Expensive.

Chez Michel – The same Michel who lent his name to the *Colony Surf* hotel also created this place. He's now retired, but the restaurant remains popular. Just outside the *Hilton Hawaiian Village* end of Waikiki in Eaton Square, it is lush with plants and heavily accented in French decor. The menu is varied, well prepared, and nicely presented. Open daily for lunch and dinner; closed Sundays for lunch. Reservations necessary. 444 Hobron Lane (phone: 955-7866). Expensive.

Musashi – Elegant decor, including miniature Japanese-style gardens, is equaled by the food that features four styles of cooking — three done at the tables. There's also a sushi bar, and typical Japanese fare can be ordered from a menu. Open for dinner daily. Reservations necessary. At the *Hyatt Regency Hotel,* 2424 Kalakaua Ave. (phone: 923-1234). Expensive.

Nicholas Nickolas – Fine dining amid soft lights and elegance at this place atop the 40-floor *Ala Moana* hotel, which affords magnificent views. The extensive menu focuses on both American and continental specialties, ranging from veal to lamb, with pasta, soup, salads, and catch-of-the-day entrées in between. Open daily from 5:30 to 11:30 PM, with live entertainment from 9:30 PM to 2:30 AM weekdays, to 3:30 AM on weekends. Reservations necessary. 410 Atkinson Dr. (phone: 955-4466). Expensive.

Nick's Fishmarket – This is one of the best fish restaurants in Honolulu. Don't let the earthy name confuse you; it is a plush establishment with individually controlled lighting systems for those customers seated at banquettes and rather too many staffers per customer. Live Maine lobsters are available at substantial cost, but this is also the ideal place to sample fresh island fish, such as opakapaka, mahimahi, and ulua. The combination seafood Louis salad is enormous and beautifully prepared. Open daily for dinner from 5:30 to 11 PM. Reservations necessary. In the *Waikiki Gateway Hotel,* 2070 Kalakaua Ave. (phone: 955-6333). Expensive.

Prince Court – This dining establishment's elegant atmosphere is duly matched by its imaginative dishes. Highlights of the menu include blackened blue ahi and kiawe grilled capon. Everything is artistically arranged, and the service is impeccable. In the *Hawaii Prince,* 100 Holomoana St. (phone: 956-1111). Expensive.

Ship's Tavern – This elegant place is decorated in an appealing mix of gray, white, and celadon green, complementing its natural backdrop of Diamond Head and the Pacific. The menu is nothing short of superb, with selections ranging from familiar standbys (such as New England clam chowder) to more unusual offerings (like sautéed filet of veal in morel sauce). Dinner nightly from 5 to 10 PM. Reservations advised. In the *Sheraton Moana Surfrider Hotel,* 2365 Kalakaua Ave. (phone: 922-3111). Expensive.

Banyan Court – The beachfront setting only adds to the enjoyment of the magnificent Sunday brunch ($32) served here. Sittings at 10 AM, noon, and 2 PM. Reservations necessary. *Sheraton Moana Surfrider Hotel,* 2365 Kalakaua Ave. (phone: 922-3111). Expensive to moderate.

Bon Appetit – Perhaps Honolulu's best French dining spot, it has the look of an elegant bistro in the French provinces with its caned-back chairs and light pink linen. The menu is imaginative and includes an unusual scallop mousse, bouillabaisse, and snails in puff pastry. The daily three- and four-course dinners are especially well priced. Closed Sundays. Reservations advised. In the *Discovery Bay* complex at 1778 Ala Moana Blvd. (phone: 942-3837). Expensive to moderate.

Ciao Mein – The *Hyatt Regency*'s original signature restaurant, *Bagwell's,* has been replaced by this gem. An eclectic menu of Italian and Chinese dishes includes delicate fried spring rolls, inspired fettuccine Alfredo, and tender pieces of lobster wrapped in noodles. Without a doubt, this is some of the finest fare in Hawaii. It offers indoor and alfresco seating nightly from 6 to 10 PM. Reservations advised. In the *Hyatt Regency Hotel,* 2424 Kalakaua Ave. (phone: 923-1234). Expensive to moderate.

Furusato – There are two branches of this Japanese eatery in Waikiki. Each has its own menu and ambience; both are comfortable if not elegant. The kitchens generally offer a range of steaks, seafood, and sushi. Open daily for lunch from 11:30 AM to 3:30 PM, and dinner from 5:30 to 10:30 PM. Reservations advised. *Hyatt Regency* (phone: 922-4991) and *Foster Tower* condominium, 2500 Kalakaua Ave. (phone: 922-5502). Expensive to moderate.

Golden Dragon – Possibly Hawaii's most elegant Chinese restaurant, the food happily lives up to the surroundings. One specialty, Imperial Beggar's chicken, is wrapped in lotus leaves with spices, then cooked for 6 hours inside a sealed clay pot to retain natural juices and flavor. Another specialty is the Peking roast duck, and be sure to leave room for the celestial desserts. Thanks to the exquisite decorative flourishes, dining indoors is as appealing as alfresco. Open daily for dinner from 6 to 9:30 PM. Reservations advised; valet parking available. *Hilton Hawaiian Village Rainbow Tower,* 2005 Kalia Rd. (phone: 949-4321). Expensive to moderate.

Hy's Steak House – Entering this place is like walking into a magnificent Victorian private library, full of velvet chairs and etched glass. But the gleaming brass broiler inside a glassed-in gazebo, where steaks and chops are prepared with loving care, demonstrates that it is something more. Although the menu indicates that chicken and seafood are available, the main attraction is steak, which is merely superb. Open daily for dinner. Reservations advised. 2440 Kuhio Ave. (phone: 922-5555). Expensive to moderate.

Matteo's – Low lighting, pleasant decor, and high-backed banquettes all combine to make this a place for quiet dining. The service is good, as is the food, which includes such highly recommended dishes as calamari, chicken, and veal. Open daily for dinner, from 6 PM to midnight; the bar is open until 2 AM. Reservations advised. In the *Marine Surf Hotel,* 364 Seaside Ave. (phone: 922-5551). Expensive to moderate.

Orchids – Sliding French doors that open onto a green lawn and expansive views of Diamond Head and the sea are a perfect backdrop for crisp white linen and tables elegantly set with silver, crystal, and fresh flowers. Breakfast is a highlight, as is the Sunday brunch from 9:30 AM to 2:30 PM, although lunch from 11 AM to 2 PM, and dinner from 5:30 to 10:30 PM are also first-rate. Reservations necessary. *Halekulani Hotel,* 2199 Kalia Rd. (phone: 923-2311). Expensive to moderate.

Baci – Linen, flatware, and crystal harmonize with the chic decor to provide an appropriate setting for the Italian specialties. Meals are complemented by a fairly priced selection of bottled wines. Open for lunch from 11:30 AM to 3 PM, and dinner from 5:30 to 10 PM daily. Reservations advised for dinner and lunch groups. Ground level, *Waikiki Trade Center,* 2255 Kuhio Ave. (phone: 924-2533). Moderate.

Mezzanine – Devotees of food that teeters on the cutting edge will appreciate the unusual "designer" pizza served here, whose toppings include everything from goat cheese to cilantro. Less adventurous folks can try the kiawe (mesquite) grilled rack of lamb, numerous pasta dishes, as well as sautéed and blackened fish dishes. There's indoor and alfresco seating to suit your fancy, as well as nightly entertainment. Open daily; on weekends, open for breakfast and dinner only. In the *Waikiki Terrace Hotel,* 2045 Kalakaua Ave. (phone: 955-6000). Moderate.

Monterrey Bay Canners – The Waikiki branch of this restaurant, located in the *Outrigger* hotel, offers a limited number of alfresco tables that take full advantage of the beachfront location. The best bet on the menu is one of the catch-of-the-day specials, which are reasonably priced and delicious. Open for breakfast,lunch, and dinner daily. Reservations advised. 2335 Kalakaua Ave. (phone: 922-5761). Moderate.

Parc Café – Although the menu is fairly limited (typically four entrées nightly, plus a buffet), the food is delicious and the prices reasonable. Pasta, catches-of-the-day, chicken, and prime ribs are the usual fare. The Sunday brunch, from 11 AM to 2 PM, is first-rate. Open daily for lunch from 11:30 AM to 2 PM, and dinner from 5:30 to 10 PM; the dinner buffets are impressive. Reservations advised. In the *Waikiki Parc Hotel,* 2198 Kalia Rd. (phone: 921-7272). Moderate.

Sergio's – Excellent Italian and continental specialties include a full range of pasta, plus veal, chicken, and shrimp in a variety of styles. Open daily for dinner from 5:30 to 11 PM. Reservations necessary. 445 Nohonani St. (phone: 926-3388). Moderate.

Siam Inn – There has been high praise for this Thai restaurant in the heart of Waikiki, where imported spices and fresh local produce and seafood are combined to advantage. Normally fiery Thai dishes are prepared with Western tastebuds in mind. Open daily for lunch from 11:30 AM to 2 PM, and dinner from 5:30 to 9:30 PM. Reservations unnecessary. 407 Seaside (phone: 926-8802). Moderate.

Spats – Dinner in a well-known disco might not sound very promising, but don't let what goes on after 9 PM deter you from coming here. The decor recalls a rather lavish speakeasy, with beveled glass, highly polished wood, and waiters in cutaways and suspenders. Try the chicken *alla cacciatore* or shrimp *all'aglio e olio* (with garlic and oil). Fettuccine Alfredo is the star attraction among the pasta dishes. Open daily from 6 to 10 PM. Reservations advised for dinner. In the *Hyatt Regency Hotel,* 2424 Kalakaua Ave. (phone: 923-1234). Moderate.

Trattoria – The chef doesn't overload the menu with tomato paste, and many dishes are cooked *al burro* — delicately, in butter — instead of doused in olive oil. The lasagna in this charmingly decorated restaurant is well worth tasting. So are *cotoletta di vitello alla parmigiana* and *pollo alla romana.* The cannelloni Milanese is definitely a "don't miss." Open for dinner daily from 5:30 to 8:30 PM. Reservations necessary. *Outrigger Edgewater Hotel,* 2168 Kalia Rd. (phone: 923-8415). Moderate.

Zuke Bistro – Formerly *Richard's Stuffed Potato,* this eatery moved to larger and fancier digs. The food remains first-rate, with a changing menu featuring all types of fish and meat specialties prepared by the owner-chef. Full wine list. Valet parking. Dinner from 5:30 to 10 PM. Closed Sundays. Reservations advised. 2171 Ala Wai (phone: 922-0102). Moderate.

California Pizza Kitchen – Wonderful pizza and other popular Italian dishes, such as calzone and eggplant parmigiana, all cooked in ovens fueled with flavor-enhancing kiawe wood. A relaxed place to eat that's deservedly popular. Reservations unnecessary. 1910 Kalakaua Ave., 2nd Floor (phone: 955-5161). Moderate to inexpensive.

Hard Rock Café – The Honolulu branch of this trendy international chain attracts a young crowd out to be part of "the scene." Food is good, crowds are standard day or night, and the noise level is decibels higher than that which allows comfortable conversation. But, then, that's intended to be part of the appeal. Guitars of famous rockers are part of the decor, as are other blasts of rock 'n' roll memorabilia, and patrons come as much to buy T-shirts and other signature souvenirs as to eat or drink. Valet parking. Open daily from 11:30 AM to midnight. No reservations. 1826 Kalakaua Ave. (phone: 955-7383). Moderate to inexpensive.

Caffè Guccini – The warm welcome at this low-key café is followed by fine pasta, rich cappuccino, and tempting desserts. Guests may bring their own wine or beer, but there's also a full bar. Open daily from 3 to 11:30 PM. Reservations unnecessary. 2139 Kuhio Ave. (phone: 922-5287). Inexpensive.

Malia's Cantina – Island-style Mexican food of mediocre quality, compensated by huge margaritas for starters. The Hawaiian entertainment can be worth a visit. Open daily for lunch from 11 AM to 3 PM, and dinner from 3 to 10 PM. No reservations. 311 Lewers St. (phone: 922-7808). Inexpensive.

Diamond Head

Like the Rock of Gibraltar, Table Mountain at Cape Town, and Sugar Loaf in Rio de Janeiro, Diamond Head is immediately recognizable, not only to sailors and airline navigators but to armchair travelers all over the world. Contrary to popular understanding, its name has nothing to do with its shape. It was christened Diamond Head by British seamen who mistook the calcite crystals they found there for diamonds. The older Hawaiian name is Leahi, brow of the ahi, or yellow-fin tuna, which it resembled in the imagination of early Hawaiians. Anyone who has seen the effigies of knights in the crypts of English and Norman churches will find a distinct likeness between them and the silhouette of the crater as seen from the high windows of Waikiki at dusk.

In geological terms, Diamond Head is a formation resulting from the titanic explosions that occurred when water came into contact with hot lava rising from a fissure 400,000 years ago, and it has been at peace, volcanically speaking, for 150,000 years.

Today, Diamond Head is a National Natural Landmark and a state monument. A road off Diamond Head Road between Makapuu Road and 18th Avenue leads through a tunnel onto the sun-baked floor of the crater, much of which today forms part of Fort Ruger and is used by the Hawaiian National Guard. To get a closer look at the terrain and at the pillboxes, gun emplacements, and warrens of tunnels built as an integral part of the Pacific defense systems in World War II, you can hike from the parking lot near the firing range through the kiawe and keahole trees to the viewing area at Point Leahi, 760 feet above sea level, the highest spot on Diamond Head. Depending on your physical condition, this should take between 30 minutes and 1 hour. The route leads along a gently graded, but occasionally rough, trail dug into the hillside. The most difficult patches have concrete steps and balustrades to make the going easier. Through a short tunnel and up 99 steps, you arrive at a gun emplacement. Beyond, three spiral staircases and a steel ladder lead up to the crater rim and a fine view of Honolulu, Waikiki, and the mountains. The trail is open from 6 AM to 6 PM, which makes sunrise and sunset hikes possible on shorter winter days.

Diamond Head's varied birdlife provides an interesting diversion for those making the climb, for it is an unofficial sanctuary for a number of cage birds, strangers to the islands, that have escaped or been released from captivity and have proliferated inside the crater and on its slopes. Species to look for include the yellow-fronted canary, the red-eared waxbill, the saffron finch with its perennial look of surprise, and the white-cheeked, pink-billed Java sparrow. Probably the most easily recognizable is the pin-tailed whydah, which, with its long, graceful tailfeathers and its black and white plumage, looks like a Dominican friar with a long train. While these birds add a dimension of color to the somewhat muted hues that characterize the crater most of the year, it should be noted that their presence among the native bird population is not without hazards, including hybridization, competition for food, and the introduction of disease.

The ocean side of Diamond Head, from Kapiolani Park to Black Point, is the start of Honolulu's Gold Coast, the most fashionable, expensive, and exclusive acres in Hawaii. The State of Hawaii has been able to obtain some property here and there, creating several vest-pocket parks. Most of the narrow ribbon of land between the outer edge of the crater and the sea is still privately owned, its cliffside and beachside villas of considerable luxury protected by high walls overrun with hibiscus, bougainvillea, poinsettia, and royal poinciana.

Easy access to the cliffs and narrow beaches on the ocean side of Diamond Head is possible from Beach Road, which turns off Diamond Head Road near the lighthouse. At Diamond Head Beach Park you will find divers fishing among the segmented reefs, though casual swimming is not recommended. Swimmers should try Kaalawai Beach, near Black Point, where volcanic lava flowed into the sea several hundred thousand years ago. There is public access from the end of Kulamanu Place, also off Diamond Head Road. Watch for net-throwing fishermen, who still practice their graceful craft in these parts.

SHOPPING: The *Kahala Mall* (phone: 732-7736) has a few standard shops, including *Liberty House* (phone: 941-2345), *Long's Drugs* (phone: 732-0784), and *Waldenbooks* (phone: 737-9550). If malls aren't your favorite milieu, this one's a lot easier to take than the larger, more crowded *Ala Moana.*

Apropos – Clothing with a European flair. *Kahala Mall* (phone: 735-1611).

As Time Goes By – Antique jewelry, paintings, and silver are showcased at this antiques shop. *Kilohana Square,* 1016 Kapahulu Ave. (phone: 732-1174).

Bailey's Antique & Thrift Shop – Prime vintage aloha shirts now fetch a cool grand here, although not all the goods are that pricey. 758 Kapahulu Ave (phone: 734-7628).

Bebe Sport – Trendy fashions are for sale at this shop. *Kahala Mall* (phone: 734-6444).

Carriage House – The mix at this store is European, Oriental, and American antiques. *Kilohana Square,* 1016 Kapahulu Ave. (phone: 737-2622).

Corner Loft – An alluring selection of antiques, silver, and jewelry. *Kahala Mall* (phone: 732-4149).

Juma – Colorful clothing for men and women, which is highlighted by the eye-popping designs of Jams, Baik Baik, and other style-conscious lines. *Kahala Mall* (phone: 739-5303).

Max Davis – High-quality Oriental antiques are the thing here. *Kilohana Square,* 1016 Kapahulu Ave. (phone: 735-2341).

Quilts Hawaii – Collectible Hawaiian quilts, as well as more contemporary designs, are sold at this shop. 2338 South King St. (phone: 942-3195).

Riches – A costume-jewelry kiosk with an impressive collection of earrings. *Kahala Mall* (phone: 737-3303).

NIGHTLIFE: Residents of Diamond Head are rarely seen in nightclubs and never at extravaganzas or luaus. If you're not joining them for a civilized evening at home, then you might spot them at the symphony or the ballet. *Bobby McGee's Conglomeration* in the *Colony East hotel* (2885 Kalakaua Ave.; phone: 922-1282), a mixed bag of stained glass, fringed velvet canopies, Tiffany lampshades, and plush banquettes, has dinner and dancing each night — the latter occasionally bordering on disco.

CHECKING IN: There are just a few hotels in the Diamond Head area, and prices are generally the same as in Waikiki. Expect to pay around $165 and up for a double in a hotel listed as expensive, from $80 to $160 at a place listed as moderate. All telephone numbers are in the 808 area code unless otherwise indicated.

Colony Surf – A true Hollywood-style condominium right on the beach, it is one of the most delightful places to stay in Honolulu. Apartments are decorated in the plush, off-white tones that many people associate with seaside living. There are no lanais, but large windows with glorious views. Kitchens are modern and fully equipped, and there is daily maid service and adequate laundry facilities. The lobby is small and elegant and chiefly famous for being the entrance to *Michel's* restaurant (see *Eating Out*). Studios with lanais and kitchenettes are available in the adjacent *Colony East* hotel, which is owned and operated by the same company at the same address. 2895 Kalakaua Ave. (phone: 923-5751; 800-252-7873). Expensive to moderate.

Diamond Head Beach – This 14-story structure on the beach was completely refurbished in 1986 to make it one of the more attractive places in terms of price and location in Honolulu. Units range from hotel rooms to 1-bedroom apartments. Rooms are smallish but comfortable, with good-size lanais. Although there is little in the way of a lobby and no shops, pool, or tour desks, these are available close by, in the *New Otani.* 2947 Kalakaua Ave. (phone: 922-1928; 800-367-6046). Expensive to moderate.

New Otani Kaimana Beach – The location is the thing here: on the Diamond Head side of Kapiolani Park, just a few minutes away from Waikiki by foot or bus. The beach is right outside, and beautiful reefs are within easy snorkeling distance. The *Hau Tree Lanai* terrace restaurant (see *Eating Out*) overlooks the beach and is edged by (and named for) large hau trees. Oceanside rooms have stunning views. Families seem to like this hotel, and women traveling alone have found it a friendly, hospitable, and safe haven. 2863 Kalakaua Ave. (phone: 923-1555; 800-657-7949). Expensive to moderate.

EATING OUT: The dinner tab in Diamond Head will generally run a bit higher than in Waikiki. For a meal for two in the restaurants listed below, $100 and up is very expensive; $65 to $95 is expensive; $25 to $60 is moderate; and under $20 is inexpensive. Prices do not include wine, tips, or drinks. All telephone numbers are in the 808 area code unless otherwise indicated.

Michel's – At most beachfront restaurants in Honolulu, the cooking takes a back seat to the view. Not here. For a start, the decor does not suggest a mere extension of sand and ocean. The dining room is elegant and subdued. Although there are occasionally deft local touches, such as prosciutto served with papaya, most of the dishes tend to be classic. Even the opakapaka is served Véronique style with a champagne sauce added. Jacket required for dinner. Open daily for breakfast from 7 to 11 AM, lunch from 11:30 AM to 3 PM, and dinner from 5:30 to 10 PM. Reservations necessary. In the *Colony Surf Hotel,* 2895 Kalakaua Aven. (phone: 923-6552). Very expensive to expensive.

Hau Tree Lanai – One of the best alfresco locales in Waikiki, with beachside patio seating beneath the ancient tree that gives this restaurant its name. Soft-shell crabs, New York strip steaks, and Cajun sashimi are some of the dinner offerings. Open for breakfast from 6:30 to 11 AM, lunch from 11:30 AM to 2:30 PM, and dinner from 5:30 to 9:00 PM. Reservations advised. In the *New Otani Kaimana Beach Hotel,* 2863 Kalakaua Ave. (phone: 923-1555). Expensive to moderate.

Miyako – Shabu shabu–style cooking (meat, vegetables, and seafood prepared in boiling water at the table) is emphasized here. Seating is either in the main dining room with its rooftop, oceanside views, or in small tatami rooms where guests sit on mats on the floor. Two days' advance notice will procure the special Kaiseiki dinner of 7, 8, or 9 courses, all making use of the freshest produce, fish, and seafood available that day. Open daily for dinner from 6 to 10 PM. Reservations advised. *New Otani Kaimana Beach Hotel,* 2863 Kalakaua Ave. (phone: 923-1555). Expensive to moderate.

Hajibaba's – Tony residential Kahala is the unlikely setting for this sophisticated Moroccan eatery. The Fassi Feast for two includes lemon chicken, lamb couscous, Moroccan pastries, and fresh mint tea. The Royal Feast ($32) goes beyond overindulgence. The portions are tremendous, so order accordingly. Most evenings there are two shows that feature the talents of belly dancers accompanied by Moroccan musicians. Open daily. Reservations necessary. 4614 Kilauea Ave. (phone: 735-5522). Moderate.

Keo's – This is a fine place to sample Thai fare, which can be flavorful and fiery, although the kitchen will prepare milder versions of its hot specialties if requested. Mint-flavored spring rolls make a delicious appetizer, and cold sweet tea is a good accompaniment for the spicier dishes. The setting is elegant and nearly drenched in orchids; the crowd, Honolulu's cognoscenti. Open daily for dinner from 5 to 10:30 PM. Reservations necessary. 625 Kapahulu Ave. (phone: 737-8240). Moderate.

Midtown Honolulu and the Ala Moana Center

This busy area — bounded by the ocean, by Ward Avenue on the *ewa* (western) side, Beretania Avenue on the mountain side, and Kalakaua Avenue and the Ala Wai Canal on the Diamond Head side — is the center of Oahu's communications and shopping. The *Ala Moana Shopping Center,* and to a lesser extent the *Ward Warehouse Shopping Center,* attracts people from all over the state. Ninety percent of the islands' radio and TV news is relayed from the studios here; *TheBus* terminal at *Ala Moana* is the busiest on Oahu; and close to Kewalo Boat Basin is one of Hawaii's most famous restaurants — *John Dominis* (see *Eating Out*). In addition, in this area are Ala Moana Park, the beach park most popular with Honolulu residents, and the *Neal S. Blaisdell Center* (Kapiolani Blvd. and Ward Ave.; phone: 521-2911), which is the scene of wrestling, basketball, and boxing events, rock concerts, and boat and automobile shows. The *Blaisdell Center*'s concert hall on South King Street is also the home of the *Honolulu Symphony Orchestra.*

Ala Moana Center – At this marketplace of the central Pacific, Asians, Australians, and South Seas Islanders can be seen as well as French, Britons, Germans, and plenty of locals indulging in that ritual that seems to unite people the world over — shopping. It's the perfect place for people watching, with fountains, statuary, and pools to relax by. And it's not just tourists who parade past: *Ala Moana Center* is the main terminus on Oahu for *TheBus,* so many island people come through as well. (For discussions of the individual stores, see *Shopping.*) Ala Moana Blvd., opposite Ala Moana Park (phone: 946-2811).

Ala Moana Park – This 76-acre recreation area was once a swampland of bulrushes, duck ponds, and islets of coconut palms and kiawe trees. Later, part of it was the city dump. Today, Ala Moana is the favorite city beach of Honolulu residents partly because of its safe swimming areas (do not venture out into the boat channels, however) and partly because it is easily accessible and away from the main hotel complexes. However, Ala Moana's beach is hard-packed sand, probably because it's manmade; plans to upgrade the park and to bring in new supplies of sand have been announced. It's great as is, with deep, sheltered waters that attract swimmers, paths that are very popular with Honolulu's fanatical joggers, picnic tables, tennis courts, a bowling green, and six softball fields. The adjacent Aina Moana Park, also known as Magic Island, affords a good view of the yachts sailing in and out of the Ala Wai Yacht Harbor across the narrow canal in Waikiki as well as a sheltered swimming beach. Between Ala Moana Blvd. and the ocean.

Contemporary Arts Center – Originally housed in the offices of the Hawaii Newspaper Agency (where it now maintains a satellite gallery), it moved to its own premises on the lower slopes of Tantalus in 1988. Top-quality, changing exhibits highlight today's best artists in a variety of disciplines (only David Hockney's work is on permanent exhibit). Among the 500 artists whose works are featured are the late Andy Warhol, Robert Arneson, and Deborah Butterfield, as well as Hawaiians Jean Charlot, Satoru Abe, and Isami Doi, and the late Madge Tennet. Notable is David Hockney's *L'Enfant et les Sortileges,* a three-dimensional work housed in its own pavilion, based on the English pop artist's sets and costumes for Ravel's 1925 opera. Open from 10 AM to 4 PM Closed Tuesdays. Admission $3; Thursdays free. 2411 Makiki Heights Dr. (phone: 526-1322; recorded information, 526-0232).

Honolulu Academy of Arts – For anyone who has ever been daunted by the sheer magnitude of the *Metropolitan Museum of Art* in New York or the *National Gallery* in Washington, DC, this human-size enclave of civilization and coolness will come as a revelation. It is possible within a couple of hours or so to savor the cultures of the West and the East without becoming mind-boggled with strange images and arcane facts. Paintings from the Italian Renaissance and Impressionist works from 19th-century France form part of the Western holdings. From the Far East there are screens, lacquerwork, and wood block prints from the 17th century. Segna di Bonaventura's *Madonna and Child* (14th century) is one of the earliest Renaissance paintings in the academy's collection. From Japan there is an ink and color handscroll dating from AD 1250. John Singleton Copley and William Guy Wall are among the several American painters represented here. Closed Mondays. 900 S. Beretania St. (phone: 538-1006).

Kewalo Boat Basin – The gleaming white hulls, polished mahogany, uniform masts, and endless bright blue tarpaulins on the boats in the Ala Wai Boat Harbor at Waikiki's western end tend to make it look like a boatyard in aspic, as though a visitor from outer space had read a book on how to construct one and couldn't get the details quite right. The Kewalo Boat Basin reminds you what boats are supposed to look like — slightly shabby and sailed in. The few remaining sampans that work out of Honolulu bring the day's catch back to the marina here, destined ultimately for the pans and broilers of *John Dominis* and *Fisherman's Wharf* restaurants in the neighborhood and other eating houses farther afield. This is also where the tour boats set off for trips along the coast to Diamond Head and Pearl Harbor.

Maui Divers Jewelry Design Center – A million dollars were spent on the museum-quality displays and to create the tour, which starts with an 8-minute video explaining the diversity of Hawaii's corals and follows with a look at the jewelry manufacturing plant where the coral is designed, cast, polished, and assembled. After the tour, you'll have a chance to spend from $150 to $15,000 on the results. Open Mondays through Saturdays from 10 AM to 3 PM. No admission charge. Near *Ala Moana Center,* at 1520 Liona St. (phone: 946-7979).

Royal Hawaiian Mint – This small mint produces some very attractive Hawaiian commemorative coins in bronze, silver, and gold. These collectibles honor the likes of Princess Kaiulani (daughter of Liliuokalani, the last reigning Queen of Hawaii) and several Hawaiian monarchs in beautiful detail. The shop, fronted by "royal guards" clad in 19th-century garb who greet you as you enter, also serves as a museum of Hawaiian coins and medals. Open Mondays through Fridays from 10 AM to 5 PM. No admission charge. 1421 Kalakaua Ave., near S. King St. (phone: 949-6468).

SHOPPING: In midtown, most shopping means a visit to the *Ala Moana Center, Ward Warehouse,* or the *Ward Center.*

ALA MOANA SHOPPING CENTER

A major expansion in 1989 upped the number of stores in this complex to 220, including large mainland operations such as *Sears* and *J. C. Penney,* plus a food court with more than 20 fast-food specialty restaurants. The center also has the main *TheBus* terminus on Oahu. The No. 8 bus leaves for and comes from Waikiki every 10 minutes, and the No. 20 bus stops here on the Airport-Waikiki run.

Artlines – All sorts of artistic to mystic collectibles from all over the globe. Plenty to browse through and maybe even be unable to resist buying (phone: 941-1445).

Banana Republic – The Hawaii branch of this outfitter of the urban adventurer is a good place for well-made, sanely priced, all-cotton clothing, as well as a location to find the unusual — especially if it's travel-related (phone: 955-2602).

Bruno Magli – A beautiful selection of Italian-style shoes and accessories for men and women (phone: 955-1448).

Cartier – This is its first boutique located in Hawaii, and stocks a full range of Cartier goods in the *Ala Moana Center.* The store is a replica of the original *Cartier's* in Paris (phone: 955-5533).

Celine – A full range of women's and men's accessories, with the Celine logo as the lure (phone: 973-3366).

Chanel – Every Chanel item ever imagined and then some at prices that maybe you hadn't. Accessories, perfumes, jewelry, and more (phone: 942-5555).

Chocolates for Breakfast – The women's clothing sold here is often elegant, sometimes daring, and occasionally counter-chic, but always sophisticated. For the pure of heart there are muslins that *look* innocent enough (phone: 947-3434).

Crack Seed Center – Preserved seeds and fruits, including dried cherries, plums, ginger, and lemon peel are featured (phone: 949-7200).

Emporio Armani – Italian men's and women's fashions in all their stylish glory (phone: 523-5020).

Foot Locker – It bills itself as America's Most Complete Athletic Store, and it might be right (phone: 944-8390).

Hale Kukui – Candles from all over the world, including scented, dripless, and/or smokeless varieties. Charming candle-powered windmills and unusual Hawaiian *Christmas* decorations are also featured (phone: 949-6500).

Honolulu Book Shop – One of the largest and most comprehensive in Hawaii (phone: 941-2274).

Iida's – This shop specializes in things Japanese, from bronze statues to porcelains to back massage rollers. It's fun to explore just to see what's being offered; there're some good gift ideas, too (phone: 973-0320).

Images International/Otsuka Gallerie – The works of Japan's Hisashi Otsuka are worth seeing, even if the price tags are high (phone: 947-8844).

Laise Adzer – The Hawaiian branch of this high-fashion designer shop offers a distinctive mix of ethnic fabrics and haute couture for women. The prices are high, but the clothes are simply beautiful (phone: 944-1564).

Liberty House – Hawaii's leading department store, of which you will find a token version in hotels on all the major islands. The emphasis is on middle-of-the-road men's, women's, and children's fashions — not quite designer creations, but not simply aloha-wear, either. The *Ala Moana* store also has housewares, toys, books, and so on. Visits to more than a dozen *Liberty House* stores indicate that the staff is on the whole more than usually helpful (phone: 941-2345).

MCM – Offering the finest in German leather goods, this shop takes its initials from designer Michael Cromer of Munich (phone: 955-8700).

Michel's Baguette – Here's the perfect place to stop for coffee, pastries, or croissants in the midst of an excursion to *Ala Moana.* Ocean side, ground level (phone: 946-6888). Inexpensive.

North Beach Leather – From coats to dresses, pants to accessories, everything you might want to wear made of leather — with high-fashion design and price tags to match (phone: 949-6719).

Pocketbook Man – Perhaps Hawaii's most complete selection of luggage and handbags, with some very elegant choices, is here (phone: 949-3535).

Polo Ralph Lauren – At three times the size of the designer's original shop in *Ward Center,* this shop carries a full collection of the Polo designs (phone: 947-7656).

Prides of New Zealand – Everything in lambskin, from stadium rugs to car seat covers, toys to golf club warmers. Golf club warmers? In Hawaii? Anyway, you'll find it all here (phone: 944-5590).

Products of Hawaii – Hawaiian perfume, Hawaiian tiki carvings, Hawaiian *lau hala* mats, Hawaiian-designed greeting cards are sold here — as advertised. It's a good spot to do all your souvenir shopping at one time (phone: 949-6866).

Royal Hawaiian Heritage – The place to visit if you've become enamored of the black and gold Hawaiian-style jewelry that graces many local women. Across from the *Ala Moana Center* at 1430 Kona St. (phone: 973-4343).

Sharper Image – This adult "toy" store is bound to have something to please, be it products of high-tech electronics or space-age imagination. The prices are neither low nor ridiculous (phone: 949-4100).

Tahiti Imports – Polynesian fashions for women, a lot of them quite classy in their brief way, are sold here. The *pareu,* in simple and elegant designs, can be turned into intriguing cover-ups and skirts (phone: 941-4539).

Waterford/Wedgwood – Here is a complete selection of England's finest porcelain and crystal (phone: 943-9630).

WARD WAREHOUSE

The *Ward Warehouse,* on Ala Moana Boulevard opposite the Kewalo Boat Basin, is a 2-story complex of 70 boutiques and restaurants constructed from stout timbers painted brown. A lot of people come here just to sip fine coffee at *The Coffee Works* and to munch on candy from *Fudge Works.*

Extra Dimension – Beautiful silk flowers and arrangements are made in this shop with the same traditional techniques used in Japan (phone: 521-5512).

Neon Leon – What started as a neon lighting specialty shop has become a place to find inexpensive, offbeat, humorous gifts, plus one of Hawaii's best selections of humorous greeting cards (phone: 545-7666).

Nohea Gallery – Superior Hawaiian arts and crafts are on display and for sale. Among these items are prints, drawings, woven goods, chimes, ceramics, pottery, and scrimshaw with nautical etchings (phone: 599-7927).

Pomegranates in the Sun – The name's a bit far-fetched, but the selection of hand-painted and ethnic clothing for men and women is intriguing (phone: 531-1108).

Waldenbooks – Offers a wide selection of best sellers and coffee-table titles, including several shelves of Hawaiiana (phone: 533-2711).

WARD CENTER

On Ala Moana Boulevard, across the street from *Ward Warehouse* and from Ala Moana Beach Park, *Ward Center* features a selection of upscale shops.

Imago – High-fashion clothing from American designers (phone: 521-1112).

Willowdale Gallery – Items featured are of the antique sort, most hailing from Europe (phone: 536-2080).

Some popular eateries here are *Monterey Bay Canners,* which features kiawe-wood charcoal-broiled fish (phone: 536-6197); *Sushi Masa* (phone: 536-1007) is self-explanatory; *Il Fresco,* with fine Italian specialties (phone: 523-5191); *Compadres,* a spacious, plant-filled place serving Mexican fare (phone: 523-1307); and *Mary Catherine's,* which serves delicious coffees and desserts (phone: 531-3525).

NIGHTLIFE: *Rumours* (at the *Ala Moana;* phone: 955-4811) is one of Honolulu's more popular discos, and gears itself to a slightly older, more sophisticated crowd. *TGI Friday's* (950 Ward Ave.; phone: 523-5841) has a lively bar, while the much quieter and more relaxed *Horatio's* (1050 Ala Moana Blvd.; phone: 521-5002) features young island musicians who perform contemporary music Wednesdays through Sundays. For just plain mingling, *Monterey Bay Canners, Compadres,* and *Ryan's,* all at *Ward Center,* are crowded and lively.

CHECKING IN: Midtown is not too close to the "action" in Waikiki, so few tourists stay in the area. That, in itself, may add to the area's appeal for some. Expect to pay $90 and up for a double in a hotel listed as expensive and from $45 to $85 in one listed as moderate. All telephone numbers are in the 808 area code unless otherwise indicated.

Ala Moana – Bright, sunny rooms in lively tropical colors and just about every kind of hotel service imaginable are two of the things that help this 36-story property compensate for not being close enough to the Waikiki beaches to be in the swing. The hotel's size can sometimes be a disadvantage; although the room staff and managers seem very helpful, a somewhat impersonal feeling pervades. 410 Atkinson Dr. (phone: 955-4811; 800-367-6025). Expensive to moderate.

Manoa Valley Inn – This may be Honolulu's most complete bed and breakfast facility, with 8 bedrooms in a beautifully restored turn-of-the-century Manoa Valley home, and it is highly recommended. Rates include an ample continental breakfast, afternoon pupus, and sunset cocktails. Bus connections to *Ala Moana Center,* and from there to all other parts of Oahu, are available. About 2 miles from Waikiki, at 2001 Vancouver Dr. (phone: 947-6019). Expensive to moderate.

Pagoda – Some people prefer to keep away from "the strip," but still within striking distance of Waikiki's sands. This is one place to fulfill both aims. A block and a half north of the *Ala Moana Center,* it's quiet and pleasant, with an informal staff that is surprisingly professional. On the hotel grounds is an attractive tropical garden with a pond of over 3,000 beautifully colored carp as well as the *Pagoda Floating* restaurant, which is quite popular with residents. 1525 Rycroft St. (phone: 941-6611; 800-367-6060). Moderate.

EATING OUT: Although not as diverse as the restaurants in Waikiki, there are a number of good places in the Ala Moana–Midtown area. For a meal for two, excluding wine, tips, and drinks, expect to pay more than $90 and up for a place listed as very expensive; $65 to $85 in a place listed as expensive, between $25 and $60 in a place listed as moderate, and under $25 in an inexpensive place. All telephone numbers are in the 808 area code.

John Dominis – One of the best (and most famous) dining spots in Honolulu, albeit expensive, at the end of an unpromising street of warehouses and light industries on a promontory overlooking the Kewalo Basin and the Pacific. Inside the dining room, at a central island lavishly laden with fruits of the sea, a chef shucks oysters, steams clams, and makes broth. In saltwater pools spiny lobsters and fresh local fish clamber and swim around. This is an ideal place to sample island seafood: ono (wahoo), onaga (red snapper), and opakapaka (white snapper) are all available in season. The cioppino (stew) of seafood and fresh fish cooked in tomatoes, herbs, and spices is unbeatable. Open daily for dinner from 5:30 to 9:30 PM; Sunday brunch from 9 AM to 1 PM. Reservations necessary. 43 Ahui St. (phone: 523-0955). Very expensive.

Andrews – The steamed clams in herbs and spices and the veal dishes are particularly noteworthy at one of Honolulu's less touted Italian restaurants. Linen, crystal, and silver set the tone for a relaxed evening in pleasant surroundings. Open daily for lunch from 11 AM to 4 PM, and dinner from 4 to 10 PM. Reservations advised. *Ward Center,* 1200 Ala Moana Blvd. (phone: 523-8677). Expensive to moderate.

Café Cambio – Northern Italian fare combines with southern highlights like cioppino and an *antipasto misto.* The owner is from Turin, which helps make this place the real thing. Open for lunch weekdays from 11 AM to 2 PM, and dinner daily from 5:30 to 10:15 PM; closed Mondays. Reservations necessary for lunch only.

1680 Kapiolani Blvd., adjacent to the *Kapiolani Theater* (phone: 942-0740). Moderate.

Café Sistina – One of Honolulu's hipper establishments, its trattoria atmosphere attracts a mixed crowd, who come for the excellent cooking and live jazz music. The menu, similar to *Café Cambio* (same owner), is northern Italian, with delicious pasta, meat, and fish specialties. Open daily. Reservations taken until 8 PM; after that, there's likely to be a wait at the door for first-come, first-served seating. 1314 S. King St. (phone: 526-0071). Moderate.

Compadres – Delicious Mexican food, a comfortable setting, and good prices make this a popular spot. Open daily for breakfast from 9:30 to 11:30 AM, lunch from 11 AM to 2:30 PM, and dinner from 5 to 10 PM. On Saturdays and Sundays, a weekend brunch is served from 10:30 AM to 2 PM. Reservations advised. *Ward Center* (phone: 523-1307). Moderate.

Fisherman's Wharf – Tuna and charter boats tie up at the dock beside this seafront place with a nautical atmosphere. Open daily. Reservations advised. 1009 Ala Moana Blvd., Kewalo Basin (phone: 538-3808). Moderate.

Il Fresco – High-tech design and tables set with crystal and linen fit its chic location. A varied menu features blackened ahi (tuna) and pasta. Open daily for dinner from 6 to 10 PM; Mondays through Fridays for lunch from 11:30 AM to 2 PM. Reservations advised. *Ward Center* (enter on Auahi St.; phone: 523-5191). Moderate.

Horatio's – The nautical decor is most appropriate in this tavern overlooking the Kewalo Boat Basin. Among the house specialties worth trying are island seafood and Nebraska beef. Freshly baked Russian rye bread accompanies each entrée. Open daily for lunch from 11 AM to 5 PM, and dinner from 5 to 10 PM. Reservations recommended Fridays and Saturdays. *Ward Warehouse,* 1050 Ala Moana Blvd. (phone: 521-5002). Moderate.

Salerno – This is like a neighborhood Italian restaurant in New York city, where generous amounts of delicious food are served (order a half portion if you're not very hungry). Just over the McCully Bridge from Waikiki. Open daily for lunch from 11 AM to 2:30 PM, and dinner from 5 to 10 PM. Reservations advised. 1960 Kapiolani Blvd., second floor (phone: 942-5273). Moderate.

Yanagi Sushi – Two Tokyo-style sushi bars serve a sushi lover's abundance of specials. The atmosphere is upbeat, the decor simple but appealing, and the sushi first-rate. Open daily. Reservations necessary. 762 Kapiolani Blvd. (phone: 537-1525). Moderate.

China House – The cavernous dining room of this Honolulu favorite is often full. If shark fin or bird nest soup is your thing, try it here. Four varieties of the former and three of the latter are served. The dim sum is famous throughout the island, and is served daily from 11 AM to 2 PM. Open daily. Reservations advised. At the top of the ramp from Kapiolani Blvd. in the *Ala Moana Center* (phone: 949-6622). Moderate to inexpensive.

Orson's – Downstairs is a coffee shop called the *Chowder House,* which serves fresh salads as well as seafood; upstairs, a dining room decorated with beautifully stained woods offers more fine seafood. Open daily for lunch and dinner; lunch menu available from 11 AM to 10 PM. Reservations advised. *Ward Warehouse,* 1050 Ala Moana Blvd. (phone: 521-5681). Upstairs moderate; downstairs inexpensive.

Ryan's Parkplace – Popular for its pasta, vegetable, and fish dishes, desserts, and coffee. Open daily for lunch from 11 AM to 5 PM, and dinner from 5 to 10 PM, with partial alfresco seating. Reservations advised. *Ward Center,* 1050 Ala Moana Blvd. (phone: 523-9132). Moderate to inexpensive.

TGI Friday's – The Honolulu version of the New York original features antique furnishings, a friendly bar, and surprisingly good food at modest prices (especially for the enormous portions served, which can easily be shared). Best known for its potato skins, this eatery also serves an array of quiches, omelettes, salads, desserts, and more. It's always lively and usually noisy. Open daily from 11 AM to midnight, Fridays and Saturdays to 1 AM. No reservations. 950 Ward Ave. (phone: 523-5841). Moderate to inexpensive.

Big Ed's Deli – This is the place to head if you've got a craving for New York–style pastrami or corned beef. Popular with the lunch crowd, it's much easier to go at dinnertime. Open Mondays through Fridays from 10:30 AM to 10 PM; Saturdays and Sundays from 8 AM to 10 PM. Reservations unnecessary. In *Ward Center* (phone: 536-4591). Inexpensive.

Downtown Honolulu

It may come as a surprise to many people, but there is a Honolulu outside the beaches and huge, windowed gravestones that line Kalakaua Avenue in Waikiki. Even if the hotels and restaurants were not there, Honolulu would thrive as a marketplace between the Far East and Australia and the United States and as the capital of a fascinating island state with a cultural past as singular as any in the Union. The high-rises housing famous corporations along Bishop Street and the surprisingly elegant promenade of the Fort Street Mall bear witness to Honolulu's importance as a Pacific marketplace and communications center. Iolani Palace and the Iolani Barracks remind us of the state's royal and independent past. The four-masted *Falls of Clyde* is a memento of the days when trade with the Sandwich Islands meant several weeks at sea, not just a few hours in the air. The city's contemporary status as the legislative and executive center of the 50th state is represented by some of the most handsome government buildings in the US, while other structures reflect the religious affiliations of their builders — Catholic, Anglican, and Congregational. There are also small enclaves of Filipinos, Koreans, and Japanese, but more significant, the city has a Chinatown, small by the standards of those in the great port cities such as San Francisco and Singapore, yet still carrying the flavor of the days when people from an exotic land came to a new place, bringing with them their traditions, dress, and cuisine. Although Hawaii managed to escape the exigencies of the British imperium, there is a distinct post-colonial feeling about downtown Honolulu in the formal 19th-century buildings around renovated Merchants Square and the hacienda-style C. Brewer and Company building, with its charming walled garden.

Downtown Honolulu — for our purposes an area bordered by Ward Avenue on the Diamond Head side, the Kapalama Stream on the *ewa* (west) side, the Lunalilo Freeway on the mountain side, and the ocean on the remaining side — leads from one culture to another and from one era to another in a matter of minutes, always with plenty of places for a bite or a sip in between. And despite efforts to alter the ambience of areas like Hotel Street — with its potted flowers and trees and its mall-style seating — the heart of downtown Honolulu retains its feel of being a sailor's port. Fortunately, gentrification and development are generally in good taste, but the sprucing up is gradually changing the area's once exotic flavor. The new Gateway Park, complete with flowing streams, graces the center of downtown. Adjacent is the classic *Hawaii Theater,* built in the 1920s and considered Hawaii's biggest and best for decades. The theater, now in the midst of a multimillion-dollar renovation, is slated for completion this year. Honolulu's old harbor is also due for redevelopment, complete with a hotel, promenades, museums, and shops.

Aloha Tower – In the old days, when first class travel meant elegant, steam-belching liners, this was what you looked for as you entered Honolulu Harbor. It was the scene of swaying hips on lithe, olive-skinned girls handing out leis and kisses to pale-faced *haoles.* Today a few luxury liners make use of its piers, including *American Hawaii Cruises'* SS *Independence* and SS *Constitution,* which dock here each Saturday. The 10th-floor observatory is still the best place to get a perspective of the city from the airport to Diamond Head, although the rapid mushrooming of high-rises can hardly be said to have improved the view. One curious phenomenon is the extraordinary sight of Honolulu Harbor as reflected in the green glass towers of the Grosvenor Center. The effect is that of a vast Japanese mural, full of stylized mountains, clouds, seascapes, boats, and cranes. The tower also affords a bird's-eye view of every deck, nook, and cranny of the few liners that still visit the port. The tower is scheduled for restoration as part of the planned redevelopment of downtown Honolulu's old port. At the bottom of *Fort Street Mall* (phone: 537-9260).

Chinatown – Chinatown is on the easternmost fringe of downtown and spills across the Nuuanu Stream into Aala Triangle Park, and across Beretania Street to the Chinese Cultural Plaza, where reverend Oriental sires can be seen playing checkers and mah-jongg or just enjoying the shade of the banyan and monkeypod trees. The real business of the community takes place on the Diamond Head side of the stream. Here, in open-air meat, fish, and vegetable markets with their esoteric produce, you will find elderly people who still dress in the costume of their native or ancestral land. You will also find barbershops with lady barbers and herb shops that dispense age-old medications for all manner of illnesses, some of them probably contracted in this neighborhood on the previous night. This is also the traditional "sin" quarter of Honolulu, known to generations of sailors and other military personnel who subsequently settled in respectable suburbs with mortgages, station wagons, and probably some fond memories. Sleazy pool bars and live sex shows compete with family-style chop suey houses for customers. A walking tour of Chinatown takes place on Tuesdays at 9:30 AM, starting from the Chinese Chamber of Commerce (42 N. King St.; phone: 533-3181). It stresses the daytime cultural and business background of the community rather than the nighttime activities, includes a visit to the famous Temple of Kuan Yin (Goddess of Mercy), and ends with an optional luncheon at the neighborhood's most famous restaurant, *Wo Fat.* Walking tours ($4) are also offered by the Hawaiian Heritage Center (1128 Smith St.; phone: 521-2749) on Wednesday and Friday mornings.

Iolani Palace – "The only royal palace on American soil," you will constantly be told. This large, gray, Victorian-rococo building was completed in 1882, when King David Kalakaua took up residence. After the Merrie Monarch's death, the palace fell to his sister, Queen Liliuokalani, who was deposed in 1893 and lived there under house arrest until 1895. Currently, it is still being restored to its former glory. Inside, the mansion has a grace that the outside does not quite achieve. The great Corinthian columns, the koa staircases, and the substantial chandeliers gleam, and eventually replicas of the original furniture will restore some life to the empty, elegant rooms. The Iolani Barracks, a sort of Disneyish replica of a Scottish baronial castle, was removed stone by stone from its original site and now stands in the palace grounds. Guided tours of the palace are conducted Wednesdays through Saturdays between 9 AM and 2:15

PM. The tours should be booked at least a day before, but since they are often sold out for several days in advance, reserve early. The charge for the 45-minute tour is $4. At the junction of King and Richard Sts. (phone: 538-1471 for information; 522-0832 for reservations).

Mission Houses Museum – These frame houses, built in 1821 from lumber that came around the Horn from Boston, used to be a school and a minister's home as well as a mission. They contain furniture and artifacts more reminiscent of New England than Hawaii as well as a rare archive of the islands' history. In the print house, constructed from coral, is a replica of the original printing press used to produce religious tracts and primers for schoolchildren, mostly in Hawaiian. On Saturdays, the Living History program populates the mission grounds with people dressed in 19th-century garb. Open daily from 9 AM to 4 PM; tours offered daily from 9:30 AM to 3 PM. Admission $3.50. 55 S. King St. (phone: 531-0481).

Kawaiahao Church – This place of worship likes to think of itself as the Westminster Abbey of Hawaii, and indeed, those remnants of the old Hawaiian royal and princely families who have retained their Congregational faith do occasionally use the church for baptisms, marriages, and funerals. It is the oldest church in Honolulu, built in 1842 on the site of Hawaii's first mission, which was a thatch-roofed hut standing close to an ancient and sacred *hao* (spring). Tall *kahilis* (feather-decorated staffs symbolic of royalty) placed on either side of the altar testify to its distinguished past. It was here that King Kamehameha III used the expression *Ua mau ke ea o ka aina i ka pono* ("The life of the land is perpetuated in righteousness"), which is now the state motto. If you would like to hear a church service with Hawaiian hymns (the one at 10:30 AM is best), this is the place. 957 Punchbowl St. (phone: 522-1333).

Judiciary Building (Aliiolane Hale) – Originally built in 1874 as a palace for Kamehameha V, the building is Iolani's match for regalness. It was never used as a royal dwelling, however, although David Kalakaua used to trip the light fantastic here at receptions every once in a while. The restored interior has brought to fuller light some very beautiful stained glass, but the building is still best known for the statue out front of King Kamehameha the Great. It is a replica of the original which was lost in an Atlantic storm en route from Italy, but was later recovered and now stands in Kohala on the Big Island, not far from Kamehameha's birthplace. The Honolulu statue is decorated each July 11 with 40-foot leis. Also inside is a small museum devoted to the history of Hawaii's judiciary system. At King and Mililani Sts.

Hawaii State Capitol – It is such a pleasure to come across an attractive government building, and the pleasure here is increased by the simple, formal layout of its grounds. The capitol, which has been recently renovated, is a massive structure whose cantilevered concrete ribs separated by glass mosaic tiles manage to suggest the form of a volcano and the rhythm of the ocean. Koa wood from the Big Island lines most of the interior, and in the house and senate chambers many pieces of art, including fabrics, rugs, and wall coverings, are patterned after tapa designs in the *Bishop Museum.* Equally riveting are the squat, bronze figure of the immortal Joseph de Veuster, Father Damien, sculpted by Marisol Escobar, which stands on the mountain side of the building and the statue of Queen Liliuokalani at the building's other entry. S. Beretania St.

St. Andrew's Cathedral – This is the seat of the Episcopalian bishop and is relentlessly Norman in style. Its outstanding feature is the front wall, a 24-by-55-foot stained glass window showing Christ with a selection of his saints and some Anglican luminaries, which manages to be modern without displaying any sign of artistic ambition. Kamehameha IV and Queen Emma were the church's patrons and among its early congregation. Beretania St. at Queen Emma St.

Our Lady of Peace Cathedral – Oddly enough, this Catholic church is less ornate than its Protestant counterpart and seems to retain a cool and airy feeling even in summer. It is chiefly famous as the place where Father Damien was ordained in May 1864 before starting the pilgrimage that led him to the leper colony on Molokai. *Fort Street Mall* at Beretania St.

Hawaii Maritime Center – The four-masted square-rigger, the *Falls of Clyde,* and the voyaging canoe *Hokulea,* both riding at anchor at Pier 7, provide the focus of activities at this museum. The captain's quarters of the *Falls of Clyde* form a nautical masterpiece of teak, birch, and mahogany fittings and furnishings, all set off by an abundance of red velvet upholstery. In contrast, visitors also see the cramped crew's quarters typical of 19th-century shipboard life. The *Hokulea* may not be boarded, but it is berthed to permit viewing from three sides. This now famous voyaging canoe has been used on several occasions to journey between the islands of Polynesia by means of stellar navigation in order to study the migration routes used by the earliest Hawaiians. A children's "hands-on" museum is housed in the Kalakaua Boat House; other exhibitions relating to Hawaii's maritime past, including a library and photo archive, are at Aloha Tower. Open daily 9 AM to 8 PM; Mondays, Tuesdays, and Thursdays until 5 PM. All-inclusive admission is $6. At Pier 7, adjacent to the Aloha Tower and off Ala Moana Blvd. (phone: 536-6373).

Foster Botanic Garden – Some 20 acres of exotic plants and trees can be found in this arboreal enclave, one of six sites across the island that make up the Honolulu Botanic Gardens. This organization is attempting to propagate plants and trees from different environments around the world in appropriate parts of Oahu. The warm, humid climate of downtown Honolulu favors the growth of orchids, and the Lyn Orchid Garden is a popular spot, where these flowers range from the tiny *(pleurothallis)* to the large *(grammatophyllum).* Orchids from both the Old and the New World grow here in rocks, on the ground, and, most exotic, on trees. Among the unusual trees are the cigar box tree from the Amazon area, which used to provide wood for cigar boxes curiously more aromatic than the tree's flowers; the sausage tree, from West Africa, the gourd-like fruit of which resembles a sausage; and the double coconut palm, which bears nuts weighing up to 50 pounds. A fascinating glimpse of the earth's past can be experienced in the Prehistoric Glen, where you will find primitive plants that thrived in the Coal Age. Fossils of these plants provide us with fuel, medicine, and fertilizer, even with plastic and paint. The gardens offer a useful view of the history of flora. And the sad-looking orchids along the garden fence that lines the freeway, devastated by gasoline fumes, tell us something about our progress. Among other importees in the garden is the Indian mongoose, discovered now and again peering from a rock. Open daily from 9 AM to 4 PM. Admission $1. N. Vineyard Blvd. (phone: 533-3214).

Dole Cannery Square/Hawaii Children's Museum – The 60-year-old cannery has been transformed into a visitor attraction, complete with restaurants, shops, and a consumer pavilion full of Dole products and gifts imprinted with the Dole logo. A visit here begins with a 10-minute multi-image presentation about the history of the pineapple in Hawaii, followed by a 45-minute tour of the cannery and free samples of pineapples and juice. Afterwards, browse through the shops and the exhibits depicting Dole's early days and the evolution of agriculture in Hawaii. Shuttle service (50¢) links the cannery to Waikiki. Word is that the cannery, a victim of competitive (read cheaper) production costs in Asia, eventually will be closed. More than half the staff had been laid off at press time, although the cannery remains open. Shops are in abundance as you exit the tour. If you're traveling with children, head to the cannery's *Hawaii Children's Museum* (phone: 522-0040), a hands-on science center with real kid appeal. Open daily; tours are conducted every 15 minutes from 9 AM to 5 PM; shuttle operates from 8:30 AM to 3 PM. Admission $3.50. 650 Iwilei Rd., just west of downtown, off Nimitz Hwy. (phone: 531-8855).

Mauna Kea Marketplace – This spot serves as a commercial centerpiece of Chinatown's renewal, and creates a sense of place through its use of Chinese architecture.

Its grand courtyard is filled with "street" vendors, shops, restaurants, and food stalls serving 17 culinary styles of Asia. On Maunakea and Pauhi Sts.

SHOPPING: The building-by-building restoration of downtown Honolulu has stimulated the opening of several galleries, antiques emporia, and quite browsable shops in the midst of a persisting honky-tonk atmosphere. It's an eclectic combination that makes a daytime walk downtown interesting. If you're looking for a high-brow approach to decor, the following stores carry some of Hawaii's best European and Oriental antiques: *Robyn Buntin* (900A Maunakea St.; phone: 523-5913); *Bushido* (936 Maunakea St.; phone: 536-5693); *Moratin Downtown-Gallery* (3 Pauahi St.; phone: 521-9669); *The Art Treasures Gallery* (9 N. Pauahi St., Suite 5; phone: 599-7792); and *Gateway Gallery* (1050 Nuuanu Ave.; phone: 599-1559). Other kinds of shops include the following:

Aala Lei Shop – Excellent selection and good prices can be found here. 1104 Maunakea St. (phone: 521-5766).

Bo Wah Trading Co. Liberty House – The offerings run from practical to kitschy at this shop. 1149 Maunakea St. (phone: 537-2017).

Pegge Hopper Gallery – Pricey outputs of this artist's palette are featured. 1164 Nuuanu St. (phone: 524-1160).

Jenny's Lei Shop – One of a number of shops downtown that specialize in the traditional Hawaiian art of lei making, with a larger and better-priced selection than that found in Waikiki. 1151 Maunakea St. (phone: 521-1595).

Honolulu Chocolate Company – Chocoholics beware, your taste buds will confirm the initial impulse to surrender to temptation. The price is steep, but the chocolates are of very high standard. Restaurant Row (phone: 531-2997) and Manoa Valley (phone: 988-4999).

Lai Fong – This long-established store features Oriental antiques and bric-a-brac. 1118 Nuuanu St. (phone: 537-3497).

Liberty House – A branch of this Hawaiian store that carries clothing for men, women, and children. 1032 Fort St. (phone: 945-5151).

Mellow's – Fans of antique jewelry will want to visit this store. 841 Bishop St. (phone: 533-6313).

Pauahi Nuuanu Gallery – The emphasis is on Hawaiian arts ranging from wood carving to feathered leis to Niihau shell jewelry. 1 North Pauahi St. (phone: 531-6088).

Penthouse – A reduced-price merchandise outlet, where some real bargains can be found. 1 N. King St. (phone: 945-5151).

Ramsey Gallery – Changing exhibits of high-quality watercolors, pen-and-ink drawings, ceramicware, and other art forms are shown here. 1128 Smith St. (phone: 537-ARTS).

Waterfall Gallery – Art photography, graphics, jewelry, and collector's quality ceramics are featured here, along with a fine selection of Balinese, Burmese, and Thai objets d'art. 1160A Nuuanu Ave. (phone: 521-6863).

NIGHTLIFE: Most people who earn their bread and butter in downtown Honolulu head for home around sundown. They may linger for a drink in the new pub-like bars around Merchant Square, but few stay for dinner. Restaurant Row has helped change that, with its cluster of shops, restaurants, the alfresco *Row Bar* (phone: 528-2345), which offers live reggae on weekends, and *Studebaker's* (phone: 526-9888) rock 'n' roll disco. The music jumps the decades, and every now and again the staff takes to the table tops to dance. In Chinatown, the Chinese and Filipino families who live or have relatives in the neighborhood can be seen until 8 or 8:30 PM, but after that, the people on the streets are either looking for each other or for some kind of substitute for each other. Hotel Street comes alive after 10

PM, when motorcyclists come by and sit on their decorated two-wheelers, watching and talking. Servicemen idle along the street, in and out of bars where the gender of the inhabitants can be indefinite at first glance and where a pool game can lead to bloodshed. The area's recently opened police substation has helped calm things down considerably, as has gentrification. Determined nightbirds can listen to rock at the *Swing Club* (35 N. Hotel St.; phone: 536-7864) and the *Shindig* (1140 Maunakea; phone: 531-1572), or watch the striptease at *Hubba Hubba* (25 N. Hotel; phone: 536-7698).

CHECKING IN: Downtown's only accommodations option is the 26-room *Town Inn,* which offers the basics at appropriate rates of $35 a day, without air conditioning, $37 with it. Weekly rates are also available. Located just beyond Chinatown at 250 N. Beretania St. (phone: 536-2377). Plans have been announced for a high-rise hotel as part of the redevelopment of Honolulu Harbor.

EATING OUT: Except for a couple of restaurants in Chinatown, downtown Honolulu used to be a culinary wasteland. It is still not exactly a diner's paradise, but some spots have better than average food, ambience, and service. And with the rise of the new Restaurant Row (500 Ala Moana Blvd. at South St., on the Waikiki side of downtown), things are definitely looking up. Lunchtime has traditionally been busier and livelier than dinnertime, but Restaurant Row is changing that trend. For a meal for two, excluding wine, tip, and drinks, expect to pay $65 or more at a restaurant listed as expensive, $30 to $60 in a place listed as moderate, and $20 or less in an inexpensive place. All telephone numbers are in the 808 area code unless otherwise indicated.

Waikiki Trolley operates a shuttle between Restaurant Row and Waikiki (50¢).

Black Orchid – American dishes are served here — both indoors and alfresco. There's also a dance floor and a large, beautifully designed lounge. Open weekdays for lunch from 11 AM to 2 PM, and dinner from 6 to 10 PM Mondays through Thursdays, 6 PM to midnight on Fridays and Saturdays. Reservations advised. Restaurant Row (phone: 521-3111). Expensive.

Ruth's Chris Steakhouse – Some of the best filets and New York steaks in town. Open daily for dinner from 5 to 10:30 PM; open Mondays through Fridays for lunch from 11 AM to 3 PM. Reservations advised. Restaurant Row (phone: 599-3860). Expensive.

Coasters – Nestled in a harborside setting at the back of the Hawaii Maritime Center, there's an excellent lunch and dinner menu, with appetizers such as clams casino and shellfish sausage nantua, plus a full range of seafood, veal, and steaks entrées. Open for lunch from 11 AM to 2:30 PM, Monday through Saturday, and dinner from 5 to 10 PM daily. Reservations advised. At Pier 7 (phone: 524-2233). Expensive to moderate.

Café Asia – This Restaurant Row version of *Keo's,* another Thai establishment owned by the same family, also offers the deliciously prepared Thai specialties that made *Keo's* a hit. The decor is upbeat and tropical, while the setting is quiet, which makes it a great place for an intense tête-à-tête. Open daily; closed for lunch on Sundays. Reservations advised on weekends. 500 Ala Moana Blvd. (phone: 536-6889). Moderate.

Café Che Pasta – Homemade pasta is only part of a menu that includes fresh grilled fish, calamari, and other nouvelle-style dishes. *Che Pasta*'s original eatery in Kaimuki established the good reputation that's maintained at this downtown branch. Open Mondays through Fridays until 8 PM for lunch, snacks, and dinner. Reservations advised. 1001 Bishop Sq. (phone: 524-0004). Moderate.

Murphy's Bar and Grill – A pleasant eatery in the revitalized Merchant Square area and a good choice for people who are tired of exotic restaurant grub. From potato skins to salads and pasta, the menu offers many tasty specials. Live sports events are beamed in courtesy of a satellite dish. Open Mondays through Saturdays for lunch, with pupus served until 7 PM. Lunch reservations advised. 2 Merchant St. (phone: 531-0422). Moderate.

Sunset Grill – The style is California-casual; the food is cooked over kiawe wood to provide a distinctive flavor. Specialties include chicken, veal, lamb, and fish with rotisserie, oven, and grill preparations. Open for lunch from 11 AM to 4 PM, and dinner from 4 to 11 PM daily, breakfast on Sundays only. Reservations advised. Restaurant Row (phone: 521-4409). Moderate.

Trattoria Manzo's – The setting is a bit disconcerting if you're seated facing the pink and green neon trim, but the service is friendly and the Italian food worth a wait and even a bit of discomfort from the lighting. The food ranks among the best Italian food in Honolulu; northern Italian specialties and traditional dishes prepared to perfection. Open daily for lunch and dinner. Reservations unnecessary. Restaurant Row (phone: 522-1711). Moderate.

Rose City Café – A 1950s-style diner, featuring outdoor dining. Good food for those seeking basic fare. Open daily for breakfast, lunch, and dinner, from 7 AM to midnight on weekdays, 8 AM to 2 AM on Fridays and Saturdays. Reservations necessary for parties of five or more. Restaurant Row (phone: 524-ROSE). Moderate to inexpensive.

Chinese Cultural Plaza – Though not quite as successful as planned, this ethnic enclave does offer a wide range of good Oriental restaurants and cuisines — Cantonese, Hakka, Mandarin, or Mongolian barbecue — as well as shops purveying Oriental bric-a-brac that are fun to browse through. Reservations unnecessary. Off S. Beretania and River Sts. Inexpensive.

Wo Fat – This granddaddy of Chinese restaurants in Honolulu will soon be 100 years old. Hong Kong chicken, beef in oyster sauce, and Wo Fat noodles draw people here from all over the island for lunch and dinner. Open daily. Reservations advised. 115 N. Hotel St. (phone: 537-6260). Inexpensive.

Greater Honolulu and Pearl Harbor

Most of what you see when you fly into town is Greater Honolulu, a sprawl of freeways and suburbs between the spines of the two mountain systems that dominate the island. To the west is the Waianae Range, which almost completely locks in leeward Oahu. To the east is the long and much-photographed Koolau Range, whose central ridges form the Honolulu watershed. Concentrated along the flatlands of the Koolau is downtown Honolulu, with its tall towers at the ocean end of Bishop Street and Fort Street; the low-rising structures along Kapiolani Boulevard behind *Ala Moana;* and then the Tombstone Mile of Waikiki, its rows of concrete skyscrapers along Kalakaua and Kuhio Avenues frowned on by Diamond Head at the eastern end.

Greater Honolulu arches around these points from blue-collar Pearl City to gold-plated Kahala with fingers of domestic urban developments, some abysmal and some magnificent, penetrating the once-pristine valleys in between. Through the sparse coconut palms that managed to survive the busy pavements of Waikiki you can see the distant mansions and villas high up in the narrow, dark green clefts, many of them the homes of the men and women who pilot the fortunes of large mid-Pacific corporations and at least one that served as the stateside residence for the late Ferdinand Marcos, former President of the Philippines.

In some ways, driving along the Lunalilo Freeway from Pearl Harbor to Kahala is like driving along any other American highway that separates the business and entertainment sections of the city from its suburbs. There are the same gas stations, the same low-slung warehouses and industrial buildings, the same pizza parlors and hamburger joints. But here you have in addition strange, wrinkled folds in the mountains, like flesh that has stayed too long in hot water; moody clouds that hang over sharp mountaintops; rainbows, sometimes three at once, diminishing in brilliance the farther away they are; and along the highway the directions to bases, forts, reservations, and cemeteries, which remind us that this is where many of our fathers, sons, brothers — yes, and sisters and mothers — stood watch in defense of the mainland.

Pearl Harbor – It is surely impossible to come here and remain unmoved. Most military monuments tend toward the vainglorious and self-serving. This one is reflective, sober, and serene. Orange buoys mark the bow and stern of the USS *Arizona,* which blew up and sank during the Japanese attack on the morning of December 7, 1941, "a day which will live in infamy." Parts of the battleship's superstructure, eroded by seawater and barnacles, still appear above the waterline. Somewhere in the ship, 1,102 officers and men of the navy and marine corps are entombed. Spanning the sunken hull is the 184-foot-long Arizona Memorial, a covered white concrete bridge sinking slightly in the middle to represent initial defeat, but firm and solid at both ends to signify ultimate victory. The memorial is divided into three parts: the museum room, containing the ship's bell; the assembly area, which can hold 200 people; and the shrine, where the names of those who died aboard the ship are inscribed on a large marble tablet. The American flag, which flies above the memorial, is not in fact anchored in the monument but in the structure of the battleship itself.

There are two ways of visiting the shrine, by sea and by land. If you come by sea, chances are that you will want to take one of the boats that leaves the Kewalo Basin opposite the *Ward Warehouse* on Ala Moana Boulevard. The Pearl Harbor Cruise, at 9:15 AM and 1:15 PM, operated by *Paradise Cruises* (350 Ward Ave., Suite 210; phone: 536-3641), heads out of Kewalo Basin, passes downtown en route to Battleship Row and past the flag and plaque above the USS *Utah.* Visitors taking a commercial cruise are not permitted to land on the Arizona Memorial, however. To do this, you must take the land route to the visitors' center, which is operated by the National Park Service. You then transfer to a US Navy launch for the trip to the memorial's dock. Although coming via land is less social than the sea voyage, with its drinks and snacks, it is in the end more informative. Here, as elsewhere in the US, the National Park Service and its personnel prove that they are among our foremost national treasures. Each day as many as 3,000 visitors pass through the center, which can get crowded, with hour-long waits for the boat to the memorial not uncommon. Rangers show a movie describing the attack and answer questions about the historic event and current operations at Pearl Harbor. A bookshop has souvenirs, among them model kits of the *Arizona* and copies of the front page of the *Honolulu Star-Bulletin* reporting the invasion. The center also houses the *Arizona*'s anchor and chain. *TheBus* Nos. 50, 51, and 52 (marked Wahiawa), which leave from *Ala Moana Center,* and No. 20 (Airport), which leaves from Waikiki, pass the gate to the memorial. *Airport Motorcoach* (phone: 926-4747) operates a shuttle between the memorial and Waikiki ($3 one way, $5 return).

USS *Bowfin*/Pacific Submarine Museum – Adjacent to the Arizona Memorial Visitors Center, the *Bowfin* provides a first-hand glimpse of the confining reality and technological innocence of World War II submarines. Submarine-related artifacts are displayed in the recently opened museum. Open daily from 8 AM to 4:30 PM; admission $6 (phone: 423-1341).

Bishop Museum – The *Bernice Pauahi Bishop Museum* is the formal name of this famous collection of Pacific anthropology and natural history, founded in memory of Princess Pauahi, the last direct descendant of the Kamehameha chieftains, by her husband, Charles Reed Bishop. The central building, in a somewhat pompous Romanesque style reminiscent of Scottish baronial mansions dating from Queen Victoria's reign, was constructed from lava rock with interiors made of koa wood. Outside there is a dome-topped modern science center with a planetarium and telescope. A great sperm whale hangs from the ceiling in the 3-story, galleried Hawaiian Hall, which displays artifacts reflecting Hawaii's rigidly structured pre-European past, the influence of European merchants and mariners in the 19th-century kingdom of Hawaii, and the influence of the various immigrant groups who have made Hawaii their home. Long feathered capes and helmets in the vivid red and yellow colors that symbolized chieftainship recall the first of these eras. The second stage is represented by thrones and decorations that show how closely the court at Honolulu tried to copy European courts, especially that of Queen Victoria at Windsor. The third development is captured in 19th-century photographs of the early Portuguese, Chinese, Japanese, and Philippine immigrants. The *Hall of Hawaiian Natural History* contains 16 exhibits depicting Hawaii's geological origins and its biological heritage. They show how some of the plants and animals that are endemic to the islands developed the idiosyncrasies of form and behavior that make them unique. The most famous example of these is the nene goose, Hawaii's state bird, whose ancestry and progress are fully described. In addition, there are materials from elsewhere in Polynesia, such as carvings, masks, tikis, tools, tapa cloths, and ceremonial clothing, indicating how the traditions of the various islands are connected. A new wing houses changing exhibits from the museum's permanent collection. The museum shop sells books, pictures, and reproductions based on Hawaiian and Pacific island themes. Hawaiian dance is performed daily at 1 PM in the *Atherton Hale,* where traditional crafts are demonstrated from 9 AM to 3 PM. Open Mondays through Saturdays from 9 AM to 5 PM. Adjacent to the museum is a state-of-the-art planetarium, with two different shows offered daily at 11 AM and 2 PM; evening shows on Fridays and Saturdays at 8 PM. The $5.95 admission ($4.95 for 6- to 17-year-olds) includes entrance to the planetarium. 1525 Bernice St. (phone: 847-3511).

Queen Emma's Summer Palace – Nuuanu Valley was Honolulu's first suburb. *Nuuanu* means "cool heights," and it was up here that Queen Emma, the wife of Kamehameha IV, was given a charming, white-frame house with generous verandahs by her aunt and uncle, which she called Hanaiakamalama. It originally had six main rooms and was surrounded by spider lilies, Castilian roses, and *maile* bushes. A major extension was added in 1869, when Queen Victoria's bad-tempered second son, Alfred, Duke of Edinburgh, was expected (he never showed). This room now houses a fascinating collection of Victorian furniture, which, except for the *kahilis* (feather-decorated staffs symbolic of royalty) that stand sentinel on either side of the door and in other spots around the room, might easily convince you that you are in Boston or London. Among smaller artifacts restored to the house — thanks to the efforts of the Daughters of Hawaii, who administer the building — are an ornate British clock, a tiny tortoise-shell brooch set in a lace handkerchief, and a beautiful necklace of tiger's claws set with seed pearls in rolled gold, a wedding gift to Emma from an Indian maharajah. There are also many mementos of Hawaii's other royalty. The palace is just one of many mansions that sprung up in the valley among the ferns, hibiscus, and ginger. Today, some of them are occupied by institutions, many with religious affiliations, that have introduced even more plant and tree life to the area, including banyans, monkeypod, kukui, mangoes, African tulips, bamboo, and eucalyptus. Open daily from 9 AM to 4 PM. Admission $4. 2913 Pali Hwy. (phone: 595-3167).

Punchbowl (The National Memorial Cemetery of the Pacific) – The ancient Hawaiians called this crater Puowaina, the Hill of Sacrifice, and the name rings true today. More than 35,000 American servicemen and servicewomen are buried here, among them 22 recipients of the Medal of Honor, as well as a civilian, the famous war correspondent Ernie Pyle (his grave number is D109). In addition, more than 26,000 names of servicemen missing in action are listed on marble walls called the Court of the Missing. Every day, but especially on Sundays, visitors and islanders come with leis and small bunches of flowers or blossoms to place against individual graves. Services are held here on *Memorial Day* and *Veterans' Day,* and there's an especially moving and popular one at dawn on *Easter Sunday,* when people by the thousands show up to honor the dead. Puowaina Dr.

Tantalus Drive – Starting on the *mauka* (inland) side of Puowaina Drive and Punchbowl, Tantalus Drive passes through the swank suburb of Makiki Heights before making its relentless, zigzag way almost to the tip of 2,013-foot Mt. Tantalus. This peak, formed millions of years ago from a volcanic fire fountain of *lapili* (glassy black lava fragments) and ash, is today covered with a tropical rain forest dense with ginger, eucalyptus, mountain apple, and bamboo trees. In the clefts and gulches that scar the mountainside, amid the profusion of flowers, taro, passion fruit vines, and avocado, banana, and guava trees, you may catch sight of a wild pig. You will certainly glimpse some of the city's most beautiful and dramatically sited houses perched on steep cliffsides, in some cases with garages on the top floor and the living quarters below. High on the mountain, at Kalaiopua Place, Tantalus Drive becomes Round Top Drive and descends in dizzying swerves down the Diamond Head side to Puu Ualakaa State Wayside. A road off the drive leads to the summit of Puu Ualakaa — known in English as Round Top — 1,048 feet high. The view of Honolulu and the surrounding valleys from this point is famous.

Manoa Valley, Paradise Park, and the Lyon Arboretum – This is another favorite residential area, where many of the attractive homes are owned by descendants of the early American settlers who came to the islands in the 19th century.

At the south end of Manoa Road, which runs the length of the valley, is the famous Punahou School, built in 1841, largely of lava rock, for the children of the missionaries. Halfway up the valley, a short side road to the left leads to the restoration of the Little Grass Shack that once was home for Robert Louis Stevenson. At the north end of the road is Paradise Park (3737 Manoa Rd.; phone: 988-6686), a 15-acre garden where the rainfall averages over 160 inches a year. A $5-million renovation completed in 1991 includes a major new exhibit of robotic dinosaurs. There is a giant walk-through aviary, a hau tree jungle, bamboo groves, and — the prime reason for a visit — more than 500 rare and exotic birds, some of which have unfortunately been taught to do tricks. Although many of the birds are quite dazzling and the flora is interesting, this is not the true Hawaii, but a version of it for tourists. Open daily from 9:30 AM to 5 PM. (phone: 988-2141). Admission $12.95.

For a more authentic and undeniably gorgeous glimpse of tropical Oahu, visit the Lyon Arboretum. Operated as a research garden by the University of Hawaii, it consists of more than 200 acres of both landscaped and wild rain forest. Open weekdays from 9 AM to 3 PM, and 9 AM to 12 noon on Saturdays, with tours offered several times monthly. 3860 Manoa Rd. (phone: 988-3177).

Kahala – If humid, forested hillsides don't appeal to you but you're thinking of settling down in Honolulu, perhaps you should head here. This wealthy community consists mostly of luxurious homes with small, beautifully kept gardens. Honolulu is, on the average, the most expensive city in the Union when it comes to buying a house and — the estates of Diamond Head aside — this is its most expensive community. Naturally, it has much to offer. It is drier than the mountains; it has a long, narrow beach that is excellent in spots for surfing, snorkeling, and swimming; and it has the poshest golf and country club on Oahu, the exclusive *Waialae Country Club,* which even the denizens of the luxurious *Kahala Hilton* may not enter unless they are members or guests of members. Another singular feature of Kahala is, along Kealaolu Avenue, what is probably the longest hibiscus hedge in the world, part of the fence that keeps the hoi polloi from the club grounds.

SHOPPING: The largest shopping center outside *Ala Moana* is at Pearl Ridge off the Kamehameha Highway at Kaonohi Street. There are more than 90 stores here, among them, *J. C. Penney, Liberty House,* and *Sears.* The main attraction of the shopping center, which is off the beaten track for most tourists, is the monorail that makes a loop through the parking area.

The *Kahala Mall* is a smaller, upscale alternative that includes shops like *Koala Blue,* which sells artistic, casual cottonwear (phone: 735-0200), and *Riches,* purveying earrings and more earrings (phone: 737-3303). A popular cinema eight-plex here will keep movie fans happy (phone: 735-9744).

Clair De Lune – A wonderful selection of high-quality art nouveau and art deco reproductions, as well as contemporary tribal arts. 2716 S. King St., near the junction with University Ave. (phone: 955-8119).

NIGHTLIFE: Danny Kaleikini sings every night except Sunday in the *Hala Terrace* room of the *Kahala Hilton* (phone: 734-2211). He is not as famous as Don Ho, and is considerably less brash, but his personal style with simple Hawaiian melodies is preferred by many *kamaainas* and visitors.

CHECKING IN: The only option is the *Kahala Hilton,* where double rooms start at about $200 a night and go steeply upward. The telephone number is in the 808 area code.

Kahala Hilton – Operated by Hilton International (which is now run by Britain's Ladbrooke group), this is one of the chain's prime showpieces. Queen Elizabeth II spent a couple of nights here, and King Juan Carlos of Spain came for part of his honeymoon with Queen Sophia. The main structure of this lavish hostelry is 12 stories high and overlooks a glorious 800-foot stretch of beach that loses nothing by being manmade. Additional beachside bungalows and a 2-story wing watch over a large lagoon in which dolphins, turtles, and penguins cavort. Rooms in the main building have charming semicircular lanais decorated with bougainvillea. Relatively recent renovation and refurbishing have put them at least on a par with those in the finest hotels. The lobby is an absolute masterpiece — with handsome chandeliers and a stunning circular carpet — that manages to look plush and airy at the same time. Guests are greeted with chilled pineapple, and an orchid is laid on each pillow when beds are turned down in the evening. Besides ocean and pool swimming, the hotel provides kayaks and snorkeling equipment and can arrange deep-sea fishing and scuba diving; and there are several fine restaurants (see *Eating Out*). "Kamp Kahala" keeps children age 6 to 12 happily occupied with a series of activities designed to entertain energetic youngsters. European efficiency at the executive level and island good humor at the service level are the keynotes here. They work together like a charm. 5000 Kahala Ave., Kahala (phone: 734-2211; 800-367-2525).

EATING OUT: Prices in Greater Honolulu are about on a par with those in Waikiki. For a meal for two, excluding wine, tips, and drinks, expect to pay more than $65 in a place listed as expensive, between $25 and $60 in a placed listed as moderate, and under $25 in an inexpensive place. All telephone numbers are in the 808 area code unless otherwise indicated.

Maile – Guests descend through a minor jungle of anthuriums, yellow heliconia, and orchids into this dining room beneath the lobby of the *Kahala Hilton,* where kimono-clad waitresses provide expert, unobtrusive service. The award-winning menu includes roast duckling Waialae and baked chicken supreme. Local fish treated somewhat exotically here include mahimahi glazed with banana and served on creamed mushrooms and baked kumu with fennel and a dash of Pernod. A classical guitarist or a pianist plays during dinner, from 6:30 to 9 PM. Live dance music begins at 9 PM. Open daily for dinner only, from 5:30 to 9 PM. Brunch is served Sundays on the *Maile Terrace* from 11 AM to 2 PM. Reservations necessary. *Kahala Hilton,* 5000 Kahala Ave., Kahala (phone: 734-2211). Expensive.

Pearl City Tavern – This Japanese-American eatery is famous for its Monkey Bar, at the back of which is a long glassed-in alley where denizens of the simian world prance and preen playfully. The Japanese dishes here tend to be better than the American, and the teriyaki and tempura are especially good. The middle-aged waitresses are downright motherly. Open weekdays for lunch from 11:30 AM to 2 PM, daily for dinner from 5:30 to 9 PM. Reservations necessary. 905 Kamehameha Hwy., Pearl City (phone: 455-1045). Expensive to moderate.

Willows – One of the most famous restaurants in the state, and *the* place to sample traditional Hawaiian dishes. The celebrated poi supper offers many of these, including poi itself, sweet potato, chicken luau, and lomilomi salmon. If all this seems too exotic, the curry dishes, leavened with coconut milk, are equally superb. It's the perfect place to don an aloha shirt or muumuu for the first time, with the rural tropical atmosphere of palm trees, thatch roofs, and strolling musicians as the backdrop. Poi Thursday lunches are legendary with islanders who come here, so be certain to arrive early (11:30 AM) to get a good seat for a taste of some authentic Hawaii. Open daily for lunch from 11:30 AM to 1:30 PM, and dinner from 5 to 9 PM. Reservations necessary. 901 Hausten St. (phone: 946-4808). Expensive to moderate.

Al Dente – Quiet and comfortable, with better than average Italian food. Steamed Manila clams are a treat, as are the well-flavored pasta, veal, and fish. And the excellent and unobtrusive service wins over patrons' hearts time and again. Open daily. Reservations suggested. In the *Nui Valley Shopping Center,* 5730 Kalanianaole Hwy. (phone: 373-8855). Moderate.

Alpine Village – Owner-chef Alex Schlemmer offers a menu of schnitzel, chicken, as well as the fresh catch of the day. The soups are delicious, as are the steamed Manila clams, the service is friendly, and the prices right. Dinner daily from 5:30 to 10 PM. Closed Sundays. Reservations advised. 2700 South King St. (phone: 949-8889). Moderate.

Castagnola's – A New York–style Italian dining spot that has drawn good reviews from the day it opened in the *Manoa Marketplace.* Delicate flavorings make for some good veal, pasta, and seafood dishes. Open daily except Sundays for lunch and dinner; lunch only on Mondays. Reservations necessary. 2752 Woodlawn Ave., Honolulu (phone: 988-2969). Moderate.

Che Pasta – Good food served at a casual café. Pasta, veal, and chicken dishes are the specialties. Open daily for dinner. Reservations recommended. 3571 Waialae Ave., Honolulu (phone: 735-1777). Moderate.

Hala Terrace – A *Kahala Hilton* restaurant and a lovely lunchtime spot. Sit in the shade and watch the Pacific across one of the loveliest beaches on Oahu. Meals here are on the light side, so it's worth ordering vichyssoise or a spring salad as a starter. Elegant sandwiches are the main item on the menu, in addition to which there are daily specials such as Kahuku prawns, which are delicious. Open daily for breakfast from 6:30 to 10:30 AM, lunch from 11:30 AM to 2:30 PM, and dinner from 6 to 9 PM. Reservations advised. *Kahala Hilton,* 5000 Kahala Ave., Kahala (phone: 734-2211). Moderate.

Phillip Paolo's – Just a 5-minute drive from Waikiki, and set in an eclectically decorated private home, this establishment receives high praise for its fine Italian fare prepared by owner-chef Phillip Paolo Sarubbi. Daily specials complement such standard features as *fettuccine Vigario* (pasta with mushrooms and spinach in a light basil cream sauce) and shrimp *parmigiano.* Open daily for lunch from 11 AM to 2 PM, and dinner from 5 to 9 PM. Reservations necessary. 2312 Beretania St. (phone: 946-1163). Moderate.

California Pizza – Pizza fans will find plenty to rave about, with specialties, such as goat cheese pizza, cooked in a kiawe wood-burning oven. They also feature an excellent selection of pasta dishes. Open daily for lunch and dinner, Sundays through Thursdays, 10:30 AM to 10:30 PM, and Fridays and Saturdays from 10:30 AM to 11 PM. No reservations. In the *Kahala Mall* (phone: 737-9446). Moderate to inexpensive.

Emilio's – Be it ever so humble, this little neighborhood-style pizza place, just outside Waikiki, has very tasty pies and other Italian dishes. The pizza is right on the mark, with crisp crusts, dense tomato sauce, and tasty cheese. 1423 Kalakaua Ave. (phone: 946-4972). Inexpensive.

Southeast Oahu

A favorite short ride out of Honolulu is the triangular drive around Oahu's east end, taking the Pali Highway, Route 61, up the Nuuanu Valley through the Nuuanu Pali Tunnel and making a right turn onto Route 72, the Kalanianaole Highway. This road brings you through Waimanalo, past Koko Crater and Koko Head, through Hawaii-Kai, and back into town. In the hills on either side of the road through Nuuanu Valley, above the churches, schools, convents, and graveyards that mark this as one of Honolulu's early suburbs, there is a herd of wallabies running wild, descendants of a group that escaped from a crate in the dockyards over 70 years ago en route from Australia to the mainland. If this is the only trip you are making outside the city, stop at the Nuuanu Pali Lookout, with its long romantic view north along the Koolau Range and the Windward Coast. Beyond the lookout, as the highway begins its southern progress, you come into a world of dramatic lava rock coastline, jagged cliffs, and clear waters covering endlessly fascinating reefs.

Waimanalo Beach – This sandy demi-paradise stretches for over 3 miles around the curve of Waimanolo Bay, making it the longest continuous beach on Oahu. Bellows Beach, as the northern part is known, is part of a military complex and therefore open only on weekends and certain holidays. The gentle but always active surf here makes it popular with people just learning to board- and body-surf. Occasionally, when the wind is in the right direction and if you have an inclination for marine life, you can spot Portuguese man-of-war jellyfish in the area. These are best not examined too closely since they impart an unpleasant sting. Farther south is Sherwood Forest, the popular name for Waimanalo Bay State Recreation Area. It received its nickname about 20 years ago when it became well known for some decidedly un–Robin Hood–like petty criminal activities in the dense groves of ironwood trees at the back of the beach, activities that have since been curtailed. At Kaiona Beach Park, farther on, you can see a rock wall that, according to legend, was constructed by a chief of the district who was especially devoted to turtle meat. Each time a turtle was caught, so the story goes, it was deposited in the pool enclosed by the rocks for the chief's sole use.

Kaupo Beach Park – This long and narrow beach south of the Waimanalo beaches is generally quite safe for swimming. It is a perfect place to relax and look longingly at two offshore islands, Kaohikaipu Island and Manana Island, commonly known as Rabbit Island, recalling its days as a rabbit farm. Today, both are bird sanctuaries, and from the shore of Oahu you may catch a glimpse of a venturesome red-tailed *koae-ula* or a friendly white tern.

Sea Life Park – Porpoises, whales, and penguins ham it up here several times a day in the entertainment part of what is a serious marine life research project at Whalers Cove. A major attraction is the Hawaiian Reef Exhibit, a 300,000-gallon tank, 3 fathoms deep and 70 feet across, in which a Pacific reef is re-created with the exotic plants and animals that would be found in the real thing. A spiral ramp winds around the tank so that visitors can observe from above the surface all the way to its depths. Clear water and direct sunlight make the denizens of this fantasy world easily visible. Manta rays and 6-foot sharks nose the glass walls of the tank, and hundreds of multicolored fish create dazzling patterns. On the reef bottom, you can see creatures that never venture to the surface and are normally not visible even to snorkelers or casual divers. The newest addition to the park is the Rocky Shores intertidal pool. Also noteworthy is the whaling museum with its excellent 19th-century artifacts. For kids, seal and sea turtle feeding and the show put on by trained porpoises and killer whales are likely to be highlights. Open daily from 9:30 AM to 5 PM, with the last complete series of shows starting at 3:15 PM; Fridays until 10 PM, the last shows beginning at 6:15 PM. Admission is $12.95 for adults, $8.50 for juniors (7–12 years), and $4.50 for children (4–6 years). Off Kalanianaole Hwy. at Makapuu Point (phone: 259-7933).

Makapuu Beach – An idyllic spot backed by sand dunes and black lava cliffs, this is the most famous body-surfing beach on Oahu, so famous that board-surfing is prohibited by law. The huge and elegant waves here are, however, lethal during the winter and even in the summer should be toyed with only by extremely experienced body-surfers. It's safer and easier to lie back, relax, and watch the hang gliders make their aerial parabolas as they catch an eddy in the air currents.

Halona Blowhole – On Kalanianaole Highway just below Koko Head Crater, there is a lookout from which you can see a natural sea geyser that spouts water in a decidedly impertinent fashion through a submerged lava tube. If the waves aren't providing the right kind of water pressure, all you see are the lava cliffs and delicious blue ocean, but if the sea is accommodating, just to the right of the lookout is a small, rock-girt beach called Halona Cove, which is not good for swimming, but perfect for getting a tan.

Hanauma Bay Beach Park – The Elvis Presley epic *Blue Hawaii* was made here. The swimming is good, especially in the sandy bottom part called the keyhole, and the snorkeling is excellent. Be advised the beach is often very crowded. The bay, an extinct volcanic crater flooded by the ocean, is a state marine conservation area. No fishing of any kind is permitted, nor is the removal of any kind of land or marine life. As a result, many of the fish gliding among the coral reefs are largely unafraid of man and will nuzzle swimmers and divers cautiously. Tall cliffs surround the bay in a horseshoe-like formation and tall coconut palms provide shade. Hanauma Bay Road leads down to the cliff tops from Kalanianaole Highway where it crosses Koko Head. Snorkeling equipment is available at the beach pavilion, but it is often not of the best quality. Gear may be rented from *Hanauma Bay Snorkeling* (phone: 944-8828), which provides equipment for snorkelers for 2½ hours on their own at Hanauma Bay. Escorted tours for a maximum of 5 hours are $55. *Hanauma* uses taxis, not vans, and is the only company allowed in-park drop-offs. It may also be necessary for divers to make their own arrangements for getting here, but once they've arrived they find it hard to leave.

Hawaii-Kai – If you have any interest in how paradise will look once planners have been allowed in, come to Hawaii-Kai. It's a conglomeration of small houses tucked inside neat little gardens, townhouses in unharmonious proximity, condominiums, and a marina that looks as though it were copied from a Hollywood backlot. True, there are the mountains in the background, the ocean nearby, and a scattering of palm trees, but the result is nevertheless depressing.

SHOPPING: There are two suburban malls that offer the expected shops and services. Of particular interest to visitors are the *Suyderhoud Water Ski Center,* which provides all that's needed for that activity (phone: 395-3773); and the misnamed *Cosmopolitan Fashion Shoppe,* for ladies who find the bikinis at *Liberty House* too puritanical (phone: 395-4269).

CHECKING IN: There are no recommended hotels in this area; see *Diamond Head* or *Waikiki* for accommodations nearby.

EATING OUT: Expect to pay $55 or more for dinner for two (drinks, wine, and tip not included) at the restaurant listed below as expensive, and from $25 to $50 at the place listed as moderate. Both telephone numbers are in the 808 area code.

Roy's – Owner Roy Yamaguchi combines Oriental and continental styles for first-rate results. Unusual dishes include pan-sautéed lemon grass calamari with Thai peanut sauce, miso-crusted ulua with fresh clams, bean sprouts, and Asian vermicelli, and mesquite-smoked, Peking-style duck with candied pecans in a lillikoi ginger sauce. Open for dinner daily; open for brunch on Sundays only. Reservations necessary. 6600 Kalanianaole Hwy., Hawaii-Kai (phone: 396-7697). Expensive to moderate.

Swiss Inn – This is the domain of ex–*Kahala Hilton* chef Martin Wyss, and the crowds tell the story. From simple dishes like Wiener schnitzel to the delightful *émince de veau zurichoise* or trout caprice (with mushrooms and bananas), your tastebuds are in for a treat. Open for lunch and dinner, from 6 to 10 PM. Closed Mondays. Reservations advised. *Nui Valley Shopping Center,* 5730 Kalanianaole Hwy. (phone: 377-5447). Moderate.

Windward Oahu

Standing in a regimental grove of papaya trees or glancing along a row of purple blooms on a vanda orchid farm, it is sometimes possible to forget the ocean on this side of the island. What cannot be ignored, however, is the long, dark green arras, with its mysterious folds formed by the precipitous windward side of the Koolau Range. For mile after mile, the fortress-like face of these fluted cliffs stretches along the eastern side of Oahu. After heavy rains, these numberless clefts are adazzle with ribbon-thin waterfalls in a display that would make even the most convinced skeptic believe that the mountains are enchanted.

Most people on this side of the island live in Kailua, a Honolulu dormitory town, and Kaneohe, where there is a big marine air corps station. Farther north are small settlements of *kamaainas* who have been here for generations, wealthy Honolulu residents who have built vacation homes along the beaches, and native Hawaiians, many of whom continue to farm and fish in rural valleys like Waiahole and Waiicane. There's a very definite feel of the South Seas once you get past suburban Kaneohe and head north to Kaaawa and Laie. Although there is a highway from Honolulu, Route 61, into Kailua, and another, Route 63, into Kaneohe, any semblance of a network of roads ends abruptly at Kahaluu. The only road north from there is the windward section of the Kamehameha Highway, winding along the coastline beneath towering *palis* and around bays. On the right as you drive north you will see boats bobbing on the water, a tie-line anchoring them to the stilts of small wooden cottages that have the Pacific for a basement. Here and there you may spot a fisherman ankle deep in water preparing to spear an octopus. On the left, between the crenelated outline of the mountains and the highway, are small farms with haphazardly growing banana trees and methodically planted acres of papayas, taro, orchids, anthuriums, and all the other exuberant paraphernalia of nature's green moments that send writers scurrying to the thesaurus looking for synonyms for the word *lush.*

Nuuanu Pali Lookout – Although barely 15 minutes from downtown Honolulu, the lookout offers a spectacular grandstand view of the vast green arena known as Windward Oahu. Kailua, Kaneohe, the ocean, the farms, twin tunnels that penetrate the mountains, and the dramatic northern sweep of the Koolau *pali* are all here at one glance. The wind on the lookout is famous, and you learn in one gasp why this side of the island is called the windward side. Even on a rainswept day, when the view is reduced to zero, the experience can be awesome. At the edge of the viewing rampart you are suddenly face to face with a cloud that is being held back by the cliffs on either side. It is rather like stepping outside an airplane in flight. Legend has it that Kamehameha the Great fought a battle here during his conquest of Oahu and sent hundreds of island warriors tumbling down the *pali* to their deaths when they chose to perish rather than submit. Their bones, the legend continues, lie by the thousands in the valleys below. It is a pious story and one you will hear repeated frequently by tour guides. Historians, however, have failed to verify the incident and the sound you hear is likely to be not the wail of the glorious dead but the wind. The Pali Lookout is reached by a side road off the Nuuanu Pali Highway, Route 61, close to the ridge of the Koolau Range. A turnoff closer to Honolulu onto the old Pali Drive brings you to the same destination by a more interesting route, along which you get some idea of what a suburb would look like surrounded by jungle.

Kailua – The beach park is the main attraction of this otherwise featureless town. The beach is wide and sandy, with excellent swimming, and is very popular with windsurfers. The park is divided into two parts by the Kaelepulu Canal. On the north side of the canal, you can walk to the end of the park and along the beaches that form the backyards of some enviable and expensive homes. On the south side, a stroll up to the pink pillar that marks the gateway to the exclusive community of Lanikai makes a pleasant diversion. From the bluff there is a good view across to the Mokulua Islands, home of the Christmas Island shearwater.

Kaneohe – The Kaneohe Bay Drive from Kailua brings you through an attractive suburban community with beachside and cliffside houses surrounded by colorful gardens. The ocean floor here is shallow and somewhat rocky and marvelously endowed with coral reefs. A glass-bottom boat, the *Coral Queen,* makes hour-long trips over the reefs five times a day from Heeia Kea Boat Harbor, just off Kamehameha Highway (phone: 235-2888; if no answer, call again, as the boat may be out). The sights from this boat might include some wonderful coral formations, such as flowery cup coral and gorgonian coral, as well as brazenly decorative fish and other marine animals with names like damselfish, long-nose hawkfish, spotted puffers, Moorish idols, lionfish, and regal slipper lobster. Cost is $7.50. Close to the pier is the ancient Heeia fishpond, a 12-foot wall enclosing 88 acres of ocean where fish were "farmed" for food for several hundred years.

Haiku Gardens – Haiku Valley was a favorite resort of the ancient Hawaiians. Nowadays *kamaainas* and visitors come here to wander by the spectacular lily and tropical fish ponds and through bamboo groves and to wonder at the unruly loveliness of the flowers, plants, and tropical trees all around. The restaurant on site is open daily for lunch and dinner (see *Eating Out*). 46-336 Haiku Rd., Kaneohe (phone: 247-6671).

Valley of the Temples – The star attraction in this memorial park is the replica of the famous Byodo-In Temple of Kyoto, Japan. Graceful and ornate and set in a classic Japanese garden with peacocks and swans, the temple has something else going for it too — the dramatic *pali* in the background. Open daily from 9 AM to 4:30 PM. Admission $2. 47-200 Kahekili Hwy., Kaneohe (phone: 239-8811).

Kualoa Regional Park – A favorite Windward Coast spot for picnics and swimming, the beach is rather narrow but long and sandy and has a beautiful view of the mountains and Kaneohe Bay. Oahu's most famous island, Mokolii, also known as Chinaman's Hat, is just offshore. When the tide is especially low, it is possible to walk the 500 yards to the island, which, although not a bird sanctuary, is a haven for several species including the frigate bird.

Sacred Falls State Park – The god to whom these falls are sacred was known as Kamapuua, the deity of swine, who could change himself into a pig or a man at will. To reach the falls, you have to hike for more than a mile along an uphill trail that is rocky in places and is best avoided in wet weather, when it becomes unpleasantly muddy. Portions of the trail follow the stream bed; for those anticipating a casual stroll — it's not! En route you will find kukui nuts, Java plums, and mountain apples. At the trail's end, in a 50-foot-wide ravine, the falls drop for 87 feet against the ever-present brocade of the green Koolau Range. The pool at the bottom of the falls is an idyllic place for swimming — cool, refreshing, and romantic. But if you have been bathing in the balmy Pacific just an hour or so before, the temperature may leave you breathless at first. From the Kamehameha Hwy. take Plantation Rd., which turns off between Punaluu and Hauula, to the trail ahead.

Hauula Beach Park – Although at first the ironwood trees along the shoreline may seem this beach's most important feature, if you happen to be here early in the day during July and August, you can witness a colorful natural phenomenon. On the ground under the many hau or beach hibiscus trees in the area, you will see red flowers that have fallen the previous night. The trees themselves will be in bloom with bright yellow flowers, which will by nightfall turn to a russet color, then later, bright red, and fall off. Photographers professional and amateur have been known to spend a day here photographing the transformation, a pastime that can be delightfully combined with picnicking and swimming in an ample, walled-in area on the beach.

Mokuauia Island – Who can resist an island, and when you are on a largish one such as Oahu, who can resist a smaller one like Mokuauia, also known as Goat Island? You can wade over from Kalani Point, off the Kamehameha Highway, through water that is sometimes waist deep but is shallow on calm days at low tide, allowing for safe and easy transit. There is a delightful small sandy beach crescent on the leeward side of the island that is good for swimming when the currents are not strong, but perhaps the main pleasure here is in quietly observing the ornithological life. Mokuauia, like most Windward Coast offshore islands, is a state bird refuge, and among the more common black noddy, brown noddy, wedge-tailed shearwater, and brown booby, you may catch a glimpse of a masked-faced booby, with its nun-like hood and black tail, and the distinguished-looking gray-backed tern, with its severe black head, white forehead and throat, and clerical gray tail. Distantly, against the sky, you may even spot a black-footed or a laysan albatross indulging in some effortless and extremely graceful aerodynamics. Mokuauia is a couple of miles north of Laie and the Polynesian Cultural Center, which are discussed in a separate section by that name.

Senator Fong's Plantation and Gardens – Hawaii's first elected US senator pays a flowery tribute to the presidents under whom he served. A 3-mile, 40-minute guided tour by open-air minibus begins at the visitors center in Eisenhower Valley, and covers Kennedy Valley, where over 15 varieties of sugarcane grow; Johnson Plateau of fruit and nut orchards, encompassing over 75 edible plants and trees; Nixon Valley, with the traditional gardens of Hawaii's main ethnic groups (Chinese, Japanese, Filipino, and Hawaiian); and Ford Plateau, which features a pine garden. The 725-acre plantation offers a lush setting and a pleasant staff, but the collection still needs time to flourish. Open daily from 10 AM to 4 PM. The last train leaves at 3 PM. Admission $6.50 adults, $3 children; under 5 free. Located in Kahaluu, a mile from the juncton of Kamemeha (83) and Kahekili Hwys., at 47-285 Pulama Rd. (phone: 239-6775).

SHOPPING: The *Kailua* and *Kaneohe* shopping centers have food marts to fill the refrigerators of these suburban communities, and at Kailua there is a branch of *Liberty House,* with its line of men's, women's, and children's clothing (phone: 941-2345). *Long's,* a statewide drugstore chain that sells most of the merchandise you find in any five-and-dime as well as pharmaceuticals and photographic equipment, has stores in the *Kailua Shopping Center* (phone: 261-8537) and in the *Kaneohe Shopping Center* (phone: 235-4511). Along the highways, a number of ramshackle stores sell papayas, pineapples, mountain apples, bananas, and occasionally some well-made local artifacts. These colorful stores offer a genuine glimpse of what is left of rural Oahu. Hawaiian artists display their works each Sunday in the *Pali Painter's Sidewalk Show,* in the 43-600 block of Kailua Rd., Kailua.

NIGHTLIFE: Mostly it's the lapping of the waves on the sand and the pounding of the surf on the reefs. If you like a mixture of Hawaiian and contemporary music with a country flavor, try *Pat's at Punaluu* (phone: 293-8502), which tends to become lively on Friday and Saturday nights; the beat turns romantic and contemporary on Thursdays and Sundays. For disco, go to *Fast Eddie's* (52 Oneawa St., Kailua; phone: 261-8561) nightly from 8 PM to 4 AM.

CHECKING IN: There is not much by way of tourist accommodations on the Windward Coast. People wishing to stay here for a month or more may find it worthwhile to check the *Honolulu Advertiser* and the *Honolulu Star-Bulletin* for home and condominium rentals. *Bed & Breakfast Hawaii* (phone: 822-7771, 536-8421, and 800-733-1632) lists several rooms and houses for rent along this stretch of the Oahu coast. All telephone numbers are in the 808 area code unless otherwise indicated.

Pat's at Punaluu – Although all the units here are privately owned, between 30 and 40 of them become available at various times of the year, often for long periods. Each is individually decorated. The building is right on Halehaha Beach, which is good for swimming, snorkeling, or just plain beachcombing. (It is sheltered from the heavy surf by a lovely reef.) There is a freshwater swimming pool and a full gym for those wanting a workout and sauna. Maid service is offered twice a week. *Bananas,* a restaurant and cocktail lounge, is adjacent (see *Eating Out*). Rates start at about $65 for a studio, with a discount for stays of 3 days or more. A private beach cottage is also available, for a modest $4 extra. 53-567 Kamehameha Hwy., Hauula (phone: 293-8111).

Plantation Spa – This 7-acre holistic retreat, owned and run by Dave and Bodil Anderson, provides a place for 18 guests to enjoy week-long programs that include kayaking, hiking, snorkeling, yoga, aquacize aerobics, massage, and evening speakers who discourse on things healthful and Hawaiian. There's no regimented schedule to follow, just a wide range of daily activities designed to get you out there and generate some nature-induced high energy. Accommodations are in the main house or in cozy nearby cottages, and all meals are prepared for strict vegetarians. Two-night programs start at $357, with the full 6-night program priced at $995 (includes two massages and an herbal wrap). 51-550 Kamehameha Hwy., Kaaawa (phone: 237-8685; 800-422-0307).

EATING OUT: Dining outside Honolulu is on the whole a less than memorable experience, and although the windward side of the island isn't quite the culinary semidesert that western Oahu appears to be, only *L'Auberge* at Kailua (below) is worth the trip just for the cooking. The chief ingredient of the others is either the setting or the view. Expect to pay $55 or more for dinner for two (drinks, wine, and tip not included) at a restaurant listed as expensive, from $25 to $50 at a place listed as moderate. All telephone numbers are in the 808 area code unless otherwise indicated.

Crouching Lion – Named for the rock formation above it, this restaurant is just across the road from Kaaawa beach. From the luncheon room watch the waves lap the white sand while you dine on mahimahi, burgers, steak teriyaki, or sandwiches. The main dining room, decorated in a Hollywood baronial style, contains a huge fireplace that is occasionally put to use to dry out the humid air. Dinner specialties include Slavonic steak, a favorite with the *kamaainas.* Open daily for lunch from 11 AM to 3:30 PM, and dinner from 5 to 9 PM. Reservations advised. 51-666 Kamehameha Hwy., Kaaawa (phone: 237-8511). Expensive to moderate.

Haiku Charthouse – A branch of the Hawaiian chain, it specializes in prime ribs, steaks, and fish, all served in a tropical setting that opens out onto lovely gardens. Open daily for dinner, which includes an impressive salad bar, from 5 to 10 PM. Reservations advised. 46-336 Haiku Rd., Kaneohe (phone: 247-6671). Expensive to moderate.

Haiku Gardens – Dining on its lanai, you take in the rain forest, gardens, and the Koolau Range. The house specialty is spareribs cooked over kiawe charcoal; steaks and seafood are also served. Sunday brunch, 10:30 AM to 2:30 PM, is a specialty. Closed Mondays. Reservations advised. 46-336 Haiku Rd., Kaneohe (phone: 247-6671). Expensive to moderate.

L'Auberge Swiss – It is a pleasant and unexpected surprise to find this bistro in an uninteresting part of downtown Kailua. The restaurant resembles a small country inn with checkered tablecloths and simple wooden chairs. The menu is substantial, with veal, beef, chicken, and fish prepared in a variety of continental styles. There is also a full range of appetizers and desserts to round out the menu. A 25-minute drive through the Pali Tunnel from Waikiki. Open Tuesdays through Saturdays from 6 to 10 PM, Sundays from 5:30 to 9 PM. Reservations advised. 117 Hekili St., Kailua (phone: 263-4663). Moderate.

Bananas – The remake of *Pat's at Punaluu* is a major improvement. Just the lack of its regular tour bus business makes the quiet seem heavenly, but the main treat is the hearty country cooking and barbecue with Pacific island–style marinades. Newly planted banana trees enhance the tropical feel. Open for lunch daily from 11 AM to 6 PM, with dinner on weekends year-round, on weekdays during the summer season. Dinner reservations advised. 53-567 Kamehameha Hwy., Hauula (phone: 293-8502). Moderate.

Buzz's Original Steakhouse – A good spot to visit for typical steakhouse fare — steaks, seafood, and salad bar. Seating is either indoors or alfresco, and the service rates among the friendliest in Hawaii. Open for dinner only, from 5 to 10 PM. Reservations advised. 413 Kawailoa Rd., Lanikai (phone: 261-4661). Moderate.

Saeng's – Excellent Thai cooking with an emphasis on vegetarian entrées, plus a fair share of beef, shrimp, and chicken dishes. Open for lunch from 11 AM to 2:30 PM on weekdays, and dinner nightly from 5 to 9:30 PM. Dinner reservations advised. 315 Hahani St., Kailua (phone: 263-9727). Moderate.

Bueno Nalo – The coconut wireless (as the local grapevine is called) gives this casual eatery high marks for its Mexican cooking. Guests bring their own wine and wait for tables. Open daily except Mondays, from 5 to 9 PM; on weekends, open at 3 PM. No reservations. 41-865 Kalanianaole Hwy., Waimanalo (phone: 259-7186). Inexpensive.

Paniolo Cafe – Big is beautiful here: half-pound burgers and chichis and mai tais served in 16-ounce mason jars. Good spot for casual dining. In Punaluu. Open for lunch daily; open for dinner Thursdays through Sundays from 5:30 to 9 PM. Reservations advised. 53-146 Kamehameha Hwy (phone: 237-8521). Inexpensive.

Smitty's Pancake House – There's lots more here than the name implies, including Hawaiian specialties, hamburgers, and desserts such as homemade blueberry pie. Open for breakfast, lunch, and dinner daily. No reservations. 46-077 Kamehameha Hwy., Kanoehe (phone: 247-8533). Inexpensive.

Polynesian Cultural Center

"A living museum of seven primitive South Sea villages" is how the promotional material describes this 42-acre cultural endeavor of the Hawaii branch of Brigham Young University in the Mormon community of Laie. Here, students from the Hawaiian Islands, Fiji, Samoa, Tonga, Tahiti, the Marquesas, and New Zealand (an Easter Island addition was in the works at press time) reproduce the skills, music, meals, ceremonies, and rituals of their homelands in fastidiously replicated South Seas villages, an activity for which they are appropriately rewarded with credit toward graduation and salaries for tuition and board. The center can be toured with guides in a festively decorated tram and by canoe on the canals that run through the villages. It is only on foot, however, that you can fully savor the flavor of each community.

Near the southern end of the complex is an Orientation Center; from this point it is best to proceed north to the Tonga Village. Here Tongan women demonstrate *ngatu,* the fashioning of the tapa cloth for which Hawaii is famous. Don't miss the Tongan House, where the walls are lined with weathered tapa decorated in clay-brown tones with ancient Tongan symbols and the floors are covered with *lau hala* carpets and pillows. In the separate kitchen is an *imu* (earth oven) and a huge, cool-looking banana leaf prepared to serve as a dining table for a meal of pig, yams, and tapioca. In the Tahiti

Village, a little farther on, serenely beautiful Tahitian girls make shell leis and grass skirts quite unlike those you will find for sale in the open-air bazaars of Waikiki. The adjacent Marquesas Village, a complex of six wooden houses with thatch roofs shaped like a narrow, upside-down "V," has a Chief's House, a house for the women and children, and a small temple with wooden tikis of tribal gods outside. Probably because it is almost totally surrounded by a wall, which in early times served as a fortification, this is easily the most successful replica in the center. "Villagers" like to point out the pictures of warriors, who are completely and elaborately tattooed. Obviously, the young Marquesan males on duty here have not felt it necessary to take authenticity this far. Crossing the bridge to the Hawaiian Village, you come to the most popular spot in the center, possibly because this is in a sense the host village. The Chief's House here boasts a raised bed with a beautiful feather cover and *kahilis* (feather-decorated staffs symbolic of royalty) on either side. You can also learn how poi, a Hawaiian and Polynesian staple, is made. Working at a low wooden table supported by a broad frame woven from pandanus leaves, a Hawaiian student pounds down a taro root. The powdered root, which is rich in vitamins and minerals, is diluted slightly with water and allowed to ferment in order to produce an acid that acts as a preservative. Poi is one of the essential ingredients of a luau. The Fiji Village, next door, is for many people the most attractive. The Chief's House is a large, handsome building divided into four separate rooms, one each for his family, his counselors, visiting common folk, and for the chief himself. His bed is covered with a splendid carpet, only slightly more luxurious than the carpet at the foot of his bed, where his current favorite slept. The walls of the rooms are formed of tapa cloth made from the bark of mulberry trees and printed with designs that appear to tell a story. Outside, Fijian music is played on bamboo pipe organs. An impressive sight in the Maori Village, just to the north, is the 40-man canoe used for coastal raids. You can learn to play the stick game *tititorea* here, although it is more amusing to watch the Maori experts themselves, who make it look like a minor juggling act. The great charm of the Samoa Village, a little farther north, is watching young ladies perform the Mauluulu dance.

In the Carver's Shop, students are reconstructing and making replicas of artifacts of all the islands. If you are lucky, you may even be present when they are carving out a war canoe, a sight that can be quite diverting.

Access to the center is available on an admission-only basis ($20) that covers the villages and the *Pageant of the Long Canoes* at the *Hale Aloha Theater.* The Admission/Buffet package ($40.50) lets you tour the grounds on your own and also includes a buffet dinner and seating at the extravagant revue, *Mana: The Spirit of the People;* the personalized Ambassador Passport package ($75) adds an escorted tour of the grounds, preferential seating for the show, and admission to the large-format IMAX movie on Polynesian history and culture. A luau is held nightly at 6 PM, and can be purchased for $50.50 along with admission and the *Mana* revue, or as an option on the Ambassador Passport package. With a cast of 150 performers from all the islands, the revue is the highlight of a visit to the center for many people. It is by far the most authentic South Seas show on Oahu since it seriously tries to represent the spirit and rhythm of the individual islands and is performed by youngsters who appear for the most part to be dedicated to their traditions.

While the performances in the various villages lack the authenticity of ritual, they do offer an understanding of life in the islands' diverse communities. As change affects these island cultures, the center has increasingly become a living museum of traditional, as opposed to modern, Hawaiian lifestyle. In fact, the center is second only to Pearl Harbor as the island's most popular tourist attraction outside Waikiki.

Souvenirs are sold in *The Marketplace.* The merchandise ranges from hula sets with plastic leis and parchment calendars with Polynesian zodiac signs to some quite good tapa wall hangings from Tonga. In between, you can find some presentable bracelet charms made from a variety of materials, such as jade, whale's teeth, and ivory. The *Gateway* restaurant serves a dinner buffet of salad, chicken, spareribs, rice, and desserts that can best be described as acceptable. This being Mormon territory, there is no liquor, wine, or beer, but there is lemonade. The center, which also offers a worthwhile trip to the grounds of the Mormon Temple, is closed Sundays (phone: 293-3333; in Waikiki, 923-1861).

The community of Laie outside the center is chiefly known for its long beach. Since it is protected from heavy surf by an offshore reef, it is good for swimming and occasionally suitable for body-surfing. From Laie Point, at the end of Naupaka Street, you can watch two pretty, small islands defend themselves against the Pacific surf. On rough days it can be quite a sight.

The *Laniloa Lodge* hotel (55-109 Laniloa; phone: 293-9282; 800-LANILOA), just outside the main entrance to the Polynesian Cultural Center, has small, pleasant rooms for about $80 and up for two people. The rooms around the swimming pool are more attractive because the tiny lanais are shaded by tall palms. An adjacent restaurant serves various kinds of chicken, hamburgers, and similar items. Again, there is no booze. *TheBus* makes a stop on its round-the-island runs at the entrance to the center. Most bus tour companies have a special Polynesian Cultural Center package leaving from Waikiki.

North Shore

"The face of this country is uncommonly beautiful," wrote Captain James Cook in his diary for 1784. He was referring to the North Shore of Oahu, an area that can be simply defined as between Kahuku Point, a protuberance in the swampy northeast corner of the island, and Kaena Point, a rocky cape in the northwest. The shoreline in between is the most famous in the world for surfing. It recedes gently to the north face of the Koolau Range in the east, the low-lying land between the ocean and the mountains supporting truck farms and small ranches. West of Haleiwa, the coastal lowlands behind Mokuleia, the old Dillingham Ranch, and the present Dillingham Air Force Base rise dramatically up the northwest arm of the Waianae Mountains, dominated by Mt. Kaala, which at 4,025 feet is the highest peak on Oahu.

In the lowland crescent between the two mountain ranges live some 10,000 inhabitants — small farmers, ranchers, a few fishermen, and people employed by the military, the COMSAT communications center near Pupukea, and the *Turtle Bay Hilton.* The recession of the late 1970s and early 1980s put many people out of work on the North Shore, and although they are not nearly so frequent as on the west coast of Oahu, there have been incidents of muggings and car thefts.

Nevertheless, well-to-do residents of Honolulu and the mainland still come to their holiday homes along the beaches. You see these properties mainly from Waialee to Haleiwa, sometimes standing on a plot adjacent to a wartime Nissen hut with a corrugated iron roof that has been converted into full-time living quarters. And since nature, unlike man, has few favorites, both types of homes seem to be surrounded with an abundance of swaying palm and ironwood trees, bougainvillea, hibiscus, and, in the winter, poinsettia.

Sunset Beach – This 2-mile-long sandy beach, averaging 200 feet in width, is one of the most attractive — and notorious — on Oahu. In the summer, swimming close to the shoreline and away from the lava rock outcrops is quite safe; swimming in the winter, when high-wave surf competitions are held, can be dangerous. Aficionados of Sunset have given different sections of it special names. The Pipeline, in front of Ke Nui Road, the residential strip that runs parallel to the Kamehameha Highway, is an area where waves form the famous tubes familiar to many people. They are spectacular to look at, very dangerous, and have in some cases proven fatal even to championship class surfers. Banzai Beach — reputedly named when an observer watching a surfer attack a particularly challenging wave called out "Banzai!" — is just a little farther west and is identified by a small group of rocks called the Banzai Rocks. Both sections of the beach have the same superbly graceful waves that climb into arcs and fall into curls. They also have a lovely view of the northwest fringes of the Waianae Mountains sinking modestly to a cape at Kaena, which, during a cloud-studded sunset, can make you gasp.

Pupukea Beach Park – The offshore coral reef here provides a memorable display of pounding surf in the winter and forms the perimeter of fascinating tidal pools in the summer. Both sights and seasons lend themselves to the photographer.

Puu o Mahuka Heiau – Here at Oahu's most famous temple are three separate enclosures, one of which contains a structure that was probably an altar where human sacrifices were performed. From the *heiau,* there is a lovely view of Waimea Bay, inlet, and beach park and of the square stone belfry of St. Peter's and St. Paul's Catholic Mission Church, which, in spite of looking like an Italian chapel tower, was once part of a rock-crushing plant.

Waimea Falls Park – This 1,800-acre canyon, with its lovely falls, rock-girt swimming pool, botanical gardens, and 7½ miles of hiking trails, is undoubtedly Oahu's most attractive tourist development. Even with its buses with well-informed guides, the park manages to remain low-key. The ancient Hawaiian games and sports that are demonstrated on the lower meadow by experts and novices do not obtrude on the visitor who wants to walk casually among the exotic plants and trees. Excavated house sites and fishing shrines remain much as they were found and have not suffered the monstrous reconstructions so beloved by developers of theme parks. Although many of the plants have been introduced from other parts of the tropics, one of the main functions of Waimea Falls Park is to preserve and propagate Hawaii's endangered flora. Among the trees here is the only known kokia cookei still in existence. Other attractions include two wild boar caught in the Waimea Valley; two wild donkeys from the Big Island, where they are known as Kona nightingales and can occasionally still be spotted on the wooded hillsides south of Kailua-Kona; peacocks; and, a special favorite, a pond with huge Amazon water lily pads that look like round, green tea trays. Daily activities include hula dancing and cliff diving into the pool at the base of Waimea Falls. On nights when the moon is full, the park offers complimentary escorted moonlight tours. For people taking *TheBus* No. 52 marked Wahiawa/Kaneohe from Honolulu, there is a 15-minute walk to the Falls Visitor Center from the Kamehameha Highway stop. The delightful hike runs through the lower part of the canyon along Kamananui Stream. Open daily from 10 AM to 5:30 PM. Admission is $12.95 for adults, $7.50 for juniors (7–12 years), and $4.50 for children (4–6 years). 59-864 Kamehameha Hwy. (phone: 638-8511).

Waimea Bay – Waimea was the home of several thousand people until 1894, when a flood destroyed homes, taro patches, livestock, and people, leaving the area desolate for many years. Nowadays there are still more visitors than residents, and they come to visit the falls and the beach park. Swimming here in the summer is wonderful, but in the winter it can be dangerous. Experienced surfers come here in December and January to test their prowess against waves that can rise as high as 25 to 30 feet, and spectators come by the hundreds to watch them.

Haleiwa – During the late 1960s and early 1970s, mainland hippies "discovered" Haleiwa, much to the chagrin of the islanders who were raised with its charms. Today, in spite of a growing number of specialty shops, it still manages to retain the feeling of being small-town Hawaii. Suburban villas facing the ocean make it too big to be a slumbering tropical village, and there aren't quite enough decorative clapboard shopfronts to compare it to cattle towns in the Old West, yet it does have character. With an emerging identity as an artists' community, Haleiwa also offers a touch of the avant-garde, with several galleries, restaurants, shops, and even a displaced Greenwich Village coffee shop, a popular haunt of artists and intellectuals.

On Kamehameha Highway diagonally across from Kewalo Lane is the Liliuokalani Church and Cemetery. In the church is the perpetual clock of Queen Liliuokalani, who had a summer home close by along the Anahulu Stream in the late 19th century. The clock, which hangs on the back wall of the church, has seven dials and seven hands. They indicate the months, days of the week, the week of the year, the day of the month, phases of the moon, and, against a dial using the 12 letters of the queen's name, the hours of the day. In the cemetery are gravestones dating from the 1830s.

Haleiwa Beach Park is one of the very few places on the North Shore where swimming is safe almost year-round, though here as elsewhere it is wise to check the water conditions before going in. *Hale"iwa* means ""home of the frigate bird," and occasionally these large, elegant fliers can be spotted off the north coast — but always in flight, in spite of the name. The Kamehameha Highway turns south at Haleiwa to proceed across central Oahu to the south coast and Honolulu. A secondary road, Route 82, continues on along the coast past Mokuleia and joins Route 930, which eventually becomes a four-wheel-drive track leading to Kaena Point, the island's extreme northwest tip. The road that leads to this section of land has been permanently blocked to protect the fragile coastal wilderness and to preserve it as a state park.

Mokuleia – The Dillingham family used to have a ranch in this quiet corner of northwest Oahu. Today, the Dillingham Air Force Base is the most visible tenant, although the polo fields here have attracted such luminaries as the Duke of Edinburgh, the Prince of Wales, and that polo-playing junkie, the Maharajah of Jaipur. Digging in the sand for shells is a favorite family pastime, as some exquisite specimens can occasionally be found. It is possible to travel beyond Mokuleia to Kaena Point, but the road is difficult and narrow and best suited to hikers.

SHOPPING: Change is coming to Haleiwa, with new restaurants and shops in place for resort growth on the North Shore. Haleiwa holds on to its old-town feel, but country stores like *Matsumoto's* and *Aoki's,* where shaved ice and T-shirts were king, now compete with upscale shops and galleries.

Barnfield's Raging Isle Sports – This is the place to witness a slice-of-the-surf-scene life. Adjacent to the *North Shore Center,* it's where some of the best custom surfboards in Hawaii are made. 66-250 Kamehameha Hwy (phone: 637-7707).

Charlie's Country Store – Apart from the distressingly familiar souvenirs, this place also sells excellent books on the flora and fauna of the islands. In Waimea Falls Park, 59-864 Kamehameha Hwy. (phone: 638-8525).

Deeni's Boutique – Good for beach towels, bikinis, and muumuus, especially when there's an "odd lot" table. 66-079 Kamehameha Hwy., Haleiwa (phone: 637-9871).

Fettig Art Gallery – Large and colorful paintings of Hawaiian rural and maritime scenes. 66-030 Kamehameha Hwy., Haleiwa (phone: 637-4933).

Kukui Nuts of Hawaii – This is the place where kukui nuts are transformed into shiny black and brown leis. Also available: an array of products, from lotions to shampoos, created from healthful kukui oil. 66-935 Kaukonahua Rd., between Haleiwa and Waialua (phone: 637-9889).

Outrigger Trading Co. – Inside *Jameson's by the Sea,* this small shop specializes in hand-crafted Hawaiian-made pottery, glass, wood, and so on. 62-540 Kamehameha Hwy., Haleiwa (phone: 637-4737).

Pacific Island Arts – Located in the *North Shore Center,* this gallery fills its 5,000 square feet with the works of some of Hawaii's finest artists. Particularly noteworthy are Dan Van Zyle (serigraphs), Norman Nagai (watercolors), Laka Morton (Hawaiian portraiture), and mother/daughter Mary Koski and Cathy Long (painting, pen and ink drawings, etchings). 66-250 Kamehameha Hwy. (phone: 637-7880).

Platinor – Oriental art and antiques, many from owner Engelbert "Angelo" Klockner's collection. In the lobby of the *Turtle Bay Hilton* (phone: 293-8777).

Wyland Gallery – Whaling Wall artist Wyland has opened a gallery featuring his primarily nautical paintings, as well as the work of other Hawaiian artists. 66-150 Kamehameha Hwy (phone: 637-7498).

NIGHTLIFE: *Steamers* (in the *Haleiwa Shopping Plaza;* phone: 637-5071) turns into a lively disco Thursdays, Fridays, and Saturdays between 10 PM and 1:30 AM. The *Bay View* at the *Turtle Bay Hilton* (phone: 293-8811) features live entertainment most evenings, while things go disco on Friday and Saturday nights from 9:30 PM to 1 AM.

CHECKING IN: The only hostelry along the North Shore offering resort amenities is the *Turtle Bay Hilton.* At press time, plans for construction of a second hotel at Turtle Bay in 1994, along with additional condominiums, had been announced. There are a few condominiums at Mokuleia Beach, but these are usually let only on fairly long leases. Expect to pay $140 and up daily for two for a place listed as expensive, and between $75 and $135 for a place listed as moderate. All telephone numbers are in the 808 area code unless otherwise indicated.

Ke Iki Hale – Set on an acre and a half of palm-fringed beachfront amid ironwood and palm trees, these cottages contain 1 or 2 bedrooms, full kitchens, and large picture windows. Recreational facilities include a volleyball court, barbecues, and picnic tables overlooking the water. Maid service is not available. 59-579 Ke Iki Rd., Haleiwa (phone: 638-8229). Expensive.

Turtle Bay Hilton – Just about everything that you could possibly want on a vacation. There are miles of beautiful beach, including tiny, idyllic Kuilima Cove, one of the few places on the North Shore where you can swim year-round. In addition, the hotel offers the new Arnold Palmer–designed course (a second Palmer course, available for play at the end of next year, will replace the original George Fazio course), tennis, scuba diving, snorkeling, and horseback riding. Tennis programs and tennis camp are offered by the *Nick Bollettieri Tennis Academy* (phone: 800-USA-NICK). The guestrooms are large and on the whole quite elegant, particularly since a property-wide renovation was completed in 1990. Winter, when it is damp and cloudy, may not be the best time to visit if you are looking for a placid ocean and a deep tan, but once you have been lulled to sleep by the pounding surf along the Kuilima beaches, any other sleeping aid will seem ineffectual. The range of accommodations here is wide, from bay-view rooms to ocean-view rooms to separate cottages, cabanas, and executive suites. Off Kamehameha Hwy., Kahuku (phone: 293-8811; 800-445-8667). Expensive.

Turtle Bay Condos – Studios, as well as 1-, 2-, and 3-bedroom condominiums adjacent to *Turtle Bay*'s expansive golf courses are available for those who prefer the privacy found here, as well as full resort amenities, that some hotels lack. Each is equipped with a full kitchen, washer/dryer, and color TV set. 1270 Ala Moana Blvd., Honolulu, HI 96814 (phone: 293-2800). Moderate.

EATING OUT: Again, the options are few and far between. For a meal for two, excluding wine, tips, and drinks, expect to pay more than $60 in a restaurant listed as expensive, between $25 and $55 at a place listed as moderate, and under $20 in an inexpensive eatery. All telephone numbers are in the 808 area code unless otherwise indicated.

Cove – At this dining room, guests at window tables gaze out at the white foam and deep blue water of Kuilima Cove as they sample the seafood and various international dishes. Reservations necessary. Open daily for dinner from 6 to 9:30 PM. Reservations advised. In the *Turtle Bay Hilton,* off Kamehameha Hwy., Kahuku (phone: 293-8811). Expensive.

Jameson's by the Sea – The setting downstairs is quite casual, while upstairs is a bit more elegant, but both provide their popular baked stuffed shrimp, fresh catch-of-the-day, steaks, or chicken specialties. Popular with North Shore residents and Honolulu day-trippers. Open daily for lunch from 11 AM to 5 PM and dinner from 5 to 10 PM. Reservations advised. 62-540 Kamehameha Hwy., Haleiwa (phone: 637-4336). Expensive to moderate.

Steamer's – Yet another seafood house paying homage to the butcher-block table. Sashimi, *poki* (raw fish, onions, and tomatoes), and steamer clams with tomatoes and onions are favorites, although there are also more substantial dishes, and all can be savored either indoors or on the deck. Open for lunch from 11:30 AM to 2:30 PM, and dinner from 5:30 PM to 10 PM. Reservations advised. In the *Haleiwa Shopping Plaza* (phone: 637-5071). Expensive to moderate.

Proud Peacock – At Waimea Falls Park, the pride of this place is a beautiful mahogany bar made in Scotland in 1814. From the terrace you can throw tidbits to the peacocks in the garden below and see some of the hundreds of rare trees and plants that stretch up to the falls and beyond. An all-you-can-eat barbecued rib special is served Tuesday and Wednesday nights; prime ribs, steaks, and seafood are nightly specials. Open daily. Reservations advised. In Waimea Falls Park, 59-864 Kamehameha Hwy. (phone: 638-8531). Moderate to inexpensive.

Rosy's Cantina – Good-quality Cal-Mex specialties, and above-par service. Open daily for breakfast from 7 to 11:30 AM, lunch from 11:30 to 2:30 PM, and dinner from 5 to 10 PM. No reservations. *Haleiwa Shopping Plaza* (phone: 637-3538). Moderate to inexpensive.

Coffee Gallery – What one fan called a "displaced Greenwich Village coffeehouse," this eatery lures the North Shore's resident artists and intellectuals with its exotic blends of coffee and sandwiches. A good place to mix lunch and people watching. Open daily for breakfast from 6 to 10 AM, with lunch and dinner menus available from 11 AM to 9 PM, and dinner specials from 5 to 9 PM. No reservations. In the *North Shore Center,* 66-250 Kamehameha Hwy, Haleiwa, (phone: 637-5571). Inexpensive.

Flavormania – The claim is 2,000 flavors of ice cream. In actuality, there are about 40, all likely to please even the most demanding ice creamaniac. No reservations. *Haleiwa Shopping Plaza* (phone: 637-9362). Inexpensive.

Kiawe-Q – Chicken, ribs, burgers, and fish flavorfully grilled over kiawe wood, Hawaiian barbecue–style. Open daily for lunch and dinner. No reservations. *Haleiwa Shopping Plaza* (phone: 637-3502). Inexpensive.

Pizza Bob's – One of Oahu's better pizza parlors. Open daily from 11 AM to 10 PM; until 11 PM, Fridays and Saturdays. Reservations advised. *Haleiwa Shopping Plaza* (phone: 637-5095). Inexpensive.

Central Oahu

Two main roads climb from the North Shore onto the Leilehua Plateau and converge in the middle of the island at Wahiawa. To the east is the Kamehameha Highway, which turns south at Haleiwa as Route 82, and to the west is the Kaukonahua Highway, or Route 99, an extension of Route 930 from Mokuleia. Kuakonahua Highway meanders along the foot of the northeast slopes of the Waianae Mountains, overlooked by Mt. Kaala. The Kamehameha Highway, the quicker and more popular route, makes an easier climb onto the 1,000-foot plateau, passing first through wide fields of sugarcane. Then, about 4 miles north of Wahiawa, the pineapple fields start, miles of them, stretching out on either side of the highway like a vast carpet of light green stripes (the plants) with dark brown stripes (the rich earth) in between. These long, narrow rows are as neat and precise as soldiers on parade — as indeed they should be in a region that is controlled almost completely by the US military.

Ever since James Dole, a New Englander like so many *haole* pioneers, opened the first cannery in 1899 to market the fruit growing on his property, pineapples and Hawaii have been synonymous. Today, the state produces 45% of the total world crop. You can sample the fruit at the modernized and expanded Dole Pineapple Pavilion from 9 AM to 6 PM daily (64-1550 Kamehameha Hwy., not far from Wahiawa; phone: 621-8408). The fruit is sold in chunks and occasionally, if there is an abundance, visitors may buy whole pineapples. At the Pineapple Variety Garden (a little closer to Wahiawa, at the junction of Kamananui Road and Kamehameha Highway, and operated by Dole's chief competitor, Del Monte), there are displays of more than 20 kinds of bromeliads, the botanic term for pineapples. You will recognize the one that looks like a large hand grenade. Those with huge cactus-like tops and others that are scarcely bigger than a golf ball may not be so familiar.

Wahiawa itself is almost totally devoid of charm. It may once have been a picturesque plantation town, but today it is a seedy commercial center with small supermarkets, chain food outlets, and unpleasant bars where fights between *haole* military personnel and *kamaaina* residents are not uncommon and sometimes fatal. Just before entering Wahiawa, at the northern side of Whitmore Avenue, a dirt track road leads through pineapple fields to the Kukaniloko Birthstones, where the wives of ancient Oahu chieftains came to bear their children to the sound of chants and the ripple of drums. In the same place, the child's umbilical cord was cut and hidden with much ritual and solemnity. There are more sacred stones in the center of Wahiawa at 108 California Avenue. These Healing Stones, as they are known, are set in a crude concrete shelter that barely makes it as a temple. Legend has it that the stones are two sisters from Kauai who flew here and were, literally, petrified by a superior deity. There are still people who firmly believe that the stones have healing powers. Ti leis, flowers, and candles are almost always left in front of them. At the Hongwanji Mission (1067 California Ave.), the temple of another culture, you will find an impressive Buddha carved from Japanese cypress and painted with gold leaf. The Wahiawa Botanical Gardens (1396 California Ave.; phone: 621-7321) is a 27-acre retreat of tropical trees, plants, shrubs, and ferns that makes a nice shelter from the sun on a hot summer day. Open daily from 9 AM to 4 PM. Just west of Wahiawa opposite the reservoir is Schofield Barracks. If you have seen *From Here to Eternity* or *Tora! Tora! Tora!* you may recognize the setting. It was through the Kolekole Pass in the Waianaes west of Schofield that the Japanese made their devastating flying raid over the barracks on December 7, 1941. The *Tropic Lightning Museum,* on the barracks grounds, exhibits artifacts and weapons from wars dating from 1812 through World War II and Korea to Vietnam. It is open Wednesdays through Sundays and is reached via the Macomb Gate entrance on Wilikina Drive.

There are three routes south from Wahiawa. The H2 expressway, which skirts the suburb of Mililani, is the fastest; it ends at the junction with H1 at Pearl City. Route 99 passes through Mililani, a completely suburban development of comfortable houses, wide streets, and attractive shade trees. The most interesting feature here is the modern Catholic Church of St. John, with its stark granite altar, cement walls, and sculptures depicting the 14 Stations of the Cross. These and the bronze statues of the Virgin Mary and St. John make the church worth a visit (95-370 Kuahelani; phone: 623-3332). Route 99 also meets H1 at Pearl City. The most interesting road into town from Wahiawa is Route 75, which turns off Route 99 just south of Schofield Barracks and passes through upland pine fields, lowland sugar plantations, and below the dark green backdrop of the Honouliuli Forest Reserve on the windward side of the Waianaes. A short detour leads to the old Japanese community of Kunia, famous for its orchids and its spring display of *ikebana* flower arranging. Route 75 also hits H1 just *ewa* (west) of Waipahu.

CHECKING IN: The first hotel at the *Ko Olina* resort, located near Ewa, about 25 minutes from Honolulu International Airport and 45 minutes west of Waikiki, is the *Ihilani,* scheduled to open late this year. Operated by Pan Pacific Hoteliers, this 394-room property is part of the first phase of development of the 640-acre resort. Facilities include a 35,000-square-foot health and fitness center, the largest and most sophisticated that Oahu has to offer. Also in place are the first of two planned 18-hole golf courses, and the nearby luau and cultural activities at Paradise Cove. The completed resort will include a series of beaches, marinas, and lagoons, additional hotels, condominiums, and private homes. The *Ihilani*'s large rooms will feature a refrigerator, a sitting room, and lanais to take in ocean or lagoon views. There will be 5 restaurants on the property, as well as a lobby bar (phone: 528-0557; 800-626-4446).

Western Oahu

This side of the island belongs to the people of Oahu. Except for a few *haoles* in the condos and resorts of Makaha Valley, the coast in the lee of the Waianae Mountains is relatively free of tourists and tourist amenities. Along the Farrington Highway, which runs *ewa* from Honolulu and turns northwest just beyond Makakilo City and then goes almost due north where it meets the ocean at Kahe Point, restaurants are few and shopping facilities confined to a couple of supermarkets and the occasional mom-and-pop store. This is the dry, leeward side of the island, where the days are usually hot and dusty and the light brown Waianae hillsides are textured with plants, shrubs, and scrub of a lusterless green. After a rainstorm these deep valleys with their steep cliffs are transformed: New vegetation springs to life and new leaves appear on old plants. The area never achieves the outrageous verdancy of the east coast, but for a few hours there is a springlike sparkle all around.

Since for the most part this is not resort or vacation country, it is the best place to get some idea of what Oahu would look like had it not been "discovered" by the military and the jet-age tourist industry. People around here are more likely to own a pickup truck than a station wagon. The few roads that penetrate the broad valleys lead to poultry farms, small flower plantations, and truck farms. The highway is lined with picturesque churches sometimes in need of a coat of paint and tumble-down houses built on stilts in order to provide some breeze and with wooden stoops for watching the famous Waianae coast sunsets. In the winter these ramshackle dwellings are surrounded by flamboyant poinsettias. In some yards, penned in by wire mesh, you can see small plots of ground where roosters strut, not the kind that awaken midwestern farmers, but nasty, demonic-looking creatures bred for battle. Cockfighting *(haka moa)* was a favorite sport among the ancient Hawaiians and is still popular today in some parts of the island, especially in western Oahu. Old-fashioned luaus are held here, too, the kind that start early in the morning and continue till late at night. These are usually family affairs celebrating weddings, birthdays, and christenings. And although the Hawaiian family is often extensive, including uncles, aunties, and cousins with no apparent blood connection, outsiders from the mainland are not likely to be invited, especially if they are known to be spending a month behind the social barriers of Makaha Valley or a week in a Waikiki hotel.

Feeling between the west coast residents and the people they consider intruders has sometimes run high in the past, with muggings and vandalism of property frequent if not commonplace. Things have improved considerably in recent years. The current major danger while visiting western Oahu beaches is that of drowning in waters where strong currents and undertows prevail from October to April. Still, what is dangerous for the swimmer can be a boon for the surfer, and Makaha Beach, the most famous on the Waianae coast, has been the site of the *International Surfing Championships* since 1952. Many people who have never been to the islands may recall seeing this coast on television or in the movie *Hawaii,* filmed just north of Makaha at Makua Beach in 1965. Farther north still, beyond Keawaula Beach, known as Yokohama Bay, the Farrington Highway ends, and the terrain from here to

Kaena Point is a coastal wilderness of rocky coast and sand dunes, which encompasses a nature preserve that's closed to vehicular traffic. Resort development in nearby Ko Olina is likely to spill over to the Waianae Coast. With plans already underway to convert agricultural lands into golf courses, it seems that this still-Hawaiian stretch of coast will change noticeably during the next decade.

Kahe Beach Park – Where the southwestern tip of the arc formed by the Waianae Mountains meets the ocean is a beach park of low rocky cliffs with kiawe trees in the background. It's not a good place to swim, but it's an excellent spot for pausing to glance north at the shapes and shades of the coastline and the mountains. Even if you venture no farther, you will have seen the Waianae coast.

Pokai Bay Beach Park – This is one of the few beaches where swimming is safe all year and also one of the few safe anchorages in times of heavy surf. If you like to sit and watch boats bobbing on placid waters in the curve of a mountain-backed bay, stop here for a picnic lunch. A *heiau* (temple) from Polynesian times sits on the bay's eastern promontory. For snorkeling or scuba, contact *Leeward Dive Center* (phone: 696-3414), which offers equipment rentals and boat dives to some of Oahu's clearest waters, where dolphin are not an uncommon sight.

Makaha Valley – While driving along the Farrington Highway, you suddenly see to your right a broad valley with modern high-rises clinging to the towering cliffs on its north side. It's no mirage, just the most developed resort area outside Waikiki. Ten miles up the valley at the head of Makaha Stream stands Mt. Kaala, at 4,025 feet the highest peak on the island. Dominating the northern ridge is Puu Keauu, 2,650 feet, and on the south side, Puu Kawiwi, 2,975 feet. Although parts of the valley have been irrigated and turned into golf courses and manicured lawns around the condominiums, much of it remains a wild, rocky, and arid land of shrubs and berry bushes where you may spot wild turkey, chukar partridge, red-necked pheasant, peacocks, and the more mundane Japanese white-eye.

A few miles up the valley is the Kaneaki Heiau, a 17th-century chiefs' temple restored by the *Sheraton Makaha* resort and the *Bishop Museum.* The temple was originally dedicated to Lono, the god of agriculture and, unlike most other *heiaus* on Oahu, it contains two thatch huts in addition to the usual platforms. One hut was used for meditation, the other to house instruments of ritual. Sometime between 1795, when Kamehameha the Great conquered Oahu, and 1812, when he established his kingdom of Hawaii, Kaneaki became a *luakini heiau,* place of human sacrifice. Today, all that disturbs the silence of the grass huts, two prayer towers, and sacrificial altar is the gurgle of the Makaha Stream and an occasional flurry of birds. Makaha Beach, at the mouth of the valley, is wide and sandy in the summer, and when the surf is calm the swimming is superb. In the winter, heavy surf erodes the sand and turns the beach into a steep narrow strip.

Yokohama Beach – The beach takes its name from the number of Japanese fishermen who used to pole fish from the attractive rocky ledges embedded along the shoreline. If you have rented a car, do not attempt to go farther than the Farrington Highway, which ends here; the road to Kaena Point is only for hikers with stout boots. Even then, the going can be rough. What you can see from Yokohama Beach — stark patches of mountain, sky, ocean, and the surf pounding on the rocks — gives you a good idea of the desolation that lies beyond, which, it must be said, many people rave about, particularly at sunset.

Kaena Point Natural Area – The sand dunes of Oahu's westernmost tip have been set aside to preserve the endangered plants, birds, and sea life native to the area. Once limited to four-wheel-drive vehicles, the roads that wound their way from Haleiwa and

Makaha to the point have been closed to all but pedestrian traffic. On foot, it's an easy 1½-mile hike from where the road ends to the point from either the Makaha and Mokuleia access roads.

SHOPPING: Most of the shopping in this area is for food and household supplies in the *Waianae Mall Shopping Center* (86-120 Farrington Hwy.; phone: 696-2690), where you will find a *Big-Way Supermarket* (phone: 696-4271), *Pay n' Save Drug Store* (phone: 696-6387), *Woolworth's* (phone: 696-8466) and, for itinerant gourmets, a *Burger King* (phone: 696-8000), *Subway Sandwiches* (phone: 696-5858), *Red Baron's Pizza* (phone: 696-2396), and *Dave's Ice Cream* (phone: 696-9294). Athletic wear and equipment are available at the *West Course Shop* of the *Sheraton Makaha* resort, 84-626 Makaha Valley Rd. (phone: 695-9544).

NIGHTLIFE: Basically it amounts to conversations among visiting mainlanders about the weather. If this doesn't interest you, try the *Sheraton Makaha* resort for contemporary music (84-626 Makaha Valley Rd., Makaha; phone: 695-9511). The lounge features karaoke singing (the audience reads from music sheets and sings along with a tape).

CHECKING IN: Accommodations on this side of the island are concentrated at Makaha, either on the beach or in the valley. In island terms, it's considered quite a long way from everywhere, although it is in fact only 40 minutes from the airport and just over an hour from Waikiki. Shops are few, and entertainment is based largely on daytime activities. If you like bright lights and kicking up your heels, forget it. Except for the *Sheraton Makaha* resort, the places listed are condominiums and usually require a stay of 2 or more nights (since people come here for exercise and rest, it is hard to see why anyone would bother to come just for a single night). Expect to pay $135 and up per night for two for the *Sheraton Makaha* hotel. At the condominiums, expect to pay $400 and up per week at places listed as expensive, and $180 to $300 for those listed as moderate. (Slightly higher rates apply in high season.) All telephone numbers are in the 808 area code unless otherwise indicated.

Sheraton Makaha – The cottages at this resort are among the most attractive accommodations on Oahu, handsomely furnished in bold tropical motifs set off by cut flowers and plants and surrounded by well-tended lawns and groves of blossoming trees. The beautiful golf course has a resident pro to help those whose game is not quite up to championship standards. There are also tennis courts, riding stables, a croquet lawn, a large swimming pool, and a beautifully restored *heiau* (ancient Hawaiian temple). From its elegant patio you can see the ocean a mile down the valley. Perhaps the only drawback is its distance from the ocean, although to compensate, the resort offers a complete beach program of scuba, snorkeling, swimming, even canoeing in an outrigger, all supervised by experts who know the caprices of the waters around here. 84-626 Makaha Valley Rd., Makaha (phone: 695-9511; 800-325-3535). Expensive.

Makaha Beach Cabanas – From the oceanside lanais of this modest-looking condominium building, you have the feeling that you could dive straight down into the surf, the water is that close. All the rooms are simple and clean, almost (but not quite) spartan. There are cooking facilities and equipment, and maid service twice weekly. 84-965 Farrington Hwy. (phone: 696-5555). Expensive.

Makaha Valley Towers – Because the apartments in this completely unexpected high-rise on the north side of the Makaha Valley are privately owned, they are all individually decorated, occasionally with some taste. Generally only 40 or so of the 500 studio and 1- and 2-bedroom units are available for rent, and these rent out rather quickly during the high season. If you are lucky enough to get one on an upper floor, the views are stupendous. Preferred minimum stay is 1 week, but daily rates are available. At the northern terminus of Kili Dr. (phone: 695-9055). Expensive.

Makaha Shores – The 40 rental units in this 6-story apartment complex on a beautiful white sand beach come with fully equipped kitchens and lanais. From the upper floors on the ocean side there's a grandstand view of champion surfers during the season. As the apartments are often occupied by their owners, there are individual touches in the decor that make them usually less impersonal than hotel rooms, but many could use an update. No maid service. A minimum stay of 1 week is required. 84-265 Farrington Hwy. (phone: 696-6400 or 696-6500). Expensive to moderate.

Makaha Valley Plantation – About a mile up Kili Drive from Farrington Highway and Makaha Beach, this condominium complex consists of 2-bedroom units in 3-story townhouses. Some of the accommodations have been decorated by their owners; others come with standard but not unattractive rattan and bamboo fixtures. All have wall-to-wall carpets; a sofa and armchairs; a dining suite; a large, well-equipped kitchen area; and comfortable beds. There are 2 swimming pools, tennis, and golf; meals are available at the *Sheraton Makaha* resort, a few minutes away by car. Minimum stay: 3 nights. 84-718 Ala Mahiku Dr. (just off Kili Dr.), Makaha (phone: 695-9758). Moderate.

EATING OUT: People searching for gastronomic nirvana will have to look elsewhere. Fast-food outlets aside, there are only a few restaurants along the coast; for a meal for two, expect to pay about $60 in a place listed as expensive, $25 to $55 in a moderate place (not including wine, tips, or drinks), and under $20 for an inexpensive restaurant. All telephone numbers are in the 808 area code unless otherwise indicated.

Kaala Room – In this elegant dining room of the *Sheraton Makaha* resort, the menu hints at *cuisine minceur* but not to the point of dogma. They have a pleasing way with simple, sautéed mahimahi, baked salmon Mauna Kea, and for something slightly more exotic, prawns are cooked in a Pernod sauce. The atmosphere here is semi-formal, though this does not extend to a jacket and tie for men. Ask for a table with a view down the valley to the ocean, and dine at sunset, when the sinking sun casts a lovely glow over the linen and sparkling crystal and flatware. Open Sundays through Thursdays from 6 to 9 PM, Fridays and Saturdays to 10 PM. Reservations advised. In the *Sheraton Makaha Resort,* 84-626 Makaha Valley Rd., Makaha (phone: 695-9511). Expensive to moderate.

Niblick – Located in the *Ko Olina* golf course clubhouse, this tri-level restaurant offers a comfortable indoor-outdoor setting with panoramic golf course views. The lunch menu highlights fresh fruits, cereals, and omelettes, while the focus is on fresh island fish and seafood at dinner. Closed Monday nights. Reservations advised. *Ko Olina Resort* (phone: 676-6703). Moderate.

Salvator's By the Sea – Steaks, seafood, and pasta are the specialties here. Open for lunch from 11 AM to 3 PM, and dinner from 5 to 9 PM nightly, with a Sunday buffet. Reservations unnecessary. At press time, the owner was considering adding a Polynesian-style show. 87-064 Farrington Hwy., Waianae (phone: 696-6121). Moderate.

E.J.s – A mix of Italian, Mexican, and local food makes up the menu here. Pizza, barbecued delicacies, and burritos are the prime fare. Also try the homemade cakes and cookies. Open daily for lunch and dinner. Reservations unnecessary. 85-773 Farrington Hwy. (phone: 696-9676). Inexpensive.

THE BIG ISLAND OF HAWAII

The Big Island sends visitors looking for superlatives. It is, as its name implies, the largest island in the Hawaiian chain, with an area of some 4,000 square miles. Geologically it is the youngest, at just over 1 million years, and the dormant volcano Mauna Kea, 13,796 feet, is the highest point in the Pacific basin and arguably the tallest mountain in the world — when measured from its base, 18,000 feet below the ocean's surface. Hilo, located on the east coast, is one of the wettest towns in the US, with a rainfall of nearly 140 inches a year. In addition, the southwest Kona Coast is one of the few areas in the nation where coffee is grown, and the ranges of Waimea support one of the largest herds of Hereford cattle in the world.

Next come the contrasts: Sweltering in the humidity of a Hilo afternoon or bathing in the clear waters off the Kona Coast, you can glimpse a snow line high up on the volcanoes and see at one glance several different climates ranging from tropical to temperate to subarctic. In less than an hour you can travel from ravines of rampant jungle to arid lava fields, from intricate green paths ablaze with exotic blossoms and fruits to vast tracts of nothing but serried grass. Although there is a dearth of good beaches on the island, among those that exist are some with jet black sand. It is this richness of topography and flora and fauna that tempts some people to refer to the Big Island as a miniature continent.

Travelers arrive on the Big Island either at Keahole Airport outside of Kailua-Kona, which is served by direct flights from the mainland, or at General Lyman Field, just outside Hilo, the county seat. A deepwater harbor has made Hilo a marketplace since the days when clippers from San Francisco carried sugar from the Hamakua Coast plantations to California and around the Horn to the East Coast. Today, Hilo is probably better known for the macadamia nuts, orchids, and anthuriums grown in cultivated fields to the south of the city which give the Big Island another of its nicknames, the Orchid Isle.

North of the city lies the Hamakua Coast, a plateau of sugar plantations where water from the top of Mauna Kea has etched out gulches of astonishing beauty, each with its own waterfalls and tropical wilderness. Straddling the mountains between the east and west coasts are the cattle ranges of Waimea, home of ranches, rodeos, and the Hawaiian cowboy, known as a *paniolo.* This is hunting country, too — the territory of wild pigs and goats and a fine sampling of game birds. The ranches stretch north from Kamuela-Waimea through the rolling green Kohala Mountains to the cape at the island's tip. This northernmost part of the island is also the oldest, coming into existence

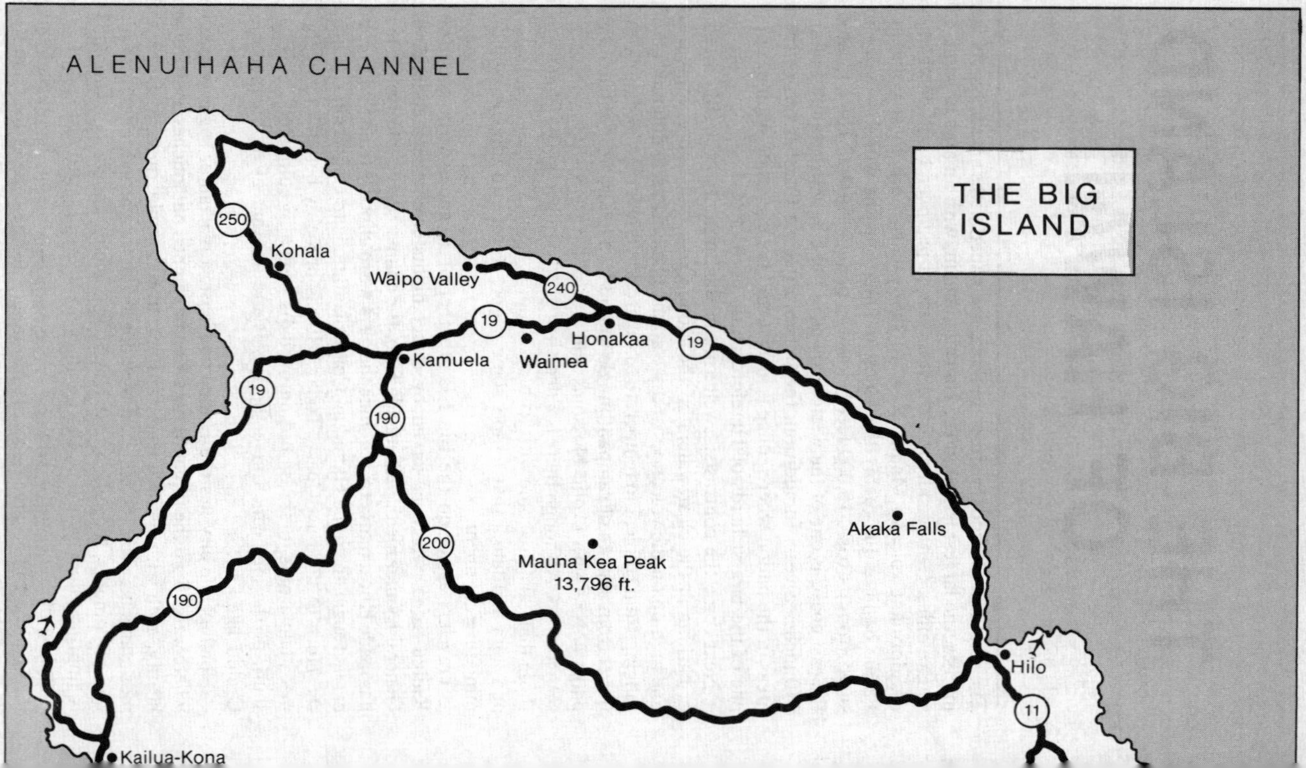
ALENUIHAHA CHANNEL
THE BIG ISLAND
250
Kohala
Waipo Valley
240
19
Honakaa
19
Kamuela
Waimea
19
190
200
Mauna Kea Peak
13,796 ft.
Akaka Falls
190
Hilo
11
Kailua-Kona

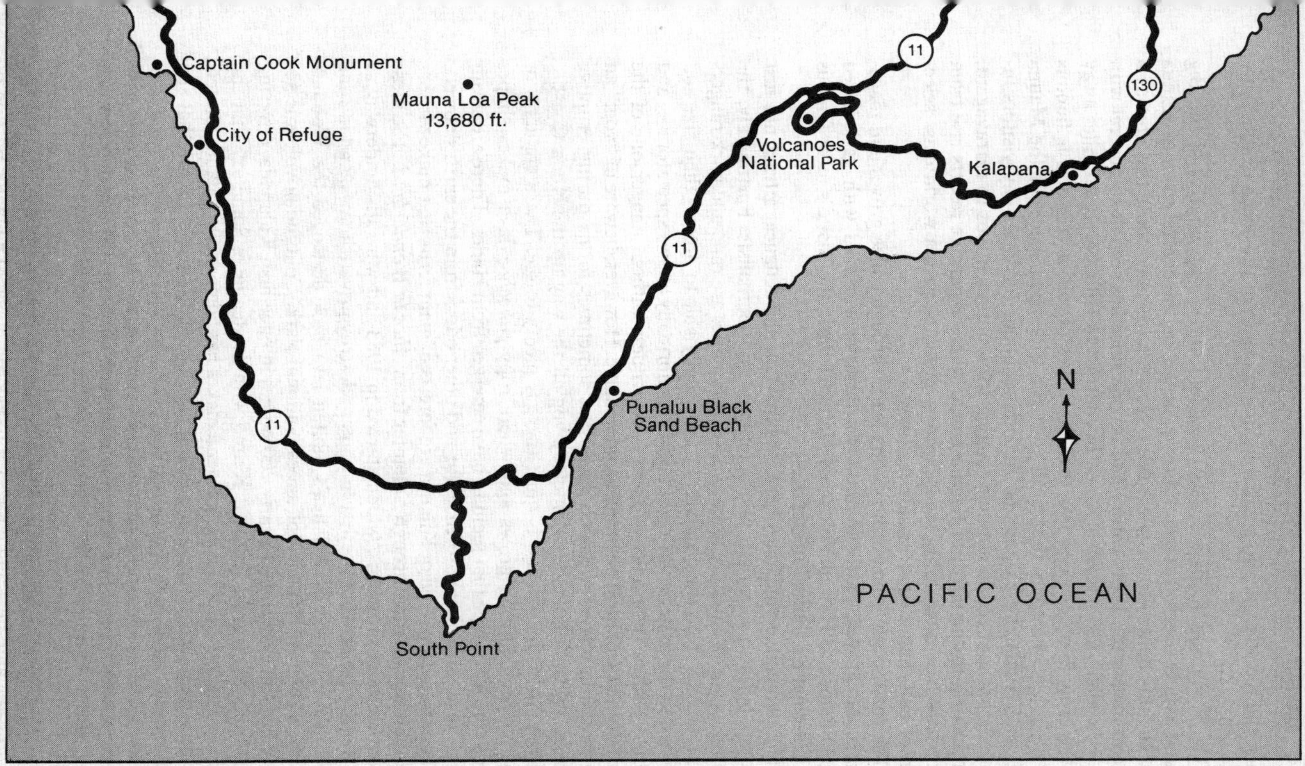
Captain Cook Monument
Mauna Loa Peak
13,680 ft.
City of Refuge
11
Volcanoes
National Park
11
130
Kalapana
11
Punaluu Black
Sand Beach
N
South Point
PACIFIC OCEAN

when the Kohala volcano spewed its first rocks from the ocean in the Cenozoic era.

The Kona and Kohala coasts (west and north, respectively) of the Big Island, where tourism reigns supreme, center on the coastal town of Kailua and the up-country town of Waimea. Hawaiian royalty chose this area as a retreat during the 19th century and no one since has seen fit to quarrel with their excellent taste. Kailua-Kona, in contrast to Hilo, barely 40 miles away as the crow flies, averages less than 30 inches of rain a year and is famous for cloudless blue skies that smile over the wide-open spaces of the Mauna Kea and Hualalai escarpments. Accommodations for latter-day visitors include hotels and condominiums ranging from unpretentious to extravagant, particularly to the north of Kailua-Kona, where expansive resorts rise from once-barren — now lushly landscaped — grounds, with a world class selection of golf, tennis, and seaside facilities.

The road south from Kailua-Kona leads through coffee groves and macadamia nut groves, past old run-down farmsteads graced with varicolored bougainvillea to Hawaii Volcanoes National Park, the island's most famous and fascinating tourist attraction.

The two active volcanoes here, Mauna Loa and Kilauea, attract not just tourists but also scientists, photographers, and journalists. Fortunately, the eruptions are so carefully monitored that fatalities are rare, and park rangers and scientists from the observatory are usually able to predict their size and extent and the path the lava will take. This normally allows spectators — and there are often thousands of them — to witness without danger one of the most dramatic natural phenomena imaginable. However, beware of "vog," an eye-irritating mix of volcanic gases that sometimes forms during eruptive phases. Prevailing winds often carry vog all the way up the Kona Coast.

Even when the volcano is quiet there is plenty to see. There are acres of desert where nothing grows and where ropy *pahoehoe* lava makes shapes across the landscape that seem to have emerged from Hades. There are steam vents constantly hissing forth sulfur and other odors from the earth's bowels, and on the eastern side of Kilauea are forests of giant ferns that make visitors feel they are walking through a chapter from *Alice in Wonderland.* The most recent series of eruptions, which started in 1983 and were still underway as we went to press, were the first in years to destroy private homes, and in June 1989, a fire caused by Kilauea's molten lava rock destroyed the Wahuala Visitor Center at Hawaii Volcanoes National Park. Continuing volcanic activity has since destroyed nearly 200 homes in once-lush Kalapana, covering its famous black sand beach at Kaimo with molten lava. Some say that the goddess Pele, who according to legend makes her home in the Kilauea Crater, has been angered by recent Big Island development. The prediction that she will one day emerge in a great explosion of lava that will form yet another island in the sea has been dramatically confirmed. The presence of a new island, named Loihi, has been photographed at about 3,000 feet below sea level, about 30 miles to the southeast of the Big Island.

Two volatile issues have emerged as the island is confronted with advanced technology and development. The first involves efforts to harness the Big Island's volcanic heat and convert it to electric power. The major portion of it would be transmitted to Maui and Oahu via what would be the world's deepest underwater cables. But there are organized groups of protesters who point out the harm that may result from this conversion: potential damage to Hawaii's last remaining lowland rain forest, the release of toxic fumes, and the spiritual affront to Pele, who still has many believers.

A second concern, also environmental, is a proposed spaceport that is being planned for isolated South Point, which will have the capacity to handle rocket launches and space probes. Opponents are concerned about potential health hazards from released rocket fuels, and also fear the intrusion of large-scale development on still-rural south Hawaii.

SOURCES AND RESOURCES

TOURIST INFORMATION: The Hawaii Visitors Bureaus (180 Kinoole St., Suite 105, Hilo, HI 96720; phone: 961-5797; and 75-5719W Alii Dr., Kailua-Kona, HI 96740; phone: 329-7787) have complete information on hotels, restaurants, sports, tours, museums, and activities. Open from 8 AM to noon and 1 to 4:30 PM, weekdays only. For detailed information on Hilo, contact *Destination Hilo* (PO Box 1391, Hilo, HI 96720; phone: 935-5294). The Hawaii Visitors Bureaus also offer an excellent self-guided walking tour map of Hilo. Those who wish to receive brochures on accommodations, special events, and sightseeing tours can contact the *Big Island Group* for further information (phone: 800-648-BIG1).

My Island B&B (PO Box 100, Volcano, HI 96785; phone: 967-7216; FAX: 967-7719) and *Bed & Breakfast Hawaii* (PO Box 449, Kapaa, HI 96746; phone: 822-7771; 800-367-8047, ext. 339) can book bed and breakfast accommodations in Big Island homes. Rates range from $55 to $100 a night for two. For a weekly stay at bargain prices in rural Kapaau, contact Lesley Patton (Box 1065, Kapaau, HI 96755; phone: 889-5735). *Hale Anvenue* (PO Box 371, Hawi, HI 96719; phone: 889-6187) provides another option for bed and breakfast establishments, as do Barbara Campbell in Kamuela (PO Box 563, Kamuela, HI 96743; phone: 885-4550) and *Hawaii's Best Bed and Breakfast* (PO Box 563, Kamuela, HI 96743; phone: 885-4550), which has more than 20 prime bed and breakfast rentals in its flier. *Mountain Meadow Ranch Bed and Breakfast* (PO Box 1361, Kamuela, HI 96743; phone: 775-9376) offers accommodations in the Waimea area and in Waipio Valley. *Waipio Wayside* (PO Box 840, Honokaa, HI 86724; phone: 775-0275) also features Waipio Valley for overnight visitors. *The Nutt House* (PO Box 852, Naalehu, HI 96772; phone: 929-9940) rents charming rooms complete with ocean views and an outdoor hot tub in a countryside setting near Naalehu (about halfway between Hilo and Kona). *Reggie's Tropical Hideaway* (PO Box 1107, Kealakekua, HI 96750; phone: 322-8888) offers accommodations in up-country rural Kealakekua, 15 minutes by car from Kona's coastal resorts. The 4-room *Holualoa Inn* (PO Box 222, Holualoa, HI 96725; phone: 324-1121), overlooking the Kona Coast, is a beautiful find, where polished wood predominates and a lovely pool and deck are on the premises. *Arnott's Lodge* (98 Apapane Rd., Hilo, HI 96720; phone: 969-7097) offers accommodations in a wildflower setting just outside of Hilo at reasonable rates. In town, check out the *Wild Ginger Inn* (100 Puueo St., Hilo, HI 96720; phone: 935-5556; 800-882-1887). In Pahoa (about 15 minutes from the current coastal eruption), *Bamboo House* (PO Box 1546, Pahoa, HI 96778; phone: 965-9340) offers an in-town bed and breakfast establishment, while *Banyan House* (PO Box 432, Keeau, HI 96749; phone: 966-8958) provides 4 lovely rooms in a large country home that's being restored to its original rural appeal.

Local Coverage – The Hawaii Visitors Bureaus also have copies of *This Week Big*

Island and *Hawaii Island Guide,* which are published weekly and available free of charge. The *Big Island Drive Guide,* with maps, itineraries, and other information of interest to visitors, is distributed free to anyone renting a car. The *Hawaii-Tribune-Herald,* published in Hilo, and *West Hawaii Today,* published in Kona, both cover international, national, and local news. The *Honolulu Advertiser* and *Honolulu Star-Bulletin* are also available. Look for the *Hawaii Charter Fishing Guide,* which offers comprehensive information on fishing, and is available free of charge at various locations. Also worth more than a glance is the *Waimea Gazette,* which scouts the areas of Kohala, Kona, and Hamakua.

TELEPHONE: The area code for Hawaii is 808.

GETTING AROUND: On this largest of the Hawaiian islands, distances correspond to those in the smaller northeastern states. Consequently, if you wish to spend any time exploring outside Kailua-Kona, Hawaii Volcanoes National Park, and Hilo, you will certainly need a car. The island has two main airports: Keahole Airport, built on hardened lava about 8 miles north of Kailua-Kona, serves Kona and Kohala coast resorts and General Lyman Field, on the outskirts of Hilo, provides access to Hilo and Hawaii Volcanoes National Park. *Aloha IslandAir* flies into Kamuela-Waimea, but there are no rental car facilities at the air strip. Another two inter-island lines that fly from Honolulu to Kona and Hilo on a regular basis are *Hawaiian Air* and *Aloha Airlines.* At press time, *United Airlines* was considering entering the inter-island market.

Taxi – Available in Hilo at the airport; radio-dispatched taxis are available from *Hilo Harry's* (phone: 935-7091). Major hotels know of individual owners with whom they like to deal and can usually find a cab within 10 minutes. Most taxi operators offer individual tours at prearranged rates. On the Kona side, the airport is usually well supplied with cabs, and they can be summoned from all major hotels. *Marina Taxi Association* in Kailua-Kona has drivers who are expert in local or all-island trips (phone: 329-2481). The fare from Hilo to hotels on Banyan Drive is about $10. The fare from Keahole Airport to Kailua-Kona runs around $20; to Keauhou-Kona, add another $10. In Kailua-Kona, *SpeediShuttle's* (phone: 329-5433) fares start at $7 to Kailua-Kona, and $21 to Kohala Coast resorts. Maximum rates apply, which means it is more economical for those traveling in groups of three or more. *SpeediShuttle* also offers fully customized tours at $30 per hour for up to seven passengers.

Bus – The bus terminal in Hilo is in downtown Mooheau Park at what also serves as a hangout for derelicts. It is merely a ticket office with outside seating facilities for those waiting. Buses serve Hilo residential areas and, to a limited extent, the surrounding area. Fares start at 75¢, and exact change is required. There are daily buses from Hilo to Naalehu-Kau, Pahoa, Honokaa, and to Kealia-Kona via Kailua. The fares are charged according to distance. The $6 fare from Hilo to Kealia, the longest route possible, has to count as one of the most extraordinary transportation bargains in the US. The buses are slow, but the company is fascinating and the scenery wonderful, and the ride is a good way to get an authentic taste of the island. Information is available from the County of Hawaii Transit Agency (25 Aupuni St.; phone: 935-8241). Bus schedules are available at the terminal. The bus to Hilo leaves Kealia at 5:45 AM and the Mokuaikaua Church in Kailua-Kona at 6:40 AM, after stopping at the *Kona Surf* and other hotels along Alii Drive. There's a rest stop at Kamuela, up-country.

Car Rental – Essential if you want to explore the island without a guide. There are over a dozen companies from which to choose, including major national firms such as

Avis (phone: 329-1745; 800-331-1212), *Budget* (phone: 935-7293; 800-527-0700), *Dollar* (phone: 329-2744; 800-342-7298), *Hertz* (phone: 329-3566; 800-654-3011), and *National* (phone: 329-1674; 800-CAR-RENT), which are represented at both Hilo and Kona airports. Also found are such regional companies as *V.I.P. Rent-A-Car* (advance reservations are required for its mid-size cars, which offer the least expensive daily rate on the island; phone: 329-7328), *Thrifty* (phone: 329-1730), *Sunshine Rent-A-Car* (phone: 329-2926, Kona; 935-1108, Hilo), and *Tropical* (phone: 935-3385; 800-678-8666).

If you want to ride up to Mauna Kea or down the hair-raising track into Waipio Valley, four-wheel-drive is mandatory, not only because of the difficult terrain, but because most car rental contracts prohibit off-road or Saddle Road use, leaving renters fully responsible for towing charges should they be required. Four-wheel-drive vehicles can be rented in Kona from *Hertz* (phone: 329-3566), and, in Hilo, from *Harper* (phone: 969-1478), the only jeep rental outfit that allows Mauna Kea summit and Saddle Road drives. The available inventory is limited, making advance reservations a must. The dry, lordly ranges of the west side of the Big Island are ideal for riding in convertibles, although heavy winter rain can make ragtops a liability in Hilo or along the Hamakua Coast. *Hertz, Budget, Dollar, National,* and *Tropical* offer convertibles.

Mopeds/Bicycles – A great way to see the Kona Coast roads at all times of the year and the Hamakua Coast roads in the dry season, though not suitable for visiting the volcanoes or the Kohala Mountains. *Rent Scooters* (phone: 329-3250) has mopeds in the Kona area. *Dave's Triathlon Shop* (phone: 329-4522) rents mountain bikes and 21-speed bicycles. Just outside of Hawaii Volcanoes National Park in Volcano Village, *Volcano's Best Gallery* (phone: 967-8644) rents bikes at $12 for 4 hours and $20 for a full day, with complimentary maps of the area, as well as helmets.

SIGHTSEEING TOURS: Bus or Van – *Gray Line* will pick you up either in Hilo (phone: 935-2835) at your hotel or the airport, or in Kailua-Kona (phone: 329-9337) at your hotel for tours around the island or to Hawaii Volcanoes National Park. Guides taking tours through the park are well versed in geology. *Kona Coast Activities* (phone: 329-2971) staffs a kiosk in the *Kona Inn Shopping Center* for a wide range of activities and tours. *SpeediShuttle* (phone: 329-5433) departs Kona and Kohala on customized van tours for up to seven passengers at $30 an hour. Local historian Russ Apple is featured on audio tour tapes of the Big Island. Rental tapes (tape decks are available with rental) are available at the *Hilo Hawaiian* hotel, *Volcano Art Center,* and *Lyman House Museum.*

Jeep – The jeep or van ride from the Waipio Valley Lookout on the Hamakua Coast north of Honokaa leads down a steep, winding cliff road into an enchanting valley that resembles a jungle hideaway. Reservations can be made through the *Waipio Valley Shuttle* (Rte. 240 at Waipio Valley Lookout; phone: 775-7121); cost is $26 for the 1½-hour tour. *Waipio Valley Wagon Tours* (phone: 775-9518) starts its outing in a four-wheel-drive van, but transfers passengers to a mule-drawn wagon for a tour of the valley. The cost is $35. Also worth considering is the deluxe mule-drawn carriage ride for two ($125) that departs at 10:00 AM and 12:30 PM, and requires reservations 24 hours in advance. *Paradise Safaris* (phone: 322-2366) offers an exciting Starfari four-wheel-drive excursion ($95), taking seven passengers to the summit of Mauna Kea in a comfortable Suburban wagon on a tour that starts at 3 PM and ends between 10 and 11 PM. Warm parkas and drinks are provided, but passengers are advised to bring their own light meals. Complimentary West Hawaii hotel and condo pickups are included from Kona and Kohala hotels.

Helicopter or Plane – When one of the volcanoes is erupting, an aerial tour is particularly worthwhile, with departures from Hawaii Volcanoes National Park via

Volcano Heli-Tours (phone: 967-7578). *Io Aviation* (phone: 935-3031), *Hilo Bay Air* (phone: 969-1545), and *Papillon* (phone: 885-5995; 800-367-7095) depart from Lyman Field in Hilo, and offer a variety of tours. Hilo is much closer to the eruption zone than Kona, so volcano aerial tours leaving from Hilo or the national park cost about half as much. *Io* flies over the Hamakua Coast, Mauna Loa's summit, and the site of the Kilauea eruption in a variety of flight combinations at prices ranging from $120 to $220. *Kenai Air Hawaii* (phone: 329-7424; 800-622-3144) and *Papillon Helicopters* (phone: 885-5995; 800-367-7095) operate from the heliport at Waikoloa on itineraries that include the tropic-hued sea, pastures of cinder cones, lava rocks, and the steep-walled valleys of the Kohala Coast. *Lacy Helicopters* (phone: 885-7272) and *Mauna Kea Helicopters* (phone: 885-6400) both depart from up-country Waimea. All feature tours that last from 1 to 2 hours, at rates that range from $130 to $275.

Even when there's no volcanic activity, the Big Island's landscape is impressive, on aerial tours that include flightseeing over the 14,000-foot summit of Mauna Loa, the dramatic Kohala Coast cliffs, and a coastal trip over colorful and historic Kailua-Kona and Puuhonua o Honaunau. *Big Island Air* (phone: 329-4868) and *Hawaii Airventures* (phone: 329-0014) leave from Keahole Airport on a series of aerial tours aboard fixed-wing aircraft at about half the cost of a helicopter tour. *Classic Aviation* (phone: 329-TOUR; 800-695-8100) is an inter-island airline that departs Keahole and Hilo on yet another aerial option, with one- or two-passenger flights aboard a reproduction of a 1935 open cockpit airplane. When the summit is cloud-free, the 70-minute morning flight to Hualalai ($150) is breathtaking. More adventurous souls can embark on the single-passenger flights, which include a series of heart-thumping acrobatics.

Boat – The volcanic reefs of the Kona Coast provide some dramatic viewing from the floor of a glass-bottom boat. *Capt. Cook VIII* (phone: 329-6411) leaves Kailua Pier each day at 8:30 AM for a 4-hour cruise down to Kealakekua Bay. The cruise is accompanied by a narrator and divers who surface occasionally with some marine specimens for examination; snorkeling gear is provided. *Captain Beans' Cruises* (phone: 329-2955) operates the *Tamure,* a stylized Polynesian catamaran. The *Tamure* makes glass-bottom boat sailings at 8:30, 10, and 11:30 AM, and evening dinner sails ($45) that feature an open bar, all the steaks you can eat, and Polynesian song and dance. The enthusiasm of *Beans'* personnel is contagious, inevitably drawing guests into the partying. The *Intuition* (phone: 885-5555), a 26-foot Excalibur sloop, departs Anaehoomalu Beach on skippered private party sails at $150 for 2 hours, $195 for 3 hours, and $275 for 6 hours, carrying up to four passengers. *Captain Zodiac* (phone: 329-3199), which pioneered zodiac rafting along the Na Pali Coast of Kauai, offers a 4-hour motorized raft trip that departs from Honokahau Harbor and heads south for Kealakekua Bay, where passengers can snorkel and snacks are provided. The $57 trip includes visits to sea caves en route.

Submarine – *Atlantis Submarine* (phone: 329-6626) submerges 155 feet below the surface in a state-of-the-art submarine with portholes. During the hour-long excursion, visitors view modest reefs and the large schools of multi-hued fish, attracted by a scuba diver with edible handouts. Depending on the fishes' appetite level and the clarity of the water (usually good), the submersion can prove either interesting or adventurous, although it's a bit pricey at $78. Groups depart the *Atlantis* office in the *King Kamehameha* hotel for the Kailua Pier, where they take the 5-minute boat trip to the submarine. The *University of Hawaii Sea Grant Extension Service* offers a 24-page, 4-color book detailing the state's 44 best dive sites ($2). Information: 1000 Pope Rd., MSB #226, Honolulu, HI 96822 (phone: 956-8191).

SPECIAL EVENTS: *The Mauna Kea Ski Meet,* a 4-day competition, is one of three ski events that take place between February and May. *Paniolos* — Hawaiian cowboys — compete in traditional rodeo events during the *Waikoloa Rodeo* in the middle of February. The *Merrie Monarch Festival,* named for Hawaii's last king, David Kalakaua, is Hawaii's premier hula competition and is celebrated in April in Hilo with flower shows, a hula contest, and pageants re-creating King David's court. *May Day,* May 1, sees everyone on the Big Island wearing leis, aloha shirts, and muumuus. *Kamehameha Day,* June 11, is observed with a procession down Alii Drive in Kona in which each island is represented by a princess wearing the ancient *pau,* a full skirt worn by female horseback riders. The same day, the king's statue at Kapaau is decorated with strands of leis. A major celebration among islanders of Japanese extraction are the *O-Bon festivals,* held from late June to September. During this period, Buddhists wearing kimonos and happi coats dance around a central tower to the music of songs, drums, and flutes in an area decorated with shrubs and lanterns. *July 4* sees *paniolos* assemble in Waimea for one of three annual rodeos (the others take place *Labor Day* and *Memorial Day*). In August, canoes compete in the *State Championship Canoe Regatta* in Hilo Bay. Polo season runs from September through early December, with matches played at both the *Kohala Ranch* (phone: 531-0505) and the *Waikii Ranch* (phone 885-6668). *Aloha Week* is celebrated on the Big Island in early October, with ceremonies using the music and dance of old Hawaii. In October or November, 4 days are set aside for the *Kona Coffee Festival* at Kailua, when you can tour coffee farms and taste some of the entries in a coffee recipe competition. October is also the month of the grueling *Ironman World Triathlon* competition, which combines a 2.4-mile rough-water swim, 112-mile bike race, and 26-mile run.

SPORTS: The Big Island is one of those rare places where visitors can proceed from skiing on a mountaintop to snorkeling in tropical waters in just about 2 hours — in minutes if transporation is via helicopter. The activities that attract most sports enthusiasts, however, are deep-sea fishing, golf, tennis, and hiking, for which the Big Island appears to be custom-made. The Kona Coast will undoubtedly become your headquarters if you are dedicated to a particular sport. The few good beaches there embellish this side of the island, and the dry climate and seemingly endless sunshine give it an unfair advantage over the humid, frequently cloudy east coast when it comes to scoring tourist points. If golf or tennis is your thing, the large resort hotels such as the *Mauna Kea Beach, Mauni Lani Bay, Hyatt Regency Waikoloa, Royal Waikoloan,* or the *Ritz-Carlton* may be what you want. Deep-sea fishing enthusiasts usually head for Kailua-Kona, close to the dock next to the *King Kamehameha* hotel, where most charter boats pick up their passengers. *Red Sails Activities* at the *Hyatt Regency Waikoloa* (phone: 885-1234) features snorkeling, whale watches (winter months), and sunset sails aboard the 50-foot catamaran *Noa Noa* for $45 to $65. Guests also can rent snorkel or scuba equipment at the hotel's oceanfront lagoon. Hikers often head for the *Volcano House* (phone: 967-7321) or *Kilauea Lodge* (phone: 967-7366) in Hawaii Volcanoes National Park, which has some of the most interesting trails on the island.

Bicycling – Alii Drive from the *King Kamehameha* hotel in Kailua down to Keauhou Bay makes a lovely, leisurely 8-mile bike ride past hotels, private homes, condominiums surrounded by extravagant tropical plants and blossoms, and small, palm-ringed beaches. Cyclists can be seen struggling along the road that climbs up to Waimea, but such jaunts are only for the fit and truly determined. In Hilo, Banyan Drive and Bayfront Highway are both flat but can be quite busy with motor traffic. The beaches and coves along Kalanianole Avenue are easily accessible by bicycle. If you didn't bring a bike with you, ask the front desk at your hotel where you might rent one. The Hawaii Volcanoes National Park offers numerous bike routes of 5 to 10 miles. Rentals are available from *Island Bicycle Adventures* (phone: 967-8644). *Red Sails Activities* at the *Hyatt Regency Waikoloa* (phone: 885-1234) offers an 8-mile downhill bicycle run from up-country Hawi (the island's northernmost town) to coastal Spencer Park, where cyclists can stop to swim or snorkel and have a picnic lunch. The 3-hour run costs $60. *Backroads Bicycle Touring* (phone: 415-527-1555; 800-245-3874) circles the Big Island at an easy pace in the course of its escorted, 8-day bicycle tours, priced at $1,650 (land only).

Deep-Sea Fishing – Connoisseurs claim that big-game fishing along the Kona Coast is among the best in the world. Tuna, mahimahi, wahoo, and barracuda are some of the fish you can do battle with in sight of land. Marlin weighing more than 1,000 pounds have been caught in spots less than an hour's boat ride from the pier at Kailua. Since 1958, the *Hawaiian International Billfish Tournament* has been held here each summer, usually at the end of July or the beginning of August, attracting anglers from all over the world. Half-, 1-, and 2-day charters are available through *Kona Coast Activities* in the *Kona Inn Shopping Village* (phone: 329-2971) or the *Kona Charter Skippers' Association* (75-5663 Palani Rd.; phone: 329-3600), both of which will put you aboard a 6-passenger boat; some full-day charters include food and drink, but most require that you buy your own. Half-day charters are also available. Several dozen independent charter boats operate out of Kona at rates that sometimes can be negotiated at less than booking service prices. If you want to sail out of Honokohau Harbor, just north of Kailua, take the *Omega* (phone: 325-7859), which has boats available for charter and sharing. Several boats also depart from Kawaihae Harbor for a full day's fishing in the calm waters between Keahole Point near Kailua and Upolu Point at the island's northernmost tip. This trip often affords passengers a marvelous view of the Haleakala Volcano on Maui. The *Hawaii Charter Fishing Guide* (free), available at numerous locations, provides comprehensive fishing information.

Golf – On the Big Island, players can tee off on a mountainside, right at the ocean's edge, or on the rim of a volcano. The most publicized golf course (recently "softened") is the one at the *Mauna Kea Beach* hotel (phone: 882-7222), wrought by the senior Robert Trent Jones from a wilderness of lava and scrub. *Mauna Kea* number 3 is notorious for the Pacific Ocean and some craggy cliffs that too often manage to attract a golf ball on its flight between the tee and the green. Windstorms in 1990 caused the loss of hundreds of trees that framed the course. Statistics for the course: 18 holes, 7,114 yards, par 72. Another course (18 holes, par 72, 6,534 yards) is due to open late this year. Close by are the two courses of the *Mauna Lani* resort. The first was the original *Francis I. Brown* course (18 holes, 6,259 yards, par 72) which closely rivaled (some say exceeded) *Mauna Kea* in terms of design and challenge (phone: 885-6655). This golf course–cum–Japanese garden was split into two 9-hole courses; then 9 additional holes were added to each course. The new courses that eventually emerged, the *North* and the *South,* are both 18-hole, par 72 courses. The *North* course (18 holes, par 72, 6,968 yards) and the *South* course (18 holes, par 72, 7,015 yards) feature dramatic oceanfront holes. On the *Waikoloa "Beach"* golf course (phone: 885-6060), designed by Robert Trent Jones, Jr. (18 holes, 5,958 yards, par 70), you play among some famous Hawaiian landmarks, which include an ocean hole and petroglyphs (ancient symbols carved into rock). In the same neighborhood are the community-owned *Waikoloa "Village"* golf course (phone: 883-9621), which was ranchland before being transformed, once again by Jones Junior (18 holes, 6,687 yards, par 72), and the marvelous 3-year-old *Kings* (phone: 885-4647). The latter is a showplace designed by Tom Weiskopf (18 holes, 7,074 yards, par 72), with six lakes and enough black lava and sand traps to provide a real challenge. *Keauhou-Kona Country Club's* (Alii Dr., about 8 miles south of Kailua; phone: 322-2595) new *Alii* course can occasionally be tough (18 holes, 6,386 yards, par 72). The *Beach* course (18 holes, 6,589 yards, par 72) is also open for play. The course at the *Volcano Golf and Country Club* (Hawaii Volcanoes National Park; phone: 967-7331) may be the only one in the world that owes its green appearance to fallout from a volcanic eruption — it was ash from a 1924 upsurge that fertilized this once-barren area (18 holes, 5,965 yards, par 72). Additional courses include *Sea Mountain at Punaluu* (phone: 928-6222; 18 holes, 6,106 yards, par 72); *Hamakua Country Club* (Rte. 19, Honokaa; phone: 775-7244; 9 holes, 2,505 yards, par 33); and *Hilo Municipal* (340 Haihai St.; phone: 959-7711; 18 holes, 6,006 yards, par 72).

Hiking – The ideal way to appreciate the wide variety of scenery, animal life, and plant life on this island is to explore it on foot, either on short walks or overnight treks. When and where to go and how to behave so as not to disturb the island's singular physical (and social) environment are answered by the Hawaii Geographic Society (PO Box 1698, 217 S. King St., Honolulu, HI 96806; phone: 538-3952), which offers a packet of maps and leaflets with suggestions and warnings for $5. For those seeking an escorted hike, contact *Hawaiian Walkways* (PO Box 2193, Kamuela, HI 96743; phone: 885-7759), which customizes hikes to suit Big Island itineraries. Most hikers visiting the island for the first time like to make for Hawaii Volcanoes National Park. Hiking trails here range from a ½-hour stroll to a 3- or 4-day trek to an overnight adventure. The 3.2-mile trail from the *Volcano House* to Halemaumau is probably the most popular, passing through dense fern forests before arriving at the crater's lava rock floor. The Devastation Trail, a surrealistic landscape of ashes and scarred trees, is a favorite short walk. The 7.2-mile Halape Trail, leading down to a rugged lava beach, is the most popular in the Kau Desert. The trail up Mauna Loa summit is one of the most ambitious on the island. It normally takes 3 to 4 days round trip and means staying at the *Red Hill Cabin,* 10,000 feet up Mauna Loa's slopes. Check-in is at park headquarters (phone: 967-7311), 7 miles from the trail head, where overnight hikers have to sign up for permits. People making 1-day or shorter trips often like to stay at the *Volcano House* (phone: 967-7321), a rustic inn with such amenities as baths and a cocktail lounge. Advance reservations are essential. Outside the park, the most popular hiking is on the Waipio/Waimanu Valley Trail, which starts at the Waipio Valley Lookout at the end of Route 240 north of Honokaa. This involves walking through true wilderness across a remote, romantic valley where thousands of Hawaiians once lived, up the northwest *pali* (cliff) of the Waipio Valley, and across numerous gulches to Waimanu. En route you'll see wild pigs, birds native to this area, butterflies, waterfalls, and a paradise of exotic trees. Permission to camp in Waipio Valley can be obtained from the Hamakua Sugar Company in Paauilo between 7:30 AM and 4 PM, weekdays (phone: 776-1211). Less rigorous, perhaps, but also more appealing and more probable for the day-tripper are the short trails at Captain Cook Monument and at the City of Refuge, on the Kona Coast south of Kailua, while a walk through the mountainside roads that link Honaunau with the small town of Captain Cook provides a memorable glimpse of pastoral, ramshackle houses in lovely, haphazard gardens and a feeling of the quiet and calm of life as it was led here 30 or 40 years ago.

Horseback Riding – A Hawaiian cowboy, called a *paniolo,* is your guide if you are lucky enough to be a horse-riding guest at the *Mauna Kea Beach Stables* in Waimea (phone: 885-4288). Riders crisscross the high, open ranges of the Parker Ranch on 1- and 2-hour rides ($30 and $55) for both guests and non-guests. *Ironwood Outfitters* (phone: 885-4941) in Waimea offers 1½- and 2½-hour long rides ($40 and $65) across Kohala's lush pastures at 8 and 10 AM, and 2 PM. This company gives experienced riders the chance to do some real riding, as well as spend some quieter time on the trail. *Waiono Meadows* (phone: 322-8466) offers 1- and 2-hour trail rides from up-country stables in Holualoa, 5 miles above Kailua-Kona. Fees run $20 for an hour's ride, and $36 for 2 hours. *King's Trail Rides O'Kona* (phone: 323-2388) offers a variety of 1½- and 2½-hour rides for $49 to $79, ranging from up-country Kealakekua Ranch lands to the beach. Customized itineraries, including overnighters, are also available. *Waipil Naalapa* (phone: 775-0419) offers trail rides into the Waipio Valley. For a glimpse of rural Pahala on horseback, contact *E-Z Riders* (phone: 928-8410), which offers excellent hourly rates.

Hunting – The sparse grasses and low scrub of the western side of the island remind some travelers of East Africa. Wild boar is the most exciting prey here, although hunters go after wild goats and sheep as well. On private lands, these can be hunted year-round. The season for game birds starts in early November and lasts till the end of January. Prey in this category includes partridge, wild turkey, quail, and several kinds of pheasant. Guests from the *Mauna Kea Beach* hotel hunt on the Parker Ranch. Eugene Ramos of *Hawaii Hunting Tours* in Paauilo (phone: 776-1666) arranges 8- to 10-hour forays across private lands looking for pigs, sheep, and goats. The company will rent guns and ammunition. A license ($20 for out-of-staters) and a permit (free) to enter certain state or county lands are required. Both are available from the State of Hawaii Conservation Enforcement Division (75 Aupuni St., Hilo, HI 96721; phone: 933-4291), and from several agents on the island whose names, addresses, and telephone numbers are available from the Hilo office. Licenses must be purchased in person at the state conservation division office on the island.

Kayaking – *Kona Kai-yak* (phone: 326-2922) in Kailua offers one- and two-passenger ocean kayak rentals for $10-$15 an hour or $50-$70 a day. They also offer half-day ($65) and full-day ($95) customized excursions. *Kayaks Kauai* (phone: 826-9844) also offers extended Big Island kayak excursions. A 5-day trip includes transfers from Keahole Airport, kayaks, an escort, all meals, and appropriate camping gear for $750. Trips are scheduled irregularly, and reservations are required well in advance.

Parasailing – *Kona Watersports* (phone: 329-1593) offers parasailing with a raft takeoff and landing in the usually calm coastal waters of Kailua-Kona. A padded harness and floatation device help calm nervous initiates. From several hundred feet up, the courageous get magnificent views of Kona and Haulalai.

Polo – With plenty of wide-open spaces, the Big Island is the heart of Hawaii's horse country. The two polo clubs on the island, the *Waikiki Polo Club* and the *Mauna Kea Polo Club,* are located in Kohala. Each club has a schedule of matches that are open to the public from mid-September through December for $3 admission. The *Waikiki Polo Club* (phone: 329-9551) hosts matches on a field off the Saddle Road. Starting time is at 1 PM. Mallets meet at the *Mauna Kea Polo Club* (phone: 885-4445) at the *Waimea Arena* on an irregular basis. *Polo Vacations* (phone: 885-0538) in Mauna Kea provides lessons for would-be polo players.

Scuba Diving and Snorkeling – The reefs along the Kona Coast make these particular activities a rare delight. At Mahukona Beach, on the west coast of North Kohala, good visibility permits you to see a wide variety of exotically colored and sometimes quite tame fish. At Puako, off Route 19 about 10 miles south of Kawaihae, you enter the water from the boat ramp. The water here is shallow and there are fascinating coral formations. The depth of the water makes it more interesting to snorkelers than to divers. Anaehoomalu Beach also has good snorkeling close to the rocks. Old Airport Beach is the best place for scuba diving near Kailua. Follow the Old Airport Highway, which swings left around the north side of the *King Kamehameha* hotel and leads right to the shore. You can also snorkel in the shallow lagoon that forms part of the hotel's backyard. South of Kailua are good scuba diving and snorkeling at Pahoehoe Beach Park and Hookena Beach Park.

If you are planning to snorkel or dive independently, you can rent or buy equipment from *Kona Watersports* (phone: 329-1593). *Jack's Diving Locker* (phone: 329-7585), *Dive Makai* (phone: 329-2025), *King Kamehameha Divers* (phone: 329-5662), *Kohala Divers Ltd.* (phone: 882-7774), *Kona Coast Divers* (phone: 329-8802), *Nautilus Dive Center* (phone: 935-6939), *Sea Dreams Hawaii* (phone: 329-8744), and *Sandwich Isle Divers* (phone: 329-9188), all located in Kailua-Kona, rent snorkel and scuba gear and offer a range of dive options, including introductory dives ($60–$65), 1- to 2-tank dives ($45–$75), night dives ($70–$80), and full certification courses ($300–$450). Most limit scuba excursions to groups of six, plus an instructor/guide. Excursions range from 2 to 4 hours, and are offered in the morning and afternoon. The *Party Boat* (phone: 329-2177) departs Kailua Pier for a 5½-hour snorkel tour to Kealakekua Bay. Scuba equipment is available. In Keauhou, call *Sea Paradise Scuba* (phone: 322-2500; 800-322-KONA) for similar options departing Keauhou Bay. The *Fairwind* sets sail from Keauhou Bay on snorkeling tours and also rents snorkeling equipment (phone: 322-

3788). Larger resort hotels, such as the *Mauna Kea Beach* (phone: 882-7222) and the *Royal Waikoloan* (phone: 885-6789), rent snorkeling equipment. *Kamanu Charters* in Kailua (phone: 329-2021) offers a 3-hour cruise aboard its sailboat, the *Kamanu,* twice daily — at 9 AM and 1:30 PM — for four or more passengers ($35). *Sea Breeze Cruises* (phone: 325-6608) sets sail from Kailua Pier at 9 and 11:30 AM and 2 PM on 2-hour snorkel sails. *Ocean Sports Waikoloa* (phone: 885-5555), in the *Royal Waikoloan* hotel, has daily scuba and snorkeling cruises aboard the 42-foot *Me A'u,* which leaves Anaehoomalu Beach daily at 8:30 AM and 1:30 PM and also offers an afternoon cocktail cruise on most days. The 55-foot *Sun Seeker* takes scuba divers down the western coast of Hawaii; contact Paul Warren (78-134 Holua Rd., Kailua-Kona, HI 96745; phone: 322-6774). Perhaps Hawaii's best dive option is the *Kona Aggressor,* a 110-foot diesel-powered craft with seven staterooms, available for week-long dive trips. Room, board, and as much diving as you have time for are included in the $1,695 cost. The *Kona Aggressor* (PO Box 2097, Kailua-Kona, HI 96745; phone: 329-2446; 800-344-KONA) has a variety of certification programs, plus underwater photography training and equipment rentals, with an on-board lab for processing and viewing each day's shoot. Kona is the fourth home port for the *Aggressor* fleet, which also operates in the Caribbean.

Skiing – No kidding: While you are happily snorkeling in clear blue 83F waters down at Kona in mid-January, somewhere in the distance you see, through swaying palm trees, people are skiing in the snow. Up on Mauna Kea from December to early May (and sometimes as late as July) there are slopes attractive enough to draw beginners, experts, and the foolhardy. It's easy to become short of breath at these altitudes — 11,000 feet and above — and badly sunburned if you are not careful. There are no lifts and a four-wheel-drive vehicle is necessary to reach the slopes. *Harper* (phone: 969-1478) can supply the vehicles, but you'll need someone willing to drop skiers at the summit and then pick them up at the end of a run. Call the Hawaii Visitors Bureau in Hilo (phone: 961-5797) for current information on summit skiing.

Surfing – Not a major sport on the Big Island since the reefs are too dangerous and the surf is quite tame by North Shore Oahu standards. But there are surfing waves year-round at Honolii Beach Park, 4 miles north of Hilo, and surfers are occasionally seen just outside the Wailuku River Estuary, at the foot of Kaiulani Street in the old part of the town. The best surfing on the Kona Coast is at Waiulua Bay, off Route 19 about 3 miles south of Kawaihae, and at Kealakekua Bay, 13 miles south of Kailua at Napoopoo. *Orchid Land Surfboards* (832 Kilauea Ave., Hilo, HI 96720; phone: 935-1533) offers board rentals and private lessons in the summer. *Ocean Sports Waikoloa* (PO Box 3291, Waikoloa, HI 96743; phone: 885-5555) has surfboard equipment, and also offers introductory, intermediate, and advanced lessons for those who wish to try windsurfing.

Swimming – Just about every major and most smaller hotels on the island have a swimming pool; this is because not many hostelries, even those at the water's edge, are near a substantial beach. The best swimming beaches are on the island's northwest coast between Anaehoomalu Bay and Kawaihae. Here as elsewhere on the island caution has to be exercised regarding strong currents and rough surf. The rule is, if the water is not what you're used to or think you can handle, stay out. Anaehoomalu Beach itself is one of the most beautiful on Hawaii. It is off Route 19, about 25 miles north of Kailua-Kona. Hapuna Beach, 3 miles south of Kawaihae just off Route 19, a great favorite with islanders, is easily accessible and beautifully looked after. North of the main beach (a short hike) is a second, less crowded beach. At Spencer Beach Park, kiawe and coconut trees surround a grassy area at the back of the beach. The swimming conditions here are among the safest on the island, and there are shower and toilet facilities. Spencer Beach is at the southern end of town on the Kawaihae Coast. Closer to Kailua is Honokohau Beach, where islanders and visitors defy the law and come to expose naked bodies to the sun. Being a nude beach, it takes a little reaching: Take Route 19 north a couple of miles out of Kailua, then take the left turn to Honokohau. Park by the small boat harbor and walk north about one-third of a mile. You'll know when you're there. In Kailua itself there is a charming small beach on the ocean side of the *King Kamehameha* hotel. At White Sands Beach, 5 miles south, the sands sometimes disappear, washing away with the tide, leaving lava rock beneath; when the sands are there, this is an idyllic spot for good, safe swimming. Kahaluu Beach Park, close to the *Keauhou Beach* hotel, is another popular small beach with picnic areas and bathroom facilities. In South Kona there is good swimming at Napoopoo Beach Park, 13 miles from Kailua, and at Hookena Beach Park, about 26 miles south. Both have picnic facilities and are ideal places for a meal alfresco. You can enjoy the buoyancy of the ocean without its hazards in the manmade tidepool at Harry K. Brown Beach Park in Puna. The black sand beaches in this neighborhood are very seductive, but swimming from them is perilous, to put it mildly. Two popular spots in Hilo are Leleiwi Beach Park and Onekahakaha Beach Park, both just off Kalanianaole Avenue. Neither has much sand, and swimming is limited to days when the surf is calm. The pool at the *Hoolulu Swim Stadium* (Kuawa and Kalanikoa Sts.; phone: 935-8907) is Olympic-size and open to the public from 1 to 4 PM and 6 to 8 PM weekdays, 10 AM to noon and 1 to 4 PM on weekends.

Tennis – There are dozens of public tennis courts on the Big Island, with the largest concentration in Hilo. *Lincoln Park, Lokahi Park,* and *Panaewa Park* are some of the locations. The eight courts at *Hoolulu Park* (phone: 935-8213) include three indoor courts, which cost $2 per hour ($4 after 4 PM), and five outdoor courts, which are free. There are five public courts at Kailua, four of them at *Old Airport Beach Park,* one in *Kailua Playground.* Other places with courts include *Kamehameha Park,* Kohala; *Honokaa Park,* Honokaa; and *Waimea Park* in Kamuela-Waimea. Public courts are under the jurisdiction of the County of Hawaii Department of Parks and Recreation (25 Aupuni St., Hilo; phone: 961-8311). In addition, many of the hotel courts are open to the public for a fee. They include the *King Kamehameha* (phone: 329-2911), *the Kona Hilton* (phone: 329-3111) in Kailua-Kona, the *Kona Surf* (phone: 322-3411) in Keauhou-Kona, the *Royal Waikoloan* (phone: 885-6789) and the *Hyatt Regency Waikoloa* (phone: 885-1234) at the *Waikoloa* resort, the *Mauna Lani Bay* (phone: 885-6622) at the *Mauna Lani* resort, and *Colony I* at *Sea Mountain* resort in Punaluu (phone: 928-8301). All have pros to service excellent tennis facilities. The *Ritz-Carlton* at Mauna Lani (phone: 885-0099) one of the latest additions to Hawaii's court inventory, is also open to the public for a fee.

AROUND THE ISLAND

The Big Island is dominated by Mauna Kea, which rises 13,796 feet above sea level, and Mauna Loa, 13,680 feet. Measured from their bases beneath the sea they are the tallest mountains in the world, both rising nearly 32,000 feet above the ocean floor. Between them, the two volcanoes give definition to the island's six main areas: Hilo and its district, which nestles among the gentle inclines where the two mountains meet; Hawaii Volcanoes National Park and the adjacent Kau area, which straddles Mauna Loa down to the ocean in the south; the Kona and Kohala coasts on the island's west side; the up-country Kamuela-Waimea district on the "saddle" between the Mauna Kea and Kohala volcanoes; the Kohala Mountains along the north coast; and the Hamakua Coast, extending from Waipio Valley in the northeast to Hilo.

Hilo and Puna District

Hilo, the largest town on the island and the county seat, is a place for travelers rather than tourists. Its attractions as a resort are few. What beaches there are are small and relatively hard to find, and the winter climate can be wet, with daily rainfall (heaviest from November through May) that adds up to 133 inches a year. Even Banyan Drive, where most of the hotels are, manages to look run-down. But for anyone in a Graham Greene frame of mind, the very seediness of the place becomes a virtue. Most of the extensive waterfront area was washed out in two *tsunamis* (tidal waves) — one in 1946, the other in 1960 — and is now a grassy public park. But the parts of the old town that remain, especially in the few blocks that straddle the Kilauea Avenue–Mamo Street junction, are a fascinating blend of frontier town and turn-of-the-century architecture with wooden façades and elegant trimming that could often do with a coat of paint. There are still soda fountains with spinning stools, and Chinese preserved-fruit shops stand among Japanese *mochi* (rice cakes) shops, saddlers, thrift shops, and swap shops, where you may find a delightful, uncomputerized world in which calculations are done by hand or even abacuses. Although the incursion of shopping malls situated on the outskirts of town had begun to draw business away from downtown, a revival is under way, centering on the shops and restaurants on Keawe Street. Hilo's authentic surroundings have begun to attract new-style émigrés, mostly big-city people who've found it the perfect antidote to urban pressure. New shops have opened, along with the gallery of the *East Hawaii Cultural Center,* and a second stage of redevelopment is now under way on Waianuenue and other nearby downtown streets. The latest architectural victory for Hilo's preservationists has been the purchase of the landmark *Palace Theater* (ca. 1927). Once Hilo's largest theater, it boasts a well-preserved interior which recently has undergone restoration, and is used for theatrical performances (phone: 969-3626). Just outside town are orchid and anthurium farms, vast fields of sugarcane, and macadamia nut groves that reach up toward the peaks of Mauna Kea where, in wintertime, the snow line is clearly visible.

The Puna District, to the southwest of Hilo, retains its funky, down-at-the-heels rural charm in towns like Keeau and Pahoa, although gentrification is beginning to alter things. The road continues from Pahoa, Kapoho, and Kalapana, where lush rain forest suddenly gives way to barren lava rock, and where recent flows have found their way to the sea. In recent years, visitors have been able to drive to within a short walk of the area for a close-up encounter with the flowing lava, sometimes under the supervision of civil defense corps, at other times unescorted. It's a 27-mile drive from Hilo to the remains of Kalapana, the town destroyed by lava in 1990, and is well worth a side trip (Rte. 130 to Kalapana heads south from Rte. 11, the Hilo Volcano Hwy., at Keaau) or a day trip if you want to explore rural Puna.

Banyan Drive – Hilo's hotel row is lined with these odd denizens of the arboreal world, each one named for a celebrated American from various walks of life. Babe Ruth and Cecil B. De Mille are among those selected for this singular honor.

Liliuokalani Gardens – If you are allergic to formal public gardens, don't let that deter you from visiting this lovely, small park close to Banyan Drive. The gardens are landscaped around a Japanese teahouse in the Edo style, and footpaths meander across ponds and graceful bridges and past stone lanterns and pagodas.

Suisan Fish Market – Just off the Bayfront Highway where the Wailoa River meets the ocean, the market is a 5- or 10-minute stroll from the Banyan Drive hotels. Compared to the vast fish markets of Pusan and Marseilles it is small, but that is its charm. Here you may find, depending on the weather and season, mahimahi, opakapaka, tuna, and many other varieties of fish destined for the table. The action begins around 7:30 AM, when traders and fishermen start to bargain in English, Japanese, Hawaiian, and a local mixture, all of which adds up to pidgin English.

Coconut Island – Reached by a small footbridge from Banyan Drive, this palm-fringed islet in Hilo Bay, surrounded by interesting, low black rocks, is probably the pleasantest picnic spot in town.

East Hawaii Cultural Center – Hawaii's growing number of resident artists exhibit their works at this spacious gallery, which features a changing exhibit of ceramics, painting, raku ware, woodcarving, and graphics. This is a grass-roots effort that succeeds with charm and sophistication. The volunteers who man the front desk are a pleasant introduction to small-town Hilo's special sense of aloha. Open Mondays through Saturdays, 9 AM to 4 PM. No admission charge. 141 Kalakaua St. (phone: 961-5711).

Rainbow Falls – This spot in the Wailuku River Park is about 5 minutes from downtown. The best time to see it is in the early morning, preferably after a heavy rainfall, when the sun's rays throw a dazzling rainbow over the pool below. Just above the falls, the river churns in a series of rock-bound pools called the Boiling Pots.

Lyman Mission House and Museum – The museum part of the complex has pictures, artifacts, and traditional clothing of all the peoples who have made the Big Island their home as well as a collection of minerals relating to the island's geology. Just as interesting is the Mission House itself, once the home of the Lymans, a missionary family from New England who came to the islands in the 1830s. The house, with its four-poster beds, quilts, pianola, and "puddled" glass brought from Boston, would be believable as the home of Louisa May Alcott's *Little Women* in Massachusetts. It is only after close examination of the koa floors and doors and the ohia wood furnishings that you realize you are somewhere more exotic. Individual tours with well-informed guides are available throughout the day. $3.50 admission. Open daily, except alternate Sundays, from 9 AM to 5 PM. 276 Haili St. (phone: 935-5021).

Onekahakaha Beach – About 3 miles from Hilo on the south shore of the bay lies this strip of white sand with a tidal pool and picnic facilities. On Kalanianaole Ave., toward Leleiwi Point.

Flower Gardens – Hilo's reputation for being one of the wettest cities in the US gives it one advantage: The public and private gardens in the area burst with luxuriant blooms most of the year. Commercially grown orchids and anthuriums are the city's chief source of income. There are a number of places where you can watch lei makers, examine arrangements of fresh flowers and displays of dried flowers, or simply stroll among many varieties of exotic flowers. Some nurseries are designed to give the impression of being ornate formal gardens; a few are open to the public. The most extensive is *Nani Mau Gardens Inc.* (421 Makalika St.; phone: 959-3541), with 20 acres and over 2,000 varieties of orchids as well as anthuriums and red ginger. Open daily, 8 AM to 5 PM for escorted or independent tours, on foot or by tram; $5 admission. There's also *Hilo Tropical Gardens* (1477 Kalanianaole Ave.; phone: 935-4957), with 2 acres of orchids and other tropical plants; *Orchids of Hawaii* (2801 Kilauea Ave., off Rte. 11; phone: 959-3581), a small nursery open weekdays only from 7:30 AM to 4:30 PM, no admission charge; and *Bloomers Hirose Nurseries Inc.* (170 Wiwoole; phone: 966-9240), open weekdays 8 AM to 5 PM, weekends 8 AM to 4 PM, no admission charge. Among the numerous anthurium nurseries in the nearby Pahoa district are *Hawaiian Greenhouse* (phone: 965-8351), open 7 AM to 3:30 PM, and *Hashimoto Nursery* (phone: 965-9522), open 6 AM to 5 PM. In Kurtistown, *Hata Farm* (phone: 966-2460) is open weekdays from 9 AM to 4 PM; no admission charge. All will ship boxed flowers to the mainland.

Hawaii Tropical Botanical Garden (phone: 964-5233) provides one of Hawaii's loveliest garden settings on magnificent coastal acreage, complete with waterfalls, pools, palm forest, and flowers in exotic and authentic profusion. The garden is on the 4-mile-long scenic route that traces the original Hamakua Coast road. From the reception office there is a shuttle down to the gardens; then a self-guided tour takes visitors through the primeval landscape. Open daily, 8:30 AM to 4:30 PM. $12 admission; under 17 free.

SHOPPING: The *Prince Kuhio Mall,* a few miles from downtown, features *Liberty House, Sears, Long's Drugs* (good prices on film), a supermarket, and more. *Honsport* (phone: 959-5816) has the Big Island's most complete selection of athletic gear, from backpacks to swimsuits. Partially destroyed by *tsunamis* several times, downtown Hilo suffered a 20-year-long decline. But downtown's distinctive ambience and a growing number of new shops have triggered a revitalization focused on residents as much as on visitors. In the streets of downtown Hilo there are functional restorations and shops with unretouched character, particularly along Keawe Street.

Basically Books – Lots to look through, including an admirable collection of Hawaiiana. 46 Waianuenue Ave. (phone: 961-0144).

Big Island Gallery – The work of Big Island artists is featured; ceramics and art photography are among the finds. 95 Waianuenue Ave. (phone: 969-3313).

Chocolate Bar – Danger for those with a mania for chocolate. Made fresh in the shop daily, including a visually and tastefully delicious selection of "sushi" with coconut for rice and sweets for the seaweed and filling. 98 Keawe St. (phone: 961-5088).

Cunningham Gallery – Hawaiian prints and artwork are the theme. 116 Keawe St. (phone: 935-9122).

Dan De Luz Woods – An inventive and unusual selection of Hawaiian wood products, such as a collection of lovely koa wood bowls. The shop also offers factory tours. 760 Kilauea Ave. (phone: 935-5587).

Dollie's Shoppe – Fun browsing in this secondhand shop overflowing with dolls, toys, silverware, and used clothing. 38 Waianeuenue Ave. (phone: 935-7444).

Futon Connection – In addition to the custom-made mattress-like futons, there's lots to appreciate, including silk kimonos and pajamas, and Bali woodcarvings — all examples of beautiful craftsmanship. 104 Keawe St. (phone: 935-8066).

Gamelan Gallery – Indonesia's the home port for most of the handicrafts, antiques, and ethnic fabrics that are on display here. Some rare and valuable items amidst lots of more ordinary offerings. 277 Keawe St. (phone: 969-7655).

Hilo Hattie's Fashion Center – This clothing store chain is famous across the islands for its muumuus, tropical tops, swimsuits, T-shirts, and alohawear. At this branch, however, the staff not only wants to show you what they have, but also how they make it. Tours are offered and pickups at Banyan Drive hotels can be arranged at no charge. 933 Kanoelehua St. (phone: 961-3077).

Image II – An attractive selection of pottery, woven baskets, and ethnic fabrics in contemporary fashions. 50-54 Waianuenue Ave. (phone: 935-7669).

King Size Men's Shop – As the name implies, clothing for those in the extra-large category. Great selections in alohawear and western clothing. 249 Keawe St. (phone: 961-2190).

The Most Irresistible Shop in Hilo – The place to pick up an elaborate doll's house or a wood-burning stove, if that's what you're hankering for. There are also handsome koa wood bowls, lace napkins, toys, jewelry, and some especially fine greeting cards "suitable for any occasion." 110 Keawe St. (phone: 935-9644).

Serendipity Bookshop – A nice selection of books, including many on the lore of Hawaii. 2100 Kanoelehua (phone: 959-5841).

Sig Zane – One of Hawaii's more inventive designers sells beautifully silk-screened cotton clothes for women. 140 Kilauea Ave. (phone: 935-7077).

Sound Advice – A place to browse amidst collectible LPs, contemporary CDs, and cassettes. 2 Main St., Keaau (phone: 966-7666).

NIGHTLIFE: While most people go to bed early in Hilo, there are a few restaurants and clubs that cater to a nighttime crowd. There's *Fiasco's* (200 Kanoelehua Ave.; phone: 935-7666) on Thursdays, Fridays, and Saturdays from 8:30 PM to 2 AM for dancing and *Stratton's* (121 Banyan Dr.; phone: 961-6815), which offers disco from 9 PM to 2 AM on Fridays and Saturdays. *D'Angora's* in the *Hilo Lagoon Center* (phone: 934-7888) has live music for dancing, Tuesdays through Thursdays from 5 to 9 PM, with disco the theme on Fridays and Saturdays from 9 PM to 1 AM. The *Menehune Lounge* (phone: 935-9361) at the *Hilo Hawaiian* offers Hawaiian musical entertainment and a chance to mingle with locals. At the *Rainbow Lounge* in the *Naniloa* (phone: 969-3333), it's karaoke (diners are invited to lip-synch to recorded songs with a microphone) from 7 PM to 1 AM; for a quieter setting, the *Sandalwood* restaurant at the *Naniloa* features piano from 6 to 9 PM nightly. *Lehua's* (Waianuenue Ave.; phone: 935-8055), a casually sophisticated restaurant and club in the heart of old downtown, is Hilo's "place to be seen." The music's Hawaiian and contemporary, with performers inbound from Honolulu. There's plenty of room for dancing for those so inclined, from 9 PM to 1 AM. *Uncle Billy's Steak and Seafood* restaurant in the *Hilo Bay* hotel (phone: 935-0861) offers a twice-nightly hula dinner show at 6 and 7:30 PM, which is popular with both *kamaainas* and visitors. Rock groups from Honolulu occasionally make forays into Hilo's *Civic Auditorium* (Manono St.; phone: 935-8213). And the *Crown Room* at the *Naniloa* (phone: 969-3333) often features Hawaii headliner shows.

CHECKING IN: Hilo's emergence during the mid-1970s as a hub for Hawaiian tourism and Big Island commerce proved short-lived: There are no longer any direct flights to Hilo from the mainland, and several of the hotels that were built in anticipation of a boom have closed. Quiet, sometimes seedy, this is Hawaii beyond the hoopla of tourism — aside from the hotels that line Banyan Drive, and even they are a comfortably pleasant retreat from the typical resort environment. Prices in Hilo are the lowest in the Hawaiian islands, $120 and up for a double room in the expensive category; $60 to $115 in a place listed as moderate; and under $60 in an inexpensive place. Aside from low rates, the beauty of the surrounding countryside and the proximity to Hawaii Volcanoes National Park make Hilo a good base for a bit of relaxed exploring, including forays to Puna, where volcanic activity was in its 7th year at press time. All telephone numbers are in the 808 area code unless otherwise indicated.

Hilo Hawaiian – There is a beautiful view of tiny Coconut Island in Hilo Bay from the hotel's large, open terrace. Recent room renovations in tasteful earth tones make these a match for the best accommodations in Hilo. There's a good-size swimming pool and a pleasant dining room, the *Queen's Court,* overlooking the bay and Mauna Kea (see *Eating Out*). 71 Banyan Dr. (phone: 935-9361; 800-272-5275). Expensive to moderate.

Naniloa – Located on a spur of Hilo Bay, its neatly trimmed gardens wrap gracefully around small lagoons and extend to the water's edge. The adjacent 9-hole golf course has been upgraded, and restaurants offer American, Japanese, and Chinese food (see *Eating Out*). Many of the accommodations are suites with expansive views of Hilo Bay and Mauna Kea. There are 2 oceanside pools, one of which leads to a separate entrance to the hotel's *Paradise Salon and Spa,* fully outfitted with workout and weight training area, steamroom, and massage. Adjacent to the golf course are 4 tennis courts, which are lighted for night play. Service is both competent and friendly. 93 Banyan Dr. (phone: 969-3333; 800-367-5360). Expensive to moderate.

Hilo Bay – Rusticity is the watchword here. The 2-wing hotel is built alongside a narrow carp pool lined with hala, bamboo, and palm trees. The lobby is a collage of thatchwork and rattan. A few rooms overlook the bay; all have air conditioning. Ground-floor rooms that open onto the tropical garden are the best bet but it's all a bit timeworn. Kitchenettes are available for a small supplement, and *Uncle Billy's* restaurant (see *Eating Out*) is on the premises. 87 Banyan Dr. (phone: 935-0861; 800-367-5102). Moderate.

Waiakea Villas – This is the only part of the lovely *Waiakea* resort that remains as a hotel. The setting is still pleasant, although nothing like it once was (but neither are the prices, which have fallen by half). Studios with kitchens and 1-bedroom suites are available, there are 2 restaurants on the property, and Hilo is easily accessible. 400 Hualani Rd. (phone: 961-2841). Moderate.

Country Club – Perhaps the most outstanding thing about this hotel is the friendliness of the staff. Many rooms have refrigerators, and a few on the ocean side of the building have decent views. 121 Banyan Dr. (phone: 935-7171). Moderate to inexpensive.

Dolphin Bay – In an old residential part of Hilo shaded by palm trees and surrounded by tropical vegetation, this 18-room apartment hotel is much favored by people who have to make extended stays. There are no room telephones, no bar, no restaurant, no swimming pool; and desk fans provide whatever cool air there might be. But the rooms are pleasant, all have kitchenettes, and the managers are quite delightful. In the front yard is a banana tree from which guests are invited to help themselves. 333 Iliahi St. (phone: 935-1466). Moderate to inexpensive.

Hilo – There has been a hotel on this site in downtown Hilo since 1888. Slightly seedy, this place has clean, comfortable rooms that are more functional than decorative, plus a swimming pool, cocktail lounge, and a fine restaurant, the *Fuji* (see *Eating Out).* The front-desk staff is very helpful. All rooms are air conditioned, and some include a TV set. 142 Kinoole St. (phone: 961-3733). Inexpensive.

Wild Ginger – A small, island-style bed and breakfast hotel, just 3 blocks from downtown. No air conditioning; no TV sets, but good value. 100 Puueo St. (phone: 935-5556). Inexpensive.

EATING OUT: While the chefs of Paris, Rome, and New York have nothing to fear from their colleagues in Hilo, there are some acceptable restaurants hereabouts. If you favor people watching, remember that eating places here tend to be at their busiest between 11:30 AM and 12:30 PM and between 6:30 and 8 PM. A meal for two, excluding wine, tips, and drinks, will cost more than $50 in a place listed as expensive, between $25 and $45 in a moderate place, and under $20 in an inexpensive place. All telephone numbers are in the 808 area code unless otherwise indicated.

Harrington's – Ensconced in a casual lagoonside setting just off Banyan Drive, many consider this Hilo's best spot for fish, seafood, and steaks, with other specialties such as delicately prepared calamari meunière and scallops chardonnay. Open nightly for dinner from 5:30 to 10 PM. Reservations advised. 135 Kalanianaole St. (phone: 961-4966). Expensive to moderate.

JP's – The island-style decor includes an ornamental carp pool and wide-open windows. Steaks are the specialty, but there are also some popular dishes such as beef teriyaki and the fresh catch of the day. Open daily for dinner from 5:30 to 10 PM. Reservations advised. 111 Banyan Dr. (phone: 961-5802). Expensive to moderate.

Nihon Saryo – This small Japanese restaurant serves patrons at sushi and teppan bars, as well as at tables. The food is good, the design of gray marble and brass appealing. Open for lunch and dinner from 5:30 to 9:30 PM. Closed Wednesdays and Thursdays. Group reservations necessary. In the *Naniloa Hotel,* 93 Banyan Dr. (phone: 969-3333). Expensive to moderate.

Pescatore – The comfortable decor is coupled with excellent northern Italian cuisine. Delicious, hot garlic bread starts things off, followed by delicately flavored *calamari fritti* (fried squid), zesty *pollo pizzaiola* (chicken with spicy tomato sauce), and a range of well-prepared veal and pasta dishes. Open for lunch and dinner. Reservations advised. 235 Keawe St. (phone: 969-9090). Expensive to moderate.

Queen's Court – A Friday night seafood buffet is the attraction here. Though it's at the *Hilo Hawaiian* hotel, it's also very popular with locals. Open daily for breakfast from 6:30 to 9 AM, lunch from 11 AM to 1 PM, and dinner from 6 to 8 PM. Reservations necessary. In the *Hilo Hawaiian Hotel,* 71 Banyan Dr. (phone: 935-9361). Expensive to moderate.

Roussel's – Hilo may seem a surprising place to find Cajun cooking, but even more surprising is the quality of this menu, which includes soft shell crab "Rising Sun," Louisiana-style boiled shrimp in a zesty creole sauce, and melt-in-your-mouth trout prepared in a variety of innovative styles. The owners are brothers, Louisiana born and bred. One of Hawaii's finest restaurants and a real find. Open daily from 5:30 to 9:30 PM. Reservations advised. 60 Keawe St. (phone: 935-5111). Expensive to moderate.

Lehua's – The food is less of a draw than are the artsy setting and the eclectic crowd, which is quite hip, especially for Hilo. Open for lunch from 11 AM to 4 PM, and dinner from 5 to 10 PM daily. Closed Sundays. Catch of the day, charbroiled prawns, and shrimp are recommended. Dancing follows dinner on Thursdays, Fridays, and Saturdays. Reservations advised. 11 Waianuenue Ave. (phone: 935-8055) Moderate.

Sandalwood – A fine eating place at the *Naniloa* hotel, which hosts a delicious, well-priced breakfast from 7 to 10:30 AM, lunch from 11:30 AM to 2 PM, and dinner from 5:30 to 10 PM. Well-prepared specialties include roast Long Island duckling flambé, curried shrimp, and chicken breast parmigiana. Sliding doors provide alfresco dining overlooking Hilo Bay. Reservations advised. *Naniloa Hotel,* 93 Banyan Dr. (phone: 969-3333). Lunch, moderate; dinner, expensive.

Uncle Billy's – This is nothing if not Polynesian, with its grass roof and abundance of tapa, batik, and bamboo. The menu is filled with steaks and seafood dishes and combinations of both. However, the food falls far short of high expectations. Breast of chicken, marinated in wine and herbs and barbecued, is a best bet. Open daily for breakfast and dinner from 5:30 to 8:30 PM. Reservations unnecessary. In the *Hilo Bay Hotel,* 87 Banyan Dr. (phone: 935-0861). Moderate.

Fuji – Unlike the rather austere hotel of which it is a part, the restaurant provides a comfortable setting of natural woods and hanging plants. Service — by waiters and busboys in traditional attire — is excellent. The beef and vegetable teppanyaki are highly recommended; the sashimi is delicate and tasty; and the tempura dishes arrive in a gossamer-thin batter retaining the flavor of what's inside. The place is something of a tradition with local Japanese families. Open daily, except Mondays, for lunch from 11 AM to 2 PM, and dinner from 5 to 9 PM. Reservations advised. In the *Hilo Hotel,* 142 Kinoole St. (phone: 961-3733). Moderate to inexpensive.

KKTEI – It's a real find for the Hilo visitor, with ample portions of tasty Japanese and American foods and very reasonable prices. A popular spot with residents. Lunch from 11 AM to 2 PM, and dinner from 5 to 9 PM daily; closed Sundays. Reservations unnecessary. 1550 Kamehameha Ave. (phone: 961-3791). Moderate to inexpensive.

Nihon – A panoramic view of Hilo Bay is the backdrop for this restaurant and sushi bar, which specializes in sukiyaki and shabu–style presentation at your table. Open daily, except Sundays, for lunch from 11 AM to 2 PM, and dinner from 5 to 8:30 PM; closed Sundays. Reservations advised. 123 Lihiwai St., across from Liliuokalani Gardens (phone: 969-1133). Moderate to inexpensive.

Paradise West Café – Surprisingly good meals, with fresh ingredients and a flair with sauces. Cream of asparagus soup, for example, followed by shrimp and scallops Moorea or charred filet of fresh ahi. The crowd looks hard-line hippie, which adds an anachronistic aspect to the setting. Open for breakfast (7 AM to noon), lunch (11 AM to 2 PM), and dinner (5:30 to 9:30 PM) daily. No reservations. On Rte. 130, Pahoa (phone: 965-8334). Moderate to inexpensive.

Bears' Coffee – Downtown's deli and espresso bar provides a good place for lingering over breakfast or lunch from 7 AM to 5 PM. This is where Hilo folks go to mingle. No reservations. Closed Sundays. 106 Keawe St. (phone: 935-0708). Inexpensive.

Ken's Pancake House – It's a lot more than the name suggests: Though the pancakes are delicious, the extensive menu, late hours, and local crowd are equal attractions. You know you've been in Hilo when you eat here and it's only a short drive (or walk) from Banyan Drive hotels. Open 24 hours a day, for breakfast, lunch, and dinner, 7 days a week. No reservations. 1730 Kamehameha Ave. (phone 935-8711). Inexpensive.

Koreana – Barbecued beef, chicken, and pork are the specialties here. Or maybe it's the free *pupus* (snacks) offered nightly in the lounge that motivate a visit. An interesting ethnic perspective of Hawaii few visitors experience. Open daily for lunch from 11 AM to 2 PM, and dinner from 5 to 9 PM. Reservations unnecessary. 200 Kanoelehua Ave., in the Waiakea Square Warehouse (phone: 961-4983). Inexpensive.

Naung Mai Thai Kitchen – The setting may be less than impressive, but delectable Thai specials such as coconut milk chicken and basil eggplant cashew more than compensate for the lack of decor. Open for lunch from 11:30 AM to 2 PM; dinner from 4:30 to 8 PM. Closed Thursdays. Reservations unnecessary. Kapoho Rd., Pahoa (phone: 965-8186). Inexpensive.

Satsuki – This prototypical, local Japanese eatery has well-prepared, well-priced food such as tempura, sashimi, and teriyaki served in an unpretentious setting. Closed Tuesdays. Reservations unnecessary. 168 Keawe St. (phone: 935-7880). Inexpensive.

Sun Sun Lau – Many locals consider this Hilo's best Chinese restaurant. The mostly Cantonese menu includes such dishes as pineapple shrimp. Open daily, except Wednesdays, for lunch from 11 AM to 2 PM, and dinner from 4 to 8 PM. Reservations advised. 1055 Kinoole St. (phone: 935-2808). Inexpensive.

Tonya's Café – The eponymous Tonya is proud of her healthful dishes, prepared with fresh, organic vegetables. Pasta with pesto, Jamaican stew (a spicy concoction with peanuts, red chilies, and rice), and other daily specials are among the excellent dishes available. Open daily from 11 AM to 7 PM. Reservations unnecessary. Main St., Keeau (phone: 966-8091). Inexpensive.

Hamakua Coast

From the air, this northeast section of the Big Island looks like a peaceful, rolling plateau, carpeted with sugarcane and dotted here and there with sleepy, one-street villages — "one-horse towns" they would be called on the mainland. Where the land abruptly embraces the ocean, the airborne traveler sees small, indented slashes of green.

From the road, these verdant slashes turn out to be small jungle canyons referred to as gulches, each with its own waterfall and a few acres of rain forest clinging to treacherously steep slopes.

Even from the main highway, Route 19, which stretches north 49 miles from Hilo to Waipio, there are gorgeous views of lacy cascades in emerald ravines. But wherever there are side roads leading down to the shore (remnants of the old Mamalahoa Highway), there are even greater rewards. These narrow lanes cross old wooden bridges and small waterfalls that have cut their way through the hillside to form stone arches. They pass by small, simple wooden cabins, the homes of the mostly Japanese and Filipino plantation workers whose forebears came to work in the sugar fields at the end of the 19th century. Eventually, they lead down to rocky coves where black volcanic rocks stand like jagged gravestones against a milk-blue sea. To savor the full flavor of the Hamakua Coast, it's necessary to explore places right on the shore as well as some a little farther inland.

The first stop traveling north from Hilo might possibly be Akaka Falls State Park, at Honomu, 15 miles north of the city, where you turn off the highway onto a small road, Route 220, which climbs for close to 4 miles through cane fields to the park, a 66-acre forest preserve of huge fan-shaped bamboo trees, plumeria, banana trees, orchids, heliconia, azaleas, ferns, bird of paradise flowers, ti plants and giant philodendrons with 2-foot leaves. Paths wind through the dense growth to the falls themselves, the lofty, ribbon-thin Akaka Falls, 442 feet high, and the lowlier, thinner Kahuna Falls, which drop a mere 400 feet into the icy bedrock pool below. Hawaiian legend has it that this is where the god Akaka fell to his death. Two smaller waterfalls farther down the gulch and crossed by one of the meandering pathways are named for his mistresses, Lehua and Maile, who turned into waterfalls when they were unable to quench their tears after Akaka's death.

Nearly 12 miles beyond the Honomu turnoff Route 19 reaches Laupahoehoe, where a small winding road leads down to Laupahoehoe Point. This narrow peninsula jutting out into the Pacific Ocean is a finger of lava — the name actually means "leaf of lava" — covered with grass and shaded by tall coconut palms, with tables and barbecue grills for picnickers. It is an ideal spot for examining the structure of the coastline, since it is one of the few places where one can see the ocean side of the cliffs and spot the gulches without going out to sea. A monument at the water's edge commemorates 20 children and three teachers who died when the 1946 tidal wave rolled over their school, which used to be part of the village located here. After the last *tsunami,* the town chose to rebuild at its present up-country site rather than along the coast.

Kalopa State Park, 13 miles north of Laupahoehoe and 2 miles up the side of Mauna Kea off Route 19, is a native forest reserve covering some 615 acres of mountainside and narrow ravines. Elevations in the park range from 2,000 to 2,572 feet. Marked trails and tags identifying various types of trees and plant life make a visit to the park ideal for the casual visitor or for someone wishing to examine the native flora and fauna in greater depth. Some simple trails to follow include the Nature Forest Trail, a .7-mile hike through the heart of an ohia rain forest with a ground cover of at least a dozen varieties of fern, and the Planted Forest, with groves of eucalyptus, silk oak, paper bark, ironwood, and tropical ash. A hike through the Kalopa Gulch Trail System offers the visitor a rare opportunity to penetrate the precipitous slopes of a Hamakua Coast gulch. The io (Hawaiian hawk) and aakuu (night heron) may be spotted. At dusk the opeapea (Hawaiian hoary bat) can be glimpsed hunting for insects. The park has picnicking and camping facilities, and there are four "group cabins" housing up to eight people in dormitory accommodations. The price for two people is around $12; reservations are essential (phone: 933-4200). For information, write to: Hawaii State Parks, PO Box 936, Hilo, HI 96720.

Just before reaching downtown Honokaa, Route 19 veers left toward Kamuela-Waimea. An extension of the highway, Route 240, stretches north to Kukuihaele and the Waipio Valley through this pleasantly old-fashioned plantation town, forming its main street. Honokaa is known as the macadamia nut capital of the world. Lime, peach, loquat, and rose apple trees adorn the front and back yards of the town, recalling the Portuguese ancestry of many of the inhabitants. The main street is lined with charming pastel shops. Signs on shop doors give some idea of the casual pace of life in this region: "Gone to the dentist" or "I'm at Charley's." There are two handsome frame churches on the main street, the United Methodist and Our Lady of Lourdes. The *Hawaiian Holiday Macadamia Nut Company* (Lehua St.; phone: 775-7201) sells its products from 9 AM to 6 PM each day; the actual candy making and nut processing usually can be seen at selected times. Call for current information. The *Honokaa Club* (Rte. 240 in downtown Honokaa; phone: 775-0678) has a restaurant serving inexpensive Japanese and American food (open for breakfast, lunch, and dinner) and clean, spartan rooms that smell strongly of disinfectant. It is not for the faint of heart, but it is a bit of small-town Hawaii, with singles for $32, doubles for $44.

The town and surrounding area have a justifiable reputation as a good place for picking up artifacts made from local materials. Just off Route 19 in Honokaa at *Kamaaina Woods* (phone: 775-7722) you can see vases, bowls, and other objects being made by craftsmen working in koa, mango, milo, and Norfolk Island pine. *Waipio Woodworks,* in nearby Kukuihaele (phone: 775-0958), sells pottery, sculpture, and woodwork made only by native Hawaiian craftsmen. Ceramics and stained and blown glass are another specialty; lovely old-fashioned wooden cradles on rockers are also carried.

Route 240 ends 10 miles beyond Honokaa at the Waipio Valley Lookout.

Here, from a height of 900 feet, you can glimpse one of the few accessible valleys on the *pali* coast of the northeast Kohala Mountains. "Accessible," however, is a relative term, since the only road to the valley floor zigzags down the mountainside for a mile at grades reaching 26% and angles of up to 45°. A four-wheel-drive vehicle is essential for the ride, but even those travelers who have one would be well advised to make a visit with either the *Waipio Valley Shuttle* (phone: 775-7121), which conducts a 90-minute excursion along the streams and taro patches of the valley floor, or *Waipio Valley Wagon Tours* (phone: 775-9518). The shuttle departs on the hour daily from 8 AM to 4 PM, using Land Rovers for the journey. Tours cost $26 for adults, $12.50 for children under 12; tickets can be purchased at *Waipio Woodworks* (phone: 775-0958), but call in advance for reservations. Wagon tours ($30) depart at 9:30 and 11:30 AM and 1:30 and 3:30 PM for a 2-hour visit that starts with a four-wheel-drive van ride to the valley floor, where a mule-drawn wagon takes over. Also worth considering are the deluxe mule-drawn carriage rides for two ($125), which depart at 10 AM and 12:30 PM. Reservations should be made a day in advance. *Waipio Naalapa* (phone: 775-0419) reaches the valley via horseback tours.

The road down the precipitous cliff can be awesome if roller-coaster-type gradients and twists are not your thing, and once down in the valley the ride can be bumpy and escorted by mosquitoes. What, then, are the compensations? For one, Waipio is spectacularly beautiful; for another, it retains the aura of old Hawaii, and guides make Waipio's natural and Polynesian history come vividly to life.

When a Protestant missionary, the Reverend William Ellis, came to the valley in 1823, there were 1,325 inhabitants farming plantations of taro, sugarcane, and bananas. Just 40 years earlier, King Kamehameha the Great had been assigned his warrior god in the valley, which still contained a *heiau,* or temple. Because of its royal associations, it became known as the Valley of the Kings. Today, about 50 people live here. Since World War II, two tidal waves and a major flood that brought rocks and debris down the steep cliffs have destroyed the taro crop. Some farmers have returned to start over, including several of the few pure-blooded Hawaiians left in the islands. Outsiders have taken an interest, too. A Philadelphia financier planned and built a restaurant that you can see as you approach the valley's bottom. He never opened it: Hawaii County residents and officials thwarted him, and today it stands empty except for a caretaker. The government was also here briefly when it selected the valley as a suitable site for training Peace Corps volunteers and built replicas of Bornean, Filipino, Malayan, and Nepalese huts for them to live in. However, time and nature have undone most of what was built.

Once on the valley floor, your vehicle travels along dirt tracks that are little more than mud, fording the Wailoa Stream just before it reaches the sea and driving up riverbeds against fast-flowing water. Along the black sand beach, outrigger canoes in many colors lie under the ironwood trees. All around, there are bananas, noni apples, guavas, and grapefruit; occasional remnants of sugarcane fields; and along the tracks, wild orchids and hibiscus. But the chief glory of the valley is its waterfalls: Hilawe, 1,300 feet high, and Nanaue, a series of cataracts that drop from pool to pool, two of which are easily reached and safe for swimming. There are hiking trails throughout the valley, one of which leads into the next valley north, Waimanu, an uninhabited place famed for its groves of hala trees, wild mountain apples, and wild pigs. The trail is about 9 miles long, climbs steeply up cliffs, and is recommended only for people with some hiking experience.

Waipio Valley even has its own motel — of sorts — for anyone who wants to spend the night, or week, in the splendid isolation of the valley. Admittedly, it's not for everyone: The *Waipio* motel imports its drinking water from Hilo; has no electricity (the three cozy bedrooms are lit with kerosene lamps), one cold shower, Coleman stoves and kitchen utensils but no refrigerator; and the nearest place to get food is the aptly named *Last Chance Store* (an uphill mile away in Kukuihaele on Rte. 240; phone: 775-9222), which is accessible from the valley only by shuttle jeep (stocking up before making your descent is not only advisable, it's essential).

But daybreak makes it all worthwhile. From the porch you can watch the sun come up over the not-so-distant cliffs, illuminating the taro patch and riot of fruit trees only steps away. Or watch the sunrise from the black sand beach, a 20-minute hike on a dirt path strewn with fallen guavas, where there's a good chance of meeting up with a black and white cow or peaceful horse. All this can be experienced at a cost of $15 per person, per night — and Tom Araki, the taro farmer who runs the motel, might throw in a starchy purple slab of boiled taro to accompany your dinner. Reservations should be made at least 3 weeks in advance (write the *Waipio Motel,* 25 Malama Pl., Hilo, HI 96720; phone: 775-0368 or, if you get no answer, 935-7466).

Kamuela-Waimea

Whether you arrive from Hilo via the subtropical Hamakua Coast or from Kona over the sparse and arid grasslands of Waikoloa, Waimea comes as a surprise. Suddenly there are meadows of soft green grass and dark green trees, white Victorian frame houses with gingerbread trimmings that recall New England. White picket fences surround gardens where camelias and magnolias bloom, and fresh, temperate-zone vegetables grow in neat rows. Farther off, in fields bordered by hardwood trees, horses and cattle graze.

This is ranch country, the home of the 225,000-acre Parker Ranch, which boasts one of the largest Hereford herds in the world on one of the largest private ranches in the United States. The Parker Ranch was started by the present owner's great-great-great-grandfather John Palmer Parker, a Massachusetts sailor who jumped ship here in the early part of the 19th century. Parker went to work for Kamehameha, rounding up cattle that had gone wild on the Big Island. Eventually he accumulated a herd for himself, which he settled on land given him by Kamehameha III in 1847. From this beginning grew the vast spread that now exists. To assist him, Parker imported cowboys from Latin America who were referred to early on as *Españolas* — the Spaniards — a word that the Hawaiian tongue adapted to *paniolos.* Today the land on which cattle graze is called *paniolo* land and the beef they produce, *paniolo* beef, even though native Hawaiians, Japanese, Chinese, Filipinos, and Caucasians now work alongside the descendants of the original cowboys. Several rodeos held every summer in Waimea prove that this pastime is as popular here as in the western part of the mainland. The most important ones are held on *Labor Day, July Fourth,* and *Memorial Day.*

Parker Ranch Visitor Center and Museum – Start with the 15-minute film about the ranch and its history, then proceed to the museum, where you will find clothes and furnishings belonging to the original Parker as well as artifacts used in ranching more than 100 years ago, such as bridles, bits, and some particularly vicious-looking forceps for delivering calves. A smaller section of the museum has a collection of materials relating to the famous Hawaiian *Olympic* swimmer and champion surfer Duke Kahanamoku. Admission is $5 each for the visitor center and museum. A $10 ticket includes both, as well as the Parker Ranch homes, and you can also buy an admission package for other Parker Ranch attractions, including the historic homes listing that follows. Open Mondays through Saturdays, 9 AM to 5 PM (phone: 885-7655).

Historic Parker Ranch Homes – Richard Smart, owner of the Parker Ranch, has opened to the public his historic family home, *Puuopelu,* along with *Mana,* the home built in 1847 by his ancestor, John Palmer Parker. As an unexpected surprise, *Puuopelu* is also a small gallery that includes Smart's fine collection of French Impressionist paintings (Degas, Pissarro, Renoir). The homes are open Tuesdays through Saturdays from 10 AM to 5 PM. Tickets for both homes may be purchased at the Parker Ranch Visitor Center for $7.50; $3.75 for children (phone: 885-5433).

Imiola Congregational Church – This charming New England–style church on the east side of town dates from 1857. The koa wood interior and the koa bowls that serve as chandeliers are especially handsome. Off Rte. 19 (phone: 885-4987).

Kamuela Museum – If you can imagine the spacious attic of a particularly favorite but slightly eccentric aunt, then you have some idea of the flavor of this museum. Few attics, however, yield treasures as rare as some to be found in this wildly eclectic collection. Ancient Hawaiian relics and robes, medals, and insignia from the days of the monarchy appear to form the nucleus of the holdings, but there is much else besides, such as German and Japanese weapons from World War II, old English and German china, rare lithographs of Old Masters, specimens of Hawaiian rocks, jewelry, priests' vestments, and rare books. Harriet Meyers Solomon, who owns the museum with her husband, is a descendant of the founder of the Parker Ranch and has to be counted among the museum's major delights. You will find a chat with her as rewarding as the collection itself. Open daily 8 AM to 5 PM. Admission is $5. At the junction of Rtes. 19 and 200 (phone: 885-4724).

Saddle Road/Mauna Kea Summit – Route 20, also called the Saddle Road, links east and west Hawaii over the plateau between Mauna Kea and Mauna Loa. Although it is the shortest route between Hilo and Kona, it is slow going in rainy weather, since portions of the road just outside of Hilo are unpaved. Most rental car companies specifically list the Saddle Road as off-limits, which means they are not responsible for towing or repair charges incurred while traveling on this route. *Harper* (phone: 969-1478) is the exception. Though *Hertz* (phone: 329-3566) also rents jeeps, the rental contract prohibits off-road travel. The Saddle Road's chief attraction is that it provides access to the road to Mauna Kea's summit observatories, a state-of-the-art complex that now includes eight major telescopes. The road is paved 9,000 feet above sea level to Hale Pohaku, where dormitories and support services for observatory staff are located. At press time, additional paving on the road to the 14,000-foot summit was still under way. Of more interest to visitors is the *Onizuka Center for International Astronomy* (phone: 961-2180), open Mondays and Fridays from 1 to 5 PM and 7 to 9 PM, Saturdays from 8 AM to 5 PM and 7 to 9 PM, and Sundays from 8 AM to 5 PM. The center is accessible by car. Exhibits explain the work being conducted atop Mauna Kea, while putting this great volcanic mountain in a Hawaiian context. Tours of the summit itself (nearly 14,000 feet above sea level) depart from the site of the University of Hawaii's 88-inch telescope Saturdays and Sundays at 2:30 PM. The rendezvous is at the visitors' center at 1:30 PM. Visitors must reach the summit on their own (four-wheel-drive is almost a necessity). On Saturday nights from 6 to 10 PM a group of 30 are given a chance to look through the university's 24-inch telescope for a bit of first class star gazing. Reservations are required (phone: 935-3371). Children under 16 are not allowed on the summit tours, and those with heart or respiratory problems are advised against going any higher than Hale Pohaku, where a small, high-quality telescope makes star gazing possible (Mondays through Fridays). Weather conditions atop Mauna Kea are quite unpredictable, so warm clothing is essential, and come prepared, as no gas, food, or lodgings are available.

Astronomy aside, a visit is also worthwhile just for the majesty of the setting: The mountainsides, streaked with red and amber at dawn and the haunting shadows at sunset, are more than memorable. Apart from the song of the lark and a glimpse of California quail, large three-ringed pheasant, and brown-black chukar, there is also the possibility that you will spot wild pigs, wild goats, and Hawaii's very own bird, the nene goose. Or you may simply want to go skiing, which is why people come here from as far away as Japan between December and May, although skiing at these altitudes — above 10,000 feet — can be very strenuous.

Hale Kea – Translated as White House, this turn-of-the-century wood frame home, built by the former manager of the Parker Ranch, A. W. Carter, is now open to visitors. Aside from the main house, which now features shops and a restaurant, there are gardens, a blacksmithy, and several interesting shops (see *Shopping*) housed in accompanying outbuildings. Off Rte. 26 (phone: 885-6094).

SHOPPING: With the opening of the shops at *Hale Kea,* the *Waimea Center,* and several shopping malls, Waimea has become something of a commercial center, aimed at both the residents and visitors.

Alihi Creations Scrimshaw – An outlet for local craftspeople who work with gold, bronze, and feathers to create some unusual jewelry and decorations. Also some offbeat carvings from Bali. The owners are the Big Island's only scrimshanders, and you can watch them at their trade in the store. *Parker Ranch Shopping Center* (phone: 885-7737).

Baskets from the Heart – Customized gift baskets featuring Hawaii-made foods and souvenirs that make distinctive presents, and can be boxed for shipping. Just off Rte. 19, across from the playing field in the center of town (phone: 885-7736).

Bentley's – Lots of browsing to be done in this store that has a great selection of gifts, including lovely pewter items for babies. *Parker Ranch Shopping Center,* on Rte. 19 (phone: 885-5565).

Big Island Natural Foods – More than just an excellent selection of health foods, vitamins, and health aids. Also hand-dipped candles and other inexpensive gifts. *Parker Ranch Shopping Center* (phone: 885-6323).

Capricorn Book Shop – A beautifully designed shop with a good collection of Hawaiiana on its shelves. In the *Waimea Center* (phone: 885-0039).

Gallery of Great Things – One of the finest arrays of contemporary and antique objets d'art in Hawaii. High-quality artifacts and handicrafts from Japan, New Guinea, Indonesia, and the US. A good place to make memorable purchases. Parker Square (phone: 885-7706).

Island Heritage Collection – Watercolors, lithographs, acrylics, and oils by island artists at reasonable prices. *Hale Kea* (phone: 885-2155).

Kamuela Hat Co. – This is a cowboy company, and its fine selection of western headgear proves the point. Would-be riders of the range can purchase a flower or feather headband with which to adorn a hat for the *paniolo* look. In town, on the Mamalahoa Hwy. (phone: 885-8875).

Kamuela Kids – American, European, and Japanese fashions for children. *Waimea Center* (phone: 885-7724).

Noa Noa – Hawaii-designed, hand-painted Balinese batik cloth in fashions for men and women. *Hale Kea* (phone: 885-5541).

Parker Ranch Store – Operated by the Parker Ranch, this shop specializes in country-and-western clothing, from cowboy shirts to belt buckles. Country edibles, such as island beef jerky and poha jam, are also delicious treats. In the *Parker Ranch Shopping Center* (phone: 885-7655).

Princess Kaiulani Fashions – The muumuu's the thing at this store, with an excellent selection of casual to elegant styles. In *Waimea Center* (phone: 885-2177).

Rice's of Hawaii – Actually three adjoining stores, crammed with Hawaiian woodcarvings, Orientalia, antiques, and Thai reproductions. You might have to devote some time to a dedicated search for the more remarkable reproductions, but you won't be disappointed. 1198 Mamane St., Honokaa (phone: 775-7703).

Rosetta Stone – Transplanted from Kauai to Waimea, with an expanded inventory of ethnic arts, books, and esoterica. Mamalahoa Hwy., on the Konokaa side of town (phone: 885-7211).

Topstitch – A wonderful selection of Hawaiian quilts, plus materials for making quilts and other hand-sewn goods. *Parker Ranch Shopping Center* (phone: 885-4482).

Tropical Dreams Gourmet Shoppe – This shop and "factory" in rural Kapaua specializes in a range of pricey, but delicious, macadamia nut butters and cookies. 91-94 Akomi Pule Hwy. (phone: 889-5386).

Tutu Nene – The nene (Hawaiian goose) is the theme of this store, with goods from potholders to planters. *Hale Kea* (phone: 885-0051).

Waimea General Store – Napkin rings, candleholders, egg cups, and boxes in a variety of shapes beautifully tooled from many native woods including koa, ohia, kiawe, and mamani are on sale here. They are made by Waimea craftsman Larry Trombly, a retired electronics engineer who sells his work nowhere else. Canvas shopping bags with Hawaiian designs and typical boutique items such as potholders, tea towels, and aprons are among the extensive inventory here. Rte. 19, across from the Hawaii Prep Academy campus (phone: 885-4479).

Woods of Kohala – Woodworker Al Heneralau produces koa bowls and other items from his shop in the North Kohala town of Kapaau (phone: 889-5001).

Wo On Gallery – Located several miles past Kapaau in rural Halaula, in a restored turn-of-the-century general store, this small gallery features hand-painted fabrics, woodcarvings, paintings, and the art of many Hawaii-based craftspeople. On Rte. 27 (phone: 889-5022).

NIGHTLIFE: Eating dinner at the *Parker Ranch Broiler* (phone: 885-7366) and listening to Hawaiian music in the *Waimea Corral* (phone: 885-7366) are about it. However, things can get lively at *Cattleman's Steak House* (phone: 885-4077), where the bar features dancing to live entertainment, weekends until 1:30 AM. From April through mid-August, Waimea's endowment-supported *Kahilu Theater* (Parker Ranch owner Richard Smart was an actor on Broadway for many years) offers both dramatic and musical productions of a surprisingly professional caliber (phone: 885-6017).

CHECKING IN: There is nothing glamorous in the way of accommodations up here on the prairie, but there are two quite comfortable places with double rooms in the $50 to $80 price range. Lodging is also available at many bed and breakfast establishments where accommodations will run between

$45 and $120 a night. There are numerous bed and breakfast options in Waimea. For information see *Tourist Information.* All telephone numbers are in the 808 area code unless otherwise indicated.

Kamuela Inn – An old favorite in early motel style, but cleaner looking and more comfortable than ever since its revamping a couple of years back. The green of the surrounding hills is astonishing on the morning after a rainstorm. Kitchenettes in some units; continental breakfast included. Rte. 19 (phone: 885-4243).

Parker Ranch Lodge – This is the newer of the two Hamakua Coast lodging places, neatly furnished, with a kitchenette in each unit. The more expensive rooms are hung with textiles and oil paintings. There are tennis courts and riding stables in the vicinity. Rte. 19 (phone: 885-4100).

EATING OUT: Given the extensive bovine population around here, beef understandably figures prominently on any menu, but rarely to the exclusion of seafood. For restaurants listed, excluding wine, drinks, and tip, expect to spend $60 and up for two in the expensive category and $30 to $60 for moderate-priced places, and under $30 at inexpensive places. All telephone numbers are in the 808 area code unless otherwise indicated.

Merriman's – Peter Merriman, formerly the chef at the *Mauna Lani Bay* hotel, now runs this restaurant, which earns high praise for its well-prepared regional specialties, such as wok-charred ahi and goat cheese in phyllo pastry and orange sauce and Kahua Ranch lamb. Chef Merriman uses locally grown produce, herbs, poultry, and meat in most of his dishes. Both the unpretentious ambience and friendly service earn an A plus. Open for lunch from 11:30 AM to 1:30 PM, and dinner from 5:30 to 9 PM. Closed Sundays and Mondays. Reservations necessary. On Rte. 19 in Opelu Plaza (phone: 885-6822). Expensive.

Cattleman's Steak House – Steaks are the predictable specialty here. Dinner served nightly from 5:30 to 9 PM. Reservations advised. At *Parker Ranch Shopping Center* (phone: 885-4077). Expensive to moderate.

Edelweiss – Owner and chef Hans Peter Hager has created a restaurant that's the perfect lunch stop on an up-country tour and worth a drive from the Kona Coast for dinner. The mostly continental menu focuses on veal dishes and wursts, though daily specials may be more exotic: Edelweiss papaya, for example, is a half papaya filled with fresh scallops and Stroganoff sauce, then baked. Lunch from 11:30 AM to 1:30 PM, and dinner from 5 to 9 PM daily, except Mondays. Closed the month of September. Dinner reservations advised. Rte. 19 (phone: 885-6800). Expensive to moderate.

Hartwell's – Part of the *Hale Kea* restoration, this lovely restaurant has five distinctive dining rooms, each in a separate room of what was once the Hartwell mansion. Lunch, served from 11:30 AM to 3:30 PM, includes a full range of appetizers, salads, and entrées. The dinner menu (served from 5 to 10 PM) includes Waimea rainbow duckling, fresh fish and other seafood, and savory grilled chicken. Customers can also eat a Lite Supper from 5 to 6:30 PM. On Kawaihae Rd., at the Kona end of town. Reservations advised (phone: 885-6095). Expensive to moderate.

Parker Ranch Broiler – The bar here, called *Waimea Corral,* is straight out of *Annie Get Your Gun,* with opulent Victorian decor and red velvet chairs. The dining room, on the other hand, recalls "As the World Turns." It is suburban and inoffensive, with koa paneling surrounding some oil paintings. The specialty, predictably, is beef, and whether you decide on New York sirloin, London broil, or a wineless and herbless *paniolo* stew, it is very good. Open daily for lunch from 11 AM to 3 PM, and dinner from 5 to 10 PM. Reservations advised. *Parker Ranch Shopping Center* (phone: 885-7366). Expensive to moderate.

Aloha Luigi's – Smack dab in the heart of Waimea, the uncomplicated fare served here is first-rate. Among the soul-satisfying selections are superb lasagna, eggplant *parmigiano,* and an interesting selection of daily specials. Open daily for lunch and dinner. Reservations advised on weekends. Lindsay Rd. (phone: 885-7277). Moderate.

Parker Square Café – Despite its cafeteria setting, good food is indisputably the lure here, with all-day breakfast and luncheon stars such as quiche, banana macadamia crêpes, and roast beef sandwiches. Closed Sundays. No reservations. Parker Square, on Rte. 19 (phone: 885-3455). Inexpensive.

Tex Drive Inn – Here's the place to sample one of Hawaii's favorite food treats. *Malasadas* — Portuguese "donuts" without the hole — are served fresh from the oven, accompanied by steaming cups of great Hawaiian coffee. Open daily from 5 AM to 10 PM. On Rte. 19 between Hilo and Waimea at the Honokaa school intersection (phone: 775-0598). Inexpensive.

Kohala

Although destination resorts are now found along the coast of the Kohala district, few tourists penetrate the mountainous peninsula that forms the northern part of the Big Island. When they do, however, they find that it is here that the Hawaii of half a century ago, sleepy and unhurried, lives on.

The area is rich in the history of both native Hawaiians and those people who settled here in more recent times. There are *heiaus* — ancient temples — and at the very northern tip of the island, the birthplace of King Kamehameha I. Handsome, simple churches recall the arrival of the missionaries from the mainland, who came with little save zeal as baggage, and cemeteries in the northeast corner salute the memory of the Chinese (mostly from Hakka province) and Japanese immigrants who came to work in the five sugar plantations that once dominated the economy of Kohala.

Geographically, there are two distinct regions. On the eastern, rainy side of the peninsula, wild ravines, gorges, valleys, and waterfalls are densely covered by rain forest that is periodically gaudy with exotic blossoms and heady with their fragrance. They're a paradise for hikers (campers need permits), or those taking a coastal drive from Hilo to Waimea.

On the western side, the Kohala Mountains drop in a lordly sweep down to the parched Kawaihae Coast, where little grows but pili grass, kiawe trees, and prickly pear cactus. Still, this side of the island also has a grandeur in the same way that the arid, open spaces of West Texas have, although there is a bonus here in that the sparse, rocky terrain meets a brilliant blue sea.

Dividing the two regions is a lesser one that blends with both. This is the high-country prairie, bisected by Route 25, which runs north from Kamuela-Waimea to Hawi. The bracing 20-mile drive along this road takes the traveler, with climbs and swoops, through cattle country, past ranches standing amid sweet grass and fennel, behind windbreaks of eucalyptus and Norfolk pine at an exhilarating altitude somewhere between 2,000 and 3,000 feet.

Hawi, the Big Island's northernmost town, provides a point of entry to the Hawaii of the plantation era, where colorful old houses stand next to rustic general stores and the derelict remains of busier times. However, a modest gentrification of the area is underway, as a result of upscale residential development in nearby Kohala Ranch lands.

Just a few miles east of Hawi on Route 27 is Kapaau, where taro patches and a pandanus forest — and a considerable increase in the humidity — indicate that you are on the wet side of the island. The pride of Kapaau is the gilt and bronze statue of Kamehameha the Great, of which the version in downtown Honolulu is merely a replica. The original Kapaau statue was sculpted in Italy in 1879–80. On its journey to Hawaii it was lost in a storm in the South Atlantic. Years later, an American sea captain discovered it in a junk shop in Port Stanley in the Falkland Islands and brought it to Hawaii. Adjacent to the statue is the Kapaau Senior Citizen Center, located in a well-maintained turn-of-the century courthouse. Stop in before noon for a real Hawaiian aloha. Kapaau's other monument is the Kalahikiola Congregational Church, built under the supervision of the Reverend Elias Bond. This white edifice with its bright red roof stands with Protestant simplicity amid trim lawns. To build it, parishioners spent 6 years hauling rocks on their shoulders from nearby ravines and taking coral from the ocean to mix with cement for making mortar. Farther into the mountains lies Halawa, where there was once a flourishing opium den not far from a charnel house, two traditional symbols of life (and presumably death) in the Chinese province of Hakka. Their former denizens now lie beneath the sod on the hillside that slopes down the Halawa Valley, their resting places marked by lichen-covered burial stones. Even farther into the dense greenery that carpets this part of the world is Niulii, where an old Japanese graveyard is partly hidden by pandanus trees. Around here you will still find waterlogged terraces of taro and sweet potatoes grown as they were before the arrival of the Europeans.

A mile and a half beyond Niulii, the road comes to an abrupt end at the Pololu Valley Lookout. From here you can see the valley floor 300 feet below and look down the northeast coastline, where dark shadows along the cliffs hint at hidden gorges full of luxuriant foliage and indigenous birds exotic to both ear and eye. The dirt trail to Pololu is easy to navigate, and if the surf looks relatively calm, you could take a swim. As elsewhere on the Big Island, beware of strong currents.

Leaving Hawi to the west, a side road, Route 271, makes a loop off Route 27 before rejoining it a few miles farther on at Puakea Ranch. Route 271 passes Upolu Point, the northernmost tip of the island, and tiny Upolu Airport before reaching Mookini Heiau, just a few hundred yards from King Kamehameha's birthplace. Part of this road is a dirt track that after a heavy rainstorm is suitable only for four-wheel-drive vehicles.

From Puakea Ranch, Route 27, known as Akoni Pule Highway between Hawi and Kawaihae, turns south along the arid Kawaihae Coast. From Kapaa Beach, which has no sand but excellent fishing and snorkeling, there is a spectacular view of Maui across the Alenuihaha Channel. The Mahukona Beach Park, a mile farther south, is also without sand, but here again the fishing is very good, especially for big redeye, threadfin, mullet, papio, and menachi.

At Lapakahi State Historical Park, a little south of Mahukona, is one of the few non-royal historical sites in Hawaii. Lapakahi is a 600-year-old seaside village partly restored by archaeologists. It is open daily for guided or self-guided tours through gnarled and thorny kiawe trees to sites once occupied by houses, the village canoe shed, and guest shelters. Marked stones indicate which were used as a fish shrine or as a *papamu,* a board for playing *konane,* the old Hawaiian form of checkers. Just off Route 27 toward the beach (phone: 889-5566, but not between noon and 2 PM).

Archaeological work is also in progress at the Puukohola Heiau, just off Route 27 at Kawaihae. Established as a National Historic Site in 1972, the *heiau* looms impressively above its 224-by-100-foot platform between the ocean and the highway. It was built in 1791 by King Kamehameha in honor of the war god Kukailimoku, following a prophecy that if he did so his victories over his rival kings and other islands would be secured. Kamehameha himself supervised the thousands of workers who built the massive, stone-lava structure. On the day of its dedication he slew his chief enemy, who was present at the ceremony, and offered the unsuspecting guest as a sacrifice to the god. The observation that after these events the king did indeed become ruler of all Hawaii is intended to be chronological, not moral. Open daily 7:30 AM to 4 PM (phone: 882-7218).

Kawaihae marks the southern outpost of the Kohala Peninsula. Until the port was constructed to handle outgoing eucalyptus and sugar products, it was possible to see cattle from the mountain ranches herded out to sea and forced to swim through the surf to boats waiting to carry them to the abattoirs of Oahu. Today you can watch them filing through gates onto barges tied up at the jetty. Ironically, it is also where cattle and horses first landed on the Big Island in 1803. For something to eat in Kawaihae, the garden terrace of the *Blue Dolphin Family Style Restaurant* (on Rte. 297, just off Rte. 19; phone: 882-7771) is a good place to get the feel of a lazy Kohala afternoon. Closed Mondays.

Modern times are making inroads, however, as the Kohala Coast resorts draw increasing numbers of visitors. Best bet for dining is at *Café Pesto,* at the back entrance to the *Kawaihae Shopping Center.* Excellent pizza and other Italian specialties, including linguine marinara, fettuccine *al pesto,* and hybrids such as Cajun shrimp and sausage. The aroma of good cooking hits you even before you enter. Open daily, 11 AM to 9 PM weekdays, until 10 PM on Fridays and Saturdays. Reservations necessary after 6 PM. Phone orders taken (phone: 882-1071). At the *Polihali Bar* (in the *Kawaihae Shopping Center;* phone: 882-7076), there's live music on Fridays and Saturdays from 9:30 PM to 1 AM.

South from Kawaihae, Kohala's west coast emerges as a flat lava plain. Geologically a part of the extinct Kohala Volcano, the Kohala Coast resorts are not really an extension of the resort-lined coast centered on the historic Kona district and the town of Kailua-Kona.

Kailua-Kona

For arrivees at Keahole Airport, the first glimpse of the Kona Coast can seem rather bleak. The Queen Kaahumanu Highway, which stretches 35 miles from Kawaihae to Kailua, crosses vast acres of lava wasteland with nothing but sparse grasses and shrubs for texture. Along the shoreline, however, there is a thin ribbon of palm trees, and here and there down the highway, bushes of bougainvillea in various shades of purple, pink, red, orange, and white leaven the barren landscape. Unlike the damp, eastern side of Mauna Kea, where the mountain is cut through with ravines and precipitous *palis,* the dry, western slope is gentle and generous, the roads and highways that traverse it at altitudes varying from a few feet to over 1,000 feet have views of the ocean that can add up occasionally to an almost implausible grandeur.

In recent years, the stretch of coastline running through the South Kohala region, about 20 miles from Kawaihae to Kaupulehu, has come to be referred to as the Kohala Coast. While a handful of resorts dot this coast that was more or less desolate until the 1960s, it is still a virtual wilderness compared with the hotels, motels, and resort condominiums that characterize the Kailua-Kona district to the south — a contrast that many visitors find welcome. The growing popularity of the more isolated Kohala Coast resorts has set a second stage of hotel and residential development in motion.

Visually, the country south of Kailua is more of a collage. There are groves of coffee trees, with white blossoms in the spring and glistening red berries in the fall, and macadamia nut plantations and terraces of mangoes that give some variety and definition to the terrain. Nestled between banana and papaya trees are ramshackle houses built on stilts with wooden stoops and corrugated iron roofs. Up in the hills of Hualalai, the 8,271-foot volcano that forms the backdrop to Kailua, you can travel up-country by jeep to within braying distance of wild donkeys — Kona nightingales, as they are known. And all along the beautiful shore are spots intimately connected with Hawaiian royalty and history: Kamehameha's royal compound at Kamakahonu, on the grounds of the present-day *King Kamehameha* hotel; Kamehameha III's birthplace close by the spot that is now Keauhou boat harbor; and a half dozen or so *heiaus* (temples) — among them, the Hikiau Heiau at Kealakekua, where Captain Cook was honored as a god. There are sandy beaches along this stretch of coast, too, though the number varies with the season because of occasional heavy winter surf that washes sand away from the lava rocks. Invariably, the sand returns. (White Sands Beach on Alii Drive is also known as Disappearing Sands Beach for this reason.) Where there is no sand, the shoreline can be even more fascinating. Just a few steps off the drive at any number of places between Kailua and Keauhou will bring you upon tidal rock pools — worlds in miniature where exotically colored and striped fish, fussbudget crabs, and other marine life are confined between high tides.

For visitors, the Kona district is generally thought of as the area along Alii Drive — the Nobles' Drive — which starts at the *King Kamehameha* hotel in the north and ends 8 miles away at Keauhou Bay. The southern portion of the drive is lined with condominium developments and private houses and is a favorite walking and biking route. The variety and color of the bushes, trees, plants, and flowers along here gives one the impression of passing through a spectacular private garden.

At the center of the Kona Coast and at the north end of the drive is Kailua; it clusters around that stretch of the road that starts at the *King Kamehameha* hotel and ends at the *Kona Hilton,* a distance of just over a mile. This was a royal haven in the 19th century. A reproduction of the temple and the home that provided Kamehameha with a royal compound is open to visitors on the grounds of the *King Kam* hotel. In town, opposite one another on Alii Drive, are the small but gracious Hulihee Palace and the Mokuaikaua Church, where royalty worshiped. These lend distinction to a historic community whose personality is being altered by shopping arcades. (In fact, several new shopping malls can be found inland of Alii Drive, bringing suburban convenience to town.) Another important element of the Kailua landscape is the sunset, which, swift though it may be by most mainland standards, usually manages to be outstanding.

There are no skyscrapers in Kailua and no flashing neon lights, so evenings tend to be low-key, a time for strolling, window shopping, or dining to quiet music on a flare-lit wooden terrace at the ocean's edge.

NORTH OF KAILUA

Holualoa and Up-country – In addition to the coastal highway, there is a beautiful up-country road that provides more than 30 miles of panoramas from 2,000- to 3,000-foot elevations. The drive is worth the time and allows for visits to small up-country towns, like Holualoa, and Kona's famous coffee farms.

Ellison Onizuka Pavilion – This recently opened museum at Kona's Keahole Airport is dedicated to Ellison Onizuka, the Big Island–born astronaut who was killed in the explosion of the space shuttle *Challenger.* It provides a pleasant hour's viewing if you've arrived at the airport early. Open daily from 8:30 AM to 4:30 PM. $2 admission (phone: 329-3441).

Hyatt Regency Waikoloa – The 65 acres landscaped with pools, lagoons, and waterfalls; the grand-scale architecture; and enough artwork to fill a fair-size museum are an attraction in their own right. Priced at $360 million, the *Hyatt Regency* is elaborate and extravagant, with motor launches and trams to shuttle you from here to there and back again. There is also a children's program ($25), which offers supervised activities such as arts and crafts, sandcastle building, and hula lessons. For all this, the property is worth a look, although it doesn't have much to do with things Hawaiian. 1 Waikoloa Beach Dr. (phone: 885-1234).

Mauna Kea Beach – One reason for visiting this latter-day Shangri-la off Route 19, 35 miles north of Kailua, is to look at the art collection. It consists of more than 1,000 art treasures, most of them antiques from the Pacific and Asia. A 7th-century Indian Buddha carved from pink granite and standing in the hotel's north garden is the outstanding piece. It comes from Nagappattinam in South India and sits in meditation atop a black granite pedestal, casting a serene eye on the foibles and frivolity all around. In the third-floor lounge is another piece of more than usual significance: the Pacifica Bell Collection, a series of antique bells from Japan, Ceylon, Singapore, and Cambodia. Japanese lacquered screens, painted masks, three-legged Indian storage chests, a hand-carved Buddhist altar from Thailand, Tongan war clubs, and Solomon Islands dance wands are some of the other things that might catch your eye. The collection of 29 original hand-stitched, antique Hawaiian quilts is especially appealing. Off Queen Kaahumanu Hwy. at *Mauna Kea Beach,* near Kawaihae (phone: 882-7222).

Mauna Lani Resort Petroglyph Fields – Hawaii's mini version of Stonehenge, this small group of upright stones bear enigmatic markings and symbolic drawings on their carved surfaces. There are several such petroglyph fields on the Big Island, and while their historical significance remains a mystery, they continue to intrigue archaeologists and travelers alike. To reach the site, follow *Mauna Lani* resort signs toward the *Ritz-Carlton* hotel. The turnoff is briefly marked by a sign just before you reach the *Ritz.*

Hapuna Beach State Park – When Laurance Rockefeller built the *Mauna Kea Beach* hotel, he donated the beachfront at neighboring Hapuna Bay to the state to be developed as a public park. Set about a mile south of the *Mauna Kea,* it has since become one of the Big Island's most popular, with an attractive beach, good swimming (although conditions may be hazardous), and rental cabins ($15 per shelter, which can accommodate one to four persons) on the grounds. Reservations should be made well in advance, although last-minute cancellations do occur. Contact Hapuna Beach Services, Hapuna Beach State Park (phone: 882-1095).

Puako – About 31 miles north of Kailua and 4 miles south of the *Mauna Kea Beach* hotel, take the coastward turn off Route 19 to Puako. Near the end of the road, past house 153, is a trail that leads through clouds of dust and groves of kiawe trees to a petroglyph field. Here, carved in ropy *pahoehoe* lava, are primitive figures of men and animals. Something special to look for are the round circles circumscribing a dot, which are supposedly where the umbilical cords of newborn babies were deposited so that tribal clairvoyants could predict the infants' destinies.

KAILUA AND SOUTH

Kamakahonu and the Ahuena Heiau – Standing at the back of the *King Kamehameha* hotel beside a small beach is the site of Kamakahonu, where Kamehameha the Great spent his last years governing all the Hawaiian islands. The rebuilt Ahuena Heiau (temple) and an authentic *hale* (house) surrounded by canoes and tikis are part of the itinerary offered in the King Kamehameha historical tours given by Aala Akana, whose considerable knowledge of the area comes a close second to her obvious affection for the place. The tour (offered weekdays, no charge) includes artifacts in the hotel's lobby and corridors, where ancient surfboards, musical instruments, and weapons are on display (phone: 329-2911).

Kailua Wharf – Just off Alii Drive next to the *King Kamehameha* hotel. Actually it's just a stone jetty, but it serves as Kailua's rialto, where you can be sure of meeting friends if they are somewhere in Kona — and where you can make friends if they are not. Between 4 and 5 PM the charter fishing boats come back to the pier with their proud (or cowed) parties, and most nights you can see landlubbers kneeling in front of lordly, defeated marlins, having their pictures taken. Later, tourists and islanders, glasses in hand and hearts pinned to sleeves, bathe themselves in the rays of the setting sun.

Hulihee Palace – It looks like a simple, late Victorian vicarage on England's Isle of Wight with its spacious rooms and vaguely gothic window frames. In fact, it was the summer residence of Hawaiian chiefs and kings from 1837 on. It is simple and handsome, and though the koa four-posters and armoires date from the stifling Victorian era, it still stays delightfully airy. No other house on the coast is quite so handsome, nor quite so lovingly tended. Tours daily from 9 AM to 4 PM; admission $4 (phone: 329-1877).

Mokuaikaua Church – This and Hulihee Palace across the road are the two focal points of old Kailua, and long may they flourish. Between them, they lend an air of benign dignity to the village and stand watch against possible architectural horrors. The church was built in 1837, of rock mortared with coral and has interior koa beams. The spire can be seen for miles and for many people symbolizes the heart of the Kona Coast.

Little Blue Church – Also known as St. Peter's, it is on a lava-strewn beach 4 miles south of Kailua on Alii Drive at Kahaluu Bay. If you are used to very ornate Catholic churches, this one will surprise you. Inside, it is bare except for a plain crucifix without a figure, in front of which a small bunch of bright red anthuriums is usually placed. This flash of color in the middle of austerity sums up the Kona Coast, where blossoms of outrageous gaudiness flourish amid an often forbidding landscape.

Kahanahou Hawaiian Foundation – Stop here to get a glimpse of contemporary Hawaiian culture presented by teacher Lanakila Brandt, who has dedicated himself to training craftspeople in the skills of the Polynesian past. In Kealakekua (phone: 322-3901).

Kona Historical Society Museum – Located in the restored *Greenwell Store* (ca. 1860) in up-country Captain Cook, the exhibits provide interesting views of life in 19th-century Kona. Open Tuesdays through Fridays from 9 AM to 3 PM. Library, manuscript, and photo collection may be viewed by appointment. No admission charge, but donations are appreciated. PO Box 398, Captain Cook, HI 96704 (phone: 323-3222).

Mrs. Fields Macadamia Nut Company – At this Kealakekua macademia nut processing plant belonging to Mrs. Fields of cookie fame, 15-minute tours are offered from 9 AM to 5 PM daily. Products may also be purchased. On Hale Kii St. (phone: 322-9515).

Kealakekua Bay – On southbound Route 11 in Captain Cook is a junction where the main highway swings east (left) and a secondary road leads off to the right. Known as the Napoopoo Road, it snakes down from Route 11, almost doubling back on itself, through avocado groves and trees heavily laden with mangoes and bright yellow papayas and eventually through acres of rough lava scrub before reaching the small township of Napoopoo, which gives its name to the lovely beach park along the shore. Napoopoo's few houses are partly hidden by arbors of luxuriant foliage often adazzle with blossoms. The stone walls surrounding them are latticed here and there with night-blooming cereus. Kealakekua Bay is famous for its clarity, and its abundant sea life, easily visible to swimmers and snorkelers, is of such variety that the park has been turned into a marine preserve where fishing is forbidden. Just offshore is the Napoopoo *heiau,* a large rock platform overlooking the beach. The bay is usually so tranquil that it is sometimes hard to remember that this is where European man had his first dramatic misadventure with the Polynesian. Here Captain James Cook made his second landing in the Sandwich Islands, as they were then newly known, on January 17, 1779. At first Cook was greeted as a god (Lono in the Hawaiian pantheon), and in due deference the natives bowed their heads and hid their faces as he passed. On February 4, Cook and his two ships, the *Discovery* and the *Resolution,* set sail, but less than a day out of the bay they ran into a winter storm off the Kohala Coast in which the *Resolution*'s foremast was damaged, forcing them to return to Kealakekua. Seeing that Cook's property was vulnerable, like that of any other mortal, the natives were less in awe of him than before. One night, the *Discovery*'s cutter was stolen, and Cook and a party of Royal Marines went ashore to take Kalaniopuu, the high chief, hostage. Enraged by this apparent arrogance, a party of native warriors attacked Cook and his companions with daggers, stones, and clubs, killing the captain and four of his followers. It is interesting to note that one of Cook's companions at Kealakekua was the notorious Captain Bligh, who later commanded the *Bounty.* A monument to Cook, a 27-foot obelisk, stands on the north side of the bay at Kaawaloa. It is best seen from one of the boats that sail daily to the spot from the pier at Kailua. If you want to get closer, take a four-wheel-drive vehicle or walk down the road that starts at a right turn about 100 feet along the Napoopoo Road from Route 11. The turnoff is signaled by the giant jacaranda tree that stands at the junction. The paved road that leads down to Napoopoo continues south, parallel to the coast, to the City of Refuge; it crosses a terrain full of nothing but air and sunshine, lava rocks and wispy grasses, and the sound of the ocean, which for many people is enough.

Kona Coffee Mill and Museum – This is the place to see at first hand what happens to all those red berries growing on the coffee trees that line some of the hillsides. You can watch coffee being dried, raked like mulch to turn it over so that all sides reap some of the sunshine, and being cleaned and graded. The museum part is really an overgrown boutique with cases of photographs showing what Kona coffee country looked like in the early 20th century. There are also examples of antique roasters and coolers. The main attraction, however, is the free sample of Kona coffee, which many experts agree is as fine as that grown under similar climatic conditions in Kenya. A pound or two of coffee will generally cost more here than in supermarkets along the coast. Napoopoo Rd. between Napoopoo and Honaunau, off Rte. 11. Open 9 AM to 5 PM daily (phone: 328-2511).

Between Kailua or Keauhou and Puuhonua O'Honaunau, along Route 11, are a number of smaller coffee roasters and retailers that offer free coffee tasting, and can handle mail-order sales of Hawaiian coffees and other products. *Bong Brothers* (phone: 328-9289), just outside Kealakekua, has the most authentic feel, with its restored turn-of-the-century mill and quotidian operations, and it's a good place to stop for fresh papaya, pineapple, and avocado, along with a well-priced pound of coffee. *Captain Cook Coffee Company* (phone: 328-9795), also outside Kealakekua, is a grower and processor of Kona beans with coffee tasting and a retail shop, as is the *Kona Plantation Coffee Company* (phone: 328-8424), located nearby, which sells a variety of locally roasted brands. Sample the all-Kona coffee at *Kona Kai Farms,* located in Kealakekua at the turnoff to Kealekekua Bay, and then select either whole beans or ground coffee to take home. Drop by during the harvest and watch local growers who bring their cherry beans in to sell (phone: 323-2911; 800-222-KONA).

Fuku-Bonsai Center – Located in up-country Keauhou (6 miles from Kailua) in a former quarry (between the 115- and 116-mile markers on Rte. 11, near the junction with Rte. 180), the world of bonsai plants is on display. Hundreds of the tiny trees adorn educational exhibits and themed gardens. Miniature plants are for sale, and can be shipped. Admission is $5. Open daily, 8 AM to 5 PM (phone: 322-9222).

St. Benedict's Church, Honaunau – On Route 16, which spirals up from the City of Refuge to Keokea on Route 11, a small country road leads off to the left. Barely 100 yards from the turnoff, standing on a foliage-clad rise next to a serene, pastoral graveyard, is a wooden edifice with a decorative, turret-like spire known all over the island as the Old Painted Church. Although the lacy, gothic fretwork on the porch is more ornate than that generally found on other island churches, it is a mere overture to the inside. The interior walls are vividly painted with religious scenes, some using Hawaiian motifs. Pillars decorated with painted scrollwork blossom into painted palm trees at the top. The wall behind the altar seems to be a gothic apse, which turns out to be a trompe l'oeil painting based on the nave of the Spanish cathedral of Burgos.

Puuhonua o Honaunau, the City of Refuge National Historical Park – Route 160 branches off Route 11 at Keokea and leads to the City of Refuge, but the undulating road that crosses the sparsely grassed lava moors girded by the Pacific can be more interesting. Even if restorations tend to leave you cold, don't let that deter you from visiting this one. The natural environment of lava beach and palm trees has been left largely intact, and parts of the 6-foot-thick walls, built of lava rock and locked in place without mortar, and some of the formidable tikis — monstrous wooden idols — are hand-crafted copies of the 16th-century originals. The coves, rock pools, and tidal lagoons here are lovely, but there is a solemnity about the park that is communicated even by the park ranger as he recalls what the place meant to his Hawaiian ancestors. In the Hawaii that Captain Cook found existed laws of *kapu,* an index of forbidden behavior. It said, for instance, that commoners might not walk in the footsteps of royalty and that women were forbidden to eat with men. Flouting a *kapu,* it was believed, led to catastrophe, which in this case might mean a lava flow or tidal wave. However, the ancient traditions held that a person reaching a *puuhonua* (place of refuge) could be purified by a priest and reinstated in normal society. Noncombatants in tribal battles and defeated warriors could also find sanctuary here. The refuge at Honaunau, where there are two *heiaus* dating from before 1550 and one built in 1650, was one of these and is today the best preserved and restored on the Big Island. It is not necessary to be fascinated by the philosophical aspects of the island's history to enjoy the City of Refuge. Canoes wrought as they were 200 years ago, the game of *konane* (checkers) set out on a rock on the beach, and *kamaainas* weaving mats and carving tikis are sufficient to hold the attention. The sunset here can be particularly magical, with the Hale O'Keawe temple silhouetted against the sky. The grounds are open from 7:30 AM to midnight and the visitor center from 7:30 AM to 5:30 PM (phone: 328-2326).

SHOPPING: The shopping scene has come to dominate Kailua in Lahaina-esque fashion. Most shops are not worth a special mention, although there are some exceptions in the small malls that now line Alii Drive. *Lanihau Center* brings shopping mall services to Kailua with *Long's Drugs* (best prices on film; phone: 329-1380); *Mail Boxes Etc.* (fax, Western Union, shipping services, stamps, photocopies; phone: 329-0038); *Waldenbooks* (phone: 329-0015); and a *Food For Less* supermarket that's open from 6 AM to midnight for the convenience of those vacationing in condos (phone: 326-2729). The *Kona Coast Shopping Center* on Palani Road opposite the Kailua-Kona Post Office (stop in at *Kim's Place,* phone: 329-4677) for the best plate lunch — the "national dish" consisting of meat, rice, shredded lettuce, and macaroni salad — in town) and the *Keauhou Shopping Village* on Alii Drive also have stores selling just about anything you'll find in a suburban shopping mall, including liquor, food, and aspirin as well as the typical array of jewelry shops, galleries, and so on of resort-town Hawaii. Some of the more interesting shops for visitors are on the road from Kailua to the City of Refuge, an up-country swing that takes you through Holualoa, Kainaliu, Kealakekua, Captain Cook, and Honaunau. Some distance north of Kailua, approaching Kawaihae, the *Mauna Lani, Mauna Kea,* and *Waikoloa* resorts have antiques shops, galleries, and boutiques aimed at wealthy buyers.

KING KAMEHAMEHA HOTEL

Hawaiian Traders – One of two branches in the neighborhood (the other is at the *Kona Surf* hotel), this shop specializes in fine wood products, etched glassware, and some interesting leis of Niihau shells, all made in the state (phone: 329-2246).

Jafar – An eclectic array of Art Deco glass lamps, paperweights, and acrylic jewelry by local artists, along with fashionable men's and women's clothing (phone: 329-5563).

Lani's Floral Shop – Not just fresh flowers but also leis and interesting arrangements of dried flowers that can be mailed back home for you (phone: 329-2551).

Liberty House – If Kona is your first stop in Hawaii, then this may be your first glance at this Honolulu chain of ready-to-wear apparel for guys, gals, and kids. The quality tends to be good, the prices by mainland standards high (phone: 329-2901).

Shellery – The place to get shell-shock if ever there was one: Here you'll find shell jewelry, shells inlaid with silver and gold, shell statuary, shell ashtrays and ornaments, and just plain shells (phone: 329-2911). A branch store is in the Kona Marketplace.

KONA MARKETPLACE

This shopping center is just across the road from the *Kona Inn Shopping Village.*

B.T. Pottery – This small gallery features the work of ceramicist Bill Traub. Kim Chong Bldg. (phone: 326-4989).

Crazy Shirts – One of the largest of this chain's numerous shops. T-shirts of every description, tasteful and otherwise (phone: 329-2176).

Crown Pearls International – A selection of natural and cultured, white and colored, freshwater and saltwater pearls; one of the best in Hawaii (phone: 329-5080).

Crystal Gallery – Hand-blown crystal is the theme, with glass artist Howard Richie working at a windowfront workbench (phone: 329-8188).

Middle Earth Book Store – Floor to ceiling books, calendars, and related goods.

It's a lot better than your average resort bookshop; here you really have some options. 75-5719 Alii Dr. (phone: 329-2123).

SEASIDE MALL/KONA BANYAN COURT

Across the road from the *King Kamehameha* hotel.

Kona's Finest Woods – The name may go a bit overboard, but some nicely crafted pieces can be found among the less unusual bric-a-brac that lines the shelves (phone: 329-1765).

Lee Sands – An astonishing variety of eelskin goods; everything from wallets to purses to shoes is for sale here (phone: 329-2285).

Neptune's Daughters – Some fine ethnic beadwork, puppets, and carvings, with Bali a prime source (phone: 326-4649).

Unison – Silk-screened sweatshirts and T-shirts are found here, well designed (phone: 329-2343).

KONA INN SHOPPING VILLAGE

Farther along Alii Drive, this shopping center has been converted from a famous old hostelry. There is a good-looking seaside restaurant here, and the walkways between the stores are made of timber.

Big Island Hat Company – From caps to dapper straw weave hats — and everything in between (phone: 329-3332).

Christel's Collectibles – Fine lingerie and feminine fashions imported from Europe (phone: 326-7577); also in Waimea at Parker Square (phone: 885-8870).

Competitive Edge Triathlon Center – As the name implies, it stocks just about anything you need for running, swimming, or bicycling, whether you plan to enter Kailua's annual triathlon or not (phone: 329-8141).

Fare Tahiti Fabrics – Not long ago it seemed as if every other shop in Hawaii sold fabrics, though today there aren't many left that do. This is one that does, and it offers the whole spectrum — from tacky to tasteful (phone: 329-2015).

Hula Heaven – A browser's heaven of vibrant aloha shirts and other Hawaiiana (phone: 329-7885).

Jim Bill's Gemfire – Owned by well-known jewelry designer Jim Bill, this is probably as close as many will ever come to a pirate's treasure trove. There are literally thousands of loose gems here — rubies, emeralds, topaz, and so forth — that you can have mounted to your own or Bill's design (329-4838).

Kona Kai Café – This shop has a nice selection of culinary gifts, as well as an outdoor coffee bar that serves fine coffees (Kona and otherwise) and pastries (phone: 329-2262).

Lowe's Rare Coins – An intriguing selection of commemorative coins of Hawaii, as well as other beautiful US gold coins and antique bills (phone: 326-2977).

KEAUHOU SHOPPING VILLAGE

The shops and restaurants at the shopping village of the Keauhou resort provide a range of resort shops and galleries as well as basics like a supermarket — useful for condo dwellers along the southern half of Kona's resort coast. Just off Alii Dr., by the turnoff for the *Kona Surf.*

Alapaki's – One of the nicest shops in town that sell collector's quality Hawaiian arts of the Polynesian past. Woodcarvings and musical instruments are among the fine offerings (phone: 322-2007). There's a second branch in town at Waterfront Row (phone: 324-0788).

Collectors Cottage – All sorts of collectibles, from limited edition plates and porcelains to dolls and music boxes (phone: 322-3154).

Dragon Fly – Beautifully simple and well-priced cotton dresses, slacks, and shorts embroidered with delicate appliqué work (phone: 329-6377).

Keauhou Village Book Shop – A good selection of reading materials, plus fax and photocopying services (phone: 322-8111).

Oscar – Fine jewelry, watches, and very stylish table clocks (phone: 322-6767).

Possible Dreams – A high-end card and gift shop with browse-worthy crystal, porcelain, and other collectibles (phone: 322-3292).

Showcase Gallery – Print art by names like Robert Lyn Nelson, Pegge Hopper, and Herb Kane, plus Hawaiian-made crafts (phone: 322-9711).

KAILUA ENVIRONS — NORTH

Exclusive Designs – A good selection of Niihau shell necklaces, muumuus, and other locally made clothing for men, women, and children. *Waikoloa Highlands Center* (phone: 883-8655).

Gallery of the Pacific – On a par with the neighboring Miller collections (see below), this shop focuses on contemporary painting and sculpture. 2 Mauna Lani Dr. (phone: 885-5757).

Herman F. Miller Museum and Gallery – One of the better antiques shops on the Big Island, and also among the best in Hawaii. The finer pieces, many of museum quality, were imported from the Orient by owner Herman Miller during the 1920s and 1930s, and are quite expensive. On the resort drive that leads from Kaahumanu Hwy. to the hotel. 2 Mauna Lani Dr. (phone: 885-7779).

Holualoa Gallery – Exquisitely wrought pottery by owner Matt Lovein, as well as the distinctive paintings of his wife, Mary, are the focus here. There is also an adjoining workshop where visitors can view the works in progress. 76-5921 Mamalahoa Hwy., Holualoa (phone: 322-8484).

Kimura Lauhala Shop – All kinds of goods, from baskets to bags to house slippers, are skillfully woven by local craftspeople from Hawaiian-grown hala leaves. Intersection of Mamalahoa and Hualalai Hwys., Holualoa (phone: 324-0053).

Lahaina Gallery – Contemporary fine arts from sculpture to painting are well represented here in the small building adjacent to the *Mauna Lani Bay* hotel (phone: 885-7244).

Waikoloa Video – This is the place to which to head if you've got a yen for a movie. A good selection of tapes, plus a helpful, friendly staff. *Waikoloa Highland Center* (phone: 883-8677).

Waikoloa Village Market – As nice a market as you'll find in Hawaii. Surprisingly well stocked with the basics, as well as deli items and delicacies you might not. 68-3916 Paniolo Ave. (phone: 883-1088).

KAILUA ENVIRONS — SOUTH

Blue Ginger – Traditional and contemporary Hawaiian arts and crafts are the main draw in this charming boutique. On Mamalahoa Hwy., Kealakekua (phone: 322-3898).

Cottage Gallery at SKEA – Sponsored by the *South Kona Educational Alliance (SKEA),* this gallery features the work of area artists, with an emphasis on pottery, ceramics, woodworking, batik, and silk clothing, and other arts. On Rte. 11, in Honaunau (phone: 328-9392).

Country Store Antiques – An interesting variety of affordable antiques can be found at this small shop in Captain Cook; perhaps you'll spot a bargain or two. Rte. 11 (phone: 323-3005).

Grass Shack – Yes, Virginia, there is a little grass shack in Hawaii. It's up in Kealakekua and has koa wood bowls, tapa cloth, tikis, jewelry made from black coral and jade, and kukui nut leis. Rte. 11 in Kealakekua (phone: 323-2877).

Little Gallery – The ceramics, woodwork, painting, and quilting of Big Island artists now on sale here were recently housed in a abandoned church in Holualoa. Now the church has been restored, and the gallery displays have taken up residence in this art center across the street. On Rte. 18, in Holualoa (no phone).

Studio Seven Galleries – A fine selection of gold jewelry, ceramics, wood sculpture, and lithographs can be purchased here. On Rte. 18 in Holualoa (phone: 324-1335).

Tropical Temptations – Hawaiian-grown bananas, pineapple, macadamia nuts, coconut, and papaya are slow-dried for 7 days to healthful, exotic perfection, or made into delicious confections. In Captain Cook (phone: 323-3131).

NIGHTLIFE: Happy hour on the Kona Coast is early by mainland standards, starting for most people at 4 PM, though for others it never seems to end — it's that kind of place. Musical entertainment runs from 5:30 to 10:30 PM in the *King Kamehameha*'s *Billfish Bar* (phone: 329-2911), and there's Hawaiian music nightly from 5:30 to 9:30 PM at the *Nalu Terrace* of the *Kona Surf* (phone: 322-3411). The *Surf*'s *Puka Bar* also features karaoke Fridays and Saturdays from 8 PM to midnight. At the *Royal Waikoloan* (phone: 885-6789), a harpist accompanies dinner at the *Tiare Room,* the hotel's deluxe restaurant. There's also nightly entertainment in the alfresco setting of the *Petroglyph Bar* from 5 to 10 PM, while there's live music on Tuesdays, Thursdays, Fridays, and Saturdays at the *Royal Terrace.* Sunset devotees sidle down to the Kailua pier, drinks and lovers in hand, to participate in the ancient ritual of watching the orange disc disappear over the horizon. Luaus are a favorite with tourists, and on the Big Island they seem to be less contrived than on Oahu. There are luaus at the *Royal Waikoloan* (phone: 885-6789) on Sundays; at the *Mauna Kea Beach* hotel (phone: 882-7222) on Tuesdays; at the *Royal Terrace* on Wednesdays; at the *Kona Village* on Fridays; at the *Kona Hilton* (phone: 329-3111) on Mondays, Wednesdays, and Fridays; and at the *King Kamehameha* (phone: 329-2911) on Sundays, Tuesdays, and Thursdays. *Mauna Kea*'s luau features Hawaiian music and dance performances (Hawaiian music is also a nightly feature in the hotel's *Café Terrace,* where complimentary *pupus* are served with cocktails). At *King Kamehameha,* the luau takes place in the shadow of the Kamakahonu restoration, where you eat by torchlight and watch a musical pageant, partly on the water, called *Hawaii Through History.* (*Note:* Since luaus are not offered every night, it's best to call ahead for the schedule in order to fit one in to your Kona visit.) *Captain Beans' Cruises* (phone: 329-2955), which offers ocean bottom–viewing cruises during the day, also runs a nightly dinner cruise that leaves the Kailua Pier at 5 PM and returns at 7. When the food is cleared away, scantily clad young ladies shake and gyrate on the dining tables to vaguely Hawaiian rhythms in a performance that would have perplexed their ancestors and outraged the missionaries. Male passengers, their inhibitions adrift in the limitless liquor that is part of the tab, are invited to join in the "fun." The resulting exhibition is one that usually manages to offend the prudish and the sophisticated in equal measure.

Conversation can be found in the bar of the *Ocean View Inn* (phone: 329-9998), the Kona Coast's neighborhood tavern, until around 10 PM most evenings; there is talk about football or baseball, depending on the season, in the bar of *Quinn's* restaurant (phone: 329-3822) and at Don Drysdale's *Club 53* (phone: 329-6651) and at its branch at the *Keauhou Shopping Village.* At the oceanfront *Jolly Roger's* (phone: 329-1344), there's dance music nightly. *Spats,* at the *Hyatt Regency Waikoloa* (phone: 885-1234), allows dancers to disco till 2 AM, 7 nights a week, in settings that would not disgrace New York's East Side. Walking along Alii Drive between the pier and the shopping village on a night when the moon is full is an affair to remember. For that rare rainy day or for an evening out, try the *World Square Theater* for good first-run films (phone: 329-4070). The *Aloha Theater,* a 1930s movie house just up-country from Keauhou-Kona, features inexpensive and well-performed theater by the *Kona Community Play-*

ers. Productions have included *Amadeus, Romeo and Juliet,* and *Annie.* For information on current performances, call 322-9924.

CHECKING IN: Because of the scarcity of sandy beaches on the Big Island, the few hotels or condominiums that have access to them tend to be very expensive. However, the success of more reasonably priced hostelries along Alii Drive, from Kailua to Keauhou Bay, proves that acres of sand are not absolutely essential for drawing visitors. For many people, the warm, dry climate, the historic appeal of Kailua-Kona, and a swimming pool on the rocks or in a landscaped garden seem to work quite well. Some places do have pocket-sized beaches adjacent or nearby, but the charm of most seagirt properties lies in the access they afford to intriguing rock pools and excellent snorkeling.

Those planning to stay a week or more on the Big Island will find a Kona Coast condo both convenient and a good bet financially as it will allow day-trip access to Kohala, Waipio, or Hawaii Volcanoes National Park, along with the luxury of eating at home or out. In selecting a condominium, be sure to specify the facilities needed to meet your personal needs and preferences. Although some are quite luxurious, well located, and well appointed, others are far simpler affairs, perhaps across the highway from the coast. Before sending a deposit, it is wise to find out if daily maid service, telephone, laundry, food shopping, restaurants, tennis, and the like are readily available.

There are four price categories for accommodations along the Kohala and Kona coasts. The *Hyatt Regency Waikoloa, Kona Village, Mauna Kea, Mauna Lani Bay,* and *Ritz-Carlton Mauna Lani* fall into a class of their own: very expensive, with rooms that begin at about $235 a day. Otherwise, expect to spend $160 to $225 for two in hotels listed as expensive, $75 to $155 in a place categorized as moderate, and under $70 for an inexpensive hostelry. All telephone numbers are in the 808 area code unless otherwise indicated.

Hyatt Regency Waikoloa – Costing nearly $400 million to build, this 1,241-room resort complex is both the largest hotel on the Neighbor Islands and one of the most extravagant in Hawaii. It is a mega-resort masterminded by the same developer (who no longer operates any hotels in Hawaii) who built the *Hyatt Regency Maui,* the *Westin Kauai,* and the *Westin Maui:* The 62 oceanfront acres have been landscaped to include manmade canals, waterfalls, and lagoons. The main wings of each of the three separate towers house a collection of works of art that can be enjoyed by strolling along the mile-long walkway that links them. Ocean views are available from 85% of the rooms, all of which have access to such amenities as 8 tennis courts, numerous swimming pools (the largest of which covers three-quarters of an acre), a lagoon-fed pool where visitors swim with dolphins who don't mind sharing their space with people, a full-service health spa, racquetball courts, and 7 restaurants, all serving excellent food. Unfortunately, not all of the much-ballyhooed spectrum of activities are available at all times. Transportation around the property is provided by trams and a fleet of passenger boats; shuttle service links the hotel with nearby golf courses, the third of which, the spectacular *Kings,* opened in February 1990. This hotel is meant to be an attraction in itself, which suggests that it will be far from the quiet getaway that some Hawaii-bound visitors seek. As dramatic as it is, it doesn't have much to do with Hawaii. *Waikoloa Resort,* Waikoloa (phone: 885-1234; 800-233-1234). Very expensive.

Kona Village – This remains a very special place, 15 miles north of Kailua, with its 125 beachcomber *hales* (cottages) scattered along the beach and lagoon. Accommodations are styled after the thatch-roofed huts found in the Pacific islands. Although equipped with beds, baths, coffee makers, and refrigerators, the more intrusive aspects of modern life — telephones and television sets — have been blissfully excluded. The resort is built around one of the few palm-shaded beaches on the island, although recent construction of the adjacent *Four Seasons* golf course and hotel (both due to open late this year) has made life less than serene. Guests can snorkel, swim, sail Sunfish; rent fishing equipment; play tennis, volleyball, Ping-Pong; or learn to shinny up a palm tree at no charge. Deep-sea fishing and scuba diving charters are also available. A complimentary children's program offers a variety of activities for restless youngsters. The daily rate includes breakfast, lunch, and dinner. There's a good luau on Friday nights. Box 1299, Kailua-Kona, HI 96745 (phone: 325-5555; 800-367-5290). Very expensive.

Mauna Kea Beach – This princely establishment was founded by Laurance Rockefeller as one of his original luxurious Rockresorts, although the present proprietor is a Japanese railroad and hotel conglomerate. Thanks to the supervision of general manager Adi Kohler, on staff since the Rockefeller days, the hotel has maintained much of its original understated elegance. The recent transfer of management from Westin to an independent group headed by Kohler should further improve operations. It stands above a crescent-shaped bay adjacent to one of the best sandy beaches on the Big Island. Flagstone terraces lined with tall pillars enhance the hotel's appealing open-air layout and lofty coconut palms tower over carp pools in the hotel's atrium. But perhaps the most outstanding decorative feature is the art and antiques collection which gives the corridors, landings, and walkways the atmosphere of a highly accessible museum. Rooms are surprisingly simple and spare. Chairs and bed frames have been made for the hotel in natural-colored wickerwork; bedspreads and cushions are brightly colored; the floors are polished brick. The lanais are large enough for a chaise longue, armchair, and table and chairs for dining, and views are memorable. The hotel is surrounded by an 18-hole golf course designed by Robert Trent Jones, Sr., and there is a 13-court tennis park. A second golf course (18 holes, par 72, 7,114 yards) is due to open late this year. Also available are excellent swimming, snorkeling, and windsurfing from the beach, fishing and scuba diving, and transportation to the stable at Parker Ranch. A complimentary children's program, which includes such activities as arts and crafts and sports, is offered here. Tariffs at the *Mauna Kea* are MAP (including breakfast and dinner) during the winter, and EP (no meals) — with a MAP option — the rest of the year. Sports activities, except for special packages, are extra. Several of the property's lordly condominiums, straddling the periphery of its golf courses, may also be rented, including use of hotel facilities, and beginning at more than $750 per day. (Ask for Property Services when dialing the hotel switchboard.) Off Queen Kaahumanu Hwy. at Mauna Kea Beach, near Kawaihae (phone: 882-7222; 800-882-6060). Very expensive.

Mauna Lani Bay – This 351-room luxury hotel is designed to appeal to the same monied clientele that frequents the nearby *Mauna Kea Beach.* Here, however, the feeling is more upscale European and contemporary in design. More than $70 million was spent building luxurious, extra-large bedrooms, a 10-court tennis garden, a health club, 4 restaurants, including a version of Honolulu's well-known *The Secret.* The *Canoe House* restaurant (see *Eating Out*) is a very special place to try the varied cuisines of the Pacific. There is also a manmade beach, as well as a private area called Keiki Beach for youngsters that offers pint-sized umbrellas, beach chairs, and surfboards. Counselor-supervised Camp Mauna Lani Bay is a complimentary program open to children ages 5 to 12, which offers beachside activities and arts and crafts. A walking trail skirts the sea, as well as fishponds restored from centuries past. There are also 2 recently built 18-hole, par 72 courses (one of which was originally the *Francis I. Brown* course), the *North* and the *South* — lush fairways surrounded by jagged black lava rock, with the sparkling Pacific Ocean as a backdrop. MAP option available. Worthy of special note are a quintet of "bungalows" along the north side of the property that are some of the most luxurious accommodations in Hawaii. Each villa contains 2 master bedrooms, a huge living/dining room, 3 baths (with steamrooms and whirlpools), a private pool, and a Jacuzzi. Butlers and maids cater to every guest whim — all for only $2,500 (volcano view) to $3,000 (oceanfront) a night. PO Box 4000, Kohala Coast, HI 96743 (phone: 885-6622; 800-367-2323). Very expensive.

Mauna Lani Terrace – Adjacent to the *Mauna Lani Bay* hotel, these luxurious 1-, 2-, and 3-bedroom units are in low-rise buildings that face nicely landscaped grounds providing direct access to the sea and two nearby beaches. Among the on-property amenities are a pool, Jacuzzi, sauna, and barbecue facilities. *Mauna Lani Resort* (phone: 885-4944; 800-882-4252). Very expensive.

Ritz-Carlton Mauna Lani – The first hotel of the Ritz-Carlton chain in Hawaii opened at the end of 1990 (the second *Ritz-Carlton,* on Maui, opened this year), just north of the *Mauna Lani Bay* property. There are 542 plushly decorated, oversize rooms, including 54 suites, and marble baths and oceanview lanais make the accommodations elegantly distinctive. The *Grill* restaurant serves very fine fare (see *Eating Out*). Also available are exclusive concierge-serviced Ritz-Carlton Club accommodations. Facilities on the hotel's 32 acres include a 10-court tennis complex, a fitness center, and two crescent beaches that lead to excellent snorkeling close to shore. There are two golf courses; the first (18 holes, par 72, 6,867 yards) is carved out of lava, lined by kiawe trees, and has strenuous ocean holes. The second course (18 holes, par 72, 7,015 yards) features ocean holes, inlets, rolling mounds, and manmade lakes. 50 Kaniku Dr., Kohala Coast, HI 96743 (phone: 885-0099; 800-241-3333). Very expensive.

Mauna Lani Point – In a lovely oceanfront setting adjacent to the sumptuous fairways of the Mauna Lani golf course, the 1-, 2-, and 3-bedroom apartments are distingushed by their quality furnishings. Other attractions include a pool, Jacuzzi, and barbecue area. 2 Kaniku Dr., Kohala Coast (phone: 885-5022; 800-642-6284). Very expensive to expensive.

Aston's Shores at Waikoloa – The prime oceanfront setting, with easy access to the beach, makes this tastefully furnished condominium worth considering. On-site facilities include a pool, Jet-Spa, and tennis; apartments have cable television linkups. Full resort facilities are nearby and a car is recommended. *Waikoloa Resort,* Waikoloa (phone: 885-5001; 800-922-7866). Very expensive to expensive.

Aston Kona by the Sea – Built on the grounds of an old estate, this low-rise condominium takes full advantage of its setting: the pool and Jacuzzi are surrounded by landscaped grounds and a line of palms that front the sea. There is also a second seawater pool and an excellent restaurant on the premises (see *Eating Out).* 75-6106 Alii Dr., Kailua-Kona (phone: 329-0200; 800-922-7866). Expensive to moderate.

Aston's Royal Sea Cliff – Artful architecture and landscaping combine to make this one of the Kona Coast's more interesting condo options, although certain units have views obstructed by other buildings. Two oceanfront pools, one saltwater, one fresh; a Jacuzzi; and a large sauna are on-property extras. So is a location just a couple of miles south of Kailua-Kona. Studio, 1- and 2-bedroom apartments with seasonal rates. 75-6040 Alii Dr., Kailua-Kona (phone: 329-8021; 800-922-7866). Expensive to moderate.

Kanaloa at Keauhou – This pleasant oceanfront condominium has several oceanfront pools, tennis facilities, and a clubhouse. Recently renovated, these 1-, 2-, and 3-bedroom apartments are private and spacious, and have been equipped with Jacuzzis. 78-261 Manukai (phone: 322-9625; 800-367-6046). Expensive to moderate.

Kona Coast – One of Keauhou's newest condominium resort properties, it has attractively furnished rooms and well-maintained grounds. There's easy access to adjacent golf and tennis and on-site activities. 78-6842 Alii Dr., Kailua-Kona (phone: 324-1721; 800-359-2566). Expensive to moderate.

Kona Hilton – Although the rooms have a certain feeling of Hilton standardization about them, the compensation is a good-sized, attractive lanai, so constructed that a guest cannot see or be seen from above or below (it also serves as an extra outdoor room, especially if you are lucky enough to have a corner room). Other assets include its tennis facilities; the smallish ocean-fed pool, handsomely screened from the full force of the main by dramatic black rocks; and its proximity to Kailua. Entertainment in the lobby area includes some voracious carp and a parrot with less dialogue than Calvin Coolidge. The friendly staff is helpful. Alii Dr., Kailua-Kona (phone: 329-3111; 800-445-8667). Expensive to moderate.

Royal Waikoloan – Not only is the broad, sandy beach a lure here — it's one of the nicest on the island — but there's also a palm-fringed lagoon, the kind that's more commonly constructed on a Hollywood back lot. The public areas are a series of indoor-outdoor terraces, their lines softened by an abundance of tropical greenery. Old Hawaiian art objects are sprinkled throughout the hotel, which has 528 rooms and 20 lagoon suites, each with its own lanai. Three 18-hole golf courses are open to guests, two adjacent and one in the Waikoloa village about 8 miles away. Tennis is also available. Taking its name from the Tahitian gardenia, the *Tiare* dining room provides a backdrop of polished koa wood, etched glass, and soothing harp music for its French and continental cuisine. Ask about the car-inclusive package prices. Off Queen Kaahumanu Hwy. at Anaehoomalu Bay, Waikoloa (phone: 885-6789; 800-537-9800). Expensive to moderate.

Casa de Emdeko – A Kona favorite because of its large living rooms, marble baths, and lanais overlooking gardens that are full of tropical flowers. The waterfront side of the building has been filled in with sand and a lava wall built along the ocean's edge to form a sun trap. There are barbecue facilities, a sauna, and 2 pools. 75-6082 Alii Dr., PO Box 1071, Kailua-Kona (phone: 329-6488 or 800-367-5168). Moderate.

Keauhou Beach – On a historic site, this recently renovated (and well-priced) hostelry now includes the old Kona lagoon. Adjoining are the remains of an ancient *heiau* complex and a reconstruction of the summer cottage of King Kamehameha III as well as some beautiful rock pools and a gray sand beach. Upper floors have panoramic views. 78-6740 Alii Dr. (phone: 322-3441; 800-367-6025). Moderate.

King Kamehameha – Built on a historic site, chosen by Kamehameha I as his royal retreat, the hotel keeps a historian on staff who gives tours of the hotel and its fabled surroundings, including the *hale* and reconstructed temple on the adjacent tiny beach. The walls of the hotel's otherwise undistinguished shopping center are lined with the ancient artifacts used in athletic contests and war, among them, *ulu maika* (stone pitching disks), *pahee* (darts), and *panaiole* (bow and arrows). The lobby contains a mural by island artist Herb Kane showing King Kamehameha at nearby Kamakahonu Bay. The rooms are bright and cheerful, especially those facing the ocean. There are 4 tennis courts on the premises. The location may be of even greater interest to deep-sea fishermen because the small wharf where billfishing charter boats tie up is next to the building. Luaus are held Tuesdays, Thursdays, and Sundays. 75-5660 Palani Rd., Kailua-Kona (phone: 329-2911; 800-367-6060). Moderate.

Kona Bay – Right in the heart of Kailua and around a pleasant courtyard and pool, the hotel is actually a remaining wing of the lovely old *Kona Inn,* now, alas, a shopping center on the waterfront across the road. The rooms here are simple and clean; some have kitchenettes and all have TV sets. For price and convenience, this is a very attractive option. 75-5739 Alii Dr., Kailua-Kona (phone: 329-1393; 800-367-5102). Moderate.

Sea Village – Pleasantly decorated rooms with some better-than-average wickerwork furniture and handsome wooden lanais make the units in this condominium attractive. Oceanside accommodations have particularly fine views. Continuous-cleaning ovens, dishwashers, and washer-dryers cut down on housekeeping time. Maid service is provided once for stays of 7 nights or longer, more frequently at extra cost; there is in-room telephone service, now available at an extra charge. A Jacuzzi and swimming pool are pleasantly situated on lava rocks just above the ocean. 75-6002 Alii Dr., Kailua-Kona (phone: 329-1000; 800-367-5205). Moderate.

Waikoloa Villas – About 25 miles north of Kailua-Kona, located near the golf course of the sprawling *Waikoloa* resort area, this 104-condominium complex, with 55 units, compensates for its relative remoteness and distance from the beach with a beautiful ranchland setting. To reach the complex, take the Waikoloa turnoff on Route 19 and drive east 6 or 7 miles (phone: 883-9144; 800-367-7042). Moderate.

Aston Islander Inn – Turn-of-the-century architecture and a beautifully shaded pool area bring a relaxing, mellow touch to this popular condo. Accommodations consist of studios; those with kitchenettes are available on request and cost $5 extra. There is daily maid service and telephones in rooms. This is a good buy, particularly during off-season. 75-5776 Kuakini Hwy., Kailua-Kona, HI 96740 (phone: 329-3181; 800-922-7866). Moderate to inexpensive.

Keauhou Resort Condominiums – Five landscaped acres surround the condominium's 1- and 2-level townhouses. Lanais have timber balustrades and outdoor carpeting, which make them more like another room than a balcony. Most face the ocean, and all have an abundance of bougainvillea trailing toward the roof or the lanai below. There are 2 swimming pools, and the famous *Keauhou-Kona* golf course is adjacent to the property. 78-7039 Kamehameha III Rd., Kailua-Kona (phone: 322-9122; 800-367-5286). Moderate to inexpensive.

Kona Riviera Villa – The 13 units of this oceanside condo are well maintained by their individual owners, each of whom visits fairly frequently. Each unit has a lanai, most with ocean views, and fully equipped kitchens. A 3-day minimum stay is required, with a discount offered on month-long stays. Cable television. Weekly maid service. 75-6124 Alii Dr., Kailua-Kona (phone: 329-1996). Moderate to inexpensive.

Kona Seaside – It would be hard to be more centrally located in Kailua than at this small, simple hotel. High standards of cleanliness and efficiency apply here, and for low-budget travelers this is an address worth remembering. Alii Dr., Kailua-Kona (phone: 329-2455; 800-367-7000). Inexpensive.

Kona Tiki – A small, modestly furnished hotel right on the water's edge — the kind of place you remember nostalgically when you have graduated to something grander. Delicious Kona coffee and rolls are served free of charge on the oceanside terrace. Some units have tiny kitchenettes. There is no room telephone, and a minimum stay of 3 days is required during high season. The managers are delightful. Alii Dr., PO Box 1567, Kailua-Kona (phone: 329-1425). Inexpensive.

Kona White Sands – This apartment hotel has only 5 units, and they are often booked a season in advance. While not luxurious, they are very comfortable and have huge picture windows with views over the ocean, across the road, deserving extravagant praise. This is the kind of place where you might want to spend a month or two. It is close enough to Kailua to provide sufficient amusement and just far enough away — about 4 miles — to avoid the hustle-bustle. No maid service. Alii Dr. at White Sands Beach, PO Box 594, Kailua-Kona (phone: 329-3210; 800-553-5035). Inexpensive.

EATING OUT: No one who comes to the Kona Coast would want to miss the opportunity of eating within sight and sound of the ocean. In Kailua-Kona alone there are at least eight restaurants where this is possible, and a couple more nearby. On the other hand, the two best restaurants in Kailua have no water view — they compensate with fine food. In general, a meal for two, excluding wine, tip, and drinks, will run more than $90 at a place listed in the very expensive category, from $55 to $85 in a restaurant listed as expensive, $25 to $50 in a moderate place, and under $25 in an inexpensive eatery. All telephone numbers are in the 808 area code.

Grill – A plush decor and a wood-panelled setting are the perfect complement to perfectly prepared steaks, veal, and lobster specialties. There is also live dinner music nightly. Open daily. Reservations advised. In the *Ritz-Carlton Mauna Lani* (phone: 885-0099). Very expensive to expensive.

Batik Room – This 2-tiered dining room in the *Mauna Kea Beach* provides an eclectic collection of Middle Eastern decor to complement its fine menu. The fragrance of the fine curry specialties is just an initial olfactory hint of the tastes to follow. Also offered are classics such as veal Oscar, tournedos of beef, and steak *au poivre.* Service is good, and the low noise level permits easy conversation. Open daily for dinner. Reservations necessary. *Mauna Kea Beach Hotel,* off the Queen Kaahumanu Hwy., just past Hapuna Beach (phone: 882-7222). Expensive.

Canoe House – The ambience alone, with evocative photos and other outrigger canoe memorabilia, makes for a very pleasant dining experience. Happily, chef Alan Wong's (formerly of *Lutèce* in New York) wonderfully varied "Pacific Rim" cooking adds substance to style with specialties such as wok-fried lilikoi shrimp, Pacific spiny lobster, and Kohala Coast snapper wrapped in nori (seaweed). Open for dinner daily from 5:30 to 10 PM. Reservations advised. *Mauna Lani Bay Hotel,* Kohala Coast (phone: 885-6622). Expensive.

Donatoni's – One of Hawaii's best Italian restaurants, the ambience is pure Mediterranean, the service impeccable. Unlike some restaurants where pretense outpaces results, just about everything tastes as good as it reads on the menu, which includes northern Italian specialties such as perfectly tender *calamari fritti* as an appetizer, linguine *al pescatore* (a perfect mix of mussels, scallops, and clams) and other pasta, pizza (with artichokes or, perhaps, smoked *pancetta*), and entrées ranging from *saltimbocca* to *osso buco alla milanese* (veal shanks braised with vegetables, white wine, and tomatoes). Open for dinner Mondays through Saturdays from 6 to 10 PM. Reservations necessary. In the *Hyatt Regency Waikoloa* (phone: 885-1234). Expensive.

Gallery – The food served supports the rave reviews it so frequently garners. The menu includes such entrées as Big Island salmon, ginger veal chops, and Brazilian chicken. The chef will also prepare the catch of the day in any style requested. Dinner daily from 6:30 to 9 PM; reservations advised. At the *Racquet Club* of the *Mauna Lani Bay Hotel,* off Queen Kaahumanu Hwy. at Manua Kea Beach, near Kawaihae (phone: 885-7777). Expensive.

Pavillion – The menu at *Mauna Kea Beach* hotel's main dining room deserves high praise for preparation and presentation. Recommended dishes include the goat cheese gnocchi, carpaccio (thinly sliced raw beef), ratatouille tartlet, sweet potato pancakes with sea scallops, and rosemary-grilled chicken. Dinner nightly. Reservations advised. At the *Mauna Kea Beach Hotel,* Kohala Coast (phone: 882-7222). Expensive.

Third Floor – Modeled on the popular Honolulu restaurant of the same name, it features some of the Big Island's best continental cuisine, with an emphasis on fresh seafood. High-back wicker chairs and strolling musicians give it a casual elegance. Dinner daily; reservations necessary. At the *Mauna Lani Bay Hotel* (phone: 885-6622). Expensive.

Eclipse – This restaurant doubles as a disco (from 10 PM to 1 AM Wednesdays through Sundays) and sports a neo-disco decor — a lot of chrome and colored lights that create a dappled effect while you dine. Considering the ambience, the food, mostly steaks and seafood, is surprisingly good. The service is slow but friendly. Open for lunch weekdays, dinner Tuesdays through Saturdays from 5 to 9 PM. Closed Mondays. Reservations advised. Across from *Foodland* on Kuakini Hwy., Kailua-Kona (phone: 329-4686). Expensive to moderate.

Fisherman's Landing – Plenty was spent to make this large restaurant tropically elegant. The menu includes catch of the day specials, steamed clams, and New Orleans–style blackened fish. Open daily with a lunch menu offered from 10:30 AM to 10 PM, and a dinner menu from 5:30 to 10 PM. Reservations advised. In the *Kona Inn Shopping Center* (phone: 326-2555). Expensive to moderate.

Imari – Elaborately Japanese in style, the specialties include sukiyaki beef, shabu shabu chicken and beef, and *yosenabe* seafood, all cooked tableside, with *teppanyaki* and *kaiseki* dinners as well. An elegant place to go Oriental. Open for dinner from 6 to 10 PM;closed Thursdays and Fridays. Reservations necessary. In the *Hyatt Regency Waikoloa* (phone: 885-1234). Expensive to moderate.

Jameson's – The first neighbor-island branch of this popular Oahu eatery has taken over the old *Dorian's* and made a few changes in the menu and decor. Now the atmosphere is tropically casual, the furnishings contemporary rattan. Catch-of-the-day specialties are a good bet, but meat and poultry dishes are also on the menu. Open weekdays for lunch from 11 AM to 3 PM, daily for dinner from 5 to 10 PM. Reservations advised. Alii Dr. at Magic Sands Beach, Kailua-Kona (phone: 329-3195). Expensive to moderate.

Kona Inn – This attractive open-air restaurant and bar boasts a decor dominated by beautifully carved koa wood and a fine vista of Kailua Bay through a silhouette of palms. The food's as tempting as the view, ranging from seafood to steaks to prime ribs. Open daily (lunch and dinner) to 1 AM. Reservations advised. *Kona Inn Shopping Center* (phone: 329-4455). Expensive to moderate.

Chart House – Beef, fish, and seafood entrées are the stars on the menu here. Dinner daily from 5 to 10 PM; reservations advised. On Alli Drive, in the *Waterfront Row* shopping complex, Kailua-Kona (phone: 329-2451). Moderate.

Kona Ranch House – There are two rooms here, of which the Lanai Room, with brass ceiling fans and white latticework, is by far the more elegant. Steaks, from island-reared cattle, and fish from local waters are faultless. Salads taste as fresh as they look, and what may be the best breakfast in Kona is served. Open daily from 6:30 AM to 9 PM. Reservations advised. At the intersection of Kuakini and Palani Hwys., Kailua-Kona (phone: 329-7061). Moderate.

Phillip Paolo's – A neighbor-island branch of the popular Honolulu restaurant of the same name. The food is flavorfully Italian, the portions large. Open daily for dinner from 4:30 to 11 PM. Reservations advised. *Waterfront Row,* Alii Dr., Kailua-Kona (phone: 329-4436). Moderate.

Rusty Harpoon – This large, California-style restaurant (there are branches at Kaanapali on Maui, and in Waikiki in Honolulu) offers a comfortable setting (with some outside tables) and an eclectic menu that includes samurai stir-fry beef, Korean ribs, shrimp tempura, and steamed Alaskan crab legs. Also available is an equally varied selection of tasty *pupus.* Open for breakfast from 7:30 to 11:30 AM (12:30 PM on weekends), lunch from 11:30 AM to 5 PM, and dinner from 5 to 10 PM. Dinner reservations advised. *Kona Village Shopping Center* overlooking Alii Dr., 2nd Floor (phone: 329-8881). Moderate.

Aloha Theater Café – Located in the historic *Aloha Theater,* 8 miles south of Kona, this place is especially great for breakfast, serving Kona coffee, freshly prepared espresso, and cappuccino; coconut, papaya, and pineapple smoothies; and homemade banana muffins alongside the fine omelettes, enjoyed alfresco on the terrace. Generous portions, deliciously prepared, are served at dinner, with dishes ranging from catch-of-the-day to filet mignon to tostadas and quesadillas. Open for breakfast from 8 to 11:30 AM, (on Sundays from 9 AM to 2 PM), lunch from 11:30 AM to 4 PM, and dinner from 4 to 8 PM. Reservations unnecessary. Rte. 11, Kainaliu (phone: 322-3383). Moderate to inexpensive.

Drysdale's Club 53 – Former baseball star Don Drysdale opened this casual and friendly alfresco restaurant where drinks, burgers, shrimp scampi, fish and chips are served. Reservations unnecessary. In the *Kona Inn Shopping Village* (phone: 329-6651) and *Drysdale's Two* at the *Keauhou Shopping Village* (phone: 322-0070). Moderate to inexpensive.

Quinn's – One of the better spots for a late-night bite. (Dinner and sandwiches are served until 1 AM.) It is popular with the kind of crowd that favors singles bars. The main dining area is an outdoor patio where scallops, shrimp, and steaks are consumed by people who seem mostly to be repeat customers. Open daily for lunch and dinner. No reservations. Opposite the *King Kamehameha Hotel* on Alii Dr., Kailua-Kona (phone: 329-3822). Moderate to inexpensive.

Daily Grind – The grind refers to fresh-brewed coffee, but the real treats are the daily lunch and dinner specials like turkey crêpes, shrimp jambalaya, and double stuffed baked potatoes. There's also a luscious lineup of desserts. Perfect for a casual meal or a meal to go. Open from 6 AM to 6 PM weekdays; 8 AM to 2 PM weekends. Reservations unnecessary. *Waikoloa Highland Center* (phone: 883-9555). Inexpensive.

Don's Family Deli – Tasty sandwiches, lasagna, and other Italian dishes. A good place for a lunch break while touring North Kohala. Closes at 6 PM. In Kapaau, on Aikona Pule Hwy. (phone: 889-5822). Inexpensive.

Ocean View Inn – If you were to canvass repeat visitors to Kailua about their favorite restaurant, odds are they would root for this spot. Large and noisy, it has a Formica–knotty pine decor reminiscent of the 1950s. Not the slightest effort has been made to exploit the view of the ocean and harbor just across the road. But it is always full, most of the time with people from the Kona and Kohala area who use it as a kind of eating club. The vast menu lists dishes of Hawaiian, Chinese, Japanese, and American persuasion with various mongrel combinations available. The cooking will never win any prizes, but on the other hand, it's hard to believe that anyone ever complains since portions are ample and the booze, by Hawaiian standards, is liberally poured. And for character and color, it merits an A plus. Open daily, except Mondays, for breakfast, lunch, and dinner. Reservations unnecessary. Right in the heart of Kailua on Alii Dr. (phone: 329-9998). Inexpensive.

Rocky's Place – If you're in the neighborhood and have a sudden craving for a pizza or veal *parmigiano,* you won't be disappointed by the fare served here. Everything is simply yet skillfully prepared, and the unpretentious decor sets the tone for a relaxed evening out. Open daily from 11 AM to 9 PM. Reservations unnecessary. *Keauhou Shopping Village* (phone: 322-3223). Inexpensive.

Sibu – The setting is like a street café, the food tastefully Indonesian, with specialties like Balinese chicken (flavored with tarragon, garlic, and onions), satés, and curries. Wine and beer available. Lunch and dinner daily. No reservations. Under the large banyan by the seawall in *Banyan Court* shops (phone: 329-1112). Inexpensive.

Wurst Place – The place to head if it's after hours and you're hungry. Featured is a local menu with specialties like short ribs, pork chops, and mushroom chicken. Open until 3 AM most nights. Open daily, except Sundays, for breakfast, lunch, and dinner. No reservations. *North Kona Shopping Center* (phone: 329-1166). Inexpensive.

Hawaii Volcanoes National Park and Environs

Make no mistake about it, the goddess Pele is alive and well in Hawaii Volcanoes National Park, the most popular tourist attraction on the Big Island. The Kilauea Caldera, where she resides deep inside the Halemaumau Crater, "erupted" no less than 30 "major" times between January 1984 and December 1986 (there is still a constant flow of lava from the rift), making Kilauea and Mauna Loa, the 13,680-foot-high "long mountain" farther up in the park (whose eruption in 1985 caused the evacuation of Hilo's western suburbs), the most active volcanoes in the world. Since records were begun 200 years ago, they have between them covered nearly 200,000 acres of land with lava, destroying trees, plants, animals, houses, and occasionally even people in the process. Generally, however, eruptions are not life threatening, and it is possible to predict with some accuracy where the lava will flow. Volcanic activity is monitored around the clock by seismographs at the Hawaii Volcanoes Observatory (call 967-7977 for eruption reports) on the western edge of the caldera, where visitors can watch them recording the minor tremors that take place each day — and the occasionally more violent tremors that indicate that Pele is restless. These safety precautions and easy accessibility have given Kilauea the nickname "the Drive-In Volcano," where people may come and watch glowing lava beside newsmen, photographers, volcanologists, geophysicists, geochemists, and geologists from around the world. Several years ago they might even have found themselves rubbing shoulders with the nation's most famous astronauts, who were brought here to give them a taste of the terrain they would face on the moon. At the *Jaeggar Museum* (open 8 AM to 5 PM), adjacent to the Hawaii Volcanoes Observatory on the rim of Halemaumau Crater, visitors can check seismic charting, speak with personnel, and learn a bit of the science of Hawaiian volcanology from displays. It is also possible to view the recently hardened lava that has been adding acreage to the Puna coast since 1983, (and destroyed more than 80 homes and the park's Wahuala Visitor Center in the process) when flows began from the Kilauea East rift zone. Since then, flowing lava wending its way to the sea has destroyed the community of Kalapana, including nearly 200 homes, as well as famous attractions like historic *Queen's* (a geologic fault filled with water that was used as a swimming pool) and the famous black sand beach at Kaimu. When conditions permit, park rangers allow visitors to view the same sight from the Wahaula side of the flow. Recently, large sections of the newly formed coastline had begun to collapse into the sea, making these coastal hikes all the more dangerous. Renewed activity near Wahaula has also brought lava to the walls of the ancient *heiau* on the site, thereby threatening its survival. This ongoing eruptive series is the longest on record for Hawaii.

Generally, however, there is no sun-red lava burgeoning from the earth's bowels, although the steam and sulfur hissing from vents inside the crater and on the surrounding mountain ridges hint at something more sinister. Certainly you sense that there is endless activity taking place beneath your feet and that the *terra* may not always be *firma.*

But steam vents and moonscape are not the whole story. The park is also a nature reserve of tropical black sand beaches, humid rain forests and fern jungles, temperate-zone acres of shrubs high up on Mauna Loa, and woods full of wild orchids, birds, and butterflies. A major delight for anyone examining the seemingly barren lava has to be the glimpse of exquisite amaumau and kupukupu ferns breaking through fissures as though determined to declare a perpetual springtime in the midst of the surrounding desolation.

The Wahaula Visitor Center, at the Kalapana entrance to the park was destroyed by fire from the molten lava of the Kilauea Volcano in June 1989. A mobile center was set up about a mile east of the *Kamoamoa Campground,* at the end of Chain of Craters Road. Until lava from several early 1987 eruptions blocked the coastal leg of the Chain of Craters Road, it was possible to continue through Puna to Hilo on Route 13. The road has been covered by lava in numerous places, and with eruptions still under way, it is unlikely that the route will be open to through traffic anytime in the near future.

The best place to get a compact and comprehensive picture of the park is the Kilauea Visitor Center (open from 7:45 AM to 5 PM; phone: 967-7311). Maps and books are available indicating roads and trails around the park, and a film (shown daily, on the hour from 9 AM to 5 PM) explains how volcanoes are formed and traces the series of eruptions that began here in 1983 and that continue as we go to press.

Some terms used in the film and literature that you may wish to memorize are: *aa,* dark, cindery, rough lava; *caldera,* the open, depressed, bowl-like area at the summit of a volcano (Kilauea Caldera is one, Mokuaweoweo Caldera on top of Mauna Loa is another); *ejecta,* cinders and other matter thrown up during an eruption; *fumarole,* a vent emitting steam, sulfur, or other matter; *kipuka,* an island of soil and vegetation surrounded but untouched by lava; *olivine,* semiprecious chrysolite, greenish yellow in color, often found among cinder fallout; *pahoehoe,* smooth, shiny lava that covers the ground in thick folds, often resembling solidified molten lead; *volcanicity,* the underground volcanic makeup of a country or area.

The Kilauea Visitor Center is close to the *Volcano House* hotel (phone: 967-7321), where you will almost certainly want to make your headquarters, whether you are visiting just for one day or for several. Bring a jacket or sweater, since at these altitudes (*Volcano House* stands at 4,077 feet) the air can get chilly, and in the winter there is snow on the summit of Mauna Loa.

It is possible to get some idea of the volcanoes and their environment by taking the 11-mile drive around the Kilauea Caldera from *Volcano House* and back again. But only by exploring some of the trails on foot can you truly appreciate the area and its wonders. Aerial tours of the park, the East rift zone, and the lava flows are offered by *Volcano Heli-Tours* (phone: 967-7578).

Chain of Craters Road – This 27-mile drive from the Kilauea Visitor Center to the coast was reopened in 1979 after parts of it had been covered by lava during a 1974 eruption and again since 1986. Stretches of the old paved road can still be seen between fingers of lava. The new road passes several pit craters dating from prehistoric times, as well as more recent *pahoehoe* lava fields, which sometimes seem to resemble deformed heads and bodies and have inspired comparisons with scenes from Dante's *Inferno.* For an unforgettable experience, visit the volcano at dusk, for at no time does Pele's wrath seem more dramatic than when the amber glow of the *pahoehoe* is highlighted by the onset of night. Be sure to bring a flashlight; take care that you stay along the perimeter of the flow — and wear comfortable, sturdy shoes. For the latest information on the volcano, call the Eruption Hotline at 967-7977. Once providing coastal access back to Hilo via Keaau, Route 13 has been covered in several places by a series of lava flows since 1986. At press time, lava had stopped flowing into the sea, although volcanic activity continued elsewhere up-country from Kaimu and 1 mile east of the site of the Wahaulu *heiau* (temple). Although ranger-led hikes to these sites had been discontinued before the lava ceased its flow into the sea, many people independently make their way across the recently hardened lava for a front-row seat, wherever volcanic activity is occurring. Warnings are posted about the dangers of the trek and of the release of laze, a toxic cloud of gas that forms when lava flows into the sea. For those contemplating such a hike, sturdy hiking shoes or sneakers are recommended, since the heat of the volcanic landscape can melt thin-soled shoes.

Some 8½ miles beyond Wahaula on the same road, just before you come to the lava roadblock formed by the 1972 eruption, a sign indicates the Puuloa petroglyph field. From the parking area you can take a 15- to 20-minute stroll toward the beach along a dusty trail, at the end of which can be found some of the oldest petroglyphs in the islands, depicting man in a variety of pursuits, weapons, fish, and a wide range of seemingly abstract symbols.

Crater Rim Drive – This road circles the Kilauea Crater in an 11-mile sweep from the Kilauea Visitor Center. It passes verdant rain forest, bleak desert, recent lava flows that gleam in the sun, and areas piled high with pumice from recent eruptions. The road is dotted with well-marked trails and parking areas overlooking significant parts of the park, among them, Kilauea Iki (Little Kilauea) Crater, Halemaumau Crater, and, from the Umekahune Bluff overlook, Kilauea Caldera from its northwest side. The small *Jaegger Museum* (phone: 967-7643), where the volcano's seismic activity is monitored, is worth a brief stop.

Thurston Lava Tube – A drive of just under 4 miles from *Volcano House* brings you to this trail, one-quarter mile long, through the most accessible lava tube on the Big Island. The tube was formed when the outer crust of a layer of flowing lava cooled while lava inside that was still molten continued to flow. Eventually the hot lava flowed right through the cool, leaving this tube-like crust, 450 yards long and from 10 to 20 feet high. All around the tube is the celebrated Fern Jungle, a humid wilderness of ohia trees surrounded by giant hapuu ferns and smaller ferns. Two native birds to look for in this neighborhood are the iiwi, a bright vermilion specimen with black wings and an orange-yellow beak, and the amakihi, identified by its blend of yellow and olive green plumage. They are often sighted among the brilliant red blossoms of the ohia, which provide them with a rich source of food. In midsummer, kahili ginger produces an almost overwhelming fragrance in the Fern Jungle.

Kipuka Puaulu – About 2 miles west of *Volcano House.* Take Route 11 west to Mauna Loa Strip Road; the park is a little way up the road on the right. A walk around the 1.1-mile loop of this enchanting *kipuka* illustrates vividly how an island of plants, birds, and insect life survives surrounded by hostile-looking petrified lava. The trail takes you through open meadows and forest studded with koa, ohia, mamani, soapberry, and kolea trees. Hawaiian raspberries, *akala,* grow in abundance along the trail. The wonderful birdlife this unusual ecosystem supports accounts for its English name, Bird Park. An extremely comprehensive exhibit at the *kipuka* entrance is worth examining.

Steam Vents and Sulfur Banks – A short, leisurely walk along the edge of Kilauea Caldera from *Volcano House* brings you to some billowing steam clouds caused by rainwater seeping into Kilauea's seething underground oven and bursting out through vents on the rim. Just a little way beyond are volcanic fumaroles emitting foul-smelling sulfur gases from the same nether regions. To reach it, you pass through a lovely forest of sandalwood, ohia lehua, and ferns.

Halemaumau Trail – The round-trip distance between *Volcano House* and the end of this trail is 6.8 miles. A steep climb down from the inn leads through dark gorges covered with vegetation into the bare, deserted Kilauea Caldera and across fresh lava flows to the Halemaumau overlook, where you can peer down into the mysterious realms where Pele dwells. If you want to walk one way and be deposited or picked up by car, there is a parking area close by on Crater Rim Road.

Devastation Trail – In 1959, an eruption in Kilauea Iki sent pumice, ash, and other ejecta shooting 1,900 feet into the air. An ohia forest on the same spot was almost completely buried. The few trees that remained were scarred and scattered and bleached by the sun. Here and there stubby bushes and brilliant yellow flowers have pushed their way through the debris, giving haphazard touches of color to this macabre landscape. A boardwalk .6 mile long crosses the area to prevent wear and tear on boots and shoes. The way to the trail is marked from Crater Rim Road and from Crater Rim Trail.

Puna – East of Hawaii Volcanoes National Park and south of Hilo, the Puna district is served by Route 13, which extends to the coast where the lava-destroyed village of Kalapana once stood. Humidly tropical Puna is home to acres of vanda orchid and anthurium farms, most of which are open to visitors. At Lava Tree State Park, on Route 132 just 2.7 miles southeast of Pahoa, you can witness the bizarre aftermath of a volcanic eruption that took place around 1790. At that time molten lava flowed through what was a dense forest of giant ferns and large ohia trees. The first waves of lava cooled and hardened around the base of the trees and plants while lava behind it built upon the first wave until there were as many as five layers. As molten lava drained away downhill or into holes in the ground, a series of grotesque pillars of petrified lava were left behind, some of them resembling unfinished tikis. Farther along Route 132 is a 420-foot-high cinder cone, the site of the village of Kapoho, which was inundated by *aa* lava in the eruption of 1960 (no lives were lost). At Kapoho you'll find tidal pools large enough for snorkeling and rife with multicolored fish. At Kaimu, where Route 13 meets the coast, is the devastation from the lava that covered the once-lush landscape until 1991, destroying the famous black sand beach of Kaimu and the village of Kalapana. The historic Star of the Sea Church was moved from its oceanfront site, and was saved from destruction only days before the lava flowed into the area. It is now temporarily relocated pending a plan for restoration, and is closed to visitors.

Kau District – On the southwest flank of the park lies Kau, a tranquil farm district whose roadsides are lined with weather-beaten rural houses surrounded by bougainvillea and eucalyptus trees. Traveling along Route 11 out of the park, you pass through fields of cattle-feeding grasses dotted here and there with yellow mamani trees and white *alahee,* a variety of coffee plant. At Punaluu there is another black sand beach. A few miles beyond Waiohinu is a left turn off Route 11, which leads to what the Hawaiians call Ka Lae (South Point). Here, at 18.58° north of the equator, is the southernmost tip of the US. This is also the site of some of the earliest Polynesian settlements (5th and 6th century) in Hawaii. For generations this has been a favorite fishing ground, even though the catch has to be hauled up over 50-foot cliffs. These are studded with the ancient iron rings used by fishermen for mooring their boats. A 3-mile hike east along the coast will bring you to Green Sand Beach, a strand formed of ground olivine particles. Just beyond the turnoff to South Point, Route 11 veers north through South Kona to Kailua.

Kau Desert – "There's no there there," Gertrude Stein is reported to have said about Oakland, California. And if the Hawaii that you seek is made up of white sands, palm trees, and women dancing the hula, then that might be your reaction to the Kau Desert, the area lying southwest of the Kilauea Caldera, between Route 11 and Chain of Craters Road. If, on the other hand, you are looking for one of the most unusual encounters with geography you are ever likely to experience, then it is here. The southwestern deserts of the mainland US, with their sparse grasses and cacti, seem a jungle compared to this. For acre upon acre there is nothing — *nothing* — but ropy, *pahoehoe* lava lying in folds, hot, shiny, and barren. Other areas consist simply of cinder parks of *aa* lava, where every step you take sends you walking through a calf-high cloud of dust. Astronaut Neil Armstrong walked here before setting foot on the moon to get some idea of the conditions he would face when he made one small step for mankind. On the desert's perimeters, between the smooth lava at its center and the shrub and grasslands that surround it, you will find Pele's hair, a thin golden substance, in the holes and fissures. Legend has it that when Pele was rampant, she would tear out her hair, scattering it to the winds, and that it would be caught in clefts and on trees. The geological version is more mundane. It states that this odd variety of natural glass is a by-product of drops of very liquid lava — known, to complicate the matter, as Pele's tears — ejected into the air. The tears take on a teardrop shape before solidifying, while the threadlike traces they leave in their wake cool quickly into hair-like strands. Something else that relieves the texture of the desert at its edges is the appearance of whitish lichen — "'Hawaiian snow" — which is the first thing that will grow on new lava.

To the traveler newly arrived from Hilo, less than 40 miles away, where it rains on average more than 130 inches a year, this aridity is astonishing. Even more remarkable is the sight of low, dense clouds dissipating their moisture on the northeastern slope of the caldera so that *Volcano House,* visible from many parts of the desert, has 100 inches of rain a year, while where you stand barely 20 inches fall.

Just inside the park's western boundary and marked with a trail sign on Route 11 is one of the few phenomena in the desert involving man: One day in 1790 a bizarre eruption of gas and dust asphyxiated a band of warriors who were crossing the desert on their way to do battle with the troops of Kamehameha the Great. A brief and altogether freakish rainstorm followed the eruption, turning the dust into damp clay so that those warriors attempting to escape left footprints behind. Footprints Trail, just under a mile long, leads to the site of this scramble, where some of the prints can still be seen, encased under glass to preserve them. It is a reminder that it is not wise to fool with Pele.

SHOPPING: Housed in the original *Volcano House,* the *Volcano Art Center* (phone: 967-7511) specializes in Hawaiian painting, sculpture, prints, and needlework. The artifacts available are among the finest in the islands. Bowls made from koa wood, quilts, watercolors, and oil paintings merit particular attention. The center also schedules cultural events during the year. Call for information. In the Kilauea Visitor Center (phone: 967-7311) at the Hawaii Volcanoes National Park are posters, dramatic slides of the volcano in eruption, and a good selection of books concerning the park and its flora and fauna.

NIGHTLIFE: *Uncle George's,* the *Volcano House* bar (phone: 967-7321), provides a place to relax. When Pele, the goddess of the volcano, is acting up in Halemaumau Crater, the view from *Uncle George's* can be spectacular.

CHECKING IN: Perhaps because Hawaii Volcanoes National Park is easily reached on a day trip from Hilo or Kona, formal accommodations are scarce, although there are many bed and breakfast options in the close vicinity of the volcanoes' park (see *Tourist Information*). *Volcano House* handles reservations for the park's cabins at Namakani Paio. These sleep four and cost $24 per night. Only one blanket is provided, which may leave you chilly. All telephone numbers are in the 808 area code unless otherwise indicated.

Colony One Condominium at Sea Mountain at Punaluu – Between the black sand and lava Kau coastline and sprawling ranchlands that climb up to Mauna Loa, this condominium complex of cottages is built, furnished, and decorated in a style that might aptly be described as rustic chic. There are tennis courts, a golf course, and a swimming pool, and the situation is ideal for those who like hiking or fishing (you won't run into many other people doing either). Daily maid service is by request and involves a surcharge; rates are based on a 2-night minimum stay. From $75 to $150 for a double. Just off Rte. 11 between Pahala and Naalehu at Punaluu; PO Box 70, Pahala, HI 98777 (phone: 928-8301; 800-488-8301).

Kilauea Lodge – Located in Volcano Village, 1 mile from the Kilauea Visitor Center of Hawaii Volcanoes National Park, this large, rustic inn, built in 1938 as a *YMCA* retreat, is now a noteworthy bed and breakfast establishment. Each of the 4 rooms is spacious, decorated with flair, with its own theme and bath, fireplace, and view of the fern forest or garden. There are 7 additional rooms in nearby cottages. Priced from $85 to $100 per night, double, including a sizable breakfast of Punaluu sweetbread French toast, pancakes, or eggs. Advance reservations are advised. PO Box 116, Volcano, HI 96785 (phone: 967-7366).

Volcano House – Although it is often mobbed by day with visitors using the bar and restaurant as a base for exploring the park, at night *Volcano House* takes on the air of a rustic lodge that in recent years has begun to look a bit worse for wear. A fire usually is kept burning in the large lobby fireplace, attracting occasional guests. *Uncle George's* bar provides another relaxing setting. Although none of the 42 rooms are large, they are all generally comfortably furnished and warm (it can be nippy up here at night). The view from the rooms overlooking the crater is memorable. There are no television sets and no swimming pool, but there is a restaurant (see *Eating Out*). Rooms are priced from $75 to $125 for a double. Advance reservations advised, particularly for crater-view rooms. Hawaii Volcanoes National Park (phone: 967-7321).

EATING OUT: Dining is limited to six possibilities. In the moderate category, expect to pay $35 and up for a dinner for two, and under $30 in inexpensive. Drinks and tips are not included. All telephone numbers are in the 808 area code unless otherwise indicated.

Black Sands – A typical range of steaks and fish highlights the menu for both lunch from 10:30 AM to 2 PM, and dinner from 5:30 to 8:30 PM. Open daily. Dinner reservations advised. A lagoonside setting and proximity to Punaluu Black Sand Beach provide appeal (phone: 928-8528). Moderate.

Kilauea Lodge – This is the place to head for dinner if you're near the national park between 5:30 and 9 PM. The dining room, with its commanding fireplace and rustic mood sets the tone. Seafood Mauna Kea and chicken Albert are among the specialties. Open daily for dinner only. Reservations advised. Old Volcano Rd. (phone: 967-7366). Moderate.

Ka Ohelo Room – The *Volcano House* has a simple dining room, with tables set with warm, deep yellow linen and candles. Dinner is usually a bit more complex than the luncheon smorgasbord: The menu includes the usual Hawaiian chicken, and the prime ribs are quite good. There's also a very reasonably priced all-you-can-eat soup and salad bar. Open daily, by reservation only. Last seating at 8 PM. *Volcano House* (phone 967-7321). Moderate to inexpensive.

Sea Mountain Broiler – The resort's golf clubhouse serves breakfast from 7:30 to 10:30 AM, and lunch from 11 AM to 2:30 PM. Reservations unnecessary. It's a good choice for a midday stop on a day trip between Hilo and Kona (phone: 928-6222). Moderate to inexpensive.

Santangelo's Pizza – The best place to stop between Hawaii Volcanoes National Park and Kona for a gooey, savory slice. Open daily. Reservations unnecessary. In Oceanview (phone: 929-9677). Inexpensive.

Volcano Store Diner – Breakfast starts the day at 8 AM, with snack-bar hamburgers and sandwiches plus lunch plate specials available until 5 PM. Open daily. On Old Volcano Hwy., attached to the *Volcano Store* (phone: 967-7707). Inexpensive.

MAUI

No one spends much time on Hawaii's second-largest and third most populated island before discovering that its residents consider themselves tops in any contest. *Maui no ka oi,* the local saying goes — Maui is the best — and they can tick off some facts to prove it. Maui is the fastest-growing island in the Hawaiian chain. Its population has increased over the years to over 100,000, and it follows Oahu (Honolulu) as the most popular tourist destination of all the neighbor islands, playing host to 2 million visitors annually. This is the place where the well-heeled want to be — Maui has more millionaires per capita than either Palm Springs or the French Riviera. Obviously, *Maui no ka oi* is no mere expression of diehard chauvinism. There must be something to it.

One reason for its popularity is Maui's topography, which accounts for scenery so beautiful that the Polynesian demigod Maui — who is credited with having fished all of the Hawaiian islands up from the sea — is thought to have called this one home. Geologists have their own version of events, however. The 729-square-mile island is actually formed by two massive volcanoes. West Maui, with its 5,788-foot summit, Puu Kukui, was the first to form, and because of this, the West Maui mountains are more deeply eroded and more rugged than East Maui, scarred with age and all but impenetrable. By comparison, the younger and larger East Maui looks almost wrinkle-free from a distance, its broad-based height often camouflaged by a cover of cloud. But appearances are deceiving, because East Maui is the massive 10,023-foot volcano Haleakala, whose crater is the centerpiece of a national park. Haleakala is now dormant, but while it was still growing, enough lava washed down its slopes to back up at the base of West Maui and form a central isthmus, which joined the two. According to one explanation, Maui's sobriquet, the Valley Isle, comes from this central valley, which is now mostly covered with fields of sugarcane bending in the wind.

Just where Maui chose to rise from the ocean floor also contributes to its beauty. Visitors to West Maui find the stunning presence of the West Maui mountains — their lower reaches swathed in more fields of bright or pale green sugarcane, their higher elevations twisting to gray-green peaks that lose themselves in smoky clouds — an unforgettable backdrop to their days. But the views in the other direction — of Molokai, Lanai, and Kahoolawe looming so close offshore at times, their medley of greens turned to blues that mimic the intervening sea — are equally heart-stopping images. Drive the length of Maui's western coast from the top of West Maui, where ribbons of red dirt thread through neat, frosty green plantations of pineapple, to the end of the road on East Maui, and the view of an island in the distance is almost always with you, the next one gathering substance as the first one disappears. If the demigod Maui did fish them from the sea, it was only yesterday, because the colors are as fresh and clean as wet paint.

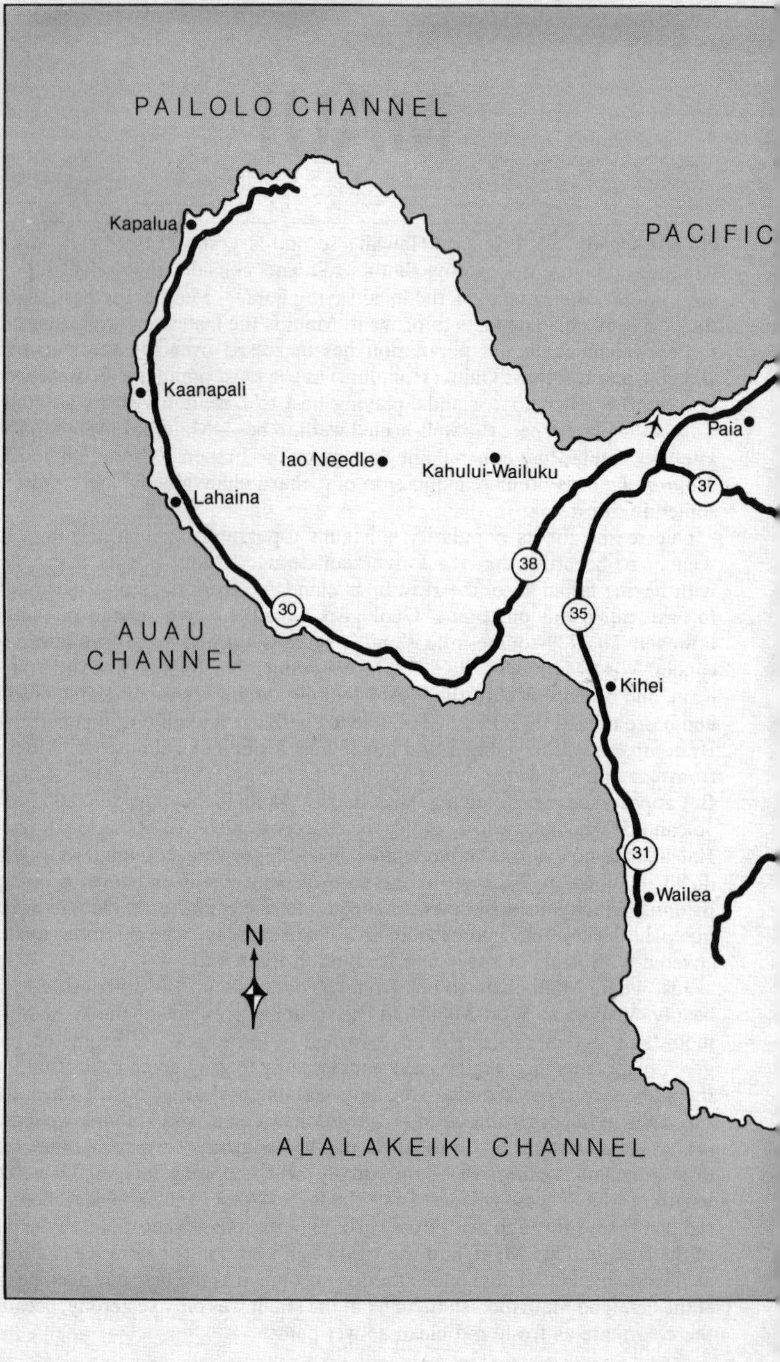
PAILOLO CHANNEL
PACIFIC
Kapalua
Kaanapali
Iao Needle
Kahului-Wailuku
Paia
Lahaina
37
38
30
35
AUAU
CHANNEL
Kihei
31
Wailea
N
ALALAKEIKI CHANNEL

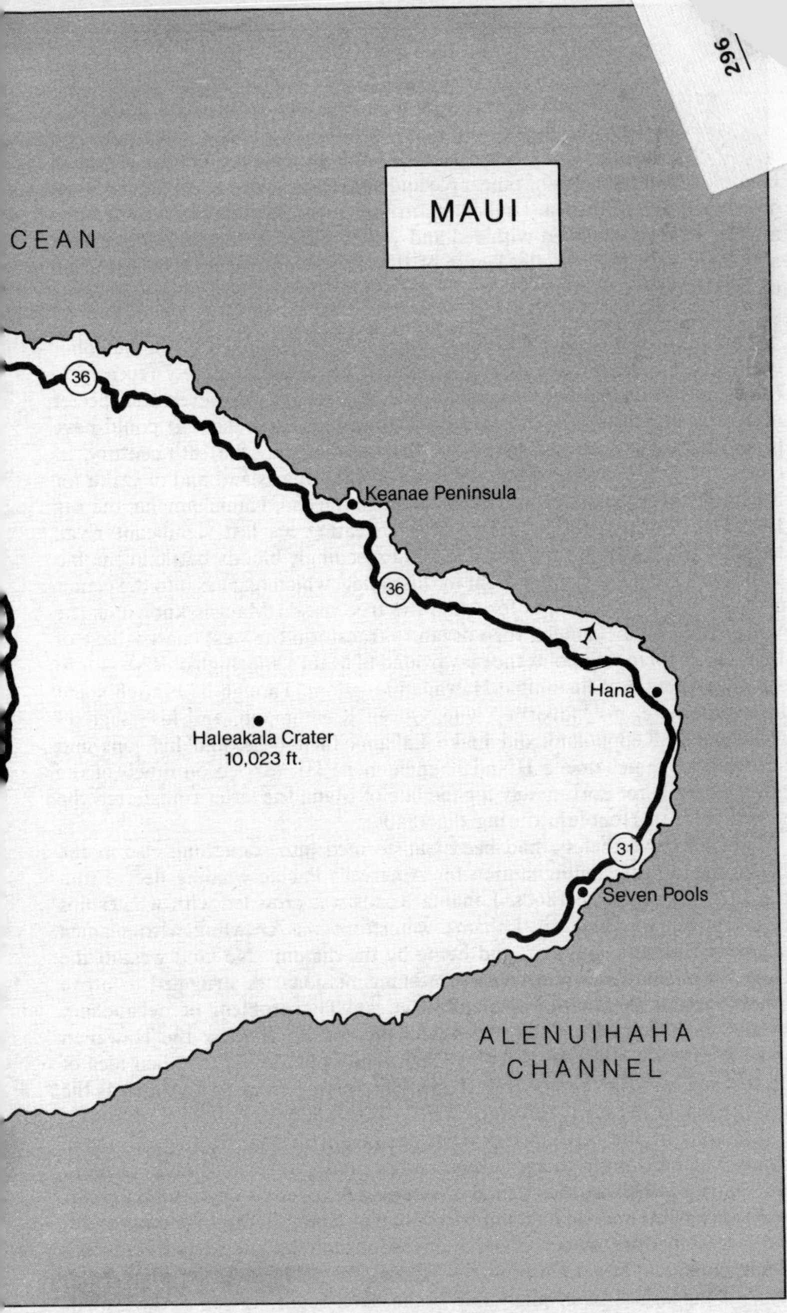
MAUI
CEAN
36
Keanae Peninsula
36
Hana
Haleakala Crater
10,023 ft.
31
Seven Pools
ALENUIHAHA
CHANNEL

Other colors accent the basic blue-green scheme — frothy white on the crest of a wave and bleached gold in strips and scallops at the edge of the water; hot, tropical reds of anthuriums in a garden or of royal poincianas lining a driveway; the pink, yellow, and white of plumeria. Sometimes the accents are surprising, as when the air cools up-country on the slopes of Haleakala and the fields of pineapple and sugarcane give way to flower farms of carnations and protea. Higher up, in the crater, the colors are ashen and muddy, at most streaked with red and yellow mineral tints and dotted here and there with the metallic leaves of the silversword plant. It is not at all unusual to see a rainbow on Maui, as though Mother Nature were keeping the palette always close at hand.

That all of this beauty still exists on the most developed of the neighbor islands is due to the fact that development has come relatively recently to Maui, most of it in an environmentally conscious age. However, the specter of overdevelopment is very much on Maui minds these days. It could have been otherwise. Maui was the island "between" during the 18th century, its chiefs at war nearly constantly with those of the Big Island and of Oahu for hegemony over the entire inhabited chain. In the end, Kamehameha, the Big Island chief, emerged the victor after defeating his last significant rival, Maui's chief Kahekili, in a decisive and exceedingly bloody battle in the Iao Valley in 1790. (The pivotal event in this valley, which reaches into the center of West Maui's volcano, is for some the true reason Maui is known as the Valley Isle.) Kamehameha then began to transform the west coast village of Lahaina — up to that point the playground of Maui's *alii* (high chiefs) — into a political center of his united Hawaiian kingdom. Though he himself spent little time here, his "favorite" wife, Queen Kaahumanu, and his "sacred" wife, Queen Keopuolani, did make Lahaina their base, and his sons and successors, Kamehameha II and Kamehameha III, carried on much of the government here. Fortunately for the fate of Maui, the latter transferred the government to Honolulu during the 1840s.

Lahaina, nevertheless, had been transformed into something else in the meantime: a provisioning station for America's Pacific whaling fleet. From the 1820s through the 1860s, Lahaina Roads was crowded with whaleships riding at anchor, and the Lahaina waterfront was crawling with seamen aflame with liquor and lust, and living by the dictum "No God west of the Horn." Lahaina's newly arrived Protestant missionaries struggled to prove otherwise and met with reasonable success. The problem of debauchery shrank to manageable proportions with the end of whaling; the Hawaiian royal family not only converted to Christianity but also to the alien idea of democracy, and the missionaries themselves, having come to do right, as the saying goes in Hawaii, "did right well" — especially in temporal matters.

The sons of the missionaries were prominent in Maui's next economic phase, which belonged to agriculture and primarily to sugar. Two in particular, Henry P. Baldwin and Samuel T. Alexander, founded a dynasty on sugar, and today Alexander & Baldwin Inc. is one of Hawaii's Big Five companies, the largest private owner of land on Maui, and its subsidiary Hawaiian Commercial and Sugar Company — whose cane fields cover the central valley — is the largest sugar plantation in the state. Sugar, as well as the growth of the pineapple industry and cattle ranching, provoked a drastic change in the makeup of Maui's population. More labor was needed than the island's declining indigenous population could provide, so during the last quarter of the 19th century, Chinese, Japanese, and Portuguese workers were brought in, followed by great numbers of Filipinos in the 20th century. Along with the native Hawaiians and the early New Englanders, all of these ethnic groups are honored in a tribute to the island's melting pot, the Kepaniwai Park and Heritage Gardens in the Iao Valley.

Maui's resort boom began 3 decades ago when Amfac, the biggest of the Big Five firms, opened the first of the super developments, the *Kaanapali* resort, on the coast of West Maui a few miles from Lahaina. Hotels, condominiums, and facilities for every conceivable kind of vacation activity materialized on land that was (but isn't much any longer) bordered by photogenic cane fields that had become only marginally productive. With the 1970s came two more planned resorts: Kapalua, surrounded by the pineapple fields of the Maui Land and Pineapple Company on the northwest corner of West Maui, and Wailea, an Alexander & Baldwin project that turned a wasteland of kiawe trees on the coast of East Maui golf-course green. The *Makena* resort, adjacent to Wailea, followed in the 1980s. Condominiums have sprung up chockablock along the coast of Kihei, northwest of Wailea, and also along the coast north of Kaanapali, through Honokowai and Kahana to Napili. And old Lahaina, whose population has doubled since 1980, is in its third incarnation as the island's major tourist attraction.

Regrettably, the early 1990s are seeing even more resort expansion, starting with new condominiums in Kihei and West Maui, and the opening of the all-suites *Kea Lani* hotel at Wailea, the new *Grand Hyatt,* the *Four Seasons Wailea,* and the *Ritz-Carlton* at Kapalua. For veteran Maui visitors, there is no joy in seeing construction cranes replace cane fields as the dominant sight on the landscape. Royal Hawaii is nearly a century past, and the only whaleboats nowadays are the ones filled with tourists out for a closer look at the humpbacks who make the waters off Maui their winter home. It's getting ever more difficult to find Hawaii on Maui.

Tourism now employs more than 50% of Maui's wage earners, few of whom can afford to buy a prime coastal condominium, but most of whom still greet visitors with the authentic welcome that demonstrates the spirit of aloha is still alive. Many deplore the changes of the last 25 years, and point with regret to the disappearance of old Hawaii as it once existed. On Maui, it now endures only in the quiet East Maui ranching district of Hana, which has few tourist facilities and is reachable only by determined driving along the most taxing paved road on the island.

But despite the rapidly encroaching presence of hotels and shopping malls, most visitors will concede that there is still some magic left in such unforgettable experiences as a Valley Isle sunset, witnessed from the privacy and comfort of one's own ocean-view lanai. As white clouds with silver linings turn to gray clouds outlined in pink, becoming formations as palpable as the neighboring islands in the sea, and as the ripples on the slate surface of the water shimmer behind the profiles of palm trees, you, too, may agree that *Maui no ka oi* — Maui is the best.

SOURCES AND RESOURCES

TOURIST INFORMATION: The first source of information most visitors encounter is the attendant at the State Visitor Information kiosk (phone: 877-6431) in Kahului Airport. Run by the State Department of Transportation and stocked with brochures on activities, sights, and hotel and condominium accommodations, the kiosk is open daily from 6 AM to 9 PM. A bit farther off the path beaten by newly arrived travelers is the Maui Visitors Bureau, which functions as a branch of the Hawaii Visitors Bureau. The office (111 Hana Hwy., Suite 112, Kahului, HI; phone: 871-8691) is open from 8 AM to 4:30 PM, Mondays through Fridays (usually closed for lunch from noon to 1 PM). Prospective visitors who need help with particularly problematical requests would do best to write ahead (mailing address: PO Box 1738, Kahului, Maui, HI 96732), but those on the spot are welcome to call (phone: 871-8691) or to drop in for assistance and brochures on everything from car rentals to windsurfing.

Bed & Breakfast Hawaii (PO Box 449, Kapaa, HI 96746; phone: 822-7771; 800-367-8047, ext. 339) provides information about bed and breakfast establishments on Maui and the other Hawaiian islands. Individual bed and breakfast lodging reservations are also taken by Jody Baldwin, who operates a lovingly restored 60-year-old home called *Kilohana* in up-country Kula (378 Kamehameiki Rd., Kula, Maui, HI 96790; phone: 878-6086). Natalie Powell runs an establishment that serves a full breakfast in rural Ulumalu (455 Kapuai Rd., Haiku, Maui, HI 96708; phone: 572-7692), and Carol Austin operates an attractive bed and breakfast establishment called *Halemanu* in up-country Kula which offers spectacular panoramic views (221 Kawehi Rd., Kula, HI 96790; phone: 878-2729). Frederick J. Fox, Jr., operates *Haikuleana,* near Hookipa, a top windsurfing spot (69 Haiku Rd., Haiku, Maui, HI 96708; phone: 575-2890).

To check out just about anything that's bookable on Maui, drop by Tom Barefoot's *Cashback Tours* (834 Front St., Lahaina; phone: 661-8889). Tom has created an informative circular file system that helps visitors make educated choices from among helicopter tours, snorkeling trips, and other, more offbeat, excursions. All reservations earn a 10% discount off published rates. In East Maui, check with *Kukui Activities Center* (phone: 875-1151) for bookings.

Local Coverage – The local newspaper, the *Maui News* (35¢), is published daily except Sunday. It's the place to find out what Maui is really talking about — local news, sports, weather, plus the tally of births, deaths, marriages, divorces, and building permits.

The island is also well supplied with free publications written with the tourist in mind. These can be found at the airport, in hotel and condominium lobbies, at shopping centers, on car rental counters, and anywhere else the distributor suspects the wandering eye of the tourist might alight. The most prominent are the weekly *Gold Coast, This Week Maui, Guide to Maui,* and the quarterly *Maui Gold.* All of them contain maps, tips on sightseeing, shopping, dining, and entertainment, and a number of coupons for discounts on goods and services. Similarly, the *Maui Drive Guide,* revised four times a year and distributed free to anyone who rents a car on the island, contains most of the above information along with more specific maps and instructions for drivers. Many hotels also distribute informative pocket-size *ResortGuides* to Kaanapali, Lahaina, and Wailea-Kihei. In addition, the weekly *Maui Bulletin* gives full listings of services and events, and is as informative for residents as it is for visitors.

For guidebooks, picture books, books on Hawaiian flora and fauna, crafts, food, history, legend, and the language, consult the Hawaiiana sections of the island's bookstores. Branches of *Waldenbooks* at the *Whalers Village* shopping complex in the *Kaanapali* resort, the *Kukui Mall* in Kihei, and at the *Maui Mall* in Kahului also have broad selections. Robert Wenkam's lusciously illustrated coffee-table book *Maui No Ka Oi* (Rand McNally; $29.95) can be bought here. The text deals with Maui and the other islands of Maui County — Molokai, Lanai, and Kahoolawe — and combines history, anecdote, and personal observation by someone who has been writing about Maui for 40 years. Other coffee-table tomes well worth considering are Rita Ariyoshi's profusely photographed, award-winning *Maui on My Mind* (Mutual Publishing; $35), and the latest elegant edition of *Under a Maui Sun* (Island Heritage; $29.95).

TELEPHONE: The area code for Hawaii is 808.

GETTING AROUND: Maui has very little in the way of public transportation, so you will have to arrange wheels, wings, or something waterborne yourself. If you arrive on the island by air, you'll land at one of Maui's three commercial airports. Kahului Airport (phone: 872-3830) is the main airfield. It is served by *Aloha Airlines, Hawaiian Airlines, Aloha IslandAir* (a sister company to *Aloha Airlines)*, and *Air Molokai.* Smaller planes provide good flightseeing opportunities en route. *American, Delta, Hawaiian,* and *United* also fly to Maui from the mainland. *Aloha IslandAir* and *Hawaiian Air* serve Kapalua/West Maui Airport (phone: 669-4866), located between the Kapalua and Kaanapali resorts. For those bound for either resort or for Kahana or Napili, this airport provides a logical — not to mention beautiful — alternative to busy Kahului. Hana Airport (phone: 248-8208), a tiny terminal outside Hana in East Maui, is served by *Aloha IslandAir.*

Bus – *Trans Hawaiian Services* (phone: 877-7308) runs shuttles from the airport to Lahaina and Kaanapali daily from 7 AM to 6 PM. The one-way fare is $13, and advance reservations are advised. The *Kaanapali Trolley,* looking like an old-fashioned, green, two-car trolley, runs through the *Kaanapali* resort daily from 7 AM to 11 PM, making stops at hotels, condominiums, the *Whalers Village* shopping complex, the golf clubhouse, and the Kaanapali station of the *Lahaina-Kaanapali and Pacific Railroad.* From 9 AM to 5 PM, the trolley offers free links between the resort and Lahaina. In addition, the trolley meets flights into and out of the Kapalua/West Maui Airport. In the *Wailea* resort area, the complimentary Wailea shuttle links hotels, condominiums, the shopping village, and sports facilities, making the rounds every 15 to 20 minutes from 6:45 AM to 10 PM. Kapalua's shuttle does not have a regular schedule, but is on call between 6 AM and midnight and upon request provides free transportation between hotels and the Kapalua/West Maui Airport. *Akina Aloha Tours* (phone: 879-2828) provides airport shuttle service daily from 8 AM to 6:30 PM. The charge is $10 one way, and advance reservations are required.

Taxi/Limousine – One of Maui's several cab companies, *Yellow Cab of Maui* (phone: 877-7000), is conveniently stationed at Kahului Airport. If your hotel is not taking care of your transfer from the airport, and if you are not renting a car, expect the fare from Kahului to a Lahaina or Kaanapali hotel to be about $40 to $50 per car (up to six people) and to an address in Kihei, Wailea, or Makena to be between $15 and $37. Once you've settled in, either consult the phone book or have your hotel call you a cab. Most taxi companies provide private sightseeing tours as well as regular service. *Alii Taxi Tours* (phone: 661-3688) provides customized limousine tours of Maui from Napili.

Car Rental – The rental counters of almost a dozen companies are in a line just outside the terminal of Kahului Airport. These include large national companies such as *Alamo* (phone: 871-6235), *Avis* (phone: 871-7575), *Budget* (phone: 871-8811), *Hertz* (phone: 877-5167), and *National* (phone: 871-8851); statewide or regional companies such as *Dollar Rent-A-Car* (phone: 877-2731), *Rainbow Rent-A-Car* (phone: 661-8734), and *Tropical Rent-A-Car* (phone: 877-0002); plus some smaller companies such as *Andres* (phone: 877-5378), *Sunshine* (phone: 871-6222), and *Kihei Rent A Car* (phone: 879-7257). Bargain basement companies — *Klunker's* (phone: 877-3197) and *Word of Mouth Rent-A-Used-Car* (phone: 877-2436), for instance — cluster in the Dairy Road–Puunene Avenue area. Still more names can be found in Lahaina and Kihei. Several companies also have rental booths at Kapalua/West Maui Airport, or they will pick up customers at the airport for a short transfer to rental outlets. These include *Avis* (phone: 661-4588), *Budget* (phone: 661-8721), *Dollar* (phone: 667-2651), *Hertz* (phone: 669-9042), *Sunrise* (phone: 661-5646), and *Tropical* (phone: 661-0061). During the peak winter and summer seasons, cars may be in short supply, so it is advisable to make a reservation. During the rest of the year, special rates are often offered on a day-to-day availability basis. Hana Airport rentals are available through *Dollar* (phone: 248-8237) at the *Hana-Maui* hotel (phone: 248-8211). In fact, most hotels and many condos on Maui have car rental desks in their lobbies for those who decide, after arrival, that they would like to have a car. (For the toll-free numbers of many of the above car rental firms, see *Touring by Car,* GETTING READY TO GO).

With the exception of portions of the Hana Highway and the road between Hana and Ulupalakua, tourist attractions themselves, the roads that visitors will encounter on Maui are well paved. The island map in the *Maui Drive Guide* (free to anyone renting a car) shows those that are not and are, therefore, off limits to rental car drivers. For those with some off-road driving in mind, four-wheel-drive vehicles are available from *Adventures Rent A Jeep* (phone: 877-6626) and *Kihei Rent A Car* (phone: 879-7257), as well as from *Budget, Hertz,* and *Rainbow*. Again, reserve well in advance, and be sure that the vehicle you get is indeed of the four-wheel-drive variety rather than two-wheel, and that off-road excursions are permitted.

Bicycle Rental – *Kukui Activities Center* (phone: 875-1151) rents bicycles for $14 a day or $65 a week. *Fun Bike Rentals* (193 Lahainaluna Rd.; phone: 661-3053) provides West Maui pick-up service. A paved bike path leads from Lahaina to the *Kaanapali* resort and on to Kapalua, but other parts of the island can present difficulties. High-speed winds in the central valley, for instance, make the going exceedingly rough for bikers. The roads that lead to the up-country offer excellent downhill runs. *Chris' Bike Adventures* (phone: 877-8000) features rentals as well as a series of escorted bike tours and bike-and-boat combination packages.

SIGHTSEEING TOURS: Bus or Van – Nearly all hotels and many condominiums have tour desks that will book guests on escorted sightseeing tours around the island. In case yours doesn't, contact one of the major tour companies — *Gray Line Maui* (phone: 877-5507), *Robert's Hawaii Tours* (phone: 871-6226), or *Trans Hawaiian Maui* (phone: 877-7308) — and count on spending anywhere from $20 to $50 per person for a 5- to 10-hour outing, which may or may not include meals. Standard half-day and full-day itineraries visit Kula, Haleakala Crater, Wailuku, Iao Valley, and Lahaina in various combinations, whereas the drive to Hana is always a full day in length. *Ekahi Tours* (phone: 572-9775) offers daily van tours to Hana for $70, including hotel/condo pickups in West or East Maui. Departures are between 7 and 8 AM, with a return via Kipahulu and the southeastern Maui coast, weather permitting. *Aloha Nui Loa Tours* (phone: 669-0000; 800-525-HANA) also offers a Hana van tour for $72 that includes a hotel/condo pickup, continental breakfast, lunch, and a round trip along the Hana Highway. *Trans Hawaiian* features a full-day tour of Hana in 11- or 14-passenger vans. Their Haleakala Sunrise tour makes a breakfast stop at scenic *Kula Lodge*. *Temptation Tours* (phone: 878-2911) offers

Haleakala and Hana itineraries in plushly outfitted vans limited to 6 passengers. *Local Guides of Maui* (phone: 877-4042; 800-228-6284) provide guides who accompany rental car visitors for up to 8 hours ($175). *Best of Maui* (phone: 871-1555) offers guided cassette tours (tapes and players included) for $25 a day from a kiosk located at 333 Dairy Road (Kahului), about 1 mile from Kahului Airport.

Helicopter/Plane – This is hardly inexpensive but it's the only way to penetrate many of the valleys of the Valley Isle to see them in all their otherwise hidden splendor. The most popular rides fly through Haleakala Crater, out to Hana, and over the Seven Pools in East Maui, or along the West Maui coast and beyond the barrier of the West Maui mountains. Costs for a 30-minute to 1½-hour flight range anywhere from $75 to $275 per person. Maui's largest helicopter-tour company, *Papillon Helicopters* (phone: 669-4884; 800-367-7095), operates a variety of tours departing from a heliport adjacent to Kahului Airport, including a West Maui/East Molokai combination aerial tour. *Papillon* also offers All-Day Hana, an excursion that includes lunch at the *Hana Ranch* and 5 hours with a rental jeep for $350. *Sunshine Helicopters* (phone: 871-0722) departs Kahului Airport for tours that run 30 to 70 minutes and start at $79. *Alex Air* (phone: 871-0192) offers a 20-minute introductory tour ($49), as well as a variety of tour itineraries, and *Blue Hawaiian* (phone: 871-8844) and *Hawaii Helicopters* (phone: 877-3900) are still other options. *Biplane Barnstormers* (phone: 878-2860) departs Kahului on open-cockpit aerial tours aboard a two-passenger makeover of a 1935 biplane. Tours run 30 to 90 minutes and cost $75 to $160 per passenger. Even more adventurous souls can try a single-passenger flight that includes a half hour of thrilling aerial aerobatics ($175). *American Pacific Air* (phone: 871-8115) offers tamer fixed-wing air tours of West Maui ($49) and Circle Island ($108).

Boat – Non-snorkelers can get a firsthand look at the fascinating underwater world through the viewing ports of the glass-bottom boat *Lin Wa* (phone: 661-3392). Done up to resemble a Chinese junk, the *Lin Wa* cruises out of Lahaina four times daily ($17.50), offering those aboard a chance to view plenty of coral. If the fish are shy, a scuba diver bearing edible gifts coaxes them into the range of vision. *Maui E-Ticket* (phone: 669-8000) also departs Lahaina on high-tech, glass-bottom boat tours for $40.

Cruises to the neighboring islands of Lanai or Molokai or both — usually costing about $60 to $90 per person for a full day out — are among the many other popular seagoing excursions from Lahaina Harbor. The Coon family of *Trilogy Excursions* (phone: 661-4743) sails to Lanai, Mondays through Fridays year-round, taking up to 40 people on the 52-foot *Trilogy I,* the 54-foot catamaran *Trilogy II,* and the 51-foot, 24-passenger *Trilogy III* for $139 per person. Breakfast is served; then there's time for snorkeling, swimming, a barbecue at Manele Bay, and a 1-hour van tour of the island before returning to Lahaina in the late afternoon. The 44-foot *Trimaran Trilogy IV* offers half-day snorkel trips to Molokini Island ($69), including continental breakfast and lunch. *Captain Zodiac* (phone: 667-5351) sails to Lanai aboard 14- and 15-passenger motorized rafts on half- ($53) and full-day ($98) tours. Both itineraries include snorkeling; full-day itineraries circle the island and land for lunch. The state-of-the-art ferry *Maui Princess* (phone: 661-8397) departs Lahaina for Molokai, where self-drive ($69) and escorted ground tours ($125) are available. Boats from the *Ocean Activities Center* (phone: 879-4485) depart Lahaina for Lanai on half-day ($60) snorkeling cruises off Lanai or Molokini picnic and snorkeling excursions aboard the *Manutea.* During winter months, they feature a 2-hour whale watching cruise for $35. These and other sails from Maui can also be booked through *Maui 800* in Kahului (phone: 877-2748; 800-367-5224). *John Keene* (phone: 874-3843) offers escorted half- and full-day kayak tours along the Maui coast. Snorkeling gear is provided.

The object of the snorkel sail is not to tour the neighbor islands, but to see their glorious coastlines — and Maui's — from the water, explore the underlying coral reefs, and swim, sun, or simply enjoy the sail itself. Molokini's popularity, unfortunately, has made a visit to this islet a crowded affair. For those craving peace and quiet, Molokini may prove something of a disappointment. The price tag can begin at $25 per person for 2 hours adrift and go up as high as $80 or $90 for a full day of sailing with a picnic lunch included. Sunset cruises, generally about 2 hours long, average $25 to $35 depending on whether the sun goes down to a cocktail toast alone or is memorialized with a full dinner. The 50-foot *Scotch Mist II* sloop carries $23 passengers on half-day snorkel sails and sunset sails from Lahaina Harbor and offers whale watching and moonlight sails from December through May (phone: 661-0386). A number of skippers do one or the other type of cruise aboard smaller boats taking no more than six people at a time. Among these boats are the 58-foot *Seasmoke*, which sails from Kaanapali Beach (phone *Captain Nemo's:* 661-5555), and the *Alihilani Yacht Charters' Makani Wiki* (phone: 871-1156), which sails out of Lahaina Harbor. Farther up the coast, at Kaanapali, *Sea Sails* (phone: 661-5244) departs from its beach shacks at the *Sheraton Maui,* the *Royal Lahaina,* the *Westin Maui,* the *Kaanapali Beach* hotels, and the *Kaanapali Shores* and *Sands of Kahana* condominiums for picnic/snorkel sails to Honolua Bay and sunset cocktail sails. In addition, the *Hyatt Regency* (phone: 661-1234) has its own catamaran, the *Kiele V,* and offers snorkel as well as sunset cocktail sails ($35 to $65). Catamarans also depart from the beach at the *Kapalua Bay* hotel (phone: 669-5656) on picnic and sunset cocktail sails.

The Kihei-Wailea coast of East Maui doesn't offer quite the number or variety of cruises for visitors as the West Maui coast, but some eye-filling adventures are possible here, too. The crescent-shaped volcanic islet of Molokini, lying offshore between Maui and the island of Kahoolawe, is a marine conservation district famed for clear waters and a multitude of fish and corals, and is a favorite destination of picnic and snorkel sails. The *Maui Sailing Center* (phone: 879-5935) has two snorkel sails daily to Molokini aboard boats departing from Maalaea Harbor. The *Pacific Whale Foundation* (phone: 879-8811; 800-WHALE-11) can take up to 49 passengers aboard the 53-foot cruiser *Whale I,* which makes a daily half-day Molokini snorkel trip from Maalaea Harbor from 7 to 11 AM, and includes continental breakfast, a *pupu* lunch, and snorkel gear for $40. The *Ocean Activities Center* (phone: 879-4485) — with a store at the *Wailea Shopping Village* and offices at the *Cannery* in Lahaina, the *Kamaole Shopping Center,* the *Mana Kai Maui,* and the *Stouffer Wailea Beach* hotels — operates the 65-foot catamarans *Wailea Kai* and *Maka Kai,* which can take 75 to 100 passengers on half-day picnic and snorkel sails departing daily from Maalaea Harbor. (The *Wailea Kai* takes snorkelers on its Molokini sails; for more on snorkel/scuba trips, see *Sports.*) Sunset cocktail cruises are also popular on this coast; the *Wailea Kai* does one out of Maalaea Harbor. The *Maui Prince* hotel (phone: 874-1111) operates a half-day catamaran sail to Molokini ($65) that features on-board continental breakfast, lunch, and an open bar. The *Four Seasons* and the *Grand Hyatt* jointly operate a 60-foot catamaran, the *Alii Nui,* for morning sails, 6:45 AM to 1:30 PM, including breakfast and a light lunch for $80 (phone: 874-8000).

Most of the above excursions are offered year-round, but in the winter a new twist appears. From December through April, many a picnic/snorkel sail turns into a whale watch — in fact, it almost seems, during this time, that a cruise by any other name does not exist. The most informative whale watches by far are the 2½-hour cruises ($30) sponsored by the *Pacific Whale Foundation* (Kealia Beach Plaza, 101 N. Kihei Rd., Suite 25, Kihei, Maui, HI 96753; phone: 879-8811; 800-WHALE-11), a nonprofit research, conservation, and education organization. Conducted by foundation experts aboard *Whale I,* a 53-foot power cruiser, they depart Maalaea Harbor daily at 1:30 and 4:15 PM during the season (tickets are available through the *PWF* and other vendors). The *Pacific Whale Foundation* also departs Slip II in Lahaina Harbor for whale watching cruises at 7:30 and 10:30 AM, and at 1:30 and 4:15 PM. If missed, the only recourse is to watch for the whale lecture on your hotel's activities board (*PWF* lecturers make the rounds of Maui hotels and some condominiums, appearing in major ones regularly) and then take a commercial whale watching cruise. Though not specialists in whale lore, *Windjammer Maui* (phone: 661-8600), *Scotch Mist* (phone: 661-0386), and others also do whale watches. The cruises depart from Lahaina (not necessarily every day), take 2½ hours, and cost $25 to $30 for adults (children under 12, half price). The *Ocean Activities Center,* in the *Lahaina Shopping Center* (phone: 879-4485), and *Maui Classic Charters* (phone: 879-8188) run whale watches out of Maalaea Harbor for $25 and $39. *Atlantis Submarines* (phone: 667-2224) offers hourly dives departing Lahaina's *Pioneer Inn* that descend 150 feet for fascinating underwater views of offshore reefs, as does the 34-passenger *Nautilus Submarine* (phone: 667-7647).

Train – The *Lahaina-Kaanapali and Pacific Railroad* (phone: 661-0089; 800-367-4753) operates the *Sugarcane Train* between Lahaina and Kaanapali six times daily. Round trip is 12 miles and takes about an hour; fare is $10 for adults, $5 one way (half price for children under 12; children under 3, free). Various excursions can be purchased together with the train ride (see *Kaanapali to Kapalua*).

SPECIAL EVENTS: During February and March, the *Maui Marine Art Expo,* at the *Stouffer Wailea Beach* resort, presents the work of numerous prominent artists in a variety of media, all with a marine theme. Runners may watch or participate in the *Maui Marathon,* which begins in Wailuku and ends in Lahaina, and is usually scheduled for early March. In late March the *Miss Maui Pageant* is sponsored by the Jaycees in the *Baldwin Auditorium,* Wailuku. The *Marui–O'Neil Invitational Windsurfing Competition* takes place at Hookipa Park in early April; the Sunday on or before *May Day* is the date for an island-wide lei competition at the *Maui Inter-Continental.* On June 11, Maui participates in the statewide celebration of *King Kamehameha Day* with a parade of floats and marching bands in either Lahaina or Kahului. *Paniolos* (Hawaiian cowboys) compete at calf-roping, bronco-busting, and steer-wrestling in an old-fashioned *Rodeo* held at *Oskie Rice Arena* in the up-country town of Makawao over *July Fourth.* In mid-July, the Jaycees sponsor their *Carnival* at the *Kahului Fairgrounds;* and in August runners compete in the *Run-to-the-Sun Marathon,* an exhausting 37½-mile race from Kanaha Beach Park to the summit of Haleakala.

Aloha Week — that statewide festival of parades, pageants, luaus, dances, crafts demonstrations, canoe races, and sports competitions — takes place on Maui during September or October. The *County Fair,* held in October, has the standard flower and produce displays, arts and crafts exhibits, and livestock shows. Late October–early November sees the *Aloha Classic Windsurfing Championships* at Hookipa Park, as well as fishermen from all across the islands participating in the *Annual Lahaina Jackpot Fishing Tournament,* headquartered in Lahaina's historic waterfront hostelry, the *Pioneer Inn,* offering a tempting purse for the heaviest marlin. Lahaina takes *Halloween* very seriously — expect shop clerks, waiters, and waitresses to be wearing something outlandish. And Kaanapali is the center of Maui's own festival, *Na Mele O Maui,* a potpourri of Hawaiian arts and crafts, music, and dance, and the high point of early November. The PGA-coordinated *Isuzu Kapalua International,* in November, is a highlight of Maui's annual series of golf tournaments. And November or December sees the *Michelob Polo Competition* at Makawao.

SPORTS: Since sunshine, sand, and the sea lure most visitors to this as well as to the other islands, it's only natural that much of Maui's active sports life takes place on the shore and in the water. Tennis is also a big draw, and golf courses actually preceded many of the major resort hotels. The following is a rundown of these and other possibilities:

Bicycling – The 38-mile road that winds its way from the 10,023-foot summit of

Haleakala to the coast (at Paia) provides cyclists with a half-day escorted excursion. Three firms operate bicycle tours on fully equipped mountain bikes. *Haleakala Downhill* (505 Front St., Lahaina; call "Cruiser Bob" at 667-7717; 800-654-7717) offers a sunrise ride that includes breakfast at *Kula Lodge,* a midday run, and an afternoon ride that includes dinner in Paia for $99. *Maui Mountain Cruisers* (353 Hanamau St., Kahawi, HI 96732; phone: 572-0195) and *Maui Downhill* (199 Dairy Rd., Kahului; phone: 871-2155) charge $96 and $99, respectively. Hotel or condo pickup is included, as is continental breakfast.

Visitors should be aware that the death of a cyclist — she lost control of her bicycle and crashed into an oncoming van — has stimulated considerable criticism of these downhill tours. Serious caution should be exerted when bicycling, and cyclers should be sure to use all of the proper equipment, such as protective helmets.

Boating – The vast majority of boats bobbing up and down in Lahaina Harbor and elsewhere around Maui are dedicated to picnic/snorkel sails, sunset cocktail trips, sightseeing cruises, whale watching expeditions, and other seagoing excursions in which you'll be a passenger. These are discussed in *Sightseeing Tours (Boat). Seabern Yachts* (PO Box 1022, Lahaina, Maui, HI 96761; phone: 661-8110), at Berth 64 in Lahaina Harbor, has two sailboats that can be rented, either on a sharing basis or for private, skippered charters by the hour. Each boat measures 42 feet, and share-boat or charter rates range from a 2-hour sunset sail ($35 share; $200 private charter) to $550 for a 6½-hour private excursion. Boats accommodate up to six people, sodas and snacks are included, and lunch is offered on full-day sails. *Island Sports Rentals* in Lahaina offers bareboat rentals, with 21-foot and 17-foot vessels for fishing, snorkeling, diving, and water skiing at rates that start at $89. *Sea Escape* (phone: 879-3721) rents twin 17½-horsepower and 25-horsepower boats in Kihei starting at $80 for 2 hours. Day rates are also available.

The *Maui Sailing Center* (Kealia Beach Village, 101 N. Kihei Rd.; phone: 879-5935) has boat rentals from Sugar Beach on Maalaea Bay. The center offers 16-foot catamarans for $40 for the first hour, $45 if an instructor is needed, and $35 per additional hour. Easy to sail 15-foot catamarans run $25 an hour. The center monitors its sailors, requiring them to stay in a designated sailing area on the bay, never more than 2 miles from shore, and it has a chase boat for emergencies. *West Maui Sailing* (phone: 667-5545) offers Hobie Cat rentals and lessons in the Kaanapali area.

Most hotels have a catamaran or two for rent. At the *Kaanapali Beach* hotel, *Sea Sails* (phone: 661-5244) rents 14-foot Hobie Cats at $35 for the first hour and $25 per hour thereafter, with lessons available for $10 an hour. The *Hyatt Regency* (phone: 661-1234) rents 16-foot Hobie Cats for $30 an hour.

Camping and Hiking – While Maui has numerous hiking trails of varying degrees of difficulty — among them, those at Honokowai Valley, Iao Valley, Kanaha Pond Wildlife Sanctuary, Keanae Arboretum, La Perouse Bay, Polipoli Springs State Park, Waikamoi Ridge, Waimoku Falls, and Waianapanapa State Park — the trails that lead into the floor of the Haleakala Crater, the island's dormant volcano, are unmatched in beauty and solitude. For overnighters, there are three cabins and two campgrounds within the crater, and another campground just inside the park entrance. More detailed descriptions of the two major trails into the crater, Halemauu and Sliding Sands, are given in the section of this chapter entitled *Haleakala National Park.*

Ken Schmidt of *Hike Maui* (PO Box 330969, Kahului, Maui, HI 96733; phone: 879-5270) guides a variety of day hikes to Maui's most scenic and interesting locales. Schmidt is well versed in Hawaiian flora, fauna, geology, and history, and his trips emphasize how best to relate to the environment. Day rates range from $60 to $100 and include lunch.

Fishing – The islands of Maui, Lanai, and Kahoolawe form a triangle that is brimful of fish waiting to be caught, and they'll put up enough of a fight to satisfy any sportsman. Fishing is a year-round activity, but the biggest prize, the Pacific blue marlin, which is generally caught off the southeast coast of Lanai, is most likely to be hooked in the fall. Other species to try for are ono (wahoo), caught throughout the year; mahimahi (dolphin fish), caught small in summer and larger in winter, and ahi (yellow-fin tuna), aku (skipjack tuna), and kawakawa (oceanic bonito or false albacore), all most abundant in summer. No license is required for saltwater fishing in the state of Hawaii.

Charter boats are as plentiful as a school of fish in Lahaina and also in Maalaea. They usually accommodate up to six people and are available on a private or share basis for a full 8-hour day or a 4-hour half day, sometimes for a 6-hour day. All gear is provided; however, you must bring your own food and refreshment. The average cost (you'll find them higher and lower) of a private charter on Maui is $450 to $500 for a full day and $350 for a half day, whereas the cost of a shared charter ranges from $100 to $125 per person for a full day and from $65 to $85 for a half day. If you're interested in sharing, most operations will organize a share boat for you if given a day or two notice in the winter, more time in the slower spring and fall seasons. If there are non-fishing members in your party, investigate the larger boats; some, while taking only six fishermen, are licensed to carry more than six passengers and will take them at half price. Remember that Hawaiian skippers keep costs down by selling the catch, so unless you come to some arrangement beforehand (they're usually very understanding about this), you'll be given only a few filets for your very own.

Among the charter captains and companies operating out of Lahaina, all available on a share or private basis for a full or half day, are *Aerial Sportfishing Charters* (phone: 667-9089), *Lahaina Charter Boats* (phone: 667-6672), *Luckey Strike Charters* (phone: 661-4606), and *Finest Kind Sportfishing* (phone: 661-0338). Outside Lahaina, contact the *Ocean Activities Center* (*Wailea Shopping Village;* phone: 879-4485), which operates the *No Ka Oi III* on fishing charters out of Maalaea Harbor.

Those interested in joining the fishermen seen along the beaches and rocky coasts of Maui should check the phone book for fishing supplies stores; the salespeople can usually be counted on for advice on how it's done in Hawaii, where to go, and what you might expect to catch.

Golf – It may be a challenge to keep your eye on the ball, because one thing almost all of Maui's golf courses have in common is the distractive power of their scenery.

At the *Kaanapali* resort, the *Royal Kaanapali* golf courses (phone: 661-3691) consist of two 18-hole championship courses, one of which, the *North* course, has been seen on TV in several tournaments, including a stop by the LPGA tour. Designed by Robert Trent Jones, Sr., the course begins close to the Pacific and climbs gently up the West Maui mountains, and from the upper holes, especially the 12th, the view of the neighboring islands of Lanai and Molokai is stunning. *Royal Kaanapali's South* course, designed by Arthur Jack Snyder, slopes mountainward more gently, encountering, along the 5th fairway, the route taken by tourists aboard the *Lahaina-Kaanapali and Pacific Railroad's Sugarcane Train.* Greens fees at either course are $90, which includes a cart. Clubs can be rented for $27. (A reduced twilight rate — $60 — goes into effect between 3 and 6:30 PM.)

At Kapalua, the *Kapalua Golf Club* (phone: 669-8044) offers a trio of spectacularly scenic 18-hole courses, including the recently completed *Plantation* course. Kapalua's newest challenge was designed by Ben Crenshaw and Bill Coore (7,100 yards, par 73), and it climbs high as it curves around streams in the bottom of small valleys and cuts through pineapple fields on West Maui's foothills.

The older and more relaxed of the three is the *Bay* course, designed by Arnold Palmer, with two holes — the 4th and the 5th — on a lava peninsula stretching dramatically into the surf-pounded blue sea. The *Village* course, designed by Palmer and Ed Seay, climbs 720 feet into the mountains, and it's rapidly gaining a reputation as one of the most demanding courses in Hawaii. The higher elevation also enhances the views, making vistas of pineapple fields, Cook and Norfolk Island pines, and the island of Molokai, across Pailolo Channel, quite simply matchless. Greens fees of $90 per player ($60 to *Kapalua* resort guests) include mandatory cart rental, and there is an afternoon rate (for play between 2 and 6:30 PM) of $50. Club rental is $25, and shoe rental is $10.

The two championship golf courses at the *Wailea Golf Club* (phone: 879-2966), called the *Blue* course and the *Orange* course, were both designed by Arthur Jack Snyder, and both are set on the lowest seaside slopes of Haleakala Volcano. Here again it's a case of the older (*Blue*) course being the more forgiving. On the *Orange* course, 4-foot-high lava rock walls, manmade but of unknown origin (they may be the remains of a 16th-century king's highway), run through the fairways — they lie along holes 5–10 and 13–18. Other distractions include *heiaus* (ancient temples), a natural rock garden, wiliwili trees, and views of the islands of Kahoolawe and Molokini. Prime time to play here is early morning, when the sun makes its dramatic entrance over Haleakala. Wailea became the new home for the *Kemper Open* on the ladies' pro tour in 1990. Greens fees for guests at the *Wailea* resort are $65; for the public the rates are $115. Club rental is $25; pro shop open daily. Maui's two newest golf courses, the *Valley* at the *Waikapu Valley Country Club* (18 holes, 7,105 yards, par 72) and the *Waikapu Sandalwood* (18 holes, 6,433 yards, par 72), are located on Route 30, adjacent to the Maui Tropical Plantation (just outside Wailuku). The Ted Robinson–designed *Valley* course (phone: 242-7090), while private, does permit play for guests at Wailea's *Four Seasons* and *Grand Hyatt* (both, along with the courses, are owned by the same Japanese developer). The *Sandalwood* course (phone: 244-7090), designed by the local firm of Nelson/Wright, is open to the public, and greens fees are $65, including cart. The course features lush green fairways on gently sloping terrain against a backdrop of 1,000 sandalwood trees. There is also a clubhouse, a restaurant, and a pro shop.

There are other courses to play on Maui. The *Makena* resort features the 18-hole *Makena* course (phone: 879-3344), across the road from the *Maui Prince* hotel, 2 miles south of Wailea. Designed by Robert Trent Jones, Jr., it, too, includes some ancient stone walls, though they don't come into play as they do at *Wailea.* Greens fees at *Makena* are $100 ($55 for guests), including a cart. (Another Robert Trent Jones, Jr.–designed 18-hole golf course is scheduled to open at press time.) The 18-hole *Silversword* course (1345 Piilani Hwy.; phone: 874-0777) charges a $60 greens fee that includes a cart, and offers a $40 twilight rate from 1:40 to 6:15 PM in summer. Clubs rent for $20. The course, on an often windy hillside overlooking Kihei, is a bit rough around the edges by Maui resort standards. The up-country location of the 18-hole course of the *Pukalani Country Club* (55 Pukalani St., Pukalani; phone: 572-1314) provides views from on high of the island's central valley with the ocean on both sides, of the back of the West Maui mountains, and up to Haleakala. Greens fees are a bit lower here ($30 for 9 holes; $55 for 18 holes, including a shared cart). Club rentals are $16. Charges are less at the *Waiehu* municipal golf course (off Hwy. 340, 5 miles north of Kahului; phone: 243-7400), 18 holes next to the ocean north of Kahului. Greens fees are $25. Cart rental (optional) is $14, clubs $12.50. The *Maui Country Club* (48 Nonohe Pl., Paia; phone: 877-0616) has a private (relatively unscenic) 9-hole course open to the public Mondays for $45 ($10 for clubs).

Hang Gliding – Hawaii's constant trade winds and mountains make for ideal hang gliding conditions. Kula-based *Maui Soaring Supplies* (RR 2, Box 780, Kula, HI 96790; phone: 878-1271) takes trained hang gliders on escorted glides and provides equipment.

Horseback Riding – Some of Maui's best scenery is beyond the paved highway, and a guided trail ride astride a four-legged mode of transportation isn't a bad way to see it. The cost is about $20 to $45 per person per hour, though longer excursions with extras such as a picnic lunch or dinner can cost more.

Rainbow Ranch (PO Box 10066, Lahaina, Maui, HI 96761; phone: 669-4991) offers mountain and plantation rides from stables situated between Kaanapali and Kapalua. For beginners to experienced riders, the 1- to 3½-hour rides cost from $30 to $80.

Two outfits in East Maui run day-long trail rides into Haleakala Crater. Tours include lunch, groups are limited to six people, and reservations should be made at least a week in advance. *Pony Express Tours* (PO Box 535, Kula, Maui, HI 96790; phone: 667-2200) charges $130 for a full-day tour, $110 for a half-day tour (both include lunch), as well as a 2-hour tour of Haleakala Ranch, across pastureland at a 4,000-foot elevation ($50). *Thompson Ranch* (RR 2, Box 203, Kula, Maui, HI 96790; phone: 878-1910) charges $150 for a tour of the crater, $200 on overnights. Less arduous 1½- and 2½-hour rides, with gentler up-country scenery, are also offered for $45 on the lower slopes of Haleakala at 3,200 feet. Two-hour private rides are $50 per person, and 1½-hour rides are $25. In Wailea/Makena, *Makena Stables* (7299 S. Makena Rd., Kihei, Maui, HI 96753; phone: 879-0244) offers up-country rides from $75 to $115 on Ulupalakua Ranch lands that include a 5½-hour ride to the Tedeschi Vineyards. There are also two sunset rides. From the Kaupo side, *Charley's Trail Rides and Pack Trips* (c/o *Kaupo Store,* Hana, Maui, HI 96713; phone: 248-8209) will take you into the crater on an overnight adventure that begins in the morning with an 8-hour trip up the Kaupo Valley and includes dinner, night lodgings in a National Park Service cabin or campground, with tents and sleeping bags provided, and a chance to see the sun set — as well as rise — over Haleakala. Rides for two to three people cost $200 per person per night, including food; for four to six, the cost is $150 with food. No treks offered on Sundays. Reservations a month in advance are advised. *Aloha Nui Loa Tours* (phone: 669-0000; 800-525-HANA) offers a combo van/horseback tour of Hana and the surrounding countryside. The $139 cost includes hotel/condo pickup and drop-off, continental breakfast, a picnic lunch, and a swim in an isolated waterfall-fed pool. For self-drive visitors to Hana, a 2-hour ride plus lunch costs $88.

In the Hana district, riding is also one of the major allures of the *Hana-Maui* hotel (phone: 248-8211), which has its own stables and organizes breakfast rides, cookout rides, sunrise rides, moonlight rides, and rides by the hour at varying prices (no rides on Sundays). Priority is given to hotel guests, but non-guests are welcome. *Adventures on Horseback* (PO Box 1771, Makawao, Maui, HI 96768; phone: 242-7445) features personalized 5½-hour excursions that depart from Halawa Bridge on the Hana Highway at 10 AM. Daily rides are limited to six participants, and include a waterfall swim and a picnic stop for $130.

Jet Skiing – On Kaanapali Beach, contact *Kaanapali Beach Jet Ski* (phone: 667-9740), which offers jet ski rentals (with lessons) for $45 per half hour, $65 per hour, and 2-passenger wave runners at $65 per hour. *Pacific Jet Ski* (phone: 667-2066) also offers jet ski rentals at $65 per hour with instruction.

Parasailing – *UFO Parasail* (phone: 661-7836) and *Parasail Kaanapali* (phone: 669-6555) offer instruction by the hour ($50). At press time, statewide implementation of thrill-craft regulations for jet skis and parasailing was being considered. The rules would allow parasailing only during the summer months, when whales are not swimming in Hawaiian offshore waters.

Snorkeling and Scuba Diving – The shores of the Valley Isle compare favorably with those of any of the other Hawaiian islands; in fact, they offer some of the best underwater sites in the state. In the vicinity of Lahaina, one of the spots favored by both divers and snorkelers is Cemetery, north of Wahikuli State Park (and just out from a cemetery). South of Lahaina, the shallow reef at Olowalu provides good snorkeling and diving (about three- quarters of a mile south of the general store rather than north of the store, where the surfers congregate), and still farther south, about three- quarters of a mile past the Scenic Lookout on Highway 30, a dirt road leads to Wash Rock, a popular diving site. The *Kaanapali* resort has Black Rock, the lava hill on which the *Sheraton Maui* hotel stands. It's ideal for either snorkeling or diving, the fish are tame enough to be fed by hand, and it's very convenient. Kapalua Beach, also extremely easy to find and endowed with a public parking lot, provides moderately good diving and snorkeling, and because of the loveliness of the beach, it would be worth a visit even if the underwater view were only fair. North of Kapalua, Honolua Bay (turn off Hwy. 30 onto the dirt road about 1½ miles north of D. T. Fleming Beach Park and after Slaughterhouse Beach) is the number one surfing spot on Maui, but as part of a coastal marine life preserve it also has excellent snorkeling and diving, particularly around the reef on the right.

The western coast of East Maui becomes interesting to snorkelers just below Kamaloe Beach Park III, in Kihei, and it's better in the morning than in the afternoon. Keawakapu Beach, near the *Mana Kai Maui,* is another morning spot. When the sea is calm, snorkeling is good in the rocky areas of Mokapu Beach (in front of *Stouffer's Wailea Beach*), excellent at Ulua Beach (between *Stouffer's Wailea Beach* and the *Inter-Continental*), and good again at Wailea Beach and Polo Beach (south of the *Inter-Continental*). From Kamaole Beach to Polo Beach, all six have the paved parking areas and other conveniences characteristic of beach parks. Five Caves, between Polo Beach and Makena Beach (but before the turnoff to Ulupalakua), is known for excellent scuba diving and snorkeling in caves below offshore rocks — which are reached by a long swim, however — and Makena Beach itself (see *Swimming and Sunning* for how to find it) has excellent snorkeling around the Puu Olai cinder cone. Farther south, via a dirt jeep trail, the rocky shores of the Ahihi-Kinau Natural Area Reserve, which runs from Ahihi Bay across Cape Kinau to La Perouse Bay, do not always allow easy access to the ocean, but the snorkeling and diving are well worth the effort.

Guided trips to nearby islands are another feature of diving on Maui. Experienced scuba divers can visit the underwater lava caves known as the Lanai Cathedrals, Mokuhooniki Rock off Molokai, and Becks Cove, off Kahoolawe, whereas everyone from the novice snorkeler to the certified diver turns up at Molokini, a volcanic islet whose crescent shape protects a great diversity of fish and coral between East Maui and the island of Kahoolawe. *Blue Water Rafting* (PO Box 1865, Kihei, Maui, HI 96753; phone: 879-RAFT) conducts snorkeling and whale watching cruises via motorized raft to the outer reef of Molokini, as well as an excursion along Maui's southern coast beyond Makena. Departures take place at 7 and 10:30 AM from the Kihei Launch Ramp. *Dive & Sea Center* (1975 S. Kihei Rd., Kihei, HI 96753; phone: 574-1952) offers a full range of dive programs, while *Capt. Nemo's Ragin' Cajun* (150 Dickenson Rd., Lahaina, HI 96761; phone: 661-5555; 800-367-8088) departs Lahaina for inter-island dives.

Beach activities concessions at most hotels have masks, fins, and snorkels for rent, occasionally with free instruction if necessary. Numerous excursion boats take passengers — anywhere from 6 to 100 people at a time — on snorkel sails, some directly from beaches in front of hotels, but most from Lahaina or Maalaea harbors. Prices range from $20 per person for a 2-hour sail up to $125 for a full-day sail, equipment included. Many such excursions feature snorkeling time along with time for swimming and sunning, a picnic on a beach, and perhaps some neighbor island sightseeing, and are listed under *Sightseeing Tours (Boat).*

Maui has a number of full-service dive shops that rent and sell snorkel and scuba gear, though most shops will rent scuba equipment to — or refill tanks for — certified divers only. Intensive, usually 5-day, courses that lead to certification by *PADI* (*Professional Association of Diving Instructors*) and/or *NAUI* (*National Association of Underwater Instructors*) or *NASDS* (*National Association of Scuba Diving Schools*) are given by several outfitters, including, in Lahaina, *Central Pacific Divers* (780 Front St.; phone: 661-8718), which also offers introductory dives for non-divers; refresher dives for certified but inactive divers; and two- and three-tank trips to Lanai or Molokini for certified divers. *Dive Maui* (*Lahaina Marketplace;* phone: 667-2080) also has 4- and 5-day certification courses and dives for beginners or certified divers, as does *Lahaina Divers* (710 Front St.; phone: 661-4505; 667-7496; 800-657-7885). *Kapalua Beach Activities,* beachfront at the *Kapalua Bay* hotel (phone: 669-5656), offers daily catamaran snorkel sails, as well as full scuba rental, lessons, and excursions. In the Kihei area, contact the *Maui Dive Shop,* in the *Azeka Place Shopping Center* (phone: 879-3388). In Wailea, the *Ocean Activities Center,* in the *Wailea Shopping Village* (phone: 879-4485; 800-869-6911), offers one- and two-tank dives, but no certification courses. The average price of a 4-day certification course is $300 to $400, and the price of a dive, whether introductory or refresher, local or inter-island, is anywhere from $40 to $90.

Surfing – Maui is not as well endowed with surf sites as Oahu, but then, neither is any other place in the world. Nevertheless, many consider Honolua Bay, on the northern coast of West Maui, one of the best surfing spots in Hawaii, certainly the best on Maui. On a good winter day, there are waves up to 15 feet, perfect tubes, and spectators watch from the cliffs above the rocky beach. Honolua is the next bay north of Slaughterhouse Beach (see *Swimming and Sunning*), accessible by dirt road off Highway 30. Other West Maui beaches that attract winter surfers are Windmill Beach and Honokohau Bay, both beyond Honolua and, because of a shallow bottom at one and submerged boulders and powerful currents at the other, both to be approached with extreme caution. Hookipa Beach Park, on the north coast of East Maui, probably has Maui's second best surf, and it's as well known as Honolua in the annals of surfing because the contemporary sport on Maui was born here. It's also as much of a surf-watching spot as Honolua, easily visible off Highway 36 just east of Paia and equipped with parking areas and picnic pavilions. This is a year-round site, though the spectacular waves — again up to 15 feet — occur in winter. Because of dangerous currents, however, Hookipa is definitely only for the experts.

On Maui's southern shores, the surf is best in the summer. Maalaea Bay, on the south side of the central valley, provides a very popular site, Maalaea Rights, considered the best break on the south shore, and though it is better in summer, there is winter surfing here, too. Maalaea Mudflats, another summer spot on the bay, is good at medium to high tide, but should be avoided at low tide because of a hazardous reef. Southeast of Maalaea, Kalama Beach Park, about midway down the Kihei coast on the western shore of East Maui, attracts its share of summer surfers; in the other direction, Olowalu, on the West Maui shore about midway between Maalaea and Lahaina, has reasonably good surfing year-round (the exact spot is one-half mile north of the village general store). In Lahaina, where the elite of pre-*haole* Hawaii rode the *papa he naru* (the wave sliding board), there are summer breaks both to the north and south of the harbor, anywhere from 2 to 10 feet.

West Maui has several places to rent surfboards and Boogie boards (a shorter surfboard), including *Sailboards Maui* (360 Papa Pl., Kahului; phone: 871-7954), *Central Pacific Divers* (780 Front St., Lahaina; phone: 661-8718), and *Hobie Sports* (in Kaanapali's *Whalers Village;* phone: 661-5455). *Sea Sails* rents only surfboards at the *Sands of Kahana* condominiums (phone: 669-6586), and Boogie boards exclusively at the *Kaanapali Beach* hotel (phone: 661-5244). *Lightning Bolt,* in the *Kahului Shopping Center* (phone: 877-3484), rents surfboards by the day and has a very economical weekly rate. In the Kihei and Wailea areas, *Maui Dive Shop* (*Kihei Town Center*; phone: 879-1919) rents Boogie boards, and at *Azeka Shopping Center* (phone: 879-3388), they rent beginner surfboards. *Tradewinds Deli* in Maalaea (phone: 242-9161) rents Boogie boards. On Maui, surfboards generally rent at $15 to $20 per 24-hour day, and Boogie boards at $5 to $10; a deposit is usually required. *Maui Surfing School* (south end of Lahaina Harbor; phone: 875-0625) will train everyone from beginners to advanced surfers. Owner Andrea Thomas specializes in providing all the basics in one lesson.

Swimming and Sunning – Nearly all and certainly the best of Maui's approximately 33 miles of beach are on West Maui and on the southwest coast of East Maui, appropriately in the same general areas with the greatest concentration of resort hotels and condominiums. Quite a number of them are beach parks, equipped by the county with paved parking areas, picnic tables and pavilions, showers, and restrooms, but they are not necessarily crowded, though the most popular ones may be on weekends. Be wary of the water at remote, deserted beaches, and even more wary if you come across a well-frequented beach, with island families ensconced thereon, but no one in for a swim. Surf conditions — and the appearance — of many beaches undergo changes from time to time, making caution always necessary.

The Lahaina area of West Maui is not overly endowed with good beaches, though it does have some picturesque ones; in fact, a stunning view of the islands of Lanai or Molokai or both is part of the beauty of all the beaches from Lahaina to Kapalua. Launiupoko State Park and Puamana Park along Highway 30 south of Lahaina both have views of Lanai across the Auau Channel guaranteed to comfort the eye, but neither is notable for swimming or sunning. The beach of Lahaina town, in the vicinity of the *Lahaina Shores* hotel, is negligible, which explains the popularity of Wahikuli State Park, along Highway 30 between Lahaina and Kaanapali, and Hanakao's Beach Park, adjacent to the *Hyatt.* Both are equipped with paved parking areas, picnic pavilions, barbecue grills, restrooms, and showers, and while most of the shoreline is edged in boulders, small beaches allow access to good swimming.

Kaanapali Beach is West Maui's resort showcase, a 2-mile stretch of golden sand that frames the hotels and condominiums of the *Kaanapali* resort, and then extends north another mile to Honokowai. There's plenty of room for everybody here, though the beach is widest where it snuggles up to Black Rock toward the center, an excellent snorkeling area. Swimming is very good, with only two provisos: Watch for the red warning flags put out by the hotels when the surf is heavy, and watch your children, because the bottom does drop quickly to depths over one's head. Access to the beach is via condos, hotels, or the *Whalers Village* shopping complex.

North of Kaanapali are two near-perfect crescents of sand curving between rocky points, both with picture-postcard views of Molokai. The first is the beach at Napili Bay, backed by condominiums hidden among palm trees, which detract little from its loveliness though they do create a parking problem (every space within a reasonable distance of the Hui Drive or Napili Place public rights of way seems to be marked for residents only). The waters of Napili are usually gentle, especially in the summer, as are the sparklingly clear aquamarine waters of the smaller beach fringing Kapalua Bay, the next bay north. Kapalua Beach is beautiful and it is easily reached (turn off Highway 30 just past the *Napili Kai Beach Club)* and has a public parking lot and restrooms.

Two more well-known beaches are north of Kapalua. The popular D. T. Fleming Beach Park, on Honokahua Bay, longer and wider than either Kapalua or Napili, provides a setting for the recently opened *Ritz-Carlton* hotel. This public park, backed by towering ironwood pines, also boasts splendid views of nearby Molokai. The park has full facilities — picnic tables, barbecue pits, restrooms, and a parking area — and it has plenty of space for sunning, but heed the sign that says it's unsafe for swimming even though you may see people in the water. Currents are dangerous here, and there have been drownings. Slaughterhouse Beach, the next beach along Highway 30, is also a dangerous beach for swimming, particularly in winter, and you'll have to be something of a mountain goat to reach it (but then so will others). After passing the first Blow Horn sign (to warn pineapple trucks coming down private roads to the right), you'll see cars parked at a clearing on the left. The beach — also known as Mokuleia — is below, a pocket of sand nearly enclosed by low cliffs that is part of a coastal marine preserve. Once nearly deserted, Mokuleia now attracts crowds who descend the short trail that leads from the road to the beach.

Considering the wealth of beaches elsewhere, there is no need to search out those in the Kahului area, but bear in mind if you are staying in Kahului that there are better local beaches than the one on the harbor by the hotels. Beaches are few and far between en route to Hana — the coast is mostly high and low sea cliffs — and in Hana, there are only two main beaches — Hana Beach Park, the safest swimming beach in the district, and Hamoa Beach, where the *Hana-Maui* hotel has its private facilities. After a 15-minute hike from the *Hana-Maui Sea Ranch* cottages, you can find relative isolation and excellent swimming off the red sands of Kaihalulu Bay. But the southern coast of East Maui is quite another thing — almost one uninterrupted stretch of sand from Maalaea Bay down to its southern tip beyond Wailea. About 3 miles at the northern end are called Maalaea Beach, a favorite with joggers because of the hard-packed sand, but also a good swimming and sunning beach — as long as you arrive early in the morning. By noon, the wind howling across the central valley will blow you straight out to Kahoolawe.

Another 6 miles of the coast, which can also become windy in the afternoon, is known as Kihei Beach, a fairly loose term that describes any beach along South Kihei Road not otherwise named. There is no shortage of pale, soft sand here, Kahoolawe and Lanai can be seen offshore, and the view of the seacoast curving north to the West Maui mountains is a grand final touch. A great deal of this stretch is lined with condominiums, and if you are not staying in one of them, your acquaintance will probably be limited to the easily accessible sections set aside as parks. Kamaole Beach Parks I, II, and III are the most popular and apt to be crowded on weekends. Kamaole Beach Park I, in the 2300 area of South Kihei Road, is a lovely, long, wide beach equipped with picnic tables, showers, restrooms, and a paved parking area. Moving south, there's Kamaole Beach Park II; and Kamaole Beach Park III, still farther south, has a playground for children, making it the most popular of all, even though its beach is the smallest. Children should be watched carefully at all three beaches (the water becomes deep rather quickly), but otherwise swimming is safe, periods of heavy surf and kona storms excepted.

The gap between Kihei and Wailea is bridged by Keawakapu Beach, a sugary soft expanse of sand lapped by translucent water. It begins at a lava point off South Kihei Road and extends a half-mile south to another lava point inside the *Wailea* resort, this latter portion constituting the first of the fabulous five Wailea beaches. (The beach can be reached either from the right of way where South Kihei Road meets Kilohana Road or from inside the resort.) Mokapu Beach, in front of *Stouffer's Wailea Beach* hotel, and Ulua Beach, between *Stouffer's Wailea Beach* hotel and the *Maui Inter-Continental* resort, are two smaller crescents, both set off by the verdant landscaping of the resort behind them, while the fourth of the five, *Wailea Beach,* is a wide expanse that is home to the *Grand Hyatt Wailea* and the *Four Seasons.* The fifth, Polo Beach, is backed by the *Polo Club* condominiums and the *Kea Lani.* Swimming is excellent at all five (and the bottom drops gently), access is clearly marked from the main road inside the resort, and all have paved parking lots and paved walks to the sand.

Pressing on past Polo Beach, there is what some consider the most beautiful beach on Maui, very long and wide, with clear waters and a view of Kahoolawe and Molokini in front, steep mountain and kiawe trees behind, and sand up to your ankles. The beach, first known as Oneloa, meaning "long sands," or Puu Olai, from the cinder cone to its right, then Hippie Beach because of the community that took up residence in the late 1960s, is now known as Makena Beach or Big Beach, to distinguish it from Little Beach, the next cove north. Reached only by walking around Puu Olai, Little Beach is Maui's foremost (but unofficial) nudist beach. Nude sunbathing is prohibited by state law, and recent police raids and arrests have discouraged total-body tanners, but our recent visit (all in the interest of research!) revealed lots of unclothed folks soaking up the sun. Be careful of Makena during heavy surf, and don't leave valuables in the car; the beach is not deserted, as the debris at its back will attest.

Tennis – Most hotels and the larger condominiums have one or a few courts, in some cases for guests only, in others open to the public. Four island installations are outstanding: The *Wailea Tennis Club* (phone: 879-1958) is not only the largest tennis complex in the state, it is also the only one with grass courts, three of them. In addition, there are 11 Plexipave courts (3 with lights) and a well-stocked pro shop. Tennis director Joe Violette and two assistant pros give private lessons and hold clinics on request. Court fees range from $15 per person per day for a Plexipave court ($15 for *Wailea* guests) to $20 per hour for grass ($15 for guests). Tennis clinics are offered on Mondays and Thursdays. The *Makena Tennis Club* (phone: 879-8777), with 4 night-lighted courts, is a pleasant smaller facility nearby. The *Royal Lahaina Tennis Ranch* (phone: 661-3611, ext. 2296), in the *Kaanapali* resort, has 10 Plexipave courts (6 with lights), 1 stadium court, and a pro shop. *Peter Burwash International* at the *Tennis Ranch* offers group and private instruction, a tennis clinic, and round-robin play. All-day court fees are $6 per person, per court, for guests of the *Royal Lahaina* and $9 for others. Fees guarantee 1 hour of play, the rest on a space-available basis. Night play is $2 additional. The *Kapalua Tennis Garden* (phone: 669-5677) provides 10 Plexipave courts, 4 lighted. Private and group lessons are available; clinics and round robins are scheduled according to demand. Play is $9 per person per day for guests of the *Kapalua Bay* hotel or the *Kapalua Villas;* others pay $10 per person per day, with 1 hour guaranteed and space available the remainder of the day.

Maui also has a number of county courts run by the Department of Parks and Recreation (phone: 243-7230) where play is free. They're in several areas frequented by visitors, but the top ones are the 5 lighted Laykold courts at the *Lahaina Civic Center* (phone: 661-4685), across Honoapiilani Highway from Wahikuli State Park, north of town. They operate on a first-come, first-served basis from 7 AM to 9:30 PM daily. Other county courts are in Kihei, Hana, Pukalani, Makawao, Wailuku, and Kahului.

Water Skiing – *Lahaina Water Ski* (phone: 661-5988) has lessons and towing time available for up to five skiers. Rates start at $30 for 15 minutes to $90 for an hour. They also take skiers offshore Kaanapali from the *Hyatt Regency Maui.*

Windsurfing – The newest water sport on Maui is growing by leaps and bounds. Experienced board sailors congregate along the north shore, between Kanaha Beach Park east of Kahului and Hookipa Beach Park east of Paia, where the *Maui International Grand Prix* of windsurfing is held and where wind conditions are ideal year round. *Sailboards Maui* (360 Papa Place, Kahului; phone: 871-7954) sells windsurfers and rents them at $45 per 24 hours, and $250 per week. Private lessons in advanced techniques can be arranged. Two hour-long introductory courses ($35) and a comprehensive 6-hour course ($75) are given by the *Maui Sailing Center* (Kealia Beach Plaza, 101 N. Kihei Rd.; phone: 879-5935). Windsurfer rentals are $15 an hour, $50 for a 4-hour time card, and $80 for an 8-hour time card. Time on these cards does not have to be used up all at once. The *Maui Windsurf Company* (phone: 877-4816) provides rentals and lessons. *Maui Magic Windsurfing Schools* (520 Keolani Pl., Kahului; phone: 877-4816; 800-872-0999) offers a full range of lessons (at $55 for 2½ hours). *Sea Sails* (phone: 661-5244) rents windsurfers for $25 for the first hour, and $15 for each additional hour, and 3- and 5-day packages for $150 to $240. Instruction is also offered at $50 for a combination 1-hour lesson, 1-hour rental. A motorized viewing board that takes the effort out of snorkeling ($25 an hour) is also available. The *Kaanapali Windsurfing School* (phone: 667-1964) offers rentals and lessons from a beachfront location south of the *Hyatt; Kapalua Beach Activities* (phone: 669-5656) offers lessons ($35) and rentals ($25) by the hour and for longer periods. *Vela Highwind Centers* (phone: 800-223-5443) offers fully packaged windsurf vacations that include accommodations and equipment.

More and more hotels are adding windsurfing to their sports rosters. In the *Kaanapali* resort, *Sea Sails,* with desks at all *Kaanapali* resort hotels and at the nearby Kaanapali Shores condominium, rents windsurfers. In Wailea, the *Ocean Activities Center* rents windsurfers at its *Stouffer's Wailea Beach* and *Maui Inter-Continental* hotel outlets. The *Four Seasons* and the *Grand Hyatt Wailea* (phone: 875-1234) offer rentals ($25 per hour) with 3- , 5- , and 10-hour multiple rental discounts. Lessons cost $35 an hour for groups or $45 for a private session. *Nick's Aquasports* (phone: 661-1234) operates out of the *Hyatt Regency* at Kaanapali with windsurfers, snorkels, and Boogie boards.

■ **Note:** The traveler seeking outdoor adventure including a variety of sports-related activities may be interested in the week-long Maui Challenge package offered by *The Challenges* (PO Box 5489, Glendale, AZ 85312; phone: 800-448-9816 for Hawaii packages) which includes a fitness-oriented diet and luxury oceanfront accommodations. For further information on outdoor adventures, see *Package Tours* and *Camping and RVs, Hiking, and Biking* in GETTING READY TO GO.

AROUND THE ISLAND

Maui looks something like the head of a steer facing east. The head is East Maui, the ear is West Maui, and where the ear is attached is the central isthmus, or valley, connecting the two. Kahului Airport is just east of the twin towns of Wailuku and Kahului, the administrative center and port respectively, on the northern coast of the central valley. Highway 38 (380 on some maps) crosses the valley north to south and meets Highway 30 above the small harbor village of Maalaea, on Maalaea Bay, which is the valley's southern shore. Highway 30 then proceeds west, circling the outer edge of West Maui in a clockwise direction, passing Lahaina, the *Kaanapali* resort, the condominium strips of Honokowai, Kahana, and Napili, and the *Kapalua* resort, beyond which the paved road ends. The interior of West Maui is mountainous, partly unexplored, and largely inaccessible, except on helicopter tours.

East Maui is the larger landmass, dominated by the dormant Haleakala volcano, which last erupted in the late 1700s. From Kahului, one main route leads south (Hwy. 35 or 350) across the central valley to the condominium strip of Maalaea and Kihei and the resorts at Wailea and Makena, which occupy East Maui's western coast. Another main route (Hwy. 37) leads inland southeast from Kahului, climbs the lower slopes of Haleakala, then veers around them through a district known as the Kula uplands or upcountry, while a branch road zigzags to the crater at the top. The third main route from Kahului leads east (Hwy. 36), and follows East Maui's northern coast past the windsurfing beach at Hookipa to the village and district of Hana, at the snout of the hypothetical steer. Highways 37 and 36 actually form a loop around East Maui, but a portion of the loop (only about 7 miles) on the southern side is still unpaved and off-limits to almost all rental cars (renters must sign an agreement with the rental companies that they will stay off this road).

Lahaina

This old waterfront town began the 19th century as the residence and playground of island *alii* (high chiefs), gradually assumed importance as the political center of the early Hawaiian kingdom, became the whaling capital of the world almost overnight, then almost as quickly sank into the oblivion from which it has only recently awakened to become Maui's prime tourist hub. Its main thoroughfare, Front Street, is lined with brightly painted (or unpainted), weatherbeaten frame buildings. They are almost all storefronts where visitors can become tropically clad *wahines* (women) and *kanes* (men), swathed in alohawear and leis of seashells or kukui nuts; shop for souvenirs; browse through art galleries (Lahaina has emerged in recent years as a major gallery town; and patronize restaurants and bars where these same visitors can watch the sunset over mai tais and a meal of mahimahi, opakapaka, or other fish brought in with the day's catch. If nothing about the town seems terribly serious today, except the cost of art in Front Street's numerous galleries, it must be said that it never was a very stuffy place.

Remnants of Lahaina's royal past are few. The village had already been a watering place for Maui's *alii* class for centuries before Kamehameha the Great arrived to spend the year in 1802, a few years after the last of the battles that assured his eventual rule over a united Hawaiian kingdom. During that year — usually taken as the date he established Lahaina as his capital — Kamehameha made his headquarters in the Brick Palace, built for him by two foreigners a few years earlier and the foundations of which can still be seen off Front Street behind the library. The Brick Palace, with four rooms and two floors, was the first Western-style building in the islands, but the king is said to have found it confining and lived in a grass house next door instead.

Kamehameha did not remain on Maui, but the two most important of his 21 wives, Queen Kaahumanu and Queen Keopuolani, both from Maui, spent most of their time here, as did the three royal children — Prince Liholiho, Prince Kauikeaouli, and Princess Nahienaena. The main residence of Liholiho, who became Kamehameha II, was an island in a pond that used to exist at the corner of Shaw and Front Streets, now marked only by a clump of palm trees in Maluuluolele Park; and while Kauikeaouli, who became Kamehameha III, spent a good part of his reign building a European-style palace of coral block — Hale Piula, or the House of the Tin Roof, which he never finished — he, too, preferred to live in what he called his private apartments, a grass house on the same little island behind the palace.

The diaries and letters of the missionaries are the best testimony of Lahaina's style of life in those days. The royal surfing grounds were in front of Princess Nahienaena's grass house, just south of today's small boat harbor, and they were well frequented, according to one missionary, who recorded that the surfboard was "an article of personal property, among all the chiefs — male and female, and among many of the common people." Another wrote of seeing the king (in this case, Kamehameha III), his wife, and others coming from the king's taro patch, which was next to the Brick Palace: "They were without shoes and stockings and hats and with a large wreath of maile and no more clothes than necessary. They were happy as any children playing in summer showers. The company had just come from performing one of those ancient acts of community interest, teaching the people the dignity of labor."

Protestant missionaries — the Reverends Charles Stewart and William

Richards were the first — arrived in Lahaina in 1823 at the invitation of Queen Keopuolani, who was the first Hawaiian chief to convert to Christianity. Almost simultaneously another set of newcomers, also mainly New Englanders, was rapidly growing from a trickle to a horde. Whalers working the lucrative sperm whale grounds off Japan began to arrive in Hawaii in 1819, and soon they discovered the safe anchorage of Lahaina's open roadstead — less enclosed than a harbor, easy to approach and leave with any wind that blew — and the abundant fruit, vegetables, and Irish potatoes grown upcountry at Kula. The town suddenly became the most important provisioning stop for America's Pacific whaling fleet, and it is not difficult to picture the wide eyes of the missionary Dr. Dwight Baldwin, who noted: "Ten days since we had two whaleships, next day ten came in, and the next day six. From that time to this, scarce an hour but we have seen from one to half a dozen coming down the channel — 50 ships now here." Lahaina had become the whaling capital of the world. When traffic was at its peak, in 1846, 429 whaleships came to call; that same year, the town census recorded 882 grass houses, 155 adobe houses, 59 houses of wood or stone, and a population of only 3,557 people.

While replenishing their stores, the whalers also replenished themselves, and it was their R&R activities that created all the fuss. Multiply a possible 50 ships at anchor by an average crew of 25 to 30 healthy men sprung from long months of confinement, and it is easy to see why the missionaries invented the muumuu. And not only the missionaries were concerned about temptations in their ersatz Garden of Eden. Maui's governor from 1823 until his death in 1840 was the high chief Hoapili, counselor to the first two Kamehamehas, the husband of the widowed Queen Keopuolani, and, like her, a Christian convert. Hoapili struggled mightily to maintain law and order, banning brothels and grog shops and putting a *kapu* (taboo) on ships and their crews, thus prohibiting native women from swimming out to visit them. His efforts were badly received from the start. In 1825, when one ship put into port and the crew discovered that women were not allowed aboard and that the grog shops were closed, a riot ensued. The life of the Reverend Mr. Richards, suspected as a moving force behind the cleanup campaign, was threatened. Two years later, another riot ended with the crew of the whaler *John Palmer* firing a few cannonballs into the same reverend's yard. Soon this tropical paradise had a curfew, a fort, and a jail; still, the problem was only resolved when the whaling era ended.

Lahaina declined as whaling declined. The discovery of oil in Pennsylvania in 1859 was the beginning of the end, the loss of whaleships to Civil War blockades contributed further, and the loss of what was left of the fleet in the ice off Alaska in 1871 was the final blow. The effect of the missionaries was more lasting. They had been instrumental in establishing schools, the most important of which, Lahainaluna, was the first high school west of the Rockies when it opened in 1831. A few years later, a printing press on its grounds was turning out the first newspaper west of the Rockies, in Hawaiian. Reverend Richards, who had instructed Queen Keopuolani in the faith, became an adviser to Kamehameha III, whom he instructed in the study of democracy; and after issuing a declaration of rights and an edict of religious toleration, the young king signed Hawaii's first written constitution in 1840. The representative body thus constituted met in Lahaina for a few years until the government was moved to Honolulu, a transfer Kamehameha accomplished gradually over the course of the decade. His successor, Kamehameha IV, rarely visited Lahaina.

Few people, in fact, came to Lahaina until the 1960s, when the *Kaanapali* resort opened, a few miles north, and tourists began to flock to Maui. At the same time, the federal government designated much of the town a National Historic Landmark, inspiring the citizenry to undertake an ongoing project of restoration. What remains of the old is not difficult to visit since the town is only a few blocks deep, and while it is about 2½ miles long, most of the points of interest are on or just off a half-mile stretch of Front Street. Sightseeing should take 2 to 3 hours or so, except for those overly entranced by shopping, which is most enjoyable during the mornings (everything is open by 10 AM) or in the evening. Lahaina means "merciless sun," and from midday until sunset, it can indeed be uncomfortably hot. Don't be put off entirely by the commercialism and hype; the authentic sights can actually be rather interesting. The County of Maui Historic Commission publishes a brochure, "Lahaina: A Walking Tour of Historic and Cultural Sites," that can be picked up at the *Baldwin House Museum* (phone: 661-3262) during a visit. (Information: Maui Historic Commission, PO Box 338, Lahaina, HI 96767.) And if you're in town on a Friday night between 6:30 and 9:30 PM, you can make the round of Lahaina's numerous galleries and sample free champagne and *pupus,* and have a chance to meet Andrea Smith, Robert Lyn Nelson, and Will Herrera, some of the Maui-based artists with international reputations, or art-world celebrities such as Peter Max. Combined with the work of masters like Chagall, the range and quality of Lahaina gallery art are quite impressive, despite pretentiously high prices and an "art as an investment" approach that sometimes makes the aesthetics of art seem secondary.

Banyan Tree – As much a center of attraction in Lahaina as the *Pioneer Inn* next to it, the banyan tree is as good a place as any to begin a walking tour and an equally good place to end one. Planted in 1873 to commemorate the 50th anniversary of the arrival of the Protestant missionaries, this tree of Indian origin has grown and grown, propping itself up when necessary by sending aerial roots downward from its many horizontal branches and turning them into subsidiary trunks to support continued expansion. By now, the banyan looks like a grove of trees and covers two-thirds of an acre — quite a lot of much-needed shade in a town as sunstruck as Lahaina. Tourists and islanders alike take shelter on park benches beneath the boughs, mynah birds congregate topside, and though signs everywhere warn against climbing the tree, nothing prevents young children from swinging on the hanging tendrils that have yet to take root. In the middle of the block bounded by Front, Hotel, Canal, and Wharf Streets.

Pioneer Inn – Across the street from the banyan tree, this hotel is the most famous manmade landmark in town. It opened in 1901, too late to accommodate the whalers, but still in time to put up travelers disembarking from the inter-island steamers plying the Lahaina Roadstead. These must have been an equally rowdy crew, judging from the rules of the house posted right from the beginning by the reception desk; to wit: "Women is not allow in you room. If you wet or burn you bed you going out. You are not allow to gambel in you room. You are not allow in the down stears in the seating room or in the dinering room or in the kitchen when you are drunk. You must use a shirt when you come to the seating room." The dark green wooden structure with the white-trimmed ground-floor arcade and second-story verandah all around is today actually two buildings — the old wing facing the harbor and, behind, a new wing, added in 1966 and looking as authentic as the original. Even if you're not staying at the hotel, you can soak up some of its atmosphere by visiting the *Snug Harbor* "dinering" room or the *Old Whaler's Grog Shop* bar, both in the old section. Hotel and Wharf Sts. (phone: 661-3636).

Carthaginian – Imagine every boat in the harbor rigged like this one and discover a picture of Lahaina in its heyday. What is now the *Carthaginian* left German shipyards in 1920 as a two-masted schooner, was converted to diesel power by Swedish owners, and for most of its life hauled cargo through the Baltic Sea. Bought in 1972 by the Lahaina Restoration Foundation, it underwent an intensive transformation, and by 1980 it had been turned into a replica of a 19th-century square-rigger, the only true-rigged brig in the world. The *Carthaginian* replaces another square-rigged vessel that was moored here (and featured in the film *Hawaii*) until 1972, when it broke up on a coral reef en route to a Honolulu dry dock. The sails are still to come for the *Carthaginian,* but in the meantime, the ship serves as a floating museum; its exhibits include the continuous showing of two videotapes on whales, phones on which to hear recorded whale songs, and an old whaleboat found preserved in Alaska in 1973. Open daily from 9 AM to 4:30 PM. Admission $3; children free with parents. The Whale Report Center on the dock beside the *Carthaginian* keeps tabs on when and where whales have last been spotted and is the place to ask where next to look for these slow-moving creatures. Lahaina Harbor, directly in front of the *Pioneer Inn* (for information on the *Carthaginian* or to report a whale, phone: 661-8527).

Wo Hing Society – Built by immigrant Chinese plantation workers in 1912 as a residence and social hall for indigent bachelors, the Lahaina Restoration Foundation has given this building new life, as a museum on Chinese culture and its links to Maui. Particularly interesting are the films — shown throughout the day on a large screen — depicting the impact of Chinese immigrants on the island's culture. Open Mondays through Saturdays from 9 AM to 4:30 PM; Sundays from 10 AM to 4:30 PM. 858 Front St. (phone: 661-5553).

Hauola Stone – A Hawaii Visitors Bureau warrior marker along the sea wall to the right of the *Pioneer Inn* and the *Carthaginian* points to several rocks in the water below. There is not much to see, but the most chair-shaped one was thought by the Hawaiians to have healing powers. They had only to sit in it and let the waves washing over them restore them to health. At your back are the foundations of Kamehameha the Great's Brick Palace and the site of the king's taro patch.

Courthouse – The Lahaina Courthouse was built in 1859 of wood and stone taken from the European-style palace that Kamehameha III had raised for himself not far away and never completed. Kamehameha's palace — Hale Piula, or the House of the Tin Roof — had already been converted into a courthouse in 1848, but 10 years later, a strong wind put an end to its usefulness and the rubble was transported here to become the new Lahaina Court and Custom House and Government Offices. Today, the building houses the District Court and offices, plus galleries of the Lahaina Art Society on the ground floor and in the basement (in the basement gallery, paintings are hung in the cells of the former jail). Open daily from 10 AM to 4 PM. Wharf St., in front of the banyan tree.

Old Fort – By the time the courthouse appeared, the fort had already been and gone. The two corners of the fort wall, now on the courthouse grounds at the Canal Street and Hotel Street intersections of Wharf Street, were reconstructed in 1964 to provide some reminder of the former landmark. The fort was built in about 1832 in an effort to restore some semblance of law and order to the R&R activities of visiting seamen, who had rioted more than once in the past upon putting into port and finding that the native women were prohibited from coming aboard and that the grog shops in town were closed, too. While the fort stood (until the early 1850s), a curfew was also in effect, and every evening at sundown a soldier stood on the ramparts beating a drum to warn all sailors ashore to return to their ships. The fort once had an inventory of 47 cannons, but the four guns now pointed at the tame fleet of pleasure boats in Lahaina Harbor were never among them. These four are believed to have come from a Russian ship that sank in Honolulu Harbor in 1816. Wharf St.

Holy Innocents Episcopal Church – As you go south on Front Street, passing Kamehameha III School on the right, this small church, dating from 1927, will also be on your right. Stop in for a look at the Hawaiian madonna on the altar, the triptych of Hawaiian scenes below it, and the other paintings in a tropical mode. Princess Nahienaena's grass house and Kamehameha III's palace, Hale Piula, were once both in this vicinity, between Front St. and the sea.

Waiola (formerly Wainee) Church and Cemetery – The first Christian services on Maui took place outdoors in June 1823, shortly after the arrival of the Protestant missionaries. It was not until 1828, however, that construction began on Wainee Church, the first stone church to be built in the islands. When it was finished in 1832, it was large enough to seat 3,000 people, though not substantial enough to survive the elements. In 1858, the same wind that damaged Kamehameha III's palace blew the steeple and part of the roof off Wainee. Then, in 1894, the whole church was torched by mobs protesting the abolition of the monarchy and the annexation of Hawaii by the US (the reverend at the time favored both developments). A subsequent church succumbed first to fire and then to a whirlwind, so that the present small, cream-colored, shake-roofed church, its name changed from Wainee to Waiola (Water of Life), dates only from 1953. The cemetery next door, surrounded by pink, red, and white plumeria trees, contains the graves of Hawaiian royalty and commoners and of missionaries and their children as well as many unmarked graves. Entering from the Waiola churchyard, a faded wooden sign points to the Royal Tomb, where two large headstones are enclosed in a black wrought-iron fence. Here lies Queen Keopuolani, wife of Kamehameha I, mother of Kamehameha II and Kamehameha III, and the first of the Hawaiian chiefs to convert to Christianity. Her daughter, Princess Nahienaena, is also buried here as is Governor Hoapili, another convert. As Governor of Maui from 1823 to 1840, he was an ally of the missionaries and the real power behind the banning of grog shops and brothels that so inflamed the early whalers. Wainee St., around the corner from Shaw St.

Hongwanji Temple – The white, slatted structure with the three gray outer-space turrets — on the left as you continue north along Wainee Street — is the church of Lahaina's largest Buddhist congregation. The Hongwanji sect has been meeting here since 1910, but the building dates from 1927.

Hale Paahao (Old Prison) – Until this prison was built, rowdy sailors were locked up inside the old fort on the waterfront. By 1852, rowdiness had evidently accelerated to an unprecedented degree in Lahaina (the gold rush was blamed for a second great influx of foreigners and the lack of moderation in their behavior) and a new prison was begun, built by the prisoners themselves. First came the wooden prison house (the small brown building that looks more like a little chapel), then the massive prison wall of coral blocks taken from the walls of the old fort, which the prison replaced. In 1988, Hale Paahao was taken apart and reconstructed, with the addition of on-site storyboards. Open daily from 9 AM to 4 PM. Prison Rd., just off Wainee St.

Episcopal Cemetery and Hale Aloha – You can return to Front Street by proceeding north along Wainee Street and turning left at Dickenson Street. En route, on the left side of Wainee, is the Episcopal Cemetery, where Walter Murray Gibson, King David Kalakaua's principal adviser during the 1880s, is buried, and if you walk into the cemetery, you will be able to see something of Hale Aloha (House of Love) behind it. This church meetinghouse, completed in 1858 and restored in 1988, was built to commemorate Maui's safe deliverance from the scourge of a smallpox epidemic that had decimated Oahu 5 years before.

Maria Lanakila Church – The large church on the corner of Wainee and Dickenson Streets is a 1928 replacement and replica of a previous one on the spot, built in 1858. An even earlier church, built in 1846, was Lahaina's first Roman Catholic house of worship. Next to the church is its cemetery, and next to that, a sign points out the Seamen's Cemetery — though only one or two slabs remain of the many that were here when the plot was in use in the 19th century.

Masters' Reading Room – In 1833, work began on what is today Maui's oldest building, the money for which came from both the Protestant mission and an assortment of ships' captains. Upon completion, the ground floor served as the mission storeroom, and the reading room upstairs was where seamen could engage in more seemly R&R activities than those that had previously strained relations between the islanders and rowdy ships' crews. The Lahaina Restoration Foundation (phone: 661-3262) is housed in the building, which is not open to the public. Corner of Dickenson and Front Sts.

Baldwin House Museum – This plastered and whitewashed coral stone house was built in 1834–35 by one of Lahaina's early missionaries, Ephraim Spaulding. From 1836 to 1868, however, it was the home of Dr. Dwight Baldwin, a missionary who was also a doctor, and his family, which grew to include six children. Through the years, the house was crowded not only with Baldwins but also with a constant parade of visitors and guests — missionaries, whaling captains, the minister's flock, and the doctor's patients. The building has been restored, furnished with period pieces (English and local), and is now a museum run by the Lahaina Restoration Foundation. The rooms open for viewing include the living room with the family's Steinway piano, the dining room set with their imported china, the master bedroom with the koa wood four-poster bed, the bathroom with the first toilet brought to Maui, the boys' bedroom with superfluous bed warmers, and the dispensary, where there is a copy of Dr. Baldwin's Hawaiian medical license, allowing him to charge $50 for "very great sickness," $40 for "less than that," $30 for "a good deal less," and so on. Note the small park next door. The home of the Reverend William Richards used to be on this spot, and this is where those cannonballs fell in 1827, fired by sailors who suspected Richards of having been the instigator of Governor Hoapili's morality drive. Museum open daily from 9:30 AM to 4 PM. Admission charge $2; children under 12 free with parents. Front St., beside the Masters' Reading Room (phone: 661-3262).

Lahaina Jodo Mission – This Japanese cultural park is too far from the center of Lahaina to be included in a walking tour, but its very distance makes it a peaceful place to visit. A small sweep of grass, pebbles, and walkways is encircled by pink and white oleander bushes and dominated by the great bronze Buddha, unveiled in 1968, on the hundredth anniversary of Japanese immigration to the Hawaiian islands. Neither the white pagoda with the three red-trimmed roofs, a memorial to the dead, nor the tiny brown and white temple is open to the public, but you can walk up the steps to the temple and peer in at its lovely flowered ceiling. Another structure houses the temple bell. Ala Moana St., near Mala Wharf.

Lahainaluna School – Also too far away to include in a walking tour, this could be the object of a short drive that will take you 2 miles uphill behind Lahaina but not as far as the giant "L" etched onto the summit of Mt. Ball (you'll be treated to the broadest possible view over the town and the Lahaina Roadstead on the way down). The "L," freshly limed twice a year to keep it visible, stands for Lahainaluna, and though the campus may not appear unusual, the school is. When it was opened by the American Board of Commissioners for Foreign Missions in 1831, it was the first secondary school west of the Rockies. Not only did the initial students, who came from mission schools all over the islands, have to build their own facilities and grow their own food, they also had to manufacture their own textbooks; Hawaiian had become a written language only a few years before, and most of the early pupils were natives. By 1834, the first newspaper printed in Hawaii (and in Hawaiian) was coming off the press at Lahainaluna, and soon Hale Pai (the printing house) was turning out histories, grammars, dictionaries, and other books, many of them first editions, that are still important to the study of Hawaiian history and culture. The school introduced a boarding program almost from the start, and though it became part of the public school system in the 1920s and is now West Maui's only public high school, it still has students who board. Traditional and vocational courses — carpentry, auto repair, agriculture, horticulture, and aquaculture — are offered, and just as the early students mixed the academic with the practical by necessity, today's boarders must fulfill a work requirement, usually farmwork (in the past they've even run their own dairy). Instruction has been in English since 1877, but the preservation of native culture is an important part of the school's heritage, as can be seen at the end of each school year on *David Malo Day,* when the students put on a program of song, dance, and ancient Hawaiian sports. The pageantry remembers Lahainaluna's most famous alumnus, a member of the first class who became a teacher and a preacher and who, as the author of the classic work of history and anthropology *Hawaiian Antiquities,* is considered to be the first Hawaiian scholar. The campus is open to the public, but if school is in session and you want to do more than drive through, stop by the vice principal's office first.

Hale Pai – The oldest building on the campus of the Lahainaluna School, Hale Pai (House of Print) has been restored to be a museum devoted to Hawaiian printing. Open to visitors Mondays through Fridays from 10 AM to 4 PM. No admission charge; donations accepted. Lahainaluna Rd. (phone: 667-7040).

Omni Theater/Hawaii Experience – The giant domed screen provides a three-dimensional view of Hawaii's natural and human history. *Hawaii: Islands of the Gods* is artistically filmed and sensitively written. Years in the making, and 40 minutes in the showing, it's worth considering at $5.95 ($3.95 for children ages 4 to 12; children under 4 are free). Shows daily every hour on the hour from 10 AM to 10 PM. 824 Front St. (phone: 661-8314).

SHOPPING: A short walk through Lahaina should be enough to convince anyone that shopkeeping is, if not the town's only business, at least its main one. The stores and galleries jammed into the length of "downtown" Front Street leave room for little else except, perhaps, restaurants, and Lahaina has several shopping centers to boot. *The Wharf Cinema Center,* toward the south of town, is an assemblage of shops, restaurants, and theaters in a 3-tiered rustic wooden structure across Front Street from the banyan tree. Most of what is for sale at *The Wharf* is meant to entice the visitor, whereas the merchandise at the *Lahaina Shopping Center,* a more prosaic agglomeration of stores and parking spaces farther north along Front Street, tends to satisfy the utilitarian needs of the islanders. Here are the post office, supermarket, variety market, drugstores, hardware stores, banks, and fast-food outlets as well as clothing stores appealing to various levels of taste. Between these two, a small indentation along Front Street of no more than several shops around a paved brick court is referred to as the *Lahaina Market Place* — not the same thing as *Lahaina Square,* which is behind the *Lahaina Shopping Center* and something of a continuation of it. At the southern end of town, are the shops and restaurants of *505 Front Street,* in a setting reminiscent of an old-fashioned New England town. The latest addition to Lahaina's commercial offerings is the mix of shops and restaurants at the *Lahaina Center,* a built-to-scale extension of Front Street's turn-of-the-century buildings that now is home to the *Hard Rock Café, Hilo Hattie's,* and more. The *Lahaina Cannery,* about a mile from downtown, in the direction of Kaanapali, is a 50-store complex. Built in the style of the pineapple cannery that was originally located here, it features *Long's Drugs* and *Safeway* as its anchor tenants, with a secondary focus on visitor-oriented shops and services, including an *Ocean Activities Center* office.

Apparels of Pauline – This boutique has been here for more than a decade catering to women who wish to slip into the aloha spirit but don't want to look as though a missionary had dressed them. Among the best sellers are lots of silks, in languorous dinner dresses, loungewear, and sarongs; popular BaikBaik-brand rayon shirts from Bali; and oversized T-shirts hand-painted on Maui. *Lahaina Market Place,* just off Front St. (phone: 661-4774).

The Bakery – It's a bit out of the way, but worth the trip, especially when the pastries and cakes are hot from the oven. 991 Limahana Pl. (phone: 667-9062).

Circle Gallery – An eclectic selection of paintings, lithographs, ceramics, and sculpture, including works by Donna Summer, Erté, and Sandro Chia. 712 Front St. (phone: 667-0344).

Crazy Shirts – Only one of Hawaii's many T-shirt shops and only one of *Crazy Shirts'* three locations on Maui. The outlet on Front Street is noteworthy not simply for the T-shirts but because it contains a museum of whaling artifacts and the figurehead of a helmeted warrior salvaged from the 1972 shipwreck of the *Carthaginian I* on the Lahaina reef. 865 Front St. (phone: 661-4775); *The Wharf* (phone: 661-4712); and *Lahaina Cannery* (phone: 661-4788).

David's – Low-cost Maui-abilia — T-shirts, shorts, sweatshirts, and Lahaina's best collection of "greeting" cards make it worth a visit. 815 Front St. (phone: 661-4009).

Down Under Lahaina – Maui's best selection of men's swimwear, plus fashionable women's shorts, tank tops, and T-shirts that are truly eclectic. *Lahaina Center,* 900 Front St. (phone: 661-1166).

Dyansen Gallery – Erté is the headliner, but there's lots more — acrylic sculptures, paintings, lithographs, and bronzes. 844 Front St. phone: 661-2055).

Elephant Walk – An interesting selection of contemporary bric-a-brac and ethnic arts and crafts. 855A Front St. (phone: 661-6129).

Endangered Species – All the animals you've every loved or worried about are symbolically represented here in colorful T-shirts, toys, and other flights of artistic fancy. 707 Front St. (phone: 661-0208).

The Gallery – One of Hawaii's best and most expensive antiques stores. Geared to Lahaina's well-heeled yachting crowd, it's especially notable for its Oriental collection and worth a visit, if only to browse. 716 Front St. (phone: 661-0696).

Hanson Gallery – Erté is the star here, but other artists are also represented by this gallery, with branches in Beverly Hills, Carmel, San Francisco, Sausalito, and elsewhere on the mainland. 839 Front St. (phone: 661-0764; 800-879-1331).

Hilo Hattie's – It may be a bit garish and fluorescent, but this is a great place to browse for gifts that are both kitsch (souvenirs, ceramic Hawaiiana and other bric-a-brac, alohawear) and contemporary (books, calendars, attire, Hawaiian food products). You're sure to find something you can't resist, and the in-store shipping department is a plus for those with long gift lists. Off Front St., in the *Lahaina Shopping Center* (phone: 667-7911).

Lahaina Camera Center – Not only film and processing, but underwater and 35mm camera rentals and repairs are available here, as well as binoculars for whale watching during the winter. *Lahaina Shopping Center,* Front St., across from the post office (phone: 661-3306).

Lahaina Galleries – Four galleries, two located in Lahaina (the others are in the Kapalua shops and Kaanapali's *Whalers Village*), that offer changing exhibits of the high-priced work of artists like Andrea Smith and Robert Lyn Nelson. One is at 117

Lahainaluna Rd. (phone: 661-0839); the galleries' showcase for a wide range of artists and their paintings, lithographs, ceramics, and acrylic art is at 841 Front St. (phone: 667-2152).

Lahaina Printsellers – Considered the best collection of antique prints and maps found in Hawaii. Especially tempting is the excellent group related to Polynesian Hawaii and the early explorers such as Cook and La Perouse, found in the shops in the *Lahaina Cannery* (phone: 667-7843) and Kaanapali's *Whalers Village* (phone: 667-7617), as well as in the *Wailea Shopping Village* (phone: 879-1567).

Lahaina Scrimshaw Factory–Pier 49 – Both collectors and the merely curious will find the largest selection of scrimshaw on Maui in the five stores of the factory. A roster of resident scrimshanders produces most of the work, which is carved or engraved less and less on the teeth of the sperm whale (protected by the Endangered Species Act of 1973, which prohibits the importation of whale products, though teeth on hand at passage may still be used) and more and more on fossilized walrus tusk. While it is possible to spend as little as $5 for a fossil walrus ivory charm, it is also possible to spend several thousand dollars for a larger, weightier, more intricately carved piece. 845 Front St. (phone: 661-8820) and at the *Lahaina Cannery* (phone: 661-3971).

Local Motion – The original Hawaiian beachwear shop for men and women, with branches on Oahu and Maui. 900 Front St., in the *Lahaina Shopping Center* (phone: 669-SURF).

Luana's – Sells resortwear for women and men, plus its own brand of Hawaiian print bikinis (tops and bottoms sold in separate sizes), to which can be added a *lavalava* (a short hip skirt) or a sarong to match. In addition, there are caftans, aloha shirts, shorts, pants. 869 Front St. (phone: 667-2275); and *The Wharf* (phone: 661-0651).

Madeline Michaels Gallery – Perhaps Lahaina's most eclectic and irreverent art gallery, with a good selection of the sculptures (mostly bronzes and ceramics) and jewelry of Mexican artist Sergio Bustamente and the multimedia work of Will Herrera as highlights. Off Front St. in the *Lahaina Shopping Center* (phone: 661-3984).

The Mail Room – Packing, gift wrapping, and shipping for what you don't want to hand-carry back home. *Lahaina Shopping Center* (phone: 661-5788).

Martin Lawrence Gallery – Paintings, sculpture, ceramics, acrylics, and more. *Lahaina Market Place,* off Lahainaluna Rd. (phone: 661-1788).

Maui Mad Hatter – Stacked hats cover every bit of wall space and more hats hang from the ceiling — straw hats from China and the Philippines, panamas from Ecuador, *lau halas* from the South Pacific islands, and more. The feathered hatbands, jewel-like in color and velvety in texture, are exquisite examples of the Hawaiian craft. *The Wharf* (phone: 661-8125).

Maui Mouse House – A wide selection of licensed merchandise, with a focus on Disney characters. 505 Front St. (phone: 661-5758).

South Seas Trading Post – This shop, which looks like a small but veritable museum of South Seas imports, stocks anything from a Marshall Islands stick chart (actually a map, with sticks showing navigation routes and cowrie shells showing the islands) to "naif" paintings by Balinese children, Tongan tapa cloth, and rare shell leis from Niihau. Objects are carefully labeled, so you know what they are and whence they came. 851 Front St. (phone: 661-3168).

Superwhale – A children's boutique that is *the* place for teeny bikinis, miniaturized muumuus, saucy small T-shirts, and dolls clad in hula skirts. The *Lahaina Cannery* (phone: 661-3424).

Village Gallery – Turn up Dickenson Street past the Masters' Reading Room and the parking lot to reach this spare contemporary showroom with the anachronistic Victorian chairs and sofa. The gallery has oils, watercolors, prints, and mixed media by some of the finest Hawaiian artists. 120 Dickenson St. (phone: 661-4402).

Watch 'n' See – A great selection of watches, upscale (Raymond Weil, Citizen) and otherwise (Swatch). Also Rayban and Serengeti sunglasses. 900 Front St., in the *Lahaina Shopping Center* (phone: 661-1776).

Waterfront Gallery – The emphasis here is on coral, pearls, scrimshaw, and gold, with many an interesting piece on display. 825 Front St. (phone: 661-3124).

Wet Seal – Casual, upbeat clothing for women on a quest for up-to-the-minute togs. 900 Front St., in the *Lahaina Center* (phone: 667-9117).

Wyland Gallery – The ethereal underwater paintings, lithographs, and prints of artist Wyland, renowned for his immense, environmentally oriented murals of whales, are displayed here. 697 Front St. (phone: 661-7099).

NIGHTLIFE: Neighbor islanders are early to bed and early to rise, and it might strike mainlanders from locales less close to nature that nightlife on Maui takes place prematurely, too. It begins at sunset, or just before, and in Lahaina, sunset watching is the ritual that kicks it off. To participate, make your way to any bar with an unobstructed view west — those of *Kimo's,* the *Oceanhouse,* and the *Lahaina Broiler* restaurants, all on the *makai* (ocean) side of Front Street, are especially nice spots, and on the opposite side of the street, *The Keg* also has a clear view over the seawall out to the blue.

The *Old Lahaina Luau* ($42) is offered Tuesdays through Saturdays, at a beachfront setting adjacent to the shops at *505 Front St.* (phone: 667-1998). With its focus on traditional hula and costume, the attention to authenticity makes this one of Hawaii's better luaus. While prime ribs cater to mainland tastes, island favorites like grilled mahimahi, shoyu chicken, pulehu ribs, lomilomi salmon, and poi are also served.

After dinner or the luau, the evening proceeds with, perhaps, a stroll, and while this part of the night is in progress, Lahaina's main drag crawls with pedestrians making their way randomly up one side of the street and down the other, with frequent enough crossings-over to slow the bumper-to-bumper traffic to well below the 15-mph speed limit. Because many stores stay open late, some of this promenade is nothing more than straightforward window-shopping, and by about 10 PM, when stores are closed and most restaurants are serving their last customers, the town begins to close down for the night. Only a few spots persevere to rend the nocturnal peace, and night owls who haven't checked their papers beforehand will be able to find them by keeping their ears open. The loudest sound is liable to be coming from *Moose McGillicuddy's* (844 Front St.; phone: 661-7758), where disco — or its live equivalent — reigns in Lahaina. The bands attract a mostly young crowd (few over-30s here), who appreciate the top-40 format. Another favorite nightspot with islanders is the *Old Whaler's Grog Shop* (just inside the swinging doors off the lobby of the *Pioneer Inn;* phone: 661-3636). Decked out with captain's chairs, whaling artifacts, and other nautical paraphernalia, the bar is the late afternoon haunt of habitués who drop in from the waterfront, and by the time the live music begins at 9 PM, the joint is ready to jump — to the beat of the top-40 tunes — until closing between midnight and 1 AM. *Longhi's* (888 Front St.; phone: 667-2288) is also a good place to stop in for an after-hours drink; weekends, there's often live music and dancing in the elegant second-story lounge. *Studio 505* (505 Front St.; phone: 661-1505), owned by Stephen Stills of *Crosby, Stills, and Nash* fame, is the newest disco hot spot in town. The nearby *Hard Rock Café* (in the *Lahaina Shopping Center*; phone: 667-7400) also has a lively bar that attracts a young and eager crowd until midnight nightly (12:30 AM on weekends). *Blackie's Bar* (at Blackie's Boat Yard on Honoapiilani Hwy.; phone: 667-7979) is the place to go for jazz Mondays, Wednesdays, Fridays, and Sundays from 5 to 8 PM. (You won't have trouble finding *Blackie's* — it's in a big house with a bright orange roof, shaped like a hexagon and built on stilts, on the main highway between Lahaina and Kaanapali.) There's also

Hawaiian music that attracts a lively weekend crowd at the *Old Lahaina Café* (505 Front St.; phone: 661-3303), from 8:30 PM to midnight. Movie buffs may want to check out what's playing at the three theaters of the *Wharf Cinema Center* (phone: 661-3347).

CHECKING IN: Lahaina may be the commercial hub of West Maui, but most people do not make it their headquarters, mainly because the town itself is without a proper beach. In addition, it tends to be hot, its backdrop of steep West Maui mountains cutting off the trade winds that ruffle the palms only a few miles up the coast. Thus, most of the hotel and condominium building has taken place north of Lahaina, where beaches and trade winds coincide, and those wishing to stay in the old whaling capital itself have a somewhat limited choice. In the suggestions below, expect to pay $145 and up to accommodate two people in places listed in the expensive category, $80 to $140 in the moderate category, and $50 to $75 in places listed in the inexpensive category. All telephone numbers are in the 808 area code unless otherwise indicated.

Lahaina – In the heart of Lahaina, this 13-room hostelry is filled with 19th-century antiques that match the 1990 restoration of this turn-of-the-century building (it was originally a feed store). Charm aplenty and temptingly priced, with room rates including a tasty continental breakfast. *David Paul's Lahaina Grill* (see *Eating Out*) is located on the ground floor. 127 Lahainaluna Rd. (phone: 661-0577; 800-669-3444). Expensive to moderate.

Lahaina Shores – This is Lahaina's major resort condominium and the only place to stay if you want to be both in town and directly on a beach. The 200-plus units occupy one 6-story building topped by a penthouse, and though the building is modern, the white columns and balustrades of 6 rows of lanais give it something of an antebellum look. The rooms — studios or 1-bedroom units, ocean or mountain views — are more prosaic, but still pleasant, with TV sets, phone, and air conditioning. A swimming pool and a Jacuzzi are on an Astroturf-covered patio, but just a few steps farther over real grass and you are on the beach, albeit a narrow one, just south of the harbor. Shops and restaurants are next door at the *505 Front Street* complex. 475 Front St. (phone: 661-4835; 800-628-6699). Expensive to moderate.

Plantation Inn – The 17 rooms and suites at this beautiful, Victorian-style hotel are situated just a block from Front Street and the ocean. *Gerard's* (see *Eating Out*) is located in the hotel and provides the breakfasts that are included in the cost of a room. Other attractions include a pool and the warm aloha spirit supplied by owners/managers Jim and Lina Patterson. 174 Lahainaluna Rd. (phone: 667-9225; 800-433-6815). Expensive to moderate.

Maui Islander – Located several blocks back from Front Street, this low-rise, air conditioned apartment complex offers both hotel and condominium accommodations. While not fancy, the comfortable facilities include tennis courts and a pool. 660 Wainee St. (phone: 667-9766; 800-367-5226). Moderate.

Pioneer Inn – This waterfront property has been a Lahaina landmark since 1901 (see description above), and it is wonderfully evocative of former times. The atmosphere begins in the tiny lobby of the original wing, replete with grandfather clock, plate rails, and a stairway that leans and creaks past a lovely stained glass window on its way to the rooms. Not everyone appreciates the stamp of yesteryear in the accommodations, however: makeshift closets, rooms without bath or with baths not quite up to snuff (showers only), ceiling fans and screen doors, but no air conditioning. Rooms in the new wing, added in 1966, are air conditioned and an improvement in other respects, too, including their distance from the *Old Whaler's Grog Shop,* a lively bar and meeting place next to the lobby in the old wing. Restaurants on the premises are the *Snug Harbor Dining Room,* the open-air

South Seas Patio, and the *Harpooner's Lanai,* serving breakfast from 7 to 11 AM, and lunch from 11:30 AM to 2 PM on the side porch. There are no TV sets, nor private lanais, but rooms in the old wing have access to the second-story verandah from which to view Lahaina Harbor, while those in the new wing open on individually railed sections of verandah overlooking the swimming pool, the banyan tree, or Front Street. 658 Wharf St. (phone: 661-3636; 800-457-5457). Moderate to inexpensive.

EATING OUT: Most restaurants in Lahaina — and on Maui in general — fall into two categories: the broiler type, where the menu stresses steaks, seafood, and one or two fresh fish-of-the-day selections; and everything else; that is, those specializing in French, Italian, or some other national cuisine — almost anything except authentic Hawaiian (though most restaurants include a few Polynesian preparations on the bill of fare). Chances are good that the prices will run a bit higher than back home. Expect to pay $75 or more for the average meal for two in any restaurant listed below as expensive and anywhere from $35 to $70 in a restaurant listed as moderate. An inexpensive listing means under $30 for two — and none of the above guidelines includes drinks, wine, or tip. There is a fourth category of eatery, the fast-food outlet, where you can spend a lot less for hamburgers, pizza, fried chicken, yogurt with toppings, and certain Oriental specialties.

The dress code is very relaxed on Maui. In no restaurant listed below would a man in an aloha shirt or comparable neat sportswear, or a woman in a simple cotton dress, skirt and blouse, or T-shirt, feel out of place at dinner. Casual dress does mean something on the formal side of shorts and rubber thongs, however, though even these usually will be fine at lunch.

All telephone numbers are in the 808 area code unless otherwise indicated.

Chez Paul – The "village" of Olowalu (halfway between Lahaina and Kahului) is the unlikely setting for this casual French restaurant. The menu features Gallic standards like pâté de foie gras and escargots, with more exotic entrées like *canard Laperousse* (boneless roast duck with Dijon mustard and a creamy sherry sauce) and for simpler tastes, filet mignon or a selection of sautéed, poached, and steamed vegetables. Dinner seatings at 6:30 and 8:30 PM, nightly. Reservations necessary. Hwy. 30, 6 miles south of Lahaina (phone: 661-3843). Expensive.

Avalon – Owner-chef Mark Ellman has created one of Maui's most popular nouvelle cuisine–style restaurants, with an imaginative menu that includes specialties like seared *sahimi,* Asian pasta (with shrimp, clams, scallops, and fish in a sauce of fragrant herbs), Indonesian *satay* with Balinese sauce, soft-shell crab, and wok-prepared whole fresh opakapaka, and desserts such as their fabled Carmel Miranda (macadamia nut ice cream with seasonal fruits glazed with caramel sauce). Same menu from noon to midnight daily. Reservations necessary. 844 Front St. (phone: 667-5559). Expensive to moderate.

Chart House – It's way, way north of the section of Front Street that could be called the beaten track, but word of mouth among visitors has made this a hit nonetheless. The building is Polynesian rustic, resembling a longhouse, but the food is no-nonsense steaks, seafood, or a combination of both, plus the best-selling prime ribs. Portions are generous, as is the salad. Open for dinner daily from 5 to 10 PM. No reservations. 1450 Front St., at the junction of Front St. and Hwy. 30 (phone: 661-0937). Expensive to moderate.

David Paul's Lahaina Grill – The decor is casual yet elegant, the menu imaginative, and the food is well prepared and well presented. Specials include tequila shrimp with firecracker rice, steamed tamalitos stuffed with shrimp and sausage, and macadamia-smoked kona yearling tenderloin with sweet chili compote and avocado relish. Open weekdays for lunch from 11:30 AM to 2:30 PM, and nightly for dinner from 6 to 11:30 PM. $15 minimum for dinner. Reservations advised. *Lahaina Hotel,* 127 Lahainaluna Rd., Lahaina (phone: 667-5117). Dinner: expensive; lunch: moderate.

Gerard's – Chef-owner Gerard Reversade has created one of Hawaii's finest restaurants with a menu that takes advantage of what's freshest in the way of seafood, meat, and produce. The results are memorable, be they appetizers like wild mushrooms in puff pastry or calamari with lime and ginger; entrées like opakapaka, tournedos *au poivre* or in lobster sauce; or luscious desserts. The ambience is a French-Hawaiian hybrid. Open daily for breakfast from 7:30 to 10 AM, and dinner from 6 to 10 PM. Reservations advised. In the *Plantation Inn,* 174 Lahainaluna Rd. (phone: 661-8939). Expensive to moderate.

Longhi's – This immensely popular Italian restaurant attracts an arty crowd that contributes as much to its cabaret atmosphere as the white and black cane-back chairs and the black-and-white checkered floor. The fellow who pulls up a chair next to your table and begins the good-humored recitative is the waiter, and the litany he's reciting is the menu, so pay attention — it's the only one you get. Homemade pastas are the ticket here, too, though you can also have fish, chicken, veal, steaks, or eggplant *alla parmigiana,* and all this is still merely a prelude to dessert. When the time comes, a tray laden with calories will sweep over the heads of the crowd, and if the array is confusing when it reaches eye level, rest assured that the mocha chocolate cheesecake will not disappoint. Open for breakfast (with some delicious fresh pastries) from 7:30 to 11:30 AM, lunch from 11:30 AM to 5:30 PM,, and dinner daily from 5 to 10 PM. No reservations. 888 Front St. (phone: 667-2288). Expensive to moderate.

Kimo's – One of the three popular waterfront restaurants, this one is a bit more sophisticated than the other two, and it is one of Lahaina's better values. Begin with a drink under one of the huge white canvas umbrellas on the open deck downstairs, and when the sun has definitely set, move on to the indoor-outdoor dining room upstairs. A basic mix of steaks, seafood, and local fresh fish of the day is served, each order with a zestfully seasoned house salad, rice, and freshly baked breads. The Polynesian chicken (marinated in a sauce of soy and ginger) and Koloa pork ribs (glazed with plum sauce in the manner of Koloa, Hawaii) are island specialties, and the hula pie (macadamia nut ice cream in an Oreo cookie crust, topped with chocolate fudge, whipped cream, and macadamia nuts) is legendary. Open daily for lunch from 11:30 AM to 2:30 PM, and dinner from 5 to 10:30 PM. Reservations advised. 845 Front St. (phone: 661-4811). Moderate.

Kobe Steak House – The sushi bar is the real draw, but the teppan-style cooking provides another reason for this restaurant's popularity with locals and visitors alike. Dinner served from 5:30 to 9:30 PM daily. Reservations advised. 136 Dickenson St. (phone: 667-5555). Moderate.

Lahaina Broiler – You'll spot this by the 100-year-old monkeypod tree, growing right through the roof. Run by the same folks who run the *Pioneer Inn,* it's a waterfront favorite. It's every bit as scenic as *Kimo's.* The bar and dining area are on one level, which is well nigh wave-pounded sea level. Steaks, prime ribs, and fresh fish of the day are the menu mainstays. Open for brunch from 10 AM to 2 PM, and dinner from 5 to 9 PM daily. Reservations advised for dinner. 889 Front St. (phone: 661-3111). Moderate.

Tasca – The decor is casual; the food is inspired by the Mediterranean, evidenced by seafood dishes like paella, as well as Asia, represented by that area's traditional saffron chicken. Most dishes are available in small, medium, or large portions, *tapas*-style, which suits all appetites and budgets. Open daily from 5:30 PM to midnight. Reservations advised for six or more people. 608 Front St. (phone: 661-8001). Moderate.

Alex's Hole in the Wall – The premises are up one flight of stairs and smallish, yes, but despite the faintly pejorative air to its name, this restaurant, run by the Didio family, is a spic and span and decorous place that manages to strike the right balance between liveliness and intimacy. The menu, too, offsets some of its more expensive veal dinners with a selection of economical spaghetti dinners, while the linguine with white clam sauce is a middle-of-the-road favorite of many a repeat customer. The pasta is made daily. Open for dinner from 5:30 to 9:45 PM; closed Sundays. Reservations advised. Wahie La., off Front St. (phone: 661-3197). Moderate to inexpensive.

Hard Rock Café – Part of the world-wide chain, the newest kid in town has 1960s decor: big surfboards, guitars, a Cadillac over the bar, concert posters, and music memorabilia. Not to be overlooked is its raison d'être, the nonstop rock music. The menu includes barbecued ribs, barbecued lime chicken, huge hamburgers, and salads, homemade soup, *pupus,* and Maui's biggest brownie à la mode. Trademark T-shirts from the restaurant make much welcome gifts. Open daily for lunch and dinner; same menu from 11:30 AM to 10:30 PM (11:30 PM on weekends). Reservations unnecessary. 900 Front St. (phone: 667-7400). Moderate to inexpensive.

J.J.'s Beach Grille – Although the atmosphere may be unassuming, the fare is soul-satisfying and solid. Excellent steaks and seafood are the mainstays of the menu, while such selections as *poisson beurre blanc* and *scampi olowalu* are as tantalizing to the eye as they are to the palate. Open daily for lunch from 10 AM to 3 PM, and dinner from 5:30 PM until midnight. Reservations advised. 505 Front St. (phone: 667-4341). Moderate to inexpensive.

Chili's Grill & Bar – Devotees of Mexican-American fare will savor the fajitas and cheese-covered nachos, and other delights such as Buffalo wings and grilled Caribbean chicken won't fail to please. Open daily for lunch and dinner from 11 AM to 10 PM. Reservations unnecessary. 900 Front St., in the *Lahaina Center* (phone: 661-3665). Inexpensive.

Happy Days Café – This 1950s-style eatery offers large portions, good prices, and tasty fare. Hearty breakfasts, served from 7 AM to 3 PM, are recommended, with a delicious selection of hamburgers and sandwiches served from 11 AM to 3 PM daily. No reservations. In the *Lahaina Marketplace* (phone: 661-3235). Inexpensive.

Sunrise Café – The fresh-baked daily French pastries and coffees are worth a gourmand's attention. Open daily from 5:30 AM to 10:30 PM. No reservations. 693-A Front St. (phone: 661-3326). Inexpensive.

And best of all, there is "Maui Pie" ice cream — a mixture of flavors including Kona coffee, chocolate fudge, coconut, macadamia nut, and chewy fudge — that's served at *Lappert's Ice Cream* on the main drag of Lahaina.

Kaanapali to Kapalua

So many of the visitors to Maui point their rented cars in the direction of West Maui that, left to their own devices, the cars could probably make the trip themselves. That trip is about to become easier as a result of the construction of a Lahaina bypass to ease passage through that high-traffic town. West Maui's gold coast of hotels and condominiums begins 4 miles north of Lahaina at the *Kaanapali* resort and ends some 10 miles farther north at another resort, *Kapalua.* In between are what local fancy and a few maps still refer to as towns, though to the uninitiated they look like a single, barely interrupted string of condominiums and homes lining both the *mauka* (inland) and *makai* (ocean) sides of the coastal road. Do not picture the concrete canyon of Waikiki, however, because the resorts at each end were planned to enhance, not overwhelm, their natural setting, and the structures between the two are sufficiently varied — here aggressively prominent, there shrinking in leaf-covered seclusion — not to blot out the view, which on West Maui, with its clean sweep from mountains to cane fields to sea, is always extraordinary.

The *Kaanapali* resort is a 500-acre playground containing six hotels (the majority of hotels on West Maui), seven condominium complexes, two golf courses, a shopping center, and an excellent whaling museum, all arranged along 3 miles of choice sandy beach divided in half by a volcanic lava outcropping called Puu Kekaa (Black Rock), and laced together by a system of neat, tree-lined driveways. Guests may not realize it, but the complex, which opened in 1962 with only a golf course and an embryonic hotel in operation and a second hotel on the way, was Hawaii's first planned resort, the prototype of an idea that no longer seems unusual, though it certainly was back in the 1950s when first proposed.

Before its development, Kaanapali was an unproductive piece of scrubland at the foot of a more productive sugarcane plantation, both owned by Lahaina's Pioneer Mill Company. During the late 19th and early 20th centuries, a sugarcane train traveled between Lahaina and a boat landing next to Black Rock. Cut cane was hauled to Lahaina; raw sugar was hauled from Lahaina and loaded onto tugboats at Black Rock and carried out to waiting ships. Pioneer eventually switched the sugar-loading operation to Lahaina, and it and its parent company, Amfac (American Factors), one of Hawaii's Big Five, began to think of a better use for the beach area. Thirty years later, Kaanapali is still growing, with additional hotels and condominiums planned for the future. The only reminder of the old days is the *Lahaina-Kaanapali and Pacific Railroad,* a replica of an old-fashioned sugarcane train that now puffs its way through the cane fields between the resort and Lahaina.

Kaanapali's beach stretches north beyond the limits of the resort as far as Honokowai, then disappears and reappears at intervals as sandy parentheses in the otherwise rocky coastline. Condominiums available for vacation rentals line the coast from Kaanapali to the north. The coastal villages of Honokowai, Kahana, and Napili are really an example of suburban sprawl pulled lengthwise, Honokowai turning into Kahana at the "S" in the road, Kahana turning into Napili in the vicinity of beautiful Napili Bay. Napili Beach is the first of two particularly lovely beaches, and Kapalua Beach, which edges Kapalua Bay around the next bend in the coast, is the second. Kapalua Beach is surrounded by the exquisite scenery of another of Maui's planned resorts, *Kapalua,* set on 750 panoramic acres formerly used to grow pineapples. Kapalua was the brainchild of the Maui Land and Pineapple Company. Its central features are the *Kapalua Bay* hotel, the *Ritz-Carlton Kapalua*, several resort condominiums, three golf courses, ten tennis courts, and a small shopping center. Construction of the *Ritz-Carlton* was delayed, and the site changed, to preserve an ancient Hawaiian burial ground that was discovered during the initial excavation at the original site.

Although the face of West Maui has in recent memory been sculpted by

Amfac, Maui Land and Pineapple Company, and other Hawaiian business interests, the area has a pre-*haole* history as well. The road that circles West Maui (Hwy. 30) is still called Honoapiilani Highway, recalling the 16th-century chief Piilani, who built the first road around Maui. Honoapiilani means "the bays of Piilani," and a drive along Highway 30 from Kaanapali to beyond Kapalua will take you past all six of the bays — Honokowai, Honokeana, Honokahua, Honolua, Honokohau, and Hononana — associated with him. And Puu Kekaa, according to ancient belief, was a sacred spot from which souls of the dead leaped into the spirit world. It was also the spot from which Maui's last chief, Kahekili, who ruled at the end of the 18th century and excelled at the sport of cliff jumping, made several of his most daring leaps. That he survived, defying death in more ways than one, reinforced his authority over his subjects. Today, the jump is repeated every evening at sundown at the *Sheraton Maui,* which sits astride Black Rock, and though the feat is less risky in thoroughly modern Maui, it can still raise a few goose bumps.

Lahaina-Kaanapali and Pacific Railroad – That is, the *Sugarcane Train,* an oil-fired turn-of-the-century steam locomotive and three open passenger coaches that now carry tourists on a pleasure excursion through golf courses and cane fields, across a 400-foot-long trestle, past views of the seashore and Lanai on one side and of the West Maui mountains on the other. The train puffs along 6 miles of 36-inch narrow-gauge track, portions of which follow the roadbed of the original cane haul line that ran between the cane fields of Kaanapali and Lahaina's Pioneer Mill from the 1880s to the early 1950s. Both of the railroad's engines — *Anaka* and *Myrtle* — were built in 1943 for a quarry in Ohio, and both have been rebuilt to resemble vintage sugarcane locomotives — circa the 1880s in the case of *Anaka,* about 1910 for *Myrtle.* The custom-made coaches are patterned after cars made in England in the late 19th century for a passenger train on the island of Hawaii. The *LK&PRR* makes six round trips daily between the Puukolii Boarding Platform and the Lahaina Station, with an interim stop at the Kaanapali Station. A one-way ride takes about 25 minutes, during which time the conductor delivers some facts and figures on the subject of sugarcane, plays the ukulele, and sings. The trip costs $6 one way, $9 round trip (half price for children ages 3 to 12), and various combination tours — such as a glass-bottom boat ride in Lahaina Harbor ($19); an Historic Lahaina itinerary, which includes admission to three museums ($12.50); and a viewing of the film *Hawaii: Islands of the Gods* on a 180° screen at the *Omni Theater* ($14) — are possible. The *Kaanapali Trolley* serves the Kaanapali Station, and a free railroad bus provides transportation between the Lahaina Station and the waterfront. The Puukolii Boarding Platform is across the highway from the *Royal Lahaina;* the Kaanapali Station is above the *Maui Eldorado* condominiums, and the Lahaina Station is 1½ blocks north of the intersection of Honoapiilani Hwy. and Lahainaluna Rd. (phone: 661-0080).

Whalers Village Museum – This is *the* place to visit if you want to know more about whales and the history of whaling. Cases full of artifacts and illustrations detail every aspect of whaling, from the construction of the ship to setting out on the voyage, life at sea, and the hunting, killing, and processing of the whale. There are tools used in sail making, harpoons, some rather horrific-looking instruments used by a ship's surgeon, and whale products — antique lamps filled with whale oil, walking canes with whale ivory handles, whale ivory letter openers, rolling pins, and pie crimpers. Scrimshaw is an important part of the collection; in fact, along with the larger *Pacific Whaling Museum* on Oahu, the best examples of old scrimshaw remaining in the

Hawaiian islands are on view here. You'll see materials for scrimshaw, comparisons of 19th-century scrimshaw with reproductions and examples of modern scrimshaw, plus some unusual pieces such as a scrimshawed ostrich egg and the jawbone of a sea lion scrimshawed with a portrait of George Washington. Open daily from 9:30 AM to 9:30 PM; no admission charge. *Whalers Village, Kaanapali* resort (phone: 661-5992).

SHOPPING: Almost everyone staying in West Maui eventually makes a shopping trip into Lahaina; the salty old town has the greatest concentration of vendibles in all the Valley Isle and no less an inclination to commerce than when whalers walked the streets to replenish their ships. Visitors don't have to make the trip, however, because almost equal opportunities to browse and buy exist closer to their Kaanapali-Kapalua homes-away-from-home. There is, first of all, Kaanapali's *Whalers Village Museum and Shopping Complex.* There, shops stock necessities as well as gifts, souvenirs, and clothing, and stay open till 9 or 10 PM daily. Hotels in the *Kaanapali* resort have lobby shops, and some have substantial shopping arcades that aim to do much more than sell guests on Hawaiian shirts. Foremost among these are the promenades at the *Hyatt Regency* and the *Maui Marriott* as well as that of the *Westin Maui.* Several miles to the north at Kapalua, the first-rate Kapalua shops practice their version of not-for-the-stingy seduction. On Mondays and Thursdays from 8 AM to 1:30 PM, the farmers' market in Kahana features locally grown produce (including sweet Hana corn and Molokai watermelon), fresh baked breads and cookies, and low prices.

WHALERS VILLAGE MUSEUM AND SHOPPING COMPLEX

Some of the more familiar names here include *Canoe* (phone: 667-2282), *Benetton* (phone: 661-8188), and *Esprit de Corps* (phone: 661-4400). Shops of a more homegrown style include the following:

Bebe Sports – One of several shops on Maui, this branch features women's contemporary fashions of bright colors and easy-to-wear styles (phone: 661-0444).

Blue Ginger – Batik is the method, Polynesian the style, for a fine selection of women's clothing (phone: 667-5433).

Cruise – Landlubbers and would-be sailors alike can find clothing with a nautical theme in this upscale women's shop (phone: 667-1974).

Hobie Sports – Bright and upbeat, this shop carries a wide range of water sports equipment as well as beach fashions, beach chairs, and all kinds of beach accessories (phone: 661-5455).

Hudson & Co. – Finely crafted jewelry is the watchword here, with an especially alluring selection of black and pink coral (phone: 661-1097).

Island Tan – Your nose will know where you are before you enter, with fragrances of tuberose, frangipani, pikake, and other tropical flowers wafting from within. This store sells tanning lotion and skin care products (all made with aloe vera), and original Hawaiian fragrances (phone: 926-5756).

Ka Honu Gift Gallery – The local and South Pacific handicrafts include lots of woodcarvings; bowls of koa, milo, hau, mango, and monkeypod; and shell leis from the island of Niihau. Browse among the large selection of Christmas ornaments, too (phone: 661-0173).

Lahaina Printsellers Ltd. – This gallery specializes in antique maps and prints of Hawaiian and South Seas scenes. Among the unusual inventory are engravings from the folio of illustrations that accompanied the official account of Cook's third voyage, as drawn by James Webber, the artist assigned to travel with Cook, and as cut into plates and published (1784) by the Admiralty in London. Other beautiful prints from diverse sources document paradises when they were truly unspoiled (phone: 667-7617).

Lahaina Scrimshaw Factory – After seeing the rare old pieces on display in the *Whalers Village Museum,* stop here to admire more modern (most of them) examples of the art of scrimshaw. The "*factory*" has a roster of resident scrimshanders producing work on whale's teeth and fossil walrus ivory for its four stores on Maui. Charms begin at $5; large, museum-quality pieces are an investment (phone: 661-4034).

Sharper Image – Perhaps the easiest shop in which to browse, with a huge inventory of high-tech gadgets. There's always something to consider buying (phone: 661-7061).

Silks Kaanapali – One of Hawaii's best selections of fashionable women's silk clothing (phone: 667-7133).

Waldenbooks – Besides all the latest paperbacks, this branch of the well-known chain provides a selection of Hawaiiana — and Mauiana — from guidebooks to folklore (phone: 661-8638).

LAHAINA CANNERY

In addition to *Long's Drugs* (phone: 667-4384), where all kinds of sundries (and Maui's best-priced film) can be purchased, a *Safeway* supermarket (phone: 667-4392), and other standard mall stores such as clothing and footwear shops, this retail complex includes the following:

Dolphin Gallery – An excellent selection of glass, jewelry, sculpture, painting, and lithographs. Although many of the items are overpriced, there are some good buys (phone: 661-5000). There's also a branch at Kaanapali's *Whaler's Village Museum and Shopping Complex* (phone: 661-5115).

Nevada Bob's – Golf and tennis are the names of the games here, with just about anything you'll need for either sport (phone: 661-3681).

HYATT REGENCY

Center Art Gallery–Hawaii – It may be the best stocked and classiest of all the art galleries in the islands, with a good selection of original paintings, lithographs, and sculpture by both American and European artists (phone: 661-1200).

Chapman's – A men's store that sells jackets, blazers, slacks, shirts, and shoes in subdued color schemes, plus a selection of flashier shirts. (phone: 661-4121).

Collections – This upscale division of *Liberty House* features an excellent selection of high-fashion women's wear (phone: 667-7785). There is also a branch at a nearby *Westin Maui* (phone: 661-5083).

Elephant Walk – Ceramics, batiks, glassware, and other items handcrafted by Hawaiian artists are among the featured collectibles and knickknacks (phone: 667-2848).

Hawaiian Island Gems – Everything (or nearly) is made of gold or ivory. Among the more interesting items are reproductions of 19th-century Hawaiian coins and Hawaiian heirloom jewelry. Bracelets and rings in this series are hand-engraved and can be enameled either with your own name in Hawaiian or as is, with a Hawaiian term of endearment (phone: 667-7788).

Lloyd and Carver – Luggage, briefcases, wallets, and ladies' handbags by French and Italian designers make up the bulk of this shop's merchandise. Swiss watches and jewelry of the only-one-piece-out-of-the-case-at-a-time variety are sold, too (phone: 667-7788).

Michele's – Elegant dresses and accessories for women. This shop sells the sort of clothing you might pick off the designer racks back home and could wear to dinner at Kapalua's *Bay Club* or *Veranda.* It's not the place to come for Polynesian styles (phone: 667-6198).

Postmark Maui – Some of it may be tacky, but some of it isn't, and at any rate, it's all made on the island, and for lovers of Maui, that may well be enough. Gifts and a wide array of souvenir trinkets, useful and otherwise (phone: 661-3408).

Sandal Tree – The name is clear: men's and women's footwear appropriate to the clime and the place; and for the opposite extreme, straw hats with feathered hatbands (phone: 661-3495).

KAPALUA

By the Bay – Quite the nicest shell shop on Maui has shells and corals from Hawaii and the rest of the Pacific. Large, lovely, pale blue coral from the Indo-Pacific; white branch, lettuce, and trumpet coral from the South Pacific; bright orange Hawaiian sea fans; and sprigs of Maui black coral make such an enticing show of the premises that all but collectors may overlook the tinier specimens, including the precious wentletrap, or spiral staircase shell, coveted by the Dutch in the 19th century. Also, distinctive shell jewelry (phone: 669-5227).

Distant Drums – It sells a small museum's worth of handicrafts, artifacts, antiques, and jewelry from Hawaii, the Pacific islands, New Guinea, Indonesia, and Asia (phone: 669-5522).

Kapalua Shop – The resort logo decorates towels, glassware, scarves, men's and women's sportswear, luggage, eyeglass cases, kimonos, and so on. Sometimes the Kapalua name appears unobtrusively in print, but mostly the butterfly logo is flying alone (phone: 669-4172).

Mandalay – Despite its name, the cottons and silks in this shop come from Thailand. There are long caftans, short dresses, smocks, blouses, and jackets for women, and a few shirts for men (phone: 669-6170).

Reyn's – This shop features both its own line of shirts, slacks, and swim trunks and sportswear by other manufacturers. The company pioneered reverse-print men's clothes — made with the bright right side of the fabric inside — more than a decade ago, and the look has become a Hawaiian classic (phone: 669-5260).

MAUI MARRIOTT

Buck's For Men – A men's clothing store that sells much more than swim trunks (phone: 667-7801).

Hawaii I.D. – Sportswear, beach gear, and other articles with the *Maui Marriott* logo are available here (phone: 667-1200, ext. 66717).

Liberty House – This branch of the Hawaii-wide chain sells men's and women's clothing and some accessories (phone: 667-6142).

Maui Sun and Surf – Masks, flippers, Boogie boards, rafts, and suntan products are offered at this store (phone: 667-9302).

NIGHTLIFE: With any number of hotel and restaurant bars strategically placed so that sight lines lead straight out to the Pacific and the offshore islands of Lanai or Molokai, sunset watching is as important here as in Lahaina. The most unusual observance takes place at the *Sheraton Maui* (phone: 661-0031) just before sunset, when a hotel employee in native dress appears brandishing fire, lights a line of tiki torches running the length of Black Rock promontory, throws his lei into the sea, and then dives from the cliff himself. Though the leap is not impressively high, it can be affecting, because the ritual recalls the ancient Hawaiian belief that Black Rock (its Hawaiian name is Puu Kekaa) was a "soul's leap," a place where the souls of the dead left Earth to rejoin the spirit world. The hotel's high *On the Rocks* bar is a splendid wide-screen vantage point for watching Kaanapali sunsets, but the *Sundowner Bar* by the pool is the best place to be for the torchlighting ceremony.

The grounds of the *Sheraton Maui* are also the site of a nightly luau, except Sundays (phone: 661-3500). The entertainment includes Hawaiian song and dance. The luau goes on at 5 PM — so beachfront sunset watching is included in the $42 cost. Shuttle service may be arranged by the time reservations are made for parties of 8 or more. Child-care service is also available upon request.

The *Royal Lahaina* (phone: 661-3611) has a competitively priced nightly luau ($40), featuring traditional foods like kalua pig and haupia (coconut pudding), as well as a variety of salads. The hour-long Polynesian revue is held on a beachfront lawn, and the luau runs from 5:30 to 8:15 PM, timed to take in the sunset. The *Maui Marriott* (phone: 661-5828) features a luau daily except Mondays. It begins at 4:30 PM with traditional Hawaiian crafts and games, followed by an *imu* ceremony and an "all-you-can-eat" buffet. Entertainment includes a Polynesian revue complete with five dancers. The beachfront luau is priced at $42. A hula and musical revue, *Maui on My Mind,* is presented in the *Discovery Room* of the *Sheraton Maui* (phone: 661-0031) at 8 PM nightly except Tuesdays, for a $5 cover charge with dinner, or $15 for cocktails only. A third option is the $42 evening package, which includes dinner and entertainment. At the *Westin* (phone: 667-2525), *Cooks at the Beach* features a prime ribs buffet ($19.75) accompanied by live Hawaiian music and hula from 6:30 to 9 PM daily (no reservations). The *Hyatt Regency* (phone: 661-1234) features the *Drums of the Pacific* dinner show on the *Sunset Terrace* ($44), with cocktail seating ($26) at 6:45 to 8 PM Monday, Wednesday, and Friday.

The *Kaanapali* resort has two popular discos, *Spats II,* at the *Hyatt Regency,* where the dancing goes on till 2 AM nightly in a cavernous space reminiscent of the gaslight era, and the *Maui Marriott*'s handsome *Banana Moon,* with two handkerchief-size dance floors, quite a few cozy seating areas conducive to conversation, and a backgammon bar. More mellow music for dancing is played in various hotel rooms around the resort, including the *Royal Ocean Terrace* at the *Royal Lahaina* and outdoors at the *Pavillion Courtyard* of the *Hyatt Regency* (nightly). Best for relaxed listening are the *Tiki Terrace* of the *Kaanapali Beach, Maui Marriott*'s *Makai Bar,* and *El Crab Catcher* restaurant at *Whalers Village.* For the early bird, the *Westin Maui* serves cocktails alfresco at its *Beach Bar* to the sounds of a Hawaiian trio, and its *Villa Restaurant Lounge* features Hawaiian music from 6 to 9 PM. At press time, a cluster of new restaurants offering evening entertainment were scheduled to open at *Whalers Village.*

Beyond the *Kaanapali* resort, nightlife is less active, though there are possibilities. The *Kapalua Bay* (phone: 669-5656) offers dancing nightly in *The Garden,* from 8 PM to midnight. The dinner show at the *Napili Kai Beach Club* (in the *Seahouse Restaurant;* phone: 669-6271) is an unusual demonstration of Hawaiiana, Fridays only, put on by children of the hotel staff. Tickets sell out quickly to *Napili Kai* guests, but you can reserve leftover seats. A Hawaiian trio holds forth with music for dancing on other nights in the same restaurant. There's nightly dancing to live contemporary and country music at the *Kahana Keys* restaurant (phone: 669-8071) at the Valley Isle resort condominiums at Kahana.

CHECKING IN: The greatest concentration of hotels and condominiums on Maui is found along the Kaanapali-Kapalua coast. North of Kaanapali, the beach narrows and gradually gives way to stretches of lava rock coast and shallow reef-lined waters that make swimming more difficult. At both Honokawai and Kahana, clusters of condominiums overwhelm the small beaches, but Napili's low-rise properties are better suited to their surroundings, taking advantage of a mix of rocky promontories and beach-lined bays. If you have just arrived from Honolulu, these accommodations may seem comparatively high priced. Expect to pay $250 and up for a double room in a place listed in the very expensive category, from $150 to $240 in expensive, $85 to $145 in moderate, and from $60 to $80 in those classed as inexpensive. There may be a slight drop in the rates off-season, which, for some properties, includes summer. The hotels below have air conditioning, a phone, a TV set, and a private lanai for every room; and while all the units in the condominiums listed are similarly endowed with the latter three amenities, they are air conditioned only as stated (the farther north you go, the less air conditioning occurs; most people find it unnecessary). Some condominiums charge extra for maid service, a few require a 3- or 4-day minimum stay, and some do not accept credit cards. All telephone numbers are in the 808 area code unless otherwise indicated.

Embassy Suites at Kaanapali – This 413-unit, all-suites hotel is situated on 7½ acres of beachfront directly north of the *Kaanapali* resort. With condominiums a well-established option in Hawaii, the all-suites concept is a less dramatic alternative to traditional accommodations. These accommodations are quite spacious, however, with each suite providing about 800 square feet of living space, a large-screen television set, and a VCR. Hotel facilities include a pool, restaurant (there have been recent complaints about food and service), lounges, and a beach-services pavilion. A 12-story waterfall adds a tropical touch to the landscaped atrium in what is otherwise designed in a Spanish Mediterranean style. Rates include a breakfast buffet. 104 Kaanapali Shores Pl., Kaanapali (phone: 661-2000; 800-462-6284). Very expensive to expensive.

Hyatt Regency – The first of Hawaii's mega-resorts, the 815-room hotel was renovated and refurbished in 1991 to mark its 10th anniversary. The years have added a landscaped softness to this huge property, enhancing its appeal. Rooms are tastefully decorated and service is excellent. There are three 7- to 9-story towers with a multimillion-dollar collection of Asian and Pacific art spilling out of teak, glass, and brass lobbies onto the grounds. And these — about 20 acres — are not only landscaped with Japanese and tropical gardens, but waterscaped, too, with streams, waterfalls, pools, and bridges around the centerpiece swimming pool, a free-form extravaganza crossed by a swinging footbridge, fed by a 130-foot lava tube water slide, and divided in two by an upcropping of rock that sends waterfalls tumbling over the swim-in or walk-in bar in its middle. Exotic birds, which glide, flutter, and perch throughout the property, are tended by a staff ornithologist. Other amenities, in addition to the beachfront location, include a 55-foot catamaran, tennis courts, a health club, a promenade of shops, a fine selection of restaurants (see *Eating Out*), and a disco. A program of supervised activities is available for children ages 3 to 15, appropriately named "Camp Hyatt," and offers cooking classes, excursions around the island, glass-bottom boat rides, hula lessons, and other recreational diversions. Costs are $5 an hour per child or $25 a day, excluding meals. *Regency Club* floors offer price-inclusive breakfasts, afternoon cocktails and *pupus,* and concierge service. This can be a crowded place to vacation during peak season. At the southern end of the *Kaanapali Resort* (phone: 661-1234; 800-233-1234). Very expensive to expensive.

Kaanapali Alii – This is one of Maui's best condo properties, with beautifully landscaped grounds, a large pool area adjacent to the beach, and modern and nicely designed and furnished apartments with fully supplied kitchens. *Kaanapali Resort* (phone: 667-1400; 800-642-6284). Very expensive to expensive.

Kaanapali Shores – Maui's largest condominium complex combines the advantages of both condo and hotel. High-rise (mostly 9 stories), the 463 units zigzag along a horseshoe that faces the sea and encloses nicely landscaped grounds. Public areas are stylish, with marble floors and contemporary works of art, while the decor upstairs reverts to the comfort of cane, rattan, and splashy prints. Studios, 1-, and 2-bedroom units are air conditioned, spacious, well maintained, and fully equipped; guests can avail themselves of the 24-hour front desk, and the activities desk, which organizes a week-round schedule of diversions. In addition, there are tennis courts, a putting green, a sundries store, the poolside *Beach Club* restaurant, and an oceanfront location just past the northern end of Kaanapali Beach (although reef-lined shallows may inhibit swimming here). 3445 Honoapilani Hwy. (phone: 667-2211; 800-922-7866). Very expensive to expensive.

Kapalua Bay – If the *Hyatt* is the southern boundary of West Maui's developed vacationland, this is its northern anchor, though the two properties are distinctively different. This one specializes in a far quieter, more restrained and stylish brand of luxury, with no glitzy gimmicks, but no less appeal. Its lobby is strikingly handsome: a 3-story open space through which birds fly amid the hanging vines as though it were the great outdoors. The hotel's fewer than 200 rooms (alike in size and decor, with generous bathrooms and his-and-her sinks) are on multiple levels of two main wings that extend seaward from the lobby like outstretched arms, one of them all but touching the exquisite crescent of Kapalua Bay beach. Views from the rooms vary, but the entire 18-acre property, with its acres of manicured lawns, occupies some of the island's most splendid topography. Equally renowned are the hotel's kitchens, which supply 3 restaurants (see *Eating Out*). Pools (including one that is an abstract copy of the resort's butterfly and pineapple logo), golf and tennis at the resort's 3 courses and 10 courts, a variety of water sports and other activities (from *ikebana* to kite flying), and an adjoining shopping arcade add to the picture. Children ages 6 to 12 can enjoy the counselor-supervised "Kamp Kapalua" program at a cost of $55 per child per day. The hotel offers both MAP and EP year-round. 1 Bay Dr., Kapalua (phone: 669-5656; 800-367-8000). Very expensive to expensive.

Kapalua Villas – The *Kapalua Bay*'s neighbors at the *Kapalua* resort. Unlike most condominium complexes, this is not a compact grouping of units on a limited lot; rather, it looks like an exclusive residential community spread out over verdant green acreage sloping to the sea, with panoramic views part of most bookings. The *Bay Villas* are clustered closest to the water, the *Ridge Villas* are higher up across the highway, and the *Golf Villas* are tucked behind the *Bay* course facing a panorama of the Pacific Ocean and the island of Molokai in the not-too-far distance through lines of neat Cook pines. Units — with 1 and 2 bedrooms — are large and comfortable, with high beamed ceilings, large bathrooms, and tiled kitchens, although some are in need of sprucing up inside. Guests have access to 3 beaches, several pools, the resort's golf and tennis facilities, room service, and they can sign up for any of the activities offered by the hotel. 500 Bay Dr., Kapalua (phone: 669-5656; 800-367-8000). Very expensive to expensive.

Maui Marriott – What meets the eye here is something of a wide "V" formed by two 9-story guest wings connected by a 4-story lobby, paved in brick and landscaped with orchids, palms, and fountains. Between the buildings and the beachfront are grassy lawns and gardens and 2 swimming pools edged in rock. The hotel's tiered main dining room, the *Moana Terrace,* faces the gardens, and so does the more intimate *Lokelani Room,* done up to resemble a plantation living room of the last century (for a third restaurant, *Nikko Steak House,* see *Eating Out*). Add several bars, a good-looking disco-nightclub, an arcade of shops, 5 tennis courts, water sports, and a full activities program (including poi pounding) to keep guests happy. Most rooms have good ocean views, but overall the hotel doesn't have quite the pizzazz of other hotels in the same price category. *Kaanapali Resort* (phone: 667-1200; 800-228-9290). Very expensive to expensive.

Ritz-Carlton Kapalua – Making its debut as the second *Ritz* in Hawaii, this lovely property promises and delivers no less than first-rate accommodations and service. Its setting is architecturally distinctive — an eclectic blend of classic elegance and contemporary luxury, with an extravagant mix of antiques, artwork, marble, and the requisite crystal chandeliers — and offers commanding views of Molokai. Guestrooms are plushly furnished (including marble baths), and most of the 551 rooms have expansive ocean views. On-site facilities include a 3-level pool, 2 restaurants, 3 lounges, easy beach access, beautifully landscaped grounds, ocean activities, and jogging and walking trails. There's also a quick shuttle bus ride to the *Kapalua* resort, which offers golf, tennis, shops, and restaurants. *Ritz-Carlton* club rooms offer the plus of a private lounge where breakfast and afternoon tea, as well as *pupus,* are served by a courteous concierge staff. *Kapalua Resort* (phone: 669-6200; 800-241-3333). Very expensive to expensive.

Sheraton Maui – The other of Kaanapali's two original hotels, this one sits on the resort area's most striking spot — atop and around Black Rock promontory, a volcanic cone whose existence gave the hotel a nice expanse of beach and two levels on which to build its lobbies, restaurants, and bars. Garden Tower, Cliff Tower, the Ocean Lanai wings at the back of the rock with panoramic views, and the low-slung beachfront cottages were all refurbished in 1991. An open-air restaurant and bar are down by one of the hotel's two pools (the one surrounded by Astroturf), but for a truly panoramic view, take the elevator or the cliffside walk up to the window-walled *On the Rocks* bar for drinks and the *Discovery Room* to enjoy the entertainment. Handsome bedrooms (435), a catamaran shared with neighboring resort hotels, tennis courts, the best snorkeling in the resort, and a luau. *Kaanapali Resort* (phone: 661-0031; 800-325-3535). Very expensive to expensive.

Westin Maui – This 761-room property features one of Hawaii's largest pool areas, a multilevel affair complete with waterfalls, islands, slides, and grottoes. Artworks (to the tune of $2 million) grace the public areas, which are among Hawaii's most appealing, designed to provide both elegance and intimacy. A lovely promenade winds past shops and the lush landscape that surrounds the pool. The hotel benefits from its central location on Kaanapali's South Beach, which allows it to offer a full water-activities program. Other amenities include a complete health spa, free to guests, and good food in its 6 restaurants and lounges. *Kaanapali Resort* (phone: 667-2525; 800-228-3000). Very expensive to expensive.

Whaler – The two stark white 12-story blocks that face each other over the swimming pool and Jacuzzi look as though they could as easily have sprouted on the Mediterranean — balconies, flower boxes, et al. The hotel comprises 360 spacious garden-view, ocean-view, or oceanfront units, from studios to 2-bedroom suites, many smashingly decorated in wicker and Polynesian prints, all air conditioned. A 24-hour front desk operates in the lobby, and tennis courts, an exercise room, a sauna, a mini-market, and the beach are right out front, but guests interested in further activity must venture beyond the enclave. Restaurants and shopping at *Whalers Village* next door. *Kaanapali Resort* (phone: 661-4861; 800-367-7052). Very expensive to expensive.

Kaanapali Beach – Expanded, refurbished, and upgraded last year, this hotel retains a more homespun appeal than most of Kaanapali's other resort hotels. The hotel, with 4 wings of 3 or 6 stories, is shaped like a horseshoe facing the beach, with a paved patio, lawn and garden, and a pool in the form of a whale among the enclosures. The 648 rooms are contemporary and appealing, and there are stores, a coffee shop, and the *Plantation Room* (see *Eating Out*) and *Tiki Terrace* restaurants, not to mention the beach shack for water sports rentals and tennis privileges at the *Royal Lahaina. Kaanapali Resort* (phone: 661-0011; 800-657-7700). Expensive to moderate.

Maui Eldorado – Were it not for a slice of the *Royal Kaanapali* golf course, this, too, would be a beachfront condominium. As it is, there's a fair bit of fairway in front of it, and while the path that weaves through the green to the hotel's own beach cabana is a lovely walk, an electric cart makes the trip hourly to spare guests the effort. The condominium consists of 200-plus air conditioned studios to 2-bedroom units in 12 low (2-story) buildings, exceedingly well-manicured grounds, 3 swimming pools, and little else. No restaurants or distracting activities, though the amenities of the *Kaanapali* resort are all around you. *Kaanapali Resort* (phone: 661-0021; 800-367-2967). Expensive to moderate.

Maui Kaanapali Villas – A 200-unit mix of mostly low-rise hotel room and condominium accommodations in an excellent location on the Kaanapali's quiet North Beach. The nicely landscaped, well-maintained grounds surround 3 swimming pools and add a luxurious spaciousness not typical of Kaanapali properties. 2805 Honoapiilani Hwy. (phone: 667-7791; 800-922-7866). Expensive to moderate.

Napili Kai Beach Club – It calls itself a hotel, one of the few in the condominium strip stretching beyond the *Kaanapali* resort to Kapalua. The rooms, however, have kitchenettes (smaller than those in the standard condo), and room service is not offered. Right on the beach, its 162 rooms spread among 11 buildings (2-story maximum) that creep along the north edge of beautiful Napili Bay; to reveal the view, you have only to slide open the shoji panels to your lanai — an appealing Japanese touch. There are 5 swimming pools, 2 tennis courts, and 2 putting greens on the property, and the *Kapalua* golf course is just across the road. There's dancing at the beachfront *Seahouse* several nights a week, a weekly mai tai party, and a weekly Polynesian show. No credit cards accepted for the room tab. 5900 Honoapiilani Rd. (phone: 669-6271; 800-367-5030). Expensive to moderate.

Napili Point – The strength of this condominium is its extraordinary long and narrow position running the length of a high point of land separating two bays, and the panorama from almost any lanai on the property is a sight to be seen. The handsome strip of low units is on two levels, fronted by a strip of lawn that drops off to boulders, but around the point a footpath leads to the beach at Napili Bay. The 108 rooms — 1- or 2-bedroom units — are attractive, and there are 2 pools, barbecue grills, and picnic tables on the grounds, but for the rest, nothing is planned except peace and quiet. A sundries store is nearby. 5295 Honoapiilani Hwy. (phone: 669-5611; 800-669-6252). Expensive to moderate.

Polynesian Shores – Two doors from the *Mahina Surf* and its twin in all but a few respects. This time there are 52 1-, 2-, and 3-bedroom condominium units in those three low wings, the pool amid the plumerias is slightly smaller, and there is the wistful addition of ironwood trees where the sweep of lawn meets the sea. A wooden deck built out over the boulders is the place for barbecuing and sunset watching, and a wooden staircase nearby leads down to a tiny, mostly rocky beachlet, good for snorkeling but not for sunning. Rooms, again individually decorated, are well above average, and it is probably for this that this condominium costs somewhat more than its neighbor. Maid service is not provided. Monthly rates are available. Minimum stay: 3 nights. 3975 Honoapiilani Rd. (phone: 669-6065; 800-433-6284). Expensive to moderate.

Royal Lahaina – On Kaanapali's northern stretch of beach, this is one of that resort area's two original hotels. Its 514 rooms — in both the 12-story Lahaina Kai Tower and in the 2 dozen 2-story cottages between the beach and the golf course — have recently been refurbished and renovated. Walk around the manicured grounds and you'll come across 3 pools, 3 restaurants (*Chopsticks,* with a well-priced international, all-appetizer menu; *Moby Dick's* for seafood (see *Eating Out*); and the *Royal Ocean Terrace* for more standard fare and a lavish Sunday brunch), a nightly luau, beachside outlets for a number of water sports, Jacuzzi, and the biggest drawing card, the *Royal Lahaina Tennis Ranch,* which has 11 courts and a stadium and is managed by *Peter Burwash International. Kaanapali Resort* (phone: 661-3611; 800-733-7777). Expensive to moderate.

Aston Maui Park – This Aston-managed property consists of 72 studios and 216 single-bedroom units, each with complete kitchen facilities, lanai, ceiling fans, and cable television. It's set north of Kaanapali, on 5 acres across from Honokowai Beach Park. 3626 Lower Honoapiilani Hwy. (phone: 669-6622; 800-92-ASTON). Moderate.

Mahina Surf – A small gem of a condo, this is for those who wish to be left to their own devices. Three 2-story buildings enclose a green lawn that sweeps down to boulders at the edge of the ocean, and beyond a good-size swimming pool, outdoor barbecue, palm trees, plumerias, bougainvillea, and banks of ginger, there is no further distraction. The 56 1- and 2-bedroom units have been individually — and nicely — decorated by their owners. You'll sun on the grass, snorkel off the rocks, but for something sandy, you'll get in the car and head up or down the road a bit. Grocery shopping is about a half mile away; maid service is extra. Minimum stay: 3 nights, with discounts for stays of 7 nights or longer. 4057 Lower Honoapiilani Rd., in the Honokowai area (phone: 669-6068; 800-367-6086). Moderate.

Kahili at Kapalua – The newest condominium property at the *Kapalua* resort, it offers nicely furnished studio and 1-bedroom units adjacent to Kapalua's fairways. Units come with complete kitchens, color sets with cable TV, and in-room washers and dryers. Kapalua and Napili beaches are within a 10-minute walk. On-site services are limited, although guests do have shuttle access to *Kapalua's* resort facilities. 5500 Honoapiilani Hwy., Kapalua (phone: 669-5635; 800-786-7387). Moderate to inexpensive.

EATING OUT: Since almost everything in the Kaanapali-Kapalua strip has been created with the tourist in mind, there is certainly no shortage of places to eat, and there are many, many more eating options than those listed below. The choice of food — continental, Italian, basic steakhouse — is much as in Lahaina and the price range also is much the same. Expect to pay $75 or more for the average meal for two in a restaurant listed as expensive; $35 to $70 in a place listed as moderate; and $30 or less in an inexpensive restaurant (prices do not include drinks, wine, or tip). The area does differ from Lahaina in two respects, however. For one thing, though the prevailing mood is still casual, there are more places where you won't feel out of place if you want to dress up, and several that strongly suggest you do. Another difference is the dearth of fast-food outlets. Those pinching pennies will find more to choose from back in town. All telephone numbers are in the 808 area code unless otherwise indicated.

Bay Club – The *Kapalua Bay*'s reputation for fine food can be tested in any of its three highly praised restaurants, and this is one of them, though it's actually a bit away from the hotel on a lava rock peninsula at the far end of Kapalua Beach. In appearance, the dining room is exceedingly well bred — pine walls with koa trim, rattan furniture cushioned in fresh batik prints, but no superfluous detail to distract from the open-air view. Lunch, from 11:30 AM to 2 PM, is relaxed (the restaurant even has a pool), with pasta, catch of the day, omelettes, sandwiches, salads, or a heaped plate from the salad bar to choose from; but dinner, from 6 to 9:30 PM, is a quiet, very softly candlelit and refined occasion to partake of the specialties of seafood, steaks, lamb, or veal. Open daily. Reservations necessary. *Kapalua Bay Hotel,* Kapalua (phone: 669-5656). Expensive.

Nikko Steak House – Diners sit with others at teppan tables (which have a grill set in the middle) nibbling appetizers, sipping miso soup and sake, until the chef arrives to bedazzle with his demonstration of the martial art of cooking. Knives flash and chop onions in midair, lobster tails pop from their skins, steaks fall into a dozen slices by sleight of hand alone. The chef cooks it all in front of you, fills your plate, and exits to applause, bowing. Don't worry if you've no room left for dessert — the fried ice cream is not so much a delicacy as a curiosity. Open for dinner daily from 6 to 9 PM. Reservations necessary. *Maui Marriott, Kaanapali Resort* (phone: 667-1200). Expensive.

Roy's Kahana Bar & Grill – Roy Yamaguchi's newest brainchild takes its theme from the original *Roy's* on Oahu by presenting a menu that combines Oriental and continental ingredients. Among the unusual concoctions are Louisiana crab cakes with spicy sesame sauce and opakapaka with roasted macadamia nut butter sauce.

Both the airy atmosphere and the unpretentious service earn an A from us. Open daily for dinner from 6 to 10 PM. Reservations necessary. *Kahana Gateway Shopping Center,* Kahana (phone: 669-6999).

Sound of the Falls – A grand entrance down a wide and lovely flight of lighted steps is an apt preparation for the elegant dining room that awaits. With much of the dining area in open air, a guest is treated to views of a waterfall, flamingos, and palm-studded pools. Perhaps a bit on the pretentious side, the menu nonetheless promises fine food, and doesn't disappoint in quality upon serving. The wine cellar is one of Maui's best, with more than 200 choices. Dessert soufflés are created in a wide variety of flavors (Grand Marnier, coconut, and chocolate being but three), and the loving table-side preparation of numerous pies and cakes provides a dramatic closing note for dinner. Open daily for dinner, from 6 to 10 PM, with dancing nightly. Reservations necessary, as are collared shirt, dress slacks, and shoes for men. *Westin Maui* (phone: 667-2525). Expensive.

Swan Court – The fine dining room of the *Hyatt Regency* has its entire façade open to the air, the mauve and dusty rose carpeted floor a mere three flagstone steps above the water of a lagoon. Guests enter by descending a grand staircase at the back, take their seats, and watch the swans glide by as though in a fairy tale. Roast duck, rack of lamb, chateaubriand, and seafood specialties like filets of Hawaiian papio and mahimahi garnished with skewered cane shrimp are typical items from the innovative menu, with service that is close to perfect. Open for breakfast from 7 to 11:30 AM, and dinner from 6 to 10 PM daily, and if you opt for the latter, remember the staircase and dress accordingly. Reservations advised. *Hyatt Regency, Kaanapali Resort* (phone: 661-1234). Expensive.

Garden Room – Another of the *Kapalua Bay*'s restaurants. The reason most non-guests have beaten a path to the door is the Mayfair Luncheon Buffet, the greatest temptation to excess since an invite from Lucullus. A fruit table, two salad tables, a cheese tray, four hot entrées with vegetables, potatoes, and rice (one day's selection: lamb curry with full garnish, island fish meunière with macadamia nuts, roast veal in cream sauce, pork tofu) and approximately 20 feet of pies, cakes, and pastries (plus wax porpoises, swans, and nene geese) are all yours at the price of $18.50 a head. The Mayfair Buffet is served Sundays from 11:30 AM to 2 PM. Reservations advised. *Kapalua Bay Hotel,* Kapalua (phone: 669-5656). Expensive to moderate.

Lahaina Provision Company – The name conjures up visions of a dusty warehouse or a folksy general store, which is unfortunate, because this open-air restaurant looking out over the rock upcropping in the *Hyatt Regency* pool is quite slick and smart. The green tile floor shines, as does the green upholstery of the rattan chairs, and so do the leaves of innumerable potted plants. The fare is basic — steaks, chops, seafood — but come dessert, diners are directed to fill a bowl with ice cream and do their own thing at a copper counterful of chocolate toppings. It's called the chocoholic bar and is offered in the evening only. Open for lunch from 11:30 AM to 2 PM, and dinner from 6 to 9:30 PM daily. Reservations advised. *Hyatt Regency, Kaanapali Resort* (phone: 661-1234). Expensive to moderate.

Lokelani – It's an elegant, plantation-style dining room, decorated with pictures of old Hawaii, antique china, and lamps. The menu focuses on seafood (lobster and scallops are the specialties) and five different varieties of fresh fish. The food's good, the presentation, appealing. Open for dinner daily from 6 to 9 PM. Reservations advised. *Maui Marriott* (phone: 667-1200). Expensive to moderate.

Maui Rose – The Sonoma County rabbit with pearl onions and herbs is one of the more unusual offerings at *Embassy Suites*' fine dining establishment. Open for dinner daily from 5 to 10 PM. Reservations advised. 104 Kaanapali Shores (phone: 661-2000). Expensive to moderate.

Moby Dick's – The name tells the tale: This eatery specializes in all manner of seafood, from Australian lobster tails to island prawns and the catch of the day. Open for dinner from 6 to 9 PM daily. Reservations advised. *Royal Lahaina* (phone: 661-3611). Expensive to moderate.

Chopsticks – Maui's first restaurant dedicated to "grazing," with a selection of appetizer-size portions that allow diners to enjoy samplings of Chinese, Japanese, continental, and Polynesian specialties all in one sitting. Open daily for dinner from 6 to 9:30 PM; closed Mondays. Reservations advised. *Royal Lahaina* (phone: 661-3611). Moderate.

El Crab Catcher – Like the *Bay Club,* this is a seaside restaurant with a pool. At lunch, you'll probably sit outside (the stretch of beach up front is a place where islanders like to see and be seen). Later, as the sun sets, white tablecloths appear, and the mood progresses from easygoing to rather romantic, diners can retreat to the glassed-in (partly) main dining area yet still be comfortably alfresco. The kitchen specializes in seafood, fresh local fishes of the day in particular, but the beer-steamed Alaskan king crab legs have been highly praised, too. Open daily for lunch from 11:30 AM to 3 PM, and dinner from 5:30 to 10 PM. Reservations advised. *Whalers Village, Kaanapali Resort* (phone: 661-4423). Moderate.

Grill & Bar – Though it's between the *Tennis Garden* and the *Golf Club* at Kapalua, this place is run by *Kimo's,* of Lahaina, rather than by the *Kapalua Bay.* This handsome redwood pavilion has windows all around to allow a view of the golf course and the bay, and given its setting, it's at once elegant and sporty. Come in tennis togs (but no cutoff jeans) if you wish, even at dinner; and then, order no more than a cheeseburger, steamed clams, or the calimari strips, if that's all you want. For others, there's the very thick and very good Portuguese bean soup, entrées ranging from pasta and salads to steaks and lobster, and a dessert of hula pie or Amaretto crème caramel. Open daily for lunch from 11:30 AM to 3 PM, and dinner from 5 to 10:30 PM. Reservations advised. Kapalua (phone: 669-5653). Moderate.

Plantation Room – Worth going to for its Sunday champagne brunch, served from 9 AM to 2 PM. Hawaiian musicians provide live entertainment ($16). Reservations advised. At the *Kaanapali Beach* (phone: 661-0011). Moderate.

Seahouse – This open-air spot right on Napili Beach has a back wall of lava rock sprouting orchids and ferns, a palm tree or two growing up through the roof, and an adjoining bar from which to watch the sun set splendidly over the bay. The ambience is tropical and the menu continental, with emphasis on seafood and light entrées. Open for breakfast from 8 to 11 AM, lunch from noon to 3 PM, and dinner from 6 to 9 PM daily; mellow Hawaiian music for dancing Mondays through Thursdays, and Saturdays. On Fridays local children put on a Hawaiian show. Reservations necessary. *Napili Kai Beach Club,* 5900 Honoapiilani Rd. (phone: 669-6271). Moderate.

Market Café – One part of this is the market, a grocery for gastronomes selling wines and spirits, pastries, meats, and cheeses. The rest of the place is a café of crisp green and white striped tablecloths, booths, and bentwood chairs. The ample menu includes everything from teriyaki beef to fried chicken, Italian dishes, and seafood. The sandwiches are huge, bursting with fresh and flavorsome ingredients; there are a dozen variations on the coffee; and as for the beer, imbibers can read through a long list of brands before getting from Anheuser-Busch to Watneys. This is an indoor, air conditioned eatery, open from 8 AM to 6 PM daily. No reservations. *Kapalua Shops,* 115 Bay Dr. (phone: 669-4888). Moderate to inexpensive.

Rusty Harpoon – An informal eatery behind the shops in *Whalers Village* in an unassuming frame structure that lets in the air and lets out sounds of much conviviality and the frequent tinkling of a piano. Sandwiches and salads are lunchtime options; at dinner, *kal bi* ribs, fresh island fish, stir-fried chicken, and pasta dishes are the specialties. Open for breakfast from 8 to 11 AM, lunch from 11 AM to 5 PM, and dinner from 5 to 10 PM daily. Reservations necessary for parties of six or more. *Whalers Village, Kaanapali Resort* (phone: 661-3123). Moderate to inexpensive.

Kihei, Maalaea, Wailea, and Makena

When the *Kaanapali* resort opened on West Maui in 1962, there was precious little on the arid leeward side of East Maui but wasteland and forests of gnarled and thorny kiawe trees. Protected by the mass of 10,023-foot Haleakala, Kihei and Wailea receive less rainfall per year than any other coast on Maui, and it was only after resort ventures began to evolve elsewhere that endless, rainless, sunny days and an edging of virgin beaches all the way from Maalaea almost to La Perouse Bay connected in anyone's mind and turned it to thoughts of resort development. Now the coastline from Kihei to Makena is the second most important resort area on Maui, and is giving the Kaanapali area serious competition — a mixed blessing at best.

But Maalaea/Kihei and Wailea/Makena are a study in contrasts. Kihei was the first to grow, and it does, like Topsy, along either side of South Kihei Road, from one end to the other, a distance of approximately 6 miles. Drive the length of this main thoroughfare and you will have seen it all: clusters of condominiums, several hotels of mostly modest size, some restaurants, numerous shopping centers, plus other by-products of life in society — the bank, the post office, the real estate office. Because its growth came about haphazardly, the result of the independent actions of many landowners and developers, Kihei is often held up as an example of what not to do in development.

Kihei, however, also has its partisans, who point to those 6 miles of almost uninterrupted golden sand, apt to be windy in the morning, at least north toward Maalaea, but not likely to be obscured by clouds or saturated with raindrops. Views of Kahoolawe, of Lanai, and of the crevassed green glory of the West Maui mountains grace the shore, and even if it is occasionally blocked by architecturally undistinguished buildings, the water's edge can be reached via rights of way and several beach parks. Though the area as a whole strikes some as an unsightly mix, Kihei has a few individual condominium complexes that are as lovely as any on West Maui — and they cost less. Kihei is also less sophisticated than Kaanapali and, because many more Mauians live on this side of the island, more homespun. Chockablock as everything is, in Kihei you'll rub shoulders — on the beach, at the gas station, in the grocery store — with *kamaainas* and visitors.

Southeast of Kihei, Wailea and Makena are, on the other hand, totally planned resorts, designed by architects and landscape artists down to the last street sign and palm tree. In 1970, Wailea was only a bright idea in the corporate mind of the landowner, Alexander & Baldwin, one of Hawaii's Big Five. Two years later, there was a golf course; a second golf course followed, along with a tennis center, six condominiums, a shopping center, and five first class hotels. Wailea is eloquent testimony to what the simple garden-variety sprinkler can do: What was once 1,450 acres of kiawe scrubland is now lushly landscaped and manicured with infinite elegance, particularly since the recent openings of the *Grand Hyatt,* the *Four Seasons,* and *Kea Lani* hotels. Wailea also has five splendid beaches among its blessings and has been applauded for making access to them via paved roads, parking areas, and paths as easy for the public as it is for resort guests, even easier than it was before development.

Wailea's resort amenities equal those of Kaanapali and Kapalua, but neither it nor Kihei can claim the diversity — of restaurants, nightlife, shopping — of West Maui (which is a 45-minute drive away). Nor does the area have its own sightseeing attractions beyond its magnificent beaches. Upcountry is just "upstairs," but Kihei-Wailea residents must take the same route via Kahului that everyone else does, because only a rugged dirt road links the two areas directly. More beaches, including the popular mile of sand at Makena, stretch south from Wailea. A four-wheel-drive vehicle is necessary to get as far as Cape Kinau, formed by the lava flow from Haleakala's last eruption in 1790 and now a nature preserve, or La Perouse Bay, named for the French explorer who landed there in 1786, the first European to set foot on Maui. Much easier to reach, actually, is the tiny islet of Molokini, offshore halfway between Maui and Kahoolawe. The exposed part of a volcanic cone, its crescent shape harbors so many kinds of fish and coral that it has been declared a marine conservation district and is the object of snorkeling and diving expeditions from both Kihei and Wailea.

SHOPPING: There are numerous shopping centers in the Kihei and Wailea area, though condo dwellers should be aware that grocery prices (already sky-high by mainland standards) are lower in Kihei than in Wailea. *Kihei Town Center,* along South Kihei Road, has a supermarket, *McDonald's,* and a few assorted shops, but has less of interest to the visitor than either the *Azeka Place Shopping Center,* which is to the north along South Kihei Road, or the *Wailea Shopping Village,* in the *Wailea* resort to the south. The newer *Rainbow Mall, Kukui Mall, Dolphin Plaza,* and *Kamaole Center* in the heart of Kihei's condominium row offer gift shops, beach boutiques, and several restaurants, mostly of the fast-food variety. On Saturdays and Wednesdays there's a Swap Meet held between 7 AM and 4 PM on South Kihei Road, just south of Azeka Place (phone: 879-8990). Open Tuesdays and Fridays from 2 to 5 PM, *Maui's Farm Market* on S. Kihei Road (by the *Suda* store) offers locally grown produce, fruit, bread, and pastries, at low prices.

The *Azeka Place Shopping Center* is a large and busy place thronged with residents buying gas and running in and out of the post office, the bank, the supermarket, the hardware store, the florist, and the health food store. In addition, it has several clothing stores, including the Kihei branch of *Liberty House* (phone: 879-7448), and *Long's Drugs* (phone: 879-2259), and a store or two selling gifts and souvenirs. The *Wailea Shopping Village* has a wide variety of boutiques carrying upscale resortwear and gift items and souvenirs. It has branches of several shops found elsewhere on the island, most notably the browse-worthy collection at *Lahaina Printsellers* (phone: 879-1567), as well as a few exclusive shops like *Native* (phone: 879-3075), with a good selection of fine-woven, hand-printed fashions. The *Grand Hyatt Wailea* includes a selection of tony shops with a focus on art, resortwear, and jewelry. The shopping village presents free Polynesian entertainment Tuesdays at 1:30 PM (phone: 879-4465); bring a camera.

Bridge Man Co. – This place offers a terrific selection of menswear, including high-fashion prints by Bali's renowned designer BaikBaik. 2439 S. Kihei Rd., *Rainbow Mall* (phone: 879-9292).

Cinnamon Roll Fair – Sweet rolls that are nothing short of heavenly. *Kamaole Center* (phone: 879-5177).

Cruise – Resortwear with a fashionable, nautical look. *Grand Hyatt Wailea* (phone: 874-4828).

For Your Eyes Only – A good selection of eye gear. *Wailea Shopping Village* (phone: 879-0545).

Lahaina Printsellers – The newest branch of this specialty shop features mostly 19th-century maps, lithographs, and prints in mint condition. *Grand Hyatt Wailea* (phone: 874-1641).

L.A. Rage – A high-fashion boutique that offers up-to-the-minute designs from the California coast. 2439 S. Kihei Rd., *Rainbow Mall* (phone: 879-7247).

Local Motion – Just about everything you might want or need related to water sports, including a great selection of swimwear and the store's own logowear. 1819 S. Kihei Rd., *Kukui Mall,* Kihei (phone: 879-7873).

Lorenzi of Italy – Nary a "Made in the USA" label to be found in this shop, which carries beautiful European leather goods. *Grand Hyatt Wailea* (phone: 874-1133).

Mango Club – Good, though small, selection of men's and women's fashions, from high-style shorts to shirts to classic aloha shirts and antique and reproduction jewelry. *Kamaole Center* (phone: 879-6898).

Maui Waterwear – More bathing suits — bikini and otherwise — than just about any other shop in Hawaii — and at prices that are a pleasant surprise. For men and women. *Kamaole Center* (phone: 879-3911).

Paradise Fruit – A craving for fruit can be satisfied here at any time of day or night — it's open 24 hours. Pineapples, papayas, and Maui onions are packaged to travel home intact; also available are such Hawaiian favorites as Maui potato chips, Kona coffee, and tropical jams and jellies. 2439 S. Kihei Rd., *Rainbow Mall* (phone: 879-1723).

Rainbow Connection – This particularly nice gift shop has beautiful silk-screen prints, a vast supply of imaginative and colorful mobiles and wind chimes, dishes, *Christmas* tree decorations, and locally handcrafted gift items such as carved koa wood whales and dolphins. *Azeka Place* (phone: 879-5188).

Richters – An exquisite selection of estate jewelry for those with an eye for the best (there are other branches in Palm Beach, Atlanta, and Nashville). *Grand Hyatt Wailea* (phone: 875-0888).

Sea and Shell – The selection of specimen shells, mounted shells and coral, and jewelry made of shells, as well as decorative ceramics and wind chimes, makes this shop worth a special look. *Wailea Shopping Village* (phone: 879-1116). Other outlets owned by the same family are in Lahaina, known as *Madeleine Michaels* (phone: 661-3984); at *Kapalua Shops,* 115 Bay Dr., where it is known as *By the Bay* (phone: 669-5227); and at *Whalers Village* (phone: 661-3730).

Superwhale – This children's boutique is only one of several locations on the island. It turns ordinary children into *keiki* in no time. *Wailea Shopping Village* (phone: 879-3636).

Wings on the Wind – The quintessential shop for initiates and enthusiasts alike. *Kukui Mall* (phone: 874-5050).

NIGHTLIFE: The Kihei-Wailea-Makena area is not exactly overcrowded with hot spots, which is one of the reasons why the route north to Lahaina and Kaanapali sees such heavy evening traffic. At the *Maui Inter-Continental* resort, there is live music for dancing nightly in the partly open-air *Inu*

Inu Lounge (phone: 879-1922), which stays awake until 1 AM. On Sundays and Mondays the tempo is disco; Tuesdays through Saturdays the music is live.

The *Inter-Continental* hosts a luau billed as Maui's merriest on Tuesday, Wednesday, and Thursday nights, though it's no less contrived than any other artificial evocation of Hawaii's past. The setting, a grassy oceanfront lawn, is certainly one of the nicest in the Islands. Dinner and Polynesian show cost $45. Kihei's *Maui Lu* resort (phone: 879-5881) features Jesse's Luau Polynesia on Saturdays, currently priced at $35 for adults and $20 for children ages 7 to 12. The luau begins at 5 PM with the requisite lei greeting and the sipping of cocktails while the oven is uncovered rock by hot rock and the pig triumphantly removed. A buffet meal and a Polynesian revue follow, with the finale at about 9 PM. The *Grand Hyatt Wailea* (phone: 875-1234) offers a luau for up to 300 with an extravagant Polynesian musical show. Mondays and Thursdays at *Stouffer Wailea Beach* resort, the luau also features the *imu* ceremony and a musical revue for $38. Reservations required (phone: 879-4900).

Elsewhere in Kihei, there's disco dancing Wednesdays and karaoke, where guests lip-synch in front of the crowd on Thursdays through Sundays from 9:30 PM until 2 AM at *Luigi's* in the *Azeka Place Shopping Center* (phone: 879-1027).

Best bet at Wailea is *Tsunami,* the glitzy new disco, awash in laser light and marble, in the *Grand Hyatt Wailea.* Open 9 AM to 2 PM weekdays; to 4 AM Fridays. Closed Sundays and Mondays. The hotel's central lobby bar, with its eclectic architecture and whimsical Botero sculptures, is a great spot to have a drink and people watch. The *Inter-Continental*'s *Inuinu* offers a quiet setting for drinks at sunset, and dancing that starts at 9 PM. Sunday is swing night here, with a musical revue of sounds of the 1930s and 1940s, from 5 to 7:30 PM. No cover. Makena's *Maui Prince* (phone: 874-1111) provides a landscaped courtyard in which a string quartet edifies with the works of Mozart and other masters. Nightly performances begin at 6:30 PM and continue until 8:30, when the music segues to the sounds of contemporary piano. In the hotel's *Molokini* lounge, there's music nightly. Tuesdays and Fridays the tempo's Hawaiian, with hulas and island music.

CHECKING IN: The price categories are the same for this area as for West Maui. Most properties have high- and low-season rates, with high season running mid-December to mid-April. In the listings that follow, very expensive means $250 and up double occupancy, expensive means $150 to $240, moderate is from $85 to $145, and inexpensive is from $45 to $80. All condominium units have full kitchens, and whether condominium or hotel, all rooms have private lanais and phone service unless otherwise stated. Hotels are air conditioned, most condominiums are not, though the afternoon trade winds that blow along this coast make air conditioning superfluous for most people. Note finally that daily maid service may not be provided free in all the condominiums, that some may require 3 or 4 days' minimum stay, and that some do not accept credit cards. All telephone numbers are in the 808 area code unless otherwise indicated.

Grand Hyatt Wailea – Maui's newest resort hotel is by far its most extravagant, with a price tag of $600 million for its 787 rooms (including 53 suites and 78 Regency Club rooms). The site includes a spectacular 2,000-foot-long river-pool, a one-third–acre formal swimming pool modeled after one at the Hearst castle at San Simeon in California, 14 tennis courts (3 of which are grass and 1 stadium, seating 1,200 people), full beach services and rentals, 5 restaurants (see *Eating Out*), a wedding chapel, a 50,000-square-foot health spa (one of the largest in the US), and lushly landscaped grounds. The hotel's artworks — wonderful bronze sculptures, inspired paintings, and frescoes and mosaics — are a marvelous blend of high art and Hawaiian tradition. The detail work here in everything from decor to lighting fixtures is the best of any new hotel in Hawaii. Youngsters tired of escorting their elders can attend "Camp Hyatt," a program of supervised activities available for children ages 3 to 15, daily during summers and holidays and on weekends the rest of the year. There's a charge of about $5 per child per hour or $25 per child per day, not including meals. Activities include sandcastle building, Hawaiian arts and crafts, cooking classes, museum tours, sports, glass-bottom boat rides, hula lessons, and treasure hunts. In addition to access to the 3 golf courses located near the hotel (the *Wailea Blue,* the *Wailea Orange,* and the one at the *Makena* resort), guests also can be shuttled 20 minutes by van to two other 18-hole golf courses near Wailuku. At the heart of the *Wailea* resort, it shares a beach with the directly adjacent *Four Seasons* hotel. 3850 Wailea Alanui Dr. (phone: 875-1234; 800-233-1234). Very expensive.

Makena Surf – Spacious, nicely decorated 2- and 3-bedroom apartments and a private beachfront setting make this condominium, the first for the *Makena* resort, one of Maui's most appealing. On-site facilities include uncrowded tennis courts and a large pool and lounge area. There is a 3-night minimum stay. 3750 Wailea Alanui Dr. (phone: 879-1595; 800-367-5246). Very expensive.

Four Seasons Wailea – The first of two Four Seasons properties in Hawaii (the other is at Kaupulehu along the Kohala Coast of the Big Island), it opened in March 1990. At an average of 620 square feet each, the 300 standard guestrooms (plus 72 suites) are among the largest conventional accommodations in Hawaii. More than 85% of the rooms boast ocean views, and every one has its own lanai, oversize closets, deluxe bathroom, and in-room VCR (with films available from the hotel's sizable video library). Other facilities include an attractive heated swimming pool with a large fountain in the center and whirlpool baths at each end. The exterior design is neo-Georgian, the interior design and decor are open, airy, and attractive — though it hardly evokes any aspect of Hawaii. The *Seasons* dining room is among the best eating places in all the islands (see *Eating Out*). The "Lobster Club" sandwich is reason in itself to check in here. There is a fully equipped spa and aerobic fitness center. The hotel also offers a children's program, "Kids for All Seasons," which includes an activities center for children from 5 to 12 years old; there are also special activities for teens. 3900 Wailea Alanui Dr. (phone: 874-8000; 800-334-6284). Very expensive to expensive.

Kea Lani – One of the most recent newcomers to the island (it opened in 1991), this establishment's architecture and decor have been the subject of much discussion. Despite its decidedly unexciting frontal view, this property's interior is a Moorish fantasy come true, complete with a lobby of great arched ceilings, as well as clusters of 2-story bungalows that lead from the main building to the beach. A large free-form pool, complete with lagoon and formal pools linked by waterslides, is perfect for a late afternoon splash. The 413 one-bedroom suites are spacious and plushly decorated, and the 2- and 3-bedroom oceanfront villas are equally appealing. Baths are large, with oversize tubs and marble vanities. There are also on-site restaurants, lounges, shops, and beach services, and the *Wailea* and *Makena* resort facilities are easily accessed by shuttle. 4100 Wailea Ala Nui Dr. (phone: 875-4100; 800-882-4100). Very expensive to expensive.

Maui Prince – The 300 rooms provided the *Makena* resort complex with its first hotel, and the Prince hotel chain (owned by Japan's Seibu railroad conglomerate) with its first property in the US. The conglomerate recently opened a second Prince hotel along Waikiki Beach in Honolulu, after purchasing the *Mauna Kea Beach* hotel on the Big Island of Hawaii. Their Maui property is adjacent to one of the string of fine Makena beaches, near the end of the paved road, where its quiet elegance is all the more unexpected. Three restaurants, including *Hakone* (see *Eating Out*), pamper tastebuds with traditional Japanese and eclectic American cooking. At night the sounds of Bach or Mozart fill the central courtyard. During the day the same courtyard echoes with the sound of running water from a series of falls and pools. Still, the overall feel of the hotel is a bit austere, with perhaps a bit too much marble and concrete. Facilities include 6 tennis courts, 2 pools (a bit small, but nicely located), golf, horseback riding, and a lovely beach. Almost all rooms have full or partial ocean views. 5400 Makena Alanui Rd. (phone: 874-1111; 800-321-6284). Very expensive to expensive.

Stouffer Wailea Beach – A multimillion-dollar renovation in 1991 has charmingly updated the decor here. With the exception of a low oceanfront wing (the only thing that comes between the hotel and Mokapu Beach), its 350 rooms are arranged in a 7-story, 3-pronged structure whose grand entrance offers a sweeping view of the ocean. Past the lobby, the sloping 15-acre grounds make use of streams, waterfalls, bridges, and tropical plantings — the latter doing so well that many an ocean view has turned into a garden view (rooms with mountain views are also available). Stay in a wing of the hotel — Mokapu Beach — for deluxe rooms, beautiful ocean views, a personal lanai, and complimentary breakfast. The hotel's *Raffles'* restaurant (see *Eating Out*) earns deservedly high praise; the activities program is a strong one (from hula lessons to windsurfing); and the 2 Wailea golf courses are just across the street. All the resort's other sports facilities (tennis and beach) are also close at hand. Wailea (phone: 879-4900; 800-9-WAILEA). Very expensive to expensive.

Wailea Condominiums – What the *Kapalua Villas* are to West Maui, these are to East Maui — condominium communities designed for comfortable, unobtrusive, vacation living. *Wailea Ekolu* village consists of rows of 2-story redwood buildings behind flowering trees on a slope above the *Blue* golf course, from where they have wonderful seaward views. *Wailea Ekahi,* also with low buildings, is lavish with bamboo, Manila hemp, and traveler's palms and plumeria, and it slopes, too, right down toward Keawakapu Beach. The most exclusive village, *Elua,* is on Ulua Beach between the *Stouffer Wailea* and the *Maui Inter-Continental.* There are 8 pools among the villages, and of the 594 units, about one-third can be rented — anything from a studio to a gorgeous 2- or 3-bedroom townhouse with cathedral ceilings. A minimum stay of 3 nights is required. Destination Resorts/Wailea, 3750 Wailea Alanui Blvd., Wailea (phone: 879-1595; 800-367-5246). Very expensive to expensive.

Maui Inter-Continental – This 600-room property, nicely refurbished and upgraded in 1991, takes advantage of an oceanfront setting that leads to Ulua and Wailea beaches. The hotel is mostly low-rise, consisting of several meandering wings surrounded by nicely landscaped, well-maintained grounds. From the entrance drive through the classic Hawaiian porte cochere and down the new Grand Staircase, the uninterrupted ocean view spreads out from Molokini Islet to Maalaea Bay and the West Maui mountains. The *Kiawe Broiler* has been expanded to encompass that view, and offers cocktails, fine dining, and traditional Hawaiian entertainment nightly. An airy lobby replaces the dark lava rock of the original, adding a contemporary look to what had become dated by a decade of use. The hotel has several restaurants, including *La Perouse* (see *Eating Out*), 3 pools, and a jogging path that winds its way around the property's expansive grounds. Children weary of escorting troublesome parents can attend *Club Gecko,* a year-round program that offers such activities as arts and crafts, swimming, and short excursions ($35 per day). Investigate reasonable off-season rates here. 3700 Wailea Alanui (phone: 879-1922; 800-367-2960). Expensive.

Kamaole Sands – There are ten 4-story buildings clustered around the pools and tennis courts (free court time for guests) at this property across the road from Kamaole Beach Park III. Available are 1-, 2-, and 3-bedroom units, with a children's pool, barbecue areas, and individual washers and dryers making this a good family choice. The only extra that's missing here is air conditioning, although the gentle, cooling trade winds usually make it unnecessary, and the units are equipped with revolving "South Seas" ceiling fans. 2695 S. Kihei Rd. (phone: 874-8700; 800-922-7866). Expensive to moderate.

Maui Hill – First impressions are reminiscent of Spain, because the condominium buildings that curve up the hillside are topped by the sort of red tile roof that so often shines in the Mediterranean sun. The pillared and arched balconies, with the wrought-iron railings that shade each unit, are downright hacienda-like, though they're actually Hawaiian lanais. Buildings are no more than 2 or 3 stories high, and the 1- to 3-bedroom units (140 all told) come with well above average furnishings (including koa cabinetry in the kitchens), 2 baths, and most have grand ocean views. The grounds — nicely landscaped, yet too new to be lush — contain a large pool, tennis and shuffleboard courts, a putting green, barbecue facilities, and nothing else — you cross the road and walk along a bit to get to the beach. 2881 S. Kihei Rd. (phone: 879-6321; 800-922-7866). Expensive to moderate.

Mana Kai Maui – Basically a condominium run as a hotel; and though the interiors are humdrum and the building — one high-rise block of 8 stories — not very handsome, consider these points in its favor. First, the location, smack on the curving far end of the same beach that runs all the way to Wailea, needs no apologies. Second, each 2-bedroom, 2-bath apartment can be split into a 1-bedroom, 1-bath unit with kitchen and a lanai overlooking the sea and a no-kitchen, no-lanai hotel unit facing the back; the latter, though small, are of interest to those on a tight budget. Third, a rental car with airport pickup comes with both hotel and condo units. On the property are a swimming pool, general store, beauty salon, apparel shop, a branch of the *Ocean Activities Center* for water sports, a bar, and a restaurant (see *Eating Out*). 2960 S. Kihei Rd. (phone: 879-1561; 800-525-2025). Moderate.

Hale Kamaole – Another attractive condominium choice on the *mauka* (inland) side of South Kihei Road. The 180-plus units are staggered in low lines around a lawn containing plumeria, a few tall palms, and walkways edged in ixora, oleander, and bougainvillea. More flowers hang on trellises between the lanais. Units of 1 and 2 bedrooms are individually decorated, and the 2-level, 2-bedroom ones are especially nice. Phones in selected units only; 2 swimming pools, a tennis court, and barbecue grills. Directly across the road, another sweep of grass ends in a small beach that is an extension south of Kamaole Beach Park III. Ask about off-season discounts. 2737 S. Kihei Rd. (phone: 879-2698; 800-367-2970). Moderate to inexpensive.

Koa – This condominium winner is made up of five 2-story buildings holding a total of 50-some units whose lanais tumble with bougainvillea and face a spacious central lawn–cum–putting green as smooth as velvet. The rattan- and bamboo-furnished rooms — units have from 1 to 3 bedrooms — are spacious, too, and as beautiful as any in a Maui condominium. Nothing more than an occasional cocktail party is planned, but to compensate, the swimming pool is large, and there are tennis courts, shuffleboard courts, barbecue facilities, and a Jacuzzi. The nearest beach is across the road. 811 S. Kihei Rd. (phone: 879-1161; 800-877-1314). Moderate to inexpensive.

Maui Lu – This Kihei hotel lacks the sophistication of its counterparts in Wailea (it's best known for its swimming pool shaped like the island of Maui) and the rooms are not flashy, but when it says it remembers "the good times of old Hawaii," it means it. The Saturday night luaus are part of it, but the key seems to be the many Hawaiian employees, whose spirit of *ohana* (family) strikes the visitor here more than elsewhere. The best of the 170 rooms on the extensive, heavily palmed grounds are the superiors in the 3-story wooden wing (Haleakala views), which repeats the architectural theme of the hotel's Polynesian longhouse-style restaurant, and the deluxes in the waterfront units across the road (where there are beachlets and access to a longer, sandier beach past the property). Most of the amenities — pool, tennis, hula lessons — of a resort hotel. 575 S. Kihei Rd. (phone: 879-5881; 800-342-1551). Moderate to inexpensive.

Nani Kai Hale – You could hardly pay less for condominium accommodations than what you'd pay for a studio unit here. The 6-story rectangular building takes up nearly the whole property (the ground floor is for parking), the only green area is a small lawn in back (with a good-size pool, picnic tables, and barbecue grill, however), but the location is on the beach and the sand stretches for miles. Larger units are available (the high front 1-bedrooms definitely have a view), and room-and-bath-only hotel units are possible, too. Phones can be put in for long-term residents. Maid service available. No air conditioning. Minimum stay, 7 nights during peak season, 3 nights off-season. Ask about off-season discounts. 73 N. Kihei Rd. (phone: 879-9120; 800-367-3705). Moderate to inexpensive.

Wailea Beachside – Small and inconspicuous, this on-the-beach property is one of Maui's best budget-conscious buys. Rooms, albeit small and utilitarian, are clean, bright, and air conditioned. Additional pluses are the nearby beach and *Carrelli's* (see *Eating Out*), which is located right next door. 2980 S. Kihei Rd. (phone: 879-7744; 800-367-5004). Moderate to inexpensive.

EATING OUT: The area won't overwhelm you with the number and diversity of its restaurants, but there are good places to eat nonetheless. In Kihei, they occur intermittently along the length of South Kihei Road; in Wailea, there are a few free-standing eating spots in addition to the restaurants and coffee shops in the hotels. As elsewhere, expect to pay $75 or more for a meal for two in a restaurant listed as expensive; $30 to $70 in a place listed as moderate; and $25 and under in an inexpensive place — drinks, wine, and tip not included. Many restaurants now offer early bird specials between 5 and 6:30 PM. For fast-food and other budget eateries, scout Kihei's shopping centers — *Azeka Place* and *Kihei Town Center* primarily. Finally, the dress code for Kihei and Wailea is on the whole casual, the top hotel restaurants excepted. All telephone numbers are in the 808 area code unless otherwise indicated.

Kincha – Modeled after its famous namesake on Tokyo's Ginza, the food is Japanese, and the menu offers a variety of dishes in three price categories, including a top rate that is astronomical to all but Japanese pocketbooks. Open for breakfast from 6 to 10:30 AM, and dinner daily from 6 to 10:30 PM. Reservations advised. In the *Grand Hyatt Wailea* (phone: 875-1234). Very expensive to expensive.

Seasons – A lovely setting, fine service, and specials such as steamed New England mussels in a saffron Tedeschi rose champagne sauce, pink abalone ceviche, pan-fried opakapaka, and roast veal chop highlight the menu, which also features several low-calorie, low-cholesterol options. Open for dinner nightly from 5:30 to 10 PM. Reservations necessary. In the *Four Seasons Wailea* (phone: 874-8000). Very expensive to expensive.

Hakone – Although the decor leans toward the ascetic, the menu is lavish. Subtly flavored dishes include *chawan mushi* (a steamed egg custard filled with chicken or shrimp and shiitake mushrooms) and egg flower soup (Japanese broth with egg), as well as beautifully presented sukiyaki, teriyaki, and sushi. Open daily for dinner from 5:30 to 10 PM. Reservations advised. In the *Maui Prince,* 5400 Makena Alanui Rd. (phone: 874-1111). Expensive.

La Perouse – Fine dining enhanced by crystal, silver, and candlelight, plus panoramic ocean views for those who choose alfresco seating. The menu stresses seafood, such as Pacific snapper with crab and dill, or sautéed scallops with black beans and cucumber. Open for dinner from 6:30 to 10:30 PM, Tuesdays through

Sundays. Reservations necessary. In the *Maui Inter-Continental* (phone: 879-1922). Expensive.

Prince Court – Both the food and the prices may raise eyebrows at the main dining room of the *Maui Prince.* The menu accent is American, with a touch of Oriental flavor found in such specialties as Hawaiian prawns, lobster, and scallops in a saffron sauce with wild rice and pecans, thinly sliced veal tenderloin, and baby chicken with Maui onion marmalade. The pleasant setting is complemented by the strains of Bach or Mozart drifting in from the string quartet playing in the courtyard outside. Service is superb, and the food is as good as it is creative. Open daily for dinner from 5 to 9:30 PM. Reservations advised. In the *Maui Prince,* 5400 Makena Alanui Rd. (phone: 874-1111). Expensive.

Raffles' – The eponymous hotel of Singapore inspired this fine dining room. Hawaiian menu standards such as mahimahi or opakapaka (served in six styles) appear on the menu, as do rack of lamb and tenderloin steaks (have these with fresh mushrooms). The chocolate mousse is scrumptious; otherwise, choose dessert from the pastry cart or the chocolate Grand Marnier soufflé. The service here is impeccable. Open for dinner nightly from 6:30 to 9 PM, and for Sunday brunch from 9 AM to 1 PM ($23.50). Reservations advised. Collared shirts or jackets suggested for men. *Stouffer Wailea Beach,* Wailea (phone: 879-4900). Expensive.

Fairway – It's in the *Wailea* golf clubhouse between the *Orange* and *Blue* courses, and quite panoramically placed so that you sit high up over the sea, either outside on a paved patio surrounded by a tropical hedge or inside behind sliding glass panels in a sporty ambience of brown wood and leather. Entrées include Polynesian chicken, steaks, chops, prime ribs, fish and seafood, and a salad bar smorgasbord stocked with lots of cold cuts in addition to greens, making it a popular main course. Open daily for breakfast from 7:30 to 10:45 AM, lunch from 11 AM to 4 PM, and dinner from 5 to 9 PM. Reservations for dinner advised. *Wailea Golf Club* (phone: 879-4060). Expensive to moderate.

Grand Dining Room – Sophistication and elegance aptly describes the decor, setting, and fine fare at the *Grand Hyatt*'s main dining enclave. The innovative chef prepares dishes that are heavily influenced by French and Oriental cooking, and the evocative Hawaiian rococo murals are hypnotically interesting. The daily breakfast buffet is transformed into a lavish brunch on Sundays. Open daily from 6 AM to noon for breakfast; 6 to 10:30 PM for dinner. Reservations advised. *Grand Hyatt Wailea* (phone: 875-1234). Expensive to moderate.

Bistro Molokini – Whether you choose to be seated indoors or at poolside alfresco, the atmosphere is refreshing and relaxing. The menu is an intriguing blend of Italian and Californian nouvelle cuisine, and there are always catch-of-the-day specials. Open daily for lunch from 11:30 AM to 3:30 PM, and dinner from 5:30 to 10:30 PM. Reservations advised. *Grand Hyatt Wailea* (phone: 875-1234). Moderate.

Carrelli's – A wonderful beachfront setting is the high point of this establishment, which offers alfresco or indoor seating. The menu is Italian, with modifications to suit Hawaiian tastes. Start with *ahi* (tuna) *carpaccio* and move on to the selection of "designer" pizza specialties such as *frutti del mare cioppino* or *pollo ripieno alla griglia.* Open daily from 5:30 to 10 PM. Reservations advised. 2980 S. Kihei Rd. (phone: 875-0001). Moderate.

Chuck's Steak House – Except for the many stained glass windows in flower patterns, the restaurant is entirely clad in redwood, so it's definitely not the place for outdoor dining or a view. Inside, plants hang, candlelight flickers, and golden oldies and more recent tunes play softly, creating a pleasantly mellow atmosphere all the same. Part of a chain that's well represented elsewhere in Hawaii (there's another at Kaanapali), this place serves steaks, ribs, fish, and seafood, and has the added attraction of an excellent salad bar. Desserts focus on cookie crust concoctions known as mud pies, hula pies, and dirt pies. Open for lunch from 11:30 AM to 5 PM and dinner daily; early bird specials from 5:30 to 6:30 PM. No reservations. *Kihei Town Center* (phone: 879-4489). Moderate.

Ferrari's – Well-prepared Italian specialties in a modern setting coupled with a cheerful and swift staff make dining here a pleasure. Among the toothsome choices are tender fried calamari, steamed clams, pizza, pasta, fish, veal, and vegetable dishes. Open daily from 5 to 10 PM. Early bird specials. Reservations advised. 1945 S. Kihei Rd. (phone: 879-1535). Moderate.

Humuhumunukukuapuaa – The name of Hawaii's colorful state fish is the tongue-twisting title of this *Grand Hyatt* eatery (we dare you to say it three times fast). While the pole-and-thatch-roof decor is casual, poolside seating provides breathtaking open-air views. The menu is an eclectic blend of Polynesian specialties with a focus on fresh fish and seafood. *Pupus* are served from 4 PM, with dinner seating from 5:30 to 10:30 PM. Open daily. Reservations advised. *Grand Hyatt Wailea* (phone: 875-1234). Moderate.

Kihei Prime Rib House – This handsome second-story room with the high-beamed ceiling is dominated by original oil paintings and several very large carvings done by master woodcraftsman Bruce Turnbull. It's known, naturally enough, for its prime ribs dinners and for its salad bar, replete with Maui onions, but a few other entrées — Polynesian chicken, teriyaki steaks, seafood brochette, shrimp, and fresh fish — also appear on the menu. Get to the restaurant early enough for the early bird special (between 5 and 6 PM), and you can have the prime ribs or the fish at a substantial reduction. Open for dinner daily from 5 to 10 PM. Reservations advised. *Kai Nani Village,* 2511 S. Kihei Rd., Kihei (phone: 879-1954). Moderate.

Lanai Terrace – The attractive decor and delicious food both make this restaurant a fine choice; alfresco dining is an added plus. Although the best buy is the daily buffet — a tempting assortment that may include steamed clams, stuffed lamb chops, or Cajun mahimahi — the evening menu offers such specialties as lamb curry and peppered steaks. Either way, a meal is aptly culminated with a wonderful selection of pies, cakes, and flambéed desserts. Breakfast is served from 6 to 11 AM, lunch from 11 AM to 5 PM, and dinner from 5 to 11 PM daily. Reservations advised. *Maui Inter-Continental* (phone: 879-1922). Moderate.

Ocean Terrace – The open-air setting is meditative, with palms overhead and the distant sound of the surf. The food is tasty and priced fairly, with fresh fish — sautéed, charbroiled, or deep fried — and prawns the house specialties. Open daily (weather permitting) for breakfast, lunch, and dinner. Reservations advised. At the *Mana Kai Maui* condos, 2960 S. Kihei Rd. (phone: 879-2607). Moderate.

Greek Bistro – Although it's a bit hidden from view, it's well worth seeking out this small gem. The assortment of delectable dishes includes sautéed Grecian chicken breast and *pastichio* (Greek lasagna). Open daily for lunch from 11 AM to 5 PM, and dinner from 5 to 10 PM. Reservations advised. 2511 S. Kihei Rd. (phone: 879-9330). Moderate to inexpensive.

New York Deli – Run by a former Manhattanite who flies authentic bagels in from a New York maker and serves everything from caviar and egg creams to authentic kosher bologna. Open daily from 9 AM to 8 PM. Reservations unnecessary. 2395 S. Kihei Rd. (phone: 879-1115). Inexpensive.

Kahului and Wailuku

Most tourists arriving at Kahului Airport jump right into a rented car and head straight for the resort hotels of West and East Maui. Barring a wrong turn somewhere along the airport road, they bypass the town of Kahului completely as well as the adjoining town of Wailuku, though they may return to Wailuku later, on their way into the Iao Valley. This is as it should be, because though Kahului and Wailuku have several features of interest to the visitor, they are not at all resort towns. The greatest concentration of Maui's population lives here (40,000 of the island's total 100,000), and while vacationers count the grains of sand along the golden beaches, it is in the everyday world of Wailuku and Kahului that much of the island's work is done.

Kahului and Wailuku flow so uninterruptedly into each other on the northern coast of Maui's central valley that they appear on the map and in reality almost one and the same. There are those who refer to them as Waikahu, but despite the flippancy, there is a division (the bridge over the Wailuku Gulch) and there is a difference. Kahului, to the east, is the newer of the two. It is a business and commercial center, and in addition to having Maui's only jet airport a few miles out of town, it has Maui's only deepwater port, right in the center of town. The island's mainland-bound sugar and pineapple production sets out from Kahului Harbor, where piers and stacked containers are part of the view from the three tourist hotels and the beach park also on the harbor. Behind them, Kahului's main thoroughfare, Kaahumanu Avenue (Hwy. 32), runs east and west, the downtown end of it dominated by three large shopping centers, and behind that — a part of town that visitors rarely see — are residential back streets lined with relatively new and pleasant-looking family homes.

Kahului's Kaahumanu Avenue proceeds west and turns into Wailuku's Main Street, and by the time Main reaches High Street, where "downtown" Wailuku is situated, the visitor is already in the foothills of the West Maui mountains. As a result, Wailuku is hillier, leafier, and more picturesque than its eastern neighbor; it is an administrative center and the county seat of Maui County (the islands of Molokai, Lanai, and Kahoolawe are part of the county) as well. While modern government structures such as the State Office Building, the Federal Building, and the 9-story Kalana O Maui — the County Office Building — line one side of High Street (the not so modern 1907 Court House is here, too), the other side is part of the Wailuku Historic District, which includes High Street between Main and Aupini Streets and a compact area toward the mountain. The 19th-century Bailey House, now the *Hale Hoikeike Museum,* and the 19th-century Kaahumanu Church are the most important buildings in this preserve, but the two white, red-roofed buildings with the brightly tiled entryways next to the church add to the picture. Some of Wailuku's side streets have the wooden and tin-roofed charm of many a Hawaiian plantation town, whereas others contain beautifully landscaped suburban hillside homes.

Main Street continues across High Street as the Iao Valley Road, the final alias of Highway 32. This is well along the tourist track and there's a reason for it. Drive along the Iao Valley Road and you are suddenly confronted by the majesty of the West Maui mountains rising in steep, dark green and brown creases on either side of the Iao Stream, their lower slopes covered in the 30ght frosty green of kukui trees that contrasts with the more somber colors above. The route is short and sweet, because 3 miles west of Wailuku, it bumps into the near-vertical crater walls of Puu Kukui, the volcano that gave birth to the island of West Maui. The scenic Iao Valley State Park is the turnaround point.

Kanaha Pond Wildlife Sanctuary – One of the state's most important waterfowl sanctuaries is the stopping place of migratory birds and the home of a great number of Hawaiian coots and stilts. Nevertheless, it may take patience and a pair of binoculars to satisfy your curiosity (the coot is the grayish-black bird with the white bill and frontal shield; the stilt is the one with the long pink legs). The pond is large, shallow, and dotted with grassy clumps, and whatever action takes place can be observed from a shelter at the end of a spit of land extending into the water. Between Kahului Airport and Kahului; the observation shelter is on Hwy. 396 and difficult to find (if you're driving east on Hwy. 32, turn right onto Hwy. 36, then left onto Hwy. 396).

Alexander & Baldwin Sugar Museum – Founded in the 19th century by descendants of Hawaii's early New England Protestant missionaries, Alexander & Baldwin grew to become one of Hawaii's Big Five corporations and Maui's predominant landowner, having planted tens of thousands of acres to sugarcane. Although the future of the sugar industry in Hawaii has lately been called into question by less-costly foreign production, it was the islands' most important economic resource for nearly a century. This museum demonstrates how and why. Located in the restored home of a plantation manager, and adjacent to a still-active sugar mill at Puunene, it houses carefully researched and well-displayed exhibits that include historic photographs, documents, and artifacts, all providing an overview of the crop's impact on Hawaii. Especially informative is the material on American entrepreneurs like Klaus Spreckels, Hawaii's "Sugar King," and that which deals with the immigrants who were brought in to work on the plantations from such locales as China, Japan, Korea, the Philippines, and Portugal, thereby recasting the demography of Hawaii. Open Mondays through Saturdays from 9:30 AM to 4:30 PM; $2 admission. Children ages 6 to 17 are admitted for $3, and those under 6 can enter free. A short drive from the airport, on Hansen Rd., Puunene (phone: 871-8058).

Maui Tropical Plantation – The cane fields that lead to the Waikapu Valley provide a setting for a wide range of tropical crops and flowers. This is the place to go if you want to see what papayas, pineapples, macadamia nuts, and avocados look like while growing. A tram takes visitors on a tour of the grounds. There is a large restaurant and a collection of very touristy shops. Open daily from 9 AM to 5 PM. No admission charge. For $8 you can take a narrated tram tour that highlights plantings of sugarcane, papaya, guava, and other tropical plantation crops. Although interesting to first-time-in-the-tropics travelers, this is a tame version of the real thing. At sunset a "country party" follows a *paniolo* (cowboy) theme, with a sunset hayride on a horse-drawn wagon, followed by a barbecue dinner and square dancing Mondays, Wednesdays, Thursdays, and Fridays from 5 to 8 PM. Off Rte. 30 at Waikapu (phone: 244-7643).

Maui Zoological and Botanical Gardens – This is probably worth a special trip only if you have restless children with you. The native Hawaiian plants in the botanical garden are somewhat upstaged by the smallish creatures of various ancestry in the zoological garden, which is actually a children's zoo. There are showy birds, such as peacocks, scarlet macaws, and salmon-crested cockatoos, and an assortment of animals, including spider monkeys and African pygmy goats. Native Hawaiian pueo owls, stilt birds, nene geese, and koloa ducks, all endangered species, are represented, and you'll also be able to see examples of the wild boar and feral goats and sheep (these last look like overworked pieces of macrame) that roam Maui's mountain fastnesses. Open from 9 AM to 4 PM daily; no admission charge. Kanaloa Ave., Kahului (phone: 243-7337).

Hale Hoikeike (Maui Historical Society Museum) – *Hale Hoikeike* means House of Display, and here the 19th-century home of a missionary is used to display a small collection of artifacts that includes items of Hawaiiana dating from both before and after the arrival of *haoles.* The plastered stone house, built in stages between 1833 and 1850, was the home of Edward Bailey, the principal of the Wailuku Female Seminary, which coexisted on the property during the 1840s. Some interesting things can be learned about tapa cloth in the museum's main-floor Hawaiian Room (that only the Hawaiians developed the art of block printing on tapa, and of beating two tapas of different colors together to make the cloth reversible, and of using various plants to give the cloth a sweet scent, for instance). The same room contains pre-Cook weapons, tools, and ornaments (including an ancient "mirror"), whereas the bedroom and sitting room upstairs are given over mainly to missionary-era furniture. A small adjoining structure (formerly the seminary dining room and the only seminary building that still stands) houses a collection of Mr. Bailey's paintings, and no matter what you think of his talent, they do show the Wailuku area as it was in its youth. Open daily except Sundays, from 10 AM to 4:30 PM. Contribution suggested. 2375A Main St., Wailuku, or Hwy. 32, on the left as you head into the Iao Valley (phone: 244-3326).

Kaahumanu Church – Queen Kaahumanu attended services in a temporary church here (actually a grass shack) in 1832 and asked that the first permanent church built on the spot be named after her. The next church was an adobe one that dissolved in the rain, but by 1837 a stone church, the predecessor of the present one, had been erected. Today's white building, dating from 1876, is half the size of the earlier version, but its green trim, the green clock in the steeple, and the cloud-covered mountains in the background make it a much-photographed landmark. Because it is locked most of the time, visitors will not see the stark interior, like an early New England church, unless they sit in the beautiful koa pews on Sundays. At the 9 AM Hawaiian Congregational services, the hymns are sung in Hawaiian. High St. (Hwy. 30), Wailuku.

Kepaniwai Park and Heritage Gardens – This lovely county park in the Iao Valley is a memorial to the Maui melting pot, and the symbol chosen to represent the various ethnic groups that settled here, appropriately enough, is the house. Scattered about the landscaped grounds you'll find a typical early Hawaiian stone-walled and grass-roofed shack, a New England saltbox with a white picket fence, a Portuguese villa with a formal garden, and picturesque Chinese, Japanese, and Philippine dwellings. The park is a pleasant setting for lunch if you want to take advantage of the picnic pavilions provided, but things were not always so peaceful here. It was in the vicinity of Kepaniwai that the forces of Kamehameha the Great defeated the forces of the Maui chief in the decisive battle of 1790. The battle assured Kamehameha of eventual hegemony over all the Hawaiian Islands, but the price paid by both sides was high. So great was the slaughter that the Iao Stream was blocked with bodies (Kepaniwai means "damming of the waters") and the village downstream got the name Wailuku (meaning "bloody river"). Iao Valley Rd. (Hwy. 32).

Tropical Gardens of Maui – Orchids are the lure here, both for viewing and buying to ship back to the mainland. The best orchid nursery on Maui, it has several acres of these showy exotics for visitors to explore. Open daily from 9 AM to 4:30 PM. Admission charge $4. Near Wailuku (phone: 244-3085; 800-367-8047, ext. 506).

John F. Kennedy Profile – It might as well be mentioned, because otherwise you'll wonder why all those cars are parked at a curve in the road. The area is called Black Gorge, and if you, too, stop and look up as indicated, you'll see that the natural rock formation does look remarkably like the late president. Iao Valley Rd. (Hwy. 32).

Iao Valley State Park – The Iao Valley Road ends here at the head of the valley, which is actually the erosion-enlarged crater of the volcano that created West Maui. The centerpiece of the beautiful park is an erosional remnant known as the Iao Needle, a green-carpeted spire that rises 1,200 feet from the valley floor (and 2,250 feet from sea level). The walk that begins at the parking lot crosses a bridge over the Iao Stream as it comes rushing down from around the needle, and more paths will take you down to where you can sit on boulders in the water's path if the day is hot or browse through the jungle of plants and sweet-smelling flowers that line it. Other paths and stairs lead up to a shelter that provides a better view of the needle and the surrounding steep valley walls or, in the opposite direction, of the mist-filled valley opening up before you, with Kahului Bay lost in the distance. Iao Valley Rd. (Hwy. 32).

SHOPPING: Kahului has three very large shopping centers all in a row on the *mauka* (inland) side of Kaahumanu Avenue. The *Kahului Shopping Center* in the middle is the oldest, and busy as it is with residents making their way from the supermarket to the dry cleaner to the auto parts shop (and to the movies at the *Maui Theater*), it has few specialty shops stocking the kinds of things visitors usually like to buy. To the east of it, the *Maui Mall Shopping Center* does have some such shops in addition to the more mundane supermarket and drugstore (it also has a *Woolworth's*), but visitors would do best to head directly to the spiffier *Kaahumanu Center,* the westernmost of the shopping centers and Maui's largest. You won't find anything here that you won't find elsewhere on the island, but if your shopping spree is going to take place in Kahului, this is the place for it. *Sears* is at one end of the complex, and the island's largest *Liberty House* is at the other. The *Holiday Theater* is also here. In Wailuku the shopping is small-town in style, with Market Street providing a surprising selection of stores worth browsing.

Able Antique Brokers – Some very nice pieces, with unique furnishings that may tempt you to ship them home. Also a fine selection of Hawaiiana. 139-A N. Market St., Wailuku (phone: 244-8012).

Alii Antiques – There's plenty to look at, and all is displayed in a way that invites discovery. Check out a broad selection of pieces from Asia, plus some interesting Hawaiiana. 160 N. Market St., Wailuku (phone: 242-4372).

Emura's – A collection of interconnected shops that offer some very good buys in eelskin, including golf bags, men's and women's shoes, and wallets. 49 Market St., Wailuku (phone: 244-0674).

Gate to the Orient – An eclectic mix that includes some collectible Orientalia and crystal. 34 Market St., Wailuku (phone: 244-6799).

Helen's Treasures – Helen Eleniki has been collecting for a while now, and her shop features a good selection of ceramics, Oriental pieces, art glass, and jewelry. 130 N. Market St., Wailuku (phone: 242-6977).

Honsport – This sporting goods emporium carries all the necessary equipment for archery, baseball, and basketball, camping, exercising, fishing, golf, hunting, running, tennis, and most other strenuous activities. *Kaahumanu Center* (phone: 877-3954).

House of Music – Hawaiian tunes are among the records, tapes, cassettes, and sheet music. Guitars and ukuleles are also sold. *Kaahumanu Center* (phone: 877-2424).

Hula Moons – A collection of five independently owned shops, whose specialties range from Hawaiiana at *Makani Ltd.* (see Bren Bailey) to Hawaiian bottles and glass at *Bird of Paradise* (see Joe Myham). 130 N. Market St., Wailuku (phone: 244-1693).

Lightning Bolt Maui – Everything needed for all sorts of water sports, plus accessories and bathing suits. 55 Kaahumanu (phone: 877-3484).

Maui Potato Chip Factory – Maui is famous for potato chips — specifically the "Kitch'n Cook'd" brand turned out at this family-owned plant. The Kobayashi family's success story began in 1957, and by 1978 had made the front page of the *Wall Street Journal,* after which orders poured in from around the world. The factory stubbornly remains a small business, however. Maui merchants get the chips first, then the rest of the state, and then a stray bag may make its way to the mainland. If you haven't found them on the local shelves, you can buy them here, 6 or 12 bags to the box. Accept no substitutes! 295 Lalo Pl., off Hwy. 36 in the Kahului industrial area (phone: 877-3652).

Memory Lane – The selection of antiques and collectibles is likely to provide more than one temptation — perhaps a bit of 1930s Hawaiiana. 158 N. Market St., Wailuku (phone: 244-4196).

Traders of the Lost Art – Tribal arts of New Guinea, the Philippines, and Oceania. Open by appointment. 65 N. Market St., Wailuku (phone: 242-7753).

Wailuku Trading Company – Odds and ends from kitsch to antiques, including vintage postcards and Hawaiiana. 42 Market St., Wailuku (phone: 242-9211).

Waldenbooks – Large and well stocked with best sellers and general books, it also carries many titles that come under the heading of Hawaiiana — books on Hawaiian flora and fauna, history, culture, crafts, the Hawaiian language, and more. In the *Maui Mall* (phone: 877-0181) and the *Kaahumanu Center* (phone: 871-6112).

NIGHTLIFE: The *Maui Theater* in the *Kahului Shopping Center* (phone: 877-3560) and the *Holiday Theater* in the *Kaahumanu Center* (phone: 877-6622) feature first-run films. The *Maui Community Theater* (phone: 242-6969) presents excellent live performances in Wailuku's *Iao Theater* on an irregular schedule. At the *Maui Tropical Plantation,* there's a sunset *paniolo* hayride and barbecue from 5:30 to 8:30 PM, Mondays, Wednesdays, Thursdays, and Fridays.

CHECKING IN: Anyone who stays in a hotel in Kahului expecting the resort of his or her dreams, including a palm-lined shore at the door, is in for a rude disappointment. The beach of Kahului Harbor is very narrow, not very appealing, and definitely not the sort of sand strand for which people come to Hawaii. Expect to pay about $60 to $100 for a double room in the moderate hotel listed below. The telephone number is in the 808 area code.

Maui Hukilau/Maui Seaside – Two parts make up this nearly 200-room hotel, which would have to be described as providing clean, adequate rooms to sleep in and a pool to swim in, but no grounds for illusion. The Hukilau wing consists of two long 2-story buildings facing each other across a lawn with palms, breadfruit trees, and the pool, while the newer Seaside wing is a 3-story row behind the Hukilau, away from the pool. The Seaside rooms are reasonably large and air conditioned but lack lanais, whereas some of the Hukilau rooms are air conditioned and all have lanais, though those on the ground floor are less private. The hotel is on the beach, such as it is, and has a restaurant. Kaahumanu Ave., Kahului (phone: 877-3311; 800-367-7000). Moderate.

EATING OUT: Since the Kahului-Wailuku area is Maui's workaday world, restaurants with visitor appeal tend to open elsewhere, but there are several exceptions. In addition to the restaurants below, there are sandwich shops, hamburger houses, and pizzerias aplenty in the shopping centers. The average dinner for two in a restaurant listed as moderate will range from $25 to $45 without drinks or tips; in an inexpensive place, about $25 for two. All telephone numbers are in the 808 area code unless otherwise indicated.

Mickey's – The popularity of the Kihei branch of this restaurant led to the opening of one here in Kahului, which has also drawn good reviews. A steady clientele of businesspeople come to lunch on the fine fish and prime ribs. Lunch weekdays only from 11 AM to 2 PM; dinner Tuesdays through Saturdays from 5 to 9 PM. Reservations advised. 33 Lono Ave., corner Kaahumanu Ave., Kahului (phone: 871-7555). Moderate.

Saeng's Thai Cuisine – Very popular, and deservedly so, with Thai specialties such as red, green, and yellow Masman curries, and spring rolls. Open Mondays through Fridays for lunch from 11 AM to 2:30 PM; daily for dinner from 5 to 9:30 PM. Dinner reservations advised. 2119 Vineyard St., Wailuku (phone: 244-1567). Moderate to inexpensive.

International House of Pancakes – The best all-day breakfasts in town. Open Sundays through Thursdays from 6 AM to midnight; Fridays and Saturdays until 2 AM. Reservations unnecessary. In the *Maui Mall* (phone: 871-4000). Inexpensive.

Luigi's – A typical neighborhood Italian restaurant that offers karaoke on Fridays and Saturdays (from 9 PM to 1 AM), and on Sundays, Mondays, and Tuesdays (from 8 PM to midnight), as well as disco on Wednesdays and Thursdays (from 10 PM to 1 AM). The fare may not make you stand up and cheer, but the basics — such as veal parmigiana — are infinitely reliable. Open daily for lunch and dinner from 11:30 AM to 10 PM. Reservations unnecessary. In the *Maui Mall* (phone: 877-3761). Inexpensive.

Ming Yuen – The location is fairly unencouraging and — as at many Chinese restaurants — the decor is utilitarian at best. However, the food is quite good (mostly Cantonese, with a bit of Szechuan) and a favorite with the island's cognoscenti. Lunch daily except Sundays from 11:30 AM to 3 PM, and dinner nightly from 5 to 9 PM. Reservations advised. 162 Alamaha St., Kahului (phone: 871-7787). Inexpensive.

Up-country

The trip from Kahului to the summit of Haleakala is an ascent from sea level to 10,023 feet in only 38 miles, an accomplishment possible on no other automobile road in the world. The drive takes about 2 hours, the last half of it one twist and turn after another on the hairpin Haleakala Crater Road. But long before the twisting and turning begins, visitors may be surprised at the beauty of the countryside going by, because up-country Maui, as the lower slopes of Haleakala are known, is a quiet rural region where sugarcane and pineapple fields give way to pastureland, eucalyptus trees, and clumps of cactus, where cattle graze, horses roam, hibiscus grows wild, jacarandas bloom by the roadside in spring, and the rolling hills are neatly carpeted with cultivated flowers. Because it is always cooler up here (average daytime temperatures are in the low 70s, and at night it's often chilly enough for a cozy fire), many Mauians happily reside up-country, far removed from the tropics and the overdeveloped resort life down below.

The uplands include the Kula district, at an average elevation of 3,000 feet, the center of vegetable, fruit, and flower farming on Maui. Rich volcanic soil and the combination of warm days (with Haleakala's cloud cover taking the sting out of the sun) and cool nights makes the area suitable for a variety of crops. The Irish potatoes that the whalers loaded onto their ships at Lahaina and that fed gold rush prospectors in California were grown in Kula, and the sweet, sweet Kula onions you'll taste at salad bars all over the island are grown here, too. So are cabbages, lettuce, tomatoes, carrots, and peas. Carnations are the leader among the flowers — there are some two dozen carnation growers up-country, the majority of whom send cut flowers to Honolulu to be strung as leis — but proteas, exotic natives of Australia and South Africa (and cousins to the macadamia nut) are the newest blossoms to be cultivated commercially. Growing conditions at Kula not only produce superior proteas, with stronger stems and richer colors, but also cause some varieties to bloom at different times of the year than they would if grown elsewhere, thus giving the Hawaiian flowers an edge in international markets.

Up-country is also ranch country. The town of Makawao, headquarters of the 20,000-acre Haleakala Ranch, has an incongruous blend of trendy shops lining the tumbledown and dusty streets of a country western town; every year, over *July Fourth,* its Wild West heritage bursts forth in a genuine rodeo. Maui's largest ranch, Ulupalakua, has 30,000 acres, about 5,000 head of Hereford and Angus cattle, and a long history besides. According to the story, one James Makee, the captain of a ship tied up at Lahaina, was struck on the head with an ax by a sailor to whom he had refused permission to go ashore. Makee stayed on in Maui to recuperate and in 1856 bought land and began to build what was known then as Rose Ranch, growing sugarcane while his wife grew roses. The Makees lived on a grand scale, and they entertained naval officers and royalty — King David Kalakaua was a frequent guest — lavishly, often heralding their arrival with torchbearers. Later, the ranch became a potato farm, then a cattle ranch, and today, a few of Ulupalakua's acres are planted with carnelian grapes to form Hawaii's only vineyard. The grounds of Ulupalakua already hold Hawaii's only winery, which produces wine from pineapples and will continue to do so even after the first grape wine is sent to market.

Even without these details of its landscape, Maui's up-country would be remarkably scenic. From some vantage points the view extends down the hills and across the central valley, where you'll see the coast on both sides and the back of the West Maui mountains. From others, you'll see the entire coastline from West Maui to Wailea, plus the islands of Molokini and Kahoolawe. Some of the marvelous scenery is visible en route from Kahului to Haleakala National Park, but a detour is well worth the trouble. To go directly to Haleakala, take Highways 37, 377 (just above Pukalani), and 378. To detour, stay on Highway 37 past Pukalani. It crosses the Kula uplands (marked on some maps now as the Kula Highway) and eventually reconnects with Highway 377, where you can turn back or continue as far as Ulupalakua Ranch. (Beyond Ulupalakua, Highway 37 becomes Highway 31 and proceeds counterclockwise around East Maui to Hana.) After suffering a landslide, the road was closed, but has since reopened. You can as easily detour around the uplands on your way down from Haleakala, and you can try out a few back roads, too: Some of the most soothing pastoral scenes occur on byways that don't appear on the *Maui Drive Guide* map.

Pukalani – The bedroom community of Pukalani, whose name means "doorway to heaven," is the first up-country town along the route from Kahului to Haleakala and the gateway to the Kula district as well. Pukalani has the only up-country golf course — and a shopping center, the *Pukalani Terrace Center,* with a supermarket, drugstore, laundromat, bank, and other stores catering mainly, but not entirely, to residents. The town also has a few places to stop for a cup of coffee or a meal (see *Eating Out*).

Church of the Holy Ghost – Continue along Highway 37 beyond Pukalani and you'll soon see this Kula landmark on a hillside to the left, with the bulk of Haleakala as a backdrop. This octagonal church was built in 1897 for the many Portuguese immigrants brought to Maui to work up-country as ranch- and farmhands. (Much farther along Highway 37, at Keokea, is St. John's Church, built to serve the Chinese, another important ethnic group among Kula's early farm laborers.)

Maui Agricultural Research Center – Just beyond the Kula Elementary School, a left turn onto Copp Road will take you to the University of Hawaii's Kula experimental station. The first proteas in Hawaii were planted here in the mid 1960s, and by now the Kula station is recognized worldwide as a center of protea research and development. The public is invited to step inside the gates for a look at these unusual flowers, whose varieties include the thumb-sized Blushing Bride and the King, as big as 8 to 12 inches across; the Sugarbush, which pours out its nectar if you tip it over; the Pink Mink, so feathery you'll want to pet it; the Pincushion; and the Hawaii Gold, the first hybrid, developed at Kula. If you do visit the garden — which is also an official All-America Rose Selection (AARS) display garden — you are required to stop by the office, where you will be given a map and asked to sign a risk sheet absolving the university of any blame in case of injury. Open weekdays from 8 AM to 3 PM. Off Hwy. 37 (phone: 878-1213).

Hui No'eau Visual Arts Center – A beautiful gallery and shop housed in Kalualani, the country estate of Henry Baldwin (ca. 1917). Run as a membership organization promoting the arts, the facility offers changing exhibits, plus classes and workshops. Well worth a visit for the exhibits and a feel of a patrician Maui home of yesteryear. Open daily from 8:30 AM to 4:30 PM weekdays; on Saturdays until 11:30 AM; closed Sundays. 2841 Baldwin Ave., just outside Makawao (phone: 572-6560).

Tedeschi Vineyards and Winery – Highway 37 crosses the western flank of Haleakala as far as Ulupalakua Ranch. Go past the ranch headquarters and you'll see a small plaster and lava rock building that was the jail of Rose Ranch, as it was known when James Makee owned it over 100 years ago and grew sugarcane. Today the jail is the tasting room and gift shop of Hawaii's only vineyard and its only winery. The prime drink is pineapple wine, which, despite its slight pineapple "nose," is surprisingly good. (The gift shop sells two- or three-bottle gift packs ready to be carried onto the plane, but you can also buy it in Maui liquor stores.) The winery has been making wine of juice bought from the Maui Land and Pineapple Company since 1977, but even before that it began to test more than 140 varieties of grapes to find the one that grew best in the upcountry climate at 2,000 feet. Twenty-five acres are now planted with the winner, the carnelian grape, which produces a sparkling Maui blanc de noir and a pale, dry Maui blush. Tasting room open — with free tours offered — from 9 AM to 5 PM daily. Ulupalakua Ranch, Hwy. 37 (phone: 878-6058).

Kula Botanical Gardens – On the way back from Ulupalakua, the entrance will be on the right, shortly after Highway 37 rejoins Highway 377. The gardens are not large, but they are quite comprehensive and entirely different from the plots of the University of Hawaii experimental station nearby. Here, trees and flowers grow in a more natural setting on landscaped mountain slopes cut by two streams, with a pond at the bottom, bridges to cross, pergolas to walk through, and picnic tables to sit at. The garden has native koa trees and early and late newcomers to Hawaii such as the kukui tree and the Norfolk Island pine. There are bamboo orchids, fragrant gingers, assorted proteas, and many more examples of the plant life you will have seen in hotel gardens and by the roadside and will now be able to identify — provided the specimen has not overgrown its marker. Open daily from 9 AM to 4 PM. Admission charge $3; 50¢ for children under 6. Hwy. 377 (phone: 878-1715).

Sunrise Protea Farm – Upcountry Kula is protea country, and this place offers a wide selection of this exotic flower for shipment to the mainland. Open daily from 8 AM to 4 PM. On Hwy. 378 (phone: 878-2119).

Maliko Certified Nursery – A sign points the way to this nursery (open 10 AM to 4 PM; closed Sundays), which features greenhouse orchids and acres of ginger, heliconia, and other tropical flora. Flowers can be boxed for shipping. About 1½ miles off Hwy. 37 (phone: 572-9292).

SHOPPING: The following shops should satisfy the most immediate buying impulses.

Coconut Classics – Collectibles and antiques, with an emphasis on kitsch, from 1900 to the present. 3647 Baldwin Ave., Makawao (phone: 572-7103).

Glass of Ages – Admirers of glass should visit this shop, which is crammed with antique and collectible pieces. 1135 Makawao Ave., Makawao (phone: 572-8344).

Hawaii Protea Co-operative – It's the best place to buy proteas; you can carry them home with you or have them sent. They last up to 4 weeks and they dry well. Hwy. 377, on *Kula Lodge* grounds (phone: 878-6273).

Heartsong – Reproductions of antiques, and toys, cards, collectibles, and memorabilia, some of which are facsimiles of things created years ago. Open daily. 3682 Baldwin Ave. (phone: 572-1101).

Holiday & Co. – High-quality cottons, silks, sweaters, jeans, and other clothing, plus gifts like baskets, vases, and craft items. 3681 Baldwin Ave. (phone: 572-1470).

Keokea Gallery – Mural-size, contemporary paintings are the focus of this gallery located in up-country Kula. On Hwy. 37 in Keokea Town, between Kula and Ulupalakua (phone: 878-3555).

Klein, Fein, and Nikki Gallery – A smallish gallery in a spruced-up plantation era home in Makawao with some interesting contemporary art. 3619 Baldwin Ave. (phone: 572-5020).

Komoda Store – It's just a little up-country store, but it's got some extra-buttery pastries and cookies that draw the locals. 3674 Baldwin Ave., Makawao (phone: 572-7261).

Maui Child Toys & Books – A great selection of children's playthings, including handmade items and inventive gifts. 3643 Baldwin Ave. (phone: 572-2765).

Maui Moorea Legends – This surprisingly elegant store sells high-style clothing and accessories. All-cotton and handmade leather garments predominate. 3639 Baldwin Ave., Makawao (phone: 572-0801).

Maui Sunburst Farm – At this working protea farm, which has 16 acres of the flowers, you can buy protea at very good prices and take them away with you or ship them to the mainland. Copp Rd., just up from the Maui Agricultural Research Center (phone: 878-1218).

The Rabbit Hole – A behind-the-scenes bookshop with an eclectic selection of new and used books. The meditatively quiet reading room overlooks a lovely patch of tropical forest. 3643 Baldwin Ave., Makawao (phone: 572-5874).

Viewpoints – The Maui Artists' Collective jointly owns this gallery with displays of members' work, from photography to ceramics, painting to sculpture. 3620 Baldwin Ave., Makawao (phone: 572-5979).

Vogue Vintage – Some excellent vintage clothing and accessories, particularly the hats, some of which are period classics. 3643 Baldwin Ave., Makawao (phone: 572-0331).

CHECKING IN: For the most part, only hikers or campers make the up-country their base, and unless you are a repeat visitor and know what you are doing, take heed. Besides the cabins in Haleakala National Park, there are very few places from which to choose. If you're interested in bed and breakfast accommodations, contact *Bed & Breakfast Hawaii* (phone: 536-8421, on Oahu). The telephone number is in the 808 area code.

Kula Lodge – This cluster of 5 rustic chalet-style cabins are set in a woodsy location on the mountainside. Most are large enough to sleep 4 people; several can accommodate 3 people only. Most have a wooden front porch or lanai, some have fireplaces, none have kitchenettes, but there is a restaurant in the main lodge open daily for breakfast and lunch, and on weekends for dinner. Rates are $120 to $140 for double occupancy. Hwy. 377, on the right going up (phone: 878-1535).

EATING OUT: Because most people come tootling around the mountain quite early in the day, especially if they've been up to watch the sunrise at Haleakala, they're usually looking for a late breakfast, lunch, or midafternoon snack rather than dinner. The restaurant listed as expensive will run $65 or more for two, those listed as moderate run between $30 and $60, while under $30 warrants an inexpensive categorization (not including drinks, wine, or tip). All telephone numbers are in the 808 area code unless otherwise indicated.

Haliimaile General Store – The former *1929 General Store* has been converted into a charming restaurant with wooden floors and tables, and some of the best food served on the island. Among the specialties are fettuccine with shrimp, vegetarian lasagna, roast duckling, and Kona-rib-eye — pure grain-fed yearling beef from the Big Island's Palani Ranch. The staff here is very friendly and helpful. Open daily for lunch from 11 AM to 3 PM, dinner from 6 to 10 PM, and Sunday brunch is served from 10 AM to 3 PM. Closed Mondays. Reservations advised. Off Hwy. 37, about 2 miles northeast of Pukalani, on Haliimaile Rd. (phone: 572-2666). Expensive.

Makawao Steak and Fish House – The setting is comfortable, and the food is good enough to attract a collection of upcountry regulars. This is a restaurant with charm and individuality. Open daily for dinner from 5 to 9:30 PM. Reservations advised. 3612 Baldwin Ave., Makawao (phone: 572-8711). Expensive to moderate.

Casanova – It's Italian, as the name implies, with appetizers such as carpaccio and calamari *fritti,* pasta, nine varieties of pizza, a chicken special of the day, *misto mare alla fra diavolo* (seafood sautéed in garlic), and an extensive wine list. Reservations suggested. Wednesdays and Thursdays, it's disco time from 9:30 PM to 1 AM, with free-form dancers given plenty of room on Maui's largest dance floor. The adjacent deli of the same name serves a tasty selection of sandwiches. Deli open daily. No reservations. Restaurant open for dinner from 5:30 to 9 PM daily; closed Sundays. Reservations advised. 1188 Makawao Ave. (phone: 572-0220). Moderate.

Pukalani Terrace – This is a simple, attractive place, with wraparound windows through which you can see the balls popping on the *Pukalani* golf course, and practically all of Maui that lies westward. Sandwiches, omelettes, and full meals are on the menu, including traditional Hawaiian food. Open daily for breakfast from 7 to 10:30 AM, lunch from 10:30 AM to 4:30 PM, and dinner from 5 to 9 PM. Reservations advised for groups. Turn right (on your way up) off Hwy. 37 just below the *Pukalani Terrace Center.* 360 Pukalani Rd. (phone: 572-1325). Moderate.

Kula Lodge – The restaurant at the lodge has windows looking down a wooded slope, with the central valley and the West Maui mountains in the distance. It's open daily for breakfast from 6:30 to 11:30 AM, lunch from 11:30 AM to 4:30 PM, and dinner from 5:30 to 9 PM. Reservations advised. Hwy. 377 (phone: 878-1535). Moderate to inexpensive.

Polli's – The original owner of Wailuku's *La Familia* has another hit in this small Mexican eatery, which serves vegetarian dishes along with more traditional fare. Open daily for lunch and dinner. Reservations advised for groups of 6 or more. 1202 Makawao Ave., Makawao (phone: 572-7808). Moderate to inexpensive.

Bullock's of Hawaii – Some might call it a greasy spoon, but complaints have yet to be heard about the moonburgers (a double han... a mustard and mayonnaise sauce) or the guava, pi... late, or coffee shakes. Open from 7:30 AM to 3 PM; ... $6.50. Open daily for lunch only. No reservations. ... (phone: 572-7220). Inexpensive.

Grandma's Maui Coffee House – Freshly baked cak... sandwiches, as well as a fine selection of espresso and c... coffee make this a great luncheon spot that attracts up-co... day as well as visitors. Open daily. Reservations unneces... Keokea Town (phone: 878-2140). Inexpensive.

Haleakala National Park

In translation, Haleakala (Hah-lay-*ah*-kah-lah) means "the house of the sun." From some points on the island it does appear that the sun rises directly from the center of Haleakala, but according to legend, the volcano gets its name from an extraordinary feat of the demigod Maui, undertaken once upon a time before ecology was a household word and the environmental impact statement was born. Back in those days, the sun used to rush rather quickly across the heavens, leaving too little daylight for Maui's mother, Hina, to finish her chores, especially the drying of tapa cloth. So one morning, well before dawn, Maui climbed the summit of Haleakala and lay in wait for the sun to come up over the eastern rim of the crater. No sooner had it appeared than Maui lassoed it (by the genitals, according to some versions of the story) and tied it to a wiliwili tree, releasing it only upon the sun's solemn promise to henceforth move more slowly across the sky.

Today, Haleakala is the centerpiece of a 27,284-acre national park dedicated to preserving nature's status quo, and visitors who make the sunrise trek to the top of the mountain huddle in the cold behind tripods trained on the eastern rim to capture the sun on film alone. The scene is indeed spectacular. Standing at the summit, the actual crater in front is only a small part of the panorama. Eighty miles away, the peaks of Mauna Loa and Mauna Kea on the Big Island of Hawaii stand up above the clouds, and as the sun slowly begins to edge the far horizon in red and gold, the earth looks like nothing so much as a giant bowl of whipped cream. Before it rises suddenly and blindingly, forcing the eyes to turn away, you may sense for a moment, at least, what Mark Twain meant when he said he felt "pinnacled in mid-heaven, a forgotten relic of a vanished world."

Curiously enough, from the central valley connecting the two, it is Maui's other volcano, the older and much-eroded Puu Kukui of West Maui, that appears the more precipitous. But Puu Kukui, once taller than Haleakala, now reaches a height of only 5,788 feet, whereas the massive Haleakala, which makes up East Maui, rises more steadily, its summit often deceptively obscured by a wreath of clouds, to 10,023 feet. Its crater — 7½ miles long by 2½ miles wide, 21 miles in circumference, and covering an area of 19 square miles — is a 3,000-foot depression in which the tallest cinder cone, Puu o Maui, stands nearly 1,000 feet high, or about four-fifths the height of the ding. The extent of Haleakala's crater is due more to erosion nic activity, processes that alternated over the course of its life. ano once stood 2,000 to 3,000 feet higher than it does today, high gh to catch the moisture of northeast trade winds and cause torrential rains to carve valleys down its slopes. Eventually, the amphitheater-like heads of two of these valleys — the Keanae Valley to the north, the Kaupo Valley to the south — met at the summit, creating one vast erosional scar. Subsequent volcanic activity filled the scar with lava and cinder cones (the result of volcanic material falling back around the vents from which it was blown), causing Haleakala finally to look like a true volcanic crater.

Haleakala's last eruption took place, it is thought, in 1790, a date arrived at (in the absence of any written firsthand account of the event) by comparing the journals of the French explorer La Perouse, who visited Maui in 1786, and the English navigator Vancouver, who visited in 1793. The eruption was forceful enough to send lava down the side of the mountain and add another peninsula to the southwest corner of East Maui in the vicinity of La Perouse Bay. Since then, the volcano has been quiet, but because the last eruption was so recent — at least according to the geological clock — Haleakala is not yet classified as extinct, but dormant.

In 1961, the summit and crater of Haleakala, which had once been part of the Big Island's Hawaii Volcanoes National Park, became a separate national park. And it was enlarged in 1969 by the addition of the Kipahulu District, a 6-mile strip following the Kipahulu Valley east from the crater to Maui's eastern coast near Hana. In both sections, the purpose is to preserve native — any plant or animal that reached Hawaii without the aid of man — flora and fauna that is rapidly being destroyed elsewhere, both by the incursion of man and by the competition of introduced species. Dry forests once covered the lower western slopes of Haleakala, for instance, but they were cleared long ago to make way for grazing cattle, and examples of the trees that grew there have now retreated to less accessible areas of the park. One hundred years ago, the rare silversword, a native plant found only in the higher alpine zones of Hawaii, carpeted the same Haleakala hillside that now contains a small, carefully enclosed stand of them. Hikers who venture to the eastern side of the crater may see the nene, or Hawaiian goose, found only here and on the island of Hawaii. The bird had been extinct on Maui until it was reintroduced in the 1960s in an international preservation effort. Even an endangered Hawaiian seabird, the dark-rumped petrel (*uau*), has taken refuge in the cliffs of Haleakala.

Before setting out for the park, it's a good idea to call 572-7749 for recorded information on weather and viewing conditions. The temperature drops about 3 degrees for every 1,000 feet in altitude, so at the summit it can be 30F (or more) colder than down on the coasts. Most likely, you will be very glad you brought a warm jacket, and if you've come for the sunrise, doubly so. Summer and fall (May through October) are generally better for viewing because they tend to be drier; winter and spring tend to be wetter, and in the winter, it can even snow, at least at the top. The crater is at its clearest in the morning, whereas from midmorning to late afternoon it may be filled with clouds, the result of heat rising from the surrounding land and pushing the volcano's wreath of clouds upward till they pour through gaps in the rim. Sunrise and sunset can both be inspiringly beautiful events, but the sunrise pilgrimage is the traditional one (see "Sightseeing Tours" in *Sources and Resources* for guided sunrise tours). Depending on the time of the year, sunrise can occur anytime from about 5:45 to 7:05 AM, and you should arrive at least a half hour before that to catch the first light. The *Maui News* prints the exact times of the next day's sunrise and sunset, and the park's recorded message gives the information as well. If you need more detailed information, call park headquarters at 572-9306 or 572-9177 (recording). In case of an after-hours emergency, call 572-9221. The only phone for visitors' use is at the visitors' center.

The trip from Kahului to the summit usually takes 1½ to 2 hours. Ask at your hotel exactly how long it takes if it's important for you to arrive by a specific time, such as sunrise. Call the National Weather Service (phone: 877-5111) for summit weather conditions and hours of sunrise and sunset. Visitors with heart disease, respiratory disease, or high blood pressure are reminded that the altitude may affect them adversely; they should consult a doctor before making the trip and they shouldn't drive alone. Finally, there are no restaurants, hotels, or shops in the park (though there are cabins and campgrounds) as at Hawaii Volcanoes National Park. For places to stop on the way up or down, see *Up-country.*

To reach the park, take Highway 37 (Haleakala Highway) from Kahului and turn left onto Highway 377 (still called Haleakala Highway) above the town of Pukalani. At an elevation of about 3,000 feet you'll bear left again onto Highway 378, or Haleakala Crater Road, and after about 10 miles of switchbacks, the road will deliver you to the park entrance — at an elevation of almost 7,000 feet — where the entry fee of $5 per car, or $1 per van or bus passenger, is paid. From there on, you'll find the following main points of interest, though if you've come to see the sunrise, waste no time in getting to the observation shelter at the summit first. For those who prefer to sleep in, the sunset offers its own rewards from atop Haleakala, allowing for a return at dusk and dinner in country-style Makawao or Paia, away from the tourist and resort restaurants along the coast.

Hosmer Grove – Just inside the park entrance, a side road to the left leads in less than one-half mile to Hosmer Grove, a campground with picnic tables and a nature trail through a stand of introduced (not native to Hawaii) trees such as North American pine, cedar, juniper, fir, and cypress as well as Australian eucalyptus. The grove honors Ralph Hosmer, a pioneering forester who in the early years of this century experimented with planting foreign trees to replace the native ones that had been cleared to make way for grazing lands, much to the detriment of the island's water supplies. Hosmer planted foreign trees because they grew faster than the native ones, and preserving the damaged watersheds was his overriding concern. Now, the protection of native vegetation, which is lower-growing and has no chance in the competition for light with the tall "exotics," is the park's prime purpose, and it is a sign of success that foreign trees such as these are in the minority within its boundaries.

Park Headquarters – About a mile from the park entrance (open daily from 7:30 AM to 4 PM), this is the place to stop for a comprehensive brochure on the park (if you don't see it, ask for it) and to buy books, slides, and posters. Those intending to use the park's campgrounds must also obtain permits here. Others may want to ask whether any crater rim walks are scheduled. These guided walks, a half-hour to 2 hours long, have been offered in the past (summer months only), but due to staff shortages they may not be offered in the future. Before leaving, go around the building to the pen containing a pair of nene, or Hawaiian geese. It may be one of your few chances to see Hawaii's state bird unless you're planning to hike into the crater.

Leleiwi Overlook – Here, at the first crater lookout point, 8,800 feet up, you might see the Brocken Specter (if conditions are right, that is, with late afternoon sun and clouds in the crater) — your own image projected on the clouds encircled by a rainbow. The name comes from one of the Harz Mountains in east Germany, where the specter also occurs.

Kalahaku Overlook – By all means, stop here. Not only can you look into the barren and blistered world of the crater, but the silversword enclosure is here, one of only two places in the park you're likely to come upon this famous native plant (the other is the Silversword Loop of the Halemauu Trail in the crater). Silverswords take some 7 to 20 years to mature, bloom once, and then die. Before the flower stalk begins to develop in May or June, the plant looks like a great pompom of silver daggers. By July or August, the flower stalk has shot up 3 to 8 feet and is covered with up to 500 individual flower heads of yellow and deep reddish purple, each shaped much like the sunflower to which it is related. Unfortunately, by autumn the plant is dead, and it lies drying on the landscape, as impressive as an old gray mop. The stone wall enclosing the collection of silverswords is meant to keep feral goats and souvenir hunters at a distance.

Haleakala Visitor Center – This glass-fronted observation building at 9,745 feet (yes, it's rounded off to 9,800 feet above the door) is 10 miles from park headquarters. It's open from 6:30 AM to 3 PM. The ranger on duty gives an hourly (9 AM to noon) introductory talk on Haleakala. You can also study the exhibits inside, which explain the geology of the crater. Outside, a footpath leads to White Hill (Pakaoao), a small hill on the crater rim adjacent to the visitor center. A short hike of about 360 yards will take you to its summit, passing stone-walled enclosures used as sleeping shelters by the early Hawaiians.

Puu Ulaula Overlook – The highest point on Maui. The glass-enclosed observation shelter with the 360-degree view is on top of Puu Ulaula, or Red Hill, which is actually a cinder cone, and the 10,023-foot summit of Haleakala. The building is open 24 hours a day, unattended, and it's the traditional spot from which to watch the sunrise. On a very clear day you can see not only the rest of Maui, but also the islands of Molokai (behind West Maui), Lanai, Kahoolawe, and Hawaii, and on a very, very clear day, even Oahu can be spotted, 130 miles away. The crater before you is less landscape than moonscape, as near perfect a lunar likeness as the earth can muster, and behind you, the five domes of Science City (see below) look exactly like any space colony you might have imagined.

Science City (Kolekole) – This research and communications center is outside the park and has nothing to do with it. The installations include solar and lunar observatories of the University of Hawaii, a Department of Defense satellite tracking station, two TV relay stations, and the equipment of a few other tenants. The scene must be admired from afar, however, because Science City is the scene of classified military laser "Star Wars" testing, and so is not open to the public.

Hiking and Horseback Riding – There is no better way to experience Haleakala than to descend the crater, and see its rim as skyline and its volcanic curiosities at close hand on all sides. The crater contains 32 miles of hiking trails, which wind past such sites as Pele's Paint Pot, where the usually gray to pinkish hills are colored with reds and yellows from the iron and sulfur imprisoned in the cold lava; Bubble Cave, formed by expanded gases that held their shape while the lava around them hardened; and the 60- to 70-foot-deep Bottomless Pit, blasted through by rising gases, into which ancient

Hawaiians threw the umbilical cords of their newborns (supposedly to prevent the infants from growing up as thieves). Making your way east, you'll pass cinder cones splattered with volcanic "bombs" (chunks of lava flung from vents and solidified in midair), cross lava flows, hear the bleating of feral goats, and, if you go to the rainy far eastern end, enter a green and grassy wilderness in considerable contrast to the rest of the crater. Here, Paliku Cabin, one of three crater cabins maintained by the National Park Service, is nestled in solitude among trees and shrubs at the base of a 1,000-foot cliff.

Two main trails lead into the crater from the western side of Haleakala. The Halemauu Trail begins along the highway 4 miles up from park headquarters, and Sliding Sands Trail begins farther up toward the summit, at the visitor center. If you set out along the Halemauu Trail, it is a 4-mile hike to Holua Cabin, another scant mile to the Silversword Loop (a half-mile detour around some good examples of the plants), and another 1½ miles to the Bottomless Pit and nearby Pele's Paint Pot. Setting out on the Sliding Sands Trail, it's 6 miles to Kapalaoa Cabin and another one-half mile to Bubble Cave, but a popular route for a full-day hike using this trail is to turn off it at the first junction and take the connecting Ka Moa O Pele Trail north, leaving the crater on the Halemauu Trail. The route leads to the Bottomless Pit, Pele's Paint Pot, the Silversword Loop, and Holua Cabin; it is a strenuous one, recommended for hikers in good physical condition only (though it does avoid climbing back up the steep and aptly named Sliding Sands Trail). A less strenuous, although still demanding, route for a day's hike is the 8-mile round trip along Halemauu to Holua and back.

No permits are necessary to hike in the park unless you stay overnight, but day hikers are requested to fill in the registration slips found at the trail heads and drop them into the box provided. And before stepping over the edge, hikers should be prepared for any kind of weather — hot and sunny or cold and rainy — with a light raincoat, sun hat, suntan lotion, and canteen as well as proper shoes. Given the distances involved, the terrain covered, and the effect of the altitude, there are no easy strolls in Haleakala.

Trail rides are another way to visit Haleakala. One possibility is a day trip entering the crater from the western side, along the Halemauu Trail or the Sliding Sands Trail. Another is an overnight adventure that begins in the morning and includes an 8-hour trip up the Kaupo Valley before entering the crater in time for sunset. For details on riding expeditions, see "Sports" in *Sources and Resources*.

Kipahulu District – This section of the park is reached by returning to the north coast of the island, driving the Hana Highway (Highway 36) east to and through the small town of Hana, and continuing 10 miles south beyond it on Highway 31. An arduous alternative route for hikers entails following the trails across the crater, leaving the Haleakala section of the park south through Kaupo Gap, and then continuing on foot, again along Highway 31, from Kaupo village 7 miles east to Kipahulu. Though evidence suggests that the early Hawaiians once used the crater as a short cut directly to Hana, this is no longer possible, not even for the daring hiker able to negotiate the terrain, because the two accessible sections of the park are separated by a part of it, the Upper Kipahulu Valley, which has been declared a scientific research preserve and closed to the public.

This makes Kipahulu a sort of park within a park, and there is a certain appropriateness to the separation. Where Haleakala is, on the whole, a cold, dry, and desert-like world of ash and cinder cones, most of Kipahulu is like a jungle, with little besides streams and waterfalls to cut the dense, tangled vegetation. Subtropical weather prevails, the humidity is high, and in the upper reaches as much as 250 inches of rain falls yearly to keep things green. Nevertheless, the rain forest is ecologically fragile. It is estimated that 90% of the plant life in the Upper Kipahulu Valley is native Hawaiian, and some very rare birds have been sighted here, too. The nukupuu, a native of Kauai and Maui that at one time was thought to be extinct, lives here, along with the akohekohe, or the crested honeycreeper, found only on Maui and only in this zone. The akohekohe is a member of a uniquely Hawaiian family of birds that evolved long curved bills to sip the nectar from Hawaiian flowers or shorter bills to feed on either nectar or insects. Another honeycreeper, the poouli, was unknown until it was discovered in 1973 in a forest on the northeast slope of Haleakala, its range confined to less than 1,000 acres.

By keeping the Upper Kipahulu Valley off-limits, except for research, its practically untouched ecosystem endures. Thus, the points of interest in the Kipahulu district that are accessible to visitors are in the coastal zone. The best known are the Seven Sacred Pools, a misnomer, because there are more than seven and they are sacred to no one. The pools are caused by the Oheo Stream as it rushes down the hillside, filling depression after depression until it overflows and cascades to the next lower level. Swimming in the pools is a popular activity among visitors, but it can be dangerous. During high water, the stream floods quickly and has been known to carry the unwary straight out to sea.

Makahiku Falls and Waimoku Falls are the objects of hiking trips in this area. The trail begins south of the bridge over Oheo Gulch and follows the left side of the stream up half a mile to Makahiku Falls, then continues through pastureland and bamboo forest another 1½ miles to the base of Waimoku Falls. (Call to see if ranger-led hikes to the falls are being offered.) For information, call the Kipahulu District Office of the National Park Service in Hana (phone: 248-8260; if no answer, try 572-9306).

CHECKING IN: Overnight camping in the park is permitted only at cabins and campgrounds, and no one may spend more than 2 consecutive nights in any one cabin or campground, nor more than 3 nights per month in the park.

Cabins – The National Park Service maintains three cabins within the crater: *Holua Cabin,* about 4 miles along the Halemauu Trail; *Kapalaoa Cabin,* 6 miles along the Sliding Sands Trail; and *Paliku Cabin,* about 10 miles in along either trail. Each cabin accommodates up to 12 people and will be rented to only one party at a time; rates are $5 per person, with a $15 nightly minimum, plus a $2.50-per-person, per-night firewood fee. There's also a refundable $15 key deposit. Reserve at least 90 days in advance with first, second, and third choices; write to the Superintendent, Haleakala National Park, PO Box 369, Makawao, Maui, HI 96768.

Campgrounds – There are three campgrounds in the Haleakala section of the park, one at Hosmer Grove and two in the crater near Holua and Paliku cabins. The number of campers is limited to 25 per campground, and the necessary permits are allotted on a first-come, first-served basis at park headquarters. The Kipahulu district's only campsite is the Oheo Campground. No permits are required, but the 3-night limit remains in effect, and you will have to bring your own water, as none is available at the site.

Hana and the Hana Highway

Put simply, Hana is a small, remote village on the eastern coast of East Maui reached by the Hana Highway (Hwy. 36), a scenic drive that follows the northern coast of East Maui, or close to it, for 52 miles from Kahului. But putting it simply does not explain Hana's mystique. The name Hana is usually preceded by the adjective "heavenly," and the appellation is far from hyperbole. Located on the windward side of Haleakala and endowed with more than 70 inches of rainfall annually (much more on the volcano's upper slopes), the Hana area is, for one thing, part dense, luxuriant rain forest, laced with waterfalls, and part open countryside, where cattle feed on meadows that are always green and dewy fresh.

In this setting, old-time Hawaii, at least on Maui, is valiantly making its last stand. The entire district is home to only some 2,500 people, many of them pure or part Hawaiians, and the village of Hana may hold about half that number. The area is agricultural, and because it is isolated and undeveloped, the tranquillity indigenous to rural spots and the simple spirit of aloha characteristic of Hawaiian towns carry on relatively undisturbed — at least for now. Outsiders have taken root in Hana, but they, mostly wealthy and many of them entertainers and movie stars — such as Jim Nabors, George Harrison, and Richard Pryor, all of whom purchased property here at one time — have come for exactly the peace, quiet, and privacy that Hana offers, and they haven't changed it one bit.

The splendid isolation that endures on this side of East Maui is due, more than anything, to the Hana Highway. This narrow, winding country road was built in 1927, and though paved since, it is so pitted and potholed, and with such ragged edges, that you'll swear it's never once been patched. By unofficial count, it contains 617 curves and 56 one-lane bridges, which explains why the drive of little more than 50 miles takes a resident expert 1½ hours at breakneck speed and everybody else at least 3 hours. The issue of improving "The Road" is a controversial one. You will hear it said that the residents are against it, to keep the tourists out, but the truth is that because road conditions have deterred no one, more recent controversy centers on the state's policy of making short stretches of the road near perfect (such as the last few miles at either end), versus the Hana residents' preference that first aid be applied to the whole course.

Those who want their Maui vacation to be a simple interlude in the country, with the added attraction of a few beaches (but not the best on the island), with no nightlife (because of Haleakala, even the sun sets early here) and no TV (reception is bad), will choose to stay in Hana. For everyone else, the road to Hana itself, and the scenery along it, is the attraction. The route runs through a jungle of subtropical vegetation, winding by damp, fern-blanketed rock walls on one side and hala trees clinging to a cliff on the other. You'll pass koa and kukui trees, mango and breadfruit trees, and, depending on the season, you'll drive over a roadway strewn with fallen guavas and the bruised red petals of the African tulip tree. Even the winding at its worst is leavened by the vision of shaded waterfalls and those one-lane bridges in the inner crooks and by sunny glimpses of sea and coast on the outer elbows. And after you've rounded the last bend to catch the last whiff of ginger or eucalyptus blown in on the breeze, the road will suddenly unwind, the jungle will open up, pastures will come into view, and blazing poinsettias and crotons will announce that you, too, have finally survived the road to Hana.

There are some rules of the road. The first is to get an early start and to keep track of the time. It will likely take at least 3 hours to make the trip — starting out from Maui's resort coast — even without stopping at all of the points of interest listed below, and you should be leaving Hana for the return trip no later than 3 PM — it's a difficult drive in the dark. Fill the gas tank — there are no gas stations between the town of Paia and Hana — and stock up on enough food and drink for the duration, because there's no place to grab a bite to eat either. Despite the scenery, keep an eye on the road, keep to your side of it, and drive very slowly around the narrow blind curves. Keep the other eye on the rearview mirror, and when you see traffic backed up behind you, pull over as a courtesy. Though most tourists take the road at speeds ranging from 15 to 30 miles per hour, locals who know it well deserve to be allowed to go on their way. Finally, if you are planning to spend the night in Hana, make sure you have firm reservations before setting out, and if you simply want to get to Hana, consider flying. There is an airport, and your hotel or condominium will pick you up if you arrange it, though unless you also arrange a rental car (through hotel or condo), you'll have no means of getting around during your stay.

Paia – Once a busy sugar plantation town, then a sleepy has-been, Paia is now emerging as an enjoyable starting point for the trip to Hana. Paint has been slapped from one end of the dusty, sun-bleached strip to the other, a few restaurants have opened or been upgraded, and shops, funky and otherwise, have appeared on the scene. The old Paia Mercantile Building has been restored and converted into the *Paia Arts Center,* with shop and studio space for artists and craftsmen, though natural cosmetics are sold and costumes are rented here, too. You will see half of the town if you keep to Highway 36, the other half if you turn right at the crossroads and drive up Baldwin Avenue, which leads to the old sugar mill owned by Henry Perrine Baldwin, one of Maui's 19th-century sugar kings and a founder of Alexander & Baldwin, one of Hawaii's historic Big Five companies. Paia does have the last gas between civilization and Hana and purveyors of box lunches for the trip, so stock up.

About 2 miles east of Paia, you will round a bend and, depending on the time of day, see cars parked on a ledge below. This is Hookipa Beach Park, where contemporary windsurfing on Maui got its start. Maui is one of the prime windsurf locales in the world, with Hookipa and Maalaea luring windsurfers from around the globe. The park contains covered picnic pavilions facing out to sea and they, or the unpaved parking areas on the cliffs, are wonderful places to sit and watch the surfers as they streak across the blue with thundering waves at their backs.

Hana Highway – Highway 36 starts out as a fast, wide, smoothly paved road, but once you've hit the 19-mile marker and the sign announces "Narrow Winding Road Next 30 Miles," you'll know you're on your way to Hana in earnest. There are many places to stop en route, but the first lookout point is Kaumahina State Park, where another sign reads that you've come 28 miles from Kahului and still have 24 miles to go. The park has picnic tables, barbecue grills, and a splendid view out to sea, down to the small beach at Honomanu Bay, and ahead to the Keanae Peninsula.

A turnoff leading to the peninsula is farther along the road, but before you reach it, the Keanae Arboretum will appear on the right. The arboretum contains sections devoted to tropical plants, Hawaiian domestic plants, and native trees, and it makes an interesting stop (provided you can spare the time). Beyond the turnstile, it is a healthy walk between yellow ginger in the gulch to the left and ferns on the bank to your right before the plantings begin, but if you persevere, you'll be able to see at first hand how taro is grown. Quite a few varieties are planted in the demonstration patches, which are irrigated with the channeled waters of a waterfall that spills from one patch to the next seeking its lowest level. The native tree section is another mile beyond the tar patches back into the valley.

The Keanae turnoff is a left fork in the road after the arboretum. If you take it, you leave the already narrow Hana Highway to go down an even narrower stretch of paved road that turns into a dirt road leading around the peninsula to a dead end. The peninsula is an ancient lava flow that issued forth from Haleakala, and the waves breaking all around it make its edging of black lava rock fairly shine through the white spray. Somewhat stranded in this location, the village of Keanae is no more than a scattering of houses and a church, a traditional Hawaiian community where taro is grown. What part of their domain is not taro field or banana patch or palms is left to grazing cattle, goats, and horses.

Whether you make the Keanae detour or not, you should stop at the small paved lookout on the highway just beyond the turnoff. The view is the classic bird's-eye shot of Keanae as it appears in all the pictures: water-logged taro fields stylized into a neat agrarian checkerboard, the whole peninsula a sparkling expanse of clear, fresh greens projecting into the sea.

An opportunity for another detour occurs farther along when you see the Wailua spur road indicated to the left. It descends into the Wailua Valley and leads through another peaceful, old-time Hawaiian village of taro farmers, while the Wailua Valley Lookout, which you'll come across back on the highway shortly after the turnoff, affords a panoramic view of this second green and taro-patched sweep of loveliness. The pebbled parking area is to the right of the road and the stone stairway leading to the actual overlook on the level above is not easy to find at first, but look for the steps under a clump of overhanging trees. Still farther along, another lookout to the left of the road surveys the same valley.

Puaa Kaa State Park is the next stop. The parking lot is just beyond a one-lane bridge, and from there a pathway will take you back to where a pretty waterfall tumbles into a natural pool (of which a swimmer or two might be taking advantage), then seeps forth as a stream and runs under the bridge and down and out through the valley. The small park contains picnic tables and is full of banana trees and ringed by eucalyptus.

The vista widens over grazing lands just after you've endured one of the remaining unimproved stretches of the Hana Highway, and by the time you see Hana Gardenland on the right — a nursery where tropical plants and seeds are sold — you'll be only 4 easy miles short of the goal. The next "landmarks" on the left are the turnoff to Hana's tiny airport and then the turnoff to Waianapanapa State Park. (Also in the vicinity is a side road to Piilanihale Heiau, the largest of the many *heiaus* (ancient temples) scattered along the coast above and below Hana and reputed to be the largest yet discovered in Hawaii. It is not easily accessible, however, with a four-wheel-drive vehicle necessary when rain turns the dirt road to mud.

Much larger than the usual wayside park, Waianapanapa contains cabins and campsites in addition to picnic tables. Tent campers must have a permit, which can be issued by any Hawaii State Park office, including the Wailuku branch on the ground floor of the State Office Building in Wailuku, which is open weekdays from 8 AM to 4 PM (phone: 243-5354). Cabins are rented through the same office (see *Checking In*). Those passing through may still want to drive in for a look at the park's two main sightseeing attractions: the black sand and pebble beach on Pailoa Bay (be careful of rough currents if you go swimming — it's not always safe even for the best of swimmers) and Waianapanapa Cave, a double cave that is actually a water-filled lava tube overhung by ferns and surrounded by flowers and legend. The legend concerns a Hawaiian princess who is supposed to have taken refuge in a hidden chamber of the cave (reachable only by swimming underwater) while fleeing her jealous husband. He found her nonetheless and killed her, and because this unfortunate event took place in April, it is claimed that every April since then the waters of the cave turn red (some blame the effect on the presence of shrimp). Waianapanapa State Park is also the starting point of a 3-mile hiking trail to Hana. It follows the path of an ancient trail along low sea cliffs, past a *heiau,* and through stands of hala trees, perilously close to the edge at times, and all but disappears at others.

Just before Hana, Highway 36 divides into a high road on the right and a low road on the left. Either one leads into town, the lower one as Uakea Road, the higher one as the Hana Highway, which goes through town and comes out the other end as Highway 31. Alii Gardens (recently opened to the public) on the Hana Hwy., about 8 miles before Hana Town (phone: 248-7217) welcomes visitors to a commercial nursery with acres and acres of heliconia, ginger, and more. Boxed flowers and dry-flower arrangements can be shipped to the mainland. Halfway between Waianapanapa and town is Helani Gardens, a 68-acre drive-through park alive with the botanical abundance of the tropics, with all plants fully labeled. The park also features Japanese koi ponds and a luncheon pavilion. Open daily from 10 AM to 4 PM; admission $2 (phone: 248-8274).

Hana – This serene and isolated village has been by turns a battleground, a sugar town, and a cow town. In the war-torn years of the 18th century, before Kamehameha the Great established the united Hawaiian kingdom, the Hana area's proximity to the Big Island (just a short canoe paddle across the Alanuihaha Channel) gave it enormous strategic importance. As the place from which Maui's chiefs launched their attacks on the neighboring island and where retaliating Hawaiian chiefs began their invasion of Maui, it was conquered and reconquered by one army after another. With the return of peace, other chapters in Hana's history began. In the mid-19th century, the first sugar was planted and numerous sugar plantations came into being that eventually coalesced into the Hana Plantation — later the Kaeleku Sugar Company — and sugar remained the basis of Hana's economy until the period between the two world wars.

Hana quickly turned into a cow town with the arrival of a San Francisco millionaire, Paul Fagan, who foresaw the end of the sugar era and in 1944 bought up 15,000 acres of sugarland. After the last crop was harvested in 1945, he began replanting the property in range grass, imported Hereford cattle from his ranch on Molokai, and called his new spread the Hana Ranch. Because this endeavor was not enough to solve Hana's unemployment problems, Fagan moved just as quickly to build a hotel, which opened in 1946 with his own baseball team, the San Francisco Seals, as the first guests. Millionaire friends followed, and the *Hana-Maui* hotel acquired a reputation as an exclusive retreat for the few, which has stuck. Today, in the post-Fagan era, the hotel is managed by Sheraton (though the entire enterprise is now owned by an American-British-Japanese corporation seriously considering future development).

Fagan died in 1960, and the memorial erected in his honor on Mt. Lyons, a cinder cone above the town, is the most panoramic spot in Hana, an ideal place to get your bearings. Don't miss the chance to take the very narrow road that begins in the parking lot across the street from the hotel and goes through pasture straight up and then around the cone to the cross at the top (hotel guests can request a key to the gate — which is always locked — that blocks the road). From here, the eye takes in one vast seaward roll of green hills and grazing cattle, a view of which the whole of Hana Bay (between Nanualele Point and Kauiki Head) is only a small part, and of which the whole of Hana, with a host of red roofs and every landmark visible, is a still smaller part.

The whole of Hana is the point, because as far as the day-tripper is concerned, the town has few specific sightseeing attractions. Kauiki Head, the cinder cone shaggy with ironwood trees to the right of Hana Bay, figured heavily in Hana's history as a fortress rock, the site of vicious battles between the armies of the Maui chief Kahekili and the Big Island chief Kalaniopuu. It was also the birthplace (ca. 1768) of Queen Kaahumanu, the favorite wife of Kamehameha the Great. Hana Beach Park, also on the right side of the bay, consists of picnic tables and the small beach itself, which offers the safest swimming in the entire district. Hana's community pavilion is the building almost in the shadow of Kauiki just across the road from the park, and at the end of the road is a T-shaped pier. From the end of the pier, there's a broad view of the town as a low line of houses tucked among trees, with two green-carpeted humps (one, Mt. Lyons) as a backdrop and the cloud-covered Haleakala behind all.

Moving inland from Hana Bay, the *Hana Cultural Center* is a small museum that provides an interesting glimpse of Hana's history and sociological present with displays of ancient Hawaiian artifacts and archival and contemporary photography. The center, which is free, is open on weekdays from 10 AM to 4 PM and is located on Uakea Road, just before the intersection that leads to Hana Bay (phone: 248-8622). Heading into town is the Wananalua Church on Haouli Street. The church was built from 1837 to 1857 on the site of an old *heiau,* and recently has been carefully restored. Across the Hana Highway from it and just a bit south is another focal point, the Hana Ranch Center complex — the ranch headquarters, a bank, the post office, and the *Hana Ranch* restaurant. The *Hasegawa General Store* (see *Shopping*), which figures in a popular song of the same name, and offers just about everything one could desire from a country store (excluding the proverbial kitchen sink), is located in what was once Hana's movie theater.

The misnamed (and now often crowded) Seven Sacred Pools (really Oheo Gulch) are the major sightseeing attraction beyond Hana. On Highway 31, in the Kipahulu district of Haleakala National Park, the pools are not known to have been sacred to anyone, and more than seven of them are formed by the Oheo Stream tumbling down the valley on its way to the sea, filling depressions at various levels like a string of overflowing champagne glasses. The pools are popular swimming holes (though high water can turn them dangerous quickly), and they are also the starting point of a hiking trail uphill to Makahiku Falls and Waimoku Falls. (For information concerning occasional Saturday morning ranger-conducted hikes to Waimoku, call 248-8260, the Kipahulu district office of the National Park Service, or 572-9307.)

The round-trip drive to the Seven Sacred Pools adds 20 rough miles to a Hana drive. Though not as winding as Highway 36, the road appears twice as narrow and twice as pockmarked — and on occasion, depressingly crowded by long lines of slow-moving cars — and the trip will take approximately 45 minutes each way. A satisfactory alternative is to drive beyond Hana far enough to sample the peaceful grazing lands on the other side and to see cattle ranging up the slopes of Haleakala and down to the frothy edge of the ocean and, offshore, the tiny island of Alau, with two tall palms standing out like a cowlick on top.

Those who want to go farther will pass Wailua Falls, 7 miles south of Hana, before they get to the pools. And about 1½ miles beyond the pools, just past an old sugar mill on the right, a sign points out the Kipahulu Congregational Church to the left, where Charles Lindbergh — a resident of Hana — was buried in 1974. A little farther, another sign announces a rough road for the next 7 miles. This is the beginning of an unpaved portion of Highway 31 which, over one surface or another, leads around East Maui to Ulupalakua. In Hana, cars can be rented from *Dollar Rent-A-Car* (phone: 944-1544; 800-367-7006) which will provide an airport pickup for customers who are flying in.

SHOPPING: Hana's few stores cater almost entirely to utilitarian needs and, therefore, close by 6 PM. In Paia, however, catering to the visitor is a growth industry. You may want to check out what's new at the *Paia Arts Center,* in addition to the shops below. Warning: You won't really find anything in this area that you won't also find elsewhere, so if you are in a rush, you might just as well save your shopping for later.

Clothes Addict – Casual wear, bikinis, and Maui's largest collection of vintage shirts are for sale in this pink building with the flowered awning. 12 Baldwin Ave., Paia (phone: 579-9266).

Eddie Flotte Studio/Gallery – Masterfully painted works (originals and prints) of

Maui's fast-changing rural lifestyle by artist Eddie Flotte. The prices are a bit steep, but the work is artistically distinctive and technically proficient. 85 Hana Hwy., Paia (phone: 579-9641).

Hana Store – A combination grocery store and five-and-dime. It sells all that you'd expect to find in such stores plus the "Road to Hana Survivor" T-shirt. Hana (phone: 248-8261).

Hasegawa General Store – This famous general store, against which all other island general stores must measure themselves, has as its motto "Almost everything," which includes groceries, clothing, hardware, souvenirs, liquor, magazines, film, cowbells, Hawaiian moon calendars, movie rentals, and gas. Hana (phone: 248-8231).

Jaggers – Women's casual fashions, with a touch of the exotic in fabrics and styles. 100 Hana Hwy., Paia (phone: 579-9221).

John of Maui and Sons – Hawaiian John Aperto is a master craftsman with Hawaiian woods, most particularly with hand-crafted bowls of all sizes and shapes. This is the factory outlet where you are likely to have a chance to talk with John and see him at work. 100 Haiku Rd., Haiku (phone: 575-2863).

Kaui's Florist – The best buy here is the selection of Niihau shell leis. 120 Hana Hwy. (phone: 579-9393).

Maui Crafts Guild – Craftspeople display everything from stained glass to photography, basketry to Hawaiian quilts, in this small Paia emporium. 43 Hana Hwy., Paia (phone: 579-9697).

Maui Sculpture Gallery – An interesting selection of sculpture, carved wood objets d'art, and painting, much of it too large to carry, but worth a look. 120 Hana Hwy., Paia (phone: 579-8844).

Paia Gifts and Collectibles – Hawaiiana, estate jewelry, and Orientalia are the main offerings. At the corner of Baldwin and Hana Hwy., Paia (phone: 579-8660).

Paia Trading Co. – A selection of collectible antique bottles, glass, and Hawaiiana. 106 Hana Hwy., Paia (phone: 579-9472).

Sandkastle Kids – An unexpectedly comprehensive selection of children's clothing and toys, including a second room with used-but-usable clothes for kids. 113 Baldwin Ave., Paia (phone: 579-8043).

Summer House – Shop here for contemporary women's clothes and accessories with a European flair. 83 Hana Hwy. (phone: 579-9201).

Things from the Past – One of Hawaii's largest selection of collectibles and near-collectibles, this shop, identified by the aloha-clothed Santa out front, has interesting estate jewelry, Orientalia, and Hawaiiana. 137 Hana Hwy., Paia (phone: 579-9115).

Ukulele – A nice selection of cotton unisex shirts, many imported from Bali. 62 Baldwin Ave., Paia (phone: 579-9960).

Yoki's – Exotic jewelry, provocative lingerie, and avant-garde clothing, including fashions by Betsey Johnson. 21 Baldwin Ave., Paia (phone: 579-9249).

NIGHTLIFE: While painting the town red is not a major priority for most of the citizenry, the *Coconut Café* (120 Hana Hwy.; phone: 579-9719) attracts crowds of area residents and visitors from the mainland and Europe for dancing in its outdoor garden on weekends from 8 PM to midnight. At press time the *Rainforest Café* (62 Baldwin Ave.; phone: 579-9391) was about to introduce nightly entertainment.

CHECKING IN: Hana can accommodate only so many people, so whether you plan to stay awhile or are simply unable to face driving the Hana Highway twice in one day, reserve accordingly. Here, the very expensive category means the *Hana Maui,* where rates start at about $300 and climb ever higher. Otherwise, a room for two in a place listed as expensive runs $100 and up;

in a place listed as moderate, $55 to $95; and in an inexpensive place, under $50. All telephone numbers are in the 808 area code unless otherwise indicated.

Hana-Maui – This is one of the world's unique hotels. Located on landscaped acres in the heart of Hana Town, the resort, managed by Sheraton since 1990, has 101 low-rise bungalows framed by flowering plumeria, heliconia, and orchids. Rooms are made luxurious with sunken bathtubs (though recent tales have reached us about an insect or two enjoying these facilities) that face private gardens, and are equipped with phone and refrigerator, but no TV sets. Diversions are provided by 2 heated outdoor pools, tennis courts, pitch-and-putt golf course, beachfront pavilion, stable of horses, and a schedule of activities that includes cookout rides and a weekly luau. The dining room is open to non-guests (see *Eating Out*). Vans, or a rebuilt 1929 Packard, shuttle guests to and from private facilities at Hamoa Beach, 3 miles away, or to and from the airport, and rental cars are also available. The hotel also offers the Sea Cottages, with 2 apartments each, that enjoy panoramic ocean views, large lanais, and individual deckside saunas in which to soak it all up. Accommodations are available inclusive of all meals, or on a room-only basis. Hana (phone: 248-8211; 800-325-3535). Very expensive.

Hana Bay Vacation Rentals – To rent a fully furnished, fully equipped home for a Hana base, Stan and Suzanne Collins are the people to contact; they handle 10 homes in the town of Hana. Some require a 3-night minimum, others are offered daily. Car rentals can also be arranged. Check for weekly discounts. The reservations office is closed Saturdays (phone: 248-7727). Expensive to moderate.

Hana Kai Maui – Two gray wooden buildings make up this 19-unit condominium — one banked with red ginger and a border of yellow allamandas, the other reached by a bridge over a stream edged in blue ginger. The rooms, while not elegant, are adequate and come equipped with cooking accessories. Each has a large lanai with a table, chairs, and lovely ocean views, which makes for perfect alfresco dining. There are, however, no phones in the units and the lack of air conditioning can prove a discomfort on occasional humid nights. It is only a short walk from the coast, where there is a rocky beach and a rough surf: Swimming is not recommended. Uakea Rd., Hana (phone: 248-8426; 800-346-2772). Moderate.

Heavenly Hana Inn – This small hostelry looks like something your great-aunt might live in — or run — were she Japanese. It has the air of a private home, hidden behind a Japanese gate hung with Japanese lanterns and guarded by two stone lions. The lobby and lounge area, too, are filled with Japanese knickknacks (plus a piano), but apart from the shoji screens everywhere, the 4 units for rent are less Oriental in their accoutrements. Each has 2 double bedrooms, a tiny TV room, a sit-in kitchen with a small refrigerator, microwave oven, and two-burner hotplate, a bathroom with stall shower, and a private porch on the encircling Japanese garden. Also available through the inn are 2 rental homes, one a beachfront cottage with kitchenette. No swimming pool. Airport transportation available at minimal charge with advance notice, however, a car is a practical necessity. On the Hana Hwy., halfway between the airport and town (phone: 248-8442). Moderate.

Waianapanapa State Park – The 12 rustic cabins here are in a forest of hala trees not quite dense enough to blot out the sun. Each has a living room, a bedroom, and kitchen facilities, and each is completely furnished with bedding, towels, and cooking and eating utensils. Prices range from $14 to $30 a day, depending on the number of occupants (the maximum is six people), so make reservations well in advance. The cabins are about 3 miles from Hana but are rented through the Department of Land and Natural Resources, Division of State Parks, 54 S. High St., Wailuku, HI 96793 (phone: 243-5354). An in-person or mail-in deposit is required. Inexpensive.

EATING OUT: There are restaurants at either end of the Hana Highway, but en route there are only picnic tables, where you'll eat what you've brought with you. (*Picnics* — at 30 Baldwin Ave. in Paia; phone: 579-8021 — packs box lunches for the road. It's open daily from 7:30 AM to 7:30 PM.) Selected restaurants in the Paia area and *all* of the places to eat in Hana are listed below; beyond these, at the Hana end, you'll have to rely on groceries or take-out service from the *Hana Store,* or on hot dogs or hamburgers from *Tutu's* lunch counter at Hana Beach Park. Dinner at the *Hana-Maui* dining room is likely to cost $75 or more for two. Elsewhere, expect to pay $25 to $30 if the establishment is listed as moderate, and under $25 if it's listed as inexpensive. All telephone numbers are in the 808 area code unless otherwise indicated.

Hana-Maui – Though currently below its once high standards of food and service, Hana's only proper restaurant is this hotel's spacious dining room. Natural woods and hanging plants, exposed beams, and teakwood tables add up to a wonderful setting for specials that include flame-seared, wok-prepared chicken breasts, bamboo-steamed opakapaka served with ginger pilaf rice, as well as a selection of meat, fish, and poultry dishes. Open daily for breakfast from 6:30 to 10 AM, lunch from 11:30 AM to 2 PM, and dinner from 6 to 8:30 PM. Dinner reservations necessary. *Hana-Maui Hotel,* Hana (phone: 248-8211). Expensive.

Mama's Fish House – Some say that Mama serves the best fish on the island, but with so many Maui restaurants serving fish, the statement would be difficult to prove. Mama also serves steaks, seafood, and a chicken dish or two, but if you do have the fish, have it sautéed, the most popular of several styles ranging from grilled to baked in tarragon sauce to teriyaki. The restaurant is enclosed, with screened windows along the *makai* (ocean) side looking across a lawn, some low palms, and the break of the surf on Kuau Cove. Open for lunch from 11 AM to 2:30 PM, and dinner from 5 to 9:30 PM daily. Reservations advised. Off the Hana Hwy. at Kuau Cove, between Paia and Hookipa Beach Park (phone: 579-8488). Moderate.

Paia Fishmarket – The name tells it like it is. The entrance has fresh fish and seafood on display in a showcase. It's come-as-you-are casual, with large portions, good prices, and tasty food. Perfect if you're in the mood for someplace simple for lunch or dinner. The same menu is offered from 11 AM to 9:30 PM, daily. Reservations unnecessary. 100 Hana Hwy., (phone 579-8030). Moderate.

Coconut Café – This lively place offers alfresco and indoor seating, and the menu is a solid bet — everything from New York steaks to fresh fish to vegetarian tofu lasagna to stir-fried chicken will leave diners sighing with pleasure. Weekend evening crowds throng here to listen to live Hawaiian music. Open for lunch from 11 AM to 2:30 PM and dinner from 5 to 9 PM. Closed Tuesdays. 120 Hana Hwy. (phone: 579-9719). Moderate to inexpensive.

Dillon's – From the street, this dusty red building looks like a Wild West saloon tarted up with yellow lace curtains. Inside, the ambience is more Polynesian, and out back there's even a tiny garden of five tables squeezed in among banana trees and a large schefflera. The menu features fresh fish, plus steaks, seafood, and Italian dishes. Open daily for breakfast from 7 to 11 AM, lunch from 11 AM to 4:30 PM, and dinner from 5 to 9 PM. Reservations advised. 89 Hana Hwy., Paia (phone: 579-9113). Moderate to inexpensive.

Kihata – The look is casual, the food mostly Japanese — which means sushi, sashimi, tempura, and the like. Open for lunch from 11 AM to 1:30 PM, and dinner from 5 to 9 PM; takeout is available. Closed Sundays. Reservations unnecessary. 117 Hana Hwy., Paia (phone: 579-9035). Moderate to inexpensive.

Hana Ranch – Take a humble cafeteria, add windows on the sides, sliding glass doors, and an outdoor dining deck with a noble view of cattle range and coastline, and you'll have an idea what this restaurant is about. Its luncheon buffet (11 AM to 3 PM daily) includes hot dishes and a salad bar. Since a lot of the people who've made it to Hana eat here, there is a certain amount of relief-related conviviality in the air. Dinner is served from 6 to 7:30 PM on Fridays and Saturdays; Thursdays it's Pizza Night from 5:30 to 7:30 PM. Reservations advised. In the *Hana Ranch Center* complex (phone: 248-8255). Inexpensive.

Picnics – This is the place for the best box lunches. All pastries and breads are baked on the premises. Open daily from 7:30 AM to 7:30 PM. Reservations unnecessary. 30 Baldwin Ave. (phone: 579-8021). Inexpensive.

Vegan – Nothing fancy, but the vegetarian, cholesterol-free specialties are quite flavorful, with delicious soups and a wide array of sandwiches and entrées from which to choose. Takeout is available for those en route from Hana or up-country. Open daily from 4 to 8:30 PM, Saturdays from noon to 9 PM. Closed Mondays. Reservations unnecessary. 115 Baldwin Ave., Paia (phone: 579-9144). Inexpensive.

MOLOKAI

The smell and feel of Molokai are, at first rush, pure prairie. The effect upon landing at Hoolehua Airport is not unlike alighting from the single daily plane in a small Texas town. Rich pasturelands and a long horizon are everywhere. A pure plains wind lifts the red dust and brings the dry air into the lungs. Only the nearby sea and the mountainous eastern half of the island hint that this is a mid-Pacific volcanic outpost.

There is, after Honolulu, tangible culture shock. Molokai is Hawaii's unsullied frontier, preserved for the time from the ravages of ambition and the pressures of population by a strange series of events. Coincidence, difficult times, and shrewd design have somehow combined to keep the island's population hovering around 6,000 and the economy almost totally based on the land. Lack of development — and lack of reason for it — has protected almost all of Molokai's beaches, forested mountains, and secluded valleys. Here is a place to leave a footprint that will be marred only by the creeping tide, to swim in a pool at the foot of a waterfall with only a floating ti leaf to bear witness, to find contentment in a trackless forest.

Kaunakakai, the only real town on the entire island, has not a single traffic light. Except for the Polynesian and Filipino faces, it could be any small town in the Southwest, right down to the single storefront street lined with pickups. The whole island, 38 miles long, has a tiny police force whose members until only recently drove their own automobiles in service to the community. From Oahu's Makapuu Point it is but 25 miles across the open water of the Kaiwi Channel to Molokai's Laau Point. The flight from Honolulu to Hoolehua takes less than 30 minutes. Yet these few miles and few ticks of time are the measure of decades.

It is not so much that time has stood still on Molokai, although it most certainly has lagged, as it is that the clock periodically has been broken. Molokai long has been more isolated than most of the seven inhabited Hawaiian islands; only Niihau and Lanai have had less contact with the outside world. The first Hawaiians, Polynesians who, it is calculated, arrived sometime in the 5th or 6th century, at first avoided Molokai. The island did not appear hospitable — its west end dry and barren (thus the Hawaiian name: *molo,* "barren"; *kai,* "sea"), its east end coastline delineated by steep-walled valleys and choked with jungle. In addition, prevailing winds and currents did not favor voyaging to or from Molokai, the island's leeward shore had no protected anchorages, and its windward coast was isolated by immense cliffs (regarded as the highest such sea cliffs in the world). Only later were the fertile north coast's valleys and the south coast's lowlands settled.

Kamehameha the Great conquered the island with a great army in a battle fought at Pakuhiwa Battleground on the south shore. The king's fleet of war canoes is said to have stretched for 4 miles. Molokai, however, was a small prize, and Hawaii's history quickly moved on and left it quiet once more.

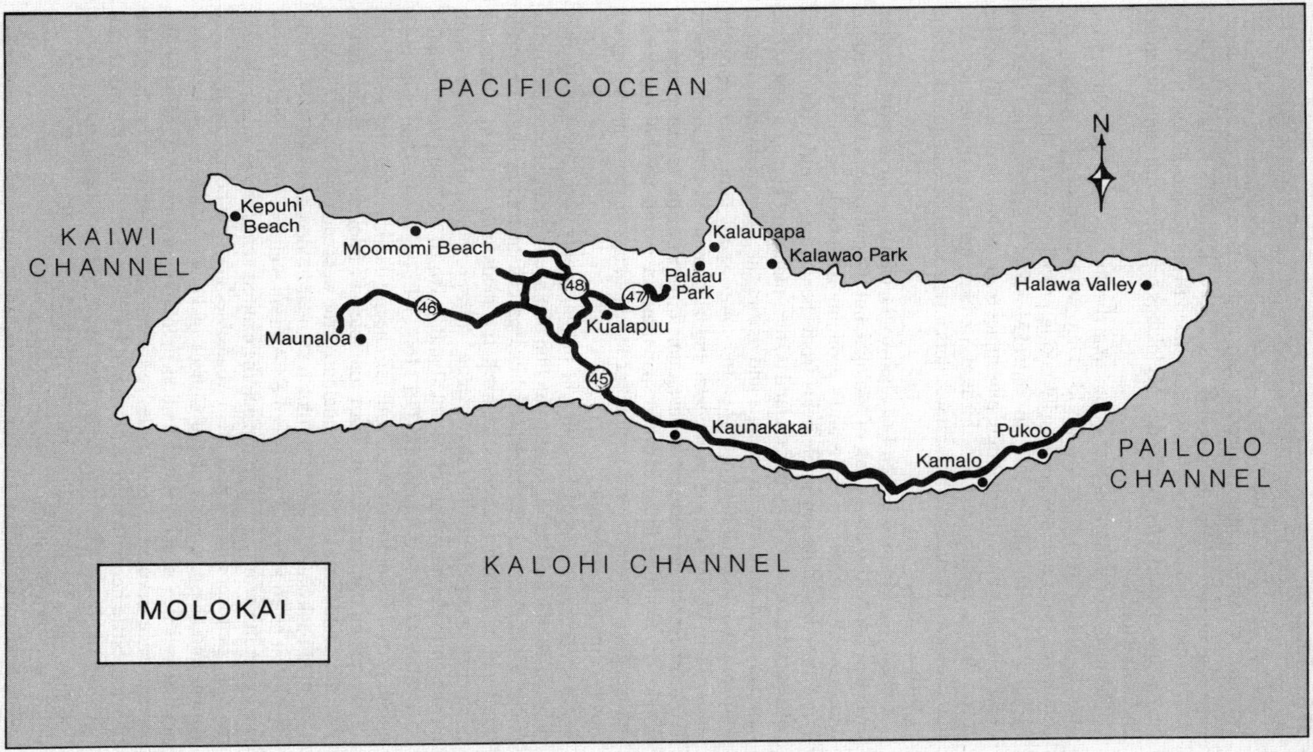
PACIFIC OCEAN
N
KAIWI CHANNEL
Kepuhi Beach
Moomomi Beach
Kalaupapa
Kalawao Park
Palaau Park
Halawa Valley
48
47
46
Kualapuu
Maunaloa
45
Kaunakakai
Pukoo
Kamalo
PAILOLO CHANNEL
KALOHI CHANNEL
MOLOKAI

Add to these factors the potent *kahunas* (priests or magic men of ancient Hawaii), which Molokai apparently had in abundance and of whom everybody else in Hawaii was scared stiff, and Father Damien's Kalaupapa leper settlement, which came much later but tended to put people off, and it is fairly easy to understand why even today Molokai is regarded with some reverence and suspicion.

The missionary families that began to arrive in the early 19th century did little to open Molokai to the world. They were interested in religion and commerce, with one not necessarily taking precedence over the other. The Meyer and Cooke families came to control Molokai, at first planting trees and eventually causing cattle to fatten, pineapples to grow, and payables to accrue. It was their dominion over two-thirds of Molokai, including the best beaches, that preserved the island's natural wonders just as isolation had guarded them in earlier times.

Until 1988, Molokai Ranch Ltd., heir to the efforts of these early families, owned or controlled about half of Molokai, but the company's voice in island affairs and its impact on the island's economy have been even more potent. Del Monte leased its pineapple fields from the company, and 6,000 head of cattle grazed on company pastureland. Green panic and guinea grasses from company land were sold to feedlots and dairies throughout Hawaii. Modern tourism came to Molokai only when the company set aside, and eventually sold, nearly 14,000 acres of prime west end beach and hill land in the middle 1970s for resort and residential development. Most of the land remains undeveloped, although in an effort to spawn an acceptable level of tourism, a master plan for resort and residential use is likely to move ahead, albeit slowly, during this decade.

There have been a small number of pivotal events in the modern history of Molokai, the first being the introduction of pineapple cultivation during the 1920s. Dole and Del Monte leased huge parcels of rolling land, imported hundreds of Filipino laborers to work the fields, and brought plantation prosperity to the island. The sharp-spiked fruit grew in geometrical precision on the entire western half of Molokai and spawned the company towns of Maunaloa (Dole) and Kualapuu (Del Monte). But as competition from pineapples grown in southeast Asia with far cheaper labor became intense in the 1970s, raising the fruit became less profitable on Molokai. Dole pulled out in 1975 and Del Monte in 1983. Maunaloa, on the west end plateau land, became a relative backwater, even by Molokai standards, despite modest efforts to establish it as an arts and crafts center. Almost everyone agrees that diversified agriculture must come to replace the expired commercial pineapple production. Lettuce, onions, and other vegetables are now being commercially grown, and the first trees of the Coffees of Hawaii coffee plantation were planted in 1989, which yielded its first profitable crop in 1992. Most of the acreage once devoted to pineapples has reverted to pasture, a boon for the reviving cattle herds that were destroyed by state decree in 1987, due to an outbreak of bovine tuberculosis. In 1989, a New Zealand ranching corporation purchased the controlling interest of the Molokai Ranch, and plans are under way to reintroduce cattle on a large scale.

The next epochal event that shaped modern Molokai, after the arrival of the pineapple, was a tidal wave that swept the east end of the island in 1946.

At that time, the verdant, peaceful Halawa Valley, which had been inhabited from ancient times, was still home to several hundred residents. Taro grew easily and the fishing was good in lovely Halawa Bay. The water rose gradually and slowly filled the valley, giving the people time to escape, but the *tsunami* receded rapidly, taking almost everything with it. Their homes and possessions lost, the people abandoned their beautiful valley and moved elsewhere on the island or left it entirely. Today, only a few families still live in Halawa, although many Hawaiians maintain weekend homes. This was the same tidal wave, says local lore, that spilled into the south shore lagoon in front of Kaunakakai and made it dull, shallow, and unfit for swimming.

The first attempt at establishing Molokai as a major resort destination came in 1977, when the *Sheraton-Molokai* (now the *Kaluakoi* hotel, jointly managed by Colony Resorts and the Castle Group) opened as the flagship hotel for the fledgling *Kaluakoi* resort. Despite a lovely setting, plus excellent, uncrowded golf and tennis, it has never really blossomed as a popular vacation spot. Since the hotel opened, two pleasant condominium properties have been added, but plans for a deluxe property at Kaluakoi have been delayed by environmental and cultural concerns and the recent state of the overall US economy. The recent sale of most of Molokai Ranch's West Molokai holdings may pave the way for future development, although an activist community is likely to bring pressure to restrain building it considers inappropriate to Molokai's rural lifestyle.

Certainly there are wonders sufficient to support far more tourism on Molokai. The island's 260 square miles include glorious (if too often unswimmable) beaches; the jungled 4,970-foot summit of Kamakou, the highest spot on the island; secluded valleys; and sacred groves and fishponds. There is Palaau Park and its famous Kalaupapa Lookout, which draws the eye down nearly 2,000 feet of sheer cliff to the flat, volcanic, tongue-like peninsula of the remote leper colony, which is now safe and open to visitors as Kalaupapa National Historic Park.

But possibly most of all, there is about Molokai its ancient Hawaiian past, a mysteriously touched history. Many believe Molokai to be the most spiritually charged of the islands — a place of powerful *kahunas,* helpful *menehunes* (little, leprechaun-like people), potent *kapus* (taboos), sacred places, myths, legends, whispers . . . The population includes the largest percentage of pure-blooded Hawaiians of all the Hawaiian islands, save off-limits Niihau. Molokai is an island of many names: In ancient times it was said to be called Puleoo (Effective Prayer). Today it is known as the Friendly Isle, but in the past it has also been the Forgotten Isle and the Lonely Isle. Molokai's direction remains today as unclear as it has for centuries.

SOURCES AND RESOURCES

TOURIST INFORMATION: The Hawaii Visitors Bureau does not have an office on Molokai, so for information contact the main office in Honolulu (2270 Kalakaua Ave., Room 801, Honolulu, HI 96815; phone: 923-1811). The Destination Molokai Association (PO Box 960, Kaunakakai, HI 96748;

phone: 553-3876; 800-367-4753) will provide brochures and information. On Molokai, your options are informal and few. Rental car offices at Hoolehua Airport have a useful guidebook and map.

Local Coverage – Also useful are the local newspapers, the twice-monthly *Molokai Advertiser-News* and the *Molokai Dispatch.* All the basics are also printed on the restaurant placemats at the *Kaluakoi* hotel, which include capsule descriptions of several tourist sites. The *Kaluakoi* hotel is also a good place to get a verbal rundown; check at the guest relations desk or tour desk in the lobby. A booklet, *Molokai, the Friendly Isle,* is available at several places on the island; also worth a look is Phil Spaulding III's booklet *Molokai.* The top of the line in books is the beautifully produced *Molokai, An Island in Time,* by Cooke family member Richard Cooke.

There are several bed and breakfast accommodations available on Molokai through *Bed & Breakfast Hawaii* (Box 449, Kapaa, HI 96746; phone: 822-7771; 800-367-8047, ext. 339). Among those offering vacation rental accommodations on the east end: Diane and Larry Swenson (Star Rte. 279, Kaunakakai, HI 96748; phone: 567-9268), Herb and Marion Mueh (pronounced *Me;* Star Rte. 128, Kaunakakai, HI 96748; phone: 558-8236), and *Honomuni House* (Star Rte. 306, Kaunakakai, HI 96748; phone: 558-8383), which offers a rental cottage.

TELEPHONE: The area code for Hawaii is 808.

GETTING AROUND: Connections among Honolulu, Maui, and Molokai are provided by *Hawaiian Air* (phone: 800-882-8811), with daily flights on its four-engine, Dash-7 turboprops. But lots of people like the service of the commuter lines with their small twin-engine craft; these include *Aloha IslandAir* (phone: 567-6115; 800-828-0806) and *Air Molokai* (phone: 553-3636), which also fly into the small airstrip that serves Kalaupapa, although visitors must arrange to be met by a guide (contact Richard Marx: phone: 567-6171) if they plan to leave the airport. *Sea Link of Hawaii* (phone: 553-5736) operates the *Maui Princess* once a day between Kaunakakai and Lahaina, Maui; seating is in air conditioned cabins or on the sun deck. The trip takes 90 minutes each way and costs $25.

There is no public transportation on Molokai. Most people arrive on the island by air at the main airport at Hoolehua. *Friendly Isle Tours* (phone: 567-6177) operates a shuttle service between the airport and hotels and condos (advance reservations required; phone: 567-6177).

Taxi – A rental car is more logical, but if you need a taxi, call Alex Puaa (phone: 553-3369) or *Teem Cab Molokai* (phone: 553-3433). Both also offer tours.

Car Rental – *Avis* (phone: 567-6814; 800-331-1212), *Budget* (phone: 567-6877; 800-527-0700), *Dollar* (phone: 567-6156; 800-367-7006; in Hawaii, outside Molokai, 800-342-7398), and *Tropical Rent-A-Car* (phone: 567-6118; 800-367-5140) have booths at Hoolehua Airport, but fleets are small, so it's advisable to reserve well in advance.

SIGHTSEEING TOURS: *Friendly Island Tours* (phone: 567-6177) and *Robert's Hawaii Tours* (phone: 552-2751) offer half- and full-day van and bus tours of the island, valuable if you're stuck without a rental car but easily duplicated if you've got one. For a real insider's view of Molokai, call Alex Puaa (phone: 553-3369), who offers ten tours with a four-wheel drive. A glimpse of Molokai at its most dramatic given by a native to the island. Tour rates are $35 an hour, with discounts offered for multiple tour bookings. *Teem Cab Molokai* (phone: 553-3433) features several itineraries, all in 7-passenger vans. *Molokai Limousine Taxi*

Service (phone: 553-3979) and Van Dale Dudoit's *Kukui Tours & Limousines* (phone: 553-5133) each offer stretch-limo luxury for island transfers or touring. *Sea Link of Hawaii* has a "Best of Molokai" day tour for $125 by boat from Maui.

Mule – *Molokai Mule Ride* mounts daily expeditions on sure-footed mules that clamber down the steep, narrow, 3⅛-mile trail from the cliffs overlooking the peninsula on which the Kalaupapa leper colony settled. The views are stupendous, and the experience itself is breathtaking. Guides meet the mule train at the bottom and conduct a tour of Kalaupapa and the Makanalua Peninsula. A simple picnic lunch is served at lovely Kalawao Park overlooking the sea cliffs of the north coast. The entire tour, including lunch, costs $90 per person. *Molokai Mule Ride* will also book hike-and-ground and round-trip air-and-ground tour visits to Kalaupapa. Contact *Molokai Mule Ride,* PO Box 200, Kaulapuu, Molokai, HI 96757 (phone: 567-6088; 800-845-9173).

Plane – *Bi-Plane Hawaii* offers open-cockpit, two-passenger biplane flights for 10, 40, and 65 minutes in the air (prices range from $90 to $500). The exhilarating east Molokai tour includes the dramatic cliffs and valleys of the North Shore, and the west Molokai tour takes in the Momomi dunes, *Kaluakoi* resort, and Kaunakakai. Contact *Bi-Plane Hawaii,* PO Box 1977, Kaunakakai, HI 96748 (phone: 567-6100).

Wagon – The horse-drawn *Molokai Wagon Ride* (phone: 558-8380) includes a visit to the sacred Iliiliopae Heiau as well as a beach stop for a picnic. The genuine Hawaiian hospitality makes this hour-and-a-half ride fly by. Daily, except Sundays. $33. *Rare Adventures,* which operates the *Molokai Mule Ride,* also offers a 2-hour ride on Meyer Ranch lands, with panoramic views of Meyer Lake, Kalaupapa, and the cliffs of the North Coast. The $35 cost includes light refreshments. Departures from the company's Kalae Stable are at 10:30 AM and 1 PM daily, except Sundays (phone: 567-6088; 800-843-5978).

SPECIAL EVENTS: A canoe race across Kaiwi Channel from Molokai to Oahu is traditionally held each year in September or October during *Aloha Week;* however, the area from which the race is launched is usually closed to visitors. A traditional Makahiki — a Polynesian-style *Olympics* — is held in Kaunakakai in mid-January. The Handcrafters and Artists of Molokai present their crafts and give workshops at various Molokai hotels and condominiums twice a month. In May, the *Molokai Ka Hula Piko,* an authentic hula festival, is held in the Kapoaiwa coconut grove and other simpatico locations. For information, contact Ginger LaVoie (phone: 558-8227).

SPORTS: Do not come to Molokai for the swimming, snorkeling, or water skiing. Come instead for the golf, hiking, tennis, hunting, exploring, and relaxing. The greatest concentration of traditional resort sports is found far out at the west end at the *Kaluakoi* resort, which boasts the island's only top-grade golf course and the best tennis courts.

Boating and Sailing – Sailing is offered at Kaunakakai aboard the 42-foot sloop *Satan's Doll* by *Molokai Charters* (PO Box 1207, Kaunakakai, HI 96748; phone: 553-5852). Options include snorkeling, sunset sails, and day trips off Lanai, with whale watching December through May. Glenn Davis of *Hokupaa Ocean Adventures* (PO Box 141, Kualapuu, HI 96757; no phone) offers cruises May through September, and the *Alyce C,* a 31-foot diesel fishing boat, (PO Box 825, Kaunakakai, HI 96748; phone: 558-8377) can be chartered for customized trips to the north shore of Lanai; fee depends on type of tour. Debbie and Jules Dudoit (phone: 558-8937) will rent boats at $400 a day to groups of up to six. Drop-offs and pickups to north coast valleys can also be arranged during the summer months.

Fishing – Although the fishing is legendary at Penguin Bank, off Molokai's southwestern tip, there is presently only one charter boat for hire: the 31-foot, twin-diesel cruiser *Alyce C,* which is fully equipped to troll for marlin, mahimahi, shark, tuna, and ono. Remember that the custom in Hawaii is that the captain, not the fisherman, gets to keep the catch. Call Joe Reich (phone: 558-8377) to arrange for charter fishing.

Golf – There are currently two golf courses on Molokai, but only one is worth playing — and it is well worth it, as it is the least crowded of all of Hawaii's resort courses. The *Kaluakoi* golf course (phone: 552-2739), a robust Ted Robinson design, has 18 holes, stretches 6,618 yards and plays to a par 72, and features 5 holes set along the sea. This is a beautiful course, equal to the best in Hawaii, with a complete pro shop, driving range, and practice putting green. It's also right at the *Kaluakoi* hotel, on the western tip of the island. Greens fee is $75, including a cart — $55 for hotel guests — and golf-inclusive packages are available (phone: 552-2555; 800-367-6046). *Ironwood Hills* golf course (phone: 567-6000), the public course (formerly owned by Del Monte) in Kualapuu in the middle of the island, has 9 holes, 3,150 yards, and is a par 34. There's a clubhouse with a pro shop and driving range. Greens fees are $10 for 9 holes and $12 for 18 holes; carts can be rented for $7 per person for 9 holes and $10 for 18 holes. To find *Ironwood,* drive up Route 47 toward Palaau State Park and look for the *Ironwood Hills* golf course sign on your left. A third course is under construction (with no completion date in sight), the 18-hole *Highlands* golf course (phone: 567-6000). *Highlands* has run into some community opposition due to plans to also include fairway-side condominiums.

Hiking – The hiking possibilities on Molokai are quite attractive — particularly up Halawa Valley or along the Wailau Trail across the entire island — but trails are poorly marked, often very difficult, and guides are unavailable. What's more, a few *pakalolo* (marijuana) growers in such isolated areas guard their territories jealously. Secure parking for hikers to Halawa Valley is sometimes available from the Dupre Dudoit family (turn right upon reaching the valley floor). The Nature Conservancy owns nearly 3,000 acres of prime mountain rain forest and dry shrubland at the Moomomi Dunes on the west end, Kamakou, and in Pelekunu Valley, along the north coast. Tours to Moomomi and Kamakou can be arranged for Nature Conservancy members ($25 annual fee). Contact Ed Misaki, Nature Conservancy of Hawaii (Molokai; PO Box 220, Kuapapuu, Kaunakakai, HI 96757; phone: 553-5326; 524-0779 from Oahu) for hike schedule. For those wishing to go on their own (not recommended), a jeep road intersecting with Route 46, just outside Kaunakakai, leads to the Kamakou Preserve, which is home to a wondrous array of rare native Hawaiian plants and birds. Most trails were created by wild boar hunters, who still use the property for this purpose. No camping is permitted within the preserve, but there is a campsite just outside the park at the Waikolu Lookout; a permit is required and can be obtained from the Department of Forestry & Wildlife (PO Box 347, Kaunakakai, HI 96748; phone: 553-5019). It's wise to keep in mind that although the hiking is good, hikers should first be sure to get good local information, directions, and perhaps permission to cross private land.

Horseback Riding – The same people who operate the *Molokai Wagon Ride* also offer 1½-hour escorted rides from Maupulehu, East Molokai. The $40 cost includes a beach picnic rendezvous with the wagon ride (phone: 558-8380). The *Molokai Mule Ride* (phone: 567-6088) offers escorted rides from its stables at Kaulapuu.

Hunting – The hunting is very good on Molokai, especially for the small axis deer (May through October), wild boar, mountain goats, and a whole flock of game birds. Deer were stocked on the island in 1850 by Kamehameha V. As elsewhere in Hawaii, the sport does not come at bargain rates. The guided hunt costs $400 per day for the first hunter, $250 for each additional hunter, $600 for each axis deer, and $1500 for each Barbary sheep, or Indian black buck of trophy caliber bagged. Bird hunting isn't quite as dear, however. Ring-necked pheasant, wild turkey, quail, doves, partridge, and other birds may be hunted on the Molokai Ranch's 40,000 acres for $50 per day, weekends only. The season runs from November through January. A state hunting license ($15) is also required. And be sure to bring your own gear since none is available on the island. For information, contact Molokai Ranch (phone: 552-2767).

Snorkeling – The best diving is at the east end of the island. Halawa Bay is a fine site when swells aren't kicking things up, and a series of coves around the area of Morris Point are fine, too. *Molokai Fish & Dive Corp.* (in Kaunakakai; phone: 553-5926), the only place on Molokai to rent or buy snorkeling gear, recommends the area between mile markers 20 and 22 on the east side for snorkeling and scuba diving. Moomomi Beach on the Pali coastline of the north shore is said to offer good diving (but it's on a dirt road, which is forbidden to all but four-wheel-drive vehicles), as does the reef about a mile from shore opposite Kaunakakai. *Molokai Charters* (phone: 553-5852) offers full-day snorkeling trips off southwest Lanai that depart at 8:30 AM from Kaunakakai Wharf. The cost is $75, and advance reservations are advised. Also contact Joe Reich (phone: 558-8377). Past the *Kaluakoi* hotel is a series of beaches with easy access and good diving close to shore. Divers must bring their own equipment as no scuba gear is available on the island. For people staying in Maui, the *Maui Princess* (phone: 661-8397 in Maui) offers snorkeling as one of its Molokai tour itineraries.

Surfing – Halawa Bay has decent surfing when conditions are right. In the winter, Kepuhi Beach often has huge waves suitable only for experienced surfers, and the action can be watched from the *Kaluakoi* hotel; during the summer, the waves here are too flat. The entire south shore is inside the reef.

Swimming and Sunning – Swimming is a sometimes proposition from the lovely beaches of the west end, but the sunning is fine in this dry area — as long as the wind isn't blowing; better swimming can be found in the isolated lagoons and coves of the east end, but the sun is iffy there. The south shore of Molokai, along which Kaunakakai is located, consists of a shallow, silty, unappetizing lagoon. The *Kaluakoi* hotel is nestled next to Kepuhi Beach, which is extremely photogenic but swimmable only during calm periods in the summer and winter; otherwise, it can be treacherous. The same goes for 2-mile-long Papohaku Beach, said to be Hawaii's longest, which stretches just south of the *Kaluakoi* — it's spectacular, but risky. Both beaches lose much of their sand in the winter, exposing wicked-looking rock and coral formations. Perhaps the best all-around beaches on the island are scattered along the western end of the north shore. The trouble is that only unpaved roads lead to these beaches — Kawakiu and Moomomi (now protected as a nature preserve) are the finest — and the car rental outfits specifically prohibit driving their vehicles off *paved* roads. Possible solutions include ignoring this instruction and hoping for the best (not recommended), or hiring Alex Puaa (phone: 533-3369), who will get you there via a four-wheel-drive vehicle. Kawakiu Beach is reached from a turnoff on Route 46 marked with a small sign that announces "Beach Access," and the drive in is a few miles. Moomomi Beach is where paved Route 48 ends and a dirt road about 3 miles long begins. Tricky as many of the west end beaches are to find, those on the east side of the island require even more patience and more than a little intuition. There's a "secret" beach (without a name, apparently) that's known only to islanders — drive along Route 45 until you reach the landmark "neighborhood grocery store," which looks like a roadside fireworks stand, on your left; just past the store on the right, take the dirt road toward the sea, where there's a protected area that's fine for swimming. There are a few more "beaches" on the east end, but they're on a very shallow lagoon. The best deep place to swim here is Halawa Bay, when the wind and swells cooperate.

Tennis – The *Kaluakoi* hotel has four Laykold courts lighted for night play, a resident pro, and a pro shop. These courts, by far the best on the island, are at the south end of the hotel complex near the 8th green of the golf course and are free for guests (phone: 555-2555). *Ke Nani Kai,* next to the *Kaluakoi* hotel, has two courts available for guests (phone: 552-2761), as does the *Wavecrest* resort, a condominium complex on the east end (phone: 558-8101). The courts at *Wavecrest* are lighted at night. In addition, there are courts at Molokai High School and the Community Center in Kaunakakai.

AROUND THE ISLAND

Molokai is half rolling lowlands, half steep mountains and deep valleys, 38 miles long and between 7 and 10 miles wide; some amateur cartographers say it resembles a shoe or moccasin. There is a central, low-lying saddle; a craggy, wild east end topped by 4,970-foot Mt. Kamakou; and a high, grassy, rolling, tableland in the west. Three volcanoes conspired to build an island of sharp contrasts; erosion then set in, carving volcanic domes into breathtaking cliffs, deeply creased jungle valleys, and cloud-scudded heights. The fishponds, of which legend says there were 58 in ancient times, lie off the eastern and southern coasts — a few are still visible today. The Makanalua Peninsula, better known as site of the Kalaupapa leper colony and Father Damien's martyrdom, is a 4½-square-mile lava flow protruding from the center of the north shore like a huge, level tongue; it seems almost not part of Molokai at all, it is so isolated. The major village of Kaunakakai, a trading town without a traffic light, pokes its single significant street south toward the reef and at the hump of Lanai, rising 9 miles away across the Kalohi Channel.

Kaunakakai, Central Molokai, and the South Shore

Kaunakakai, Molokai's "capital," is best known for the song written about a supposed individual of some civic note, "The Cock-eyed Mayor of Kaunakakai." Yet Kaunakakai has no mayor; the seat of government is actually on Maui, since Molokai is part of Maui County. Still, Kaunakakai is an important place even though its population probably doesn't exceed 2,500. It was here that Kamehameha V chose to build a summer home (only the barely distinguishable foundations remain.) And it is here that everyone on the island comes to shop, eat, drink, and gossip — Ala Malama Street, though it is only 3 blocks long, is the commercial heart of Molokai.

The south shore of Molokai, although important in Hawaiian history for its collection of royal fishponds, has mostly drowsed in modern times. Apart from Kaunakakai and its underused pier that stretches a half mile offshore in search of deep water, there is little but the historical sights to interest a visitor. In fact, the entire western half of the south shore has only a rough dirt track, and permission must be obtained to use it. The eastern part of the south shore is nicely paved, however, and Route 45 rolls past points of historical interest and a picnic ground or two before proceeding into the verdant mysteries of the east end. Central Molokai, above and beyond Kaunakakai, contains the airport and homestead area of Hoolehua, agricultural and pasture lands, the town of Kualapuu, and Palaau State Park, the windswept outlook over Kalaupapa and the staging point for mule expeditions down the sheer cliffs.

Kapuaiwa Grove – Originally a grove of 1,000 coconut palms, said to have been planted for Kamehameha V, beside the lagoon just west of Kaunakakai and across the street from Molokai's famous Church Row (see below), in an area considered sacred. Although there are far fewer palms now, their effect is still striking. Next to the grove is a small park.

Church Row – Six churches and a mission school are lined up in an impressive display of the island's regard for religion just west of Kaunakakai and across Route 46 from the Kapuaiwa Grove. Most of the churches are tiny clapboard affairs and combine on Sunday mornings to produce Molokai's weekly "traffic jam."

Palaau State Park – This cool, whispery park, with trails, a picnic area, and campgrounds, is forested with cypress, koa, ironwood, and paperbark trees on a high bluff over the ocean pounding the northern shore. There's also Kauleonanahoa, the well-known Phallic Rock, which seems anatomically perfect enough and to which ancient Hawaiians attributed magical powers to combat barrenness. But the most famous feature here is the Kalaupapa Lookout, from which the leper colony and its buildings 2,000 feet below can be clearly seen and the totality of its isolation fully comprehended.

Hoolehua – This residential area of homesteads also holds the island's airport. But blink and you'll miss it. At *Purdy's Nuts* (phone: 567-6601 or 567-6495), a small macadamia nut farm, an enjoyable tour is offered, with a chance to meet the charming Harry Purdy and to taste and buy afterward. Open daily, 9 AM to 1 PM.

R. W. Meyer Sugar Mill – This excellent restoration of one of Molokai's original steam-run sugar mills (ca. 1878) also includes well-documented displays and memorabilia of Rudolph Wilhelm Meyer. The German immigrant settled on Molokai in the 1850s, and his numerous descendants (he reportedly had 110 children) are to be found all over Molokai. Open daily from 10 AM to noon. The $2.50 admission fee includes a tour. On Route 47, between Kualapuu and Palaau State Park (phone: 567-6436).

Kualapuu – Del Monte's former pineapple town was said to have a population of 550 prior to the company's pull-out. Kualapuu Reservoir, visible from the road, is claimed to be the largest manmade rubber-lined reservoir in the world, built to hold 1.4 million gallons to irrigate the pineapple fields.

Sandalwood Pit – More than 100 years ago, when sandalwood trees grew on Molokai, sailing vessels would come to the island to load the precious cargo. This pit was dug to simulate the size of a ship's hold so the amount of wood could be measured for a single load. The dirt road that leads here forks off from Route 46 and heads bumpily inland several miles west of Kaunakakai before the turnoff to Route 47; be prepared for a tough jeep ride.

Waikolu Lookout – As long as you've made it to the Sandalwood Pit, you might as well continue along the same rutted track a couple of miles more, where you'll be rewarded with one of Molokai's most inspiring views. The Waikolu Lookout reveals wooded valleys and a 3,000-foot-deep gorge. It's only about 12 miles from the paved road, but it'll seem much more. Beyond Waikolu is a 3,000-acre nature preserve, with several partially obscured trails.

Kamehameha V's Summer House – Just west of the pier outside Kaunakakai is the rubble and foundation of the monarch's getaway during his reign from 1863 to 1872. There's so little left to see that it's just about impossible to find.

The Pier – The solid concrete structure once used for loading pineapples is one of the island's proudest achievements, yet it seems destined to fall into disuse. It's possible to drive one-half mile out on it.

Kakahaia Park – A pleasant, well-kept beach strip park on the lagoon a few miles east of Kaunakakai and past the *Molokai* hotel. There are picnic tables, grass, and a fine view of Lanai, but not a swimmable beach.

One Alii Park – A bigger park with more facilities and closer to Kaunakakai than Kakahaia. This is one of very few places on Molokai where it's possible to camp. Permits are available in Kaunakakai from the County Parks Office (phone: 553-5141).

SHOPPING: Resort clothing and tourist trinkets are not common items on Molokai — you're more likely to find farm implements and basic household products. This is particularly true in the Kaunakakai area, where most of the residents come to shop. There are, however, a few interesting exceptions. Molokai kiawe tree honey is an excellent local product.

Imports Gift Shop – For the dedicated browser, a surprising array of souvenirs, jewelry, and ladies clothing will be found here. Puali St., off Ala Malama (phone: 553-5734).

Lourdes – Casual clothing for men, women, and children. Ala Malama St. Closed Sunday afternoons (phone: 553-9998).

Molokai Fish and Dive – This is the place to head for Molokai's largest selection of T-shirts and other Molokai-emblazoned souvenirs. Open daily. Ala Malama St. (phone: 553-5926).

Molokai Gift Shop – A well-stocked hotel shop that has a good selection of Hawaiian print muumuus, aloha shirts, and swimsuits. Also on hand is quite a bit of unusual Hawaiiana. *Molokai* hotel (phone: 553-5801).

Molokai Island Creations – Kaunakakai's most contemporary shop has an interesting selection of women's and children's wear, toys, lingerie, books, hats, jewelry, and more. Ala Malama St. (phone: 553-5926).

Shop 2 – Clothing, along with Chinese herbs and other fun-to-browse items, are sold at this small boutique. On Ing Rd. off Ala Malama at *Pascual Store* (phone: 553-5888).

NIGHTLIFE: Nightlife in and around Kaunakakai is so limited, it's easy to find. The *Molokai* hotel's *Holo Holo Kai* (phone: 553-5347) features simple guitar-and-voice entertainment next to the bar and restaurant on Thursdays, Fridays, and Saturdays. But the best bet is at the *Pau Hana Inn* (phone: 553-5342), whose bar is *the* place locally, especially on Friday and Saturday nights. There's usually a dance band, and things often get very Hawaiian and sometimes very enthusiastic. Those in search of local color will find it here.

CHECKING IN: Room rates on Molokai are among the lowest in the islands. Expensive accommodations run \$95 or more for a double room; moderate hotels cost \$45 to \$90, and inexpensive prices range from \$35 to \$45. All telephone numbers are in the 808 area code unless otherwise indicated.

Molokai – The first classy hostelry on the island, opened in 1966. A real Polynesian flavor clings to this place, from the island-style, 2-story wooden buildings to the open bar and restaurant area. The grounds are compact but filled with flowers, coconut palms, and lots of tranquillity, except when a boisterous crowd is at the bar. All rooms (insects can be a problem) have a lanai swing and a refrigerator. There's a small pool that faces right on the unswimmable lagoon. And there's very low-key dinner music most nights. The *Holo Holo Kai* restaurant in the hotel has a good, standard menu (see *Eating Out*). PO Box 546, Kaunakakai, HI 96748 (phone: 553-5347; 800-367-8047). Expensive to moderate.

Pau Hana Inn – Molokai's oldest hotel is a relaxed, very basic place that has a real charm for those who appreciate the native way of doing (or not doing) things. It's so laid back that its own brochure admits the hotel is "content to do business in an aimless, languid, southseas sort of way." And that goes double. There's an assortment of 39 units with ages and prices that bounce all over the place and amenities reflected in the price. It's on the beach, but the beach is awful so most people opt for congregating around the nice, medium-size pool instead. The best buy is the 2-room oceanfront cottage for $90. Kitchenettes are also available. The hotel is within easy walking distance of Kaunakakai and, as it advertises, it does "cater to *kamaainas,*" as can easily be discerned at the bar and in the restaurant (where prime ribs are the best bet). This hotel is truly "action central," particularly on Friday and Saturday evenings. PO Box 860, Kaunakakai, HI 96748 (phone: 553-5342; 800-531-4004). Expensive to moderate.

Molokai Shores – Here is a very pleasant condominium with 101 one- and two-bedroom units, all with full kitchens, in three 3-story buildings. It's less than 2 miles east of Kaunakakai, and boasts lovely grounds facing an unfortunately unswimmable lagoon. There's a pool, picnic tables, and barbecues, a 9-hole putting green, lots of lawn, laundry facilities, and even a hair salon. But there's no bar, no restaurant, and no grocery store. Maid service is available for an extra charge. A Molokai condo caution is to bring anything fancy with you since Kaunakakai's markets are seldom super nor very well stocked with luxury items. PO Box 1037, Kaunakakai, HI 96748 (phone: 553-5954; 800-367-7042). Moderate.

EATING OUT: The food served on Molokai is unexceptional despite menus that aspire to more discriminating tastes. Expect to pay about $20 to $30 for two people in establishments listed as moderate, less than $20 in an inexpensive place. These prices do not include wine, drinks, or tip. All telephone numbers are in the 808 area code unless otherwise indicated.

Holo Holo Kai – Simple but generally good food is served in this lagoon-front restaurant. Breakfast (try French toast made with Molokai bread), lunch (finished at 1:30 PM), and dinner, served from 5 to 10 PM (a good place for alfresco sunset dining), are offered daily. Catch of the day and teriyaki chicken are the best bets. There's a bar and entertainment Thursdays, Fridays, and Saturdays. Open daily. Dinner reservations advised. *Molokai Hotel* (phone: 553-5347). Moderate.

Pau Hana Inn – Meals are served inside near the fireplace or outside under the huge banyan tree, depending on the season and weather. Breakfast, lunch, and dinner, from 5 to 9:30 PM, are on a par with Molokai's best. The Portuguese bean soup is fine, though, as are the prime ribs, sautéed shrimp, and catch of the day. The bar is active, especially on Friday and Saturday nights. Open daily. Reservations advised. At the *Pau Hana Inn* (phone: 553-5342). Moderate.

Hop Inn – The island's Chinese restaurant looks a bit shabby from Ala Malama Street, but the food is good. Open daily to dish out lunch and dinner, which runs from 5 to 9 PM. No reservations. Kaunakakai (phone: 553-5465). Inexpensive.

Kanemitsu Bakery – This is the source of the wonderful Molokai cheese and onion bread. There are a few tables in back, and breakfast, lunch, and dinner are served. Closed Tuesdays. Reservations unnecessary. Kaunakakai (phone: 553-5855). Inexpensive.

Outpost Natural Food – Off Ala Malama Street, good sandwiches and a range of health-related dishes are the offerings here. There's a juice bar, and picnic tables are outside. Open Mondays through Fridays from 10 AM to 2 PM for lunch. Reservations unnecessary. Just off Ala Malama, next to the Molokai Library. (phone: 553-3377). Inexpensive.

West Molokai

It really is, as they say, "out island" here. This is the turf of the *paniolo,* the Hawaiian cowboy — the word is said to be a corrupted form of *Español,* referring to the Mexicans who were the first cowboys to come to Molokai early in this century. Most of the western portion of Molokai is owned or leased by the Molokai Ranch Ltd. It is largely grazing land or empty spaces awaiting the future, perhaps tourism and residential development. The arid, high tableland that is the dominant feature of West Molokai once was heavily planted in pineapple, but that ended in 1975, when Dole gave up its lease. Molokai Ranch has since planted these fields in hay, which it sells as cattle feed in Hawaii and Japan. There is fine bird hunting upland here, and fringes of attractive beaches, most of which cannot be reached without a four-wheel-drive vehicle (hard to find) and Molokai Ranch permission (difficult to get). On the 6,700 acres of Kaluakoi are the *Molokai Kaluakoi* hotel and a golf course. There are several small condominiums on the property, now owned by Castle Resorts. Kaluakoi and its regulated development, centered around the slow phasing in of tourism and secondary residences, is thought by many to contain the germ of economic salvation for Molokai as the island's agricultural base dwindles; others see it as the initial step in the destruction of the Hawaiian way of life treasured by the people.

Molokai Ranch Wildlife Park – This 800-acre wildlife preserve with more than 300 animals native to India and Africa was begun in 1977 by Molokai Ranch Ltd. to stock and breed exotic and endangered species for the world's zoos and parks. But the business venture turned into something more when guests at the nearby *Kaluakoi* hotel showed an interest in visiting the park. Now there is a very low-key 1½-hour van tour that bumps and lurches into the park and affords glimpses, often close ones, of axis deer, sable antelope, Indian black buck, Barbary sheep, oryx, ibex, and zebra — all grass eaters, no predators, who thrive in the dry brush and hills that duplicate so well their native habitat. The office for the tour is at the tour desk of the *Kaluakoi;* the cost is $30 plus tax for adults, $20 for children up to age 12. Refreshments are served at the giraffe compound on this 1½-hour tour. Departures at 8 and 10 AM and at 1 and 3 PM daily (weather permitting). *Kaluakoi Hotel,* PO Box 8, Maunaloa, HI 96770 (phone: 552-2767).

Maunaloa – After emerging in the 1920s as the company town for Dole, of pineapple fame, it remained one of the most important towns on Molokai for half a century. Then Dole abandoned its pineapple fields and left Maunaloa in 1975. For several years, the town — left still and nearly empty on a high plateau about a mile from the ocean, yet near the modern development of Kaluakoi — seemed to be dying. But lately it has seen a modest revival thanks to the combined efforts of new arrivals and the few old-time residents. A forlorn post office, a ramshackle general store called the *Friendly Market,* and rows of plantation housing are reminders of the past. This is the end of the paved road — only fields of grass that once were covered in pineapple plants lie beyond.

SHOPPING: There are three shops at the *Kaluakoi* hotel: *Liberty House* (a branch of the Hawaiian store chain), *Molokai Gems* (a jewelry boutique), and *Kepuhi Sundries* (reading matter, liquor, snack foods, and so on). In all of West Molokai, there are only three other shops, all in Maunaloa — *Dolly Hale,* for Hawaiian dolls (no phone); *Plantation Gallery,* with deer-horn scrimshaw, silver jewelry, woodcarvings, and Balinese imports, as well as Molokai's best selection of Hawaiian books and cards (phone: 552-2364); and the *Big Wind Kite Factory,* whose motto is "Come fly a kite" (phone: 552-2364).

NIGHTLIFE: There is no nightlife outside the *Kaluakoi.* The hotel's *Ohia Lounge* (phone: 552-2555) features an active bar and a Hawaiian group that plays during the cocktail and dinner hours. On Saturday nights, the hotel features a buffet and *Moana's Polynesian Revue,* a hometown-style event that features youngsters in vibrant costumes in the *Paniolo Broiler* for $25. Dinner seating is at 7 PM; cocktail show seating (one drink minimum) is at 8 PM (phone: 552-2555).

CHECKING IN: Room rates in West Molokai are more moderate than at most destination resorts. For a room at the properties listed below, above $125 is considered expensive, from $80 to $120 is considered moderate. All telephone numbers are in the 808 area code unless otherwise indicated.

Ke Nani Kai – This resort condominium has 170 1- and 2-bedroom units with full kitchens and lanais offering views across the golf course and beach. There's a pool, Jacuzzi, and 2 tennis courts; a short walk leads to the beach, restaurants, and shops at the *Kaluakoi.* PO Box 126, Maunaloa, HI 96770 (phone: 552-2761; 800-888-2791). Expensive.

Villas at Kaluakoi – The Castle Group manages approximately 100 of *Kaluakoi*'s units, and most of its accommodations are studio and 1-bedroom resort condominium apartments, with a small number of traditional hotel rooms. Guests check in at an apartment converted to front office use, and Castle Group guests have full access to the Colony-operated restaurant and services, as well as an adjacent golf course and tennis courts (phone: 552-2721; 800-525-1470: The Castle Group, 552-2721; 800-525-1470). Expensive.

Colony's Kaluakoi – The 150 units at Kaluakoi operated by Colony Resorts make up Molokai's only resort-style hotel. Beautifully set on photogenic Kepuhi Beach (not, unfortunately, usually suitable for swimming) with a first-rate 18-hole golf course curling around it; there are 2 restaurants and a lounge. There's also a small swimming pool, 4 lighted tennis courts, and several shops, including a branch of *Liberty House.* The 292 rooms include hotel and condo accommodations in 32 1- and 2-story villas scattered over broad areas of lawn, all nicely decorated in South Seas motifs, and all with TV sets (not common on Molokai). Here you will be isolated (a rental car is a necessity, unless you want to make this a retreat), but in comfortable surroundings. For golf enthusiasts, there's the *Colony Club* golf package ($189 per person, double occupancy) that includes a room, all meals, wine, tennis, and one round of golf per day. PO Box 200, Maunaloa, HI 96770 (phone: Colony Resorts, 552-2555; 800-777-1700). Expensive to moderate.

Paniolo Hale – The property is adjacent to the *Kaluakoi* hotel and separated from the beach only by a fairway of the golf course. There are 77 studio, 1-, and 2-bedroom units (although not all are in the rental pool) in a well-designed community of 1- and 2-story structures; all have full kitchens (there's a small market 6 miles away in Maunaloa), and some have indoor hot tubs (extra charge for heating). There is a pool, a paddle tennis court, outdoor gas barbecues, and weekly maid service. No restaurant or bar (use the *Kaluakoi*'s), and you'll feel lost without a car (phone: 552-2731; 800-367-2984). Expensive to moderate.

EATING OUT: There isn't much to choose from in the way of restaurants on this side of Molokai. In the expensive range, expect to pay about $20 to $25 per person; $15 to $20 at a place listed as moderate; less than that at an inexpensive place — not including wine, drinks, or tip. All telephone numbers are in the 808 area code unless otherwise indicated.

Ohia Lodge – The *Kaluakoi*'s main restaurant, an attractive, high-ceilinged, lodge-like affair above the crashing surf, serves breakfast, lunch, and dinner; most call it the best restaurant on the island, with a decent wine list, a limited but good dinner menu. Open daily. Dinner reservations necessary. *Kaluakoi* hotel (phone: 552-2555). Expensive to moderate.

Jojo's Café – Decent lunches and West Molokai's least expensive dinners, with 1950s mood and prices. Open daily for lunch and dinner until 7:45 PM. Reservations unnecessary. Maunaloa (phone: 552-2803). Inexpensive.

Kualapuu Cookhouse – A bright and airy place that serves great French toast for breakfast, and hamburgers, sandwiches, and plate lunches until 5 PM. Closed Sundays. Reservations unnecessary. In the plantation town of Kualapuu. (phone: 567-6185). Inexpensive.

Snack Shop – Near poolside at the *Kaluakoi.* Fast foods (including good burgers) from 11 AM to 5 PM daily and 6 to 8 PM on weekends. Reservations unnecessary. *Kaluakoi* hotel (phone: 552-2555). Inexpensive.

Kalaupapa and the Makanalua Peninsula

One of the most awe-inspiring sights in all Hawaii is also its most deeply moving spiritual experience. Makanalua is the isolated volcanic tongue of slightly more than 12 square miles spewed out eons ago and separated from the rest of the world by the vigorous sea on three sides and by sheer cliffs said to be the highest in the world on the fourth. This natural prison became an actual one on January 6, 1866, when the first lepers were dumped into the sea and left to drown or begin a harsh existence on the barren peninsula. Leprosy — called *mai-Pake,* the "Chinese disease" — had come to Hawaii sometime in the early 19th century, and the government, fearing widespread contagion, responded by hunting down and exiling the lepers to the most inaccessible place they could find. The Makanalua Peninsula was it, and the lepers who survived established a crude settlement at Kalawao. Father Damien Joseph de Veuster, a Belgian priest who served in Hawaii, heard of the ugly, lawless colony of condemned people and came here permanently in 1873 to tend the lepers and bring organization and justice. Often called the Martyr of Molokai, Father Damien died of the disease in 1889 at age 49 and one day may be officially canonized a saint: Locally he is already considered one.

The settlement moved to Kalaupapa (once a native fishing village) from Kalawao in 1888, when water was piped in to this more pleasant west side of the peninsula. Kalaupapa offers a score of weathered structures, a modern hospital, a kind of general store, and several historic churches and monuments. The main attraction at Kawalao, aside from the landscape, is Father Damien's St. Philomena Church, completed in the late 1870s. Kalawao Park, on a beautiful but rugged portion of the peninsula's east coast, is the site of the original colony. The victims of Hansen's disease (the proper term for leprosy) who live on the peninsula today number fewer than 100 (there were 1,200 early in this century), and their condition has been arrested through the use of sulfone drugs, introduced in the 1940s. But they chose to remain at

Kalaupapa, which was declared a National Historic Park (phone: 567-6102), although it remains under state control.

There are several ways to reach Kalaupapa. *Aloha IslandAir* (phone: 567-6115; 800-255-7198 in Hawaii; 800-828-0806 elsewhere in the continental US) and *Air Molokai* (phone: 553-3636; 524-0090 on Oahu) fly into Kalaupapa's tiny airstrip from Hoolehua Airport topside on Molokai and to Kalaupapa from Oahu and the other Neighbor Islands. It's also possible to hike in, down the steep 3-mile trail from the top of the 2,000-foot cliff at Palaau State Park, but hikers must be experienced and ready for a strenuous climb; before heading down the trail they must have a sponsor who will obtain the required permit from the state's Department of Communicable Diseases and will arrange for a tour guide to meet them at the base of the cliffs. *Damien Tours* (PO Box 1, Kalaupapa, HI 96748; phone: 567-6171 or 567-6675) will arrange a land tour (including a mule ride) for visitors arriving by air or on foot. Usually led by the company's owner and resident curmudgeon, Richard Marks (the third generation of his family to be settled at Kalaupapa), the tours are interesting, informative, and enjoyable. Remember to bring your own lunch.

Most visitors reach Kalaupapa as part of a mule train. From a bluff 2,000 feet above the peninsula, the mule train winds down a 3⅛-mile trail studded with 26 hairpin switchbacks. The view is thrilling and the adventure is, well, stimulating. But be comforted that no mule has yet missed a step. At the bottom, each excursion is met by a tour conductor who is also a Kalaupapa resident for a close look at the settlement. A box lunch is served at Kalawao Park, the site of the original colony. The entire trip takes about 7 hours. Reservations are required, as permits must be obtained for you; the minimum age is 16, the maximum weight, 225. Trips begin about 9 AM at the stables near the Kalaupapa Lookout and return around 3:30 PM. The price is $115 per person. Contact *Molokai Mule Rides* (phone: 567-6088; 800-843-5978 in the continental US).

Makanalua Peninsula and Kalaupapa are not the usual tourist attractions. There are no hotels, shops, or restaurants. Though there is no chance of being exposed to or contracting Hansen's disease, you're not permitted to leave the tour and wander around on your own. No children under the age of 16 are allowed, and none will be seen living here. The experience is a somber yet uplifting one.

East Molokai to the Halawa Valley

It is only about 30 miles from Kaunakakai to the end of Route 45 at the luxuriant Halawa Valley, but it is the distance of time. Every mile farther east takes you a step back into Hawaiian history as the landscape changes gradually from dry and hilly to lush and mountainous. This east end once was thickly populated, at least for Molokai, and was a center of island life. Now things are different. There are few residents, no gasoline, no restaurants, no bars, only a single lonely condo complex. This is the part of Molokai being protected, held back from development and encroachment by modern ways. There is much sacred here to many Hawaiians, much that is *kapu* — locked and off-limits. It is the mysterious and fascinating part of Molokai.

Places of historical interest are numerous in this east end of Molokai, although many are nearly impossible to find without local help and a few are behind locked gates or otherwise on private land. Heritage is sometimes jealously guarded out here.

Fishponds – These traps once supplied fish for royal tables. In the old days it is said there were 58, some perhaps one-half mile long, ringing the east and southeast shoreline. They were built of lava rock and worked by allowing in small fish that, when fattened, would be too large to escape through the chinks in the walls. Historians have speculated that fishponds existed on Molokai as early as AD 1000, but positive records indicate them in the 15th century. Some ponds have been restored and are in use today — they can easily be seen as you drive along Route 45. Two, Keawanui and Ualapue, are part of a National Historic Landmark.

Halawa Valley – The road ends at the entrance to this beautiful, verdant valley, once the home of many of the island's people. A tidal wave (*tsunami*) forced Halawa's evacuation in 1946, and most of the residents never returned; it echoes with ghosts today. Yet it remains a lovely, tranquil, very tropical place popular with hikers and nature lovers. It's 4½ miles long, and a 2-hour hike that isn't too difficult (there are several streams to ford) leads to Moaula and Hipuapua falls, which cascade 250 feet down into the head of the valley. The freshwater pool at Moaula Falls is cool but safe for swimming, according to legend, if a ti leaf floats.

Kalanikaula Grove (also spelled Lanikaula) – This sacred grove of kukui trees is said to have been planted for a very powerful *kahuna* (priest and magic man) around his grave. Hawaiians say the aura is potent. The grove is on private land just before reaching the Halawa Valley.

Mapulehu Mango Grove – The trees are venerably old in what may be Hawaii's largest mango grove. For an unusual visit to the grove in a horse-drawn wagon, take the *Molokai Wagon Ride* (phone: 558-8380).

Iliiliopae Heiau – One of the largest religious shrines of ancient Hawaii is more than 100 yards long and nearly 40 yards wide. Only the stone platform and terraces may be seen, but the scale is impressive. It's near Pukoo on private land, yet it's possible to pay a visit. *Molokai Wagon Tours* (phone: 558-8380) includes the *heiau* as part of its 3-hour itinerary ($33).

Kawela – This "city of refuge," similar to the more famous one on the Big Island of Hawaii, was where Hawaiians accused of crimes fled. Little remains today. It's just before Kamalo.

Pakuhiwa Battlefield – The area west of Kamalo is where Kamehameha the Great landed with a force of war canoes said to have stretched for 4 miles. It is here the warrior-conqueror vanquished Molokai. Artifacts of the battle are still found today.

Our Lady of Sorrows Church – Mass is celebrated in this church, which was founded by Father Damien before he moved to Kalaupapa and is now brightly restored. A life-size statue of the Martyr of Molokai is in a screened pavilion next to the church, which is on the inland side of the road at Kaluaaha.

St. Joseph's Catholic Church – Another of Father Damien's churches, a tiny, white clapboard structure, is right next to the road on the lagoon side at mile marker 10 near Kamalo.

Smith and Bronte Landing – Ernest Smith and Emory Bronte made a somewhat less than dignified emergency landing just past the lagoon in a stand of kiawe trees at Kamalo after the first civilian transpacific flight in 1927. A roadside marker notes their ignominious contribution to history.

Moanui Sugar Mill – The ruins of a sugar mill operated between 1870 and 1900 by a Norwegian lie inland a short distance from Halawa. The crumpled stack and rubble can be seen from the road.

Wailau Trail – A rough hiking trail that crosses the entire rugged east end of Molokai from south to north leads to the idyllic Wailau Valley, once heavily populated. Permission must be obtained for crossing private property, and grumpy islanders may not be overly pleased by an intrusion — best to get good advice on this trek from the state-run Department of Land and Natural Resources (phone: 553-5019).

SHOPPING: Nary a single boutique out here.

NIGHTLIFE: You guessed it.

CHECKING IN: The only option is the *Wavecrest* resort, with 1- and 2-bedroom apartments which rent from $61 to $96. The telephone number is in the 808 area code.

Wavecrest – A 125-unit condominium complex, at mile marker 13 between Kamalo and Pukoo, with 35 1- and 2-bedroom suites, all of which have kitchens and an ocean view, but no maid service. The 5½-acre resort is on the lagoon, but the water is not suitable for swimming or diving. There is a pool, lighted tennis courts, a putting green, and a reasonably well-stocked general store, but no restaurant, though a snack bar has opened at the *Neighborhood Store,* several miles away in Pukoo. Things are tranquil indeed at *Wavecrest,* and also neat and orderly; the climate here is considerably more damp than in the central and western parts of the island. Star Rte. 155, Kaunakakai, HI 96748 (phone: 558-8101; 800-367-2980).

EATING OUT: The only eatery worth the name on the entire east end of Molokai is the snack bar listed below. The nearest restaurant is in the *Molokai* hotel, west of Kamalo. The telephone number is in the 808 area code.

Neighborhood Store – The snack counter here provides take-out foods for a Halawa Valley picnic, or a place to stop for lunch en route. Stock up. It's the last store in East Molokai. Open daily from 7 AM to 6 PM (phone: 558-8933).

LANAI

Despite its location at the heart of the archipelago, Lanai is the least known of the major Hawaiian islands, with a history of being shunned that stretches back into the mists of Polynesian colonization. The old legends identify Lanai as haunted by evil spirits and consequently hostile to men until Kaululaau, the precocious son of a West Maui king, was exiled to Lanai — just 8 miles across the Auau Channel — for his harmful hijinks, such as pulling up breadfruit trees. Kaululaau proceeded either to hunt down and kill or to drive off the demons, and when he'd made Lanai safe (Lanai means Day of Conquest), he lit a signal fire to inform a watching Maui that Lanai was ready for habitation. The brat became a hero and Hawaiians moved to Lanai.

Apparently, however, not too many came to the vaguely pear-shaped island, 13 miles across at its widest and 18 miles long. Geography did not favor Lanai. The wet mountains of the east side contained precipitous gulches and other largely uninhabitable areas, while the rest of the island was dry, mostly devoid of vegetation and unsuitable for any agriculture. Anthropologists have estimated that the inhabitants of old Lanai never exceeded 2,500 (though some figures estimate as many as 4,000), and populated periods were interspersed with long intervals during which the island was nearly deserted. When Captain James Cook's expedition sailed past the island in the last part of the 18th century (after Cook himself had been killed on the island of Hawaii), it was described in logs as a brown, barren, and inhospitable place. Yet it was on Lanai at Kaunolu Bay that King Kamehameha I (Kamehameha the Great) chose to make his summer home in the early 19th century.

History moved sluggishly, in fits and starts, on Lanai. Battles were fought when Kamehameha and his forces swept through during his conquest and unification of Hawaii; important petroglyphs were left; some old *heiaus* (ancient shrines and temples) were built. A faint ripple was felt in 1854, when a group of Mormons arrived to colonize Lanai and began farming the fertile but arid Palawai Basin — a large flatland that is all that's left of the ancient volcano Palawai, which formed Lanai. But the endeavor failed and the Mormons left a decade later.

It wasn't until 1921, when Jim Dole purchased the entire island (with the exception of a few small parcels granted by Hawaiian royalty to local families) for $1.1 million to raise pineapples, that Lanai gained a new identity. There had been short-lived attempts to grow sugarcane and raise cattle, but both had been unsuccessful. Pineapples were perfect for the island's climate, and grew furiously once water was piped in from the mountains and pumped up from underground. The Palawai Basin was quickly planted in pineapple fields of military precision, turning Lanai into one of the largest pineapple plantations in the world.

Consequently, Lanai quickly became known as the Pineapple Island. Yet

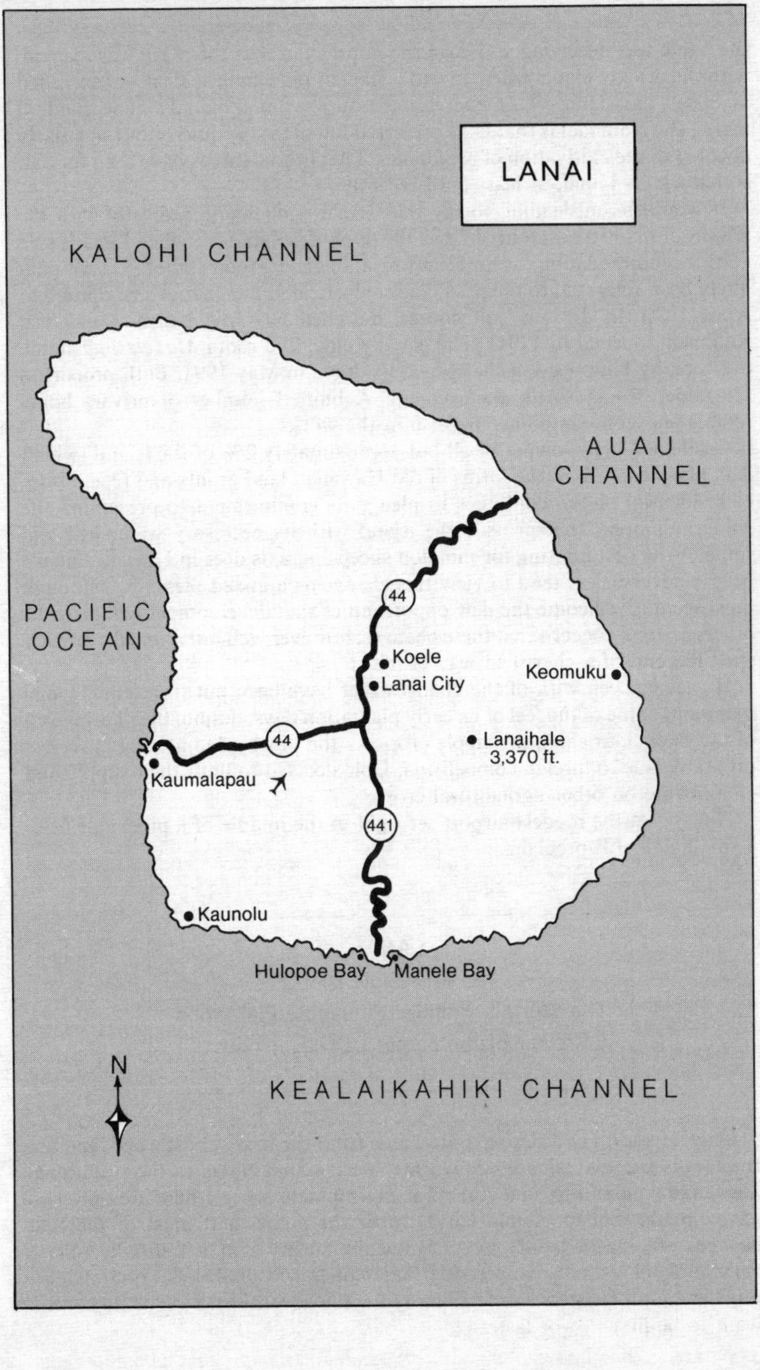
LANAI
KALOHI CHANNEL
AUAU CHANNEL
PACIFIC OCEAN
44
Koele
Lanai City
Keomuku
44
Lanaihale 3,370 ft.
Kaumalapau
441
Kaunolu
Hulopoe Bay
Manele Bay
N
KEALAIKAHIKI CHANNEL

the name was deceiving and gave the impression that the place was overrun with the prickly plants when, in truth, Lanai's pineapple fields never exceeded 16,000 of the island's 90,000 acres, and now are found on only a few hundred acres. The plain fact is that Dole preferred Lanai to stay quietly and singularly devoted to the cultivation of pineapples. That is how things have been for half a century on Lanai, at least until recently.

It would be misleading to say that Lanai is changing radically with the advent of mainstream tourism, but the days of isolation — when Lanai's sole guest accommodations were found in a single 10-room hotel — have definitely been relegated to the past. The sophisticated *Lodge at Koele* opened in April 1990 (its 18-hole golf course, designed by Greg Norman and Ted Robinson, opened in 1991). The equally chic, 250-room *Manele Bay* hotel, overlooking Hulopoe Beach, opened its doors in May 1991. Both properties are under Rockresort's management. A limited number of private home rentals and condominiums are also in the works.

Castle & Cooke, owner of all but approximately 2% of the island (which is in private hands in the forms of old Hawaiian land grants and recent sales of residential plots), continues to pledge its commitment to preserving the wilderness areas that provide the island with its necessary watershed and some of the best hunting for mouflon sheep and axis deer in Hawaii. Lanai's people nevertheless tend to view this change as a mixed blessing: Although most seem to welcome the new opportunities that development will provide, others express concern that these changes, however well intentioned, can only spell the end of a cherished way of life.

However, even with of the changes that have been put in motion, Lanai maintains some of the feel of its early plantation days, despite the phasing-out of the once-flourishing pineapple crop. As the pineapple industry grew less profitable due to foreign competition, Dole decided to limit their supply and concentrate on other agricultural crops.

And yet at the modest airport set right in the middle of a pineapple field, a small sign still proclaims:

LANAI
The Pineapple Island
The World's Premier Pineapple Plantation
Grower of the Famous DOLE Products

Only a handful of miles separate Lanai from the tourist bustle of Maui, but the fact is the two islands are worlds apart. Lanai clings to the traditional Hawaiian style of life, in a still-rural environment where there are only two paved roads (outside Lanai City) worth the name, and most of the best beaches are reached only after significant buffeting in a four-wheel-drive vehicle. Rockresort's two recently built hotels will doubtless bring change, but Lanai still remains a true getaway for the adventurous — for those who want to be first . . . or last.

SOURCES AND RESOURCES

TOURIST INFORMATION: The Hawaii Visitors Bureau has no office on Lanai, but information can be obtained from the main office (2270 Kalakaua Ave., Room 801, Honolulu, HI 96815; phone: 923-1811). On Lanai, talk to Glen Oshiro of *Oshiro's* (the gas station, car and jeep rental agency, and taxi service); the folks at *Lanai City Service* (another gas station and car rental agency); or a ranger with the *Koele Company,* the Castle & Cooke division that manages Lanai's wildlands. The best book for background and insights is *Survey of the Island of Lanai,* by Kenneth Emory; if you can't find it here, try the *Bishop Museum* in Honolulu. Another good book to consult is Ruth Tabrah's *Lanai. Oshiro's* and *Lanai City Service* have maps, which you'll need, and the best map of all is found in the gift shops at the *Lodge at Koele* and the *Manele Bay.*

TELEPHONE: The area code for Hawaii is 808.

GETTING AROUND: *Hawaiian Air, Aloha Air, Aloha IslandAir,* and *Air Molokai* offer scheduled flights to Lanai from Honolulu, Maui, Molokai, and the Big Island. Work is currently under way to enlarge Lanai Airport with the runway extended to accommodate jet planes.

Lanai has absolutely no public transportation. There's a taxi shuttle to and from the airport run by *Oshiro's* (phone: 565-6952) for $7, which brings you into the heart of town; and *Lanai City Service* (phone: 565-7227). Lanai's two newest hotels provide their own shuttle between the hotels and the airport.

Car and Jeep Rental – Glen Oshiro has a small fleet of Pontiac sedans ($49–$55 daily plus gas), four-wheel-drive vehicles ($99 daily plus gas), and assorted other vehicles for hire (*Oshiro's;* phone: 565-6952). Credit card required. Reserve ahead if you want a specific vehicle. *Lanai City Service* (phone: 565-7227), now a *Dollar Rent A Car* affiliate, also rents compacts for $49–$59 per day plus gas, and four-wheel-drive vehicles for $100 per day plus gas. Lanai only has 20 miles of paved roads, so if you want to do more than drive to the beach you'll need a jeep ($100) or a van ($130). Rentals are available via the concierge desks at *Manele Bay* and the *Lodge.*

SIGHTSEEING TOURS: Again, very little is offered in the way of prepared tours. *Lanai City Service* (phone: 565-7227) offers a daily, hour-long van tour that includes Lanai City; however, individuals would do just as well to rent a car and just follow the map. The *Lodge at Koele* and the *Manele Bay* hotel also offer tour itineraries, the best of which are led by Sol Kahoohalahala (at the *Lodge*), a fifth-generation Lanaian.

Boat – Several Maui-based operators, including *Trilogy* (phone: 661-4743) and *Ocean Activities Center* (phone: 879-4485) offer day sails to Lanai. *Trilogy* stops at Manele Bay, with time for snorkeling and sunbathing; also included is a 1-hour land excursion ($139). *Ocean Activities Center* offers a sailing trip from 8 AM to 1 PM for $60, which includes an open bar and lunch. Lahaina's *Seabern Yachts* will customize skippered day tours or overnighters to Lanai (PO Box 1022, Lahaina, HI 96761; phone: 661-8110). *Ocean Riders* (PO Box 367, Lahaina, HI 96767; phone: 661-3586) offers a full-day power boat excursion departing Lahaina that circles Lanai. While it's fun and informative, the length of the trip, plus seas that are often choppy for portions of the tour, make it a good choice for only those with sea legs and stamina.

SPORTS: Lanai offers good swimming, beachcombing, scuba, and snorkeling; fair fishing; superb hunting; and some golf and tennis.

Boating – *C & Sea Ocean Sports* (phone: 565-7227), operated by *Trilogy Excursions,* offers sightseeing, snorkeling, and scuba excursions, as well as some equipment rentals. Their main headquarters is located at *Lanai City Service,* with an additional desk in the *Manele Bay* hotel.

Fishing – No charter fishing boats are available for hire on Lanai. Surf and shore fishing are usually only fair and depend on tides and time of year. Skillful fishermen may be successful with reef fish, divers with lobsters at the north end of the island.

Golf – With the arrival of the two Rockresorts hotels on Lanai have come two 18-hole championship courses. Adjacent to the *Lodge at Koele* lies the 6,127-yard, par 72 course called *The Experience* (phone: 565-7300). Designed by Greg Norman and Ted Robinson, the course opened in 1991, complete with downhill holes, forest hazards, and panoramic views of Lanaihale and nearby mountains. Construction on a second course, dubbed the *Challenge of Manele,* has been delayed due to environmental considerations, and will not be ready for play until next year. Created by Jack Nicklaus, this course (phone: 565-7700; 800-223-7637) will have several holes overlooking the ocean, with several over-the-water carries promised. Full pro shop services and club rentals are available at both courses. Visitors also can play at the upgraded 9 holes of the island's original *Cavendish* course, next to the *Lodge at Koele.* In addition, Castle & Cooke plans to convert 160 acres around Manele-Hulopoe Bay into a new golf course, also to be designed by Jack Nicklaus.

Hiking – Camping is allowed only at Hulopoe. Prepayment is required via the *Koele Company.* Hiking is permitted in certain areas, but discouraged in others — remember, this is practically all private land. The Munro Trail loop of 7 to 8 miles, up and over the ridge of mountains behind Lanai City, is one of the most beautiful hikes in Hawaii. From various viewpoints on clear days almost all of the Hawaiian islands are visible, and the trail leads through lush foliage and past the haunts of axis deer and numerous birds. Just be sure you have a well-marked map — *Oshiro's* has a good one. It's also a good idea to check with hunting sources (see below) to make sure you won't be hiking in a hunting area.

Horseback Riding – The equestrian center (phone: 565-7300) affiliated with the *Lodge at Koele* offers a number of topnotch riding options, including a *paniolo* (cowboy) trail ride through Pu'uale'ole'a. There's a 1-hour trail ride ($25) through the plantation fields to the Palawai Basin that departs at 1:30 PM Tuesdays through Fridays, and on Saturdays at 8:30 and 10:30 AM. A 2-hour ride ($50), limited to eight riders, is conducted Tuesdays through Fridays at 8:30 AM, on Saturdays at 1:30 PM, and on Sundays at 8:30 AM and 1:30 PM.

Hunting – Lanai is a hunter's paradise. The prized axis deer, a small but treasured trophy animal native to India and imported from Japan in the 1920s, outnumbers humans on Lanai by at least two to one. They currently exist in such numbers that they are seriously threatening island vegetation. Mouflon sheep are hunted in August, with two Sundays limited to bow-and-arrow hunting and from two to six Sundays (depending on the sheep population) to high-powered rifle. Hunters are selected by lottery for this popular game opportunity. State lands enforce hunting seasons — for seasons, licenses, and requirements, check with the State Department of Land and Natural Resources, Division of Forestry and Wildlife (PO Box 1, Lanai City, HI 96763; phone: 565-6688), but there are none for axis deer on the private land of the *Koele Company.* (Trophy axis deer, however, are usually taken between May and November.) Guide service is normally required by the company. The $750-per-day fee includes guide, permit, transfers, and vehicle; there is no "trophy" fee, as is so often charged elsewhere.

For information: Chief Ranger, *Lanai Company* (PO Box L, Lanai City, HI 96763; phone: 565-7203). Game birds such as Gambel's quail, chukar partridge, Rio Grande turkey, ring-necked pheasant, and francolin are also hunted on Lanai — get information from the State Department of Land and Natural Resources in Honolulu. Note that there are no professional outfitters on Lanai. Accommodations for those on guided tours are arranged by the *Lanai Company.*

Snorkeling and Scuba – Hulopoe Bay and adjacent Manele Bay (a small boat harbor) constitute the Manele-Hulopoe Marine Life Conservation District, with spear- and boat-fishing prohibited. Generally calm water with many coral formations means superb diving on good days, with visibility in many places along this south coast to 100 feet. Puupehe, a rocky outcropping just offshore, is popular with dive boats from Maui. Other good dive areas, all of which require a four-wheel-drive vehicle to reach, are Kaunolu Bay and Three Stone Bay. *C & Sea Ocean Sports* (phone: 565-7227) offers snorkel and scuba excursions departing Manele Harbor. Information and bookings are also available through the concierge desks at the *Manele Bay* hotel and the *Lodge at Koele*. These two hotels also offer snorkeling and scuba diving trips, and rent equipment.

Surfing – Rarely is the surf very good. Hulopoe Bay sometimes gets decent waves, as do some stretches of Shipwreck Beach. Lopa, on the east coast, is another hopeful surfing location.

Swimming and Sunning – Hulopoe Bay beach (also called White Manele), 7 miles down a twisting but paved road from the Lanai City, is one of the best in Hawaii. Virtually surfless, except when storms kick up from the south, it has fine, beige sand and shower and picnicking facilities. Although Shipwreck Beach has reef-lined shallows that make swimming difficult, if you follow the dirt road past Keomuku Village, the beach widens and offers access to somewhat clearer waters. There is a small, nice campsite at the far end of the small cove — advance reservations are required. Apply to the *Lanai Company* (PO Box L, Lanai City, HI 96763; phone 565-7233) for permission. Fees are $5 for a permit, $5 per person per night, with a maximum stay of 7 nights.

Tennis – The *Lodge at Koele* features three courts, none of which are lighted. Tennis also is available at the *Manele Bay,* which features six courts that are available only for day use. There are four public courts on 7th Street in Lanai City; two are lighted for night play (stroll over to the electric company and ask them to turn on the lights). The courts are not in great shape, but are playable.

AROUND THE ISLAND

Lanai is shaped much like a pear or avocado balanced on its fat end. The lower, plumper portion contains the verdant mountains and gorges as well as the pineapple fields laid out in the depression of the Palawai Basin, while the upper part comprises largely arid, rolling tableland. Lanai City is almost in the exact center of the 140-square-mile island.

Lanai City

This is a plantation town and looks it: Rows of single-story, wooden buildings and houses cluster in a grid pattern around a central park square. The only commercial enterprises on Lanai, outside of the new hotels and plantation and government offices, also surround this square, with the *Lanai* hotel on a low knoll above it.

Yet it is an oddly satisfying little town, out of step with both modern times and with the rest of Hawaii. And it seems like a pleasant, if *very* tranquil, place. At 1,650 feet above sea level, Lanai City is above the pineapple fields and below the 3,370-foot peak of Lanaihale, the highest point on the island, and so enjoys an unusually temperate climate, enhanced by the old Cook and Norfolk Island pines that shade and cool the town — at night, even in summer, it can be foggy and chilly. It was founded in 1923 by Dole and even today shelters virtually the entire island population of perhaps 2,600, almost all of whom were once connected with the pineapple industry. There are three general stores, one bank, two restaurants (try the hamburgers at the *S&T* (see *Eating Out*), one bar (in the *Lanai* hotel), and it is closed by 10 PM — the sidewalks roll up rather early here.

Lanai City contains little of significance except the quaint, tidy, terribly uncontemporary aspect of the town itself; it thrives in its own kind of time warp.

Ito's Garden – A retired pineapple worker spent his time meticulously putting together a plant and rock garden on the edge of town just a short stroll from the *Lanai* hotel. Mr. Ito is now gone, but his personal statement of tropical flowers and foliage remains.

Lanai Art Program – In response to the recent agricultural changes sweeping the island, the president of Dole has opened an innovative community art studio designed to benefit Lanai's residents. Supplies for painting, photography, and a number of other applied arts are offered free of charge to the public, and native artwork is displayed in the island's two Rockresort hotels. Pay a visit and you may meet one of the artists in residence at work. Open daily (phone: 565-7503).

Old Plantation Manager's House – It's just above town and has been restored, providing a public reception hall and a glimpse of the vanished grand plantation style.

SHOPPING: The only things you'd want to buy on Lanai are what you've run out of unexpectedly, since there are few local arts and crafts or other kinds of industries. Fortunately, Dole has taken great pains to preserve Lanai's authenticity (the lack of commerce on the island is one of the reasons why the atmosphere is very relaxed here), and more shops will be added slowly — if at all.

Akamai Trading – Their business card says "Hawaii's smallest department store," and so it is, with its collection of useful and artistic goods. Not much you might not have seen elsewhere, although not on Lanai. 408 8th Ave. (phone: 565-6587).

Pine Isle Market – A general store combining groceries, booze, and dry goods with a hardware section — the top of the local retail scene. 365 8th Ave. (phone: 565-6488).

Richard's Shopping Center – This is another general store, and it sells the best selection of Lanai T-shirts. 434 8th Ave. (phone: 565-6065).

Shop at Koele – As upscale as shopping gets on Lanai, it offers casual resortwear and gifts. At the *Lodge at Koele* (phone: 565-7300).

Shop at Manele – Logo wear and classy souvenirs are the mainstay of this shop. At the *Manele Bay* (phone: 565-7700).

NIGHTLIFE: The various hotels are apt to present such low-key entertainment as Hawaiian trios and the like; check with them for schedules. Check out the *Tea Room Bar* at the *Lodge at Koele* or the classical music at the hotel's elegant *Music Room* (phone: 565-7300). Despite the new trend toward sophistication, things still close early; 11 PM is apt to find most people asleep hereabouts. There are local shindigs and dances if you can find them, and the town's bachelors get together almost nightly to gossip and drink beer, usually around the barbecue behind the electric company. That's the kind of island Lanai is. Starting late afternoon and running until 10 PM, the bar at the *Lanai* hotel (phone: 565-7211) is the hotspot in town, and attracts a usually raucous but friendly mix of locals and visitors.

CHECKING IN: Lanai's accommodations are either rustic or elegant, with nothing in between. Elegant means expensive, and for such accommodations, rates begin at $300 for a double room and run significantly higher. Moderate (read rustic) indicates something in the $100 range. All telephone numbers are in the 808 area code unless otherwise indicated.

Lodge at Koele – Hawaii's first upscale, up-country resort hotel is located adjacent to Lanai City at Koele, at the base of Lanaihale's mountainous heights. The setting is every bit as appealing as the palm-tree-and-beach variety of Hawaiian surroundings. With each of its 102 rooms situated in garden surroundings, the *Lodge* provides a sophisticated version of a country inn. A massive living room at the center of the main floor — complete with a pair of 50-foot fireplaces, high-beamed ceilings, and an impressive collection of art and artifacts (including a wonderful selection of Polynesian relics discovered on Lanai) — sets a decorative theme that recalls the island's ranching and plantation eras. As for this Rockresort's amenities, all guestrooms have top-grade cosmetics and beauty aids, a hair dryer, and extra-plush robes and towels. There's easy access to its 18-hole, par 72 championship golf course named *The Experience* (designed by Greg Norman and Ted Robinson) and to an older 9-hole layout, an executive putting course, croquet, impressive garden walks, and an archaeological tour. Adjacent facilities include 4 tennis courts and stables that offer tame yet enjoyable rides. The hotel's 2 restaurants are quite sophisticated and serve elegant fare (see *Eating Out*). If you see something on the menu called "grilled pastrami of striped marlin," order it without delay. No TV sets in the rooms, but there's a large projection set in the library with which to keep track of world events (if you must). Shuttle service links the *Lodge* with Lanai City (1 mile away), the *Manele Bay* hotel, Hulopoe Beach (20 minutes away), and the airport. Lanai City (phone: 565-7300; 800-321-4666). Expensive.

Manele Bay – With access to such assets as Lanai's best beach, excellent snorkeling and scuba, and some of Hawaii's sunniest weather, this 250-room hotel is difficult to leave. This second Rockresort property on Lanai opened in 1991, and between its chic contemporary architecture and decor and its beautiful setting overlooking Hulopoe Beach, it's first rate. Set amid a variety of Oriental gardens, pools, and streams, the spacious rooms are exquisitely decorated, with marble baths and lanais with gorgeous views overlooking the beach and ocean. Other niceties include a private library and a spa facility that offers customized workouts and one-on-one training sessions. Also planned is an 18-hole, par 72 championship golf course, designed by Jack Nicklaus, with several holes that will require carrying significant water hazards. Dubbed the *Challenge of Manele,* this course is scheduled to open early next year. Tennis, horseback riding, and swimming are nearby. The *Hulopoe Court* restaurant (see *Eating Out*) affords an intimate setting for dinner, nightly musical entertainment and dancing. Manele Bay (phone: 565-7700; 800-321-4666). Expensive.

Lanai – This rustic clapboard example of authentic Hawaiiana was constructed in 1923 as a boardinghouse for Dole supervisors and a temporary lodging for visitors. In the course of its checkered existence, it has been the *Lanai Inn,* then the *Lanai Lodge.* Currently owned and operated by Castle & Cooke, the simple, 1-story frame structure contains 10 rooms, some better than others, but all nicely redecorated and all with private baths. The dining room is wood-panelled and cozy (see *Eating Out*), and the popular bar is comfortably set on the glass-enclosed lanai. Expect a basic but comfortable room, decent food, and personal attention. Beach towels are supplied for excursions to Hulopoe Beach. PO Box A-119, Lanai City, HI 96763 (phone: 565-7211;800-624-8849). Moderate.

■ **Private Home Rentals:** *Oshiro's* (PO Box 67, Lanai City, HI 96763; phone: 565-6952) can arrange the rental of three fully equipped private homes on Lanai. One home has 3 bedrooms available on a daily ($150) or weekly basis, with a 3-day minimum and a 10% discount for stays of a week of more; the other two houses have 3 bedrooms each and rent for $85 to $95 per day, with a 2-day minimum and the same longer-term discount. Lucille Graham runs a homey bed and breakfast establishment for about $50 a night (312 Mahana Pl., Lanai City, HI 96763; phone: 565-6378).

EATING OUT: The two new restaurants at the *Manele Bay* hotel, *Hulopoe Court* and the *Ihilani Room,* cater to refined and sophisticated tastes, serving haute cuisine at prices that are equally haute. Under the direction of John Farnsworth, who runs the kitchen at the *Lodge at Koele* as well, the food is a treat. For the rest of the island, the options are limited to places where a down-home atmosphere prevails. Expect to pay $45 to $60 at the *Lodge* or *Manele Bay* per person without drinks or tips; $25 to $30 for two at the *Lanai* hotel; under $15 at the inexpensive establishments. All telephone numbers are in the 808 area code unless otherwise indicated.

Hulopoe Court – The surroundings are refined (yet not overly pretentious), crowned by high ceilings and an adjacent lanai for alfresco dining. The wonderful fare ranges from appetizers such as duck with prosciutto, watermelon and red onion salad to entrées such as Palawai pork medallions with roasted pumpkin sauce, tiger prawns in lemon olive oil, and grilled opah with black Thai rice and stir-fried vegetables. Open for breakfast, lunch, and dinner (5:30 to 9:30 PM). Reservations suggested. In the *Manele Bay* hotel (phone: 565-7700). Expensive.

Ihilani Room – Lavishly decorated with satin tablecloths and lovely china, this sophisticated establishment serves Pacific Rim fare with distinctive flair. Open daily. Reservations suggested. In the *Manele Bay* (phone: 565-7700). Expensive.

Koele Dining Room – The main restaurant at the *Lodge at Koele,* it features continental cuisine with a local twist — most of the herbs and vegetables served here are grown in gardens not far from the hotel, and the eggs and pork products are locally produced as well. At breakfast, concentrate on such local specialties as the pineapple/orange juice, Palawai sugar pineapple, papaya, Kaunolu bananas in coconut cream, Koala bacon, Lanai axis deer sausage, macadamia nut butter, and Kona coffee. Open daily for breakfast, lunch, and dinner. Reservations advised. At the *Lodge at Koele* (phone: 565-7300). Expensive.

Lanai – Good, solid, home cooking in a rustic setting. Expect hearty breakfasts, uninspired lunches, decent dinners centered around meat-and-potatoes dishes. Nothing fancy, certainly, but the homemade pies are great, and there is bar service. Open daily. Reservations advised. *Lanai* hotel (phone: 565-7211). Moderate.

Blue Ginger Café – Breakfast, lunch, and dinner served in a bright, cheery atmosphere. Closed Sundays. No reservations. 409 7th Ave. (phone: 565-6363). Inexpensive.

S&T Properties – An unlikely name for a counter service luncheonette, but breakfast and lunch (plate lunches mostly) are served. The hamburgers are very tasty. Open daily except Wednesdays. No reservations. 409 7th Ave. (phone: 565-6537). Inexpensive.

Elsewhere on the Island

A number of rewarding tourist sites are spread around Lanai, but be forewarned that most of them will require a sturdy four-wheel-drive vehicle. And even thus equipped, you may find many of the rutted dirt roads impossible to maneuver. It's best to check first at *Oshiro's* (phone: 565-6952) or *Lanai City Service* (phone: 565-7227) to see which roads are passable and then make your plans. For the sake of those unwilling to take the four-wheel-drive plunge, the sites listed first below can be reached by nice, civilized, paved roads.

Hulopoe Bay (paved road) – A lovely, white sand beach in a small, protected cove. Not only the best beach on Lanai, it's the *only* swimmable one (most north coast beaches generally front shallow reefs). There are gentle waves, good snorkeling, picnic tables, showers, and a campsite. Even when it's cool and cloudy 1,650 feet higher up and inland in Lanai City, it's likely to be clear, dry, hot, and sunny here. Besides, this is one of the most pleasant beaches in all Hawaii.

Manele Bay (paved road) – This is the bay right next to Hulopoe, a small boat harbor and marina where most of the tour boats from Maui dock and disgorge their passengers for a few hours at the beach.

Kaumalapau Harbor (paved road) – The pineapples have to leave Lanai from somewhere, and this is it. This pineapple loading port is at its most interesting during the height of the summer picking season.

Munro Trail – George C. Munro was a New Zealander who in the early 1900s was the manager of the ill-fated Lanai Ranch during the cattle experiment phase of the island (ironically, cattle recently have been reintroduced — this time successfully — to Lanai). But Munro was also an amateur botanist who imported seeds for Lanai's now-signature Cook and Norfolk Island pines from his native land, and sowed them (along with those of other trees and plants) along the 7-mile ridge above what is today Lanai City. That ridge is now crowned by a tough trail (and a road suitable only for four-wheel-drive vehicles) bearing Munro's name that winds through Cook and Norfolk Island pine, eucalyptus, ironwood, silver oak, and koa trees. From the trail on clear days all the Hawaiian islands except Kauai and Niihau can be glimpsed, along with the deep, spectacular gulches (particularly Hauola and Maunalei) on the wild and rugged east slope. Along the way you will crest the 3,370-foot peak of Lanaihale, the island's highest point. A four-wheel-drive vehicle is a necessity for this exploration, as are detailed instructions on how to find the beginning of the trail.

Luahiwa Petroglyphs – These fascinating rock carvings, only a mile or so outside Lanai City off the Manele Road (Route 441) to Hulopoe and Manele bays, are difficult to find, but you'll be rewarded with some of the best examples of petroglyphs left in the islands. Boulders containing the drawings march up a steep hillside next to pineapple fields, and are deeply scratched with likenesses of men, animals, and ships. Getting here means traveling on dirt pineapple roads, so you'll need good instructions and a sturdy vehicle.

Garden of the Gods – An unusual, austere tumble of boulders and lava formations near Kanepuu, off the beaten path, about 7 miles from Lanai City. Ask at one of the hotels or car rental companies for assistance in locating the garden. Even with good instructions, it may prove difficult to find. The colors and severe beauty are locally celebrated, and well worth searching out.

Kaunolu Bay – King Kamehameha I, the warrior king who united Hawaii by force of arms, kept a summer home and built a small village at the southwestern tip of Lanai in the early 19th century. This archaeological site is one of the most interesting in Hawaii, although only stone foundations remain. Next to Kaunolu Village is Kahekili's Leap, where the king, as a test of loyalty and bravery, ordered his warriors to jump 62 feet past a protruding ledge and into the sea. The road here is a very difficult, four-wheel-drive–only track. It's also visited on *C & Sea Ocean Sports* raft excursions (see *Snorkeling and Scuba*).

Shipwreck Beach – The breezy northern coast of Lanai, the portion facing Molokai, is protected by coral reefs and swept by strong currents. Numerous ships have been driven onto the reefs and some hulks remain visible today. The beach stretches for 8 miles, provides excellent beachcombing (glass Japanese balls used to float nets are often found), decent diving, and fine lobstering, but the sea is shallow and dangerous. There is a good paved road that leads to the north shore, but not along it — for that you'll need a jeep. A dirt track parallels the coastline westward from the end of the road.

Keomuku Village – If, when you reach the end of the paved road at Shipwreck Beach, you drive straight ahead rather than turning left and then bend eastward along the shoreline, eventually you'll reach the overgrown ruins of the sugar town that was abandoned in 1903 when the irrigation water turned brackish. The old church (partially restored at press time) and a lovely palm grove are about all that's left to see. The church is being repaired by a group of village descendants. A sign on the altar (frequently covered by coins dedicated to the restoration) reveals that the church was built in 1903. The trek here is difficult but well worth it for those with an interest in island history.

Lopa Beach – Although Lanai is not blessed with many beaches, the ones that do exist are wonderful. Lopa Beach in particular is a lovely strand of fine, white sand (although the water here is not swimmable). Just beyond earshot of Keomoku, this is another good reason to rent a four-wheel-drive to reach out-of-the-way spots, for it is the perfect definition of island escape. The view from the beach looks out over the Pacific to both East and West Maui and Kahoolawe.

KAUAI

While the Kings of Maui, Oahu, and Hawaii bloodily battled each other for control of the Hawaiian islands, Kauai, the westernmost of the major islands, stayed peacefully out of the fray. Twice, by sheer luck or divine intervention, Kauai was spared invasion by King Kamehameha, who had already subdued — and with no light hand — all the other islands. The first attempt, in 1796, was thwarted by rough seas in the channel between Oahu and Kauai, and the second, 6 years later, by an epidemic of cholera (or perhaps typhoid) that ravaged Kamehameha's army as it waited on Oahu's shores for propitious weather to make the crossing to Kauai. Although Kauai eventually became part of Kamehameha's kingdom, it was as a semi-independent state. Kauai's King Kaumualii, smart enough to realize his people might not be so lucky if the persistent conqueror tried a third time, agreed to acknowledge him as King of all Hawaiian Islands, and was so able to keep much of his autonomy.

In many respects, Kauai still retains a sense of separateness from the other islands. Kauai is the Hawaii most visitors seek but never find. Many of its attractions are quaint — a mountain that resembles a sleeping giant, a rubbly wall that is barely recognizable as the Russian fort it once briefly was. Slow to make use of its tourist resources, which are considerable, developers have until recently had a tough go with planning and zoning boards on Kauai. Many are now concerned that the possible demise of sugar and the lure of tourist dollars may be undoing decades of caution. Even low-rise development can be an intrusion if it goes too far, and while Kauai's resort hotels and condominiums are generally well planned and nicely designed, they tend to surrender authenticity in order to service the increasing flow of visitors.

While the population of Kauai is still mostly rural, living in villages where the grocery store and post office make up most of the business district, shopping malls and convenience stores have sprung up, implanting contemporary suburbia in a setting of unparalleled natural beauty. Even the Na Pali Coast and Waimea Canyon, once the preserve of hikers alone, now echo with the engines of the helicopters, planes, and motorized boats bringing increasing numbers of visitors to Kauai's primeval wilderness. Conflicts over use of the wilderness have been brewing for years, and access limitations have been implemented. Although tourism and the cultivation of taro, guava, papaya, and macadamia nuts have somewhat broadened the island's economic base, sugarcane still dominates the landscape, as it has since the first cane plantation was started at Koloa in 1835. Everywhere you see cane at one stage or another: newly plowed fields waiting to be planted; young seedlings green against the red furrows of earth; mature cane, taller than corn in August. At night, fires burning the leaves off the harvested cane blaze orange before the dark, impenetrable mountains of the interior. By day, huge cane trucks,

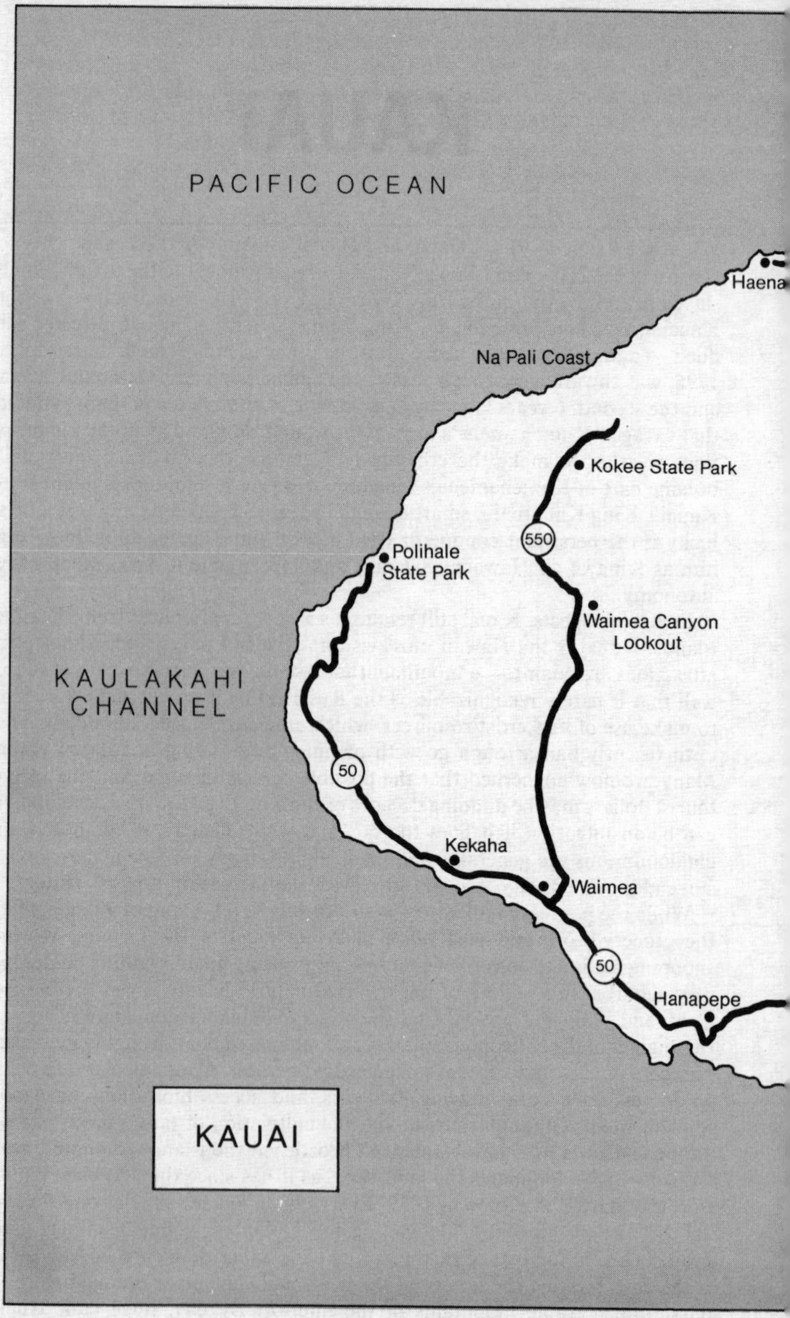
PACIFIC OCEAN
Haena
Na Pali Coast
Kokee State Park
550
Polihale
State Park
Waimea Canyon
Lookout
KAULAKAHI
CHANNEL
50
Kekaha
Waimea
50
Hanapepe
KAUAI

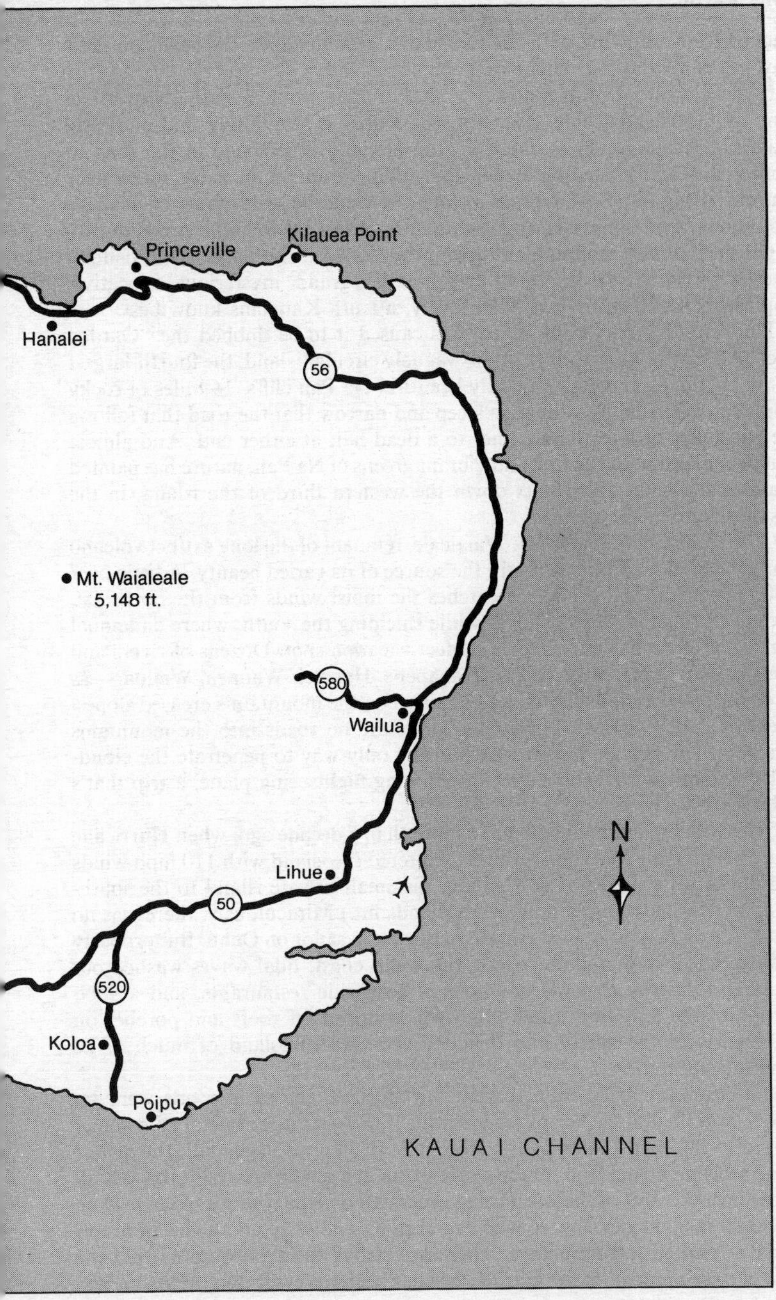
Kilauea Point
Princeville
Hanalei
56
Mt. Waialeale
5,148 ft.
580
Wailua
N
Lihue
50
520
Koloa
Poipu
KAUAI CHANNEL

stacked to overflowing with the raw stalks, rumble down the roads on their way to one of the four sugar mills on the island.

It was almost inevitable, however, that tourism would eventually overtake cane as the island's chief industry, for Kauai is stunningly and endlessly beautiful. A newcomer is likely to stop at every other bend in the road to admire a beach glistening under the midday sun or an early missionary church sitting small and pious before the majestic wilderness of Kauai's mountains. And while islanders, who have jobs to get to and errands to run, might find all this stopping annoying, they can hardly blame their visitors. There's rarely a view that isn't breathtaking, grand, mysterious, evocative, inspiring, charming, or just plain lovely, a truth Kauaians know best.

The verdancy pervading Kauai has caused it to be dubbed the "Garden Isle." Along the North Shore of this vaguely circular island, the fourth-largest in the chain, are the extravagantly beautiful Na Pali cliffs, 14 miles of rocky heights punctuated by valleys so steep and narrow that the road that follows the perimeter of the island comes to a dead halt at either end. And almost as if to contrast with the rich and vibrant greens of Na Pali, nature has painted Waimea Canyon, which cuts down the western third of the island, in the pastel palette of the desert.

In the center of Kauai is Mt. Waialeale, remnant of the long extinct volcano that gave birth to Kauai and still the source of its varied beauty. A little over 5,000 feet high, Mt. Waialeale catches the moist winds from the northeast, feeding the lushness of the north while shielding the south, where an annual rainfall of 20 inches makes for a perfect vacation spot. Dozens of rivers and streams rise on Mt. Waialeale — Hanapepe, Hanalei, Waimea, Wailua — as do countless waterfalls that hang like tinsel on the mountain's creased slopes. Like Na Pali, Waialeale is remote. There are no roads into the mountains (besides a few private jeep trails), and the only way to penetrate the cloud-veiled summit is by helicopter or fixed-wing flightseeing plane, a trip that's well worth its cost.

Quiet little Kauai made the news more than a decade ago, when Hurricane Iwa, sweeping in from the southwest, battered the island with 110 mph winds and devastating tidal waves. (Niihau, the small private island to the southwest, and Oahu were the only other islands hit.) Miraculously, there was no loss of life on Kauai — Iwa's single victim was a sailor on Oahu. But property loss exceeded $100 million. Along the south coast, tidal waves washed out roads and destroyed numerous houses, beachside restaurants, and a good portion of the *Sheraton* hotel. High winds ripped off roofs and porches on other parts of the island and denuded the Garden Island of much of its luxuriant vegetation.

The cleanup started immediately: within days, the main roads were repaired, and the foliage began regenerating. Six weeks after Iwa, fertile Kauai started to bud and bloom again. Except in the stories locals tell, the visitor today will find no evidence of the worst storm in a generation to hit this island.

These days, most of the wind being generated on Kauai seems to come from the residents and developers who are arguing endlessly about the future of Kauai's tourism infrastructure. There are strong feelings by some that the pace of development on the Garden Isle has been too swift, too extensive, and lacking in recognition of development's impact on the delicate local balance of nature.

The debate has become increasingly complicated, and lately has focused on new zoning laws meant to inhibit operation of motorized rafts, boats, and helicopters that visit the wild Na Pali Coast and other inaccessible portions of the Kauai wilderness. At press time, the state's efforts to limit wilderness access have been held up by court battles among state and county governments, boating and helicopter operators, and environmentalists. Developers also face stiff opposition by the county government to new projects that are not deemed beneficial to Kauai's environment, atmosphere, or its economy.

There's no telling where these disputes will end, but it seems clear that considerable numbers of Kauai residents are intent on preserving the unique appeal of their remarkable island, and that can't be bad for visitors.

SOURCES AND RESOURCES

TOURIST INFORMATION: The Hawaii Visitors Bureau is at 3016 Umi St., Rm. 207, Lihue, HI 96766 (phone: 245-3971). It also operates a visitor information booth at Lihue Airport. The *Kauai Drive Guide,* with excellent maps and other useful information, is one of the best visitor publications. Pick up the free guide, which includes good maps and itineraries as well as entries on restaurants, shops, sights, and sports, at most car rental agencies.

Local Coverage – Other useful free visitor publications include *This Week on Kauai, Kauai Beach Press,* and *Spotlight Kauai.* The two local newspapers are the weekly *Kauai Times* and the *Garden Island,* published five times a week. Many hotels and condominiums also offer copies of the excellent *Beach Guide* series on Poipu, East Kauai, and Princeville. The *Sandwich Islands Quarterly* and *Kauai* (also a quarterly publication) feature Kauai in four-color, magazine format.

TELEPHONE: The area code for Hawaii is 808.

GETTING AROUND: Several inter-island airlines provide service to Kauai: *Aloha Airlines* and *Hawaiian Air* both fly into Lihue Airport, while *Aloha IslandAir* has daily service to Princeville Airport at Hanalei. The only major airline with scheduled flights to Kauai via Honolulu is *United.* While on the island, you can choose one of many modes of travel to see it — bus, van, jeep, car, taxi, boat, rubber raft, or helicopter.

Taxi – All taxis are metered, and because there's a fair distance between sights in Kauai, they're not an economical way to travel. From Lihue Airport to the Wailua area, expect to pay between $10 and $14 (excluding tip); to Poipu Beach, about $25; and to Princeville, around $55. Some reputable services to call: *Kauai Cab* (phone: 246-9554), *Aloha Taxi* (phone: 245-4609), and *ABC Taxi* (phone: 822-7641).

Several taxi companies also offer custom limousine tour services which charge passengers on an hourly basis. *North Shore Cab & Tours* (phone: 826-6189) serves the Princeville/Hanalei area; *Lorenzo's* (phone: 245-6331) departs from Lihue, and *Poipu Taxi & Tours* (phone: 651-7140) serves south Kauai.

Car Rental – Despite the proliferation of rental companies — nearly a score now — demand can outstrip supply, particularly during the peak winter season and when convention business is heavy. While excess availability discounts may be offered on arrival, it is still a good idea to book in advance, especially for the jeeps and convertibles that are an increasingly popular rental option for touring the Garden Isle. While many companies have check-in counters at the Lihue Airport terminal, most cars are picked up at lots nearby, with company vans providing transfers.

Cars here are a bargain, though, and the best way to get around. Although the roads get curvy at the Waimea end and narrow past Hanalei, they are very good in between.

In addition to the national chains — *Alamo* (phone: 246-0645), *Avis* (phone: 245-3512), *Budget* (phone: 245-1901), *Dollar* (phone: 245-3651), *Hertz* (phone: 245-3356), *National* (phone: 245-5636), and *Thrifty* (phone: 245-7388) — there are also regional and local agencies at or near Lihue Airport: *Sunshine* (phone: 245-9541 on Kauai; 800-522-8440 on other islands); and *Tropical Rent-A-Car* (phone: 245-6988). Check for daily and weekly specials.

If you fly into Princeville, your choice is more limited — *Avis* (phone: 826-9773) or *Hertz* (phone: 826-7455).

Bicycle/Mountain Bike/Moped Rental – In the Poipu area contact *Outfitters Kauai* (phone: 742-9667) for mountain bikes that are great for off-road and beach riding. Their 4-hour Ecotour ($58) offers an escorted mountain bike excursion to Kokee Park. In Hanalei call *Pedal & Paddle* (phone: 826-9069) for bikes and mopeds. *North Shore Bike, Cruise and Snorkel* (phone: 822-1582) offers a 6-mile escorted bike tour along the North Shore, followed by snorkeling and a beach barbecue ($99). *Kauai Downhill* (phone: 245-1774) offers a 12-mile escorted run to the coast from Waimea Canyon that includes a sunrise breakfast ($60).

SIGHTSEEING TOURS: By Bus or Van – Tour options consist of half-day trips to Waimea Canyon, Hanalei and the North Shore, or Wailua and the Fern Grotto, and are offered by a number of companies. Full-day itineraries usually combine two of these half-day options. Many tours are by van rather than big bus, and most companies will pick you up at your hotel or condo.

One of the best van tours is operated by *Chandler's Kauai Tours* (phone: 245-5675), which offers half- and full-day tours to Waimea Canyon. Full-day itineraries include a boat trip to the Fern Grotto. *Chandler's* also runs special half- and full-day tours to Hanalei and Haena. Another company, *TransHawaiian* (phone: 245-5108), does sightseeing tours to Waimea, the Fern Grotto, and Hanalei. *Gray Line Kauai* (phone: 245-3344; 800-367-2420) offers both van and bus tours, as does *Robert's Hawaii* (phone: 245-9558). The most off-the-beaten-path option is the four-wheel-drive excursion into Kauai's magnificent wilderness interior via *Kauai Mountain Tours* (phone: 245-7224). The 7-hour ($75) tour (with continental breakfast and picnic lunch) of Kokee State Park includes exploration of up-country forests and streams, with stops at isolated overviews of the Waimea Canyon. Guides are well-versed in Hawaiiana and provide interesting insights into the Polynesian past and the Hawaiian present. Hotel transfers from various Kauai resorts are included.

A visitor can also hire a car and driver/guide through some of the taxi companies. *Akiko's Taxi,* for instance, charges $35 an hour with a 1-hour minimum (phone: 822-3613). *Best of Kauai* (phone: 826-6189) features a full-day excursion that includes a helicopter tour, a visit to the Kilauea Lighthouse and bird sanctuary, and a boat trip to the Fern Grotto ($109). On the North Shore call *North Shore Cab and Tours* (phone: 826-6189), where the charter rate is $55 an hour per person for a 15-passenger van (with a 1-hour minimum) and $60 an hour for a stretch-limo (with a 2-hour minimum). *LimoLimo* (phone: 822-0393) offers deluxe Rolls Royce and Cadillac limousine tours.

Kimo Cassette Tour Guide (phone: 245-6721) provides a stop-by-stop tour of Kauai on two cassette tapes for $20 a day; a tape player is included.

Boat – Two companies — *Smith's Boat Tours* (phone: 822-4111) and *Waialeale Boat Tours* (phone: 822-4908) — ply the Wailua River up to the Fern Grotto. It's a short ride (about 2 miles), and although Hawaiian music and local legend are used to make it interesting, the experience is more a cliché than a true adventure. Numerous companies take visitors along the 19-mile Na Pali Coast in an assortment of Zodiac rafts and hard-hull vessels. In most cases, landings are not made, this being conservation property. There are, however, opportunities to enter sea caves and snorkel offshore at several locations. Starting in October, strong currents and waves can make the Na Pali Coast dangerous for boating, and many companies shift their operations to Kauai's South Shore, where the highlights are the magnificent beach and fish at Kipukai and the Spouting Horn.

An unusual boat tour is offered by *Captain Zodiac* (phone: 826-9772 or 826-9371), which uses rubber rafts seating up to 15 people to cruise the Na Pali Coast year-round, although during winter months when the surf is high, trips may be rerouted to the calmer waters of the southeast coast from Nawiliwili to Kipukai. From May through September, there are morning, full-day, and sunset cruises, plus a drop-off service for Na Pali hikers and campers. Prices range from about $50 for the 2-hour sunset cruise to $105 for the 5-hour day trip. In winter, for $65 per person, *Blue Odyssey Adventures* (phone: 826-9033) takes its customized raft from Kukuiula Harbor near Poipu for snorkeling and a visit to Kipukai, perhaps the single most exotic and idyllic bit of the tropics in Hawaii. During the summer months, *Blue Odyssey* also offers raft and snorkeling excursions along the Na Pali Coast ($70), as does *Na Pali Adventures* (phone: 826-6804) aboard its fleet of motorized catamarans ($85); *Paradise Adventure Cruises* (phone: 826-9999) has two tours daily on 22- and 25-foot, 6-passenger Boston Whalers ($80) and catamaran-style boats ($85). *Na Pali Coast Cruises* (phone: 335-5078), with its 135-foot *Na Pali Queen, Na Pali Adventures* (phone: 826-6804), with 13-, 17-, and 18-passenger power cats ($85), and *Hanalei Sea Tours* (phone: 826-7254; 800-733-7997) ply coastal waters in motorized pleasure craft, making en-route stops for snorkeling. *Pacific Safari* (phone: 742-7033) offers Na Pali and south coast excursions aboard 38-foot glass-bottom boats. Due to occasional high surf in winter, all Na Pali boat trips are weather conditional from October through May. *Captain Andy's Sailing Adventures* (phone: 822-7833) runs snorkel (with lunch) and sunset tours in a 46-foot catamaran from Kukuiula Harbor near Poipu. *Captain Sundown* (phone: 822-3359) departs Nawiliwili on half-day snorkel/picnic catamaran sails ($75) and 3-hour sunset sails ($45) aboard a 40-foot catamaran. *Brennecke Ocean Sports* (phone: 742-6570) can book a wide range of boat options, including some of those listed above. The state-of-the-art racing catamaran *Kiele VI* (phone: 245-5050, ext. 5232) departs Kalapaki Beach (in front of the *Westin*) on 1-hour, high-speed ocean sails. Mahogany power launches depart Kauai Lagoons Visitor Center from 8 AM to sunset on 45-minute tours of the lagoon complex, which is rife with wildlife (phone: 246-5060).

Kayak – There's no easier way to enjoy the Kauai wilderness than by kayak. *Kayak Kauai,* with offices in Hanalei (phone: 826-9844) and Kapaa (phone: 822-9179), offers rentals ($48 for a 2-passenger kayak for the day), complete with car roof rack for on-your-own rentals. Kayaking is possible along the coast and inland, up one of Kauai's numerous small rivers. In Koloa, river and ocean kayak rentals are available from *Outfitters Kauai* (phone: 742-9667), which also offers full-day escorted Na Pali Coast excursions ($110) during the summer. *Island Adventures* (phone: 245-9662) runs trips up the Huleia River off Nawiliwili Bay (scenes from *Raiders of the Lost Ark* were filmed here) in royaks — 1-passenger, kayak-like vessels. *Luana of Hawaii* (phone: 826-9195) sets out in hawayaks — glass-bottom, fiberglass, single-passenger kayaks.

Glider – *Tradewinds Glider* (phone: 335-5086) features 20- and 40-minute glider flights that depart Port Allen and take in the south coast from Poipu to Hanapepe, heading inland (weather permitting) for views of isolated canyons and valleys. Costs range from $75 to $125 for a single, $90 to $150 double.

Helicopter – Without a doubt, the best way to see Kauai is by helicopter, for there's no other way to get close to much of the island, and there's nothing to match the exhilaration of hovering over the jagged cliffs of Na Pali or sweeping into the heart of Waialeale. Several companies fly daily, all charging about $135 for a 50-minute spin around the island, or $185 for a 70-75 minute itinerary. (Check tourist publications for discount coupons.) They are *Kenai Helicopter Tours* (phone: 245-8591), *Island Helicopters Kauai* (phone: 245-8588), *Papillon Helicopters* (phone: 826-6591), *South Seas Helicopters* (phone: 245-7781), *Air Kauai Helicopters* (phone: 246-4666), *Bali Hai Helicopters* (phone: 332-7331), *Ohana Helicopters* (phone: 245-3996), *Jack Harter Helicopters* (phone: 245-3774), *Bruce Needham Helicopters* (phone: 335-3115), and *InterIsland Helicopters* (phone: 335-5009). In addition to Lihue Airport, there are helipads at Princeville Airport (*Papillon*), and at Port Allen, on the south side, where *Bruce Needham, Bali Hai,* and *InterIsland* provide service. *Papillon* offers a special 2½-hour tour ($150) that includes an hour-long lunch break in Hanalei. *Jack Harter* offers an exciting 90-minute helicopter tour ($160). Those interested in flightseeing over the nearby island of Niihau should contact *Niihau Helicopter* (phone: 335-3500), which departs from Port Allen Airport. Called the "Forbidden Island," the privately owned jewel (Kauai's Robinson family are the owners) until recently has been off limits to all but a select few invited guests (see *Niihau,* ISLAND-BY-ISLAND HOPPING). The tour ($200) is offered Mondays through Fridays. Visitors should not expect to see any Niihauans, however; the single landing on the island is at its isolated north end.

Plane – For those who prefer the familiarity of a fixed-wing plane or an aerial tour at about half the typical helicopter rate, *Fly Kauai* (phone: 246-9123) offers tours that start at $39. Its circle island tour ($69) is actually a bit more comprehensive than the helicopter options, tying in the south coast in a fly-by that includes Kipukai, Poipu, and Waimea before heading inland for a circuit of Waimea Canyon and the Na Pali Coast. At press time, *Classic Aviation* (phone: 329-TOUR; 800-695-8100, inter-island) planned tours over Kauai in a 1935-era open-cockpit biplane.

Jeep – For scenic views of Waimea Canyon by the back roads, *Kauai Mountain Tours* (phone: 245-7224) offers a tour of Kokee State Park in a four-wheel-drive vehicle. There's time to explore up-country streams and the chance to learn about native and exotic forest flora. A contintental breakfast, picnic lunch, and hotel pickup are included ($75).

SPECIAL EVENTS: Waimea marks the anniversary of Captain James Cook's arrival in the Hawaiian islands with reenactments, a parade, parties, and a foot race during the *Captain Cook Celebration* in February. The most special of special events on Kauai is the *Prince Kuhio Festival* held at the end of March, honoring native son Prince Jonah Kuhio Kalanianaole, who for many years was the Hawaiian Territory's delegate to the US Congress. There's lots of Hawaiian pageantry, canoe races, and a royal ball to cap the festivities. With the Japanese constituting the largest segment of Kauai's population, *Buddha Day* in early April, celebrating the birth of Buddha, is an occasion for pageants, flower festivals, and dance across the island. On May 1, locals celebrate *Lei Day* with flowers, music, and song. July is a good month to watch Kauai celebrate itself, not the least of reasons being the week-long (July 5–11) *King Kamehameha Celebration,* which culminates in a festive parade in Lihue, with exhibits of local foods, flowers, and arts and crafts. The *Miss Native Hawaiian Pageant* happens in September; in late September or early October the *Aloha Week* activities — canoe races, luaus, dances, pageants, and parades — get under way. Check with *CJM Ranch* (phone: 245-6666) for information on their annual November rodeo.

SPORTS: Boating – There are no bareboat charters on Kauai because of insurance problems, but most tour operators offer customized charters in addition to their listed tours. So most of the boating that visitors do on Kauai is as passengers. *Blue Water Sailing* (phone: 822-0525) provides skippered charters (full-day, $850; half-day, $600; and sunset, $350) aboard its 42-foot ketch. *True Blue Charters* (phone: 246-6333) rents Hobie Cats and small sailing craft at $45 for the first hour, $25 each additional hour. The rate includes a check-out ride with an instructor and a short refresher lesson if required. *Na Pali Coast Cruise Lines* (phone: 335-5078), *Hanalei Sea Tours* (phone: 826-9686; 800-733-7997), and *Captain Zodiac* (phone: 826-9772 or 826-9371) are among those who offer snorkeling along the Na Pali Coast in an armada that ranges from diesel-powered launches to rubber Zodiac rafts. Tours also depart the south coast from Nawiliwili, Poipu, or Port Allen. At press time, the *Na Pali Coast Cruise Line* (phone: 335-5078), departing Port Allen for the Na Pali Coast, was scheduled to add a 150-passenger SWATH vessel to its fleet. The state-of-the-art SWATH's hull is designed to provide a steady ride even in rough seas. *Captain Andy's Sailing Adventures* (phone: 822-7833) departs Kukuiula Harbor in Poipu aboard a 46-foot, 48-passenger catamaran for snorkel and sunset cruises along the south coast, as well as the Na Pali Coast. *Aloha Destinations* in Koloa (phone: 742-7548) and *Brennecke Ocean Sports* (phone: 742-6570) can make reservations for a number of water activities.

Camping – Between state and county parks, there are several attractive places to camp on Kauai, from the green forests high in Kokee State Park to the stark beach at Polihale. For permits to camp in state parks, go to the Division of State Parks (3060 Eiwa St., Lihue; phone: 241-3444); for county parks, to the Parks Permit Section (4193 Hardy St., Lihue; phone: 245-1881) from 7:45 AM to 4:30 PM on weekdays. Equipment rentals are available from *Jungle Bob's* (phone: 826-6664) and *Kayak Kauai* in Kapaa (phone: 822-9179) and Hanalei (phone: 826-9844).

Fishing – The best season is from May to August, when 100-pound-plus yellow-fin tuna is the big catch, but year-round fishing is good, too, with a plentitude of marlin, ono, mahimahi, and bonito. Charter rates run $90 per person for a half day (4 hours), $120 for 6 hours, and $500 for the entire boat (holding up to six people) for a half day. Among the operators: *Gent-Lee Fishing Charters* (phone: 245-7504) and *Alana-Lynn Too* (phone: 245-7446), both operating from Nawiliwili. *Sport Fishing Kauai* (phone: 742-7013) offers fishing charters from Kukuiula Harbor near Poipu. *Sea Breeze Sport Fishing Charters* (phone: 828-1285) offers less expensive charter rates and departs from Anini or Port Allen.

Golf – There are six distinctive golf complexes on Kauai. At the 27-hole *Princeville Makai* golf course (par 72, 6,116 yards), fees range from $75 (for guests) to $100 (non-guests) for 18 holes (phone: 826-3580). The recently completed 18 holes of the adjacent *Prince* course (par 72, 7,309 yards), considered the best new resort course in the US in 1990 by *Golf Digest,* are strung through the paradisiacal landscape near Hanalei (phone: 826-3240). The new *Prince* clubhouse includes Hawaii's largest pro shop, as well as a full-service, multimillion-dollar spa. The *Kiahuna Plantation* golf course's (phone: 742-9595) 18 holes (par 70, 6,353 yards) — 9 more are scheduled to open later this year — wrap around various archaeological sites in Poipu. Greens fees are $62 to $70 for 18 holes. At the Jack Nicklaus–designed 18-hole *Kiele Lagoons* (par 72, 7,070 yards) at the *Kauai Lagoons* resort, fees range from $95 to $135. (In 1989 *Golf Digest* voted the *Kiele* course the best new resort course in the US.) The 18-hole *Kauai Lagoons* course (par 72, 6,942 yards), also at the *Kauai Lagoons* resort, charges from $70 to $105 in greens fees (phone: 246-5061). The 18-hole *Poipu Bay* resort course at Poipu, adjacent to the *Hyatt Regency Kauai* (phone: 742-8711), which opened in early 1991, is the newest on the island (par 72, 6,969 yards). Its wide, open fairways cover dozens of coastal hills. Greens fees are $85 to $115. At the 18-hole *Wailua* golf course (par 72, 6,585 yards), considered one of the best municipal courses in the country, greens fees range from $18 to $20 (phone: 245-2163). The charming 9-hole *Kukui o Lono Park* course is on a hill from which the ancient Hawaiians signaled fishermen along the south coast.

Hiking – Kauai is a hiker's dream. There are miles of well-marked trails in the state parks at Kokee, Waimea Canyon, and along the Na Pali Coast, threading through areas so wild and remote as to challenge the imagination as well as the body. Get maps of trails and good advice from the Division of State Parks (3060 Eiwa St., Lihue, HI 96766; phone: 241-3444), and from the Division of Forestry (same address and telephone number as the Division of State Parks), which maintains trails in forest reserves throughout the island. There are also three excellent guidebooks: *Hiking Kauai,* by Robert Smith (Hawaiian Outdoor Adventures Press, Huntington Beach, CA; $7.95), *Hawaiian Hiking Trails,* by Craig Chisholm (Fernglen Press, Lake Oswego, OR; $12.95), and *Kauai Hiking Trails,* also by Chisholm ($12.95). Each includes maps, descriptions, and pertinent commentary on both well-known and less-traveled trails. If the timing is right, you could join one of the *Sierra Club*'s twice-monthly outings. Call the *Sierra Club*'s Hawaii chapter in Oahu (phone: 946-8494) for local officers' numbers.

Horseback Riding – In Poipu, *CJM Country Stables* (phone: 742-6096) offers escorted rides along the South Shore's wild coastline. The 3-hour Breakfast Ride includes coast and valleys, with a beach breakfast ($70). Midday options are the 1-hour ($27) and 2-hour ($48) coastal rides. Private rides can also be arranged at $65 an hour (2-hour minimum). *Pooku Stables* (phone: 826-6777) in Princeville offers three daily rides, ranging from a 1-hour Valley Ride (daily at 2:15 PM; $25), a 2-hour ride that follows the ridgeline above Hanalei Valley ($46), and a 3-hour Waterfall/Picnic Ride (it requires a bit of hiking to get to the waterfall) that departs daily at 10:30 AM ($75). *Garden Island Ranch* offers both 1- and 2-hour scheduled rides ($35 an hour per person) in the vicinity of Waimea Canyon, as well as customized rides of 3 and 4 hours, priced at $125 to $150. Shorter rides are limited to 6 people, and longer rides are limited to 2 people. A 3-hour ride along the Waimea Canyon rim is offered in conjunction with the *Hyatt Regency,* which includes lunch. Departures are from the ranch corral (hotel pickups can be arranged at an additional charge). On Kaumuakii Hwy., just west of Waimea town (phone: 338-0052).

Polo – Sunday matches are held at the *Anini Beach Polo Field* at 3 PM, from March through August. Admission is $3 per person or $6 per car. Off Kaumaukii Hwy. (phone: 245-6731).

Snorkeling and Scuba Diving – The best beaches for these sports are Kee, Haena, and Anini in the north; Anahola and Moloaa in the east; and Palama, Sheraton Caves, and Koloa Landing in the south. Though most resort hotels and condominiums provide snorkeling equipment (fins, masks, and snorkel) gratis to guests, if you plan to do a lot of snorkeling, it's worthwhile to ask whether hotels offer this amenity. Otherwise, expect to pay between $5 and $15 a day for snorkeling equipment. Hotels will also arrange for snorkeling or scuba lessons. The *Waiohai* (phone: 742-9511) and *Sheraton Poipu Beach* (phone: 742-1661) hotels, for instance, give a free hour-long mini-scuba lesson in the hotel pool. Dive shops in Koloa, Wailua/Kapaa, and Hanalei feature shore and boat dives at the introductory, intermediate, and advanced levels, although most boat dives are limited to certified divers or to those involved in the 4- or 5-day certification courses that are available. One- and two-tank dives are featured at an average of $55 to $75. Certification courses range from $300 to $350, inclusive of dive time, equipment, and instruction books, while private certification courses range from $400 to $500. A 1½- to 3-hour snorkeling tour will cost about $55, including equipment, and half-day scuba dives cost around $70. Since prices vary so much on package courses, it pays to shop around.

In the Poipu area, *Kauai Sea Sports* at the *Sheraton* (phone: 742-1661) rents snorkel equipment; its Koloa office (phone: 742-9303) and *Fathom Five* (phone: 742-6991) both rent snorkel gear, as well as offering shore dives, instruction, and courses in diving certification. *Sea Sports* also rents Snuba, an apparatus with air supplied from an inflatable raft, for a scuba-like experience without the heavy gear. In the Wailua/Kapaa area, *Ocean Odyssey* (phone: 245-8681), *Get Wet* (phone: 822-4884), *Aquatics Kauai* (phone: 822-9213; 800-822-9422), and *Sea Sage Diving Center* (phone: 822-3841) all offer escorted dives and certification courses, the least expensive of which is *Odyssey*, with certification courses at $300 to $350. *Sea Sage* also rents scuba equipment and offers use of underwater scooters on dives for an additional $75. Dives and rentals can also be arranged through *Aloha Destinations* in Koloa (phone: 742-7548). In Hanalei, *Pedal & Paddle* (phone: 826-9069) and *Sand People* (phone: 826-6981) offer snorkeling equipment rentals. *Luana of Hawaii* (phone: 826-9195) provides personalized snorkeling excursions in Wailua/Kapaa or Hanalei Bay ($45).

Surfing – Tyros should stick to the beaches on the east and south side of the island: Anahola, Wailua (across from the *Coco Palms*), Kalapaki, and Poipu. All have steady, gentle waves just right for beginners. More experienced surfers may want to tackle the rougher waves at Kekaha and Polihale on the south coast or at Hanalei Bay and Anini on the north coast. Unless you're an exceptionally good surfer, however, don't surf the North Shore in winter. Rollers as high as 30 feet make even boats that call this home in other seasons take refuge in the south during winter.

You can rent surf and Boogie boards (a shorter version of the surfboard) from most big hotels and condominium resorts, or from *Kauai Sea Sports* (phone: 742-9303) in Koloa, *Pedal & Paddle* (phone: 826-9069) and *Sand People* (phone: 826-6981) in Hanalei, and *Sea Sage Diving Center* in Kapaa (phone: 822-3841), which also offers instruction. Surfboards rent for between $10 and $16 a day; Boogie boards, between $5 and $10. *Sea Sage* and *True Blue Charters* (phone for both: 246-6333), adjacent to the *Westin Kauai*, offer surfboard rentals, as do *Hanalei Surf Co.* (phone: 826-9000) and *Progressive Expressions*, with shops in Koloa (phone: 742-6041) and Kapaa (phone: 822-9211). *Progressive Expressions* also rents both Boogie boards and surfboards by the hour and day. If you're interested in lessons, contact the *Margo Oberg Surfing School* (phone: 742-6411), which operates on the grounds of the *Kiahuna Plantation* daily except Sunday. One-hour lessons ($40) include a half-hour board rental after the lesson.

Swimming and Sunning – To make it easier to enjoy its miles of beautiful beaches, Kauai County has built numerous beach parks that provide restrooms, showers, and picnicking facilities right next to the water. But there are plenty of other beaches unnamed on maps and unmarked on the road that would make for a lovely day of swimming or sunning, often in solitude.

Starting as far west as civilization will carry you is Polihale Beach — wide, long, bone white, and dry, a good swimming beach with state camping and picnicking facilities nearby. Kekaha Beach, in the southwestern corner of the island, and Waimea Beach, about 5 miles on, are also long, sunstruck beaches with parks. The most popular beach on the south coast is Poipu; "popular," on weekends, can mean crowded.

Since the east coast is the most developed, the beaches here are, naturally enough, the most populous. But they are also ample and easily accommodate the growing number of visitors. Kalapaki Beach, a graceful scimitar of sand on Nawiliwili Bay, is always bustling with both guests of the *Westin Kauai* and residents, who like the protected waters for windsurfing. No more than 15 minutes up the coast is Hanamaulu Beach, as serene as Kalapaki is lively, although swimming here is more difficult because of an offshore reef.

The coast from Lydgate State Park at Wailua River to Kapaa is one long series of beaches that vary from good to very good for swimming, sunning, or splashing around. Those along the several resorts at Wailua and Waipouli tend to get a fair number of bathers, but toward Kapaa Beach Park, roughly midway through the town of Kapaa, the bathers are fewer and, for the most part, local. Some 3 miles north of Kapaa is Anahola Beach, another excellent swimming beach with good picnicking facilities.

The north coast is studded with small and not-so-small beaches that aren't marked on maps and don't have the amenities offered by more popular spots. And although swimming on the north coast, especially in the winter, can be iffy (asking islanders is usually a good way to find out if a beach is safe for swimming), don't pass up those tempting jewels of beaches just because there's no sign pointing the way. Even the better-known North Shore beaches offer a quiet and seclusion few others can boast. Anini Beach, a few miles outside Kilauea; Hanalei Bay; Lumahai Beach, where *South Pacific* was filmed; Haena and Kee beaches, at the end of the road, are all splendid strips of sand, often with few fellow bathers around. Anini, Hanalei, and Haena have showers, restrooms, picnic tables, and barbecue pits. If it's a wilderness setting you want, hike the Kalalau Trail, to the otherwise inaccessible beaches of Na Pali — Hanakapiai, a beach that is often washed out in winter; Hanakoa; or Kalalau, where not only the beach but the whole valley is likely to be yours. Just be cautious when swimming in the coastal waters — that current can be rough, and there have been injuries.

Tennis – If it's a tennis vacation you're after, the best bets are *Kiahuna Plantation*, the *Westin Kauai, Hanalei Bay* resort, *Poipu Kai* resort, or the *Hyatt Regency Kauai* at Poipu, none of which charges guests court fees and have full-time professional staffs. Other resorts that have good tennis facilities, but do charge court fees (ranging from $5 to $10), are the *Waiohai, Coco Palms,* and the *Princeville* resort. In addition, many smaller hotels and condominiums have courts, and there are free public courts at Kapaa, Wailua, Lihue, Koloa, Kalaheo, Kekaha, Hanapepe, and Waimea.

Water Skiing – Despite several wide rivers on Kauai, this sport hasn't caught on here, at least with tourists. There's only one company, *Kauai Water Ski and Sports* (phone: 822-3574), that offers it, for $45 per half hour or $90 per hour (not per person, but for boat time), on the Wailua River. A single run down the river costs $25.

Windsurfing – *True Blue Charters* (adjacent to the *Westin Kauai;* phone: 246-6333), on *Kauai Lagoons* resort's Kalapaki Beach, offers windsurfing rentals at $15 an hour. Lessons are also available. *Hanalei Sailboards* (phone: 826-9000) offers hourly or day rentals (surfboards for $12 to $15, snorkel gear for $8, and Boogie boards for $7 to $10), and lessons. Three-hour sessions are available for beginning, intermediate, and advanced windsurfers for $60.

AROUND THE ISLAND

The westernmost of the major Hawaiian islands, Kauai looks like a circle drawn by a small child, bulging or concave in spots, but essentially round. Lihue, the county seat and the point of arrival for most island visitors, is on the southeast coast, about 60 miles from Oahu, Kauai's nearest neighbor besides the private island of Niihau. Midway up the east coast is the resort area of Wailua/Kapaa. To the north are the *Princeville* resort and historic Hanalei, the wettest and greenest part of the island, and to the northwest, the breathtaking Na Pali Coast. Poipu, a popular and growing resort, sits along the island's sunny south coast; and running up the dry west side of the island are long stretches of beach and the 10-mile-long Waimea Canyon.

Lihue

It's an indication of Kauai's slow pace that Lihue, a populated crossroads on the southeast coast, is the commercial and governing center of the island. With some 6,000 people calling it home, it's just a larger version of the plantation it was to begin with, although a restoration of portions of the town, new housing, and a shopping center on the outskirts of town have given it a more contemporary look. The sugar mill still processes cane on the outskirts of town. Government offices, a small museum, and the county court are clustered around the little square that is the heart of "downtown." Nawiliwili, the island's main harbor, is 2 miles distant, and Kalapaki Beach provides the setting for the extravagant *Westin Kauai,* located at the *Kauai Lagoons* resort. Lihue is also the site of the island's main commercial airport, so most travelers see some of the town even though their destination is one of the resorts up or down the coast. Lihue offers a funky kind of charm, and it has some interesting sights and several good restaurants.

Kauai Museum – The museum has a permanent natural history collection as well as changing exhibits on current art and culture and a good gift and book shop. There's also a 10-minute videocassette about Kauai at the museum that visitors can view, which is a good way to get your bearings before exploring the island yourself. Open Mondays through Fridays 9 AM to 4:30 PM, Saturdays 9 AM to 1 PM. Adult admission, $3; children under 18 free, when accompanied by an adult. 4428 Rice St. (phone: 245-6931).

Grove Farm Homestead – Founded as a sugarcane plantation in 1864 by the son of a Hanalei missionary family, *Grove Farm* was a flourishing plantation for three-quarters of a century. (The company is still in existence, but moved from this site in the 1930s.) Now the farm — the main house, plantation office, workers' cottages and various outbuildings, orchards, gardens, and pastures — is a carefully preserved museum of early plantation life. The 2-hour tour, conducted by well-informed guides and limited to two or three groups of six (depending on how many guides are available), often sells out, so it's a good idea to call or write for a reservation in advance (PO Box 1631, Lihue, Kauai, HI 96766; phone: 245-3202). One bit of advice to parents: This isn't the place to bring small children since you're on the move the whole 2 hours of the tour. Open Mondays, Wednesdays, and Thursdays, with tours starting at 10 AM and 1 PM. Admission for adults, $3; for children between 5 and 12 years old, $1. Nawiliwili Rd.

Nawiliwili Bay – Well-protected Nawiliwili Bay is one of two deepwater harbors on the island (Port Allen on Hanapepe Bay is the other). A lot of cane is shipped from here, and many fishing and pleasure boats call this home. At the ocean end of the harbor are beautiful Kalapaki Beach and Kalapaki Beach Park. Farther inland, at the mouth of the Huleia Stream, is Niumalu Beach Park.

Alakoko (or Menehune) Fishpond – The pond, off Hulemalu Road to Nawiliwili Bay, is a portion of the Huleia Stream walled off by a 900-foot-long stone wall to create a fishpond. It's nothing much to look at; the interest in it is mostly generated by the legend that it was constructed by the semi-mythical Menehune, who once lived on the island. As the lore has it, the Menehune, like Irish leprechauns, were a race of tiny people possessing supernatural powers and who, in addition, were prodigious workers capable of building the likes of the Alakoko pond in a single night. More likely, the Menehune were the Marquesans, the first inhabitants of Hawaii, who were conquered by the later Tahitians and put to work serving them. (The Tahitian word for "commoner" is very similar to Menehune.)

Wailua Falls – Just north of Lihue is the Maalo Road, which will take you to Wailua Falls, on the southern branch of the river by the same name. The twin falls are lovely to look at, and, for the hardy, there's a rather steep trail down to the pool at the bottom. For the less adventurous, a more accessible pool is some 200 yards beyond the falls.

Kilohana Estate – Standing on some 35 acres of landscaped grounds is the *Wilcox House,* renovated to look as it did when it was built in 1935 and housing collections of Oceanic and Hawaiian artifacts. There is also a restored section of sugar plantation homes, displays, a selection of shops, a restaurant, and a 20-minute carriage ride around the grounds pulled by powerful Clydesdales. Off Rte. 50, on the outskirts of Lihue (phone: 245-5608).

Kauai Lagoons/Westin Kauai – With hundreds of landscaped acres, oceanside lagoons, extravagant displays of art, mosaic beachside promenade, pools, and colonnades more reminiscent of Las Vegas than Hawaii, the *Kauai Lagoons* resort and its *Westin Kauai* flagship hotel (phone: 245-5050) are attractions in their own right. Elegant carriages drawn by Clydesdales traverse miles of trails, while canolas (outrigger canoe/gondola hybrids) and a fleet of seven mahogany launches make 45-minute tours ($14) of the lagoons, whose small islands are home to kangaroos, wallabies, and monkeys. Both make stops at the resort's lagoonside shopping village, health spa, and restaurants. If you're headed to one of these lagoonside facilities rather than just sightseeing, the launch ride is complimentary.

SHOPPING: Shopping in Lihue improved considerably with the addition of the *Kukui Grove Center* on Route 50 just south of town. With *Liberty House, Sears, Woolworth, Long's Drugs* (for Kauai's best buy on film), *Waldenbooks,* and a collection of shops and restaurants, it's a good place to go for alohawear, beach clothes and supplies, and incidentals. Among the special shops in *Kukui Grove Center* are the following:

Alexandra Christian – Women's fashions, from casual to dressy. Discounts on some items found at higher prices at Kauai's resort shops. *Kukui Grove Center* (phone: 246-8806).

Crazy Shirts – One of the ubiquitous T-shirt shops in this chain *Anchor Cove* (phone: 245-7073).

Foot Locker – Running gear that didn't get packed can be purchased here. *Kukui Grove Center* (phone: 245-7162).

Great Gourmet! – For cooks — gourmet or otherwise — there's quality kitchenware and a good selection of cheeses, specialty foods, and California wines. *Kukui Grove Center* (phone: 245-7162).

Jewelry Box – A surprisingly large and tempting selection of gold and silver jewelry. Kilohana (phone: 245-3445).

Kahn Galleries – Fine art ranging from sculpture to paintings is the big draw here. In *Anchor Cove,* adjacent to the *Kauai Lagoons* resort (phone: 245-5397).

Kapaia Stitchery – Just to the east of Lihue in the once-upon-a-time town of Kapaia (you'll miss it if you take the airport bypass road), it features Hawaiian prints and patchwork quilts, cotton kimonos, fabric, and needlework. On the old Kuhio Hwy. (phone: 245-2281).

Kilohana Galleries – Specializing in laser-etched scrimshaw and Niihau shell jewelry. Kilohana, just off Hwy. 50 (phone: 245-9352).

Robyn Buntin's Oriental Gallery – Japanese and Chinese antiques, including kimonos, lacquerware, porcelain bowls, and sculpture, all dazzle the eye here. Kilohana (phone: 245-4922).

Stones at Kilohana – Affiliated with *Stones Gallery* at *Kukui Grove Center,* it features Hawaiian arts and crafts. Kilohana, just off Hwy. 50 (phone: 245-6684).

Stones Gallery – Displays the best of contemporary Hawaiian art — fine silkscreens, etchings, pastels, and oils from artists all over the state. *Kukui Grove Center* (phone: 245-6653).

Hanamaulu offers a cluster of old plantation-style buildings that house a variety of shops and eateries. Don't take the new bypass that heads from the airport toward Kapaa and Hanalei if you want to go to Kapaia and Hanamaulu; take the old road instead.

WESTIN KAUAI

The shops at the *Westin Kauai,* as suits this extravagant showplace, make for interesting browsing and may even tempt a purchase or two, although the prices may inspire caution. In addition to the hotel shops, the resort also features a lagoonside commercial theme village, *Fashion Landing,* that focuses on clothing and accessories. The village was designed as a visitor attraction in its own right, and can be reached by boat, horse-drawn carriage, or resort limousine. Adjacent to the resort, on Nawiliwili Harbor, are the recently opened shops and restaurant of the *Anchor Cove* commercial complex.

Carol & Mary – High-fashion clothing and accessories for women. *Fashion Landing* (phone: 245-7289).

Chapman's – Contemporary menswear, including European-style shirts fashioned in Balinese fabrics. *Fashion Landing* (phone: 246-4420).

DFS Cosmetics – A full selection of beauty aides from Lancôme, Yves Saint Laurent, Givenchy, and others. *Fashion Landing* (phone: 245-6884).

Elephant Walk – An eclectic grouping of avant-garde jewelry, ceramics, and marvelous Kosage kaleidoscopes. *Westin Kauai* lobby (phone: 245-9398).

Giorgio Armani – The latest styles from Italy are available at this world-renowned designer's shop. *Fashion Landing* (phone: 245-7301).

Hemmeter Collection – A fine selection of well-priced originals and high-quality reproductions of classic decor pieces for home and garden. *Westin Kauai* lobby (phone: 246-8896) and at nearby *Kilohana Plantation* (phone: 245-6634).

Kula Bay Tropical Clothing – An upscale *Banana Republic*–style logo shop. *Fashion Landing* (phone: 246-9492).

Loewe – High fashion for women with a European flair. *Fashion Landing* (phone: 245-8638).

Lorenzi of Italy – Exotic leather accessories, made from ostrich, alligator, lizard, and buffalo, at prices bound to raise eyebrows. *Fashion Landing* (phone: 245-6646).

Louis Vuitton – The famous name — and equally famous monogram — appears on all the high-quality leather goods on display here. *Fashion Landing* (phone: 245-7025).

Pua Lani Kauai – Distinctive handbags, accessories, and women's fashions. *Westin Kauai* lobby (phone: 245-8784).

NIGHTLIFE: Nawiliwili is the headquarters for nightlife in the Lihue area. *Club Jetty* (phone: 245-4970), on the wharf, is the liveliest spot, with a bar popular with the local folks, a restaurant, and a disco with dancing until 4 AM Wednesdays through Saturdays. At the *Westin Kauai,* the *Colonnade Lounge* (phone: 245-5050) — where the music is Hawaiian — is open from 8 to 11 PM nightly, with a trio on weekends and a piano bar on Tuesdays, Wednesdays, and Thursdays. Check out the *Kauai Lagoon* resort's *Inn on the Cliffs* (phone: 245-5054) for live jazz Tuesdays through Saturdays.

CHECKING IN: The only hotel worth mentioning in Lihue is the *Westin Kauai.* It took several hundred million dollars to transform the old *Kauai Surf* into one of Hawaii's most extravagant resort properties, an 849-room blend of eclectic elegance and contemporary glitz. The 1,400-foot beachfront is backed by landscaped lagoons and a Copacabana-style mosaic promenade. Facilities include a large, half-acre swimming pool complete with waterfalls and 5 Jacuzzis, 2 golf courses, an 11-court tennis complex (plus a 1,000-seat stadium court), stables, a full health spa (containing everything from Nautilus equipment to racquetball courts, saunas and massages), a Japanese garden, a wedding chapel on an island in a lagoon, and a theme shopping village (jewelry and fashion). Though smallish and less impressive than the public areas, the guestrooms are nicely furnished, using pastels and white to create a tropical feel. There are also several topnotch restaurants (see *Eating Out*). While there's plenty of space to wander about, this is not your quiet Kauai hideaway; it tries to operate at a low-key level, but the decor clearly has been designed for high-powered impact. With rates that start at about $200 a night, it is clearly pitched toward an affluent trade and a healthy proportion of convention business. Glitz is king here, and it's hard to find much of authentic Hawaii in these halls. Royal Beach Club accommodations include concierge service and many extras and upgrades. *Kauai Lagoons* resort, *Westin Kauai,* Lihue, HI 96766 (phone: 245-5050; 800-228-3000). Expensive.

EATING OUT: A typical dinner tab in Lihue tends to be substantial, though there are some noteworthy exceptions. For a meal for two, excluding wine, tip, and drinks, expect to pay around $80 or more in the restaurant listed as very expensive, $50 in those noted as expensive, $30 to $45 in a moderate place, and under $25 in an inexpensive eating place. All telephone numbers are in the 808 area code unless otherwise indicated.

Inn on the Cliffs – Within the stylish decor, seafood and the day's catch are the house specialties, with a wide variety of familiar and innovative combinations from which to choose. Diners twirl their forks while they enjoy views of Nawiliwili Bay and the *Westin Kauai.* Open daily for lunch and dinner. Reservations advised. At the *Kauai Lagoons Resort* (phone: 245-5050). Expensive.

Gaylord's – Dining is alfresco, on the verandah facing the grassy lawn that is the back yard of Kilohana, the restored Wilcox mansion. Views of Kauai's central core of mountains add to the feeling of *la dolce vita.* Sunday brunch is particularly pleasant. Dinner choices include fresh lamb, venison, veal, and chicken stuffed with prawns and cream cheese — overpriced for the quality. Dinner from 5 to 9:30 PM. Reservations necessary. On Kaumualii Hwy., 2 miles south of Lihue toward Poipu (phone: 245-9593). Expensive to moderate.

Sharky's – Lest anyone wonder about the type of food served here, the live shark in the tank that serves as a centerpiece to this *Kauai Lagoons* eatery leaves no doubt that this is a place for fish and seafood. The appealing decor is complemented by an innovative mix of indoor and outdoor seating. Open for dinner daily. Reservations advised. In the *Kauai Lagoons Resort* complex (phone: 246-4470). Expensive to moderate.

Tempura Garden – An attractive Japanese garden, complete with waterfalls, a rock garden, and live cranes, creates a serene atmosphere in keeping with the menu, which features tempura, sushi, and sashimi, all served Kyoto-style. There's table seating as well as sushi and tempura bars. Open daily for dinner. Reservations advised. On the grounds of the *Westin Kauai* (phone: 245-5050). Expensive to moderate.

Dukes – The owners of *Kimo's* in Lahaina, Maui, have made this a very Hawaiian place. In the boathouse of the *Westin Kauai,* it has a beachfront setting that suits a distinctive collection of racing canoes and paddling memorabilia. The menu is basic and casual, the food good. Downstairs, the restaurant's *Kau Kau Grill* serves cocktails and light meals from 4 PM to midnight. Open daily. Reservations advised. *Westin Kauai* (phone: 246-9599). Moderate.

JJ's Broiler – Long the leading restaurant of its kind on Kauai, its kitchen serves steaks, steaks, and more steaks — plus the catch of the day, simply broiled. Dinner only, 5 to 9:30 PM. Reservations for six or more necessary. In the *Anchor Cove* shopping complex on Nawiliwili Harbor, adjacent to the *Westin Kauai* (phone: 246-4422). Moderate.

Portofino Café – If the courteous and attentive service don't sway you, then the excellent northern Italian specialties will. Dishes include carpaccio and antipasti appetizers and seafood pasta, as well as rabbit, veal, eggplant, and shrimp prepared with flair. There is indoor and alfresco seating. Open for lunch on weekdays from 11 AM to 2:30 PM; dinner daily from 5 to 10 PM. Reservations advised. On the second floor of the *Pacific Ocean Plaza,* across from the *Kauai Lagoons Resort* (phone: 245-2121). Moderate.

Prince Bill's – Tiled floors, blond wood, and soothing pastels create a relaxing setting that is enhanced by panoramic views of Kalapaki Beach and Nawiliwili Harbor. The menu features northern Italian specialties such as *fettuccine alla pescatore* (shrimp, scallops, and mussels in a garlic cream sauce), veal with porcini mushrooms, and breast of chicken with prosciutto and Bel Paese cheese, as well as deliciously marinated tenderloin. Open daily. Reservations advised. Atop the Surf Tower of the *Westin Kauai* (phone: 245-5050). Moderate.

Barbecue Inn – Halfway down what looks like a deserted street, this popular place is short on atmosphere but offers an international menu where yakitori rubs elbows with knockwurst and down-home favorites like pot roast. The food is tasty, and the low price includes everything — soup, vegetables, drinks, and dessert. Open for breakfast, lunch, and dinner; closed Sundays. Reservations unnecessary. 2982 Kress St., Lihue (phone: 245-2921). Inexpensive.

Eggbert's – Back when it was known as the *Egg and I,* this eatery served omelettes only. Now it has added fish, beef, chicken, and pork dishes to its menu and stays open for all three meals. Still, what you come for are the omelettes, which you can get in an almost endless combination of ingredients. Open daily until 3 PM. Reservations advised. 4481 Rice St., Lihue (phone: 245-9025). Inexpensive.

Hamura Saimin – Perfect for those tired of the tourist glitz and ready to experience Kauai as a local. The steaming bowls of noodles and broth are best appreciated when extras like ham, beef, egg, and a dab of hot mustard are added. All the more authentic for being located in the heart of Lihue's old shopping district. Open daily. No reservations. 2956 Kress St. (phone: 245-3271). Inexpensive.

Kiibo – Japanese atmosphere and food: tempura, teriyaki, sukiyaki, and sushi. Open daily except Sundays for lunch and dinner. Reservations unnecessary. 2991 Umi St. (phone: 245-2650). Inexpensive.

Yokuzuna Ramen – If you like *ramen* (hot Japanese noodles cooked in shrimp, chicken, or beef broth), this is the place. Try their take-out lunches if it's a sushi or *bento* (a Japanese box lunch) picnic you've got in mind. Open daily, 10 AM to 10 PM. No reservations. 4444 Rice St. (phone: 246-1008). Inexpensive.

Hanamaulu, Wailua, and Kapaa: East Kauai's Coconut Coast

Hawaii's royalty, the *alii,* claimed Wailua, midway along the east coast, as their own. It had everything those of regal temperament and expectations could want: a superb beach to indulge their love of sunning and surfing, a stately river that winds through tropical forests hiding grottoes and waterfalls, and dependable weather all year. It wasn't beset by the rain and angry seas that winter brought to the north; nor did it bake in summer, as the south coast did. To the pleasures that nature bestowed, the *alii* added a few of their own. They dug freshwater lagoons to sweeten and fatten up their fish and planted magnificent groves of towering coconut palms. And they kept it all to themselves. Commoners were forbidden, on pain of death, to enter Wailua except at the *alii*'s pleasure.

In these democratic times, Wailua is a gracious host to thousands of commoners a year. There's still much of old Hawaii here, if not in buildings, then in legend, and, not surprisingly, the site attracts a fair number of visitors. Happily, the resorts that have grown up around Wailua have used the natural beauty that drew royalty here to good advantage.

The town of Kapaa, Kauai's second-largest, is adjacent to Wailua. In recent years they've kind of grown together by way of small shopping malls and development along the Kuhio Highway. Kapaa has some fairly good restaurants, clothing and dive shops, and a stretch of condominiums that front its several miles of white sand beach.

Lydgate State Park – At the mouth of the Wailua River, this park is a good place to start a tour of the area's historical sites. Here are the remains of an ancient place of refuge, where Hawaiians sentenced to death for breaking one of the many *kapus* could find sanctuary and where women and children sought safety during war. Nearby is one of the many *heiaus* (temples) along the river, Hikina O Kala, which, like the place of refuge, is now a low stone wall enclosing a coconut grove.

Holoholoku Heiau – Royal mothers traveled to this important *heiau* a mile or so up the north bank of the river to give birth and thereby ensure the royalty of the child. All that's left of the old temple is the birthstone, against which women in labor leaned; the bellstone, which rang to announce the birth of another royal Hawaiian; and a more ominous relic of old Hawaii, a large stone upon which human sacrifices reputedly were made.

Coconut Grove at Coco Palms – Planted in the mid-1800s by a German doctor who wanted to start a coconut plantation, now the center of one of Hawaii's most famous resorts, this serene grove of towering palms has the feel of a public garden, an impression the hotel, happily, does nothing to discourage. Palms have a relatively short life span — about 100 years — and as the original trees grow old, the *Coco Palms* hotel plants replacements in the names of its many illustrious guests. The plaques identifying the trees' namesakes are a record of recent Hawaiian history. In addition to Hawaiian politicians, writers, athletes, and philanthropists, there are representatives of corporate Hawaii. And there are a few distinguished *haoles* too, such as writer James Michener and crooner Bing Crosby, who earned honorary citizenship for their fondness for the islands.

Wailua River State Park – A 2½-mile drive up Route 580 leads to Opaekaa Falls and the Wailua River State Park. Continue along Route 580 till it ends, another 3 miles or so, and you'll come to the Keahua Arboretum. Hike along here (the Division of Forestry has a leaflet identifying the tree plantings), picnic, and swim in a secluded swimming hole.

Smith's Tropical Paradise – Smith's is a cross between a garden and a cultural center. Scattered throughout its 23-acre tropical garden are full-scale models of Polynesian, Filipino, and Japanese villages, complete with ducks and chickens — visit them on a self-guided walking tour or via a narrated tram tour. A luau, dance, and musical revue, which focuses on the cultural legacy of Polynesia, are offered Mondays through Fridays ($45). Admission to the park is $5; it's open daily from 8:30 AM to 4 PM. Adjacent to Wailua Boat Marina (phone: 822-4654).

Opaekaa Falls – While this isn't one of one Kauai's largest waterfalls, it is the most easily accessible and certainly lovely. Just 2 miles inland from the Kuhio Highway are several scenic lookouts that offer a view of the falls as well as Wailua River and the surrounding mountains.

Fern Grotto – A cave draped with ferns, this popular attraction is incontestably beautiful. But to get here you have to endure a 20-minute boat ride ($10) during which you're relentlessly entertained with corny tourist jokes. And once there, you share this lovely spot with literally hundreds of others, since two boats leave every half hour. If you *must* go, take the very first cruise and carry a cane so you'll have an excuse to lag behind the crowds. Boats leave from Wailua Marina. Contact *Smith's Boat Tours* (phone: 822-4111) or *Waialeale Boat Tours* (phone: 822-4908).

Kamokila Hawaiian Village – Located on a bend of the Wailua River and accessible via a road adjacent to the Opaekaa Falls lookout, this cluster of Hawaiian grass houses, display areas, and taro patches provides a glimpse of the ancient Polynesian lifestyle, authentically replicated by staff. This reconstruction is near the site of the ruins of an old Hawaiian village. You can either drive to the riverside village site or take a boat from the Wailua Marina. Admission is $5 or $8, respectively, including the boat ride. Plans are in the making for stops by boats en route to and from the Fern Grotto. Open 9 AM to 4 PM; closed Sundays (phone: 822-1192).

Kauai Village Museum – This small charmer, a labor of love by owner Serge King, contains exhibits of the arts, crafts, history, and culture of Hawaii, as well as artifacts from Polynesia. After viewing, visit the adjacent shops for a good selection of gifts and Hawaiian souvenirs. *Kauai Village Center,* 4-831 Kuhio Hwy., Kapaa (phone: 822-9272).

Coconut Plantation – Between Wailua and Kapaa at Waipouli is the Coconut Plantation, a collection of several resort hotels sharing a rocky beach, a shopping center called the *Market Place,* and a number of restaurants ranging from fast-food noodle shops to leisurely dining spots.

SHOPPING: A full selection of shops can be found at the *Market Place* at Coconut Plantation. There's a wide selection of resortwear, jewelry, scrimshaw, wooden bowls, wicker, pottery, other island crafts, and plenty of souvenirs and T-shirts, not to mention 1-hour photo service. Numerous shops and restaurants are also to be found in small shopping malls along the highway that provide residents with supermarkets, services, and such standards as *Pizza Hut, Sizzler,* and *McDonald's*. The town of Kapaa has been undergoing a commercial revival, with the restoration of many of its early-20th-century buildings attracting a variety of crafts shops.

Art to Wear – A broad selection of hand-painted clothing, mostly for women and children. Artists work on projects at the adjacent studio. 1435 Kuhio Hwy., Kapaa (phone: 822-1125).

Classical Glass – Besides great browsing, there are demonstrations by glass workers Meg and John. Closed Sundays and Mondays. 4523 Niu St., Kapaa (phone: 822-5515).

Clear Path – The theme is crystals, with some interesting browsing — or buying — for the metaphysically inclined. 1596 Kuhio Hwy., Kapaa (phone: 822-2745)

For Your Eyes Only – Everything you need to shade your eyes from the tropical sun, and fashionably. Coconut Plantation (phone: 822-5922).

Hot Rocket – Hip and flashy describes much of the casual clothing (mostly shirts and shorts) shown here. 4-1354 Kuhio Hwy. (phone: 822-7848).

Island Images – The name says it all. Lithographs, acrylics, and watercolors are the primary media of the local artists on display. At the *Market Place* (phone: 822-3636).

Jim Saylor Jewelers – One of Kauai's more innovative jewelry makers, this shop carries distinctive designs for both men and women. 1318 Kuhio Hwy., Kapaa (phone: 822-3591).

Kahn Gallery – A real find, with beautifully — and locally — made ceramics, woodwork, jewelry (including an excellent selection of Niihau shell necklaces), lithographs, paintings, and much more. Coconut Plantation (phone: 822-4277).

Lady Jane's Company – An interesting selection of quality Hawaiian crafts, including some particularly noteworthy hand-crafted wood bowls. 3-4684 Kuhio Hwy., near Hanamaulu (phone: 245-1814).

Nighten' Gales – Fine handicrafts are imported, mainly from Indonesia: batiks, woven Borneo bags, shell work, and more. 4-1413 Kuhio Hwy., Kapaa (phone: 822-3729).

The Only Show in Town – It's pleasant to browse among the antiques and curiosities here, which include Hawaii's best selection of old bottles. On Kuhio Hwy., just at the bridge on the Hanalei side of Kapaa (phone: 822-1442).

Plantation Stitchery – This small craft shop carries a wide selection of needlecraft supplies and some lovely all-cotton Hawaiian fabrics at about $6 a yard and up. Coconut Plantation (phone: 822-3570).

Progressive Expressions – All kinds of swimwear and water-related gear. 4-1354 Kuhio Hwy., Kapaa (phone: 822-9211).

Tahiti Imports – Here's Kauai's best selection of silk-screened fabrics with a South Seas flavor, including a nice collection of pareos (cloth wraps). Coconut Plantation (phone: 822-9342).

Tropical Tantrum – The largest of three family-owned shops (the others are in Hanapepe and Hanalei) that specialize in hand-painted clothing for men, women, and children, some of it quite tasteful. 4-1296 Kuhio Hwy., Kapaa (phone: 822-1882).

Wyland Collection – Artist Wyland, who uses only his last name professionally, shows his own paintings, as well as the work of other artists. His claim to fame, the environmentally conscious Whaling Wall murals (there are currently 32 around the world), are vast panels covered with life-size whales. *Kauai Village Shopping Center,* 4-831 Kuhio Hwy., Kapaa (phone: 822-2888).

NIGHTLIFE: For Polynesian entertainment there is a nightly luau ($45) at the *Kauai Coconut Beach* (closed Mondays; phone: 822-3455), and Mondays through Fridays at *Smith's Tropical Paradise* (phone: 822-4654). All feature typical Hawaiian foods (kalua pig, lomilomi salmon, and poi) plus a musical revue including the dances of the various Pacific island groups. The *Coconut Beach* luau is the most popular. There is also a Polynesian revue following family-style dining Tuesdays, Fridays, and Saturdays, from 8:30 to 11:30 PM at the *Coco Palms Lagoon* dining room (phone: 822-4921). Cost is $5 if you're also having dinner, $10 (which includes two drinks) if you're not. The menu is more traditionally American here, highlighting catch of the day and prime ribs for those anxious to steer clear of more exotic culinary offerings. The *Aston Kauai* resort (phone: 245-3931) also features a prime ribs buffet and dinner show of Polynesian music and dance on Mondays, Wednesdays, and Fridays from 7 to 8 PM ($18). On Tuesdays and Saturdays it's a prime ribs/seafood buffet and contemporary Hawaiian entertainment (7:30 to 8:30 PM) for $25.

Dance action centers on the *Kauai Hilton*'s *Gilligan's* (phone: 245-1955), where disco reigns 8 PM to 2 AM weekdays, 8 PM to 4 AM weekends. There's a nightly Comedy Show ($12 or $23, including dinner) from 8:30 to 10 PM, followed by dancing, with live music.

The *Kauai Coconut Beach* features listening music from 8:30 to 11:30 PM nightly in its *Cook's Landing* restaurant (phone: 822-3455). There's Hawaiian and contemporary music nightly from 4 to 9:30 PM at the *Terrace Lounge* at the *Coco Palms* (phone: 822-4921), which also occasionally plays host to Honolulu headliners.

And if you're in the mood for a film, check the schedule at the *Plantation Cinema* (phone: 822-9391).

CHECKING IN: For accommodations listed here, $150 and above for two people is considered expensive, $75 to $145 moderate, and less than $70 inexpensive. These figures are based on the tariffs for a typical double hotel room or 1-bedroom condominium apartment. All telephone numbers are in the 808 area code unless otherwise indicated.

Aston Kauai – Among the most spacious hotel accommodations on Kauai, its 242 rooms are tastefully decorated in pastel hues with rattan furniture; the cabana units feature kitchenettes. Facilities include a pool, 2 tennis courts, restaurants, and a magnificent beachfront setting backed by 10 acres of landscaped grounds. Located at the mouth of the Wailua River. 3-5920 Kuhio Hwy. (phone: 245-3931; 800-922-7866). Expensive to moderate.

Kauai Coconut Beach – A comfortable property on Waipouli Beach (better for beachcombing than swimming, thanks to the rocky shore break), it has a white-washed atrium lobby, elevated walkways, and serried terraces. The grounds, which include a nice stretch of beachfront, are lovely. Its luau is one of Kauai's most popular. Coconut Plantation (phone: 822-3455; 800-325-3535). Expensive to moderate.

Kauai Hilton – This 350-room property features a lovely beachfront setting, several restaurants, including *Midori,* which serves continental and Japanese dishes, and a 3-section pool complete with waterfalls, Jacuzzis, and sauna. Another plus is its central location along miles of undeveloped beach. Hanamaulu (phone: 245-1955; 800-445-8667). Expensive to moderate.

Lae Nani – This low-rise luxury condominium complex faces the coast, with tidal pools and a private stretch of beach. The oceanfront pool is surrounded by grassy lawns and landscaped grounds. On the Wailua beachfront (phone: 822-4938; 800-367-6046). Expensive to moderate.

Coco Palms – On the royal grounds of the *alii* is the hotel that made Wailua a resort destination. It has been the scene of numerous movies (*Blue Hawaii* and *Sadie Thompson* among them) and television shows ("Fantasy Island"), and has played host to celebrities of every rank. It's such an institution that even if you're not staying here you should at least visit. The theme is Polynesian Hawaii, and every night Hawaiian runners race through the coconut grove and across the three lovely lagoons in an elaborate torch-lighting ceremony. As for the rooms, some are tastefully decorated in tropical pastels, and others are a bit more garish in bright blues and greens. There's little that this place doesn't offer in the way of activities: tennis, swimming (3 pools, and the beach is just across the street), croquet, billiards, fishing, a museum, a zoo, and, just in case you need it, a thatch-roofed wedding chapel amid the coconut trees. Wailua (phone: 822-4921; 800-542-2626). Moderate.

Kauai Beachboy – Managed by Aston Resorts, this is a quiet oasis in the middle of Kauai's busiest tourist center. The courtyard opening onto the beach encloses a pool, shuffleboard, volleyball, and tennis courts. There's a nearby 18-hole golf course. The beach is lovely; the rooms, good-size and well kept, each with a view of the beach from a private balcony. Coconut Plantation (phone: 822-3441). Moderate.

Plantation Hale – This pleasant little condominium property in the Coconut Plantation complex joined the Outrigger chain in 1990. Just a short walk from the beach, its large 1-bedroom, 1-bath suites include a full kitchen and terrace and sleep up to four. There are 3 swimming pools and a volleyball court on the property. Coconut Plantation (phone: 822-4941; 800-367-5170). Moderate.

Wailua Bay View Apartments – On a slight rise over Wailua Beach and with easy access down, this small complex couldn't be better located. The 1-bedroom apartments, with full kitchen and balconies, all face the beach. Each unit has a washer and dryer, and room rates include a rental car. Weekly and monthly rates available. Wailua (phone: 822-3651). Moderate.

EATING OUT: For a meal for two, excluding wine, tips, and drinks, expect to pay around $70 in a place listed as expensive, between $30 and $65 in moderate, and about $20 (sometimes less) in inexpensive. All telephone numbers are in the 808 area code unless otherwise indicated.

Kintaro – A typical Tokyo blend of light wood, white rice paper shoji screens, and black trim provides a comfortable setting. The food is well prepared, with nightly specials in addition to teriyaki, tempura, and sushi standards. The fact that this place has more than doubled in size since opening several years ago attests to its popularity with both residents and visitors. Open for dinner from 5:30 to 9:30 PM. Closed Sundays. Reservations advised. 4-370 Kuhio Hwy. (phone: 822-3341). Expensive to moderate.

A Pacific Café – High praise for the nouvelle cuisine menu prepared by chef Jean Marie Josselin. Delicate sauces and unexpected garnishes make for memorable meals, including lemon chicken soup with barbecue chicken wonton, steamed shrimp and chicken Siu Mai with teriyaki dip, and grilled Australian lamb served with tamarind plum sauce. Avant-garde decor and an eclectic crowd help to make this one of Kauai's more interesting eateries. Open nightly for dinner from 5:30 to 10 PM. Reservations advised. *Kauai Village Shopping Center,* 4-831 Kuhio Hwy., Kapaa (phone: 822-0013). Expensive to moderate.

Sea Shell – An open pavilion right on Wailua Beach, this *Coco Palms* restaurant has a good selection of seafood specialties and steaks. Open daily for dinner only from 5:30 to 9 PM. Reservations advised. *Coco Palms,* Wailua (phone: 822-3632). Expensive to moderate.

Bull Shed – As you might guess, this eatery, a little north of Coconut Plantation, specializes in beef and prime ribs, but it also offers teriyaki chicken and the seafood catch of the day. The setting on the water and tropical decor are also nice. Open daily for dinner only from 5:30 to 10 PM. Reservations advised for groups of six or more. 796 Kuhio Hwy. (phone: 822-3791). Moderate.

Dragon Inn – Kauai's best Chinese restaurant specializes in Szechuan cooking. Dinner Tuesdays through Sundays from 4:30 to 9:30 PM; lunch Tuesdays through Saturdays 11 AM to 2 PM. Reservations advised. In Waipuoli Plaza (phone: 822-3788). Moderate.

Hanamaulu Café – From the highway, this place doesn't look like anything special, but just head through the main room, which is pleasant enough, and you'll find shoji-screened rooms, tatami mats and on-the-floor seating, plus a lovely garden landscaped around a free-flowing brook and ponds. The food is good, featuring Japanese and Chinese specialties. It's a pleasant place to spend a few hours over dinner. Open for lunch from 11 AM to 1 PM and dinner from 4:30 to 9 PM Tuesdays through Fridays; dinner only on Saturdays and Sundays. Reservations advised. 3-4291 Kuhio Hwy. (phone: 245-2511). Moderate to inexpensive.

Jimmy's Grill – Sand on the floor and a surfer decor create an upbeat — if somewhat noisy — setting for dinners of ribs, fresh island fish, homemade pasta, and hamburgers. Open daily for lunch from 11:30 AM to 3 PM, and dinner from 5:30 to 10 PM. Reservations unnecessary. 4-1354 Kuhio Hwy., in the center of Kapaa (phone: 822-7000). Moderate to inexpensive.

The King And I – Indisputably one of the best Thai food places on Kauai, it specializes in spring rolls, curries, eggplant, chicken, and shrimp. Open daily for dinner; open for lunch weekdays, except Wednesdays, 11 AM to 2 PM. Reservations advised. Off Kuhio Hwy. in Waipuoli Plaza (phone: 822-1642). Moderate to inexpensive.

Kountry Kitchen – This small unpretentious restaurant in Kapaa serves tasty food (breakfast, lunch, and dinner) in plentiful proportions. Breakfast is the best bet. Try the omelettes. Open daily from 6 AM to 2:30 PM for breakfast; 5 to 8:30 for dinner. No reservations. 1485 Kuhio Hwy., Kapaa (phone: 822-3511). Moderate to inexpensive.

Makai Mediterranean – Despite the incurably rustic setting, the menu selections are quite good. Specialties include ginger chicken, moussaka, gyros, and chicken in phyllo pastry and garlic prawns. Open for breakfast (8 to 11:30 AM), lunch (11:30 AM to 2:30 PM), and dinner (6 to 9:30 PM). Reservations unnecessary. On the Kuhio Hwy, in the heart of Kapaa (phone: 822-3955). Moderate to inexpensive.

Deco Gecko – The setting is casual, the food (from lasagna to falafel) prepared with fine, fresh, healthful ingredients with an eye toward what's good for you. That is, until you're faced with the incredible urge to sample one of the pies and cakes. Open daily for breakfast (7 AM to 2 PM) and lunch. Reservations unnecessary. 1384 Kuhio Hwy., Kapaa (phone: 822-5969). Inexpensive.

Violet's Place – Coffee shop devotees flock to this unusual spot, which features a range of American, Hawaiian, Filipino, and vegetarian dishes. Locals are attracted to its back-to-basics approach, as well as its friendly atmostphere. Open daily from 8 to 1 AM. *Kauai Village Shopping Center* (phone: 822-2456). Inexpensive.

Princeville and Hanalei: The Magnificent North Shore

The standard cliché is "sleepy," and if that includes a fully conscious desire to remain quiet and unhurried, then it fits Hanalei, the northern district of Kauai. North Shore folk have a kind of perverse pride that there's no nightlife to speak of, and it doesn't bother them one iota that their single-lane bridges are too narrow for tour buses. In fact, they prefer it that way, resisting efforts to widen the bridges that maintain the North Shore's slow pace. And although the bridges are finally being rebuilt to accommodate larger vehicles, they will retain their country appeal.

If in the past Princeville's reputation for quiet and its rather wet winter weather have made the North Shore a less popular overnight destination than the Coconut Coast or Poipu — with their sunny skies — the tropic beauty of the setting and an expanding range of activities and options have begun to draw those who prefer its uncrowded beaches (some of the best anywhere in Hawaii) and sense of Hawaiian authenticity. Still, due to the limited number of accommodations, most visitors see the North Shore on a morning or afternoon swing up the coast by car or van tour, or aboard one of the numerous boats and rafts that provide access to the spectacular wilderness of the Na Pali Coast.

Those who linger longer do so to take in the abundance of the riches that nature saw fit to bestow on this corner of the Pacific. For here are a string of long, sandy beaches splendidly isolated at the foot of towering cliffs, a broad luminous bay backed by mountains whose forms seem to change with the light of day, numerous waterfalls, rainbows, a wide fertile valley of taro fields that serves as a bird sanctuary, and the Na Pali cliffs, jagged and lofty, virtually inaccessible and achingly beautiful.

You can have your nature both ways, too — from the inside of a pup tent on an isolated Na Pali beach or from the luxury of a hotel or your own apartment at the *Princeville* resort. And besides the sports that nature affords — camping, hiking, swimming, surfing, snorkeling, sailing, fishing, horseback riding — are those that require the civilizing hand of man — tennis and golf.

The good life as envisioned by the golf and tennis set is the guiding principle behind the development of the *Princeville* resort — the North Shore's mix of single-family homes, resort condominiums, and the *Princeville,* reopened in 1991 after a $100-million face-lift that stripped the 4-year-old hotel to its concrete shell for a total remake. Development of its second 1,000 acres is well under way. At present, there are 45 holes of golf, a score of tennis courts, a dozen swimming pools, and 3 restaurants, plus an attractive shopping complex. Even non-golfers can't help but like *Princeville.* On a rolling plateau overlooking Hanalei Bay, with mountains rising behind it, this is one of the most gorgeously situated resorts in the world.

Kilauea Point – Naturalists gravitate to this craggy point at the northernmost tip of the island for the rare chance of seeing some of the Pacific's seabirds at close range. The point, under the protection of the US Fish and Wildlife Service, is home to the wedge-tailed shearwater, the red-and-white-tailed tropic bird, and the frigate; just across the bay, within easy sight, is a colony of the red-footed booby. There's a good self-guided tour on the point's bird, plant, and sea life. The lighthouse here, out of use since 1967, isn't open to the public. Kilauea Point is open from noon to 4 PM every day but Saturday. No admission charge.

Guava Kai Plantation – A video at this visitor center-cum-products shop traces the history of the guava in Hawaii (it was imported to the islands early in the 19th century) and shows current production plans. Visitors who stroll through part of the plantation will find a group of picnic tables at the end of their walk. There is also a garden of native Hawaiian plants. No admission charge for a 30-minute escorted tour of the grounds. Open daily from 9 AM to 5 PM. Just off Rte. 56, outside Kilauea (phone: 828-1925).

Hanalei Valley Lookout – Just past the entrance to Princeville is a lookout that spreads the treasures of the North Shore before you. In one direction is a patchwork of taro fields cut through by the placid Hanalei River, along which farmers tether their horses without fear of thieving. Seaward is Hanalei Bay, with lips of white beaches and the shrouded Na Pali Coast looming beyond. Most of what you see from here is part of the Hanalei National Wildlife Refuge. Taro farmers get special permission to use the land because their fields provide a good habitat for the endangered birds the refuge is meant to protect: the Hawaiian stilt, gallinule, koot, and duck. With binoculars, it's possible to see them from the lookout.

Hanalei – The town of Hanalei stretches from the line of shops on Kuhio Highway toward the bay. Despite recent development, Hanalei retains a lazy charm, exemplified by several historic buildings, a number of older buildings renovated as shops, and a lack of high-rises. Hanalei Beach Park and Pavilion, near the wharf where the Hanalei River enters the Pacific, is a perfect spot for picnicking and swimming. The sunset from the end of the pier is as sublime an experience as a Polynesian sunset should be, and according to residents of many years, repeated exposure doesn't jade the senses to it.

Waioli Mission House Museum – At first glance you might mistake this trim white frame building for a private home. But the house, built in 1841 by early Protestant missionaries, has been a museum for over 60 years, containing furniture and artifacts of the missionary period of Hawaiian history. The guided tour, given Tuesdays, Thursdays, and Saturdays from 9 AM to 3 PM, is an interesting mix of the founding family's history and that of Hanalei. No admission charge. Hanalei town (phone: 245-3202).

Lumahai Beach – There's rarely a travel brochure of Kauai that doesn't include a picture of this beach, about 2 miles outside Hanalei town. This is Polynesia, as pictured by Hollywood in *South Pacific,* and although pretty, it's really no lovelier than a number of other beaches that ring the North Shore like a necklace.

Wet and Dry Caves – Just before you come to Haena State Park is the Maniniholo Dry Cave, so called to distinguish it from the Waikapalae Wet Cave a jot down the road or the Waikanaloa Wet Cave farther on. These sea caves, wide-mouthed and shallow, so there's no need for a guide or artificial light to see them, were probably formed when the sea stood at a higher level. Hawaiian legends ascribe them to the work of Pele and other mythical beings.

Haena State Park – This is the terminus for vehicles and the jumping-off point for hikers and campers headed into Na Pali. There's an exquisite little beach — Kee Beach — at the very end of the road, and just around the promontory that curls over it is the Hula Halau Heiau, where the goddess Pele was thought to dance and where in earlier times young women came to learn the ancient art of hula. Wade out into the water at Kee and you can see the Na Pali cliffs shimmering in the distance.

SHOPPING: The *Princeville Center* (currently being expanded), low redwood buildings connected by white-railed walkways, is a pleasant place to catch your breath if you're day-tripping to the North Shore. Since it serves a resident community as well as tourists, it's more than a collection of souvenir and gift shops. There is also a butcher shop, supermarket, beauty shop, and bank in addition to a well-stocked camera shop; *Toucans* (phone: 826-7332), an enjoyable stop for swimwear, resortwear, and other women's apparel; the *Mail Service Center* for shipping and fax services (phone: 826-7331); *Kauai Kite and Hobby Company* (phone: 826-9144), for high-fliers and do-it-yourselfers; and *Montage Galleries* (phone: 826-9151) for artworks.

Near Kilauea (about 8 miles before Princeville on the Kuhio Hwy.) are *Moloaa Sunrise* (phone: 822-7552), *Mango Mama's Fruit Stand* (phone: 828-1020), and *Waiakalua Fruits and Flowers* (phone: 828-2164). All three are open-air shops that feature exotic fresh fruits and other Hawaiian delicacies. Try the tropical "smoothies," delicious fruit shakes. *Banana Joe's Tropical Fruit Farm,* in Kilauea, features a similar range of items (phone: 828-1092). The *Wainiha Store* (phone: 826-6251) provides sundries as well as tasty sandwiches for those headed to end-of-the-road beaches.

Also notable are some of the shops in the town of Hanalei and in the plantation town of Kilauea, about 10 miles southeast of Hanalei.

Aarozz – Lovely hand-painted silk dresses, scarves, and wall hangings adorn this shop. In *Ching Young Village,* Hanalei town (phone: 826-6441).

Artisans Guild of Kauai – Showcased here are the work of local painters, potters, woodworkers, and jewelers at prices usually lower than those in Kauai's resort shops. In *Ching Young Village,* Hanalei town (phone: 826-6441).

Checkers Beach Gear – Just about anything you might need to head to the beach, from swimwear to sunscreen, towels to snorkel equipment. In the *Old Hanalei School Center* on Kuhio Hwy. (phone: 826-9555).

Jungle Bob's – Camping supplies, for sale and rent, and a full range of sporting goods and books on Hawaii. *Ching Young Center,* Hanalei town (phone: 826-6664).

Kong Lung – This surprisingly sophisticated place carries custom-made arts and crafts, clothing, Hawaiiana, antiques, and Oriental objets d'art. Keneke St. and Lighthouse Rd. (phone: 828-1822).

Ola's – A wide range of imaginative gifts and top-quality woodwork, ceramics, dolls, and other crafts, as well as one of Hawaii's best selections of humorous greeting cards. 5-5016 Kuhio Hwy. (phone: 826-6937).

On the Road to Hanalei – An intriguing mix of ethnic Asian arts and crafts, local pottery, glass, and paintings, hand-painted silks, and Hawaiian and esoteric books are among the offerings here. In *Ching Young Village,* Hanalei town (phone: 826-7360).

Princeville Logo Shop – A small yet appealing selection of fashionable silks and outwear for men and women. In the lobby of the *Princeville* (phone: 826-2781).

Puu Hale Creations – Quilter extraordinaire Barbara Jossem-Naud produces charming made-to-order, Hawaiian-style quilts. 2288 Kolo Rd., in Kilauea (phone: 828-1455).

Sand People – Contemporary resort wear, plus a small selection of beach gear. On Kuhio Hwy. at the entrance to Hanalei, with a second shop in Old Koloa Town (phone: 826-6981).

NIGHTLIFE: Your best bet is the *Tahiti Nui* (phone: 826-6277), on the main highway in Hanalei, where most nights there's impromptu Hawaiian entertainment, country-and-western music, rock and roll, as well as Wednesday and Friday night luaus. The *Hanalei Gourmet,* in the old *Hanalei School Center,* features live Hawaiian music on weekends and cable TV sports on other nights. At Princeville, the *Lanai* restaurant in the *Princeville* clubhouse occasionally features Hawaiian and contemporary music live (phone: 826-6226). In the *Princeville Center, Café Zelo's* features live music on Fridays and Saturdays, from 8:30 to 11 PM (phone: 826-9700). For specifics on the nightly entertainment at the *Living Room* lounge at the *Princeville,* call 826-9644.

CHECKING IN: For accommodations listed here, $250 and up for two people is considered very expensive; $160 to $245 is expensive; and $75 to $145 is moderate. These categories are based on a typical double hotel room or 1-bedroom condominium. *Hale Maha* (phone: 826-4447), a bed and breakfast establishment, provides a lovely, quiet setting quite close to North Shore beaches, as does *Bed, Breakfast, and Beach* (phone: 826-6111) on Hanalei Bay. Room costs range from $50 to $75 for a double. All telephone numbers are in the 808 area code unless otherwise indicated.

Sheraton Princeville – This 252-room property, the only hotel at the *Princeville* resort, reopened in mid-1991 after a $100-million renovation that virtually reduced the original building to its shell and rebuilt it into one of Hawaii's most elegant hostelries. Cooled by green and white marble and given a European flavor in the classic style of its furnishings, this place now offers luxurious surroundings both inside and out. The views from its beautifully decorated rooms are nothing short of spectacular, taking in the expanse of Hanalei Bay and the first cliffs of the nearby Na Pali Coast. Paths on various levels lead to an enlarged pool, a small health spa, and a beach on Hanalei Bay. Guests have access to and preferential times and rates at the resort's tennis and golf facilities. Several first-rate restaurants (see *Eating Out*) and the *Living Room* lounge, where afternoon tea and sunset cocktails are served each evening, make this hotel a true standout. Princeville (phone: 826-9644; 800-325-3535). Very expensive.

Hanalei Bay – More like a hotel than the other condominiums at Princeville, this resort has a bustling central area with a full-service front desk, shops, a restaurant and lounge overlooking 8 tennis courts, and a free-form swimming pool complete with waterfalls and lush landscaping. The recently refurbished hotel rooms, studios, and the fully equipped 1-, 2-, and 3-bedroom condominium apartments have terraces opening onto beautifully gardened grounds. The resort is just a walk down a paved footpath to the beach, where there's a telephone to summon the jitney if you don't want to walk back. Princeville (phone: 826-6522; 800-827-4427). Very expensive to expensive.

Puu Poa – A sense of privacy pervades this condominium resort. The 2-bedroom/2-bath apartments are large, with all appliances and even *furo*-style tubs (Japanese tubs to soak in after bathing); all units feature panoramic ocean views. Maid service is provided daily. Other amenities include a tennis court, swimming pool, and a pathway to the beach. Princeville (phone: 826-9602). Expensive.

Cliffs – Named for its dramatic setting over the Pacific, it is one of Princeville's more handsome properties. Its big, breezy apartments (from 1 to 4 bedrooms) feature balconies off both the living rooms and master bedrooms and soaring 2-story living rooms with spacious sleeping lofts. And because the design allows the apartment to be divided into single rooms, staying here can be very economical. There's daily maid service, a front desk, a swimming pool, tennis courts, and Jacuzzis on the property. The kitchens aren't as well equipped as you might like, but this is only a minor drawback. Request a unit with a telephone if that matters to you. Princeville (phone: 826-6219; 800-523-0411). Expensive to moderate.

Hanalei Colony – This appealing condominium just a few miles from the end of the road at Haena State Park is a country cousin to Princeville's sophisticated brood. The 2-bedroom apartments are essentially 1 bedroom with a sleeping niche separated by folding louvered doors. But the whole is open, large, and comfortable. Right on the beach (the only North Shore resort that is), it also has a swimming pool and Jacuzzi. What you get in spades here is quiet. There are no telephones or TV sets in the apartments, and you're away from what little community the North Shore can claim. Don't even consider this secluded haven unless you have a car. Hanalei (phone: 826-6235; 800-628-3004). Moderate.

Pali Ke Kua – Panoramic views are offered at this cliff-top condominium. Its 1- and 2-bedroom units (some feature an additional loft) have full kitchen facilities, TV sets, and telephones. There's a pool, an on-site restaurant, and a paved path that leads down the Princeville cliffside to a private beach. Princeville (phone: 826-9066; 800-657-7751). Moderate to inexpensive.

Hanalei Bay Inn – A collection of bed and breakfast-style cottages just a short walk from the beach. Comfortable and casual. In Hanalei, just off Rte. 56 (phone: 826-9333). Inexpensive.

EATING OUT: For a meal for two, excluding wine, tip, and drinks, expect to pay around $65 and up at a place listed as expensive, between $25 and $60 in a moderate place, and under $25 in an inexpensive one. All telephone numbers are in the 808 area code unless otherwise indicated.

Bali Hai – Panoramic views of the surrounding mountains include the profile of famous Bali Hai peak, from which this restaurant at the *Hanalei Bay* resort takes its name. Breakfast is tasty and reasonably priced; the dinner menu highlights sautéed breast of duck, medallions of pork, and lighter fare, including a delicious shrimp, chicken, or vegetable stir fry. Open daily for dinner from 5:30 to 10 PM. Dinner reservations advised. *Hanalei Bay Resort* (phone: 826-6522). Expensive.

Café Hanalei – The panoramic views of Hanalei Bay and the surrounding mountains are spectacular, but they are almost outdone by the fine food. Dishes include poached onaga (a tender, flaky fish) in saffron almond sauce, smoked veal chops with red pepper flan, coffee-roasted lamb, and New York sirloin steaks for those longing for a reminder of Gotham's fare. Open daily for breakfast, lunch, and dinner. Reservations advised. In the *Princeville Hotel* (phone: 826-9644). Expensive.

La Cascata – Also located in the *Princeville Hotel,* this establishment offers such fare as herb and vinegar oysters on the half shell, steamed shrimps and artichokes, oven-baked sea bass, veal scaloppine, and *saltimbocca alla romana.* It is considered one of the islands' finest restaurants, and the views overlooking Hanalei Bay and Bali Hai are gorgeous. Open daily for dinner. Reservations necessary. In the *Princeville Hotel* (phone: 826-9644). Expensive.

Charo's – Owned by the entertainer of the same name, its seaside setting halfway between Hanalei and Haena and the rattan-and-tile interior are pleasant enough, but the menu, featuring fish, steaks, prime ribs, and specialties like shrimp breaded in macadamia nut crumbs, draws mixed reviews. "Monday Night Football" and other sports events are aired on a large-screen TV set in the adjacent *Coochie Coochie Cantina.* Open for lunch and dinner daily. Dinner reservations advised. *Hanalei Colony Resort* (phone: 826-6422). Expensive to moderate.

Dolphin – Deliciously prepared fish, steaks, and chicken are the mainstays at this small eatery on the banks of the Hanalei River. Complete dinners include generous salads served family style, vegetables, and hot bread. Dinner only, nightly from 6 to 10 PM. No reservations. Hanalei town (phone: 826-6113). Expensive to moderate.

Hanalei Shell House – A very relaxed place with a beach-shack atmosphere enlivened by hanging plants, it serves fresh seafood (catch of the day prepared in several styles), pasta dishes, and lavish salads bursting with fresh ingredients. Open daily for breakfast (the best on the North Shore, with great macadamia nut pancakes), lunch, and dinner from 5 to 10 PM. Dinner reservations advised. Hanalei town (phone: 826-7977). Expensive to moderate.

Lanai – Located in the *Princeville* resort's clubhouse, the panoramic views and good food are both pluses, although service may be a little slow. Seafood, pasta, steaks, and combinations of all three are menu specialties. A strolling ukulele player entertains. Open nightly from 5:30 to 9:30 PM. Reservations advised. (phone: 826-6226). Expensive to moderate.

Beamreach – Dark and nautical, this Princeville restaurant offers standard fare — steaks, seafood, and chicken dinners that include salad and vegetables. Dinner only, nightly, from 6 to 9:45 PM. Reservations advised. *Pali Ke Kua Condominium,* Princeville (phone: 826-9131). Moderate.

Casa di Amici – In an out-of-the-way setting in the middle of the plantation town of Kilauea (9 miles southeast of Princeville), this Italian restaurant features sliding walls that allow it to enjoy the night breezes. Prices are reasonable, but the food gets mixed reviews. Open daily, except Sundays, for lunch from 11:30 AM to 2:30 PM; daily for dinner from 5:30 to 9 PM. Reservations necessary. 2484 Keneke St. (phone: 828-1388). Moderate.

Chuck's Steakhouse – A branch of the Hawaiian steakhouse chain, it is worth a visit for its good steaks, prime ribs, teriyaki, and seafood dishes. Dinner daily from 6 to 10 PM, lunch on weekdays only from 11:30 AM to 3 PM. Reservations unnecessary. *Princeville Shopping Center* (phone: 826-6211). Moderate.

Tahiti Nui – If you want to experience a real Hawaiian luau, skip the elaborate dos put on by the big resorts and come here for the Wednesday and Friday night luaus. For $30 you can get the traditional fare — kalua pig, taro, poi, lomilomi salmon, sweet potato — in the company of islanders and in a setting that is distinctly old Hawaii, including traditional Hawaiian musical entertainment. Saturday nights are dedicated to rock and roll from 10 PM to 2 AM, while Mondays are Paniolo night from 9:30 AM to 1 AM. Unusual dishes here include Tahitian raw marinated fish, Papeete-style calamari with sautéed mushrooms, and taro burgers, all of which are prepared with organically grown herbs and spices. The bar, with its wide verandah made for sipping a beer at sunset, is open from 11 AM to 2 AM. Reservations necessary at the restaurant. Hanalei town (phone: 826-6277). Moderate.

Black Pot Luau Hut – A popular hangout among locals, it serves such traditional Hawaiian dishes as poki, kalua pig, and chicken long rice, as well as American staples including hamburgers and pork chops. Open daily for lunch and dinner (same menu). Reservations unnecessary. In *Kauhale Center,* Hanalei (phone: 826-9871). Moderate to inexpensive.

Hanalei Gourmet – Once an old schoolroom, this cheerful eatery was converted into an upscale bistro with an on-site bakery. Those who shun roast quail in favor of deli sandwiches will find true happiness with the *pupus,* pasta, and fresh fish dishes. Picnic lovers can arrange for a basket of goodies to be ready and waiting by early afternoon. Live music most evenings. Open daily for lunch and dinner. Reservations advised. In the old Hanalei school (phone: 826-2524). Moderate to inexpensive.

Café Zelo's – Breakfast includes delicious omelettes and frittatas, while lunch focuses on hefty sandwiches, fresh salads, and specialties like spinach lasagna and stuffed potatoes. Dinner features a Mediterranean menu, with pasta and seafood specialties. Open daily, with live music Fridays and Saturdays from 8:30 to 11 PM. Reservations unnecessary. *Princeville Center* (phone: 826-9700). Inexpensive.

Farmer's Market – The perfect lunch stop, serving homemade soups, salads, and sandwiches. Open daily from 9 AM to 9 PM. No reservations. In Kilauea, en route to the Kilauea Lighthouse (phone: 828-1512). Inexpensive.

Jacques' Bakery – Fresh croissants and pastries for a fast breakfast or a midday snack en route. French expatriate Jacques Atlan has created a Kauai tradition here. Milk and fresh coffee are also available. Don't be surprised if you have to wait in line a few minutes to be served. Word of Jacques' baking talent has spread far and wide, despite the out-of-the-way setting in Kilauea. Open daily from 6 AM to 6 PM. No reservations. Oka St. (phone: 828-1393). Inexpensive.

Pizzaburger – This very informal eatery makes good pizza, subs, and other standards of fast food — fries, onion rings, and such. It's a little pricey (because of the neighborhood) for what's offered, but one of the few casual places to eat on the North Shore. Open 11 AM to 10 PM daily. No reservations. *Princeville Center* (phone: 826-6070). Inexpensive.

Na Pali Coast

Unless you possess extraordinary powers of imagination, it's hard to picture the dazzling beauty of this 14-mile stretch of coast. Wind, rain, and the centuries have cut deep valleys into the windward face of Kauai, leaving sharp pleats of land as lush as they are mysterious. And between the great knuckles of cliffs that jut out into the surf are beaches, pristine and isolated from all but the most determined adventurers.

The Na Pali Coast has never offered easy access. Early Polynesians settled in these vertiginous valleys because the formidable natural barriers offered a measure of protection from belligerent neighboring tribes. They've long since departed, and only the remnants of stone-walled taro fields built up in the narrow valleys recall their tenure.

Because there are no paved roads into Na Pali, most people see it from a helicopter or boat. But a few penetrate its tropical valleys on foot. For day hikers, there's a 2-mile trail starting from Haena Beach Park and ending at Hanakapiai Beach, with an additional 4-mile (round-trip) trail up the valley to towering Hanakapiai Falls. More experienced backpackers hike the 11-mile trail to Kalalau Beach. But it's a vigorous hike requiring at least one overnight stop at Kalalau, and none but the hardy should attempt it. Swimmers, too, are advised to use extreme caution on entering the water either at Hanakapiai or Kalalau, particularly when winter surf is high and dangerous currents make for unsafe swimming conditions.

Poipu: The Sunny South Coast

It's no surprise that the south coast of Kauai has become the most popular destination for visitors on the island. Its nearly perpetual sunshine, broad swaths of white sand beaches, usually calm seas, and exuberant plant life that scents the air with intoxicating fragrance make it irresistible. Poipu, a series of scalloped beaches along the southernmost tip of the island, is where the resorts took root, providing such amenities as golf, tennis, good restaurants, and handsome lodgings to complement the area's excellent swimming, snorkeling, scuba diving, and surfing.

But except for the developments at Poipu and the gentrified plantation town of Koloa, sugarcane is still king in the south, and the villages owe their existence to it rather than to tourism, although that is beginning to change as resort development continues. Still, driving down a road between tall fields of mature cane or following a lumbering cane truck still links Poipu to its 19th-century past.

The south coast is hot, too, especially after the shaded cool of Hanalei, and it becomes hotter the farther west you go. The long, treeless beaches of Waimea, Kekaha, and Polihale should be visited before the day heats up. Swimmers should be careful, too. Strong currents and surf can be dangerous along this stretch of coast.

This coast was particularly hard hit when Hurricane Iwa ripped through the island in November 1982. A number of buildings along the shore — from the resorts at Poipu to the sugarcane town of Kekaha — were simply swept off their foundations by tidal waves. Portions of coast roads were washed out, as was much coastal vegetation.

Recovery was remarkably fast. Main roads were repaired within days. Resorts cleared the sand and rocks from swimming pools and lobbies, rebuilt rooms, replaced furnishings, and started to reopen 6 weeks after the storm. Replanting began immediately, too, replacing the salt-soaked soil with fresh earth. And the landscape today looks as luxuriant as ever. The only lasting damage done by Iwa was to the reefs off Poipu Beach, which were damaged by the storm. In the decade since, the *Poipu Bay* resort has opened and added a new *Hyatt* hotel, an 18-hole golf course (Poipu's second course), and stables.

Koloa – About 3 miles from Poipu's condominiums and hotels on Kaumualii Highway, Koloa was Hawaii's first plantation town, built around a mill that started refining sugar in 1835 — and its residents still plant and harvest sugarcane from surrounding fields or work in the mill a few miles outside town. An artistically appealing and informative monument to Hawaii's sugar workers is found at the entrance to the town, adjacent to the chimney that is all that remains of the plantation's original mill. In recent years, shop-by-shop restoration has made Koloa a popular attraction, outwardly maintaining its plantation town feel, although increasingly compromising its authenticity in the process. Despite an increasingly gentrified façade, however, Koloa remains a village of old plantation houses and churches — Protestant, Catholic, and Buddhist — that reflect the diverse origins of Kauai's people.

Poipu Beach – The series of beaches that line the Poipu coast are what attracted resorts to this southernmost portion of Kauai. Shower and restroom facilities are on Poipu Beach itself, attracting a mix of locals and visitors. Hotels and condos provide right-of-way access to the other beaches. Surfers head this way for offshore waves, snorklers for multicolored waters, and swimmers for reef-sheltered waters which can, however, be quite rough on occasion. Hobie Cat rentals and catamaran sails depart from here. A newly opened road now bypasses Koloa town for those who wish to go directly to Poipu without delay.

Olu Pua Gardens – Japanese gardens, palms, jungle plants, and orchids are some of the many themes that appear throughout these 12½ acres. Tours are offered on weekdays on the hour from 9:30 AM to 1:30 PM. Admission charge, $10; children under 12, $5. Just off Hwy. 50, near Kalaheo, en route to Waimea Canyon (phone: 332-8182).

Kukuiula Harbor – This pretty bay about 2 miles west of Poipu is the home of many small pleasure crafts as well as a center for water sports.

Spouting Horn – If you have a taste for sea geysers, this fountain — created by waves pushing water through a submerged lava tube — may interest you. A popular visitor attraction, it is reached by a coastal road from Poipu. Nearby hawkers peddle a surprisingly complete selection of well-priced coral jewelry and Niihau shell leis: Shop around and negotiate.

National Tropical Botanical Garden – A research garden to study the prodigious variety of plants that thrive in the tropics, this is also one of the most rewarding side trips you can take on the island. The tour of the 186-acre garden — it lasts 2 hours and includes a 2-mile walk that demands a comfortable pair of walking shoes — is conducted by a knowledgeable volunteer. In addition to the research garden, the tour includes an adjoining private garden which once belonged to John Gregg Allerton, a local patron and millionaire whose family established the First National Bank of Chicago. Allerton, an architect by training, created an exquisite garden on the spot where Queen Emma, the wife of King Kamehameha IV, started one in the last century. There's a serene outdoor "room" walled by tall, thin-trunked trees, a lovely bamboo grove, and an ingenious series of pools, fountains, and waterfalls. Tours of the gardens are offered daily at 9 AM and 1 PM. The tour includes a visit to the grounds of the adjoining Allerton Estate. Cost is $15, with tours limited to 12 people. Call well in advance for reservations or write: PO Box 340, Lawai, Kauai, HI 96765. 2 miles south of Lawai, off Rte. 53 (phone: 332-7361).

Hanapepe Lookout – About a mile and a half before you come to Hanapepe town, stop here to get a panoramic view of the valley. Upvalley are the taro fields; downvalley, the town itself, picturesque clapboard buildings ranging along both sides of the Hanapepe River. Just outside the town, off the main road, is Salt Pond Beach Park, named after the nearby salt ponds that are still harvested.

Waimea – Captain Cook landed here in 1778 at the mouth of the river that carved the magnificent Waimea Canyon. The town was also the winter home of the Kauaian royalty, who, when summer heated up, moved their court to Wailua on the eastern side of the island. There's a plaque to commemorate Captain Cook's landing, a neat little beach park, and the remains of a Russian fort on a point of land opposite the town. Don't waste your time looking for Ft. Elizabeth, built in 1816 by a German adventurer employed by a Russian shipping company; it's not much more than a low wall of red rubble with a tangle of dead-looking trees inside.

Kekaha – Kekaha is the last town of any size before the Kaumualii Highway stops at the western end of the Na Pali cliffs and is as dry as Haena is wet. There's a sugar mill here, and you can pull off the road to watch the cane trucks disgorge their load into what looks like a giant Cuisinart.

Polihale State Park – At the literal end of the road (and a rutted cane road at that) is Polihale State Park, where a quarter-mile-wide beach of bone white sand stretches on for miles nearly unbroken by shade trees. Polihale is a fine beach for swimming and body-surfing and a good vantage point for seeing the Na Pali cliffs. You can camp and picnic here, too. But it *is* hot on this side of the island, and there's precious little in the way of shade, manmade or otherwise. Those planning to spend the day should stock up on food and drink ahead of time.

SHOPPING: In recent years quite a number of shops and restaurants have opened to serve south Kauai's growing number of visitors.

Old Koloa Town

After many quiet years as a lazy plantation town, Koloa has been transformed into a small Lahaina, complete with restored buildings from the turn of the century and earlier, and the usual array of souvenir shops, resort and water attire, activities desks, and restaurants. The planned addition of the *Koloa Plantation Marketplace* may mean commercial overkill for a small town.

Crazy Shirts – Unisex shirts, shorts, and jackets are for sale here. 5356 Koloa Rd. (phone: 742-7161).

Fathom Five Dive Shop – A full line of snorkel and scuba gear, plus accessories, T-shirts, and Boogie boards are offered. On Poipu Rd. (phone: 742-9791).

Gallery – Paintings and watercolors by noted Hawaiian artists, as well as delicate Japanese porcelain, scrimshaw, and woodcarvings of local birds. *Stouffer Waiohai* (phone: 742-9211).

Indo-Pacific Trading Company – Specializing in Balinese arts. 3432 Poipu Rd. (phone: 742-7655).

Island Images – One of several art galleries in Koloa, it displays oils, lithographs, serigraphs, prints and watercolors. Located at the end of the Boardwalk, Old Koloa Town (phone: 742-7447).

Progressive Expressions – *The* place in Kauai for swimwear and surfboard and Boogie board rentals. 5428 Koloa Rd. (phone: 742-6041).

Ralston Gallery – With shops in Koloa and the *Kiahuna Shopping Village,* this place offers a wide selection of oils, lithographs, prints and watercolors. In Old Koloa Town (phone: 742-6366); in the *Kiahuna Shopping Village* (phone: 742-9755).

Sgt. Leisure – Interesting collection of logowear with a military twist. A second shop is in the *Coconut Plantation Market Place* (phone: 822-2021). On the Boardwalk, Old Koloa Town (phone: 742-7992).

Sueoka Store – The last holdout from pre-gentrified Koloa, this typical, small-town, all-purpose market carries groceries, liquor, T-shirts, and sundries. 5392 Koloa Rd. (phone: 742-1611).

KIAHUNA SHOPPING VILLAGE

This nicely designed cluster of shops provides Poipu with a commercial core. A free Polynesian revue is offered Thursdays at 5 PM in the center's grassy central courtyard. A major expansion is scheduled for this year.

Black Pearl Collection – Rare Japanese black pearls are the focus of this store's custom-made jewelry (phone: 822-7170).

Garden Isle Bake Shop – Macadamia nut and cinnamon rolls, bran-mango muffins (in season), chocolate- and macadamia-filled croissants, and macadamia cream pies, all baked fresh daily (phone: 742-6070).

Joelle's Collection – Coral provides a centerpiece for many of the custom-designed pieces that are artfully displayed (phone: 742-1303).

Ship Shore Gallery – Everything from ships-in-a-bottle to antique guns; from paintings to shipboard brass (phone: 742-7123).

Whalers' General Store – As its "old general store" atmosphere suggests, the inventory includes attractive casual clothes at good prices, Hawaiian fabrics, jewelry, and a slew of tasteful, inexpensive gifts, such as bath oils, hair ornaments, straw bags, Chinese purses, and stationery (phone: 742-9431).

HYATT REGENCY KAUAI

H.F. Wichman – A fine selection of gold jewelry and gemstones in tasteful settings (phone: 742-1863).

Merrill Chase Galleries – Kauai's finest art gallery contains wonderful Belle Epoque lithographs by Toulouse-Lautrec, Mucha, and other masters of the art, as well as paintings, glasswork, and sculpture (phone: 742-7666).

NIGHTLIFE: The *Sheraton*'s *Drum Lounge* (phone: 742-1661) starts the evening with Hawaiian music. Dancing to more contemporary sounds from 9 PM to midnight weekdays, 9 PM to 1 AM weekends. For "easy listening," a guitarist plays daily at the *Waiohai*'s *Terrace* restaurant (phone: 742-9511) and a pianist performs at the hotel's *Tamarind Lounge* (phone: 742-9511). Right next door, at the *Poipu Beach* hotel's *Poipu Beach Café* (phone: 742-1681), there's live music for dancing from 8:30 PM to midnight. Some nights it's rock and roll, some nights it's reggae, and other nights it's contemporary. Cover charge is $3. On Mondays, the café airs football games on its big-screen TV set (phone: 742-1681). At the *Hyatt Regency* on Fridays and Saturdays from 9 PM to 2 AM you can check out *Kuhio's* nightclub. The hotel also features live entertainment in several lounges, including the *Seaview* lounge, which plays Hawaiian music from 5:30 to 9:30 PM daily. The most elaborate room in the house is the ornate *Stevenson's Library,* a bar–cum–reading room reminiscent of a 19th-century English club. Hot spots for mingling are the bars at *Keoki's Paradise* (phone: 742-7534), *Pancho and Lefty's* (phone: 742-7377), and *Brennecke's* (phone: 742-7588). Looking for something truly Hawaiian? Try the Polynesian revue and dinner buffet at the *Sheraton* (phone: 742-1611) Wednesdays or the luau on the grounds of the *Waiohai* (phone: 742-9511) Mondays, both from 6 to 9 PM.

Otherwise, Poipu nights are best appreciated with a stroll along the beach under Kauai's usually star-filled skies, which explains why Poipu has become a popular destination with honeymooners.

CHECKING IN: Beachfront hotels and condominiums are generally at a premium. Smaller, often less expensive off-beach condominiums are found at either end of its central beaches. It is advisable to ask about location and facilities as well as price when making reservations. Expect to pay $250 and up for two for accommodations listed as very expensive; $160 to $245 for expensive; $75 to $155 at those places listed as moderate; and under $75 at an inexpensive place. These categories are based on a typical 1-bedroom condominium apartment or double hotel room. For bed and breakfast bookings, call *Bed & Breakfast Hawaii* (phone: 822-7771; 800-733-1632) or *Poipu Bed and Breakfast Inn Reservations* (phone: 742-1146; 800-552-0095). All telephone numbers are in the 808 area code unless otherwise indicated.

Kiahuna Plantation – A first-rate tennis and golf resort, offering a prime beachfront location, expansive lawns, and landscaped grounds. White beachfront cottages and low-rise, plantation-style buildings with balconies blend comfortably with the setting. Inside, the 1- and 2-bedroom apartments follow a tropical scheme — high ceilings, louvered windows, redwood-trimmed walls, patterned pastel fabrics, and rattan furnishings. Be prepared to walk: The grounds are expansive and it's a good distance to the pool, which is actually part of the tennis complex. Poipu Beach (phone: 742-6411; 800-367-7052). Very expensive.

Hyatt Regency Kauai – Poipu's largest and most extravagant ($220-million) property, its architecture is reminiscent of that of Hawaii's territorial days. In the course of construction, a number of archaeological sites were discovered — including human bones and other artifacts. Of the 600 rooms in these mid-rise buildings, 80% have ocean views. One unusual feature is its saltwater swimming lagoon, complete with Polynesian-style islets. Three restaurants (northern Italian, seafood, and continental — see *Eating Out*), 2 pools (including the saltwater lagoon), 4 tennis courts, the Robert Trent Jones, Jr. 18-hole golf course, adjacent stables, a full health spa, and 1,500 feet of beachfront round out the total resort experience. During the summer, *Christmastime, Easter,* and most weekends, "Camp Hyatt" offers a series of children's programs that include activities such as sandcastle building, Hawaiian arts and crafts, cooking classes, museum tours, glass-bottom boat rides, hula lessons, and treasure hunts. Meanwhile adults can enjoy the hotel's "Discover Kauai" programs on local legends and history, Hawaiian salt-making, poi pounding, coconut weaving, quilting, and the creation of Niihau shell leis, as well as guided horseback rides along beautiful Waimea Canyon. Regency Club rooms available. It's the flagship of the *Poipu Bay* resort, and compared with other Hyatt properties in Hawaii, it is surprisingly subdued and tasteful. In Poipu (phone: 742-1234; 800-233-1234). Very expensive to expensive.

Poipu Kapili – Neighbor to the *Sheraton Kauai,* this small (60-unit) condominium offers privacy and is beautifully maintained, with a pool and tennis on-property. Poipu Beach (phone: 742-6449; 800-443-7714). Very expensive to expensive.

Sheraton Kauai and Towers – Recent additions and renovations have upgraded the oceanfront half of this Poipu hotel (its Garden Wing is across the street). Although this is a large property (456 rooms), its low-rise layout, the landscaped grounds and gardens, and direct access to one of Poipu's crescent beaches make it an enjoyable place to stay. Guestrooms are decorated in pleasing, subtle earth tones and pastels. Facilities include several restaurants (see *Naniwa* in *Eating Out*), a fitness center, and 3 tennis courts. Nearby, the 4-story *Towers* boasts 117 upgraded rooms, a complimentary breakfast, a cocktail hour, after-dinner drinks and movies, as well as concierge service. Poipu Beach (phone: 742-1661; 800-325-3535). Very expensive to expensive.

Stouffer Waiohai – Quiet elegance, a prime beachfront setting, a small spa, tennis, and excellent food are the hallmarks of this resort. Rooms are redecorated in pastels, with wicker and rattan furnishings, creating a tropical atmosphere. Lanais, the majority of which offer partial sea views, face landscaped gardens that lead to swimming pools (there are three on the property) and the beach. It also offers myriad guest activities, among them snorkeling lessons, botanical tours of the grounds, petroglyph drawing, aerobics, hula lessons, a children's program, and golf packages at the *Kiahuna Golf Village.* Poipu Beach (phone: 742-9511; 800-426-4122). Very expensive to expensive.

Whaler's Cove – Nine-foot ceilings make for spacious interiors that open onto ocean views in this 39-unit property. Though each of the 1-, 2-, and 3-bedroom suites is individually decorated, rates are a bit pricey. Poipu (phone: 742-7571; 800-367-7050). Very expensive to expensive.

Poipu at Makahuena – An oceanfront site provides these 1-, 2-, and 3-bedroom units with lovely views; the courtyard units that surround the pool afford less privacy. The place is well maintained and offers front desk service, but no maid service is provided. Weekly rates available. Poipu (phone: 742-5500; 800-367-8022). Expensive to moderate.

Poipu Bed and Breakfast Inn – Set in Koloa, this ca. 1933 hostelry offers a dose of plantation-scale charm and comfort. Rounding out the rentable options are 6 rooms, plus a large house, a condo apartment, several cottages, and some oceanfront accommodations. Guests can use the pool and courts gratis at the *Kiahuna Tennis Club.* Rates start at $75 per room. 2720 Hoonani Rd. (phone: 742-1146; 800-552-0095). Expensive to moderate.

Poipu Kai – It consists of 4 separate condominiums — *Poipu Sands, Makanui, Kahala, Manualoha* — each different in style, but all having telephones, daily maid service, tennis courts, and swimming pools. There's a lot of attractive architecture here; many of the 1- and 2-bedroom apartments have cathedral ceilings, sleeping lofts, and 2-level living areas. A number of private homes are also available for rent. And though a bit underdecorated, all the units are comfortably furnished. None of the buildings is on the beach, however — it's a few minutes' walk away. Poipu (phone: 742-6464; 800-777-1700). Expensive to moderate.

Kuhio Shores – The beach may be small, but the ocean views from the apartments at sunset can be spectacular. The 1- and 2-bedroom units are comfortably furnished and well priced. No daily maid service. Weekly rates available. Poipu (phone: 742-7555; 800-367-8022). Moderate.

Nihi Kai Villas – Near Brennecke's Beach (popular with body-surfers) and Poipu's public beach, its fully equipped 2-bedroom apartments are also within walking distance of Poipu's hotels and restaurants. Weekly rates available. Check for off-season discounts. Even without specials this is a very well priced property. Poipu (phone: 742-6459; 800-331-8076). Moderate.

Stouffer Poipu Beach – Those seeking tranquillity as well as an attractive environment need look no further. Here are a lovely spacious courtyard facing the beach, a poolside grill where guests can cook their own lunches, and a lively café with Hawaiian entertainment and dancing. The large rooms all have ocean views, terraces, and kitchenettes. One of Poipu's best buys. Next door to the *Waiohai* at Poipu Beach (phone: 742-1681; 800-426-4122). Moderate.

Koloa Landing Cottages – A good buy, this small oceanfront property provides simple and comfortable accommodations, with cable TV, full kitchens, and in-unit telephones. 2740-B Hoonani Rd. (phone: 742-1470). Inexpensive.

EATING OUT: For a meal for two, excluding wine, tips, and drinks, expect to pay $70 or more in a place listed as expensive; $30 to $65, moderate; under $25, inexpensive. All telephone numbers are in the 808 area code unless otherwise indicated.

Dondero's – Patterned tilework, marble, and trompe l'oeil murals of the Mediterranean provide a charming background for the equally upscale fare. Dishes ranging from sautéed shrimp in garlic, carpaccio, grilled shrimp wrapped in *pancetta,* and saltimbocca are among the offerings. Open nightly for dinner from 6 to 10 PM. Reservations advised. At the *Hyatt Regency Kauai* (phone: 742-6260). Expensive.

Tamarind – A first class place, with Szechuan-style shrimp and chicken, rack of lamb or veal, and catch of the day and seafood dishes. The decor is equal to the food: Subtly colored Thai silk and striking brass pillars add the flavor of the Orient to the banquette seating and very French table settings. Open daily for dinner only. Reservations advised. In the *Stouffer Waiohai,* Poipu Beach (phone: 742-9511). Expensive.

Terrace – Not only does the restaurant at the *Waiohai* serve a fabulous Sunday brunch ($25), with over 100 selections, but it may be the best place for dinner in Poipu, if not on the whole island. Open daily. Reservations advised. At the *Stouffer Waiohai* (phone: 742-9511). Expensive.

House of Seafood – For food, ambience, and truly hospitable service, this ranks as one of Kauai's best restaurants. It's made all the more appealing by a menu that includes a wide variety of fresh fish prepared in a diversity of styles — perfectly cooked calamari and Hawaiian abalone — and excellent soups and salads. Potted plants, lots of wicker, and pastel fabrics give it a breezy, island look. Open daily from 5:30 to 9:30 PM. Reservations advised. Located at the entrance to the *Poipu Kai Resort* (phone: 742-6433). Expensive.

Beach House – Fresh fish and seafood and prime ribs are dishes of choice, and the sunset is the entertainment. Open daily for dinner from 5 to 9 PM. Reservations necessary. Poipu Beach (phone: 742-7575). Expensive to moderate.

Keoki's Paradise – Owner Keoki left little to the imagination in putting together a Garden of Eden setting, complete with waterfalls, streams, and lush plantings of orchids and ferns. The ambience belies its setting at the entrance to a shopping center. Seafood and taco bar open from 4:30 to 11 PM; dinner, nightly from 4:30 to 10 PM, includes steaks, seafood, and fresh fish. Reservations advised. *Kiahuna Shopping Village* (phone: 742-7534). Expensive to moderate.

Naniwa – This dining room in the *Sheraton Kauai* features Osaka-style fare (Naniwa is the ancient name of Osaka). Specialties include sushi, *tori yasaimaki* (grilled chicken roll with teriyaki sauce), beef *yasai make age* (sesame-flavored vegetables wrapped with thinly sliced beef and fried), and more standard dishes such as New York steaks. Open nightly from 6 to 9:30 PM. Reservations advised. *Sheraton Kauai* (phone: 742-1661). Expensive to moderate.

Plantation Gardens – Housed in a charming plantation manager's house from the 1930s, it withstood the wrath of Hurricane Iwa, which so ravaged the surrounding gardens. The culinary emphasis here is on seafood — appetizers of sashimi, entrées of crab, shrimp, lobster, and abalone as well as deliciously prepared fresh catch of the day. Open for dinner daily from 5:30 to 10:30 PM. Reservations advised. *Kiahuna Plantation,* Poipu Beach (phone: 742-1695). Expensive to moderate.

Tidepools – If Polynesian resort decor, complete with thatch huts floating in a lagoon, appeals to your imagination, then this establishment could be a small slice of heaven. The menu provides such fare as Kula onion soup and steamed Kauai-grown clams, as well as fresh fish and grilled steaks. A truly relaxed place to dine. Open nightly from 5:30 to 10:30 PM. Reservations advised. In the *Hyatt Regency Kauai* (phone: 742-6260). Expensive to moderate.

Brennecke's – Kiawe broiled steaks, chicken and seafood, fresh fish, pasta, and a generous salad bar are the specialties. Good food and service and a friendly atmosphere attract a spirited mix of locals and visitors, making it worth a recommendation. Hamburgers are the popular lunch item. Open daily from noon to 4 PM for lunch; 2 to 4 PM for happy hour; and 4 to 10:30 PM for dinner. Reservations advised. Poipu Beach (phone: 742-7588). Moderate.

Flamingo's Cantina – People rave about the *fajitas* and other Mexican specialties served in this place decorated with pink flamingos and huge tropical fish in *Sea World*-size tanks. Open for dinner daily from 5 to 9:30 PM. From 11:30 AM to 2 PM there's lunch and an all-you-can-eat taco bar. Reservations unnecessary. On

Nalu Rd.: Take the first left past Brennecke's Beach (phone: 742-9505). Moderate to inexpensive.

Anara Café – This eatery is actually a part of the *Hyatt*'s elegant Anara Spa (see *Sybaritic Spas,* DIVERSIONS), but it is open to those not using the spa's first-rate facilities. Delicious light lunches composed of healthful ingredients are the main draw, as well as a wide variety of baked goods that will help keep a diet regimen in tow. Open daily for breakfast and lunch from 8 AM to 2:30 PM. Reservations unnecessary. In the *Hyatt Regency Kauai* (phone: 742-6260). Inexpensive.

D.J.'s Last Resort – The pizza alone would be worth a recommendation, but the lasagna is even more noteworthy. The perfect place to head for a casual, inexpensive lunch or dinner. Open daily from 11:30 AM to 9:30 PM. No reservations. Koloa (phone: 742-9096). Inexpensive.

Koloa Ice House – A great place for lunch or a light dinner, serving an interesting selection of sandwiches, soup, salads, and hot specials, such as nachos, lasagna, and chili. Open daily. No reservations. Koloa (phone: 742-6063). Inexpensive.

Mustard's Last Stand – The specialty is the hot dog, with lots of styles from which to choose. This is a good place for a quick midday snack. Open daily from 8:30 AM to 6:30 PM. No reservations. On Lawai Rd., just before it joins the main highway, next to *Lee Sand*'s eelskin shop (phone: 332-7245) Inexpensive.

Taqueria Norteños – Don't be fooled by the low-key decor and infinitesimal size of this self-service establishment. Inside is a wonderful selection of the best Mexican food found on Kauai. Open Mondays through Saturdays from 11 AM to 11 PM, and on Wednesday from 11 AM to 5:30 PM. Closed Sundays. 2827A Poipu Rd. (phone: 742-7222) Inexpensive.

Waimea Canyon

Down the western third of the island runs a 10-mile-long gash known as Waimea Canyon. The sculptor of this monumental work is the modest Waimea River, which, viewed from the rim of the canyon, looks like nothing more than a slim silver ribbon curled on the canyon floor. The river rises in the Alakai swamp, which, in turn, is fed by Mt. Waialeale. But on its way to the sea it cuts through much drier terrain. Instead of the jungle greens of the mountains, Waimea's tones are of the desert — the pink of the iron-rich soil and the pale green of the vegetation.

There are two roads leading to Waimea Canyon (and Kokee State Park beyond). The Waimea Canyon Road, starting in Waimea, affords some lovely backward glances at Waimea Bay and the flatlands of sugarcane fields. The Kokee Road, starting at Kekaha, leads through dry, scrubby land with lots of dog-eared cactus. Since it's interesting to see the change that just a few miles makes in the landscape of the island, drive up one road and down the other. Both are full of curves and hairpin turns, but are wide, well marked, and well graded. Go early in the morning before the traffic gets heavy. It's cooler then, too; the drive up can get warm by midmorning, even though it's always cool at the top of the canyon. Some days the canyon is enveloped in mist, which makes it difficult, if not impossible, to view anything from the lookouts. To avoid this, call ahead to Kokee State Park for the day's weather conditions (phone: 335-5871). If there's no answer, try the *Kokee Lodge* (phone: 335-6061).

About 12 miles up, from either Waimea or Kekaha, is the first lookout, from which you can see smaller canyons link up with Waimea. Another 2 or 3 miles beyond is Puu Hinahina lookout. Because people tend to stop at the first lookout, this one is a little less crowded. There are two views from here: one of the canyon and another facing southwest toward the island of Niihau.

If you want a close look at Waimea, the Kukui Trail, just a few miles before the first lookout, leads to the canyon floor. The hike down and back (5 miles round trip) can be made in a day, but there is an overnight shelter, the *Wiliwili Camp,* at the end of the trail where you can spend the night.

SHOPPING: The old plantation towns of Hanapepe and Waimea are beginning to attract artists and artisans who appreciate their authenticity and charm.

Andy Lopez – You may well catch artist Andy painting in the morning light of his studio/gallery in the heart of Hanapepe Town. 3878 Hanapepe Rd. (phone: 335-3853).

Collectibles & Fine Junque – Lots of Hawaiiana, plus odds and ends for antiques hunters. Unlike most shops in the area, it's closed on Sundays. On Kaumalii Hwy. (phone: 338-9855).

Gazebo – This in-home gallery features the work of Jean Jack, a friendly septuagenarian whose hand-painted plates are offered in limited editions. On Koloa Rd., Lawai (phone: 332-9203).

James Hoyle Gallery – Impressionist-style paintings by one of Hawaii's well-known artists are sold here. 3900 Hanapepe Rd. (phone: 335-3582).

Kahsuba Fine Arts – Hawaiiana in books and handicrafts, as well as ethnic and esoteric items from around the world. The adjacent *Captain Cook and Natural History Museum* includes artifacts from HMS *Discovery,* one of Captain Cook's ships. The museum (no admission charge) commemorates Cook's first Hawaiian landfall in Waimea in 1778. 9883 Waimea Rd., Waimea (phone: 338-1750).

Kauai Fine Arts – A first-rate collection of antique maps, prints, lithographs, and book illustrations that focus on exploration and travel from the 16th century onward. 3848 Hanapepe Rd., Hanapepe town (phone: 335-3778).

Lele Aka Gallery – Local crafts and paintings. 3876 Hanapepe Rd. (no phone).

Station – An unusual selection of Hawaiian-designed needlepoint kits and supplies. On Hwy. 50 just outside Hanapepe (phone: 332-7533).

CHECKING IN: The best choice for accommodations in the area are the *Waimea Plantation Cottages.* Expect to pay between $100 to $155 for an individual cottage.

Waimea Plantation Cottages – One of Hawaii's most unique properties, it gives a sense of the plantation lifestyle that dominated on Kauai for nearly a century. Beautifully restored and modernized, these comfortable cottages (41 at press time, with a dozen more to come) are set amid towering palms. The beachside pool is lovely, as are the new clubhouse reception area (in a restored plantation manager's home) and restaurant. Advance reservations are required much of the year. At the edge of Waimea town (phone: 338-1625; 800-992-4632). Moderate.

EATING OUT: There's not much to choose from, but if you're headed to Waimea Canyon or the beaches of the west coast, Hanapepe and Waimea provide a few inexpensive (under $20 for two, wine excluded) and moderate ($25 to $40) eateries for en route lunch or dinner. All telephone numbers are in the 808 area code unless otherwise indicated.

Kalaheo Steak House – Creditable steaks in a country-casual setting, this place is a hit with locals. Open nightly from 5 to 10 PM. No reservations. 4444 Papalina Rd. (phone: 332-9780). Moderate.

Brick Oven Pizza – Some say it's the best pizza on Kauai. Local color abounds. Open from 11 AM to 11 PM. Closed Mondays. Reservations advised. 2488A Kaumualii Hwy., in Kalaheo (phone: 332-8561). Moderate to inexpensive.

Camp House Grill – Good hamburgers and local-style barbecued chicken are the stars of the menu. Open daily for breakfast (6:30 to 10:30 AM), lunch, and dinner; closed Wednesdays for breakfast only. The same lunch and dinner menu is offered from 11 AM to 9 PM. No reservations. On Kaumualii Hwy. in Kalaheo (phone: 332-9755). Moderate to inexpensive.

Wrangler – An Old West mood pervades this place, and island-grown beef and Mexican fare, both well prepared, make up the menu. Open daily, except Sundays, for lunch (11 AM to 9 PM) and dinner. Reservations advised. In the renovated Ako Building, on Waimea's main drag (phone: 338-1218). Moderate to inexpensive.

Green Garden – The look is cinderblock and fluorescent lights, the food cafeteria-style, with lilikoi pie the best treat on the menu, but this family-run eatery is a popular en route stop for lunch. Open daily for breakfast (7:30 AM to 11 AM), lunch (11 AM to 2 PM), and dinner (5 PM to 9 PM); closed Tuesdays for dinner only. Reservations for dinner only. On Kaumualii Hwy. in Hanapepe (phone: 335-5422). Inexpensive.

Toi's Travelers Den – This unexpectedly good Thai place is open daily for lunch (11 AM to 2:30 PM) and dinner (5:30 to 8:30 PM). Closed Saturdays.Reservations advised. Next to the post office in out-of-the-way Kekaha. (phone: 337-9922). Inexpensive.

Kokee State Park

Another few miles along this road will bring you to Kokee State Park, a 4,345-acre nature reserve that's a magnet for picnickers, hikers, campers, and others who just appreciate the sights and smells of nature at its purest.

There are more than a dozen hiking trails — ranging from one-tenth of a mile to 3½ miles — that lead through fragrant forests of koa, pine, and redwood trees, and hibiscus, mokihana, and maile, the vine and berries used to make Kauai brides' wedding leis. Native forest birds flit in and out, and wild goats roam at will. At the end of most trails, you're rewarded with a scenic vista and a secluded picnicking spot. Since some trails are still closed as a result of damage from Hurricane Iwa, it's best to call the ranger station in advance (phone: 335-5871).

You can camp here, in tents or in trailers, or rent one of the park's cabins for $35 ($45 for a newer, cedar cabin); an additional $6.25 gets you firewood for the wood-burning stove. There are a dozen cabins and they're very popular, so make reservations in advance (holidays are booked up to a year in advance), although a call *may* find cabins available even at the last minute (*Kokee Lodge,* PO Box 819, Waimea, Kauai, HI 96796; phone: 335-6061). You can also, with permission of the park rangers (their headquarters is at the entrance to the park), pick up 10 pounds of the small, tart plums that grow wild on Kauai. The season usually starts in June or July and lasts from a few weeks to 2 months.

If you have less time to give to Kokee, follow the road to the end of the park to Kalalau Valley Lookout. At 4,000 feet, the air is sweet and cool, and the view of the broad green valley opening out to the sea is dramatic. The small slip of surf at the foot of the valley is Kalalau Beach, the end of the 11-mile trail that starts at Haena State Park on the northern side of the island. The only other way to reach it is by sea. There are picnic tables and fireplaces at the lookout. A second lookout a mile farther (at the end of the road) offers equally expansive views and serves as a trailhead for several hikes along the ridge.

Kokee has its own small restaurant, *Kokee Lodge* (phone: 335-6061), serving modestly priced breakfasts and lunches daily, and excellent dinners on Fridays and Saturdays (try the fine, light homemade cornbread). Next door is the Kokee *Natural History Museum* (phone: 335-9975), a pocket-size museum with a large relief map of western Kauai and exhibits of native birds, animals, and shells. The museum bookstore focuses on natural history, but also carries Hawaiian literature and poetry books. Open daily from 10 AM to 4 PM. No admission charge.

NIIHAU

For over a century, this small, private island, 17 miles off the leeward coast of Kauai, has been closed to the world. Besides an occasional doctor or government official, only invited guests of Niihau's 225 inhabitants are allowed to visit, and then only at the discretion of the owners, the Robinson family of Kauai. The only regular transportation to Niihau is a World War II landing craft that makes weekly runs to Port Allen on Kauai's southern shore, and securing passage on it is more difficult than getting an audience with the pope. Curious outsiders who try to land their own boats on Niihau are firmly turned away. Today that isolation has been modestly compromised by helicopter tours offered by *Niihau Helicopters* (PO Box 370, Makaweli, HI 96769; phone: 335-3500). The helicopter was purchased by the Robinson family for use in medical emergencies and the tours are their way of subsidizing the cost of purchase and maintenance. After a sightseeing flight over the island — the 3-hour tour costs $200 — the helicopter lands near both the northern and southern ends of Niihau, far from the island's only village, thereby maintaining Niihau's isolation and its uniquely Hawaiian lifestyle.

Niihau wasn't always so reclusive. When Captain Cook's ships, the *Discovery* and *Resolution,* drifted from anchorage in Kauai's Waimea Bay to neighboring Niihau, the islanders welcomed the strange white men from the "floating islands," as the Hawaiians referred to Cook's massive ships, and traded local yams and salt for seeds of foods then unknown in Hawaii — onions, melons, and pumpkins. Niihau went on supplying whalers and trading ships with yams, which were thought to be of superior quality to those grown on Kauai or Oahu, well into the 19th century.

Its isolation began in 1864, when King Kamehameha V sold the entire island for $10,000 to Eliza Sinclair, the daughter of a wealthy Scottish merchant and the widow of a New Zealand rancher. Mrs. Sinclair and her grown children (including Helen Sinclair Robinson, whose descendants now own the estate) turned the 46,000-acre island into a cattle and sheep ranch, employing the Hawaiians — who until then had worked their own yam and taro patches — as ranch hands and building a grand manor house with wood shipped from Boston around Cape Horn. Although Niihau's flat grassy meadows and numerous freshwater lakes — a rarity in the Hawaiian islands — proved ideal for ranching, the Sinclair clan soon tired of the heat and humidity and after a few years moved to Kauai, where they continued to run the Niihau ranch from the green valleys of that more temperate island.

Somewhere along the way, Mrs. Sinclair decided that the traditional Hawaiian way of life on Niihau should be preserved, which to her meant the lifestyle of the white ranchers, not the easygoing existence of the pre-Cook Hawaiians who lived on fish and poi and happily abandoned fields and labors whenever the waves were good for surfing. Succeeding generations have

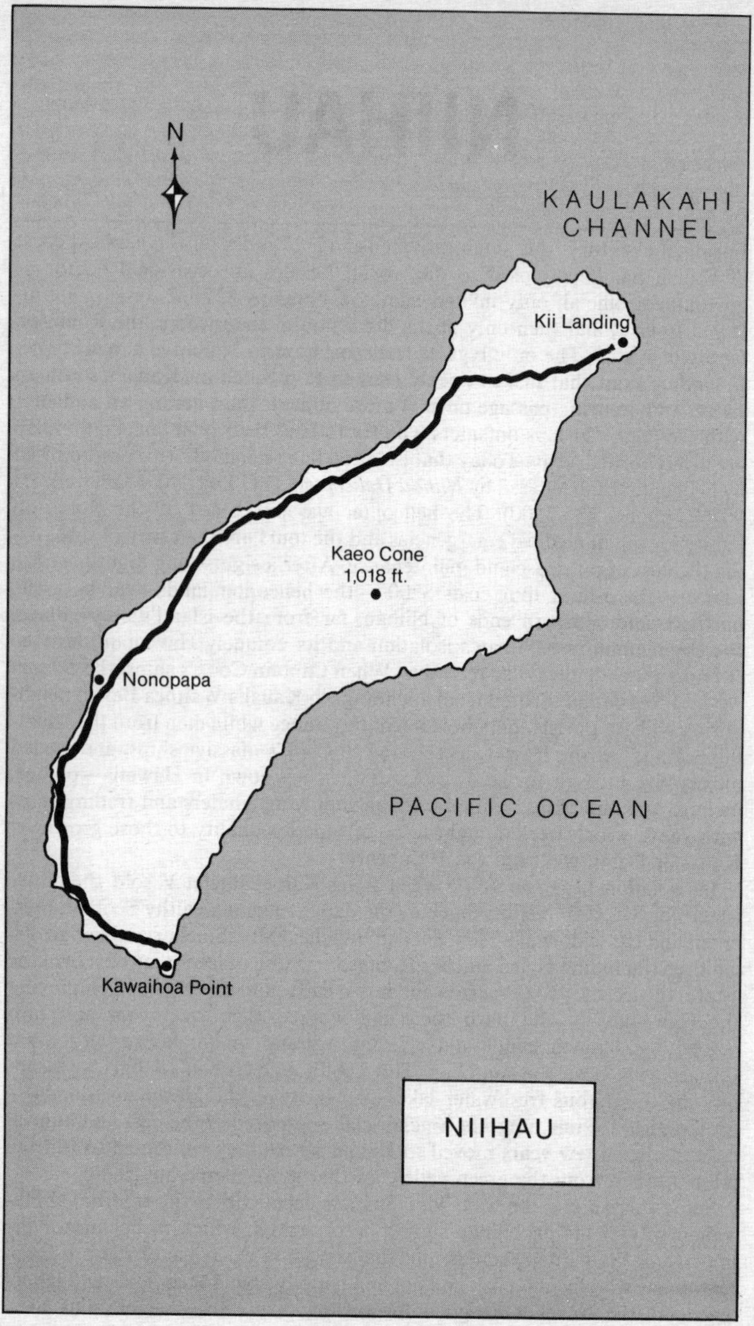
N
KAULAKAHI
CHANNEL
Kii Landing
Kaeo Cone
1,018 ft.
Nonopapa
PACIFIC OCEAN
Kawaihoa Point
NIIHAU

faithfully observed the old woman's wish, so that today Niihau still belongs to the 19th century.

The islanders, most of whom are full-blooded Hawaiians, all work for the ranch, living in small wooden houses more reminiscent of the Kansas frontier than Polynesia and sending their children to the ranch-run school. Life is simple and, by modern standards, backward. There's electricity at the school and the homestead kept by the Robinsons, but elsewhere oil lamps illuminate houses at night. There are no telephones or television sets, no shops, cinemas, or restaurants, and few motorized vehicles, with the medical helicopter a fairly recent addition. The staples of life are provided by the ranch, although each family keeps a garden, fishes, and hunts wild pigs and turkeys to supplement the beef and mutton produced on the ranch. What Niihauans can't grow or hunt they often do without, even though they could catch the barge to Kauai to shop for commonplace luxuries.

The only private industry allowed is the making of Niihau shell leis, intricately worked garlands that often fetch thousands of dollars in galleries on the major islands. Every October the work stops and the islanders comb the beaches for the tiny, multicolored shells used to make the leis. The shells, which range from beige to hot pink, are then painstakingly sorted by size and quality and strung into necklaces of exquisite beauty. It takes weeks to fashion the more complex designs, such as the many-stranded kipona lei or the pikake lei, whose clusters resemble the pikake blossom. An intricate, multicolored strand can cost thousands of dollars; however, there are enough Niihauans practicing this old art that it's possible to get a simple lei for $75.

Because Niihau is a living example of Hawaii's recent past, it arouses a great deal of curiosity. But fearing a deluge of requests for access, the Robinsons resolutely refuse to allow any visits or interviews, and they have rebuffed attempts by the Hawaiian legislature to buy the island so it could be turned over to native Hawaiians for homesteading. There may come a time, however, when the family may have to reconsider the state's offer. The population of Niihau has been steadily dwindling over the years. No newcomers are allowed to settle, and youngsters, who attend high school on Kauai or at the Kamehameha School in Honolulu, seldom return permanently to the island once they've had a taste of the outside world. But for the present, Niihau remains an enigma, a mysterious outline on the horizon.

KAHOOLAWE

To an outsider, Kahoolawe seems a Hawaiian anomaly — an undesirable piece of real estate. Seven miles off the south coast of East Maui, Kahoolawe is a barren, windswept island whose only inhabitants are wild goats barely able to subsist on its sparse and scrubby vegetation and streams that dry up after the winter rains. Kahoolawe lies in the shadow of Maui's looming Haleakala, the dormant volcano that blocks most of the rain and cool breezes borne by the trade winds. Consequently, it's hot and humid during the day and cold at night. And to add to its natural disadvantages, for more than 50 years it was pounded by naval artillery and bombers, using this bleak, unhappy island for target practice until 1990, when a 2-year moratorium was put into effect by Congress. One of the most dangerous results is that hundreds of unexploded shells lie hidden in the island's red soil.

Yet Kahoolawe is one of the most hotly contested parcels of land in the state. Native Hawaiians want it back, partially because it's the most blatant example of *haole* disregard for their homeland and, more practically, because in an island state, land of any kind is valuable. Since 1976, when a group called Protect Kahoolawe Ohana ("family" in Hawaiian) occupied the island against the express orders of the navy, Kahoolawe has become the symbol of native Hawaiian consciousness. Due to activist pressure, the US Navy granted Hawaiians fishing and visitation rights. Today, there is an ongoing movement by Hawaiians to have the US government remove the unexploded ordnance that litters much of the island, while everyone waits for a decision to be made as to who will eventually have jurisdiction over the territory.

The Ohana wants the island to be set aside for cultural and educational purposes. Kahoolawe, named in ancient times after Kanaloa, one of the four major Hawaiian gods, is a sacred island, mentioned often in the chants and legends passed down through the ages. At one time, all travelers to Tahiti stopped here to perform rituals before continuing on their way. And as late as 1874, King David Kalakaua was sent here by his *kahuna* (priest) to purge himself before he ascended the throne. Thanks to the isolation imposed by the navy's bombing, many of the ancient temples and fishing shrines are in excellent repair, and the Ohana sees the island as an unprecedented opportunity to add to the knowledge of their past.

The Ohana has scored some impressive successes in its efforts to regain civilian control of Kahoolawe. It forced the navy to make a comprehensive study of the environmental impact of the bombing and to conduct a survey of the archaeological sites. It also managed, in March 1981, to get the island named a National Historic Site. The Ohana also won the right to visit the island 4 days a month for 10 months of the year. During these times, men, women, and children gather on Kahoolawe's northeast shore to establish their claim to the island and to explore, with military guides, the old ruins; or to

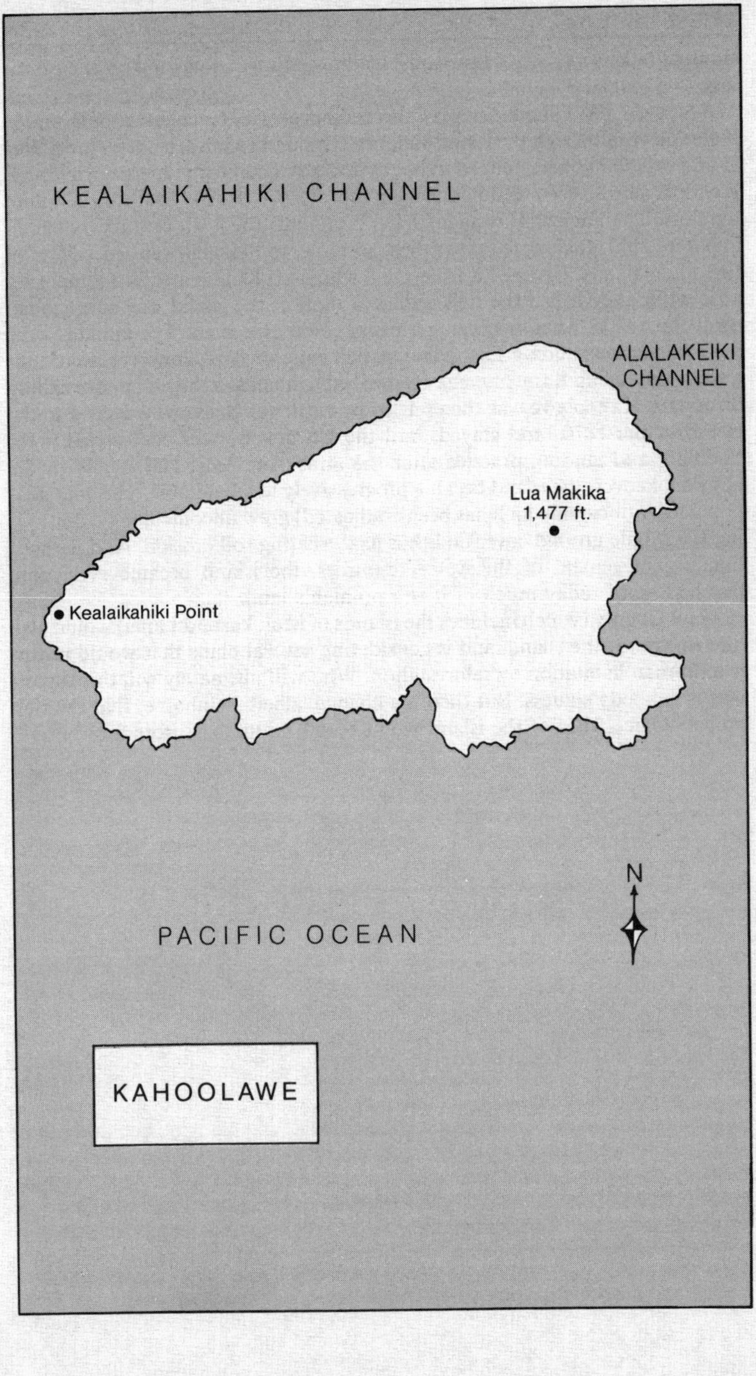
KEALAIKAHIKI CHANNEL
ALALAKEIKI
CHANNEL
Lua Makika
1,477 ft.
Kealaikahiki Point
N
PACIFIC OCEAN
KAHOOLAWE

simply "talk story," the Hawaiians' traditional way of passing on their heritage.

Not even the Ohana foresees the return of a permanent population to Kahoolawe, although the island supported modest ranches before World War II and its soil has been judged to be particularly good for modern agriculture. Kahoolawe has been uninhabited for more years than it has been home to humans. The ancient Hawaiians lived here until the 13th century, when an apparent shift in climate forced them to move to the well-watered valleys of the other islands. Except for fishermen, who used Kahoolawe as a temporary base while they fished the rich waters around it, the island was uninhabited until the 1830s, when it became a penal colony for men. The inmates were so brazen about raiding East Maui settlements for food, however, that after a short time King Kamehameha III decided to abandon the practice of exiling criminals. Kahoolawe was then settled by cattle ranchers, who moved to the island in the 1870s and stayed until the US government confiscated it for bombing and landing practice after the attack on Pearl Harbor. With the navy's takeover, the island became progressively less habitable. The wild goat population (most of which has been eradicated) grew uncontrollably, destroying the fragile ground cover and thus exacerbating soil erosion. And without man's management of the water resources, the island became ever more parched, until today much of it is a no-man's-land.

Maui County (which includes the islands of Molokai and Lanai) would also like control of the island, and is considering several plans that would return it to human habitation by reforestation. Who will ultimately win this tug-of-war is anybody's guess. But there's a chance, albeit a slim one, that the rich archaeological sites of the island won't be off limits to visitors forever.

DIVERSIONS

For the Experience

Quintessential Hawaii

You've sat on the beach at Waikiki until you're nut-brown and watched a succession of glorious sunsets from your private lanai. You've quaffed many a mai tai; donned a muumuu or aloha shirt; and sampled opakapaka, *pupus,* and three-finger poi. You've even decided that morning coffee will never again taste as good unless there's a tiny orchid floating in it. But while all of the foregoing are a pleasant part of any Hawaiian vacation, only after visiting the places described below — which allow a visitor to be a part of the real Hawaii — can a trip to these unique islands be considered a complete experience.

WAIMEA FALLS PARK, Haleiwa, Oahu: This is among the most beautiful spots on Oahu, with a gem of a cascade that tumbles into a rock-girt pool straight out of *Tarzan* or *The Blue Lagoon.* Even when the pathways through the gardens and around the natural, waterfall-fed pool are fairly crowded, which they often are on weekends and holidays, it's easy to escape the human traffic by walking rather than taking the park's motorized tram, which tends to drop large numbers of people at its more popular (and crowded) sections only. Apart from its considerable scenic charm, Waimea Falls Park inspires both historical and botanical fascination. The land once belonged to the high priest who served Kamehameha the Great, a man said to be buried hereabouts, though no one is quite sure where. Just off the main path are remnants of an ancient Hawaiian village, terraces where fruit and vegetables were cultivated, temple platforms, and fishing shrines. Psychics tell of feeling distinct vibrations in this area, although whoever is trying to relay a message seems to be placated by the sight and sound of old Hawaiian games such as *ulu maika,* a form of lawn bowling, which is taught and played in a meadow close by. The Waimea Arboretum and Botanical Gardens, on the meadows and hillsides between the visitors' entrance and the falls, is a wonderland of tropical flora. Amid this paradise of trees, shrubs, and plants are plots devoted to heliconia and ginger, hibiscus, ferns, bamboo, and exotic vegetation from such distant places as Bermuda, the Canary Islands, Sri Lanka, and Madagascar. A favorite conversation piece among visitors is the world's only known specimen of a tree called *kokia cookei.* Another is the 35 varieties of banana plants. The park is also home to some species of Hawaiian wildlife, including nene geese, Kona nightingales — wild donkeys — from the Big Island, peacocks, and wild boar. The annual *Makahiki Festival,* held during the first weekend in October, is recommended Hawaiiana. Also worthy of note: The park opens on nights when the moon is full, and free guided walks are conducted. Information: *Waimea Falls Park,* 59-864 Kamehameha Hwy., Haleiwa, HI 96712 (phone: 638-8511).

POLYNESIAN CULTURAL CENTER, Laie, Oahu: Like the Polynesian people themselves, their artifacts, dance, and music exemplify grace, beauty, and a highly refined artistic imagination. A dazzling array of all these qualities can be seen at the Polynesian Cultural Center on Brigham Young University's Hawaiian campus at Laie, on Oahu's windward coast. Students from many distinct Polynesian backgrounds, working in replicas of their native villages, explain the life, customs, rituals, ceremonies, habits, arts, crafts, and food of their homelands to visitors. The things to see, and sometimes participate in, include Tongan women making *ngatu,* or tapa cloth; Tahitian girls, lovely as moonlight, making shell leis and grass skirts; elaborate pint-size wooden tikis outside a small Marquesan village temple; Fijians playing music on pipe organs; Maoris from New Zealand throwing spears in their own unique manner; Samoan men walking unscathed through a curtain of flame; and Hawaiians making poi, something no one should leave the islands without seeing. The villages, authentic in every detail, have been built by students of the university, who are very friendly and carry a storehouse of detailed information in their heads. Fortunately, they also talk about up-to-date clothes, modern music, and baseball scores, which infuse a little real life into this museum village community. Don't miss the Tongan House and the Chief's House in the Fiji village. A film on the cultures of Polynesia is shown at the state-of-the-art (IMAX) theater, with its oversize screen. The center also features a series of musical performances throughout the day, including *Mana: Spirit of Our People,* a canoe spectacle that is included in the $25 entry fee, as well as an extravagant song-and-dance revue performed evenings and selected afternoons. The entry fee, dinner, and show package, at $40.50, is a good buy. For an additional $10, you can substitute the nightly luau for the dinner buffet. Front-row "VIP" seating and dinner cost $80.50. Motorcoach transfers are also available from Waikiki. Information: *Polynesian Cultural Center,* 55-370 Kamehameha Hwy., Laie, HI 96762 (phone: 293-3333).

SEA LIFE PARK, Waimanalo, Oahu: "An educational experience" may sound like just the sort of thing you've come to Hawaii to escape, but the didactic side of Sea Life Park is riveting, far more appealing than the show-biz side. The outstanding feature of the park is the Hawaiian Reef Tank, a 300,000-gallon re-creation of an undersea Pacific reef. Spiraling around the tank's transparent sides from top to bottom is a ramp with illuminated panels above the windows. These displays help visitors to identify some of the more obscure marine species, such as hermit crabs, which normally exist at depths of 200 to 300 feet; saddleback fish; and vivid butterfly and banded-angel fish. The panels also give the scientific names of some specimens that may be vaguely familiar already, such as the hammerhead shark, reef shark, brown sting rays, eagle rays, and moray eels. In the *Science Theater,* dolphins and penguins perform, while the recently opened Rocky Shores Exhibit shows a cross section of tidal ecology. At Whaler's Cove, porpoises wearing leis and whales towing a rowboat also take part in a sub-Disneyish scenario, which is about as edifying as watching a poodle turn somersaults. A number of small pools hold sea turtles, whiskered harbor seals, and a variety of seabirds normally found in the chain of islets strung out for 1,000 miles northwest of Hawaii. The *Pacific Whaling Museum* displays the largest collection of whaling artifacts and scrimshaw in the Pacific, not to mention the skeleton of a 38-foot sperm whale. Walls full of brightly illustrated explanatory texts inspire a desire to go probing around full fathom five and deeper. Sea Life Park's location at the foot of a sheer Koolau cliff and beside the ocean at Makapuu Beach is exceptionally beautiful. On Fridays, the park is open until 10 PM; every other day until 5 PM. The last series of shows starts at 6:15 PM, and includes Hawaiian music and dance as well as marine shows. Admission is $14.95 for adults, $7.95 for children 6 to 12, and $4.50 for those 4 to 7 years old. Information: *Sea Life Park,* Makapuu Point, Waimanalo, HI 96795 (phone: 259-7933).

HAWAII VOLCANOES NATIONAL PARK, the Big Island of Hawaii: The Hawaiian islands are rich in myth and legend, and among the pantheon of gods frequently mentioned, none looms so large, so tangible, or so memorable as Pele. This capricious firebrand has dwelt on all the major islands, and now makes her uneasy home on the Big Island in the very active Kilauea Crater, 4,077 feet above sea level, which is the dramatic focal point of the park. Pele has been repeatedly displaying her irascible temper during the series of eruptions that have been nearly constant since 1983. In a succession of fiery events that began toward the end of 1986, she sent waves of sun-red lava pouring down the hillsides and into the ocean along the island's south coast. The lava Pele sent heading for the sea has destroyed more than 200 homes and covered Route 13, closing the Hilo–Chain of Craters Road circuit via Wahaula several times during the eruptions. Pele has repeated her performance soon after each time the road has been restored to use (at press time, the route was closed and there was little likelihood of its being reopened in the near future).

In 1990, the village of Kalapana and the famous black sand beach at Kaimu were destroyed by flowing lava, which has added more than 200 acres to the adajcent coast. Ranger-led tours occasionally depart from Wahuaula to the eruption zone. And even when the goddess is resting, hissing steam vents and evil-smelling sulfur vents in the crater and on the surrounding bluffs confirm her presence and her readiness to rumble at any moment. Evidence of her wrath is everywhere: in the Kau Desert, where shiny folds of lava look like burnished chrome; along the surrealistic Devastation Trail, where scarred, gray wrecks of trees lie abandoned like driftwood on an ocean of cinders; and in the ohia forests, where molten droplets of lava have frosted branches and leaves and crystallized into gossamer forms, a phenomenon known as "Pele's hair."

In other parts of the park, the world seems to have turned topsy-turvy and dreamlike: The Thurston Lava Tube looks like a tunnel burrowed by a giant earthworm; giant ferns tower over Lilliputian visitors in the Fern Jungle; and all along the beaches, beneath familiar palm trees, are unfamiliar sands of jet black. For the botanist, ornithologist, paleontologist, geologist, and volcanologist, the park is a vast and bountiful laboratory. To laypeople it is almost always beautiful, frequently eerie, and invariably full of wonders. Because the park is so easily accessible by road, and Kilauea Crater and some smaller craters can frequently be seen by car, it has been dubbed "the Drive-in Volcano." Information: *Hawaii Volcanoes National Park,* PO Box 52, Hawaii National Park, HI 96785 (phone: 967-7311; for eruption reports, 967-7977).

HAWAII TROPICAL BOTANICAL GARDEN, Hilo, the Big Island of Hawaii: This once private garden and nature preserve, located on scenic acreage along the Hamakua Coast just 4 miles north of Hilo, offers one of Hawaii's most successful blends of native rain forest and formal garden. Palm groves lead to waterfalls and coastal lookouts, with lush plantings of heliconia, bromeliads (the pineapple family), banana, hibiscus, and orchids en route. A visit starts at the visitors' center, one-quarter mile from the gardens. From here, a van transports visitors to the garden, where two trails provide both beauty and privacy. Open daily, from 8:30 AM to 4:30 PM. Admission is $12 (no admission charge for children under 16). Information: *Hawaii Tropical Botanical Garden,* RR 143-A, Papaikou, HI 96781 (phone: 964-5233).

NANI MAUI GARDENS, Hilo, the Big Island of Hawaii: Nani Maui's 20 acres contain an abundance of flowering orchids and exotic trees and shrubs planted so that blooms are showing off no matter what the season. Well-marked plants and a short brochure make a self-guided tour both pleasant and informative, and at the end of the visit a selection of tropical fruits from Nani Maui's trees and plants, including several likely to be first-time experiences, are served. Located just off the highway linking Hilo with Hawaii Volcanoes National Park. The turnoff is marked by a visitors' bureau sign. Open daily from 8 AM to 5 PM. Admission is $5. Information: *Nani Maui Gardens,* 421 Makalika St., Hilo, HI 96720 (phone: 959-3541).

WAIPIO VALLEY, the Big Island of Hawaii: Secret gardens, desert islands, and Shangri-las of various kinds have always had a fascination for the traveler. Unfortunately, they are becoming harder and harder to find. One such place still exists on the northeast coast of the Big Island of Hawaii, about 50 miles north of Hilo. Called Waipio Valley, it's a broad, deep cleft in the Kohala Mountains rampant with as much floral exuberance as can be gathered in one place. On its three landward sides, it is flanked by precipitous cliffs many hundreds of feet high. Its oceanfront is guarded by often pernicious surf. Although there are taro patches here and there and remnants of sugarcane plots and rice paddies, most of the valley is an entangled umbrage of banana, guava, passion fruit, noni apple, avocado, mango, papaya, and grapefruit trees, with ginger, hibiscus, and orchids adding to the tumult of color and tall ferns with arabesque fronds lending a touch of mystery. Clear, fast-flowing streams run through these luxuriant groves, fed by the narrow, lacy Hiilawe Falls, which plunge 1,300 feet down from the mountains. Legend has it that in the late 18th century, the chief priest gave Kamehameha the Great custody of his war god here before embarking on his conquest of the islands.

In 1823, a traveler recorded that 1,325 people lived in the valley, and as scattered dwellings and multicolored outrigger canoes along the beach indicate, some still do. But their numbers have dwindled dramatically as tidal waves and other natural disasters have, albeit infrequently, made a hell of this paradise, driving many people to higher, safer ground. This lovely wilderness is penetrable on foot — allow a day to take full advantage — or with a four-wheel-drive vehicle, the only kind that can safely maneuver the steep grades and angles of the road. Perhaps the best way to explore the valley is in one of the jeeps operated by the *Waipio Valley Shuttle,* whose colorful drivers know the local lore, history, flora and fauna, or with *Waipio Wagon Tours,* which makes 2-hour visits in mule-drawn wagons that follow the four-wheel-drive descent to the valley floor. For those who wish to spend the night, which is magnificently alive with fragrant tropical breezes and stars, there's the *Waipio* motel — not so much a motel as a retreat, where a room costs $15 a night per person. The few bedrooms are lit with kerosene lamps, and drinking water is hauled in from Hilo. Unless you're fasting or are prepared to search the valley for some of its abundant fruits, remember to bring your own food, which can be prepared on the propane burners in the kitchen. Information: *Waipio Valley Shuttle,* PO Box 5128, Kukuihaele, HI 96727 (phone: 775-7121); *Waipio Wagon Tours,* PO Box 1340, Honokaa, HI 96727 (phone: 775-9518); *Waipio Motel,* 25 Malama Pl., Hilo, HI 96720 (phone: 775-0368 or 935-7466; advance reservations necessary).

MAUNA KEA SUMMIT, the Big Island of Hawaii: At 13,796 feet, Mauna Kea is not only the tallest mountain in Hawaii but, measured from its base 18,000 feet under the surface of the Pacific, it is also the tallest, most massive mountain on Earth. The summit — usually well above the clouds — is home to one of the most important astronomical observatory complexes in the world. *Paradise Safaris* runs day trips in four-wheel-drive vehicles that make easy work of the long road of flattened cinders which climbs to the summit and includes an observatory tour and remarkable panoramas. (Those who prefer to make the trip on their own should rent a four-wheel-drive vehicle.) In winter, there's likely to be snow covering the cinder cones dotting the summit, making the road extra difficult to navigate. Information: *Paradise Safaris,* Box A-D, Kailua-Kona, HI 96745 (phone: 322-2366).

At 9,000 feet, adjacent to the Hale Pohaku dormitories and facilities for the summit observatories' staff and astronomers, is the visitors' center of the Onizuka Center for International Astronomy, named for the late Hawaiian-born astronaut, which offers interesting displays on Mauna Kea and its state-of-the-art observatories. It also invites visitors to stargaze through its small (11-inch) but effective telescope on Fridays starting at 7 PM, and Saturdays starting at 6 PM. The sessions last for 2 hours. Those with respiratory or heart conditions are advised not to go higher than Hale Pohaku, and children under 16 are not permitted on tours. The center (phone: 961-2180) is open on an erratic schedule, so it's best to call for current hours and the status of weekend tours to the summit observatory. Summit tours are also offered by the Institute for Mauna Kea Support Services that depart the visitors' center at 2 PM Saturdays and Sundays.

You'll need a four-wheel-drive vehicle to participate. Information: *Institute for Mauna Kea Support Services,* 177 Makaala St., Hilo, HI 96720 (phone: 935-3371).

SUNRISE AT HALEAKALA NATIONAL PARK, Maui: Those folks seen staggering into your hotel at around 10 o'clock in the morning, looking tired but happy and weighed down by heavy sweaters, jackets, and blankets, have just returned from one of Maui's classic excursions — the trip to the top of Haleakala to see the sun rise. Haleakala, meaning "House of the Sun," is Maui's huge dormant volcano, and it has been known by that name at least since the Polynesian demigod Maui climbed to its 10,023-foot summit to lasso the rising sun and force it to move more slowly across the sky, thereby providing his mother with a few more hours of warm daylight in which to dry her tapa cloth. Latter-day visitors who retrace Maui's steps do it in a more reverent spirit. Mark Twain, in fact, wrote that it was the "sublimest spectacle" he ever saw, the memory of which would remain with him always.

The first requirement for the Haleakala pilgrimage is warm clothing. Temperatures at the summit can drop to as low as 35F in the summer and another 10 degrees lower in the winter, though the average is about 30 degrees lower than the temperature at sea level. A further requirement is the willpower to roll out of bed while the rest of the world is asleep. Sunrise occurs anywhere between about 5:45 AM in the summer and 7 AM in the winter, and it's necessary to be on the scene at least a half hour before dawn to witness the full spectacle. (Check the *Maui News* for the exact time of the next day's sunrise, or call the park's recorded information number, 572-7749, or the Maui Recreational Forecast, 871-5054.) *Papillon Helicopters* (phone: 669-4884) offers a sunrise itinerary ($195) and the Hana Crater Odyssey ($130). Both include a ground tour of Hana, along with a champagne breakfast or a deli-style lunch. Sunrise ground tours are offered by *Trans Maui* ($42; phone: 877-7308). Several companies offer downhill bicycle runs (38 miles from summit to sea). Information: *Pacific Island Cruisers,* 505 Front St., Lahaina, HI 96767 (phone: 579-8444; 800-654-7714). In addition, you can ride into the crater on horseback ($100). Contact *Pony Express Tours*, PO Box 535, Kula, HI 96790 (phone: 667-2200).

The road from Kahului to the top of the volcano is the only road on earth that rises from sea level to above 10,000 feet in a distance of only 40 miles. It will take about 1½ hours to drive and will deposit you above the cloud layer at the highest point on Maui, Puu Ulaula, a volcanic cone on which the glass-walled observation shelter that is the traditional spot for sunrise watching is perched. The shelter provides relative warmth and, poised as it is on the western rim of Haleakala's vast 19-square-mile crater, presents no obstruction of the view. Outside, as fellow pilgrims shiver and set their tripods pointing east, the sky brightens and the far edge of the sea of fluffy clouds takes on a border of spreading red and gold. When the sun finally appears, it comes up quickly (though portions of the crater do remain in shadow until late in the the day), but in the meantime, the play of light at the top of the world will have left an indelible impression. Afterward, there's plenty of time to observe the crater's barren landscape of cinder cones and ash from several vantage points and still make it out of the park before the visitor center opens and the day's tourists arrive. Information: Haleakala National Park, PO Box 369, Makawao, HI 96768 (phone: 572-9306, 572-9177).

MOLOKAI RANCH WILDLIFE PARK, Molokai: A square mile resembling Africa's open game land was carved out of the Friendly Island's dry, rolling western hills in 1977 and stocked with such exotic and endangered species of animals native to India and Africa as axis deer, sable antelope, Indian black buck, Barbary sheep, oryx, zebra (including a rare all-white zebra), giraffe, and ibex. Molokai Ranch Ltd.'s plan was to use an area similar to the animals' native habitat to breed them, thus serving as a transition supply point for the world's zoos and parks. But when guests at the nearby *Kaluakoi* hotel (which opened in 1977) heard of the park and expressed an interest in touring it, the company realized it had an automatic tourist attraction in what really is a working animal preserve. A very low-key van tour that lasts 1½ hours is now available; check with the *Kaluakoi*'s tour desk. The tour route runs over rough, rutted dirt roads (no pampering here), and affords good views of many of the 300 animals in the park. A picnic lunch is included, with resident giraffes as guests. Tickets are $30 plus tax; $20 for children 7 to 12; under age 7, free. Information: PO Box 1977, Maunaloa, HI 96770 (phone: 552-2555).

DAY SAILS TO LANAI: Several boats leave Maui daily for sails to what was once called the Pineapple Island — Lanai, where the attractions are a get-away-from-it-all setting and crystal clear waters that provide some of Hawaii's best snorkeling and scuba. Among those sailing are *Trilogy Excursions* from Lahaina, and *Ocean Activities Center* out of Maalaea. The cost ranges from $70 to $105, with more expensive sails that include a land tour of Lanai. *Trilogy* and *Ahilani Yacht Charters* head to Hulopoe Bay, where a crescent beach faces waters that are perfect for snorkeling. Lunch is served here. *Ocean Activities* offers snorkeling and swimming packages, as well as cruises off Lanai. Information: *Trilogy Excursions,* PO Box 1121, Lahaina, HI 96767 (phone: 661-4743; 800-874-2666); *Ahilani Yacht Charters,* Kahului Heliport 107, Kahului, HI 96732 (phone: 871-1156; 800-544-2520); *Ocean Activities Center,* 1325 S. Kihei Rd., Suite 212, Kihei, HI 96753 (phone: 879-4485; 800-367-8047, ext. 448).

NA PALI COAST STATE PARK, Kauai: No roads run through Na Pali; the ridges and valleys etched into the northwest coast of Kauai are so steep and narrow that they've even confounded the master builders of the last few decades, who've strung challenging highways elsewhere over the world. To see Na Pali, therefore, the adventurous must take a boat, skirting massive cliffs occasionally broken by isolated beaches; hire a helicopter to fly deep into the densely forested valleys; or hike in on foot, using the trail left by the ancient Hawaiians. Despite this inconvenience, most people who spend any time on Kauai get to Na Pali, for not to experience the awesome beauty of these jagged cliffs and hanging valleys is like visiting Paris and missing the *Louvre.*

Most people choose to see Na Pali by boat or helicopter, but for those who have the time — and stamina — to see it on foot, it's by far the best choice. The Kalalau Trail, starting at Haena State Park on the north coast and ending at Kalalau Valley 11 miles away, plunges into an Eden rich with fruit trees, wild orchids, sweet-smelling ginger, and Hawaii's majestic monkeypod, kukui, and koa trees. It's possible to camp overnight in a mango grove, pick sweet guava, bananas, and mountain apples for your breakfast, and bathe in a pristine pool at the foot of a waterfall. Scattered up the valleys, some so narrow a trekker hardly reaches the bottom before beginning the ascent up the other side, are the remains of stone-walled taro fields built by the early Polynesians, who chose this rugged and isolated terrain for the protection it offered from warring neighbors. Indeed, Na Pali has always offered refuge to those threatened from outside. One entire tribe is said to have fled into a valley west of Kalalau, never to be seen or heard of again. In more recent times, Koolau, a cowboy condemned to the Molokai leper colony, escaped with his family to one of Na Pali's valleys, where he successfully fought off the troops sent to take him back.

The first 2 miles of the trail to Hanakapiai Beach can be done in less than 2 hours by a walker in reasonable shape. From Hanakapiai, a 4-mile-long trail that fords streams and includes some strenuous portions heads toward the cliffs and a magnificent waterfall that is an authentic piece of paradise. The 8-mile circuit to Hanakapiai Valley and falls is a demanding day's hike. Beyond that, the trek to Kalalau requires an overnight stay and a good deal of stamina. *Captain Zodiac* (PO Box 5612, Kailua-Kona, HI 96745 (phone: 826-9371; 800-247-9484) provides hiker drop-offs or pickups in Kalalau. For those planning to cover the entire trail, camping equipment (and permission from the state parks department) is necessary, since the hike to Kalalau and back takes at least 2 to 3 days. Equipment for purchase or rent is available from *Jungle Bob's* (*Ching Young Shopping Center,* Hanalei, HI 96714; phone: 826-6664). For information on boat and helicopter tours, see "Sightseeing Tours" in *Kauai,* ISLAND-BY-ISLAND HOPPING. Hiking and camping information (and camping permits) can be obtained from the Division of State Parks, State Bldg. (3060 Eiwa St., Lihue, HI 96766; phone: 241-3444). Permits are issued by mail when applicants send a photocopy of their driver's license as I.D.

NATIONAL TROPICAL BOTANICAL GARDEN, Lawai, Kauai: Gardens are a special pleasure in Hawaii, where *everything* grows quickly and profusely. This garden, which runs down sunny Lawai Valley on the south side of Kauai, offers more than most since it's the only tropical research garden in the US and cultivates plants as rare as the white Tahitian mountain apple alongside hundreds of variations of the ubiquitous palm. (At last count, the garden had 800 different palms, about one third of the known varieties.)

In addition to studying and preserving tropical plant life, the garden conducts regular tours to acquaint the public with its work. The 2-hour tour, which includes 2 miles on foot, is limited to about a dozen people, who are led by knowledgeable volunteers who take the time to explain what's being seen and to answer visitors' questions. The result is an intimate and expert introduction for the layman to the staggering abundance of tropical flora.

For a young garden — just over 23 years old — its collections are extensive. In a section devoted to plants used for clothing, housing, food, and building, there are some 20 varieties of the hau tree, a member of the hibiscus family, which was important to early Polynesians both as a source of cordage (from the bark) and lightweight lumber for their outriggers. Among the many edible plants and spices raised by the garden are bananas (in a mere 60 varieties), coconuts, breadfruit, jackfruit, taro, Java plums, ginger, clove, allspice, cardamom, cinnamon, turmeric, and peppercorns.

Much of the garden is devoted to ornamental plants — red, waxy-leaved bromeliads; anthuriums; coral erythrinas; bamboos; and flowering trees, bushes, and ground covers in a multitude of shades and shapes. But the biggest crowd-pleaser is the fantastically large (big enough to support the weight of a small child) Victoria Amazonica, a green and pink water lily that rightfully belongs on the other side of Alice's looking glass.

Adjoining the Pacific Garden is the Allerton estate. The work of Robert Allerton, a wealthy Chicago banker, and his son John Gregg Allerton, it is an enchanting combination of formal gardens and tropical jungle. The younger Allerton, an architect by training, created outdoor "rooms" using living nature as his building material. The walls of his Thanksgiving Room, for instance, are formed by panax trees, slim-trunked trees used by Tahitians to support vanilla bean vines, while two sheltering monkeypod trees, flanking a classical water fountain, serve as a leafy roof.

The National Tropical and Allerton gardens are open to the public daily, with tours departing at 9 AM and 1 PM. Reservations are required. The tour costs $15. Membership in the garden costs $35 for two and includes the tour charge for the holder and immediate family members. Membership also allows entry to Satellite Gardens at Limahuli (on the north shore of Kauai) and in Hana, Maui. Information: *National Tropical Botanical Garden,* PO Box 340, Lawai, HI 96765 (phone: 332-7361).

Whale Watching

Every year from November to May, Hawaii plays host to some unusually distinguished guests, humpback whales who leave their summer home in the Gulf of Alaska to winter in the warm waters off Hawaii. The greatest congregation (properly called pods), between 500 to 800 whales, heads to the large shallow basin formed by the islands of Maui, Lanai, Molokai, and Kahoolawe, an area called, appropriately enough, the "bedroom of the whales," since it is here that they mate and give birth to their calves. Whales have also been sighted off south Kauai, south Oahu, and the west coast of the Big Island. Except for those glimpsed in southern California waters, the humpbacks in Hawaii constitute the largest gathering of whales routinely visible to humans, and in recent years, watching the aquatic antics of these remarkable creatures has been delighting thousands of visitors to the islands.

Measuring from 40 to 50 feet long and weighing about 40 tons, the humpback has distinctive characteristics that make it easily identifiable: bumps on its snout, unusually long flippers, and a scalloped tail fin, called a fluke, that is often 18 feet across. For all its bulk, the humpback is an agile and even graceful swimmer. In one incredible display, known as "breaching," the whale will propel its entire body up out of the water and then land on its back or side, sending up a wall of spray. Whether it breaches to communicate its location, to dislodge the many barnacles and lice that cling to its ample body, or simply to express a natural exuberance, no one knows for certain. But the display is undeniably impressive.

What fascinates biologists and laymen alike about whales is their intelligence and their highly developed social structure. A mother and her calf are always accompanied by a third whale, usually male, perhaps the father, who helps teach the newborn the necessities of life — diving, breathing, breaching — and runs interference for the mother and calf should anything threaten them.

The most striking evidence of their sense of community is their singing — sonorous, otherworldly sounds thought to be mating calls or communications to whales hundreds of miles away. The songs are complicated sequences, lasting anywhere from 6 to 30 minutes, repeated over and over. Not only do all the whales in a given community sing the same song (North Pacific humpbacks sing a different song from humpbacks in the North Atlantic), but the song changes, subtly, from year to year, and everybody learns the new verses. Just how they do it is something that no doubt will baffle and challenge scientists for years to come.

Maui is by far the best island base for whale watching. They can easily be seen from several spots along the shore, and because Maui is a popular tourist destination, there are a number of whale watching cruises that leave from Lahaina and Maalaea harbors. The cruise sponsored by the *Pacific Whale Foundation* (101 N. Kihei Rd., Kealia Beach Plaza, Kihei, HI 96753; phone: 879-8811), a research organization, is perhaps the most informative, but others run by residents well acquainted with the waters can be just as fruitful. (If you book your cruise through the *Pacific Whale Foundation,* a portion of your fare will go to its efforts on behalf of the whales.)

Don't, however, take a boat out on your own. There are strict federal regulations regarding the observation of whales, and fines of up to $20,000 for violating them. Although the humpback has been a protected animal since 1966, its numbers have continued to drop until today there are only an estimated 1,000 to 1,500 left in the Pacific. Some think that one of the reasons for the decline is human-generated activity, such as the buzz of a boat's motor around their breeding grounds, which interferes with mating. Since females give birth to a single calf only once every 2 years, it's not hard to appreciate how perilously close to extinction the humpback is.

Because of these concerns, naturalists are encouraging people to watch whales from the shore. Shore-spotting is excellent on Maui, from Kaanapali to Maalaea Bay on West Maui, and down the coast of East Maui to Makena. There are a number of high spots where observers can pull off the road to watch them, but the scenic lookout at McGregor Point, near the town of Maalaea, offers the best viewing.

Whales are also visible from Molokai and Lanai, but the best viewing spots are difficult for tourists to reach. A small group of whales spends time at Kawaihae Bay, on the northwest side of the Big Island, and, with a little patience, it's possible to spot them from one of several elevated places along the coast. There are some winter sightings from Kauai's south coast, but April and May are the better months, when great numbers pass offshore on their trek back north. Any high spot along Poipu, especially Makahuena and Nukumoi points, is likely to reward a patient observer with the sight of a group of two or three humpbacks swimming along the surface at a good clip. If they're not cavorting around, there's plenty of spray coming from their blowholes to track them by. *Kauai Sea Sports* (phone: 742-9303) offers motorized raft whale watch tours during winter months from Poipu's Kukuiula Harbor. On Oahu, whales are occasionally spotted from lookouts between Diamond Head and Makapuu.

There's no great trick to successful shore-spotting, but a few tips should help first-timers get started. To begin with, use elevated ground for your observation point. Then go early in the morning or late in the afternoon. By midday, the wind is stronger and churns up the water, making it more difficult to spot the whales, but a few hours before sunset, which comes between 6 and 7 PM, the whales tend to come closer to shore, sometimes as near as 50 feet away. Finally, be patient. Scan the horizon till you see what looks like an explosion of smoke about 18 feet high. That's the blow of the humpback. If you have binoculars, by all means, take them along. They're especially good for spotting the light blow of a calf. When a humpback lifts its head out of the water, an activity dubbed "spy hopping" since its eyes are just above the surface, it's just playing around. But when it lifts its tail straight up out of the water (called a fluke-up dive), it's going under for a prolonged dive and won't surface again for another 20 minutes or so.

To bone up on humpbacks before setting off on a watch, the *Pacific Whale Foundation* gives a number of lectures at hotels and condominiums around Maui. (Call 879-8811 for a schedule of upcoming lectures.) It's also possible to catch two films on whales at the *Carthaginian,* a boat–cum–whaling museum anchored at Lahaina Harbor. And at the Whale Report Center, on the dock next to the *Carthaginian,* there's updated news on where whales have been sighted most recently. Also worth a visit is the *Whalers Village Whale Museum* at Kaanapali, the *Pacific Whale Museum* at Oahu's *Sea Life Park,* Honolulu's *Bishop Museum,* and the *Hawaii Maritime Center* adjacent to Aloha Tower in downtown Honolulu, all of which feature excellent displays on the great whales and artifacts of the hunt. If you come away as fascinated by these creatures as most people do, treat yourself to Richard Ellis's beautiful and comprehensive work, *The Book of Whales* (Knopf; $25); Bob Goodman's interesting book, *Whale Song;* or a Robert Lyn Nelson, Wyland, or Christian Lassen painting (very expensive), lithograph (affordable), or print (very affordable).

Hawaii's Heavenly Hotels

Contrary to popular conception, Hawaii does not have a long innkeeping tradition. In fact, most of its hotels, resorts, and condominiums have been constructed in the decades since World War II, when the islands experienced a tremendous boom in tourism. Many of these facilities were ill planned and hastily constructed, resulting in too many faceless concrete high-rises and such hodgepodge developments as Waikiki (on Oahu) and Kihei (on Maui). Still, the state has several very fine hostelries, notable for their history, architecture, ambience, setting, or luxury, and it is in this context that they are discussed below.

BED AND BREAKFAST: Just a few years ago, there were no bed and breakfast accommodations in Hawaii. Today, several hundred island families open their homes to visitors at per person rates that start at $35, average $70, and climb to over $150, depending on location, amenities, and room size. Most bed and breakfast accommodations include a private bath, and many have a private entrance. In some cases, entire apartments are available. Four Hawaii-based agencies now handle bookings. Oldest and largest is *Bed & Breakfast Hawaii,* which includes properties on all the islands and sells a book listing bed and breakfast options. Information: *Bed & Breakfast Hawaii,* PO Box 449, Kapaa, HI 96746 (phone: 822-7771; on Oahu, 536-8421; 800-733-1632); *Bed & Breakfast Honolulu,* 3242 Kaohinani Dr., Honolulu, HI 96817 (phone: 595-7533; 800-288-4666); *Bed and Breakfast Connection Maui Style,* PO Box 98, Puunene, Kihei, HI 96784 (phone: 879-7865, 800-848-5567); *Pacific Hawaii Bed & Breakfast,* 970 N. Kalaheo, Kailua, HI 96734 (phone: 262-6026; 254-5030; 800-999-6026); and *Hawaii's Best Bed and Breakfast Statewide* (PO Box 563, Kamuela, HI 96743; phone: 885-0550; 800-262-9912). For individual bed and breakfast recommendations, see *Checking In* in each island chapter.

KAHALA HILTON INTERNATIONAL, Honolulu, Oahu: There is something about staying here that is reminiscent of spending a few days at a superbly run country house; considering that there are 370 rooms in the complex; this is no mean feat. It may be the hotel's comparative isolation, surrounded as it is by the *Waialae* golf course and the ocean, or it may be the subdued harmony that exists between the polite, friendly, Hawaiian staff and the rather more formal European management. Whatever the individual ingredients, they add up to an operation that manages to be scrupulously (but unobtrusively) attentive to detail. News of the *Kahala*'s singular reputation and the seductive beauty of its setting has been brought to ears influential enough to persuade the Queen of England and her consort and the King of Spain and his wife to spend a few days here, as well as a host of other celebrities. Besides the main building, with its bright and airy rooms, there are oceanside bungalows and a 2-story wing overlooking the hotel lagoon. The 30-foot-high lobby is filled with orchids and dominated by two huge chandeliers. The lagoon and adjacent ponds hold sea turtles, more than 1,000 reef fish, and dolphins that are constantly on the lookout for mischief and perform for guests during feedings at 11 AM, and at 2 and 3 PM. Among the more than 50 varieties of flora are hau and autograph trees; traveler's and bottle palms; heliconia, bird of paradise, hibiscus, and ginger, Tahitian gardenias (called *tiare*), and spider lilies. The *Maile* restaurant, under the hotel lobby, is one of the best known, most elegant eating places in Honolulu. The *Hala Terrace,* where scrumptious lunch snacks and delicious Sunday brunches are served, looks out on the ocean and palm trees. Information: *Kahala Hilton International,* 5000 Kahala Ave., Honolulu, HI 96816 (phone: 734-2211; 800-367-2525).

HILTON HAWAIIAN VILLAGE, Honolulu, Oahu: With close to 2,600 rooms, Hawaii's largest hotel has been totally renovated and rebuilt (at a cost of nearly $100 million), with very appealing results, not least of which is the comfortable lounging area by the free-form, beachside pool, complete with waterfalls and grottoes. The posh Alii Tower provides guests with a private pool, luxurious furnishings, and full concierge services. But the best rooms in terms of spectacular views of Diamond Head are those facing the ocean in the Rainbow Tower. Fine dining (the *Golden Dragon* and *Bali by the Sea* are both worthy of note), a full complement of shops and boutiques, two showrooms with headliner entertainment, one nightclub, a catamaran pier, full beach services, and a tranquil location at the west end of Waikiki Beach are also among its many assets. Throughout the week, Hawaiian dance, music, song, and crafts are offered on the hotel's expansive grounds, culminating in fireworks on Friday evenings. Information: *Hilton Hawaiian Village,* 2005 Kalia Rd., Honolulu, HI 96815 (phone: 949-4321; 800-445-8667).

HYATT REGENCY WAIKIKI, Honolulu, Oahu: The builders set out to prove that all tall concrete hostelries on famous seaside avenues do not have to be totally devoid of character, and they have largely succeeded. The structure is easily recognized from a distance because of the two octagonal towers that have become a Honolulu landmark.

In the atrium, it is possible to forget that Kalakaua Avenue is just steps away and to enjoy the cool spray from the 3-story-high waterfall that cascades dramatically into a garden pool. All the guestrooms have spacious lanais with panoramic views, but the most luxurious of rooms are in the Regency Club, on floors 37 through 40, for which a special elevator key is required. A penthouse suite in each tower provides Regency Club guests with a lounge where breakfast is served each morning and cocktails are served in the evening. A concierge is on duty daily. Culinary talent is exhibited at *Caio Mein,* the hotel's new restaurant that serves Italian and Chinese dishes, and at the elegant *Musashi,* which offers a serene Oriental atmosphere and Japanese cuisine. Action of a noisier sort can be found in *Spats,* a disco that looks like an upper-crust speakeasy designed for preppy gangsters. The late-evening jazz at *Trapper's* lounge draws night owls. *Hyatt Regency,* 2424 Kalakaua Ave., Honolulu, HI 96815 (phone: 923-1234; 800-233-1234).

SHERATON MOANA SURFRIDER, Honolulu, Oahu: When the *Moana* was built in 1901 on Waikiki Beach, there were only a few seaside cottages here, along with a number of mansions used by Hawaiian royalty and a handful of wealthy merchants. In spite of predictions that it was too far from downtown to attract customers, it quickly became *the* place to stay, and was preferred by the blue-blood set even when the *Royal Hawaiian* was attracting millionaires and silent-movie stars. In the era of flappers and Bright Young Things, the Prince of Wales (later Duke of Windsor) and his cousin Lord Louis Mountbatten (later Earl Mountbatten of Burma) stayed at the hotel. In keeping with its historic past the *Moana* was completely restored, at a cost of more than $50 million. The original Greek Revival portico was reconstructed and the rooms redesigned with a combination of turn-of-the-century elegance and contemporary chic. The clutter that nearly obscured the great beachfront banyan was removed, re-creating the atmosphere of bygone days that once inspired Robert Louis Stevenson, who used to sit and write here even before the *Moana* was imagined. The *Moana* has been joined with the neighboring *Surfrider* into a single hotel, and although the Surfrider wing offers rooms with spectacular views of Diamond Head, the historic charm and elegance of the original hotel provides its guests with a more unique experience. Information: *Sheraton Moana Surfrider,* 2365 Kalakaua Ave., Honolulu, HI 96815 (phone: 922-3111; 800-325-3535).

ROYAL HAWAIIAN, Honolulu, Oahu: It is from Waikiki Beach that the Pink Lady, as she is affectionately known, is seen best. Most of the surrounding buildings tower over her rudely, but the hotel's Spanish-Moorish hacienda lines and gaudy pink color still catch the eye immediately. When it was opened in 1927, amid much pomp and circumstance, the Pink Lady was only the second hotel of any note along Waikiki, a kind of flashy Hollywood rival to the *Moana,* the prim, New England–style, seaside hotel just down the street. But the years when steamer trunks were carried to the *Royal Hawaiian* by Chinese coolies riding on the backs of trucks, when *kamaaina* servants stood around the dining rooms waiting on *haole* ladies wearing vast brimmed hats and flowery frocks, have gone. The restaurants have efficient staffs now, and jogging shorts, jeans, and tennis togs are the current fashions for guests. But some nostalgic touches still linger, such as Sunday tea dances, at which elderly swains whirl handsome matrons around the floor, and the romantic pink decor, which is so pervasive that one feels an obligation to blush in order not to appear conspicuous. And visitors sitting on the porch at sunset, listening to the palms rustling in the breeze and the faint music wafting up from the bars along the beach, can't help but imagine that they belong — however fleetingly — to an earlier and much different time. Information: *Royal Hawaiian Hotel,* 2259 Kalakaua Ave., Honolulu, HI 96815 (phone: 923-7311; 800-325-3535).

HALEKULANI, Honolulu, Oahu: Considered by many (including us) to be Waikiki's finest, most luxurious hostelry. Incorporating several of the buildings of the original bungalow hotel, the *Halekulani* features 2 restaurants and beautifully landscaped grounds consisting of 5 acres of prime Waikiki beachfront. Facing the beach is the hotel's *House Without a Key* open-air lounge — a perfect place to sip cocktails at day's end, listen to Hawaiian music, and admire the fine views of Diamond Head. The oceanfront *La Mer* is one of Waikiki's finest restaurants, and service throughout the hotel provides a personal touch. Altogether, this property seems to provide a sense of exclusivity and romance. Information: *The Halekulani,* 2199 Kalia Rd., Honolulu, HI 96815 (phone: 923-2311; 800-367-2343).

SHERATON MAKAHA, Makaha Valley, Oahu: The precipitous valley walls soaring up to jagged peaks suggest a fortress. Along these mysterious ramparts, mists linger in the early mornings, then later tumble in rivulets down the steep mountainsides, along which there is also a daily display of ever-changing light and shadow. In the middle of this diorama is the *Sheraton Makaha,* a complex of attractively furnished bungalows and low Polynesian-style buildings set amid green lawns, palm trees, and a striking jumble of bougainvillea, plumeria, and hibiscus 40 miles from the hustle and bustle of Waikiki. Sports are a major attraction here. There are jogging and hiking trails, tennis courts, and horses to ride up into the remoter parts of the valley, where peacocks screech and wild turkeys gobble. The main pastime, however, is golf: The challenging 7,200-yard West Course is one of the best in Hawaii. Watching the sunset beside the pool is a favorite evening entertainment, for the setting sun sinks slowly over the Pacific horizon and casts a haunting, roseate glow over Makaha Beach, a mile or so away at the foot of the valley. Afterward, there is dinner in the elegant *Kaala Room,* and a postprandial stroll under a blanket of stars is simply a must. Information: *Sheraton Makaha Resort,* PO Box 896, Makaha, HI 96792 (phone: 695-9511; 800-325-3535).

ASTON WAIKIKI BEACHSIDE, Honolulu, Oahu: Small and regal, this charmer radiates 18th-century Oriental and European elegance. All 79 guestrooms are decorated with panache, and are so tastefully appointed that you might be inspired to begin humming a Noël Coward tune. Even the lobby is pure swank from floor to ceiling, and is filled with fine Oriental and European pieces. A crackerjack staff, impeccably and formally clad, practically jumps to respond to guests' needs — no matter the hour. Other small luxuries include in-room VCRs and French toiletries. There are no restaurant facilities on the premises, but there is easy access to the *Hyatt Regency* and other resort complexes in the area. Information: *Aston Waikiki,* 2552 Kalakaua Ave., Honolulu, HI 96815; phone: 931-2100; 800-922-7866).

TURTLE BAY HILTON, the North Shore, Oahu: Miles of beach, stables for horseback riding, tennis, golf (a new 18-hole course, designed by Arnold Palmer, has recently opened; the old George Fazio layout is currently being revamped as another Palmer course), helicopter tours, snorkeling, and scuba add up to a self-contained, neighbor island–style resort an hour's drive from Waikiki. Hub of a much larger resort now in the planning stages, the recently renovated *Turtle Bay Hilton* features accommodations in a mid-rise tower and in a lovely low-rise, seafront wing that are spacious and private. The location provides easy access to the famous North Shore surfing beaches (some of Hawaii's most beautiful), the Polynesian Cultural Center, and Waimea Falls Park. The only drawback is an occasional high wind that sends sand flying and makes the surf dangerous. The Towers Concept of concierge services, preferential reservations, and special amenities is available to guests staying in rooms on the west wing of the 6th floor. Information: *Turtle Bay Hilton and Country Club,* PO Box 187, Kahuku, HI 96831 (phone: 293-8811; 800-445-8667).

PLANTATION SPA, Kawaa, Oahu: Seven lovely acres at the foot of the verdant, saw-edged Koolau Mountains provide a setting perfectly in keeping with this spa's commitment to psychological and physical well-being. Guests visit for a day, a weekend, or a full week-long program of activities that includes everything from kayaking to hiking to aerobics to lectures on subjects both holistic and Hawaiian. You can do all or nothing; the choice is yours. Owners Dave and Bodil Anderson, he from Hawaii, she from Sweden, run a superbly efficient, hands-on operation. Accommodations in the main house (ca. 1935) are quite comfortable, and there are several cottages on the grounds that lead to turquoise waters. The guest list is limited to 18 people at any given time, which further enhances a sense of serenity and privacy. Information: *Plantation Spa,* 51-550 Kamehameha Hwy., Kawaa, HI 96730 (phone: 237-8685; 800-422-0307).

VOLCANO HOUSE/KILAUEA LODGE, Hawaii Volcanoes National Park, the Big Island of Hawaii: The *Volcano House* is a small, rustic lodge (37 units) and adjacent bungalow with compact but comfortable rooms, an unpretentious restaurant serving satisfactory food, a bar where guests can listen to relaxing music in the evenings, and a flagstone sitting room–lobby where a fire burns to lessen the summer humidity and remove the winter chill. But by far its main allure is its site above the Halemaumau Crater. Usually all there is to see are vapors rising from steam and sulfur vents. But sometimes there are the more dramatic pyrotechnic demonstrations of the goddess Pele, when she begins spouting molten lava into the sky from the nearby Kilauea firepit. When this happens, guests and sightseers by the hundreds watch the show from the restaurant, the bar, or, if you're on the crater side, your own room. Although in recent years, the hotel has gotten a bit worn, it still retains its easy access to the park's numerous wonders. Just a mile outside the park in Volcano Village is a more charming option, the 4-room *Kilauea Lodge* (ca. 1930). Rustic appeal abounds, from the blazing fire to the fine restaurant that serves a breakfast (included in the room rate) and a dinner worth the anticipation. Information: *Kilauea Lodge,* PO Box 116, Volcano, HI 96785 (phone: 967-7366); *Volcano House,* Hawaii Volcanoes National Park, HI 96718 (phone: 967-7321).

MAUNA LANI BAY, Kawaihae, the Big Island of Hawaii: Guests who arrive at this elegant hotel are greeted with leis in a lobby complete with waterfalls, palm trees, garden, and pool. The guestrooms, with their ivory and burgundy color schemes, are no less striking, though a tad more sedate. Downstairs, there are 4 restaurants, including the attractive *Canoe House,* with its "Pacific Rim" menu; the elegant French-accented *Le Soleil;* and the *Third Floor,* which serves mullet from the hotel's ancient fish ponds (which once belonged to Kamehameha I). Amateur archaeologists will enjoy exploring the 15th-century rock shelters that were left standing under orders from Ken Brown, the hotel's president and a direct descendant of Hawaiian royalty. Those of a less studious bent may opt for swimming at the pool or beach, outrigger canoe rides, helicopter tours, or, most often, golf. The two 18-hole courses, the *North* and the *South,* offer green fairways that snake through black lava fields broken by coastal inlets. Though the courses aren't quite as formidable as they first appear, players often find themselves distracted by the occasional cavorting of migrating whales, jumping out of the ocean less than half a mile from the sixth tee of the *North* course. The most luxurious of all the accommodations here are the five ultra-posh 2-bedroom "bungalows" where no expense has been spared to swathe guests in plush surroundings — as might be expected in digs that cost $2,000 to $2,500 a night. Everything from the private pool to the personal staff of maids and butlers ready to respond at the drop of a lei to guests' wishes radiates extravagance. Information: *Mauna Lani Bay Hotel,* Box 4000, Kohala Coast, HI 96743 (phone: 885-6622; 800-367-2323).

RITZ-CARLTON MAUNA LANI, Mauna Lani, the Big Island of Hawaii: One of two Hawaiian properties belonging to the very upscale Ritz-Carlton group, its 542 spacious rooms offer marble baths, elegant decor, and oceanview lanais. In addition, visitors can enjoy the extra pampering (for an extra price) offered by *Ritz-Carlton* Club accommodations. Guests can take advantage of the many activities the 32-acre property offers, including a 10-court tennis complex, two 18-hole golf courses, a fitness center, and a lovely white sand beach. Information: *Ritz-Carlton Mauna Lani Resort,* 50 Kaniku Dr., Kohala Coast, HI 96743 (phone: 885-0099; 800-241-3333).

HYATT REGENCY WAIKOLOA, Waikoloa, the Big Island of Hawaii: With 1,241 rooms and 62 oceanfront acres, this nearly $400-million resort is one of Hawaii's most extravagant. Perfectly manicured grounds provide the background for a tapestry of manmade canals, waterfalls, and lagoons. Millions of dollars in artwork grace the hotel's 3 separate wings and the mile-long walkway that meanders through corridors and landscaped grounds. The majority of the guestrooms have ocean views. Facilities include three 18-hole golf courses, tennis and racquetball courts, a health spa, several swimming pools (the largest of which covers three-quarters of an acre), and 7 restaurants. Information: *Hyatt Regency Waikoloa,* Waikoloa, Kamuela, HI 96743 (phone: 885-1234; 800-223-1234).

MAUNA KEA BEACH, Kamuela, the Big Island of Hawaii: There is little doubt that the Hawaiian gods smiled on *Mauna Kea.* This monument to luxury and good taste is built above the Big Island's most beautiful sand beach. The first luxury resort built on the island, it has aged gracefully, and retains a sense of quiet sophistication. The grounds are meticulously landscaped, and there are hundreds of Hawaiian, Oriental, and South Pacific antiques — relics of the original Rockefeller (Rockresorts) stewardship — that grace the cool and elegant lobbies and landings and line the corridor walls. Room furnishings are relatively simple, with brightly polished tile floors covered by handsome carpets, bleached wicker bedsteads and armchairs, and no television sets. Lanais are generous enough to accommodate a dining table for two and a chaise longue. Breakfast out here, on eggs Benedict and Kona coffee, or sipping a cocktail as the sun sets, is enough to inspire genuine feelings of despair at the thought of leaving. And if there is a beach in heaven, it probably looks like this one. The *North* golf course is one of Hawaii's most scenic, and a second course, called the *South,* opened early this year. Other sports facilities are similarly first-rate. Information: *Mauna Kea Beach Hotel,* PO Box 218, Kamuela, HI 96743 (phone: 882-7222; 800-882-6060).

KONA VILLAGE, Kaupulehu, the Big Island of Hawaii: If you've ever dreamed of a South Seas retreat, this is the place. *Kona Village* is marvelously situated in a private oasis surrounded by thousands of acres of semi-barren lava fields. The beach and lagoon, however, are fringed with palm trees and tropical vegetation and interspersed with 125 rustic *hales* (houses) in Hawaiian, Tahitian, Samoan, Fijian, and Tongan designs. Guests staying a week or more can select accommodations in the island style of their choice, otherwise you accept what's available. Rustic they may be without, but there's considerably more comfort within, with grass mats, louvered doors, wicker furniture, crisp, colorful coverings on the beds, plants, and paintings. There are no in-room telephones or television sets or newspapers. If you are hyperactive, there are tennis courts, sailboats, volleyball, shuffleboard, outrigger canoes, and a helipad for tours. For the more sedate, there are lessons in lei making and flower-arranging, and for those blessed with true slothfulness, hammocks are slung between palm trees on the beach. There are rotating dinner menus, and weekly specials include a *paniolo* steak panfry and a Friday night luau. A favorite conversation corner is the *Shipwreck Bar,* which is named with wry precision. It was constructed from the remains of a 42-foot sloop that sank in a storm before the resort was developed. Although the *Four Seasons Kona* threatened to spoil the splendid isolation of this prime property, the golf course (owned by the *Four Seasons*) that separates the two hotels maintains the resort's sense of privacy. Information: *Kona Village Resort,* PO Box 1299, Kaupulehu-Kona, HI 96745 (phone: 325-5555; 800-367-5290).

FOUR SEASONS WAILEA, Wailea Resort, Maui: Formal yet welcoming, this beachfront property provides a perfect mix of sophisticated architecture, service, and the creature conforts that make for a memorable stay. The 380 rooms are spacious, decorated in earth tones and pastels, and the public areas are filled with paintings and sculpture, more in the style of a creatively decorated villa than of a hotel. Most of the rooms have full or partial ocean views, and the remainder face beautifully landscaped, flower-filled grounds. On-site facilities include a small spa and workout room, a children's activity center for guests ages 5 to 12, and a year-round baby-sitting service that is free for guests, allowing parents the opportunity to enjoy the golf, tennis, and the shops of Wailea and other nearby resorts. The heated pool, while not large, is enhanced by large fountains and two adjacent open-air Jacuzzis and direct access to crescent Wailea Beach (pool attendants pamper guests with plush towels and Evian spritzers). Your taste buds won't be neglected thanks to the hotel's 2 fine restaurants. Don't miss the Lobster Club sandwich. Information: *Four Seasons Wailea,* 3900 Wailea Alanui Dr., Wailea, HI 96753 (phone: 874-8000; 800-334-6284).

GRAND HYATT WAILEA, Wailea Resort, Maui: The most expensive resort property built to date in Hawaii, this $500-million hostelry, like other mega-resorts in Hawaii, offers surroundings that amount to a self-contained vacation spot. The 787-room hotel (with 53 suites and 78 Regency Club rooms) includes a 2,000-foot-long river pool, a formal swimming pool that's one-third of an acre and is modeled on the Roman-style one at the Hearst Castle at San Simeon in California, Hawaii's largest health spa, several excellent restaurants, and a high-tech disco. The hotel is filled with contemporary artwork, from mosaics to sculpture to paintings. Visually, this property is a tour de force. In addition to *Wailea*'s two 18-hole golf courses, players can take the shuttle to the additional 18-hole courses minutes away at Makena. Information: *Grand Hyatt Wailea,* Wailea Alanui Dr., Kihei, HI 96753 (phone: 875-1234).

HANA-MAUI, Hana, Maui: This distinctive hostelry is on the eastern coast of East Maui, in the isolated ranching village of Hana, a settlement with a worldwide reputation for peace, quiet, and the simple spirit of old-time Hawaii. The hotel embraces this ideal and elaborates on it with a definitively understated interpretation of luxury. Under Sheraton management since 1990, the hotel maintains a level of luxury that does not come inexpensively. Public areas are handsome, particularly the large dining room, lobby, and poolside lounge, and the grounds are colorfully alive with Hana's flowers. This is *the* place for horse lovers; it has its own stables and offers an assortment of breakfast rides, cookout rides, sunrise rides, and moonlight rides, as well as English and Western riding lessons. There are 2 heated outdoor pools, a fitness center, private beach facilities and services at Hamoa Beach, 3 miles away, and the prettiest beach in the district — albeit with occasionally rough surf. The rebuilt 1929 Packard that transports guests to the beach is another *Hana-Maui* touch. This is not the place for folks who crave action and excitement; it is Eden for the self-sufficient who like a bit of pampering and truly wish to get away from it all. Information: *Hana-Maui Hotel,* Hana HI 96713 (phone: 248-8211; 800-325-3535).

HYATT REGENCY MAUI, Kaanapali Resort, Maui: Hawaii's first mega-resort, this one has benefited from a property-wide refurbishing that makes it the equal of the even more elaborate destination resorts that have followed. The hotel's appeal has been enhanced by landscaping that has had time to fill in, providing a setting that is both lavish and natural looking. The hotel's pool, one of Hawaii's largest, features grottoes, waterfalls, a Japanese garden alongside, and a 130-foot lava tube water slide. The central Atrium Tower, open to the sky, is one of three towers (housing a total of 815 guestrooms). A multimillion-dollar collection of Asian and Pacific art is distributed throughout the lobbies and promenades with seeming disregard for security. The property offers the *Swan Court* restaurant with a front-row-center view of the eponymous birds gliding on the lagoon, as well as several other dining spots, the most popular disco on the island (*Spats II*), and its showiest Polynesian revue ("Drums of the Pacific"). The 16-inch telescope sequestered on a remote rooftop corner, complete with a resident astronomer, allows a glimpse of stars, planets, galaxies, and nebulae. Throw in the beachfront location with beach service pavilion, the 55-foot catamaran for snorkel sails and cocktail cruises, the Regency Health Club with exercise room and sauna, tennis courts, 2 adjacent 18-hole golf courses, hula lessons, and lei making demonstrations, shops, and you've got the picture. The place for those who like glitz in their getaway. Information: *Hyatt Regency Maui,* 200 Nohea Kai Dr., Lahaina, HI 96761 (phone: 661-1234; 800-233-1234).

WESTIN MAUI, Kaanapali Resort, Maui: This 761-room property has emerged as a low-key version of the neighboring *Hyatt Regency.* Millions of dollars in art are set amidst magnificently landscaped grounds surrounding an exceptional 5-level pool, with grottoes, waterslides, and waterfalls connecting its 5 levels, each of which has plenty of space for lounging. Although somewhat on the small side, the recently refurbished rooms make up for their lack of spaciousness with very stylish decor. Six restaurants, a supper club (with dancing on a marble floor between a grand staircase and a romantic waterfall), a grotto bar, some prime beachfront, and a fully equipped spa also are offered in conjunction with Kaanapali's golf, tennis, and water activities. Information: *Westin Maui,* 2365 Kaanapali Pkwy., Lahaina, HI 96761 (phone: 667-2525; 800-228-3000).

KAPALUA BAY, Kapalua, Maui: The 750-acre *Kapalua* resort, on the northwestern corner of West Maui, is as magnificent a plot of land as exists anywhere in Hawaii. Pineapple fields bordered by rows of neat Cook and Norfolk Island pines stretch behind the development, velvety fairways and clipped lawns roll through it to the edge of the water, and across the Pailolo Channel, the island of Molokai looms like a large mirage. The *Kapalua Bay,* the focal point of the resort, is an elegant showplace that is quieter in its approach to luxury. While it doesn't strive for flashy effects, it is eye-catching nonetheless. The hotel has fewer than 200 rooms, all alike in size and rust or blue decor, in two main wings, one of which reaches out from the lobby toward the beach at Kapalua Bay, a picturesque, palm-lined crescent. Other beaches surround the *Kapalua* property, so there is no shortage of opportunities for water sports such as scuba diving, snorkeling, or surfing. The resort also has a 10-court Tennis Garden, as well as three of the most distractingly scenic island golf courses in existence. In addition, the hotel has two of Maui's most respected restaurants: the *Bay Club,* at the far end of Kapalua Beach and the *Plantation Veranda,* the site of a spectacular Sunday luncheon buffet — its groaning tables are an invitation to excess eagerly accepted by visitors from all over the island. And for some of the most tempting merchandise on the island, *Kapalua* guests have to go no farther than the adjacent *Kapalua Shops*. Information: *Kapalua Bay Hotel,* 1 Bay Dr., Kapalua, HI 96761 (phone: 669-5656; 800-367-8000).

KAPALUA VILLAS, Kapalua, Maui: Nearly half the accommodations available on Maui are condominiums. Most often these units are a solid, multi-story block of apartments or a low line of attached apartments shaped in a U or V, facing the sea. The *Kapalua Villas* fit neither description, but cluster in various spots around the *Kapalua* resort property — the *Bay Villas* close to the water, the *Ridge Villas* above and behind them, and the *Golf Villas* still farther up behind one of 3 golf courses — and the overall effect is that of an exclusive residential community in a supremely fortunate setting. It's possible to buy 1- or 2-bedroom units with a fully equipped tiled kitchen, an enormous bathroom fit for a sybarite, a living room with wicker and rattan furniture, and a wraparound lanai facing the islands of Lanai and Molokai. For a sum more within the grasp of a mortal traveler, these exact same opulent apartments can be rented for a day, a week, or longer. The various condominium clusters have their own recreation facilities — pools, tennis courts, Jacuzzis, barbecue pits — in addition to their proximity to the resort's Tennis Garden, the 3 courses of the *Kapalua Golf Club,* and 3 beaches. Villa residents may also take part in the activities offered by the *Kapalua Bay.* Information: *Kapalua Villas,* 500 Bay Dr., Kapalua, HI 96761 (phone: 669-5656; 800-367-8000).

MAUI INTER-CONTINENTAL, Wailea, Maui: Not too long ago, the Wailea coast of East Maui was a dry scrub forest of kiawe trees with a scalloped edge of wonderful beaches. Then developers turned on the sprinklers, made the land green, and the *Wailea* resort emerged. The *Inter-Continental,* the first of Wailea's hotels, has recently been upgraded at a cost of $37 million. The initial impression of clean white surfaces and simple lines continues through the rest of the hotel. Its large, stylish rooms are in a tower and a series of low structures scattered across the grounds that seem much more extensive than they could possibly be. A detailed map of the property is provided at check-in to help guests find their way around the sprawling landscape. Also provided is a *Flowers and Plants* guide, which is very useful while touring the grounds. There are 3 small swimming pools on site, with 14 tennis courts, 3 championship golf courses, and a shopping village just a short sprint away, and the nearest of the resort's 5 fine beaches only a short walk to the north or south edge of the property. The *Ocean Activities Center* takes care of guests' snorkeling, scuba diving, deep-sea fishing, surfing, and sailing needs, while the hotel provides the volleyball net, the shape-up and yoga exercises, the hula lessons, and the weekly luau. The elegant *La Perouse* is one of the island's best restaurants, and on Sundays, the *Makani Room* serves up an excellent champagne brunch. And to round out an active day, there is the *Inu Inu Lounge,* a cocktail lounge with a dance floor that features a sushi bar. Information: *Maui Inter-Continental,* PO Box 779, Wailea, HI 96753 (phone: 879-1922; 800-367-2960).

STOUFFER WAILEA BEACH, Wailea, Maui: The 350-room *Wailea Beach* works hard at cultivating an air of sophisticated refinement. Rooms are in three wings of 7 stories projecting from a central lobby; the entrance is flanked by reflecting pools and two concrete walls with sculptures that depict events in the life of the demigod Maui. Nicely landscaped grounds include a waterfall that drops from the lobby level and splits into streams that flow under bridges and form cascades. A wing of low suites operated as the deluxe Mokapu Club, a swimming pool, and an arbor-shaded poolside café (the *Maui Onion*) lead from the hotel to Mokapu Beach, a lovely pocket of sand that is the smallest of the five Wailea beaches. The *Ocean Activities Center* here is charged with supplying guests with the equipment and instruction necessary for a variety of water sports (including windsurfing), and the resort's tennis courts and golf courses are just across the road. Demonstrations of Hawaiian arts and crafts and other activities take place regularly. The *Lost Horizon* nightspot and the first class *Raffles',* one of Maui's best restaurants, are additional options. Information: *Stouffer Wailea Beach Resort,* Wailea, HI 96753 (phone: 879-4900; 800-9-WAILEA).

MAKENA SURF, Wailea, Maui: These spacious, nicely furnished, 2- and 3-bedroom condominium apartments offer oceanfront privacy, adjacent beaches, beautifully landscaped grounds alive with birds of paradise and hibiscus, and amenities that include a large pool and tennis courts. Nearby are the golf courses of the *Wailea* and *Makena* resorts. Daily maid service, 24-hour front desk. Information: *Makena Surf,* 3750 Wailea Alanui Dr., Makena, HI 96753 (phone: 879-1331/1595; 800-367-5246).

MAUI PRINCE, Makena Resort, Maui: This 300-room hotel is often overlooked by Maui-bound visitors, but behind the low profile are tastefully decorated rooms, a beachfront setting, and adjacent golf and tennis facilities that are among Maui's best. The pervading away-from-the-crowd feeling is a prime asset at a time when even resorts in "low-density" destinations are becoming overdeveloped. Information: *Maui Prince,* 5400 Makena Alanui Rd., Kihei, HI 96753 (phone: 874-1111; 800-321-6284).

WAILEA CONDOMINIUMS, Wailea, Maui: Wailea's condo options include three low-rise properties. *Wailea Elua,* right on Ulua Beach between two of the resort's hotels, is the most exclusive. *Wailea Ekolu,* on a sloping site above a plush golf course, consists of 1- and 2-bedroom apartments and 2-bedroom, 2½-bath townhouses. The upstairs units have grand vaulted ceilings, and all the units have wonderful views down to the sea. Closer to the shoreline, the sand-colored stucco buildings of *Wailea Ekahi* lie amid a variety of palm trees on ground that tilts gently toward Keawakapu Beach. Its units, which include some economical studios, have tiled kitchens behind swinging doors, high, high, second-story ceilings, and ocean and garden views from lanais lavish with bougainvillea. Whereas *Wailea Ekolu* has 2 swimming pools, *Wailea Ekahi* has 3, plus a beautifully tiled beach pavilion with a full kitchen for those who don't want to budge from the beachfront to fix lunch. *Wailea Elua* has its own beach pavilion and pool, as well as access to golf, tennis, shops, and nearby restaurants. Information: *Destination Resorts/Wailea,* Wailea Villas, 3750 Wailea Alanui Blvd., Kihei, HI 96753 (phone: 879-1595; 800-367-5246).

LAHAINA, Lahaina, Maui: This 13-room, Victorian-style inn (10 rooms, 3 suites), in a beautifully restored turn-of-the-century building (it was once a feed store) in the center of the bustling town of Lahaina, is decorated with $3 million worth of period antiques. A generous continental breakfast is included in room rates, which are considerably lower than those at Maui's better resort hotels. Rooms are air conditioned (Lahaina can be quite hot), and will please those appreciative of quality and authentic style. Though there is no beach or pool, the relaxing ambience offers guests an opportunity to reflect on Maui's bygone days. *David Paul's Lahaina Grill* bar is a perfect spot to meet locals. Information: *Lahaina Hotel,* 127 Lahainaluna Rd., Lahaina, HI 96761 (phone: 661-0577; 800-669-3444).

PLANTATION INN, Lahaina, Maui: Although this modest inn does not boast an imposing marble and gilt lobby like some of its bolder and brassier brethren, it remains a resounding success in terms of comfort and understated elegance. Accommodations are ample and sophisticated, and all 17 rooms and suites are deftly decorated with Victorian antiques and flowing curtains. Air conditioning provides an extra level of comfort, as does the lovely pool on a sizzling summer day. Dining is a chic and delicious affair at *Gerard's,* considered one of the island's best restaurants. An alfresco breakfast on the inn's front porch is included in the room rate. Information: *Plantation Inn,* 174 Lahainaluna Rd., Lahaina, HI 96766; 667-9225; 800-433-6815).

LODGE AT KOELE, Lanai City, Lanai: This up-country inn, which offers authentic elegance in a rustic setting, is one of two Rockresorts properties in Hawaii (the other is the *Manele Bay,* also on Lanai). It is Hawaii's first deluxe off-beach hotel (there is a shuttle that goes to the crescent beach at Manele, where a second Rockresorts property is located). Rooms are large and elegantly furnished in Laura Ashley–style country decor and face the forested hillsides of Lanaihale or expansive pastures and fields of pineapple. The Great Hall features two 50-foot fireplaces and exquisite stenciling and floor-to-ceiling murals. Adjacent to the hotel are stables, an 18-hole golf course, and tennis courts. Lanai City, the island's only town, is just a mile away. Information: *The Lodge at Koele,* Lanai City, HI 96763 (phone: 565-7300; 800-223-7636).

MANELE BAY, Manele Bay, Lanai: Guests won't want to leave this property that sits on a spectacular setting on red lava cliffs overlooking Hulopoe Bay, Lanai's best beach. This Rockresorts property features stylish, contemporary architecture and an eclectic decor that ranges from west to east, with a lavish use of objets d'art. Accommodations are situated in low-rise wings (2 to 4 stories high) that are linked by covered walkways, courtyards, gardens, and flowery streams. All the 250 rooms are spacious, beautifully appointed, and open out onto lanais with panoramic views. A large pool overlooks the ocean and beach. Both the *Ihilani Room* and *Hulapoe Court,* the hotel's two upscale restaurants, proffer fine fare. The unique Jack Nicklaus–designed golf course, called the *Experience,* offers distinct challenges for both the beginner and the master golfer. Lest you feel too isolated in paradise, a shuttle links the hotel to Lanai City, tennis courts, stables, and the *Lodge at Koele.* Information: *Manele Bay Hotel,* Lanai City, HI 96763 (phone: 565-7700; 800-223-7637).

KIAHUNA PLANTATION, Poipu Beach, Kauai: One of Hawaii's most complete condominium resorts, on Kauai's sunny South Shore. Handsome 1- and 2-bedroom apartments, excellent tennis and golf facilities, superb beachfront, and first-rate restaurant are reasons enough for the loyal clientele. But what really sets *Kiahuna* apart are the grounds, 50 lushly landscaped acres.

Among this luxuriant growth are low white buildings with steep roofs hanging over the balconies. High ceilings and long louvered windows keep the apartments comfortably cool without air conditioning, so guests can smell the heady fragrance of the gardens inside, too. The apartments are big (a 1-bedroom can easily accommodate four people) and have fully equipped kitchens. They're smartly decorated, too, in pastel prints and rattan furniture.

There's daily maid service and other hotel amenities — beach sports (including surfing lessons from champion Margo Oberg) and tennis are the main draws. The plantation has a very attractive tennis complex: 10 courts, a good pro shop, and a courtside café. Best of all, guests play for free. The golf course across the road (owned by the *Hyatt Regency*) will add golf enthusiasts to *Kiahuna*'s long list of regulars. Information: *Kiahuna Plantation,* 2253 Poipu Rd., Koloa, HI 96756 (phone: 742-6411; 800-367-7052).

WESTIN KAUAI, Kauai Lagoons Resort, Kauai: "Extravagant" is the only word to describe this showplace that combines grand scale, millions of dollars in artwork, a made-to-order beachfront setting, and facilities that rival those of any resort anywhere. Whether all this is necessary in a place as naturally beautiful as Kauai is the question. Those seeking a quiet retreat had best head elsewhere, as just a glimpse of the 800 lounge chairs surrounding the oversize pool will quickly tell them. On-site facilities include 36 holes of Jack Nicklaus–designed golf, fully equipped men's and women's spas, 8 tennis courts, restaurants, shops and lounges galore, and hundreds of landscaped acres that sport lagoons, gardens, and seemingly endless lawns. The lagoons are traversed by canolas (outrigger canoe/gondola hybrids), and the grounds, by miles of carriage trails served by a fleet of elegant horse-drawn carriages. Last, but by no means least, guests can also enjoy a full range of water sports activities. Special off-season rates are a plus. Information: *Westin Kauai,* Kalapaki Beach, Lihue, HI 96766 (phone: 245-5050; 800-228-3000).

HYATT REGENCY KAUAI, Poipu, Kauai: This 220-million beachfront property features low-rise buildings built in Hawaii's tile-roofed style, elaborately decorated with inlaid marble, teak, and koa, and lit by exquisite chandeliers. There are 2 large pools, including one with beachfront sections linked by waterslides, 4 tennis courts, and an 18-hole golf course, a full spa and fitness center, and stables on adjacent acreage. Although not quite as overwhelming as some of Hawaii's other mega-resorts, the *Hyatt* certainly is the most extravagant hostelry in Poipu. Information: *Hyatt Regency Kauai,* Poipu, Kauai (phone: 742-1234; 800-233-1234).

STOUFFER WAIOHAI, Poipu Beach, Kauai: From the stone-paved porte-cochere to decor rich in travertine marble, brass, and polished teak, this establishment is the epitome of elegance. Guestrooms, which have spacious sitting areas discreetly set off from the beds by slim bamboo panels, are done in cool, contemporary pastels.

The *Waiohai* has also made an impressive show in the culinary field. *The Tamarind,* a restaurant strikingly decorated in salmon banquettes, a brass ceiling, and Thai silks, features various continental and Asian dishes, including a sublime Thai curry.

Like all resort hotels, the *Waiohai* offers a host of activities. There are 3 swimming pools (one with a bar built into it and one on a terrace over the hotel's lovely beach), poolside Jacuzzis, tennis courts, a full health club, and snorkeling and scuba lessons. For those who prefer diversions of a less rigorous nature, hotel hostesses give lessons in Hawaiian crafts and conduct botanical tours of the 2 courtyard gardens. The property's chief pleasure is its atmosphere of unruffled calm, and there's no shortage of friendly staff to help guests enjoy it. Information: *Stouffer Waiohai,* 2249 Poipu Rd., Koloa, HI 96756 (phone: 742-9511; 800-426-4122).

PRINCEVILLE, Princeville, Kauai: There are several attractive places to stay at the golfer's paradise known as *Princeville,* the resort on the 11,000-acre ranch overlooking Kauai's Hanalei Bay. Three condominiums are worthy of note, as is the *Sheraton Princeville.*

The *Hanalei Bay* resort, *Pali Ke Kua,* and *Puu Poa* are each very special condominium complexes, each distinguished by spaciousness, appealing decor, and an excellent location. *Puu Poa,* the smallest of the three, has the greatest sense of privacy, oversize lanais, and cliff-top views of the ocean. Ocean and mountain views can be had at *Pali Ke Kua,* though the apartments are a bit older and less airy, and a walkway connects *Pali Ke Kua* to a small private beach frequented by surfers who approach it from a precipitous cliffside trail. The recently renovated *Hanalei Bay* resort, a hotel/condominium mix situated on a perfectly manicured hillside that winds its way down to a small beach and Hanalei Bay, offers large, nicely decorated accommodations (from hotel rooms to 3-bedroom apartments), beautifully landscaped grounds, a free-form pool complete with waterfalls, 8 tennis courts, a complimentary beach jitney, and panoramic views. The best views at Princeville are undoubtedly those offered at the *Sheraton Princeville.* Rebuilt at a cost of $100 million, it is one of Hawaii's most elegant hotels. Tiled in green and white marble and furnished in an eclectic mix of classic and contemporary styles, its real asset are rooms that face Hanalei Bay from a cliff-top perspective that is perhaps Hawaii's most dramatically beautiful. Its kitchens offer some of Kauai's finest food. Aside from golf, Princeville guests enjoy tennis, a wide range of water sports, and a chance to explore the magnificent coast from Princeville to the end of the road at Kee Beach. Information: *Pali Ke Kua* and *Puu Poa,* Hawaiian Island Resorts, PO Box 212, Honolulu, HI 96810 (phone: 826-9602); *Hanalei Bay Resort,* PO Box 220, Hanalei, HI 96714 (phone: 826-6522; 800-827-4427); *Sheraton Princeville,* Princeville, HI 96722 (phone: 826-9644; 800-325-3535).

WAIMEA PLANTATION COTTAGES, Waimea, Kauai: Located in the old plantation town of Waimea on Kauai's sunny southwest coast, and consisting of more than 40 restored plantation homes from the 1920s, 1930s, and 1940s, this is truly one of Hawaii's more unusual properties. Many of the homes were brought to the site from other parts of Kauai as part of a comprehensive preservation plan that ultimately will offer 52 restored cottages in the complex. Ranging from 1 to 6 bedrooms, all of the cottages are tastefully furnished and are situated in an expansive, beachfront palm grove where the deco-style pool and clubhouse are located. The *Grove* dining room is the latest addition to the on-site facilities. A laid-back, private setting offers access to miles of undeveloped beach. Information: *Waimea Plantation Cottages,* PO Box 367, Waimea, HI 96796 (phone: 338-1625; 800-992-4632).

Delightful Island Dining

Although the islands are better known for volcanoes and black sand beaches, today's Hawaii offers a wide variety of first class restaurants and a broad spectrum of ethnic cuisines. Reflecting its history, Hawaii's culinary repertoire embraces traditional Polynesian, American, and continental dishes, as well as those from other nations around the world, including China, Japan, Korea, the Philippines, Thailand, and Vietnam. Thus menus will often feature a variety of dishes, including lomilomi salmon, sashimi, Portuguese bean soup, egg rolls, veal Oscar, teriyaki steaks, *coquilles St.-Jacques,* Korean *kal bi* ribs, macadamia nut ice cream, and lots of fresh fruit. The following selection of restaurants represents the very best of island eateries. Reservations are essential at all dining spots.

CAFÉ SISTINA, Honolulu, Oahu: Michelangelo and a magnificent menu are the major attractions at this energetic establishment. An unfinished re-creation of a section of the Sistine Chapel hangs above the bar, presumably to emphasize the fact that good art is at home anywhere. Plentiful portions of hearty northern Italian fare are served, with numerous antipasti and pasta dishes to tempt the fickle tongue, and simply superb entrées. On weekends the place is jammed, and currently considered an "in" spot with hip Honoluluans and their friends. After 10 PM, noise reaches a high-decibel pitch, when the owner's wife, a superb jazz vocalist, provides upbeat entertainment. Information: *Café Sistina,* 1314 S. King St., Honolulu, HI 96822 (phone: 526-0071).

CIAO MEIN, Honolulu, Oahu: The restaurant that replaced the far-more-formal *Bagwell's* is an unlikely mix of Italian and Chinese cuisines. The masterful results prepared by the restaurant's two chefs are superb from either menu. Appetizers include savory sesame asparagus and black mushrooms in oyster sauce, antipasto misto (buffalo mozzarella, copa ham, calamaza olives, roasted onions, and sun-dried tomato croutons), and hearty minestrone soup with braised sausage. Entrées include roast duck served with carrots and cucumber, broiled prawns with Italian tomato butter sauce, and salmon baked in parchment in sea salt crust. There is indoor as well as alfresco seating on the *Hyatt*'s third-floor deck. Dinner is accompanied by live music. Information: *Caio Mein, Hyatt Regency,* 2424 Kalakaua Ave., Honolulu, HI 96815 (phone: 923-1234).

HAJIBABA'S, Honolulu, Oahu: A bit out of the way in tony, residential Kahala (10 minutes by car from Waikiki), this Moroccan restaurant offers oversize portions of eat-more-than-you-should, delicious specialties such as lamb couscous and pastilla lemon chicken. Seating is low to the floor, decor appropriately Moroccan (the owners are the real thing, so this isn't a formula restaurant), and the belly dancers and musicians who entertain during dinner add immeasurably to the sense of place and an enjoyable evening that provides you with more than your money's worth. Information: *Hajibaba's,* 4614 Kilauea Ave. (adjacent to Kahala Mall), Honolulu, HI 96816 (phone: 735-5522).

JOHN DOMINIS, Honolulu, Oahu: Every town has one restaurant that attracts local power brokers and politicos, and this is Honolulu's. Approaching this restaurant can make a first-timer want to turn back: It is surrounded by small factories and warehouses on a street of zero charm. But once inside, there's the pleasure of dining on a promontory overlooking the Kewalo Boat Basin, with a view clear down to Diamond Head, and the restaurant's tiered structure gives nearly everyone at least a glimpse of the ocean. And even if you don't have one, you are probably sitting next to a saltwater pool brimming with tropical fish and Hawaiian spiny lobsters that eventually end up on one of the restaurant's stout tables.

The cooking is first-rate. While there are steaks, Chinese dishes, and the odd Italian specialty on the menu, to come here and not eat seafood is a sacrilege. Island specialties such as opelu (mackerel), hapuu (grouper), and ono (wahoo) are all available in season. When decision making becomes too difficult, diners often compromise with a cioppino (stew) of soft-shell crabs, seafood, and fresh island fish cooked in tomatoes, herbs, and spices. The bar is another bonus, one of the few in Honolulu restaurants where the drinks are good and the atmosphere inviting enough to make a cocktail or after-dinner drink a pleasure. Information: *John Dominis,* 43 Ahui St., Honolulu, HI 96813 (phone: 523-0955).

KEO'S, Honolulu, Oahu: Famed for its reputation as the first restaurant to put Thai food on Honolulu's map, this is one of five Thai restaurants owned by the same family. This particular spot offers the prettiest decor, which is a lush background of bamboo, potted palms, parasols, flowers, and paintings. An eclectic menu offers such delicacies as the establishment's signature dish, evil jungle prince (either chicken or prawns bathed in coconut milk, basil, and red chili), panang curry (chicken baked in kaffir lime leaves, fresh ground lemon grass, peas, and coconut milk), and Thai noodles made from sticky rice and stir-fried with bean spouts, chives, and tofu. Unusual desserts include Thai banana chips with coconut ice cream and iced Thai tea, a traditional drink that tastes something like a milkshake. Just outside Waikiki, at the base of Diamond Head. Information: *Keo's,* 625 Kapahulu Ave., Honolulu, HI 96815 (phone: 737-8240).

MAILE, Honolulu, Oahu: To compensate for the lack of a view, the *Maile* (named for a leaf often made into leis and always worn by a Hawaiian bridegroom on his wedding day) has a sumptuous decor of pools, heliconia, anthuriums, orchids, and a variety of tropical plants. Here the maile motif is seen on the gold-rimmed china, a patrician touch that is further underlined by tablecloths of Belgian lace. Among the items on the menu are some native specialties that receive opulent treatment: mahimahi glazed with bananas served on creamed mushrooms; spicy ahi on balsamic mango coulis with curried wild rice; filet of opakapaka (pink snapper) with *beurre blanc* sauce; and luscious dessert soufflés. Petits fours and chocolate are served with coffee, and unobtrusive background music is provided by a classical guitarist or pianist. Meals are deftly served by ladies in kimonos who seem to sum up all that is traditionally feminine and graceful about the East. There is a touch of enchantment about dining here. Information: *Maile, Kahala Hilton,* 5000 Kahala Ave., Kahala, HI 96816 (phone: 734-2211).

LA MER, Honolulu, Oahu: The *Halekulani*'s fine dining room is elegantly subdued, with a menu that is innovative and delicious. Appetizers include salad of sautéed foie gras and sautéed Kahuku prawns, with standard fare turned exotic — entrées such as whole onaga baked in a thyme and rosemary rock salt crust and *papillote* of kumu with shiitake mushrooms and basil — both dishes enhanced with *ogo,* also known as Hawaiian seaweed. Those longing for Paris should order the cheese course; in due time, a cart laden down with the finest cheese this side of the Left Bank arrives for your perusal. Service is attentive and professional. This is a match for the best when it comes to intimate dining. Information: *La Mer, Halekulani,* 2199 Kalia Rd., Honolulu, HI 96815 (phone: 923-2311).

MICHEL'S, Honolulu, Oahu: Scattered across the south of France are scores of medium-size restaurants that scornfully eschew the "folksy-rustic" look in favor of an ambience that suggests upper-middle-class prosperity. The cooking in these places is usually impeccable. So it is with *Michel's.* Diners sit under crystal chandeliers on banquettes or chairs upholstered in Belgian velvet with Regency stripes, at tables elegantly set with fine china, brilliantly polished glass, and crisp, snow-white napery. Quiet and skillful service is civilized, without fuss or pressure. Most of the dishes on the menu are classics, such as lobster bisque with brandy and roast rack of veal. When local produce is used, it is treated in a classic fashion. Fresh opakapaka, for instance, is poached in champagne and served with hollandaise sauce and grapes to become *opakapaka poche au champagne Véronique* — triumphantly. Information: *Michel's,* 2895 Kalakaua Ave., Honolulu, HI 96815 (phone: 923-6552).

PRINCE COURT, Honolulu, Oahu: Two indisputable facts about this dining establishment are its charming, airy surroundings and its polite, unobtrusive staff. A third is the superb menu, whose specialties range from kiawe grilled capon to pan sautéed tenderloin of veal with porcini mushrooms to blackened blue ahi to Hawaiian bouillabaisse. Everything is flavorfully prepared, and the fare is so artistically arranged on the plate that you might be tempted to take a photo to preserve the memory. The Sunday brunch is a knockout. Information: *Prince Court, Hawaii Prince,* 100 Holomoana St., Honolulu, HI (phone: 956-1111).

ROY'S/ROY'S PARK BISTRO, Honolulu, Oahu: Master chef Roy Yamaguchi has created an eclectic Eurasian menu that has catapulted this eponymous place to fame as one of Honolulu's most popular eateries. The lively ambience, with the kitchen on display, the casually elegant dining room, the prompt service, and specialties such as Mongolian loin of Niihau lamb with island vinaigrette and cabernet sauce, and smoked Peking-style duck with candied pecans and a lilikoi ginger sauce, are first-rate reasons to come here. *Roy's Park Bistro* (6600 Kalanianaole Hwy., *Waikiki Park Plaza* hotel, Honolulu, HI 96825; phone: 396-ROYS) in Waikiki has an equally eclectic menu. Specialties include salmon with a goat cheese crust and sun-dried tomato sauce, Muscovy duck in a blueberry hazelnut cabernet sauce, and lobster with macadamia nut butter sauce. Maui-bound visitors may also want to check out *Roy's Kahana Bar & Grill,* a creative culinary counterpart to its Oahu cousins. Information: *Roy's,* Hawaii Kai Corporate Plaza, 6600 Kalanianaole Hwy. (phone: 396-ROYS).

WILLOWS, Honolulu, Oahu: Ah, *The Willows!* Outdoors, indoors, in a grass shack–like longhouse, under thatch umbrella roofs, by a carp pond, or surrounded by palms and hibiscus, wherever you sit you experience the graceful flavor of a bygone era — not the one that existed before the missionaries arrived, but something akin to that found by the early passengers on the Pacific liners that used to call at Honolulu en route from San Francisco to the Far East. While dining, listen to old Hawaiian songs accompanied only by the bass and the ukulele and the intense hush of a tropical night.

A specialty of the house is the Poi Supper, which includes most of the ingredients of a real luau on a smaller scale, such as laulau, a mixture of fish and pork wrapped in ti leaves and steamed; chicken luau, simmered with ti leaves and coconut milk; lomilomi salmon, chopped salt salmon mixed with onions and tomatoes; sweet potatoes; and poi itself, the bland, smooth paste made from the taro root that is a Hawaiian staple. Desserts are a specialty, so indulge yourself with the coconut cream pie or chocolate gâteau. An indisputable way to appreciate *The Willows* is to come for Poi Thursday's spirit of aloha. Hawaiian entertainment here is full of spontaneity and is well-attended by many old-timers. It's one of the few places where visitors can experience Hawaiian hospitality at its best. Information: *The Willows,* 901 Hausten St., Honolulu, HI 96826 (phone: 946-4808).

FUJI, Hilo, the Big Island of Hawaii: The *Fuji* has atmosphere — the kind that no amount of trendy design or other artifice can produce, the kind that just happens. Tourists are irrelevant here. They are welcome, but the *Fuji* exists mostly for islanders. There are *kamaaina* ladies enjoying a weekday lunch together and Japanese families celebrating a birthday or anniversary. Residents with business in the area — the sort who always have favorite obscure eating places — are seen here. The food is served with the same attention to aesthetic detail, each platter looking like a delicate arrangement of flower petals. It is also excellently prepared. The sashimi seems to melt on contact with the palate, and the tempura dishes boast a batter that is ephemerally thin. Information: *Fuji,* 142 Kinoole St., Hilo, HI 96720 (phone: 961-3733).

ROUSSELS, Hilo, the Big Island of Hawaii: Even more surprising than the Cajun style of the cooking is the high quality of the food, which — from breads and appetizers to entrées and desserts — is unfailingly first-rate. The brothers who own *Roussels* are Louisiana born and bred, bringing recipes from home like oysters Bienville (baked in a creamy shrimp and mushroom sauce), seafood gumbo, shrimp creole (in a rich, piquant tomato sauce), chicken Pontalba (boned, sautéed, and served with bearnaise sauce), soft shell crab, and a mouthwatering selection of duck and vegetarian dishes. From light lunches to full dinners, this is not only one of Hawaii's finest eateries, but it is also reasonably priced. A real find. Information: *Roussels,* 60 Keawe St., Hilo, HI 96720 (phone: 935-5111).

BATIK ROOM, Kohala Coast, the Big Island of Hawaii: The 2-tiered dining room is host to an eclectic menu, highlighted by excellent curries, as well as veal Oscar, tournedos of beef, and steak *au poivre.* Chef Klaus Mayr offers such specialties as rice-paper rolls dipped in tiger beef with chorizo, refried beans, avocado, cilantro-flavored rice noodles, and *molcajete* sauce, *achiote*-flavored smoked tiger prawns with salsa cruda and jalapeño-corn muffins, and deep-fried bananas in won ton wrappers with a confit of gingered azuki beans. The decor is Middle Eastern, the service attentive, and the noise level perfect for dinner conversation. Information: *Batik Room, Mauna Kea Beach Hotel,* Kohala Coast, HI 96743 (phone: 882-7222).

CANOE HOUSE, Kohala Coast, the Big Island of Hawaii: Polynesian artifacts adorn this beachfront dining spot, which is located in an open-sided, longhouse-style building. Chef Alan Wong, formerly of New York's famed *Lutèce,* concocts mouth-watering appetizers such as curried chicken with coconut ginger cream, and nori-wrapped tempura ahi with soy mustard sauce and tomato ginger relish. Adventurous folks can snack on the sushi sampler. Entrées include grilled tenderloin with shiitake mushrooms and coconut chili sauce, braised opakapaka with Chinese sausages in black bean sauce, and roast rack of lamb with berry glaze and sweet potatoes. The pièce de résistance is the dessert sampler, which proffers macadamia nut fudge cake, lilikoi ohelo berry cheesecake, banana papaya strudel, ginger crème brûlée, frozen Hanaoka lime mousse, and Oriental cookies. The service is warm yet unobtrusive. Information: *Canoe House, Mauna Lani Bay,* One Mauna Lani Dr., Kohala Coast, HI (phone: 885-6622).

DONATONI'S, Kohala Coast, the Big Island of Hawaii: One of Hawaii's best Italian restaurants, it truly does justice to its extensive menu that ranges from appetizers such as tender *calamari fritti* to *linguine al pescatore,* with its mouth-watering melange of mussels, scallops, and clams to entrées such as *osso buco alla milanese* (veal shanks with vegetables, white wine, and tomatoes). Service is impeccable, as is the decor, which boasts an elegantly Mediterranean theme. *Donatoni's, Hyatt Regency Waikoloa,* Kohala Coast, HI 96743 (phone: 885-1234).

GRILL, Kohala Coast, the Big Island of Hawaii: Henry James would have been right at home in this sophisticated dining room, whose wood-paneled walls create the feel of a private club's reading room. The fare is straightforward, and focuses on perfectly grilled veal, steaks, lamb, and fish complemented by delicate sauces and fresh garnishes. Standouts include New York steaks with mustard herb sauce, double colorado lamb chops with papaya mint relish, veal chop with creamy tomato tarragon sauce, and filet of onaga with mushroom tomato salsa. Service is English proper without being presumptuous. A well-orchestrated trio provides background music that harmonizes beautifully with the meal. Information: *Grill, Ritz-Carlton Mauna Lani,* One N. Kaniku Dr., Kohala Coast, HI (phone: 885-0099).

IMARI, Kohala Coast, the Big Island of Hawaii: Everything Japanese, from the cuisine to the decor, is presented here. Selections range from shabu shabu chicken to sukiyaki beef, from teppanyaki to *kaiseki* dinners. Shoji screens open to take in the setting: free-running streams and meticulous gardens. *Imari, Hyatt Regency Waikoloa,* Kohala Coast, HI 96743 (phone: 885-1234).

EDELWEISS, Waimea, the Big Island of Hawaii: The perfect place to make a midday or end-of-day stop when passing through up-country Waimea. It's even worth the drive from the Kohala Coast resorts for flavorful German and continental specialties with a tasteful focus on veal. Try the Edelweiss Papaya — an imaginative dish consisting of scallops and Stroganoff sauce, baked in a half-papaya. Closed Sundays, Mondays, and in September. Information: *Edelweiss,* Route 19, Waimea, HI 96743 (phone: 885-6800).

MERRIMAN'S, Waimea, the Big Island of Hawaii: The chef of this fine restaurant uses locally grown and harvested produce, herbs, poultry, fish, and beef to make specialties such as wok-charred marlin, Kahua Ranch lamb, and sweet red peppers with Puna goat cheese. Excellent service and ambience. Information: *Merriman's,* Rte. 19, Opelu Plaza, Waimea, HI 96743 (phone: 885-6822).

HALIIMAILE GENERAL STORE, Haliimaile, Maui: This former general store off the beaten path is now a charming restaurant with some of the best food on Maui. Specialties include goat cheese and sun-dried tomato tart, vegetarian lasagna, roast duckling, fettuccine with scallops, and rack of lamb Hunan-style. Great place to stop on the way to or from Haleakala's summit. Information: *Haliimaile General Store,* Haliimaile Rd., Haliimaile, HI 96768 (phone: 572-2666).

ROY'S KAHANA BAR & GRILL, Kahana, Maui: Following in the venerable footsteps of the original *Roy's* on Oahu, this dining establishment proffers fine fare that deftly combines Oriental and continental flavors. The results are unusual and quite delicious, and include such tasty dishes as rack of lamb with a parmesan crust, Louisiana crab cakes with spicy sesame sauce, and fresh-seared opakapaka with roasted macadamia nut butter sauce. The decor is cheerful and bright, dominated by a 30-foot-high copper ceiling and an open kitchen from which tempting scents waft into the dining room. Information: *Roy's Kahana Bar & Grill, Kahana Gateway Shopping Center,* Kahana, Maui (phone: 669-6999).AVALOÑ, Lahaina, Maui

Owner-chef Mark Ellman has created one of Maui's most popular dining establishments, which focuses on Asian nouvelle cuisine. An imaginative menu includes specialties such as seared *sahimi,* Asian pasta (with shrimp, clams, scallops, and fish in a sauce of fragrant herbs), Indonesian *satay* with Balinese sauce, soft shell crabs, and wok-prepared whole fresh opakapaka, and desserts such as their fabled Carmel Miranda (macadamia nut ice cream with seasonal fruits glazed with caramel sauce). Information: *Avalon,* 844 Front St., Lahaina, Maui 96761 (phone: 667-5559).

DAVID PAUL'S LAHAINA GRILL, Lahaina, Maui: Right around the corner from *Avalon,* chef David Paul Johnson makes a delicious tempest in a stewpot. Johnson relies on strong, powerful ingredients which he boldly mixes in highly unusual combinations that may confuse your common sense but will certainly awaken the palate. Dishes such as macadamia-smoked Kona tenderloin with sweet chili compote and avocado relish, tequila shrimp with firecracker rice, and steamed tamalitos stuffed with shrimp and sausage will satisfy taste buds aching for variety. Information: *David Paul's Lahaina Grill, Lahaina Hotel,* 127 Lahainaluna Rd., Lahaina, Maui 96761 (phone: 667-5117).

BAY CLUB, Kapalua, Maui: More than one visit is necessary to sample the products of the famed kitchens of the *Kapalua Bay* hotel, at West Maui's *Kapalua* resort. More than one visit could be devoted just to the *Bay Club,* which, though part of the hotel, is at the other end of the crescent-shaped beach on a point of lava rock jutting out into the water. This is an open-air restaurant decorated with rattan furniture and the handsomest of batik prints, completed at lunch by a color scheme of nature's own sea and sky blue; of the hotel's three eating spots, this is the one with the view. At the *Bay Club,* lunch can be as exotic as a papaya boat stuffed with shrimp and crabmeat in a sauce of Rémy Martin, or as simple as a good wiener. Dinner, however, is soft lights and sophistication all the way, with three rotating fixed-price menus — featuring chateaubriand, lamb, and veal chops — and a varied selection of continental and nouvelle cuisine entrées available à la carte. Information: *Bay Club, Kapalua Bay Hotel,* One Bay Dr., Kapalua, HI 97653 (phone: 874-1111).

HAKONE, Kihei, Maui: The decor is a bit spartan, as befits a purist's Japanese restaurant, and the food is beautifully presented and delicious. The menu starts with delicately flavored specialties such as *chawan mushi* (steamed egg custard with chicken, shrimp, shiitake mushrooms, and ginko nuts), egg flower soup (Japanese broth with egg beaten in), and elegant sushi, then continues with sukiyaki, teriyaki, and *kaiseki* dinners. There's a sushi bar as well as table seating. Information: *Hakone, Maui Prince Hotel,* 5400 Makena Alanui, Kihei, HI 96753 (phone: 874-1111).

GERARD'S, Lahaina, Maui: The French-born chef and owner of this dining spot, in the Victorian-style *Plantation Inn,* has created a restaurant that would draw raves in New York or Paris. The decor is reminiscent of Provence and the service is friendly and competent. One of Hawaii's best eateries, food choices include wild mushrooms in puff pastry, calamari with lime and ginger, venison in a white pepper sauce, and a seafood ragout with vegetables and fresh pasta. Indoor and alfresco seating. Information: *Gerard's, Plantation Inn,* 174 Lahainaluna Rd., Lahaina, HI 96761 (phone: 661-8939).

LONGHI'S, Lahaina, Maui: Beloved by islanders and mainlanders alike, this dining spot's time-honored reputation remains pristine. Classic Italian specialties such as *antipasti* and veal *parmigiano* provide the backbone of its menu, which emphasizes veal, pasta, and seafood dishes accompanied by — and sometimes awash in — hearty sauces. Printed menus are unavailable, so the waiters' *modus operandi* is to recite each dish, which proves to be no mean feat. The joint usually is jumping, and since they don't take reservations, expect to wait a bit for a choice table. Information: *Longhi's,* 888 Front St., Lahaina, Maui (phone: 667-2288).

GRAND DINING ROOM, Wailea, Maui: Elegant decor complemented by vast Hawaiian murals only heightens the pleasure of dining in this chic spot. Panoramic views of sea are soothing to the eye, while the fare proves exhilarating to the palate. The menu offers most dishes in both appetizer and entrée portions, which makes it possible to enjoy a mini-smorgasbord. Succulent dishes include crispy Asian squid with lemon grass and baby bok choy, tossed Kula greens with sherry walnut vinaigrette, hoisin crusted rack of lamb with Oriental ratatouille, and roasted pork tenderloin with pine nut chutney and Maui sweet potato cake. The daily breakfast is transformed into Maui's most lavish brunch on Sundays. Information: *Grand Dining Room, Grand Hyatt Wailea,* 3850 Wailea Alanui Dr., Wailea, HI 96753 (phone: 875-1234).

LA PEROUSE, Wailea, Maui: An elegant restaurant, complete with sparkling crystal, table linen, fine service, alfresco seating (for those so inclined), and an eclectic menu. For instance, for starters there is a gâteau of grilled sea scallops and seafood with wild mushrooms. Soups include seafood minestrone and bonito broth, while sautéed crab cakes, baked onaga in a potato crust, and baked lamb chops with eggplant purée are the highlights among the entrées. When it's time for dessert, the waiter will wheel out the pastry cart or set fire to something scrumptious, and rest assured that he'll do it with perfect aplomb. Information: *La Perouse, Maui Inter-Continental Resort,* Wailea, HI 96753 (phone: 879-1922).

RAFFLES', Wailea, Maui: The restaurant aims for a mix of East and West in its menu, with consistently fine entrées ranging from island fish — mahimahi and opakapaka — to noisette of lamb Sir Stamford Raffles and *suprême* of duck breast cassis. The lobster with watercress sauce and nasturtiums is a delicious cold appetizer; other appetizers, hot and cold, include oyster cassoulet with fresh sea urchin and riesling, fresh sautéed goose liver in sherry vinegar and honey, and gravlax (salmon marinated in dill and anise with mustard sauce). After a dessert of chocolate mousse, a confection from the pastry cart, or some flamboyant flambéed fruit, there are petits fours to nibble and an after-dinner liqueur to sip slowly. Light and airy decor provides a relaxed setting. Information: *Raffles', Stouffer Wailea Beach Resort,* Wailea, HI 96753 (phone: 879-4900).

LA CASCATA, Princeville, Kauai: Couples and other admirers of gorgeous landscapes should request a table by the window to gaze out at the view, especially as the sun goes down, just to watch that orb's spectacular descent behind Bali Hai Mountain. Inside, the Mediterranean-style decor is simple and unassuming, as is its menu, which nevertheless concocts such tasty fare as *saltimbocca alla romana,* warm oysters with grilled radicchio, roasted guinea fowl with spinach, pine nuts, and raisins, and salmon cutlets. Service is superb and discreet, as is the wine list. Information: *La Cascata, Princeville Hotel, Princeville Resort,* Kauai, HI 96722 (phone: 826-9644).

DONDERO'S, Poipu, Kauai: Elaborate tilework and distinctive trompe l'oeil murals of the Mediterranean characterize this charming spot. As one might surmise, fine Italian fare graces the menu, with selections that include shrimp wrapped in *pancetta* (a kind of bacon), sautéed scallops, cioppino (hearty seafood fish soup or stew), grilled calamari, and blackened veal chops, as well as pizza topped with everything from green peppers and sausage to anchovies. Information: *Dondero's, Hyatt Regency Kauai,* 1571 Poipu Dr., Koloa, HI 96756 (phone: 742-1234).

TIDEPOOLS, Poipu, Kauai: Considered a first-rate steak and seafood restaurant, the wonderful food frequently is upstaged by the stunning setting. The collection of Polynesian-style dining rooms are built along the *Hyatt's* oceanfront lagoon and overlook verdant vistas. While the food may lack a certain flair for the dramatic, dishes such as filet mignon, mahimahi, and lobster are ably presented and succulent. Don't miss the exceptional apple tart, which is individually baked and served at table in a 6-inch iron skillet. Information: *Tidepools, Hyatt Regency Kauai,* 1571 Poipu Dr., Koloa, HI 96756 (phone: 742-1234).

HOUSE OF SEAFOOD, Poipu, Kauai: An eponymous title if there ever was one, this establishment provides ichthyophagous souls with plenty to crow about. Everything from ia ula ahi (sautéed at the table with enoki mushrooms and Dijon mustard) to broiled scallops to Hawaiian spiny lobster tail to shrimp scampi is lovingly and expertly prepared. Additional niceties are a low-key setting complete with polished wood and hanging plants, a relaxing ambience, and gracious Hawaiian hospitality. Information: *House of Seafood, Poipu Kai Resort,* 1941 Poipu Dr., Koloa, HI 96756 (phone: 742-6433).

A PACIFIC CAFÉ, Kapaa, Kauai: Owner-chef Jean Marie Josselin receives high praise for his Pacific Rim nouvelle cuisine — and deservedly so. Josselin's winning menu relies on his unusual combinations and delicate sauces. Delectable choices range from barbecued chicken wontons to Australian lamb served with tamarind sauce. Don't miss his signature dish dubbed deep-fried sashimi, which combines layers of raw tuna and wasabi which are fried in a delectable tempura batter. Contemporary and avant-garde art adorns the walls of this spacious establishment, which is frequently packed to its proverbial gills with the trendiest of patrons. Information: *A Pacific Café, Kauai Village Center,* 4-831 Kuhio Hwy., Kapaa, HI 96746 (phone: 822-0013).

TEMPURA GARDEN, Nawiliwili, Kauai: A perfect place to regain peace of mind, this establishment's exquisite, all-wood interior faces out on two soothing gardens. The first is a meditative, Zen-style rock garden, and the other is a lush landscape of waterfalls, bamboo, and several resident cranes. Those who insist on authenticity will appreciate the sushi bar with several chefs in attendance, as well as Japanese seating on tatami mats (Western-style seating is also available). Kyoto specialties are the mainstay of the menu, which include miso soup, sashimi, and tempura dishes. Information: *Tempura Garden, Westin Kauai,* Lihue, HI 96766 (phone: 245-5050).

INN ON THE CLIFFS, Nawiliwili, Kauai: True to its appellation, this dining place adjacent to the *Westin Kauai* perches on a cliff top overlooking the Pacific. Patrons can leave their car in the parking lot just past the entrance to the *Westin Kauai* and take a mahogany launch across the lagoon, which lands just outside the front door. Inside, such dishes as broiled pepper scallops with Maui onion salsa, avocado, and sour cream, blackened ahi with Hawaiian ginger salsa, and grilled black Angus filet with rosemary Dijon sauce round out the menu nicely. Those with an appetite for the sweeter things in life should sample the exotic papaya and pineapple cheese cake or chocolate *ganache* with citrus raspberry *couli.* Information: *Inn on the Cliffs, Kauai Lagoons Resort,* Lihue, Kauai 96766 (phone: 245-5050).

Shopping Spree

Most people do more shopping in Hawaii than they originally intended, and not simply because shopping is an integral part of any holiday. It probably won't be long after you've stepped from the plane before you begin to feel constricted and lackluster in your mainland clothing, chic as it was at home. Just as you conclude that absolutely everybody is wearing something loose and billowy, its surface rampant with splashy birds, flowers, and leaves, you'll notice that some commercially minded citizen has had the prescience to place, if not a shopping center, at least a shop, exactly where you happen to be. Before you know it, you will have outfitted yourself in a manner you never dreamed possible, in something you will probably never find occasion to wear again. Moreover, you will more than likely never regret your purchase and, once transformed, will look around to find what else is for sale. The only warning offered here is to plan for these purchases before you go — and leave room in your suitcase for the souvenirs you'll inevitably acquire.

Most of what Hawaii's merchants have to offer falls into the souvenir and gift category — T-shirts, shell leis, woven hats, Polynesian bric-a-brac — or alohawear, a designation that includes any clothes with the casual island look, from elegant evening skirts of hand-painted silk to inexpensive muumuus. These items are in alarming abundance virtually everywhere. As expected, hotel boutiques and shops near popular tourist attractions tend to be more expensive than stores catering to a resident clientele. But if you're only buying a $4.95 T-shirt or carved keychain, it's probably not worth wasting precious vacation time looking for the very best prices.

Beyond the mountains of trinkets and flowered shirts, however, are some goods of a distinctly higher caliber, and chances are there will come a time to contemplate a more serious purchase. Thanks to heightened native Hawaiian consciousness, there has been a revival of interest in traditional crafts. Niihau shell leis, intricately worked garlands of the tiny, lustrous shells found on the leeward beaches of the island of Niihau, and elaborate feather leis are highly prized collector's items found in galleries on all the major islands. There has also been a flowering of contemporary art: Painters, sculptors, ceramists, jewelers, woodturners, and glass-blowers are producing a prodigious amount of island-inspired work. Much of it is amateurish, to be sure, but some is attracting the attention of the serious art world.

Because of its whaling past, Hawaii also does a lively trade in scrimshaw, the art of etching on whale bone practiced by 19th-century sailors to relieve the tedium of long voyages. Most of what is in the shops is contemporary and is done on the fossilized mammoth and walrus bone unearthed by the ton during the digging of the Alaska pipeline. (Trading in whale ivory has been illegal since whales came under the protection of the Endangered Species Act of 1973.) Very few of the pieces created when Hawaii was the center of the Pacific whaling industry still exist. The work of licentious sailors, much of the early scrimshaw depicted bawdy scenes and was destroyed by priggish missionaries. However, there are some 40 scrimshanders working in Hawaii today, turning out pieces that range from quickly etched pendants the size of a postage stamp to exquisitely worked pieces that fetch thousands of dollars. Some very good work also comes from scrimshanders living in Washington State.

Since Hawaii has always been a trading center between East and West, it is also the place to pick up such treasures as jade from Myanma and Taiwan, Japanese porcelain, Cambodian and Tibetan antiques, Thai silks, or hand-embroidered linen from China. Though not easily found, shops selling Oriental antiques do exist on all the main islands. Ivory carvings are also found in abundance, though visitors are advised against buying them because of the damage trafficking in ivory has caused to remaining wild elephant herds.

BEST BUYS

Following is an item-by-item guide to the best shopping in the islands. More comprehensive discussions of shopping appear in the chapter on each island.

Alohawear – Any loose-fitting, casual garment made in a bright floral print qualifies as alohawear. *Liberty House,* Hawaii's best-known retailer, and *Chapman's* are well known for good-quality island attire. *Collections* has numerous resort shops on each of the major islands. *W. H. Smith's* is another big name. *Hilo Hattie's* offers warehouse merchandise, and sells a wide range of muumuus and aloha shirts. Its larger outlets on Oahu, the Big Island of Hawaii, and Maui are factory and store combined; so eager are they to dress you up in Polynesian patterns that they operate a bus to take you there. The *Goodwill Thrift Shop* (780 S. Beretania St., Honolulu) is a good place to pick up nearly new shirts and muumuus at very low prices. For alohawear a cut above average, try *Apparels of Pauline, Lahaina Marketplace* (Lahaina, Maui, and at the *Royal Hawaiian* hotel and *Hilton Hawaiian Village,* both in Waikiki, Oahu). For vintage aloha shirts, drop in at the *Clothes Addict* (in Paia, Maui); *Bailey's Antique Clothing* (Kapahulu St., Honolulu, Oahu), where prices range from $25 to $1,250; *Reminisce* (Waikiki, Oahu); the *Best Show in Town* (Kapaa, Kauai); *Paradise Thrift Shop* (Kapaa, Kauai); *Collectibles* (Hanapepe, Kauai). Other shops to browse include *Princess Kaiulani Fashions* (in Kamuela, the Big Island of Hawaii), *Helen's Treasures* (Wailuku, Maui), and *Exclusive Designs (Waikoloa Highlands Center,* Big Island of Hawaii).

Arts and Crafts – Paintings, watercolors, prints, sculpture, ceramics, hand-blown glasswork, jewelry, and carved wood, much of it by local artists and inspired by island themes, can be found at a number of galleries. Among them: *Artists Guild* (*Ward Warehouse,* Honolulu, Oahu); *Hawaiian Antiquities* (Honolulu, Oahu); *Jafar, King Kamehameha Mall* (Kona, Hawaii); *Volcano Art Center* (Hawaii Volcanoes National Park, the Big Island of Hawaii); *The Gallery of Great Things* (*Waimea Village Green,* Waimea, Hawaii); *Elephant Walk* (*Hyatt Regency,* Kaanapali, Maui; *Grand Hyatt,* Wailea, Maui; and *Westin Kauai,* Lihue, Kauai); *Wailea Shopping Village* (Wailea, Maui) and *Ala Moana Center* (Honolulu, Oahu); *Maui Crafts Guild* (Paia, Maui); *Dolphin Gallery* (*Whaler's Village,* Kaanapali), and the *Cannery* (Lahaina, Maui); *Distant Drums, The Shops* (Kapalua, Maui); *Village Gallery* (120 Dickenson St., Lahaina, Maui); *Stones Printsellers and Gallery* (*Kukui Grove Center,* Lihue, Kauai); *Viewpoints-The Maui Artists Collective* (Makawao, Maui); *Hui No'eau* (Makawao, Maui); *Kahn Gallery* (*Market Place* at Coconut Plantation, Wailua, Kauai, and four other Kauai locations); *Wyland Gallery* (Haleiwa, Oahu, and Kapaa, Kauai); *The Gallery* (*Waiohai* hotel, Poipu, Kauai); *Artisans Guild* (Hanalei, Kauai); *Ola's* (Hanalei, Kauai); *Ship's Store Gallery* — for marine arts — (in the *Kiahuna Shopping Village,* Kauai); *Hawaiian Handcraft* (760 Kilauea Ave., Hilo, Hawaii); *Island Bamboo* (Makawao, Maui); *Akemi Daniells* (Haiku, Maui).

Coral – All those necklaces of pinkish orange bunched twigs are white coral from Japan and Taiwan, dyed to give the coral effect; they are not precious coral. The pink precious coral in island shops comes from the Kaiwi Channel between Molokai and Oahu, and so does the gold coral, which is found only in the Hawaiian Islands. (There is something similar in Alaska, but it is not quite the same color.) Black coral is harvested off the coast of Maui, while the dark, oxblood red coral, considerably more expensive, is a Mediterranean import. *Coral Grotto* (*Hyatt Regency Waikiki,* 2424 Kalakaua Ave., Honolulu, Oahu; *Ala Moana Shopping Center* in Honolulu; Front St., Lahaina, Maui); *Golden Reef* (*Sheraton Maui,* Maui); *The Necklace Gallery* (*Market Place* at Coconut Plantation, Wailua, Kauai); *Jim Saylor Jewelers* (Kapaa, Kauai); *Jewels Kauai* (*Kiahuna Shopping Village,* Poipu, Kauai); outdoor vendors at the *Spouting Horn* (Poipu, Kauai); *Maui Divers* (Lahaina, Maui, and *Kona Inn Shopping Center,* Kailua-Kona, Hawaii).

Eastern Art and Artifacts – Exquisite jade and ivory carvings, Japanese ceramics, and Chinese cloisonné are some of the Eastern arts that have found their way to Polynesian America. *Bushido Antiques* (Eaton Sq., Honolulu, Oahu); *Robyn Buntin* (Maunakea St., Honolulu, Oahu; Hale Kea, Waimea, Hawaii; and Kilohana, Lihue, Kauai); *Nomad* (Hanapepe, Kauai); and *Yugen* (Waimea, Hawaii); *Garakuta-do* and *Sweet By-Gones* (Maunakea St., Honolulu, Oahu); *Bernard Hurtig's Oriental Treasures* (*Kahala Hilton,* Oahu); *Iida's* (*Ala Moana Shopping Center,* Honolulu, Oahu); *Orientations* (Honolulu, Oahu); *Herman Miller Antiques* (*Mauna Lani Bay Hotel,* Kawaihae, Hawaii); *Gallery* (*Mauna Kea Beach Hotel,* Kawaihae, Hawaii); *Raintree Gallery* (Hilo, Hawaii); *The Gallery* (716 Front St., Lahaina, Maui); *Kong Lung* (Kilauea, Kauai); *Half Moon Japanese Antiques* (Kilohana, Kauai); *Gate to the Orient* (Wailuku, Maui); and *Alii Antiques* (Wailuku, Maui).

Edibles – Papayas, avocados, and bananas must be treated before they can be taken to the mainland; coconuts and pineapples may go as they are. Even so, it's best to buy all fruit from airport shops on your way home (so you won't have to lug your lovely bunch of coconuts around the islands) or from "take home" stores elsewhere, many of which will deliver to your flight. Coconuts can also be labeled, stamped, and sent "as is" through the mail. Macadamia nuts, Kona coffee, Maui potato chips (be sure to get "Kitch'n Cook'd"), taro chips, and crack seed — preserved fruits, nuts, and seeds — can be found in many shops catering to tourists, as can the Hawaiian Plantations line of products, including tropical fruit jams and mango chutney. *Hawaiian Holidays Macadamia Nut Company* (Honokaa, Hawaii, and Front St., Lahaina, Maui); *Guava Kai Plantation* (Kilauea, Kauai); *Tropical Temptations* (Captain Cook, Hawaii); *Lani Truffles Chocolate Factory* (Hilo, Hawaii); *Baskets from the Heart* (Kamuela, Hawaii); *Maui Potato Chip Factory* (295 Lalo St., Kahului, Maui); *Bong Brothers Coffee* (Captain Cook, Hawaii); *Captain Cook Coffee Co.* (Kealakekua, Hawaii); *Honolulu Chocolate Co.* (Manoa Ave. and Restaurant Row, Honolulu, Oahu); *Lappert's Ice Cream* (*Ala Moana Center,* Oahu, and numerous locations on the neighboring islands); *Matsumoto's* (for shaved ice, Haleiwa, Oahu); *Crack Seed Center* (*Ala Moana Center,* Oahu); *Woolworth's* (2222 Kalakaua Ave., Waikiki, Oahu); *Duty Free Shops* (Honolulu International Airport, Oahu); *Maaloa Sunrise* (Kilauea, Kauai); *Mapulehu Mango Grove* (South Shore, Molokai.)

Enameled Jewelry – During the 19th century, Hawaii's royal ladies developed a liking for this jewelry, black enamel on gold inscribed with their names. Modern examples of the art can cost between $100 and $400 for a ring and between $300 and $1,200 for a bracelet. *Precious Metals Hawaii* (Pan Am Building, 1600 Kapiolani Blvd., Suite 616, Honolulu, Oahu); *Rainbow Bazaar* (*Hilton Hawaiian Village,* Honolulu, Oahu); *Royal Hawaiian Heritage* (1430 Kona St., across from the *Ala Moana Center,* Honolulu, Oahu).

Fabrics – Silks from Europe and the Far East, hand-painted Hawaiian panels, and untold yards of tropical prints fill boutiques and department stores across the islands. *Plantation Stitchery* (*Market Place* at Coconut Plantation, Wailua, Kauai); *Singer* (*Kukui Grove Shopping Center,* Lihue, Kauai); *Sew Special* (*Kaahumanu Center,* Kahului, Maui); *Fare Tahiti* (*Kona Inn Shopping Village,* Kailua-Kona, Hawaii); *Kapaia Stitchery* (Lihue, Kauai); *Tahiti Imports* (*Market Place* at Coconut Plantation, Wailua, Kauai and *Kona Shopping Village,* Kailua, Hawaii); *Creative Fibers* (Piikoi St., Honolulu, Oahu).

Feather Leis – This ancient Hawaiian art has been revived and updated, using the feathers of peacocks and pheasants to create beautiful and fanciful hatbands. A feather lei can cost from $50 to $1,000. *Maui Mad Hatter* (*The Wharf,* Lahaina, Maui); *The Gallery* (*Waiohai Hotel,* Poipu Beach, Kauai); *Stone's Gallery* (*Kukui Grove Shopping Center,* Lihue, Kauai); *Royal Feather Co.* (Aiea, Oahu).

Flower Leis – The symbol of Hawaiian hospitality and a joy to indulge in as often as possible during your stay, flower leis are sold at airports, by street vendors, and at hotels and shops all over the islands. There's a fine selection at *Lani's Floral Shoppe* (*King Kamehameha Hotel,* Kailua, Hawaii). Also try the lineup of lei stands at Honolulu International Airport in Oahu, a short walk from the main terminal. Honolulu's Chinatown also features small lei shops on Mauna Kea, Nuuanu, and King Streets, where prices are generally less than at the airport or Waikiki lei stands. For special *haku* leis (dried flowers), try *Ah Lan's* (at the Hilo Airport, Hawaii); *Lotus Blossom* (Koloa, Kauai); *Joe Rossi's* (Kihei, Maui); *Exotica* (Wailuku, Maui).

Hawaiian Music – At first hearing, the falsetto singing of traditional Hawaiian music may sound peculiar to Western ears, but before long most people are seduced by its sweet and strange melodiousness. Musicians and groups for which to look include the *Brothers Cazimero,* Eddie Kamae, Palani Vaughn, the *Beamer Brothers,* the *Sons of Hawaii,* and the *Makaha Sons of Niihau. Jack Wada's* (Lihue, Kauai); *Larry's Music*

(Kapaa, Kauai); *House of Music* (*Kaahumanu Center,* Kahului, Maui and *Ala Moana Center,* Honolulu, Oahu); *J.R.'s Music Shop* (*Maui Mall,* Kahului and *Kukui Plaza,* Kihei, Maui); *Tower Records* (Keaumoku St., Honolulu, Oahu).

Hawaiian Quilts – Introduced by New England missionaries, local quilt making quickly developed a unique Hawaiian style by introducing designs of native flora and motifs from the royal era. It's almost impossible to buy an authentic antique example, but quilt kits and patterns are widely available. *Volcano Art Center* (Volcanoes National Park, Hawaii); *Topstitch* (Parker Ranch Center, Kamuela, Hawaii); *Pineapple Patch* (Holualoa, Hawaii); *Kapaia Stitchery* (Lihue, Kauai); Hawaii Quilts (King St., Honolulu, Oahu). For made-to-order quilts, contact Barbara Jossem-Naud (2288 Kolo Rd., Kilauea, HI 96754) or Elaine Kaopuiki (PO Box K, Lanai City, HI 96763). On Oahu, the *Hawaiian Quilt Collection* (PO Box 632, Kailua, Oahu 96734) offers a small catalogue with pictures for custom-made quilts.

Hawaiiana – Guides, maps, books on Hawaiian flora, fauna, history, culture, legends, language, food, crafts — any printed material to feed the curiosity of the new Hawaiiphile comes under this heading. *Waldenbooks* (*Waikiki Shopping Plaza* and *Ward Warehouse,* Honolulu, Oahu); *Honolulu Book Shop* (*Ala Moana Shopping Center* and 1001 Bishop St., Honolulu, Oahu); *Shop Pacifica* (1525 Bernice St., Honolulu, Oahu) at the *Bishop Museum*; *The Museum Shop* at the Honolulu Academy of Arts (900 S. Beretania St., Honolulu, Oahu); *Little Hawaiian Craft Shop* (*Royal Hawaiian Center,* Waikiki, Oahu); *Huki Like* (Banyan Dr., Hilo, Hawaii); *Kilauea Visitors Center* (Hawaii Volcanoes National Park, Hawaii); *Middle Earth Book Shop* (75-5719 Alii Dr., Kailua-Kona, Hawaii); *Artisans Guild* (Hanalei, Kauai); *Kauai Museum Gift and Book Shop* (4428 Rice St., Lihue, Kauai); *Stone's Gallery* (*Kukui Grove Center,* Lihue, Kauai); *Hawaiian Arts and Museum* (Kilauea, Kauai); *Paia Gifts & Collectibles* (Paia, Maui); *Kihei Town Antiques* (Kihei, Maui); *Things from the Past* (Wailuku, Maui); *Hula Moons* (Wailuku, Maui).

■ **Book Mark:** We immodestly suggest that in addition to *BIRNBAUM'S Hawaii 1993,* you can also pick up a copy of our first-time-ever *BIRNBAUM'S Honolulu 1993.*

Jade – Much of the jade jewelry and objets d'art in the islands is from Myanma or Taiwan. Burmese jade, which comes in a rainbow of greens, reds, and lavenders, is the connoisseur's choice. *Alberta's Gazebo* (*The Wharf,* Lahaina, Maui); *Monarch Jade* (Honolulu, Oahu); *Goldsmith's Gallery* (*Kinipopo Shopping Village,* Kapaa, Kauai); *Security Diamond* (*Ala Moana Center,* Honolulu, Oahu).

Kukui Nut Jewelry – Called the candlenut because its oil was used in lamps, the nut of the ubiquitous kukui tree is polished to a high sheen and made into necklaces, bracelets, and other jewelry. Black is the least expensive ($8 for a plain choker); brown, slightly higher; and jewelry made of the rare white nut, the most expensive. *Kukui Nuts of Hawaii* (66-935 Kaukonohua Rd., Waialua, Oahu; phone: 637-5620), Hawaii's only manufacturer of kukui nut jewelry, also offers the widest selection. Also available at *The Museum Shop* (*Bishop Museum,* 1355 Kalihi St., Honolulu, Oahu); *The Little Grass Shack* (Rte. 11, Captain Cook, Hawaii).

Lau Hala – Products woven from the leaves of the pandanus tree range from big-weave placemats, napkin rings, baskets, and boxes to finely textured hats of distinction. *The Little Grass Shack* (Rte. 11, Captain Cook, Hawaii); *Sugawara Lauhala & Gift Shop* (59 Kalakaua Ave., Hilo, Hawaii); *Hale Manucraft* (195 Kinoole St., Hilo, Hawaii); *Products of Hawaii* (*Ala Moana Shopping Center,* Honolulu, Oahu); *Maui Mad Hatter* (*The Wharf,* Lahaina, Maui).

Leather Goods – Like any ranching country, Hawaii has its share of shops that cater to the needs of cowboys and would-be cowboys who simply appreciate fine leatherwork.

Lee Sands Eel Skin (Lawai, Kauai); *Yokahama-Okadaya* (*Royal Hawaiian Shopping Center,* Waikiki, Oahu); *Bebe's* (*Waikiki Trade Center,* Waikiki, Oahu); *Raku Leather* (*Royal Hawaiian Shopping Center,* Waikiki, Oahu); *Escada* (*Ala Moana Center,* Oahu); *Louis Vuitton* (*Royal Hawaiian Shopping Center,* Waikiki, Oahu); *Paniolo* (*Ala Moana Center,* Oahu); *Gucci* (*Ala Moana Center,* Oahu); *North Beach Leather* (*Ala Moana Center,* Oahu); *Shibumi Leather* (624 Front St., Lahaina, 7 Market St., Wailuku, and *Azeka Place,* Kihei, all on Maui).

Niihau Leis – The most prized of permanent leis, Niihau leis are made from hundreds of tiny shells that wash up on the shore of Niihau, the small private island off Kauai. A simple choker can cost as little as $15, but more complicated designs, such as the pikake lei — so called because its clusters resemble the pikake flower — can cost several thousand dollars. *Koloa Gallery* (*Sheraton Kauai,* Poipu Beach, Kauai); the outdoor vendors at the *Spouting Horn Lookout* (Poipu, Kauai); *Kahn Gallery* (*Market Place* at Coconut Plantation, Kapaa, Kauai); *Kong Lung* (Kilauea, Kauai); *Kilohana Gallery* (Kilohana, Kauai); *Pendragon* (Koloa, Kauai); *Ka Honu Gift Gallery* (*Whalers Village,* Kaanapali, Maui); *Hawaiian Traders* (*King Kamehameha Hotel* and *Kona Surf Hotel,* Kailua, Hawaii); *Kaui's Florist* (Paia, Kauai).

Pacific Art and Artifacts – Balinese paintings, antiques from Borneo and the Marshall Islands, and Malaysian kites are among the many imports from Hawaii's Pacific neighbors. *South Seas Trading Post* (851 Front St., Lahaina, Maui); *The Lady Jane Company* (Hanamaulu, Kauai); *Traders of the Lost Art* (Wailuku, Maui); *Waipio Woodworks* and *Kamaaina Woods* (Kukuihaele, Hawaii); *Woods of Kohala* (Kapaau, Hawaii); *The Little Grass Shack* (Rte. 11, Captain Cook, Hawaii); *The Little Hawaiian Shop* (*Royal Hawaiian Shopping Center,* Waikiki, Oahu); *John of Maui & Son* (Haiku, Maui); *Ka Honu* (*Whaler's Village,* Kaanapali, Maui).

Plants – Seeds, cuttings, and potted specimens of Hawaii's abundant and exotic plant life — plumeria, ginger, orchids, birds of paradise, protea, anthuriums, hibiscus, ti, bamboo — inspected by the Department of Agriculture and packed to travel, are available at several airport shops, as well as at other places around the islands. Some of the larger stores will mail plants. *Hana Gardenland* (Hana Hwy., 4 miles from the town of Hana, Maui); *Hawaii Protea Co-operative* (Hwy. 37, Kula, Maui); *Maui Sunburst* (Kula, Maui); *Nani Mau Gardens* (421 Makalika St., Hilo, Hawaii); *Fuku-Bonsai Center* (Keauhou, Hawaii); *Orchids of Hawaii* (2801 Kilauea Ave., Hilo, Hawaii); *Shimunishi Nursery* (Hanapepe, Kauai); *Likelike Florist* (Waianvenue Av., Hilo, Hawaii); *Rainbow Forest* (Pahoa, Hawaii).

Scrimshaw – The 19th-century whalers' art of carving ivory (whalebone) is alive and well in Hawaii these days. It's possible to spend as little as $10 for a small pendant or ring, or as much as $10,000 for an elaborately etched display piece. Lahaina is the center of Hawaiian scrimshaw, with the largest selection and most competitive prices. *Lahaina Scrimshaw Factory–Pier 49* (845 Front St., Lahaina, Maui); and *Whalers Village,* Kaanapali, Maui); *Alihi Creations* (*Parker Ranch Shopping Center,* Kamuela, Hawaii); *Kahn Gallery* (*Market Place,* Coconut Plantation, Wailua, Kauai); and *Kilohana Gallery* (Kilohana, Kauai).

Swimwear – As expected, there's a dizzying selection. *Liberty House*, on all islands; *Down Under Honolulu* (Kuhio Ave., Waikiki, Oahu); *Reyn's* (*Kapalua Shops,* Kapalua, Maui); *Surf Sports* (Front St., Lahaina, Maui); *Bikini Company* (Front St., Lahaina, Maui); *Bikini Discount* (*Kamaole Center,* Kihei, Maui); *Shops of the Market Place* (Coconut Plantation, Wailua, Kauai); *Suits Me* (*Waiohai Hotel,* Poipu, Kauai).

Tapa Cloth – Also called kapa, tapa is the bark fabric worn by Hawaiians before Westerners introduced them to cotton. Most of the tapa found in Hawaii today, in the form of wall hangings, table linen, placemats, boxes, and purses, comes from Samoa and Tonga, although it's possible to get an old piece of Hawaiian tapa for $100 and up. *The Museum Shop* (*Bishop Museum,* 1355 Kahili St., Honolulu, Oahu); *The Lady*

Jane Company (Hanamaulu, Kauai); and Coconut Plantation *Market Place* (Kapaa, Kauai).

T-Shirts – Even the most out-of-the-way places have them, emblazoned with an endless variety of designs and messages. *Crazy Shirts,* with dozens of shops, is the big name, but there are numerous others, including *Novelty World* (*Ward Warehouse,* Honolulu, Oahu); *Tropical Dreams* (Kapaa, Kauai); and *Tropical Shirts* (*Kiahuna Shopping Village* and Coconut Plantation, Kauai).

Wood Items – Out of the islands' native woods, woodturners make beautiful art of everyday objects, such as bowls, trays, and boxes. The best known wood, koa, is often called Hawaiian mahogany because of its rich, reddish tone and lustrous finish. Mango wood, whitish to tan in color, is shot through with streaks of pink, yellow, and sometimes green, producing what one artisan calls rainbow wood. Monkeypod ranges from light to dark brown, while milo wood is reddish with patches of beige. A very rare and lovely wood is kaimani, which is light to reddish pink in tone and is finely grained. *Martin & MacArthur Koa Wood Furnishings* (Honolulu, Oahu); *Nohea* (Honolulu, Oahu); *Waimea General Store* (across from the Hawaii Prep Academy Campus, Rte. 19, Kamuela, Hawaii); *Hawaiian Traders* (*King Kamehameha Hotel,* Kailua, Hawaii); *Kamaaina Woods, Inc.* (Kukuihaele, Hawaii); *Waipio Woodworks* (Kukuihaele, Hawaii); *Kahn Gallery* (*Market Place,* Coconut Plantation, Wailua, Kauai); *Kong Lung Center* (Kilauea, Kauai); *Stone's Gallery* (at Kiahana, Lihue, Kauai); *Ola's* (Hanalei, Kauai); *The Lady Jane Company* (Hanamaulu, Kauai); *Artisans Guild* (Hanalei, Kauai); *John of Maui & Son* (Haiku, Maui); *Maui Sculpture Gallery* (Paia, Maui).

For the Body

Dream Beaches

The best beaches of Hawaii? Even the ones considered only ordinary by *akamai* (in-the-know) residents are often exquisite by mainland standards, with their bright seascapes of blue skies and even bluer waters, strands of white or black sand ringed by sea palms, pandanus, and ironwood pines, and ocean surf ranging from gentle baby swells to monster rollers up to 30 feet high.

The beachcombing possibilities in Hawaii are endless. More than 1,500 varieties of shells wash up on the islands' beaches, and in some areas the remnants of wrecked ships can also be found. Some coastlines have wave-washed rocky shores and lava ledges, as well as exposed tide pools and shallow reef flats. Exploring these areas for marine invertebrates can be a fascinating alternative to sun worshiping. Protective gloves and shoes are recommended for wading in tide pools and walking on the reefs.

To avoid angering residents by trespassing on private property, look for Public Access to Beach signs. If you're searching for secluded beaches, check around; an unmarked road cut through a sugar plantation will often lead to an isolated, heavenly oceanside site.

Be mindful of sea conditions in Hawaii. Riptides, dangerous undertows, sharp coral bottoms, and other such hazards are not always readily discernible to *malihinis* (newcomers). So check with lifeguards, surfers, or residents before entering the water.

OAHU

WAIKIKI: This 2-mile arc of sand lined with resort hotels is probably the single most famous beach in the world. Waikiki is relatively clean and free of litter but is often carpeted instead with large numbers of sunbathers. Replacement sand that's been trucked in to bolster "the Beach" is constantly washed out to sea and has altered the contour of the offshore ocean floor. Consequently, the shape and size of Waikiki's famous surfing waves are changing. Surfboard rentals, catamaran sails, and outrigger canoe rides are available at concession stands up and down the beach. The best sections of beach lie closer to Diamond Head, a 15-minute walk from central Waikiki. An acquired taste by day, Waikiki is a great place to go for a moonlight stroll, and the hour immediately after dawn makes rising early worth the effort.

ALA MOANA PARK: Honolulu residents and Waikiki exiles flock to this 76-acre park to build sand castles, fly kites, or spread a picnic in a grassy area. Safe, reef-sheltered waters make it a popular place to bring kids. Deep offshore channels makes it a favorite spot with swimmers. Those bored with sun and surf activities can walk across the street to the *Ala Moana Shopping Center,* a huge complex of more than 200 stores.

HANAUMA BAY BEACH PARK: An extinct volcanic crater shaped into a huge outdoor aquarium by sea erosion, Hanauma Bay is one of Oahu's top areas for underwater exploration, a fact that brings almost ruinous crowds to this once quiet spot. Now a designated marine preserve, it has sand pockets within the reef that provide good swimming, especially the Keyhole and a small inlet with a natural rock-carved hole called the Toilet Bowl. Bring food: The fish will eat out of your hand on the reef. In addition, the tide pools contain many fascinating creatures. Snorkelers should be wary of a turbulent area of the bay known as Witches Brew, as well as the Molokai Express, a strong current that sweeps across the outer edge of the bay. Movie buffs (especially Elvis Presley fans) will recognize Hanauma as the backdrop for the 1961 film *Blue Hawaii.*

GOAT ISLAND (MOKUAUIA BEACH): Simply wade across a narrow strait of water — on a calm day, at low tide — to reach this small island off the North Shore's Kalanai Point. (Wear sneakers to protect your feet from the coral, and don't attempt to cross if the surf is rough.) The island's sandy beach is protected by an offshore reef that makes swimming ideal, especially for children. Goat Island is a state bird refuge, with many bird species in its ironwood trees.

NORTH SHORE: SUNSET, PIPELINE, WAIMEA, AND EHUKAI: Along with other legendary North Shore surf sites such as Waimea Bay, Banzai Beach (home of the deadly "Pipeline"), and Ehukai Beach Park, Sunset is where towering mountains of water crash into shore during the winter. One of Oahu's largest tracts of sand, Sunset Beach stretches for 2 miles. Be aware that swimming in certain stretches can be dangerous, except for a few weeks in the summer. It may be wiser just to pack a picnic lunch and bring a pair of binoculars to watch the world's most daring surfers challenge the largest surfable waves on earth.

MOKULEIA: This mile-long stretch of beach at the western end of Oahu is often nearly deserted, except for local fishermen, picnicking families, and military personnel on a day off (much of the beach is military-owned land). The Waianae Mountains provide a lovely green backdrop, and while swimming is complicated by close-to-shore reefs, there are coastal pools where you can cool off, as well as pockets of deeper water.

KAILUA: Powder-white sand and vibrantly turquoise water make this miles-long beach one of the island's most beautiful. Although houses line much of the shoreline, there is a beach park with shower and picnic facilities on the eastern end and numerous public access points elsewhere along the coast. Steady winds make this a favorite spot for windsurfers.

HAWAII

PUNALUU BEACH PARK: In the Kau district between Kona and Hilo, Punaluu is a black sand beach adjacent to a lagoon. Despite an occasional stop by tour buses, it attracts few swimmers or sunbathers. Check with the lifeguard or with residents before wading in; strong currents can make swimming dangerous here. A short distance away is Ninole Cove, a miniature (and secluded) version of its big brother that is ideal for private outings.

OLD AIRPORT: This is one of the few fine beaches Mother Nature deposited along the Big Island's Kona Coast. The skin diving in this area is unrivaled for underwater beauty. Protected from prevailing trade winds by the twin volcanic peaks of Mauna Loa and Mauna Kea, the water at Old Airport (and its neighboring beaches) is usually smooth. Near the *King Kamehameha* hotel and Kailua's former airport, this white sand beach is guarded by a rocky entrance. Skin divers who negotiate it successfully are rewarded by marine life and coral formations that are mesmerizing.

ANAEHOOMALU: A wide crescent of beach separates an iridescent bay from ancient coastal fish ponds. Full beach services are available, including snorkel gear and Hobie Cat rentals. A road provides public access to this central beach within the *Waikoloa* resort.

MILOLII: On the southern Kona Coast near the fishing village of the same name is one of the state's most authentically Hawaiian villages. Fishermen still salt and dry their day's catch in the hot sun, usually in the front yards of their ramshackle homes. And though the rough-hewn beach does not have acres of sand, the coastal reef offers good snorkeling and the tide pools along the shoreline are worlds unto themselves. (To reach the nearby sandy beach, pick up the coastal trail at the end of the Milolii Beach road, a 10-minute walk.)

HAPUNA: About half an hour north of Kailua, this double-crescent beach has fine sunbathing and swimming, although the current is strong. Full picnic, shower, and barbecue facilities make it a popular family beach. Just south of the *Mauna Kea Beach* hotel.

MAUI

KAPALUA BAY: This small crescent of golden sand at the foot of the *Kapalua Bay* hotel on West Maui is lovely. Coconut palms surround the beach, an entrancing view of Molokai faces it, and rocky points reach out into the bay on either side, creating gentle, sparkling, and clear inshore waters that attract snorkelers and divers in addition to swimmers. Given its location in the midst of civilization, it's not a beach where sunbathers will ever be alone, but it's one worth sharing.

KAANAPALI: Hotels and condominiums line most of this beach, which edges the *Kaanapali* resort for 2 miles and then extends north for another mile. Hotels and condos notwithstanding, the strip of sand remains pretty as a picture, with the less crowded north beach providing a backdrop of lawns, golf courses, sugarcane fields, and the West Maui mountains. The offshore islands are visible across the azure water. Black Rock, an outcropping of lava on which the *Sheraton Maui* is built, divides the beach in two, and the skin diving in this vicinity rivals that of the Big Island's Kona Coast for undersea splendor. Most of the beach is good for swimming, as long as bathers heed the warning signs that hotels put up when the surf is rough.

KAMAOLE PARKS I, II, III: Conveniently set along South Kihei Road on East Maui are three fine, wide sandy beaches framed from afar by the blue-green mass of the West Maui mountains. The Kamaole beaches are especially popular with families and new swimmers and may be quite crowded on weekends. The stretch of beach at the Maalaea end of the coast is much less crowded, though the shallower waters are less appealing to swimmers. The parks have picnic areas, showers, and restrooms, and there's even a playground for kids at Kamaole III.

WAILEA: Besides its hotels and a host of plush condominiums, the *Wailea* resort has five lovely beaches — Keawakapu, Mokapu, Ulua, Wailea, and Polo — strung along 2 miles of coastline. Like the Kamaole beaches to the north, they have no protective reef. Swimming is possible, however, as long as the kona winds aren't blowing. All have clear water for snorkeling, which is especially good around the rocky points that separate them. Because of its position between the two hotels, Ulua Beach is the most heavily trafficked, but a backing of dunes and a certain amount of seclusion can be found by heading toward the beaches to the south. Limited public access parking is available.

MAKENA: It used to be known as Oneloa Beach, and since Oneloa is Hawaiian for "long sands," that was the perfect moniker for this very long, very wide swath of beachfront south of Wailea. Bounded by cliffs and a scrub forest of kiawe trees, Makena is possibly Maui's most beautiful beach. It's blessed with good underwater visibility for snorkelers, but it, too, has no protective reef and is, therefore, to be approached with care during heavy surf. Makena was a popular hippie hangout during the 1960s and 1970s (it was even called Hippie Beach for a while), but the impromptu settlements built by the counterculture crowd are long gone, replaced in part by nearby resort development. Fortunately, the beach remains undeveloped — a result, no doubt, of continuing efforts to protect it by making it a state park. A rocky outcrop separates Oneloa from Little Makena, long a peaceful nudist hideaway. A court ruling has stopped unwarranted police raids against the nudists.

SEVEN POOLS: A few miles south of Hana, in the Kipahulu section of Haleakala National Park, are the well-known plunge pools that are often referred to as the Seven Sacred Pools. There are more than seven of them, and though there is no evidence that they were ever sacred, ancient Hawaiians certainly must have splashed around in them. The rocks bordering the pools are slippery when wet, but the water is refreshingly cool, however you manage to enter. The grove of kamani trees bordering the pools, the view down the Oheo Stream to the rough ocean (too rough for swimming), and the view upstream toward Haleakala make this an enchanting spot in one of Maui's most beautiful regions.

MOLOKAI

MOOMOMI: Moomomi Bay is a sizable indentation along Molokai's west coast, sheltering one of the finest beaches and congregations of sand dunes in the state. Freshwater pools are nestled in some of the dunes, though most folks spend their time snorkeling along the reef or beachcombing for driftwood. (Swimming may be prohibited when the surf is high.) Moomomi is rarely crowded because it is difficult to find: The right fork of Farrington Avenue (a dirt road near the beach) must be followed to the park.

PAPOHAKU: This is one of the largest and widest (and prettiest) sandy beaches in Hawaii. The vast expanse of sand is offset by undulating dunes covered by scrub growth. Near the *Kaluakoi* hotel on the west coast of the island, Papohaku is not always safe for swimming (rip currents are prevalent), but the beach is simply too beautiful to pass up.

HALAWA: For those heading to rural Halawa Valley on Molokai's east end, this horseshoe-shaped, dark sand beach provides a perfect picnic locale for an isolated luncheon. The water is often turbulent here, and swimmers are advised to be cautious. Halawa Stream cuts the beach in half as it enters the Pacific sea.

LANAI

HULOPOE: Though by no means its least crowded park, Hulopoe is probably Lanai's finest beach. A long, wide arc of sand fringed by kiawe trees and marked by a pair of lava points, Hulopoe has a partially protected swimming area, as well as a large tidal pool blasted out of the lava shoreline that serves as a children's swimming pool. Colorful tropical fish are trapped in the shoreline's tidal pools each day by the outgoing tide. Good snorkeling and scuba diving can be found just offshore. There are also beachfront tables for picnics. Hotel and condominium development is under way on adjacent land, but the beach has been set aside as a park with public access.

SHIPWRECK: By driving along Keomuku Road until it forks near the shoreline, visitors can discover 8 miles of undisturbed berm and dunes stretching from Polihua Beach to Kahokunui. Powerful winds off Lanai's north coast have driven many boats up on the reef, from great wooden schooners to World War II tankers, and the flotsam from these wrecks eventually drifts in to shore. In addition to the free pickings on the beach, lobsters can be taken near the reef by snorkelers with quick hands.

KAUAI

MAHAULEPU: Once-isolated Mahaulepu now has the *Hyatt Regency Kauai* as a neighbor. Still, the setting remains somewhat wild, with dramatic coastal panoramas that are best seen from the promontory on the eastern border of the beach. Winds and currents deposit beach glass and driftwood on the shore, and who knows, you might even find a bottle with a message in it. Mahaulepu's reef-protected water offers ideal swimming conditions, too. The film *Islands in the Stream,* starring George C. Scott, was shot here.

POLIHALE STATE PARK: At the end of a long, winding (and bumpy) cane road on the west end of Kauai, Polihale is a great place to soak up the rays in relative peace. The beach, one of Hawaii's widest, longest, and wildest, is known for its extraordinary sunsets, a great variety of seashells, a distant view of the island of Niihau, and its unique geographical position as the westernmost park in America. Coastal waters, however, can be dangerous for swimmers.

ANINI PARK: In the Hanalei area, with a protective reef 200 yards offshore that provides placid waters for safe swimming. That, and its picnic area, make Anini especially popular with families. Shell collectors also find it rewarding. Folks looking for a place to get away from it all should take the shore road, on either side of Anini, to one of the numerous unnamed, rarely visited, very secluded small beaches.

LUMAHAI: This is where Mitzi Gaynor tried to wash that man right out of her hair in the movie version of *South Pacific.* Lumahai is a jewel of a beach tucked into a small cove surrounded by lush green hills and hala trees. Beachgoers must descend a dirt trail that winds down the hillside, but it's worth the effort. Black lava rock formations at either end of the beach create fairly protected swimming waters, and, pity poor Mitzi, the setting is certainly not conducive to forgetting. If you had to pick the single most beautiful beach in Hawaii, Lumahai would probably be it. Two even more isolated beaches can be reached on foot from Lumahai.

KEE BEACH: At the end of Kuhio Highway, nestled at the base of the Na Pali cliffs, is one of Kauai's most accessible "wilderness" beaches. Reef-sheltered swimming and good snorkeling near the shore are surpassed only by the lush, towering mountains and a forest of venerable ironwood pines. The Na Pali Coast trail begins within a few feet of the beach, and a short hike on a trail that leads from the beach takes you to the remains of an ancient *heiau* (temple) and panoramic coastal views.

Sensational Surfing

"Let's go surfing now, everybody's learning how, come on a safari with me." So sang *Jan and Dean* and the *Beach Boys* of surfing's heyday during the 1960s, when "woodies" (old wood-sided station wagons loaded with surfboards), "hanging ten" (putting all ten toes over the front edge of the board), and bleached-blond surfers were the rage. Interest in the sport may have peaked on the mainland, but in Hawaii surfing remains an endless summer of sandy beaches, open-air snack bars, and near-perfect surfing conditions.

The individual Hawaiian islands are actually the tops of volcanic mountains rising from the ocean floor, and without a continental shelf to slow them down or shrink them, the North Pacific's winter swells attain monstrous proportions by the time they reach Hawaii's coastline. The raw energy of these great rollers combines with the contour of the ocean bottom to create the biggest (and best-shaped) surfing waves in the world.

But the beginning surfer need not feel left out in Hawaii. Oahu's Waikiki Beach, as well as some ocean parks on neighbor islands, have relatively tame conditions where, in a short time, a novice can learn how to balance the board — and ultimately how to catch a wave. (It takes years to refine technique and develop a personal style.)

One-hour group instruction rates cost about $25, including the use of a board. Private lessons are higher. Surfboard rentals start at $5 per hour and go to $25 per day. The Morey Doyle boards — made from a soft fiber foam that is more buoyant and stable than the hard, fiberglass boards — are recommended for "gremlins" (novice surfers). (A hard stringer running from tip to tail makes these boards firm enough to stand on.) "Boogie boards," short body-surfing boards made of soft polyurethane that are ridden in a kneeling or prone position, are also popular in the islands. Rental fees range from $7.50 to $15 for a full day.

The appeal of surfing escapes definition. It is a spontaneous, creative activity that is never the same twice because each wave has its own characteristics. Surfboards have come a long way from the long flat wooden planks used by Hawaiian royalty, who surfed to prove the worthiness of their leadership, but the sensation hasn't changed in 200 years. Said Captain Cook of a surfer he observed in 1777: "I could not help concluding that this man felt the most supreme pleasure while he was driven so fast and so smoothly by the sea." So if the surf's up and you're so inclined, go catch a wave.

OAHU: Just the thought of this island is guaranteed to raise goose pimples on any serious surfer's surface. In part because of its fortuitous location, Oahu has some of the finest surfing breaks in the world. The North Shore, where giant 30-foot waves arrive in the winter, is still the ultimate proving ground for professionals and top amateurs.

Beginners confine themselves to the mellow swells at Waikiki Beach, where professional "beach boys" are available for surfing lessons at a number of concessions along the beach. The instructors at *Waikiki Beach Services,* for example, go through the motions of surfing on land with students before wading into the "soup" (foamy white water) to get the feel of the board underfoot. "We eliminate the fear aspect of the sport," said one teacher. Once gremlins learn to stand with their feet parallel and wide apart, their knees bent, and their weight forward, they are in position to ride a wave. Willing students with good balance can learn to surf in an hour. Catching a wave takes a bit more practice, but the sensation of being carried along on the board is indescribably exhilarating. Information: *Waikiki Beach Services,* c/o *Outrigger Reef Hotel,* 2169 Kalia Rd., Honolulu, HI 96815 (phone: 924-4940 or 924-4941), or *Sheraton Waikiki,* 2255 Kalakaua Ave., Honolulu, HI 96815 (phone: 922-4422).

In addition to Waikiki, Oahu's other top beginner and intermediate beaches include Ala Moana, Diamond Head, and Koko Head. Black Point near Diamond Head, with the great brown and green slopes of the eroded volcanic cone overlooking the surf, is one of the most beautiful settings for wave riding in the islands.

The *Haleiwa Surf Center* at the Alii Beach Park on Oahu's North Shore is a water sports center run by the island's Department of Parks and Recreation where surfing (including using the board) is taught *free of charge* on weekends. The beach park is well south of the more famous North Shore sites, where the waves are often higher than most of the homes in the area! The surf at Alii Beach averages 2 to 4 feet, ideal for beginners. Information: *Haleiwa Surf Center,* 66167 Haleiwa Rd., Haleiwa, HI 96712 (phone: 637-5051).

When the great North Pacific swells roll in from Alaska and Siberia in late fall and early winter, the cream of the sport gathers on the North Shore for pro tournaments and competitions. The three top sites, strictly for experts, are Sunset Beach, Waimea Bay, and the Banzai Pipeline. Waves break in a curl and envelop surfers in a tube at the famed Pipeline, but this is probably the most dangerous surfing site on earth, as surfers risk being thrown onto the sharp coral reef bottom. Mistakes here are costly — and painful.

HAWAII: The Big Island is rarely mentioned as a top place to surf, but Kona winds and northern swells can produce exceptional conditions in the vicinity of Hilo Bay.

Orchid Land Surfboards (see below) is one of the few board rental outlets on the island. Private lessons (Sundays are best) are a summer possibility. Good surfing sites can also be found on the Big Island's South Shore beaches.

With few exceptions, the island's Kona coastline is not suitable for novices. There is lots of lava, but unfortunately very little sand for soft landings on the leeward side of the island. Top surfers gravitate to Banyans at Kailua Bay, where a *Masters Tournament* is held in the winter. Lyman's Cove also has excellent surf up to 10 feet.

"Boogie boarders" and body-surfers usually head to Magic Sands Beach Park, where wave riders can glide into a near fluorescent white sandy beach. Information: *Orchid Land Surfboards,* 832 Kilauea Ave., Hilo, HI 96720 (phone: 935-1533); *Pacific Vibra-*

tions, 75-5755 Alii Dr., Kailua-Kona, HI 96740 (phone: 329-4140); *Hobie Sports Kona, Kona Inn Shopping Village,* Kailua-Kona, HI 96740 (phone: 329-1001).

MAUI: Though windsurfing has swept the island, stalwart wave riders still frequent a number of top surfsites on the Valley Isle, depending on the season. In the winter, capable surfers head north to Honolua Bay and Hookipa Beach Park near Paia. (*Hookipa* means "hospitality" in Hawaiian, but this surfsite is anything but gracious when the swells rise up in huge walls of rolling water.) Come summer, the action gravitates to Maui's more southerly shores, where the Kihei Coast of Maalaea Bay and the town of Lahaina are the top gathering spots. Ambitious surfers fasten their boards to overhead car racks and travel the coast road between Kaanapali and Makena in search of uncrowded beaches with perfect waves. They are seldom disappointed. Little-known hot spots, with names like Shark Pit, Hot Sands, and Breakwall, are the places to check out.

Gremlins should head to Lahaina, where *Indian Summer Surf Shop* rents Morey Doyle boards, which simplify the beginner's first encounter with surfing. Inquire at the shop about lessons. Information: *Indian Summer Surf Shop,* 193 Lahainaluna Rd., Lahaina, HI 96761 (phone: 661-3794). For Kihei or Wailea, contact *Lightning Bolt,* 55 Kaahumanu Ave., Kahului, HI 96732 (phone: 877-3484).

KAUAI: The Garden Isle is only a step or two behind Oahu as the best surfing destination in the state. It is also the state's best-kept surfing secret, with few professional tournaments and little media exposure. Aging surfers retire to Kauai because of its lovely waves, ideal weather, and uncrowded beaches.

Surf shops (and good surf) are concentrated in two areas. On the south shore, Poipu Beach near Makahuena Point has several fine surfing sites that come to life in July and August, when summer swells of 6 to 8 feet attract advanced practitioners.

Kapaa, on Kauai's windward coast, also has fine surfing. The mouth of the Wailua River south of Anahola Bay has good waves in the summer for surfers who have mastered the basics. On Kauai's north shore, the ferocious winter surf challenges the best and most daring riders. The top surf site is Hanalei Bay, where the rollers scrape the sky from October through January. Tunnels, a site frequented by locals near Na Pali Coast State Park, has winter surf conditions similar to those at the famous Banzai Pipeline on Oahu's North Shore.

Pedal & Paddle in Hanalei (phone: 826-9069), *Kauai Sea Sports* at the *Sheraton Kauai* in Poipu (phone: 742-1221), *Progressive Expressions* in Koloa (phone: 742-6041) and Kapaa (phone: 822-9211), and the *Hanalei Surf Co.* (phone: 826-9000) in Hanalei all rent surfboards and can probably arrange lessons. Your best bet for lessons is the *Margo Oberg Surfing School* (RR1, Box 73, Koloa, HI 96756; phone: 742-6411, ext. 2510), which operates on the grounds of the *Kiahuna Plantation* condo resort. Marge herself is an ex-surfing champion who charges $40 for an hour-long lesson (plus a half-hour's use of a surfboard following the lesson) designed to suit everyone from beginners to expert surfers. Surfboard rentals are also available.

Windsurfing

The fastest growing sport in the world, windsurfing has found a special home in Hawaii. This is because the ideal learning conditions for beginners include a bay with a wide sandy beach, smooth warm water, and a light breeze; Hawaii has all of these elements in abundance. Most of the islands also have prevailing onshore, or sea, breezes that blow at an angle to shore and prevent a careless novice from being swept out to sea.

In addition to its ideal beginner conditions, Hawaii has some of the best expert and competition waters in the world. "Surf-sailing" and wave-jumping, advanced techniques using wind *and* waves to produce an exciting (and often airborne) ride, are among the windsurfing variations that have been pioneered in Hawaii.

Instructors say novices require a minimum of 2 hours of lessons to acquaint themselves with the rudiments of the sport; dancers, sailors, and skiers tend to pick it up most quickly. One Oahu instructor thinks that women often make rapid improvement because they "plug into the feel of the wind and its effect on the sail without trying to resort to sheer strength." Windsurfing lessons start at $30 for a 2-hour session. A half hour is usually spent on a ground simulator to learn wind theory. Windsurfer rentals start at $10 per hour with half- and full-day discounts available.

OAHU: The Kailua Beach Park area, on the windward side of the island, lays claim to some of the finest windsurfing grounds in the world. A mere 30 minutes by car from Honolulu, Kailua is a gathering place for hot shots, gurus, and top board and sail designers, all of whom congregate in much the same way that surfers did on the North Shore in the 1950s to test-ride new fiberglass boards. *World Cup* windsurfing competitions are held here each year.

Windsurfing Hawaii's *Kailua Beach School* offers private lessons for $50, including a 1½-hour lesson and a 2½-hour rental, and group lessons for $35 for the same lesson/rental package, and provides equipment rentals for beginner and advanced sailors. Because there are no hotels on its beaches, the Kailua area is relatively uncrowded and, therefore, ideal for windsurfing. From the water, sailors see a white sand beach ringed by palm trees, with the vivid green and often cloud-encircled peaks of the Koolau Range in the distance. For those who want to purchase a sailboard, the *Windsurfing Hawaii* shop, 5 minutes from the beach, probably has the best selection of beginner and high-performance custom boards and accessories in the islands. Information: *Kailua Beach School,* 155A Hamakua Dr., Kailua, HI 96734 (phone: 261-3539).

HAWAII: *Ocean Sports Waikoloa,* which runs a windsurfing concession from the *Royal Waikoloan* on the Kona Coast, is on a large crescent beach that serves as an ideal launching point for novices. A reef across the entrance of tiny Anaehoomalu Bay protects the waters and keeps surf activity to a minimum. The mountains behind the bay shield it from strong winds. Sailors have views of Mauna Loa and Mauna Kea, the island's two large volcanic cones that are snow-capped in winter. The area typically receives a light breeze in the morning, a moderate wind at midday, and calmer winds again in late afternoon. Good onshore winds prevail most of the year, though conditions are best in the spring, summer, and fall. *Ocean Sports* has equipment for children 12 years and older who want to try the sport. Introductory lessons and certification courses are available. Information: *Ocean Sports Waikoloa,* PO Box 3291, Waikoloa, HI 96743 (phone: 885-5555).

MAUI: The *Maui Sailing Center* teaches windsurfing on Maalaea Bay, on the southern shore of Maui's central valley. Since this is on the leeward side of the island, windsurfers must contend with offshore, or land, breezes, which are more fitful and less constant than prevailing onshore breezes. For this reason, the school's 2-hour introductory course starts out with an hour spent on a land simulator and an hour spent in the bay on a sailboard tethered to an underground line.

The school claims a 100% success rate for novices. Within an hour, most students can pull up the boom and sail back and forth in a straight line. The sight of the tiny volcanic island of Molokini, as well as the feathery kiawe trees shading some of Maui's best sandy beaches, makes Maalaea Bay one of the loveliest places to sail. The season runs year-round, though there are periods when strong winds make it impossible to take beginners out. Information: *Maui Sailing Center,* 101 N. Kihei Rd., Kihei, HI 96753 (phone: 879-5935). *Windsurfing West Tours,* 460 Dairy Rd., West Maui, HI 96732 (phone: 871-8733), offers rentals and lessons.

KAUAI: *Hanalei Sailboards* (5-5161 Kuhio Hwy., Hanalei, HI 96714; phone: 826-

9000) and *True Blue Charters* (3500 Rice St., Lihue, HI 96766; phone: 246-6333) can each arrange for windsurfing rentals and lessons.

MOLOKAI: If you're proficient, give George Peabody a call for escorted runs, departing his Waialua lagoon-front home for windsurfing along Molokai's south coast. Information: *George Peabody,* Star Rte. 329, Kaunakakai, HI 96748 (phone: 558-8253).

Best Depths: Snorkeling and Scuba Diving

As beautiful as the Hawaiian landscape is, some of the islands' most ravishing scenery is found beneath the sea. A fascinating kaleidoscope of coral-lined caves, great lava tubes, and cathedral-size archways, Hawaii's underwater terrain is also home to a varied and interesting marine life, with a cast of characters ranging from giant spiny puffers to barber pole shrimp. The overall effect of this sensate world on the visiting snorkeler or scuba diver is one of nonstop, wide-eyed wonder, for nowhere are nature's gifts of life, movement, and beauty more concentrated than around the islands' coral reefs.

Underwater visibility, especially in the outer islands, is usually 100 feet or more. Water temperature is 74 to 80F, ideal for extended explorations. A scuba diver can bring his or her own mask, fins, snorkel, wet suit, regulator with pressure gauge, and buoyancy compensator. Heavier equipment (tanks, weights, backpack, etc.) can be rented, though most dive shops make scuba equipment available only to certified divers. Certification courses, that is, those accredited by the *National Association of Underwater Instructors* (*NAUI*) or the *Professional Association of Diving Instructors* (*PADI*), are offered by most major dive concessions.

Scuba prices range from $45 for an introductory dive to $350 and up for a 5-day scuba certification class. One-, two- or three-tank dives can be arranged. Most excursions are run from 25- to 42-foot boats with open decks, from which diving is easy. Because a good portion of Hawaii's sea life is nocturnal, night dives are popular. Underwater camera rentals are available at most dive shops.

Snorkelers can bring their own masks, fins, and snorkels, or rent all necessary gear from local dive shops. Beach or boat snorkel tours start at $20, with standard half-day tours at $40 to $50.

Because of the fragility of the underwater environment, undersea explorers are strongly reequested to "take only pictures, leave only bubbles."

OAHU: Oahu is the most "dived" island in the Hawaiian chain, and is especially good for novices seeking instruction. (There is an abundance of reputable dive shops in Honolulu.) Hanauma Bay, on the island's southeast shore between Koko Head and Makapuu Point, is probably Oahu's best snorkeling and scuba divesite. Though daily conditions on this side of the island are variable, Hanauma Bay is protected from water-disturbing winds and enjoys near-perfect dive conditions year-round. Most divers make a beach entry to the inner reef lagoon, though visibility and the variety of fish increase dramatically in the outer bay, where a maze of canyon-life surge channels can be explored. The fish here are quite tame and can be fed from your hand. Hanauma Bay is ideal for the beginning skin or scuba diver. *Hanauma Bay Snorkeling Tours* (phone: 944-8828) provides four round trips a day (6:30, 8:30, and 11:15 AM, and 1:45 PM) from Waikiki hotels for $14, including gear. Separate rental gear is available.

Another top site on the southeast shore is Fantasy Reef, off Kahala, where intermediate and advanced divers can ride the back of a turtle or watch manta rays glide effortlessly through the water.

Because of the great distance between beach and reef, diving on Oahu's windward shore is best accomplished from a boat. Manana (Rabbit) Island and Makapuu Point attract experienced divers to depths of 60 feet, where the basalt rock bottom is overgrown with coral. Sharks are sighted here occasionally, but seldom threaten divers.

Oahu's North Shore offers good diving opportunities from late spring to late summer, especially for beginners. (In the winter, the waves at Waimea Bay and other top surfing beaches reach gigantic proportions, creating unsafe conditions.) Large fish and brightly colored sponges can be identified at Pupukea (Shark's Cove), known for its many caves and steep drop-offs (but not its sharks; few are ever sighted here). Nearby Three Tables, accessible by beach entry, has several pockmarked caves and is inhabited by schools of small fish.

In addition to Waikiki Beach, Oahu's top snorkeling sites include Black Point near Diamond Head, where ancient lava flows protrude into the ocean and form the basis of a coral reef teeming with life, the nearby Waikiki marine preserve, and Kahe Point on the Waianae (leeward) coast, where the large shallow-water coral reef gives skin divers enough underwater terrain to keep them happy all day. *Aikane Catamarans*' Bare Foot snorkel sail heads from Kewalo Basin to the marine preserve off Diamond Head on half-day excursions.

Information: *Dan's Dive Shop,* 660 Ala Moana Blvd., Honolulu, HI 96813 (phone: 536-6181); *Waikiki Diving Center,* 1734 Kalakaua Ave., Honolulu, HI 96815 (phone: 955-5151); *Aloha Dive Shop,* Koko Marina, Hawaii Kai, Honolulu, HI 96825 (phone: 395-5922); *South Seas Aquatics,* 870 Kapahulu Ave., Honolulu, HI 96816 (phone: 735-0437); *Steve's Diving Adventures,* 1860 Ala Moana Blvd., Honolulu, HI 96814 (phone: 947-8900); *Leeward Dive Center,* 87-066 Farrington Hwy., Maili, HI 96792 (phone: 696-3414); *Aikane Catamarans,* 677 Ala Moana Blvd., Honolulu, HI 96813 (phone: 522-1569; 800-522-1538).

HAWAII: The Big Island's Kona Coast offers visiting divers some of the most exciting underwater formations and marine life in the Pacific. Because the Kona Coast is protected from trade winds by three high volcanic peaks, surface conditions are usually placid — and, therefore, ideal for diving. The shallow reefs along the coastline are especially good for snorkeling, though most sites accommodate both snorkelers and scuba divers.

Working south from Kawaihae, Hawaii's top sites for skin diving include: Puako Boat Ramp (lovely coral formations); Keauhou Cliffs (large chunks of lava shaped like giant blocks of granite); Anaehoomalu Bay (a beautiful beach with clear, calm water; be sure to duck under the windsurfers); Kahaluu Beach Park (popular with families who like to feed cheese to the fish inside a natural breakwater); and Hookena Beach Park (worth the bumps and grinds caused by the tortuous access road).

Even though some of the Big Island's top scuba diving sites suffered damage from hurricane Iwa in 1982 and still bear the scars, they remain the stuff of legends: Kaumoo Bay, its lava arches and deep ravines inhabited by Hawaiian lobster and Kona crabs; Red Hills, once part of an ancient volcanic cinder cone, its bottom decorated with large flat lava mesas; the Tubes, an offshore area honeycombed with long lava tunnels, some of them as large as a two-car garage; the Arches, named for eight sculptured lava archways formed by the rapid cooling of molten lava poured into the sea long ago; and Old Airport Beach Park near Kailua, known for its coral archways, lava tubes, and excellent spearfishing.

Other top dive sites south of Kailua include: Magic Sands Beach Park, where the sand disappears in winter and miraculously returns in summer; Kealakekua Bay, the landing site of Captain Cook and the current home of a pair of tame moray eels (named Orville and Wilbur by locals) who love to pose for photographs (provided you feed them some squid); and City of Refuge, the former religious sanctuary for defeated warriors where diving is popular behind the visitors' center and off the boat ramp.

Night dives along the Kona Coast give adventurous scubaphiles equipped with hand-held lights a chance to visit caverns to see creatures that only emerge at night. There is something eerily exciting about scuba diving after dark. It is also a flash photographer's delight. Information: *Dive Makai Charters,* PO Box 2955, Kailua-Kona, HI 96745 (phone: 329-2025); *Jack's Diving Locker,* 75-5819 Alii Dr., Kailua-Kona, HI 96740 (phone: 329-7585); *Kona Activities Center,* PO Box 70, Kailua-Kona, HI 96745 (phone: 329-3171); *Kohala Divers Ltd.,* PO Box 4935, Kawaihae, HI 96743 (phone: 882-7774); *Kona Coast Divers,* 75-5614 Palani Rd., Kailua-Kona, HI 96745 (phone: 329-8802); and *Nautilus Dive Center,* 382 Kamehameha Ave., Hilo, HI 96720 (phone: 935-6939).

MAUI: Because of its proximity to the surrounding islands of Molokai, Lanai, Kahoolawe, and Molokini, the Valley Isle offers some of the most varied and exciting dive sites in the state. Weather conditions usually determine which island is dived on any given day. The top dive sites likely to be visited on a guided two- or three-tank inter-island trip include: Mokuhooniki Rock off Molokai, where strong currents sweep in tremendous numbers of fish; the famous Lanai Cathedrals, a series of open-ended and well-lit lava caves and grottoes frequented by Japanese barracuda and small sharks; and Becks Cove off Kahoolawe, known for its black coral forest and large jacks.

On Maui, the top underwater spots for novice and intermediate divers are Kaanapali's Black Rock, where there is a small cave with many varieties of fish accessible to beginners; and La Perouse Bay, where huge lava caves shelter very large fish. Honolua Bay, a protected marine preserve, also offers excellent diving and snorkeling. Another popular locale is the island of Molokini, lying between Wailea, on Maui, and the neighboring island of Kahoolawe. Molokini is accessible via Maui dive shop excursions or aboard the *Wailea Kai* catamaran, with Maalaea Harbor departures, or the *Kai Karani* catamaran, which sails from Makena beach in front of the *Maui Prince*. In addition, the west coast of Maui off Lahaina is known for the Outside Drift Drive, where whaling artifacts are littered across the ocean floor. Schools of goatfish numbering in the thousands can be seen here. Black Rock, at Kaanapali, and the promontories at Wailea are easily accessible and offer excellent snorkeling.

Snorkeling enthusiasts have a wide range of beach parks from which to choose. Honolua Bay, near Kapalua, is a large, protected bay with good visibility to the right and left of the harbor mouth. The large shallow reef at Olowalu is ideal for snorkeling, with a great variety of fish found in the deeper waters surrounding it. Five Caves near Makena Beach demands a long surface swim to offshore rocks, but below them are five caves worth exploring.

A small caveat to divers visiting Maui in the winter: You may find yourself sharing space in the sea with humpback whales, which visit from November through May.

Information: *Dive Maui, Lahaina Marketplace,* Lahainaluna Rd., Lahaina, HI 96761 (phone: 667-2080); *Lahaina Divers,* 710 Front St., Lahaina, HI 96761 (phone: 667-7496; 661-4505; toll-free, 800-657-7885); *Maui Dive Shop,* PO Box 1018, Kihei, HI 96753 (phone: 879-3388), with shops in Lahaina, Kahului, and Kihei; *Ocean Activities Center,* 1325 S. Kihei Rd., Suite 212, Kihei, HI 96753 (phone: 879-4485; 800-869-6911).

KAUAI: The Garden Isle has some of the finest dive sites in Hawaii. As the oldest major island, Kauai has a great diversity of marine life and coral formations. A lack of good beach entry and exit points, however, make a boat dive imperative on Kauai.

Kauai divers usually frequent the south shore (Poipu Beach) in the fall, winter, and spring, moving up to the north shore (Hanalei Bay, where *South Pacific* was filmed) in the summer, when underwater visibility is at its best. Top north shore dive sites include the Shell Graveyard, a cave at Hanalei Bay where a great number of mollusks and crustaceans have abandoned their calcium homes; King's Reef, a large underwater canyon lined with coral growth; and Tunnels Beach, near the dry cave.

Divers on the south shore can explore Sheraton Caverns, the home of many graceful sea turtles, and Oasis Reef, an underwater playground where divers can arm-wrestle small octopi. Nearby, thousands of yellow butterfly fish feed on the plankton-covered reef. Perhaps the most entertaining dive site on Kauai is Koloa Landing, where tame fish will accompany divers on their trek across the reef. Here divers can meet tame moray eels who, for a morsel of squid, will pose for a photo coiled around your neck. *Captain Andy's* makes its way from Kukuiula harbor to the magnificent beach, bay, and valley at Kipukai. Still privately owned, Kipukai is Hawaii at its best. When waters are calm, there's good snorkeling and diving off the bay's western arm. Information: *Fathom Five Divers,* PO Box 907, Koloa, HI 96756 (phone: 742-6991); *Sea Sage Diving Center,* 4-1378 Kuhio Hwy., Kapaa, HI 96746 (phone: 822-3841); *Nawiliwili Dive and Snorkel,* 3501 Rice St., Lihue, HI 96766 (phone: 245-6919); *Captain Andy's,* PO Box 1291, Koloa, HI 96756 (phone: 822-7833); *Dive Kauai,* 4-976 Kuhio Hwy., Wailua, HI 96746 (phone: 822-0452).

LANAI: Most of the boats that head to Lanai from Maui dock at Manele harbor and provide a quick transfer to the waters off Hulopoe, which are perfect for snorkeling. Those staying on Lanai can make a beachfront entry from Hulopoe or take one of several 2- and 2½-hour sails and raft trips down the cliff-lined south shore, where several excellent bays offer sheltered snorkeling and diving in some of Hawaii's most tropically vibrant waters. Information: *C & Sea Ocean Sports,* 1036 Lanai Ave., Lanai City, HI 96763 (phone: 565-7227).

Gone Fishing

Because of its serendipitous position at the crossroads of game fish migration paths, Hawaii enjoys some of the best deep-sea fishing in the world. And though the smooth, glassy waters off the Big Island's Kona Coast are revered as the finest Pacific blue marlin grounds on the planet, the Waianae coast of Oahu, the southwest coast of Maui, and the waters off Kauai's Na Pali cliffs are also very productive.

Visitors who want to try their hands at deep-sea fishing need not be old salts. As one Kona captain noted, "If we had to depend on experienced anglers for all our business, we'd all be broke." The main thing for *malihinis* (newcomers) to remember is to follow the instructions of the captain and the mate when a fish is hooked.

Most of Hawaii's top game-fishing ports have both private and share charters. Obviously, a private charter is the way to go, especially if there are three or more people in your party. (Most boats accommodate up to six.) Private charters run from $450 to $650 for a full day (8 hours), $350 to $450 for three-quarters of a day (6 hours), and $275 to $400 for a half day (4 hours). Rates vary according to the type of vessel.

On share charters, anglers pay an individual rate of from $75 to $125 and share time with up to five other cohorts. All boats have a democratic rotation system, where anglers draw lots for position and take turns minding the rods. On all charters, fishing tackle and equipment are supplied; anglers usually bring their own lunch and beverages (don't, however, take a banana on board, as they're considered bad luck for fishing). And don't forget your camera, sunscreen, and broad-brimmed hat.

Deep-sea fishing in Hawaii is good year-round, but for folks serious about hooking a marlin, chances of success are best from late June to November. No fishing license is required for saltwater fishing in Hawaii.

Though Pacific blue marlin is *the* premier game fish, the supporting cast of heavy-weights is also impressive. Hawaiian waters are rich with ahi (yellow-fin tuna), an extremely fast, torpedo-like fish ranging up to 300 pounds; mahimahi (dolphin fish), a beautiful phosphorescent fish known for its leaping, spirited battles; ono (wahoo), a fast swimmer averaging 30 pounds, with a mouthful of sharp teeth; and aku (skipjack tuna), a school fish highly prized by sashimi lovers. Black and striped marlin, as well as sailfish, are also taken in Hawaiian waters.

Unless previous arrangements are made, it is customary in Hawaii for the catch to be left with the crew, which usually fillets enough fish for the client's party and then sells the rest at the market. This arrangement permits charter captains to keep prices down. (Most of the larger marlin are ground up into fishcakes. Better-tasting dolphin and wahoo are sold to restaurants.)

A word of advice for the prospective deep-sea angler with time to spare: Go to the harbor in the area you plan to fish and talk to the captain and crews of each charter boat. You'll hear some tall stories, but you'll also get a good feel for who's hot — and who's not.

Because Hawaiian charters are among the least expensive and most accessible to top fishing grounds, deep-sea fishing excursions throughout the state are considered a bargain. If you've only tried freshwater stream or lake fishing for pan fish, the feeling of a large game fish tugging powerfully at the rod while it tail-dances across the surface of the water may render you speechless for the rest of your vacation.

OAHU: Honolulu's Kewalo Basin (Fisherman's Wharf), only 10 minutes by car from Waikiki hotels, is the base for a fleet of sportfishing boats ranging from 35 to over 60 feet. These cruisers sail off Koko Head to the Penguin Banks southwest of Molokai or off the Waianae Coast. (The world's largest Pacific blue marlin caught on rod and reel, a 1,805-pound monster now on display at the *International Market Place* in Waikiki, was taken off the Waianae Coast by a Kewalo charter vessel in 1971.)

Boats on Oahu can be chartered for 1- or 2-day trips by reserving them in advance. Although the custom is for a group to book the entire boat for a day, single anglers are placed with private parties when space is available. Honolulu boats stalk a mixed bag of game fish — depending on the size and species of fish running, a variety of artificial plugs and live swimming baits are used to capture marlin, tuna, wahoo, and dolphin. For North Shore fishing, charters are available at Pokai Bay and Haleiwa at slightly lower rates than at Kewalo Basin. Information: *Island Charters,* Kewalo Basin, Honolulu, HI 96814 (phone: 536-1555); *Coreene C's Sport Fishing,* Kewalo Basin, Honolulu, HI 96814 (phone: 226-8421); *Golden Eagle Marine Charter Services,* Kewalo Basin, Honolulu, HI 96814 (phone: 531-4966).

HAWAII: Sheltered from the northeast trade winds by the twin volcanoes of Mauna Kea and Mauna Loa, the Big Island's Kona Coast is world-renowned for its huge marlin. In recent years, no less than 20 au (marlin) weighing more than 1,000 pounds have been taken off the Kona Coast. Record weights top 1,400 pounds. In 1981, about half of Kona's 60-odd charter boats landed more than 100 marlin! The great fish is attracted by schools of smaller fish that breed rapidly in these plankton-rich waters.

Unlike in other deep-sea fishing ports, Kona marlin and other game fish are usually taken within 10 miles of the harbor mouth and along 20 miles of the Kona coastline marked by the Keahole Lighthouse. This means anglers get the most for their money and spend very little time getting to and from the fishing grounds.

The sleepy fishing town of Kailua hosts the *Hawaiian International Billfish Tournament* every summer, an angling extravaganza that is considered the world's premier marlin fishing event. Teams from around the world compete for world championship honors in an *Olympics*-style format. In addition, jackpot tournaments are held from March to November. Anglers put up a cash entry fee in a gamble to collect more than $35,000 for landing the largest fish.

Though a small, live skipjack tuna or bonito is occasionally harnessed with a heavy marlin hook and set free to swim at the end of a line, the choice method of fishing in

Hawaii is with large, plastic, rubber-skirted lures. These Kona Head plugs are trolled at 8 to 10 knots for marlin and tuna. The lures are attached to specially designed heads that create trails of bubbles and give the mini–hula skirts a wiggling action. Experienced captains say the fish strike out of anger or curiosity, not hunger.

For a longer trip, take a 2-day run past extinct lava flows to South Point, the southernmost point in the US, where the right tide conditions can produce some of the fastest and most furious fishing action in the world. Ahi (yellow-fin tuna, known for their blistering 60 mph "freight train" runs), ulua (jack crevalle, a large reef fish ranging up to 100 pounds), and mahimahi (dolphin fish) can be taken here in great numbers.

A visitor's chance of landing a trophy game fish off the Kona Coast is probably just as good as his or her chance of winning money in Las Vegas. Kailua's expert charter captains, however, can slant the odds in your favor. Look for the *Hawaii Fishing* guide in local bookstores, which focuses primarily on the Big Island. Information: *Kona Coast Activities,* PO Box 5397, Kailua-Kona, HI 96745 (phone: 329-2971; 800-367-5105); *Kona Charter Skippers Association,* 75-5663 Palani Rd., Kailua-Kona, HI 96745 (phone: 329-3600; 800-762-7546); *Kona Marina Sport Fishing Charters,* PO Box 2398, Kailua-Kona, HI 96740 (phone: 329-1115).

MAUI: The colorful missionary outpost and former whaling center of Lahaina, on Maui's west coast near Kaanapali Beach, is the game fishing center of the Valley Isle. Maui charter boats head for waters in the triangle formed by Lanai, Kahoolawe, and Maui, and troll near fish aggregation buoys placed by the state at strategic locations. Waters at the southeast tip of Lanai produce good marlin runs during the fall months, though the island's best all-around fishing is from May to August. Mahimahi (dolphin fish), pound for pound one of the toughest (and prettiest) fish in the ocean; ono (wahoo), a very good eating fish — ono is the Hawaiian word for "good" or "delicious"; and various species of small tuna are what anglers expect to catch in Maui's waters. Because the chances of landing a trophy fish are best in early morning, Maui captains prefer to leave port at 6:30 AM in the spring and summer, and at 7 AM in the fall and winter. Full-day charters are recommended for the serious angler, as marlin are usually found quite a distance from Maui, in deep water off Lanai. Information: *Ocean Activities Center,* 1325 S. Kihei Rd., Suite 212, Kihei, HI 96753 (phone: 879-4485; 800-367-8047, ext. 448); *Lahaina Charter Boats,* PO Box 12, Lahaina, HI 96767 (phone: 667-6672).

KAUAI: In addition to the great schools of tackle-smashing ahi (yellow-fin tuna), weighing up to 250 pounds, that cruise into Kauai waters in late spring, the island's charter captains troll for mahimahi (dolphin fish) and smaller tuna year-round. There are also unusually large bonefish, a near translucent game fish prized for its fighting abilities, found on the flats off Hanalei on the north shore. (Kauai held the world record for bonefish — 19 pounds, 2 ounces — for many years.)

Information: *Sea Breeze Sport Fishing Charters,* PO Box 594, Kilauea, HI 96754 (phone: 828-1285); *Gent-Lee Fishing Charters,* PO Box 1691, Lihue, HI 96766 (phone: 245-7504); *Sport Fishing Kauai,* PO Box 1195, Koloa, HI 96756 (phone: 742-7013).

Sailing the South Seas

Experienced sailors, diehard adventurers, and even carefree day-trippers who delight mostly in watching fish wriggle in the water through the glass bottom of a Polynesian canoe may all find their respective pleasures in Hawaii. Bareboat charters are available to seamen worthy of the challenge of open ocean sailing, while raft rides along Kauai's Na Pali Coast usually attract the shoot-the-rapids crowd. Theme cruises aboard diesel-powered craft or catamarans are popular on Oahu, the Big Island, and Maui, with morning snorkeling tours and late afternoon sunset sails leading the list of favorites. In the end, boating opportunities in Hawaii are as diverse as the islands themselves.

OAHU: Outrigger Canoe Rides – An ideal way to get the feel of surfing, without mastering board-balancing skills, is to take an outrigger canoe ride on the modest breakers off Waikiki Beach. By paddling hard at the right moment, passengers can assist the two crewmen in putting the 30-foot surfing canoe on the crest of a wave. A pontoon jutting out from the side of these long banana-shaped boats gives them stability. Paddlers get a good workout, along with three thrilling rides during the 30- to 40-minute experience. The price is $6 to $10. (Several of the canoe concessions also have hour-long catamaran rides.) Information: *Waikiki Beach Services,* c/o *Outrigger Reef Hotel,* 2169 Kalia Rd., Honolulu, HI 96815 (phone: 923-3111); *Beach Services,* c/o *Waikiki Outrigger Hotel,* 2335 Kalakaua Ave., Honolulu, HI 96815 (phone: 923-0711); *Waikiki Beach Services,* c/o *Sheraton Waikiki,* 2255 Kalakaua Ave., Honolulu, HI 96815 (phone: 922-4422).

Cruises – Several companies offer cruises off Waikiki beaches; others provide transportation from Waikiki, with departures set from Kewalo Basin. The following outfits include both free hotel pickups and drop-offs:

Hilton Hawaiian Village offers sails aboard the glass-bottom catamaran *Hilton Rainbow I,* departing from the *Hilton* end of Waikiki Beach. The breakfast sail is from 8 to 9:30 AM. Information: *Hilton Catamaran,* 2005 Kalia Rd., Honolulu, HI 96815 (phone: 949-4321).

The state-of-the-art Swath vessel *Navatek* offers an upscale cruise from Kewalo Basin past Diamond Head to offshore Kahala. The 150-passenger ship, designed for comfort and stability, offers a variety of day and evening sails, which include buffet luncheons and formal dinners. Information: *Royal Hawaiian Cruises,* PO Box 29816, Honolulu, HI 96820 (phone: 848-6360).

The *Hyatt Regency*'s 48-passenger catamaran *Mani Kai* heads out for hour-long sails and 1½-hour-long cocktail sails from a beachfront location. Information: *Hyatt Regency Waikiki,* 2424 Kalakaua Ave., Honolulu, HI 96815 (phone: 923-1234).

Windjammer offers a sunset dinner sail ($45) and a moonlight cruise ($45, including buffet; $24, cocktails only) aboard the 1,000-passenger *Rella Mae.* Those seeking quiet, romantic moments should look elsewhere: The sunset sail includes a Polynesian revue, and the moonlight sail comes complete with a Broadway-style musical. A less noisy option for the sunset sail is first class seating on the upper deck. It's worth the $65 charge for full service, two drinks, and tranquillity if you take the dinner cruise. Information: *Windjammer Cruises,* 2222 Kalakaua Ave., Honolulu, HI 96815 (phone: 521-0036).

Aikane Catamarans operates three 150-passenger cats on two nightly dinner sails, with 5:15 and 7:45 departures from Kewalo Basin. The sails, at $41 and $48 per person, respectively, both include table service dinner, an open bar, and Polynesian entertainment inviting audience participation. Other sails include an SOS dinner show, which is priced at $52.50. Those in a romantic mood may wish to make a getaway to the upper deck and enjoy the breezes, moonlight, and relative quiet. Information: *Aikane Catamarans,* 677 Ala Moana Blvd., Honolulu, HI 96813 (phone: 522-1533; 800-522-1538).

Yacht Charters – *Jada Yacht Charters* offers a two-boat fleet for charter service on 4-hour morning and 4½-hour afternoon sails. Charter options include the 62-foot *Jada I,* a teak-and-mahogany classic sailboat, and the 71-foot, 48-passenger *Jada II,* complete with captain, hostess, and crew of two. *Cloud Nine Limousine* offers crewed charters aboard its custom-built 45-foot sloop. A 3-hour minimum, starting at $400, is required. A Wetsail 43 and a Hunter 54 round out the fleet. Information: *Cloud Nine*

Limousine, 45-656 Halekou Pl., Kaneohe, HI 96744 (phone: 524-7999); *Jada Sailing Adventures,* 1860 Ala Moana Blvd., Suite 413, Honolulu, HI 96815 (phone: 955-0772).

HAWAII: Ocean Sports Waikoloa – *Me A'u* is a 42-foot catamaran owned by *Ocean Sports* and moored in Anaehoomalu Bay near the *Royal Waikoloan.* Used for morning snorkel/lunch sails as well as afternoon cocktail sails, the *Me A'u* accommodates up to 36 passengers and has plenty of deck space.

The morning snorkel cruises are often run to Kiholo Bay, 5 miles south of Waikoloa at the edge of an 1859 lava flow. Underwater visibility at the site exceeds 100 feet. Excursions are also run to Makaiwa to the north, where skin diving offshore of the black sand beach is superb. *Pupus* are served on board, and when the wind picks up in the afternoon, the boat sails back to port. The morning snorkel cruise costs $55 per person, which includes all equipment and instruction. A shorter afternoon dive costs $29, and a one-tank scuba sail is available for $89.

In the winter (the best time of year for sighting humpback whales), afternoon sails start at 1:30 PM ($19.50); in summer, they start at 4 PM, when the *Me A'u* is used for cocktail trips that cruise by lava formations found along the rugged Kona coastline. Drinks and *pupus* (Hawaiian hors d'oeuvres) are included. The price is $35 per person. *Me A'u* can be chartered for sunset or evening cruises. Information: *Ocean Sports Waikoloa,* PO Box 5000, Kohala Coast, HI 96743 (phone: 885-5555).

Kona Coast Activities – A mixed bag of boating adventures is available through this all-purpose sports complex. *Captain Beans'* cruises, held aboard an 85-foot Polynesian canoe with a glass-bottom viewing area, are the perennial favorites. The craft departs from Kailua pier daily for cruises of the Kona Coast. The 4½-hour cruise to Kealakekua Bay is a highlight. Underwater divers feed fish at reef sites so that armchair frogmen can see marine activity without getting wet.

In the evening, *Captain Beans'* offers a dinner cruise. The 2-hour sail, for $42, departs at 5:15 PM and features an open bar, lots of good food, and a starlit Hawaiian dancing and music show.

The Captain Cook cruise, a narrated 3-hour history/water sports tour of Kealakekua Bay, is run daily from Kailua pier at 8:30 AM. The *Captain Cook VIII,* a craft with four decks that hold up to 150 passengers, moors near the Captain Cook Monument, where swimming and snorkeling are available off the boat. The tour price is $40 for adults, $20 for children under 12.

One of the center's more popular cruises is its 4-hour morning sail ($56 for adults, $31 for children under 12, including lunch) from lovely Keauhou Bay (near the *Kona Surf* hotel) to Kealakekua Bay aboard the *Fairwind,* a 50-foot trimaran equipped with a water slide and bar. Snorkelers sit down to a barbecue lunch when they return to the boat. The *Fairwind* also offers a 3-hour afternoon cruise with snacks. The price is $36 for adults, $21 for children. *Kamanu Charters* offers two 3-hour-long catamaran sails for up to 24 passengers from Honokahau Harbor to Kaiwi Point for $30, $15 for children under 12. Information: *Kona Coast Activities,* PO Box 5397, Kailua-Kona, HI 96745 (phone: 329-2971; 800-367-5105).

MAUI: Ocean Activities Center – A smorgasbord of sailing excursions is offered by this sports packager. The best trips are run on the 65-foot catamarans *Wailea Kai* and *Maka Kai.* The tours, which depart from Maalaea Harbor, include a snorkeling cruise to the marine preserves of Molokini and La Perouse Bay, where sea life is varied and abundant. Visitors need bring only a towel — all equipment is provided. The buffet lunch (preceded by fresh Maui pineapple and papaya) is quite good. The price is $60 for adults, $40 for children. Day trips to Lanai (half-day; $60) depart Lahaina Harbor daily. During whale season, which lasts from the fall through the winter, 2-hour whale watch cruises on the *Manutea* also leave Lahaina, with daily departures at 2 PM during winter months ($35 includes open bar and snacks).

Other whale watching trips include 2-hour cruises aboard the *Wailea Kai* and the

Maka Kai from December through April, with a marine biologist on hand to provide information about the magnificent humpbacks who visit Hawaii each year to mate. Drinks and *pupus* are available. The tour departs at noon, 1:30, and 3 PM from Maalaea Harbor, and free transportation is provided from Wailea hotels and selected Kihei condominiums.

The center's 2-hour sunset dinner cruise (also known as the "champagne sail") features an open bar (try a mai-tai) and a buffet dinner. There is perhaps no more romantic way to take in a Maui sunset than from the deck of the *Wailea Kai.* The tour costs $45 for adults and children, who get soft drinks in lieu of champagne. The tour leaves Maalaea Harbor at 5:30 PM (5 PM in the winter). The *Stardancer Floating Restaurant* features a substantial buffet and Art Deco cocktail lounge for sunset and moonlight dinner cruises, and the *High Seas Nightclub,* on the top deck, is open from 10 PM to 2 AM, and has a shuttle every 20 minutes from Lahaina Harbor (phone: 871-1144). Information: *Ocean Activities Center,* 1325 S. Kihei Rd., Suite 212, Kihei 96753 (phone: 879-4485; 800-869-6911).

Seabern Yachts – Two 42-foot, 6-passenger sailboats are available for skippered charters out of Lahaina. Rates start at $220 for a 2-hour sail (sunset sails include *pupus* and champagne); a full-day charter costs $650. Shared-boat rates are also available. Half-day sails cruise along the Maui coast, while full-day charters usually set course for Lanai and Hanalua Bay. The sailing season runs throughout the year. Information: *Seabern Yachts,* PO Box 1022, Lahaina, HI 96767 (phone: 661-8110).

KAUAI: Captain Zodiac Raft Expeditions – Aboard large inflatable rafts similar to those used by Jacques Cousteau, passengers explore portions of the rugged Na Pali Coast that are accessible only by air or water. From the craft, wild goats can be seen picking their way along the brown cliffs that rise 3,000 feet from the water's edge. Schools of dolphin and flying fish break the water, as do the humpback whales in the winter. When a fish hits, the rod is handed to a passenger. The rafts, powered by twin outboard engines, are anchored over a virgin reef, where razorback turtles (an endangered species) and other sea life can be seen by snorkelers. The tour also explores the many sea caves found along the coast.

The expedition boats hold up to 15 persons, and advance reservations are required. The 3-hour sunrise tour from Hanalei is priced at $65; morning and afternoon excursions cost $85; 5-hour tours that include a 2-hour landing at Nualolokai and lunch cost $115. This is probably one of the most exciting boating adventures in the islands.

For those interested in camping along the Na Pali Coast, the expedition company runs a camper and backpacker drop-off service May through September. The cost is $60 one way, $120 round trip. Information: *Captain Zodiac,* PO Box 456, Hanalei, HI 96714 (phone: 826-9772 or 826-9371; 800-422-7824).

Captain Andy's – This Poipu adventure group uses a 40-passenger catamaran on 4-hour snorkel and pleasure cruises along the south shore, including visits to beautiful Kipukai. The $65 cost includes lunch and snorkeling equipment. Information: *Captain Andy's,* PO Box 1291, Koloa, HI 96756 (phone: 822-7833).

The Islands' Top Tennis

While Hawaii's warm sun, blue canopy of a sky, and prevailing trade winds create almost perfect year-round playing conditions, visiting tennis players — novice and advanced alike — can find themselves too easily distracted by court settings that range from simply beautiful to dramatically spectacular. Windbreaks, for example, are often bedecked with oleander and bougainvillea, and vistas of green cliffs, blue surf, and white sandy beaches are the rule, not the exception.

Tennis courts in the islands are generally very well kept and constructed with all-weather Laykold or Plexipave surfaces, though the *Wailea Tennis Club* in Maui features the state's only grass courts.

In addition to hotel and resort tennis complexes, where hourly rates range from $5 to $10 per hour or are free to guests, several of the islands have well-maintained county courts, where playing time is usually free of charge. Details on county courts are available from local parks and recreation departments. Information on tournaments can be supplied by the *Hawaii Pacific Tennis Association,* 2615 S. King St., Suite 2A, Honolulu, HI 96826 (phone: 955-6696).

Most hotels and resorts with tennis facilities will arrange a match for an unattached visiting player. Individual lessons for players of all abilities range from $20 to $25 per hour, while group lessons and clinics usually average about $6 per hour. Videotaping and playback are also available.

A list of the best public and private tennis facilities around the state follows.

OAHU: The top three municipal facilities in the Honolulu/Waikiki area are the 10 Laykold courts at *Ala Moana Tennis Center,* all of which are lighted for night play until 9 PM (phone: 522-7031), the unlighted, 9-court *Diamond Head Tennis Center* in Kapiolani Park (phone: 971-7150), and the 4 lighted *Kapiolani Park Courts,* also in Kapiolani Park, which are open until 2:30 AM (no phone). Free classes are offered at the Ala Moana facility. Courts are available on a first-come, first-served basis, with a 45-minute cap on play if other players are waiting.

Also in the Honolulu area are the noteworthy *Honolulu Tennis Club* and the *Ilikai* hotel courts. The former is a good place to go to avoid the crowds of *malihinis* (newcomers) that mainland snowstorms have driven to the islands in search of sun. Its 4 Laykold courts have a third-floor rooftop location atop a department store, from which players have a view of the Waikiki skyline on the *makai* (ocean) side of the building and a panorama of the Manoa Valley on the *mauka* (mountain) side. The courts, which are at their busiest from the end of November through April, have a pro on hand for lessons. For the four-wall crowd, there are also 3 racquetball courts. A free pick-up service is available to and from Waikiki hotels from 10 AM to 5 PM. Information: *Honolulu Tennis Club,* 2220 S. King St., Honolulu, HI 96826 (phone: 944-9696).

The *Ilikai* has 6 Plexipave tennis courts, including the lighted Yacht Harbor court (open until 10 PM) on top of the hotel's main ballroom, overlooking the Ala Wai yacht harbor. The hotel's other showcase court is the Diamond Head court, with the famous extinct volcano providing background distraction. The remaining courts, on the hotel's seventh floor, provide players with fine views of the ocean and marina below.

All reservations for court time and lessons at the *Ilikai,* which is staffed by two tennis pros, are made through the hotel's Sports Desk. A final note: The *Ilikai* has one of the best-stocked tennis shops on the island. Information: *Ilikai Hotel,* 1777 Ala Moana Blvd., Honolulu, HI 96815 (phone: 949-3811).

Outside Honolulu, two Oahu resorts are standout tennis destinations. On the North Shore, the *Turtle Bay Hilton* has 10 Plexipave courts (4 lighted at night) set in a grove of coconut palms near the golf course. The courts, cooled by ocean breezes, are within sight of stark volcanic peaks in the Koolau Range. In the interests of privacy, there are no adjoining courts. The resort's player matching service pairs off partners of equal ability based on its rating system. Clinics and social doubles events are also part of the program. The best times to visit are spring and summer — washouts are not uncommon in late fall and winter. Information: *Turtle Bay Hilton and Country Club,* Kahuku, HI 96731 (phone: 293-8811).

On Oahu's leeward coast, in the vast natural arena of Makaha Valley, is the *Sheraton Makaha* resort, a secluded hotel in a country club setting. Four Plexipave courts, 2 lighted, are set in this horseshoe-shaped development. Because there is little wind or rain on the leeward coast, *Sheraton Makaha* guests enjoy near-perfect playing conditions year round, and since the resort is 40 miles from the bustle of Honolulu, its tennis facilities are not pressed to the limit. The *Sheraton Makaha* is a great place to perfect your backhand without fear of discovery by rivals. "It's just you and the tennis here," commented the resident pro. "People come for the quiet." Information: *Sheraton Makaha Resort,* 84-626 Makaha Valley Rd., Makaha, HI 96792 (phone: 695-9511).

HAWAII: Among the Big Island's excellent county tennis courts is Hilo's *Hoolulu Park.* A mile from Hilo Bay, the complex boasts 8 courts, 3 of them lighted. The peak of Mauna Kea, snow-covered in winter, smiles down on the serve-and-volley crowd, and those having trouble with their ground strokes can later seek comfort in the city's many luxuriant public and commercial gardens (Hilo is the orchid-growing capital of the world). For those who perform best in front of an audience, the covered tennis stadium at Hoolulu Park seats 2,000 fans and admirers. Hoolulu is one of the few county facilities that charges an hourly rate ($2 to $4 per court, depending on the time of day; phone: 935-8213).

The queen of the Big Island's resorts is the *Mauna Kea Beach,* a world class property first developed by Laurance Rockefeller on the Kona Coast at the base of the dormant volcano for which it is named. The *Mauna Kea* has 13 Plexipave courts and, like the *Wailea Tennis Center* on Maui, it is listed among the top 50 US tennis complexes by *Tennis* magazine. In addition to magnificent ocean views, players at the tennis park will find such nice touches as an ice machine courtside, a juice bar, and lots of thick, thirsty towels. Daily clinics and round-robin tournaments are also part of the *Mauna Kea* tennis program. The 13 courts are open to guests and non-guests. Note that this super-deluxe approach to the sport does not come inexpensively: The *Mauna Kea*'s tennis packages are some of the most expensive in the state. Information: *Mauna Kea Beach Hotel,* PO Box 218, Kamuela, HI 96743 (phone: 882-7222).

The *Mauna Lani Bay* hotel features 10 Laykold courts, a pro shop, and a restaurant. Information: *Mauna Lani Bay Hotel,* One Mauna Lani Bay Dr., Kohala Coast, HI 96743 (phone: 885-6622). The *Mauna Lani* resort's *Racquet Club* has an additional 8 courts, including 2 clay courts. Information: *Mauna Lani Bay Hotel,* PO Box 4959, Kohala Coast, HI 96743 (phone: 885-7765).

In Waikoloa, the *Royal Waikoloan* features 6 courts, open to guests, and a pro shop. Lessons are also available. Information: *Royal Waikoloan,* PO Box 5000, Waikoloa, HI 96743 (phone: 885-6789).

Unfortunately, enthusiasts will likely find the 8 courts at the 1,244-room *Hyatt* monopolized by guests.

In Kona, the *King Kamehameha* has 4 Laykold courts (2 lighted) set on Kailua Bay at the base of 8,271-foot Mt. Hualalai. Because of its top-flight staff and dependably fine weather — little rain and wind, lots of sun — the *King Kamehameha* offers a tennis experience as fine as that available anywhere in the islands. As an extra bonus, after a rigorous match, overheated players can cool off in the ocean at Kailua Bay. Information: *Hotel King Kamehameha,* Kailua-Kona, HI 96740 (phone: 329-2911).

The *Kona Hilton* also has commendable tennis facilities. Information: *Kona Hilton,* PO Box 1179, Kailua-Kona, HI 96745 (phone: 329-3111). *The Kona Surf* (78-128 Ehukai St., Kailua-Kona, HI 96740; phone: 322-3411) offers play to guests only.

MAUI: The Valley Isle's top public courts are situated between the sea and the West Maui peak of Puu Kukui in Lahaina, a former whaling center and missionary outpost. The *Lahaina Civic Center*'s 5 Laykold courts (all lighted), within walking distance of the beach, are free and operate on a first-come, first-served basis. Courts are open from 7 AM to 10 PM (phone: 661-4685).

Kaanapali's *Royal Lahaina Tennis Ranch* has 11 Plexipave tennis courts, plus one practice wall; 6 courts are lighted for night play. Available on request is the stadium court. The hotel's tennis director is Bernard Gusman, who heads a staff chosen and trained by the *Peter Burwash* tennis organization. *Royal Lahaina*'s courts are surrounded by the fairways of the *Royal Kaanapali* golf courses on a 500-acre planned resort that was once a sugar plantation. The hotel stresses that proper tennis attire is required at all times. No cutoffs, aloha shirts, or bikinis on the courts, please. Open daily from 7 AM to 9 PM. Information: *Royal Lahaina Tennis Ranch, Kaanapali Resort,* Kaanapali, HI 96761 (phone: 661-3611, ext. 2296).

Kapalua's 10-court *Tennis Garden* gives the *Royal Lahaina* a good run for its money. Information: *Kapalua Tennis Garden,* Kapalua, HI 96761 (phone: 669-5677).

On the lower slopes of Haleakala, where the sun shines 355 days a year, is Hawaii's largest tennis complex, the *Wailea Tennis Club.* On a typical crystal clear day, the islands of Lanai, Molokini, and Kahoolawe can be spotted from the court complex. During the winter, players run the very real risk of being distracted by humpback whales frolicking offshore.

In addition to *Wailea*'s 11 Plexipave courts (3 lighted) and an amphitheater-style tennis stadium with lava rock seats, the resort's 3 grass courts (the only ones in the state) afford players a surface that does not radiate heat (a definite plus in the tropics) and are easier on the joints, not to mention having more aesthetic appeal. Like the *Mauna Kea Beach* on the Big Island, Wailea is listed by *Tennis* magazine as one of the top 50 tennis resorts in the US. Information: *Wailea Tennis Club,* 131 Wailea Iki Pl., Wailea, HI 96753 (phone: 879-1958).

There are 6 courts at the *Makena* resort, as well as a pro shop and lounge. Information: *Makena Tennis Club,* 5415 Makena Ala Nui, Kihei, HI 96753 (phone: 879-8777).

KAUAI: Taken together, the Garden Isle's tennis facilities are some of the most beautiful in the state. The island's county courts, for the most part modest double-court facilities, include *New Park* in Kapaa, where the 2 lighted courts are bordered by coconut palms and favored by a cool breeze. Near Kokee State Park, within sight of the ocean, are 2 lighted courts at Kekaha. The courts are patronized by residents, but visitors are welcome on a first-come, first-served basis. A $10 deposit, payable at the Parks Permit Section (Finance Department, 4280A Rice St., Lihue; phone: 245-1881), is required for night play.

One of the shining stars of Hawaiian tennis is the *Hanalei Bay* resort on Kauai's north shore, which has 8 Laykold courts (2 lighted) overlooking Hanalei Bay, of *South Pacific* film fame. The setting of the tennis courts, among bougainvillea flowers and coconut trees, is a Bali Hai all its own. When they're not hitting the ball, players see the velvety outlines of the Wainiha *palis* (cliffs) and long furrows of surf breaking against the old rice and taro piers in Hanalei Bay. There is perhaps no more breathtaking spot in which to smack a fuzzy yellow ball past an opponent. The teaching program includes videotape playback. Showers in the morning and evening feed the hundred or so waterfalls in the vicinity of the resort and keep everything lush, though heavy rain can frustrate play in midwinter. Residents claim, however, it is impossible to get rained out for an entire day. There is a $15 charge for non-guests. Information: *Hanalei Bay Resort,* PO Box 220, Hanalei, HI 96714 (phone: 826-6522).

The *Coco Palms* resort in Wailea offers uncrowded play in the middle of a palm grove on 9 courts (4 lighted), including 3 clay courts. There is a $10 fee for non-guests. Information: *Coco Palms Resort,* PO Box 631, Lihue, HI 96766 (phone: 822-4921).

Though hallowed ground for golfers (the 5 *Princeville* nines comprise one of the world's great golf courses), tennis players flock to the *Princeville* resort's 6 Plexipave courts for the stunning view of the Wainiha Mountains and general *bonhomie* of the place. Players convene at *Princeville*'s clubhouse, one of the classiest watering holes in the islands, to discuss the finer points of the game. Players looking for partners will be matched up by clubhouse personnel. The best time to visit is from April through November, when clear weather is more likely. The cost is $7 for *Princeville* guests, $9 for non-guests. Information: *Princeville at Hanalei,* Hanalei, HI 96714 (phone: 826-9823).

Kauai's other top tennis resort is the Kiahuna Plantation, a series of airy and handsome beachfront condominiums at Poipu Beach on the island's south shore. Kiahuna (Polynesian for "a special place") has 10 tennis courts set in splendid gardens and bordered by blue and white pavilions, as well as a courtside restaurant. There is a $9 per hour charge for non-guests. Weekly rates are also available. For information, contact *Kiahuna Tennis Club,* PO Box 334, Koloa, HI 96756 (phone: 742-9533). The *Stouffer Waiohai* has 6 courts (4 nightlit) and charges guests $8 a day and non-guests $15 a day, which includes use of the fitness center. Information: *Stouffer Waiohai,* 2249 Poipu Rd., Koloa, HI 96756 (phone: 742-9511).

In addition to 8 Plexipave courts, the *Kauai Lagoons* resort also includes a tennis stadium. Guests and non-guests pay $20 an hour per court, which includes use of the adjacent spa for hotel guests only. Information: *Kauai Lagoons Golf and Racquet Club,* PO Box 3330, Lihue, HI 96766 (phone: 246-5063).

LANAI: There are 6 Plexipave courts at the *Manele Bay,* and 3 Plexipave courts at the *Lodge at Koele,* with lessons available at *Manele.* While the oceanview courts at *Manele* are lovely, the lodge in up-country Koele is a lot cooler for play. Since both are Rockresorts' properties, guests at one hotel can use the courts at the other. Information: *Manele Bay,* PO Box 774, Lanai City, HI 96763 (phone: 565-7700); *Lodge at Koele,* PO Box 774, Lanai City, HI 96763 (phone: 565-7300; 800-321-4666).

MOLOKAI: There are 4 nightlit Laykold courts for play at Colony Resorts' *Kaluakoi* hotel. Information: *Kaluakoi Hotel and Golf Club,* Maunaloa, HI 96770 (phone: 552-2555).

Great Golf

The problem with playing golf in Hawaii is that the scenery that surrounds golf holes in the 50th state is as dramatic as can be imagined, and keeping your head down requires a very determined act of will. In all candor, we're not sure it's worth the effort: The normal run of duffer may enjoy looking at the snow-capped peak behind the Mauna Kea golf course much more than watching his or her errant shot dive into the crashing surf.

But if you take your golf game seriously, there are now nearly 5 dozen layouts scattered around the islands, only about a dozen of which are private. In fact, there is a golf course boom in the making with more than 100 new courses (many of them private) in one phase or another of proposal and development. Restrictions on land and water use will ultimately cancel many of these proposals, but it is likely that several dozen new courses will open during the next decade. Regrettably, the *Waialae Country Club* (4997 Kahala Ave., Honolulu; 734-2151), probably the most familiar Hawaiian course to visitors (it's the site of the televised *Hawaiian Open* each winter), is one of the private oases for members only, as is the *Oahu Country Club* (150 Country Club Rd., Honolulu; 595-6331). The *Mid-Pacific Country Club* (266 Kaelepulu Dr., Kailua; 262-8161) occasionally allows outsiders to play. There are, however, at least two (often successful) gambits for gaining access to these otherwise exclusive enclaves, the most productive of which is to ask the manager of your Honolulu hotel to try to intercede on your behalf. Alternatively, you might present a letter from your own club president and/or resident pro requesting course privileges — a good idea, incidentally, whenever you travel — and you may be pleasantly surprised at the result. In any event, there's no harm in asking.

TURTLE BAY HILTON, Kahuku, Oahu: *Turtle Bay*'s new course, designed by Arnold Palmer (18 holes, 7,000 yards, par 72), which opened in 1992, provides a challenge even for longtime golf mavens. Built amidst an oceanside grove of ironwood pines, it includes numerous water hazards, as well as demanding, forest-lined fairways on the back nine. The old George Fazio layout will be replaced by another Palmer-designed course, and will be ready for play next year. Though golf dominates this remote resort complex, there are many other activities to enjoy: tennis, scuba diving, snorkeling, and horseback riding. And the setting, with the ocean in one direction and the peaks of the Koolau Range in the other, is nearly as memorable as the golf itself. Course: 18 holes, par 70, 6,400 yards; resident pro, Jody Shaw. Information: *Turtle Bay Hilton and Country Club,* Kahuku, HI 96731 (phone: 293-8811).

MAKAHA VALLEY, Makaha, Oahu: The two William Bell–designed courses here — the *West* course and the *Makaha Valley Country Club* — lie in a deep valley well within view of notorious Makaha Beach, where championship surfers regularly pit their tanned bodies against some of the planet's most violent waves. The golf courses are slightly safer, though the tougher *West* course requires a combination of cool temperament and substantial power. The greens on both courses are undulating and difficult to read, and the fairness of the fairways (and their usually superb condition) will provide scant solace for soaring scores. *Makaha Valley Country Club:* 18 holes, par 71, 6,369 yards; managed by Nitto Kogyo, 84-627 Makaha Valley Rd., Waianae, HI 96792 (phone: 695-9578). *West Course:* 18 holes, par 72, 6,398 yards; resident pro, Ron Kiaaina; managed by the *Sheraton Makaha Resort,* 84-626 Makaha Valley Rd., Makaha, HI 96792 (phone: 695-9511).

KO OLINA, Ewa Beach, Oahu: Designed by Ted Robinson, the course at this resort complex is set on a beautiful plain, filled with coconut palm trees, banyans, monkeypods, silver buttonwood trees, flowering bougainvillea, and other flora. Built to accommodate a wide range of players, there are water hazards at eight different holes, making a round even more interesting. Opened at the end of 1990 as the first component of the resort, the course offers exciting play in unusually scenic surroundings. Course: 18 holes, par 72, 6,867 yards, resident pro, Craig Williamson. *Ko Olina Golf Club,* 92-1220 Farrington Hwy., Ewa Beach, HI 96707 (phone: 676-5300).

PALI, Kaneohe, Oahu: Located at the base of the lush, vertical *pali* (cliff) is one of the best municipal courses you'll find anywhere. The magnificent setting and the expert maintenance make it a bargain at $18 for greens fees (an additional $11 for a non-mandatory cart). Open from 6 AM to 6 PM daily. It's necessary to get there early for a decent tee time, as this course is a favorite with residents. Course: 18 holes, par 72, 6,950 yards; operated by the City and County of Honolulu, Department of Parks. 45-050 Kamehameha Hwy., Kaneohe, HI 96744 (phone: 261-9784).

KEAUHOU-KONA, Kailua-Kona, the Big Island of Hawaii: The Big Island's black lava rock poses real challenges at this oceanside course designed by William Bell. After your ball lands in the deep crags of the mini-canyons here, you'll pray for rough that's just long grass. There are compensations, however: The surrounding Kona Coast scenery is breathtaking, and the weather the best in the islands. Course: 27 holes, par 36 nines, approximately 6,800 yards, depending on choice of nines. Information: *Keauhou-Kona Country Club,* 78-7000 Alii Dr., Kailua-Kona, HI 96740 (phone: 322-2595).

MAUNA KEA BEACH, Kohala Coast, the Big Island of Hawaii: It would be worth the 30-minute flight from Honolulu to Kona just to play a round on this magnificent Pacific gem designed by Robert Trent Jones, Sr. Cloudless skies and incredible vistas of the 13,800-foot dormant volcano for which the resort is named are the primary reasons why this golf course may be the most photographed anywhere. The course is also quite challenging, despite a recent "softening" to make it more compatible with the skills of resort visitors. Course: 18 holes, par 72, 7,114 yards; golf director, John Ebersberger. Another course (18 holes, par 72, 7,114 yards) is in the works, with play set for late this year. Information: *Mauna Kea Beach Hotel,* PO Box 218, Kamuela, HI 96743 (phone: 882-7222).

MAUNA LANI BAY, Kohala Coast, the Big Island of Hawaii: Built atop jagged black lava flows, using thousands of tons of imported topsoil, the *North* and *South* courses are among the most beautiful in the islands. In 1991, the original Francis I. Brown course was split to create two new 18-hole courses. Panoramic vistas can be seen from all the holes and there are many dramatic settings, including a 150-yard carry from a cliff top over a small bay. Hazards range from the conventional complement of sand traps to huge lava boulders that evoke images of Japanese gardens. Beauty aside, the courses provide a true test of golfing skill. Pro shop and restaurant are at the clubhouse. *North Course:* 18 holes, par 72, 6,968 yards. *South Course:* 18 holes, par 72, 7,015 yards. Information: *Mauna Lani Resort,* Box 4959, Kohala Coast, HI 96743 (phone: 885-6655).

WAIKOLOA, Waikoloa, the Big Island of Hawaii: Course designer Robert Trent Jones, Jr. describes his *Beach* layout as "a unique golf course . . . a contrast of Eden-like green grass amidst black lava." Jones began as a landscape architect, and the way in which this seaside layout is sculpted reflects his training. His marriage of landscape technique and golf course design craft has produced dramatically beautiful results. The fairways adjacent to the *Royal Waikoloan* hotel are lush with palm trees, bougainvillea, wedelia, oleander, and plumeria, providing a sharp contrast to the moonlike black lava that serves as rough here. Shots hit toward the sea — such as the drive at number 17 — often have the added background of a whale cavorting out in the Pacific. Course: 18 holes, par 70, 6,566 yards. Tom Weiskopf's *Kings* layout is merely marvelous, using the local lava fields as stunning course highlights. Two "drivable" par 4s — number 5 (293 yards) and number 13 (318 yards) — are highlights, and there is a huge double green that serves both the 3rd and 6th holes. This is the tougher of the two Waikoloa layouts. Course: 18 holes, par 72, 7,074 yards. Information: *Waikoloa Golf Courses,* Box 5100, Waikoloa, HI 96743 (phone: 885-6060).

ROYAL KAANAPALI, Kaanapali, Maui: The golf courses here serve a resort strip that is among the most popular in the neighbor islands. Among the hazards in this less than pastoral place are resort guests who shouldn't, but do, cut through the fairways en route to the beach and the distraction of a tourist-filled sugarcane train, which chugs along tracks cut through the layout en route to and from Lahaina. Still, the long *North* course, designed by Robert Trent Jones, Sr., is one of Hawaii's best; Arthur Jack Snyder's *South* course is shorter and flatter and doesn't range as far from the sea. *North Course:* 18 holes, par 72, 6,704 yards. *South Course:* 18 holes, par 72, 6,250 yards. Golf director, Ray DeMello. Information: *Royal Kaanapali Golf Courses, Kaanapali Resort,* Kaanapali, HI 96761 (phone: 661-3691).

KAPALUA, Kapalua, Maui: Arnold Palmer and Francis Duane designed the *Kapalua* resort's original, spectacular *Bay* course on hilly seaside acres formerly dedicated to the growing of pineapples. The newer *Village* course, created by Palmer and Ed Seay, pushes up even farther into the mountains, and sidehill lies are a constant here. Several holes thread through groves of Norfolk and Cook pines, the latter of which is an unusual species whose "needles" appear to grow upside down, which creates a scenic frame along the fairways. A third course designed by Bill Coore and Ben Crenshaw, the *Plantation* course (opened in March 1991), has made Kapalua a triple threat. This magnificent layout wanders up hills and down valleys. After a round on any one of these courses, however, you'll welcome an escape to the lavish luncheon buffet put on Sundays by the adjacent *Kapalua Bay* hotel. The *Isuzu Kapalua International* tournament is held here in November. *Bay Course:* 18 holes, par 72, 6,160 yards. *Village Course:* 18 holes, par 71, 6,194 yards. *Plantation Course:* 18 holes, par 73, 7,100 yards. Golf director, Gary Planos. Information: *Kapalua Golf Club,* 300 Kapalua Dr., Kapalua, HI 96761 (phone: 669-8044).

WAILEA, Wailea, Maui: Try to arrange to tee it up on the *Orange* course at exactly 2 minutes before dawn, and if this seems a bit early to crank up your body, be aware that watching the sun come up over the Haleakala crater is one of the most spectacular sights in the Pacific. Especially in winter, the *Blue* course (home of the women's

Kemper Open) often offers its own fine views, in this case of the humpback whales that come to this area of the world to mate and calve. Arthur Jack Snyder is responsible for the design of both courses, and the golf's pretty darn good — as are the pro shop and the clubhouse restaurant. We think the *Orange* is the tougher track. *Blue Course:* 18 holes, par 72, 6,152 yards. *Orange Course:* 18 holes, par 72, 6,304 yards. Information: *Wailea Golf Club,* 120 Kaukahi St., Kihei, HI 96753 (phone: 879-2966).

MAKENA, Makena, Maui: A beautifully maintained 18 holes (with 18 more scheduled to open next year), made more challenging by narrow fairways. *Makena* skirts the sea and climbs uphill for panoramic views. Number 15, an oceanside par 3, number 10, and number 6, with views that range from the island of Molokini to the West Maui mountains, are three of the more scenic holes of this Robert Trent Jones, Jr. design. Course: 18 holes, par 72, 6,389 yards. Information: *Makena Golf Course,* 5415 Makena Alanui, Kihei, HI 96753 (phone: 879-3344).

SANDALWOOD, Waikapu, Maui: This is Maui's newest course, which made its debut in 1991 in conjunction with the opening of the *Grand Hyatt Wailea* (owned by the same Japanese corporation that manages the *Four Seasons*). Located just outside Wailuku (about 25 minutes from the Wailea and West Maui resorts) at the base of the imposing West Maui Mountains, it offers play amidst 1,000 native sandalwood (now almost extinct in the wild) trees that have been planted on the course, adding to its aesthetic appeal and eventually (when the trees mature) to the difficulty of play. Course: 18 holes, 6,433 yards, par 72. Information: *Sandalwood Golf Course,* Waikapu, HI 96793 (phone: 244-7090).

KALUAKOI, Kaluakoi, Molokai: The western end of Molokai was first developed during the late 1970s, and its resort area thus far consists only of Colony Resorts' *Kaluakoi* hotel, the *Kaluakoi Villas* condominiums, and two independent condominium developments. However, for the golfer who appreciates solitude, *Kaluakoi* offers a very special bonus — a first-rate golf course, designed by Ted Robinson, that curls along the sea and ranks among the best in the islands. Course: 18 holes, par 72, 6,618 yards. Golf director, Ben Neely. Information: *Kaluakoi Golf Course,* PO Box 26, Maunaloa, HI 96770 (phone: 552-2739).

KOELE, Lanai City, Lanai: Operated by one of Lanai's two new Rockresorts' hotels, this 18-hole, up-country course, adjacent to the *Lodge at Koele,* was designed by Greg Norman and Ted Robinson, and is built on the forested slopes of Lanaihale's ridges. Named the *Experience,* the course offers challenging play and astounding views of mountains and the sea. The eighth hole, which lies in a ravine at the bottom of a 200-foot drop with incredible views of the water and forest on either side, will help you redefine the definition of spectacular. Pro shop and instruction services available. Course: 18 holes, par 72, 7,013 yards. Information: The *Lodge at Koele,* Lanai City, HI 96763 (phone: 565-7300; 800-321-4666).

PRINCEVILLE, Hanalei, Kauai: The risks of golfing on Kauai almost equal the allures, for this island includes the wettest spot on earth — and is also one of the most verdant. Still, the golf opportunities at *Princeville,* on the north shore, far outweigh most other considerations, and it has become normal to add the word "unbelievable" to any description of this extraordinary golf site. The original three nines were created by Robert Trent Jones, Jr., son of golf's best-known resort course creator, and each has a distinctive personality. There's an *Ocean* nine, a *Woods* nine, and a *Lake* nine, the last complete with a Zen garden bunker, jungle caverns gaping between tee and green, and lots of pounding sea to complement the other hazards. The latest addition to *Princeville's* golf inventory are the 18 holes of the *Prince* course. You owe yourself at least one crack at *Princeville,* if just to see what all the raving is about. Three original 9-hole, par-36 courses, 3,058, 3,098, and 3,018 yards, and the 18-hole *Prince Course:* par 72, 7,309 yards; resident pro, Neil Finch. Information: *Princeville Makai Course,* PO Box 3040, Princeville, HI 96722 (phone: 826-3580).

KIAHUNA, Poipu, Kauai: This nicely maintained course, built as part of the

Kiahuna resort, covers flat terrain and skirts several important historic Polynesian sites. The holes are relatively straightforward, and the pace on the course is relaxed. Course: 18 holes, par 70, 5,631 yards; resident pro, Cheryl Hayes. A 9-hole addition is planned, with opening set for later this year. Information: *Kiahuna Golf Club,* RR1, Box 73, Koloa, HI 96756 (phone: 742-9595).

KAUAI LAGOONS GOLF & RACQUET CLUB, Kauai Lagoons Resort, Kauai: This pair of 18-hole resort courses was designed by Jack Nicklaus, who also serves as the resort's non-resident director of golf. Manmade lagoons and the ocean require plenty of carries over water. The 190-acre *Kauai Lagoons* course (18 holes, 6,942 yards, par 72) is a country club–style links, relatively straight and well manicured. The sprawling, 262-acre *Kiele Classic* (18 holes, 7,070 yards, par 72) is a tournament class brute of a layout, with substantial room for a spectator gallery. The 18 hole at *Kiele* typifies its challenge: A normal approach shot must carry at least 210 yards into the wind or splash into the lake that surrounds the green. The *Kiele* course was named one of the best new resort courses in the US for 1989 by *Golf Digest* magazine. The courses are part of the resort's *Golf & Racquet Club,* which also includes a driving range, instruction, and a pro shop. Information: *Kauai Lagoons Golf & Racquet Club,* PO Box 3330, Lihue, HI (phone: 246-5063).

POIPU BAY RESORT, Poipu, Kauai: Kauai's newest golf layout (18 holes, 6,959 yards, par 72) opened in 1991. Designed by Robert Trent Jones, Jr., and dubbed the "Pebble Beach of the South Pacific," it offers play over rolling hills that front the ocean along with numerous elevated greens that increase the degree of difficulty. The course also has inland and coastal water holes, as well as preserved archeological sites on some holes. During the winter, humpback whales cavort in the Pacific and monk seals and green sea turtles often soak in the sun on neigboring beaches. There is also a clubhouse, a driving range, instruction, and a pro shop. Information: *Poipu Bay Resort Golf Course,* 2250 Ainako St., Koloa, HI 96756 (phone: 742-8711).

Hiking the Hawaiian Wilderness

The only way to experience Hawaii fully is to walk along its more remote trails. The paradise of picture postcards and mournful legends reveals itself to those willing to explore regions beyond the vision of resort-bound vacationers. However, visitors need not be able to leap tall cliffs in a single bound. The trails listed below include easy strolls and nature walks less than a mile long, some with swimming holes and picnic tables along the way. One of the best books to read before you go is *Hawaiian Hiking Trails* by Craig Chisholm (published by Fernglen Press), which features 49 trails on the five major islands, along with useful information about relative difficulty, time, altitude, and average calories expended on each hike. (Chisholm has also written books on the individual islands.)

The key to Hawaiian hiking is variety: Trekkers can sample humid rain forests and moonlike volcanic craters, as well as deserted beaches scattered with the flotsam and jetsam of shipwrecks. Sights along the way include groves of sweet mountain apples, slim waterfalls cascading into deep pools, and fertile valleys where nature has all but reclaimed the remnants of earlier civilizations.

Hikers should be aware of Hawaii's unique hiking conditions. For example, climbing should not be attempted on volcanic surfaces, which tend to crumble when pressure is applied by hand or foot. (Be sure to wear sturdy boots for hiking in volcanic areas.) In the tropics, night drops like a curtain after sunset; plan to be off the trail a few minutes before twilight unless you're going to spend the night. Carry a canteen — not all of Hawaii's water is potable. Bring insect repellent for all hikes on terrain below

3,000 feet — the mosquitoes in low-lying regions can be fierce. As a final note, it is wise to stick to marked trails, since taking shortcuts can disturb the delicate ecological balance of the environment.

Malihinis (newcomers) seeking guidance and companionship can contact the various organizations listed below that arrange group hiking trips. These provide an excellent introduction to the state's wilderness regions. To return home without discovering one or two of them is to miss seeing the real Hawaii.

OAHU

Though it offers few extended wilderness treks for an advanced hiker, Oahu has several fine day hikes, many of them just a few miles from Honolulu. To hike with a group, contact the *Hawaiian Trail and Mountain Club* (PO Box 2238, Honolulu, HI 96804; phone: 247-3922) or the *Sierra Club* (212 Merchant St., Suite 201, Honolulu, HI 96813; phone: 538-6616; 235-8330). The *Hawaii Nature Center* (2131 Makiki Heights Dr., Honolulu, HI 96822; phone: 955-0100) offers detailed trail maps and escorted hikes in the Koolau Mountains urban watershed, which overlooks the city. For trail information and maps: Department of Land and Natural Resources, Division of Forestry, 1151 Punchbowl St., Honolulu, HI 96813 (phone: 587-0166).

DIAMOND HEAD: Though most visitors know it only as the big green and brown landmark at the far end of Waikiki Beach, Diamond Head also is a fine place for a short hike. Inside this extinct volcano is a trail cut into the crater's interior walls (a flashlight is recommended) that climbs 760 feet to the top of the rim (Point Leahi), where hikers are treated to a panoramic view of Honolulu and the surrounding mountains. Military fortifications built inside the crater during World War II are still there. The trail starts at the parking area near the firing range in the middle of the crater, and is open from 6 AM to 6 PM daily, allowing sunrise and sunset climbs from late November through April. Information: Department of Land and Natural Resources, Division of State Parks, 1151 Punchbowl St., Honolulu, HI 96813 (phone: 587-0300).

KAHANA VALLEY STATE PARK: A 5,220-acre preserve that includes picnic grounds and a variety of valley and mountain trails that head into the windward coast's portion of the Koolau Mountains. No camping is allowed here, but the city and county maintain campsites nearby at the Kahana Bay Beach Park. Information: Department of Land and Natural Resources, Division of State Parks, 1151 Punchbowl St., Room 310, Honolulu, HI 96813 (phone: 587-0300).

JUDD MEMORIAL: This 1.3-mile loop trail, in the Nuuanu Valley, may well be the most entertaining hike in the state. After passing through a stand of eucalyptus, Norfolk pine, and bamboo trees, the trail comes upon one of the best mud-sliding chutes on the island. In the rainy winter months, bring a sheet of heavy plastic for a slick ride down a muddy hill. A fork in the trail leads to Jackass Ginger Pool, a fine place to swim (or wash off the mud). There is a short waterfall slide at the pool for the clean fun crowd.

MANOA VALLEY: One of the more popular and easiest hikes on Oahu, this trail begins at the end of Manoa Road, just past Paradise Park, and winds through a rain forest amid lush tropical plants, mountain apples, and passion fruit vines. The reward at the end of the 1-mile trail is Manoa Falls, with its crisp, clear pool.

BLOWHOLE TO HANAUMA BAY: This seaside trail (2 miles, one way) follows a rock shelf past a variety of fascinating formations created by the erosive action of the sea, including caves and tidal pools. Wear a bathing suit and sneakers for this hike — waves wash over the shelf in some places. Start the hike at the Blowhole and walk back to Hanauma Bay, where a tide pool known as the Toilet Bowl can be seen filling and flushing with each wave. Caution is urged: Several people have been killed diving into its surging waters.

LANIPO TRAIL: An all-day hike on this 7-mile trail affords enough spectacular views of Windward Oahu to convince anyone of the island's great beauty. On the climb up to 1,600 feet, hikers can cool off in one of the many swimming holes found in Waimano Stream. The *palis* (cliffs) of the Koolau Range rise up majestically along this trail. Hikers should be in good shape for this trek.

For the more robust hiker, the Mauumae Trail offers a 6-hour jaunt through groves of ohia and koa trees to a 2,500-foot elevation. Along the southeastern edge of the Kookau Range, the hike provides a rare look at Kaau Crater. Other popular Oahu hikes include Makua Gulch on the northern Windward slopes of the Koolaus, an easy trek in Makaha Valley, and the 2-mile Koko Head Cliff Walk near Hanauma Bay.

MAUNAWILI: Originating at a point near the Pali Highway's hairpin turn, this trail meanders through the Maunawili Valley highlands and ascends to the Aniani ridgeline atop the Koolau Mountains. It is being built by the *Sierra Club,* and while the ultimate completion of the 15-mile complex is still several years away, the first 2½ miles are now open to hikers. Higher portions of the trail display panoramic views of the windward coast, and at one point, the trail passes by the 200-foot-long O'Shaughnessy Tunnel.

HAWAII

The Big Island has some of the most dramatic volcanic trails in the Pacific. Because of its size, hiking routes are longer and the variety of trails is greater on Hawaii than on other islands. Nowhere else in the state can trekkers walk the hot-bedded floor of an active volcano — and live to talk about it. For guided hikes, check with the *Sierra Club* (212 Merchant St., Suite 201, Honolulu, HI 96813; phone: 538-6616; 235-8330). For trail information and maps: Department of Land and Natural Resources, Division of Forestry, 1643 Kilauea Ave., Hilo, HI 96720 (phone: 961-7221).

HAWAII VOLCANOES NATIONAL PARK: The state's most fascinating volcanic trails crisscross the area around the Kilauea Crater, considered the most active volcanic crater in the world. The easiest of the lot is *Devastation Trail,* a short jaunt of less than a mile that passes through the skeletal remains of an ohia forest that was rained on by volcanic showers in 1959. There is a per-vehicle or -person charge for park entry.

The 4-mile *Kilauea Iki Trail* leaves from a large volcanic tunnel known as the Thurston Lava Tube and descends a few hundred feet onto the crater floor. To the uninitiated, walking on the thick lava crust that blankets a red-hot molten pool of liquid rock can be like walking on eggs. The soles of your shoes will really heat up from this hike.

Experienced hikers seeking a good overview of the park itself should take a full-day tour on *Crater Rim Trail,* encircling the Kilauea Crater. The 11.6-mile route starts at the park's *Volcano House* and passes through the barren Kau Desert, skirting several steam vents along the way (hold your breath; the sulfurous clouds of smoke smell like rotten eggs). Make a detour off the trail to see the Halemaumau "fire pit," a hellish lake of steam. Good views can also be had on a hike to the summit of Mauna Loa, which takes 2 to 3 days and requires overnighting at park-run cabins. At press time, the lava had stopped flowing into the sea and was re-surfacing along an isolated up-country vent. A remarkable sight is the Wahaula *heiau* (temple), surrounded to the base of its walls by lava yet otherwise untouched, the only thing spared for miles along the coast. The area remains active, and when lava flows into the sea, creating a poisonous steam, the air can be dangerous to breathe. Visitors should take all warnings seriously. The entry fee is $5 per car. Contact the center for current information (phone: 967-7311) or call the 24-hour volcano hotline (phone: 967-4977).

WAIPIO/WAIMANU VALLEY TRAILS: On the Big Island's northern tip are a pair of green, green valleys at the base of the rugged Kohala Mountains, where time stands still. A rich and fertile land once planted with acres of taro and favored by Hawaiian royalty, the valleys today are virtually unpopulated. A 2-to-3-day trip is necessary to penetrate this verdant retreat, far removed from the island's volcanic regions. In addition to the twin 1,000-foot waterfalls of Hiilawe, the four-wheel-drive road of the Waipio Valley takes hikers past ancient ruins, as well as by homes flattened by two *tsunami* (tidal waves) in the 1940s. Ambitious trekkers can scale the Z-shaped trail leading from Waipio Valley to the smaller and more secluded Waimanu Valley, where magnificent waterfalls and numerous beachfront campsites greet the backpacker.

MAUI

From the luxuriant rain forests of Hana to the otherworldly moonscape of Haleakala Crater, the Valley Isle has a superb variety of trails. Resort and condominium development may have inundated several coastal areas, but Maui's interior regions and the Hana coastline remain as untamed as ever for those willing to forgo civilized comforts in favor of natural wonders, at least for an afternoon. Walks and hikes in Haleakala National Park are led by park rangers on a seasonal, weather-permitting schedule. Call park headquarters, open 7:30 AM to 4 PM (phone: 572-9306), for information on any scheduled walks, and the Kipahulu District office (phone: 248-8260) for details of the Saturday hikes to Waimoku Falls. At press time, walks were scheduled on Tuesdays and Thursdays at 10 AM, and Mondays and Thursdays from Hosmer Grove at 9 AM. Non-members may join the guided hikes of the *Sierra Club,* usually held on Saturdays and Sundays. They're announced in the Datebook section of the *Maui News* or you can call the *Sierra Club* Hawaii chapter on Oahu (phone: 538-6616) for the telephone numbers of the Maui group's officers. *Hike Maui* (PO Box 33096, Kahuluai, HI 96733; phone: 808-879-5270) provides guided excursions to Haleakala Crater, Hana Falls, the West Maui Mountains, and other areas. For trail information and maps: Department of Land and Natural Resources, Division of Forestry, 54 High St., Wailuku, HI 96793 (phone: 243-5352).

HALEAKALA NATIONAL PARK: Thirty-two miles of trails crisscross the crater depths of the massive dormant volcano known as "the House of the Sun." Trails lead down the crater walls or stretch across the crater floor 3,000 feet below the rim. Multicolored cinder cones and rare silversword plants punctuate this infernal landscape. The three main trail systems within the volcano are *Sliding Sands Trail,* a steep path of ash and cinders that drops precipitously to the crater floor; *Kaupo Trail,* which leaves the crater through Kaupo Gap and continues several miles south to the sea; and *Halemauu Trail,* a lovely path bordered by red and green ferns that winds past volcanic vents, large cones, and ancient lava flows. In addition to wild goats, hikers may spot the nene, a virtually extinct variety of Hawaiian goose that's been designated as Hawaii's state bird. Park headquarters has a brochure with a map, and also can provide details on the best trails for individual hikers. Ranger-led hikes also are offered occasionally (phone: 572-9306). Most of Haleakala's trails have steep grades and are fairly strenuous. The park charges a small entrance fee.

KEANAE ARBORETUM: This short hike (a half mile) above the Keanae Peninsula on the road to Hana is a perfect spot for a relaxed family outing. The garden contains domestic Hawaiian plants, native trees, and non-native tropical species. Several varieties of taro are grown (poi, a traditional Hawaiian food, is made from the taro corm, or root) as well as papayas, bananas, and sweet potatoes. Picnics are popular along the Piinaau Stream, which makes a fine swimming hole; but beware: signs now warn of the danger of intestinal infection from natural pollutants in the water.

WAIKAMOI RIDGE: This is the shortest, easiest, and one of the most pleasurable trails on the island. Leading up an evenly graded slope to a grassy area with picnic tables overlooking Kolea Reservoir, the ridge trail passes bamboo and eucalyptus trees as well as large ferns. *Waikamoi Ridge Trail* is off the Hana Highway near Kailua; the hiking trail is convenient to good swimming and picnic areas at Twin Falls and Puohokamoa Falls.

MOLOKAI

Though most of its land is restricted, the Friendly Isle has several fine trails cut through four north coast valleys. One of the best (and the only one accessible by car) is the *Halawa Valley Trail,* a half-day hike for intermediate trekkers that leads to a pair of lovely waterfalls at the valley's end. These are Moaula Falls, two successive cascades that drop 250 feet to a large clear pool ideal for swimming, and Hipupua Falls, a high ribbon of water that tumbles over a *pali* (cliff) into a pool in the shape of a dog bone. This second waterfall is reached by hopping rocks leading up the Halawa Stream, an approach that should not be attempted if rain has made the rocks slippery. Another find is the Kamakou Preserve, which is marked by a four-wheel-drive vehicle track that intersects Route 46 (ask for directions at any service station), and is thick with native Hawaiian plants and birds. Wild boar hunters are to be thanked for creating the trails here.

LANAI

In addition to three rather arduous trails that meander around the rim of its spectacular interior gorge, Lanai has one of the best beachcombing hikes in the state. Polihua Beach, a trackless expanse of sand on the island's northwest shore, invites hikers to travel as many miles as they please along an almost endless stretch of berm and dunes. Hikers can discover the remnants of shipwrecks (the area has been appropriately dubbed "Shipwreck Beach"), as well as myriad seashells along the way. The island of Molokai is plainly visible across the Kalohi Channel from the beach. Polihua is accessible by foot or jeep only; four-wheel-drive vehicles are available from rental agencies in Lanai City. There's a short trail that leads from the eastern end of Hulopoe Beach to beautiful views of the hills, emerald and sapphire sea, and legend-haunted Sweetheart Rock.

Behind Lanai City, the 7-to-8-mile *Munro Trail* loop is considered one of the most beautiful hikes in all Hawaii. From the trail, almost all of the Hawaiian islands are visible. A good map is available from *Oshiro U-Drive & Taxi,* a *Dollar* franchise, at PO Box 516, Lanai, HI 96763 (phone: 565-6952).

KAUAI

Only 20 minutes by air from Honolulu, the Garden Isle's top hiking trails are nevertheless far removed from civilization. The Hawaii of most people's fantasies can be seen on treks into the spectacular Waimea Canyon, along the plunging seacliffs of the Na Pali Coast, or on the fringes of the primordial Alakai Swamp. For trail information and maps: Department of Land and Natural Resources, Division of Forestry, 3060 Eiwa St., Lihue, HI 96766 (phone: 241-3444).

KALALAU TRAIL: One of the finest wilderness hiking trails on earth. A strenuous and incredibly scenic route that winds above the massive seacliffs of the Na Pali Coast, the trail follows an ancient Hawaiian path for 11 miles through dense rain forests and groves of wild fruit trees. Day-trippers can turn back along the *Hanakapiai Valley Loop Trail* after stopping for a breather at Hanakapiai Falls and the sandy beach nearby. Hardy backpackers can continue along the *Kalalau Trail* to Hanakoa Valley, where the grade steepens considerably and their efforts are rewarded by the lovely sight of

Hanakoa Falls, as well as marvelous views of the coastline. Snacks of wild guava and mountain apple can be enjoyed before descending Kalalau Valley, where there are several fine campsites near the beach. For those up to the challenge, this may well be the most beautiful and exciting hike in the state.

KUKUI TRAIL: This rugged 2½-mile trail descends 2,000 feet to the Waimea River, along the western edge of the famed "Grand Canyon of the Pacific," which originally received its nickname from Samuel Clemens, that is, Mark Twain. Though ideal for intermediate day hikers, the *Kukui Trail* provides access to the network of trails found on the Waimea Canyon floor, where experienced backpackers can continue on to campsites. Multicolored rocks that change in hue throughout the day, lush tropical forests, and many rare and colorful birds are among the sights glimpsed along this trail.

PIHEA LOOKOUT TRAIL: Here's a short trail (1.7 miles) that can be traversed in 2 hours, and yet provides the novice hiker with an excellent view of Kalalau Valley from a series of high *palis.* The path also skirts Alakai Swamp, sparing hikers the necessity of sinking in mud. Try taking this trail in the early morning hours, when wild goats can be seen hopping along the cliffs. The trail begins at Puu O Kila Lookout, where the 3,000-foot-high Na Pali sea cliffs reach down like brown fingers to the crashing surf. The views along this modest trail are as wondrous as the floral profusion alongside it.

Camping from Crater to Coastline

Better known for its extravagant resorts that pamper guests with every luxury, Hawaii also boasts a generous supply of campgrounds for visitors who prefer more primitive accommodations. The range of environments is remarkable: Only in Hawaii can a camper spend one night in the eerie netherworld of a volcanic crater and the next in a beachfront park where tents are pulled taut on a grassy lawn within a stone's throw of pounding surf.

Camping in Hawaii is permitted in two national parks, 11 state parks, and 37 county parks. There is more than one way to go: It's possible to hike to a secluded campsite and pitch a tent (or sleep out under the stars). Camping equipment can be brought from home or rented at a number of sporting goods stores around the islands. Lightweight tents with a sewn-in floor are best for Hawaiian camping. Pack warm clothing for mountain camping; the weather is anything but tropical at 10,000 feet.

With the exception of three cabins in Haleakala Crater on Maui and cabins at the Namakani Paio campsite in Hawaii Volcanoes National Park, camping at Hawaii's federal parks is free. State park permits are free and usually allow camping for up to 1 week. Cabins at state parks are free or range from $3 per person to $25 per cabin per night. County park permits cost $1 for adults per night and 50¢ for children under 12. These permits are issued for stays of from 3 to 7 days.

If you want to stay in a cabin on the Big Island of Hawaii, there are several in Hawaii Volcanoes National Park (PO Box 52, Hawaii National Park, HI 96718), Mauna Kea State Park, Kalopa State Recreation Area, and Kilauea State Recreation Area. Information on state parks: State Parks Division, 75 Aupuni St., Hilo, HI 96720; phone: 933-4200. On Maui, you can rent a cabin in Haleakala National Park (PO Box 369, Makawao, HI 96768; phone: 572-8306) or at Polipoli Spring State Recreation Area, and Waianapanapa State Park (Department of Land and Natural Resources, Division of State Parks, 54 High St., 1st Floor, Wailuku, Maui, HI 96793; phone: 243-5354). On Kauai, cabins can be rented in Kokee State Park (c/o *Kokee Lodge,* PO Box 819, Waimea, HI 96796; phone: 335-6061) and Kahili Mountain Park (PO Box 298, Koloa, HI 96756).

A small caveat for Hawaiian campers: Don't leave valuables unprotected. Theft is not uncommon at campsites. On the bright side, there are no snakes, poisonous insects, or poison ivy in the islands. A review of the top camping sites in the state follows.

OAHU

KEAIWA HEIAU STATE PARK: In the foothills of the Koolau Range, a few miles from Pearl Harbor, this up-country park has a decidedly non-tropical climate, as well as a fascinating history. Keaiwa Heiau (a *heiau* is an ancient temple) is where Hawaiian medicine men cultivated herbs and other plants used to heal the sick. The campground here is a few hundred yards from temple ruins and herb gardens, all of it surrounded by dense forests of pine and eucalyptus trees. Keaiwa Heiau is best for tent camping; RVs can stay overnight with a permit. Reservations cannot be made more than 30 days in advance. Closed Wednesdays and Thursdays. Information: Department of Land and Natural Resources, Division of State Parks, 1151 Punchbowl St., Room 310, Honolulu, HI 96813 (phone: 587-0300).

BELLOWS FIELD BEACH PARK: Though limited to weekend and holiday use, this lovely park, 20 miles east of Waikiki, is actually the small oceanfront corner of a large military base. Its barbecue pits and picnic tables make it popular with day-trippers, and the white sandy beach and calm sea make it a favorite of campers who also like to swim and snorkel. Visitors pitch tents near the forest of ironwood trees that rings the beach. A wonderful pastime here is watching the Pacific mole crabs ("sand turtles") burrow into the sand between waves. Bellows is convenient to Hanauma Bay, a designated marine preserve much enjoyed by snorkelers, and to Sea Life Park, where leaping porpoises and trained whales are the main attractions. A permit is required and must be obtained in person. Open weekends only. Information: Department of Parks and Recreation, 650 S. King St., Honolulu, HI 96813 (phone: 523-4525).

The Division of State Parks operates the *Waimanalo Bay State Recreational Area* adjacent to Bellows Field. Camping is allowed daily, except Wednesdays and Thursdays, and permits are required. Information: Department of Land and Natural Resources, Division of State Parks, 1151 Punchbowl St., Room 310, Honolulu, HI 96813 (phone: 587-0300).

KAHANA BAY BEACH PARK: A beautiful grove of ironwood pines on a wide crescent beach, with sawtooth mountains as a backdrop, makes this park on windward Oahu particularly inviting. The beach is very popular and safe for swimming, with a sandy ocean bottom and a gentle slope. Kahana Bay also offers shoreline fishing, and the park provides shower and barbecue facilities. There is beachfront camping (daily except Wednesdays and Thursdays; permit required) at Malaekahana Beach, several miles up the coast from Kahana. Information: Department of Land and Natural Resources, Division of State Parks, 1151 Punchbowl St., Room 310, Honolulu, HI 96813 (phone: 587-0300). Other top campsites in this region include *Nanakuli Beach Park* (tent and trailer camping allowed) and *Lualualei Beach Park* (tent camping only). Permits required for all parks. No camping allowed on Wednesdays and Thursdays. Information: Department of Parks and Recreation, 650 S. King St., Honolulu, HI 96813 (phone: 587-0300).

HAWAII

HAWAII VOLCANOES NATIONAL PARK: Even hardened scoutmasters have been known to react like tenderfeet at the sight of this ethereal volcanic parkland. Some 30 miles from Hilo, the park is centered around 13,680-foot Mauna Loa and the flat, sloping volcano of Kilauea, the legendary home of Pele, Hawaiian goddess of fire. From the rim of the Halemaumau Firepit, campers can watch as Kilauea Crater belches sulfurous clouds of steam — recently it has erupted often to offer a far more spectacular show. The contrasts here are nearly surreal: giant fern forests not far from hardened lava flows punctuated by scorched trees.

The park maintains three fine drive-in campsites. At *Namakani Paio,* large eucalyptus trees shade individual RV camping slots. The campsite also has 10 cabins, as well as room for several tents. Temperatures here can drop below freezing at night. Even during the summer, campers curl up in down sleeping bags and often spend the night around large fireplaces near the site's pavilions. Reservations for cabins ($24 per day for up to four people) can be made at the *Volcano House.* You may need to bring an extra blanket, as only one is provided.

Kipuka Nene, a secluded campsite favored by residents, is surrounded by a ghostly forest of dead trees, all overshadowed by the volcanic cone of Mauna Loa. At the upper rim of Kilauea, off Chain of Craters Road, the site has a flat grassy area for tent campers and a parking lot for RVs. Like all of the park campsites, *Kipuka Nene* can be windy and rainy, but there are few more dramatic camping sites in the state.

In the lower reaches of the park, near Kalapana, is *Kamoamoa,* an oceanfront campsite bordered by a stand of ohia lehua trees ablaze with red pompom blossoms. The ruins of an ancient Hawaiian village can be explored here, and petroglyphs (pictures and ideographs carved in rock) can be found along the rugged lava coastline. There is a pleasant stretch of grass within earshot of the pounding surf where campers like to spread their picnics. *Kamoamoa* is quiet, private, and hauntingly beautiful. The lava flows of late 1986 and 1987 entered the sea not far from here. Check with park administration for feasibility of hiking in this area if eruptions are nearby. Information for all three sites: Hawaii Volcanoes National Park, PO Box 52, Hawaii National Park, HI 96718 (phone: 967-7311).

MAUNA KEA STATE PARK: Mauna Loa's volcanic twin sister is the 13,796-foot peak of Mauna Kea. The 500-acre state park on the slopes of the mountain can be reached by negotiating the Saddle Road (rent a four-wheel-drive vehicle for this excursion) to an elevation of 6,500 feet, where the state maintains 15 cozy log cabins. Five of the cabins have fireplaces, and all have bedding and kitchen utensils. (Advance reservations are advised.) Though the sun is intense during the day, the weather turns sharply colder at night. (The cabins are popular with skiers during the winter.) The night sky at Mauna Kea is so dense with stars that it's worth rolling out of bed to see; the cabins are a great place to stay if you plan to make a night visit to the *Onizuka Center* for a look through their telescope, or Mauna Kea's summit for a look through one of the telescopes set up for visitors. Information: Division of State Parks, 75 Aupuni St., Hilo, HI 96720 (phone: 933-4200).

HAPUNA BEACH STATE PARK: Though often a bit crowded, Hapuna has 6 screened A-frame cabins across the street from one of the finest white sand beaches in the state. Each cabin (they cost $15) accommodates four people on rather spartan wooden platforms (bring your own bedding). Like most Kona Coast beaches, Hapuna has abundant and varied marine life and coral formations; it is especially popular with campers who like to snorkel. In addition, there are spacious picnic areas shaded by coconut palms and hala trees. Maui's volcano, Haleakala, is plainly visible from the park. Advance reservations are advised. Information: Division of State Parks, 75 Aupuni St., Hilo, HI 96720 (phone: 882-1095).

MAUI

HALEAKALA NATIONAL PARK: Though the opportunities are limited, the fortunate few who get to camp inside Haleakala Crater are said to be transformed by the experience. Whether from excitement or the cold, campers usually awaken early to see the crater's red cinder cones and spiny silversword plants bathed in the purplish light that appears just before dawn.

There are two campgrounds inside this vast dormant volcano: *Holua* and *Paliku* are both wilderness sites 3,000 feet below the crater rim, accessible by trail. Each campground is limited to 25 persons. Overnight stays are limited to 2 days at one site and 3 days' total at both, and a permit is required. There is also a 12-person cabin at each campsite, but these shelters are so popular that a monthly lottery is held to determine their use. If you're lucky enough to make it to "the House of the Sun," dress warmly; temperatures regularly drop below freezing inside the moonlike crater.

In addition to the crater campsites, a tent campground and picnic facilities are in a forested area near the park entrance at Hosmer Grove. In marked contrast to the arid crater landscape, Hosmer is lush, wooded, and serene. No permit is required, but camping is limited to 3 days. Information: Haleakala National Park, PO Box 369, Makawao, HI 96768 (phone: 572-9306).

POLIPOLI SPRINGS STATE PARK: On the slopes of Haleakala in central Maui, Polipoli has cabin and tent camping for those who manage to survive a hair-raising 10-mile drive on a bumpy dirt road leading to the campsite (a four-wheel-drive vehicle is suggested). This secluded up-country retreat is nestled in a dense forest of redwood, pine, and cypress trees, and is usually blanketed by a morning fog that lifts in the afternoon to reveal a stunning view of several surrounding islands. The 3-bedroom cabin at the site sleeps 10 people. Dress warmly; the weather (by Hawaiian standards) can be very damp and cold. A permit is required, as is an advance deposit. Information: Department of Land and Natural Resources, Division of State Parks, 54 High St., 1st Floor, Wailuku, HI 96793 (phone: 243-5354).

WAIANAPANAPA STATE PARK: On a grassy bluff overlooking a black sand beach along the Hana coast, this 120-acre park has both tent sites and cabins. The ocean is too rough for swimming here, but the opportunities for hiking and exploring are unsurpassed. The list of natural attractions includes ancient lava flows, dramatic sea arches, shallow lava caves, a small blowhole, and a lovely footpath that winds along the coastline to Hana. With its exuberant vegetation and fine facilities, Waianapanapa is considered one of the state's top campsites. A permit is required, also an advance deposit. Information: Division of State Parks, 54 High St., Wailuku, HI 96793 (phone: 243-5354).

MOLOKAI

PALAAU STATE PARK: A 34-acre mountain wilderness of koa, paperbark, ironwood, and cypress trees, this north coast park is known for its spectacular view of Makanalua, the peninsula where Father Damien founded his famous leper colony. In addition to having a series of petroglyphs carved in rock near the campground, the site is just a few hundred yards from a 6-foot-high phallic symbol that was visited long ago by infertile women hoping to change their luck. There is tent camping only at Palaau. A permit is required. Information: Division of State Parks, PO Box 627, Kaunakakai, HI 96748 (phone: 567-6083).

KAUAI

KOKEE STATE PARK: Tent and trailer camping is available at this tropical mountain forest of silver oak and wild plum trees marked off by Waimea Canyon and Kalalau Lookout. The views of Kauai and the blue ocean that surrounds it, as seen from Kokee's 45 miles of trails, are simply breathtaking. In addition to rustic campsites with minimal facilities along these hiking trails, the state maintains 12 cabins, each of which can accommodate three or seven people. Reservations for the latter should be sent to *Kokee Lodge* (PO Box 819, Waimea, HI 96796; phone: 335-6061). Kokee also accommodates trailer campers (a permit is required for RVs). Plan your trip during the summer; heavy rains can turn Kokee's trails to mud at other times of the year. Permits are required. Information: Division of State Parks, PO Box 1671, Lihue, HI 96766 (phone: 241-3444).

HAENA BEACH PARK: This county-run site on Kauai's north shore, sandwiched between the raging ocean (strong currents and rip tides make swimming dangerous here) and steep lava cliffs, is a good base from which to see a variety of attractions. Just across the street from the park is the Maniniholo Dry Cave, a lava tube worth exploring. Up the road a piece are the Waikapalae and Waikanaloa Wet Caves, both ideal for a bracing swim. Ocean bathers are advised to go to Kee Beach, at the head of the Kalalau trail. Adventurous beachgoers can hike a 2-mile trail to Hanakapiai Beach, or a more difficult 11-mile trail to Kalalau Beach, or follow the dirt roads leading off Route 56 to any number of unnamed (and uncrowded) beaches. Haena has tent camping, and a permit is required. As with other Kauai County parks, including Anini (see below), mail-in reservations are *not* accepted. In person payment for out-of-staters ($3 per night, per adult) must be made at the park's permit section, or, if they are closed, at the Lihue police station (3060 Umi St.), which can accept payments from campers 24 hours a day. Information: Parks Permit Section, 4193 Hardy St., Lihue, HI 96766 (phone: 245-1881).

ANINI PARK: Take the turnoff 2 miles past Kilauea Village to this large beach park which is set amid ancient ironwood pines and grassy lawns, with two camping areas that can accommodate up to 200 people at a time. Facilities include cold showers, picnic and barbecue sites, and uncovered pavilions for eating. Safe swimming and a large, uncrowded beach are the lures. Camping is permitted for 7 consecutive nights. Information: Parks Permit Section, 4193 Hardy St., Lihue, HI 96766 (phone: 245-1881).

Hawaii on Horseback

For those partial to four-legged means of transportation, Hawaii's riding facilities offer the adventurous equestrian all-day or overnight treks, as well as horses on an hourly basis. Even for rank beginners, there are few more delightful ways to explore dormant volcanoes, mountain rain forests, or hidden waterfalls than on horseback or mule.

MAUI: Overnight trail rides into the crater of Haleakala, the 10,023-foot "House of the Sun," where the legendary demigod Maui lassoed the sun and held it captive in a primitive form of daylight saving time, gives visiting cowpokes a firsthand look at the natural wonders that spawned island mythology. The vast crater (Manhattan would easily fit inside it) is creased with trails that descend to a moonlike surface littered with multicolored cinder cones. Within this volcanic netherworld are several more miles of marked trails that meander through exotic vegetation and grazing areas for the horses. Travelers stay at one of three cabins maintained by park rangers, and since the air turns cool at night in the crater, sweaters or heavy sleepwear is recommended. The trek, limited to two to six riders, costs $175 per person, with meals included ($225 per person if the ride is limited to two or three riders), although it's said that the trail leader's wife packs a fried chicken and potato salad dinner that far surpasses freeze-dried trail food. The 8-hour ride up Kaupo Gap from the ranch to Haleakala is a rather arduous ride, but the chance to chase the rising sun across the crater on horseback is not soon forgotten. Rides must be booked a month or two in advance. Tents and sleeping bags provided. Information: *Charley's Trail Rides and Pack Trips,* c/o *Kaupo Store,* Hana,

HI 96713 (phone: 248-8209). For those with something a bit less exhaustive in mind, day trips into the crater are offered by *Pony Express Tours,* PO Box 535, Kula, HI 96790 (phone: 667-2200).

Rainbow Ranch makes tame ascents to west Maui's panoramic up-country. *Adventures on Horseback* meets riders at the Halawa Bridge on the Hana Highway for rides inland and to the sea. *Aloha Nui Loa Tours* also offers Hana horseback tours departing the *Hana-Maui* hotel. Information: *Rainbow Ranch,* PO Box 10066, Lahaina, HI 96761 (phone: 669-4991); *Adventures on Horseback,* PO Box 1771, Makawao, HI 96768 (phone: 242-7445); *Aloha Nui Loa Tours,* PO Box 10582, Lahaina, HI 96761 (phone: 669-0000; 800-525-HANA).

MOLOKAI: On the isolated Makanalua Peninsula, accessible only by plane, boat, or mule, is Kalaupapa, the famed 19th-century leper colony where Father Damien, the Belgian priest, settled. After a brief stop at Kalaupapa Lookout, 1,600 feet above the peninsula, riders on sure-footed mules edge down a steep 3-mile trail cut from a rain forest. The lacy waterfalls and sheer *palis* (cliffs) seen during the descent make up some of Hawaii's most dramatic scenery. At trail's end, a 3-hour minibus tour of this historic settlement gives visitors an insight into the life of the unfortunate leper outcasts of the past. (The disease has since been largely arrested.) The group breaks for a picnic lunch at Kalawao Park before returning their mounts to the Kalae corral.

Mule rides to the Makanalua Peninsula are limited to visitors over 16 years and under 225 pounds. The price for the all-day trek is $115. Information: *Molokai Mule Ride,* PO Box 200, Kualapuu, HI 96757 (phone: 567-6088; 800-843-5978).

KAUAI: In addition to a 1-hour ride ($27) across ranchlands bordering the upper reaches of beautiful Hanalei Valley on Kauai's north shore, visitors can saddle up for a 2-hour Hawaiian country ride ($48) that crisscrosses the famous Princeville Ranch and affords impressive views of the coast. Wrangler Les Miles also offers a peaceful sunset beach ride for $100 for an hour. Apprehensive first-time riders will be relieved to know that his Appaloosas, Arabians, and palominos are unusually gentle "critters." Reservations should be made at least 24 hours in advance (phone: 338-0052). One of the more popular trips on the island is a 3½-hour Waterfall Picnic Ride ($75), which stops at the 70-foot Kalihiwai waterfall for a cool swim followed by a picnic lunch. Children or adults with mobility problems are excluded because the hike to the waterfall, though short, is strenuous. Information: *Pooku Stables,* PO Box 888, Hanalei, HI 96714 (phone: 826-6777).

In Poipu, *CJM Country Stables* offers three types of rides. In the morning, there is the 3-hour Breakfast Ride ($70 per person), which heads inland before stopping for breakfast on a secluded beach, and in the afternoons, there are 1- and 2-hour beach rides ($25 and $45, respectively). Information: *CJM Country Stables,* 5598 Tapa St., Koloa, HI 96756 (phone: 742-6096).

LANAI: The stables adjacent to the *Lodge at Koele* offer a number of escorted 1- and 2-hour rides out onto the flatlands of the Palawai Basin (once studded with rows of pineapple plants, they are now being groomed for alfalfa and pastureland) or into the hills above Lanai City, where the views, framed by signature Cook pines, are simply stunning. Information: *Lodge at Koele,* PO Box 774, Lanai City, HI 96763 (phone: 565-7300).

HAWAII: West Hawaii's ranchland provides beautiful up-country pastures for horseback riding. *Ironwood Outfitters* (PO Box 832, Kamuela, HI 96743; phone: 885-4941) offers the best rides in Hawaii, both for the scenic grandeur of the Kohala Mountains and the chance for riders to let loose and gallop. The first-light ride (8 to 9:30 AM) catches the sunrise over Mauna Kea, while the 2½-hour morning ride (10 AM to 1 PM) reaches panoramic heights 5,000 feet above sea level. Riders are more tamely escorted at the *Mauna Kea Beach Stables* (PO Box 218, Kamuela, HI 96743; phone: 885-4288), whose routes rove Parker Ranch land on the slopes of Hualalai.

King's Trail Rides O'Kona departs Kealakekua Ranch on 2- ($59) and 4½-hour rides (2 hours in the saddle, with a 2½-hour tour of a working ranch; $79). The longer rides start at a 4,200-foot elevations, which ensure magnificent views. Information: *Long Rides,* PO Box 1366, Kealakekua, HI 96750; phone: 323-2388).

Hunting

Hawaii, believe it or not, has some of the most productive hunting grounds in the world. In the cool mountain uplands roam wild boar descended from the pigs first brought to Hawaii by the original Polynesian settlers. Feral sheep and wild goats are found on the high slopes of the Big Island's dormant volcanoes, while axis deer are hunted on Molokai. In addition, game birds ranging from pheasant and quail to wild turkey and chukar partridge challenge the buckshot artist.

The state hunting license and permit for non-residents is $20, and there are usually trophy fees for game taken. Though there are nearly 20 public hunting areas in the state, the best hunting opportunities are found on private lands, for which guide services are available. Rates for these services are $400 for the first hunter per day and $150 per person for additional hunters, and usually include a guide, transportation, and meals. Rifles and ammunition are available at $30 per day. A maximum of four hunters per party is the rule.

HAWAII: The finest hunting in the state is found on the slopes of Mauna Kea and Mt. Hualalai on the Kona Coast. Eugene Ramos, who is *Hawaii Hunting Tours* and to whom the *Mauna Kea Beach* hotel refers prospective hunters, has access to 20,000 acres of the Parker Ranch, on the slopes of Mauna Kea. Corsican sheep and wild goats are the main quarry. Wild boar, weighing up to 300 pounds, with short curling tusks, are found in wet areas. Hunters travel by jeep to selected sites and then stalk game on foot. Ramos claims that nowhere else in the world can a big-game hunter be "successful" and return to his hotel the same day. He also notes that hunters can be stalking game in the snows of Mauna Kea in the morning and go swimming in the afternoon. Bird hunting on the Big Island is especially good for Nepal Kaliz pheasant, Erckel's francolin (a type of grouse), chukar partridge, and Japanese quail. The game bird season runs from the first Saturday in November through the third Sunday in January. Information: *Hawaii Hunting Tours,* PO Box 58, Paauilo, HI 96776 (phone: 776-1666).

LANAI: The *Lanai Company* offers guided hunts on Mt. Lanaihale for $750 a day, all-inclusive. Hunters can track axis deer, mouflon sheep, quail, and partridge. Information: *Lanai Company,* PO Box L, Lanai City, HI 96763 (phone: 565-7233).

MAUI: Maui's best hunting grounds are found in the forest reserves of East Maui, on the slopes of Haleakala. Here the feral goat and wild boar are the choice game mammals, though wild boar are also found in the forests below the Eke Crater on West Maui. Valley Isle hunters conduct their searches on fertile territory, where the air is often scented by pine and eucalyptus trees. *Hunting Adventures of Maui* (645 Kapakalua Rd., Haiku, HI 96708; phone: 572-8214), looks for wild boar and Spanish goats on Kaupo, Haleakala, and Ulupalakua ranchlands. Cost is $400 per day for the first hunter, $275 for each additional one, to a maximum of three. Rifle rentals are available for $30, plus $20 for a permit.

Individual hunters with state-issued permits can go after game, although this may be difficult and risky without a guide.

MOLOKAI: Modeled after the commercial hunting preserves in Texas, the *Molokai Ranch* offers year-round hunting for axis deer (bucks weigh up to 200 pounds) and

Barbary sheep on a fee basis. (There is a $400 daily fee for the first hunter, and $250 for each additional hunter. There is a $600 fee for each axis deer that is bagged, and a whopping $1,500 for a trophy caliber Barbary sheep or Indian black buck.) Exclusivity is guaranteed: The number of hunters on the ranch is limited to five for deer and three for big game on any given day.

From November through January, weekends and holidays only, the ranch permits hunting for upland game birds. The fee is $50 per day. A detailed map is provided in lieu of a guide. Hunters must bring their own equipment. Information: *Molokai Ranch,* PO Box 8, Maunaloa, HI 96770 (phone: 552-2767).

Gliding and Hang Gliding

HANG GLIDING: Thanks to recent aerodynamic improvements in flying equipment, hang gliding is no longer considered a "fringe" sport, suited only for potential kamikaze pilots. Hawaii, in fact, has some of the world's most beautiful sites for this highly individual pursuit. The *Tradewinds Hang Gliding Center* runs a beginner program for those interested in savoring the immediate and thrilling sense of flight unavailable to those inside an aircraft. According to the *US Hang Gliding Association,* the sport is "great physical and mental therapy for those frustrated by the daily constraints of modern living." (The *USHGA* also believes that hang gliding most closely realizes the flying imagined in dreams.)

Following *USHGA* guidelines, Lani Akiona and state champion Mike Benson of *Tradewinds* organizes small classes (no more than six pupils in a group) for introductory lessons, during which novices "tackle some pretty good-size sand dunes." The 2- to 3-hour sessions cost $50. Akiona emphasizes that achieving great height is not necessary to experience the exhilaration of hang gliding. Whether you are 12 inches or 1,200 feet in the air, the excitement of lifting off the ground on a pair of wings is the same. Only the view is different.

Tradewinds' emphasis during the introductory lessons is on fun. The basic course is designed to show beginners how hang gliders fly, to familiarize them with the glider and its equipment, and to enable them to experience the thrill of launching themselves into the air safely. Novices can look forward to 10 mini-flights during the first session. Akiona only teaches when the weather is good, which is about 75% of the time. (In the same way that a surfer needs waves to surf, a hang glider needs wind to fly.) Safety is the overriding concern, but Akiona insists the only injury incurred during her classes was a blister someone received from holding on to the control bar too tightly.

In further support of the sport, Akiona says hang glider equipment at present is vastly improved over "wings" made less than 5 years ago, which are now considered unsafe. The flying characteristics of new certified gliders permit pilots to climb higher, go farther, and land more safely. Turning, handling, and performance are all greatly improved on new models. Accidents caused by design inadequacies are virtually nonexistent these days.

Tradewinds runs excursions for advanced flyers to the main ridge of Makapuu, among the velvety green *palis* (cliffs) of the Koolau Range. Waimanalo is also a favorite ridge-soaring site of accomplished hang glider pilots. Back to the beginners: Akiona says that many visitors who take the introductory lesson pursue the sport back home. No finer setting could be provided for a first taste of do-it-yourself flying, though the timid need not apply. Information: *Tradewinds Hang Gliding Center* (phone: 396-8557).

GLIDING: Those who feel more secure flying *inside* even a motorless aircraft can book a *Glider Rides* flight at Dillingham Airfield, near the Mokuleia polo grounds in northwest Oahu. The 15-to-20-minute flights, narrated and piloted by veterans who have logged more than a million miles in gliders, soar to mountain range heights of up to 3,000 feet, depending on lift conditions. Visibility extends more than 30 miles from Kahuku and the patchwork sugarcane plantations at Waialua to Kaena Point, at the western tip of the island. Sights include the famous North Shore surfing playgrounds, brilliant coral reefs, and various Oahu resort complexes as well as the US Air Force Satellite Tracking Station and leaping schools of dolphin and humpback whales. On a clear day, 80-mile-distant Kauai may be spotted.

The bubble-top gliders seat one or two passengers and leave Dillingham Airfield every 20 minutes from 10:30 AM to 5:30 PM. Rides are $50 for one person, $75 for two. Glider pilot instruction is available by appointment. The service operates year-round; pilots report no more than 30 unflyable days a year. Gliders provide a tranquil, safe, and almost noiseless high-altitude view of Oahu. Information: *Glider Rides,* PO Box 626, Waialua, HI 96791 (phone: 677-3404).

On Kauai, *Tradewinds Gliders* departs Burns Field for 20-minute ($75 for one person, $90 for two) and 40-minute ($125 for one person, $150 for two) flights over the south coast, from Waimea to Poipu. Weather permitting, gliders head inland for views of the waterfalls and canyons of Hanapepe. Information: *Tradewinds Gliders,* PO Box 2099, Lihue, HI 96766 (phone: 335-5086).

Flightseeing

Perhaps the most interesting aspect of either helicopter or fixed-wing flightseeing tours of the Hawaiian islands is each visitor's reaction to being borne aloft over sections of paradise inaccessible to all but the air traveler. "Too beautiful to describe," "Absolutely unreal," and "Purely and uniquely of the Lord" are among the entries found in the ledger of one Maui helicopter company.

There is no more glamorous tour in Hawaii than a flightseeing excursion. With their champagne picnics at secluded spots and drops on deserted beaches, the helicopter companies are the ultimate trailblazers. "We're not in the transportation business — we're in the 'experience-providing' business," says one company owner, who calls his trips "adventures set to music." Most helicopters and tour planes are equipped with headsets, through which passengers hear the pilot's narration or music appropriate to the natural wonder below.

Yes, flightseeing prices are high, but many travelers consider them a relative bargain for the quality of the experience delivered. Prices range from under $50 for a short hop along the Waikiki coast to $250 to $300 for some island touring or a volcano tour departing West Hawaii's Keahole Airport. The helicopters, most of them flown by former air force fighter pilots, seat four to six passengers. By all means, bring your camera; you'll have rare opportunities to capture crater rims, deep gorges, sheer cliffs, and other sights to which only birds and other privileged sightseers are usually privy. See *A Shutterbug's Hawaii,* in this section, for advice on how best to take photos aloft. In general, March through October is the best season for flightseeing, though it's possible year-round.

Apart from the more publicized helicopter services whose tours are extensively described below, there are several smaller competing flightseeing services over Hawaii. Sometimes they offer significant discounts. Check local listings. Fixed-wing commuter aircraft are also used for aerial tours. For those uncomfortable with the thought of helicopter flying, this may be the answer. It also costs less, on the average.

OAHU: Though the dramatic scenery of Hawaii's outer islands draws most of the flightseeing raves, Oahu is also worth seeing. In addition to its famous surfing beaches on the North Shore and beautiful interior valleys, the island has points of historical interest that take on a new dimension from the air.

Papillon Helicopters runs a series of three tours ranging from a half hour ($79) to an hour. The hour-long Oahu Experience ($99) provides an excellent condensed tour of the island. Passengers fly over Waikiki Beach, the extinct volcano of Diamond Head, and the exclusive residential community of Kahala before hovering near Hanauma Bay, where the love scenes of *From Here to Eternity* were filmed. The helicopter follows the rugged coastline to Makapuu Beach before passing over Sea Life Park near the *palis* (cliffs) of the Koolau Range. Here the aircraft rises suddenly to climb over the twin peaks of 1,643-foot tall Olomana. The scenic highlight of the trip may well be the visit to Nuuanu Pali, where sheer 1,000-foot drop-offs, sawtooth mountains blanketed in green, and waterfalls whose cascades are blown upward by the wind are sprawled out in the Nuuanu Valley. It is a magnificent vista.

The Oahu Epic ($187) skips Nuuanu Pali but visits the North Shore. Sunset and the Banzai Pipeline, the famous surfing beaches where the waves reach a height of 30 feet in winter, and Waimea Bay, known for its beautiful valley and 45-foot waterfall, also are included. Large fields of pineapple and sugarcane, stretching to the fuzzy blue peaks of the Waianae Mountains, signal the approach to Pearl Harbor, where the elegant, white Arizona Memorial can be seen, marking the resting place of the sunken battleship. Information: *Papillon Hawaiian Helicopters,* 421 Aowena Pl., Honolulu, HI 96819 (phone: 836-1566; 800-367-7095).

Cherry Helicopters offers two tour itineraries that depart from the helipad at the *Turtle Bay* resort. There's a 15-minute look at the North Shore beaches ($50) and a 30-minute visit to Sacred Falls ($100). Information: *Cherry Helicopters,* 441 Aowena Pl., Honolulu, HI 96819 (phone: 293-7588).

HAWAII: Departing from the *Waikoloa* resort, on the Big Island's west coast, *Kenai Air*'s Volcano, Kohala Mountains, and Kona Coast helicopter tours fly over some of the most dramatic volcanic scenery in the world. On the Volcano tour, passengers soar above lava flows that stretch from the sea to the top of Kilauea, and the pilot guides the whirling craft over the eruption zone, passing by 13,680-foot Mauna Loa and its neighbor, 13,796-foot Mauna Kea, for a bird's-eye view of this great volcano — the highest point in Hawaii. The vista from this mountaintop perspective is absolutely awesome. The observant sightseer may spot feral goats, sheep, and wild boar on the slopes of Mauna Loa. The Kona Coast tour includes Kailua-Kona and the coast down to Puuhonua O Honaunau (City of Refuge), a sanctuary set in a lush coconut grove. It was in this asylum that defeated warriors, and those excommunicated from their tribes for violating sacred *kapus* (taboos), sought refuge. While the pilot narrates the enclave's fascinating history, look for the tall stone tikis depicting Polynesian gods located inside the thick lava stone walls encircling the temple grounds.

The next stop is Kealakekua Bay. Here the Captain Cook Monument juts out into the water where the great British navigator, who discovered the Hawaiian islands, died. The helicopter then skims over the shiny green coffee plantations on the Kona Coast, pausing at lovely Keauhou Bay to see how lava flows created this sparkling body of water. The great size of the Big Island (comparable in landmass to Connecticut) is best appreciated from the air. Information: *Kenai Air Hawaii,* PO Box 4118, Kailua-Kona, HI 96745 (phone: 329-7424; 800-622-3144). Similar tour itineraries are offered by *Papillon Helicopters* (PO Box 55, Kamuela, HI 96743; phone: 885-5995, 329-0551; 800-562-5641 from other islands), which departs from the Waikoloa helipad, and by *Mauna Kea Helicopters* (PO Box 1713, Waimea, HI 96743; phone: 885-6400), which goes up-country for tours of the Kohala Mountains, Parker ranchlands, and the volcano.

For tours that focus on Hawaii Volcanoes National Park, there are *Io Aviation* and *Hilo Bay Air,* which depart from Hilo's General Lyman Field, and *Volcano Helitours,* which leaves from the helipad at the national park. Due to their proximity to the park, these volcano viewing tours are much less expensive than Kailua-Kona departures and a lot shorter, with more air time over the actual site. *Io* also offers tours of the Hamakua Coast, with its dramatic gullies, sea cliffs, and a rain forest, and a 2-hour combination tour that goes all the way to Waipio Valley. Information: *Io Aviation,* Commuter Air terminal, Hilo International Airport, Hilo, HI 96720 (phone: 935-3031); *Hilo Bay Air,* PO Box 4278, Hilo, HI 96720 (phone: 969-1545 or 969-1547); *Volcano Heli-Tours,* PO Box 626, Volcano, HI 96785 (phone: 967-7578).

Big Island Air offers twin-prop aircraft departures from Keahole Airport. Its 2-hour Circle Island itinerary ($150) is about the most comprehensive aerial view of the Big Island offered by anyone. Charters are also available. Information: *Big Island Air,* PO Box 1476, Kailua-Kona, HI 96745 (phone: 329-4868). *Classic Aviation* offers aerial tours and acrobatics in a modern remake of a 1935-era open-cockpit biplane. It's a bit noisy at times, but the views are exhilarating (even though it's difficult to take photographs due to the position of the struts). Departures are from Keahole Airport. Information: *Classic Aviation,* PO Box 1899, Kailua-Kona, HI 96745; phone: 329-TOUR; 800-695-8100, inter-island).

MAUI: *Alex Air* operates five air tours of the island, plus custom charters, departing from the helicopter air terminal at Kahului. The company's most popular trip is its Panoramic Journey, which combines a number of Maui highlights.

After lifting off in Kahului and passing over the lava flows and coral reefs along the Kihei shoreline, the four-passenger helicopter swings over Makena Beach. From late November to May, passengers may catch sight of a humpback whale breaking the surface offshore. The pilot then steers the craft away from the sea, moving inland up the steep incline of Haleakala. The helicopter climbs to the rim of this 10,023-foot volcano and then flies over the crater to explore an unearthly moonscape that stretches for 19 square miles. Passengers can see vividly colored cinder cones, cavernous pits, and winding footpaths cut through this desolate caldera.

Emerging from the interior of the crater, the pilot steers directly to Hana, the heavenly region on the eastern slope of Haleakala, where the great profusion of jungles, waterfalls, and cliffs is spellbinding. Creeping up the north shore, the helicopter flies over waterfalls, countless unnamed valleys, and rain forests before touching down on the Kahului's helipad. Information: *Alex Air,* PO Box 330626, Kahalui, HI 96733 (phone: 871-0792; 800-462-2281).

"I'll never stop smiling again!" and "High point of my life" are among the comments made by passengers on returning from *Papillon Helicopters'* top-of-the-line Maui Odyssey flight. The 2-hour excursion, departing from Kahalui Heliport, is an air/land experience: In addition to extensive exploration of the West Maui mountains and other sites where green velvet walls soar to 5,000 feet, the helicopter sets down in the Kaupo Gap for a picnic lunch. The flight also includes Iao Needle and the pinwheel of valleys and cliffs that surrounds it, the tropical geometry of the taro fields of the Keanae Peninsula, and the lunar reality of Haleakala.

Papillon also runs a spectacular Haleakala Sunrise flight, which lasts 2 hours and includes a stop on ranchland in the Kaupo Gap, where a champagne continental breakfast is served. Information: *Papillon Helicopters,* PO Box 1478, Kahului, HI 96732 (phone: 669-4884; 800-367-7095).

MOLOKAI: Formed thousands of years ago by the upsurge of two volcanic domes, Molokai is paradise preserved. It is a perfect flightseeing destination for those who prefer the quiet seclusion of an isolated beach between their airborne adventures. *Kenai Air* (see above) departs Kahului, Maui for tours of Molokai's north coast valleys, circling over Kalaupapa. The hour-long trip costs $180.

Papillon Helicopters (see above) runs a 1-hour West Maui/Molokai ($185) trip departing from Kahului Airport. After crossing the Pailolo Channel (watch for humpback whales in the winter), the whirlybirds fly over southeast Molokai, where deep valleys stretch like so many fingers to a sea that seems bluer than anywhere else in Hawaii. On the northern coastline, the pilot flies close to Molokai's famous *palis,* the sheer 2,000-foot sea cliffs creased with waterfalls that crash triumphantly into the surf. The photographic opportunities here are unsurpassed. The heli-tour continues on to the Makanalua Peninsula, the flat volcanic plateau where the Belgian priest Father Damien founded his leper colony in 1873. It includes a half-hour ground tour at Kalaupapa, on the peninsula's west coast, where the colony has resided since 1888. While it's interesting to explore Kalaupapa on foot, the settlement's geographic isolation from the rest of the island can be best appreciated from the air.

KAUAI: One airborne trip over Kauai is enough to convince anyone that the Garden Isle is one of Mother Nature's masterpieces. Seen from the air, Kauai is Hawaii at its best — lush, serene, and spectacularly beautiful.

Papillon Helicopters, which has transported entire wedding parties to remote coastline settings, runs five tours of the island. These range from 30 minutes to 2 hours in length and from $90 to $180 per person in price, taking in those twin splendors of Kauai — Waimea Canyon, the island's smaller version of Arizona's Grand Canyon, and the Na Pali Coast, where cliffs rise 3,000 feet from the sea. Looking down at this untamed coastline from the air is known to make people ecstatically giddy or unusually silent. Departures from Princeville Airport. Information: *Papillon Helicopters,* Princeville Airport, PO Box 339, Hanalei, HI 96714 (phone: 826-6591; 800-367-7095).

Kenai Air Hawaii's most popular air tour of Kauai is its 1-hour Garden Island Deluxe trip ($129 per person). The airborne theme is one of contrast: The helicopter flies over the 5,000-foot rim of Waialeale Crater to enter a world of thin streaming waterfalls and leafy green cliffs half-shrouded in mist. Passengers next view the vast barren insides of the 10-mile-long Waimea Canyon, where mountain goats leaping among the rocks and the ever-changing hues of the landscape are the main sources of wonder. The tour passes over Hanalei Valley, the "birthplace of rainbows," before traversing the sacred valleys of the ancient Hawaiians along the Na Pali Coast. Here, forbidding 3,000-foot mountain walls shelter a string of isolated beaches and hidden valleys. Departures from Lihue Airport. Information: *Kenai Air Hawaii,* PO Box 3270, Lihue, HI 96766 (phone: 245-8591; 800-622-3144).

South Sea Helicopter also offers a range of aerial tours of the garden isle. Information: *South Sea Helicopter,* PO Box 1445, Lihue, HI 96766 (phone: 245-7781; 800-367-2914).

Fly Kauai flies several Cessna aircraft on ½- and 1-hour tours for considerably less than their helicopter counterparts: $39 and $69, respectively. The 1-hour Circle Island itnierary includes a fly-by of Kipukai and Poipu, which are not included on helicopter tours. The ½-hour tour heads straight from Lihue Airport to Waimea Canyon and the Na Pali Coast. Information: *Fly Kauai,* PO Box 3778, Lihue, HI 96766 (phone: 246-9123).

NIIHAU: The only way you'll see the "forbidden isle" is to take a 3-hour aerial tour ($200) that departs from Kauai's Port Allen airfield Mondays through Fridays at 9 and 11 AM and again at 3 PM. The plane alights at both the northern and southern ends of the island so that visitors can take a brief stroll around this uninhabited property. Information: *Niihau Helicopters,* PO Box 370, Makaweli, HI 06769 (phone: 335-3500; 800-338-1234).

For the Mind

Museums, Churches, and Mission Houses

The Hawaiian culture is an ancient one, reaching back more than 1,400 years to its South Seas roots, and several noteworthy museums stand as testimony to the state's cultural diversity. Like the islands themselves, they are small in size but full of delightful surprises. Our museum selection traces the islands' multiracial heritage and development, ranging from the early Polynesian settlers to European traders and American whalers, then on to the various Asian groups imported to till the soil. It includes several churches and mission houses, which so poignantly chronicle Hawaii's conversion to Christianity, as well as the homestead of a former sugarcane plantation, which provides a glimpse into the lives of those who shaped Hawaii's present.

BISHOP MUSEUM, Honolulu, Oahu: On three separate levels plus a newly opened wing, the museum traces the story of the islands from prehistoric times. Among the exhibits: "Hawaii: The Royal Isles," tracing the islands' monarchy. This section of the museum has portraits of all the islands' kings and queens, together with thrones, crowns, and regalia, plus examples of their uniforms and clothes. Also on display is a fine collection of artifacts common to the islands before the arrival of Captain Cook. A shallow bowl supported by humanoid figurines, an ornate bone fishhook that would be commendable as a brooch, and feather cloaks, capes, and helmets in the royal colors of yellow, red, and black catch the eye here. The second level features a lovely collection of tapa cloth, as well as exhibits on 19th-century whaling. In the Polynesian Hall is a magnificent display of materials from other islands of the Pacific. Look particularly for an elaborate mourning costume from the Society Islands, an ornamental headdress from Samoa, and a highly decorated mask from Melanesia. For a real whale of a time, enjoy all 55 feet, 22 tons, of one right here. A sperm whale is suspended from the ceiling in the Hawaiian Hall, recalling the days when whaling brought Hawaii much of its reputation and prosperity. A stunning array of exquisitely formed mollusks is displayed next to the Hall of Natural History. In the Science Center is an exhibit of rainbow-colored insects arranged like bracelets and necklaces in a jeweler's window. There is more besides: hula and Hawaiian crafts at the Atherton Halau, astronomy shows in the planetarium, special exhibits, classes, lectures, and examples of indigenous trees and shrubs in the charming Garden Courtyard. Admission charge ($6). Information: *Bishop Museum,* 1525 Bernice St., Honolulu, HI 96817 (phone: 847-3511; 848-4129 for a recorded message).

HONOLULU ACADEMY OF ARTS, Honolulu, Oahu: A special delight for connoisseurs of small art museums. But even for those who never give paintings or sculpture a second glance, a worthwhile hour or two can be spent here, particularly if you take in one of the excellent special exhibits. The academy's Spanish Court and Chinese

Courtyard, both cloistered patios, are the most civilized oases in Honolulu, the perfect escape from the hectic trading in the merchant houses of downtown and from the hedonistic throng on Waikiki. Handsome as the gallery's design and architecture are — and they are very handsome indeed — it is the collections that give the academy its nationwide reputation. Among the most celebrated of these are its Asian holdings, consisting of ceramics, paintings, furniture, bronzes, lacquerwork, and sculpture; the Kress Collection of Italian Renaissance paintings; and the Michener Collection of Japanese prints. Among items that remain vividly in one's memory are a bronze and silver mirror from the T'ang dynasty of China, between the 7th and 10th centuries; the 14th-century statue *Kuan Yin,* also from China; Segna de Bonaventura's painting *Madonna and Child,* from the early Italian Renaissance; Paul Gauguin's *Two Nudes on a Tahitian Beach;* and one of Monet's superb studies of *Water Lilies.* There's also an intriguing collection of Roman glass and an elegant English drawing room with a table set for tea. Open Tuesdays through Saturdays 10 AM to 4:30 PM; Sundays from 1 to 4 PM. Closed Mondays. Tie in a visit with an alfresco lunch at the *Garden Café* (open Tuesdays through Sundays from 11:30 AM to 1:15 PM (phone: 531-8865). Information: *Honolulu Academy of Arts,* 900 S. Beretania St., Honolulu, HI 96814 (phone: 538-3693).

MISSION HOUSES MUSEUM, Honolulu, Oahu: "The clapboards are bare and admit quantities of dust which the trade winds bring in such fearful clouds as to suggest the fate of Pompeii. We have three chairs, a table, a bedstead, and a nice little secretary." So wrote Laura Fish Judd, wife of the evangelist Gerrit P. Judd, in August 1828 of the house they shared with the despotic Reverend Hiram Bingham, the first of the Protestant missionaries who were to leave an indelible imprint on Hawaiian life, both socially and architecturally. As if to underscore their uncompromising moral attitudes, the missionaries rejected the practical, relaxed, and airy grass shacks inhabited by the Hawaiians, including the king, in favor of the prim and proper (and stuffy and dusty) dwellings that replicated those they had known in Massachusetts. All over the islands, postage-stamp-size versions of New England hamlets sprung up, looking incongruous among the exotic tropical trees and shrubs that surrounded and overshadowed them. The *Mission Houses* are the most elaborate complex remaining that recalls this typical example of Yankee obstinacy. The Frame House, which Mrs. Judd described, was shipped to Hawaii in 1820 from Boston and is the oldest existing house in Hawaii. In the parlors, bedrooms, and kitchen is a collection of the original furniture and utensils. The Printing House next door, built from coral blocks in 1831, contains a replica of the old-fashioned Rampage handpress used by the printer, Elisha Loomis, to produce a Hawaiian translation of the Bible, schoolbooks, and hymnals. On the *makai* (ocean) side of the Chamberlain House, built in 1841 — the latest and largest in the complex — the block and tackle used to haul missionary supplies up to the second-floor storehouse is still visible. Also in the Chamberlain House is a model of the mission station in 1850, which graphically illustrates how Honolulu has changed. Living history events, when visitors mingle with costumed volunteers, are offered twice monthly. Occasionally, candlelit evening walks are also scheduled on the calendar. Information: *Mission Houses Museum,* 553 S. King St., Honolulu, HI 96813 (phone: 531-0481).

LYMAN MISSION HOUSE AND MUSEUM, Hilo, the Big Island of Hawaii: Like their mentors, the Binghams and the Judds, the Reverend David and Mrs. Lyman built themselves a New England–style homestead when they arrived in the rain-sodden town of Hilo in 1832. The house is currently arranged much as it was from 1840 to 1880, which suggests that missionary life must have had its compensations, for the sturdy, simple furnishings are quite lovely. The whole house has an atmosphere of merriment and comfort totally different from the feeling of austerity that one associates with strict religious households. "Puddled" glass is used in the windows, antique wallpaper covers the walls, and the bedrooms, with their four-posters, marble-topped washstands, and handmade quilts and throw rugs, are as cozy and quaint as in any New England inn.

The floors throughout the house are made from unevenly cut planks of native koa and look unusually fine. As a gesture to the tropical environment, the stools and tables in the conservatory are made from ohia wood and stand on legs fashioned from crooked branches. The *Lyman Museum,* in a modern building adjacent to the *Mission House,* is stuffed with haphazardly arranged collections relating to ancient Hawaii, the missionaries, immigrants to the islands, volcanology, geology, and mineralogy. The collections need considerable pruning and rearranging to make the museum truly rewarding as an educational and aesthetic experience; too much is currently exhibited in too small a space. There are some quite remarkable artifacts, however, among which must be counted the more than 400 glass paperweights. Closed Sundays. Admission charge ($4.50). Information: *Lyman Mission House and Museum,* 276 Haili St., Hilo, HI 96720 (phone: 935-5021).

HISTORIC PARKER RANCH HOMES, Kamuela, the Big Island of Hawaii: Both *Puuopelu,* the family home of Parker Ranch owner Richard Smart, and *Mana,* the 1847 home of Smart's ancestor John Palmer Parker, are open to the public. Surrounded by rich and beautiful up-country pasture, the real surprise is found inside *Puuopelu,* where an art collection that includes works by Degas, Renoir, and Chagall is housed in six rooms. (Open Tuesdays through Saturdays, 10 AM to 5 PM). Tickets are available at the Parker Ranch Visitor Center; a visit to both homes will take at least an hour. Admission charge ($5); closed Sundays. Information: *Parker Ranch,* PO Box 458, Kamuela, Hawaii, HI 96743 (phone: 885-5433).

GROVE FARM HOMESTEAD, Lihue, Kauai: Perhaps nothing so profoundly shaped modern Hawaii as sugarcane. From the 1840s on, ambitious settlers looked to cane to make their fortunes, turning vast tracts of forest and jungle into cultivated fields and bringing in thousands of foreign laborers — from Portugal, Japan, Korea, China, and the Philippines — who would make Hawaiians a minority in their own country. And until inexpensive and frequent air travel established Hawaii as a prime tourist destination after World War II, cane was the prime source of livelihood for the majority of islanders.

Grove Farm Homestead on Kauai offers a fascinating glimpse into Hawaii's plantation past. Founded in 1864 by 25-year-old George Wilcox, a Yale engineering graduate and the son of missionaries in Hawaii, *Grove Farm* was the center of a thriving cane plantation for nearly 75 years and, after the company headquarters moved, was a self-sufficient family estate for another 40 years. It was Mabel Wilcox, a niece of George and the last occupant of the house, who determined that the homestead should become a museum. Two years after her death, in 1978, *Grove Farm* opened to the public.

Everything within the low stone wall enclosing the main compound has been carefully restored: from a modest worker's cottage, furnished with belongings donated by the Wilcox family laundress, to the fernery, a small louver-sided building whose sole purpose is to house ferns too delicate to tolerate direct sunlight. The main house contains much of the furniture Wilcox commissioned local cabinetmakers to build out of koa wood. An interesting example of the planter's resourcefulness is the old wood stove that covers the entire back wall of the kitchen — which, incidentally, is still used to bake cookies for museum guests. By running the water pipes behind it, the family was able to heat its water supply without burning extra fuel. The homestead's spacious grounds, rich with pines, palms, ironwoods, and numerous fruit trees, as well as vegetable and flower gardens, also help illuminate a past that is all too quickly fading.

Grove Farm is open Mondays, Wednesdays, and Thursdays. Reservations for the 2-hour tour (scheduled at 10 AM and 1 PM), limited to two or three groups of six, are required. Admission charge ($3). *Grove Farm* also operates the *Waioli Mission Home* in Hanalei, a furnished missionary home on lovely, landscaped grounds (see below). Information: *Grove Farm Homestead,* Nawiliwili Rd., Lihue, HI 96766 (phone: 245-3202).

WAIOLI MISSION HOUSE MUSEUM, Hanalei, Kauai: Missionary links to New

England are evident in this trim white home set amid Hawaii's lush landscape. Built in 1841 by early Protestant missionaries, it has been a museum for more than 60 years. A short guided tour of the mission house is given on Tuesdays, Thursdays, and Saturdays, and it provides a glimpse of old Hawaii as well as of the founding family's history and that of Hanalei. Waioli Huiia Church, the still-active mission church that once was associated with the house, is nearby. No admission charge. Open from 9 AM to 3 PM. Information: *Waioli Mission House Museum,* Hanalei, Kauai, HI 96714 (phone: 245-3202).

CHURCHES, Island-wide: Along with their zeal and religious convictions, the missionaries who came to the islands in the 19th century brought with them a determination to see their beliefs made solidly manifest in the form of churches. Though architecturally unimpressive, their historical associations and/or decorative details make them noteworthy.

The Episcopal *St. Andrew's Cathedral* (at Beretania and Queen Emma Sts., Honolulu) was the inspiration of Kamehameha IV and his wife, Queen Emma, anglophiles both, who adopted the religion of English aristocracy. Although the cathedral's design, and some of its building materials, were imported from Britain, it was the *Kawaiahao Church* (957 Punchbowl St., Honolulu), built by New Englanders and dedicated by Kamehameha III, that became known as the "Westminster Abbey of Hawaii" for the number of royal baptisms, weddings, and funerals held there. In the church gallery is the Hoffstot Collection, 21 portraits of all of Hawaii's rulers and most of their consorts. Especially moving is the portrait of King Kamehameha III, who in the church sanctuary first used the words that were to become Hawaii's motto: "*Ua mau ke ea o ka aina i ka pono*" ("The life of the land is perpetuated in righteousness"). Today, *kahilis* (feather standards) adorn both sides of the sanctuary, and at most Sunday services at least one hymn is sung in Hawaiian. Also in Honolulu, at the Fort Street Mall, is *Our Lady of Peace Cathedral,* where Joseph de Veuster, Father Damien, was ordained in 1864. The *Queen Liliuokalani Church* (66-090 Kamehameha Hwy., Haleiwa) is special for its old clock with seven dials and seven hands showing the month, day of the week, week of the year, and phases of the moon, and a dial indicating the hours of the day that uses the 12 letters of the queen's name instead of numbers. *St. John the Apostle and Evangelist Church* (95-370 Kuahelani Ave., Mililani Town) is as austere as an early Christian abbey, with its stark granite altar and concrete walls. Highlights are the sculptures depicting the 14 Stations of the Cross, the modernistic stained glass windows, and the bronze statues of the Blessed Virgin Mary and St. John.

The most famous of the churches on the Big Island is *Mokuaikaua Church* (Alii Dr., Kailua), which stands across the road from Hulihee Palace. Built in 1837 using cornerstones that were reputedly hewn in the 16th century, *Mokuaikaua* is the oldest and most historic church in the state. Walls made from lava rock and cemented with coral, and beams and posts constructed from ohia wood brought down from the mountains, give this church its distinctly Hawaiian character. Standing on a small side road off Route 16, which branches from the main highway (Route 11) a few miles south of Captain Cook, is *St. Benedict's,* known as "the Painted Church," the most celebrated Catholic church in the islands. Although this small church has a humble frame exterior, its interior is brightly decorated with Hawaiian scenes and, behind the altar, a quite unexpected trompe l'oeil rendering of the nave of Burgos Cathedral in Spain. Another small Catholic house of worship in this painted tradition is the *Star of the Sea Church,* which had to be uprooted when the Kalapana Coast was recently covered by lava. This tiny house of worship now sits on supports several miles north of Kalapana on Route 130. The community rallied to preserve it from the molten tides issuing from the Kilauea volcano, and towed it to its current (though temporary) spot. Severe termite damage was discovered when the church was moved, and it is now closed and undergoing restoration. At Kapaau, on the north side of the island, is *Kalahikiola Church,* which was truly a labor of love. Stones were brought to the site on men's backs from nearby gulches. Others went out in canoes to dive for coral, and ohia wood was brought down from the mountains to make pillars and beams. Today, this white edifice stands amid trim lawns, witness to the faith of the parishioners who built it.

One of the most photographed churches on Maui is the *Church of the Holy Ghost,* set on a gentle, green hillside below the summit of Haleakala, just off the highway near Waiakoa. The interior of this octagonal church contains wooden, gold-leaf bas-reliefs and an altar that was brought around Cape Horn from Austria. At Wailuku is the equally photogenic *Kaahumanu Church,* named for Queen Kaahumanu, who asked that the first permanent church on this spot be named after her. The present structure, built in 1876, replaces a stone church that was erected in 1837. The svelte form of the present New England–style building is delightfully emphasized by its dark green trim. This is probably the most elegant of the many graceful wooden churches in the islands. From Huelo (near Paia) to Kanaio (just past Ulupalakua) are a series of circuit churches, each a day's mule ride apart. Several have been restored in 1989, including the *Wainanalua Church* in Hana (1857), the *Kipahulu Congregational Church* (1858), and *Hualaha Church* at Kaupo (1859).

Among the most moving experiences in Hawaii is visiting the tiny, restored *St. Philomena Church* at Kalawao, Molokai, which was completed by Father Damien during the late 1870s. It was here, during a morning mass on the first Sunday in June 1885, that Damien began his sermon not with the customary "My brethren," but with the significant salutation "We lepers." Close by is the beautifully constructed Protestant *Siloama Church,* whose white, geometric simplicity and spare green spire contrast vividly with the surrounding soft tapestry of tropical foliage.

Ancient Ruins and Historic Sites

Unlike the Celts and Romans in Europe, the Polynesians built no tombs or burial chambers, no forts or castles, no great walls or monuments. For the most part, nature, not man, still dominates the Hawaiian landscape, and many of the most critical events in Hawaiian history — the death of Captain Cook, the abandonment of the *kapus,* the arrival of the first missionaries and whalers, the overthrow of the monarchy — are marked in memory, not in stone. Listed below are a few of the important historical sites still extant, ranging from the ruins of two ancient *heiaus* (temples) to the modern memorial at Pearl Harbor.

IOLANI PALACE, Honolulu, Oahu: This neo-Florentine edifice, with its stone verandahs and Corinthian columns, is the only former royal palace in the United States. It was completed for King David Kalakaua in 1882 and cost more than $350,000. Kalakaua had traveled around the world and had been received by a number of reigning monarchs. He was particularly attracted by the courts of Europe, and he set out to copy their customs, clothes, and houses in his Polynesian homeland. He instituted Royal Household Guards with formal uniforms, complete with epaulets and ribbons; he built a coronation stand, where today the smartly turned out *Royal Hawaiian Band* gives concerts; he had crowns made for himself and his queen, Kapiolani; and on February 12, 1883, he began a coronation ceremony that continued for 2 weeks. Thereafter the palace, with its Victorian armoires and settees, became the scene of balls, receptions, dinners, and musical soirees. These displays of what they perceived as an effete way of life, as well as Kalakaua's high-handed style of government, disturbed and offended the American entrepreneurs in Hawaii. Kalakaua's successor, his sister Liliuokalani, reigned for only 2 years before she was deposed in 1893 by a provisional government headed by the pineapple magnate Samuel B. Dole. For the next 3 years, Iolani was periodically a prison for the ex-queen.

In 1898, sovereignty of the islands was transferred to the government of the United States, and the American flag flew above the former royal residence. The Territory of Hawaii was administered from here, and when the islands became the 50th state, the palace became the executive building. In 1969, the splendid new state capitol was opened, and a group called the Friends of Iolani Palace began looking for funds to restore it to its original opulence. Many of the furnishings and artifacts had been dispersed among Liliuokalani's family, as well as to collectors and museums. But little by little, donations and purchases have enabled a growing number of items to return to their original setting. The mirrored throne room, with its gilt trim and crystal chandeliers, once again evokes a sense of 19th-century court elegance. The main stairwell, made of highly polished koa wood and trimmed with ohia and cedar carvings, glows as it did when Robert Louis Stevenson stopped by to pay his respects and to note that Kalakaua could demolish five bottles of champagne in an afternoon. The walls of the king's bedroom still retain the silver-leaf decoration and eggshell blue paint of his day; and a portrait of Louis Philippe, King of France, which he presented to Kamehameha III in 1848, still hangs on the first-floor landing. From time to time, people can be seen sipping champagne on the verandahs. Usually these are visiting chieftains from other Polynesian islands being entertained by Edward Kawanankoa, the pretender to the Hawaiian throne. Although Mr. Kawanankoa receives no official recognition from the state, he is extended these minor courtesies in memory of the Kamehamehas, from whom he is descended. Although much remains to be done before the house regains its original palatial status, it nevertheless offers a glimpse of how a semi-Europeanized Polynesian court thought it ought to live. Tours last 45 minutes and are offered from 9 AM to 2:15 PM, Wednesdays through Saturdays; call for reservations. Admission is $4. Information: *Iolani Palace,* Box 2259, Honolulu, HI 96804 (phone: 538-1471; for reservations, 522-0832).

QUEEN EMMA'S SUMMER PALACE, Honolulu, Oahu: Unlike the ornate Iolani Palace, Queen Emma's summer retreat up in the Nuuanu Valley above Honolulu looks like the home of a well-to-do plantation owner. Built sometime between 1847 and 1850, it is a simple square building with Doric columns supporting the roof over the front lanai. Queen Emma, wife of Kamehameha IV, inherited the property in 1857, and in 1869 she added a large back room in the expectation of throwing a party for Queen Victoria's second son, Alfred, Duke of Edinburgh. The prince never showed up, but the room is still called the Edinburgh Room. After 1872, Emma no longer lived there. Following her death in 1885, the house fell into disrepair and was about to be torn down when the Daughters of Hawaii rescued it in 1913. Since 1915, they have operated it as a museum, displaying many of the artifacts that belonged to Emma and her family, as well as materials relating to that period in Hawaiian history. Some exotic pieces that visitors find especially appealing among the *kahilis* (feather standards) and Victorian furniture are an elaborate, three-tiered Gothic cabinet bordered with cruciform fretwork and finials, a gift from Queen Victoria's consort, Prince Albert; a stereopticon, presented to the queen by Napoleon III; and a necklace hung with tiger claws decorated with seed pearls embedded in rolled gold. Queen Emma's only son, Albert, died when he was 4 years old. His christening robe, embroidered with the royal coat of arms, hangs in his mother's bedroom, not far from the simple red jacket and brass megaphone given to the infant prince when he was made an honorary member of the Honolulu Volunteer Fire Department. Many of the plants found here in Emma's day still flourish on the grounds, and a delightful view of the house is seen from the driveway, framed by kukui and koa trees and surrounded by roses, geraniums, spider lilies, and serpentine ferns. Admission is $4. Information: *Queen Emma's Summer Palace,* 2913 Pali Hwy., Honolulu, HI 96817 (phone: 595-3167).

ARIZONA MEMORIAL, Pearl Harbor, Oahu: The Arizona Memorial is a perfect example of what a material tribute to those who died in the service of their country should be: simple, graceful, and intensely moving. The white concrete structure, in the blue-green water off the tip of Ford Island in Pearl Harbor, spans the battleship USS *Arizona,* whose sunken hull lies beneath the memorial, entombing the 1,102 servicemen who were aboard on the morning of December 7, 1941, when Japanese planes attacked the base. The memorial is divided into three parts. There is a museum room, containing among other mementos the *Arizona*'s ship's bell; an open assembly area, from which visitors may look down at the battleship's rusted and barnacled hull; and the shrine, where a marble tablet is inscribed with the names of those who died on the *Arizona.* It reads like a cross section of the immigrant groups who traveled to America in search of freedom, prosperity, and peace: Aarons, Abercrombie, Blake, Blanchard, Blankenship, Jastremski, Le Gros, Lynch, McGuire, Tambolleo, Van Horn, Vosti, Zimmerman. The American flag that flies above the memorial is attached to a flagpole anchored in the ship's hull. Each morning and evening, the flag is raised and lowered by an honor guard. Alfred Preis, architect of the memorial, said of it: "The overall effect is one of serenity. Overtones of sadness have been omitted to permit the individual to contemplate . . . his own innermost feelings." The US Navy operates the short boat trip to the memorial from the USS *Arizona* Visitor Center — which is run by National Park Rangers — from 8 AM to 3 PM daily; the visitors' center itself is open from 7:30 AM to 5 PM. Commercial sea tours from Kewalo Basin sail along "battleship row," past where other battleships were sunk during the raid. Only passengers on US Navy boats, however, are allowed to disembark at the Arizona Memorial. As it is Hawaii's most popular tourist attraction, a wait of 1 hour or longer for tours to the memorial is not uncommon. No admission charge. Information: *Arizona Memorial Navy Boat Tours,* Pearl Harbor, HI 96701 (phone: 422-0561).

PUUHONUA O HONAUNAU NATIONAL HISTORICAL PARK, Honaunau, the Big Island of Hawaii: There are many things that attract visitors to the Kona Coast: swaying palms, tide pools with live corals, and the ocean surging into rocky coves. But here is the most complete restoration in the islands of an ancient Hawaiian place of sanctuary for defeated warriors and for people who had broken a *kapu,* or taboo. Here the ground was sacred to both the pursued and the pursuer, and any miscreant who reached it and received absolution from a *kahuna* (temple priest) was considered a free man once more. There were, however, certain impediments involved in getting here. The only access in ancient days was by swimming across a bay known as the shark's den, and once on the temple grounds, a 10-foot-high wall had to be scaled. The wall, built during the 16th century, still stands, 1,000 feet long and 6 feet wide, like a monstrous three-dimensional abstract jigsaw puzzle. Around a splendidly reconstructed *heiau* (temple) at the ocean's edge stands a half circle of tall tikis, with countenances suggesting growls and grimaces. Even in the water, close to an old outrigger canoe carved from ohia wood, a smaller figure stands sentinel to warn the common folk that this part of the shoreline is for the *alii* (nobles) only. In the palace ruins on the non-sacred side of the wall are the skeletons of two A-frame buildings, one with just enough dried grass attached to indicate how thatching was performed. Local handicraft workers demonstrate how to make tapa cloth, fishnets, poi, and feather leis, helmets, and capes. For a change of pace, visitors can sit on smooth stone and play *konane,* the ancient Hawaiian game of checkers, which is set out on a rock on the beach. Here, as elsewhere in the US, the National Park Rangers prove that they are among our best informed and dedicated public servants. Rangers are on duty from 8 AM to 5 PM daily. The site remains open until midnight, and memorable sunsets silhouette the temple and palm grove against the sky. Information: *Puuhonua O Honaunau National Historical Park,* PO Box 129, Honaunau, HI 96726 (phone: 328-2326).

HULIHEE PALACE, Kailua-Kona, the Big Island of Hawaii: This is another gem of a house that owes its preservation to the Daughters of Hawaii, who rescued it from near ruin in 1925. Hulihee was built in 1838 by John Adams Kuakini, Governor of the Big Island and a cousin of Kamehameha the Great, and was inherited in the 1850s by Princess Ruth Keelikolani. The palace stands by the ocean with landscaped lawns, palm trees, and a lovely garden of tropical plants. Apart from one mock-Gothic window in the upstairs sitting room above the front entrance, the building is classically simple. Princess Ruth, known for her generosity, used the palace for entertaining and housing guests. Among these were Queen Emma, her husband, Kamehameha IV, and their son, Prince Albert, who used it frequently as a vacation retreat from Honolulu; King Lunalilo; and King David Kalakaua, who bought the palace after Ruth's death and filled it with rugs, china, glassware, sofas, satin cushions, prints, paintings, and family mementos similar to those he had seen in Europe. Today the house is more simply furnished, with some representative pieces from the royal era, and the floors are covered with handsome *lau hala* mats. In the north bedroom there is a beautifully made bed and a fine crib that belonged to the infant Prince Albert. In the Kuakini Room are several ancient artifacts, including a huge round stone used by Kamehameha the Great as an exercise ball. Everywhere there is the smooth, lustrous sheen of koa and other natural hardwoods. Many visitors come here again and again just to see the collection of koa bowls, although there is much else besides: Victorian marble busts of the Hawaiian royals; old prints of Hawaii; old *kahilis* (feather standards) that used to accompany the monarchs wherever they went; and David Kalakaua's helmet, medals, and guitar. Admission is $4. Information: *Hulihee Palace,* 75-5718 Alii Dr., Kailua-Kona, HI 96740 (phone: 329-1877).

PUUKOHOLA HEIAU, Kawaihae, the Big Island of Hawaii: One of the goals of the 19th-century New England missionaries was to eradicate Hawaii's ancient *heiaus* (temples). Among the most famous and best preserved of these is the Puukohola Heiau, which stands impressively between the ocean and the highway at Kawaihae. It was built in 1791 on the remains of a 16th-century temple by Kamehameha the Great, following a prophecy that if he constructed a temple to his war god, Kukailimoku, he would become conqueror of all the islands. On the day of the *heiau*'s dedication, the king slew his chief enemy, who was at the ceremony, and offered him to the god as a sacrifice. The Reverend Hiram Bingham, the most famous of the Protestant missionaries, commented on the 224-foot-long, 100-foot-wide, and 15-foot-high *heiau* built of ominous black lava and set in a hill overlooking the sea:

> I visited Puukohola, the large heathen temple at that place, a monument of folly, superstition, and madness, which the idolatrous conqueror [Kamehameha] and his murderous priests had consecrated with human blood to the senseless deities of Pagan Hawaii. . . . The frowning structure is so large and prominent, that it can be distinctly seen with the naked eye, from the top of Maunakea, a distance of about 32 miles. As a fortification of Satan's kingdom, its design was more for war against the human species than the worship of the Creator. [From *A Residence of Twenty-One Years in the Sandwich Islands* (New York: Converse, 1847).]

After a review like that, who could resist a visit? Open from 7:30 AM to 4 PM. No admission charge. Information: *Puukohola Heiau National Historic Site,* Kawaihae, HI 96743 (phone: 882-7218).

MOOKINI HEIAU, the Big Island of Hawaii: Still preserved by the family that was responsible for its upkeep in the days of Kamehameha the Great, this coastal *heiau,* or temple, is among the best preserved in Hawaii, retaining more architectural detail than most others that survive. This is where Kamehameha was taken for the celebration of his birth rites, and the site of his birth is within walking distance of the *heiau.* A visitors' center has recently opened here. Located off Rte. 227, between Upolu Point and Lapakahi.

LAPAKAHI STATE HISTORICAL PARK, Kawaihae, the Big Island of Hawaii: Though this archaeological site is composed mostly of simple rock walls and walkways, these remains of a 14th-century Hawaiian fishing village supply a fascinating idea of how things were way back when. Guided and self-guided tours traverse the fascinating sun-dried landscape that is relieved only by gnarled kiawe trees and the bits of shade they provide. No admission charge. Information: *Lapakahi State Historical Park,* Kawaihae, Hawaii, HI 96744 (phone: 889-5566).

LAHAINA, Maui: Since its designation as a National Historic Landmark in 1962, this waterfront town of 10,000 people has become West Maui's main attraction. Before the European discovery of Hawaii, Lahaina was the haunt of Maui's ruling elite, and with the advent of Kamehameha the Great, the native village became an early political center of the united Hawaiian kingdom. Protestant missionaries arrived in the 1820s, just as Lahaina was about to lose its innocence: The whaling era, which was to have the greatest impact upon the town, was under way. From approximately 1820 to 1860, this tiny Hawaiian port turned into the most important provisioning stop for America's entire Pacific whaling fleet, becoming the whaling capital of the world, in fact. While the ships took on stores and their hard-bitten crews indulged themselves with women and grog, the missionaries tried to save souls, and these two sets of foreign intruders (ironically, both mainly New Englanders) fought — like the virtual forces of good and evil — for the hearts and minds of the Hawaiian people.

Today, Lahaina is no Williamsburg, but a good deal of restoration of its largely wood (and some coral stone) buildings has been carried out by concerned citizens and the Lahaina Restoration Foundation. The town consists of shopfronts along Front Street, the main thoroughfare, and the grid of streets between Front Street and the Honoapiilani Highway. Although shopping has become the main draw, there are more things to see than the average tourist on a shopping spree might imagine. Located just off Route 27, a recently opened visitor center (phone: 377-5000) is the first phase of a comprehensive educational complex planned by *heiau* guardian priestess, Momi Lum. The *Baldwin House Museum,* home of the medical missionary Dr. Dwight Baldwin during the mid-19th century, is furnished as it was when he lived there. Not far away, a huge banyan tree, planted in 1873 to commemorate 50 years of missionary work on the island, flourishes in the town's main square. Across the street is the *Pioneer Inn,* an old hotel that opened at the turn of the century and is still in use. It appeared on the scene after the whaling ships had gone, but around the harbor in front of it, there's the *Carthaginian,* a ship of relatively recent vintage, true-rigged like the brigs of whaling days. Other remains of the past are the Courthouse, some rubble of the Old Fort that Lahaina was forced to build to deal with rioting seamen, and the reconstructed Hale Paahoa, or Old Prison, which also became necessary as rowdiness increased. The Wo Hing Society Hall, also on Front St., provides a perspective on the lives led by the Chinese immigrants who came to work West Maui's cane fields. The grave of Queen Keopuolani, the wife of Kamehameha the Great and the first Hawaiian chief to be converted to Christianity, along with the graves of other members of the royal family, are in Waiola Cemetery, next to Waiola Church, which stands where the first stone church to be built in the islands once stood. On the grounds of historic Lahainaluna School is Hale Pai (printing house), where some of the first Hawaiian-language books were printed during the 1830s. Information: *Lahaina Restoration Foundation,* PO Box 338, Lahaina, HI 96767 (phone: 661-3262); or *Maui Visitors Bureau,* 250 Alamaha, Suite 1116, Kahului, HI 96732 (phone: 871-8691).

KALAUPAPA NATIONAL HISTORIC MONUMENT, Kalaupapa, Molokai: Leprosy appeared in the Hawaiian islands during the middle of the 19th century and, by 1860, fear of the terrible new disease convinced Hawaii's rulers that something had to be done. As a result, the most remote and inaccessible place in the islands was found, Molokai's Makanalua Peninsula, windblown and deserted, and lepers were exiled there in a horrible "prison" from which no escape was possible — cliffs 1,600 feet high backed the 12-square-mile tongue of volcanic rock, and the raw power of the sea enclosed it on the three other sides. The first lepers were dumped overboard off the peninsula on January 6, 1866, and those who made it ashore commenced a life of lawlessness and hardship. The first settlement was at Kalawao, a harsh spot on the east coast, but one with drinking water; the colony did not move to Kalaupapa, on the more pleasant west coast of the peninsula, until 1888, when water was first piped in. It was into this corner of hell that Father Damien Joseph de Veuster came in 1873 to tend a flock of perhaps 1,000 damned souls. Father Damien brought not only religion — he carried with him order, organization, and justice. The Belgian priest himself eventually contracted leprosy and died of it at Kalaupapa in 1889, at the age of 49.

Today, leprosy (renamed Hansen's disease) has been tamed by the sulfone drugs introduced during the 1940s, and Kalaupapa's residents, now fewer than 100, are free to leave. But they stay to live out their lives in the simple, state-supported settlement founded in such terror a century ago. Kalaupapa itself was named a National Historical Monument in 1976, and it became part of the National Park System in 1980.

It has been possible for some years to visit Kalaupapa and the peninsula, since the disease is no longer contagious as a result of medical advances (although children under 16 are not allowed on the peninsula). Still, visitors must obtain an entry permit issued by the State Department of Health in Honolulu. If you participate in a tour, the permit is included. There is a small airstrip to which several commuter lines fly small, twin-engined craft from Oahu, the Hoolehua Airport on topside Molokai, and other points in the islands. Experienced trekkers may also hike down the 3-mile-plus trail from overlooking Palaau State Park, but it is a steep and difficult hike; a mandatory tour at the bottom must be arranged in advance with *Damien Tours* (phone: 567-6171). *Aloha IslandAir* (phone: 800-652-6541 in Hawaii; 800-323-3345 elsewhere in the continental US) and *Air Molokai* (phone: 521-0090 on Oahu; 567-6881 on Molokai) offer service to Kalaupapa. Connections can be made for Honolulu, Maui, and Lanai. When booking a flight, it is very important to indicate Kalaupapa, not Molokai. Most Molokai-bound flights head for the main airport at Hoolehua. *Damien Tours* offers trips both in conjunction with arrivals on these airlines and independently.

The most popular method of visiting Kalaupapa, however, is on muleback. *Molokai Mule Ride* runs a mule train down a 3⅛-mile trail that takes more than two dozen hairpin switchbacks to descend the 1,600-foot cliffs. The full-day trips, which include a tour of the settlement, leave the stable site near the Kalaupapa lookout at 9 AM and return around 3:30 PM. Reservations are necessary; rides are limited to visitors over 16 years and under 225 pounds. Information: *Rare Adventures,* PO Box 200, Kualapuu, HI 96757 (phone: 567-6088; 537-1845 from Oahu; 800-843-5978 from the mainland).

A Shutterbug's Hawaii

The dramatic juxtaposition of land and sea, vibrant color, beautiful weather, and a diverse and exotic population are Hawaii's photographic stock in trade. Even a beginner can achieve remarkable results with a surprisingly basic set of lenses and filters or a camcorder. Equipment is, in fact, only as valuable as the imagination that puts it into use. (For further information on equipment, see *Cameras and Equipment* in GETTING READY TO GO.)

Don't be afraid to experiment. Use what knowledge you have to explore new possibilities. Don't limit yourself by preconceived ideas of what's hackneyed or corny. Because a hibiscus has been photographed hundreds of times before doesn't make it any less worthy of your attention.

In Hawaii, as elsewhere, spontaneity is one of the keys to good photography. Whether it's a sudden shaft of light bursting through the clouds or workers in a taro field in the midst of harvesting, don't hesitate to shoot if the moment is right. If photography is indeed capturing a moment and making it timeless, success lies in judging just when a moment worth capturing occurs and reacting quickly.

A good picture reveals an eye for detail, whether it's a matter of lighting, of positioning your subject, or of taking time to crop a picture carefully. The better your grasp of the importance of details, the better your results will be photographically.

Patience is often necessary. Don't shoot a view of Diamond Head if a cloud suddenly covers it with shadows. A dead tree in a panorama of Hanalei Valley? Reframe your image to eliminate the obvious distraction. People walking toward a scene that would benefit from their presence? Wait until they're in position before you shoot. After the fact, many of the flaws will be self-evident. The trick is to be aware of the ideal and have the patience to allow it to happen. If you are part of a group, you may well have to trail behind a bit in order to shoot properly. Not only is group activity distracting, but bunches of people hovering nearby tend to stifle spontaneity and overwhelm potential subjects.

A camera or camcorder provides an opportunity, not only to capture Hawaii's straightforward beauty, but to interpret it. What it takes is a sensitivity to the surroundings, a knowledge of the capabilities of your equipment, and a willingness to see things in new ways.

LANDSCAPES AND SEASCAPES: The Hawaiian landscape is of such compelling beauty that it is often the photographer's primary focus. Even Honolulu and Waikiki are best captured in the context of their setting, sandwiched between the lush, saw-toothed Koolaus and the variegated blues and greens of the Pacific.

Color and form are the obvious ingredients here, and how you frame your pictures can be as important as getting the proper exposure. Study the shapes, angles, and colors that make up the scene and create a composition that uses them to best advantage.

Lighting is a vital component in landscapes and seascapes. Take advantage of the richer colors of early morning and late afternoon whenever possible. The overhead light of midday is often harsh and without the shadowing that can add to the drama of a scene. This is when a polarizer is used to best effect. Most polarizers come with a mark on the rotating ring. If you can aim at your subject and point that marker at the sun, the sun's rays are likely to be right for the polarizer to work for you. If not, stick to your skylight filter, underexposing slightly if the scene is particularly bright. Most light meters respond to an overall light balance, with the result that bright areas may appear burned out.

Although a standard 50mm to 55mm lens may work well in some landscape situations, most will benefit from a 20mm to 28mm wide-angle. Waikiki, Hanauma Bay, Haleakala Crater, Kilauea, Waimea Canyon, and the Pali Lookout are just some of the panoramas that fit beautifully into a wide-angle format, allowing not only the overview, but the opportunity to include people or other points of interest in the foreground. A flower, for instance, may be used to set off a view of Diamond Head; or people can provide a sense of perspective in a shot of Haleakala.

To isolate specific elements of any scene, use your telephoto lens. Perhaps there's a particular segment of Kauai's Hanalei Valley that would make a lovely shot, or it might be the interplay of light and shadow on Oahu's Pali, or a distant waterfall cascading down the side of Waimea Canyon. The successful use of a telephoto means developing your eye for detail.

PEOPLE: As with taking pictures of people anywhere, there are going to be times in Hawaii when a camera is an intrusion. Your approach is the key: Consider your own reaction under similar circumstances, and you have an idea as to what would make others comfortable enough to be willing subjects. People are often sensitive to having a camera suddenly pointed at them, and a polite request, while getting you a share of refusals, will also provide a chance to shoot some wonderful portraits that capture the spirit of the islands as surely as the scenery does. For candids, an excellent lens is a zoom telephoto in the 70mm to 210mm range; it allows you to remain unobtrusive while the telephoto lens draws the subject closer. And for portraits, a telephoto can be used effectively as close as 2 or 3 feet.

For authenticity and variety, select a place likely to produce interesting subjects. Waikiki is an obvious spot for visitors, but if it's local color you're after, visit Chinatown, wander into a pineapple field, or go to one of the North Shore beaches that are popular with surfers. Aim for shots that tell what's different about Hawaii. In portraiture, there are several factors to keep in mind. Morning or afternoon light will add richness to skin tones, emphasizing tans. To avoid the harsh facial shadows cast by direct sunlight, shoot in the shade or in an area where the light is diffused. The only filter to use is a skylight.

SUNSETS: Not every Hawaiian night is preceded by a brilliant sunset, but there are likely to be some that will seem to typify every magical impression ever dreamed of the tropics.

Since many of the major resort areas face the setting sun, it's not difficult to be in the right place at the right time. Waikiki, Ko Olina, Makaha, Kona, the Kohala Coast, Kaanapali, Wailea, Makena, Kapalua, Kihei, Napili, Poipu, Princeville, and Kaluakoi all offer excellent opportunities to catch the sun as it slips below the horizon.

When shooting sunsets, keep in mind that the brightness will distort meter readings. When composing a shot directly into the sun, frame the picture in the viewfinder so that only half of the sun is included. Read the meter, set, and shoot. Whenever there is this kind of unusual lighting, shoot a few frames in half-step increments, both over and under the meter reading. Bracketing, as this is called, can provide a range of images, the best of which may well be other than the one shot at the meter's recommended setting.

Use any lens for sunsets. A wide-angle is good when the sky is filled with color-streaked clouds, when the sun is partially hidden, or when you're close to an object that silhouettes dramatically against the sky.

Telephotos also produce wonderful silhouettes, either with the sun as a backdrop or against the palette of a brilliant sunset sky. Bracket again here. For the best silhouettes, wait 10 to 15 minutes after sunset. Unless using a very fast film, a tripod is recommended.

Orange, magenta, and split screen filters are often used to accentuate a sunset's picture potential. Orange will help turn even a gray sky into something approaching a photogenic finale to the day and can provide particularly beautiful shots linking the sky with the sun reflected on the ocean. A pale magenta, as in a flourescent or daylight correction filter, can add subtle color to dull or brilliant sunsets. If the sunset is already bold in hue, the orange will overwhelm the natural colors. A red filter will produce dramatic, highly unrealistic results.

NIGHT: If you think that picture possibilities end at sunset, you're presuming that night photography is the exclusive domain of the professional. If you've got a tripod, all you'll need is a cable release to attach to your camera to assure a steady exposure (which is often timed in minutes rather than fractions of a second).

For situations such as luaus, Polynesian revues, and other nighttime entertainments, a strobe does the trick, but beware: Flash units are often used improperly. You can't take a view of Diamond Head with a flash. It may reach out 30 to 50 feet, but that's it. On the other hand, a flash used too close to your subject may result in overexposure, resulting in a "blown out" effect. With most cameras, strobes will work with a maximum shutter speed of 1/125 or 1/250 of a second. If you set the exposure properly and shoot within range, you should come up with pretty sharp results.

CLOSE-UPS: Whether of people or of objects such as lava, close-ups can add another dimension to your photography. There are a number of shooting options, one of which is to use a 70mm or a 210mm lens at its closest focusable distance. Unless you're working in bright sunlight, a tripod will be worthwhile. If you are very near your subject and there is a good deal of reflective light, it may pay to underexpose a bit in relation to the meter reading.

If you do not have a telephoto lens, you can still shoot close-ups using a set of magnification filters. Filter packs of one-, two-, and three-time magnification are available, converting your lens into a close-up lens. Even better is a special macro lens designed for close-up photography.

AERIAL VIEWS: An inter-island flight or a helicopter tour can inspire some great pictures, but you have to be prepared. Get your equipment ready as soon as you're seated, test the meter against the horizon's light, and set for the proper exposure. Have spare film unpackaged and handy so you can change it quickly, and try to start off with a full roll rather than waste time (and photo opportunities) while airborne.

You can use a wide-angle lens from the air, although it will flatten things out and may well include sections of the plane in the picture. A 50mm can be used, and a telephoto will pick out details. Don't shoot through glass (or plexiglass) that is curved or at too extreme an angle; it will cause distortion. If there's bright sunlight, it's possible to underexpose a bit, yet still have enough light to shoot at speeds of 1/500 or 1/1000: fast enough to get results. Below 1/125 the outcome is questionable.

A SHORT PHOTOGRAPHIC TOUR

OAHU: For people shots, you can't beat Chinatown, particularly the early morning market on King Street. A visit to any of Oahu's beaches will also provide lots of subjects: Try Waikiki for all sorts and shapes of sunbathers; Diamond Head and Kailua Beach for windsurfers; Sunset and the Banzai Pipeline for championship surfboarders; Hanauma Bay for snorkelers, marine life, and one of Hawaii's largest reefs. For the latter, you'll need an underwater casing. You might try an 81B (brown) filter to warm up beach shots or underexpose a bit if you're using a skylight to compensate for reflective glare.

A drive to the Tantalus Lookout offers spectacular cityscapes that include Diamond Head, Waikiki, and downtown Honolulu. The lookout at Punchbowl National Cemetery also features panoramas of the city. Early morning is the best time to shoot unless you're after sunsets, in which case the obvious time is late afternoon.

For the definitive shot of Diamond Head, wait until afternoon and head down the beach to the jetty in front of the *Outrigger Reef.* The beach to the right of the *Hilton Hawaiian Village* and the Magic Island section of Ala Moana Beach Park also have clear, uncluttered views. So do the lounge and restaurant atop the *Sheraton Waikiki.*

The view from the Pali Lookout is one of the most encompassing in Hawaii, offering picture possibilities anytime during the day before 4 PM, when the Windward Coast becomes covered in shadow. Even better is a morning's drive up the Windward Coast to the North Shore and beyond for its 2-hour sweep of rugged mountains, ribbon beaches, ever-changing seas, and thick green vegetation. Also noteworthy are the pineapple fields of the Schofield Plains — especially if a harvest is taking place — and the charming town of Haleiwa, which sees some beautiful sunsets.

THE BIG ISLAND OF HAWAII: For volcanoes and Hawaiiana, visit the Big Island. Hawaii Volcanoes National Park provides access to the active Kilauea Volcano's Halemaumau Crater and lava-scarred East Rift zone along the Chain of Craters Road and down to the coast near the Wahaula *heiau* (temple) now completely surrounded by molten lava. A wide-angle lens will capture the vastness of the setting, while a telephoto will help record the exciting detail. Don't expect jets of flaming lava; it could happen, but it's unlikely. There will, however, be powerful images of the living earth and the scars it leaves behind after moments of eruptive fury. The best lookouts are behind the *Volcano House* hotel, as well as those along the Rim Road, which encircles the crater, allowing a direct look into the central pit itself.

Several easy trails lead to portions of the crater floor, passing through thick fern forest before opening upon the barren crust of newly hardened lava. The rim-level Devastation Trail has an easy walk through the site of a major eruption in 1959. Stark shapes and colors are the major elements here. Depending on conditions, you may be able to photograph flowing lava from lookouts along the Puna Coast near Kalapana.

The Big Island is at its scenic best along the Hamakua Coast — 40 miles of cane fields, up-country, and dusty old towns beginning in Hilo and ending at Waipio Valley Overlook. Hire a jeep (and a driver) to go down into the valley to see its 1,500-foot waterfall, black sand beach, and marshy taro plots.

The area between Waimea and Hawi provides still another Hawaiian perspective, with volcanic craters now covered by lush grass cropped slowly by grazing cattle. Long views of the Kohala Coast all the way to Kona are part of the drive south; morning or afternoon light is best.

The City of Refuge, south of Kona, is a reconstruction of an important temple complex, with crafts and lifestyle exhibits. Try shooting the major temples and tikis silhouetted against the setting sun.

MAUI: Haleakala is not to be missed. One of the world's largest dormant volcanoes, its crater is 19 square miles of colorful cliffs, cinder cones, and slides of lava ash. From its 10,023-foot summit there are often views of the distant peaks of the Big Island, neighboring Molokai, Lanai, and Kahoolawe.

Sunrise and sunset offer some dramatic long distance shots, but the best views into the crater are seen several hours after sunrise or before sunset when the sunlight hits the crater floor. By midday, crater light can be flat. Wide-angles, telephotos, and standard lenses will all prove useful. The best vistas are from the Haleakala Visitor Center and from the summit overlook. Since weather may be a problem here (frequent rain and clouds), call park headquarters before making the long drive to the top.

The Hana Highway is Maui's other great photographic asset. This 50-mile road from Kahului to Hana ties together such disparate scenery as the "artsy" town of Paia, the taro fields of Keanae, the pastures of Hana, and the forests and waterfalls of the Seven Pools. Morning and afternoon are equally good for picture-taking.

On West Maui is Lahaina, with its old whaling town architecture. An afternoon's walk on the rock jetty that surrounds the yacht harbor will yield some good views of the town and the mountains, as well as of boats, surfers, and windsurfers.

Along the drive from Kapalua to Lahaina and Maalaea to Makena are impressive vistas of distant Molokai, Lanai, and Kahoolawe. Early morning and afternoon are best.

MOLOKAI: The Makanalua Peninsula, majestically situated beneath 2,000-foot cliffs, has been the home of Kalaupapa, the famous leper colony, for almost a century. At the eastern end of the island, reached via four-wheel-drive vehicle through the mountains and along the coast, are Halawa Valley's twin waterfalls and beach.

LANAI: While most of the pineapple fields have now been phased out, crops such as wheat and alfalfa still provide gorgeous landscapes of the Palawai Basin. The best views are from the Lanaihale Road. At 3,500 feet above sea level, this view offers some breathtaking looks at neighboring Molokai and Maui that are easy to frame with the unusual silhouettes of Cook pines. The route, however, is rocky and rutted and can be difficult even with four-wheel-drive vehicles.

KAUAI: Thought by many to be the most photogenic of the Hawaiian islands, Kauai offers both variety and beauty. And with its range of blues and greens, this Garden Isle reproduces especially well with a polarizer.

The Princeville and Na Pali Coast areas are perfect for those *South Pacific* shots. Some places to watch for are the taro fields in Hanalei Valley, the overlook for Hanalei Bay, the Lumahai Beach Lookout, and the towering cliffs of the Na Pali Coast. For the best view of the coast, walk around the rocks to the left of Haena Beach or, if you've got the energy and time, hike to the half-mile marker on the Kalalau Trail, which also begins at Haena.

The highway from Lihue to Waimea Canyon runs through some of Kauai's quaintest towns; Hanapepe and Waimea, for example. If you take the back road up to Waimea Canyon, the panoramas may include neighboring Niihau, Hawaii's "forbidden island." The best natural light for shots of the canyon itself occurs in the afternoon, when the sun hits the canyon's east wall directly, drawing out the rich mix of purples and reds. The view of Kalalau Valley and the sea can be wonderful if the weather is clear; however, mist and heavy clouds frequently roll in to block it. Have patience: Strong winds can clear the view within minutes, providing some dramatic images as the clouds roll by.

INDEX

Index